Human Anatomy & Physiology Laboratory Manual

RAT VERSION

Elaine N. Marieb, R.N., Ph.D.
Holyoke Community College

Susan J. Mitchell, Ph.D.
Onondaga Community College

Rat Dissection authored by **Robert J. Sullivan,** Ph.D.
Marist College

PhysioEx™ Version 8.0 authored by

Peter Z. Zao
North Idaho College

Timothy Stabler, Ph.D.
Indiana University Northwest

Lori Smith, Ph.D.
American River College

Greta Peterson
Middlesex Community College

Andrew Lokuta, Ph.D.
University of Wisconsin–Madison

Benjamin Cummings

Boston Columbus Indianapolis New York San Francisco Upper Saddle River
Amsterdam Cape Town Dubai London Madrid Milan Munich Paris Montréal Toronto
Delhi Mexico City São Paulo Sydney Hong Kong Seoul Singapore Taipei Tokyo

Make the Most of Your Lab Time

with the new edition of Marieb's Lab Manuals

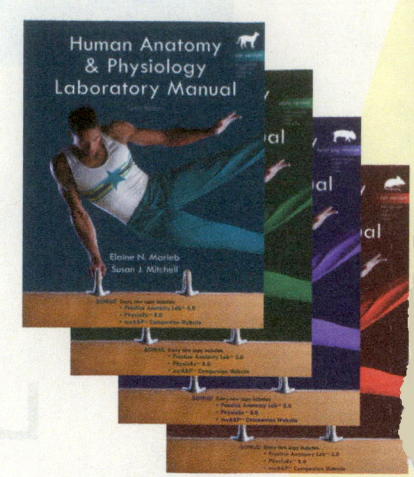

New! Pre-lab Quizzes

Brand-new pre-lab quizzes motivate your students to prepare for lab by asking them basic information they should know before doing the lab. *For example, see page 145.*

New! Electronic Test Bank of Pre-lab and Post-lab Quizzes

This brand-new electronic Test Bank of pre-lab and post-lab quizzes, different from those found in the lab manual and on myA&P, allows you to assign these quizzes for homework or extra-credit. The quizzes can be downloaded from the Instructor Resources section of the myA&P website and imported into WebCT, BlackBoard, CourseCompass, and other course management systems.

Practice Anatomy Lab 2.0 and IRDVD with Test Bank

These tools give you and your students access to lab specimens and assessments 24/7. *See next page.*

Other Key Improvements

Expanded Histology

New and improved histology images have been added. Images from the Histology Atlas have been integrated into the lab exercises so that students can review relevant histology images within the context of the exercise.

See page vi for a complete listing of histology figures.

All-new Art Program

Brand-new art program uses three-dimensional, realistic styles with dramatic views and perspectives and rich, vibrant colors. The art includes key anatomy figures that are rendered with detail, depth, and a clear focus on key anatomical structures. Also included are new cadaver photos and all new surface anatomy photos showing superb muscle definition and clear surface landmarks for skeletal, muscular, and vascular structures.

BONUS!

CUSTOMIZATION OPTION

You can now customize this lab manual any way you want to meet your needs. For more information, go to **www.pearsoncustom/integrate.**

FOR STUDENTS

Practice Anatomy Lab 2.0

Everything you need to prepare for your lab practicals

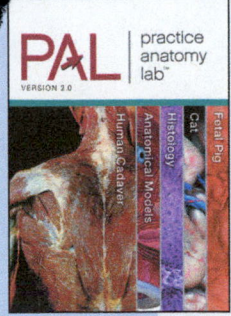

Practice Anatomy Lab (PAL) 2.0 is an indispensable virtual anatomy study and practice tool that gives you 24/7 access to the most widely used lab specimens including **human cadaver, anatomical models, histology, cat, and fetal pig.**

PAL 2.0 features:

- **Hundreds of images** and interactive tools for reviewing and learning the names of anatomical structures

- **Built-in audio pronunciation** of anatomical terms

- Rich variety of **multiple choice quizzes and fill-in-the-blank lab practical exams**

- **3D Anatomy Animations** of Origins, Insertions, Actions, and Innervations of over 65 muscles in the Human Cadaver module

- **Fully rotatable human skull** and 17 other rotatable skeletal structures

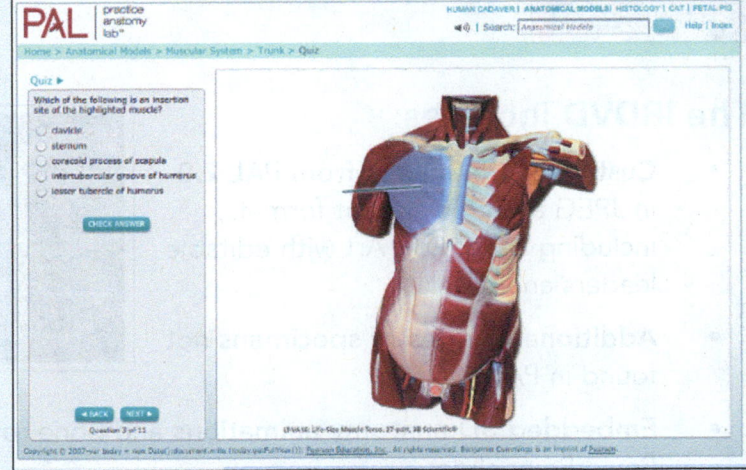

PAL 2.0 is available on this book's companion website at www.myaandp.com.

FOR INSTRUCTORS

Instructor Resource DVD with Updated Test Bank for PAL 2.0

Everything you need to customize PAL 2.0 for lecture, pre-lab assignments, or testing

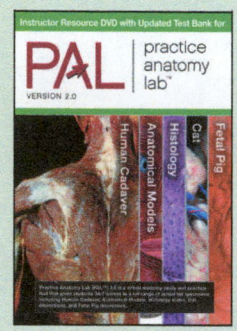

This DVD includes everything you need to present and assign PAL 2.0 in your lecture and lab. Whether it's used for lecture presentation, pre-lab assignments, or testing, this invaluable resource makes it easy for you to use PAL 2.0 to fit <u>your</u> course.

The IRDVD includes:

- **Customizable images from PAL 2.0** in JPEG and PowerPoint formats, including Label-Edit Art with editable leaders and labels

- **Additional images of specimens** not found in PAL 2.0

- **Embedded 3D anatomy animations** and bone rotations in relevant PowerPoint slides

- **Active Lecture Questions** (for use with or without clickers)

- **Index of anatomical structures** covered in PAL 2.0

- **Updated Test Bank** allows you to modify multiple choice quiz questions and fill-in-the-blank lab practical questions to reflect the content you want your students to be quizzed and tested on. Test Bank includes more than 3,400 questions. Avalible in PDF and TestGen format. Test item files can be imported into **WebCT, Blackboard,** and **CourseCompass**

PhysioEx™ 8.0 sets the standard in lab simulation

PhysioEx 8.0 laboratory simulations

This easy-to-use software consists of 11 modules containing 79 physiology lab simulations that may be used to supplement or substitute for wet labs. **PhysioEx 8.0** allows students to repeat labs as often as they like, perform experiments without harming live animals, and conduct experiments that may be difficult to perform in a wet lab environment due to time, cost, or safety concerns.

The seven PhysioEx 8.0 videos show students how to relate their PhysioEx simulation to a real wet lab experience and demonstrate the following experiments: Skeletal Muscle, Blood Typing, Cardiovascular Physiology, Water-Filled Spirometry, Nerve Impulses, BMR Measurement, and Cell Transport.

Additional illustrations relate the

onscreen lab equipment to the corresponding human body structures in certain labs to help students understand the relationship.

Editor-in-Chief: Serina Beauparlant
Project Editor: Sabrina Larson
Development Manager: Barbara Yien
Art Development Manager: Laura Southworth
Assistant Editor: Nicole Graziano
Editorial Assistant: John Maas
Managing Editor: Deborah Cogan
Production Manager: Michele Mangelli
Production Supervisor: Janet Vail
Art Editor: Karen Gulliver
Art and Photo Coordinator: Jean Lake
Photo Researcher: Kristin Piljay
Interior and Cover Designer: Riezebos Holzbaur Design Group
Copyeditor: Antonio Padial
Compositor: S4Carlisle Publishing Services
Media Producer: Erik Fortier
PhysioEx Developer: Cadre Design
Senior Manufacturing Buyer: Stacey Weinberger
Marketing Manager: Derek Perrigo

Cover photograph credit: Masterfile

Credits and acknowledgments borrowed from other sources
and reproduced, with permission, in this textbook appear on
the appropriate page within the text or on p. BM-2.

Benjamin Cummings gratefully acknowledges Carolina
Biological Supply for the use of numerous histology images
found on the PhysioEx™ CD-ROM.

The Benjamin Cummings Series in Human Anatomy & Physiology

By R.A. Chase
The Bassett Atlas of Human Anatomy (1989)

By Kapit/Elson
The Anatomy Coloring Book, Third Edition (2002)

By Kapit/Macey/Meisami
The Physiology Coloring Book, Second Edition (2000)

By E.N. Marieb and S.J. Mitchell
*Human Anatomy & Physiology Laboratory Manual,
Main Version,* Ninth Edition (2011)

*Human Anatomy & Physiology Laboratory Manual,
Cat Version,* Tenth Edition (2011)

*Human Anatomy & Physiology Laboratory Manual,
Fetal Pig Version,* Tenth Edition (2011)

*Human Anatomy & Physiology Laboratory Manual,
Rat Version* (2011)

*Human Anatomy Laboratory Manual with Cat
Dissections,* Sixth Edition (2011)

By E.N. Marieb
*The A&P Coloring Workbook: A Complete Study
Guide,* Ninth Edition (2009)

Laboratory Manual for Anatomy & Physiology,
Fourth Edition (2011)

By Lafferty/Panella
A.D.A.M.® Interactive Anatomy Student Package,
Third Edition, with Windows DVD or with Windows
CD-ROM (2006)

A.D.A.M.® Interactive Anatomy Student Lab Guide,
Third Edition (2006)

The Authors and Publisher believe that the lab experiments
described in this publication, when conducted in conformity with the
safety precautions described herein and according to the school's
laboratory safety procedures, are reasonably safe for the student to
whom this manual is directed. Nonetheless, many of the described
experiments are accompanied by some degree of risk, including
human error, the failure or misuses of laboratory or electrical
equipment, mismeasurement, chemical spills, and exposure to sharp
objects, heat, bodily fluids, blood, or other biologics. The Authors
and Publisher disclaim any liability arising from such risks in
connection with any of the experiments contained in this manual. If
students have any questions or problems with materials, procedures,
or instructions on any experiment, they should always ask their
instructor for help before proceeding.

Benjamin Cummings
is an imprint of

ISBN 10: 0-321-76561-3
ISBN 13: 978-0-321-76561-1

Contents

THE ENDOCRINE SYSTEM

THE CIRCULATORY SYSTEM

THE RESPIRATORY SYSTEM

THE DIGESTIVE SYSTEM

THE URINARY SYSTEM

THE REPRODUCTIVE SYSTEM, DEVELOPMENT, AND HEREDITY

SURFACE ANATOMY

DISSECTION EXERCISES

HISTOLOGY FIGURES

Preface to the Instructor

The philosophy behind this manual mirrors that of its companion versions. It reflects a still-developing sensibility for the way teachers teach and students learn, engendered by years of teaching the subject and by listening to the suggestions of other instructors as well as those of students enrolled in multifaceted health-care programs. *Human Anatomy & Physiology Laboratory Manual, Rat Version* was developed to facilitate and enrich the laboratory experience for both teachers and students.

This manual, intended for students in introductory human anatomy and physiology courses, presents a wide range of laboratory experiences for students concentrating in nursing, physical therapy, dental hygiene, pharmacology, respiratory therapy, and health and physical education, as well as biology and premedical programs. It differs from *Human Anatomy & Physiology Laboratory Manual, Main Version* (Ninth Edition, 2011) in that it contains detailed guidelines for dissecting a laboratory animal. The manual's coverage is intentionally broad, allowing it to serve both one- and two-semester courses.

BASIC APPROACH AND FEATURES

The generous variety of experiments in this manual provides flexibility that enables instructors to gear their laboratory approach to specific academic programs, or to their own teaching preferences. The manual is still independent of any textbook, so it contains the background discussions and terminology necessary to perform all experiments. Such a self-contained learning aid eliminates the need for students to bring a textbook into the laboratory.

Each of the 46 exercises leads students toward a coherent understanding of the structure and function of the human body. The manual begins with anatomical terminology and an orientation to the body, which together provide the necessary tools for studying the various body systems. The exercises that follow reflect the dual focus of the manual—both anatomical and physiological aspects receive considerable attention. As the various organ systems of the body are introduced, the initial exercises focus on organization, from the cellular to the organ system level. As indicated by the table of contents, the anatomical exercises are usually followed by physiological experiments that familiarize students with various aspects of body functioning and promote the critical understanding that function follows structure. Homeostasis is continually emphasized as a requirement for optimal health. Pathological conditions are viewed as a loss of homeostasis; these discussions can be recognized by the homeostatic imbalance logo within the descriptive material of each exercise. This holistic approach encourages an integrated understanding of the human body.

Features

- The numerous physiological experiments for each organ system range from simple experiments that can be performed without specialized tools to more complex experiments using laboratory equipment, computers, and instrumentation techniques.

- The laboratory Review Sheets following each exercise are designed to accompany that lab exercise. The Review Sheets provide space for recording and interpreting experimental results and require students to label diagrams and answer multiple-choice and short-answer questions.

- In addition to the figures, isolated animal organs such as the sheep heart and pig kidney are employed because of their exceptional similarity to human organs.

- All exercises involving body fluids (blood, urine, saliva) incorporate current Centers for Disease Control and Prevention (CDC) guidelines for handling human body fluids. Because it is important that nursing students, in particular, learn how to safely handle bloodstained articles, the human focus has been retained. However, the decision to allow testing of human (student) blood or to use animal blood in the laboratory is left to the discretion of the instructor in accordance with institutional guidelines. The CDC guidelines for handling body fluids are reinforced by the laboratory safety procedures described on the inside front cover of this text, in Exercise 29A: Blood, and in the *Instructor Guide*. You can photocopy the inside front cover and post it in the lab to help students become well versed in laboratory safety.

- Six logos alert students to special features or instructions. These include:

The dissection scissors icon appears at the beginning of activities that entail the dissection of isolated animal organs.

The homeostatic imbalance icon directs the student's attention to conditions representing a loss of homeostasis.

A safety icon notifies students that specific safety precautions must be observed when using certain equipment or conducting particular lab procedures. (For example, when working with ether, a hood is to be used, or when handling body fluids such as blood, urine, or saliva, gloves are to be worn.)

BIOPAC The BIOPAC icon in the materials list for an exercise clearly identifies use of the BIOPAC Student Lab System and alerts you to the equipment needed. BIOPAC is used in Exercises 16A, 20, 21, 22, 31, 33A, 34A, and 37A. The instructions in the lab manual are for use with the BIOPAC MP36 (or MP35/30) data acquisition unit. New versions of the BSL software (3.7.5 and higher for Windows, 3.7.4 and higher for Mac OS X) require different channel settings and collection strategies. Instructions for their use can be found in the Instructor Resources at myA&P. There you can also find instructions for the use of the new 2-channel data acquisition unit, the MP45.

PEx The PhysioEx icon at the end of the materials list for an exercise directs students to the corresponding PhysioEx computer simulation exercise found in the back of the lab manual.

• Other data aquisition instructions are available on myA&P, including:

PowerLab Instructions

For Exercises 16A, 22, 31, 33A, 34A, and 37A, instructors using PowerLab equipment may print these exercises for student handouts.

iWorx Instructions

For Exercises 16A, 20, 22, 31, 33A, 34A, and 37A, instructors using iWorx equipment in their laboratory may print these exercises for student handouts.

Intelitool Instructions

Four physiological experiments (Exercises 16i, 22i, 31i, and 37i) using Intelitool® equipment are available. Instructors using Intelitool equipment in their laboratory may print these exercises for student handouts.

WHAT'S NEW

In this revision, we have continued to try to respond to reviewers' and users' feedback concerning trends that are having an impact on the anatomy and physiology laboratory experience, most importantly:

• The growing demand for student-based experimentation

• The increased use of computers in the laboratory and in students' homes, and hence the continuing desire for more computer simulation and practice exercises

• The replacement of older recording equipment with computerized data acquisition and analysis systems

• The continued importance of visual learning for today's student

• The need to reinforce writing, computation, and critical thinking skills across the curriculum

The specific changes implemented to address these trends are described next.

Pre-lab Quizzes

Brand new pre-lab quizzes at the beginning of each Exercise motivate your students to prepare for lab by asking them basic information they should know before doing the lab. These quizzes are different than those found on myA&P and those in the Instuctor Test Bank.

All-new Art Program

This brand-new art program uses three-dimensional, realistic styles with dramatic views and perspectives, and rich, vibrant colors. The art includes key anatomy figures that are rendered with detail, depth, and a clear focus on key anatomical structures. Ten new and improved histology images have been added. Images from the Histology Atlas have been integrated into the lab exercises so that students can review relevant histology images all in one place. See page vi for a complete listing of histology figures.

Also included are five new cadaver photos and all new surface anatomy photos showing superb muscle definition and clear surface landmarks for skeletal, muscular, and vascular structures.

New! Electronic Test Bank of Pre-lab and Post-lab Quizzes

See "Supplements for the Instructor" on page xi.

Customization Options

With Integrate, our custom laboratory publishing program for anatomy and physiology, you have the freedom to choose labs from our library of highly regarded Pearson Benjamin Cummings lab manuals and other collections to build the right manual for your course. You'll find excellent, class-tested labs—many printed in full color—for one- and two-semester anatomy and physiology laboratories, and one-semester human anatomy or physiology courses. Use our online Book-Build system to select just the labs you need, in the sequence you want—your students pay only for the labs you choose. You can also add your own original labs. With Integrate, you're in control. For more information, visit our Integrate website at www.pearsoncustom/integrate, or contact your Pearson sales representative for details.

SUPPLEMENTS FOR THE STUDENT

Practice Anatomy Lab 2.0

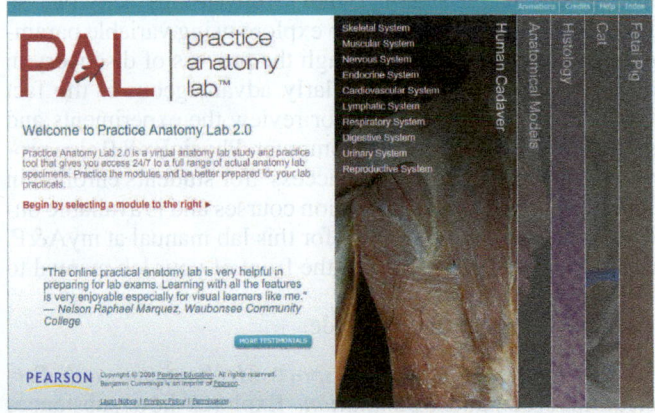

Practice Anatomy Lab (PAL) 2.0 is an indispensable virtual anatomy study and practice tool that gives students 24/7 access to the most widely used lab specimens including **human cadaver, anatomical models, histology, cat, and fetal pig.**

PAL 2.0 features:

• **Hundreds of images** and interactive tools for reviewing and learning the names of anatomical structures

• **Built-in audio pronunciation** of anatomical terms

• Rich variety of **multiple choice quizzes** and **fill-in-the-blank lab practical exams**

- **3D anatomy animations** of origins, insertions, actions, and innervations of over 65 muscles in the Human Cadaver module
- **Fully rotatable human skull** and 17 other rotatable skeletal structures

The Instructor's Resource DVD for PAL 2.0 includes labeled and unlabeled images from PAL 2.0 in both JPEG and PowerPoint® formats. The PowerPoint Label Edit feature, with editable labels and leader lines, is built into every image. PowerPoint image slides include embedded links to the relevant 3D animations of origins, insertions, actions, and innervations.

PAL 2.0 is available on the myA&P Lab Manual Website at www.myaandp.com. The PAL 2.0 CD-ROM can also be packaged with Marieb's lab manual at no additional charge.

PhysioEx 8.0 CD-ROM

The PhysioEx CD-ROM, packaged with every lab manual, consists of 11 modules containing 79 physiology lab simulations that may be used to supplement or substitute for wet labs. PhysioEx 8.0 allows you to repeat labs as often as you like, perform simulated animal experiments and conduct simulated wet lab experiments either in or out of the laboratory.

PhysioEx 8.0 also includes videos of laboratory experiments that demonstrate the actual experiments simulated on the screen, making it easier for students to understand and visualize the laboratory context of the simulations. The seven videos demonstrate the following experiments: Skeletal Muscle, Blood Typing, Cardiovascular Physiology, Use of a Water-Filled Spirometer, Nerve Impulses, BMR Measurement, and Cell Transport.

Unlike the typical tutorial-based computer supplements that usually target anatomy, the 79 physiology activities on PhysioEx 8.0 allow students to explore using variable parameters while being guided through the process of discovery in a laboratory exercise. Particularly advantageous is the fact that the students can conduct or review the experiments and slides at home on a personal computer. PhysioEx 8.0 also provides convenient "laboratory access" for students enrolled in Internet-based distance education courses and is available online at the companion website for this lab manual at myA&P. (Use the access code found at the front of your lab manual to log onto the site.)

PhysioEx 8.0 topics include:

- Exercise 5B, *Cell Transport Mechanisms and Permeability: Computer Simulation.* Explores how substances cross the cell's membrane. Simple and facilitated diffusion, osmosis, filtration, and active transport are covered.
- Exercise 6B, *Histology Atlas and Review Supplement.* Includes over 200 histology images, viewable at various magnifications, with accompanying descriptions and labels.

- Exercise 16B, *Skeletal Muscle Physiology: Computer Simulation.* Provides insights into the complex physiology of skeletal muscle. Electrical stimulation, isometric contractions, and isotonic contractions are investigated.
- Exercise 18B, *Neurophysiology of Nerve Impulses: Computer Simulation.* Investigates stimuli that elicit action potentials, stimuli that inhibit action potentials, and factors affecting nerve conduction velocity.
- Exercise 28B, *Endocrine System Physiology: Computer Simulation.* Investigates the relationship between hormones and metabolism; the effect of estrogen replacement therapy; the diagnosis of diabetes; and the relationship between the levels of cortisol and adrenocorticotropic hormone and a variety of endocrine disorders.
- Exercise 29B, *Blood Analysis: Computer Simulation.* Covers hematocrit determination, erythrocyte sedimentation rate determination, hemoglobin determination, blood typing, and total cholesterol determination.
- Exercise 33B, *Cardiovascular Dynamics: Computer Simulation.* Allows students to perform experiments that would be difficult if not impossible to do in a traditional laboratory. Topics of inquiry include vessel resistance and pump (heart) mechanics.
- Exercise 34B, *Frog Cardiovascular Physiology: Computer Simulation.* Variables influencing heart activity are examined. Topics include setting up and recording baseline heart activity, the refractory period of cardiac muscle, and an investigation of factors that affect heart rate and contractility.
- Exercise 35B, *Serological Testing: Computer Simulation* **(available online only at myA&P).** Investigates antigen-antibody reactions and their role in clinical tests used to diagnose a disease or an infection.
- Exercise 37B, *Respiratory System Mechanics: Computer Simulation.* Investigates physical and chemical aspects of pulmonary function. Students collect data simulating normal lung volumes. Other activities examine factors such as airway resistance and the effect of surfactant on lung function.
- Exercise 39B, *Chemical and Physical Processes of Digestion: Computer Simulation.* Turns the student's computer into a virtual chemistry lab where enzymes, reagents, and incubation conditions can be manipulated (in compressed time) to examine factors that affect enzyme activity.
- Exercise 41B, *Renal System Physiology: Computer Simulation.* Simulates the function of a single nephron. Topics include factors influencing glomerular filtration, the effect of hormones on urine function, and glucose transport maximum.
- Exercise 47, *Acid-Base Balance: Computer Simulation.* Topics include respiratory and metabolic acidosis/alkalosis, and renal and respiratory compensation.

myA&P

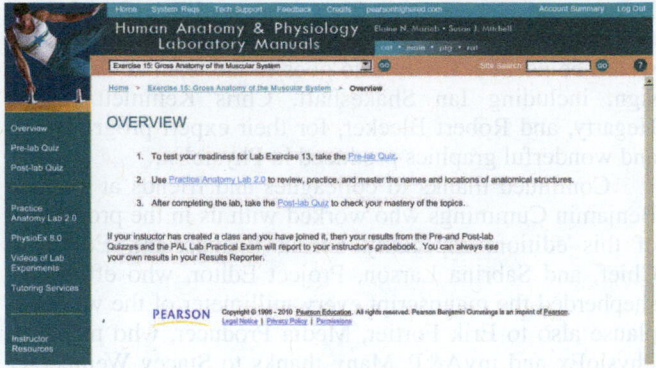

From the home page of myA&P (www.myaandp.com), you and your students can access the companion website for the Human Anatomy & Physiology Laboratory Manuals, which features the following resources and activities:

- **Access to Practice Anatomy Lab 2.0**
- **Gradable pre- and post-lab quizzes** for each of the 46 lab exercises in the lab manual. These quizzes are different than those found in the lab manual.
- **PhysioEx 8.0**

Instructor tools:

- **Gradebook** allows pre- and post-lab quizzes and PAL Lab Practical Exams to be reported to the instructor's online gradebook.
- **Instructor Resources** include the Instructor Guide, procedures for using **PowerLab®**, **iWorx®**, and **Intelitool®** equipment with certain lab exercises, and more.

A 12-month subscription to this powerful website is included with each new copy of the lab manual. Access directions, along with access codes, are included at the front of the book.

Also Available

A Brief Atlas of the Human Body, Second Edition (0-321-66261-X)

This full-color atlas includes 107 bone and 47 soft-tissue photographs with easy-to-read labels. This edition of the atlas contains a brand-new, comprehensive histology photomicrograph section with more than 50 slides of basic tissue and organ systems. Featuring photos taken by renowned biomedical photographer Ralph Hutchings, this high-quality photographic atlas makes an excellent resource for the classroom and laboratory. Available for purchase from Pearson Education.

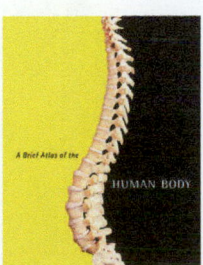

SUPPLEMENTS FOR THE INSTRUCTOR

New! Electronic Test Bank of Pre-lab and Post-lab Quizzes

This brand-new electronic Test Bank of pre-lab and post-lab quizzes, different than those found in the lab manual and on myA&P, allows you to assign these quizzes for homework or extra credit. These quizzes can be downloaded from the Instructor Resources section of my A&P and imported into **WebCT, BlackBoard, CourseCompass,** and other course-management systems.

New! PAL 2.0 IRDVD with Updated Test Bank

This DVD includes everything you need to present and assign PAL 2.0 in your lecture and lab. Whether it's used for lecture presentation, pre-lab assignments, or testing, this invaluable resource makes it easy for you to use PAL 2.0 to fit *your* course.

The IRDVD with Updated Test Bank for PAL 2.0 includes:

- Additional images of specimens not found in PAL 2.0
- Embedded 3D anatomy animations and bone rotations in relevant PowerPoint slides
- Active Lecture Questions (for use with or without clickers)
- Index of anatomical structures covered in PAL 2.0
- Updated Test Bank allows you to modify multiple-choice quiz questions and fill-in-the-blank lab practical questions to reflect the content you want your students to be quizzed and tested on. Test Bank includes more than 3400 questions. Available in PDF and TestGen format. Test item files can be imported into **WebCT, Blackboard,** and **CourseCompass.**

myA&P Instructor Resources

Instructor Resources include the Instructor Guide, procedures for using **PowerLab®, iWorx®,** and **Intelitool®** equipment with certain lab exercises, and instructions for BIOPAC exercises using the newest software (3.7.5 for Windows and 3.7.4 for Mac) and data acquisition unit (MP45).

Instructor Guide (0-321-64415-8)

This guide accompanies all versions of the *Human Anatomy & Physiology Laboratory Manual* and contains a wealth of information for those teaching this course, including answers to the new pre-lab quizzes. Instructors can find help in planning the experiments, ordering equipment and supplies, anticipating pitfalls and problem areas, and locating audiovisual material. The probable in-class time required for each lab is indicated by an hourglass icon. Another useful resource is the Trends in Instrumentation section, which describes the latest laboratory equipment and technological teaching tools available.

Human Anatomy & Physiology Videotapes

These tapes are available free of charge to qualified adopters. Produced by University Media Services and scripted by Rose Leigh Vines, Rosalee Carter, and Ann Motekaitis of California State University, Sacramento, these excellent videotapes reinforce many of the concepts covered in this manual and represent a valuable addition to any multimedia library.

Student Video Series Vol. I (0-8053-4110-2)

Student Video Series Vol. II (0-8053-6115-4)

ACKNOWLEDGMENTS

We wish to thank the following reviewers for their contributions to this edition: C. Thomas G. Appleton, University of Western Ontario; Richard Connett, Monroe Community College; Smruti Desai, Lone Star College CyFair; Jose Fierro, Florida State College at Jacksonville; Katelijne Flies, Central New Mexico Community College; Lynn Gargan, Tarrant County College Northeast; Lori Garrett, Parkland College; Fran Hardin, Ivy Tech Community College—Kokomo; DJ Hennager, Kirkwood Community College; William Hoover, Bunker Hill Community College; Sandra Hsu, Skyline College; William Huber, St. Louis Community College; Jesse Lang, Holyoke Community College; Stephen Lebsack, Linn Benton Community College; Linda Mackie, St. Johns River Community College; Cherie McKeever, Montana State University—Great Falls, College of Technology; Judy Megaw, Indian River Community College; Ellen Ott-Reeves, Blinn Community College; Steve Perry, Liberty University; Jean Revie, South Mountain Community College; Laura Ritt, Burlington Community College; Josephine Rogers, University of Cincinnati; Dale Smoak, Piedmont Technical College; Pam Strong, Quincy College; Diane Teter, South Texas College; Harriett Tresham, Kennesaw Community College; Maureen Tubbiola, St. Cloud State; Wendy Waters, Wharton Junior College.

We would like to extend a special thank you to the following authors of our outstanding companion website and Practice Anatomy Lab 2.0: Ruth Heisler, University of Colorado; Nora Hebert, Red Rocks Community College; Yvonne Baptiste-Szymanski, Niagara County Community College; Deanna Denault, New Hampshire Community Technical College—Claremont; Steve Downing, University of Minnesota Medical School—Duluth; Marjorie Johnson, University of Western Ontario; Leif Saul, University of Colorado; Charles J. Venglarik, Jefferson State Community College; and Nina Zanetti, Siena College.

Special thanks to Josephine Rogers of the University of Cincinnati for authoring the brand new pre-lab quizzes featured in this edition of the lab manual.

The excellence of PhysioEx reflects the expertise of Peter Zao, Timothy Stabler, Lori Smith, Greta Peterson, Andrew Lokuta, and Nina Zanetti. They generated the ideas behind the equipment graphics and envisioned the animations that would be needed. Credit also goes to the team at Cadre Design, including Ian Shakeshaft, Chris Kemmett, David Hegarty, and Robert Bleeker, for their expert programming and wonderful graphics produced in PhysioEx.

Continued thanks to colleagues and friends at Pearson Benjamin Cummings who worked with us in the production of this edition, especially Serina Beauparlant, Editor-in-Chief, and Sabrina Larson, Project Editor, who efficiently shepherded the manuscript every millimeter of the way. Applause also to Erik Fortier, Media Producer, who managed PhysioEx and myA&P. Many thanks to Stacey Weinberger for her manufacturing expertise. Finally, our Marketing Manager, Derek Perrigo, has efficiently kept us in touch with the pulse of the market place.

Kudos also to Michele Mangelli and her production team, who did their usual great job. Janet Vail, production editor for this project, got the job done in jig time. Laura Southworth, Art Development Manager, and Karen Gulliver, Art Editor, were in charge of overseeing the entire art program. Jean Lake acted as art and photo coordinator, and Kristin Piljay conducted photo research. Our fabulous interior and cover designs were created by Yvo Riezebos. Antonio Padial brought his experience to copyediting the text.

We are grateful to the team at BIOPAC, especially to Jocelyn Kremer, who was extremely helpful in making sure we had the latest updates and answering all of our questions.

Last but not least, thank you to Robert Sullivan of Marist College for authoring the rat dissection exercises found in this brand-new Rat Version of the lab manual.

Elaine N. Marieb

Susan J. Mitchell

Elaine N. Marieb and
Susan J. Mitchell
Anatomy and Physiology
Pearson Benjamin Cummings
1301 Sansome Street
San Francisco, CA 94111

Preface to the Student

We hope you will enjoy your laboratory experiences. As with any unfamiliar experience, it really helps if you know in advance what to expect and what will be expected of you.

LABORATORY ACTIVITIES

The A&P laboratory exercises in this manual are designed to help you gain a broad understanding of both anatomy and physiology. You can anticipate examining models, dissecting a specimen, and using a microscope to look at tissue slides (anatomical approaches). You will also investigate chemical interactions in both living and nonliving systems, manipulate variables in computer simulations, and conduct experiments that examine responses of living organisms to various stimuli (physiological approaches).

Preserved organ specimens used in the anatomy and physiology labs are *not* harvested from animals raised specifically for dissection purposes. Organs that are of no use to the meat packing industry (such as the brain, heart, or lungs) are sent from slaughterhouses to biological supply houses for preparation.

Included with this edition is a companion website designed to help you practice for lab practical exams outside of class. Also included with the manual is the PhysioEx CD-ROM, with 11 simulation exercises that allow you to convert a computer into a virtual laboratory. You will be able to manipulate variables to investigate physiological phenomena.

There is little doubt that computer simulations offer many advantages, however an animated frog muscle or heart on a computer screen is not really a substitute for observing the responses of actual muscle tissue. Consequently, living animal experiments remain an important part of the approach of this manual to the study of human anatomy and physiology. However, we use the minimum number of animals needed.

If you use living animals for experiments, you are required to handle them humanely. Inconsiderate treatment of laboratory animals will not be tolerated in your anatomy and physiology laboratory.

ICONS/VISUAL MNEMONICS

We have tried to make this manual easy for you to use by employing different icons (visual mnemonics) throughout:

The *Dissection* head is orange and is accompanied by the **dissection scissors icon** at the beginning of activities that require you to dissect isolated animal organs.

The **homeostatic imbalance icon** directs your attention to conditions representing a disruption of homeostasis.

The **safety icon** alerts you to special precautions that you should take when handling lab equipment or conducting certain procedures. For example, it alerts you to use a ventilating hood when using volatile chemicals and signifies that you should take special measures to protect yourself when handling blood or other body fluids (e.g., saliva, urine).

BIOPAC The **BIOPAC icon** in the materials list for an exercise clearly identifies use of the BIOPAC Student Lab System. BIOPAC is used in Exercises 16A, 20, 21, 22, 31, 33A, 34A, and 37A.

PEx The **PhysioEx icon** at the end of the materials list for an exercise directs you to the corresponding PhysioEx computer simulation exercise found in the back of the lab manual.

HINTS FOR SUCCESS IN THE LABORATORY

Most students can use helpful hints and guidelines to ensure that they have successful lab experiences.

1. Perhaps the best bit of advice is to attend all your scheduled labs and to participate in all the assigned exercises. Learning is an *active* process.

2. Scan the scheduled lab exercise and the questions in the Review Sheet following it *before* going to lab, then complete the pre-lab quiz.

3. Be on time. Most instructors explain what the lab is about, pitfalls to avoid, and the sequence or format to be followed at the beginning of the lab session. If you are late, not only will you miss this information, you also will not endear yourself to the instructor.

4. Follow the instructions in the order in which they are given. If you do not understand a direction, ask for help.

5. Review your lab notes after completing the lab session to help you focus on and remember the important concepts.

6. Keep your work area clean and neat. Move books and coats out of the way. This reduces confusion and accidents.

7. Assume that all lab chemicals and equipment are sources of potential danger to you. Follow directions for equipment use and observe the laboratory safety guidelines provided inside the front cover of this manual.

8. Keep in mind the real value of the laboratory experience—a place for you to observe, manipulate, and experience hands-on activities that will dramatically enhance your understanding of the lecture presentations.

We hope that this lab manual makes learning about intricate structures and functions of the human body a fun and rewarding process. We are always open to constructive criticism and suggestions for improvement in future editions. If you have any, please write to us.

Elaine N. Marieb and
Susan J. Mitchell
Anatomy and Physiology
Pearson Benjamin Cummings
1301 Sansome Street
San Francisco, CA 94111

Getting Started—What to Expect, The Scientific Method, and Metrics

Two hundred years ago science was largely a plaything of wealthy patrons, but today's world is dominated by science and its technology. Whether or not we believe that such domination is desirable, we all have a responsibility to try to understand the goals and methods of science that have seeded this knowledge and technological explosion.

The biosciences are very special and exciting because they open the doors to an understanding of all the wondrous workings of living things. A course in human anatomy and physiology (a minute subdivision of bioscience) provides such insights in relation to your own body. Although some experience in scientific studies is helpful when beginning a study of anatomy and physiology, perhaps the single most important prerequisite is curiosity.

Gaining an understanding of science is a little like becoming acquainted with another person. Even though a written description can provide a good deal of information about the person, you can never really know another unless there is personal contact. And so it is with science—if you are to know it well, you must deal with it intimately.

The laboratory is the setting for "intimate contact" with science. It is where scientists test their ideas (do research), the essential purpose of which is to provide a basis from which predictions about scientific phenomena can be made. Likewise, it will be the site of your "intimate contact" with the subject of human anatomy and physiology as you are introduced to the methods and instruments used in biological research.

For many students, human anatomy and physiology is taken as an introductory-level course; and their scientific background exists, at best, as a dim memory. If this is your predicament, this prologue may be just what you need to fill in a few gaps and to get you started on the right track before your actual laboratory experiences begin. So—let's get to it!

THE SCIENTIFIC METHOD

Science would quickly stagnate if new knowledge were not continually derived from and added to it. The approach commonly used by scientists when they investigate various aspects of their respective disciplines is called the **scientific method.** This method is *not* a single rigorous technique that must be followed in a lockstep manner. It is nothing more or less than a logical, practical, and reliable way of approaching and solving problems of every kind—scientific or otherwise—to gain knowledge. It comprises five major steps.

Step 1: Observation of Phenomena

The crucial first step involves observation of some phenomenon of interest. In other words, before a scientist can investigate anything, he or she must decide on a *problem* or focus for the investigation. In most college laboratory experiments, the problem or focus has been decided for you. However, to illustrate this important step, we will assume that you want to investigate the true nature of apples, particularly green apples. In such a case you would begin your studies by making a number of different observations concerning apples.

Step 2: Statement of the Hypothesis

Once you have decided on a focus of concern, the next step is to design a significant question to be answered. Such a question is usually posed in the form of a **hypothesis,** an unproven conclusion that attempts to explain some phenomenon. (At its crudest level, a hypothesis can be considered to be a "guess" or an intuitive hunch that tentatively explains some observation.) Generally, scientists do not restrict themselves to a single hypothesis; instead, they usually pose several and then test each one systematically.

We will assume that, to accomplish step 1, you go to the supermarket and randomly select apples from several bins. When you later eat the apples, you find that the green apples are sour, but the red and yellow apples are sweet. From this observation, you might conclude *(hypothesize)* that "green apples are sour." This statement would represent your current understanding of green apples. You might also reasonably predict that if you were to buy more apples, any green ones you buy will be sour. Thus, you would have gone beyond your initial observation that "these" green apples are sour to the prediction that "all" green apples are sour.

Any good hypothesis must meet several criteria. First, *it must be testable*. This characteristic is far more important than its being correct. The test data may or may not support the hypothesis, or new information may require that the hypothesis be modified. Clearly the accuracy of a prediction in any scientific study depends on the accuracy of the initial information on which it is based.

In our example, no great harm will come from an inaccurate prediction—that is, were we to find that some green apples are sweet. However, in some cases human life may depend on the accuracy of the prediction; thus: (1) Repeated testing of scientific ideas is important, particularly because scientists working on the same problem do not always agree in their conclusions. (2) Careful observation is essential, even at the very outset of a study, because conclusions drawn from scientific tests are only as accurate as the information on which they are based.

A second criterion is that, even though hypotheses are guesses of a sort, *they must be based on measurable, describable facts. No mysticism can be theorized.* We cannot conjure up, to support our hypothesis, forces that have not been shown to exist. For example, as scientists, we cannot say that the tooth fairy took Johnny's tooth unless we can prove that the tooth fairy exists!

Third, a hypothesis *must not be anthropomorphic*. Human beings tend to anthropomorphize—that is, to relate all experiences to human experience. Whereas we could state that bears instinctively protect their young, it would be anthropomorphic to say that bears love their young, because love is a human emotional response. Thus, the initial hypothesis must be stated without interpretation.

Step 3: Data Collection

Once the initial hypothesis has been stated, scientists plan experiments that will provide data (or evidence) to support or disprove their hypotheses—that is, they *test* their hypotheses. Data are accumulated by making qualitative or quantitative observations of some sort. The observations are often aided by the use of various types of equipment such as cameras, microscopes, stimulators, or various electronic devices that allow chemical and physiological measurements to be taken.

Observations referred to as **qualitative** are those we can make with our senses—that is, by using our vision, hearing, or sense of taste, smell, or touch. For some quick practice in qualitative observation, compare and contrast* an orange and an apple.

Whereas the differences between an apple and an orange are obvious, this is not always the case in biological observations. Quite often a scientist tries to detect very subtle differences that cannot be determined by qualitative observations; data must be derived from measurements. Such observations based on precise measurements of one type or another are **quantitative observations**. Examples of quantitative observations include careful measurements of body or organ dimensions such as mass, size, and volume; measurement of volumes of oxygen consumed during metabolic studies; determination of the concentration of glucose in urine; and determination of the differences in blood pressure and pulse under conditions of rest and exercise. An apple and an orange could be compared quantitatively by analyzing the relative amounts of sugar and water in a given volume of fruit flesh, the pigments and vitamins present in the apple skin and orange peel, and so on.

A valuable part of data gathering is the use of experiments to support or disprove a hypothesis. An **experiment** is a procedure designed to describe the factors in a given situation that affect one another (that is, to discover cause and effect) under certain conditions.

Two general rules govern experimentation. The first of these rules is that the experiment(s) should be conducted in such a manner that every **variable** (any factor that might affect the outcome of the experiment) is under the control of the experimenter. The **independent variables** are manipulated by the experimenter. For example, if the goal is to determine the effect of body temperature on breathing rate, the independent variable is body temperature. The effect observed or value measured (in this case breathing rate) is called the **dependent** or **response variable**. Its value "depends" on the value chosen for the independent variable. The ideal way to perform such an experiment is to set up and run a series of tests that are all identical, except for one specific factor that is varied.

One specimen (or group of specimens) is used as the **control** against which all other experimental samples are compared. The importance of the control sample cannot be overemphasized. The control group provides the "normal standard" against which all other samples are compared relative to the dependent variable. Taking our example one step further, if we wanted to investigate the effects of body temperature (the independent variable) on breathing rate (the dependent variable), we could collect data on the breathing rate of individuals with "normal" body temperature (the implicit control group), and compare these data to breathing-rate measurements obtained from groups of individuals with higher and lower body temperatures.

The second rule governing experimentation is that valid results require that testing be done on large numbers of subjects. It is essential to understand that it is nearly impossible to control all possible variables in biological tests. Indeed, there is a bit of scientific wisdom that mirrors this truth—that is, that laboratory animals, even in the most rigidly controlled and carefully designed experiments, "will do as they damn well please." Thus, stating that the testing of a drug for its painkilling effects was successful after having tested it on only one postoperative patient would be scientific suicide. Large numbers of patients would have to receive the drug and be monitored for a decrease in postoperative pain before such a statement could have any scientific validity. Then, other researchers would have to be able to uphold those conclusions by running similar experiments. *Repeatability* is an important part of the scientific method and is the primary basis for support or rejection of many hypotheses.

During experimentation and observation, data must be carefully recorded. Usually, such initial, or raw, data are recorded in table form. The table should be labeled to show the variables investigated and the results for each sample. At this point, *accurate recording* of observations is the primary concern. Later, these raw data will be reorganized and manipulated to show more explicitly the outcome of the experimentation.

Some of the observations that you will be asked to make in the anatomy and physiology laboratory will require that a drawing be made. Don't panic! The purpose of making drawings (in addition to providing a record) is to force you to observe things very closely. You need not be an artist (most biological drawings are simple outline drawings), but you do need to be neat and as accurate as possible. It is advisable to use a 4H pencil to do your drawings because it is easily erased and doesn't smudge. Before beginning to draw, you should examine your specimen closely, studying it as though you were going to have to draw it from memory. For example, when looking at cells you should ask yourself questions such as "What is their shape—the relationship of length and width? How are they joined together?" Then decide precisely what you are going to show and how large the drawing must be to show the necessary detail. After making the drawing, add labels in the margins and connect them by straight lines (leader lines) to the structures being named.

Step 4: Manipulation and Analysis of Data

The form of the final data varies, depending on the nature of the data collected. Usually, the final data represent information converted from the original measured values (raw data)

---

* *Compare* means to emphasize the similarities between two things, whereas *contrast* means that the differences are to be emphasized.

to some other form. This may mean that averaging or some other statistical treatment must be applied, or it may require conversions from one kind of units to another. In other cases, graphs may be needed to display the data.

Elementary Treatment of Data

Only very elementary statistical treatment of data is required in this manual. For example, you will be expected to understand and/or compute an average (mean), percentages, and a range.

Two of these statistics, the mean and the range, are useful in describing the *typical* case among a large number of samples evaluated. Let us use a simple example. We will assume that the following heart rates (in beats/min) were recorded during an experiment: 64, 70, 82, 94, 85, 75, 72, 78. If you put these numbers in numerical order, the **range** is easily computed, because the range is the difference between the highest and lowest numbers obtained (highest number minus lowest number). The **mean** is obtained by summing the items and dividing the sum by the number of items. What is the range and the mean for the set of numbers just provided?

1. *

The word *percent* comes from the Latin meaning "for 100"; thus *percent,* indicated by the percent sign, %, means parts per 100 parts. Thus, if we say that 45% of Americans have type O blood, what we are really saying is that among each group of 100 Americans, 45 (45/100) can be expected to have type O blood. Any ratio can be converted to a percent by multiplying by 100 and adding the percent sign.

$$.25 \times 100 = 25\% \qquad 5 \times 100 = 500\%$$

It is very easy to convert any number (including decimals) to a percent. The rule is to move the decimal point two places to the right and add the percent sign. If no decimal point appears, it is *assumed* to be at the end of the number; and zeros are added to fill any empty spaces. Two examples follow:

$$0.25 = 0.25 = 25\%$$

$$5 = 5 = 500\%$$

Change the following to percents:

2. 38 = _____   **4.** 1.6 = _____

3. .75 = _____

Note that although you are being asked here to convert numbers to percents, percents by themselves are meaningless. We always speak in terms of a percentage *of* something.

To change a percent to decimal form, remove the percent sign, and divide by 100. Change the following percents to whole numbers or decimals:

5. 800% = _____   **6.** 0.05% = _____

Making and Reading Line Graphs

For some laboratory experiments you will be required to show your data (or part of them) graphically. Simple line

graphs allow relationships within the data to be shown interestingly and allow trends (or patterns) in the data to be demonstrated. An advantage of properly drawn graphs is that they save the reader's time because the essential meaning of a large amount of statistical data can be seen at a glance.

To aid in making accurate graphs, graph paper (or a printed grid in the manual) is used. Line graphs have both horizontal (X) and vertical (Y) axes with scales. Each scale should have uniform intervals—that is, each unit measured on the scale should require the same distance along the scale as any other. Variations from this rule may be misleading and result in false interpretations of the data. By convention, the condition that is manipulated (the independent variable) in the experimental series is plotted on the X-axis (the horizontal axis); and the value that we then measure (the dependent variable) is plotted on the Y-axis (the vertical axis). To plot the data, a dot or a small x is placed at the precise point where the two variables (measured for each sample) meet; and then a line (this is called the **curve**) is drawn to connect the plotted points.

Sometimes, you will see the curve on a line graph extended beyond the last plotted point. This is (supposedly) done to predict "what comes next." When you see this done, be skeptical. The information provided by such a technique is only slightly more accurate than that provided by a crystal ball! When constructing a graph, be sure to label the X-axis and Y-axis and give the graph a legend (see Figure G.1).

To read a line graph, pick any point on the line, and match it with the information directly below on the X-axis and with that directly to the left of it on the Y-axis. Figure G.1 is a graph that illustrates the relationship between breaths per minute (respiratory rate) and body temperature. Answer the following questions about this graph:

7. What was the respiratory rate at a body temperature of 96°F? _____

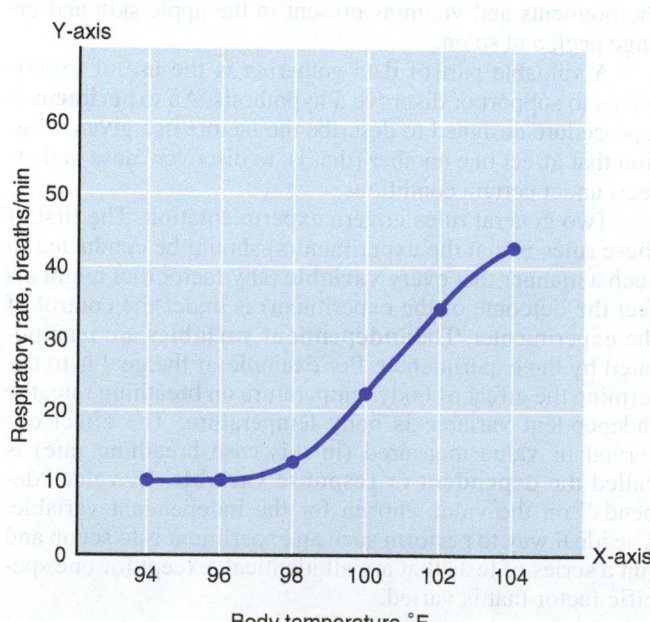

FIGURE G.1   Example of graphically presented data. Respiratory rate as a function of body temperature.

8. Between which two body temperature readings was the increase in breaths per minute greatest? _____

Step 5: Reporting Conclusions of the Study

Drawings, tables, and graphs alone do not suffice as the final presentation of scientific results. The final step requires that you provide a straightforward description of the conclusions drawn from your results. If possible, your findings should be compared to those of other investigators working on the same problem. (For laboratory investigations conducted by students, these comparative figures are provided by classmates.)

It is important to realize that scientific investigations do not always yield the anticipated results. If there are discrepancies between your results and those of others, or what you expected to find based on your class notes or textbook readings, this is the place to try to explain those discrepancies.

Results are often only as good as the observation techniques used. Depending on the type of experiment conducted,

---

LAB REPORT

Cover Page

- Title of Experiment
- Author's Name
- Course
- Instructor
- Date

Introduction

- Provide background information.
- Describe any relevant observations.
- State hypotheses clearly.

Materials and Methods

- List equipment or supplies needed.
- Provide step-by-step directions for conducting the experiment.

Results

- Present data using a drawing (figure), table, or graph.
- Analyze data.
- Summarize findings briefly.

Discussion and Conclusions

- Conclude whether data gathered support or do not support hypotheses.
- Include relevant information from other sources.
- Explain any uncontrolled variables or unexpected difficulties.
- Make suggestions for further experimentation.

Reference List

- Cite the source of any material used to support this report.

you may need to answer several questions. Did you weigh the specimen carefully enough? Did you balance the scale first? Was the subject's blood pressure actually as high as you recorded it, or did you record it inaccurately? If you did record it accurately, is it possible that the subject was emotionally upset about something, which might have given falsely high data for the variable being investigated? Attempting to explain an unexpected result will often teach you more than you would have learned from anticipated results.

When the experiment produces results that are consistent with the hypothesis, then the hypothesis can be said to have reached a higher level of certainty. The probability that the hypothesis is correct is greater.

A hypothesis that has been validated by many different investigators is called a **theory.** Theories are useful in two important ways. First, they link sets of data; and second, they make predictions that may lead to additional avenues of investigation. (OK, we know this with a high degree of certainty; what's next?)

When a theory has been repeatedly verified and appears to have wide applicability in biology, it may assume the status of a **biological principle.** A principle is a statement that applies with a high degree of probability to a range of events. For example, "Living matter is made of cells or cell products" is a principle stated in many biology texts. It is a sound and useful principle, and will continue to be used as such—unless new findings prove it wrong.

We have been through quite a bit of background concerning the scientific method and what its use entails. Because it is important that you remember the phases of the scientific method, they are summarized here:

1. Observation of some phenomenon

2. Statement of a hypothesis (based on the observations)

3. Collection of data (testing the hypothesis with controlled experiments)

4. Manipulation and analysis of the data

5. Reporting of the conclusions of the study (routinely done by preparing a lab report—see page xvii)

Writing a Lab Report Based on the Scientific Method

A laboratory report is not the same as a scientific paper, but it has some of the same elements and is a formal way to report the results of a scientific experiment. The report should have a cover page that includes the title of the experiment, the author's name, the name of the course, the instructor, and the date. The report should include five separate, clearly marked sections: Introduction, Materials and Methods, Results, Discussion and Conclusions, and References. Use the previous template to guide you through writing a lab report.

METRICS

No matter how highly developed our ability to observe, observations have scientific value only if we can communicate them to others. Without measurement, we would be limited to qualitative description. For precise and repeatable communication of information, the agreed-upon system of measurement used by scientists is the **metric system.**

A major advantage of the metric system is that it is based on units of 10. This allows rapid conversion to workable numbers so that neither very large nor very small figures need be used in calculations. Fractions or multiples of the standard units of length, volume, mass, time, and temperature have been assigned specific names. Table G.1 shows the commonly used units of the metric system, along with the prefixes used to designate fractions and multiples thereof.

To change from smaller units to larger units, you must *divide* by the appropriate factor of 10 (because there are fewer of the larger units). For example, a milliunit (*milli* = one-thousandth), such as a millimeter, is one step smaller than a centiunit (*centi* = one-hundredth), such as a centimeter. Thus to change milliunits to centiunits, you must divide by 10. On the other hand, when converting from larger units to smaller ones, you must *multiply* by the appropriate factor of 10. A partial scheme for conversions between the metric units is shown on the next page.

TABLE G.1	Metric System			
A. Commonly used units		**B. Fractions and their multiples**		
Measurement	**Unit**	**Fraction or multiple**	**Prefix**	**Symbol**
Length	Meter (m)	10^6 one million	mega	M
Volume	Liter (L; l with prefix)	10^3 one thousand	kilo	k
Mass	Gram (g)	10^{-1} one-tenth	deci	d
Time*	Second (s)	10^{-2} one-hundredth	centi	c
Temperature	Degree Celsius (°C)	10^{-3} one-thousandth	milli	m
		10^{-6} one-millionth	micro	μ
		10^{-9} one-billionth	nano	n

* The accepted standard for time is the second; and thus hours and minutes are used in scientific, as well as everyday, measurement of time. The only prefixes generally used are those indicating *fractional portions* of seconds—for example, millisecond and microsecond.

$$\underset{\text{smallest}}{\text{microunit}} \underset{\times 1000}{\overset{\div 1000}{\rightleftharpoons}} \text{milliunit} \underset{\times 10}{\overset{\div 10}{\rightleftharpoons}} \text{centiunit} \underset{\times 100}{\overset{\div 100}{\rightleftharpoons}} \text{unit} \underset{\times 1000}{\overset{\div 1000}{\rightleftharpoons}} \underset{\text{largest}}{\text{kilounit}}$$

The objectives of the sections that follow are to provide a brief overview of the most-used measurements in science or health professions and to help you gain some measure of confidence in dealing with them. (A listing of the most frequently used conversion factors, for conversions between British and metric system units, is provided in Appendix A.)

Length Measurements

The metric unit of length is the **meter (m).** Smaller objects are measured in centimeters or millimeters. Subcellular structures are measured in micrometers.

To help you picture these units of length, some equivalents follow:

One meter (m) is slightly longer than one yard (1 m = 39.37 in.).

One centimeter (cm) is approximately the width of a piece of chalk. (Note: There are 2.54 cm in 1 in.)

One millimeter (mm) is approximately the thickness of the wire of a paper clip or of a mark made by a No. 2 pencil lead.

One micrometer (µm) is extremely tiny and can be measured only microscopically.

Make the following conversions between metric units of length:

9. 12 cm = _____ mm

10. 2000 µm = _____ mm

Now, circle the answer that would make the most sense in each of the following statements:

11. A match (in a matchbook) is (0.3, 3, 30) cm long.

12. A standard-size American car is about 4 (mm, cm, m, km) long.

Volume Measurements

The metric unit of volume is the liter. A **liter** (l, or sometimes L, especially without a prefix) is slightly more than a quart (1 L = 1.057 quarts). Liquid volumes measured out for lab experiments are usually measured in milliliters (ml). (The terms *ml* and *cc,* cubic centimeter, are used interchangeably in laboratory and medical settings.)

To help you visualize metric volumes, the equivalents of some common substances follow:

A 12-oz can of soda is a little less than 360 ml.

A fluid ounce is about 30 (it's 29.57) ml (cc).

A teaspoon of vanilla is about 5 ml (cc).

Compute the following:

13. How many 5-ml injections can be prepared from 1 liter of a medicine? _____

14. A 450-ml volume of alcohol is _____ L.

Mass Measurements

Although many people use the terms *mass* and *weight* interchangeably, this usage is inaccurate. **Mass** is the amount of matter in an object; and an object has a constant mass, regardless of where it is—that is, on earth, or in outer space. However, weight varies with gravitational pull; the greater the gravitational pull, the greater the weight. Thus, our astronauts are said to be weightless* when in outer space, but they still have the same mass as they do on earth.

The metric unit of mass is the **gram (g).** Medical dosages are usually prescribed in milligrams (mg) or micrograms (µg); and in the clinical agency, body weight (particularly of infants) is typically specified in kilograms (kg) (1 kg = 2.2 lb).

The following examples are provided to help you become familiar with the masses of some common objects:

Two aspirin tablets have a mass of approximately 1 g.

A nickel has a mass of 5 g.

The mass of an average woman (132 lb) is 60 kg.

Make the following conversions:

15. 300 g = _____ mg = _____ µg

16. 4000 µg = _____ mg = _____ g

17. A nurse must administer to her patient, Mrs. Smith, 5 mg of a drug per kg of body mass. Mrs. Smith weighs 140 lb. How many grams of the drug should the nurse administer to her patient?

_____ g

Temperature Measurements

In the laboratory and in the clinical agency, temperature is measured both in metric units (degrees Celsius, °C) and in British units (degrees Fahrenheit, °F). Thus it helps to be familiar with both temperature scales.

The temperatures of boiling and freezing water can be used to compare the two scales:

The freezing point of water is 0°C and 32°F.

The boiling point of water is 100°C and 212°F.

* Astronauts are not *really* weightless. It is just that they and their surroundings are being pulled toward the earth at the same speed; and so, in reference to their environment, they appear to float.

As you can see, the range from the freezing point to the boiling point of water on the Celsius scale is 100 degrees, whereas the comparable range on the Fahrenheit scale is 180 degrees. Hence, one degree on the Celsius scale represents a greater change in temperature. Normal body temperature is approximately 98.6°F or 37°C.

To convert from the Fahrenheit scale to the Celsius scale, the following equation is used:

$$°C = \frac{5(°F - 32)}{9}$$

To convert from the Celsius scale to the Fahrenheit scale, the following equation is used:

$$°F = (9/5 \ °C) + 32$$

Perform the following temperature conversions:

18. Convert 38°C to °F: _____

19. Convert 158°F to °C: _____

Answers

1. range of 94–64 or 30 beats/min; mean 77.5

2. 3800%

3. 75%

4. 160%

5. 8

6. 0.0005

7. 10 breaths/min

8. interval between 100–102° (went from 22 to 36 breaths/min)

9. 12 cm = 120 mm

10. 2000 μm = 2 mm

11. 3 cm long

12. 4 m long

13. 200

14. 0.45 L

15. 300 g = 3 × 10⁵ mg = 3 × 10⁸ μg

16. 4000 μg = 4 mg = 4 × 10⁻³ g (0.004 g)

17. 0.32 g

18. 100.4°F

19. 70°C

The Language of Anatomy

MATERIALS

- ☐ Human torso model (dissectible)
- ☐ Human skeleton
- ☐ Demonstration: sectioned and labeled kidneys [three separate kidneys uncut or cut so that (a) entire, (b) transverse sectional, and (c) longitudinal sectional views are visible]
- ☐ Gelatin-spaghetti molds
- ☐ Scalpel

OBJECTIVES

1. To describe the anatomical position verbally or by demonstration, and to explain its importance.
2. To use proper anatomical terminology to describe body directions, planes, and surfaces.
3. To name the body cavities and indicate the important organs in each.

PRE-LAB QUIZ

1. Circle True or False. In anatomical position, the body is recumbent (lying down).
2. Circle the correct term. With regard to surface anatomy, abdominal / axial refers to the division relating to the head, neck, and trunk of the body.
3. The term *superficial* refers to a structure that is:
   a. attached near the trunk of the body
   b. toward or at the body surface
   c. toward the head
   d. toward the midline
4. The _____ plane runs longitudinally and divides the body into right and left parts.
   a. frontal   c. transverse
   b. sagittal   d. ventral
5. Circle the correct terms. The dorsal body cavity can be divided into the cranial / thoracic cavity, which contains the brain, and the sural / vertebral cavity, which contains the spinal cord.
6. What organ would you expect to find in the thoracic cavity surrounded by the pericardium? _____

Most of us are naturally curious about our bodies. This fact is amply demonstrated by infants, who are fascinated with their own waving hands or their mother's nose. Unlike the infant, however, the student of anatomy must learn to observe and identify the dissectible body structures formally.

When beginning the study of any science, the student is often initially overcome by jargon unique to the subject. The study of anatomy is no exception. But without this specialized terminology, confusion is inevitable. For example, what do *over, on top of, superficial to, above,* and *behind* mean in reference to the human body? Anatomists have an accepted set of reference terms that are universally understood. These allow body structures to be located and identified with a minimum of words and a high degree of clarity.

This exercise presents some of the most important anatomical terminology used to describe the body and introduces you to basic concepts of **gross anatomy,** the study of body structures visible to the naked eye.

For practice quizzes on this lab, go to www.myaandp.com.

Anatomical Position

When anatomists or doctors refer to specific areas of the human body, they do so in accordance with a universally accepted standard position called the **anatomical position.** It is essential to understand this position because much of the body terminology employed in this book refers to this body positioning, regardless of the position the body happens to be in. In the anatomical position the human body is erect, with the feet only slightly apart, head and toes pointed forward, and arms hanging at the sides with palms facing forward (Figure 1.1a).

• Assume the anatomical position, and notice that it is not particularly comfortable. The hands are held unnaturally forward rather than hanging partially cupped toward the thighs.

Surface Anatomy

Body surfaces provide a wealth of visible landmarks for study. There are two major divisions of the body:

Axial: Relating to head, neck, and trunk, the axis of the body

Appendicular: Relating to limbs and their attachments to the axis

Anterior Body Landmarks

Note the following regions in Figure 1.1a:

Abdominal: Pertaining to the anterior body trunk region inferior to the ribs

Acromial: Pertaining to the point of the shoulder

Antebrachial: Pertaining to the forearm

Antecubital: Pertaining to the anterior surface of the elbow

Axillary: Pertaining to the armpit

Brachial: Pertaining to the arm

Buccal: Pertaining to the cheek

Carpal: Pertaining to the wrist

Cephalic: Pertaining to the head

Cervical: Pertaining to the neck region

Coxal: Pertaining to the hip

Crural: Pertaining to the leg

Digital: Pertaining to the fingers or toes

Femoral: Pertaining to the thigh

Fibular (peroneal): Pertaining to the side of the leg

Frontal: Pertaining to the forehead

Hallux: Pertaining to the great toe

Inguinal: Pertaining to the groin

Mammary: Pertaining to the breast

Manus: Pertaining to the hand

Mental: Pertaining to the chin

Nasal: Pertaining to the nose

Oral: Pertaining to the mouth

Orbital: Pertaining to the bony eye socket (orbit)

Palmar: Pertaining to the palm of the hand

Patellar: Pertaining to the anterior knee (kneecap) region

Pedal: Pertaining to the foot

Pelvic: Pertaining to the pelvis region

Pollex: Pertaining to the thumb

Pubic: Pertaining to the genital region

Sternal: Pertaining to the region of the breastbone

Tarsal: Pertaining to the ankle

Thoracic: Pertaining to the chest

Umbilical: Pertaining to the navel

Posterior Body Landmarks

Note the following body surface regions in Figure 1.1b:

Acromial: Pertaining to the point of the shoulder

Brachial: Pertaining to the arm

Calcaneal: Pertaining to the heel of the foot

Cephalic: Pertaining to the head

Dorsum: Pertaining to the back

Femoral: Pertaining to the thigh

Gluteal: Pertaining to the buttocks or rump

Lumbar: Pertaining to the area of the back between the ribs and hips; the loin

Manus: Pertaining to the hand

Occipital: Pertaining to the posterior aspect of the head or base of the skull

Olecranal: Pertaining to the posterior aspect of the elbow

Otic: Pertaining to the ear

Pedal: Pertaining to the foot

Perineal: Pertaining to the region between the anus and external genitalia

Plantar: Pertaining to the sole of the foot

Popliteal: Pertaining to the back of the knee

Sacral: Pertaining to the region between the hips (overlying the sacrum)

Scapular: Pertaining to the scapula or shoulder blade area

Sural: Pertaining to the calf or posterior surface of the leg

Vertebral: Pertaining to the area of the spinal column

Cephalic
- Frontal
- Orbital
- Nasal
- Buccal
- Oral
- Mental

Cervical

Thoracic
- Sternal
- Axillary
- Mammary

Abdominal
- Umbilical

Pelvic
- Inguinal

Pubic

Upper limb
- Acromial
- Brachial
- Antecubital
- Olecranal
- Antebrachial
- Carpal

Manus (hand)
- Pollex
- Palmar
- Digital

Lower limb
- Coxal
- Femoral
- Patellar
- Popliteal
- Crural
- Sural
- Fibular or peroneal

Pedal (foot)
- Tarsal
- Calcaneal
- Digital
- Plantar
- Hallux

Cephalic
- Otic
- Occipital

Cervical

Dorsum
- Scapular
- Vertebral
- Lumbar
- Sacral
- Gluteal
- Perineal

Thorax
Abdomen
Back (Dorsum)

(a) Anterior/Ventral

(b) Posterior/Dorsal

FIGURE 1.1 Surface anatomy. (a) Anatomical position. **(b)** Heels are raised to illustrate the plantar surface of the foot.

ACTIVITY 1

Locating Body Regions

Locate the anterior and posterior body landmarks on yourself, your lab partner, and a human torso model before continuing. ■

Body Orientation and Direction

Study the terms below, referring to Figure 1.2. Notice that certain terms have a different meaning for a four-legged animal (quadruped) than they do for a human (biped).

Superior/inferior *(above/below):* These terms refer to placement of a structure along the long axis of the body. Superior structures always appear above other structures, and inferior structures are always below other structures. For example, the nose is superior to the mouth, and the abdomen is inferior to the chest.

Anterior/posterior *(front/back):* In humans the most anterior structures are those that are most forward—the face, chest, and abdomen. Posterior structures are those toward the backside of the body. For instance, the spine is posterior to the heart.

Medial/lateral *(toward the midline/away from the midline or median plane):* The sternum (breastbone) is medial to the ribs; the ear is lateral to the nose.

The terms of position just described assume the person is in the anatomical position. The next four term pairs are more absolute. Their applicability is not relative to a particular body position, and they consistently have the same meaning in all vertebrate animals.

Cephalad (cranial)/caudal (*toward the head/toward the tail*): In humans these terms are used interchangeably with *superior* and *inferior,* but in four-legged animals they are synonymous with *anterior* and *posterior,* respectively.

Dorsal/ventral (*backside/belly side*): These terms are used chiefly in discussing the comparative anatomy of animals, assuming the animal is standing. *Dorsum* is a Latin word meaning "back." Thus, *dorsal* refers to the animal's back or the *back*side of any other structures; for example, the posterior surface of the human leg is its dorsal surface. The term *ventral* derives from the Latin term *venter,* meaning "belly," and always refers to the belly side of animals. In humans the terms *ventral* and *dorsal* are used interchangeably with the terms *anterior* and *posterior,* but in four-legged animals *ventral* and *dorsal* are synonymous with *inferior* and *superior,* respectively.

Proximal/distal (*nearer the trunk or attached end/farther from the trunk or point of attachment*): These terms are used primarily to locate various areas of the body limbs. For example, the fingers are distal to the elbow; the knee is proximal to the toes. However, these terms may also be used to indicate regions (closer to or farther from the head) of internal tubular organs.

Superficial (external)/deep (internal) (*toward or at the body surface/away from the body surface*): These terms lo-

cate body organs according to their relative closeness to the body surface. For example, the skin is superficial to the skeletal muscles, and the lungs are deep to the rib cage.

ACTIVITY 2

Practicing Using Correct Anatomical Terminology

Before continuing, use a human torso model, a human skeleton, or your own body to specify the relationship between the following structures when the body is in the anatomical position.

1. The wrist is _____ to the hand.

2. The trachea (windpipe) is _____ to the spine.

3. The brain is _____ to the spinal cord.

4. The kidneys are _____ to the liver.

5. The nose is _____ to the cheekbones.

6. The thumb is _____ to the ring finger.

7. The thorax is _____ to the abdomen.

8. The skin is _____ to the skeleton. ▬

Body Planes and Sections

The body is three-dimensional, and in order to observe its internal structures, it is often helpful and necessary to make use of a **section,** or cut. When the section is made through the body wall or through an organ, it is made along an imaginary surface or line called a **plane.** Anatomists commonly refer to three planes (Figure 1.3), or sections, that lie at right angles to one another.

FIGURE 1.2 Anatomical terminology describing body orientation and direction.
(a) With reference to a human. **(b)** With reference to a four-legged animal.

Frontal plane

Median (midsagittal) plane

Transverse plane

(a) Frontal section (through torso)

(b) Transverse section (through torso, inferior view)

(c) Median (midsagittal) section

Left and right lungs   Liver   Heart   Stomach   Spleen   Arm

Liver   Spinal cord   Subcutaneous fat layer   Aorta   Body wall   Pancreas   Spleen

Rectum   Vertebral column   Intestines

FIGURE 1.3 **Planes of the body with corresponding magnetic resonance imaging (MRI) scans.**

Sagittal plane: A plane that runs longitudinally and divides the body into right and left parts is referred to as a sagittal plane. If it divides the body into equal parts, right down the midline of the body, it is called a **median,** or **midsagittal, plane.**

Frontal plane: Sometimes called a **coronal plane,** the frontal plane is a longitudinal plane that divides the body (or an organ) into anterior and posterior parts.

Transverse plane: A transverse plane runs horizontally, dividing the body into superior and inferior parts. When organs are sectioned along the transverse plane, the sections are commonly called **cross sections.**

On microscope slides, the abbreviation for a longitudinal section (sagittal or frontal) is l.s. Cross sections are abbreviated x.s. or c.s.

As shown in Figure 1.4, a sagittal or frontal plane section of any nonspherical object, be it a banana or a body organ, provides quite a different view than a transverse section.

(a) Cross section

(b) Midsagittal section

(c) Frontal sections

FIGURE 1.4 Objects can look odd when viewed in section. This banana has been sectioned in three different planes **(a–c),** and only in one of these planes **(b)** is it easily recognized as a banana. If one cannot recognize a sectioned organ, it is possible to reconstruct its shape from a series of successive cuts, as from the three serial sections in **(c).**

ACTIVITY 3

Observing Sectioned Specimens

1. Go to the demonstration area and observe the transversely and longitudinally cut organ specimens (kidneys). Pay close attention to the different structural details in the samples because you will need to draw these views in the Review Sheet at the end of this exercise.

2. After completing instruction 1, obtain a gelatin-spaghetti mold and a scalpel and bring them to your laboratory bench. (Essentially, this is just cooked spaghetti added to warm gelatin, which is then allowed to gel.)

3. Cut through the gelatin-spaghetti mold along any plane, and examine the cut surfaces. You should see spaghetti strands that have been cut transversely (x.s.), some cut longitudinally, and some cut obliquely.

4. Draw the appearance of each of these spaghetti sections below, and verify the accuracy of your section identifications with your instructor.

Body Cavities

The axial portion of the body has two large cavities that provide different degrees of protection to the organs within them (Figure 1.5).

Dorsal Body Cavity

The dorsal body cavity can be subdivided into the **cranial cavity,** in which the brain is enclosed within the rigid skull,

Transverse cut   Longitudinal cut   Oblique cut

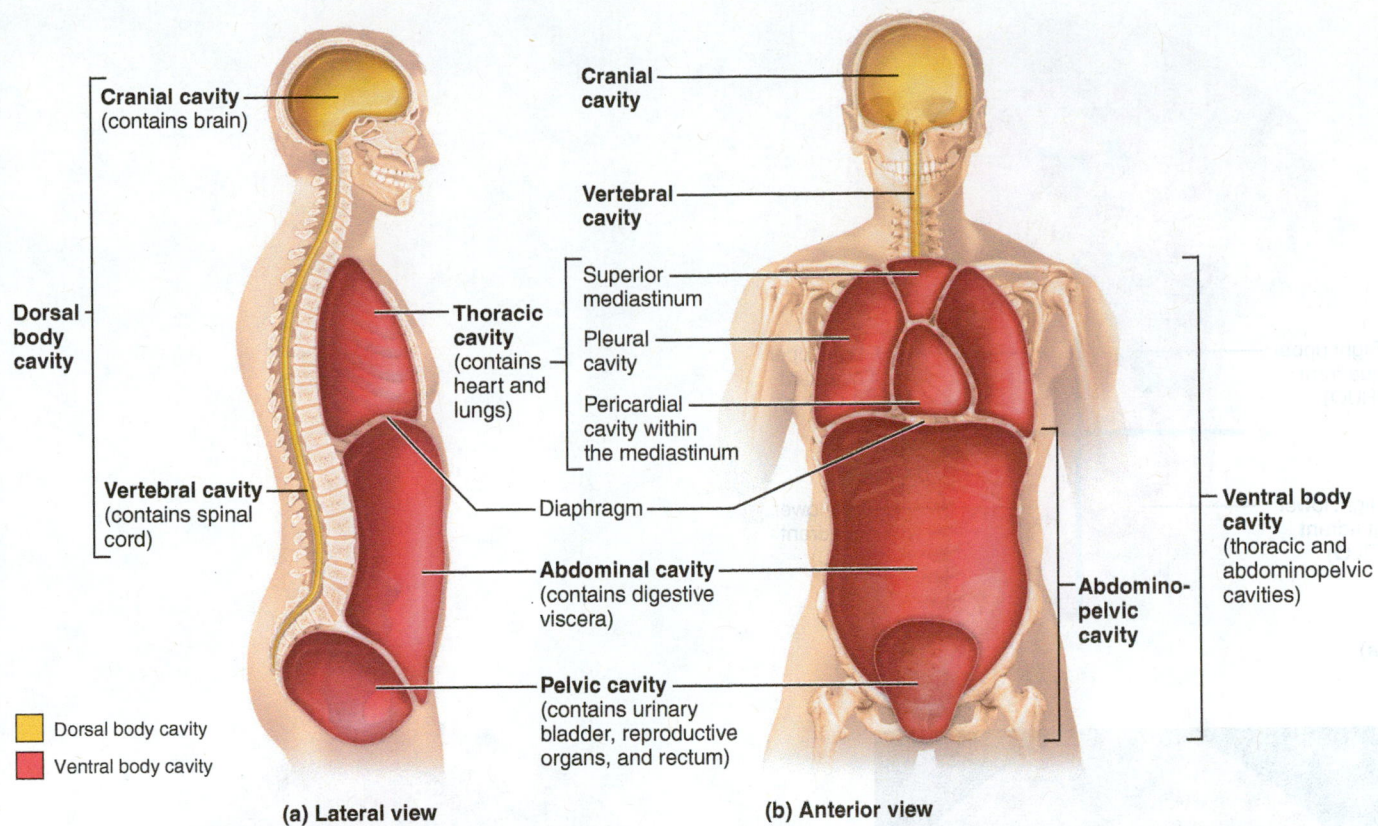

(a) Lateral view

(b) Anterior view

FIGURE 1.5 **Dorsal and ventral body cavities and their subdivisions.**

and the **vertebral** (or **spinal**) **cavity,** within which the delicate spinal cord is protected by the bony vertebral column. Because the spinal cord is a continuation of the brain, these cavities are continuous with each other.

Ventral Body Cavity

Like the dorsal cavity, the ventral body cavity is subdivided. The superior **thoracic cavity** is separated from the rest of the ventral cavity by the dome-shaped diaphragm. The heart and lungs, located in the thoracic cavity, are afforded some measure of protection by the bony rib cage. The cavity inferior to the diaphragm is often referred to as the **abdominopelvic cavity.** Although there is no further physical separation of the ventral cavity, some prefer to describe the abdominopelvic cavity in terms of a superior **abdominal cavity,** the area that houses the stomach, intestines, liver, and other organs, and an inferior **pelvic cavity,** the region that is partially enclosed by the bony pelvis and contains the reproductive organs, bladder, and rectum. Notice in Figure 1.5 that the abdominal and pelvic cavities are not continuous with each other in a straight plane but that the pelvic cavity is tipped away from the perpendicular.

Serous Membranes of the Ventral Body Cavity

The walls of the ventral body cavity and the outer surfaces of the organs it contains are covered with an exceedingly thin, double-layered membrane called the **serosa,** or **serous mem-**

brane. The part of the membrane lining the cavity walls is referred to as the **parietal serosa,** and it is continuous with a similar membrane, the **visceral serosa,** covering the external surface of the organs within the cavity. These membranes produce a thin lubricating fluid that allows the visceral organs to slide over one another or to rub against the body wall with minimal friction. Serous membranes also compartmentalize the various organs so that infection of one organ is prevented from spreading to others.

The specific names of the serous membranes depend on the structures they envelop. Thus the serosa lining the abdominal cavity and covering its organs is the **peritoneum,** that enclosing the lungs is the **pleura,** and that around the heart is the **pericardium** (see Figure 8.1).

Abdominopelvic Quadrants and Regions

Because the abdominopelvic cavity is quite large and contains many organs, it is helpful to divide it up into smaller areas for discussion or study.

A scheme used by most physicians and nurses divides the abdominal surface (and the abdominopelvic cavity deep to it) into four approximately equal regions called **quadrants.** These quadrants are named according to their relative position—that is, *right upper quadrant, right lower quadrant, left upper quadrant,* and *left lower quadrant* (see Figure 1.6a). Note that the terms left and right refer to the left and right of the figure, not your own. The left and right of the figure are referred to as **anatomical left and right.**

(a)

Right upper quadrant (RUQ)

Left upper quadrant (LUQ)

Right lower quadrant (RLQ)

Left lower quadrant (LLQ)

(b)

Right hypochondriac region	Epigastric region	Left hypochondriac region
Right lumbar region	Umbilical region	Left lumbar region
Right iliac (inguinal) region	Hypogastric (pubic) region	Left iliac (inguinal) region

(c)

Liver

Gallbladder

Ascending colon of large intestine

Small intestine

Cecum

Appendix

Diaphragm

Stomach

Transverse colon of large intestine

Descending colon of large intestine

Initial part of sigmoid colon

Urinary bladder

FIGURE 1.6 Abdominopelvic surface and cavity. (a) The four quadrants, showing superficial organs in each quadrant. **(b)** Nine regions delineated by four planes. The superior horizontal plane is just inferior to the ribs; the inferior horizontal plane is at the superior aspect of the hip bones. The vertical planes are just medial to the nipples. **(c)** Anterior view of the abdominopelvic cavity showing superficial organs.

ACTIVITY 4

Identifying Organs in the Abdominopelvic Cavity

Examine the human torso model to respond to the following questions.

Name two organs found in the left upper quadrant.

_____ and _____

Name two organs found in the right lower quadrant.

_____ and _____

What organ (Figure 1.6a) is divided into identical halves by

the median plane line? _____ ■

A different scheme commonly used by anatomists divides the abdominal surface and abdominopelvic cavity into nine separate regions by four planes, as shown in Figure 1.6b. Although the names of these nine regions are unfamiliar to you now, with a little patience and study they will become easier to remember. As you read through the descriptions of these nine regions and locate them in Figure 1.6b, also look at Figure 1.6c to note the organs the regions contain.

Umbilical region: The centermost region, which includes the umbilicus

Epigastric region: Immediately superior to the umbilical region; overlies most of the stomach

Hypogastric (pubic) region: Immediately inferior to the umbilical region; encompasses the pubic area

Iliac (inguinal) regions: Lateral to the hypogastric region and overlying the superior parts of the hip bones

Lumbar regions: Between the ribs and the flaring portions of the hip bones; lateral to the umbilical region

Hypochondriac regions: Flanking the epigastric region laterally and overlying the lower ribs

ACTIVITY 5

Locating Abdominal Surface Regions

Locate the regions of the abdominal surface on a human torso model and on yourself before continuing. ■

Other Body Cavities

Besides the large, closed body cavities, there are several types of smaller body cavities (Figure 1.7). Many of these are in the head, and most open to the body exterior.

Oral cavity: The oral cavity, commonly called the mouth, contains the tongue and teeth. It is continuous with the rest of the digestive tube, which opens to the exterior at the anus.

Nasal cavity: Located within and posterior to the nose, the nasal cavity is part of the passages of the respiratory system.

Orbital cavities: The orbital cavities (orbits) in the skull house the eyes and present them in an anterior position.

Middle ear cavities: Each middle ear cavity lies just medial to an eardrum and is carved into the bony skull. These cavities contain tiny bones that transmit sound vibrations to the organ of hearing in the inner ears.

Synovial (sĭ-no′ve-al) **cavities:** Synovial cavities are joint cavities—they are enclosed within fibrous capsules that surround the freely movable joints of the body, such as those between the vertebrae and the knee and hip joints. Like the serous membranes of the ventral body cavity, membranes lining the synovial cavities secrete a lubricating fluid that reduces friction as the enclosed structures move across one another.

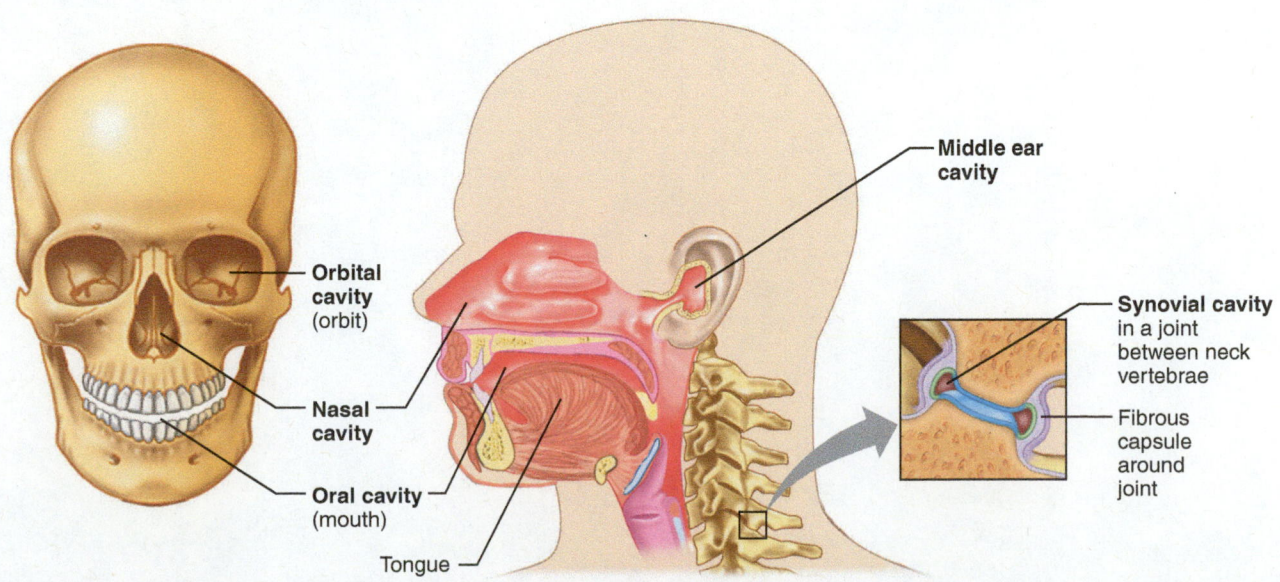

Middle ear cavity

Orbital cavity (orbit)

Nasal cavity

Oral cavity (mouth)

Tongue

Synovial cavity in a joint between neck vertebrae

Fibrous capsule around joint

FIGURE 1.7 Other body cavities. The oral, nasal, orbital, and middle ear cavities are located in the head and open to the body exterior. Synovial cavities are found in joints between many bones such as the vertebrae of the spine, and at the knee, shoulder, and hip.

NAME _____

LAB TIME/DATE _____

The Language of Anatomy

Surface Anatomy

1. Match each of the following descriptions with a key equivalent, and record the key letter or term in front of the description.

Key: a. buccal   c. cephalic   e. patellar
       b. calcaneal   d. digital   f. scapular

_____ 1. cheek   _____ 4. anterior aspect of knee

_____ 2. pertaining to the fingers   _____ 5. heel of foot

_____ 3. shoulder blade region   _____ 6. pertaining to the head

2. Indicate the following body areas on the accompanying diagram by placing the correct key letter at the end of each line.

Key:

a. abdominal
b. antecubital
c. brachial
d. cervical
e. crural
f. femoral
g. fibular
h. gluteal
i. lumbar
j. occipital
k. oral
l. popliteal
m. pubic
n. sural
o. thoracic
p. umbilical

3. Classify each of the terms in the key of question 2 above into one of the large body regions indicated below. Insert the appropriate key letters on the answer blanks.

_____ 1. appendicular   _____ 2. axial

Body Orientation, Direction, Planes, and Sections

4. Describe completely the standard human anatomical position. _____

_____

5. Define *section*. _____

6. Several incomplete statements are listed below. Correctly complete each statement by choosing the appropriate anatomical term from the key. Record the key letters and/or terms on the correspondingly numbered blanks below.

Key: a. anterior d. inferior g. posterior j. superior
b. distal e. lateral h. proximal k. transverse
c. frontal f. medial i. sagittal

In the anatomical position, the face and palms are on the __1__ body surface; the buttocks and shoulder blades are on the __2__ body surface; and the top of the head is the most __3__ part of the body. The ears are __4__ and __5__ to the shoulders and __6__ to the nose. The heart is __7__ to the vertebral column (spine) and __8__ to the lungs. The elbow is __9__ to the fingers but __10__ to the shoulder. The abdominopelvic cavity is __11__ to the thoracic cavity and __12__ to the spinal cavity. In humans, the dorsal surface can also be called the __13__ surface; however, in quadruped animals, the dorsal surface is the __14__ surface.

If an incision cuts the heart into right and left parts, the section is a __15__ section; but if the heart is cut so that superior and inferior portions result, the section is a __16__ section. You are told to cut a dissection animal along two planes so that both kidneys are observable in each section. The two sections that will always meet this requirement are the __17__ and __18__ sections. A section that demonstrates the continuity between the spinal and cranial cavities is a __19__ section.

1. _____ 8. _____ 14. _____

2. _____ 9. _____ 15. _____

3. _____ 10. _____ 16. _____

4. _____ 11. _____ 17. _____

5. _____ 12. _____ 18. _____

6. _____ 13. _____ 19. _____

7. _____

7. Correctly identify each of the body planes by inserting the appropriate term for each on the answer line below the drawing.

(a) _____medial_____ (b) _____transverse_____ (c) _____

8. Draw a kidney as it appears when sectioned in each of the three different planes.

Transverse   Sagittal   Frontal
section   section   section

9. Correctly identify each of the nine areas of the abdominal surface by inserting the appropriate term for each of the letters indicated in the drawing.

a. _____

b. _____

c. _____

d. _____

e. _____

f. _____

g. _____

h. _____

i. _____

(a)
(b)
(c)
(d)
(e)
(f)
(g)
(h)
(i)

Body Cavities

10. Which body cavity would have to be opened for the following types of surgery or procedures? (Insert letter of key choice in same-numbered blank. More than one choice may apply.)

Key: a. abdominopelvic   c. dorsal   e. thoracic
      b. cranial   d. spinal   f. ventral

_____ 1. surgery to remove a cancerous lung lobe   _____ 4. appendectomy

_____ 2. removal of the uterus, or womb   _____ 5. stomach ulcer operation

_____ 3. removal of a brain tumor   _____ 6. delivery of pre-operative "saddle" anesthesia

11. Name the muscle that subdivides the ventral body cavity. _____

12. Which organ system would not be represented in any of the body cavities? _____

13. What are the bony landmarks of the abdominopelvic cavity? _____

_____

14. Which body cavity affords the least protection to its internal structures? _____

15. What is the function of the serous membranes of the body? _____

_____

16. Using the key choices, identify the small body cavities described below.

Key: a. middle ear cavity   c. oral cavity   e. synovial cavity
      b. nasal cavity   d. orbital cavity

_____ 1. holds the eyes in an anterior-facing position   _____ 4. contains the tongue

_____ 2. houses three tiny bones involved in hearing   _____ 5. lines a joint cavity

_____ 3. contained within the nose

17. On the incomplete flowchart provided below:

- Fill in the cavity names as appropriate to boxes 3–8.
- Then, using either the name of the cavity or the box numbers, identify the descriptions in the list that follows.

Body cavities

1 Dorsal body cavity	**3** _____ cavity (superior)
	4 _____ cavity (inferior)
2 Ventral body cavity	**5** _____ cavity (superior)
	6 _____ cavity (inferior) → **7** _____ cavity (superior)
	8 _____ cavity (inferior)

_____ a. contained within the skull and vertebral column   _____ e. contains the heart

_____ b. houses female reproductive organs   _____ f. contains the small intestine

_____ c. the most protective body cavity   _____ g. bounded by the ribs

_____ d. its name means belly   _____ h. its walls are muscular

Organ Systems Overview

OBJECTIVES

1. To name the human organ systems and indicate the major functions of each.
2. To list two or three organs of each system and categorize the various organs by organ system.
3. To identify these organs in a dissected rat or human cadaver or on a dissectible human torso model.
4. To identify the correct organ system for each organ when presented with a list of organs (as studied in the laboratory).

PRE-LAB QUIZ

1. Name the basic unit or building block of all living things. _____
2. The small intestine is an example of a(n) _____, because it is composed of two or more tissue types performing a specific function for the body.
   a. epithelial tissue   c. organ
   b. muscular tissue   d. organ system
3. The _____ system is responsible for maintaining homeostasis of the body via rapid transmission of electrical signals.
4. The _____ system keeps the blood continuously supplied with oxygen while removing carbon dioxide.
5. The kidneys are part of the _____ system.
6. The thin muscle that separates the thoracic and abdominal cavities is the _____.

The basic unit or building block of all living things is the **cell.** Cells fall into four different categories according to their structures and functions. Each of these corresponds to one of the four tissue types: epithelial, muscular, nervous, and connective. A **tissue** is a group of cells that are similar in structure and function. An **organ** is a structure composed of two or more tissue types that performs a specific function for the body. For example, the small intestine, which digests and absorbs nutrients, is composed of all four tissue types.

An **organ system** is a group of organs that act together to perform a particular body function. For example, the organs of the digestive system work together to break down foods moving through the digestive system and absorb the end products into the bloodstream to provide nutrients and fuel for all the body's cells. In all, there are 11 organ systems, which are described in Table 2.1. The lymphatic system also encompasses a *functional system* called the immune system, which is composed of an army of mobile *cells* that act to protect the body from foreign substances.

Read through this summary of the body's organ systems before beginning your rat dissection or examination of the predissected human cadaver. If a human cadaver is not available, Figures 2.3 through 2.6 will serve as a partial replacement.

TABLE 2.1	Overview of Organ Systems of the Body	
Organ system	**Major component organs**	**Function**
Integumentary (Skin)	Epidermal and dermal regions; cutaneous sense organs and glands	• Protects deeper organs from mechanical, chemical, and bacterial injury, and desiccation (drying out) • Excretes salts and urea • Aids in regulation of body temperature • Produces vitamin D
Skeletal	Bones, cartilages, tendons, ligaments, and joints	• Body support and protection of internal organs • Provides levers for muscular action • Cavities provide a site for blood cell formation
Muscular	Muscles attached to the skeleton	• Primary function is to contract or shorten; in doing so, skeletal muscles allow locomotion (running, walking, etc.), grasping and manipulation of the environment, and facial expression • Generates heat
Nervous	Brain, spinal cord, nerves, and sensory receptors	• Allows body to detect changes in its internal and external environment and to respond to such information by activating appropriate muscles or glands • Helps maintain homeostasis of the body via rapid transmission of electrical signals
Endocrine	Pituitary, thymus, thyroid, parathyroid, adrenal, and pineal glands; ovaries, testes, and pancreas	• Helps maintain body homeostasis, promotes growth and development; produces chemical "messengers" (hormones) that travel in the blood to exert their effect(s) on various "target organs" of the body
Cardiovascular	Heart, blood vessels, and blood	• Primarily a transport system that carries blood containing oxygen, carbon dioxide, nutrients, wastes, ions, hormones, and other substances to and from the tissue cells where exchanges are made; blood is propelled through the blood vessels by the pumping action of the heart • Antibodies and other protein molecules in the blood act to protect the body
Lymphatic/ Immunity	Lymphatic vessels, lymph nodes, spleen, thymus, tonsils, and scattered collections of lymphoid tissue	• Picks up fluid leaked from the blood vessels and returns it to the blood • Cleanses blood of pathogens and other debris • Houses lymphocytes that act via the immune response to protect the body from foreign substances (antigens)
Respiratory	Nasal passages, pharynx, larynx, trachea, bronchi, and lungs	• Keeps the blood continuously supplied with oxygen while removing carbon dioxide • Contributes to the acid-base balance of the blood via its carbonic acid–bicarbonate buffer system.
Digestive	Oral cavity, esophagus, stomach, small and large intestines, and accessory structures (teeth, salivary glands, liver, and pancreas)	• Breaks down ingested foods to minute particles, which can be absorbed into the blood for delivery to the body cells • Undigested residue removed from the body as feces
Urinary	Kidneys, ureters, bladder, and urethra	• Rids the body of nitrogen-containing wastes (urea, uric acid, and ammonia), which result from the breakdown of proteins and nucleic acids by body cells • Maintains water, electrolyte, and acid-base balance of blood
Reproductive	Male: testes, prostate gland, scrotum, penis, and duct system, which carries sperm to the body exterior	• Provides germ cells (sperm) for perpetuation of the species
	Female: ovaries, uterine tubes, uterus, mammary glands, and vagina	• Provides germ cells (eggs); the female uterus houses the developing fetus until birth; mammary glands provide nutrition for the infant

DISSECTION AND IDENTIFICATION:

The Organ Systems of the Rat

Many of the external and internal structures of the rat are quite similar in structure and function to those of the human, so a study of the gross anatomy of the rat should help you understand our own physical structure. The following instructions complement and direct your dissection and observation of a rat, but the descriptions for organ observations in Activity 4 ("Ex-

amining the Ventral Body Cavity," which begins on page 18) also apply to superficial observations of a previously dissected human cadaver. In addition, the general instructions for observing external structures can easily be extrapolated to serve human cadaver observations. The photographs in Figures 2.3 to 2.6 will provide visual aids.

Note that four of the organ systems listed in Table 2.1 (integumentary, skeletal, muscular, and nervous) will not be studied at this time, as they require microscopic study or more detailed dissection.

FIGURE 2.1 Rat dissection: Securing for dissection and the initial incision. (a) Securing the rat to the dissection tray with dissecting pins. **(b)** Using scissors to make the incision on the median line of the abdominal region. **(c)** Completed incision from the pelvic region to the lower jaw. **(d)** Reflection (folding back) of the skin to expose the underlying muscles.

(a) (b)

(c) (d)

ACTIVITY 1

Observing External Structures

1. If your instructor has provided a predissected rat, go to the demonstration area to make your observations. Alternatively, if you and/or members of your group will be dissecting the specimen, obtain a preserved or freshly killed rat (one for every two to four students), a dissecting tray, dissecting pins or twine, scissors, probe, forceps, and disposable gloves, and bring them to your laboratory bench.

If a predissected human cadaver is available, obtain a probe, forceps, and disposable gloves before going to the demonstration area.

⚠ 2. Don the gloves before beginning your observations. This precaution is particularly important when handling freshly killed animals, which may harbor internal parasites.

3. Observe the major divisions of the body—head, trunk, and extremities. If you are examining a rat, compare these divisions to those of humans. ▮

ACTIVITY 2

Examining the Oral Cavity

Examine the structures of the oral cavity. Identify the teeth and tongue. Observe the extent of the hard palate (the portion underlain by bone) and the soft palate (immediately posterior to the hard palate, with no bony support). Notice that the posterior end of the oral cavity leads into the throat, or pharynx, a passageway used by both the digestive and respiratory systems. ▮

ACTIVITY 3

Opening the Ventral Body Cavity

1. Pin the animal to the wax of the dissecting tray by placing its dorsal side down and securing its extremities to the wax with large dissecting pins as shown in Figure 2.1a.

If the dissecting tray is not waxed, you will need to secure the animal with twine as follows. (Some may prefer

FIGURE 2.2 Rat dissection: Making lateral cuts at the base of the rib cage.

this method in any case.) Obtain the roll of twine. Make a loop knot around one upper limb, pass the twine under the tray, and secure the opposing limb. Repeat for the lower extremities.

2. Lift the abdominal skin with a forceps, and cut through it with the scissors (Figure 2.1b). Close the scissor blades and insert them flat under the cut skin. Moving in a cephalad direction, open and close the blades to loosen the skin from the underlying connective tissue and muscle. Now, cut the skin along the body midline, from the pubic region to the lower jaw (Figure 2.1c). Finally, make a lateral cut about halfway down the ventral surface of each limb. Complete the job of freeing the skin with the scissor tips, and pin the flaps to the tray (Figure 2.1d). The underlying tissue that is now exposed is the skeletal musculature of the body wall and limbs. It allows voluntary body movement. Notice that the muscles are packaged in sheets of pearly white connective tissue (fascia), which protect the muscles and bind them together.

3. Carefully cut through the muscles of the abdominal wall in the pubic region, avoiding the underlying organs. Remember, to *dissect* means "to separate"—not mutilate! Now, hold and lift the muscle layer with a forceps and cut through the muscle layer from the pubic region to the bottom of the rib cage. Make two lateral cuts at the base of the rib cage (Figure 2.2). A thin membrane attached to the inferior boundary of the rib cage should be obvious; this is the **diaphragm,** which separates the thoracic and abdominal

cavities. Cut the diaphragm where it attaches to the ventral ribs to loosen the rib cage. Cut through the rib cage on either side. You can now lift the ribs to view the contents of the thoracic cavity. Cut across the flap, at the level of the neck, and remove it. ▬

ACTIVITY 4

Examining the Ventral Body Cavity

1. Starting with the most superficial structures and working deeper, examine the structures of the thoracic cavity. Refer to Figure 2.3, which shows the superficial organs, as you work. Choose the appropriate view depending on whether you are examining a rat (a) or a human cadaver (b).

Thymus: An irregular mass of glandular tissue overlying the heart (not illustrated in the human cadaver photograph).

With the probe, push the thymus to the side to view the heart.

Heart: Medial oval structure enclosed within the pericardium (serous membrane sac).

Lungs: Flanking the heart on either side.

Now observe the throat region to identify the trachea.

Trachea: Tubelike "windpipe" running medially down the throat; part of the respiratory system.

Follow the trachea into the thoracic cavity; notice where it divides into two branches. These are the bronchi.

Bronchi: Two passageways that plunge laterally into the tissue of the two lungs.

To expose the esophagus, push the trachea to one side.

Esophagus: A food chute; the part of the digestive system that transports food from the pharynx (throat) to the stomach.

Diaphragm: A thin muscle attached to the inferior boundary of the rib cage; separates the thoracic and abdominal cavities.

Follow the esophagus through the diaphragm to its junction with the stomach.

Stomach: A curved organ important in food digestion and temporary food storage.

2. Examine the superficial structures of the abdominopelvic cavity. Lift the **greater omentum,** an extension of the peritoneum that covers the abdominal viscera. Continuing from the stomach, trace the rest of the digestive tract (Figure 2.4).

Small intestine: Connected to the stomach and ending just before the saclike cecum.

Large intestine: A large muscular tube connected to the small intestine and ending at the anus.

Cecum: The initial portion of the large intestine.

Trachea

Thymus

Heart

Lung

Diaphragm

Liver

(a)

Trachea

Superior
vena cava

Pericardium (cut
and reflected)

Lungs

Heart

Diaphragm

(b)

FIGURE 2.3 Superficial organs of the thoracic cavity. (a) Dissected rat. **(b)** Human
cadaver.

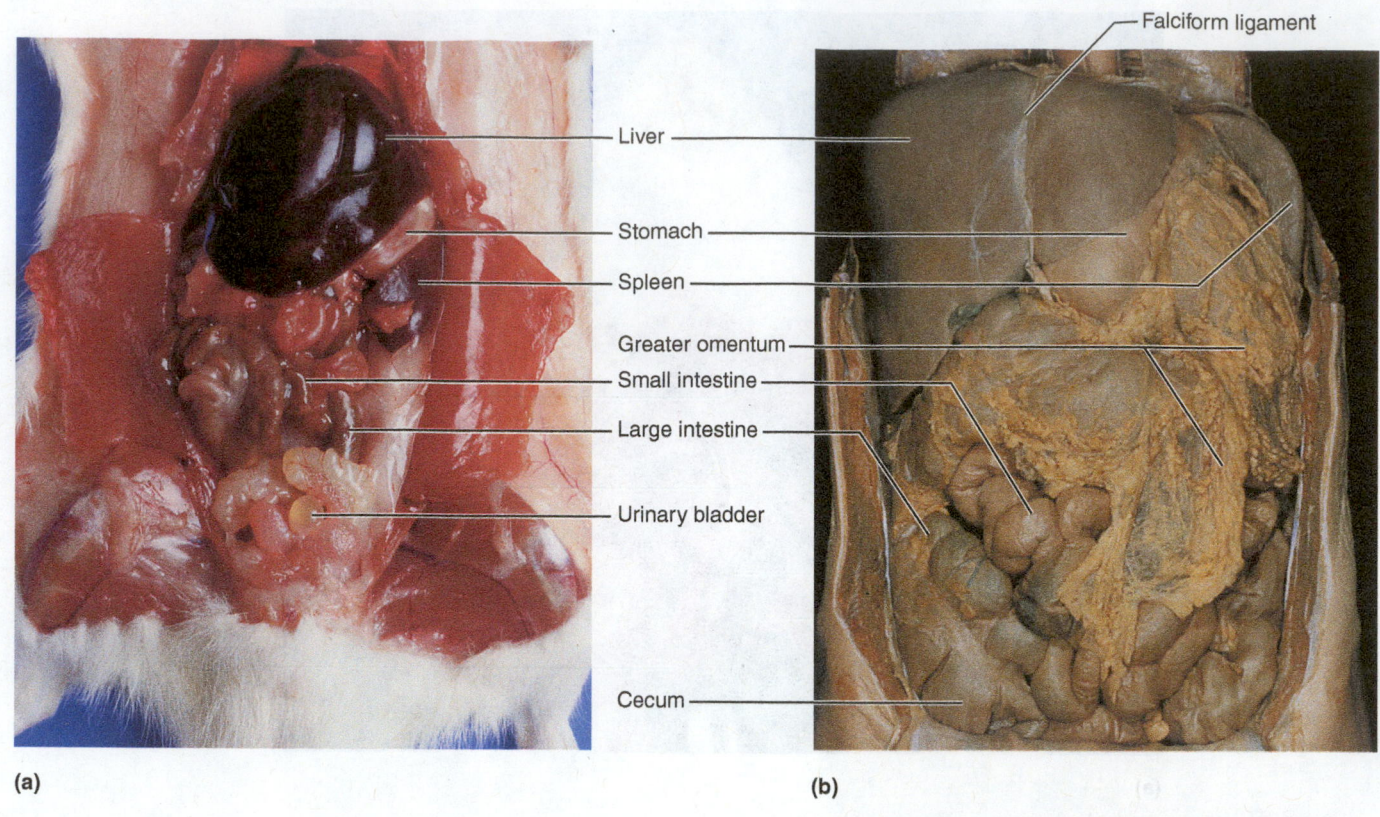

FIGURE 2.4 Abdominal organs. (a) Dissected rat, superficial view. **(b)** Human cadaver, superficial view. **(c)** Human cadaver, intermediate view. Stomach reflected superiorly to reveal the pancreas, spleen, and duodenum.

Follow the course of the large intestine to the rectum, which is partially covered by the urinary bladder (Figure 2.5).

Rectum: Terminal part of the large intestine; continuous with the anal canal.

Anus: The opening of the digestive tract (through the anal canal) to the exterior.

Now lift the small intestine with the forceps to view the mesentery.

Mesentery: An apronlike serous membrane; suspends many of the digestive organs in the abdominal cavity. Notice that it is heavily invested with blood vessels and, more likely than not, riddled with large fat deposits.

Locate the remaining abdominal structures.

Pancreas: A diffuse gland; rests dorsal to and in the mesentery between the first portion of the small intestine and the stomach. You will need to lift the stomach to view the pancreas.

Spleen: A dark red organ curving around the left lateral side of the stomach; considered part of the lymphatic system and often called the red blood cell graveyard.

Liver: Large and brownish red; the most superior organ in the abdominal cavity, directly beneath the diaphragm.

3. To locate the deeper structures of the abdominopelvic cavity, move the stomach and the intestines to one side with the probe.

Examine the posterior wall of the abdominal cavity to locate the two kidneys (Figure 2.5).

(a)

FIGURE 2.5 Deep structures of the abdominopelvic cavity. (a) Human cadaver.

(Figure continues on page 22.)

Kidneys: Bean-shaped organs; retroperitoneal (behind the peritoneum).

Adrenal glands: Large endocrine glands that sit astride the superior margin of each kidney; considered part of the endocrine system.

Carefully strip away part of the peritoneum with forceps and attempt to follow the course of one of the ureters to the bladder.

Ureter: Tube running from the indented region of a kidney to the urinary bladder.

Urinary bladder: The sac that serves as a reservoir for urine.

4.   In the midline of the body cavity lying between the kidneys are the two principal abdominal blood vessels. Identify each.

Inferior vena cava: The large vein that returns blood to the heart from the lower regions of the body.

Descending aorta: Deep to the inferior vena cava; the largest artery of the body; carries blood away from the heart down the midline of the body.

5.   Only a cursory examination of reproductive organs will be done. If you are working with a rat, first determine if the animal is a male or female. Observe the ventral body surface beneath the tail. If a saclike scrotum and an opening for the anus

are visible, the animal is a male. If three body openings—urethral, vaginal, and anal—are present, it is a female.

Male Animal

Make a shallow incision into the **scrotum.** Loosen and lift out one oval **testis.** Exert a gentle pull on the testis to identify the slender **ductus deferens,** or **vas deferens,** which carries sperm from the testis superiorly into the abdominal cavity and joins with the urethra. The urethra runs through the penis and carries both urine and sperm out of the body. Identify the **penis,** extending from the bladder to the ventral body wall. Figure 2.5b indicates other glands of the male rat's reproductive system, but they need not be identified at this time.

Female Animal

Inspect the pelvic cavity to identify the Y-shaped **uterus** lying against the dorsal body wall and superior to the bladder (Figure 2.5c). Follow one of the uterine horns superiorly to identify an **ovary,** a small oval structure at the end of the uterine horn. (The rat uterus is quite different from the uterus of a human female, which is a single-chambered organ about the size and shape of a pear.) The inferior undivided part of the rat uterus is continuous with the **vagina,** which leads to the body exterior. Identify the **vaginal orifice** (external vaginal opening).

If you are working with a human cadaver, proceed as indicated next.

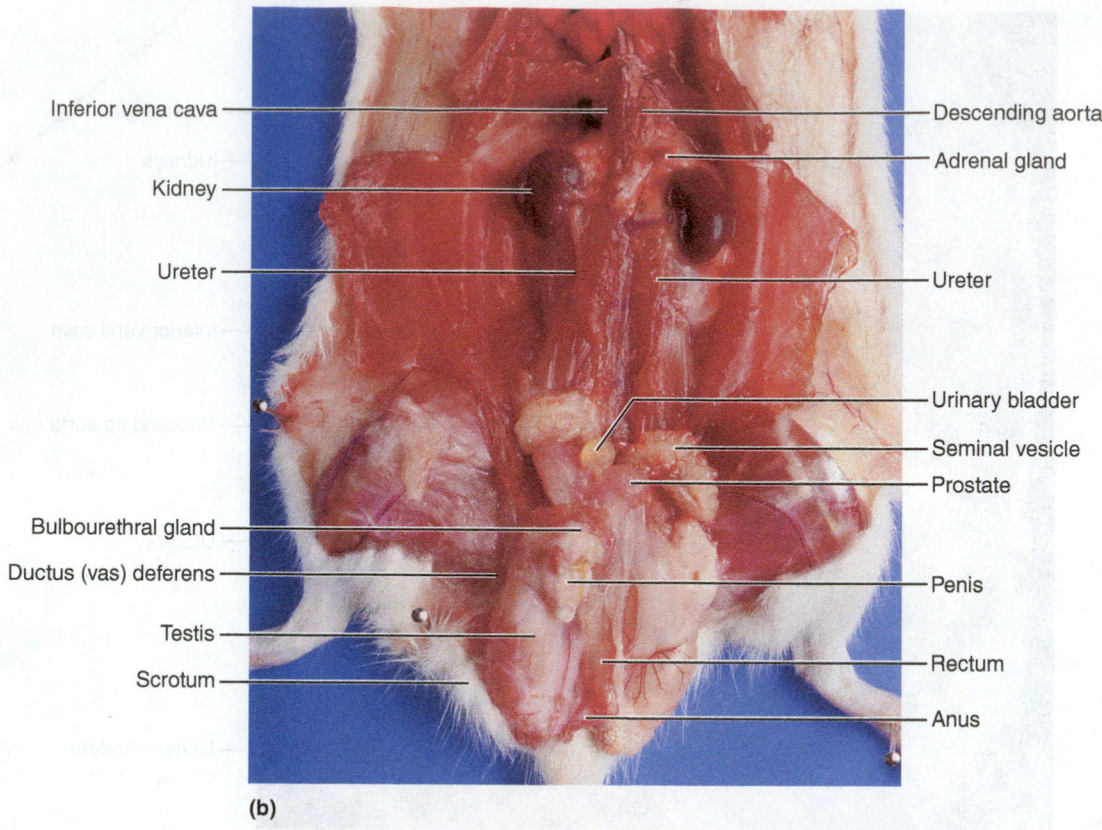

Inferior vena cava
Kidney
Ureter
Bulbourethral gland
Ductus (vas) deferens
Testis
Scrotum

Descending aorta
Adrenal gland
Ureter
Urinary bladder
Seminal vesicle
Prostate
Penis
Rectum
Anus

(b)

Kidney
Uterine horns
Urinary bladder
Urethral opening

Adrenal gland
Descending aorta
Ureter
Ovary
Uterus
Vagina
Vaginal orifice
Anus

(c)

FIGURE 2.5 (*continued*) Deep structures of the abdominopelvic cavity.
(b) Dissected male rat. (Some reproductive structures also shown.) **(c)** Dissected female rat. (Some reproductive structures also shown.)

Colon

Ureter

Seminal vesicle

Ductus deferens

Bladder

Pubis

Prostate

Penis

Testis

(a)

(b)

Colon

End of uterine tube

Ovary

Uterus

Bladder

Pubis

Vagina

External opening of vagina

(c)

FIGURE 2.6 Human reproductive organs. (a) Male external genitalia. **(b)** Sagittal section of the male pelvis. **(c)** Sagittal section of the female pelvis.

Male Cadaver

Make a shallow incision into the **scrotum** (Figure 2.6a). Loosen and lift out the oval **testis.** Exert a gentle pull on the testis to identify the slender **ductus (vas) deferens,** which carries sperm from the testis superiorly into the abdominal cavity and joins with the urethra (Figure 2.6b). The urethra runs through the penis and carries both urine and sperm out of the body. Identify the **penis,** extending from the bladder to the ventral body wall.

Female Cadaver

Inspect the pelvic cavity to identify the pear-shaped **uterus** lying against the dorsal body wall and superior to the bladder. Follow one of the **uterine tubes** superiorly to identify an **ovary,** a small oval structure at the end of the uterine tube (Figure 2.6c). The inferior part of the uterus is continuous with the **vagina,** which leads to the body exterior. Identify the **vaginal orifice** (external vaginal opening).

6. When you have finished your observations, rewrap or store the dissection animal or cadaver according to your instructor's directions. Wash the dissecting tools and equipment with laboratory detergent. Dispose of the gloves. Then wash and dry your hands before continuing with the examination of the human torso model. ▬

ACTIVITY 5

Examining the Human Torso Model

1. Examine a human torso model to identify the organs listed adjacent to Figure 2.7. Some model organs will have to be removed to see the deeper organs. If a torso model is not available, Figure 2.7 may be used for this part of the exercise.

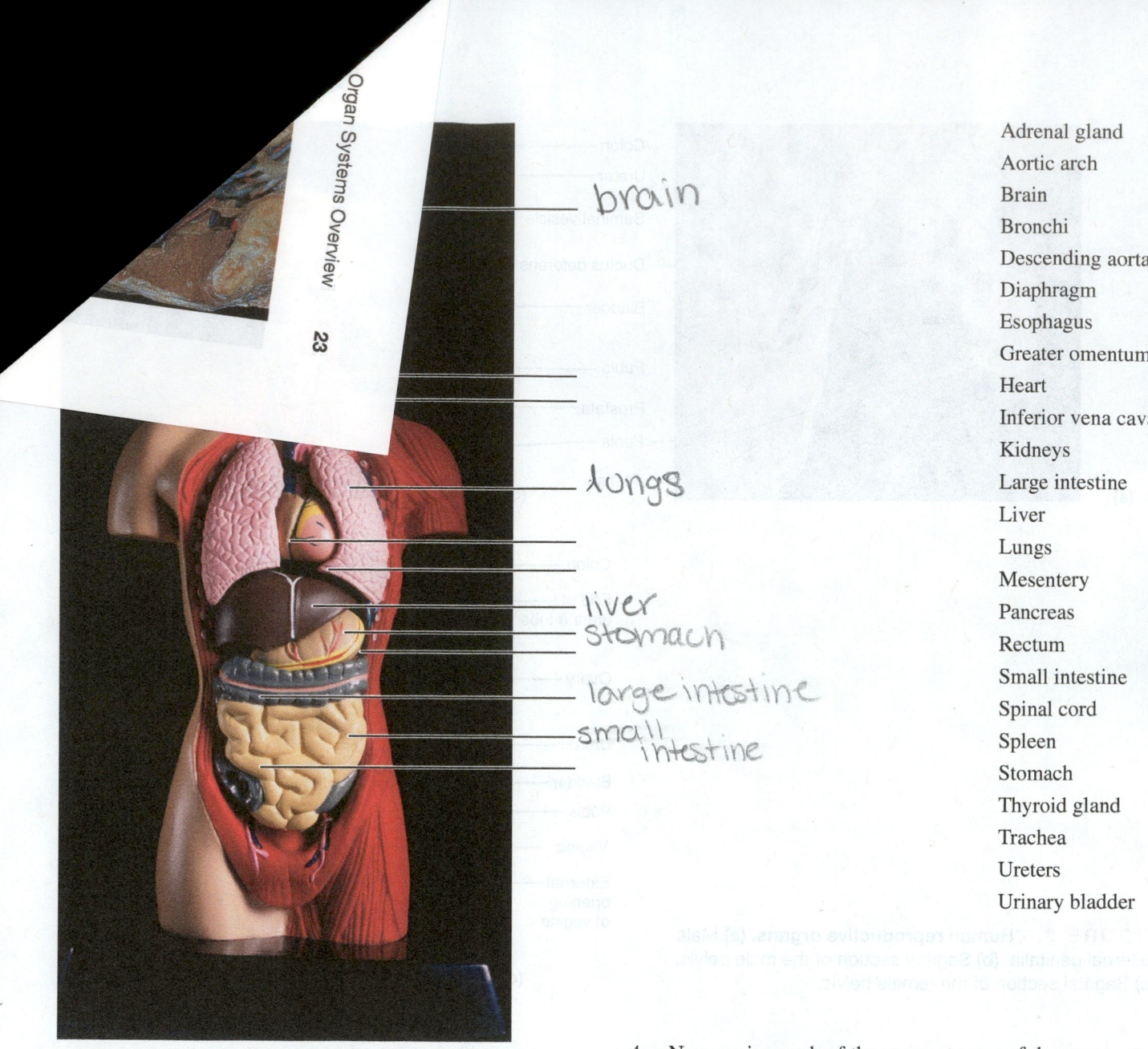

brain

lungs

liver

stomach

large intestine

small intestine

Adrenal gland
Aortic arch
Brain
Bronchi
Descending aorta
Diaphragm
Esophagus
Greater omentum
Heart
Inferior vena cava
Kidneys
Large intestine
Liver
Lungs
Mesentery
Pancreas
Rectum
Small intestine
Spinal cord
Spleen
Stomach
Thyroid gland
Trachea
Ureters
Urinary bladder

FIGURE 2.7 Human torso model.

2. Using the terms at the right of Figure 2.7, label each organ supplied with a leader line in Figure 2.7.

3. Place each of the listed organs in the correct body cavity or cavities. For organs found in the abdominopelvic cavity, also indicate which quadrant they occupy.

Dorsal body cavity _____

Thoracic cavity _____

_____

Abdominopelvic cavity _____

_____

_____

4. Now, assign each of the organs to one of the organ system categories listed below.

Digestive: _____

_____

Urinary: _____

Cardiovascular: _____

Endocrine: _____

Reproductive: _____

Respiratory: _____

Lymphatic/Immunity: _____

Nervous: _____

Organ Systems Overview

1. Use the key below to indicate the body systems that perform the following functions for the body. Then, circle the organ systems (in the key) that are present in all subdivisions of the ventral body cavity.

Key: a. cardiovascular   d. integumentary   g. nervous   j. skeletal
      b. digestive   e. lymphatic/immunity   h. reproductive   k. urinary
      c. endocrine   f. muscular   i. respiratory

_____ 1. rids the body of nitrogen-containing wastes

_____ 2. is affected by removal of the thyroid gland

_____ 3. provides support and levers on which the muscular system acts

_____ 4. includes the heart

_____ 5. causes the onset of the menstrual cycle

_____ 6. protects underlying organs from drying out and from mechanical damage

_____ 7. protects the body; destroys bacteria and tumor cells

_____ 8. breaks down ingested food into its building blocks

_____ 9. removes carbon dioxide from the blood

_____ 10. delivers oxygen and nutrients to the tissues

_____ 11. moves the limbs; facilitates facial expression

_____ 12. conserves body water or eliminates excesses

_____ and _____ 13. facilitate conception and childbearing

_____ 14. controls the body by means of chemical molecules called hormones

_____ 15. is damaged when you cut your finger or get a severe sunburn

2. Using the above key, choose the *organ system* to which each of the following sets of organs or body structures belongs.

_____ 1. thymus, spleen, lymphatic vessels

_____ 2. bones, cartilages, tendons

_____ 3. pancreas, pituitary, adrenals

_____ 4. trachea, bronchi, alveoli

_____ 5. epidermis, dermis, and cutaneous sense organs

_____ 6. testis, ductus deferens, urethra

_____ 7. esophagus, large intestine, rectum

_____ 8. muscles of the thigh, postural muscles

3. Using the key below, place the following organs in their proper body cavity.

Key:

    a. abdominopelvic   b. cranial   c. spinal   d. thoracic

_____ 1. stomach   _____ 4. liver   _____ 7. heart

_____ 2. esophagus   _____ 5. spinal cord   _____ 8. trachea

_____ 3. large intestine   _____ 6. urinary bladder _____ 9. rectum

4. Using the organs listed in question 3 above, record, by number, which would be found in the abdominal regions listed below.

_____ 1. hypogastric region   _____ 4. epigastric region

_____ 2. right lumbar region   _____ 5. left iliac region

_____ 3. umbilical region   _____ 6. left hypochondriac region

5. The levels of organization of a living body are chemical, _____, _____,

_____, _____, and organism.

6. Define *organ.*_____

_____

7. Using the terms provided, correctly identify all of the body organs provided with leader lines in the drawings shown below. Then name the organ systems by entering the name of each on the answer blank below each drawing.

Key: blood vessels   heart   nerves   spinal cord   urethra
          brain   kidney   sensory receptor   ureter   urinary bladder

a. _____   b. _____   c. _____

8. Why is it helpful to study the external and internal structures of the rat? _____

_____

The Microscope

MATERIALS

- ☐ Compound microscope
- ☐ Millimeter ruler
- ☐ Prepared slides of the letter e or newsprint
- ☐ Immersion oil
- ☐ Lens paper
- ☐ Prepared slide of grid ruled in millimeters (grid slide)
- ☐ Prepared slide of three crossed colored threads
- ☐ Clean microscope slide and coverslip
- ☐ Toothpicks (flat-tipped)
- ☐ Physiologic saline in a dropper bottle
- ☐ Iodine or methylene blue stain (dilute) in a dropper bottle
- ☐ Filter paper or paper towels
- ☐ Beaker containing fresh 10% household bleach solution for wet mount disposal
- ☐ Disposable autoclave bag
- ☐ Prepared slide of cheek epithelial cells

Note to the Instructor: The slides and coverslips used for viewing cheek cells are to be soaked for 2 hours (or longer) in 10% bleach solution and then drained. The slides and disposable autoclave bag (containing coverslips, lens paper, and used toothpicks) are to be autoclaved for 15 min at 121°C and 15 pounds pressure to ensure sterility. After autoclaving, the disposable autoclave bag may be discarded in any disposal facility, and the slides and glassware washed with laboratory detergent and reprepared for use. These instructions apply as well to any bloodstained glassware or disposable items used in other experimental procedures.

my A&P *For practice quizzes on this lab, go to www.myaandp.com.*

OBJECTIVES

1. To identify the parts of the microscope and list the function of each.
2. To describe and demonstrate the proper techniques for care of the microscope.
3. To define *total magnification* and *resolution*.
4. To demonstrate proper focusing technique.
5. To define *parfocal, field,* and *depth of field*.
6. To estimate the size of objects in a field.

PRE-LAB QUIZ

1. The microscope slide rests on the _____ while being viewed.
   a. base
   b. condenser
   c. iris
   d. stage
2. Your lab microscope is *parfocal*. This means that:
   a. The specimen is clearly in focus at this depth.
   b. The slide should be in focus at higher magnifications once it is properly focused at lower magnifications.
   c. You can easily discriminate two close objects as separate.
3. If the ocular lens magnifies a specimen 10×, and the objective lens used magnifies the specimen 35×, what is the total magnification being used to observe the specimen? _____
4. How do you clean the lenses of your microscope?
   a. with a paper towel
   b. with soap and water
   c. with special lens paper and cleaner
5. Circle True or False. You should always start your observation of specimens with the oil-immersion lens.
6. Circle True or False. It is always necessary to use a coverslip with a wet mount to prevent soiling or damaging the objective lens.

With the invention of the microscope, biologists gained a valuable tool to observe and study structures (like cells) that are too small to be seen by the unaided eye. The information gained helped in establishing many of the theories basic to the understanding of biological sciences. This exercise will familiarize you with the workhorse of microscopes—the compound microscope—and provide you with the necessary instructions for its proper use.

Care and Structure of the Compound Microscope

The **compound microscope** is a precision instrument and should always be handled with care. *At all times you must observe the following rules for its transport, cleaning, use, and storage:*

- When transporting the microscope, hold it in an upright position with one hand on its arm and the other supporting its base. Avoid swinging the instrument during its transport and jarring the instrument when setting it down.

- Use only special grit-free lens paper to clean the lenses. Use a circular motion to wipe the lenses, and clean all lenses before and after use.

- Always begin the focusing process with the lowest-power objective lens in position, changing to the higher-power lenses as necessary.

- Use the coarse adjustment knob only with the lowest-power lens.

- Always use a coverslip with temporary (wet mount) preparations.

- Before putting the microscope in the storage cabinet, remove the slide from the stage, rotate the lowest-power objective lens into position, wrap the cord neatly around the base, and replace the dust cover or return the microscope to the appropriate storage area.

- Never remove any parts from the microscope; inform your instructor of any mechanical problems that arise.

ACTIVITY 1

Identifying the Parts of a Microscope

1. Obtain a microscope and bring it to the laboratory bench. (Use the proper transport technique!)

- Record the number of your microscope in the summary chart on page 30.

Compare your microscope with the illustration in Figure 3.1 and identify the following microscope parts:

Base: Supports the microscope. (**Note:** Some microscopes are provided with an inclination joint, which allows the instrument to be tilted backward for viewing dry preparations.)

Substage light or **mirror:** Located in the base. In microscopes with a substage light source, the light passes directly upward through the microscope: light controls are located on the microscope base. If a mirror is used, light must be reflected from a separate free-standing lamp.

Stage: The platform the slide rests on while being viewed. The stage has a hole in it to permit light to pass through both it and the specimen. Some microscopes have a stage equipped with *spring clips;* others have a clamp-type *mechanical stage* as shown in Figure 3.1. Both hold the slide in position for viewing; in addition, the mechanical stage has two adjustable knobs that control precise movement of the specimen.

Condenser: Small substage lens that concentrates the light on the specimen. The condenser may have a *rack and pinion knob* that raises and lowers the condenser to vary light delivery. Generally, the best position for the condenser is close to the inferior surface of the stage.

Iris diaphragm lever: Arm attached to the base of the condenser that regulates the amount of light passing through the condenser. The iris diaphragm permits the best possible contrast when viewing the specimen.

Coarse adjustment knob: Used to focus on the specimen.

Fine adjustment knob: Used for precise focusing once coarse focusing has been completed.

Head or **body tube:** Supports the objective lens system (which is mounted on a movable nosepiece) and the ocular lens or lenses.

Arm: Vertical portion of the microscope connecting the base and head.

Ocular (or *eyepiece*): Depending on the microscope, there are one or two lenses at the superior end of the head or body tube. Observations are made through the ocular(s). An ocular lens has a magnification of 10×. (It increases the apparent size of the object by ten times or ten diameters.) If your microscope has a **pointer** (used to indicate a specific area of the viewed specimen), it is attached to one ocular and can be positioned by rotating the ocular lens.

Nosepiece: Rotating mechanism at the base of the head. Generally carries three or four objective lenses and permits sequential positioning of these lenses over the light beam passing through the hole in the stage. Use the nosepiece to change the objective lenses. Do not directly grab the lenses.

Objective lenses: Adjustable lens system that permits the use of a **scanning lens,** a **low-power lens,** a **high-power lens,** or an **oil immersion lens.** The objective lenses have different magnifying and resolving powers.

2. Examine the objective lenses carefully; note their relative lengths and the numbers inscribed on their sides. On many microscopes, the scanning lens, with a magnification between 4× and 5×, is the shortest lens. If there is no scanning lens, the low-power objective lens is the shortest and typically has a magnification of 10×. The high-power objective lens is of intermediate length and has a magnification range from 40× to 50×, depending on the microscope. The oil immersion objective lens is usually the longest of the objective lenses and has a magnifying power of 95× to 100×. Some microscopes lack the oil immersion lens.

- Record the magnification of each objective lens of your microscope in the first row of the summary chart on page 30. Also, cross out the column relating to a lens that your microscope does not have. Plan on using the same microscope for all microscopic studies.

3. Rotate the lowest-power objective lens until it clicks into position, and turn the coarse adjustment knob about 180 degrees. Notice how far the stage (or objective lens) travels during this adjustment. Move the fine adjustment knob 180 degrees, noting again the distance that the stage (or the objective lens) moves. ▪

Head

Arm

Mechanical
stage

Coarse
adjustment
knob

Fine
adjustment
knob

Condenser
rack and
pinion knob
(regulates
height of
condenser)

Base

Power
switch

Ocular lenses

Rotating
nosepiece

Stage

Objective lenses

Condenser

Iris diaphragm
lever

Substage light

Light control

FIGURE 3.1 Compound microscope and its parts.

Magnification and Resolution

The microscope is an instrument of magnification. In the compound microscope, magnification is achieved through the interplay of two lenses—the ocular lens and the objective lens. The objective lens magnifies the specimen to produce a **real image** that is projected to the ocular. This real image is magnified by the ocular lens to produce the **virtual image** seen by your eye (Figure 3.2).

The **total magnification** (TM) of any specimen being viewed is equal to the power of the ocular lens multiplied by the power of the objective lens used. For example, if the ocular lens magnifies $10\times$ and the objective lens being used magnifies $45\times$, the total magnification is $450\times$ (or 10×45).

• Determine the total magnification you may achieve with each of the objectives on your microscope, and record the figures on the third row of the chart.

The compound light microscope has certain limitations. Although the level of magnification is almost limitless, the

resolution (or resolving power), that is, the ability to discriminate two close objects as separate, is not. The human eye can resolve objects about 100 µm apart, but the compound microscope has a resolution of 0.2 µm under ideal conditions. Objects closer than 0.2 µm are seen as a single fused image.

Resolving power is determined by the amount and physical properties of the visible light that enters the microscope. In general, the more light delivered to the objective lens, the greater the resolution. The size of the objective lens aperture (opening) decreases with increasing magnification, allowing less light to enter the objective. Thus, you will probably find it necessary to increase the light intensity at the higher magnifications.

ACTIVITY 2

Viewing Objects Through the Microscope

1. Obtain a millimeter ruler, a prepared slide of the letter *e* or newsprint, a dropper bottle of immersion oil, and some lens paper. Adjust the condenser to its highest position and switch

③ Retina

Ocular lens

① **Real image**

Objective lens

Object

② **Virtual image**

Light

FIGURE 3.2 Image formation in light microscopy.
Step ① The objective lens magnifies the object, forming the real image. **Step** ② The ocular lens magnifies the real image, forming the virtual image. **Step** ③ The virtual image passes through the lens of the eye and is focused on the retina.

on the light source of your microscope. (If the light source is not built into the base, use the curved surface of the mirror to reflect the light up into the microscope.)

2. Secure the slide on the stage so that you can read the slide label and the letter *e* is centered over the light beam passing through the stage. If you are using a microscope with spring clips, make sure the slide is secured at both ends. If your microscope has a mechanical stage, open the jaws of its slide retainer (holder) by using the control lever, typically located at the rear left corner of the mechanical stage. Insert the slide squarely within the confines of the slide retainer. Check that the slide is resting on the stage (and not on the mechanical stage frame) before releasing the control lever.

3. With your lowest-power (scanning or low-power) objective lens in position over the stage, use the coarse adjustment knob to bring the objective lens and stage as close together as possible.

4. Look through the ocular lens and adjust the light for comfort using the iris diaphragm. Now use the coarse adjustment knob to focus slowly away from the *e* until it is as clearly focused as possible. Complete the focusing with the fine adjustment knob.

5. Sketch the letter *e* in the circle on the summary chart on page 31 just as it appears in the **field** (the area you see through the microscope).

How far is the bottom of the objective lens from the specimen? In other words, what is the **working distance**? Use a millimeter ruler to make this measurement.

Record the working distance in the summary chart.

How has the apparent orientation of the *e* changed top to bottom, right to left, and so on?

_____

_____

6. Move the slide slowly away from you on the stage as you view it through the ocular lens. In what direction does the image move?

_____

Move the slide to the left. In what direction does the image move?

_____

At first this change in orientation may confuse you, but with practice you will learn to move the slide in the desired direction with no problem.

7. Today most good laboratory microscopes are **parfocal;** that is, the slide should be in focus (or nearly so) at the higher magnifications once you have properly focused. *Without touching the focusing knobs,* increase the magnification by rotating the next higher magnification lens (low power or high power) into position over the stage. Make sure it clicks into position. Using the fine adjustment only, sharpen the focus.* Note the decrease in working distance. As you can see, focusing with the coarse adjustment knob could drive the objective lens through the slide, breaking the slide and possibly damaging the lens. Sketch the letter *e* in the summary chart. What new details become clear?

_____

_____

As best you can, measure the distance between the objective and the slide.

_____

Record the working distance in the summary chart.

Is the image larger or smaller? _____

Approximately how much of the letter *e* is visible now?

_____

Is the field larger or smaller? _____

Why is it necessary to center your object (or the portion of the slide you wish to view) before changing to a higher power?

_____

*If you are unable to focus with a new lens, your microscope is not parfocal. Do not try to force the lens into position. Consult your instructor.

Summary Chart for Microscope # _____

	Scanning	Low power	High power	Oil immersion
Magnification of objective lens	_____ ×	_____ ×	_____ ×	_____ ×
Magnification of ocular lens	__10__ ×	__10__ ×	__10__ ×	__10__ ×
Total magnification	_____ ×	_____ ×	_____ ×	_____ ×
Working distance	_____ mm	_____ mm	_____ mm	_____ mm
Detail observed Letter e	◯	◯	◯	◯
Field size (diameter)	____ mm ____ μm	____ mm ____ μm	____ mm ____ μm	____ mm ____ μm

---

Move the iris diaphragm lever while observing the field. What happens?

_____

Is it more desirable to increase *or* decrease the light when changing to a higher magnification?

_____ Why? _____

8.   If you have just been using the low-power objective, repeat the steps given in direction 7 using the high-power objective lens. What new details become clear?

_____

_____

Record the working distance in the summary chart.

9.   Without touching the focusing knob, rotate the high-power lens out of position so that the area of the slide over the opening in the stage is unobstructed. Place a drop of immersion oil over the *e* on the slide and rotate the oil immersion lens into position. Set the condenser at its highest point (closest to the stage), and open the diaphragm fully. Adjust the fine focus and fine-tune the light for the best possible resolution.

Note: If for some reason the specimen does not come into view after adjusting the fine focus, do not go back to the 40× lens to recenter. You do not want oil from the oil immersion

lens to cloud the 40× lens. Turn the revolving nosepiece in the other direction to the low-power lens and recenter and refocus the object. Then move the immersion lens back into position, again avoiding the 40× lens. Sketch the letter *e* in the summary chart, What new details become clear?

_____

_____

Is the field again decreased in size? _____

As best you can, estimate the working distance, and record it in the summary chart. Is the working distance less *or* greater than it was when the high-power lens was focused?

_____

Compare your observations on the relative working distances of the objective lenses with the illustration in Figure 3.3. Explain why it is desirable to begin the focusing process at the lowest power.

_____

_____

_____

10. Rotate the oil immersion lens slightly to the side and remove the slide. Clean the oil immersion lens carefully with

10× 45× 100×

Stage

FIGURE 3.3 Relative working distances of the 10×, 45×, and 100× objectives.

TABLE 3.1	Comparison of Metric Units of Length	
Metric unit	Abbreviation	Equivalent
Meter	m	(about 39.3 in.)
Centimeter	cm	10^{-2} m
Millimeter	mm	10^{-3} m
Micrometer (or micron)	μm (μ)	10^{-6} m
Nanometer (or millimicrometer or millimicron)	nm (mμ)	10^{-9} m
Ångstrom	Å	10^{-10} m

Refer to the "Getting Started" exercise (page xv) for tips on metric conversions.

lens paper, and then clean the slide in the same manner with a fresh piece of lens paper. ▬

The Microscope Field

By this time you should know that the size of the microscope field decreases with increasing magnification. For future microscope work, it will be useful to determine the diameter of each of the microscope fields. This information will allow you to make a fairly accurate estimate of the size of the objects you view in any field. For example, if you have calculated the field diameter to be 4 mm and the object being observed extends across half this diameter, you can estimate that the length of the object is approximately 2 mm.

Microscopic specimens are usually measured in micrometers and millimeters, both units of the metric system. You can get an idea of the relationship and meaning of these units from Table 3.1. A more detailed treatment appears in Appendix A.

ACTIVITY 3

Estimating the Diameter of the Microscope Field

1. Obtain a grid slide (a slide prepared with graph paper ruled in millimeters). Each of the squares in the grid is 1 mm on each side. Use your lowest-power objective to bring the grid lines into focus.

2. Move the slide so that one grid line touches the edge of the field on one side, and then count the number of squares you can see across the diameter of the field. If you can see only part of a square, as in the accompanying diagram, estimate the part of a millimeter that the partial square represents.

~2.5 mm

Record this figure in the appropriate space marked "field size" on the summary chart (page 31). (If you have been using the scanning lens, repeat the procedure with the low-power objective lens.)

Complete the chart by computing the approximate diameter of the high-power and oil immersion fields. The general formula for calculating the unknown field diameter is:

Diameter of field A × total magnification of field A = diameter of field B × total magnification of field B

where A represents the known or measured field and B represents the unknown field. This can be simplified to

$$\text{Diameter of field } B =$$

$$\frac{\text{diameter of field } A \times \text{ total magnification of field } A}{\text{total magnification of field } B}$$

For example, if the diameter of the low-power field (field A) is 2 mm and the total magnification is 50×, you would compute the diameter of the high-power field (field B) with a total magnification of 100 × as follows:

Field diameter B = (2mm × 50)/100
Field diameter B = 1mm

3. Estimate the length (longest dimension) of the following microscopic objects. *Base your calculations on the field sizes you have determined for your microscope.*

Object seen in low-power field:

approximate length:

_____ mm

Object seen in high-power field:

approximate length:

_____ mm

or _____ μm

Object seen in oil immersion field:

approximate length:

_____ µm

4. If an object viewed with the oil immersion lens looked as it does in the field depicted just below, could you determine its approximate size from this view?

If not, then how could you determine it? _____

_____

_____ ▬

Perceiving Depth

Any microscopic specimen has depth as well as length and width; it is rare indeed to view a tissue slide with just one layer of cells. Normally you can see two or three cell thicknesses. Therefore, it is important to learn how to determine relative depth with your microscope. In microscope work the **depth of field** (the depth of the specimen clearly in focus) is greater at lower magnifications.

ACTIVITY 4

Perceiving Depth

1. Obtain a slide with colored crossed threads. Focusing at low magnification, locate the point where the three threads cross each other.

2. Use the iris diaphragm lever to greatly reduce the light, thus increasing the contrast. Focus down with the coarse adjustment until the threads are out of focus, then slowly focus upward again, noting which thread comes into clear focus first. (You will see two or even all three threads, so you must be very careful in determining which one first comes into clear focus.) Observe: As you rotate the adjustment knob forward (away from you), does the stage rise or fall? If the stage rises, then the first clearly focused thread is the top one; the last clearly focused thread is the bottom one.

If the stage descends, how is the order affected? _____

_____

Record your observations, relative to which color of thread is uppermost, middle, or lowest:

Top thread _____

Middle thread _____

Bottom thread _____ ▬

Viewing Cells Under the Microscope

There are various ways to prepare cells for viewing under a microscope. Cells and tissues can look very different with different stains and preparation techniques. One method of preparation is to mix the cells in physiologic saline (called a wet mount) and stain them with methylene blue stain.

If you are not instructed to prepare your own wet mount, obtain a prepared slide of epithelial cells to make the observations in step 10 of Activity 5.

ACTIVITY 5

Preparing and Observing a Wet Mount

1. Obtain the following: a clean microscope slide and coverslip, two flat-tipped toothpicks, a dropper bottle of physiologic saline, a dropper bottle of iodine or methylene blue stain, and filter paper (or paper towels). Handle only your own slides throughout the procedure.

2. Place a drop of physiologic saline in the center of the slide. Using the flat end of the toothpick, *gently* scrape the inner lining of your cheek. Transfer your cheek scrapings to the slide by agitating the end of the toothpick in the drop of saline (Figure 3.4a).

FIGURE 3.4 Procedure for preparation of a wet mount. (a) The object is placed in a drop of water (or saline) on a clean slide, **(b)** a coverslip is held at a 45° angle with the fingertips, and **(c)** it is lowered carefully over the water and the object.

FIGURE 3.5 Epithelial cells of the cheek cavity (surface view, 750×).

Obtain the following: a clean microscope slide and cov...

Immediately discard the used toothpick in the disposable autoclave bag provided at the supplies area.

3. Add a tiny drop of the iodine or methylene blue stain to the preparation. (These epithelial cells are nearly transparent and thus difficult to see without the stain, which colors the nuclei of the cells and makes them look much darker than the cytoplasm.) Stir again.

Immediately discard the used toothpick in the disposable autoclave bag provided at the supplies area.

4. Hold the coverslip with your fingertips so that its bottom edge touches one side of the fluid drop (Figure 3.4b), then *carefully* lower the coverslip onto the preparation (Figure 3.4c). *Do not just drop the coverslip,* or you will trap large air bubbles under it, which will obscure the cells. *A coverslip should always be used with a wet mount* to prevent soiling the lens if you should misfocus.

5. Examine your preparation carefully. The coverslip should be closely apposed to the slide. If there is excess fluid around its edges, you will need to remove it. Obtain a piece of filter paper, fold it in half, and use the folded edge to absorb the excess fluid. (You may use a twist of paper towel as an alternative.)

Before continuing, discard the filter paper in the disposable autoclave bag.

6. Place the slide on the stage, and locate the cells at the lowest power. You will probably want to dim the light with the iris diaphragm to provide more contrast for viewing the lightly stained cells. Furthermore, a wet mount will dry out quickly in bright light because a bright light source is hot.

7. Cheek epithelial cells are very thin, six-sided cells. In the cheek, they provide a smooth, tilelike lining, as shown in Figure 3.5. Move to high power to examine the cells more closely.

8. Make a sketch of the epithelial cells that you observe.

Use information on your summary chart (page 31) to estimate the diameter of cheek epithelial cells.

_____ mm

Why do *your* cheek cells look different than those illustrated in Figure 3.5? (Hint: What did you have to *do* to your cheek to obtain them?)

_____

_____

9. When you complete your observations of the wet mount, dispose of your wet mount preparation in the beaker of bleach solution, and put the coverslips in an autoclave bag.

10. Obtain a prepared slide of cheek epithelial cells, and view them under the microscope.

Estimate the diameter of one of these cheek epithelial cells using information from the summary chart (page 31).

_____ mm

Why are these cells more similar to those seen in Figure 3.5 and easier to measure than those of the wet mount?

_____

_____

11. Before leaving the laboratory, make sure all other materials are properly discarded or returned to the appropriate laboratory station. Clean the microscope lenses and put the dust cover on the microscope before you return it to the storage cabinet. ▪

NAME_____

LAB TIME/DATE_____

The Microscope

Care and Structure of the Compound Microscope

1. Label all indicated parts of the microscope.

2. Explain the proper technique for transporting the microscope.

_____

_____

3. The following statements are true or false. If true, write *T* on the answer blank. If false, correct the statement by writing on the blank the proper word or phrase to replace the one that is underlined.

_____ 1. The microscope lens may be cleaned <u>with any soft tissue</u>.

_____ 2. The microscope should be stored with the <u>oil immersion</u> lens in position over the stage.

_____ 3. When beginning to focus, use the <u>lowest-power</u> lens.

_____ 4. When focusing, always focus <u>toward</u> the specimen.

_____ 5. A coverslip should always be used <u>with wet mounts and the high-power and oil lenses</u>.

4. Match the microscope structures given in column B with the statements in column A that identify or describe them.

Column A

_____ 1. platform on which the slide rests for viewing

_____ 2. used to increase the amount of light passing through the specimen

_____ 3. secure(s) the slide to the stage

_____ 4. delivers a concentrated beam of light to the specimen

_____ 5. used for precise focusing once initial focusing has been done

_____ 6. carries the objective lenses; rotates so that the different objective lenses can be brought into position over the specimen

Column B

a. coarse adjustment knob
b. condenser
c. fine adjustment knob
d. iris diaphragm
e. mechanical stage or spring clips
f. movable nosepiece
g. objective lenses
h. ocular
i. stage

5. Define the following terms.

virtual image: _____

_____

resolution: _____

Viewing Objects Through the Microscope

6. Complete, or respond to, the following statements:

_____ 1. The distance from the bottom of the objective lens in use to the specimen is called the _____.

_____ 2. Assume there is an object on the left side of the field that you want to bring to the center (that is, toward the apparent right). In what direction would you move your slide?

_____ 3. The area of the specimen seen when looking through the microscope is the _____.

_____ 4. If a microscope has a 10× ocular and the total magnification at a particular time is 950×, the objective lens is use at that time is _____×.

_____ 5. Why should the light be dimmed when looking at living (nearly transparent) cells?

_____ 6. If, after focusing in low power, only the fine adjustment need be used to focus the specimen at the higher powers, the microscope is said to be _____.

_____ 7. If, when using a 10× ocular and a 15× objective, the field size is 1.5 mm, the approximate field size with a 30× objective is _____ mm.

_____ 8. If the size of the high-power field is 1.2 mm, an object that occupies approximately a third of that field has an estimated diameter of _____ mm.

7. You have been asked to prepare a slide with the letter _k_ on it (as shown below). In the circle below, draw the _k_ as seen in the low-power field.

k

8. Figure out the magnification of fields 1 and 3, and the field size of 2. (_Hint:_ Use your ruler.) Note that the numbers for the field sizes below are too large to represent the typical compound microscope lens system, but the relationships depicted are accurate.

5 mm	____ mm	0.5 mm
1. ➤◯◄	2. ➤◯◄	3. ➤•◄
_____×	100×	_____×

9. Say you are observing an object in the low-power field. When you switch to high-power, it is no longer in your field of view.

Why might this occur? _____

_____

What should be done initially to prevent this from happening? _____

_____

10. Do the following factors increase or decrease as one moves to higher magnifications with the microscope?

resolution: _____   amount of light needed: _____

working distance: _____   depth of field: _____

11. A student has the high-dry lens in position and appears to be intently observing the specimen. The instructor, noting a working distance of about 1 cm, knows the student isn't actually seeing the specimen.

How so? _____

12. Describe the proper procedure for preparing a wet mount.

_____

_____

_____

13. Indicate the probable cause of the following situations arising during use of a microscope.

a.   Only half of the field is illuminated: _____

_____

b.   Field does not change as mechanical stage is moved: _____

_____

The Cell: Anatomy and Division

MATERIALS

- ☐ Three-dimensional model of the "composite" animal cell or laboratory chart of cell anatomy
- ☐ Compound microscope
- ☐ Prepared slides of simple squamous epithelium, teased smooth muscle (l.s.), human blood cell smear, and sperm
- ☐ Animation/video of mitosis
- ☐ Three-dimensional models of mitotic stages
- ☐ Prepared slides of whitefish blastulae

Note to the Instructor: See directions for handling wet mount preparations and disposable supplies on page 33, Exercise 3. For suggestions on the animation/video of mitosis, see the Instructor Guide.

OBJECTIVES

1. To define *cell, organelle,* and *inclusion.*
2. To identify on a cell model or diagram the following cellular regions and to list the major function of each: nucleus, cytoplasm, and plasma membrane.
3. To identify and list the major functions of the various organelles studied.
4. To compare and contrast specialized cells with the concept of the "generalized cell."
5. To define *interphase, mitosis,* and *cytokinesis.*
6. To list the stages of mitosis and describe the events of each stage.
7. To identify the mitotic phases on slides or appropriate diagrams.
8. To explain the importance of mitotic cell division and its product.

PRE-LAB QUIZ

1. Define *cell.* _____
   _____
2. When a cell is not dividing, the genetic material is loosely dispersed throughout the nucleus in a threadlike form called:
   a. chromatin   c. cytosol
   b. chromosomes   d. ribosomes
3. The plasma membrane not only provides a protective barrier for the cell but also determines which substances enter or exit the cell. We call this characteristic:
   a. diffusion   c. osmosis
   b. membrane potential d. selective permeability
4. Name the organelles that are the sites of protein synthesis.
   _____
5. Because these organelles are responsible for providing the bulk of ATP needed by the cell, they are often referred to as the "powerhouses" of the cell. They are the:
   a. centrioles   c. mitochondria
   b. lysosomes   d. ribosomes
6. Circle the correct term. During <u>cytokinesis</u> / <u>interphase</u> the cell grows and carries out its usual activities.
7. Circle True or False. The end product of mitosis is four genetically identical daughter cells.
8. How many stages of mitosis are there? _____
9. DNA replication occurs during:
   a. cytokinesis   c. metaphase
   b. interphase   d. prophase
10. Circle True or False. All animal cells have a cell wall.

The **cell,** the structural and functional unit of all living things, is a complex entity. The cells of the human body are highly diverse, and their differences in size, shape, and internal composition reflect their specific roles in the body. Nonetheless, cells do have many common anatomical features, and all cells must carry out certain functions to sustain life. For example, all cells can maintain their boundaries, metabolize, digest nutrients and dispose of wastes, grow and reproduce, move, and respond to a stimulus. Most of these functions are considered in detail in later exercises. This exercise focuses on structural similarities that typify the "composite," or "generalized," cell and considers only the function of cell reproduction (cell division). Transport mechanisms (the means by which substances cross a cell's external membrane) are dealt with separately in Exercise 5.

Anatomy of the Composite Cell

In general, all cells have three major regions, or parts, that can readily be identified with a light microscope: the **nucleus,** the **plasma membrane,** and the **cytoplasm.** The nucleus is typically a round or oval structure near the center of the cell. It is surrounded by cytoplasm, which in turn is enclosed by the plasma membrane. Since the advent of the electron microscope, even smaller cell structures—organelles—have been identified. Figure 4.1a is a diagrammatic representation of the fine structure of the composite cell; Figure 4.1b depicts cellular structure (particularly that of the nucleus) as revealed by the electron microscope.

Nucleus

The nucleus contains the genetic material, DNA, sections of which are called "genes." Often described as the control center of the cell, the nucleus is necessary for cell reproduction. A cell that has lost or ejected its nucleus (for whatever reason) is programmed to die.

When the cell is not dividing, the genetic material is loosely dispersed throughout the nucleus in a threadlike form called **chromatin.** When the cell is in the process of dividing to form daughter cells, the chromatin coils and condenses, forming dense, darkly staining rodlike bodies called **chromosomes**—much in the way a stretched spring becomes shorter and thicker when it is released. (Cell division is discussed later in this exercise.) Carefully note the appearance of the nucleus—it is somewhat nondescript when a cell is healthy. A dark nucleus and clumped chromatin are indications that the cell is dying and undergoing degeneration.

The nucleus also contains one or more small round bodies, called **nucleoli,** composed primarily of proteins and ribonucleic acid (RNA). The nucleoli are assembly sites for ribosomal particles (particularly abundant in the cytoplasm), which are the actual protein-synthesizing "factories."

The nucleus is bound by a double-layered porous membrane, the **nuclear envelope.** The nuclear envelope is similar in composition to other cellular membranes, but it is distinguished by its large **nuclear pores.** Although they are spanned by diaphragms, these pores permit easy passage of protein and RNA molecules.

(a)

(b) Mitochondria   Chromatin   Nucleolus

FIGURE 4.1 Anatomy of the composite animal cell. (a) Diagrammatic view. **(b)** Transmission electron micrograph (10,000×).

ACTIVITY 1

Identifying Parts of a Cell

As able, identify the nuclear envelope, chromatin, nucleolus, and the nuclear pores in Figure 4.1a and b and Figure 4.3. ■

Plasma Membrane

The **plasma membrane** separates cell contents from the surrounding environment. Its main structural building blocks are phospholipids (fats) and globular protein molecules, but some of the externally facing proteins and lipids have sugar (carbohydrate) side chains attached to them that are important in cellular interactions (Figure 4.2). Described by the fluid-mosaic model, the membrane is a bilayer of phospholipid molecules in which the protein molecules float. Occasional cholesterol molecules dispersed in the fluid phospholipid bilayer help stabilize it.

Besides providing a protective barrier for the cell, the plasma membrane plays an active role in determining which substances may enter or leave the cell and in what quantity. Because of its molecular composition, the plasma membrane is selective about what passes through it. It allows nutrients to

Extracellular fluid (watery environment)

Polar head of phospholipid molecule

Cholesterol

Glycolipid

Glycoprotein

Nonpolar tail of phospholipid molecule

Carbohydrate of glycocalyx

Bimolecular lipid layer containing proteins

Outward-facing layer of phospholipids

Inward-facing layer of phospholipids

Integral proteins

Filament of cytoskeleton

Peripheral proteins

Cytoplasm (watery environment)

FIGURE 4.2 Structural details of the plasma membrane.

enter the cell but keeps out undesirable substances. By the same token, valuable cell proteins and other substances are kept within the cell, and excreta or wastes pass to the exterior. This property is known as **selective permeability.** Transport through the plasma membrane occurs in two basic ways. In *active transport,* the cell must provide energy (adenosine triphosphate, ATP) to power the transport process. In *passive transport,* the transport process is driven by concentration or pressure differences.

Additionally, the plasma membrane maintains a resting potential that is essential to normal functioning of excitable cells, such as neurons and muscle cells, and plays a vital role in cell signaling and cell-to-cell interactions. In some cells the membrane is thrown into minute fingerlike projections or folds called **microvilli** (see Figure 4.3 on page 42). Microvilli greatly increase the surface area of the cell available for absorption or passage of materials and for the binding of signaling molecules.

ACTIVITY 2

Identifying Components of a Plasma Membrane

Identify the phospholipid and protein portions of the plasma membrane in Figure 4.2. Also locate the sugar (*glyco* = car-

bohydrate) side chains and cholesterol molecules. Identify the microvilli in the orientation diagram at the top of Figure 4.2 and in Figure 4.3. ■

Cytoplasm and Organelles

The cytoplasm consists of the cell contents between the nucleus and plasma membrane. It is the major site of most activities carried out by the cell. Suspended in the **cytosol,** the fluid cytoplasmic material, are many small structures called **organelles** (literally, "small organs"). The organelles are the metabolic machinery of the cell, and they are highly organized to carry out specific functions for the cell as a whole. The organelles include the ribosomes, endoplasmic reticulum, Golgi apparatus, lysosomes, peroxisomes, mitochondria, cytoskeletal elements, and centrioles.

ACTIVITY 3

Locating Organelles

Each organelle type is summarized in Table 4.1 and described briefly below. Read through this material and then, as best you can, locate the organelles in both Figures 4.1b and 4.3. ■

* **Ribosomes** are densely staining, roughly spherical bodies composed of RNA and protein. They are the actual sites of

Chromatin

Nucleolus

Smooth endoplasmic reticulum

Cytosol

Mitochondrion

Lysosome

Centrioles

Centrosome matrix

Microvilli

Microfilament

Microtubule

Cytoskeletal elements

Intermediate filaments

Nuclear envelope

Nucleus

Plasma membrane

Rough endoplasmic reticulum

Ribosomes

Golgi apparatus

Secretion being released from cell by exocytosis

Peroxisome

FIGURE 4.3 Structure of the generalized cell. No cell is exactly like this one, but this composite illustrates features common to many human cells. Not all organelles are drawn to the same scale in this illustration.

protein synthesis. They are seen floating free in the cytoplasm or attached to a membranous structure. When they are attached, the whole ribosome-membrane complex is called the *rough endoplasmic reticulum.*

• The **endoplasmic reticulum (ER)** is a highly folded system of membranous tubules and cisternae (sacs) that extends throughout the cytoplasm. The ER is continuous with the nuclear envelope. Thus, it is assumed that the ER provides a system of channels for the transport of cellular substances (primarily proteins) from one part of the cell to another. The ER exists in two forms; a particular cell may have both or only one, depending on its specific functions. The **rough ER,** as noted earlier, is studded with ribosomes. Its cisternae modify and store the newly formed proteins and dispatch them to other areas of the cell. The external face of the rough ER is involved

in phospholipid and cholesterol synthesis. The amount of rough ER is closely correlated with the amount of protein a cell manufactures and is especially abundant in cells that make protein products for export—for example, the pancreas cells that produce digestive enzymes destined for the small intestine.

The **smooth ER** does not participate in protein synthesis but is present in conspicuous amounts in cells that produce steroid-based hormones—for example, the interstitial cells of the testes, which produce testosterone. Smooth ER is also abundant in cells that are active in lipid metabolism and drug detoxification activities—liver cells, for instance.

• The **Golgi apparatus** is a stack of flattened sacs with bulbous ends that is generally found close to the nucleus. Within its cisternae, the proteins delivered to it by transport vesicles from the rough ER are modified (by attachment of sugar groups), segregated, and packaged into membranous vesicles that ultimately (1) are incorporated into the plasma membrane, (2) become secretory vesicles that release their contents from the cell, or (3) become lysosomes.

- **Lysosomes,** which appear in various sizes, are membrane-bound sacs containing an array of powerful digestive enzymes. A product of the packaging activities of the Golgi apparatus, the lysosomes contain *acid hydrolases,* enzymes capable of digesting worn-out cell structures and foreign substances that enter the cell via vesicle formation through phagocytosis or endocytosis (see Exercise 5A). Because they have the capacity of total cell destruction, the lysosomes are often referred to as the "suicide sacs" of the cell.

- **Peroxisomes,** like lysosomes, are enzyme-containing sacs. However, their *oxidases* have a different task. Using oxygen, they detoxify a number of harmful substances, most importantly free radicals. Peroxisomes are particularly abundant in kidney and liver cells, cells that are actively involved in detoxification.

- **Mitochondria** are generally rod-shaped bodies with a double-membrane wall; the inner membrane is thrown into folds, or *cristae.* Oxidative enzymes on or within the mitochondria catalyze the reactions of the Krebs cycle and the electron transport chain (collectively called oxidative respiration), in which end products of food digestion are broken down to produce energy. The released energy is captured in the bonds of ATP molecules, which are then transported out of the mitochondria to provide a ready energy supply to power the cell. Every living cell requires a constant supply of ATP for its many activities. Because the mitochondria provide the bulk of this ATP, they are referred to as the "powerhouses" of the cell.

- **Cytoskeletal elements** ramify throughout the cytoplasm, forming an internal scaffolding called the *cytoskeleton* that supports and moves substances within the cell. The **microtubules** are slender tubules formed of proteins called *tubulins,* which have the ability to aggregate and then disaggregate spontaneously. Microtubules organize the cytoskeleton and direct formation of the spindle formed by the centrioles during cell division. They also act in the transport of substances down the length of elongated cells (such as neurons), suspend organelles, and help maintain cell shape by providing rigidity to the soft cellular substance. **Intermediate filaments** are *stable* proteinaceous cytoskeletal elements that act as internal guy wires to resist mechanical (pulling) forces acting on cells. **Microfilaments,** ribbon or cordlike elements, are formed of contractile proteins, primarily *actin.* Because of their ability to shorten and then relax to assume a more elongated form, these are important in cell mobility and are very conspicuous in cells that are specialized to contract (such as muscle cells). A cross-linked network of *lamin* microfilaments braces and strengthens the internal face of the plasma membrane.

The cytoskeletal structures are changeable and minute. With the exception of the microtubules of the spindle, which are very obvious during cell division (see pages 46–47), and the microfilaments of skeletal muscle cells, they are rarely seen, even in electron micrographs, and are not depicted in Figure 4.1b. However, special stains can reveal the plentiful supply of these important organelles.

- The paired **centrioles** lie close to the nucleus in all animal cells capable of reproducing themselves. They are rod-shaped bodies that lie at right angles to each other. Internally each centriole is composed of nine triplets of microtubules. During cell division, the centrioles direct the formation of the mitotic spindle. Centrioles also form the cell projections called cilia and flagella, and in that role are called basal bodies.

The cell cytoplasm contains various other substances and structures, including stored foods (glycogen granules and lipid droplets), pigment granules, crystals of various types, water vacuoles, and ingested foreign materials. However, these are not part of the active metabolic machinery of the cell and are therefore called **inclusions.**

ACTIVITY 4

Examining the Cell Model

Once you have located all of these structures in Figure 4.3, examine the cell model (or cell chart) to repeat and reinforce your identifications. ■

Differences and Similarities in Cell Structure

ACTIVITY 5

Observing Various Cell Structures

1. Obtain a compound microscope and prepared slides of simple squamous epithelium, smooth muscle cells (teased), human blood, and sperm.

2. Observe each slide under the microscope, carefully noting similarities and differences in the cells. See photomicrographs for simple squamous epithelium (Figure 3.5 in Exercise 3) and teased smooth muscle (Figure 6A.7c in Exercise 6A). (The oil immersion lens will be needed to observe blood and sperm.) Distinguish the limits of the individual cells, and notice the shape and position of the nucleus in each case. When you look at the human blood smear, direct your attention to the red blood cells, the pink-stained cells that are most numerous. The color photomicrographs illustrating a blood smear (Figure 29A.3 in Exercise 29A) and sperm (Figure 43.3 in Exercise 43) may be helpful in this cell structure study. Sketch your observations in the circles provided on page 45.

3. Measure the length or diameter of each cell, and record below the appropriate sketch.

4. How do these four cell types differ in shape and size?

_____

_____

_____

_____

TABLE 4.1	Summary of Structure and Function of Cytoplasmic Organelles
Organelle	**Location and function**
Ribosomes	Tiny spherical bodies composed of RNA and protein; actual sites of protein synthesis; floating free or attached to a membranous structure (the rough ER) in the cytoplasm
Endoplasmic reticulum (ER)	Membranous system of tubules that extends throughout the cytoplasm; two varieties—rough ER is studded with ribosomes (tubules of the rough ER provide an area for storage and transport of the proteins made on the ribosomes to other cell areas; external face synthesizes phospholipids and cholesterol) and smooth ER, which has no function in protein synthesis (rather it is a site of steroid and lipid synthesis, lipid metabolism, and drug detoxification)
Golgi apparatus	Stack of flattened sacs with bulbous ends and associated small vesicles; found close to the nucleus; plays a role in packaging proteins or other substances for export from the cell or incorporation into the plasma membrane and in packaging lysosomal enzymes
Lysosomes	Various-sized membranous sacs containing digestive enzymes (acid hydrolases); function to digest worn-out cell organelles and foreign substances that enter the cell; have the capacity of total cell destruction if ruptured
Peroxisomes	Small lysosome-like membranous sacs containing oxidase enzymes that detoxify alcohol, hydrogen peroxide, and other harmful chemicals
Mitochondria	Generally rod-shaped bodies with a double-membrane wall; inner membrane is thrown into folds, or cristae; contain enzymes that oxidize foodstuffs to produce cellular energy (ATP); often referred to as "powerhouses of the cell"
Centrioles	Paired, cylindrical bodies lie at right angles to each other, close to the nucleus; direct the formation of the mitotic spindle during cell division; form the bases of cilia and flagella
Cytoskeletal elements: microfilaments, intermediate filaments, and microtubules	Provide cellular support; function in intracellular transport; microfilaments are formed largely of actin, a contractile protein, and thus are important in cell mobility (particularly in muscle cells); intermediate filaments are stable elements composed of a variety of proteins and resist mechanical forces acting on cells; microtubules form the internal structure of the centrioles and help determine cell shape

How might cell shape affect cell function? _____

_____

_____

_____

_____

_____

Which cells have visible projections? _____

_____

How do these projections relate to the function of these cells?

_____

_____

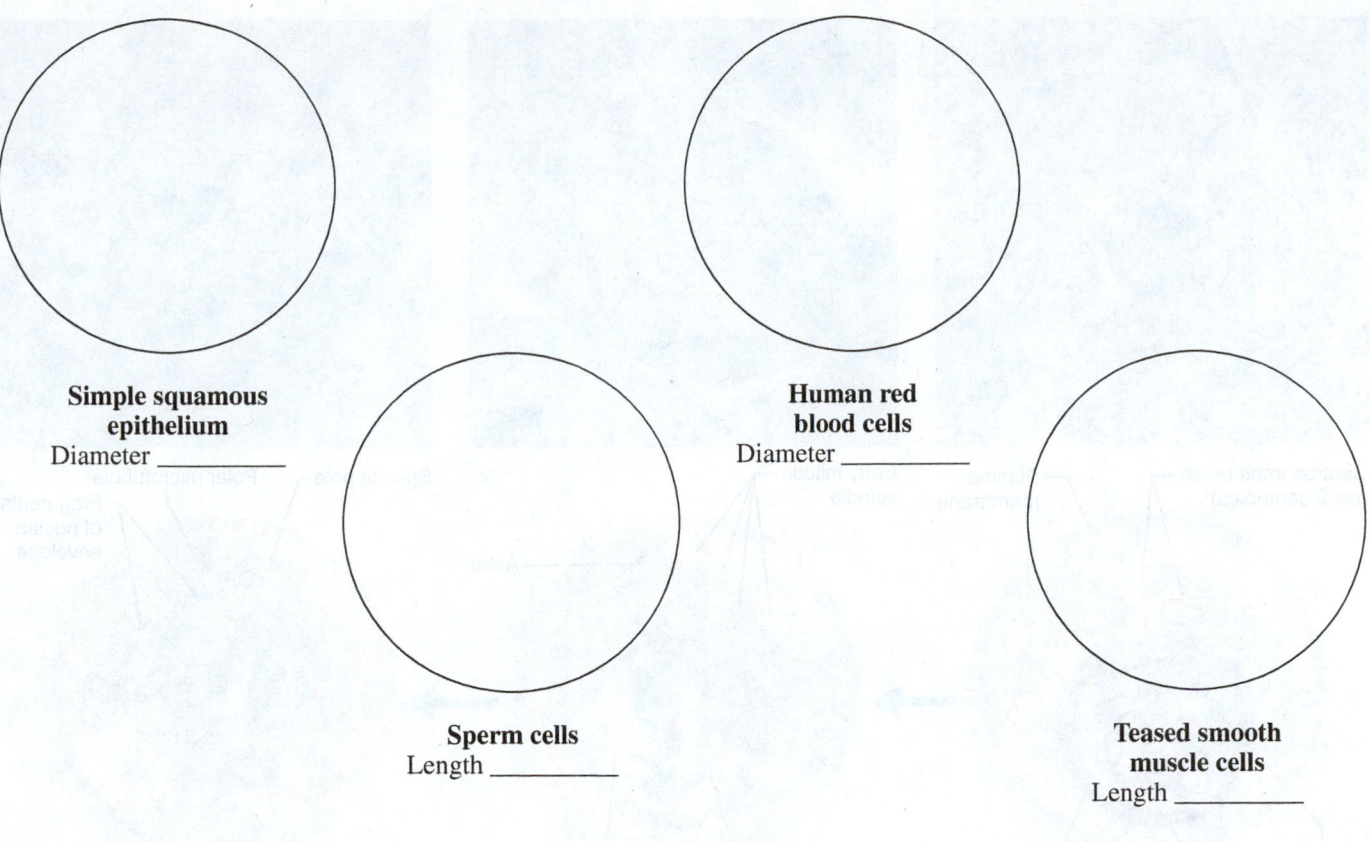

**Simple squamous
epithelium**
Diameter _____

**Human red
blood cells**
Diameter _____

Sperm cells
Length _____

**Teased smooth
muscle cells**
Length _____

Do any of these cells lack a plasma membrane? _____

A nucleus? _____

In the cells with a nucleus, can you discern nucleoli?

_____

Were you able to observe any of the organelles in these cells?

_____ Why or why not? _____

_____

_____

_____

_____

Cell Division: Mitosis and Cytokinesis

A cell's *life cycle* is the series of changes it goes through from the time it is formed until it reproduces itself. It encompasses two stages—**interphase,** the longer period during which the cell grows and carries out its usual activities (Figure 4.4a), and **cell division,** when the cell reproduces itself by dividing. In an interphase cell about to divide, the genetic material

(DNA) is replicated (duplicated exactly). Once this important event has occurred, cell division ensues.

Cell division in all cells other than bacteria consists of a series of events collectively called mitosis and cytokinesis. **Mitosis** is nuclear division; **cytokinesis** is the division of the cytoplasm, which begins after mitosis is nearly complete. Although mitosis is usually accompanied by cytokinesis, in some instances cytoplasmic division does not occur, leading to the formation of binucleate (or multinucleate) cells. This is relatively common in the human liver.

The product of **mitosis** is two daughter nuclei that are genetically identical to the mother nucleus. This distinguishes mitosis from **meiosis,** a specialized type of nuclear division (covered in Exercise 43) that occurs only in the reproductive organs (testes or ovaries). Meiosis, which yields four daughter nuclei that differ genetically in composition from the mother nucleus, is used only for the production of gametes (eggs and sperm) for sexual reproduction. The function of cell division, including mitosis and cytokinesis in the body, is to increase the number of cells for growth and repair while maintaining their genetic heritage.

The stages of mitosis illustrated in Figure 4.4 include the following events:

Prophase (Figure 4.4b and c): At the onset of cell division, the chromatin threads coil and shorten to form densely staining, short, barlike **chromosomes.** By the middle of prophase the chromosomes appear as double-stranded structures (each strand is a **chromatid**) connected by a small median body called a **centromere** and an adhesive protein called *cohesin*. The centrioles separate from one another and act as focal points for the assembly of two systems of microtubules: the

Text continues on page 48.

Centrosomes (each has 2 centrioles) — Plasma membrane

Nucleolus

Nuclear envelope

Chromatin

(a)

Early mitotic spindle

Aster

Chromosome consisting of two sister chromatids

Centromere

(b)

Spindle pole — Polar microtubule

Fragments of nuclear envelope

Kinetochore

Kinetochore microtubule

(c)

Interphase

Interphase is the period of a cell's life when it carries out its normal metabolic activities and grows.

• During interphase, the DNA-containing material is in the form of chromatin. The nuclear envelope and one or more nucleoli are intact and visible.

• There are three distinct periods of this phase:
  G_1: The centrioles begin replicating.
  S: DNA is replicated.
  G_2: Final preparations for mitosis are completed and centrioles finish replicating.

Early Prophase

• The chromatin condenses, forming barlike *chromosomes* that are visible with a light microscope.

• Each duplicated chromosome appears as two identical threads, now called *sister chromatids*, held together at a small, constricted region called a *centromere*. (After the chromatids separate, each is considered a new chromosome.)

• As the chromosomes appear, the nucleoli disappear, and the two centrosomes separate from one another.

• The centrosomes act as focal points for growth of a microtubule assembly called the **mitotic spindle**. As these microtubules lengthen, they propel the centrosomes toward opposite ends (poles) of the cell.

• Microtubule arrays called *asters* ("stars") are seen extending from the matrix around the centrosomes.

Late Prophase

• While the centrosomes are still moving apart, the nuclear envelope fragments, allowing the spindle to interact with the chromosomes.

• Some of the growing spindle microtubules attach to *kinetochores* (ki-ne′-to-korz), special protein structures at each chromosome's centromere. Such microtubules are called *kinetochore microtubules*.

• The remaining spindle microtubules (not attached to any chromosomes) are called *polar microtubules*. The microtubules slide past each other, forcing the poles apart.

• The kinetochore microtubules pull on each chromosome from both poles in a kind of tug-of-war that ultimately draws the chromosomes to the exact center or equator of the cell.

FIGURE 4.4 The interphase cell and the stages of mitosis. The cells shown are from an early embryo of a whitefish. Photomicrographs are above; corresponding diagrams are below. (Micrographs approximately 1210×).

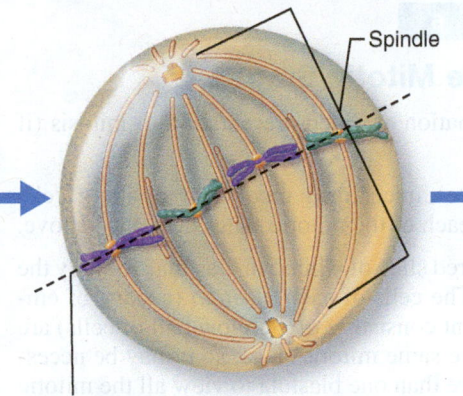

Spindle

Metaphase plate

(d)

Daughter chromosomes

(e)

Nuclear envelope forming   Nucleolus forming   Contractile ring at cleavage furrow

(f)

Metaphase

Metaphase is the second phase of mitosis.

• The two centrosomes are at opposite poles of the cell.

• The chromosomes cluster at the middle of the cell, with their centromeres precisely aligned at the *equator* of the spindle. This imaginary plane midway between the poles is called the *metaphase plate*.

Anaphase

Anaphase is the third and shortest phase of mitosis. Anaphase begins abruptly as the centromeres of the chromosomes split simultaneously. Each chromatid now becomes a chromosome in its own right.

• The kinetochore microtubules, moved along by motor proteins in the kinetochores, gradually pull each chromosome toward the pole it faces.

• At the same time, the polar microtubules slide past each other, lengthen, and push the two poles of the cell apart.

• Anaphase is easy to recognize because the moving chromosomes look V-shaped. The centromeres lead the way, and the chromosomal "arms" dangle behind them.

• This process of moving and separating the chromosomes is helped by the fact that the chromosomes are short, compact bodies. Diffuse threads of chromatin would tangle, trail, and break, resulting in imprecise "parceling out" to the daughter cells.

Telophase

Telophase begins as soon as chromosomal movement stops. This final phase is like prophase in reverse.

• The identical sets of chromosomes at the opposite poles of the cell uncoil and resume their threadlike chromatin form.

• A new nuclear envelope forms around each chromatin mass, nucleoli reappear within the nuclei, and the spindle breaks down and disappears.

• Mitosis is now ended. The cell, for just a brief period, is binucleate (has two nuclei) and each new nucleus is identical to the original mother nucleus.

Cytokinesis

• As a rule, as mitosis draws to a close, cytokinesis completes the division of the cell into two identical daughter cells. Cytokinesis occurs as a contractile ring of actin microfilaments forms the *cleavage furrow* and pinches the cell apart. It begins during late anaphase and continues through and beyond telophase.

FIGURE 4.4 *(continued)*

mitotic spindle, which forms between the centrioles, and the **asters** ("stars"), which radiate outward from the ends of the spindle and anchor it to the plasma membrane. The spindle acts as a scaffolding for the attachment and movement of the chromosomes during later mitotic stages. Meanwhile, the nuclear envelope and the nucleolus break down and disappear.

Metaphase (Figure 4.4d): A brief stage, during which the chromosomes migrate to the central plane or equator of the spindle and align along that plane in a straight line (the so-called *metaphase plate*) from the superior to the inferior region of the spindle (lateral view). Viewed from the poles of the cell (end view), the chromosomes appear to be arranged in a "rosette," or circle, around the widest dimension of the spindle.

Anaphase (Figure 4.4e): At the beginning of anaphase the enzyme *separase* cleaves cohesin, and the centromeres split. The chromatids (now called chromosomes again) separate from one another and then progress slowly toward opposite ends of the cell. The chromosomes are pulled by the kinetochore microtubules attached to their centromeres, their "arms" dangling behind them. Anaphase is complete when poleward movement ceases.

Telophase (Figure 4.4f): During telophase, the events of prophase are essentially reversed. The chromosomes clustered at the poles begin to uncoil and resume the chromatin form, the spindle breaks down and disappears, a nuclear envelope forms around each chromatin mass, and nucleoli appear in each of the daughter nuclei.

Mitosis is essentially the same in all animal cells, but depending on the tissue, it takes from 5 minutes to several hours to complete. In most cells, centriole replication occurs during interphase of the next cell cycle.

Cytokinesis, or the division of the cytoplasmic mass, begins during late anaphase and continues through telophase (Figure 4.4f). In animal cells, a *cleavage furrow* begins to form approximately over the spindle equator and eventually splits or pinches the original cytoplasmic mass into two portions. Thus at the end of cell division, two daughter cells exist—each with a smaller cytoplasmic mass than the mother cell but genetically identical to it. The daughter cells grow and carry out the normal spectrum of metabolic processes until it is their turn to divide.

Cell division is extremely important during the body's growth period. Most cells divide until puberty, when normal body size is achieved and overall body growth ceases. After this time in life, only certain cells carry out cell division routinely—for example, cells subjected to abrasion (epithelium of the skin and lining of the gut). Other cell populations—such as liver cells—stop dividing but retain this ability should some of them be removed or damaged. Skeletal muscle, cardiac muscle, and mature neurons almost completely lose this ability to divide and thus are severely handicapped by injury. Throughout life, the body retains its ability to repair cuts and wounds and to replace some of its aged cells.

ACTIVITY 6

Identifying the Mitotic Stages

1. Watch an animation or video presentation of mitosis (if available).

2. Using the three-dimensional models of dividing cells provided, identify each of the mitotic states described above.

3. Obtain a prepared slide of whitefish blastulae to study the stages of mitosis. The cells of each *blastula* (a stage of embryonic development consisting of a hollow ball of cells) are at approximately the same mitotic stage, so it may be necessary to observe more than one blastula to view all the mitotic stages. A good analogy for a blastula is a soccer ball in which each leather piece making up the ball's surface represents an embryonic cell. The exceptionally high rate of mitosis observed in this tissue is typical of embryos, but if it occurs in specialized tissues it can indicate cancerous cells, which also have an extraordinarily high mitotic rate. Examine the slide carefully, identifying the four mitotic stages and the process of cytokinesis. Compare your observations with Figure 4.4, and verify your identifications with your instructor. ■

NAME_____

LAB TIME/DATE_____

The Cell: Anatomy and Division

Anatomy of the Composite Cell

1. Define the following terms:

   organelle: _____

   _____

   cell: _____

2. Although cells have differences that reflect their specific functions in the body, what functions do they have in common?

   _____

3. Identify the following cell parts:

   _____ 1. external boundary of cell; regulates flow of materials into and out of the cell; site of cell signaling

   _____ 2. contains digestive enzymes of many varieties; "suicide sac" of the cell

   _____ 3. scattered throughout the cell; major site of ATP synthesis

   _____ 4. slender extensions of the plasma membrane that increase its surface area

   _____ 5. stored glycogen granules, crystals, pigments, and so on

   _____ 6. membranous system consisting of flattened sacs and vesicles; packages proteins for export

   _____ 7. control center of the cell; necessary for cell division and cell life

   _____ 8. two rod-shaped bodies near the nucleus; direct formation of the mitotic spindle

   _____ 9. dense, darkly staining nuclear body; packaging site for ribosomes

   _____ 10. contractile elements of the cytoskeleton

   _____ 11. membranous system; involved in intracellular transport of proteins and synthesis of membrane lipids

   _____ 12. attached to membrane systems or scattered in the cytoplasm; synthesize proteins

   _____ 13. threadlike structures in the nucleus; contain genetic material (DNA)

   _____ 14. site of free radical detoxification

4. In the following diagram, label all parts provided with a leader line.

Differences and Similarities in Cell Structure

5. For each of the following cell types, list (a) *one* important structural characteristic observed in the laboratory, and (b) the function that the structure complements or ensures.

squamous epithelium   a. _____

  b. _____

sperm   a. _____

  b. _____

smooth muscle   a. _____

  b. _____

red blood cells   a. _____

                       b. _____

6. What is the significance of the red blood cell being anucleate (without a nucleus)? _____

_____

Did it ever have a nucleus? _____ If so, when? _____

7. Of the four cells observed microscopically (squamous epithelial cells, red blood cells, smooth muscle cells, and sperm) which

has the smallest diameter? _____ Which is longest? _____

Cell Division: Mitosis and Cytokinesis

8. Identify the three phases of mitosis in the following photomicrographs.

a. _____   b. _____   c. _____

9. What is the importance of mitotic cell division? _____

_____

10. Draw the phases of mitosis for a cell that contains four chromosomes as its diploid or 2*n* number.

11. Complete or respond to the following statements:

Division of the __1__ is referred to as mitosis. Cytokinesis is division of the __2__. The major structural difference between chromatin and chromosomes is that the latter are __3__. Chromosomes attach to the spindle fibers by undivided structures called __4__. If a cell undergoes mitosis but not cytokinesis, the product is __5__. The structure that acts as a scaffolding for chromosomal attachment and movement is called the __6__. __7__ is the period of cell life when the cell is not involved in division. Two cell populations in the body that do not routinely undergo cell division are __8__ and __9__.

1. _____

2. _____

3. _____

4. _____

5. _____

6. _____

7. _____

8. _____

9. _____

12. Using the key, categorize each of the events described below according to the phase in which it occurs.

Key: a. anaphase   b. interphase   c. metaphase   d. prophase   e. telophase

_____ 1. Chromatin coils and condenses, forming chromosomes.

_____ 2. The chromosomes are V-shaped.

_____ 3. The nuclear envelope re-forms.

_____ 4. Chromosomes stop moving toward the poles.

_____ 5. Chromosomes line up in the center of the cell.

_____ 6. The nuclear envelope fragments.

_____ 7. The mitotic spindle forms.

_____ 8. DNA synthesis occurs.

_____ 9. Centrioles replicate.

_____ 10. Chromosomes first appear to be duplex structures.

_____ 11. Chromosomal centromeres are attached to the kinetochore fibers.

_____ 12. Cleavage furrow forms.

_____ and _____ 13. The nuclear envelope(s) is absent.

13. What is the physical advantage of the chromatin coiling and condensing to form short chromosomes at the onset of mitosis?

_____

_____

The Cell: Transport Mechanisms and Cell Permeability—Wet Lab

MATERIALS

Passive Processes

Diffusion of Dye Through Agar Gel

- ☐ Petri dish containing 12 ml of 1.5% agar-agar
- ☐ Millimeter-ruled graph paper
- ☐ Wax marking pencil
- ☐ 3.5% methylene blue solution (approximately 0.1 M) in dropper bottles
- ☐ 1.6% potassium permanganate solution (approximately 0.1 M) in dropper bottles
- ☐ Medicine dropper

Diffusion and Osmosis Through Nonliving Membranes

- ☐ Four dialysis sacs or small Hefty® "alligator" sandwich bags
- ☐ Small funnel
- ☐ 25-ml graduated cylinder
- ☐ Wax marking pencil
- ☐ Fine twine or dialysis tubing clamps
- ☐ 250-ml beakers
- ☐ Distilled water
- ☐ 40% glucose solution
- ☐ 10% sodium chloride (NaCl) solution
- ☐ 40% sucrose solution colored with Congo red dye
- ☐ Laboratory balance
- ☐ Paper towels
- ☐ Hot plate and large beaker for hot water bath
- ☐ Benedict's solution in dropper bottle
- ☐ Silver nitrate (AgNO₃) in dropper bottle
- ☐ Test tubes in rack, test tube holder

Text continues on next page.

OBJECTIVES

1. To define *differential permeability* and explain the difference between *active* and *passive processes* of cellular transport.
2. To define *diffusion (simple diffusion)* and *osmosis; isotonic, hypotonic,* and *hypertonic solutions; active transport; vesicular transport;* and *exocytosis, phagocytosis,* and *pinocytosis.*
3. To describe the processes that account for the movement of substances across the plasma membrane and to indicate the driving force for each.
4. To determine which way substances will move passively through a differentially permeable membrane (given appropriate information on concentration differences).

PRE-LAB QUIZ

1. Circle the correct term. A passive process, <u>diffusion</u> / <u>osmosis</u> is the movement of solute molecules from an area of greater concentration to an area of lesser concentration.
2. A solution surrounding a cell is *hypertonic* if:
   a. it contains fewer nonpenetrating solute particles than the interior of the cell.
   b. it contains more nonpenetrating solute particles than the interior of the cell.
   c. it contains the same amount of nonpenetrating solute particles as the interior of the cell.
3. Which of the following would require an input of energy?
   a. diffusion
   b. filtration
   c. osmosis
   d. vesicular transport
4. Circle the correct term. In <u>pinocytosis</u> / <u>phagocytosis</u>, parts of the plasma membrane and cytoplasm expand and flow around a relatively large or solid material and engulf it.
5. Circle the correct term. In <u>active</u> / <u>passive</u> processes, the cell provides energy in the form of ATP to power the transport process.

B ecause of its molecular composition, the plasma membrane is selective about what passes through it. It allows nutrients to enter the cell but keeps out undesirable substances. By the same token, valuable cell proteins and other substances are kept within the cell, and excreta or wastes pass to the exterior. This property is known as **differential,** or **selective, permeability.** Transport through the plasma membrane occurs in two basic ways. In **passive processes,** concentration or pressure differences drive the movement. In **active processes,** the cell provides energy (ATP) to power the transport process.

(materials list continued)

Experiment 1

☐ Deshelled eggs

☐ 400-ml beakers

☐ Wax marking pencil

☐ Distilled water

☐ 30% sucrose solution

☐ Laboratory balance

☐ Paper towels

☐ Graph paper

☐ Weigh boat

Experiment 2

☐ Clean microscope slides and coverslips

☐ Medicine dropper

☐ Compound microscope

☐ Vials of animal (mammalian) blood obtained from a biological supply house or veterinarian—at option of instructor

☐ Freshly prepared physiologic (mammalian) saline solution in dropper bottle

☐ 5% sodium chloride solution in dropper bottle

☐ Distilled water

☐ Filter paper

☐ Disposable gloves

☐ Basin and wash bottles containing 10% household bleach solution

☐ Disposable autoclave bag

☐ Paper towels

Diffusion Demonstrations

1: Diffusion of a dye through water

Prepared the morning of the laboratory session with setup time noted. Potassium permanganate crystals are placed in a 1000-ml graduated cylinder, and distilled water is added slowly and with as little turbulence as possible to fill to the 1000-ml mark.

2: Osmometer

Just before the laboratory begins, the broad end of a thistle tube is closed with a differentially permeable dialysis membrane, and the tube is secured to a ring stand. Molasses is added to approximately 5 cm above the thistle tube bulb, and the bulb is immersed in a beaker of distilled water. At

the beginning of the lab session, the level of the molasses in the tube is marked with a wax pencil.

Filtration

☐ Ring stand, ring, clamp

☐ Filter paper, funnel

☐ Solution containing a mixture of uncooked starch, powdered charcoal, and copper sulfate ($CuSO_4$)

☐ 10-ml graduated cylinder

☐ 100-ml beaker

☐ Lugol's iodine in a dropper bottle

Active Processes

☐ Videotape showing phagocytosis (if available)

☐ Videotape viewing box

☐ **PEx** PhysioEx™ 8.0 Computer Simulation on page PEx-5

Note to the Instructor: See directions for handling wet mount preparations and disposable supplies on page 33, Exercise 3.

Passive Processes

The two important passive processes of membrane transport are *diffusion* and *filtration*. Diffusion is an important transport process for every cell in the body. By contrast, filtration usually occurs only across capillary walls.

Recall that all molecules possess *kinetic energy* and are in constant motion. At a specific temperature, given molecules have about the same average kinetic energy. Since kinetic energy is directly related to both mass and velocity ($KE = \frac{1}{2}mv^2$), smaller molecules tend to move faster. As molecules move about randomly at high speeds, they collide and ricochet off one another, changing direction with each collision (Figure 5A.1).

Diffusion

When a **concentration gradient** (difference in concentration) exists, the net effect of this random molecular movement is that the molecules eventually become evenly distributed throughout the environment; that is, the process called diffusion occurs. Hence, **diffusion** is the movement of molecules from a region of their higher concentration to a region of their lower concentration. Its driving force is the kinetic energy of the molecules themselves.

There are many examples of diffusion in nonliving systems. For example, if a bottle of ether was uncorked at the front of the laboratory, very shortly thereafter you would be nodding as the ether molecules became distributed throughout the room. The ability to smell a friend's cologne shortly after he or she has entered the room is another example.

The diffusion of particles into and out of cells is modified by the plasma membrane, which constitutes a physical barrier. In general, molecules diffuse passively through the plasma membrane if they can dissolve in the lipid portion of

FIGURE 5A.1 Random movement and numerous collisions cause molecules to become evenly distributed. The small spheres represent water molecules; the large spheres represent glucose molecules.

the membrane (for example CO_2 and O_2). The unassisted diffusion of solutes (dissolved substances) through a differentially permeable membrane is called **simple diffusion.**

Certain molecules (for example, glucose) are transported across the plasma membrane with the assistance of a protein carrier molecule. The glucose binds to the carrier and is ferried across the membrane. Small ions cross the membrane by moving through water-filled protein channels. In both cases, the substances move by a passive transport process called **facilitated diffusion.** As with simple diffusion, the substances move from an area of higher concentration to one of lower concentration, that is, down their concentration gradients.

Osmosis

The flow of water across a differentially permeable membrane is called **osmosis.** During osmosis, water moves down its concentration gradient. The concentration of water is inversely related to the concentration of solutes. If the solutes can diffuse across the membrane, both water and solutes will move down their concentration gradients through the membrane. If the particles in solution are nonpenetrating solutes (prevented from crossing the membrane), water alone will move by osmosis and in doing so will cause changes in the volume of the compartments on either side of the membrane.

Diffusion of Dye Through Agar Gel and Water

The relationship between molecular weight and the rate of diffusion can be examined easily by observing the diffusion of two different types of dye molecules through an agar gel. The dyes used in this experiment are methylene blue, which has a molecular weight of 320 and is deep blue in color, and potassium permanganate, a purple dye with a molecular weight of 158. Although the agar gel appears quite solid, it is primarily (98.5%) water and allows free movement of the dye molecules through it.

ACTIVITY 1

Observing Diffusion of Dye Through Agar Gel

1.   Work with members of your group to formulate a hypothesis about the rates of diffusion of methylene blue and potassium permanganate through the agar gel. Justify your hypothesis.

2.   Obtain a petri dish containing agar gel, a piece of millimeter-ruled graph paper, a wax marking pencil, dropper bottles of methylene blue and potassium permanganate, and a medicine dropper. (See Figure 5A.2.)

3.   Using the wax marking pencil, draw a line on the bottom of the petri dish dividing it into two sections. Place the petri dish on the ruled graph paper.

4.   Create a well in the center of each section using the medicine dropper. To do this, squeeze the bulb of the medicine dropper, and push it down into the agar. Release the bulb as you slowly pull the dropper vertically out of the agar. This should remove an agar plug, leaving a well in the agar.

5.   Carefully fill one well with the methylene blue solution and the other well with the potassium permanganate solution.

Record the time. _____

6.   At 15-minute intervals, measure the distance the dye has diffused from each well. Continue these observations for 1 hour, and record the results in the adjacent chart.

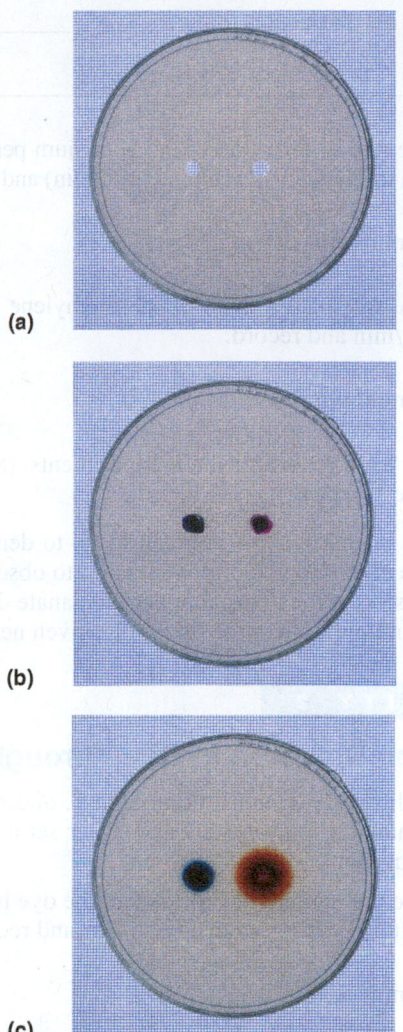

(a)

(b)

(c)

FIGURE 5A.2 Comparing diffusion rates. Agar-plated petri dish as it appears after the diffusion of 0.1 *M* methylene blue placed in one well and 0.1 *M* potassium permanganate placed in another.

Time (min)	Diffusion of methylene blue (mm)	Diffusion of potassium permanganate (mm)
15		
30		
45		
60		

Which dye diffused more rapidly? _____

What is the relationship between molecular weight and rate of molecular movement (diffusion)?

_____

Why did the dye molecules move? _____

_____

Compute the rate of diffusion of the potassium permanganate molecules in millimeters per minute (mm/min) and record.

_____ mm/min

Compute the rate of diffusion of the methylene blue molecules in mm/min and record.

_____ mm/min

7. Prepare a lab report for these experiments. (See Getting Started, page xv.) ▬

Make a mental note to yourself to go to demonstration area 1 at the end of the laboratory session to observe the extent of diffusion of the potassium permanganate dye through water. At that time, follow the directions given next.

ACTIVITY 2

Observing Diffusion of Dye Through Water

1. Go to diffusion demonstration area 1, and observe the cylinder containing dye crystals and water set up at the beginning of the lab.

2. Measure the number of millimeters the dye has diffused from the bottom of the graduated cylinder and record.

_____ mm

3. Record the time the demonstration was set up and the time of your observation. Then compute the rate of the dye's diffusion through water and record below.

Time of setup _____

Time of observation _____

Rate of diffusion _____ mm/min

4. Does the potassium permanganate dye move (diffuse) more rapidly through water or the agar gel? (Explain your answer.)

_____

_____ ▬

ACTIVITY 3

Observing Diffusion and Osmosis Through Nonliving Membranes

The following experiment provides information on the movement of water and solutes through differentially permeable membranes called dialysis sacs. Dialysis sacs have pores of a particular size. The selectivity of living membranes depends on more than just pore size, but using the dialysis sacs will allow you to examine selectivity due to this factor.

1. Read through the experiments in this activity, and develop a hypothesis for each part.

2. Obtain four dialysis sacs, a small funnel, a 25-ml graduated cylinder, a wax marking pencil, fine twine or dialysis tubing clamps, and four beakers (250 ml). Number the beakers 1 to 4 with the wax marking pencil, and half fill all of them with distilled water except beaker 2, to which you should add 40% glucose solution.

3. Prepare the dialysis sacs one at a time. Using the funnel, half fill each with 20 ml of the specified liquid (see below). Press out the air, fold over the open end of the sac, and tie it securely with fine twine or clamp it. Before proceeding to the next sac, rinse it under the tap, and quickly and carefully blot the sac dry by rolling it on a paper towel. Weigh it with a

Data from Experiments on Diffusion and Osmosis Through Nonliving Membranes						
Beaker	Contents of sac	Initial weight	Final weight	Weight change	Tests— beaker fluid	Tests— sac fluid
Beaker 1 ½ filled with distilled water	Sac 1, 20 ml of 40% glucose solution				Benedict's test:	Benedict's test:
Beaker 2 ½ filled with 40% glucose solution	Sac 2, 20 ml of 40% glucose solution					
Beaker 3 ½ filled with distilled water	Sac 3, 20 ml of 10% NaCl solution				AgNO₃ test:	
Beaker 4 ½ filled with distilled water	Sac 4, 20 ml of 40% sucrose solution containing Congo red dye				Benedict's test:	

laboratory balance. Record the weight in the data chart on page 56, and then drop the sac into the corresponding beaker. Be sure the sac is completely covered by the beaker solution, adding more solution if necessary.

- Sac 1: 40% glucose solution
- Sac 2: 40% glucose solution
- Sac 3: 10% NaCl solution
- Sac 4: Congo red dye in 40% sucrose solution

Allow sacs to remain undisturbed in the beakers for 1 hour. (Use this time to continue with other experiments.)

4. After an hour, boil a beaker of water on the hot plate. Obtain the supplies you will need to determine your experimental results: dropper bottles of Benedict's solution and silver nitrate solution, a test tube rack, four test tubes, and a test tube holder.

5. Quickly and gently blot sac 1 dry and weigh it. (**Note:** Do not squeeze the sac during the blotting process.) Record the weight in the data chart.

Has there been any change in weight? _____

Conclusions: _____

_____

Place 5 ml of Benedict's solution in each of two test tubes. Put 4 ml of the beaker fluid into one test tube and 4 ml of the sac fluid into the other. Mark the tubes for identification and then place them in a beaker containing boiling water. Boil 2 minutes. Cool slowly. If a green, yellow, or rusty red precipitate forms, the test is positive, meaning that glucose is present. If the solution remains the original blue color, the test is negative. Record results in the data chart.

Was glucose still present in the sac? _____

Was glucose present in the beaker? _____

Conclusions: _____

_____

_____

6. Blot gently and weigh sac 2. Record the weight in the data chart.

Was there an *increase* or *decrease* in weight? _____

With 40% glucose in the sac and 40% glucose in the beaker, would you expect to see any net movement of water (osmosis) or of glucose molecules (simple diffusion)?

_____ Why or why not? _____

_____

7. Blot gently and weigh sac 3. Record the weight in the data chart.

Was there any change in weight? _____

Conclusions: _____

_____

Take a 5-ml sample of beaker 3 solution and put it in a clean test tube. Add a drop of silver nitrate. The appearance of a white precipitate or cloudiness indicates the presence of silver chloride (AgCl), which is formed by the reaction of $AgNO_3$ with NaCl (sodium chloride). Record results in the data chart.

Results: _____

Conclusions: _____

8. Blot gently and weigh sac 4. Record the weight in the data chart.

Was there any change in weight? _____

Did the beaker water turn pink? _____

Conclusions: _____

_____

Take a 1-ml sample of beaker 4 solution and put the test tube in boiling water in a hot water bath. Add 5 drops of Benedict's solution to the tube and boil for 5 minutes. The presence of glucose (one of the hydrolysis products of sucrose) in the bath water is indicated by the presence of a green, yellow, or rusty colored precipitate.

Did sucrose diffuse from the sac into the bath water? _____

Conclusions: _____

_____

9. In which of the test situations did net osmosis occur?

_____

_____

In which of the test situations did net simple diffusion occur?

_____

_____

What conclusions can you make about the relative size of glucose, sucrose, Congo red dye, NaCl, and water molecules?

_____

_____

_____

With what cell structure can the dialysis sac be compared?

_____

10. Prepare a lab report for the experiment. (See Getting Started, page xv.) Be sure to include in your discussion the answers to the questions proposed in this activity. ▬

Observing Osmometer Results

Before leaving the laboratory, observe demonstration 2, the *osmometer demonstration* set up before the laboratory session to follow the movement of water through a membrane (osmosis). Measure the distance the water column has moved during the laboratory period and record below. (The position of the meniscus [the surface of the water column] in the thistle tube at the beginning of the laboratory period is marked with wax pencil.)

Distance the meniscus has moved: _____ mm

Did net osmosis occur? Why or why not?

_____

_____

_____ ▬

Investigating Diffusion and Osmosis Through Living Membranes

To examine permeability properties of plasma membranes, conduct the following experiments. As you read through the experiments in this activity, develop a hypothesis for each part.

Experiment 1

1. Obtain two deshelled eggs and two 400-ml beakers. Note that the relative concentration of solutes in deshelled eggs is about 14%. Number the beakers 1 and 2 with the wax marking pencil. Half fill beaker 1 with distilled water and beaker 2 with 30% sucrose.

2. Carefully blot each egg by rolling it gently on a paper towel. Place a weight boat on a laboratory balance and tare the balance (that is, make sure the scale reads 0.0 with the weigh boat on the scale). Weigh egg 1 in the weigh boat, record the initial weight in the data chart below, and gently place it into beaker 1. Repeat for egg 2, placing it in beaker 2.

3. After 20 minutes, remove egg 1 and gently blot it and weigh it. Record the weight, and replace it into beaker 1. Repeat for egg 2, placing it into beaker 2. Repeat this procedure at 40 minutes and 60 minutes.

4. Calculate the change in weight of each egg at each time period, and enter that number in the data chart below. Also calculate the percent change in weight for each time period and enter that number in the data table.

How has the weight of each egg changed?

Egg 1 _____

Egg 2 _____

Make a graph of your data by plotting the percent change in weight for each egg versus time.

How has the appearance of each egg changed?

Egg 1 _____

Egg 2 _____

A solution surrounding a cell is **hypertonic** if it contains more nonpenetrating solute particles than the interior of the cell. Water moves from the interior of the cell into a surrounding hypertonic solution by osmosis. A solution surrounding a cell is **hypotonic** if it contains fewer nonpenetrating solute particles than the interior of the cell. Water moves from a hypotonic solution into the cell by osmosis. In both cases, water moved down its concentration gradient. Indicate in your conclusions whether distilled water was a hypotonic or hypertonic solution and whether 30% sucrose was hypotonic or hypertonic.

Data from Experiment 1 on Diffusion and Osmosis Through Living Membranes						
Time	Egg 1 (in distilled H$_2$O)	Weight change	% Change	Egg 2 (in 30% sucrose)	Weight change	% Change
Initial weight (g)		—	—		—	—
20 min.						
40 min.						
60 min.						

(a) **Isotonic solutions**	(b) **Hypertonic solutions**	(c) **Hypotonic solutions**
Cells retain their normal size and shape in isotonic solutions (same solute/water concentration as inside cells; no net osmosis).	Cells lose water by osmosis and shrink in a hypertonic solution (contains a higher concentration of solutes than are present inside the cells).	Cells take on water by osmosis until they become bloated and burst (lyse) in a hypotonic solution (contains a lower concentration of solutes than are present in cells).

FIGURE 5A.3 **Influence of isotonic, hypertonic, and hypotonic solutions on red blood cells.**

Conclusions: _____

_____

_____

Experiment 2

Now you will conduct a microscopic study of red blood cells suspended in solutions of varying tonicities. The objective is to determine if these solutions have any effect on cell shape by promoting net osmosis.

1. The following supplies should be available at your laboratory bench to conduct this experimental series: two clean slides and coverslips, a vial of animal blood, a medicine dropper, physiologic saline, 5% sodium chloride solution, distilled water, filter paper, and disposable gloves.

 Wear disposable gloves at all times when handling blood (steps 2–5).

2. Place a very small drop of physiologic saline on a slide. Using the medicine dropper, add a small drop of animal blood to the saline on the slide. Tilt the slide to mix, cover with a coverslip, and immediately examine the preparation under the high-power lens. Notice that the red blood cells retain their normal smooth disclike shape (see Figure 5A.3a). This is because the physiologic saline is **isotonic** to the cells. That is, it contains a concentration of nonpenetrating solutes (e.g., proteins and some ions) equal to that in the cells (same solute/water concentration). Consequently, the cells neither gain nor lose water by osmosis. Set this slide aside.

3. Prepare another wet mount of animal blood, but this time use 5% sodium chloride (saline) solution as the suspending medium. Carefully observe the red blood cells under high power. What is happening to the normally smooth disc shape of the red blood cells?

_____

_____

_____

This crinkling-up process, called **crenation,** is due to the fact that the 5% sodium chloride solution is hypertonic to the cytosol of the red blood cell. Under these circumstances, water tends to leave the cells by osmosis. Compare your observations to Figure 5A.3b.

4. Add a drop of distilled water to the edge of the coverslip. Fold a piece of filter paper in half and place its folded edge at the opposite edge of the coverslip; it will absorb the saline solution and draw the distilled water across the cells. Watch the red blood cells as they float across the field. Describe the change in their appearance.

_____

_____

Distilled water contains *no* solutes (it is 100% water). Distilled water and *very* dilute solutions (that is, those containing less than 0.9% nonpenetrating solutes) are hypotonic to the cell. In a hypotonic solution, the red blood cells first "plump up" (Figure 5A.3c), but then they suddenly start to disappear. The red blood cells burst as the water floods into them, leaving "ghosts" in their wake—a phenomenon called **hemolysis.**

⚠️ 5. Place the blood-soiled slides and test tube in the bleach-containing basin. Put the coverslips you used into the disposable autoclave bag. Obtain a wash (squirt) bottle containing 10% bleach solution, and squirt the bleach liberally over the bench area where blood was handled. Wipe the bench down with a paper towel wet with the bleach solution and allow it to dry before continuing. Remove gloves, and discard in the autoclave bag.

6. Prepare a lab report for experiments 1 and 2. (See Getting Started, page xv.) Be sure to include in the discussion answers to the questions proposed in this activity. ▪

Filtration

Filtration is a passive process by which water and solutes are forced through a membrane by hydrostatic (fluid) pressure. For example, fluids and solutes filter out of the capillaries in the kidneys and into the kidney tubules because the blood pressure in the capillaries is greater than the fluid pressure in the tubules. Filtration is not selective. The amount of filtrate (fluids and solutes) formed depends almost entirely on the pressure gradient (difference in pressure on the two sides of the membrane) and on the size of the membrane pores.

ACTIVITY 6

Observing the Process of Filtration

1. Obtain the following equipment: a ring stand, ring, and ring clamp; a funnel; a piece of filter paper; a beaker; a 10-ml graduated cylinder; a solution containing uncooked starch, powdered charcoal, and copper sulfate; and a dropper bottle of Lugol's iodine. Attach the ring to the ring stand with the clamp.

2. Fold the filter paper in half twice, open it into a cone, and place it in a funnel. Place the funnel in the ring of the ring stand and place a beaker under the funnel. Shake the starch solution, and fill the funnel with it to just below the top of the filter paper. When the steady stream of filtrate changes to countable filtrate drops, count the number of drops formed in 10 seconds and record.

_____ drops

When the funnel is half empty, again count the number of drops formed in 10 seconds and record the count.

_____ drops

3. After all the fluid has passed through the filter, check the filtrate and paper to see which materials were retained by the paper. (Note: If the filtrate is blue, the copper sulfate passed. Check both the paper and filtrate for black particles to see whether the charcoal passed. Finally, using a 10-ml graduated cylinder, put a 2-ml filtrate sample into a test tube. Add several drops of Lugol's iodine. If the sample turns blue/black when iodine is added, starch is present in the filtrate.)

Passed: _____

Retained: _____

What does the filter paper represent? _____

During which counting interval was the filtration rate

greatest? _____

Explain: _____

_____

_____

What characteristic of the three solutes determined whether or not they passed through the filter paper?

_____ ▪

Active Processes

Whenever a cell uses the bond energy of ATP to move substances across its boundaries, the process is an *active process.* Substances moved by active means are generally unable to pass by diffusion. They may not be lipid soluble; they may be too large to pass through the membrane channels; or they may have to move against rather than with a concentration gradient. There are two types of active processes: *active transport* and *vesicular transport.*

Active Transport

Like one form of facilitated diffusion, **active transport** requires carrier proteins that combine specifically with the transported substance. Active transport may be primary, driven directly by hydrolysis of ATP, or secondary, driven indirectly by energy stored in ionic gradients. In most cases the substances move against concentration or electrochemical gradients or both. Some of the substances that are moved into the cells by such carriers are amino acids and some sugars. Both solutes are insoluble in lipid and too large to pass through membrane channels but are necessary for cell life. However, sodium ions (Na^+) are ejected from cells by active transport. Carrier-mediated active transport is difficult to study in an A&P laboratory and will not be considered further here.

Vesicular Transport

Large particles and molecules are transported across the membrane by **vesicular transport.** Movement may be into the cell (**endocytosis**) or out of the cell (**exocytosis**).

Most types of endocytosis utilize clathrin protein–coated pits to engulf the substance to be carried into the cell. Once engulfed, the substance is transported in the cell within a clathrin-coated vesicle.

In **phagocytosis** (cell eating), parts of the plasma membrane and cytoplasm expand and flow around a relatively large or solid material (for example, bacteria or cell debris) and engulf it (Figure 5A.4a). The membranous sac thus

(a) Phagocytosis

(b) Pinocytosis

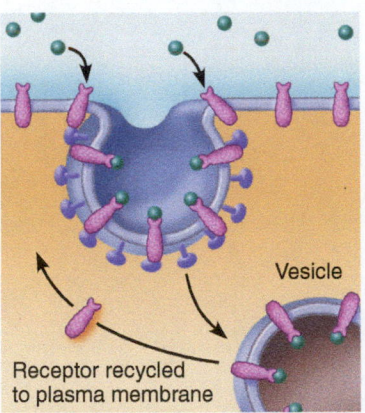

(c) Receptor-mediated endocytosis

FIGURE 5A.4 Three types of endocytosis. (a) In phagocytosis, cellular extensions (pseudopodia) flow around the external particle and enclose it within a vacuole. **(b)** In pinocytosis, dissolved proteins gather on the external surface of the plasma membrane, causing the membrane to invaginate and to incorporate a droplet of the fluid in a tiny vesicle. Most vesicles are protein coated. **(c)** In receptor-mediated endocytosis, plasma membrane proteins bind only with certain substances in regions of coated pits. The pits form protein-coated vesicles.

formed, called a *phagosome,* is then fused with a lysosome and its contents are digested. In the human body, phagocytic cells are mainly found among the white blood cells and macrophages that act as scavengers and help protect the body from disease-causing microorganisms and cancer cells.

In **pinocytosis,** also called **fluid-phase endocytosis,** the cell membrane sinks beneath the material to form a small vesicle, which then pinches off into the cell interior (see Figure 5A.4b). Pinocytosis is most common for taking in liquids containing protein or fat.

A more selective type of endocytosis uses plasma membrane receptors and is called **receptor-mediated endocytosis** (Figure 5A.4c). As opposed to the phagocytosis used by the body's scavenger cells, this type of endocytosis is exquisitely selective and is used primarily for cellular uptake of specific molecules, such as cholesterol, iron, and some hormones, and for transfer of substances from one side of the cell to the other.

ACTIVITY 7

Observing Phagocytosis

Go to the videotape viewing area and watch the videotape demonstration of phagocytosis (if available). ▬

Note: If you have not already done so, complete Activity 2 ("Observing Diffusion of Dye Through Water," page 56), and Activity 4 ("Observing Osmometer Results," page 58).

NAME_____

LAB TIME/DATE _____

The Cell: Transport Mechanisms and Permeability—Wet Lab

Choose all answers that apply to questions 1 and 2, and place their letters on the response blanks to the right.

1. Molecular motion _____.

    a. reflects the kinetic energy of molecules   c. is ordered and predictable

    b. reflects the potential energy of molecules   d. is random and erratic

2. Velocity of molecular movement _____.

    a. is higher in larger molecules   d. decreases with increasing temperature

    b. is lower in larger molecules   e. reflects kinetic energy

    c. increases with increasing temperature

3. Summarize the results of Activity 3, diffusion and osmosis through nonliving membranes, below. List and explain your observations relative to tests used to identify diffusing substances, and changes in sac weight observed.

Sac 1 containing 40% glucose suspended in distilled water

_____

_____

Sac 2 containing 40% glucose suspended in 40% glucose

_____

_____

Sac 3 containing 10% NaCl suspended in distilled water

_____

_____

Sac 4 containing 40% sucrose and Congo red dye suspended in distilled water

_____

_____

4. What single characteristic of the differentially permeable membranes *used in the laboratory* determines the substances that

can pass through them? _____

In addition to this characteristic, what other factors influence the passage of substances through living membranes?

_____

_____

5. A semipermeable sac containing 4% NaCl, 9% glucose and 10% albumin is suspended in a solution with the following composition: 10% NaCl, 10% glucose, and 40% albumin. Assume that the sac is permeable to all substances except albumin. State whether each of the following will (a) move into the sac, (b) move out of the sac, or (c) not move.

glucose: _____   albumin: _____

water: _____   NaCl: _____

6. Summarize the results of Activity 5, Experiment 1 (diffusion and osmosis through living membranes—the egg), below. List and explain your observations.

Egg 1 in distilled water: _____

_____

_____

Egg 2 in 30% sucrose: _____

_____

_____

7. The diagrams below represent three microscope fields containing red blood cells. Arrows show the direction of net osmosis.

Which field contains a hypertonic solution? _____ The cells in this field are said to be _____. Which

field contains an isotonic bathing solution? _____ Which field contains a hypotonic solution? _____ What is happening

to the cells in this field? _____

_____

     (a)   (b)   (c)

8. Assume you are conducting the experiment illustrated in the next figure. Both hydrochloric acid (HCl) with a molecular weight of about 36.5 and ammonium hydroxide (NH$_4$OH) with a molecular weight of 35 are volatile and easily enter the gaseous state. When they meet, the following reaction will occur:

$$HCl + NH_4OH \rightarrow H_2O + NH_4Cl$$

Ammonium chloride (NH$_4$Cl) will be deposited on the glass tubing as a smoky precipitate where the two gases meet. Predict which gas will diffuse more quickly and indicate to which end of the tube the smoky precipitate will be closer.

a.   The faster-diffusing gas is _____.

b.   The precipitate forms closer to the _____ end.

9. What determines whether a transport process is active or passive? _____

_____

10. Characterize membrane transport as fully as possible by choosing all the phrases that apply and inserting their letters on the answer blanks.

Passive processes: _____ Active processes: _____

a.   account for the movement of fats and respiratory gases through the plasma membrane

b.   explain solute pumping, phagocytosis, and pinocytosis

c.   include osmosis, simple diffusion, and filtration

d.   may occur against concentration and/or electrical gradients

e.   use hydrostatic pressure or molecular energy as the driving force

f.   move ions, amino acids, and some sugars across the plasma membrane

11. For the osmometer demonstration (Activity 4), explain why the level of the water column rose during the laboratory session.

_____

_____

12. Define the following terms.

diffusion: _____

_____

osmosis: _____

_____

simple diffusion: _____

_____

filtration: _____

_____

active transport: _____

_____

phagocytosis: _____

_____

fluid-phase endocytosis: _____

_____

Classification of Tissues

MATERIALS

- ☐ Compound microscope
- ☐ Immersion oil
- ☐ Prepared slides of simple squamous, simple cuboidal, simple columnar, stratified squamous (nonkeratinized), stratified cuboidal, stratified columnar, pseudostratified ciliated columnar, and transitional epithelium
- ☐ Prepared slides of mesenchyme; of adipose, areolar, reticular, and dense (both regular and irregular connective tissues); of hyaline and elastic cartilage; of fibrocartilage; of bone (x.s.); and of blood
- ☐ Prepared slides of skeletal, cardiac, and smooth muscle (l.s.)
- ☐ Prepared slide of nervous tissue (spinal cord smear)
- **PEx** PhysioEx™ 8.0 Computer Simulation on page PEx-21

 myA&P *For practice quizzes on this lab, go to www.myaandp.com.*

PAL *For access to anatomical models and more, check out Practice Anatomy Lab.*

OBJECTIVES

1. To name the four primary tissue types in the human body and the major subcategories of each.
2. To identify the tissue subcategories through microscopic inspection or inspection of an appropriate diagram or projected slide.
3. To state the location of the various tissue types in the body.
4. To list the general functions and structural characteristics of each of the four major tissue types.

PRE-LAB QUIZ

1. Groups of cells that are similar in structure and function are called:
   a. organ systems
   b. organisms
   c. organs
   d. tissues
2. How many primary tissue types are found in the human body? _____
3. Circle True or False. Endocrine and exocrine glands are classified as epithelium because they usually develop from epithelial membranes.
4. Epithelial tissues can be classified according to cell shape. _____ epithelial cells are scalelike and flattened.
   a. Columnar
   b. Cuboidal
   c. Squamous
   d. Transitional
5. This type of epithelium lines the digestive tract from stomach to anus.
   a. simple cuboidal
   b. simple columnar
   c. stratified squamous
   d. transitional
6. All connective tissue is derived from an embryonic tissue known as:
   a. cartilage
   b. ground substance
   c. mesenchyme
   d. reticular
7. All the following are examples of connective tissue except:
   a. bones
   b. ligaments
   c. neurons
   d. tendons
8. Circle True or False. Blood is a type of connective tissue.
9. Circle the correct term. Of the two major cell populations in nervous tissue, <u>neurons</u> / <u>neuroglial cells</u> are highly specialized to receive stimuli and conduct waves of excitation to all parts of the body.
10. How many basic types of muscle tissue are there? _____
11. This type of muscle tissue is found in the walls of hollow organs. It has no striations, and its cells are spindle shaped. It is:
    a. cardiac muscle
    b. skeletal muscle
    c. smooth muscle

Exercise 4 describes cells as the building blocks of life and the all-inclusive functional units of unicellular organisms. However, in higher organisms, cells do not usually operate as isolated, independent entities. In humans and other multicellular organisms, cells depend on one another and cooperate to maintain homeostasis in the body.

With a few exceptions, even the most complex animal starts out as a single cell, the fertilized egg, which divides almost endlessly. The trillions of cells that result become specialized for a particular function; some become supportive bone, others the transparent lens of the eye, still others skin cells, and so on. Thus a division of labor exists, with certain groups of cells highly specialized to perform functions that benefit the organism as a whole. Cell specialization carries with it certain hazards, because when a small specific group of cells is indispensable, any inability to function on its part can paralyze or destroy the entire body.

Groups of cells that are similar in structure and function are called **tissues.** The four primary tissue types—epithelium, connective tissue, nervous tissue, and muscle—have distinctive structures, patterns, and functions. The four primary tissues are further divided into subcategories, as described shortly.

To perform specific body functions, the tissues are organized into **organs** such as the heart, kidneys, and lungs. Most organs contain several representatives of the primary tissues, and the arrangement of these tissues determines the organ's structure and function. Thus **histology,** the study of tissues, complements a study of gross anatomy and provides the structural basis for a study of organ physiology.

The main objective of this exercise is to familiarize you with the major similarities and dissimilarities of the primary tissues, so that when the tissue composition of an organ is described, you will be able to more easily understand (and perhaps even predict) the organ's major function. Because epithelium and some types of connective tissue will not be considered again, they are emphasized more than muscle, nervous tissue, and bone (a connective tissue), which are covered in more depth in later exercises.

Epithelial Tissue

Epithelial tissue, or **epithelium,** covers surfaces. For example, epithelium covers the external body surface (as the epidermis), lines its cavities and tubules, and generally marks off our "insides" from our outsides. Since the various endocrine (hormone-producing) and exocrine glands almost invariably develop from epithelial membranes, glands, too, are logically classed as epithelium.

Epithelial functions include protection, absorption, filtration, excretion, secretion, and sensory reception. For example, the epithelium covering the body surface protects against bacterial invasion and chemical damage; that lining the respiratory tract is ciliated to sweep dust and other foreign particles away from the lungs. Epithelium specialized to absorb substances lines the stomach and small intestine. In the kidney tubules, the epithelium absorbs, secretes, and filters. Secretion is a specialty of the glands.

The following characteristics distinguish epithelial tissues from other types:

• Polarity. The membranes always have one free surface, called the *apical surface,* and typically that surface is significantly different from the *basal surface.*

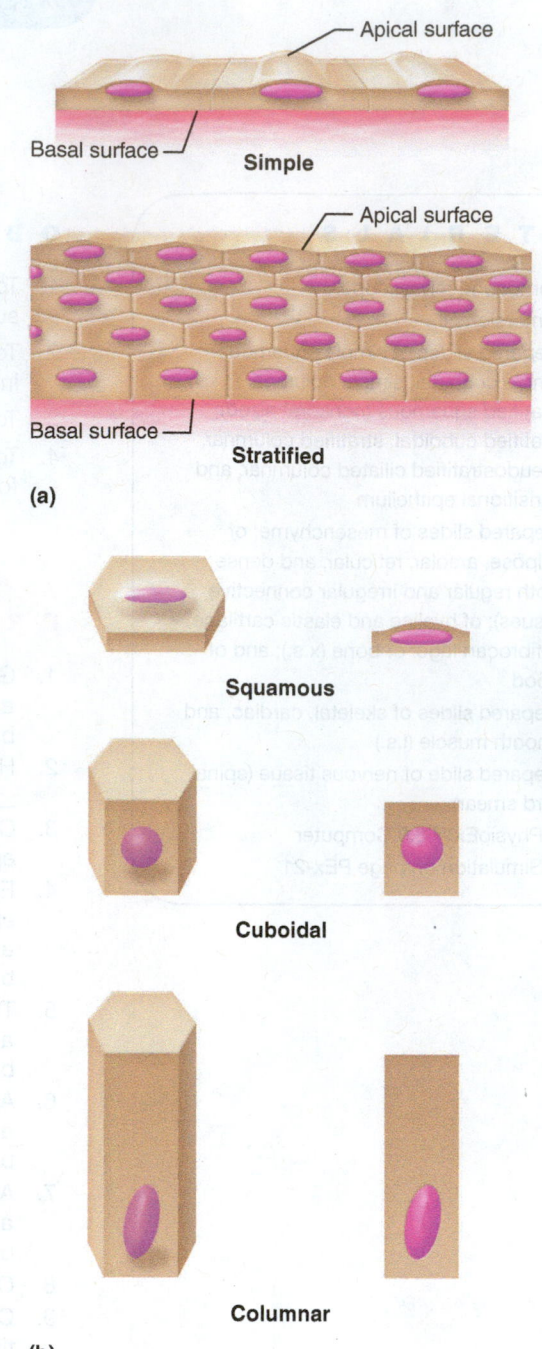

FIGURE 6A.1 Classification of epithelia.
(a) Classification on the basis of arrangement (relative number of layers). **(b)** Classification on the basis of cell shape. For each category, a whole cell is shown on the left and a longitudinal section is shown on the right.

• Cellularity and specialized contacts. Cells fit closely together to form membranes, or sheets of cells, and are bound together by specialized junctions.

• Supported by connective tissue. The cells are attached to and supported by an adhesive **basement membrane,** which is an amorphous material secreted partly by the epithelial cells (*basal lamina*) and connective tissue cells (*reticular lamina*) that lie adjacent to each other.

• Avascularity. Epithelial tissues have no blood supply of their own (are avascular) but instead depend on diffusion of nutrients from the underlying connective tissue. (Glandular epithelia, however, are very vascular.)

• Regeneration. If well nourished, epithelial cells can easily regenerate themselves. This is an important characteristic because many epithelia are subjected to a good deal of friction.

The covering and lining epithelia are classified according to two criteria—arrangement or relative number of layers and cell shape (Figure 6A.1). On the basis of arrangement, there are **simple** epithelia, consisting of one layer of cells attached to the basement membrane, and **stratified** epithelia, consisting of two or more layers of cells. The general types based on shape are **squamous** (scalelike), **cuboidal** (cubelike), and **columnar** (column-shaped) epithelial cells. The terms denoting shape and arrangement of the epithelial cells are combined to describe the epithelium fully. *Stratified epithelia are named according to the cells at the apical surface of the epithelial membrane,* not those resting on the basement membrane.

There are, in addition, two less easily categorized types of epithelia. **Pseudostratified epithelium** is actually a simple columnar epithelium (one layer of cells), but because its cells vary in height and the nuclei lie at different levels above the basement membrane, it gives the false appearance of being stratified. This epithelium is often ciliated. **Transitional epithelium** is a rather peculiar stratified squamous epithelium formed of rounded, or "plump," cells with the ability to slide over one another to allow the organ to be stretched. Transitional epithelium is found only in urinary system organs subjected to periodic distension, such as the bladder. The superficial cells are flattened (like true squamous cells) when the organ is distended and rounded when the organ is empty.

Epithelial cells forming glands are highly specialized to remove materials from the blood and to manufacture them into new materials, which they then secrete. There are two types of glands, as shown in Figure 6A.2. **Endocrine glands** lose their surface connection (duct) as they develop; thus they are referred to as ductless glands. Their secretions (all hormones) are released into the extracellular fluid, from which they enter the blood or the lymphatic vessels that weave through the glands. **Exocrine glands** retain their ducts, and their secretions empty through these ducts to an epithelial surface. The exocrine glands—including the sweat and oil glands, liver, and pancreas—are both external and internal; they will be discussed in conjunction with the organ systems to which their products are functionally related.

The most common types of epithelia, their characteristic locations in the body, and their functions are described in Figure 6A.3.

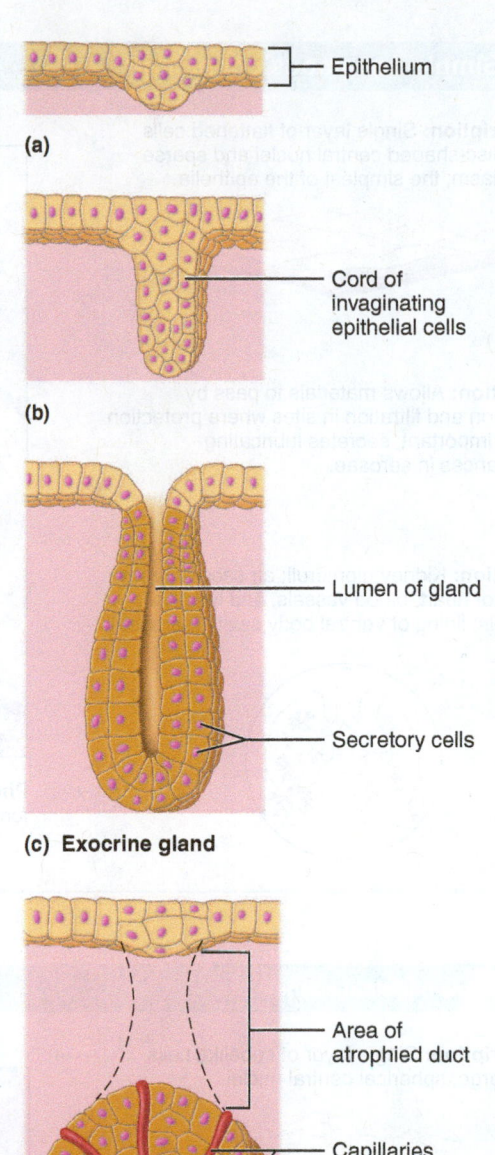

(a)

(b)

(c) Exocrine gland

(d) Endocrine gland

Epithelium

Cord of invaginating epithelial cells

Lumen of gland

Secretory cells

Area of atrophied duct

Capillaries

Secretory cells

FIGURE 6A.2 Formation of endocrine and exocrine glands from epithelial sheets. (a) Epithelial cells grow and push into the underlying tissue. **(b)** A cord of epithelial cells forms. **(c)** In an exocrine gland, a lumen (cavity) forms. The inner cells form the duct, the outer cells produce the secretion. **(d)** In a forming endocrine gland, the connecting duct cells atrophy, leaving the secretory cells with no connection to the epithelial surface. However, they do become heavily invested with blood and lymphatic vessels that receive the secretions.

Text continues on page 74.

(a) Simple squamous epithelium

Description: Single layer of flattened cells with disc-shaped central nuclei and sparse cytoplasm; the simplest of the epithelia.

Function: Allows materials to pass by diffusion and filtration in sites where protection is not important; secretes lubricating substances in serosae.

Location: Kidney glomeruli; air sacs of lungs; lining of heart, blood vessels, and lymphatic vessels; lining of ventral body cavity (serosae).

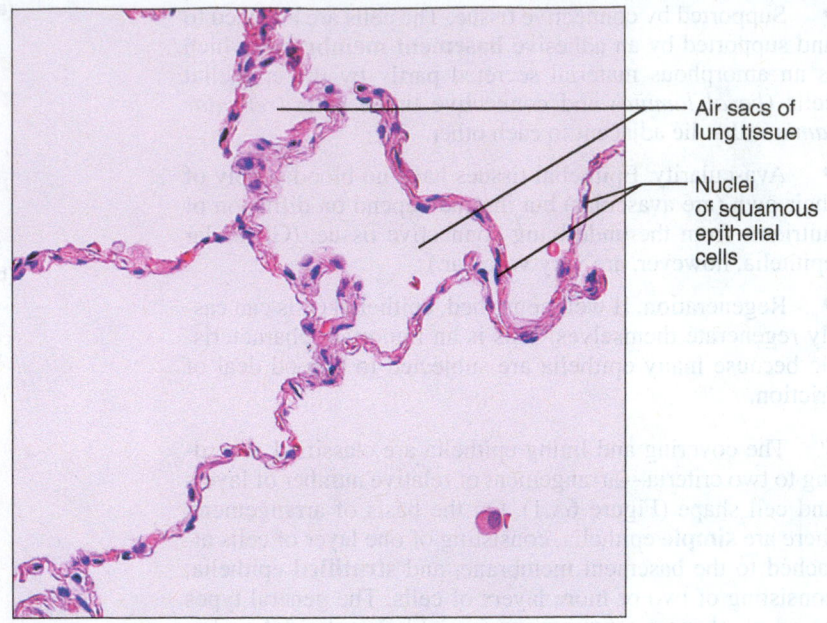

Air sacs of lung tissue

Nuclei of squamous epithelial cells

Photomicrograph: Simple squamous epithelium forming part of the alveolar (air sac) walls (140×).

(b) Simple cuboidal epithelium

Description: Single layer of cubelike cells with large, spherical central nuclei.

Function: Secretion and absorption.

Location: Kidney tubules; ducts and secretory portions of small glands; ovary surface.

Simple cuboidal epithelial cells

Basement membrane

Connective tissue

Photomicrograph: Simple cuboidal epithelium in kidney tubules (430×).

FIGURE 6.3 Epithelial tissues. Simple epithelia (**a** and **b**).

(c) Simple columnar epithelium

Description: Single layer of tall cells with *round* to *oval* nuclei; some cells bear cilia; layer may contain mucus-secreting unicellular glands (goblet cells).

Function: Absorption; secretion of mucus, enzymes, and other substances; ciliated type propels mucus (or reproductive cells) by ciliary action.

Location: Nonciliated type lines most of the digestive tract (stomach to anal canal), gallbladder, and excretory ducts of some glands; ciliated variety lines small bronchi, uterine tubes, and some regions of the uterus.

Goblet cells

Mucus secretion

Microvilli (brush border)

Photomicrograph: Simple columnar epithelium containing goblet cells from the small intestine (1150×).

(d) Pseudostratified columnar epithelium

Description: Single layer of cells of differing heights, some not reaching the free surface; nuclei seen at different levels; may contain mucus-secreting cells and bear cilia.

Function: Secretion, particularly of mucus; propulsion of mucus by ciliary action.

Location: Nonciliated type in male's sperm-carrying ducts and ducts of large glands; ciliated variety lines the trachea, most of the upper respiratory tract.

Trachea

Cilia
Mucus of goblet cell

Pseudo-stratified epithelial layer

Basement membrane

Photomicrograph: Pseudostratified ciliated columnar epithelium lining the human trachea (570×).

FIGURE 6A.3 (*continued*) Simple epithelia (**c** and **d**).

(e) Stratified squamous epithelium

Description: Thick membrane composed of several cell layers; basal cells are cuboidal or columnar and metabolically active; surface cells are flattened (squamous); in the keratinized type, the surface cells are full of keratin and dead; basal cells are active in mitosis and produce the cells of the more superficial layers.

Function: Protects underlying tissues in areas subjected to abrasion.

Location: Nonkeratinized type forms the moist linings of the esophagus, mouth, and vagina; keratinized variety forms the epidermis of the skin, a dry membrane.

Stratified squamous epithelium

Nuclei

Basement membrane

Connective tissue

Photomicrograph: Stratified squamous epithelium lining the esophagus (285×).

(f) Stratified cuboidal epithelium

Description: Generally two layers of cubelike cells.

Function: Protection

Location: Largest ducts of sweat glands, mammary glands, and salivary glands.

Basement membrane

Cuboidal epithelial cells

Duct lumen

Photomicrograph: Stratified cuboidal epithelium forming a salivary gland duct (285×).

FIGURE 6A.3 (continued) Epithelial tissues. Stratified epithelia (**e** and **f**).

(g) Stratified columnar epithelium

Description: Several cell layers; basal cells usually cuboidal; superficial cells elongated and columnar.

Function: Protection; secretion.

Location: Rare in the body; small amounts in male urethra and in large ducts of some glands.

Urethra

— Basement membrane

— Stratified columnar epithelium

— Underlying connective tissue

Photomicrograph: Stratified columnar epithelium lining of the male urethra (315×).

(h) Transitional epithelium

Description: Resembles both stratified squamous and stratified cuboidal; basal cells cuboidal or columnar; surface cells dome shaped or squamouslike, depending on degree of organ stretch.

Function: Stretches readily and permits distension of urinary organ by contained urine.

Location: Lines the ureters, urinary bladder, and part of the urethra.

— Transitional epithelium

— Basement membrane
— Connective tissue

Photomicrograph: Transitional epithelium lining the urinary bladder, relaxed state (360×); note the bulbous, or rounded, appearance of the cells at the surface; these cells flatten and become elongated when the bladder is filled with urine.

FIGURE 6A.3 *(continued)* Stratified epithelia **(g** and **h)**.

Source of (g): Kessel and Kardon/Visuals Unlimited.

FIGURE 6A.4 Areolar connective tissue: A prototype (model) connective tissue. This tissue underlies epithelia and surrounds capillaries. Note the various cell types and the three classes of fibers (collagen, reticular, elastic) embedded in the ground substance.

Cell types

- Macrophage
- Fibroblast
- Lymphocyte
- Fat cell
- Mast cell
- Neutrophil

Extracellular matrix

- Ground substance
- Fibers
  - • Collagen fiber
  - • Elastic fiber
  - • Reticular fiber
- Capillary

ACTIVITY 1

Examining Epithelial Tissue Under the Microscope

Obtain slides of simple squamous, simple cuboidal, simple columnar, stratified squamous (nonkeratinized), pseudostratified ciliated columnar, stratified cuboidal, stratified columnar, and transitional epithelia. Examine each carefully, and notice how the epithelial cells fit closely together to form intact sheets of cells, a necessity for a tissue that forms linings or covering membranes. Scan each epithelial type for modifications for specific functions, such as cilia (motile cell projections that help to move substances along the cell surface), and microvilli, which increase the surface area for absorption. Also be alert for goblet cells, which secrete lubricating mucus. Compare your observations with the descriptions and photomicrographs in Figure 6A.3.

While working, check the questions in the Exercise 6A Review Sheet. A number of the questions there refer to some of the observations you are asked to make during your microscopic study. ■

Connective Tissue

Connective tissue is found in all parts of the body as discrete structures or as part of various body organs. It is the most abundant and widely distributed of the tissue types.

Connective tissues perform a variety of functions, but they primarily protect, support, and bind together other tis-sues of the body. For example, bones are composed of connective tissue (**bone,** or **osseous tissue**), and they protect and support other body tissues and organs. The ligaments and tendons (**dense connective tissue**) bind the bones together or bind skeletal muscles to bones.

Areolar connective tissue (Figure 6A.4) is a soft packaging material that cushions and protects body organs. **Adipose** (fat) tissue provides insulation for the body tissues and a source of stored food. Blood-forming (**hematopoietic**) tissue replenishes the body's supply of red blood cells. Connective tissue also serves a vital function in the repair of all body tissues, since many wounds are repaired by connective tissue in the form of scar tissue.

The characteristics of connective tissue include the following:

- With a few exceptions (cartilages, tendons, and ligaments, which are poorly vascularized), connective tissues have a rich supply of blood vessels.

- Connective tissues are composed of many types of cells.

- There is a great deal of noncellular, nonliving material (matrix) between the cells of connective tissue.

The nonliving material between the cells—the **extracellular matrix**—deserves a bit more explanation because it distinguishes connective tissue from all other tissues. It is produced by the cells and then extruded. The matrix is primarily responsible for the strength associated with connective tissue, but there is variation. At one extreme, adipose tissue is composed mostly of cells. At the opposite extreme, bone and cartilage have few cells and large amounts of matrix.

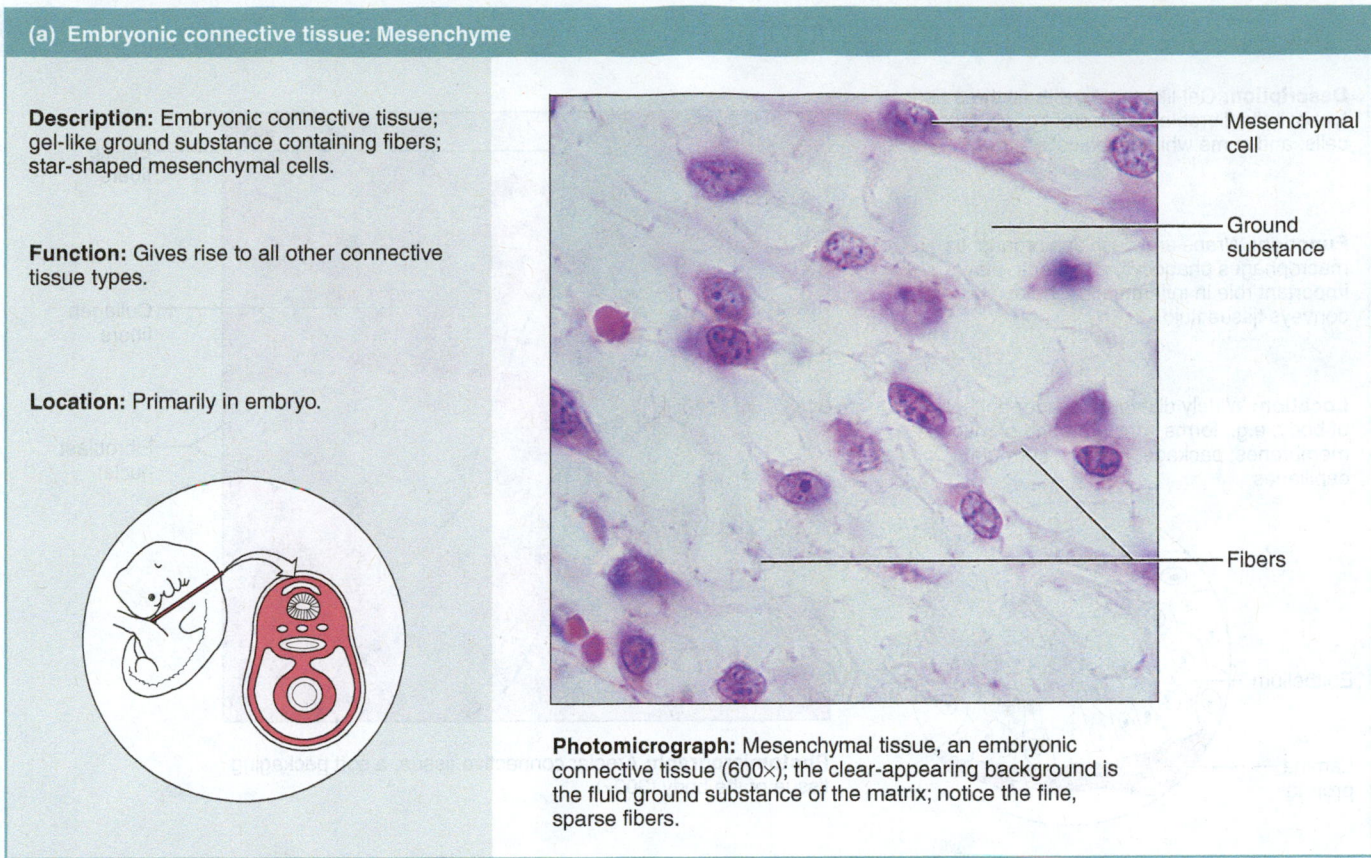

(a) Embryonic connective tissue: Mesenchyme

Description: Embryonic connective tissue; gel-like ground substance containing fibers; star-shaped mesenchymal cells.

Function: Gives rise to all other connective tissue types.

Location: Primarily in embryo.

Mesenchymal cell

Ground substance

Fibers

Photomicrograph: Mesenchymal tissue, an embryonic connective tissue (600×); the clear-appearing background is the fluid ground substance of the matrix; notice the fine, sparse fibers.

FIGURE 6A.5 Connective tissues. Embryonic connective tissue **(a).**

The matrix has two components—ground substance and fibers. The **ground substance** is composed chiefly of interstitial fluid, cell adhesion proteins, and proteoglycans. Depending on its specific composition, the ground substance may be liquid, semisolid, gel-like, or very hard. When the matrix is firm, as in cartilage and bone, the connective tissue cells reside in cavities in the matrix called *lacunae*. The fibers, which provide support, include **collagen** (white) **fibers, elastic** (yellow) **fibers,** and **reticular** (fine collagen) **fibers.** Of these, the collagen fibers are most abundant.

Generally speaking, the ground substance functions as a molecular sieve, or medium, through which nutrients and other dissolved substances can diffuse between the blood capillaries and the cells. The fibers in the matrix hinder diffusion somewhat and make the ground substance less pliable. The properties of the connective tissue cells and the makeup and arrangement of their matrix elements vary tremendously, accounting for the amazing diversity of this tissue type. Nonetheless, the connective tissues have a common structural plan seen best in *areolar connective tissue* (Figure 6A.4), a soft packing tissue that occurs throughout the body. Since all other connective tissues are variations of areolar, it is considered the model or prototype of the connective tissues. Notice in Figure 6A.4 that areolar tissue has all three varieties of fibers, but they are sparsely arranged in its transparent gel-like ground substance. The cell type that secretes its matrix is the *fibroblast,* but a wide variety of other cells (including phagocytic cells like macrophages and certain white blood cells and mast cells that act in the inflammatory response) are

present as well. The more durable connective tissues, such as bone, cartilage, and the dense fibrous varieties, characteristically have a firm ground substance and many more fibers.

There are four main types of adult connective tissue, all of which typically have large amounts of matrix. These are **connective tissue proper** (which includes areolar, adipose, reticular, and dense [fibrous] connective tissues), **cartilage, bone,** and **blood.** All of these derive from an embryonic tissue called *mesenchyme.* Figure 6A.5 lists the general characteristics, location, and function of some of the connective tissues found in the body.

ACTIVITY 2

Examining Connective Tissue Under the Microscope

Obtain prepared slides of mesenchyme; of adipose, areolar, reticular, dense regular, elastic, and irregular connective tissue; of hyaline and elastic cartilage and fibrocartilage; of osseous connective tissue (bone); and of blood. Compare your observations with the views illustrated in Figure 6A.5.

Distinguish between the living cells and the matrix and pay particular attention to the denseness and arrangement of the matrix. For example, notice how the matrix of the dense regular and irregular connective tissues, respectively making up tendons and the dermis of the skin, is packed with collagen fibers. Note also that in the *regular* variety (tendon), the

Text continues on page 81.

(b) Connective tissue proper: loose connective tissue, areolar

Description: Gel-like matrix with all three fiber types; cells: fibroblasts, macrophages, mast cells, and some white blood cells.

Function: Wraps and cushions organs; its macrophages phagocytize bacteria; plays important role in inflammation; holds and conveys tissue fluid.

Location: Widely distributed under epithelia of body, e.g., forms lamina propria of mucous membranes; packages organs; surrounds capillaries.

Epithelium

Lamina propria

Elastic fibers

Collagen fibers

Fibroblast nuclei

Photomicrograph: Areolar connective tissue, a soft packaging tissue of the body (300×).

(c) Connective tissue proper: loose connective tissue, adipose

Description: Matrix as in areolar, but very sparse; closely packed adipocytes, or fat cells, have nucleus pushed to the side by large fat droplet.

Function: Provides reserve fuel; insulates against heat loss; supports and protects organs.

Location: Under skin; around kidneys and eyeballs; within abdomen; in breasts.

Vacuole containing fat droplet

Nuclei of fat cells

Photomicrograph: Adipose tissue from the subcutaneous layer under the skin (350×).

FIGURE 6A.5 *(continued)* Connective tissues. Connective tissue proper (**b** and **c**).

(d) Connective tissue proper: loose connective tissue, reticular

Description: Network of reticular fibers in a typical loose ground substance; reticular cells lie on the network.

Function: Fibers form a soft internal skeleton (stroma) that supports other cell types, including white blood cells, mast cells, and macrophages.

Location: Lymphoid organs (lymph nodes, bone marrow, and spleen).

Spleen

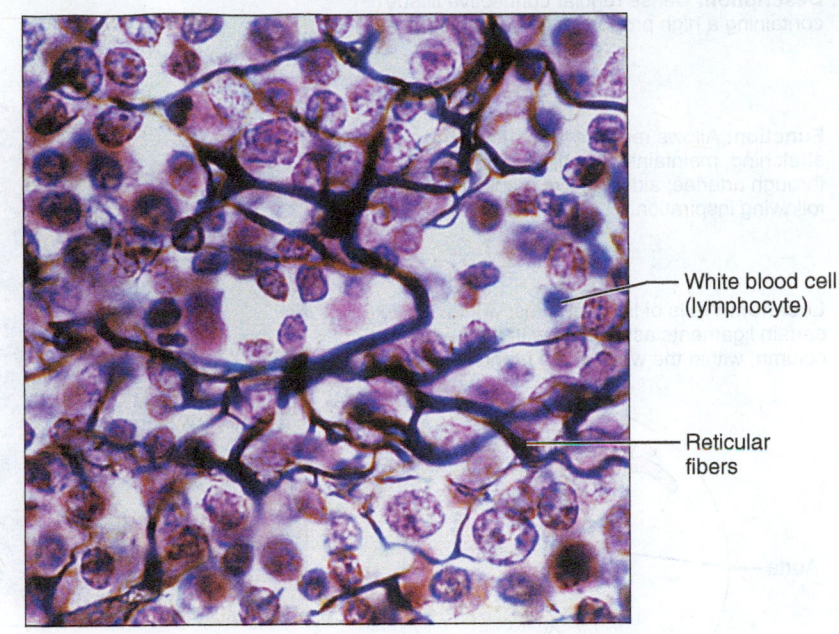

White blood cell (lymphocyte)

Reticular fibers

Photomicrograph: Dark-staining network of reticular connective tissue fibers forming the internal skeleton of the spleen (350×).

(e) Connective tissue proper: dense connective tissue, dense regular

Description: Primarily parallel collagen fibers; a few elastic fibers; major cell type is the fibroblast.

Function: Attaches muscles to bones or to muscles; attaches bones to bones; withstands great tensile stress when pulling force is applied in one direction.

Location: Tendons, most ligaments, aponeuroses.

Shoulder joint

Ligament

Tendon

Collagen fibers

Nuclei of fibroblasts

Photomicrograph: Dense regular connective tissue from a tendon (500×).

FIGURE 6A.5 *(continued)* Connective tissue proper **(d** and **e).**

(f) Connective tissue proper: dense connective tissue, elastic

Description: Dense regular connective tissue containing a high proportion of elastic fibers.

Function: Allows recoil of tissue following stretching; maintains pulsatile flow of blood through arteries; aids passive recoil of lungs following inspiration.

Location: Walls of large arteries; within certain ligaments associated with the vertebral column; within the walls of the bronchial tubes.

Aorta

Heart

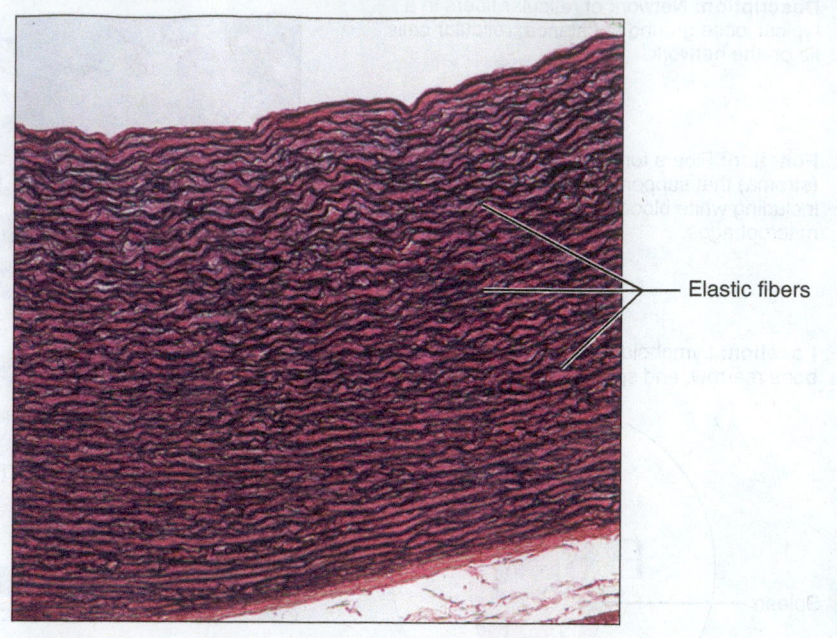

Elastic fibers

Photomicrograph: Elastic connective tissue in the wall of the aorta (250×).

(g) Connective tissue proper: dense connective tissue, dense irregular

Description: Primarily irregularly arranged collagen fibers; some elastic fibers; major cell type is the fibroblast.

Function: Able to withstand tension exerted in many directions; provides structural strength.

Location: Fibrous capsules of organs and of joints; dermis of the skin; submucosa of digestive tract.

Fibrous joint capsule

Nuclei of fibroblasts

Collagen fibers

Photomicrograph: Dense irregular connective tissue from the dermis of the skin (400×).

FIGURE 6A.5 *(continued)* Connective tissues. Connective tissue proper **(f)** and **(g)**.

(h) Cartilage: hyaline

Description: Amorphous but firm matrix; collagen fibers form an imperceptible network; chondroblasts produce the matrix and when mature (chondrocytes) lie in lacunae.

Function: Supports and reinforces; has resilient cushioning properties; resists compressive stress.

Location: Forms most of the embryonic skeleton; covers the ends of long bones in joint cavities; forms costal cartilages of the ribs; cartilages of the nose, trachea, and larynx.

Costal cartilages

Chondrocyte in lacuna

Matrix

Photomicrograph: Hyaline cartilage from the trachea (750×).

(i) Cartilage: elastic

Description: Similar to hyaline cartilage, but more elastic fibers in matrix.

Function: Maintains the shape of a structure while allowing great flexibility.

Location: Supports the external ear (pinna); epiglottis.

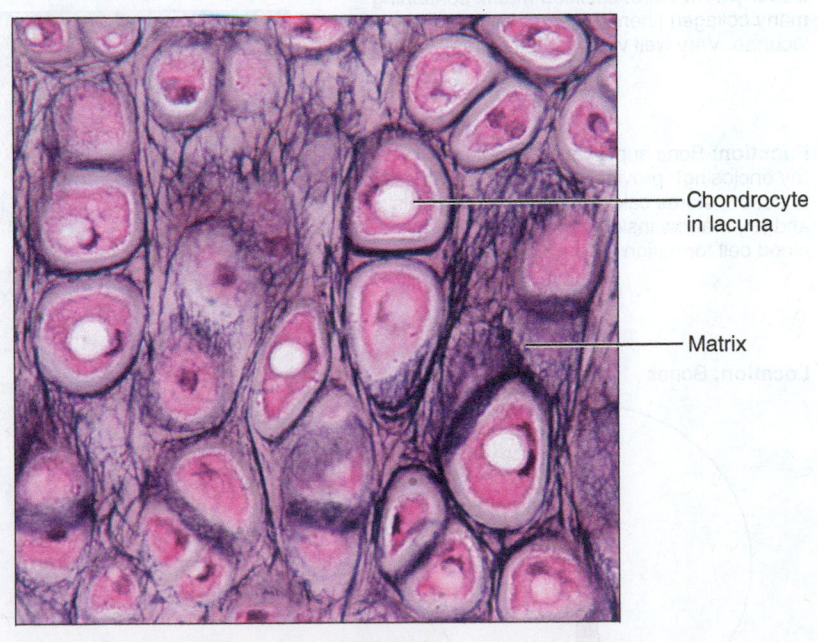

Chondrocyte in lacuna

Matrix

Photomicrograph: Elastic cartilage from the human ear pinna; forms the flexible skeleton of the ear (800×).

FIGURE 6A.5 (continued) Cartilage (**h** and **i**).

(j) Cartilage: fibrocartilage

Description: Matrix similar to but less firm than that in hyaline cartilage; thick collagen fibers predominate.

Function: Tensile strength with the ability to absorb compressive shock.

Location: Intervertebral discs; pubic symphysis; discs of knee joint.

Intervertebral discs

Chondrocytes in lacunae

Collagen fiber

Photomicrograph: Fibrocartilage of an intervertebral disc (125×). Special staining produced the blue color seen.

(k) Bones (osseous tissue)

Description: Hard, calcified matrix containing many collagen fibers; osteocytes lie in lacunae. Very well vascularized.

Function: Bone supports and protects (by enclosing); provides levers for the muscles to act on; stores calcium and other minerals and fat; marrow inside bones is the site for blood cell formation (hematopoiesis).

Location: Bones

Central canal

Lacunae

Lamella

Photomicrograph: Cross-sectional view of bone (125×).

FIGURE 6A.5 (continued) Connective tissues. Cartilage **(j)** and bone **(k)**.

(I) Blood

Description: Red and white blood cells in a fluid matrix (plasma).

Function: Transport of respiratory gases, nutrients, wastes, and other substances.

Location: Contained within blood vessels.

Plasma

Neutrophil

Red blood cells

Lymphocyte

Photomicrograph: Smear of human blood (1860×); two white blood cells (neutrophil in upper left and lymphocyte in lower right) are seen surrounded by red blood cells.

FIGURE 6A.5 *(continued)* Blood **(I).**

fibers are all running in the same direction, whereas in the dermis they appear to be running in many directions.

While examining the areolar connective tissue, notice how much empty space there appears to be (*areol* = small empty space), and distinguish between the collagen fibers and the coiled elastic fibers. Identify the starlike fibroblasts. Also, try to locate a **mast cell,** which has large, darkly staining granules in its cytoplasm (*mast* = stuffed full of granules). This cell type releases histamine, which makes capillaries more permeable during inflammatory reactions and allergies and thus is partially responsible for that "runny nose" of some allergies.

In adipose tissue, locate a "signet ring" cell, a fat cell in which the nucleus can be seen pushed to one side by the large, fat-filled vacuole that appears to be a large empty space. Also notice how little matrix there is in adipose (fat) tissue. Distinguish between the living cells and the matrix in the dense fibrous, bone, and hyaline cartilage preparations.

Scan the blood slide at low and then high power to examine the general shape of the red blood cells. Then, switch to the oil immersion lens for a closer look at the various types of white blood cells. How does blood differ from all other connective tissues?

Nervous Tissue

Nervous tissue is composed of two major cell populations. The **neuroglia** are special supporting cells that protect, support, and insulate the more delicate neurons. The **neurons** are highly specialized to receive stimuli (irritability) and to conduct waves of excitation, or impulses, to all parts of the body (conductivity). They are the cells that are most often associated with nervous system functioning.

The structure of neurons is markedly different from that of all other body cells. They all have a nucleus-containing cell body, and their cytoplasm is drawn out into long extensions (cell processes)—sometimes as long as 1 m (about 3 feet), which allows a single neuron to conduct an impulse over relatively long distances. More detail about the anatomy of the different classes of neurons and neuroglia appears in Exercise 17.

ACTIVITY 3

Examining Nervous Tissue Under the Microscope

Obtain a prepared slide of a spinal cord smear. Locate a neuron and compare it to Figure 6A.6. Keep the light dim—this

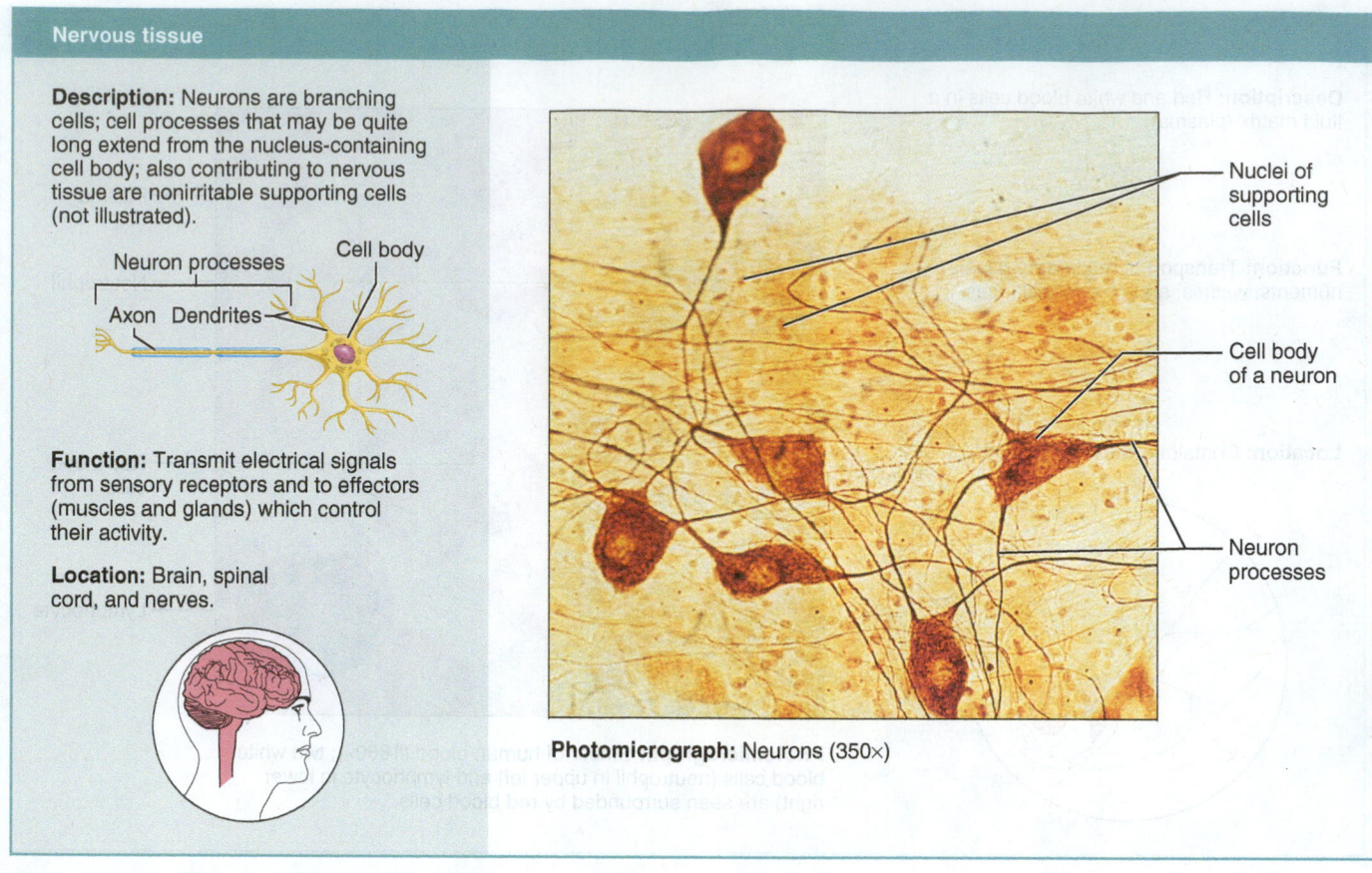

Nervous tissue

Description: Neurons are branching cells; cell processes that may be quite long extend from the nucleus-containing cell body; also contributing to nervous tissue are nonirritable supporting cells (not illustrated).

Neuron processes — Axon   Dendrites   Cell body

Function: Transmit electrical signals from sensory receptors and to effectors (muscles and glands) which control their activity.

Location: Brain, spinal cord, and nerves.

Nuclei of supporting cells

Cell body of a neuron

Neuron processes

Photomicrograph: Neurons (350×)

FIGURE 6A.6 Nervous tissue.

Muscle Tissue

Muscle tissue (Figure 6A.7) is highly specialized to contract and produces most types of body movement. As you might expect, muscle cells tend to be elongated, providing a long axis for contraction. The three basic types of muscle tissue are described briefly here. Cardiac and skeletal muscles are treated more completely in later exercises.

Skeletal muscle, the "meat," or flesh, of the body, is attached to the skeleton. It is under voluntary control (consciously controlled), and its contraction moves the limbs and other external body parts. The cells of skeletal muscles are long, cylindrical, and multinucleate (several nuclei per cell), with the nuclei pushed to the periphery of the cells; they have obvious *striations* (stripes).

Cardiac muscle is found only in the heart. As it contracts, the heart acts as a pump, propelling the blood into the blood vessels. Cardiac muscle, like skeletal muscle, has striations, but cardiac cells are branching uninucleate cells that interdigitate (fit together) at junctions called **intercalated**

discs. These structural modifications allow the cardiac muscle to act as a unit. Cardiac muscle is under involuntary control, which means that we cannot voluntarily or consciously control the operation of the heart.

Smooth muscle, or *visceral muscle,* is found mainly in the walls of hollow organs (digestive and urinary tract organs, uterus, blood vessels). Typically it has two layers that run at right angles to each other; consequently its contraction can constrict or dilate the lumen (cavity) of an organ and propel substances along predetermined pathways. Smooth muscle cells are quite different in appearance from those of skeletal or cardiac muscle. No striations are visible, and the uninucleate smooth muscle cells are spindle-shaped.

ACTIVITY 4

Examining Muscle Tissue Under the Microscope

Obtain and examine prepared slides of skeletal, cardiac, and smooth muscle. Notice their similarities and dissimilarities in your observations and in the illustrations in Figure 6A.7. ▮

(a) Skeletal muscle

Description: Long, cylindrical, multinucleate cells; obvious striations.

Function: Voluntary movement; locomotion; manipulation of the environment; facial expression; voluntary control.

Location: In skeletal muscles attached to bones or occasionally to skin.

Striations

Nuclei

Part of muscle fiber (cell)

Photomicrograph: Skeletal muscle (approx. 460×). Notice the obvious banding pattern and the fact that these large cells are multinucleate.

(b) Cardiac muscle

Description: Branching, striated, generally uninucleate cells that interdigitate at specialized junctions (intercalated discs).

Function: As it contracts, it propels blood into the circulation; involuntary control.

Location: The walls of the heart.

Striations

Intercalated discs

Nucleus

Photomicrograph: Cardiac muscle (500×); notice the striations, branching of cells, and the intercalated discs.

FIGURE 6A.7 Muscle tissues. Skeletal muscle **(a)** and cardiac muscle **(b).**

(c) Smooth muscle

Description: Spindle-shaped cells with central nuclei; no striations; cells arranged closely to form sheets.

Function: Propels substances or objects (foodstuffs, urine, a baby) along internal passageways; involuntary control.

Location: Mostly in the walls of hollow organs.

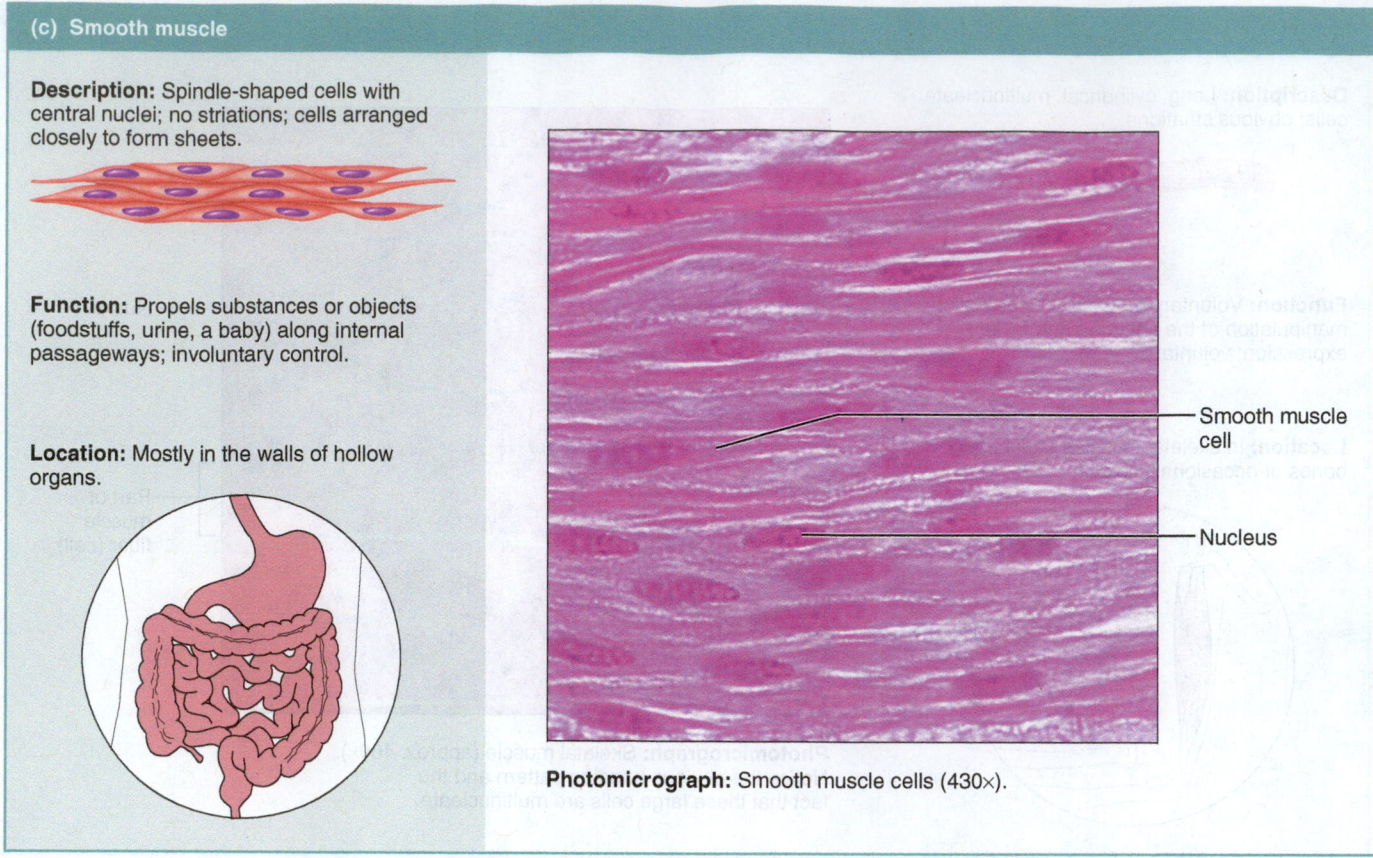

Photomicrograph: Smooth muscle cells (430×).

Smooth muscle cell

Nucleus

FIGURE 6A.7 *(continued)* Muscle tissues. Smooth muscle **(c)**.

NAME_____

LAB TIME/DATE _____

Classification of Tissues

Tissue Structure and Function—General Review

1. Define *tissue*. _____

_____

2. Use the key choices to identify the major tissue types described below.

Key: a.   connective tissue   b.   epithelium   c.   muscle   d.   nervous tissue

_____   1. lines body cavities and covers the body's external surface

_____   2. pumps blood, flushes urine out of the body, allows one to swing a bat

_____   3. transmits electrochemical impulses

_____   4. anchors, packages, and supports body organs

_____   5. cells may absorb, secrete, and filter

_____   6. most involved in regulating and controlling body functions

_____   7. major function is to contract

_____   8. synthesizes hormones

_____   9. the most durable tissue type

_____   10. abundant nonliving extracellular matrix

_____   11. most widespread tissue in the body

_____   12. forms nerves and the brain

Epithelial Tissue

3. Describe five general characteristics of epithelial tissue. _____

_____

_____

_____

4. On what basis are epithelial tissues classified? _____

5. List five major functions of epithelium in the body, and give examples of each.

Function 1: _____ Example: _____

Function 2: _____ Example: _____

Function 3: _____ Example: _____

Function 4: _____ Example: _____

Function 5: _____ Example: _____

6. How does the function of stratified epithelia differ from the function of simple epithelia? _____

_____

_____

7. Where is ciliated epithelium found? _____

_____

What role does it play? _____

_____

8. Transitional epithelium is actually stratified squamous epithelium with special characteristics.

How does it differ structurally from other stratified squamous epithelia? _____

_____

How does the structural difference support its function? _____

_____

_____

9. How do the endocrine and exocrine glands differ in structure and function? _____

_____

_____

_____

10. Respond to the following with the key choices.

Key: a. simple squamous   c. simple columnar   e. stratified squamous
     b. simple cuboidal   d. pseudostratified ciliated columnar   f. transitional

_____ 1. lining of the esophagus

_____ 2. lining of the stomach

_____ 3. alveolar sacs of lungs

_____ 4. tubules of the kidney

_____ 5. epidermis of the skin

_____ 6. lining of bladder; peculiar cells that have the ability to slide over each other

_____ 7. forms the thin serous membranes; a single layer of flattened cells

Connective Tissue

11. What are three general characteristics of connective tissues? _____

_____

_____

12. What functions are performed by connective tissue? _____

_____

13. How are the functions of connective tissue reflected in its structure? _____

_____

_____

14. Using the key, choose the best response to identify the connective tissues described below.

_____ 1. attaches bones to bones and muscles to bones

_____ 2. acts as a storage depot for fat

_____ 3. the dermis of the skin

_____ 4. makes up the intervertebral discs

_____ 5. forms the hip bone

_____ 6. composes basement membranes; a soft packaging tissue with a jellylike matrix

_____ 7. forms the larynx, the costal cartilages of the ribs, and the embryonic skeleton

_____ 8. provides a flexible framework for the external ear

_____ 9. firm, structurally amorphous matrix heavily invaded with fibers; appears glassy and smooth

_____ 10. matrix hard owing to calcium salts; provides levers for muscles to act on

_____ 11. insulates against heat loss

_____ 12. walls of large arteries

Key: a. adipose connective tissue
       b. areolar connective tissue
       c. dense fibrous connective tissue
       d. elastic cartilage
       e. elastic connective tissue
       f. fibrocartilage
       g. hematopoietic tissue
       h. hyaline cartilage
       i. osseous tissue

15. Why do adipose cells remind people of a ring with a single jewel? _____

_____

Nervous Tissue

16. What two physiological characteristics are highly developed in neurons (nerve cells)? _____

_____

17. In what ways are neurons similar to other cells? _____

_____

How are they different? _____

18. Describe how the unique structure of a neuron relates to its function in the body.

_____

_____

Muscle Tissue

19. The three types of muscle tissue exhibit similarities as well as differences. Check the appropriate space in the chart to indicate which muscle types exhibit each characteristic.

Characteristic	Skeletal	Cardiac	Smooth
Voluntarily controlled			
Involuntarily controlled			
Striated			
Has a single nucleus in each cell			
Has several nuclei per cell			
Found attached to bones			
Allows you to direct your eyeballs			
Found in the walls of the stomach, uterus, and arteries			
Contains spindle-shaped cells			
Contains branching cylindrical cells			
Contains long, nonbranching cylindrical cells			
Has intercalated discs			
Concerned with locomotion of the body as a whole			
Changes the internal volume of an organ as it contracts			
Tissue of the heart			

For Review

20. Label the tissue types illustrated here and on the next pages, and identify all structures provided with leaders.

(a) _____

(b) _____

(c) _____

(d) _____

(e) _____

(f) _____

(g) _____

(h) _____

(i) _____

(j) _____

(k) _____

(l) _____

The Integumentary System

MATERIALS

- ☐ Skin model (three-dimensional, if available)
- ☐ Compound microscope
- ☐ Prepared slide of human scalp
- ☐ Prepared slide of skin of palm or sole
- ☐ Sheet of #20 bond paper ruled to mark off cm² areas
- ☐ Scissors
- ☐ Betadine® swabs, or Lugol's iodine and cotton swabs
- ☐ Adhesive tape
- ☐ Disposable gloves
- ☐ Data collection sheet for plotting distribution of sweat glands
- ☐ Porelon fingerprint pad or portable inking foils
- ☐ Ink cleaner towelettes
- ☐ Index cards (4 in. × 6 in.)
- ☐ Magnifying glasses

myA&P *For practice quizzes on this lab, go to www.myaandp.com.*

PAL *For access to anatomical models and more, check out Practice Anatomy Lab.*

OBJECTIVES

1. To list several important functions of the skin, or integumentary system.
2. To recognize and name during observation of an appropriate model, diagram, projected slide, or microscopic specimen the following skin structures: epidermis, dermis (papillary and reticular layers), hair follicles and hair, sebaceous glands, and sweat glands.
3. To name the layers of the epidermis and describe the characteristics of each.
4. To compare the properties of the epidermis to those of the dermis.
5. To describe the distribution and function of the skin derivatives— sebaceous glands, sweat glands, and hairs.
6. To differentiate between eccrine and apocrine sweat glands.
7. To enumerate the factors determining skin color.
8. To describe the function of melanin.
9. To identify the major regions of nails.

PRE-LAB QUIZ

1. All the following are functions of the skin except:
   a. excretion of body wastes
   b. insulation
   c. protection from mechanical damage
   d. site of vitamin A synthesis
2. The skin has two distinct regions. The superficial layer is the _____ and the underlying connective tissue, the _____.
3. These cells produce a brown-to-black pigment that colors the skin and protects DNA from the damaging effects of ultraviolet radiation. The cells are:
   a. epidermal dendritic cells
   b. keratinocytes
   c. melanocytes
   d. tactile cells
4. Circle True or False. Nails are hornlike derivatives of the epidermis.
5. The portion of a hair that you see that projects from the scalp surface is known as the _____.
   a. bulb   c. root
   b. matrix   d. shaft
6. Circle the correct term. The ducts of <u>sebaceous</u> / <u>sweat</u> glands usually empty into a hair follicle but may also open directly on the skin surface.
7. Circle the correct term. <u>Eccrine</u> / <u>Apocrine</u> glands are found primarily in the genital and axillary areas.

The **skin,** or **integument,** is considered an organ system because of its extent and complexity. It is much more than an external body covering; architecturally the skin is a marvel. It is tough yet pliable, a characteristic that enables it to withstand constant insult from outside agents.

The skin has many functions, most (but not all) concerned with protection. It insulates and cushions the underlying body tissues and protects the entire body from mechanical damage (bumps and cuts), chemical damage (acids, alkalis, and the like), thermal damage (heat), and bacterial invasion (by virtue of its acid mantle and continuous surface). The hardened uppermost layer of the skin (the cornified layer) prevents water loss from the body surface. The skin's abundant capillary network (under the control of the nervous system) plays an important role in regulating heat loss from the body surface.

The skin has other functions as well. For example, it acts as a mini-excretory system; urea, salts, and water are lost through the skin pores in sweat. The skin also has important metabolic duties. For example, like liver cells, it carries out some chemical conversions that activate or inactivate certain drugs and hormones, and it is the site of vitamin D synthesis for the body. Finally, the cutaneous sense organs are located in the dermis.

Basic Structure of the Skin

The skin has two distinct regions—the superficial *epidermis* composed of epithelium and an underlying connective tissue *dermis* (Figure 7.1). These layers are firmly "cemented" together along an undulating border. But friction, such as the rubbing of a poorly fitting shoe, may cause them to separate, resulting in a blister. Immediately deep to the dermis is the **hypodermis,** or **superficial fascia** (primarily adipose tissue), which is not considered part of the skin. The main skin areas and structures are described below.

ACTIVITY 1

Locating Structures on a Skin Model

As you read, locate the following structures in Figure 7.1 and on a skin model.

Epidermis

Structurally, the avascular epidermis is a keratinized stratified squamous epithelium consisting of four distinct cell types and four or five distinct layers.

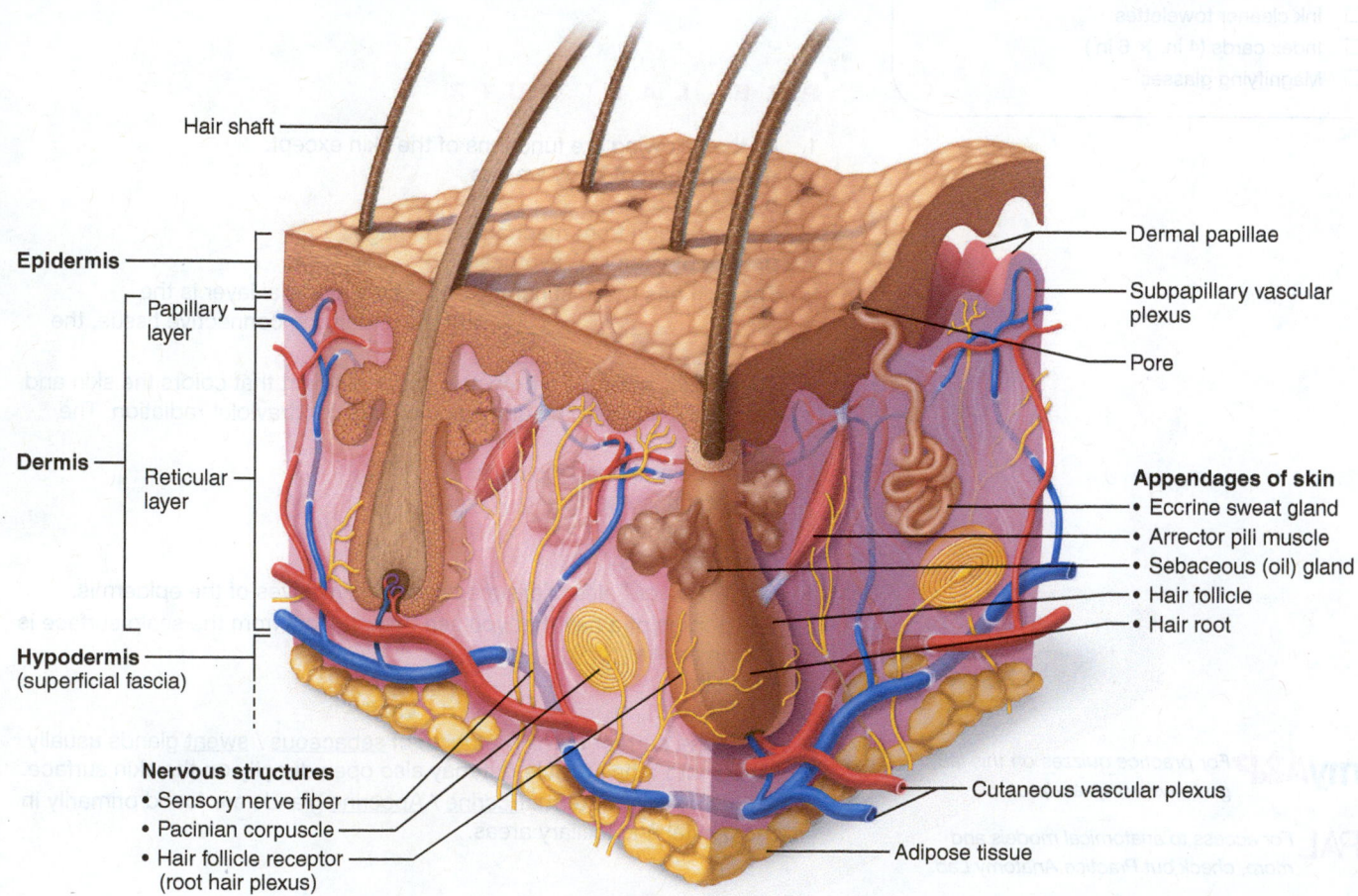

Hair shaft

Epidermis

Papillary layer

Dermis

Reticular layer

Hypodermis (superficial fascia)

Nervous structures
• Sensory nerve fiber
• Pacinian corpuscle
• Hair follicle receptor (root hair plexus)

Dermal papillae

Subpapillary vascular plexus

Pore

Appendages of skin
• Eccrine sweat gland
• Arrector pili muscle
• Sebaceous (oil) gland
• Hair follicle
• Hair root

Cutaneous vascular plexus

Adipose tissue

FIGURE 7.1 Skin structure. Three-dimensional view of the skin and the underlying hypodermis. The epidermis and dermis have been pulled apart at the right corner to reveal the dermal papillae.

Cells of the Epidermis

- **Keratinocytes** (literally, keratin cells): The most abundant epidermal cells, they function mainly to produce keratin fibrils. **Keratin** is a fibrous protein that gives the epidermis its durability and protective capabilities. Keratinocytes are tightly connected to each other by desmosomes.

Far less numerous are the following types of epidermal cells (Figure 7.2):

- **Melanocytes:** Spidery black cells that produce the brown-to-black pigment called **melanin.** The skin tans because melanin production increases when the skin is exposed to sunlight. The melanin provides a protective pigment umbrella over the nuclei of the cells in the deeper epidermal layers, thus shielding their genetic material (deoxyribonucleic acid, DNA) from the damaging effects of ultraviolet radiation. A concentration of melanin in one spot is called a *freckle.*

FIGURE 7.2 **The main structural features in epidermis of thin skin. (a)** Photomicrograph depicting the four major epidermal layers (200 ×). **(b)** Diagram showing the layers and relative distribution of the different cell types. Keratinocytes (orange), melanocytes (gray), epidermal dendrite cells (purple), and tactile cells (blue). A sensory nerve ending (yellow) extending from the dermis is associated with a tactile cell forming a tactile disc (touch receptor). Notice that the keratinocytes are joined by numerous desmosomes. The stratum lucidum, present in thick skin, is not illustrated here.

Stratum corneum
Most superficial layer; 20–30 layers of dead cells represented only by flat membranous sacs filled with keratin. Glycolipids in extracellular space.

Stratum granulosum
Three to five layers of flattened cells, organelles deteriorating; cytoplasm full of lamellated granules (release lipids) and keratohyaline granules.

Stratum spinosum
Several layers of keratinocytes unified by desmosomes. Cells contain thick bundles of intermediate filaments made of pre-keratin.

Stratum basale
Deepest epidermal layer; one row of actively mitotic stem cells; some newly formed cells become part of the more superficial layers.

Keratinocytes

Dermis

Melanin granule

Sensory nerve ending

Tactile (Merkel) cell

Desmosomes

Melanocyte

Epidermal dendritic cell

(a)

Dermis

(b)

FIGURE 7.3 Photograph of a deep (stage III) decubitus ulcer.

- **Epidermal dendritic cells:** Also called *Langerhans cells,* these cells play a role in immunity.

- **Tactile (Merkel) cells:** Occasional spiky hemispheres that, in conjunction with sensory nerve endings, form sensitive touch receptors called *tactile* or *Merkel discs* located at the epidermal-dermal junction.

Layers of the Epidermis

The epidermis consists of four layers in thin skin, which covers most of the body. Thick skin, found on the palms of the hands and soles of the feet, contains an additional layer, the stratum lucidum. From deep to superficial, the layers of the epidermis are the stratum basale, stratum spinosum, stratum granulosum, stratum lucidum, and stratum corneum (Figure 7.2).

- **Stratum basale** (basal layer): A single row of cells immediately adjacent to the dermis. Its cells are constantly undergoing mitotic cell division to produce millions of new cells daily, hence its alternate name *stratum germinativum.* From 10% to 25% of the cells in this stratum are melanocytes, which thread their processes through this and the adjacent layers of keratinocytes. Note also the tactile cells of this layer (Figure 7.2).

- **Stratum spinosum** (spiny layer): A stratum consisting of several cell layers immediately superficial to the basal layer. Its cells contain thick weblike bundles of intermediate filaments made of a pre-keratin protein. The stratum spinosum cells appear spiky (hence their name) because as the skin tissue is prepared for histological examination, they shrink but their desmosomes hold tight. Cells divide fairly rapidly in this layer, but less so than in the stratum basale. Cells in the basal and spiny layers are the only ones to receive adequate nourishment via diffusion of nutrients from the dermis. So as their daughter cells are pushed upward and away from the source of nutrition, they gradually die. Note the epidermal dendritic cell (Figure 7.2).

- **Stratum granulosum** (granular layer): A thin layer named for the abundant granules its cells contain. These granules are of two types: (1) *lamellated granules,* which contain a waterproofing glycolipid that is secreted into the extracellular space; and (2) *keratohyaline granules,* which combine with the intermediate filaments in the more superficial layers

to form the keratin fibrils. At the upper border of this layer, the cells are beginning to die.

- **Stratum lucidum** (clear layer): A very thin translucent band of flattened dead keratinocytes with indistinct boundaries. It is not present in regions of thin skin.

- **Stratum corneum** (horny layer): This outermost epidermal layer consists of some 20 to 30 cell layers, and accounts for the bulk of the epidermal thickness. Cells in this layer, like those in the stratum lucidum (where it exists), are dead, and their flattened scalelike remnants are fully keratinized. They are constantly rubbing off and being replaced by division of the deeper cells.

Dermis

The dense irregular connective tissue making up the dermis consists of two principal regions—the papillary and reticular areas. Like the epidermis, the dermis varies in thickness. For example, it is particularly thick on the palms of the hands and soles of the feet and is quite thin on the eyelids.

- **Papillary layer:** The more superficial dermal region composed of areolar connective tissue. It is very uneven and has fingerlike projections from its superior surface, the **dermal papillae,** which attach it to the epidermis above. These projections lie on top of the larger dermal ridges. In the palms of the hands and soles of the feet, they produce the *fingerprints,* unique patterns of *epidermal ridges* that remain unchanged throughout life. Abundant capillary networks in the papillary layer furnish nutrients for the epidermal layers and allow heat to radiate to the skin surface. The pain (free nerve endings) and touch receptors (*Meissner's corpuscles* in hairless skin) are also found here.

- **Reticular layer:** The deepest skin layer. It is composed of dense irregular connective tissue and contains many arteries and veins, sweat and sebaceous glands, and pressure receptors (*Pacinian corpuscles*).

Both the papillary and reticular layers are heavily invested with collagenic and elastic fibers. The elastic fibers give skin its exceptional elasticity in youth. In old age, the number of elastic fibers decreases, and the subcutaneous layer loses fat, which leads to wrinkling and inelasticity of the skin. Fibroblasts, adipose cells, various types of macrophages (which are important in the body's defense), and other cell types are found throughout the dermis.

The abundant dermal blood supply allows the skin to play a role in the regulation of body temperature. When body temperature is high, the arterioles serving the skin dilate, and the capillary network of the dermis becomes engorged with the heated blood. Thus body heat is allowed to radiate from the skin surface. If the environment is cool and body heat must be conserved, the arterioles constrict so that blood bypasses the dermal capillary networks temporarily.

Any restriction of the normal blood supply to the skin results in cell death and, if severe enough, skin ulcers (Figure 7.3). **Bedsores (decubitus ulcers)** occur in bedridden patients who are not turned regularly enough. The weight of the body exerts pressure on the skin, especially over bony projections (hips, heels, etc.), which leads to restriction of the blood supply and tissue death. ■

The dermis is also richly provided with lymphatic vessels and a nerve supply. Many of the nerve endings bear highly specialized receptor organs that, when stimulated by environmental changes, transmit messages to the central nervous system for interpretation. Some of these receptors—free nerve endings (pain receptors), a Pacinian corpuscle, and a hair follicle receptor (also called a *root hair plexus*)—are shown in Figure 7.1. (These receptors are discussed in depth in Exercise 23.)

Skin Color

Skin color is a result of the relative amount of melanin in skin, the relative amount of carotene in skin, and the degree of oxygenation of the blood. People who produce large amounts of melanin have brown-toned skin. In light-skinned people, who have less melanin pigment, the dermal blood supply flushes through the rather transparent cell layers above, giving the skin a rosy glow. *Carotene* is a yellow-orange pigment present primarily in the stratum corneum and in the adipose tissue of the hypodermis. Its presence is most noticeable when large amounts of carotene-rich foods (carrots, for instance) are eaten.

Skin color may be an important diagnostic tool. For example, flushed skin may indicate hypertension, fever, or embarrassment, whereas pale skin is typically seen in anemic individuals. When the blood is inadequately oxygenated, as during asphyxiation and serious lung disease, both the blood and the skin take on a bluish or cyanotic cast. **Jaundice,** in which the tissues become yellowed, is almost always diagnostic for liver disease, whereas a bronzing of the skin hints that a person's adrenal cortex is hypoactive (**Addison's disease**). ∎

Accessory Organs of the Skin

The accessory organs of the skin—cutaneous glands, hair, and nails—are all derivatives of the epidermis, but they reside in the dermis. They originate from the stratum basale and grow downward into the deeper skin regions.

Nails

Nails are hornlike derivatives of the epidermis (Figure 7.4). Their named parts are:

- **Body:** The visible attached portion.

- **Free edge:** The portion of the nail that grows out away from the body.

- **Root:** The part that is embedded in the skin and adheres to an epithelial nail bed.

- **Nail folds:** Skin folds that overlap the borders of the nail.

- **Eponychium:** The thick proximal nail fold commonly called the cuticle.

- **Nail bed:** Extension of the stratum basale beneath the nail.

- **Nail matrix:** The thickened proximal part of the nail bed containing germinal cells responsible for nail growth. As the matrix produces the nail cells, they become heavily keratinized and die. Thus nails, like hairs, are mostly nonliving material.

- **Lunule:** The proximal region of the thickened nail matrix, which appears as a white crescent. Everywhere else,

(a)

Lateral nail fold   Lunule

Free edge of nail   Body of nail   Eponychium (cuticle)   Root of nail

Proximal nail fold   Nail matrix

Hyponychium   Nail bed   Phalanx (bone of fingertip)

(b)

FIGURE 7.4 Structure of a nail. (a) Surface view of the distal part of a finger showing nail parts. The nail matrix that forms the nail lies beneath the lunule; the epidermis of the nail bed underlies the nail. **(b)** Sagittal section of the fingertip.

nails are transparent and nearly colorless, but they appear pink because of the blood supply in the underlying dermis. When someone is cyanotic because of a lack of oxygen in the blood, the nail beds take on a blue cast.

ACTIVITY 2

Identifying Nail Structures

Identify the nail structures shown in Figure 7.4 on yourself or your lab partner. ∎

Hairs and Associated Structures

Hairs, enclosed in hair follicles, are found all over the entire body surface, except for thick-skinned areas (the palms of the hands and the soles of the feet), parts of the external genitalia, the nipples, and the lips.

- **Hair:** Structure consisting of a medulla, a central region surrounded first by the *cortex* and then by a protective *cuticle* (Figure 7.5). Abrasion of the cuticle results in split ends. Hair color is a manifestation of the amount and kind of melanin pigment within the hair cortex. The portion of the hair enclosed within the follicle is called the **root;** that portion projecting from the scalp surface is called the **shaft.** The **hair bulb** is a collection of well-nourished germinal epithelial

Follicle wall
- Connective tissue root sheath
- Glassy membrane
- External epithelial root sheath
- Internal epithelial root sheath

Hair
- Cuticle
- Cortex
- Medulla

(a)

Follicle wall
- Connective tissue root sheath
- Glassy membrane
- External epithelial root sheath
- Internal epithelial root sheath

Hair root
- Cuticle
- Cortex
- Medulla
- Hair matrix
- Hair papilla
- Melanocyte
- Subcutaneous adipose tissue

(b)

Hair shaft
Arrector pili muscle
Sebaceous gland
Hair root
Hair bulb

(c)

FIGURE 7.5 Structure of a hair and hair follicle. (a) Diagram of a cross section of a hair within its follicle. **(b)** Diagram of a longitudinal view of the expanded hair bulb of the follicle, which encloses the matrix, the actively dividing epithelial cells that produce the hair. **(c)** Photomicrograph of longitudinal view of the hair bulb in the follicle (105×).

cells at the basal end of the follicle. As the daughter cells are pushed farther away from the growing region, they die and become keratinized; thus the bulk of the hair shaft, like the bulk of the epidermis, is dead material.

- **Follicle:** A structure formed from both epidermal and dermal cells (see Figure 7.5). Its inner epithelial root sheath, with two parts (internal and external), is enclosed by a thick-

ened basement membrane, the glassy membrane, and a connective tissue root sheath, which is essentially dermal tissue. A small nipple of dermal tissue that protrudes into the hair bulb from the connective tissue sheath and provides nutrition to the growing hair is called the **papilla.**

- **Arrector pili muscle:** Small bands of smooth muscle cells connect each hair follicle to the papillary layer of the dermis (Figures 7.1 and 7.5). When these muscles contract (during cold or fright), the slanted hair follicle is pulled upright, dimpling the skin surface with goose bumps. This phenomenon is especially dramatic in a scared cat, whose fur actually stands on end to increase its apparent size. The activity of the arrector pili muscles also exerts pressure on the sebaceous glands surrounding the follicle, causing a small amount of sebum to be released.

Comparison of Hairy and Relatively Hair-Free Skin Microscopically

While thick skin has no hair follicles or sebaceous (oil) glands, thin skin typical of most of the body has both. The scalp, of course, has the highest density of hair follicles.

1.   Obtain a prepared slide of the human scalp, and study it carefully under the microscope. Compare your tissue slide to the view shown in Figure 7.6a, and identify as many of the structures diagrammed in Figure 7.1 as possible.

How is this stratified squamous epithelium different from that observed in Exercise 6A or 6B?

_____

_____

How do these differences relate to the functions of these two similar epithelia?

_____

_____

_____

2.   Obtain a prepared slide of hairless skin of the palm or sole (Figure 7.6b). Compare the slide to Figure 7.6a. In what ways does the thick skin of the palm or sole differ from the thin skin of the scalp?

_____

_____

Cutaneous Glands

The cutaneous glands fall primarily into two categories: the sebaceous glands and the sweat glands (Figure 7.1 and Figure 7.7).

Sebaceous (Oil) Glands

The sebaceous glands are found nearly all over the skin, except for the palms of the hands and the soles of the feet. Their ducts usually empty into a hair follicle, but some open directly on the skin surface.

Sebum is the product of sebaceous glands. It is a mixture of oily substances and fragmented cells that acts as a lubricant to keep the skin soft and moist (a natural skin cream) and

Sloughing stratum corneum cells   Epidermis
Hair follicle   Hair shaft   Dermis

(a)

Epidermis

• Stratum corneum

• Stratum lucidum

• Stratum granulosum

• Stratum spinosum

• Stratum basale

Dermis

(b)

FIGURE 7.6 Photomicrographs of skin. (a) Thin skin with hairs (115×). **(b)** Thick hairless skin (120×).

FIGURE 7.7 Cutaneous glands. (a) Photomicrograph of a sebaceous gland (220×).
(b) Photomicrograph of eccrine sweat gland (140×).

keeps the hair from becoming brittle. The sebaceous glands become particularly active during puberty when more male hormones (androgens) begin to be produced; thus the skin tends to become oilier during this period of life.

Blackheads are accumulations of dried sebum, bacteria, and melanin from epithelial cells in the oil duct. **Acne** is an active infection of the sebaceous glands. ■

Sweat (Sudoriferous) Glands

These exocrine glands are widely distributed all over the skin. Outlets for the glands are epithelial openings called *pores*. Sweat glands are categorized by the composition of their secretions.

- **Eccrine glands:** Also called **merocrine sweat glands,** these glands are distributed all over the body. They produce clear perspiration consisting primarily of water, salts (mostly NaCl), and urea. Eccrine sweat glands, under the control of the nervous system, are an important part of the body's heat-regulating apparatus. They secrete perspiration when the external temperature or body temperature is high. When this water-based substance evaporates, it carries excess body heat with it. Thus evaporation of greater amounts of perspiration provides an efficient means of dissipating body heat when the capillary cooling system is not sufficient or is unable to maintain body temperature homeostasis.

- **Apocrine glands:** Found predominantly in the axillary and genital areas, these glands secrete a milky protein- and fat-rich substance (also containing water, salts, and urea) that is an excellent nutrient medium for the microorganisms typically found on the skin. Because these glands enlarge and recede with the phases of a woman's menstrual cycle, the apocrine

glands may be analogous to the pheromone-producing scent glands of other animals.

ACTIVITY 4

Differentiating Sebaceous and Sweat Glands Microscopically

Using the slide *thin skin with hairs*, and Figure 7.7 as a guide, identify sebaceous and eccrine sweat glands. What characteristics relating to location or gland structure allow you to differentiate these glands?

_____

_____

_____

ACTIVITY 5

Plotting the Distribution of Sweat Glands

1. Form a hypothesis about the relative distribution of sweat glands on the palm and forearm. Justify your hypothesis.

2. For this simple experiment you will need two squares of bond paper (each 1 cm × 1 cm), adhesive tape, and a Betadine (iodine) swab *or* Lugol's iodine and a cotton-tipped swab. (The bond paper has been preruled in cm²—put on disposable gloves and cut along the lines to obtain the required squares.)

3. Paint an area of the medial aspect of your left palm (avoid the crease lines) and a region of your left forearm with the iodine solution, and allow it to dry thoroughly. The painted area in each case should be slightly larger than the paper squares to be used.

4. Have your lab partner *securely* tape a square of bond paper over each iodine-painted area, and leave them in place for 20 minutes. (If it is very warm in the laboratory while this test is being conducted, good results may be obtained within 10 to 15 minutes.)

5. After 20 minutes, remove the paper squares, and count the number of blue-black dots on each square. The presence of a blue-black dot on the paper indicates an active sweat gland. (The iodine in the pore is dissolved in the sweat and reacts chemically with the starch in the bond paper to produce the blue-black color.) Thus "sweat maps" have been produced for the two skin areas.

6. Which skin area tested has the greater density of sweat glands?

_____

_____

_____

7. Tape your results (bond paper squares) to a data collection sheet labeled "palm" and "forearm" at the front of the lab. Be sure to put your paper squares in the correct columns on the data sheet.

8. Once all the data has been collected, review the class results.

9. Prepare a lab report for the experiment. (See Getting Started, page xv) ▬

Dermography: Fingerprinting

As noted previously, each of us has a unique genetically determined set of fingerprints. Because of the usefulness of fingerprinting for identifying and apprehending criminals, most people associate this craft solely with criminal investigations. However, civil fingerprints are invaluable in quickly identifying amnesia victims, missing persons, and unknown deceased such as those killed in major disasters.

The friction ridges responsible for fingerprints appear in several patterns, which are clearest when the fingertips are inked and then pressed against white paper. Impressions are also made when perspiration or any foreign material such as blood, dirt, or grease adheres to the ridges and the fingers are then pressed against a smooth, nonabsorbent surface. The three most common patterns are *arches, loops,* and *whorls* (Figure 7.8). The *pattern area* in loops and whorls is the only area of the print used in identification, and it is delineated by the *type lines*—specifically the two innermost ridges that start parallel, diverge, and/or surround or tend to surround the pattern area.

ACTIVITY 6

Taking and Identifying Inked Fingerprints

For this activity, you will be working as a group with your lab partners. Though the equipment for professional fingerprinting is fairly basic, consisting of a glass or metal inking plate,

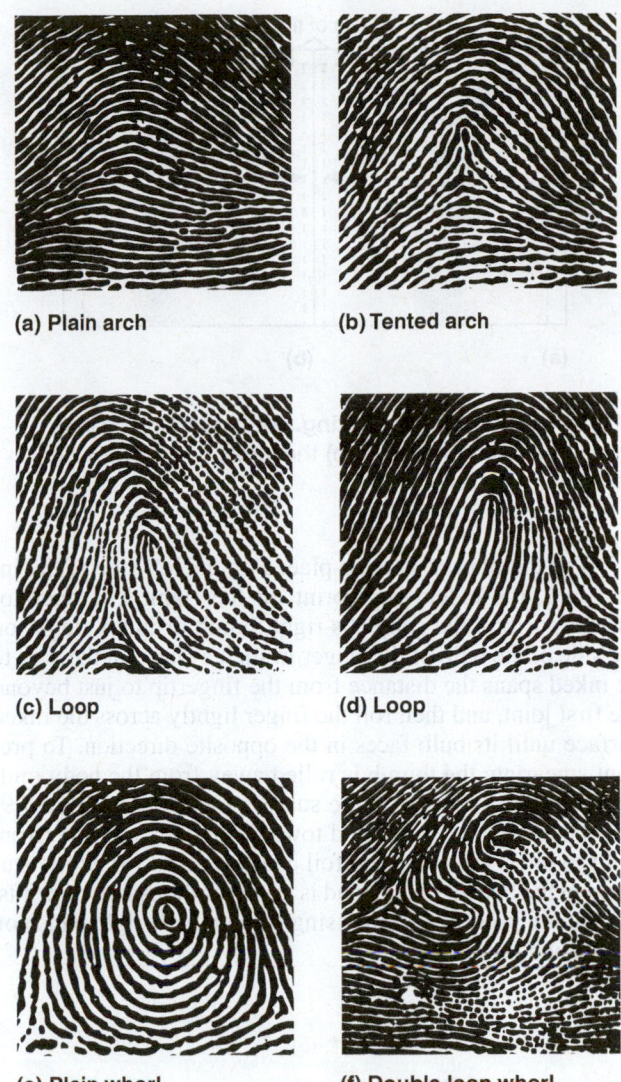

(a) Plain arch   **(b) Tented arch**

(c) Loop   **(d) Loop**

(e) Plain whorl   **(f) Double loop whorl**

FIGURE 7.8 Main types of fingerprint patterns.
(a–b) Arches. **(c–d)** Loops. **(e–f)** Whorls.

printer's ink (a heavy black paste), ink roller, and standard 8 in. × 8 in. cards, you will be using supplies that are even easier to handle. Each student will prepare two index cards, each bearing his or her thumbprint and index fingerprint of the right hand.

1. Obtain the following supplies and bring them to your bench: two 4 in. × 6 in. index cards per student, Porelon fingerprint pad or portable inking foils, ink cleaner towelettes, and a magnifying glass.

2. The subject should wash and dry the hands. Open the ink pad or peel back the covering over the ink foil, and position it close to the edge of the laboratory bench. The subject should position himself or herself at arm's length from the bench edge and inking object.

3. A second student, called the *operator,* stands to the left of the subject and with two hands holds and directs movement of the subject's fingertip. During this process, the subject should look away, try to relax, and refrain from trying to help the operator.

Bulb of finger

Start roll here
Roll →
← Roll
Ink
Ink
Start roll here

(a)   (b)

FIGURE 7.9 Fingerprinting. Method of inking and printing **(a)** the thumb and **(b)** the index finger of the right hand.

4.   The thumbprint is to be placed on the left side of the index card, the index fingerprint on the right. The operator should position the subject's right thumb or index finger on the side of the bulb of the finger in such a way that the area to be inked spans the distance from the fingertip to just beyond the first joint, and then roll the finger lightly across the inked surface until its bulb faces in the opposite direction. To prevent smearing, the thumb is rolled away from the body midline (from left to right as the subject sees it; see Figure 7.9) and the index finger is rolled toward the body midline (from right to left). The same ink foil can be reused for all the students at the bench; the ink pad is good for thousands of prints. Repeat the procedure (still using the subject's right hand) on the second index card.

5.   If the prints are too light, too dark, or smeary, repeat the procedure.

6.   While subsequent members are making clear prints of their thumb and index finger, those who have completed that activity should clean their inked fingers with a towelette and attempt to classify their own prints as arches, loops, or whorls. Use the magnifying glass as necessary to see ridge details.

7.   When all members at a bench have completed the above steps, they are to write their names on the backs of their index cards, then combine their cards and shuffle them before transferring them to the bench opposite for classification of pattern and identification of prints made by the same individuals.

How difficult was it to classify the prints into one of the three categories given?

_____

Why do you think this is so?

_____

_____

Was it easy or difficult to identify the prints made by the same individual?

_____

Why do you think this was so?

_____

NAME_____

LAB TIME/DATE_____

The Integumentary System

Basic Structure of the Skin

1. Complete the following statements by writing the appropriate word or phrase on the correspondingly numbered blank:

   The two basic tissues of which the skin is composed are dense irregular connective tissue, which makes up the dermis, and __1__, which forms the epidermis. The tough water-repellent protein found in the epidermal cells is called __2__. The pigments melanin and __3__ contribute to skin color. A localized concentration of melanin is referred to as a __4__.

   1. _____

   2. _____

   3. _____

   4. _____

2. Four protective functions of the skin are

   a. _____   c. _____

   b. _____   d. _____

3. Using the key choices, choose all responses that apply to the following descriptions.

   Key: a. stratum basale   d. stratum lucidum   g. reticular layer
           b. stratum corneum   e. stratum spinosum   h. epidermis as a whole
           c. stratum granulosum   f. papillary layer   i. dermis as a whole

   _____ 1. translucent cells in thick skin containing keratin fibrils

   _____ 2. dead cells

   _____ 3. dermal layer responsible for fingerprints

   _____ 4. vascular region

   _____ 5. major skin area that produces derivatives (nails and hair)

   _____ 6. epidermal region exhibiting the most rapid cell division

   _____ 7. scalelike dead cells, full of keratin, that constantly slough off

   _____ 8. mitotic cells filled with intermediate filaments

   _____ 9. has abundant elastic and collagenic fibers

   _____ 10. location of melanocytes and tactile (Merkel) cells

   _____ 11. area where weblike pre-keratin filaments first appear

   _____ 12. region of areolar connective tissue

...ures and areas indicated in the accompanying diagram of thin skin. Then, complete the statements that

epidermis

dermis

Subcutaneous
tissue or
hypodermis

pacinian corpuscle
(deep pressure receptor)

Stratum corneum
Stratum lucidum
Stratum granulosum
Stratum basale
(layers)
Papillary layer

hair root
Sebaceous gland

arrector pili muscle

Reticular layer

endocrine gland

Blood vessel

hair bulb

Adipose cells

a. _____ granules extruded from the keratinocytes prevent water loss by diffusion through the epidermis.

b. Fibers in the dermis are produced by _____.

c. Glands that respond to rising androgen levels are the _____ glands.

d. Phagocytic cells that occupy the epidermis are called _____.

e. A unique touch receptor formed from a stratum basale cell and a nerve fiber is a _____.

f. What layer is present in thick skin but not in thin skin? _____

g. What cell-to-cell structures hold the cells of the stratum spinosum tightly together? _____

5. What substance is manufactured in the skin that plays a role in calcium absorption elsewhere in the body?

_____

6. List the sensory receptors found in the dermis of the skin. _____

_____

_____

7. A nurse tells a doctor that a patient is cyanotic. Define *cyanosis*. _____

What does its presence imply? _____

8. What is a bedsore (decubitus ulcer) ? _____

Why does it occur? _____

_____

Accessory Organs of the Skin

9. Match the key choices with the appropriate descriptions.

Key: a.   arrector pili
     b.   cutaneous receptors
     c.   hair

d.   hair follicle
e.   nail
f.   sebaceous glands

g.   sweat gland—apocrine
h.   sweat gland—eccrine

_____ 1. produces an accumulation of oily material that is known as a blackhead

_____ 2. tiny muscles, attached to hair follicles, that pull the hair upright during fright or cold

_____ 3. perspiration glands with a role in temperature control

_____ 4. sheath formed of both epithelial and connective tissues

_____ 5. less numerous type of perspiration-producing gland; found mainly in the pubic and axillary regions

_____ 6. found everywhere on the body except the palms of hands and soles of feet

_____ 7. primarily dead/keratinized cells

_____ 8. specialized nerve endings that respond to temperature, touch, etc.

_____ 9. secretes a lubricant for hair and skin

_____ 10. "sports" a lunule and a cuticle

10. Describe two integumentary system mechanisms that help in regulating body temperature. _____

_____

_____

11. Several structures or skin regions are listed below. Identify each by matching its letter with the appropriate area on the figure.

a. adipose cells

b. dermis

c. epidermis

d. hair follicle

e. hair shaft

f. sloughing stratum corneum cells

Plotting the Distribution of Sweat Glands

12. With what substance in the bond paper does the iodine painted on the skin react? _____

13. Based on class data, which skin area—the forearm or palm of hand—has more sweat glands? _____

Was this an expected result? _____ Explain. _____

_____

Which other body areas would, if tested, prove to have a high density of sweat glands? _____

_____

14. What organ system controls the activity of the eccrine sweat glands? _____

Dermography: Fingerprinting

15. Why can fingerprints be used to identify individuals?

_____

16. Name the three common fingerprint patterns.

_____, _____, and _____

Classification of Covering and Lining Membranes

MATERIALS

- ☐ Compound microscope
- ☐ Prepared slides of trachea (x.s.), esophagus (x.s.), and small intestine (x.s.)
- ☐ Prepared slide of serous membrane (for example, mesentery artery and vein [x.s.] or small intestine [x.s.])
- ☐ Longitudinally cut fresh beef joint (if available)

OBJECTIVES

1. To compare the structure and function of the major membrane types.
2. To list the general functions of each membrane type and indicate its location in the body.
3. To recognize by microscopic examination cutaneous, mucous, and serous membranes.

PRE-LAB QUIZ

1. Body membranes fall into two major categories: _____ and
   _____.
   a. epithelial and cutaneous
   b. epithelial and synovial
   c. connective and cutaneous
   d. serous and synovial
2. The _____ membrane is the skin, a dry membrane with a keratinizing epithelium.
   a. cutaneous
   b. mucous
   c. serous
3. The mucous membranes are made up of a layer of epithelial cells resting on a layer of loose connective tissue called the _____
   _____.
   a. goblet cells
   b. lamina propria
   c. visceral pericardium
4. Circle True or False. Mucous membranes line body cavities that open to the surface.
5. Circle the correct terms. The serous membranes generally occur in twos and are actually continuous. The parietal / visceral layer lines a body cavity, and the parietal / visceral layer covers the outside of the organs in that cavity.
6. Unlike mucous and serous membranes, _____ membranes contain no epithelial cells and are composed entirely of connective tissue.
   a. cutaneous
   b. parietal
   c. synovial
   d. visceral

The body membranes, which cover surfaces, line body cavities, and form protective (and often lubricating) sheets around organs, fall into two major categories. These may be designated as *epithelial membranes* and *synovial membranes*.

Epithelial Membranes

Most of the covering and lining epithelia take part in forming one of the three common varieties of epithelial membranes: cutaneous, mucous, or serous. The term "epithelial membrane" is used in various ways. Here we will define an **epithelial membrane** as a simple organ consisting of an epithelial sheet bound to an underlying layer of connective tissue proper.

myA&P For practice quizzes on this lab, go to www.myaandp.com.

105

(a) Cutaneous membrane

Cutaneous membrane (skin)

(b) Mucous membranes

Mucosa of nasal cavity

Mucosa of mouth

Esophagus lining

Mucosa of lung bronchi

(c) Serous membranes

Parietal peritoneum

Visceral peritoneum

Parietal pleura

Visceral pleura

Parietal pericardium

Visceral pericardium

FIGURE 8.1 Classes of epithelial membranes. Epithelial membranes are composite membranes with epithelial and connective tissue elements. **(a)** The cutaneous membrane, or skin, covers and protects the body surface. **(b)** Mucous membranes line body cavities (hollow organs) that open to the exterior. **(c)** Serous membranes line the closed ventral cavity of the body. Three examples, the peritoneums, pericardia, and pleurae, are illustrated here.

The **cutaneous membrane** (Figure 8.1a) is the skin, a dry membrane with a keratinizing epithelium (the epidermis). Since the skin is discussed in some detail in Exercise 7, we focus on the mucous and serous membranes here.

Mucous Membranes

The **mucous membranes (mucosae)*** are composed of epithelial cells resting on a layer of loose connective tissue called the **lamina propria.** They line all body cavities that open to the body exterior—the respiratory, digestive (Figure 8.1b), and urogenital tracts. In most cases mucosae are "wet" membranes,

---

*Notice the spelling difference between *mucous*, an adjective describing the membrane type, and *mucus*, a noun indicating the product of glands.

(a)

Villus

Simple columnar epithelium with microvilli

Lamina propria within villus

(c)

Stratified squamous epithelium

Lamina propria

(b)

FIGURE 8.2 Photomicrographs of mucosae. (a) Cross section through the mucosa of the trachea showing a pseudostratified columnar epithelium with lamina propria beneath (315×). **(b)** Section through the esophageal mucosa showing a stratified squamous epithelium with lamina propria beneath (140×). **(c)** Section through several villi of the small intestine. Intestinal mucosa has a simple columnar epithelium with microvilli and goblet cells. The lamina propria lies between the epithelia in the center of the villus (30X).

Which mucosae contain goblet cells?

_____

Compare and contrast the roles of these three mucous membranes.

_____

_____

_____

which are continuously bathed by secretions (or, in the case of urinary mucosa, urine). Although mucous membranes often secrete mucus, this is not a requirement. The mucous membranes of both the digestive and respiratory tracts secrete mucus; that of the urinary tract does not.

ACTIVITY 1

Examining the Microscopic Structure of Mucous Membranes

Using Figure 8.2 as a guide, examine slides made from cross sections of the trachea, esophagus, and small intestine. Draw the mucosa of each in the appropriate circle, and fully identify each epithelial type. Remember to look for the epithelial cells at the free surface. Also search the epithelial sheets for **goblet cells**—columnar epithelial cells with a large mucus-containing vacuole (goblet) in their apical cytoplasm.

Serous Membranes

The **serous membranes (serosae)** are also epithelial membranes (Figure 8.1c). They are composed of a layer of simple squamous epithelium on a scant amount of areolar connective tissue. The serous membranes generally occur in twos and are actually continuous. The *parietal layer* lines a body cavity, and the *visceral layer* covers the outside of the organs in that cavity. In contrast to the mucous membranes, which line open body cavities, the serous membranes line body cavities that are closed to the exterior (with the exception of the female peritoneal cavity and the dorsal body cavity). These double-layered serosae secrete a thin fluid (serous fluid) that lubricates the organs and body walls and thus reduces friction as the organs slide across one another and against the body cavity walls. Inflammation of these membranes typically results in less serous fluid being produced and excruciating pain.

The labels in (a): **Pseudostratified columnar epithelium** with cilia; Goblet cell; Lamina propria.

Mucosa of trachea

Mucosa of esophagus

Mucosa of small intestine

A serous membrane also lines the interior of blood vessels (endothelium) and the heart (endocardium). In capillaries, the entire wall is composed of serosa that serves as a selectively permeable membrane between the blood and the tissue fluid of the body.

ACTIVITY 2

Examining the Microscopic Structure of a Serous Membrane

Using Figure 8.3 as a guide, examine a prepared slide of a serous membrane and diagram it in the circle provided here.

Serosa of blood vessel

What are the specific names of the serous membranes covering the heart and lining the cavity in which it resides (respectively)?

_____ and _____

Of the abdominal viscera and visceral cavity (respectively)?

_____ and _____

Simple squamous epithelium (endothelium)

FIGURE 8.3 Photomicrograph of a serosa. Cross section of a blood vessel showing the simple squamous epithelium that forms its endothelial lining (200×).

Synovial Membranes

Synovial membranes, unlike mucous and serous membranes, are composed entirely of connective tissue; they contain no epithelial cells. These membranes line the cavities surrounding the joints, providing a smooth surface and secreting a lubricating fluid. They also line smaller sacs of connective tissue (bursae and tendon sheaths), which cushion structures moving against each other, as during muscle activity. See Figure 13.2C, which illustrates a synovial membrane in the joint cavity.

ACTIVITY 3

Examining the Gross Structure of a Synovial Membrane

If a freshly sawed beef joint is available, visually examine the interior surface of the joint capsule to observe the smooth texture of the synovial membrane. A more detailed study of synovial membranes is done in Exercise 13.

NAME_____

LAB TIME/DATE_____

Classification of Covering and Lining Membranes

1. Complete the following chart.

Membrane	Tissue types: membrane composition (epithelial/connective)	Common locations	General functions
cutaneous			
mucous			
serous			
synovial			

2. Respond to the following statements by choosing an answer from the key.

Key: a. cutaneous   b. mucous   c. serous   d. synovial

_____ 1. membrane type in joints, bursae, and tendon sheaths

_____ 2. epithelium of this membrane is always simple squamous epithelium

_____, _____ 3. membrane types *not* found in the ventral body cavity

_____ 4. the only membrane type in which goblet cells are found

_____ 5. the dry membrane with keratinizing epithelium

_____, _____, _____ 6. "wet" membranes

_____ 7. adapted for absorption and secretion

_____ 8. has parietal and visceral layers

3. Using terms from the key above the figure, identify the different types of body membranes (cutaneous, mucous, and serous) by writing the terms at the end of the leader lines.

Key: a. cutaneous membrane (skin) g. parietal pericardium
b. esophageal mucosa h. parietal pleura
c. gastric mucosa i. tracheal mucosa
d. mucosa of lung bronchi j. visceral pericardium
e. nasal mucosa k. visceral pleura
f. oral mucosa

4. The suffix -itis means "inflammation of." What do peritonitis, pleurisy, and pericarditis (pathological conditions) have in common?

_____

5. Why are these conditions accompanied by a great deal of pain? _____

_____

Overview of the Skeleton: Classification and Structure of Bones and Cartilages

OBJECTIVES

1. To list five functions of the skeletal system.
2. To locate and identify the three major types of skeletal cartilages.
3. To identify the four main groups of bones.
4. To identify surface bone markings and functions.
5. To identify the major anatomical areas on a longitudinally cut long bone (or diagram of one).
6. To identify the major regions and structures of an osteon in a histologic specimen of compact bone (or diagram of one).
7. To explain the role of the inorganic salts and organic matrix in providing flexibility and hardness to bone.

PRE-LAB QUIZ

1. All the following are functions of the skeleton except:
   a. attachment for muscles
   b. production of melanin
   c. site of red blood cell formation
   d. storage of lipids
2. Circle the correct term. The <u>axial</u> / <u>appendicular</u> skeleton consists of bones that surround the body's center of gravity.
3. This type of cartilage has great tensile strength and is found in the knee joint and intervertebral discs.
   a. elastic
   b. fibrocartilage
   c. hyaline
4. Circle the correct term. <u>Compact</u> / <u>Spongy</u> bone looks smooth and homogeneous.
5. _____ bones are generally thin, with two waferlike layers of compact bone sandwiching a layer of spongy bone.
   a. Flat   c. Long
   b. Irregular d. Short
6. The femur is an example of a(n) _____ type of bone.
   a. flat   c. long
   b. irregular d. short
7. Circle the correct term. The shaft of a long bone is known as the <u>epiphysis</u> / <u>diaphysis</u>.
8. A central canal and all the concentric lamellae surrounding it are referred to as:
   a. an osteon
   b. canaliculi
   c. lacunae
9. Circle True or False. Embryonic skeletons consist primarily of elastic cartilage, which is gradually replaced by bone during development and growth.

The **skeleton,** the body's framework, is constructed of two of the most supportive tissues found in the human body—cartilage and bone. In embryos, the skeleton is predominantly composed of hyaline cartilage, but in the adult, most of the cartilage is replaced by more rigid bone. Cartilage persists only in such isolated areas as the external ear, bridge of the nose, larynx, trachea, joints, and parts of the rib cage (see Figure 9.2).

Besides supporting and protecting the body as an internal framework, the skeleton provides a system of levers with which the skeletal muscles work to move the body. In addition, the bones store lipids and many minerals (most importantly calcium). Finally, the red marrow cavities of bones provide a site for hematopoiesis (blood cell formation).

The skeleton is made up of bones that are connected at *joints,* or *articulations.* The skeleton is subdivided into two

(a) Anterior view

(b) Posterior view

FIGURE 9.1 The human skeleton. The bones of the axial skeleton are colored green to distinguish them from the bones of the appendicular skeleton.

FIGURE 9.2 Cartilages in the adult skeleton and body. Additional cartilages that support the respiratory tubes and larynx are shown separately at the upper right.

Bones of skeleton
- Axial skeleton
- Appendicular skeleton

Cartilages
- Hyaline cartilages
- Elastic cartilages
- Fibrocartilages

divisions: the **axial skeleton** (those bones that lie around the body's center of gravity) and the **appendicular skeleton** (bones of the limbs, or appendages) (Figure 9.1).

Before beginning your study of the skeleton, imagine for a moment that your bones have turned to putty. What if you were running when this metamorphosis took place? Now imagine your bones forming a continuous metal framework within your body, somewhat like a network of plumbing pipes. What problems could you envision with this arrangement? These images should help you understand how well the skeletal system provides support and protection, as well as facilitating movement.

Cartilages of the Skeleton

As mentioned earlier, cartilaginous regions of the skeleton have a fairly limited distribution in adults (Figure 9.2). The most important of these skeletal cartilages are (1) **articular cartilages,** which cover the bone ends at movable joints; (2) **costal cartilages,** found connecting the ribs to the sternum (breastbone); (3) **laryngeal cartilages,** which largely construct the larynx (voice box); (4) **tracheal** and **bronchial cartilages,** which reinforce other passageways of the respiratory system; (5) **nasal cartilages,** which support the external nose; (6) **intervertebral discs,** which separate and cushion bones of the spine (vertebrae); and (7) the cartilage supporting the external ear.

The skeletal cartilages consist of some variety of *cartilage tissue,* which typically consists primarily of water and is fairly resilient. Cartilage tissues are also distinguished by the fact that they contain no nerves and very few blood vessels. Like bones, each cartilage is surrounded by a covering of dense connective tissue, called a *perichondrium* (rather than a *periosteum*), which acts to resist distortion of the cartilage when it is subjected to pressure, and plays a role in cartilage growth and repair.

The skeletal cartilages have representatives from each of the three cartilage tissue types—hyaline, elastic, and fibrocartilage. Since you have already studied cartilage tissues (Exercise 6A), we will only briefly discuss that information here.

- **Hyaline cartilage** provides sturdy support with some resilience or "give." As easily seen in Figure 9.2, most skeletal cartilages are composed of hyaline cartilage.

- **Elastic cartilage** is much more flexible than hyaline cartilage, and it tolerates repeated bending better. Only the cartilages of the external ear and the epiglottis (which flops over and covers the larynx when we swallow) are elastic cartilage.

- **Fibrocartilage** consists of rows of chondrocytes alternating with rows of thick collagen fibers. Fibrocartilage, which has great tensile strength and can withstand heavy compression, is used to construct the intervertebral discs and the cartilages within the knee joint (see Figure 9.2).

Classification of Bones

The 206 bones of the adult skeleton are composed of two basic kinds of osseous tissue that differ in their texture. **Compact bone** looks smooth and homogeneous; **spongy** (or *cancellous*) **bone** is composed of small *trabeculae* (bars) of bone and lots of open space.

Bones may be classified further on the basis of their relative gross anatomy into four groups: long, short, flat, and irregular bones.

Long bones, such as the femur and phalanges (bones of the fingers) (Figure 9.1), are much longer than they are wide, generally consisting of a shaft with heads at either end. Long bones are composed predominantly of compact bone. **Short bones** are typically cube shaped, and they contain more spongy bone than compact bone. The tarsals and carpals in Figure 9.1 are examples.

Flat bones are generally thin, with two waferlike layers of compact bone sandwiching a layer of spongy bone between them. Although the name "flat bone" implies a structure that is level or horizontal, many flat bones are curved (for example, the bones of the skull). Bones that do not fall into one of the preceding categories are classified as **irregular bones.** The vertebrae are irregular bones (see Figure 9.1).

Some anatomists also recognize two other subcategories of bones. **Sesamoid bones** are special types of short bones formed in tendons. The patellas (kneecaps) are sesamoid bones. **Wormian** or **sutural bones** are tiny bones between cranial bones. Except for the patellas, the sesamoid and Wormian bones are not included in the bone count of 206 because they vary in number and location in different individuals.

Bone Markings

Even a casual observation of the bones will reveal that bone surfaces are not featureless smooth areas but are scarred with an array of bumps, holes, and ridges. These **bone markings** reveal where bones form joints with other bones, where muscles, tendons, and ligaments were attached, and where blood vessels and nerves passed. Bone markings fall into two categories: projections, or processes that grow out from the bone and serve as sites of muscle attachment or help form joints;

and depressions or cavities, indentations or openings in the bone that often serve as conduits for nerves and blood vessels. The bone markings are summarized in Table 9.1 on page 116.

Gross Anatomy of the Typical Long Bone

ACTIVITY 1

Examining a Long Bone

1. Obtain a long bone that has been sawed along its longitudinal axis. If a cleaned dry bone is provided, no special preparations need be made.

⚠ Note: If the bone supplied is a fresh beef bone, don disposable gloves before beginning your observations.

With the help of Figure 9.3, identify the **diaphysis** or shaft. Observe its smooth surface, which is composed of compact bone. If you are using a fresh specimen, carefully pull away the **periosteum,** or fibrous membrane covering, to view the bone surface. Notice that many fibers of the periosteum penetrate into the bone. These fibers are called **perforating (Sharpey's) fibers.** Blood vessels and nerves travel through the periosteum and invade the bone. *Osteoblasts* (bone-forming cells) and *osteoclasts* (bone-destroying cells) are found on the inner, or osteogenic, layer of the periosteum.

2. Now inspect the **epiphysis,** the end of the long bone. Notice that it is composed of a thin layer of compact bone that encloses spongy bone.

3. Identify the **articular cartilage,** which covers the epiphyseal surface in place of the periosteum. Because it is composed of glassy hyaline cartilage, it provides a smooth surface to prevent friction at joint surfaces.

4. If the animal was still young and growing, you will be able to see the **epiphyseal plate,** a thin area of hyaline cartilage that provides for longitudinal growth of the bone during youth. Once the long bone has stopped growing, these areas are replaced with bone and appear as thin, barely discernible remnants—the **epiphyseal lines.**

5. In an adult animal, the central cavity of the shaft (*medullary cavity*) is essentially a storage region for adipose tissue, or **yellow marrow.** In the infant, this area is involved in forming blood cells, and so **red marrow** is found in the marrow cavities. In adult bones, the red marrow is confined to the interior of the epiphyses, where it occupies the spaces between the trabeculae of spongy bone.

6. If you are examining a fresh bone, look carefully to see if you can distinguish the delicate **endosteum** lining the shaft. The endosteum also covers the trabeculae of spongy bone and lines the canals of compact bone. Like the periosteum, the endosteum contains both osteoblasts and osteoclasts. As the bone grows in diameter on its external surface, it is constantly being broken down on its inner surface. Thus the thickness of the compact bone layer composing the shaft remains relatively constant.

⚠ 7. If you have been working with a fresh bone specimen, return it to the appropriate area and properly dispose of your gloves, as designated by your instructor. Wash your hands before continuing to the microscope study. ▪

FIGURE 9.3 The structure of a long bone (humerus of the arm). (a) Anterior view with longitudinal section cut away at the proximal end. **(b)** Pie-shaped, three-dimensional view of spongy bone and compact bone of the epiphysis. **(c)** Cross section of diaphysis (shaft). Note that the external surface of the diaphysis is covered by a periosteum, but the articular surface of the epiphysis is covered with hyaline cartilage.

Longitudinal bone growth at epiphyseal plates (growth plates) follows a predictable sequence and provides a reliable indicator of the age of children exhibiting normal growth. In cases in which problems of long-bone growth are suspected (for example, pituitary dwarfism), X rays are taken to view the width of the growth plates. An abnormally thin epiphyseal plate indicates growth retardation. ■

Chemical Composition of Bone

Bone is one of the hardest materials in the body. Although relatively light, bone has a remarkable ability to resist tension and shear forces that continually act on it. An engineer would tell you that a cylinder (like a long bone) is one of the strongest structures for its mass. Thus nature has given us an

extremely strong, exceptionally simple (almost crude), and flexible supporting system without sacrificing mobility.

The hardness of bone is due to the inorganic calcium salts deposited in its ground substance. Its flexibility comes from the organic elements of the matrix, particularly the collagen fibers.

ACTIVITY 2

Examining the Effects of Heat and Hydrochloric Acid on Bones

Obtain a bone sample that has been soaked in hydrochloric acid (HCl) (or in vinegar) and one that has been baked. Heating removes the organic part of bone, while acid dissolves out the minerals. Do the treated bones retain the structure of untreated specimens?

TABLE 9.1	Bone Markings	
Name of bone marking	Description	Illustration

Projections That Are Sites of Muscle and Ligament Attachment

Tuberosity (too"be-ros'ĭ-tē)	Large rounded projection; may be roughened
Crest	Narrow ridge of bone; usually prominent
Trochanter (tro-kan'ter)	Very large, blunt, irregularly shaped process (the only examples are on the femur)
Line	Narrow ridge of bone; less prominent than a crest
Tubercle (too'ber-kl)	Small rounded projection or process
Epicondyle (ep"ĭ-kon'dīl)	Raised area on or above a condyle
Spine	Sharp, slender, often pointed projection
Process	Any bony prominence

Projections That Help Form Joints

Head	Bony expansion carried on a narrow neck
Facet	Smooth, nearly flat articular surface
Condyle (kon'dīl)	Rounded articular projection
Ramus (ra'mus)	Armlike bar of bone

Depressions and Openings for Passage of Blood Vessels and Nerves

Groove	Furrow
Fissure	Narrow, slitlike opening
Foramen (fo-ra'men)	Round or oval opening through a bone
Notch	Indentation at the edge of a structure

Others

Meatus (mē-a'tus)	Canal-like passageway
Sinus	Bone cavity, filled with air and lined with mucous membrane
Fossa (fos'ah)	Shallow basinlike depression in a bone, often serving as an articular surface

Gently apply pressure to each bone sample. What happens to the heated bone?

_____

_____

What happens to the bone treated with acid?

_____

What does the acid appear to remove from the bone?

_____

What does baking appear to do to the bone?

_____

_____

In rickets, the bones are not properly calcified. Which of the demonstration specimens would more closely resemble the bones of a child with rickets?

_____

Microscopic Structure of Compact Bone

As you have seen, spongy bone has a spiky, open-work appearance, resulting from the arrangement of the **trabeculae** that compose it, whereas compact bone appears to be dense and homogeneous. However, microscopic examination of compact bone reveals that it is riddled with passageways carrying blood vessels, nerves, and lymphatic vessels that provide the living bone cells with needed substances and a way to eliminate wastes. Indeed, bone histology is much easier to

FIGURE 9.4 Microscopic structure of compact bone. (a) Diagrammatic view of a pie-shaped segment of compact bone, illustrating its structural units (osteons). **(b)** Higher-magnification view of a portion of one osteon. Note the position of osteocytes in lacunae. **(c)** Photomicrograph of a cross-sectional view of an osteon (160×). Veins, lymphatic vessels, and nerves that also occupy bone canals are not illustrated.

understand when you recognize that bone tissue is organized around its blood supply.

Examining the Microscopic Structure of Compact Bone

1. Obtain a prepared slide of ground bone and examine it under low power. Using Figure 9.4 as a guide, focus on a central canal. The **central** (Haversian) **canal** runs parallel to the long axis of the bone and carries blood vessels, nerves, and lymph vessels through the bony matrix. Identify the **osteocytes** (mature bone cells) in **lacunae** (chambers), which are arranged in concentric circles (**concentric lamellae**) around the central canal. Because bone remodeling is going on all the time, you will also see some *interstitial lamellae,* remnants of *circumferential lamellae* that have been broken down (Figure 9.4c).

A central canal and all the concentric lamellae surrounding it are referred to as an **osteon,** or Haversian system. Also identify **canaliculi,** tiny canals radiating outward from a central canal to the lacunae of the first lamella and then from lamella to lamella. The canaliculi form a dense transportation network through the hard bone matrix, connecting all the living cells of the osteon to the nutrient supply. The canaliculi allow each cell to take what it needs for nourishment and to pass along the excess to the next osteocyte. You may need a higher-power magnification to see the fine canaliculi.

2. Also note the **perforating (Volkmann's) canals** in Figure 9.4. These canals run into the compact bone and marrow cavity from the periosteum, at right angles to the shaft. With the central canals, the perforating canals complete the communication pathway between the bone interior and its external surface.

3. If a model of bone histology is available, identify the same structures on the model. ▬▬

Ossification: Bone Formation and Growth in Length

Except for the collarbones (clavicles), all bones of the body inferior to the skull form in the embryo by the process of **endochondral ossification,** which uses hyaline cartilage "bones" as patterns for bone formation. The major events of this process, which begins in the (primary ossification) center of the shaft of a developing long bone, are:

• The fibrous membrane covering the hyaline cartilage model is vascularized and converted to a periosteum.

• Osteoblasts at the inner surface of the periosteum secrete bone matrix around the hyaline cartilage model, forming a bone collar.

• Cartilage in the shaft center calcifies and then hollows out, forming an internal cavity.

A *periosteal bud* (blood vessels, nerves, red marrow elements, osteoblasts, and osteoclasts) invades the cavity, which becomes the medullary cavity. This process proceeds in both directions from the *primary ossification center.*

Resting zone

① **Proliferation zone**
Cartilage cells undergo mitosis.

② **Hypertrophic zone**
Older cartilage cells enlarge.

③ **Calcification zone**
Matrix becomes calcified; cartilage cells die; matrix begins deteriorating.

④ **Ossification zone**
New bone formation is occurring.

Calcified cartilage spicule

Osteoblast depositing bone matrix

Osseous tissue (bone) covering cartilage spicules

FIGURE 9.5 Growth in length of a long bone occurs at the epiphyseal plate. The side of the epiphyseal plate facing the epiphysis (distal face) contains resting cartilage cells. The cells of the epiphyseal plate proximal to the resting cartilage area are arranged in four zones—proliferation, hypertrophic, calcification, and ossification—from the region of the earliest stage of growth ① to the region where bone is replacing the cartilage ④ (150×).

As bones grow longer, the medullary cavity gets larger and larger. Chondroblasts lay down new cartilage matrix on the epiphyseal face of the epiphyseal plate, and it is eroded away and replaced by bony spicules on the side facing the medullary cavity (Figure 9.5). This process continues until late adolescence when the entire epiphyseal plate is replaced by bone.

Examination of the Osteogenic Epiphyseal Plate

Obtain a slide depicting endochondral ossification (cartilage bone formation) and bring it to your bench to examine under the microscope. Using Figure 9.5 as a reference, identify the growth, hypertrophic, calcification, and ossification zones of the epiphyseal plate. Then, also identify the area of resting cartilage cells distal to the growth zone, some hypertrophied chondrocytes, bony spicules, the periosteal bone collar, and the medullary cavity. ▬▬

NAME_____

LAB TIME/DATE_____

Overview of the Skeleton: Classification and Structure of Bones and Cartilages

Bone Markings

1. Match the terms in column B with the appropriate description in column A.

Column A

_____ 1. sharp, slender process*

_____ 2. small rounded projection*

_____ 3. narrow ridge of bone*

_____ 4. large rounded projection*

_____ 5. structure supported on neck[†]

_____ 6. armlike projection[†]

_____ 7. rounded, articular projection[†]

_____ 8. narrow opening[‡]

_____ 9. canal-like structure

_____ 10. round or oval opening through a bone[‡]

_____ 11. shallow depression

_____ 12. air-filled cavity

_____ 13. large, irregularly shaped projection*

_____ 14. raised area on or above a condyle*

_____ 15. projection or prominence

_____ 16. smooth, nearly flat articular surface[†]

Column B

a. condyle

b. crest

c. epicondyle

d. facet

e. fissure

f. foramen

g. fossa

h. head

i. meatus

j. process

k. ramus

l. sinus

m. spine

n. trochanter

o. tubercle

p. tuberosity

*a site of muscle and ligament attachment
[†]takes part in joint formation
[‡]a passageway for nerves or blood vessels

Classification of Bones

2. The four major anatomical classifications of bones are long, short, flat, and irregular. Which category has the least amount

of spongy bone relative to its total volume? _____

3. Place the name of each labeled bone in Figure 9.1, page 112, into the appropriate column of the chart here.

Long	Short	Flat	Irregular

Gross Anatomy of the Typical Long Bone

4. Use the terms below to identify the structures marked by leader lines and braces in the diagrams (some terms are used more than once).

Key: a. articular cartilage   e. epiphyseal line   i. periosteum
       b. compact bone   f. epiphysis   j. red marrow cavity
       c. diaphysis   g. medullary cavity   k. trabeculae of spongy bone
       d. endosteum   h. nutrient artery   l. yellow marrow

(a)   (b)   (c)

5. Match the terms in question 4 with the information below.

_____ 1. contains spongy bone in adults   _____ 5. scientific term for bone shaft

_____ 2. made of compact bone   _____ 6. contains fat in adult bones

_____ 3. site of blood cell formation   _____ 7. growth plate remnant

_____ 4. major submembranous site of osteoclasts _____ 8. major submembranous site of osteoblasts

6. What differences between compact and spongy bone can be seen with the naked eye? _____

_____

7. What is the function of the periosteum? _____

_____

Microscopic Structure of Compact Bone

8. Trace the route taken by nutrients through a bone, starting with the periosteum and ending with an osteocyte in a lacuna.

Periosteum ___→_____ → _____ _____

_____ → _____ → _____ osteocyte

9. Several descriptions of bone structure are given below. Identify the structure involved by choosing the appropriate term from the key and placing its letter in the blank. Then, on the photomicrograph of bone on the right (365✕), identify all structures named in the key and bracket an osteon.

Key: a. canaliculi   b. central canal   c. concentric lamellae   d. lacunae   e. matrix

_____ 1. layers of bony matrix around a central canal

_____ 2. site of osteocytes

_____ 3. longitudinal canal carrying blood vessels, lymphatics, and nerves

_____ 4. minute canals connecting osteocytes of an osteon

_____ 5. inorganic salts deposited in organic ground substance

Chemical Composition of Bone

10. What is the function of the organic matrix in bone? _____

11. Name the important organic bone components. _____

12. Calcium salts form the bulk of the inorganic material in bone. What is the function of the calcium salts?

_____

13. Baking removes _____ from bone. Soaking bone in acid removes _____.

Ossification: Bone Formation and Growth in Length

14. Compare and contrast events occurring on the epiphyseal and diaphyseal faces of the epiphyseal plate.

Epiphyseal face: _____

Diaphyseal face: _____

Cartilages of the Skeleton

15. Using the key choices, identify each type of cartilage described (in terms of its body location or function) below.

Key: a.   elastic   b.   fibrocartilage   c.   hyaline

_____ 1. supports the external ear   _____ 6. meniscus in a knee joint

_____ 2. between the vertebrae   _____ 7. connects the ribs to the sternum

_____ 3. forms the walls of   _____ 8. most effective at resisting
           the voice box (larynx)   compression

_____ 4. the epiglottis   _____ 9. most springy and flexible

_____ 5. articular cartilages   _____ 10. most abundant

The Axial Skeleton

OBJECTIVES

1. To identify the three bone groups composing the axial skeleton.
2. To identify the bones composing the axial skeleton, either by examining isolated bones or by pointing them out on an articulated skeleton or a skull, and to name the important bone markings on each.
3. To distinguish the different types of vertebrae.
4. To discuss the importance of intervertebral discs and spinal curvatures.
5. To distinguish three abnormal spinal curvatures.

PRE-LAB QUIZ

1. The axial skeleton can be divided into the skull, the vertebral column, and the _____.
   - a. bony thorax
   - b. femur
   - c. hip bones
   - d. humerus
2. Eight bones make up the _____, which encloses and protects the brain.
   - a. cranium
   - b. face
   - c. skull
3. How many bones compose the face? _____
4. Circle the correct term. The lower jawbone, or <u>maxilla</u> / <u>mandible</u>, articulates with the temporal bones in the only freely movable joints in the skull.
5. Circle the correct term. The <u>body</u> / <u>spinous process</u> of a typical vertebra forms the rounded, central portion that faces anteriorly in the human vertebral column.
6. The seven bones of the neck are called _____ vertebrae.
   - a. cervical
   - b. lumbar
   - c. spinal
   - d. thoracic
7. The _____ vertebrae articulate with the corresponding ribs.
   - a. cervical
   - b. lumbar
   - c. spinal
   - d. thoracic
8. The _____, commonly referred to as the breastbone, is a flat bone formed by the fusion of three bones: the manubrium, the body, and the xiphoid process.
   - a. coccyx
   - b. sacrum
   - c. sternum
9. Circle True or False. The first seven pairs of ribs are called floating ribs because they have only indirect cartilage attachments to the sternum.

The **axial skeleton** (the green portion of Figure 9.1 on page 112) can be divided into three parts: the skull, the vertebral column, and the bony thorax.

The Skull

The **skull** is composed of two sets of bones. Those of the **cranium** enclose and protect the fragile brain tissue. The **facial bones** present the eyes in an anterior position and form the base for the facial muscles, which make it possible for us to present our feelings to the world. All but one of the bones of the skull are joined by interlocking joints called *sutures*. The mandible, or lower jawbone, is attached to the rest of the skull by a freely movable joint.

ACTIVITY 1

Identifying the Bones of the Skull

The bones of the skull, shown in Figures 10.1 through 10.7, are described below. As you read through this material, identify each bone on an intact and/or Beauchene skull (see Figure 10.6c).

Note: Important bone markings are listed beneath the bones on which they appear, and a color-coded dot before each bone name corresponds to the bone color in the figures. ◼◼

The Cranium

The cranium may be divided into two major areas for study—the **cranial vault** or **calvaria,** forming the superior, lateral, and posterior walls of the skull, and the **cranial floor** or **base,** forming the skull bottom. Internally, the cranial floor has three distinct concavities, the **anterior, middle,** and **posterior cranial fossae** (see Figure 10.3). The brain sits in these fossae, completely enclosed by the cranial vault.

Eight bones construct the cranium. *With the exception of two paired bones (the parietals and the temporals), all are single bones.* Sometimes the six ossicles of the middle ear are also considered part of the cranium. Because the ossicles are functionally part of the hearing apparatus, their consideration is deferred to Exercise 25, Special Senses: Hearing and Equilibrium.

● *Frontal Bone* See Figures 10.1, 10.3, 10.6, and 10.8. Anterior portion of cranium; forms the forehead, superior part of the orbit, and floor of anterior cranial fossa.

Supraorbital foramen (notch): Opening above each orbit allowing blood vessels and nerves to pass.

Glabella: Smooth area between the eyes.

● *Parietal Bone* See Figures 10.1 and 10.6. Posterolateral to the frontal bone, forming sides of cranium.

Sagittal suture: Midline articulation point of the two parietal bones.

Coronal suture: Point of articulation of parietals with frontal bone.

● *Temporal Bone* See Figures 10.1 through 10.3 and 10.6. Inferior to parietal bone on lateral skull. The temporals can be divided into four major parts: the **squamous region** abuts the parietals; the **tympanic region** surrounds the external ear opening; the **mastoid region** is the area posterior to the ear; and the **petrous region** forms the lateral portion of the skull base.

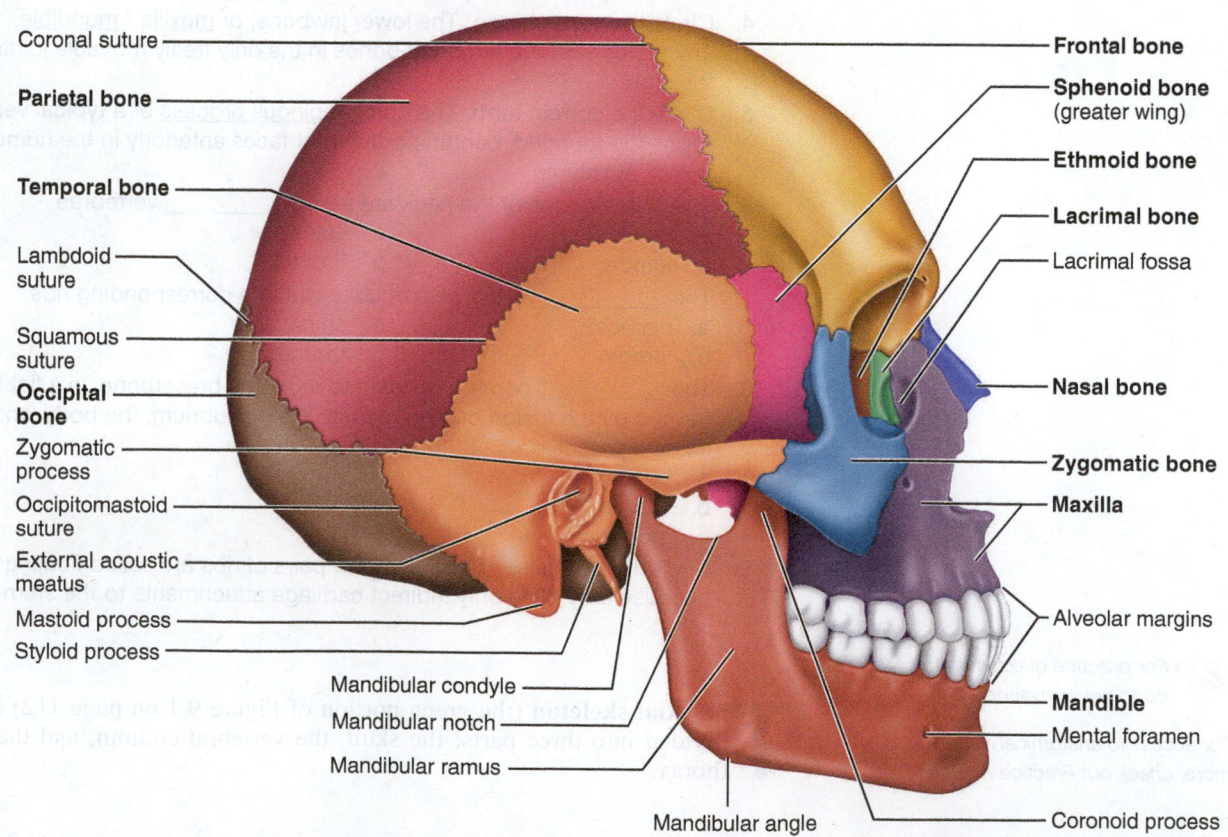

Coronal suture — Frontal bone

Parietal bone — Sphenoid bone (greater wing)

Temporal bone — Ethmoid bone

Lambdoid suture — Lacrimal bone

Squamous suture — Lacrimal fossa

Occipital bone — Nasal bone

Zygomatic process

Occipitomastoid suture — Zygomatic bone

External acoustic meatus — Maxilla

Mastoid process — Alveolar margins

Styloid process

Mandibular condyle — Mandible

Mandibular notch — Mental foramen

Mandibular ramus

Mandibular angle — Coronoid process

FIGURE 10.1 External anatomy of the right lateral aspect of the skull.

Maxilla
(palatine process)

Hard
palate

Palatine bone
(horizontal plate)

Zygomatic bone

Temporal bone
(zygomatic process)

Vomer

Mandibular
fossa

Styloid process

Mastoid process

Temporal bone
(petrous part)

Pharyngeal tubercle
of basilar region of
the occipital bone

Parietal bone

External occipital crest

External occipital
protuberance

Incisive fossa

Intermaxillary suture

Median palatine suture

Infraorbital foramen

Maxilla

Sphenoid bone
(greater wing)

Foramen ovale

Foramen spinosum

Foramen lacerum

Carotid canal

External acoustic meatus

Stylomastoid
foramen

Jugular foramen

Occipital condyle

Inferior nuchal line

Superior nuchal line

Foramen magnum

FIGURE 10.2 Inferior view of the skull, mandible removed.

Important markings associated with the flaring squamous region (Figures 10.1 and 10.2) include:

Squamous suture: Point of articulation of the temporal bone with the parietal bone.

Zygomatic process: A bridgelike projection joining the zygomatic bone (cheekbone) anteriorly. Together these two bones form the *zygomatic arch.*

Mandibular fossa: Rounded depression on the inferior surface of the zygomatic process (anterior to the ear); forms the socket for the mandibular condyle, the point where the mandible (lower jaw) joins the cranium.

Tympanic region markings (Figures 10.1 and 10.2) include:

External acoustic meatus: Canal leading to eardrum and middle ear.

Styloid (*stylo*=stake, pointed object) **process:** Needlelike projection inferior to external acoustic meatus; attachment point for muscles and ligaments of the neck. This process is often broken off demonstration skulls.

Prominent structures in the mastoid region (Figures 10.1 and 10.2) are:

Mastoid process: Rough projection inferior and posterior to external acoustic meatus; attachment site for muscles.

The mastoid process, full of air cavities and so close to the middle ear—a trouble spot for infections—often becomes infected too, a condition referred to as **mastoiditis.** Because the mastoid area is sepa-

rated from the brain by only a thin layer of bone, an ear infection that has spread to the mastoid process can inflame the brain coverings, or the meninges. The latter condition is known as **meningitis.** ■

Stylomastoid foramen: Tiny opening between the mastoid and styloid processes through which cranial nerve VII leaves the cranium.

The petrous part (Figures 10.2 and 10.3), which helps form the middle and posterior cranial fossae, exhibits several obvious foramina with important functions:

Jugular foramen: Opening medial to the styloid process through which the internal jugular vein and cranial nerves IX, X, and XI pass.

Carotid canal: Opening medial to the styloid process through which the internal carotid artery passes into the cranial cavity.

Internal acoustic meatus: Opening on posterior aspect (petrous region) of temporal bone allowing passage of cranial nerves VII and VIII (Figure 10.3).

Foramen lacerum: A jagged opening between the petrous temporal bone and the sphenoid providing passage for a number of small nerves and for the internal carotid artery to enter the middle cranial fossa (after it passes through part of the temporal bone).

● ***Occipital Bone*** See Figures 10.1, 10.2, 10.3, and 10.6. Most posterior bone of cranium—forms floor and back wall. Joins sphenoid bone anteriorly via its narrow basioccipital region.

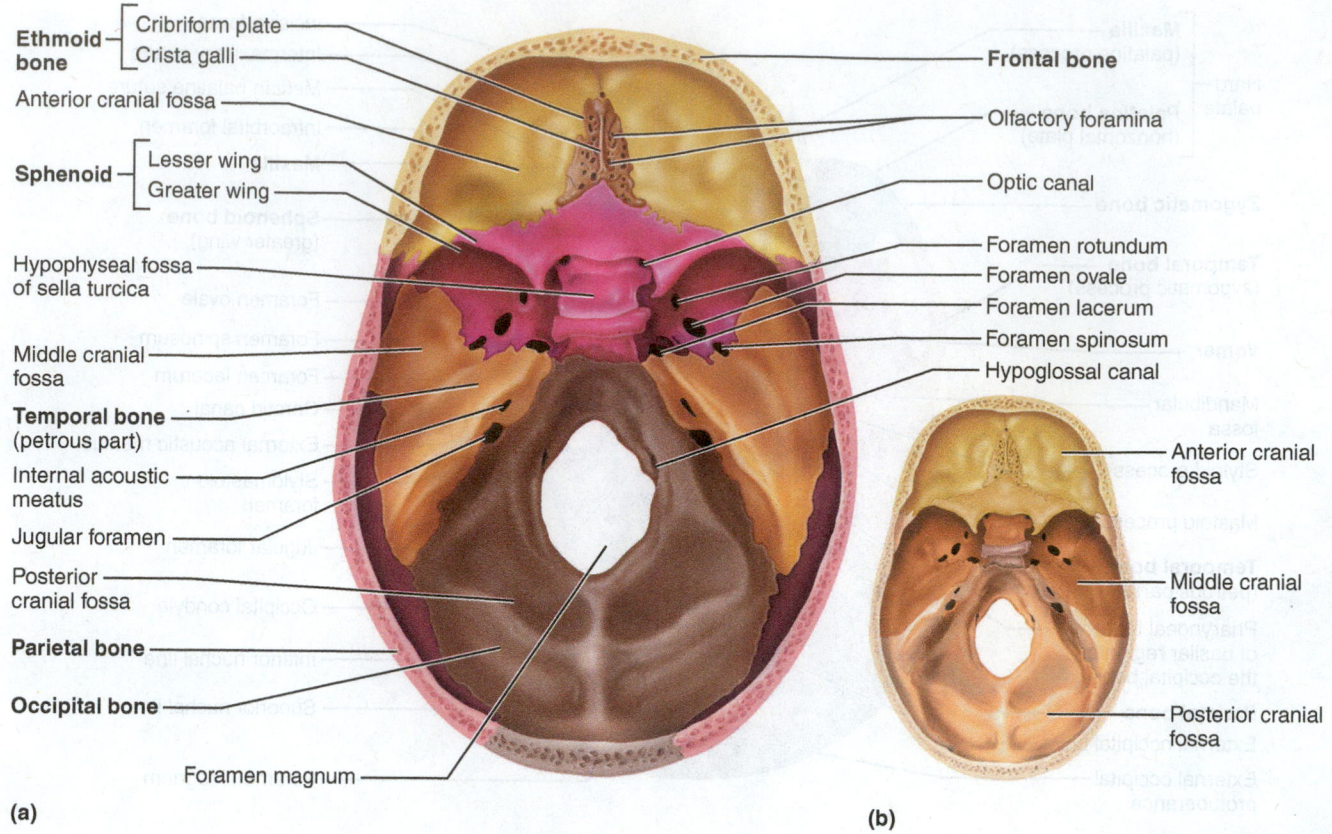

Ethmoid bone
Cribriform plate
Crista galli
Anterior cranial fossa
Sphenoid
Lesser wing
Greater wing
Hypophyseal fossa of sella turcica
Middle cranial fossa
Temporal bone (petrous part)
Internal acoustic meatus
Jugular foramen
Posterior cranial fossa
Parietal bone
Occipital bone
Foramen magnum

Frontal bone
Olfactory foramina
Optic canal
Foramen rotundum
Foramen ovale
Foramen lacerum
Foramen spinosum
Hypoglossal canal

Anterior cranial fossa
Middle cranial fossa
Posterior cranial fossa

(a)   (b)

FIGURE 10.3 **Internal anatomy of the inferior portion of the skull. (a)** Superior view of the floor of the cranial cavity, calvaria removed. **(b)** Schematic view of the cranial cavity floor showing the extent of its major fossae.

Lambdoid suture: Site of articulation of occipital bone and parietal bones.

Foramen magnum: Large opening in base of occipital, which allows the spinal cord to join with the brain.

Occipital condyles: Rounded projections lateral to the foramen magnum that articulate with the first cervical vertebra (atlas).

Hypoglossal canal: Opening medial and superior to the occipital condyle through which the hypoglossal nerve (cranial nerve XII) passes.

External occipital crest and protuberance: Midline prominences posterior to the foramen magnum.

● *Sphenoid Bone* See Figures 10.1 through 10.4, 10.6, and 10.8. Bat-shaped bone forming the anterior plateau of the middle cranial fossa across the width of the skull. The sphenoid bone is the keystone of the cranium because it articulates with all other cranial bones.

Greater wings: Portions of the sphenoid seen exteriorly anterior to the temporal and forming a part of the eye orbits.

Pterygoid processes: Inferiorly directed trough-shaped projections from the junction of the body and the greater wings.

Superior orbital fissures: Jagged openings in orbits providing passage for cranial nerves III, IV, V, and VI to enter the orbit where they serve the eye.

The sphenoid bone can be seen in its entire width if the top of the cranium (calvaria) is removed (Figure 10.3).

Sella turcica (Turk's saddle): A saddle-shaped region in the sphenoid midline. The seat of this saddle, called the **hypophyseal fossa,** surrounds the pituitary gland (hypophysis).

Lesser wings: Bat-shaped portions of the sphenoid anterior to the sella turcica.

Optic canals: Openings in the bases of the lesser wings through which the optic nerves enter the orbits to serve the eyes.

Foramen rotundum: Opening lateral to the sella turcica providing passage for a branch of the fifth cranial nerve. (This foramen is not visible on an inferior view of the skull.)

Foramen ovale: Opening posterior to the sella turcica that allows passage of a branch of the fifth cranial nerve.

● *Ethmoid Bone* See Figures 10.1, 10.3, 10.5, 10.6, and 10.8. Irregularly shaped bone anterior to the sphenoid. Forms the roof of the nasal cavity, upper nasal septum, and part of the medial orbit walls.

Crista galli (cock's comb): Vertical projection providing a point of attachment for the dura mater, helping to secure the brain within the skull.

Cribriform plates: Bony plates lateral to the crista galli through which olfactory fibers pass to the brain from the nasal

Optic canal

Lesser wing

Superior orbital fissure

Greater wing

Foramen rotundum

Hypophyseal fossa of sella turcica

Foramen ovale

Foramen spinosum

Body of sphenoid

(a) Superior view

Body of sphenoid

Lesser wing

Greater wing

Superior orbital fissure

Pterygoid process

(b) Posterior view

FIGURE 10.4 The sphenoid bone.

Olfactory foramina

Crista galli

Cribriform plate

Orbital plate

Left lateral mass

Ethmoidal air cells

Perpendicular plate

Middle nasal concha

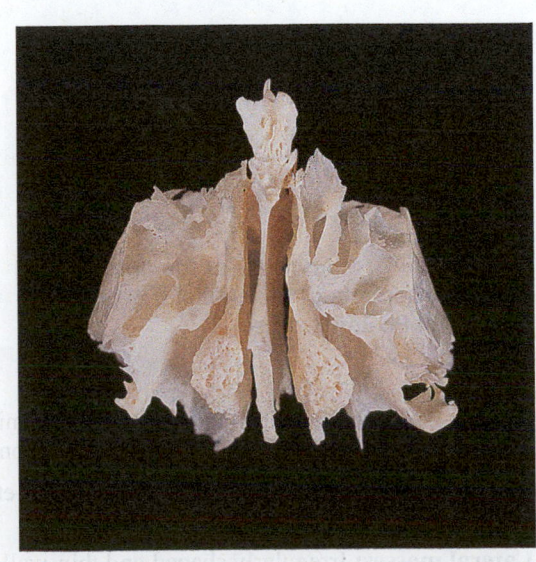

FIGURE 10.5 The ethmoid bone. Anterior view.

Parietal bone

Squamous part of frontal bone

Nasal bone

Sphenoid bone (greater wing)

Temporal bone

Ethmoid bone

Lacrimal bone

Zygomatic bone

Infraorbital foramen

Maxilla

Mandible

Mental foramen

Frontal bone

Glabella

Frontonasal suture

Supraorbital foramen (notch)

Supraorbital margin

Superior orbital fissure

Optic canal

Inferior orbital fissure

Middle nasal concha ⎤ **Ethmoid**
Perpendicular plate ⎦ **bone**

Inferior nasal concha

Vomer

Mandibular symphysis

(a)

Sagittal suture

Parietal bone

Sutural bone

Lambdoid suture

Occipital bone

Superior nuchal line

External occipital protuberance

Occipitomastoid suture

External occipital crest

Occipital condyle

Mastoid process

Inferior nuchal line

(b)

FIGURE 10.6 Anatomy of the anterior and posterior aspects of the skull. (a) Anterior aspect. **(b)** Posterior aspect.

mucosa. Together the cribriform plates and the midline crista galli form the *horizontal plate* of the ethmoid bone.

Perpendicular plate: Inferior projection of the ethmoid that forms the superior part of the nasal septum.

Lateral masses: Irregularly shaped and thin-walled bony regions flanking the perpendicular plate laterally. Their lateral surfaces (*orbital plates*) shape part of the medial orbit wall.

Superior and middle nasal conchae (turbinates): Thin, delicately coiled plates of bone extending medially from the lateral masses of the ethmoid into the nasal cavity. The conchae make air flow through the nasal cavity more efficient and greatly increase the surface area of the mucosa that covers them, thus increasing the mucosa's ability to warm and humidify incoming air.

Parietal bone

Frontal bone

Sphenoid bone

Ethmoid bone

Nasal bones

Temporal bone

Zygomatic bone

Maxilla

Mandible

(c)

FIGURE 10.6 *(continued)* **(c)** Frontal view of the Beauchene skull.

Facial Bones

Of the 14 bones composing the face, 12 are paired. *Only the mandible and vomer are single bones.* An additional bone, the hyoid bone, although not a facial bone, is considered here because of its location.

● *Mandible* See Figures 10.1, 10.6, and 10.7. The lower jawbone, which articulates with the temporal bones in the only freely movable joints of the skull.

Mandibular body: Horizontal portion; forms the chin.

Mandibular ramus: Vertical extension of the body on either side.

Mandibular condyle: Articulation point of the mandible with the mandibular fossa of the temporal bone.

Coronoid process: Jutting anterior portion of the ramus; site of muscle attachment.

Mandibular angle: Posterior point at which ramus meets the body.

Mental foramen: Prominent opening on the body (lateral to the midline) that transmits the mental blood vessels and nerve to the lower jaw.

Mandibular foramen: Open the lower jaw of the skull to identify this prominent foramen on the medial aspect of the mandibular ramus. This foramen permits passage of the nerve involved with tooth sensation (mandibular branch of cranial nerve V) and is the site where the dentist injects Novocain to prevent pain while working on the lower teeth.

Alveolar margin: Superior margin of mandible; contains sockets in which the teeth lie.

Mandibular symphysis: Anterior median depression indicating point of mandibular fusion.

● *Maxillae* See Figures 10.1, 10.2, 10.6, and 10.7. Two bones fused in a median suture; form the upper jawbone and part of the orbits. All facial bones, except the mandible, join the maxillae. Thus they are the main, or keystone, bones of the face.

FIGURE 10.7 Detailed anatomy of the mandible and maxilla.

Articulates with frontal bone

Orbital surface

Frontal process

Zygomatic process (cut)

Infraorbital foramen

Anterior nasal spine

Alveolar margin

(a) Maxilla, right lateral view

Temporomandibular joint

Mandibular notch

Mandibular condyle

Ramus of mandible

Mandibular angle

Mandibular fossa of temporal bone

Coronoid process

Mandibular foramen

Alveolar margin

Mental foramen

Body of mandible

(b) Mandible, right lateral view

Alveolar margin: Inferior margin containing sockets (alveoli) in which teeth lie.

Palatine processes: Form the anterior hard palate; meet medially in the intermaxillary suture.

Infraorbital foramen: Opening under the orbit carrying the infraorbital nerves and blood vessels to the nasal region.

Incisive fossa: Large bilateral opening located posterior to the central incisor tooth of the maxilla and piercing the hard palate; transmits the nasopalatine arteries and blood vessels.

● *Lacrimal Bone* See Figures 10.1 and 10.6a. Fingernail-sized bones forming a part of the medial orbit walls between the maxilla and the ethmoid. Each lacrimal bone is

Roof of orbit

• Lesser wing of sphenoid bone

• Orbital plate of frontal bone

Lateral wall of orbit

• Zygomatic process of frontal bone

• Greater wing of sphenoid bone

• Orbital surface of zygomatic bone

Inferior orbital fissure

Infraorbital groove

Zygomatic bone

Supraorbital notch

Superior orbital fissure

Optic canal

Infraorbital foramen

Medial wall

• Sphenoid body

• Orbital plate of ethmoid bone

• Frontal process of maxilla

• Lacrimal bone

Nasal bone

Floor of orbit

• Orbital process of palatine bone

• Orbital surface of maxillary bone

• Zygomatic bone

FIGURE 10.8 Bones that form the orbit. Seven skull bones form the orbit, the bony cavity that surrounds the eye. They are frontal, sphenoid, ethmoid, lacrimal, maxilla, palatine, and zygomatic.

(a)

(b)

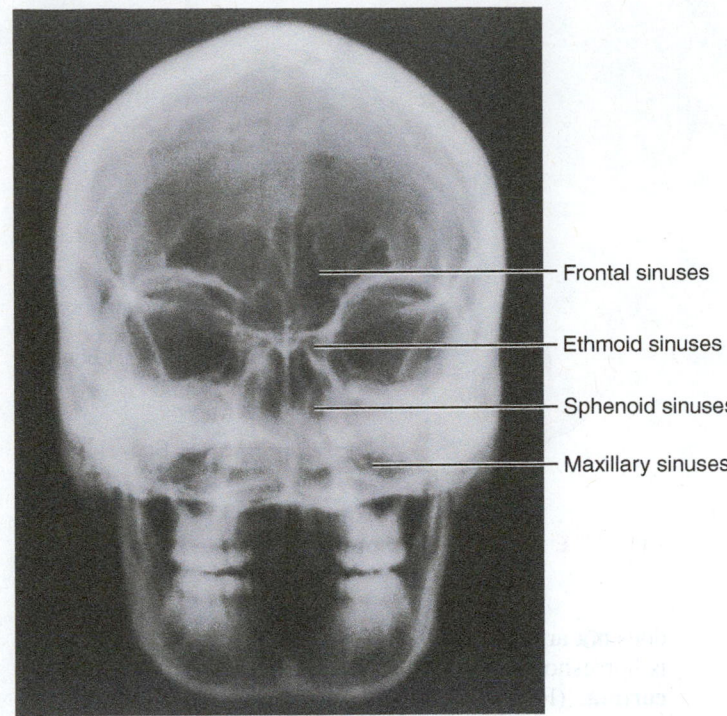

(c)

FIGURE 10.9 **Paranasal sinuses. (a)** Anterior aspect.
(b) Medial aspect. **(c)** Skull X ray showing the paranasal
sinuses, anterior view.

- *Vomer* See Figures 10.2 and 10.6. Blade-shaped bone
(*vomer* = plow) in median plane of nasal cavity that
forms the posterior and inferior nasal septum.

- *Inferior Nasal Conchae (Turbinates)* See Figure 10.6a.
Thin curved bones protruding medially from the lateral
walls of the nasal cavity; serve the same purpose as the
turbinate portions of the ethmoid bone (described earlier).

Paranasal Sinuses

Four skull bones—maxillary, sphenoid, ethmoid, and frontal—
contain sinuses (mucosa-lined air cavities) that lead into the
nasal passages (see Figures 10.5 and 10.9). These paranasal sinuses lighten the facial bones and may act as resonance chambers for speech. The maxillary sinus is the largest of the sinuses
found in the skull.

Sinusitis, or inflammation of the sinuses, sometimes occurs as a result of an allergy or bacterial invasion of the sinus cavities. In such cases, some of the
connecting passageways between the sinuses and nasal passages may become blocked with thick mucus or infectious
material. Then, as the air in the sinus cavities is absorbed, a
partial vacuum forms. The result is a sinus headache localized
over the inflamed sinus area. Severe sinus infections may require surgical drainage to relieve this painful condition. ■

Hyoid Bone

Not really considered or counted as a skull bone, the hyoid
bone is located in the throat above the larynx. It serves as a
point of attachment for many tongue and neck muscles. It

pierced by an opening, the **lacrimal fossa,** which serves as
a passageway for tears (*lacrima* = tear).

- *Palatine Bone* See Figure 10.2 and 10.8. Paired bones
posterior to the palatine processes; form posterior hard
palate and part of the orbit; meet medially at the median
palatine suture.

- *Zygomatic Bone* See Figures 10.1, 10.2, 10.6, and 10.8.
Lateral to the maxilla; forms the portion of the face commonly called the cheekbone, and forms part of the lateral
orbit. Its three processes are named for the bones with
which they articulate.

- *Nasal Bone* See Figures 10.1 and 10.6. Small rectangular bones forming the bridge of the nose.

FIGURE 10.10 Hyoid bone.

does not articulate with any other bone and is thus unique. It is horseshoe-shaped with a body and two pairs of **horns,** or **cornua.** (Figure 10.10)

ACTIVITY 2

Palpating Skull Markings

Palpate the following areas on yourself:

- Zygomatic bone and arch. (The most prominent part of your cheek is your zygomatic bone. Follow the posterior course of the zygomatic arch to its junction with your temporal bone.)

- Mastoid process (the rough area behind your ear).

- Temporomandibular joints. (Open and close your jaws to locate these.)

- Greater wing of sphenoid. (Find the indentation posterior to the orbit and superior to the zygomatic arch on your lateral skull.)

- Supraorbital foramen. (Apply firm pressure along the superior orbital margin to find the indentation resulting from this foramen.)

- Infraorbital foramen. (Apply firm pressure just inferior to the inferomedial border of the orbit to locate this large foramen.)

- Mandibular angle (most inferior and posterior aspect of the mandible).

- Mandibular symphysis (midline of chin).

- Nasal bones. (Run your index finger and thumb along opposite sides of the bridge of your nose until they "slip" medially at the inferior end of the nasal bones.)

- External occipital protuberance. (This midline projection is easily felt by running your fingers up the furrow at the back of your neck to the skull.)

- Hyoid bone. (Place a thumb and index finger beneath the chin just anterior to the mandibular angles, and squeeze gently. Exert pressure with the thumb, and feel the horn of the hyoid with the index finger.) ▬▬▬

Anterior view   Right lateral view

FIGURE 10.11 The vertebral column. Notice the curvatures in the lateral view. (The terms *convex* and *concave* refer to the curvature of the posterior aspect of the vertebral column.)

The Vertebral Column

The **vertebral column,** extending from the skull to the pelvis, forms the body's major axial support. Additionally, it surrounds and protects the delicate spinal cord while allowing the spinal nerves to issue from the cord via openings between adjacent vertebrae. The term *vertebral column* might suggest a rather rigid supporting rod, but this is far from the truth. The vertebral column consists of 24 single bones called **vertebrae** and two composite, or fused, bones (the sacrum and coccyx) that are connected in such a way as to provide a flexible curved structure (Figure 10.11). Of the 24 single vertebrae, the seven bones of the neck are called *cervical vertebrae;* the next 12 are *thoracic vertebrae;* and the 5 supporting the lower back are *lumbar vertebrae.* Remembering common mealtimes for breakfast, lunch, and dinner (7 A.M., 12 noon, and 5 P.M.) may help you to remember the number of bones in each region.

The vertebrae are separated by pads of fibrocartilage, **intervertebral discs,** that cushion the vertebrae and absorb shocks. Each disc is composed of two major regions, a central gelatinous *nucleus pulposus* that behaves like a fluid, and an outer ring of encircling collagen fibers called the *annulus fibrosus* that stabilizes the disc and contains the pulposus.

As a person ages, the water content of the discs decreases (as it does in other tissues throughout the body), and the discs become thinner and less compressible. This situation, along with other degenerative changes such as weakening of the ligaments and tendons of the vertebral column, predisposes older people to **ruptured discs.** In a ruptured disc, the nucleus pulposus herniates through the annulus portion and typically compresses adjacent nerves. ■

The presence of the discs and the S-shaped or springlike construction of the vertebral column prevent shock to the head in walking and running and provide flexibility to the body trunk. The thoracic and sacral curvatures of the spine are referred to as *primary curvatures* because they are present and well developed at birth. Later the *secondary curvatures* are formed. The cervical curvature becomes prominent when the baby begins to hold its head up independently, and the lumbar curvature develops when the baby begins to walk.

FIGURE 10.12 Abnormal spinal curvatures

Scoliosis   Kyphosis   Lordosis

Structure of a Typical Vertebra

Although they differ in size and specific features, all vertebrae have some features in common (Figure 10.13).

ACTIVITY 3

Examining Spinal Curvatures

1. Observe the normal curvature of the vertebral column in the articulated vertebral column or laboratory skeleton, and compare it to Figure 10.11. Then examine Figure 10.12, which depicts three abnormal spinal curvatures—*scoliosis, kyphosis,* and *lordosis.* These abnormalities may result from disease or poor posture. Also examine X-rays, if they are available, showing these same conditions in a living patient.

2. Then, using the articulated vertebral column (or an articulated skeleton), examine the freedom of movement between two lumbar vertebrae separated by an intervertebral disc.

When the fibrous disc is properly positioned, are the spinal cord or peripheral nerves impaired in any way?

_____

Remove the disc and put the two vertebrae back together. What happens to the nerve?

_____

What would happen to the spinal nerves in areas of malpositioned or "slipped" discs?

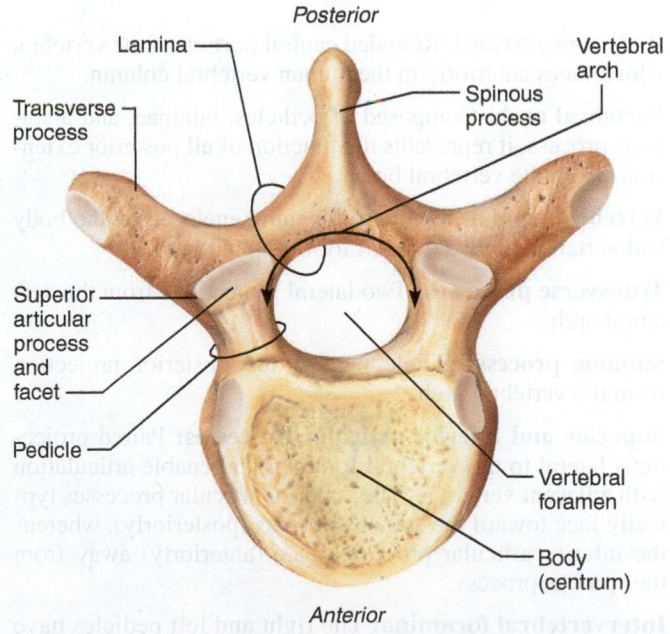

FIGURE 10.13 A typical vertebra, superior view. Inferior articulating surfaces not shown.

Posterior

Lamina — Vertebral arch
Transverse process — Spinous process
Superior articular process and facet
Pedicle — Vertebral foramen
Body (centrum)

Anterior

(a) Superior view of atlas (C₁)

(b) Inferior view of atlas (C₁)

FIGURE 10.14 The first and second cervical vertebrae.

(c) Superior view of axis (C₂)

Body (or **centrum**): Rounded central portion of the vertebra, which faces anteriorly in the human vertebral column.

Vertebral arch: Composed of pedicles, laminae, and a spinous process, it represents the junction of all posterior extensions from the vertebral body.

Vertebral (spinal) foramen: Opening enclosed by the body and vertebral arch; a conduit for the spinal cord.

Transverse processes: Two lateral projections from the vertebral arch.

Spinous process: Single medial and posterior projection from the vertebral arch.

Superior and inferior articular processes: Paired projections lateral to the vertebral foramen that enable articulation with adjacent vertebrae. The superior articular processes typically face toward the spinous process (posteriorly), whereas the inferior articular processes face (anteriorly) away from the spinous process.

Intervertebral foramina: The right and left pedicles have notches (see Figure 10.15) on their inferior and superior surfaces that create openings, the intervertebral foramina, for spinal nerves to leave the spinal cord between adjacent vertebrae.

Figures 10.14 through 10.16 and Table 10.1 show how specific vertebrae differ; refer to them as you read the following sections.

Cervical Vertebrae

The seven cervical vertebrae (referred to as C_1 through C_7) form the neck portion of the vertebral column. The first two cervical vertebrae (atlas and axis) are highly modified to perform special functions (see Figure 10.14). The **atlas** (C_1) lacks a body, and its lateral processes contain large concave depressions on their superior surfaces that receive the occipital condyles of the skull. This joint enables you to nod "yes." The **axis** (C_2) acts as a pivot for the rotation of the atlas (and skull) above. It bears a large vertical process, the **dens,** or **odontoid process,** that serves as the pivot point. The articulation between C_1 and C_2 allows you to rotate your head from side to side to indicate "no."

The more typical cervical vertebrae (C_3 through C_7) are distinguished from the thoracic and lumbar vertebrae by several features (see Table 10.1 and Figure 10.15). They are the smallest, lightest vertebrae, and the vertebral foramen is triangular. The spinous process is short and often bifurcated (divided into two branches). The spinous process of C_7 is not branched, however, and is substantially longer than that of the other cervical vertebrae. Because the spinous process of C_7 is visible through the skin, it is called the *vertebra prominens* (Figure 10.11) and is used as a landmark for counting the vertebrae. Transverse processes of the cervical vertebrae are wide, and they contain foramina through which the vertebral arteries pass superiorly on their way to the brain. Any time you see these foramina in a vertebra, you can be sure that it is a cervical vertebra.

● Palpate your vertebra prominens.

Thoracic Vertebrae

The 12 thoracic vertebrae (referred to as T_1 through T_{12}) may be recognized by the following structural characteristics. As shown in Figure 10.15, they have a larger body than the cervical vertebrae. The body is somewhat heart-shaped, with two small articulating surfaces, or **costal facets,** on each side (one superior, the other inferior) close to the origin of the vertebral arch. Sometimes referred to as *costal demifacets* because of their small size, these facets articulate with the heads of the corresponding ribs. The vertebral foramen is oval or round, and the spinous process is long, with a sharp downward hook. The closer the thoracic vertebra is to the lumbar region, the less sharp and shorter the spinous process. Articular facets on the transverse processes articulate with the tubercles of the

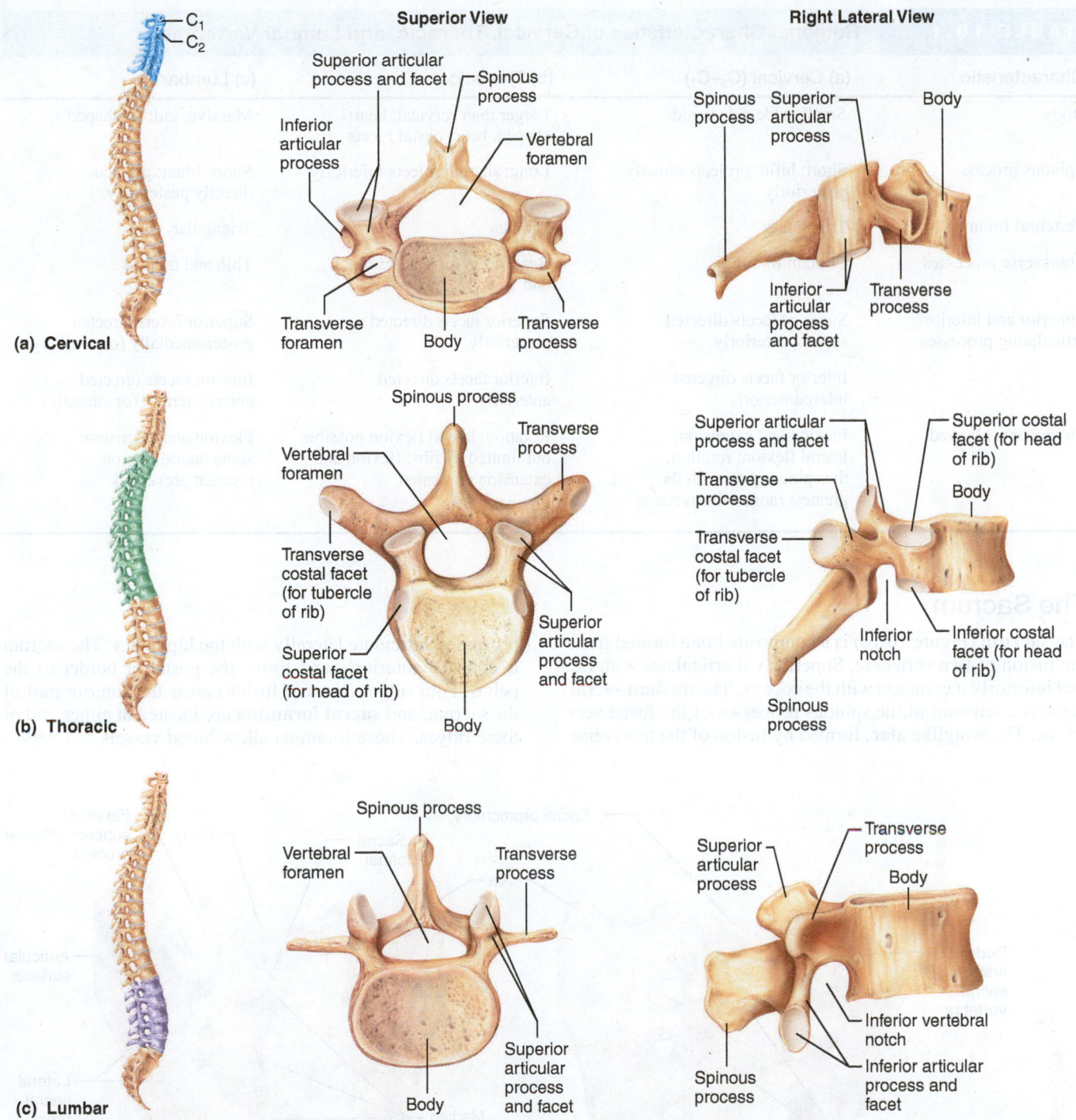

Superior View   **Right Lateral View**

(a) Cervical

- C₁
- C₂

Superior articular process and facet
Inferior articular process
Transverse foramen
Spinous process
Vertebral foramen
Body
Transverse process

Spinous process
Superior articular process
Body
Inferior articular process and facet
Transverse process

(b) Thoracic

Spinous process
Vertebral foramen
Transverse process
Transverse costal facet (for tubercle of rib)
Superior costal facet (for head of rib)
Superior articular process and facet
Body

Superior articular process and facet
Transverse process
Transverse costal facet (for tubercle of rib)
Superior costal facet (for head of rib)
Body
Inferior notch
Inferior costal facet (for head of rib)
Spinous process

(c) Lumbar

Spinous process
Vertebral foramen
Transverse process
Superior costal facet (for head of rib)
Superior articular process and facet
Body

Superior articular process
Transverse process
Body
Inferior vertebral notch
Inferior articular process and facet
Spinous process

FIGURE 10.15 Superior and right lateral views of typical vertebrae. (a) Cervical. **(b)** Thoracic. **(c)** Lumbar.

ribs. Besides forming the thoracic part of the spine, these vertebrae form the posterior aspect of the bony thorax. Indeed, they are the only vertebrae that articulate with the ribs.

Lumbar Vertebrae

The five lumbar vertebrae (L_1 through L_5) have massive blocklike bodies and short, thick, hatchet-shaped spinous processes extending directly backward (see Table 10.1 and Figure 10.15). The superior articular facets face posteromedially; the inferior ones are directed anterolaterally. These

structural features reduce the mobility of the lumbar region of the spine. Since most stress on the vertebral column occurs in the lumbar region, these are also the sturdiest of the vertebrae.

The spinal cord ends at the superior edge of L_2, but the outer covering of the cord, filled with cerebrospinal fluid, extends an appreciable distance beyond. Thus a *lumbar puncture* (for examination of the cerebrospinal fluid) or the administration of "saddle block" anesthesia for childbirth is normally done between L_3 and L_4 or L_4 and L_5, where there is little or no chance of injuring the delicate spinal cord.

TABLE 10.1	Regional Characteristics of Cervical, Thoracic, and Lumbar Vertebrae		
Characteristic	**(a) Cervical (C$_3$–C$_7$)**	**(b) Thoracic**	**(c) Lumbar**
Body	Small, wide side to side	Larger than cervical; heart-shaped; bears costal facets	Massive; kidney-shaped
Spinous process	Short; bifid; projects directly posteriorly	Long; sharp; projects inferiorly	Short; blunt; projects directly posteriorly
Vertebral foramen	Triangular	Circular	Triangular
Transverse processes	Contain foramina	Bear facets for ribs (except T$_{11}$ and T$_{12}$)	Thin and tapered
Superior and inferior articulating processes	Superior facets directed superoposteriorly	Superior facets directed posteriorly	Superior facets directed posteromedially (or medially)
	Inferior facets directed inferoanteriorly	Inferior facets directed anteriorly	Inferior facets directed anterolaterally (or laterally)
Movements allowed	Flexion and extension; lateral flexion; rotation; the spine region with the greatest range of movement	Rotation; lateral flexion possible but limited by ribs; flexion and extension prevented	Flexion and extension; some lateral flexion; rotation prevented

The Sacrum

The **sacrum** (Figure 10.16) is a composite bone formed from the fusion of five vertebrae. Superiorly it articulates with L$_5$, and inferiorly it connects with the coccyx. The **median sacral crest** is a remnant of the spinous processes of the fused vertebrae. The winglike **alae,** formed by fusion of the transverse processes, articulate laterally with the hip bones. The sacrum is concave anteriorly and forms the posterior border of the pelvis. Four ridges (lines of fusion) cross the anterior part of the sacrum, and **sacral foramina** are located at either end of these ridges. These foramina allow blood vessels and nerves

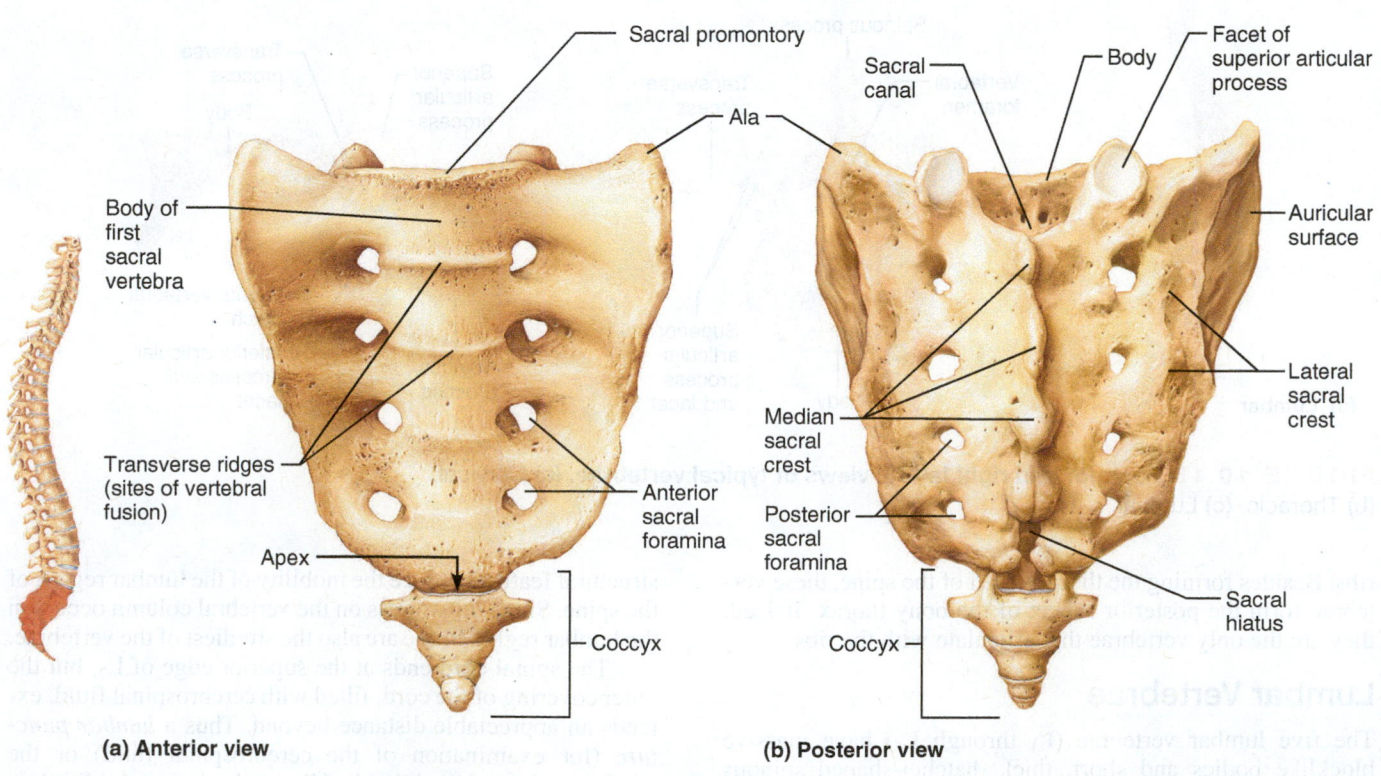

(a) Anterior view

(b) Posterior view

FIGURE 10.16 Sacrum and coccyx.

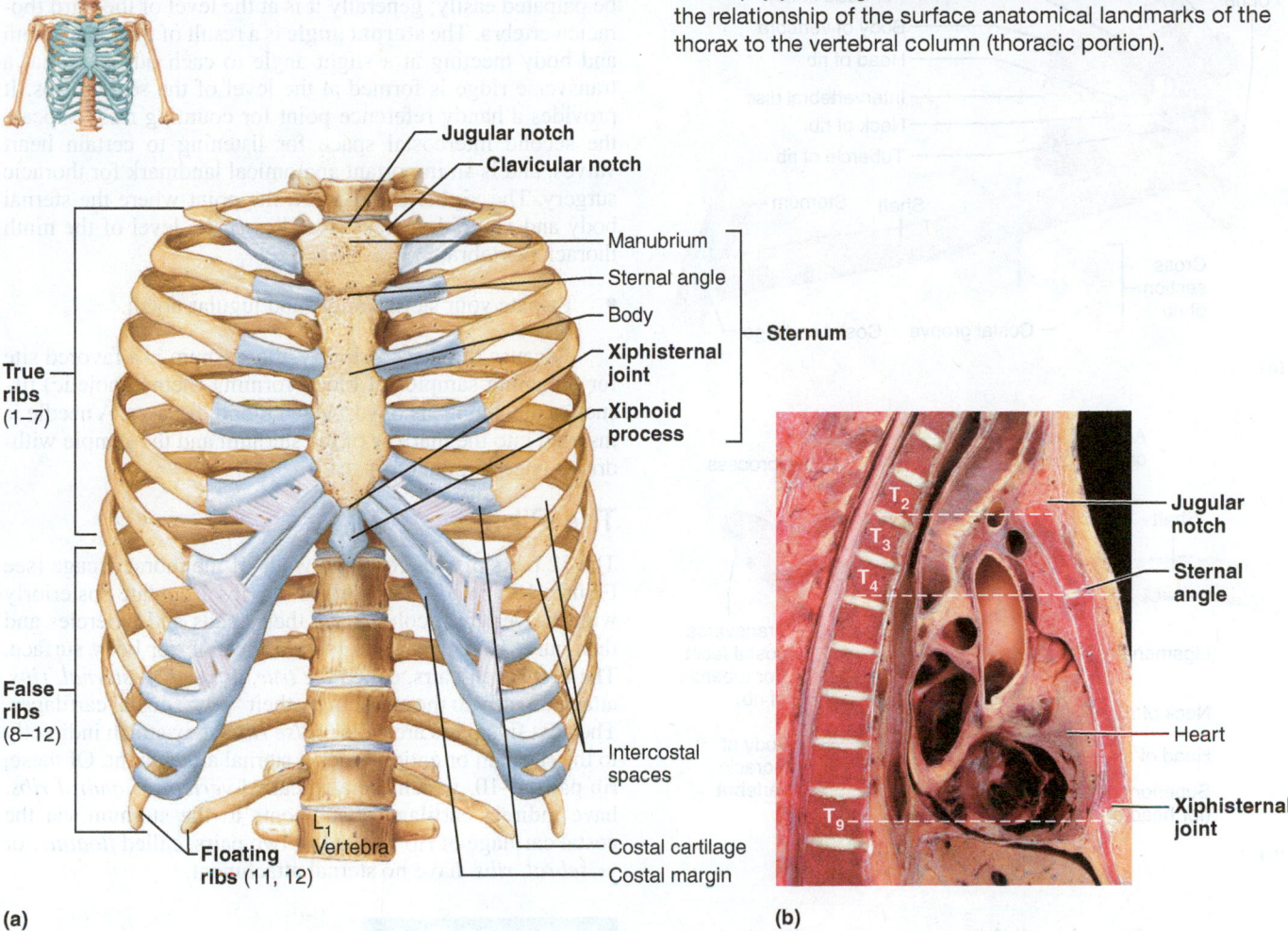

Figure labels (a): Jugular notch, Clavicular notch, Manubrium, Sternal angle, Body, Xiphisternal joint, Xiphoid process, Sternum, True ribs (1–7), False ribs (8–12), Floating ribs (11, 12), L₁ Vertebra, Intercostal spaces, Costal cartilage, Costal margin

Figure labels (b): T₂, T₃, T₄, T₉, Jugular notch, Sternal angle, Heart, Xiphisternal joint

(a)   **(b)**

to pass. The vertebral canal continues inside the sacrum as the **sacral canal** and terminates near the coccyx via an enlarged opening called the **sacral hiatus.** The **sacral promontory** (anterior border of the body of S₁) is an important anatomical landmark for obstetricians.

- Attempt to palpate the median sacral crest of your sacrum. (This is more easily done by thin people and obviously in privacy.)

The Coccyx

The **coccyx** (see Figure 10.16) is formed from the fusion of three to five small irregularly shaped vertebrae. It is literally the human tailbone, a vestige of the tail that other vertebrates have. The coccyx is attached to the sacrum by ligaments.

ACTIVITY 4

Examining Vertebral Structure

Obtain examples of each type of vertebra and examine them carefully, comparing them to Figures 10.14, 10.15, 10.16 and Table 10.1, and to each other. ■

The Thoracic Cage

The bony thorax is composed of the sternum, ribs, and thoracic vertebrae (Figure 10.17). Combined with the costal cartilages, it is referred to as the **thoracic cage** because of its appearance and because it forms a protective cone-shaped enclosure around the organs of the thoracic cavity (heart and lungs, for example).

The Sternum

The **sternum** (breastbone), a typical flat bone, is a result of the fusion of three bones—the manubrium, body, and xiphoid process. It is attached to the first seven pairs of ribs. The superiormost **manubrium** looks like the knot of a tie; it articulates with the clavicle (collarbone) laterally. The **body (gladiolus)** forms the bulk of the sternum. The **xiphoid process** constructs the inferior end of the sternum and lies at the level of the fifth intercostal space. Although it is made of hyaline cartilage in children, it is usually ossified in adults.

In some people, the xiphoid process projects dorsally. This may present a problem because physical trauma to the chest can push such a xiphoid into the heart or liver (both immediately deep to the process), causing massive hemorrhage. ■

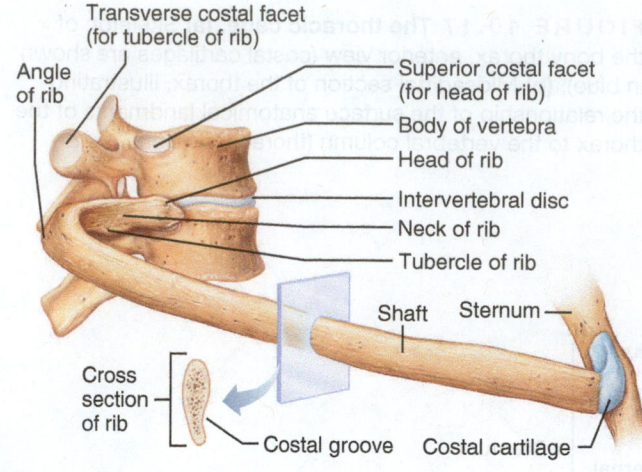

(a)

Transverse costal facet
(for tubercle of rib)

Angle
of rib

Superior costal facet
(for head of rib)

Body of vertebra

Head of rib

Intervertebral disc

Neck of rib

Tubercle of rib

Shaft

Sternum

Cross
section
of rib

Costal groove

Costal cartilage

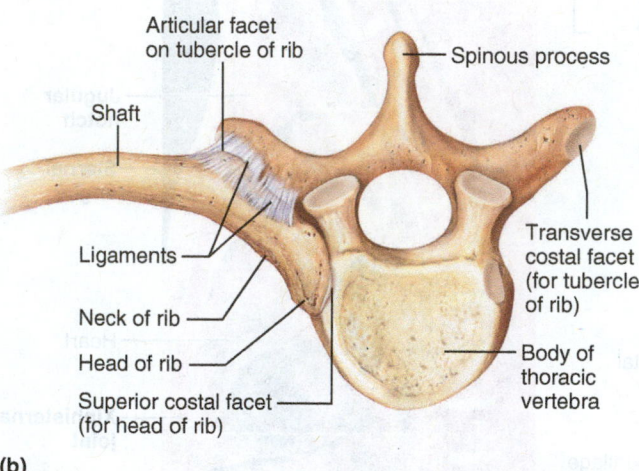

(b)

Articular facet
on tubercle of rib

Spinous process

Shaft

Ligaments

Transverse
costal facet
(for tubercle
of rib)

Neck of rib

Head of rib

Superior costal facet
(for head of rib)

Body of
thoracic
vertebra

(c)

Shaft

Facets for articulation
with vertebrae

Head Neck

Articular facet
on tubercle

Junction with
costal cartilage

Costal groove Costal angle

FIGURE 10.18 Structure of a typical true rib and its articulations. (a) Vertebral and sternal articulations of a typical true rib. **(b)** Superior view of the articulation between a rib and a thoracic vertebra, with costovertebral ligaments shown on left side only. **(c)** Right rib 6, posterior view.

The sternum has three important bony landmarks—the jugular notch, the sternal angle, and the xiphisternal joint. The **jugular notch** (concave upper border of the manubrium) can be palpated easily; generally it is at the level of the third thoracic vertebra. The **sternal angle** is a result of the manubrium and body meeting at a slight angle to each other, so that a transverse ridge is formed at the level of the second ribs. It provides a handy reference point for counting ribs to locate the second intercostal space for listening to certain heart valves, and is an important anatomical landmark for thoracic surgery. The **xiphisternal joint,** the point where the sternal body and xiphoid process fuse, lies at the level of the ninth thoracic vertebra.

• Palpate your sternal angle and jugular notch.

Because of its accessibility, the sternum is a favored site for obtaining samples of blood-forming (hematopoietic) tissue for the diagnosis of suspected blood diseases. A needle is inserted into the marrow of the sternum and the sample withdrawn (sternal puncture).

The Ribs

The 12 pairs of **ribs** form the walls of the thoracic cage (see Figures 10.17 and 10.18). All of the ribs articulate posteriorly with the vertebral column via their heads and tubercles and then curve downward and toward the anterior body surface. The first seven pairs, called the *true,* or *vertebrosternal, ribs,* attach directly to the sternum by their "own" costal cartilages. The next five pairs are called *false ribs;* they attach indirectly to the sternum or entirely lack a sternal attachment. Of these, rib pairs 8–10, which are also called *vertebrochondral ribs,* have indirect cartilage attachments to the sternum via the costal cartilage of rib 7. The last two pairs, called *floating,* or *vertebral, ribs,* have no sternal attachment.

ACTIVITY 5

Examining the Relationship Between Ribs and Vertebrae

First take a deep breath to expand your chest. Notice how your ribs seem to move outward and how your sternum rises. Then examine an articulated skeleton to observe the relationship between the ribs and the vertebrae.

Refer to Activity 3 (Palpating Landmarks of the Trunk) and Activity 4 (Palpating Landmarks of the Abdomen) in Exercise 46, Surface Anatomy Roundup. ■

The Axial Skeleton

The Skull

1. First, match the bone names in column B with the descriptions in column A (the items in column B may be used more than once). Then, circle the bones in column B that are cranial bones.

Column A

_____ 1. forehead bone

_____ 2. cheekbone

_____ 3. lower jaw

_____ 4. bridge of nose

_____ 5. posterior bones of the hard palate

_____ 6. much of the lateral and superior cranium

_____ 7. most posterior part of cranium

_____ 8. single, irregular, bat-shaped bone forming part of the cranial floor

_____ 9. tiny bones bearing tear ducts

_____ 10. anterior part of hard palate

_____ 11. superior and middle nasal conchae formed from its projections

_____ 12. site of mastoid process

_____ 13. site of sella turcica

_____ 14. site of cribriform plate

_____ 15. site of mental foramen

_____ 16. site of styloid processes

_____, _____, _____

_____ 17. four bones containing paranasal sinuses

_____ 18. condyles here articulate with the atlas

_____ 19. foramen magnum contained here

_____ 20. small U-shaped bone in neck, where many tongue muscles attach

_____ 21. middle ear found here

_____ 22. nasal septum

_____ 23. bears an upward protrusion, the "cock's comb," or crista galli

_____ 24. contain alveoli bearing teeth

Column B

a. ethmoid

b. frontal

c. hyoid

d. lacrimal

e. mandible

f. maxilla

g. nasal

h. occipital

i. palatine

j. parietal

k. sphenoid

l. temporal

m. vomer

n. zygomatic

2. Using choices from the numbered key to the right, identify all bones (⎯⎯•), sutures (⎯⎯►), and bone markings provided with various leader lines in the two diagrams below.

Key:
1. carotid canal
2. coronal suture
3. ethmoid bone
4. external occipital protuberance
5. foramen lacerum
6. foramen magnum
7. foramen ovale
8. frontal bone
9. glabella
10. incisive fossa
11. inferior nasal concha
12. inferior orbital fissure
13. infraorbital foramen
14. jugular foramen
15. lacrimal bone
16. mandible
17. mandibular fossa
18. mandibular symphysis
19. mastoid process
20. maxilla
21. mental foramen
22. middle nasal concha of ethmoid
23. nasal bone
24. occipital bone
25. occipital condyle
26. palatine bone
27. palatine process of maxilla
28. parietal bone
29. sagittal suture
30. sphenoid bone
31. styloid process
32. stylomastoid foramen
33. superior orbital fissure
34. supraorbital foramen
35. temporal bone
36. vomer
37. zygomatic bone
38. zygomatic process of temporal bone

3. Define *suture*. _____

4. With one exception, the skull bones are joined by sutures. Name the exception. _____

_____

5. What bones are connected by the lambdoid suture?

_____

What bones are connected by the squamous suture?

_____

6. Name the eight bones of the cranium.

_____   _____   _____

_____   _____   _____

7. Give two possible functions of the sinuses.

_____

_____

8. What is the orbit? _____

What bones contribute to the formation of the orbit? _____

_____

9. Why can the sphenoid bone be called the keystone of the cranial floor? _____

_____

The Vertebral Column

10. The distinguishing characteristics of the vertebrae composing the vertebral column are noted below. Correctly identify each described structure by choosing a response from the key.

Key: a.   atlas   d.   coccyx   f.   sacrum
　　　 b.   axis   e.   lumbar vertebra   g.   thoracic vertebra
　　　 c.   cervical vertebra—typical

_____ 1.   vertebral type containing foramina in the transverse processes, through which the vertebral arteries ascend to reach the brain

_____ 2.   dens here provides a pivot for rotation of the first cervical vertebra (C_1)

_____ 3.   transverse processes faceted for articulation with ribs; spinous process pointing sharply downward

_____ 4.   composite bone; articulates with the hip bone laterally

_____ 5.   massive vertebrae; weight-sustaining

_____ 6.   "tail bone"; vestigial fused vertebrae

_____ 7.   supports the head; allows a rocking motion in conjunction with the occipital condyles

11. Using the key, correctly identify the vertebral parts/areas described below. (More than one choice may apply in some cases.)
Also use the key letters to correctly identify the vertebral areas in the diagram.

Key: a. body   d. pedicle   g. transverse process
       b. intervertebral foramina   e. spinous process   h. vertebral arch
       c. lamina   f. superior articular facet i. vertebral foramen

_____ 1. cavity enclosing the nerve cord

_____ 2. weight-bearing portion of the vertebra

____, ____ 3. provide levers against which muscles pull

____, ____ 4. provide an articulation point for the ribs

_____ 5. openings providing for exit of spinal nerves

____, ____ 6. structures that form an enclosure for the spinal cord

12. Describe how a spinal nerve exits from the vertebral column. _____

_____

13. Name two factors/structures that permit flexibility of the vertebral column. _____

_____ and _____

14. What kind of tissue composes the intervertebral discs? _____

15. What is a herniated disc? _____

What problems might it cause? _____

_____

16. Which two spinal curvatures are obvious at birth? _____ and _____

Under what conditions do the secondary curvatures develop? _____

_____

_____

17. On this illustration of an articulated vertebral column, identify each curvature indicated and label it as a primary or a secondary curvature. Also identify the structures provided with leader lines, using the letters of the terms listed in the key below.

Key: a. atlas
     b. axis
     c. intervertebral disc
     d. sacrum
     e. two thoracic vertebrae
     f. two lumbar vertebrae
     g. vertebra prominens

_____ (curvature)

_____ (curvature)

_____ (curvature)

_____ (curvature)

The Thoracic Cage

18. The major bony components of the thorax (excluding the vertebral column) are the _____

and the _____.

19. Differentiate between a true rib and a false rib. _____

_____

_____

Is a floating rib a true or a false rib? _____.

20. What is the general shape of the thoracic cage? _____

21. Using the terms in the key, identify the regions and landmarks of the bony thorax.

L₁ vertebra

Key: a. body

b. clavicular notch

c. costal cartilage

d. false ribs

e. floating ribs

f. jugular notch

g. manubrium

h. sternal angle

i. sternum

j. true ribs

k. xiphisternal joint

l. xiphoid process

The Appendicular Skeleton

MATERIALS

☐ Articulated skeletons
☐ Disarticulated skeletons (complete)
☐ Articulated pelves (male and female for comparative study)
☐ X rays of bones of the appendicular skeleton

OBJECTIVES

1. To identify on an articulated skeleton the bones of the pectoral and pelvic girdles and their attached limbs.
2. To arrange unmarked, disarticulated bones in proper relative position to form the entire skeleton.
3. To differentiate between a male and a female pelvis.
4. To discuss the common features of the human appendicular girdles (pectoral and pelvic), and to note how their structure relates to their specialized functions.
5. To identify specific bone markings in the appendicular skeleton.

PRE-LAB QUIZ

1. The _____ skeleton is composed of 126 bones of the appendages and pectoral and pelvic girdles.
2. Circle the correct term. The <u>pectoral</u> / <u>pelvic</u> girdle attaches the upper limb to the axial skeleton.
3. The _____ or shoulder blades are generally triangular in shape. They have no direct attachment to the axial skeleton but are held in place by trunk muscles.
4. The arm consists of one long bone, the _____.
   a. femur   c. tibia
   b. humerus   d. ulna
5. The hand consists of three groups of bones. The carpals make up the wrist. The _____ make up the palm, and the phalanges make up the fingers.
6. You are studying a pelvis that is wide and shallow. The acetabula are small and far apart. The pubic arch/angle is rounded and greater than 90°. It appears to be tilted forward, with a wide, short sacrum. Is this a male or a female pelvis? _____
7. The strongest, heaviest bone of the body is in the thigh. It is the
   a. femur
   b. fibula
   c. tibia
8. The _____, or "knee cap," is a sesamoid bone that is enclosed in the quadriceps tendon. It guards the knee joint anteriorly and improves leverage of the thigh muscles acting across the knee joint.
9. Circle True or False. The fingers of the hand and the toes of the foot— with the exception of the great toe and the thumb—each have three phalanges.

myA&P For practice quizzes on this lab, go to www.myaandp.com.

PAL For access to anatomical models and more, check out Practice Anatomy Lab.

The **appendicular skeleton** (the gold-colored portion of Figure 9.1) is composed of the 126 bones of the appendages and the pectoral and pelvic girdles, which attach the limbs to the axial skeleton. Although the upper and lower limbs differ in their functions and mobility, they have the same fundamental plan, with each limb composed of three major segments connected together by freely movable joints.

Examining and Identifying Bones of the Appendicular Skeleton

Carefully examine each of the bones described throughout this exercise and identify the characteristic bone markings of each. The markings aid in determining whether a bone is the right or left member of its pair; for example, the glenoid cavity is on the lateral aspect of the scapula and the spine is on its posterior aspect. *This is a very important instruction because you will be constructing your own skeleton to finish this laboratory exercise.* Additionally, when corresponding X rays are available, compare the actual bone specimen to its X-ray image. ▬

Bones of the Pectoral Girdle and Upper Limb

The Pectoral (Shoulder) Girdle

The paired **pectoral,** or **shoulder, girdles** (Figure 11.1) each consist of two bones—the anterior clavicle and the posterior scapula. The shoulder girdles function to attach the upper limbs to the axial skeleton and provide attachment points for many trunk and neck muscles.

The **clavicle,** or collarbone, is a slender doubly curved bone—convex forward on its medial two-thirds and concave laterally. Its *sternal* (medial) *end,* which attaches to the sternal manubrium, is rounded or triangular in cross section. The sternal end projects above the manubrium and can be felt and (usually) seen forming the lateral walls of the *jugular notch* (see Figure 10.17, page 137). The *acromial* (lateral) *end* of the clavicle is flattened where it articulates with the scapula to form part of the shoulder joint. On its posteroinferior surface is the prominent **conoid tubercle** (Figure 11.2b). This projection anchors a ligament and provides a handy landmark for determining whether a given clavicle is from the right or left side of the body. The clavicle serves as an anterior brace, or strut, to hold the arm away from the top of the thorax.

The **scapulae** (Figure 11.2c–e), or shoulder blades, are generally triangular and are commonly called the "wings" of humans. Each scapula has a flattened body and two important processes—the **acromion** (the enlarged, roughened end of the spine of the scapula) and the beaklike **coracoid process** (*corac* = crow, raven). The acromion connects with the clavicle; the coracoid process points anteriorly over the tip of the shoulder joint and serves as an attachment point for some of the upper limb muscles. The **suprascapular notch** at the base of the coracoid process allows nerves to pass. The scapula has no direct attachment to the axial skeleton but is loosely held in place by trunk muscles.

The scapula has three angles: superior, inferior, and lateral. The inferior angle provides a landmark for auscultating (listening to) lung sounds. The **glenoid cavity,** a shallow socket that receives the head of the arm bone (humerus), is located in the blunted lateral angle. The scapula also has three named borders: superior, medial (vertebral), and lateral (axillary). Several shallow depressions (fossae) appear on both sides of the scapula and are named according to location; there are the anterior *subscapular fossa* and the posterior *infraspinous* and *supraspinous fossae.*

FIGURE 11.1 Articulated bones of the pectoral (shoulder) girdle. The right pectoral girdle is articulated to show the relationship of the girdle to the bones of the thorax and arm.

The shoulder girdle is exceptionally light and allows the upper limb a degree of mobility not seen anywhere else in the body. This is due to the following factors:

- The sternoclavicular joints are the *only* site of attachment of the shoulder girdles to the axial skeleton.

- The relative looseness of the scapular attachment allows it to slide back and forth against the thorax with muscular activity.

- The glenoid cavity is shallow and does little to stabilize the shoulder joint.

However, this exceptional flexibility exacts a price: the arm bone (humerus) is very susceptible to dislocation, and fracture of the clavicle disables the entire upper limb.

The Arm

The arm (Figure 11.3) consists of a single bone—the **humerus,** a typical long bone. Proximally its rounded *head* fits into the shallow glenoid cavity of the scapula. The head is separated from the shaft by the *anatomical neck* and the more constricted *surgical neck,* which is a common site of fracture. Opposite the head are two prominences, the **greater** and **lesser tubercles** (from lateral to medial aspect), separated by

Text continues on page 148.

(a) **Right clavicle, superior view**

Acromial (lateral) end
Sternal (medial) end
Posterior
Anterior

(b) **Right clavicle, inferior view**

Acromial end
Anterior
Sternal end
Conoid tubercle
Posterior

Supraspinous fossa
Infraspinous fossa
Subscapular fossa
Posterior
Anterior

(c) **Right scapula, anterior aspect**

Acromion
Suprascapular notch
Superior border
Superior angle
Coracoid process
Glenoid cavity in lateral angle
Lateral border
Subscapular fossa
Medial border
Inferior angle

(d) **Right scapula, posterior aspect**

Suprascapular notch
Coracoid process
Acromion
Superior angle
Supraspinous fossa
Spine
Infraspinous fossa
Medial border
Lateral border
Inferior angle

(e) **Right scapula, lateral aspect**

Supraspinous fossa
Acromion
Coracoid process
Glenoid cavity
Infraspinous fossa
Infraglenoid tubercle
Subscapular fossa

FIGURE 11.2 Individual bones of the pectoral (shoulder) girdle. View **(e)** is accompanied by a schematic representation of its orientation.

FIGURE 11.3 Bone of the right arm. Humerus in **(a)** anterior view, **(b)** posterior view. Detailed views illustrate **(c)** anterior and **(d)** posterior extended elbow.

a groove (the **intertubercular sulcus,** or **bicipital groove**) that guides the tendon of the biceps muscle to its point of attachment (the superior rim of the glenoid cavity). In the midpoint of the shaft is a roughened area, the **deltoid tuberosity,** where the large fleshy shoulder muscle, the deltoid, attaches. Nearby, the **radial groove** runs obliquely, indicating the pathway of the radial nerve.

At the distal end of the humerus are two condyles—the medial **trochlea** (looking rather like a spool), which articulates with the ulna, and the lateral **capitulum,** which articulates with the radius of the forearm. This condyle pair is flanked medially by the **medial epicondyle** and laterally by the **lateral epicondyle.**

The medial epicondyle is commonly called the "funny bone." The ulnar nerve runs in a groove beneath the medial epicondyle, and when this region is sharply bumped, we are likely to experience a temporary, but excruciatingly painful, tingling sensation. This event is called "hitting the funny bone," a strange expression, because it is certainly *not* funny!

Above the trochlea on the anterior surface is the **coronoid fossa;** on the posterior surface is the **olecranon fossa.** These two depressions allow the corresponding processes of the ulna to move freely when the elbow is flexed and extended. The small **radial fossa,** lateral to the coronoid fossa, receives the head of the radius when the elbow is flexed.

The Forearm

Two bones, the radius and the ulna, compose the skeleton of the forearm, or antebrachium (see Figure 11.4). When the body is in the anatomical position, the **radius** is in the lateral position in the forearm, and the radius and ulna are parallel. Proximally, the disc-shaped head of the radius articulates with the capitulum of the humerus. Just below the head, on the medial aspect of the shaft, is a prominence called the **radial tuberosity,** the point of attachment for the tendon of the biceps muscle of the arm. Distally, the small **ulnar notch** reveals where it articulates with the end of the ulna.

(c) **Proximal portion of ulna, lateral view**

(d) **Distal ends of the radius and ulna at the wrist, anteroinferior view**

(a) **Anterior view**   (b) **Posterior view**

FIGURE 11.4 Bones of the right forearm. Radius and ulna in **(a)** anterior view, **(b)** posterior view. Structural details in **(c)** and **(d)** illustrate articular surfaces between these bones and between radius and bones of the wrist.

The **ulna** is the medial bone of the forearm. Its proximal end bears the anterior **coronoid process** and the posterior **olecranon process,** which are separated by the **trochlear notch.** Together these processes grip the trochlea of the humerus in a plierslike joint. The small **radial notch** on the lateral side of the coronoid process articulates with the head of the radius. The slimmer distal end, the ulnar **head,** bears a small medial **styloid process,** which serves as a point of attachment for the ligaments of the wrist.

The Hand

The skeleton of the hand, or manus (Figure 11.5), includes three groups of bones, those of the carpus (wrist), the metacarpals (bones of the palm), and the phalanges (bones of the fingers).

The wrist is the proximal portion of the hand. It is referred to anatomically as the **carpus;** the eight bones composing it are the **carpals.** (So you actually wear your wristwatch over the distal part of your forearm.) The carpals are arranged in two irregular rows of four bones each, which are illustrated in Figure 11.5. In the proximal row (lateral to medial) are the *scaphoid, lunate, triquetral,* and *pisiform bones;* the scaphoid and lunate articulate with the distal end of the radius. In the distal row are the *trapezium, trapezoid,*

capitate, and *hamate.* The carpals are bound closely together by ligaments, which restrict movements between them.

The **metacarpals,** numbered 1 to 5 from the thumb side of the hand toward the little finger, radiate out from the wrist like spokes to form the palm of the hand. The *bases* of the metacarpals articulate with the carpals of the wrist; their more bulbous *heads* articulate with the phalanges of the fingers distally. When the fist is clenched, the heads of the metacarpals become prominent as the knuckles.

Like the bones of the palm, the fingers are numbered from 1 to 5, beginning from the thumb *(pollex)* side of the hand. The 14 bones of the fingers, or digits, are miniature long bones, called **phalanges** (singular: *phalanx*) as noted above. Each finger contains three phalanges (proximal, middle, and distal) except the thumb, which has only two (proximal and distal).

ACTIVITY 2

Palpating the Surface Anatomy of the Pectoral Girdle and the Upper Limb

Before continuing on to study the bones of the pelvic girdle, take the time to identify the following bone markings on the

FIGURE 11.5 Bones of the left hand. (a) Posterior view showing the relationships of the carpals, metacarpals, and phalanges. The pisiform bone is obscured by the triquetrum. **(b)** X ray. White bar on the proximal phalanx of the left ring finger shows the position at which a ring would be worn.

skin surface of the upper limb. It is usually preferable to palpate the bone markings on your lab partner since many of these markings can only be seen from the dorsal aspect.

• Clavicle: Palpate the clavicle along its entire length from sternum to shoulder.

• Acromioclavicular joint: The high point of the shoulder, which represents the junction point between the clavicle and the acromion of the scapular spine.

• Spine of the scapula: Extend your arm at the shoulder so that your scapula moves posteriorly. As you do this, your scapular spine will be seen as a winglike protrusion on your dorsal thorax and can be easily palpated by your lab partner.

• Lateral epicondyle of the humerus: The inferiormost projection at the lateral aspect of the distal humerus. After you have located the epicondyle, run your finger posteriorly into the hollow immediately dorsal to the epicondyle. This is the site where the extensor muscles of the hand are attached and is a common site of the excruciating pain of tennis elbow, a condition in which those muscles and their tendons are abused physically.

• Medial epicondyle of the humerus: Feel this medial projection at the distal end of the humerus.

• Olecranon process of the ulna: Work your elbow—flexing and extending—as you palpate its dorsal aspect to feel the olecranon process of the ulna moving into and out of the olecranon fossa on the dorsal aspect of the humerus.

• Styloid process of the ulna: With the hand in the anatomical position, feel out this small inferior projection on the medial aspect of the distal end of the ulna.

• Styloid process of the radius: Find this projection at the distal end of the radius (lateral aspect). It is most easily located by moving the hand medially at the wrist. Once you have palpated the styloid process, move your fingers just medially onto the anterior wrist. Press firmly and then let up slightly on the pressure. You should be able to feel your pulse at this pressure point, which lies over the radial artery (radial pulse).

• Pisiform: Just distal to the styloid process of the ulna, feel the rounded pealike pisiform bone.

• Metacarpophalangeal joints (knuckles): Clench your fist and find the first set of flexed-joint protrusions beyond the wrist—these are your metacarpophalangeal joints. ▬

Bones of the Pelvic Girdle and Lower Limb

The Pelvic (Hip) Girdle

As with the bones of the pectoral girdle and upper limb, pay particular attention to bone markings needed to identify right and left bones.

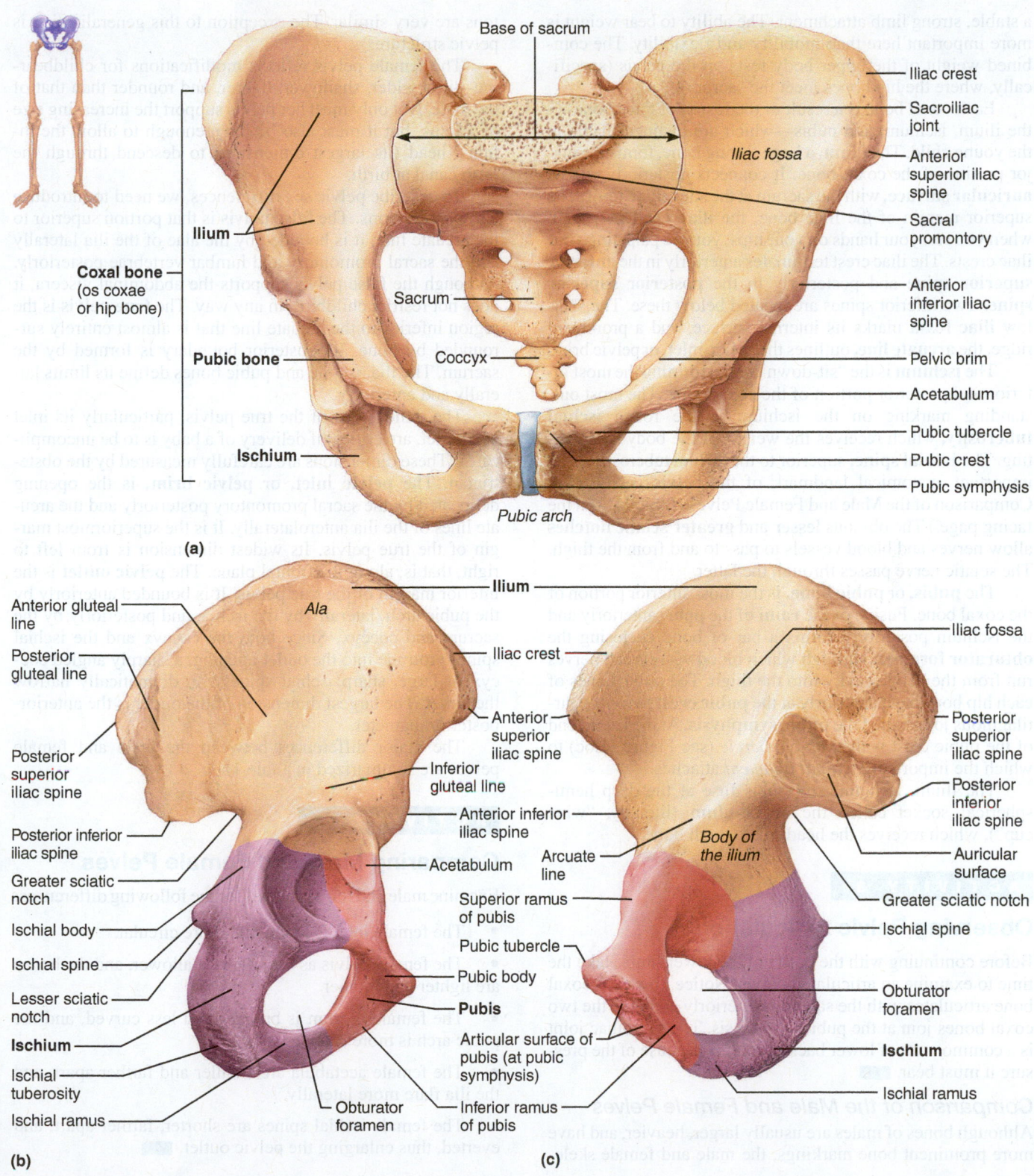

FIGURE 11.6 Bones of the pelvic girdle. (a) Articulated bony pelvis, showing the two hip bones (coxal bones), which together comprise the pelvic girdle, the sacrum, and the coccyx. **(b)** Right hip bone, lateral view, showing the point of fusion of the ilium, ischium, and pubic bones. **(c)** Right hip bone, medial view.

The **pelvic girdle**, or **hip girdle** (Figure 11.6), is formed by the two **coxal** (*coxa* = hip) **bones** (also called the **ossa coxae**, or hip bones). The two coxal bones together with the sacrum and coccyx form the **bony pelvis.** In contrast to the

bones of the shoulder girdle, those of the pelvic girdle are heavy and massive, and they attach securely to the axial skeleton. The sockets for the heads of the femurs (thigh bones) are deep and heavily reinforced by ligaments to ensure a stable, strong limb attachment. The ability to bear weight is more important here than mobility and flexibility. The combined weight of the upper body rests on the pelvis (specifically, where the hip bones meet the sacrum).

Each coxal bone is a result of the fusion of three bones—the ilium, ischium, and pubis—which are distinguishable in the young child. The **ilium,** a large flaring bone, forms the major portion of the coxal bone. It connects posteriorly, via its **auricular surface,** with the sacrum at the **sacroiliac joint.** The superior margin of the iliac bone, the **iliac crest,** is rough; when you rest your hands on your hips, you are palpating your iliac crests. The iliac crest terminates anteriorly in the **anterior superior spine** and posteriorly in the **posterior superior spine.** Two inferior spines are located below these. The shallow **iliac fossa** marks its internal surface, and a prominent ridge, the **arcuate line,** outlines the pelvic inlet, or pelvic brim.

The **ischium** is the "sit-down" bone, forming the most inferior and posterior portion of the coxal bone. The most outstanding marking on the ischium is the rough **ischial tuberosity,** which receives the weight of the body when sitting. The **ischial spine,** superior to the ischial tuberosity, is an important anatomical landmark of the pelvic cavity. (See Comparison of the Male and Female Pelves, Table 11.1 on the facing page.) The obvious **lesser** and **greater sciatic notches** allow nerves and blood vessels to pass to and from the thigh. The sciatic nerve passes through the latter.

The **pubis,** or **pubic bone,** is the most anterior portion of the coxal bone. Fusion of the **rami** of the pubis anteriorly and the ischium posteriorly forms a bar of bone enclosing the **obturator foramen,** through which blood vessels and nerves run from the pelvic cavity into the thigh. The pubic bones of each hip bone meet anteriorly at the **pubic crest** to form a cartilaginous joint called the **pubic symphysis.** At the lateral end of the pubic crest is the *pubic tubercle* (see Figure 11.6c) to which the important *inguinal ligament* attaches.

The ilium, ischium, and pubis fuse at the deep hemispherical socket called the **acetabulum** (literally, "wine cup"), which receives the head of the thigh bone.

ACTIVITY 3

Observing Pelvic Articulations

Before continuing with the bones of the lower limbs, take the time to examine an articulated pelvis. Notice how each coxal bone articulates with the sacrum posteriorly and how the two coxal bones join at the pubic symphysis. The sacroiliac joint is a common site of lower back problems because of the pressure it must bear. ■

Comparison of the Male and Female Pelves

Although bones of males are usually larger, heavier, and have more prominent bone markings, the male and female skeletons are very similar. The exception to this generalization is pelvic structure.

The female pelvis reflects modifications for childbearing—it is wider, shallower, lighter, and rounder than that of the male. Not only must her pelvis support the increasing size of a fetus, but it must also be large enough to allow the infant's head (its largest dimension) to descend through the birth canal at birth.

To describe pelvic sex differences, we need to introduce a few more terms. The **false pelvis** is that portion superior to the arcuate line; it is bounded by the alae of the ilia laterally and the sacral promontory and lumbar vertebrae posteriorly. Although the false pelvis supports the abdominal viscera, it does not restrict childbirth in any way. The **true pelvis** is the region inferior to the arcuate line that is almost entirely surrounded by bone. Its posterior boundary is formed by the sacrum. The ilia, ischia, and pubic bones define its limits laterally and anteriorly.

The dimensions of the true pelvis, particularly its inlet and outlet, are critical if delivery of a baby is to be uncomplicated. These dimensions are carefully measured by the obstetrician. The **pelvic inlet,** or **pelvic brim,** is the opening delineated by the sacral promontory posteriorly and the arcuate lines of the ilia anterolaterally. It is the superiormost margin of the true pelvis. Its widest dimension is from left to right, that is, along the frontal plane. The **pelvic outlet** is the inferior margin of the true pelvis. It is bounded anteriorly by the pubic arch, laterally by the ischia, and posteriorly by the sacrum and coccyx. Since both the coccyx and the ischial spines protrude into the outlet opening, a sharply angled coccyx or large, sharp ischial spines can dramatically narrow the outlet. The largest dimension of the outlet is the anterior-posterior diameter.

The major differences between the male and female pelves are summarized in Table 11.1.

ACTIVITY 4

Comparing Male and Female Pelves

Examine male and female pelves for the following differences:

• The female inlet is larger and more circular.

• The female pelvis as a whole is shallower, and the bones are lighter and thinner.

• The female sacrum is broader and less curved, and the pubic arch is more rounded.

• The female acetabula are smaller and farther apart, and the ilia flare more laterally.

• The female ischial spines are shorter, farther apart, and everted, thus enlarging the pelvic outlet. ■

Text continues on page 154.

TABLE 11.1	Comparison of the Male and Female Pelves	
Characteristic	**Female**	**Male**
General structure and functional modifications	Tilted forward; adapted for childbearing; true pelvis defines the birth canal; cavity of the true pelvis is broad, shallow, and has a greater capacity	Tilted less far forward; adapted for support of a male's heavier build and stronger muscles; cavity of the true pelvis is narrow and deep
Bone thickness	Less; bones lighter, thinner, and smoother	Greater; bones heavier and thicker, and markings are more prominent
Acetabula	Smaller; farther apart	Larger; closer
Pubic angle/arch	Broader (80°–90°); more rounded	More acute (50°–60°)
Anterior view		
Sacrum	Wider; shorter; sacrum is less curved	Narrow; longer; sacral promontory more ventral
Coccyx	More movable; straighter	Less movable; curves ventrally
Left lateral view		
Pelvic inlet (brim)	Wider; oval from side to side	Narrow; basically heart shaped
Pelvic outlet	Wider; ischial spines shorter, farther apart, and everted	Narrower; ischial spines longer, sharper, and point more medially
Posteroinferior view		

FIGURE 11.7 Bones of the right knee and thigh. (a) The patella (kneecap). **(b)** The femur (thigh bone).

The Thigh

The **femur,** or thigh bone (Figure 11.7b), is the sole bone of the thigh. It is the heaviest, strongest bone in the body. The ball-like head of the femur articulates with the hip bone via the deep, secure socket of the acetabulum. Obvious in the femur's head is a small central pit called the **fovea capitis** ("pit of the head"), from which a small ligament runs to the acetabulum. The head of the femur is carried on a short, constricted *neck,* which angles laterally to join the shaft. The neck is the weakest part of the femur and is a common fracture site (an injury called a broken hip), particularly in the elderly. At the junction of the shaft and neck are the **greater** and **lesser trochanters** (separated posteriorly by the **intertrochanteric crest** and anteriorly by the **intertrochanteric line**). The trochanters and trochanteric crest, as well as the **gluteal tuberosity** and the **linea aspera** located on the shaft, are sites of muscle attachment.

The femur inclines medially as it runs downward to the leg bones; this brings the knees in line with the body's center of gravity, or maximum weight. The medial course of the femur is more noticeable in females because of the wider female pelvis.

Distally, the femur terminates in the **lateral** and **medial condyles,** which articulate with the tibia below, and the **patellar surface,** which forms a joint with the patella (kneecap) anteriorly. The **lateral** and **medial epicondyles,** just superior to the condyles, are separated by the **intercondylar fossa.** On the superior part of the medial epicondyle is a bump, the **adductor tubercle,** to which the large adductor magnus muscle attaches.

The **patella** (Figure 11.7a) is a triangular sesamoid bone enclosed in the (quadriceps) tendon that secures the anterior thigh muscles to the tibia. It guards the knee joint anteriorly and improves the leverage of the thigh muscles acting across the knee joint.

FIGURE 11.8 Bones of the right leg. Tibia and fibula, anterior view on left; posterior view on right.

Labels in figure:
- Intercondylar eminence
- Lateral condyle
- Head
- Proximal tibiofibular joint
- Articular surface of medial condyle
- Medial condyle
- Tibial tuberosity
- Interosseous membrane
- Anterior border
- Fibula
- Tibia
- Distal tibiofibular joint
- Lateral malleolus
- Medial malleolus
- Articular surface
- **(a) Anterior view**
- Articular surface of lateral condyle
- Head of fibula
- Fibula
- Lateral malleolus
- **(b) Posterior view**

The Leg

Two bones, the tibia and the fibula, form the skeleton of the leg (see Figure 11.8). The **tibia,** or *shinbone,* is the larger and more medial of the two leg bones. At the proximal end, the **medial** and **lateral condyles** (separated by the **intercondylar eminence**) receive the distal end of the femur to form the knee joint. The **tibial tuberosity,** a roughened protrusion on the anterior tibial surface (just below the condyles), is the site of attachment of the patellar (kneecap) ligament. Small facets on the superior and inferior surface of the lateral condyle of the tibia articulate with the fibula. Distally, a process called the **medial malleolus** forms the inner (medial) bulge of the ankle. The more medial articular surface of the tibia articulates with the talus bone of the foot. The anterior surface of the tibia bears a sharpened ridge that is relatively unprotected by muscles. This so-called **anterior border** is easily felt beneath the skin.

The **fibula,** which lies parallel to the tibia, takes no part in forming the knee joint. Its proximal head articulates with the lateral condyle of the tibia. The fibula is thin and sticklike with a sharp anterior crest. It terminates distally in the **lateral malleolus,** which forms the outer part, or lateral bulge, of the ankle.

The Foot

The bones of the foot include the 7 **tarsal** bones, 5 **metatarsals,** which form the instep, and 14 **phalanges,** which form the toes (see Figure 11.9). Body weight is concentrated on the two largest tarsals, which form the posterior aspect of the foot. These are the *calcaneus* (heel bone) and the *talus,* which lies between the tibia and the calcaneus. The other tarsals are named and identified in Figure 11.9. The metatarsals are numbered 1 through 5, medial to lateral. Like the fingers of the hand, each toe has three phalanges except the great toe, which has two.

(a) Superior view

(b) Lateral view

FIGURE 11.9 Bones of the right foot. (a) Superior view. **(b)** Lateral view showing arches of the foot.

The bones in the foot are arranged to produce three strong arches—two longitudinal arches (medial and lateral) and one transverse arch (Figure 11.9b). Ligaments, binding the foot bones together, and tendons of the foot muscles hold the bones firmly in the arched position but still allow a certain degree of give. Weakened arches are referred to as fallen arches or flat feet.

ACTIVITY 5

Palpating the Surface Anatomy of the Pelvic Girdle and Lower Limb

Locate and palpate the following bone markings on yourself and/or your lab partner.

• Iliac crest and anterior superior iliac spine: Rest your hands on your hips—they will be overlying the iliac crests. Trace the crest as far posteriorly as you can and then follow it anteriorly to the anterior superior iliac spine. This latter bone marking is easily felt in almost everyone and is clearly visible through the skin (and perhaps the clothing) of very slim people. (The posterior superior iliac spine is much less obvious and is usually indicated only by a dimple in the overlying skin. Check it out in the mirror tonight.)

• Greater trochanter of the femur: This is easier to locate in females than in males because of the wider female pelvis; also it is more likely to be clothed by bulky muscles in males. Try to locate it on yourself as the most lateral point of the proximal femur. It typically lies about 6 to 8 inches below the iliac crest.

• Patella and tibial tuberosity: Feel your kneecap and palpate the ligaments attached to its borders. Follow the inferior patellar ligament to the tibial tuberosity.

• Medial and lateral condyles of the femur and tibia: As you move from the patella inferiorly on the medial (and then the lateral) knee surface, you will feel first the femoral and then the tibial condyle.

• Medial malleolus: Feel the medial protrusion of your ankle, the medial malleolus of the distal tibia.

• Lateral malleolus: Feel the bulge of the lateral aspect of your ankle, the lateral malleolus of the fibula.

• Calcaneus: Attempt to follow the extent of your calcaneus or heel bone. ▪

ACTIVITY 6

Constructing a Skeleton

1. When you finish examining yourself and the disarticulated bones of the appendicular skeleton, work with your lab partner to arrange the disarticulated bones on the laboratory bench in their proper relative positions to form an entire skeleton. Careful observation of bone markings should help you distinguish between right and left members of bone pairs.

2. When you believe that you have accomplished this task correctly, ask the instructor to check your arrangement to ensure that it is correct. If it is not, go to the articulated skeleton and check your bone arrangements. Also review the descriptions of the bone markings as necessary to correct your bone arrangement. ▪

NAME_____

LAB TIME/DATE _____

The Appendicular Skeleton

Bones of the Pectoral Girdle and Upper Limb

1. Match the bone names or markings in column B with the descriptions in column A.

Column A

_____ 1. raised area on lateral surface of humerus to which deltoid muscle attaches

_____ 2. arm bone

_____, _____, 3. bones of the shoulder girdle

_____, _____, 4. forearm bones

_____ 5. scapular region to which the clavicle connects

_____ 6. shoulder girdle bone that is unattached to the axial skeleton

_____ 7. shoulder girdle bone that articulates with and transmits forces to the bony thorax

_____ 8. depression in the scapula that articulates with the humerus

_____ 9. process above the glenoid cavity that permits muscle attachment

_____ 10. the "collarbone"

_____ 11. distal condyle of the humerus that articulates with the ulna

_____ 12. medial bone of forearm in anatomical position

_____ 13. rounded knob on the humerus; adjoins the radius

_____ 14. anterior depression, superior to the trochlea, that receives part of the ulna when the forearm is flexed

_____ 15. forearm bone involved in formation of the elbow joint

_____ 16. wrist bones

_____ 17. finger bones

_____ 18. heads of these bones form the knuckles

_____, _____, 19. bones that articulate with the clavicle

Column B

a. acromion

b. capitulum

c. carpals

d. clavicle

e. coracoid process

f. coronoid fossa

g. deltoid tuberosity

h. glenoid cavity

i. humerus

j. metacarpals

k. olecranon fossa

l. olecranon process

m. phalanges

n. radial tuberosity

o. radius

p. scapula

q. sternum

r. styloid process

s. trochlea

t. ulna

2. How is the arm held clear of the widest dimension of the thoracic cage?

_____

_____

3. What is the total number of phalanges in the hand? _____

4. What is the total number of carpals in the wrist? _____

Name the carpals (medial to lateral) in the proximal row. _____

In the distal row, they are (medial to lateral) _____

5. Using items from the list at the right, identify the anatomical landmarks and regions of the scapula.

(socket)

(fossa)

(fossa)

Key:

a. acromion

b. coracoid process

c. glenoid cavity

d. inferior angle

e. infraspinous fossa

f. lateral border

g. medial border

h. spine

i. superior angle

j. superior border

k. suprascapular notch

l. supraspinous fossa

6. Match the terms in the key with the appropriate leader lines on the drawings of the humerus and the radius and ulna. Also decide whether the bones shown are right or left bones and whether the view shown is an anterior or a posterior view.

(fossa)

Key:

a. anatomical neck

b. coronoid process

c. distal radioulnar joint

d. greater tubercle

e. head of humerus

f. head of radius

g. head of ulna

h. lateral epicondyle

i. medial epicondyle

j. olecranon fossa

k. olecranon process

l. proximal radioulnar joint

m. radial groove

n. radial notch

o. radial tuberosity

p. styloid process of radius

q. styloid process of ulna

r. surgical neck

s. trochlea

t. trochlear notch

Circle the correct term for each pair in parentheses:

The humerus is a (right/left) bone in (an anterior/a posterior) view. The radius and ulna are (right/left) bones in (an anterior/a posterior) view.

Bones of the Pelvic Girdle and Lower Limb

7. Compare the pectoral and pelvic girdles by choosing appropriate descriptive terms from the key.

Key: a. flexibility most important   d. insecure axial and limb attachments
       b. massive   e. secure axial and limb attachments
       c. lightweight   f. weight-bearing most important

Pectoral: _____, _____, _____ Pelvic: _____, _____, _____

8. What organs are protected, at least in part, by the pelvic girdle? _____

_____

9. Distinguish between the true pelvis and the false pelvis. _____

_____

_____

10. Use letters from the key to identify the bone markings on this illustration of an articulated pelvis. Make an educated guess as to whether the illustration shows a male or female pelvis and provide two reasons for your decision.

(fossa)

(socket)

Key:

a. acetabulum

b. ala of sacrum

c. anterior superior iliac spine

d. iliac crest

e. iliac fossa

f. ischial spine

g. pelvic brim

h. pubic crest

i. pubic symphysis

j. sacroiliac joint

k. sacrum

This is a _____ (female/male) pelvis because:

_____

_____

11. Deduce why the pelvic bones of a four-legged animal such as the cat or pig are much less massive than those of the human.

_____

_____

12. A person instinctively curls over his abdominal area in times of danger. Why? _____

_____

13. For what anatomical reason do many women appear to be slightly knock-kneed? _____

_____

How might this anatomical arrangement contribute to knee injuries in female athletes?

_____

14. What does *fallen arches* mean? _____

_____

15. Match the bone names and markings in column B with the descriptions in column A.

Column A

_____, _____ , and

_____ 1. fuse to form the coxal bone

_____ 2. "sit-down" bone of the coxal bone

_____ 3. point where the coxal bones join anteriorly

_____ 4. superiormost margin of the coxal bone

_____ 5. deep socket in the coxal bone that receives the head of the thigh bone

_____ 6. joint between axial skeleton and pelvic girdle

_____ 7. longest, strongest bone in body

_____ 8. thin lateral leg bone

_____ 9. heavy medial leg bone

_____, _____ 10. bones forming knee joint

_____ 11. point where the patellar ligament attaches

_____ 12. kneecap

_____ 13. shinbone

_____ 14. medial ankle projection

_____ 15. lateral ankle projection

_____ 16. largest tarsal bone

_____ 17. ankle bones

_____ 18. bones forming the instep of the foot

_____ 19. opening in hip bone formed by the pubic and ischial rami

_____ and _____ 20. sites of muscle attachment on the proximal femur

_____ 21. tarsal bone that "sits" on the calcaneus

_____ 22. weight-bearing bone of the leg

_____ 23. tarsal bone that articulates with the tibia

Column B

a. acetabulum

b. calcaneus

c. femur

d. fibula

e. gluteal tuberosity

f. greater and lesser trochanters

g. greater sciatic notch

h. iliac crest

i. ilium

j. ischial tuberosity

k. ischium

l. lateral malleolus

m. lesser sciatic notch

n. linea aspera

o. medial malleolus

p. metatarsals

q. obturator foramen

r. patella

s. pubic symphysis

t. pubis

u. sacroiliac joint

v. talus

w. tarsals

x. tibia

y. tibial tuberosity

16. Match the terms in the key with the appropriate leader lines on the drawings of the femur and the tibia and fibula. Also decide if these bones are right or left bones and whether the view shown is an anterior or a posterior view.

Key:

a. distal tibiofibular joint

b. fovea capitis

c. gluteal tuberosity

d. greater trochanter

e. head of femur

f. head of fibula

g. intercondylar eminence

h. intertrochanteric crest

i. lateral condyle

j. lateral epicondyle

k. lateral malleolus

l. lesser trochanter

m. medial condyle

n. medial epicondyle

o. medial malleolus

p. neck of femur

q. proximal tibiofibular joint

r. tibial anterior border

s. tibial tuberosity

Circle the correct term for each pair in parentheses:

The femur is a (right/left) bone in (an anterior/a posterior) view. The tibia and fibula are (right/left) bones in (an anterior/ a posterior) view.

Summary of Skeleton

17. Identify all indicated bones (or groups of bones) in the diagram of the articulated skeleton on page 163.

partial bone

tumporal bone

occiptal bone

sternum

true ribs

radis

ulna

corpals

metacarpals

ischium

patella

tibia

fibia

tarsals

frontal bone

maxilla

mandible

clavicle

scapula

humerus

vertebrae

felonges

femur

planter

metatarsals

digits

The Fetal Skeleton

MATERIALS

☐ Isolated fetal skull
☐ Fetal skeleton
☐ Adult skeleton

OBJECTIVES

1. To define *fontanel* and discuss the function and fate of fontanels in the fetus.
2. To demonstrate important differences between the fetal and adult skeletons.

myA&P *For practice quizzes on this lab, go to www.myaandp.com.*

PRE-LAB QUIZ

1. Circle the correct term. The fetal skeleton has <u>more</u> / <u>fewer</u> bones than the adult skeleton.
2. A fontanel
   a. is an indentation between bones of the fetal skull
   b. is a fibrous membrane
   c. allows for compression of the skull during birth
   d. all of the above
3. The fetal skull has _____ fontanel(s).
   a. 1   c. 3
   b. 2   d. 4 or more
4. Ossification is
   a. the process of bone formation
   b. the development of fontanels in the skull
   c. the process of red blood cell formation
   d. the process of white blood cell formation

A human fetus about to be born has 275 bones, many more than the 206 bones found in the adult skeleton. This is because many of the bones described as single bones in the adult skeleton (for example, the coxal bone, sternum, and sacrum) have not yet fully ossified and fused in the fetus.

ACTIVITY

Examining a Fetal Skeleton and Skull

1. Obtain a fetal skeleton or use Figure 12.1, and examine it carefully, noting differences between it and an adult skeleton. Pay particular attention to the vertebrae, sternum, frontal bone of the cranium, patellae (kneecaps), coxal bones, carpals and tarsals, and thoracic cage.

2. Obtain a fetal skull and study it carefully. Make observations as needed to answer the questions on page 166.

FIGURE 12.1 The fetal skeleton.
Anterior view.

(a) Superior view

(b) Left lateral view

(c) Anterior view

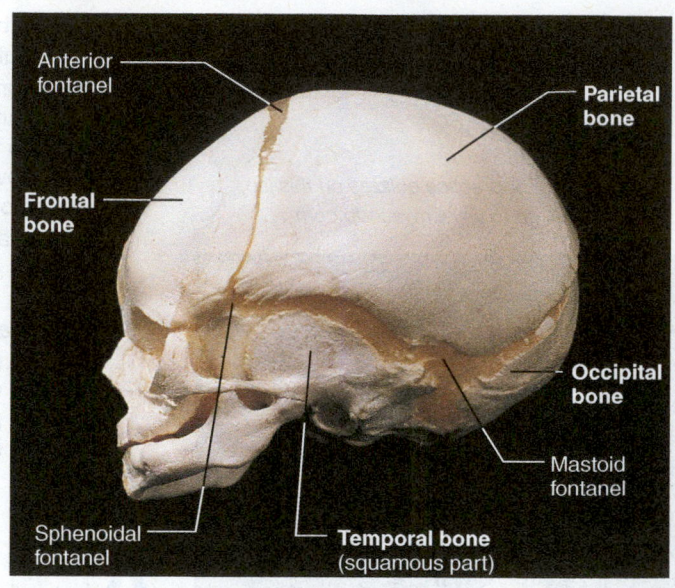

(d) Left lateral view

FIGURE 12.2 Skull of a newborn.

- Does it have the same bones as the adult skull?
- How does the size of the fetal face relate to the cranium?
- How does this compare to what is seen in the adult?

3. Indentations between the bones of the fetal skull, called **fontanels,** are fibrous membranes. These areas will become bony (ossify) as the infant ages, completing the process by the age of 20 to 22 months. The fontanels allow the fetal skull to be compressed slightly during birth and also allow for brain growth during late fetal life. Locate the following fontanels on the fetal skull with the aid of Figure 12.2: *anterior* (or *frontal*)

fontanel, mastoid fontanel, sphenoidal fontanel, and *posterior* (or *occipital*) *fontanel.*

4. Notice that some of the cranial bones have conical protrusions. These are **ossification (growth) centers.** Notice also that the frontal bone is still bipartite, and the temporal bone is incompletely ossified, little more than a ring of bone.

5. Before completing this study, check the questions on the review sheet at the end of this exercise to ensure that you have made all of the necessary observations. ◼

NAME_____

LAB TIME/DATE_____

The Fetal Skeleton

1. Are the same skull bones seen in the adult also found in the fetal skull? _____

2. How does the size of the fetal face compare to its cranium?_____

   _____

   How does this compare to the adult skull?_____

   _____

   _____

3. What are the outward conical projections on some of the fetal cranial bones?_____

4. What is a fontanel? _____

   What is its fate?_____

   What is the function of the fontanels in the fetal skull?_____

   _____

5. Describe how the fetal skeleton compares with the adult skeleton in the following areas:

   vertebrae:_____

   _____

   coxal bones:_____

   _____

   carpals and tarsals:_____

   sternum:_____

   frontal bone:_____

   patella:_____

   thoracic cage:_____

   _____

6. How does the size of the fetus's head compare to the size of its body?_____

_____

7. Using the terms listed, identify each of the fontanels shown on the fetal skull below.

Key:

a. anterior fontanel

b. mastoid fontanel

c. posterior fontanel

d. sphenoidal fontanel

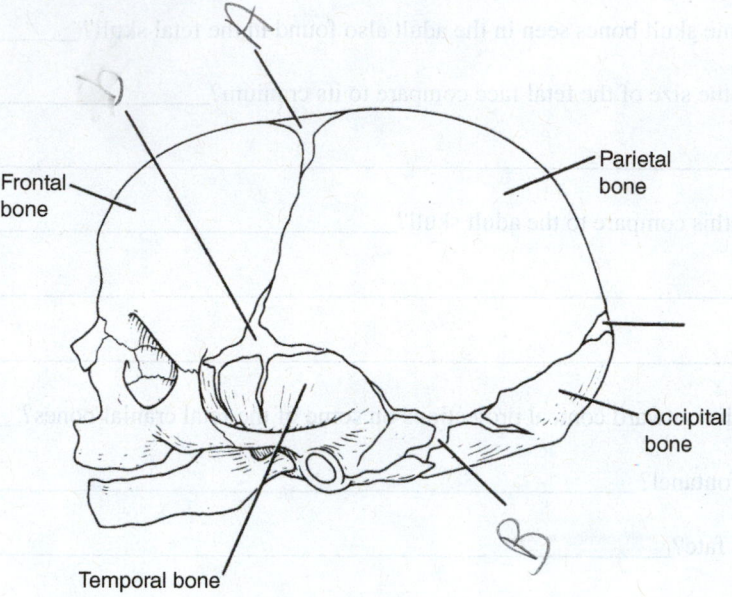

Articulations and Body Movements

MATERIALS

- ☐ Skull
- ☐ Articulated skeleton
- ☐ X ray of a child's bone showing the cartilaginous growth plate (if available)
- ☐ Anatomical chart of joint types (if available)
- ☐ Diarthrotic joint (fresh or preserved), preferably a beef knee joint sectioned sagittally (Alternatively, pig's feet with phalanges sectioned frontally could be used)
- ☐ Disposable gloves
- ☐ Water balloons and clamps
- ☐ Functional models of hip, knee, and shoulder joints (if available)
- ☐ X-rays of normal and arthritic joints (if available)

OBJECTIVES

1. To name and describe the three functional categories of joints.
2. To name and describe the three structural categories of joints, and to compare their structure and mobility.
3. To identify the types of synovial joints.
4. To define origin and insertion of muscles.
5. To demonstrate or identify the various body movements.

PRE-LAB QUIZ

1. Name one of the two functions of an articulation, or joint. _____
   _____

2. The functional classification of joints is based on
   a. a joint cavity
   b. amount of connective tissue
   c. amount of movement allowed by the joint

3. Structural classification of joints includes fibrous, cartilaginous, and _____, which have a fluid-filled cavity between articulating bones.

4. Circle the correct term. Sutures, which have their irregular edges of bone interlocked by short fibers of connective tissue, are an example of fibrous / cartilaginous joints.

5. Circle True or False. All synovial joints are diarthroses, or freely movable joints.

6. Circle the correct term. Every muscle of the body is attached to a bone or other connective tissue structure at two points. The origin / insertion is the more movable attachment.

7. The hip joint is an example of a _____ synovial joint.
   a. ball-and-socket   c. pivot
   b. hinge   d. plane

8. Movement of a limb *away* from the midline or median plane of the body in the frontal plane is known as
   a. abduction   c. extension
   b. eversion   d. rotation

9. Circle the correct term. This type of movement is common in ball-and-socket joints and can be described as the movement of a bone around its longitudinal axis. It is rotation / flexion.

10. Circle True or False. The knee joint is the most freely movable joint in the body.

myA&P *For practice quizzes on this lab, go to www.myaandp.com.*

PAL *For access to anatomical models and more, check out Practice Anatomy Lab.*

With rare exceptions, every bone in the body is connected to, or forms a joint with, at least one other bone. **Articulations,** or joints, perform two functions for the body. They (1) hold the bones together and (2) allow the rigid skeletal system some flexibility so that gross body movements can occur.

FIGURE 13.1 Types of joints. Joints to the left of the skeleton are cartilaginous joints; joints above and below the skeleton are fibrous joints; joints to the right of the skeleton are synovial joints. **(a)** Synchondrosis (joint between costal cartilage of rib 1 and the sternum). **(b)** Symphyses (intervertebral discs of fibrocartilage connecting adjacent vertebrae). **(c)** Symphysis (fibrocartilaginous pubic symphysis connecting the pubic bones anteriorly). **(d)** Suture (dense fibrous connective tissue connecting interlocking skull bones). **(e)** Syndesmosis (ligament of dense fibrous connective tissue connecting the distal ends of the tibia and fibula). **(f)** Synovial joint (multiaxial shoulder joint). **(g)** Synovial joint (uniaxial elbow joint). **(h)** Synovial joint (biaxial radiocarpal joint of the hand).

Joints may be classified structurally or functionally. The structural classification is based on the presence of connective tissue fiber, cartilage, or a joint cavity between the articulating bones. Structurally, there are *fibrous, cartilaginous,* and *synovial joints.*

The functional classification focuses on the amount of movement allowed at the joint. On this basis, there are **synarthroses,** or immovable joints; **amphiarthroses,** or slightly movable joints; and **diarthroses,** or freely movable joints. Freely movable joints predominate in the limbs, whereas immovable and slightly movable joints are largely restricted to the axial skeleton, where firm bony attachments and protection of enclosed organs are priorities.

As a general rule, fibrous joints are immovable, and synovial joints are freely movable. Cartilaginous joints offer both rigid and slightly movable examples. Since the structural categories are more clear-cut, we will use the structural classification here and indicate functional properties as appropriate.

Fibrous Joints

In **fibrous joints,** the bones are joined by fibrous tissue. No joint cavity is present. The amount of movement allowed depends on the length of the fibers uniting the bones. Although some fibrous joints are slightly movable, most are synarthrotic and permit virtually no movement.

The two major types of fibrous joints are sutures and syndesmoses. In **sutures** (Figure 13.1d) the irregular edges of the bones interlock and are united by very short connective tissue fibers, as in most joints of the skull. In **syndesmoses** the articulating bones are connected by short ligaments of dense fibrous tissue; the bones do not interlock. The joint at the distal end of the tibia and fibula is an example of a syndesmosis (Figure 13.1e). Although this syndesmosis allows some give, it is classed functionally as a synarthrosis. Not illustrated here is a **gomphosis,** in which a tooth is secured in a bony socket by the periodontal ligament (see Figure 38.12).

ACTIVITY 1

Identifying Fibrous Joints

Examine a human skull again. Notice that adjacent bone surfaces do not actually touch but are separated by fibrous connective tissue. Also examine a skeleton and anatomical chart of joint types and Table 13.1 (pp. 176–177) for examples of fibrous joints. ▄▄▄

Cartilaginous Joints

In **cartilaginous joints,** the articulating bone ends are connected by a plate or pad of cartilage. No joint cavity is present. The two major types of cartilaginous joints are synchondroses and symphyses. Although there is variation, most cartilaginous joints are *slightly movable* (amphiarthrotic) functionally. In **symphyses** (*symphysis* = a growing together), the bones are connected by a broad, flat disc of fibrocartilage. The intervertebral joints and the pubic symphysis of the pelvis are symphyses (see Figure 13.1b and c). In **synchondroses** the bony portions are united by hyaline cartilage. The articulation of the costal cartilage of the first rib with the sternum (Figure 13.1a) is a synchondrosis, but perhaps the best examples of synchon-

droses are the epiphyseal plates seen in the long bones of growing children. View an X ray of the cartilaginous growth plate (epiphyseal disc) of a child's bone if one is available. The epiphyseal plates are flexible during childhood, but eventually they are totally ossified.

ACTIVITY 2

Identifying Cartilaginous Joints

Identify the cartilaginous joints on a human skeleton, Table 13.1, and on an anatomical chart of joint types. ▄▄▄

Synovial Joints

Synovial joints are those in which the articulating bone ends are separated by a joint cavity containing synovial fluid (see Figure 13.1f–h). All synovial joints are diarthroses, or freely movable joints. Their mobility varies, however; some synovial joints can move in only one plane, and others can move in several directions (multiaxial movement). Most joints in the body are synovial joints.

All synovial joints have the following structural characteristics (Figure 13.2):

• The joint surfaces are enclosed by a two-layered *articular capsule* (a sleeve of connective tissue), creating a joint cavity.

- Periosteum
- Ligament
- Joint cavity (contains synovial fluid)
- Articular (hyaline) cartilage
- Fibrous capsule ⎱ Articular
- Synovial membrane ⎰ capsule

FIGURE 13.2 General structure of a synovial joint. The articulating bone ends are covered with articular cartilage, and enclosed within an articular capsule that is typically reinforced by ligaments externally. Internally the fibrous capsule is lined with a smooth synovial membrane that secretes synovial fluid.

a Plane joint (intercarpal joint)

b Hinge joint (elbow joint)

c Pivot joint (proximal radioulnar joint)

d Condyloid joint (metacarpophalangeal joint)

e Saddle joint (carpometacarpal joint of thumb)

f Ball-and-socket joint (shoulder joint)

Nonaxial
Uniaxial
Biaxial
Multiaxial

FIGURE 13.3 Types of synovial joints. Dashed lines indicate the articulating bones.

- The inner layer is a smooth connective tissue membrane, called the *synovial membrane,* which produces a lubricating fluid (synovial fluid) that reduces friction. The outer layer, or *fibrous capsule,* is dense irregular connective tissue.

- *Articular* (hyaline) *cartilage* covers the surfaces of the bones forming the joint.

- The articular capsule is typically reinforced with ligaments and may contain *bursae* (fluid-filled sacs that reduce friction where tendons cross bone).

- Fibrocartilage pads *(articular discs)* may be present within the capsule.

ACTIVITY 3

Examining Synovial Joint Structure

Examine a beef or pig joint to identify the general structural features of diarthrotic joints as listed above.

⚠️ If the joint is freshly obtained from the slaughterhouse and you will be handling it, don disposable gloves before beginning your observations. ▬

ACTIVITY 4

Demonstrating the Importance of Friction-Reducing Structures

1. Obtain a small water balloon and clamp. Partially fill the balloon with water (it should still be flaccid), and clamp it closed.

2. Position the balloon atop one of your fists and press down on its top surface with the other fist. Push on the balloon until your two fists touch and move your fists back and forth over one another. Assess the amount of friction generated.

3. Unclamp the balloon and add more water. The goal is to get just enough water in the balloon so that your fists cannot come into contact with one another, but instead remain separated by a thin water layer when pressure is applied to the balloon.

4. Repeat the movements in step 2 to assess the amount of friction generated.

How does the presence of a sac containing fluid influence the amount of friction generated?

_____

_____

What anatomical structure(s) does the water-containing balloon mimic?

_____

_____

What anatomical structures might be represented by your fists?

_____

Types of Synovial Joints

Because there are so many types of synovial joints, they have been divided into the following subcategories on the basis of movements allowed (Figure 13.3):

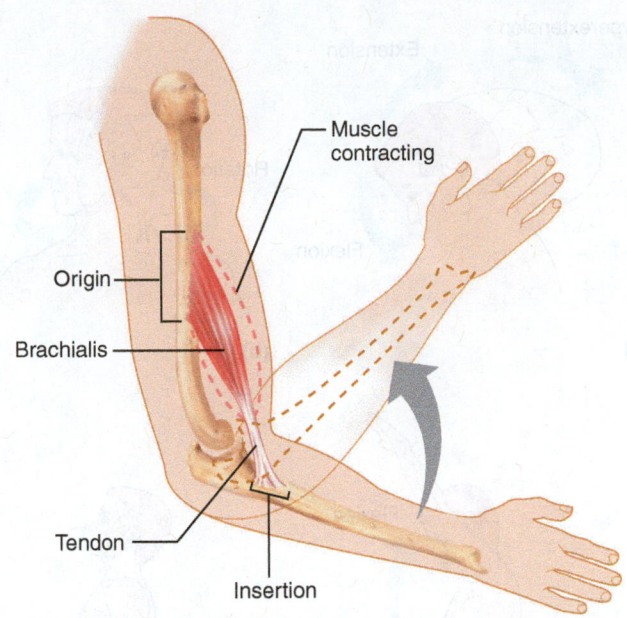

FIGURE 13.4 Muscle attachments (origin and insertion). When a skeletal muscle contracts, its insertion moves toward its origin.

- Plane (Gliding): Articulating surfaces are flat or slightly curved, allowing sliding movements in one or two planes. Examples are the intercarpal and intertarsal joints and the vertebrocostal joints of ribs 2–7.

- Hinge: The rounded process of one bone fits into the concave surface of another to allow movement in one plane (uniaxial), usually flexion and extension. Examples are the elbow and interphalangeal joints.

- Pivot: The rounded or conical surface of one bone articulates with a shallow depression or foramen in another bone. Pivot joints allow uniaxial rotation, as in the proximal radioulnar joint and the joint between the atlas and axis (C_1 and C_2).

- Condyloid (Ellipsoidal): The oval condyle of one bone fits into an ellipsoidal depression in another bone, allowing biaxial (two-way) movement. The radiocarpal (wrist) joint and the metacarpophalangeal joints (knuckles) are examples.

- Saddle: Articulating surfaces are saddle-shaped; the articulating surface of one bone is convex, and the reciprocal surface is concave. Saddle joints, which are biaxial, include the joint between the thumb metacarpal and the trapezium of the wrist.

- Ball and socket: The ball-shaped head of one bone fits into a cuplike depression of another. These are multiaxial joints, allowing movement in all directions and pivotal rotation. Examples are the shoulder and hip joints.

Movements Allowed by Synovial Joints

Every muscle of the body is attached to bone (or other connective tissue structures) at two points—the **origin** (the stationary, immovable, or less movable attachment) and the **insertion** (the movable attachment). Body movement occurs when muscles contract across diarthrotic synovial joints (Figure 13.4). When the muscle contracts and its fibers shorten, the insertion moves toward the origin. The type of movement depends on the construction of the joint (uniaxial,

FIGURE 13.5 Movements occurring at synovial joints of the body. (a) Flexion and extension of the head. **(b)** Rotation of the head. **(c)** Flexion and extension of the knee and shoulder.

biaxial, or multiaxial) and on the placement of the muscle relative to the joint. The most common types of body movements are described below and illustrated in Figure 13.5.

Demonstrating Movements of Synovial Joints

Attempt to demonstrate each movement as you read through the following material:

Flexion (Figure 13.5a and c): A movement, generally in the sagittal plane, that decreases the angle of the joint and reduces

the distance between the two bones. Flexion is typical of hinge joints (bending the knee or elbow) but is also common at ball-and-socket joints (bending forward at the hip).

Extension (Figure 13.5a and c): A movement that increases the angle of a joint and the distance between two bones or parts of the body (straightening the knee or elbow); the opposite of flexion. If extension is greater than 180 degrees (bending the trunk backward), it is termed *hyperextension.*

Abduction (Figure 13.5d): Movement of a limb away from the midline or median plane of the body, generally on the frontal plane, or the fanning movement of fingers or toes when they are spread apart.

Adduction (Figure 13.5d): Movement of a limb toward the midline of the body or drawing the fingers or toes together; the opposite of abduction.

Rotation (Figure 13.5b and e): Movement of a bone around its longitudinal axis without lateral or medial displacement. Rotation, a common movement of ball-and-socket joints, also describes the movement of the atlas around the odontoid process of the axis.

Circumduction (Figure 13.5e): A combination of flexion, extension, abduction, and adduction commonly observed in ball-and-socket joints like the shoulder. The proximal end of the limb remains stationary, and the distal end moves in a circle. The limb as a whole outlines a cone. Condyloid and saddle joints also allow circumduction.

Pronation (Figure 13.5f): Movement of the palm of the hand from an anterior or upward-facing position to a posterior or downward-facing position. The distal end of the radius moves across the ulna.

Supination (Figure 13.5f): Movement of the palm from a posterior position to an anterior position (the anatomical position); the opposite of pronation. During supination, the radius and ulna are parallel.

The last four terms refer to movements of the foot:

Inversion (Figure 13.5g): A movement that results in the medial turning of the sole of the foot.

Eversion (Figure 13.5g): A movement that results in the lateral turning of the sole of the foot; the opposite of inversion.

Dorsiflexion (Figure 13.5h): A movement of the ankle joint in a dorsal direction (standing on one's heels).

Plantar flexion (Figure 13.5h): A movement of the ankle joint in which the foot is flexed downward (standing on one's toes or pointing the toes). ▬

Demonstrating Uniaxial, Biaxial, and Multiaxial Movements

Using the information gained in the previous activity, perform the following demonstrations and complete the three charts.

(d)

(e)

(f)

(g)

(h)

FIGURE 13.5 *(continued)*
(d) Abduction and adduction of the upper limb. **(e)** Circumduction of the upper limb and lateral and medial rotation of the lower limb around its long axis. **(f)** Supination and pronation of the forearm. **(g)** Eversion and inversion of the foot. **(h)** Dorsiflexion and plantar flexion of the foot.

1. Demonstrate movement at two joints that are uniaxial.

Name of joint	Movement allowed

2. Demonstrate movement at two joints that are biaxial.

Name of joint	Movement allowed	Movement allowed

3. Demonstrate movement at two joints that are multiaxial.

Name of joint	Movement allowed	Movement allowed	Movement allowed

TABLE 13.1	Structural and Functional Characteristics of Body Joints

Illustration	Joint	Articulating bones	Structural type*	Functional type; movements allowed
	Skull	Cranial and facial bones	Fibrous; suture	Synarthrotic; no movement
	Temporo-mandibular	Temporal bone of skull and mandible	Synovial; modified hinge† (contains articular disc)	Diarthrotic; gliding and uniaxial rotation; slight lateral movement, elevation, depression, protraction, and retraction of mandible
	Atlanto-occipital	Occipital bone of skull and atlas	Synovial; condyloid	Diarthrotic; biaxial; flexion, extension, lateral flexion, circumduction of head on neck
	Atlantoaxial	Atlas (C_1) and axis (C_2)	Synovial; pivot	Diarthrotic; uniaxial; rotation of the head
	Intervertebral	Between adjacent vertebral bodies	Cartilaginous; symphysis	Amphiarthrotic; slight movement
	Intervertebral	Between articular processes	Synovial; plane	Diarthrotic; gliding
	Vertebrocostal	Vertebrae (transverse processes or bodies) and ribs	Synovial; plane	Diarthrotic; gliding of ribs
	Sternoclavicular	Sternum and clavicle	Synovial; shallow saddle (contains articular disc)	Diarthrotic; multiaxial (allows clavicle to move in all axes)
	Sternocostal (first)	Sternum and rib 1	Cartilaginous; synchondrosis	Synarthrotic; no movement
	Sternocostal	Sternum and ribs 2–7	Synovial; double plane	Diarthrotic; gliding
	Acromio-clavicular	Acromion of scapula and clavicle	Synovial; plane (contains articular disc)	Diarthrotic; gliding and rotation of scapula on clavicle
	Shoulder (glenohumeral)	Scapula and humerus	Synovial; ball and socket	Diarthrotic; multiaxial; flexion, extension, abduction, adduction, circumduction, rotation of humerus
	Elbow	Ulna (and radius) with humerus	Synovial; hinge	Diarthrotic; uniaxial; flexion, extension of forearm
	Radioulnar (proximal)	Radius and ulna	Synovial; pivot	Diarthrotic; uniaxial; rotation of radius around long axis of forearm to allow pronation and supination
	Radioulnar (distal)	Radius and ulna	Synovial; pivot (contains articular disc)	Diarthrotic; uniaxial; rotation (radius moves around ulna in ulnar notch of radius)
	Wrist (radiocarpal)	Radius and proximal carpals	Synovial; condyloid	Diarthrotic; biaxial; flexion, extension, abduction, adduction, circumduction of hand
	Intercarpal	Adjacent carpals	Synovial; plane	Diarthrotic; gliding
	Carpometacarpal of digit 1 (thumb)	Carpal (trapezium) and metacarpal 1	Synovial; saddle	Diarthrotic; biaxial; flexion, extension, abduction, adduction, circumduction, opposition of metacarpal 1
	Carpometacarpal of digits 2–5	Carpal(s) and metacarpal(s)	Synovial; plane	Diarthrotic; gliding of metacarpals
	Knuckle (metacarpo-phalangeal)	Metacarpal and proximal phalanx	Synovial; condyloid	Diarthrotic; biaxial; flexion, extension, abduction, adduction, circumduction of fingers
	Finger (interphalangeal)	Adjacent phalanges	Synovial; hinge	Diarthrotic; uniaxial; flexion, extension of fingers

TABLE 13.1	*(continued)*			

Illustration	Joint	Articulating bones	Structural type*	Functional type; movements allowed
	Sacroiliac	Sacrum and coxal bone	Synovial; plane	Diarthrotic; little movement, slight gliding possible (more during pregnancy)
	Pubic symphysis	Pubic bones	Cartilaginous; symphysis	Amphiarthrotic; slight movement (enhanced during pregnancy)
	Hip (coxal)	Hip bone and femur	Synovial; ball and socket	Diarthrotic; multiaxial; flexion, extension, abduction, adduction, rotation, circumduction of thigh
	Knee (tibiofemoral)	Femur and tibia	Synovial; modified hinge† (contains articular discs)	Diarthrotic; biaxial; flexion, extension of leg, some rotation allowed
	Knee (femoropatellar)	Femur and patella	Synovial; plane	Diarthrotic; gliding of patella
	Tibiofibular (proximal)	Tibia and fibula (proximally)	Synovial; plane	Diarthrotic; gliding of fibula
	Tibiofibular (distal)	Tibia and fibula (distally)	Fibrous; syndesmosis	Synarthrotic; slight "give" during dorsiflexion
	Ankle	Tibia and fibula with talus	Synovial; hinge	Diarthrotic; uniaxial; dorsiflexion, and plantar flexion of foot
	Intertarsal	Adjacent tarsals	Synovial; plane	Diarthrotic; gliding; inversion and eversion of foot
	Tarsometatarsal	Tarsal(s) and metatarsal(s)	Synovial; plane	Diarthrotic; gliding of metatarsals
	Metatarso-phalangeal	Metatarsal and proximal phalanx	Synovial; condyloid	Diarthrotic; biaxial; flexion extension, abduction, adduction, circumduction of great toe
	Toe (interpha-langeal)	Adjacent phalanges	Synovial; hinge	Diarthrotic; uniaxial; flexion, extension of toes

***Fibrous joint** indicated by orange circles; **cartilaginous joints**, by blue circles; **synovial joints**, by purple circles.
†These modified hinge joints are structurally bicondylar.

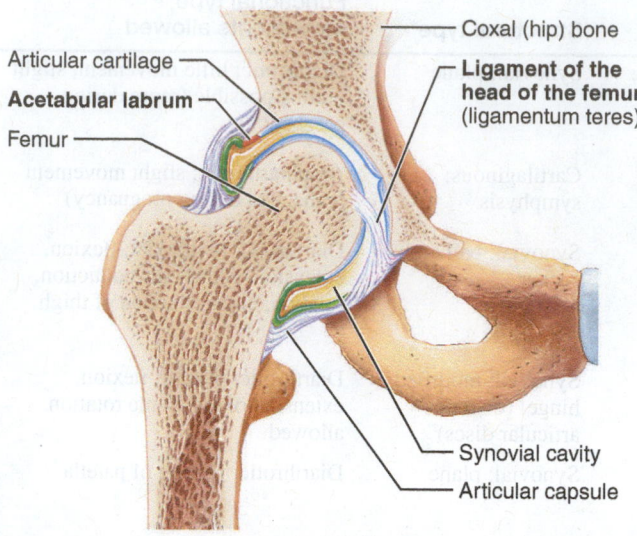

Coxal (hip) bone

Articular cartilage

Ligament of the head of the femur (ligamentum teres)

Acetabular labrum

Femur

Synovial cavity

Articular capsule

(a)

Anterior inferior iliac spine

Iliofemoral ligament

Pubofemoral ligament

Greater trochanter

(b)

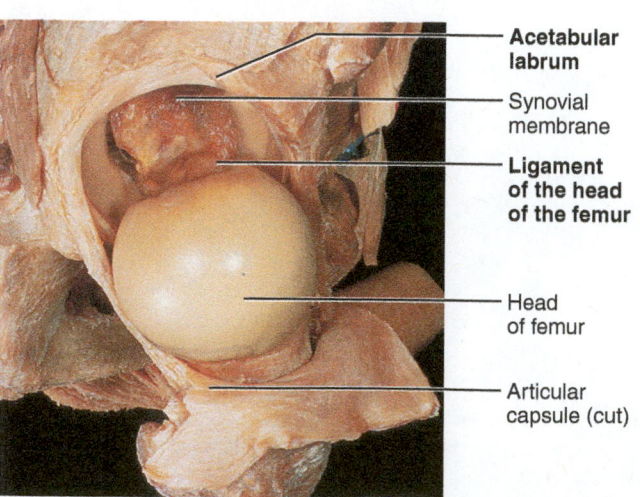

Acetabular labrum

Synovial membrane

Ligament of the head of the femur

Head of femur

Articular capsule (cut)

(c)

Selected Synovial Joints

Now you will have the opportunity to compare and contrast the structure of the hip and knee joints and to investigate the structure and movements of the temporomandibular joint and shoulder joint.

The Hip and Knee Joints

Both of these joints are large weight-bearing joints of the lower limb, but they differ substantially in their security. Read through the brief descriptive material below, and look at the questions in the review sheet at the end of this exercise before beginning your comparison.

The Hip Joint

The hip joint is a ball-and-socket joint, so movements can occur in all possible planes. However, its movements are definitely limited by its deep socket and strong reinforcing ligaments, the two factors that account for its exceptional stability (Figure 13.6).

The deeply cupped acetabulum that receives the head of the femur is enhanced by a circular rim of fibrocartilage called the **acetabular labrum.** Because the diameter of the labrum is smaller than that of the femur's head, dislocations of the hip are rare. A short ligament, the **ligament of the head of the femur** or **ligamentum teres,** runs from the pitlike **fovea capitis** on the femur head to the acetabulum where it helps to secure the femur. Several strong ligaments, including the **iliofemoral** and **pubofemoral** anteriorly and the **ischiofemoral** that spirals posteriorly (not shown), are arranged so that they "screw" the femur head into the socket when a person stands upright.

ACTIVITY 7

Demonstrating Actions at the Hip Joint

If a functional hip joint model is available, identify the joint parts and manipulate it to demonstrate the following movements: flexion, extension, abduction, and inner and outer rotation that can occur at this joint.

Reread the information on what movements the associated ligaments restrict, and verify that information during your joint manipulations. ■

The Knee Joint

The knee is the largest and most complex joint in the body. Three joints in one (Figure 13.7), it allows extension, flexion, and a little rotation. The **tibiofemoral joint,** actually a duplex joint between the femoral condyles above and the **menisci** (semilunar cartilages) of the tibia below, is functionally a hinge joint, a very unstable one made slightly more secure by the menisci (Figure 13.7b and d). Some rotation occurs when the knee is partly flexed, but during extension, rotation and side-to-side movements are counteracted by the menisci and ligaments. The other joint is the **femoropatellar joint,** the intermediate joint anteriorly (Figure 13.7a and c).

FIGURE 13.6 Hip joint relationships. (a) Frontal section through the right hip joint. **(b)** Anterior superficial view of the right hip joint. **(c)** Photograph of the interior of the hip joint, lateral view.

(a)

Femur
Articular capsule
Posterior cruciate ligament
Lateral meniscus
Anterior cruciate ligament
Tibia

Tendon of quadriceps femoris
Suprapatellar bursa
Patella
Subcutaneous prepatellar bursa
Synovial cavity
Lateral meniscus
Infrapatellar fat pad
Deep infrapatellar bursa
Patellar ligament

(b)

Fibular collateral ligament
Lateral condyle of femur
Lateral meniscus
Tibia
Fibula

Posterior cruciate ligament
Medial condyle
Tibial collateral ligament
Anterior cruciate ligament
Medial meniscus
Patellar ligament
Patella
Quadriceps tendon

(c)

Quadriceps femoris muscle
Tendon of quadriceps femoris muscle
Patella
Lateral patellar retinaculum
Fibular collateral ligament
Fibula

Medial patellar retinaculum
Tibial collateral ligament
Patellar ligament
Tibia

(d)

Medial femoral condyle
Anterior cruciate ligament
Medial meniscus on medial tibial condyle
Patella

(e)

Tendon of adductor magnus
Medial head of gastrocnemius muscle
Popliteus muscle
Tibial collateral ligament
Tendon of semimembranosus muscle

Femur
Articular capsule
Oblique popliteal ligament
Lateral head of gastrocnemius muscle
Bursa
Fibular collateral ligament
Arcuate popliteal ligament
Tibia

FIGURE 13.7 Knee joint relationships. (a) Midsagittal section of right knee joint. **(b)** Anterior view of slightly flexed right knee joint showing the cruciate ligaments. Articular capsule has been removed; the quadriceps tendon has been cut and reflected distally. **(c)** Anterior superficial view of the right knee. **(d)** Photograph of an opened knee joint corresponds to view in (b). **(e)** Posterior superficial view of the ligaments clothing the knee joint.

FIGURE 13.8 Shoulder joint relationships. (a) Frontal section through the shoulder.
(b) Right shoulder joint, cut open and viewed from the lateral aspect; humerus removed.
(c) Photograph of the interior of the shoulder joint, anterior view. **(d)** Anterior superficial
view of the right shoulder.

The knee is unique in that it is only partly enclosed by an articular capsule. Anteriorly, where the capsule is absent, are three broad ligaments, the **patellar ligament** and the **medial** and **lateral patellar retinacula** (retainers), which run from the patella to the tibia below and merge with the capsule on either side.

Capsular ligaments including the **fibular** and **tibial collateral ligaments** (which prevent rotation during extension) and the **oblique popliteal** and **arcuate popliteal ligaments** are crucial in reinforcing the knee. The knees have a built-in locking device that must be "unlocked" by the popliteus muscles (Figure 13.7e) before the knees can be flexed again. The **cruciate ligaments** are intracapsular ligaments that cross (cruci = cross) in the notch between the femoral condyles. They prevent anterior-posterior displacement of the joint and overflexion and hyperextension of the joint.

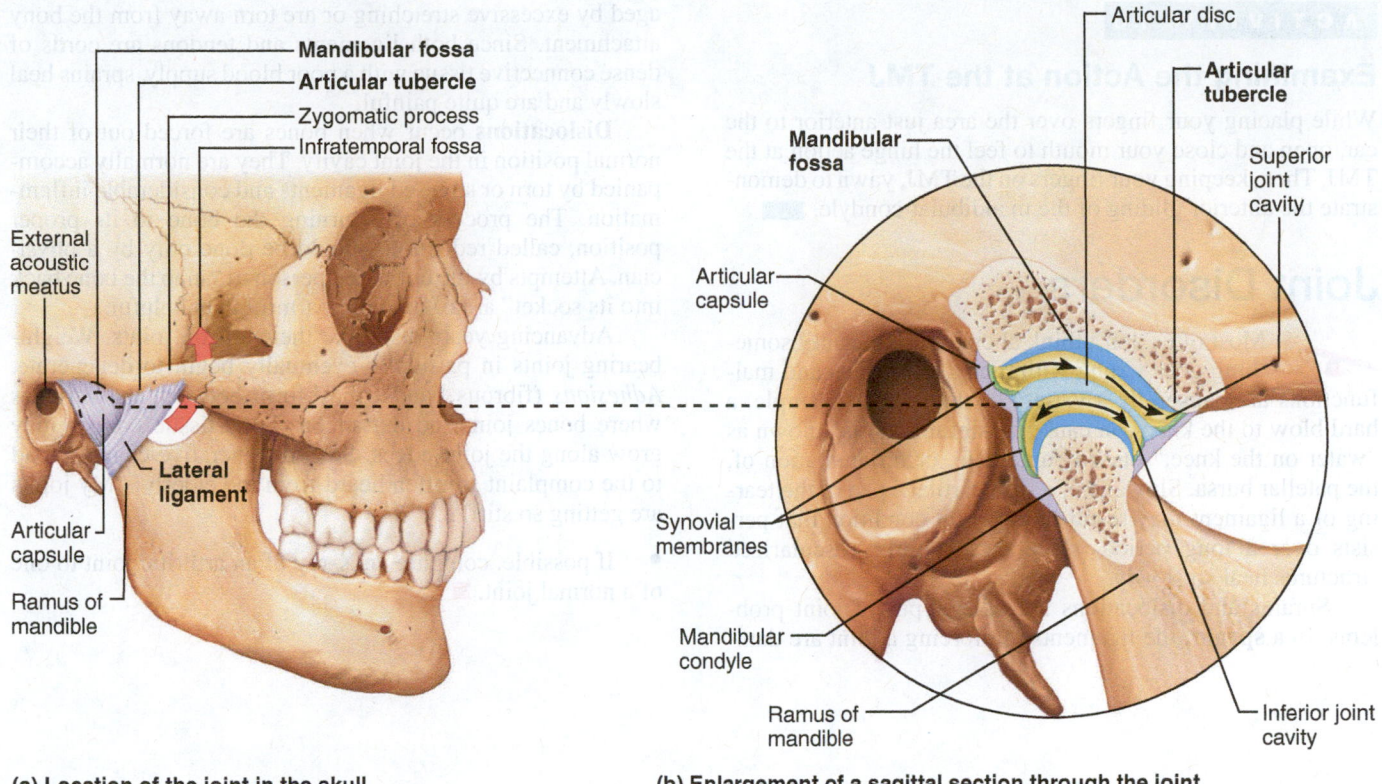

(a) Location of the joint in the skull

(b) Enlargement of a sagittal section through the joint

FIGURE 13.9 The temporomandibular (jaw) joint relationships. Note that the superior and inferior compartments of the joint cavity allow different movements indicated by arrows.

Demonstrating Actions at the Knee Joint

If a functional model of a knee joint is available, identify the joint parts and manipulate it to illustrate the following movements: flexion, extension, and inner and outer rotation.

Reread the information on what movements the various associated ligaments restrict, and verify that information during your joint manipulations.

The Shoulder Joint

The shoulder joint or **glenohumeral joint** is the most freely moving joint of the body. The rounded head of the humerus fits the shallow glenoid cavity of the scapula (Figure 13.8). A rim of fibrocartilage, the **glenoid labrum,** deepens the cavity slightly.

The articular capsule enclosing the joint is thin and loose, contributing to ease of movement. Few ligaments reinforce the shoulder, most of them located anteriorly. The **coracohumeral ligament** helps support the weight of the upper limb, and three weak **glenohumeral ligaments** strengthen the front of the capsule. In some people they are absent. Muscle tendons from the biceps brachii and **rotator cuff** muscles (subscapularis, supraspinatus, infraspinatus, and teres minor) contribute most to shoulder stability.

Demonstrating Actions at the Shoulder Joint

If a functional shoulder joint model is available, identify the joint parts and manipulate the model to demonstrate the following movements: flexion, extension, abduction, adduction, circumduction, and inner and outer rotation.

Note where the joint is weakest and verify the most common direction of a dislocated humerus.

The Temporomandibular Joint

The **temporomandibular joint (TMJ)** lies just anterior to the ear (Figure 13.9), where the egg-shaped condyle of the mandible articulates with the inferior surface of the squamous region of the temporal bone. The temporal bone joint surface has a complicated shape: posteriorly is the **mandibular fossa** and anteriorly is a bony knob called the **articular tubercle.** The joint's articular capsule, though strengthened by the **lateral ligament,** is slack; an articular disc divides the joint cavity into superior and inferior compartments. Typically, the mandibular condyle–mandibular fossa connection allows the familiar hingelike movements of elevating and depressing the mandible to open and close the mouth. However, when the mouth is opened wide, the mandibular head glides anteriorly and is braced against the dense bone of the articular tubercle so that the mandible is not forced superiorly when we bite hard foods.

Examining the Action at the TMJ

While placing your fingers over the area just anterior to the ear, open and close your mouth to feel the hinge action at the TMJ. Then, keeping your fingers on the TMJ, yawn to demonstrate the anterior gliding of the mandibular condyle. ■

Joint Disorders

Most of us don't think about our joints until something goes wrong with them. Joint pains and malfunctions are caused by a variety of things. For example, a hard blow to the knee can cause a painful bursitis, known as "water on the knee," due to damage to, or inflammation of, the patellar bursa. Slippage of a fibrocartilage pad or the tearing of a ligament may result in a painful condition that persists over a long period, since these poorly vascularized structures heal so slowly.

Sprains and dislocations are other types of joint problems. In a **sprain,** the ligaments reinforcing a joint are damaged by excessive stretching or are torn away from the bony attachment. Since both ligaments and tendons are cords of dense connective tissue with a poor blood supply, sprains heal slowly and are quite painful.

Dislocations occur when bones are forced out of their normal position in the joint cavity. They are normally accompanied by torn or stressed ligaments and considerable inflammation. The process of returning the bone to its proper position, called reduction, should be done only by a physician. Attempts by the untrained person to "snap the bone back into its socket" are often more harmful than helpful.

Advancing years also take their toll on joints. Weight-bearing joints in particular eventually begin to degenerate. *Adhesions* (fibrous bands) may form between the surfaces where bones join, and extraneous bone tissue (*spurs*) may grow along the joint edges. Such degenerative changes lead to the complaint so often heard from the elderly: "My joints are getting so stiff. . . ."

- If possible, compare an X-ray of an arthritic joint to one of a normal joint. ■

Articulations and Body Movements

Fibrous, Cartilaginous, and Synovial Joints

1. Use key responses to identify the joint types described below.

   Key: a. cartilaginous   b. fibrous   c. synovial

   _____ 1. typically allows a slight degree of movement

   _____ 2. includes joints between the vertebral bodies and the pubic symphysis

   _____ 3. essentially immovable joints

   _____ 4. sutures are the most remembered examples

   _____ 5. characterized by cartilage connecting the bony portions

   _____ 6. all characterized by a fibrous articular capsule lined with a synovial membrane surrounding a joint cavity

   _____ 7. all are freely movable or diarthrotic

   _____ 8. bone regions united by fibrous connective tissue

   _____ 9. include the hip, knee, and elbow joints

2. Describe the tissue type and function of the following structures in relation to a synovial joint and label the structures indicated by leader lines in the diagram.

   ligament: _____

   _____

   tendon: _____

   _____

   articular cartilage: _____

   _____

   synovial membrane: _____

   _____

   _____

   bursa: _____

   _____

3. Match the synovial joint categories in column B with their descriptions in column A.

Column A   **Column B**

_____ 1. joint between the axis and atlas   a. ball and socket

_____ 2. hip joint   b. condyloid

_____ 3. intervertebral joints (between articular processes)   c. gliding

_____ 4. joint between forearm bones and wrist   d. hinge

_____ 5. elbow   e. pivot

_____ 6. interphalangeal joints   f. saddle

_____ 7. intercarpal joints

_____ 8. joint between talus and tibia/fibula

_____ 9. joint between skull and vertebral column

_____ 10. joint between jaw and skull

_____ 11. joints between proximal phalanges and metacarpal bones

_____ 12. a multiaxial joint

_____, _____ 13. biaxial joints

_____, _____ 14. uniaxial joints

4. Indicate the number of planes in which each joint can move.

_____ uniaxial joints   _____ biaxial joints   _____ multiaxial joints

5. What characteristics do all joints have in common? _____

_____

Selected Synovial Joints

6. Which joint, the hip or the knee, is more stable? _____

Name two important factors that contribute to the stability of the hip joint.

_____ and _____

Name two important factors that contribute to the stability of the knee.

_____ and _____

7. The diagram shows a frontal section of the hip joint. Identify its major structural elements by using the key letters.

Key:

a. acetabular labrum

b. articular capsule

c. articular cartilage

d. coxal bone

e. head of femur

f. ligamentum teres

g. synovial cavity

8. The shoulder joint is built for mobility. List four factors that contribute to the large range of motion at the shoulder:

1. _____

2. _____

3. _____

4. _____

9. In which direction does the shoulder usually dislocate? _____

Movements Allowed
by Synovial Joints

10. Which letter of the adjacent diagram marks the origin

of the muscle? _____ Which letter marks the inser-

tion? _____

Insert the words *origin* and *insertion* into the following sentence:

During muscle contraction, the _____ moves

toward the _____.

11. Complete the descriptions below the diagrams by inserting the type of movement in each answer blank.

(a) _____ of the elbow

(b) _____ of the knee

(c) _____ of the shoulder

(d) _____ of the hip

(e) _____ of the shoulder

(f) _____ of the foot

(g) _____ of the head

(h) _____ of the hand

Joint Disorders

12. What structural joint changes are common to the elderly? _____

_____

13. Define the following terms.

sprain: _____

dislocation: _____

14. What types of tissue damage might you expect to find in a dislocated joint?

_____

_____

14

Microscopic Anatomy and Organization of Skeletal Muscle

MATERIALS

☐ Three-dimensional model of skeletal muscle cells (if available)
☐ Forceps
☐ Dissecting needles
☐ Clean microscope slides and coverslips
☐ 0.9% saline solution in dropper bottles
☐ Chicken breast or thigh muscle (freshly obtained from the meat market)
☐ Compound microscope
☐ Prepared slides of skeletal muscle (l.s. and x.s. views) and skeletal muscle showing neuromuscular junctions
☐ Three-dimensional model of skeletal muscle showing neuromuscular junction (if available)

OBJECTIVES

1. To describe the structure of skeletal muscle from gross to microscopic levels.

2. To define and explain the role of the following:

fiber	aponeurosis
myofibril	tendon
myofilament	epimysium
actin	perimysium
myosin	endomysium

3. To describe the structure of a neuromuscular junction and to explain its role in muscle function.

PRE-LAB QUIZ

1. Which is *not* true of skeletal muscle?
   a. It enables you to manipulate your environment.
   b. It influences the body's contours and shape.
   c. It is one of the major components of hollow organs.
   d. It provides a means of locomotion.

2. Circle the correct term. Because the cells of skeletal muscle are relatively large and cylindrical in shape, they are also known as <u>fibers</u> / <u>tubules</u>.

3. Circle True or False. Skeletal muscle cells have more than one nucleus.

4. The two contractile proteins that make up the myofilaments of skeletal muscle are _____ and _____.

5. Each muscle cell is surrounded by thin connective tissue called the
   a. aponeuroses   c. epimysium
   b. endomysium   d. perimysium

6. A strong cordlike structure that connects a muscle to another muscle or bone is
   a. a fascicle
   b. a tendon
   c. deep fascia

7. The junction between a nerve fiber and a muscle cell is called a
   _____.

8. Circle True or False. The neuron and muscle fiber membranes do not actually touch but are separated by a fluid-filled gap.

The bulk of the body's muscle is called **skeletal muscle** because it is attached to the skeleton (or associated connective tissue structures). Skeletal muscle influences body contours and shape, allows you to grin and frown, provides a means of locomotion, and enables you to manipulate the environment. The balance of the body's muscle—smooth and cardiac muscle, the major components of the walls of hollow organs and the heart, respectively—is involved with the transport of materials within the body.

myA&P For practice quizzes on this lab, go to www.myaandp.com.

PAL For access to anatomical models and more, check out Practice Anatomy Lab.

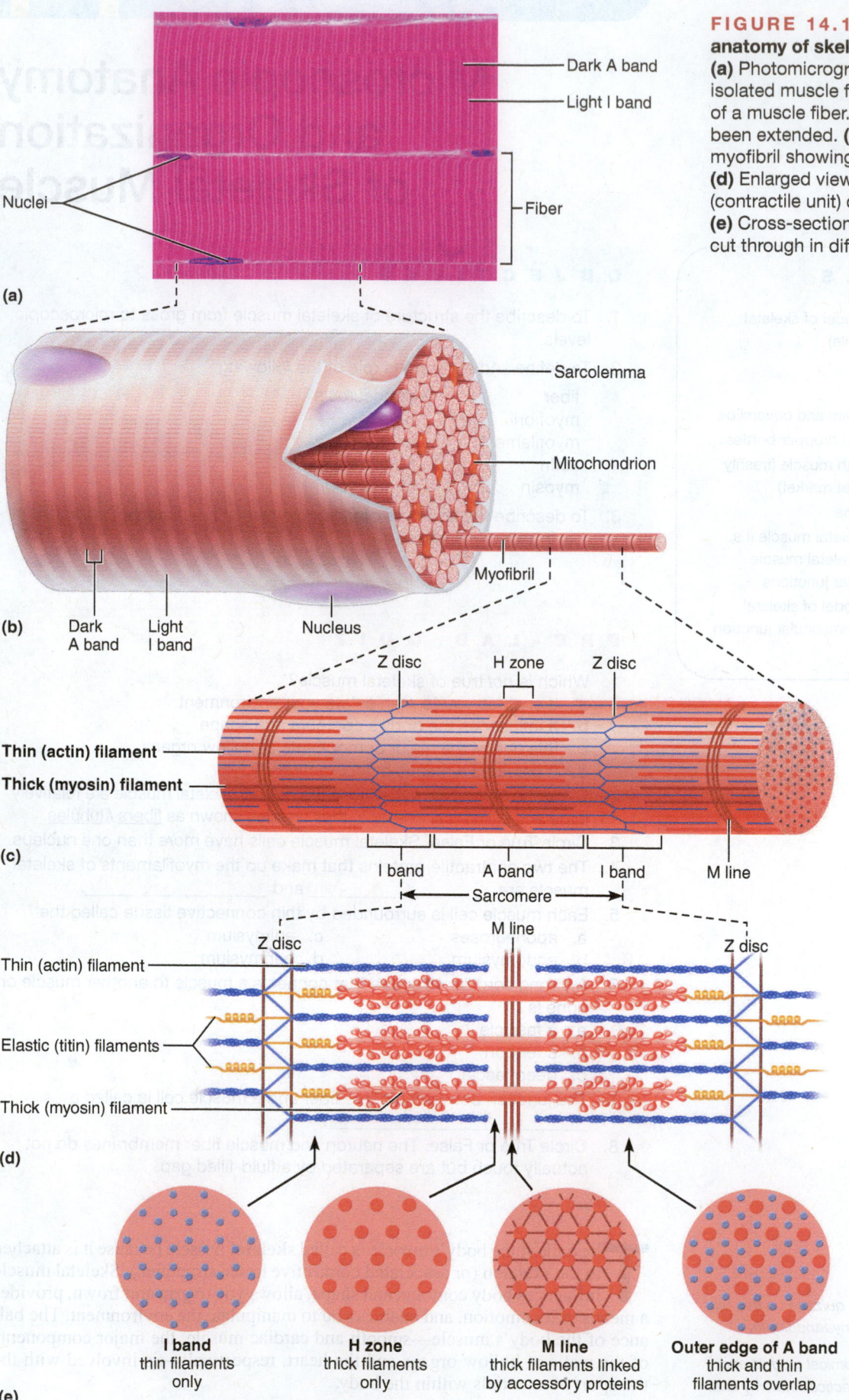

(a)

Nuclei

Dark A band

Light I band

Fiber

(b)

Sarcolemma

Mitochondrion

Myofibril

Dark
A band

Light
I band

Nucleus

(c)

Z disc   H zone   Z disc

Thin (actin) filament

Thick (myosin) filament

I band   A band   I band   M line

Sarcomere

(d)

Z disc   M line   Z disc

Thin (actin) filament

Elastic (titin) filaments

Thick (myosin) filament

(e)

I band
thin filaments
only

H zone
thick filaments
only

M line
thick filaments linked
by accessory proteins

Outer edge of A band
thick and thin
filaments overlap

FIGURE 14.1 Microscopic anatomy of skeletal muscle.
(a) Photomicrograph of portions of two isolated muscle fibers (700×). **(b)** Part of a muscle fiber. One myofibril has been extended. **(c)** Enlarged view of a myofibril showing its banding pattern. **(d)** Enlarged view of one sarcomere (contractile unit) of a myofibril. **(e)** Cross-sectional view of a sarcomere cut through in different areas.

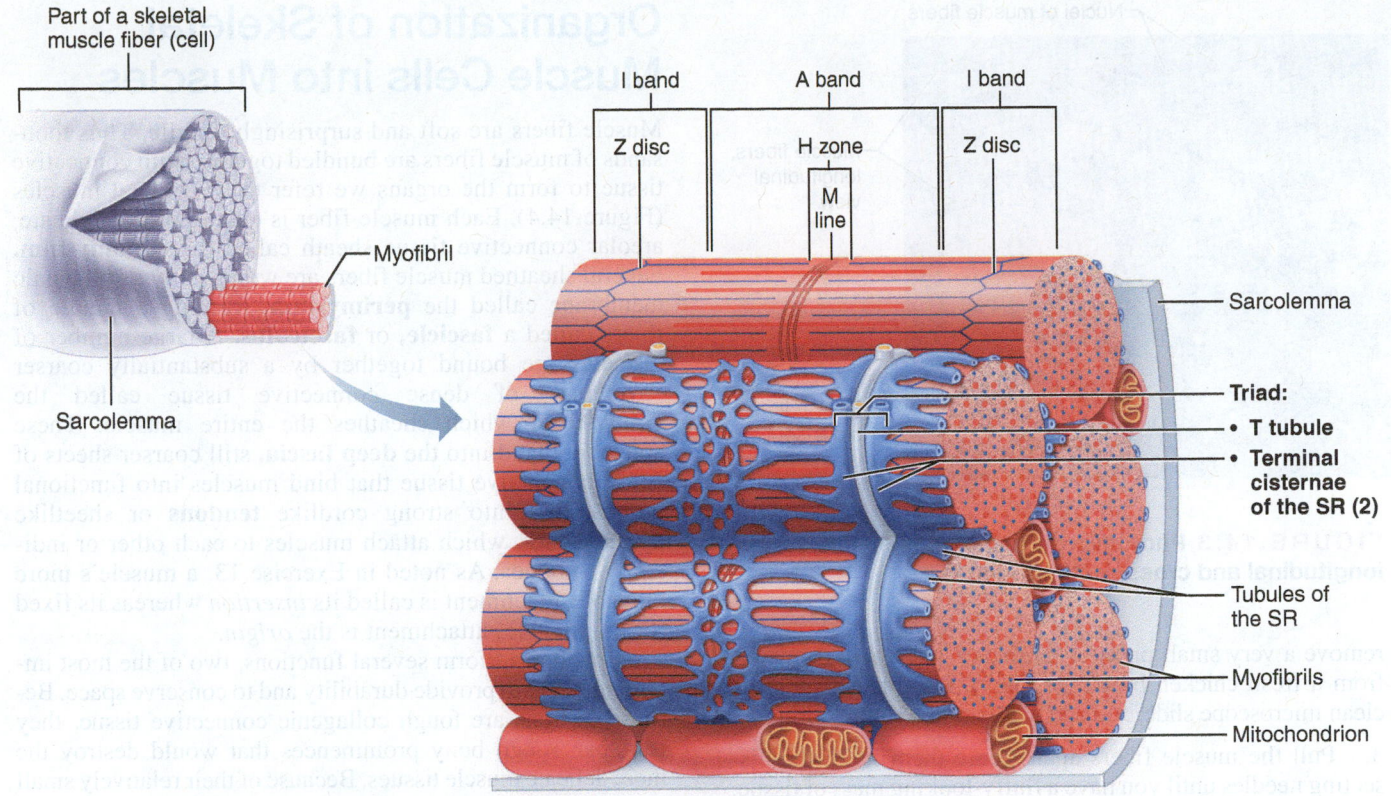

FIGURE 14.2 Relationship of the sarcoplasmic reticulum and T tubules to the myofibrils of skeletal muscle.

Each of the three muscle types has a structure and function uniquely suited to its task in the body. However, because the term *muscular system* applies specifically to skeletal muscle, the primary objective of this unit is to investigate the structure and function of skeletal muscle.

Skeletal muscle is also known as *voluntary muscle* (because it can be consciously controlled) and as *striated muscle* (because it appears to be striped). As you might guess from both of these alternative names, skeletal muscle has some special characteristics. Thus an investigation of skeletal muscle should begin at the cellular level.

The Cells of Skeletal Muscle

Skeletal muscle is composed of relatively large, long cylindrical cells, sometimes called **fibers,** ranging from 10 to 100 μm in diameter and up to 6 cm in length. However, the cells of large, hard-working muscles like the antigravity muscles of the hip are extremely coarse, ranging up to 25 cm in length, and can be seen with the naked eye.

Skeletal muscle cells (Figure 14.1a and b) are multinucleate; multiple oval nuclei can be seen just beneath the plasma membrane (called the *sarcolemma* in these cells). The nuclei are pushed peripherally by the longitudinally arranged **myofibrils,** which nearly fill the sarcoplasm. Alternating light (I) and dark (A) bands along the length of the perfectly aligned myofibrils give the muscle fiber as a whole its striped appearance.

Electron microscope studies have revealed that the myofibrils are made up of even smaller threadlike structures called **myofilaments** (Figure 14.1d). The myofilaments are

composed largely of two varieties of contractile proteins—**actin** and **myosin**—which slide past each other during muscle activity to bring about shortening or contraction of the muscle cells. It is the highly specific arrangement of the myofilaments within the myofibrils that is responsible for the banding pattern in skeletal muscle. The actual contractile units of muscle, called **sarcomeres,** extend from the middle of one I band (its Z disc) to the middle of the next along the length of the myofibrils (Figure 14.1c and d.) Cross sections of the sarcomere in areas where **thick** and **thin filaments** overlap show that each thick filament is surrounded by six thin filaments; each thin filament is enclosed by three thick filaments (Figure 14.1e).

At each junction of the A and I bands, the sarcolemma indents into the muscle cell, forming a **transverse tubule (T tubule).** These tubules run deep into the muscle cell between cross channels, or **terminal cisternae,** of the elaborate smooth endoplasmic reticulum called the **sarcoplasmic reticulum (SR)** (Figure 14.2). Regions where the SR terminal cisternae abut a T tubule on each side are called **triads.**

Examining Skeletal Muscle Cell Anatomy

1. Look at the three-dimensional model of skeletal muscle cells, noting the relative shape and size of the cells. Identify the nuclei, myofibrils, and light and dark bands.

2. Obtain forceps, two dissecting needles, slide and coverslip, and a dropper bottle of saline solution. With forceps,

Nuclei of muscle fibers

Muscle fibers, longitudinal view

Muscle fibers, cross-sectional view

FIGURE 14.3 Photomicrograph of muscle fibers, longitudinal and cross sections (400×).

remove a very small piece of muscle (about 1 mm diameter) from a fresh chicken breast (or thigh). Place the tissue on a clean microscope slide, and add a drop of the saline solution.

3.   Pull the muscle fibers apart (tease them) with the dissecting needles until you have a fluffy-looking mass of tissue. Cover the teased tissue with a coverslip, and observe under the high-power lens of a compound microscope. Look for the banding pattern by examining muscle fibers isolated at the edge of the tissue mass. Regulate the light carefully to obtain the highest possible contrast.

4.   Now compare your observations with Figure 14.3 and with what can be seen with professionally prepared muscle tissue. Obtain a slide of skeletal muscle (longitudinal section), and view it under high power. From your observations, draw a small section of a muscle fiber in the space provided below. Label the nuclei, sarcolemma, and A and I bands.

What structural details become apparent with the prepared slide?

_____

_____

Organization of Skeletal Muscle Cells into Muscles

Muscle fibers are soft and surprisingly fragile. Thus thousands of muscle fibers are bundled together with connective tissue to form the organs we refer to as skeletal muscles (Figure 14.4). Each muscle fiber is enclosed in a delicate, areolar connective tissue sheath called the **endomysium.** Several sheathed muscle fibers are wrapped by a collagenic membrane called the **perimysium,** forming a bundle of fibers called a **fascicle,** or **fasciculus.** A large number of fascicles are bound together by a substantially coarser "overcoat" of dense connective tissue called the **epimysium,** which sheathes the entire muscle. These epimysia blend into the **deep fascia,** still coarser sheets of dense connective tissue that bind muscles into functional groups, and into strong cordlike **tendons** or sheetlike **aponeuroses,** which attach muscles to each other or indirectly to bones. As noted in Exercise 13, a muscle's more movable attachment is called its *insertion* whereas its fixed (or immovable) attachment is the *origin.*

Tendons perform several functions, two of the most important being to provide durability and to conserve space. Because tendons are tough collagenic connective tissue, they can span rough bony prominences that would destroy the more delicate muscle tissues. Because of their relatively small size, more tendons than fleshy muscles can pass over a joint.

In addition to supporting and binding the muscle fibers, and providing strength to the muscle as a whole, the connective tissue wrappings provide a route for the entry and exit of nerves and blood vessels that serve the muscle fibers. The larger, more powerful muscles have relatively more connective tissue than muscles involved in fine or delicate movements.

As we age, the mass of the muscle fibers decreases, and the amount of connective tissue increases; thus the skeletal muscles gradually become more sinewy, or "stringier." ■

ACTIVITY 2

Observing the Histological Structure of a Skeletal Muscle

Obtain a slide showing a cross section of skeletal muscle tissue. Using Figure 14.4 as a reference, identify the muscle fibers, their peripherally located nuclei, and their connective tissue wrappings, (the endomysium, perimysium, and epimysium, if visible). ■

The Neuromuscular Junction

The voluntary skeletal muscle cells are always stimulated by motor neurons via nerve impulses. The junction between a nerve fiber (axon) and a muscle cell is called a **neuromuscular,** or **myoneural, junction** (Figure 14.5).

FIGURE 14.4 Connective tissue coverings of skeletal muscle. (a) Diagrammatic view. **(b)** Photomicrograph of a cross section of skeletal muscle (30x).

Bone

Epimysium

Tendon

Epimysium

Perimysium

Endomysium

Muscle fiber in middle of a fascicle

(b)

Blood vessel

Fascicle (wrapped by perimysium)

Endomysium (between individual muscle fibers)

Muscle fiber

Perimysium   Fascicle

(a)

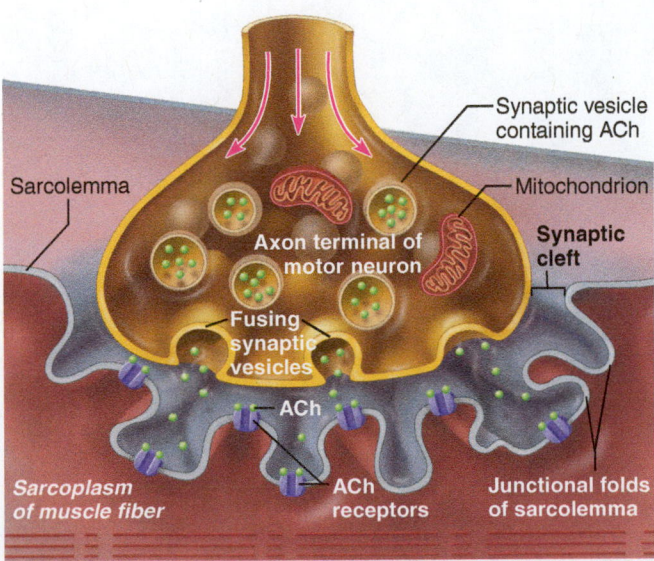

FIGURE 14.5 The neuromuscular junction.
Red arrows indicate arrival of the nerve impulse (action potential), which ultimately causes vesicles to release ACh. The ACh receptor is part of the ion channel that opens briefly, causing depolarization of the sarcolemma.

Synaptic vesicle containing ACh

Mitochondrion

Synaptic cleft

Axon terminal of motor neuron

Sarcolemma

Fusing synaptic vesicles

ACh

Sarcoplasm of muscle fiber

ACh receptors

Junctional folds of sarcolemma

Each axon of the motor neuron breaks up into many branches called *axon terminals* as it approaches the muscle, and each of these branches participates in forming a neuromuscular junction with a single muscle cell. Thus a single neuron may stimulate many muscle fibers. Together, a neuron and all the muscle fibers it stimulates make up the functional structure called the **motor unit.** Part of a motor unit, showing two neuromuscular junctions, is shown in Fig. 14.6. The neuron and muscle fiber membranes, close as they are, do not actually touch. They are separated by a small fluid-filled gap called the **synaptic cleft** (see Figure 14.5).

Within the axon terminals are many mitochondria and vesicles containing a neurotransmitter chemical called acetylcholine (ACh). When a nerve impulse reaches the axon terminal, some of these vesicles release their contents into the synaptic cleft. The ACh rapidly diffuses across the junction and combines with the receptors on the sarcolemma. When receptors bind ACh, a change in the permeability of the sarcolemma occurs. Channels that allow both sodium (Na^+) and potassium (K^+) ions to pass open briefly. Because more Na^+ diffuses into the muscle fiber than K^+ diffuses out, depolarization of the sarcolemma and subsequent contraction of the muscle fiber occurs.

Branch of
an axon

Axon
terminal at
neuromuscular
junctions

Muscle fibers

FIGURE 14.6 Photomicrograph of neuromuscular junctions (160×).

Studying the Structure of a Neuromuscular Junction

1.   If possible, examine a three-dimensional model of skeletal muscle cells that illustrates the neuromuscular junction. Identify the structures just described.

2.   Obtain a slide of skeletal muscle stained to show a portion of a motor unit. Examine the slide under high power to identify the axon fibers extending leashlike to the muscle cells. Follow one of the axon fibers to its terminus to identify the oval-shaped axon terminal. Compare your observations to Figure 14.6. Sketch a small section in the space provided below. Label the axon of the motor neuron, its terminal branches, and muscle fibers. ■

Microscopic Anatomy and Organization of Skeletal Muscle

Skeletal Muscle Cells and Their Packaging into Muscles

1. Use the items in the key to correctly identify the structures described below.

_____ 1. connective tissue ensheathing a bundle of muscle cells

_____ 2. bundle of muscle cells

_____ 3. contractile unit of muscle

_____ 4. a muscle cell

_____ 5. thin reticular connective tissue surrounding each muscle cell

_____ 6. plasma membrane of the muscle fiber

_____ 7. a long filamentous organelle with a banded appearance found within muscle cells

_____ 8. actin- or myosin-containing structure

_____ 9. cord of collagen fibers that attaches a muscle to a bone

Key:

a. endomysium

b. epimysium

c. fascicle

d. fiber

e. myofibril

f. myofilament

g. perimysium

h. sarcolemma

i. sarcomere

j. sarcoplasm

k. tendon

2. List three reasons why the connective tissue wrappings of skeletal muscle are important.

_____

_____

_____

3. Why are there more indirect—that is, tendinous—muscle attachments to bone than there are direct attachments?

_____

_____

_____

4. How does an aponeurosis differ from a tendon structurally? _____

_____

How is an aponeurosis functionally similar to a tendon? _____

_____

5. The diagram illustrates a small portion of several myofibrils. Using letters from the key, correctly identify each structure indicated by a leader line or a bracket.

Key: a. A band   d. myosin filament   g. triad
b. actin filament   e. T tubule   h. sarcomere
c. I band   f. terminal cisterna   i. Z disc

6. On the following figure, label a blood vessel, endomysium, epimysium, a fascicle, a muscle cell, perimysium, and the tendon.

The Neuromuscular Junction

7. Complete the following statements:

The junction between a motor neuron's axon and the muscle cell membrane is called __1__ junction. A motor neuron and all of the skeletal muscle cells it stimulates is called a __2__. The actual gap between the axon terminal and the muscle cell is called a __3__. Within the axon terminal are many small vesicles containing a neurotransmitter substance called __4__. When the __5__ reaches the ends of the axon, the neurotransmitter is released and diffuses to the muscle cell membrane to combine with receptors there. The combining of the neurotransmitter with the muscle membrane receptors causes the membrane to become permeable to both sodium and potassium. The greater influx of sodium ions results in __6__ of the membrane. Then contraction of the muscle cell occurs.

1. _____

2. _____

3. _____

4. _____

5. _____

6. _____

8. The events that occur at a neuromuscular junction are depicted below. Identify by labeling every structure provided with a leader line.

Key:

a.   axon terminal

b.   mitochondrion

c.   muscle fiber

d.   myelinated axon

e.   sarcolemma

f.   synaptic cleft

g.   T tubule

h.   vesicle containing ACh

Action potential

Nucleus

(a)

Junctional folds of the sarcolemma

Part of a myofibril

(b)

Gross Anatomy of the Muscular System

MATERIALS

- ☐ Human torso model or large anatomical chart showing human musculature
- ☐ Human cadaver for demonstration (if available)
- ☐ Disposable gloves
- ☐ *Human Musculature* videotape
- ☐ Tubes of body (or face) paint
- ☐ 1″ wide artist's brushes
- For instructions on animal dissections, see the dissection exercises starting on page 697 in the cat, fetal pig, and rat editions of this manual.

OBJECTIVES

1. To define *agonist* (prime mover), *antagonist, synergist, fixator, origin,* and *insertion.*
2. To cite criteria used in naming skeletal muscles.
3. To name and locate the major muscles of the human body (on a torso model, a human cadaver, lab chart, or diagram) and state the action of each.
4. To explain how muscle actions are related to their location.
5. To name muscle origins and insertions as required by the instructor.
6. To identify antagonists of the major prime movers.

PRE-LAB QUIZ

1. A prime mover or _____ is responsible for producing a particular type of movement.
   a. agonist   c. fixator
   b. antagonist   d. synergist
2. Skeletal muscles are named on the basis of many criteria. Name one.
   _____
3. Circle True or False. Muscles of facial expression differ from most skeletal muscles because they insert into the skin or other muscles rather than into bone.
4. The _____ musculature includes muscles that move the vertebral column and muscles that move the ribs.
   a. head and neck   b. lower limb   c. trunk
5. Muscles that act on the _____ cause movement at the hip, knee, and foot joints.
   a. lower limb   b. trunk   c. upper limb
6. This two-headed muscle bulges when the forearm is flexed. It is the most familiar muscle of the anterior humerus. It is the
   a. biceps brachii   c. flexor carpii radialis
   b. extensor digitorum   d. triceps brachii
7. These abdominal muscles are responsible for giving me my "six-pack." They also stabilize my pelvis when walking. They are the _____ muscles.
   a. internal intercostal   c. rectus abdominis
   b. quadriceps   d. triceps femoris
8. Circle the correct term. This lower limb muscle, which attaches to the calcaneus via the calcaneal tendon and plantar flexes the foot when the knee is extended, is the <u>sartorius</u> / <u>gastrocnemius</u>.
9. The _____ is the largest and most superficial of the gluteal muscles.
   a. gluteus internus   c. gluteus medius
   b. gluteus maximus   d. gluteus minimus

myA&P *For practice quizzes on this lab, go to www.myaandp.com.*

PAL *For access to anatomical models and more, check out Practice Anatomy Lab.*

Skeletal muscles cause movement. Among the movements are smiling, frowning, speaking, singing, breathing, dancing, running, and playing a musical instrument. Most often, purposeful movements require the coordinated action of several skeletal muscles.

Classification of Skeletal Muscles

Types of Muscles

Muscles that are primarily responsible for producing a particular movement are called **prime movers,** or **agonists.** Muscles that oppose or reverse a movement are called **antagonists.** When a prime mover is active, the fibers of the antagonist are stretched and in the relaxed state. The antagonist can also regulate the prime mover by providing some resistance, to prevent overshoot or to stop its action. Antagonists can be prime movers in their own right. For example, the biceps muscle of the arm (a prime mover of elbow flexion) is antagonized by the triceps (a prime mover of elbow extension).

Synergists aid the action of agonists by reducing undesirable or unnecessary movement. Contraction of a muscle crossing two or more joints would cause movement at all joints spanned if the synergists were not there to stabilize them. For example, you can make a fist without bending your wrist only because synergist muscles stabilize the wrist joint and allow the prime mover to exert its force at the finger joints.

Fixators, or fixation muscles, are specialized synergists. They immobilize the origin of a prime mover so that all the tension is exerted at the insertion. Muscles that help maintain posture are fixators; so too are muscles of the back that stabilize or "fix" the scapula during arm movements.

Naming Skeletal Muscles

Remembering the names of the skeletal muscles is a monumental task, but certain clues help. Muscles are named on the basis of the following criteria:

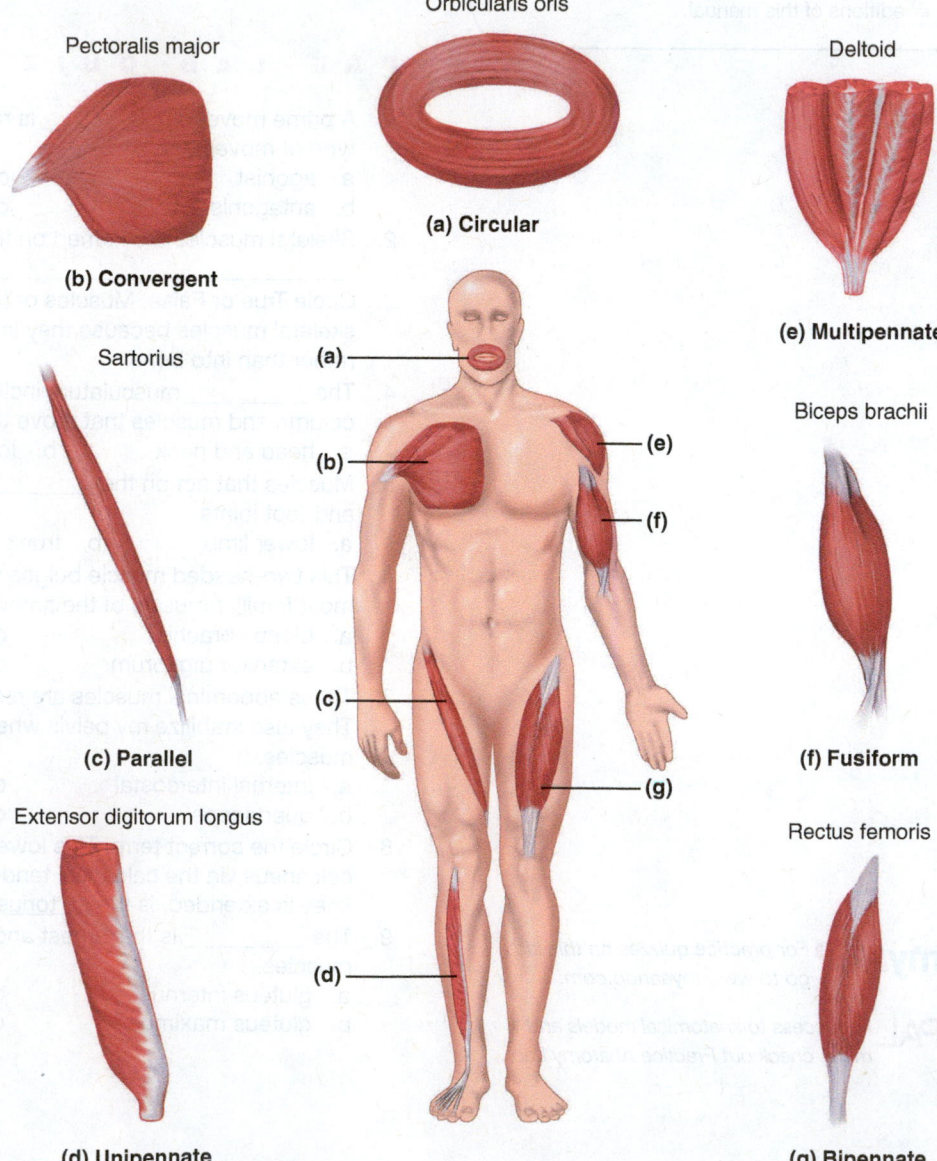

Pectoralis major

Orbicularis oris

Deltoid

(a) Circular

(b) Convergent

(e) Multipennate

Sartorius

Biceps brachii

(c) Parallel

(f) Fusiform

Extensor digitorum longus

Rectus femoris

FIGURE 15.1 Patterns of fascicle arrangement in muscles.

(d) Unipennate

(g) Bipennate

- **Direction of muscle fibers:** Some muscles are named in reference to some imaginary line, usually the midline of the body or the longitudinal axis of a limb bone. A muscle with fibers (and fascicles) running parallel to that imaginary line will have the term *rectus* (straight) in its name. For example, the rectus abdominis is the straight muscle of the abdomen. Likewise, the terms *transverse* and *oblique* indicate that the muscle fibers run at right angles and obliquely (respectively) to the imaginary line. Figure 15.1 shows how muscle structure is determined by fascicle arrangement.

- **Relative size of the muscle:** Terms such as *maximus* (largest), *minimus* (smallest), *longus* (long), and *brevis* (short) are often used in naming muscles—as in gluteus maximus and gluteus minimus.

- **Location of the muscle:** Some muscles are named for the bone with which they are associated. For example, the temporalis muscle overlies the temporal bone.

- **Number of origins:** When the term *biceps, triceps,* or *quadriceps* forms part of a muscle name, you can generally assume that the muscle has two, three, or four origins (respectively). For example, the biceps muscle of the arm has two heads, or origins.

- **Location of the muscle's origin and insertion:** For example, the sternocleidomastoid muscle has its origin on the sternum *(sterno)* and clavicle *(cleido),* and inserts on the mastoid process of the temporal bone.

- **Shape of the muscle:** For example, the deltoid muscle is roughly triangular *(deltoid = triangle),* and the trapezius muscle resembles a trapezoid.

- **Action of the muscle:** For example, all the adductor muscles of the anterior thigh bring about its adduction, and all the extensor muscles of the wrist extend the wrist.

Identification of Human Muscles

While reading the tables and identifying the various human muscles in the figures, try to visualize what happens when the muscle contracts. Since muscles often have many actions, we have indicated the primary action of each muscle in blue type in the tables. Then, use a torso model or an anatomical chart to again identify as many of these muscles as possible. (If a human cadaver is available for observation, your instructor will provide specific instructions for muscle examination.) Then carry out the instructions for demonstrating and palpating muscles.

Muscles of the Head and Neck

The muscles of the head serve many specific functions. For instance, the muscles of facial expression differ from most skeletal muscles because they insert into the skin (or other muscles) rather than into bone. As a result, they move the facial skin, allowing a wide range of emotions to be shown on the face. Other muscles of the head are the muscles of masti-

cation, which manipulate the mandible during chewing, and the six extrinsic eye muscles located within the orbit, which aim the eye. (Orbital muscles are studied in Exercise 24.)

ACTIVITY 1

Identifying Head and Neck Muscles

Neck muscles are primarily concerned with the movement of the head and shoulder girdle. Figures 15.2 and 15.3 are summary figures illustrating the superficial musculature of the body as a whole. Head and neck muscles are discussed in Tables 15.1 and 15.2 and shown in Figures 15.4 and 15.5.

Demonstrating Operations of Head Muscles

1. Raise your eyebrow to wrinkle your forehead. You are using the *frontal belly* of the *epicranius* muscle.

2. Blink your eyes; wink. You are contracting *orbicularis oculi.*

3. Close your lips and pucker up. This requires contraction of *orbicularis oris.*

4. Smile. You are using *zygomaticus.*

5. To demonstrate the temporalis, place your hands on your temples and clench your teeth. The masseter can also be palpated now at the angle of the jaw. ▬

Muscles of the Trunk

The trunk musculature includes muscles that move the vertebral column; anterior thorax muscles that act to move ribs, head, and arms; and muscles of the abdominal wall that play a role in the movement of the vertebral column but more importantly form the "natural girdle," or the major portion of the abdominal body wall.

ACTIVITY 2

Identifying Muscles of the Trunk

The trunk muscles are described in Tables 15.3 and 15.4 and shown in Figures 15.6 through 15.9. As before, identify the muscles in the figure as you read the tabular descriptions and then identify them on the torso or laboratory chart.

Demonstrating Operation of Trunk Muscles

Now, work with a partner to demonstrate the operation of the following muscles. One of you can demonstrate the movement (the following steps are addressed to this partner). The other can supply resistance and palpate the muscle being tested.

1. Fully abduct the arm and extend the elbow. Now adduct the arm against resistance. You are using the *latissimus dorsi.*

2. To observe the *deltoid,* try to abduct your arm against resistance. Now attempt to elevate your shoulder against resistance; you are contracting the upper portion of the *trapezius.*

3. The *pectoralis major* is used when you press your hands together at chest level with your elbows widely abducted. ▬

Text continues on page 213.

Head
- Temporalis
- Masseter

Facial
- Epicranius, frontal belly
- Orbicularis oculi
- Zygomaticus
- Orbicularis oris

Neck
- Platysma
- Sternohyoid
- Sternocleidomastoid

Shoulder
- Trapezius
- Deltoid

Thorax
- Pectoralis minor
- Pectoralis major
- Serratus anterior
- Intercostals

Arm
- Triceps brachii
- Biceps brachii
- Brachialis

Abdomen
- Rectus abdominis
- External oblique
- Internal oblique
- Transversus abdominis

Forearm
- Pronator teres
- Brachioradialis
- Flexor carpi radialis
- Palmaris longus

Pelvis/thigh
- Iliopsoas
- Pectineus

Thigh
- Tensor fasciae latae
- Sartorius
- Adductor longus
- Gracilis

Thigh
- Rectus femoris
- Vastus lateralis
- Vastus medialis

Leg
- Fibularis longus
- Extensor digitorum longus
- Tibialis anterior

Leg
- Gastrocnemius
- Soleus

FIGURE 15.2 Anterior view of superficial muscles of the body. The abdominal surface has been partially dissected on the left side of the body to show somewhat deeper muscles.

Neck
Epicranius, occipital belly
Sternocleidomastoid
Trapezius

Shoulder
Deltoid
Infraspinatus
Teres major
Rhomboid major
Latissimus dorsi

Hip
Gluteus medius
Gluteus maximus

Thigh
Adductor magnus
Hamstrings:
Biceps femoris
Semitendinosus
Semimembranosus

Arm
Triceps brachii
Brachialis

Forearm
Brachioradialis
Extensor carpi radialis longus
Flexor carpi ulnaris
Extensor carpi ulnaris
Extensor digitorum

Iliotibial tract

Leg
Gastrocnemius
Soleus
Fibularis longus
Calcaneal (Achilles) tendon

FIGURE 15.3 Posterior view of superficial muscles of the body.

TABLE 15.1	Major Muscles of Human Head (see Figure 15.4)			
Muscle	**Comments**	**Origin**	**Insertion**	**Action**
Facial Expression (Figure 15.4a)				
Epicranius— frontal and occipital bellies	Bipartite muscle consisting of frontal and occipital parts, which covers dome of skull	Frontal belly—galea aponeurotica (cranial aponeurosis); occipital belly—occipital and temporal bones	Frontal belly—skin of eyebrows and root of nose; occipital belly—galea aponeurotica	With aponeurosis fixed, frontal belly raises eyebrows; occipital belly fixes aponeurosis and pulls scalp posteriorly
Orbicularis oculi	Tripartite sphincter muscle of eyelids	Frontal and maxillary bones and ligaments around orbit	Encircles orbit and inserts in tissue of eyelid	Various parts can be activated individually; closes eyes, produces blinking, squinting, and draws eyebrows inferiorly
Corrugator supercilii	Small muscle; activity associated with that of orbicularis oculi	Arch of frontal bone above nasal bone	Skin of eyebrow	Draws eyebrows medially and inferiorly; wrinkles skin of forehead vertically
Levator labii superioris	Thin muscle between orbicularis oris and inferior eye margin	Zygomatic bone and infraorbital margin of maxilla	Skin and muscle of upper lip and border of nostril	Raises and furrows upper lip; opens lips
Zygomaticus— major and minor	Extends diagonally from corner of mouth to cheekbone	Zygomatic bone	Skin and muscle at corner of mouth	Raises lateral corners of mouth upward (smiling muscle)
Risorius	Slender muscle; runs inferior and lateral to zygomaticus	Fascia of masseter muscle	Skin at angle of mouth	Draws corner of lip laterally; tenses lip; zygomaticus synergist
Depressor labii inferioris	Small muscle from lower lip to mandible	Body of mandible lateral to its midline	Skin and muscle of lower lip	Draws lower lip inferiorly
Depressor anguli oris	Small muscle lateral to depressor labii inferioris	Body of mandible below incisors	Skin and muscle at angle of mouth below insertion of zygomaticus	Zygomaticus antagonist; draws corners of mouth downward and laterally
Orbicularis oris	Multilayered muscle of lips with fibers that run in many different directions; most run circularly	Arises indirectly from maxilla and mandible; fibers blended with fibers of other muscles associated with lips	Encircles mouth; inserts into muscle and skin at angles of mouth	Closes lips; purses and protrudes lips (kissing and whistling muscle)
Mentalis	One of muscle pair forming V-shaped muscle mass on chin	Mandible below incisors	Skin of chin	Protrudes lower lip; wrinkles chin
Buccinator	Principal muscle of cheek; runs horizontally, deep to the masseter	Molar region of maxilla and mandible	Orbicularis oris	Draws corner of mouth laterally; compresses cheek (as in whistling); holds food between teeth during chewing

(Continues on page 204.)

FIGURE 15.4 Muscles of the head (left lateral view). (a) Superficial muscles.
(b) Photo of superficial structures of head and neck.

TABLE 15.1	Major Muscles of Human Head *(continued)*			
Muscle	**Comments**	**Origin**	**Insertion**	**Action**
Mastication (Figure 15.4c,d)				
Masseter	Covers lateral aspect of mandibular ramus; can be palpated on forcible closure of jaws	Zygomatic arch and maxilla	Angle and ramus of mandible	Prime mover of jaw closure; elevates mandible
Temporalis	Fan-shaped muscle lying over parts of frontal, parietal, and temporal bones	Temporal fossa	Coronoid process of mandible	Closes jaw; elevates and retracts mandible
Buccinator	(See muscles of facial expression.)			
Medial pterygoid	Runs along internal (medial) surface of mandible (thus largely concealed by that bone)	Sphenoid, palatine, and maxillary bones	Medial surface of mandible, near its angle	Synergist of temporalis and masseter; elevates mandible; in conjunction with lateral pterygoid, aids in grinding movements
Lateral pterygoid	Superior to medial pterygoid	Greater wing of sphenoid bone	Mandibular condyle	Protracts jaw (moves it anteriorly); in conjunction with medial pterygoid, aids in grinding movements of teeth

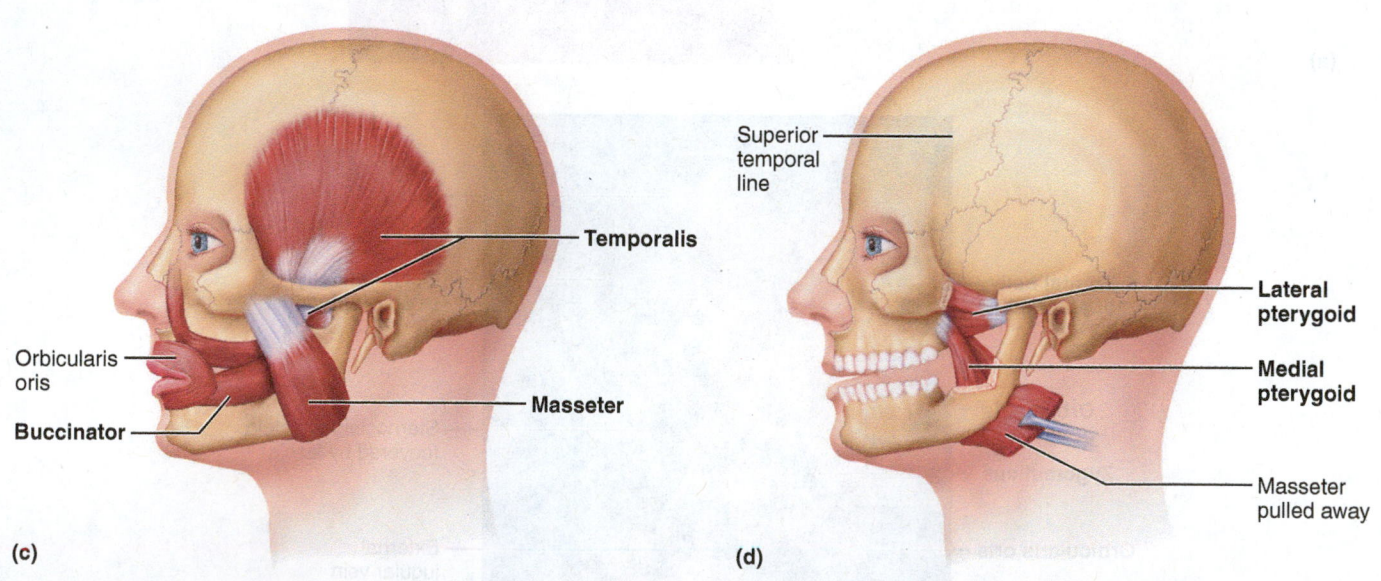

(c)

(d)

Orbicularis oris

Buccinator

Temporalis

Masseter

Superior temporal line

Lateral pterygoid

Medial pterygoid

Masseter pulled away

FIGURE 15.4 *(continued)* **Muscles of the head: mastication. (c)** Lateral view of the temporalis, masseter, and buccinator muscles. **(d)** Lateral view of the deep chewing muscles, the medial and lateral pterygoid muscles.

TABLE 15.2	Anterolateral Muscles of Human Neck (see Figure 15.5)			
Muscle	**Comments**	**Origin**	**Insertion**	**Action**
Superficial				
Platysma	Unpaired muscle: thin, sheetlike superficial neck muscle, not strictly a head muscle but plays role in facial expression (see also Fig. 15.4a)	Fascia of chest (over pectoral muscles) and deltoid	Lower margin of mandible, skin, and muscle at corner of mouth	Tenses skin of neck; depresses mandible; pulls lower lip back and down (i.e., produces downward sag of the mouth)
Sternocleidomastoid	Two-headed muscle located deep to platysma on anterolateral surface of neck; fleshy parts on either side indicate limits of anterior and posterior triangles of neck	Manubrium of sternum and medial portion of clavicle	Mastoid process of temporal bone and superior nuchal line of occipital bone	Simultaneous contraction of both muscles of pair causes flexion of neck forward, generally against resistance (as when lying on the back); acting independently, rotate head toward shoulder on opposite side
Scalenes—anterior, middle, and posterior	Located more on lateral than anterior neck; deep to platysma and sternocleidomastoid (see Fig. 15.5c)	Transverse processes of cervical vertebrae	Anterolaterally on ribs 1–2	Flex and slightly rotate neck; elevate ribs 1–2 (aid in inspiration)

(continues)

(a)

FIGURE 15.5 Muscles of the anterolateral neck and throat. (a) Cadaver photo of the anterior and lateral regions of the neck.

TABLE 15.2	Anterolateral Muscles of Human Neck (continued)			
Muscle	Comments	Origin	Insertion	Action
Deep (Figure 15.5a,b)				
Digastric	Consists of two bellies united by an intermediate tendon; assumes a V-shaped configuration under chin	Lower margin of mandible (anterior belly) and mastoid process (posterior belly)	By a connective tissue loop to hyoid bone	Acting in concert, elevate hyoid bone; open mouth and depress mandible
Stylohyoid	Slender muscle parallels posterior border of digastric; below angle of jaw	Styloid process of temporal	Hyoid bone	Elevates and retracts hyoid bone
Mylohyoid	Just deep to digastric; forms floor of mouth	Medial surface of mandible	Hyoid bone and median raphe	Elevates hyoid bone and base of tongue during swallowing
Sternohyoid	Runs most medially along neck; straplike	Manubrium and medial end of clavicle	Lower margin of body of hyoid bone	Acting with sternothyroid and omohyoid depresses larynx and hyoid bone if mandible is fixed; may also flex skull
Sternothyroid	Lateral and deep to sternohyoid	Posterior surface of manubrium	Thyroid cartilage of larynx	(See Sternohyoid above)
Omohyoid	Straplike with two bellies; lateral to sternohyoid	Superior surface of scapula	Hyoid bone; inferior border	(See Sternohyoid above)
Thyrohyoid	Appears as a superior continuation of sternothyroid muscle	Thyroid cartilage	Hyoid bone	Depresses hyoid bone; elevates larynx if hyoid is fixed

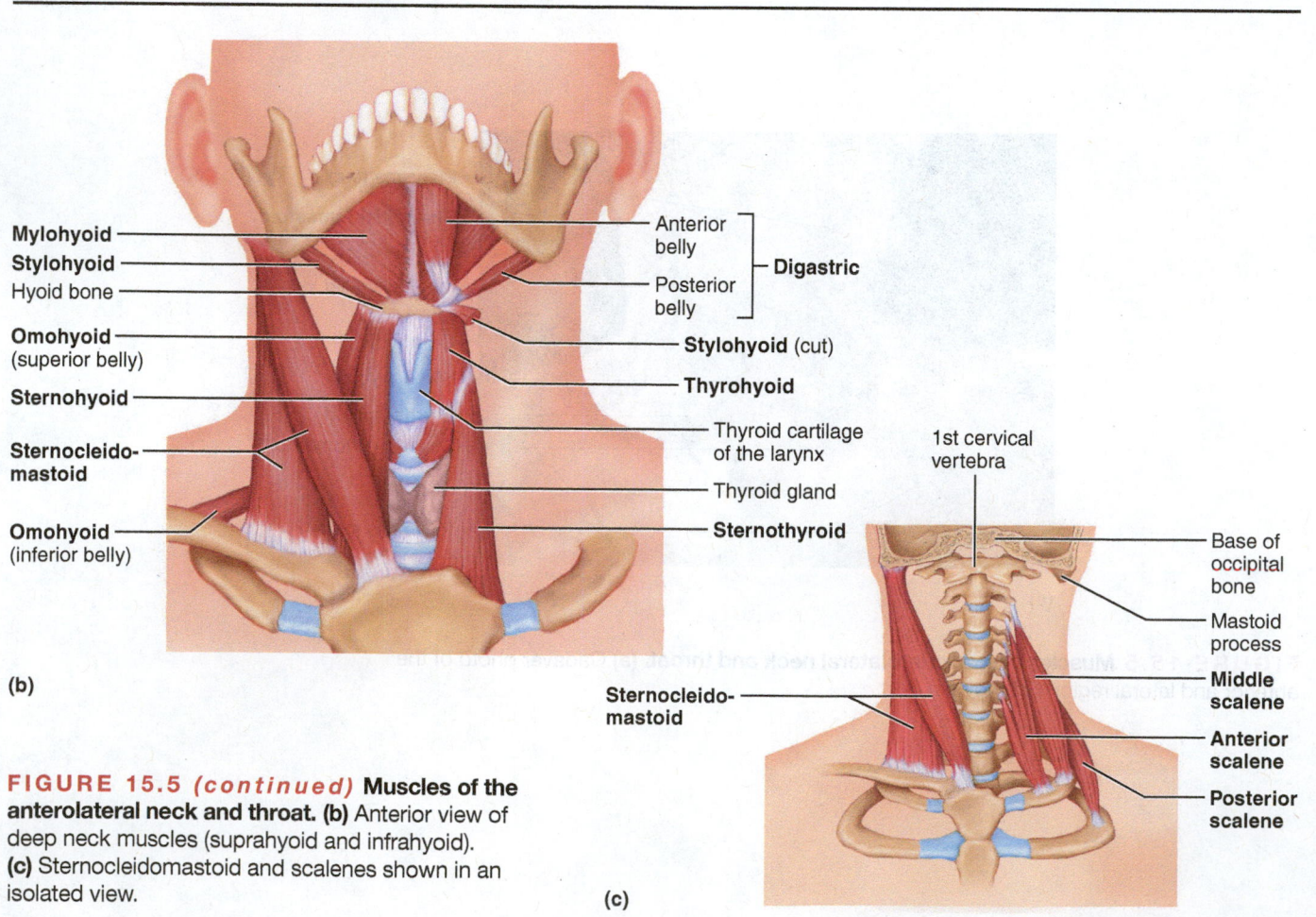

(b)

FIGURE 15.5 (continued) Muscles of the anterolateral neck and throat. (b) Anterior view of deep neck muscles (suprahyoid and infrahyoid). **(c)** Sternocleidomastoid and scalenes shown in an isolated view.

(c)

TABLE 15.3	**Anterior Muscles of Human Thorax, Shoulder, and Abdominal Wall (see Figures 15.6, 15.7, and 15.8)**			
Muscle	**Comments**	**Origin**	**Insertion**	**Action**
Thorax and Shoulder, Superficial (Figure 15.6)				
Pectoralis major	Large fan-shaped muscle covering upper portion of chest	Clavicle, sternum, cartilage of ribs 1–6 (or 7), and aponeurosis of external oblique muscle	Fibers converge to insert by short tendon into intertubercular sulcus of humerus	Prime mover of arm flexion; adducts, medially rotates arm; with arm fixed, pulls chest upward (thus also acts in forced inspiration)
Serratus anterior	Fan-shaped muscle deep to scapula; beneath and inferior to pectoral muscles on lateral rib cage	Lateral aspect of ribs 1–8 (or 9)	Vertebral border of anterior surface of scapula	Prime mover to protract and hold scapula against chest wall; rotates scapula, causing inferior angle to move laterally and upward; essential to raising arm; fixes scapula for arm abduction
Deltoid	Fleshy triangular muscle forming shoulder muscle mass; intramuscular injection site	Lateral ⅓ of clavicle; acromion and spine of scapula	Deltoid tuberosity of humerus	Acting as a whole, prime mover of arm abduction; when only specific fibers are active, can aid in flexion, extension, and rotation of humerus

(continues)

FIGURE 15.6 Muscles of the thorax and shoulder acting on the scapula and arm (anterior view). The superficial muscles, which effect arm movements, are shown on the left. These muscles have been removed on the right side of the figure to show the muscles that stabilize or move the pectoral girdle.

TABLE 15.3	Anterior Muscles of Human Thorax, Shoulder, and Abdominal Wall *(continued)*			
Muscle	Comments	Origin	Insertion	Action

Thorax and Shoulder, Superficial *(continued)*

Muscle	Comments	Origin	Insertion	Action
Pectoralis minor	Flat, thin muscle directly beneath and obscured by pectoralis major	Anterior surface of ribs 3–5, near their costal cartilages	Coracoid process of scapula	With ribs fixed, draws scapula forward and inferiorly; with scapula fixed, draws rib cage superiorly

Thorax, Deep: Muscles of Respiration (Figure 15.7)

Muscle	Comments	Origin	Insertion	Action
External intercostals	11 pairs lie between ribs; fibers run obliquely downward and forward toward sternum	Inferior border of rib above (not shown in figure)	Superior border of rib below	Pull ribs toward one another to elevate rib cage; aid in inspiration
Internal intercostals	11 pairs lie between ribs; fibers run deep and at right angles to those of external intercostals	Superior border of rib below	Inferior border of rib above (not shown in figure)	Draw ribs together to depress rib cage; aid in forced expiration; antagonistic to external intercostals
Diaphragm	Broad muscle; forms floor of thoracic cavity; dome-shaped in relaxed state; fibers converge from margins of thoracic cage toward a central tendon	Inferior border of rib and sternum, costal cartilages of last six ribs and lumbar vertebrae	Central tendon	Prime mover of inspiration flattens on contraction, increasing vertical dimensions of thorax; increases intra-abdominal pressure

Abdominal Wall (Figure 15.8a and b)

Muscle	Comments	Origin	Insertion	Action
Rectus abdominis	Medial superficial muscle, extends from pubis to rib cage; ensheathed by aponeuroses of oblique muscles; segmented	Pubic crest and symphysis	Xiphoid process and costal cartilages of ribs 5–7	Flexes and rotates vertebral column; increases abdominal pressure; fixes and depresses ribs; stabilizes pelvis during walking; used in sit-ups and curls
External oblique	Most superficial lateral muscle; fibers run downward and medially; ensheathed by an aponeurosis	Anterior surface of last eight ribs	Linea alba,* pubic crest and tubercles, and iliac crest	See rectus abdominis, above; compresses abdominal wall; also aids muscles of back in trunk rotation and lateral flexion; used in oblique curls
Internal oblique	Most fibers run at right angles to those of external oblique, which it underlies	Lumbar fascia, iliac crest, and inguinal ligament	Linea alba, pubic crest, and costal cartilages of last three ribs	As for external oblique
Transversus abdominis	Deepest muscle of abdominal wall; fibers run horizontally	Inguinal ligament, iliac crest, cartilages of last five or six ribs, and lumbar fascia	Linea alba and pubic crest	Compresses abdominal contents

*The linea alba (white line) is a narrow, tendinous sheath that runs along the middle of the abdomen from the sternum to the pubic symphysis. It is formed by the fusion of the aponeurosis of the external oblique and transversus muscles.

FIGURE 15.7 Deep muscles of the thorax: muscles of respiration. (a) The external intercostals (inspiratory muscles) are shown on the left and the internal intercostals (expiratory muscles) are shown on the right. These two muscle layers run obliquely and at right angles to each other. **(b)** Inferior view of the diaphragm, the prime mover of inspiration. Notice that its muscle fibers converge toward a central tendon, an arrangement that causes the diaphragm to flatten and move inferiorly as it contracts. The diaphragm and its tendon are pierced by the great vessels (aorta and inferior vena cava) and the esophagus.

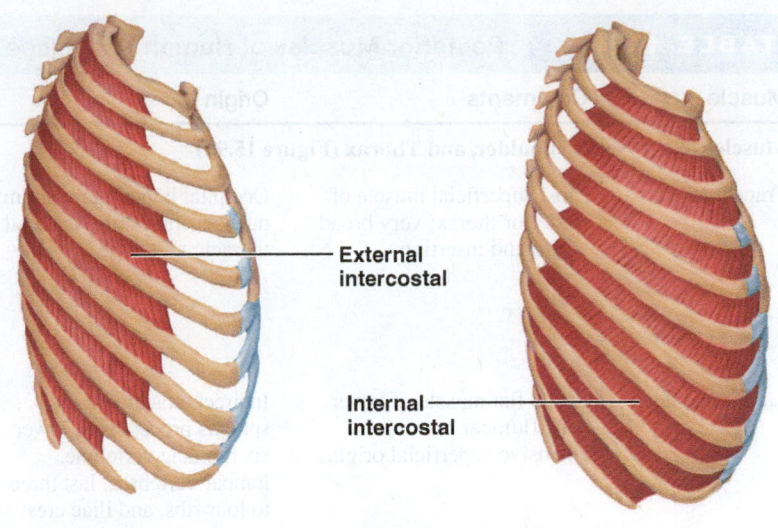

External intercostal

Internal intercostal

(a)

Foramen for inferior vena cava

Central tendon of diaphragm

Foramen for aorta

12th rib

Xiphoid process of sternum

Foramen for esophagus

Costal cartilage

Diaphragm

Lumbar vertebra

(b)

Pectoralis major

Serratus anterior

Linea alba

Tendinous intersection

Transversus abdominis

Rectus abdominis

Internal oblique

External oblique

Aponeurosis of the external oblique

Inguinal ligament (formed by free inferior border of the external oblique aponeurosis)

(a)

FIGURE 15.8 Anterior view of the muscles forming the anterolateral abdominal wall. (a) The superficial muscles have been partially cut away on the left side of the diagram to reveal the deeper internal oblique and transversus abdominis muscles.

TABLE 15.4 Posterior Muscles of Human Trunk (see Figure 15.9)

Muscle	Comments	Origin	Insertion	Action
Muscles of the Neck, Shoulder, and Thorax (Figure 15.9a)				
Trapezius	Most superficial muscle of posterior thorax; very broad origin and insertion	Occipital bone; ligamentum nuchae; spines of C_7 and all thoracic vertebrae	Acromion and spinous process of scapula; lateral third of clavicle	Extends head; raises, rotates, and retracts (adducts) scapula and stabilizes it; superior fibers elevate scapula (as in shrugging the shoulders); inferior fibers depress it
Latissimus dorsi	Broad flat muscle of lower back (lumbar region); extensive superficial origins	Indirect attachment to spinous processes of lower six thoracic vertebrae, lumbar vertebrae, last three to four ribs, and iliac crest	Floor of intertubercular sulcus of humerus	Prime mover of arm extension; adducts and medially rotates arm; brings arm down in power stroke, as in striking a blow
Infraspinatus	Partially covered by deltoid and trapezius; a rotator cuff muscle	Infraspinous fossa of scapula	Greater tubercle of humerus	Lateral rotation of humerus; helps hold head of humerus in glenoid cavity; stabilizes shoulder
Teres minor	Small muscle inferior to infraspinatus; a rotator cuff muscle	Lateral margin of scapula	Greater tubercle of humerus	As for infraspinatus
Teres major	Located inferiorly to teres minor	Posterior surface at inferior angle of scapula	Intertubercular sulcus of humerus	Extends, medially rotates, and adducts humerus; synergist of latissimus dorsi

Serratus anterior

External oblique

Rectus abdominis

Internal oblique

Transversus abdominis

Inguinal ligament

(b)

FIGURE 15.8 (continued)
Anterior view of the muscles forming the anterolateral abdominal wall.
(b) Photo of the anterolateral abdominal wall.

TABLE 15.4	(continued)			
Muscle	**Comments**	**Origin**	**Insertion**	**Action**
Supraspinatus	Obscured by trapezius; a rotator cuff muscle	Supraspinous fossa of scapula	Greater tubercle of humerus	Initiates abduction of humerus; stabilizes shoulder joint
Levator scapulae	Located at back and side of neck, deep to trapezius	Transverse processes of C_1–C_4	Medial border of scapula superior to spine	Elevates and adducts scapula; with fixed scapula, laterally flexes neck to the same side
Rhomboids— major and minor	Beneath trapezius and inferior to levator scapulae; rhomboid minor is the more superior muscle	Spinous processes of C_7 and T_1–T_5	Medial border of scapula	Pull scapula medially (retraction); stabilize scapula; rotate glenoid cavity downward
Muscles Associated with the Vertebral Column (Figure 15.9b)				
Semispinalis	Deep composite muscle of the back—thoracis, cervicis, and capitis portions	Transverse processes of C_7–T_{12}	Occipital bone and spinous processes of cervical vertebrae and T_1–T_4	Acting together, extend head and vertebral column; acting independently (right vs. left) causes rotation toward the opposite side

(continues)

(a)

FIGURE 15.9 Muscles of the neck, shoulder, and thorax (posterior view).
(a) The superficial muscles of the back are shown for the left side of the body, with a corresponding photograph. The superficial muscles are removed on the right side of the illustration to reveal the deeper muscles acting on the scapula and the rotator cuff muscles that help to stabilize the shoulder joint.

TABLE 15.4	Posterior Muscles of Human Trunk (continued)			
Muscle	Comments	Origin	Insertion	Action
Erector spinae	A long tripartite muscle composed of iliocostalis (lateral), longissimus, and spinalis (medial) muscle columns; superficial to semispinalis muscles; extends from pelvis to head	Iliac crest, transverse processes of lumbar, thoracic, and cervical vertebrae, and/or ribs 3–6 depending on specific part	Ribs and transverse processes of vertebrae about six segments above origin; longissimus also inserts into mastoid process	Extend and bend the vertebral column laterally; fibers of the longissimus also extend head

Mastoid process of temporal bone

Longissimus capitis

Iliocostalis cervicis
Longissimus cervicis

Iliocostalis thoracis

Longissimus thoracis

Spinalis thoracis

Erector spinae
— Iliocostalis
— Longissimus
— Spinalis

Iliocostalis lumborum

External oblique

Semispinalis capitis

Semispinalis cervicis

Semispinalis thoracis

Multifidus

Quadratus lumborum

FIGURE 15.9 (continued)
Muscles of the neck, shoulder, and thorax (posterior view). (b) The erector spinae and semispinalis muscles, which respectively form the intermediate and deep muscle layers of the back associated with the vertebral column.

(b)

TABLE 15.4	(continued)			
Muscle	**Comments**	**Origin**	**Insertion**	**Action**
Splenius (see Figure 15.9c)	Superficial muscle (capitis and cervicis parts) extending from upper thoracic region to skull	Ligamentum nuchae and spinous processes of C_7–T_6	Mastoid process, occipital bone, and transverse processes of C_2–C_4	As a group, extend or hyperextend head; when only one side is active, head is rotated and bent toward the same side
Quadratus lumborum	Forms greater portion of posterior abdominal wall	Iliac crest and lumbar fascia	Inferior border of rib 12; transverse processes of lumbar vertebrae	Each flexes vertebral column laterally; together extend the lumbar spine and fix rib 12; maintains upright posture

- Mastoid process

Splenius capitis

Spinous processes of the vertebrae

Splenius cervicis

(c)

FIGURE 15.9 *(continued)* Muscles of the neck, shoulder, and thorax (posterior view). (c) Deep (splenius) muscles of the posterior neck. Superficial muscles have been removed.

Muscles of the Upper Limb

The muscles that act on the upper limb fall into three groups: those that move the arm, those causing movement at the elbow, and those effecting movements of the wrist and hand.

The muscles that cross the shoulder joint to insert on the humerus and move the arm (subscapularis, supraspinatus and infraspinatus, deltoid, and so on) are primarily trunk muscles that originate on the axial skeleton or shoulder girdle. These muscles are included with the trunk muscles.

The second group of muscles, which cross the elbow joint and move the forearm, consists of muscles forming the musculature of the humerus. These muscles arise primarily from the humerus and insert in forearm bones. They are responsible for flexion, extension, pronation, and supination.

The third group composes the musculature of the forearm. For the most part, these muscles insert on the digits and produce movements at the wrist and fingers.

ACTIVITY 3

Identifying Muscles of the Upper Limb

The origins, insertions, and actions of muscles that move the forearm are summarized in Table 15.5 and the muscles are shown in Figure 15.10.

In general, muscles acting on the wrist and hand are more easily identified if their insertion tendons are located first. These muscles are described in Table 15.6 and illustrated in Figure 15.11.

First study the tables and figures, then see if you can identify these muscles on a torso model, anatomical chart, or cadaver. Complete this portion of the exercise with palpation demonstrations as outlined next.

Demonstrating Operations of Upper Limb Muscles

1.   To observe the *biceps brachii,* attempt to flex your forearm (hand supinated) against resistance. The insertion tendon of this biceps muscle can also be felt in the lateral aspect of the antecubital fossa (where it runs toward the radius to attach).

2.   If you acutely flex your elbow and then try to extend it against resistance, you can demonstrate the action of your *triceps brachii.*

3.   Strongly flex your wrist and make a fist. Palpate your contracting wrist flexor muscles (which originate from the medial epicondyle of the humerus) and their insertion tendons, which can be easily felt at the anterior aspect of the wrist.

4.   Flare your fingers to identify the tendons of the *extensor digitorum* muscle on the dorsum of your hand. ■

Text continues on page 218.

TABLE 15.5	Muscles of Human Humerus That Act on the Forearm (see Figure 15.10)			
Muscle	Comments	Origin	Insertion	Action
Triceps brachii	Sole, large fleshy muscle of posterior humerus; three-headed origin	Long head—inferior margin of glenoid cavity; lateral head—posterior humerus; medial head—distal radial groove on posterior humerus	Olecranon process of ulna	Powerful forearm extensor; antagonist of forearm flexors (brachialis and biceps brachii)
Anconeus	Short triangular muscle blended with triceps	Lateral epicondyle of humerus	Lateral aspect of olecranon process of ulna	Abducts ulna during forearm pronation; extends elbow
Biceps brachii	Most familiar muscle of anterior humerus because this two-headed muscle bulges when forearm is flexed	Short head: coracoid process; tendon of long head runs in intertubercular sulcus and within capsule of shoulder joint	Radial tuberosity	Flexion (powerful) of elbow and supination of forearm; "it turns the corkscrew and pulls the cork"; weak arm flexor
Brachioradialis	Superficial muscle of lateral forearm; forms lateral boundary of antecubital fossa	Lateral ridge at distal end of humerus	Base of styloid process of radius	Synergist in forearm flexion
Brachialis	Immediately deep to biceps brachii	Distal portion of anterior humerus	Coronoid process of ulna	A major flexor of forearm

FIGURE 15.10 Muscles causing movements of the arm and forearm. (a) Superficial muscles of the anterior thorax, shoulder, and arm, anterior view. **(b)** Posterior aspect of the arm showing the lateral and long heads of the triceps brachii muscle.

TABLE 15.6	Muscles of Human Forearm That Act on Hand and Fingers (see Figure 15.11)			
Muscle	Comments	Origin	Insertion	Action
Anterior Compartment (Figure 15.11a, b, c)				
Superficial				
Pronator teres	Seen in a superficial view between proximal margins of brachioradialis and flexor carpi radialis	Medial epicondyle of humerus and coronoid process of ulna	Midshaft of radius	Acts synergistically with pronator quadratus to pronate forearm; weak elbow flexor
Flexor carpi radialis	Superficial; runs diagonally across forearm	Medial epicondyle of humerus	Base of metacarpals 2 and 3	Powerful flexor of wrist; abducts hand
Palmaris longus	Small fleshy muscle with a long tendon; medial to flexor carpi radialis	Medial epicondyle of humerus	Palmar aponeurosis; skin and fascia of palm	Flexes wrist (weak); tenses skin and fascia of palm

(continues)

FIGURE 15.11 Muscles of the forearm and wrist. (a) Superficial anterior view of right forearm and hand. **(b)** The brachioradialis, flexors carpi radialis and ulnaris, and palmaris longus muscles have been removed to reveal the position of the somewhat deeper flexor digitorum superficialis. **(c)** Deep muscles of the anterior compartment. Superficial muscles have been removed. *Note:* The thenar muscles of the thumb and the lumbricals that help move the fingers are illustrated here but are not described in Table 15.6.

TABLE 15.6	Muscles of Human Forearm That Act on Hand and Fingers *(continued)*			
Muscle	**Comments**	**Origin**	**Insertion**	**Action**
Flexor carpi ulnaris	Superficial; medial to palmaris longus	Medial epicondyle of humerus and olecranon process and posterior surface of ulna	Base of metacarpal 5; pisiform and hamate bones	Powerful flexor of wrist; adducts hand
Flexor digitorum superficialis	Deeper muscle (deep to muscles named above); visible at distal end of forearm	Medial epicondyle of humerus, coronoid process of ulna, and shaft of radius	Middle phalanges of fingers 2–5	Flexes wrist and middle phalanges of fingers 2–5
Deep				
Flexor pollicis longus	Deep muscle of anterior forearm; distal to and paralleling lower margin of flexor digitorum superficialis	Anterior surface of radius, and interosseous membrane	Distal phalanx of thumb	Flexes thumb (*pollex* is Latin for "thumb")
Flexor digitorum profundus	Deep muscle; overlain entirely by flexor digitorum superficialis	Anteromedial surface of ulna, interosseous membrane, and coronoid process	Distal phalanges of fingers 2–5	Sole muscle that flexes distal phalanges; assists in wrist flexion
Pronator quadratus	Deepest muscle of distal forearm	Distal portion of anterior ulnar surface	Anterior surface of radius, distal end	Pronates forearm
Posterior Compartment (Figure 15.11d, e, f)				
Superficial				
Extensor carpi radialis longus	Superficial; parallels brachioradialis on lateral forearm	Lateral supracondylar ridge of humerus	Base of metacarpal 2	Extends and abducts wrist
Extensor carpi radialis brevis	Deep to extensor carpi radialis longus	Lateral epicondyle of humerus	Base of metacarpal 3	Extends and abducts wrist; steadies wrist during finger flexion
Extensor digitorum	Superficial; medial to extensor carpi radialis brevis	Lateral epicondyle of humerus	By four tendons into distal phalanges of fingers 2–5	Prime mover of finger extension; extends wrist; can flare (abduct) fingers
Extensor carpi ulnaris	Superficial; medial posterior forearm	Lateral epicondyle of humerus; posterior border of ulna	Base of metacarpal 5	Extends and adducts wrist
Deep				
Extensor pollicis longus and brevis	Muscle pair with a common origin and action; deep to extensor carpi ulnaris	Dorsal shaft of ulna and radius, interosseous membrane	Base of distal phalanx of thumb (longus) and proximal phalanx of thumb (brevis)	Extend thumb
Abductor pollicis longus	Deep muscle; lateral and parallel to extensor pollicis longus	Posterior surface of radius and ulna; interosseous membrane	Metacarpal 1 and trapezium	Abducts and extends thumb
Supinator	Deep muscle at posterior aspect of elbow	Lateral epicondyle of humerus; proximal ulna	Proximal end of radius	Acts with biceps brachii to supinate forearm; antagonist of pronator muscles

Brachioradialis

Extensor carpi radialis longus

Insertion of triceps brachii

Anconeus

Extensor carpi radialis brevis

Flexor carpi ulnaris

Extensor digitorum

Extensor carpi ulnaris

Abductor pollicis longus

Extensor digit minimi

Extensor pollicis brevis

Extensor indicis

Extensor pollicis longus

Tendons of extensor carpi radialis brevis and longus

Tendons of extensor digitorum

Extensor expansion

(d)

Olecranon process of ulna

Anconeus

Supinator

Abductor pollicis longus

Extensor pollicis longus

Extensor pollicis brevis

Extensor indicis

Interossei

(e)

Abductor pollicis longus

Extensor pollicis brevis

Brachioradialis

Extensor carpi radialis longus

Extensor carpi radialis brevis

Extensor digitorum

Extensor carpi ulnaris

Extensor digiti minimi

Tendon of extensor digitorum

(f)

FIGURE 15.11 (continued) **Muscles of the forearm and wrist. (d)** Superficial muscles, posterior view. **(e)** Deep posterior muscles; superficial muscles have been removed. The interossei, the deepest layer of intrinsic hand muscles, are also illustrated. **(f)** Photo of deep posterior muscles of the right forearm. The superficial muscles have been removed.

Muscles of the Lower Limb

Muscles that act on the lower limb cause movement at the hip, knee, and foot joints. Since the human pelvic girdle is composed of heavy, fused bones that allow very little movement, no special group of muscles is necessary to stabilize it. This is unlike the shoulder girdle, where several muscles (mainly trunk muscles) are needed to stabilize the scapulae.

Muscles acting on the thigh (femur) cause various movements at the multiaxial hip joint (flexion, extension, rotation, abduction, and adduction). These include the iliopsoas, the adductor group, and others.

Muscles acting on the leg form the major musculature of the thigh. (Anatomically the term *leg* refers only to that portion between the knee and the ankle.) The thigh muscles cross the knee to allow its flexion and extension. They include the hamstrings and the quadriceps.

The muscles originating on the leg act on the foot and toes.

ACTIVITY 4

Identifying Muscles of the Lower Limb

Muscles acting on the thigh are summarized in Tables 15.7 and 15.8 and illustrated in Figures 15.12 and 15.13.

Muscles acting on the leg are described in Tables 15.7 and 15.8 and illustrated in Figures 15.12 and 15.13. Since some of these muscles can also have attachments on the pelvic girdle, they can cause movement at the hip joint.

Muscles acting on the foot and toes are described in Table 15.9 and shown in Figures 15.14 and 15.15.

TABLE 15.7	**Muscles Acting on Human Thigh and Leg, Anterior and Medial Aspects (see Figure 15.12)**			
Muscle	Comments	Origin	Insertion	Action
Origin on the Pelvis				
Iliopsoas—iliacus and psoas major	Two closely related muscles; fibers pass under inguinal ligament to insert into femur via a common tendon; iliacus is more lateral	Iliacus—iliac fossa and crest, lateral sacrum; psoas major—transverse processes, bodies, and discs of T_{12} and lumbar vertebrae	On and just below lesser trochanter of femur	Flex trunk on thigh; flex thigh; lateral flexion of vertebral column (psoas)
Sartorius	Straplike superficial muscle running obliquely across anterior surface of thigh to knee	Anterior superior iliac spine	By an aponeurosis into medial aspect of proximal tibia	Flexes, abducts, and laterally rotates thigh; flexes knee; known as "tailor's muscle" because it helps effect cross-legged position in which tailors are often depicted
Medial Compartment				
Adductors—magnus, longus, and brevis	Large muscle mass forming medial aspect of thigh; arise from front of pelvis and insert at various levels on femur	Magnus—ischial and pubic rami and ischial tuberosity; longus—pubis near pubic symphysis; brevis—body and inferior ramus of pubis	Magnus—linea aspera and adductor tubercle of femur; longus and brevis—linea aspera	Adduct and medially rotate and flex thigh; posterior part of magnus is also a synergist in thigh extension
Pectineus	Overlies adductor brevis on proximal thigh	Pectineal line of pubis (and superior ramus)	Inferior from lesser trochanter to linea aspera of femur	Adducts, flexes, and medially rotates thigh
Gracilis	Straplike superficial muscle of medial thigh	Inferior ramus and body of pubis	Medial surface of tibia just inferior to medial condyle	Adducts thigh; flexes and medially rotates leg, especially during walking

(Continues on page 220.)

12th thoracic vertebra

12th rib

Quadratus lumborum

Psoas minor

Iliac crest

Iliopsoas — **Psoas major**

Iliacus

Anterior superior iliac spine

Tensor fasciae latae

Pectineus

Sartorius

Quadriceps femoris
• **Rectus femoris**

• **Vastus lateralis**

• **Vastus medialis**

Tendon of quadriceps femoris

5th lumbar vertebra

Adductor longus

Gracilis

Adductor magnus

Patella

Patellar ligament

(a)

Pectineus (cut)

Adductor brevis

Adductor longus

Femur

Adductor magnus

O = origin
I = insertion

(b)

Vastus lateralis

Vastus intermedius

Vastus medialis

Rectus femoris tendon (cut)

Patella

Patellar ligament

(c)

FIGURE 15.12 Anterior and medial muscles promoting movements of the thigh and leg. (a) Anterior view of the deep muscles of the pelvis and superficial muscles of the right thigh. **(b)** Adductor muscles of the medial compartment of the thigh. **(c)** The vastus muscles (isolated) of the quadriceps group.

TABLE 15.7	Muscles Acting on Human Thigh and Leg, Anterior and Medial Aspects *(continued)*			
Muscle	**Comments**	**Origin**	**Insertion**	**Action**
Anterior Compartment				
Quadriceps femoris*				
Rectus femoris	Superficial muscle of thigh; runs straight down thigh; only muscle of group to cross hip joint	Anterior inferior iliac spine and superior margin of acetabulum	Tibial tuberosity and patella	Extends knee and flexes thigh at hip
Vastus lateralis	Forms lateral aspect of thigh; intramuscular injection site	Greater trochanter, intertrochanteric line, and linea aspera	Tibial tuberosity and patella	Extends and stabilizes knee
Vastus medialis	Forms inferomedial aspect of thigh	Linea aspera and intertrochanteric line	Tibial tuberosity and patella	Extends knee; stabilizes patella
Vastus intermedius	Obscured by rectus femoris; lies between vastus lateralis and vastus medialis on anterior thigh	Anterior and lateral surface of femur	Tibial tuberosity and patella	Extends knee
Tensor fasciae latae	Enclosed between fascia layers of thigh	Anterior aspect of iliac crest and anterior superior iliac spine	Iliotibial tract (lateral portion of fascia lata)	Flexes, abducts, and medially rotates thigh; steadies trunk

*The quadriceps form the flesh of the anterior thigh and have a common insertion in the tibial tuberosity via the patellar tendon. They are powerful leg extensors, enabling humans to kick a football, for example.

TABLE 15.8	Muscles Acting on Human Thigh and Leg, Posterior Aspect (see Figure 15.13)			
Muscle	**Comments**	**Origin**	**Insertion**	**Action**
Origin on the Pelvis				
Gluteus maximus	Largest and most superficial of gluteal muscles (which form buttock mass); intramuscular injection site	Dorsal ilium, sacrum, and coccyx	Gluteal tuberosity of femur and iliotibial tract*	Complex, powerful thigh extensor (most effective when thigh is flexed, as in climbing stairs—but not as in walking); antagonist of iliopsoas; laterally rotates and abducts thigh
Gluteus medius	Partially covered by gluteus maximus; intramuscular injection site	Upper lateral surface of ilium	Greater trochanter of femur	Abducts and medially rotates thigh; steadies pelvis during walking
Gluteus minimus (not shown in figure)	Smallest and deepest gluteal muscle	External inferior surface of ilium	Greater trochanter of femur	Abducts and medially rotates thigh; steadies pelvis
Posterior Compartment				
Hamstrings† Biceps femoris	Most lateral muscle of group; arises from two heads	Ischial tuberosity (long head); linea aspera and distal femur (short head)	Tendon passes laterally to insert into head of fibula and lateral condyle of tibia	Extends thigh; laterally rotates leg; flexes knee

(continues)

TABLE 15.8 (continued)

Muscle	Comments	Origin	Insertion	Action
Semitendinosus	Medial to biceps femoris	Ischial tuberosity	Medial aspect of upper tibial shaft	Extends thigh; flexes knee; medially rotates leg
Semimembranosus	Deep to semitendinosus	Ischial tuberosity	Medial condyle of tibia; lateral condyle of femur	Extends thigh; flexes knee; medially rotates leg

* The iliotibial tract, a thickened lateral portion of the fascia lata, ensheathes all the muscles of the thigh. It extends as a tendinous band from the iliac crest to the knee.

† The hamstrings are the fleshy muscles of the posterior thigh. The name comes from the butchers' practice of using the tendons of these muscles to hang hams for smoking. As a group, they are strong extensors of the hip; they counteract the powerful quadriceps by stabilizing the knee joint when standing.

(a)

Gluteus medius

Gluteus maximus

Adductor magnus

Gracilis

Iliotibial tract

Long head ⎤
            ⎬ **Biceps femoris**
Short head ⎦

Semitendinosus

Semimembranosus

(b)

Gluteus maximus

Adductor magnus

Semitendinosus

Semimembranosus

Gracilis

Biceps femoris (long head)

Iliotibial tract

Sartorius

Gastrocnemius

FIGURE 15.13 Muscles of the posterior aspect of the right hip and thigh.
(a) Superficial view showing the gluteus muscles of the buttock and hamstring muscles of the thigh. **(b)** Photo of muscles of the posterior thigh.

TABLE 15.9	Muscles Acting on Human Foot and Ankle (see Figures 15.14 and 15.15)			
Muscle	Comments	Origin	Insertion	Action
Lateral Compartment (Figure 15.14a, b and Figure 15.15b)				
Fibularis (peroneus) longus	Superficial lateral muscle; overlies fibula	Head and upper portion of fibula	By long tendon under foot to metatarsal 1 and medial cuneiform	Plantar flexes and everts foot; helps keep foot flat on ground
Fibularis (peroneus) brevis	Smaller muscle; deep to fibularis longus	Distal portion of fibula shaft	By tendon running behind lateral malleolus to insert on proximal end of metatarsal 5	Plantar flexes and everts foot, as part of fibularis group
Anterior Compartment (Figure 15.14a, b)				
Tibialis anterior	Superficial muscle of anterior leg; parallels sharp anterior margin of tibia	Lateral condyle and upper ⅔ of tibia; interosseous membrane	By tendon into inferior surface of first cuneiform and metatarsal 1	Prime mover of dorsiflexion; inverts foot; supports longitudinal arch of foot
Extensor digitorum longus	Anterolateral surface of leg; lateral to tibialis anterior	Lateral condyle of tibia; proximal ¾ of fibula; interosseous membrane	Tendon divides into four parts; inserts into middle and distal phalanges of toes 2–5	Prime mover of toe extension; dorsiflexes foot
Fibularis (peroneus) tertius	Small muscle; often fused to distal part of extensor digitorum longus	Distal anterior surface of fibula and interosseous membrane	Tendon inserts on dorsum of metatarsal 5	Dorsiflexes and everts foot
Extensor hallucis longus	Deep to extensor digitorum longus and tibialis anterior	Anteromedial shaft of fibula and interosseous membrane	Tendon inserts on distal phalanx of great toe	Extends great toe; dorsiflexes foot

(Continues on page 224.)

Patella

Head of fibula

Gastrocnemius

Soleus

Fibularis longus

Extensor digitorum longus

Tibialis anterior

Fibularis brevis

Flexor hallucis longus

Fibular retinaculum

Lateral malleolus

Extensor hallucis longus

Fibularis tertius

Superior and inferior extensor retinacula

Extensor hallucis brevis

Extensor digitorum brevis

(a)

5th metatarsal

Fibularis longus

Gastrocnemius

Tibia

Tibialis anterior

Extensor digitorum longus

Soleus

Extensor hallucis longus

Fibularis tertius

Superior and inferior extensor retinacula

(b)

FIGURE 15.14 Muscles of the anterolateral aspect of the right leg. **(a)** Superficial view of lateral aspect of the leg, illustrating the positioning of the lateral compartment muscles (fibularis longus and brevis) relative to anterior and posterior leg muscles. **(b)** Superficial view of anterior leg muscles.

TABLE 15.9		Muscles Acting on Human Foot and Ankle *(continued)*		
Muscle	Comments	Origin	Insertion	Action

Posterior Compartment

Superficial (Figure 15.15a)

Triceps surae	Refers to muscle pair below that shapes posterior calf		Via common tendon (calcaneal, or Achilles) into heel	Plantar flex foot
Gastrocnemius	Superficial muscle of pair; two prominent bellies	By two heads from medial and lateral condyles of femur	Calcaneus via calcaneal tendon	Plantar flexes foot when knee is extended; crosses knee joint; thus can flex knee (when foot is dorsiflexed)
Soleus	Deep to gastrocnemius	Proximal portion of tiba and fibula; interosseous membrane	Calcaneus via calcaneal tendon	Plantar flexion; is an important muscle for locomotion

(Continues on page 226.)

Demonstrating Operations of Lower Limb Muscles

1. Go into a deep knee bend and palpate your own *gluteus maximus* muscle as you extend your hip to resume the upright posture.

2. Demonstrate the contraction of the anterior *quadriceps femoris* by trying to extend your knee against resistance. Do this while seated and note how the patellar tendon reacts. The *biceps femoris* of the posterior thigh comes into play when you flex your knee against resistance.

3. Now stand on your toes. Have your partner palpate the lateral and medial heads of the *gastrocnemius* and follow it to its insertion in the calcaneal tendon.

4. Dorsiflex and invert your foot while palpating your *tibialis anterior* muscle (which parallels the sharp anterior crest of the tibia laterally). ▆▆▆

ACTIVITY 5

Review of Human Musculature

Review the muscles by watching the *Human Musculature* videotape. ▆▆▆

ACTIVITY 6

Making a Muscle Painting

1. Choose a male student to be "muscle painted."

2. Obtain brushes and water-based paints from the supply area while the "volunteer" removes his shirt and rolls up his pant legs (if necessary).

3. Using different colored paints, identify the muscles listed below by painting his skin. If a muscle covers a large body area, you may opt to paint only its borders.

- biceps brachii
- deltoid
- erector spinae
- pectoralis major
- rectus femoris
- tibialis anterior
- triceps brachii
- vastus lateralis
- biceps femoris
- extensor carpi radialis longus
- latissimus dorsi
- rectus abdominis
- sternocleidomastoid
- trapezius
- triceps surae
- vastus medialis

4. Check your "human painting" with your instructor before cleaning your bench and leaving the laboratory. ▆▆▆

✂ For instructions on animal dissections, see the dissection exercises starting on page 697 in the cat, fetal pig, and rat editions of this manual.

Plantaris

Gastroc-
nemius

Medial
head

Lateral
head

Soleus

Tendon of
gastrocnemius

Calcaneal
tendon

Medial
malleolus

Lateral
malleolus

Calcaneus

(a)

Plantaris (cut)

Gastrocnemius
lateral head (cut)

Gastroc-
nemius
medial head
(cut)

Popliteus

Soleus (cut)

Tibialis posterior

Fibula

Fibularis
longus

Flexor
digitorum
longus

**Flexor hallucis
longus**

Fibularis brevis

Tendon of
tibialis posterior

Medial
malleolus

Calcaneal
tendon (cut)

Calcaneus

(b)

FIGURE 15.15 Muscles of the posterior aspect of the right leg. (a) Superficial
view of the posterior leg. **(b)** The triceps surae has been removed to show the deep
muscles of the posterior compartment.

TABLE 15.9	Muscles Acting on Human Foot and Ankle (continued)			
Muscle	Comments	Origin	Insertion	Action
Deep (Figure 15.15b–e)				
Popliteus	Thin muscle at posterior aspect of knee	Lateral condyle of femur and lateral meniscus	Proximal tibia	Flexes and rotates leg medially to "unlock" extended knee when knee flexion begins
Tibialis posterior	Thick muscle deep to soleus	Superior portion of tibia and fibula and interosseous membrane	Tendon passes obliquely behind medial malleolus and under arch of foot; inserts into several tarsals and metatarsals 2–4	Prime mover of foot inversion; plantar flexes foot; stabilizes longitudinal arch of foot
Flexor digitorum longus	Runs medial to and partially overlies tibialis posterior	Posterior surface of tibia	Distal phalanges of toes 2–5	Flexes toes; plantar flexes and inverts foot
Flexor hallucis longus (see also Figure 15.14a)	Lies lateral to inferior aspect of tibialis posterior	Middle portion of fibula shaft; interosseous membrane	Tendon runs under foot to distal phalanx of great toe	Flexes great toe (*hallux* = great toe); plantar flexes and inverts foot; the "push-off muscle" during walking

O = origin
I = insertion

Tibialis posterior

Popliteus

Flexor hallucis longus

Flexor digitorum longus

(c)   (d)   (e)

FIGURE 15.15 (continued) Muscles of the posterior aspect of the right leg. (c–e) Individual muscles are shown in isolation so that their origins and insertions may be visualized.

Gross Anatomy of the Muscular System

Classification of Skeletal Muscles

1. Several criteria were given for the naming of muscles. Match the criteria (column B) to the muscle names (column A). Note that more than one criterion may apply in some cases.

Column A

_____ 1. gluteus maximus

_____ 2. adductor magnus

_____ 3. biceps femoris

_____ 4. transversus abdominis

_____ 5. extensor carpi ulnaris

_____ 6. trapezius

_____ 7. rectus femoris

_____ 8. external oblique

Column B

a. action of the muscle

b. shape of the muscle

c. location of the origin and/or insertion of the muscle

d. number of origins

e. location of the muscle relative to a bone or body region

f. direction in which the muscle fibers run relative to some imaginary line

g. relative size of the muscle

2. Match the key terms to the muscles and movements described below.

Key: a. prime mover (agonist)   b. antagonist   c. synergist   d. fixator

_____ 1. term for the biceps brachii during elbow flexion

_____ 2. term that describes the relation of brachialis to biceps brachii during elbow flexion

_____ 3. term for the triceps brachii during elbow flexion

_____ 4. term for the iliopsoas during hip extension

_____ 5. term for the gluteus maximus during hip extension when walking up stairs

_____ 6. term for the rotator cuff muscles and deltoid when the elbow is flexed and the hand grabs a tabletop to lift the table

Muscles of the Head and Neck

3. Using choices from the key at the right, correctly identify muscles provided with leader lines on the diagram.

Key:

a. buccinator

b. corrugator supercilii

c. depressor anguli oris

d. depressor labii inferioris

e. epicranius (frontal belly)

f. epicranius (occipital belly)

g. levator labii superioris

h. masseter

i. mentalis

j. orbicularis oculi

k. orbicularis oris

l. platysma

m. trapezius

n. zygomaticus major and minor

Galea aponeurotica

4. Using the key provided in question 3, identify the muscles described next.

_____ 1. used in smiling

_____ 2. used to suck in your cheeks

_____ 3. used in blinking and squinting

_____ 4. used to pout (pulls the corners of the mouth downward)

_____ 5. raises your eyebrows for a questioning expression

_____ 6. used to form the vertical frown crease on the forehead

_____ 7. your "kisser"

_____ 8. prime mover to raise the mandible

_____ 9. tenses skin of the neck during shaving

Muscles of the Trunk

5. Correctly identify both intact and transected (cut) muscles depicted in the diagram, using the key given at the right. (Not all terms will be used in this identification.)

Coracoid process

Bursa

Clavicle

Sternum

Key:

a.   biceps brachii

b.   brachialis

c.   deltoid (cut)

d.   external intercostals

e.   external oblique

f.   internal oblique

g.   latissimus dorsi

h.   pectoralis major

i.   pectoralis minor

j.   rectus abdominis

k.   rhomboids

l.   serratus anterior

m.   subscapularis

n.   transversus abdominis

o.   trapezius

6. Using the key provided in question 5 above, identify the major muscles described next.

_____ 1. a major spine flexor

_____ 2. prime mover for arm extension

_____ 3. prime mover for arm flexion

_____ 4. assume major responsibility for forming the abdominal girdle (three pairs of muscles)

_____ 5. prime mover of shoulder abduction

_____ 6. important in shoulder adduction; antagonists of the shoulder abductor (two muscles)

_____ 7. moves the scapula forward and rotates scapula upward

_____ 8. small, inspiratory muscles between the ribs; elevate the ribs

_____ 9. extends the head

_____ 10. pull the scapulae medially

Muscles of the Upper Limb

7. Using terms from the key on the right, correctly identify all muscles provided with leader lines in the diagram. (Not all the listed terms are used in this exercise.)

Medial epicondyle of humerus

Flexor retinaculum

Palmar aponeurosis

Key:

a. biceps brachii

b. brachialis

c. brachioradialis

d. extensor carpi radialis longus

e. extensor digitorum

f. flexor carpi radialis

g. flexor carpi ulnaris

h. flexor digitorum superficialis

i. flexor pollicis longus

j. palmaris longus

k. pronator quadratus

l. pronator teres

m. supinator

n. triceps brachii

8. Use the key provided in question 7 to identify the muscles described next.

_____ 1. flexes the forearm and supinates the hand

_____ 2. synergist for supination of hand

_____ 3. forearm flexors; no role in supination (two muscles)

_____ 4. elbow extensor

_____ 5. power wrist flexor and abductor

_____ 6. flexes wrist and middle phalanges

_____ 7. pronate the hand (two muscles)

_____ 8. flexes the thumb

_____ 9. extends and abducts the wrist

_____ 10. extends the wrist and digits

_____ 11. flat muscle that is a weak wrist flexor; tenses skin of the palm

Muscles of the Lower Limb

9. Using the terms from the key on the right, correctly identify all muscles provided with leader lines in the diagram below. (Not all listed terms are used in this exercise.)

Patella

Head of fibula

Superior and inferior extensor retinacula

Fibular retinaculum

Lateral malleolus

5th metatarsal

Key:

a. adductor group

b. biceps femoris

c. extensor digitorum longus

d. fibularis brevis

e. fibularis longus

f. flexor hallucis longus

g. gastrocnemius

h. gluteus maximus

i. gluteus medius

j. rectus femoris

k. semimembranosus

l. semitendinosus

m. soleus

n. tensor fasciae latae

o. tibialis anterior

p. tibialis posterior

q. vastus lateralis

10. Use the key terms in question 9 to respond to the descriptions below.

_____ 1. flexes the great toe and inverts the foot

_____ 2. lateral compartment muscles that plantar flex and evert the foot (two muscles)

_____ 3. abduct the thigh to take the "at ease" stance (two muscles)

_____ 4. used to extend the hip when climbing stairs

_____ 5. prime movers of plantar flexion (two muscles) of the foot

_____ 6. prime mover of inversion of the foot

_____ 7. prime mover of dorsiflexion of the foot

_____ 8. adduct the thigh, as when standing at attention

_____ 9. extends the toes

_____ 10. extend thigh and flex knee (three muscles)

_____ 11. extends knee and flexes thigh

General Review: Muscle Recognition

11. Identify the lettered muscles in the diagram of the human anterior superficial musculature by matching its letter with one of the following muscle names:

_jj_ 1. adductor longus

_g_ 2. biceps brachii

_____ 3. brachioradialis

_e_ 4. deltoid

_____ 5. extensor digitorum longus

_ee_ 6. external oblique

_b_ 7. fibularis longus

_____ 8. flexor carpi radialis

_i_ 9. flexor carpi ulnaris

_b_ 10. frontalis

_ll_ 11. gastrocnemius

_____ 12. gracilis

_____ 13. iliopsoas

_____ 14. internal oblique

_____ 15. latissimus dorsi

_____ 16. masseter

_v_ 17. orbicularis oculi

_x_ 18. orbicularis oris

_____ 19. palmaris longus

_____ 20. pectineus

_aa_ 21. pectoralis major

_y_ 22. platysma

_____ 23. pronator teres

_ff_ 24. rectus abdominis

_____ 25. rectus femoris

_____ 26. sartorius

_____ 27. serratus anterior

_mm_ 28. soleus

_z_ 29. sternocleidomastoid

_____ 30. sternohyoid

_a_ 31. temporalis

_____ 32. tensor fasciae latae

_____ 33. tibialis anterior

_gg_ 34. transversus abdominis

_d_ 35. trapezius

_f_ 36. triceps brachii

_____ 37. vastus lateralis

_____ 38. vastus medialis

_w_ 39. zygomaticus

12. Identify each of the lettered muscles in this diagram of the human posterior superficial musculature by matching its letter to one of the following muscle names:

_____ 1. adductor magnus

_____ 2. biceps femoris

_____ 3. brachialis

_____ 4. brachioradialis

_m_ 5. deltoid

_____ 6. extensor carpi radialis longus

_____ 7. extensor carpi ulnaris

_____ 8. extensor digitorum

_____ 9. external oblique

_____ 10. flexor carpi ulnaris

_____ 11. gastrocnemius

_S_ 12. gluteus maximus

_r_ 13. gluteus medius

_____ 14. gracilis

_____ 15. iliotibial tract (tendon)

_____ 16. infraspinatus

_____ 17. latissimus dorsi

_____ 18. occipitalis

_____ 19. semimembranosus

_____ 20. semitendinosus

_k_ 21. sternocleidomastoid

_____ 22. teres major

_l_ 23. trapezius

_a_ 24. triceps brachii

General Review: Muscle Descriptions

13. Identify the muscles described by completing the following statements.

1. The _____, _____, _____, and _____

   are commonly used for intramuscular injections (four muscles).

2. The insertion tendon of the _____ group contains a large sesamoid bone, the patella.

3. The triceps surae insert in common into the _____ tendon.

4. The bulk of the tissue of a muscle tends to lie _____ to the part of the body it causes

   to move.

5. The extrinsic muscles of the hand originate on the _____.

6. Most flexor muscles are located on the _____ aspect of the body; most

   extensors are located _____. An exception to this generalization is the

   extensor-flexor musculature of the _____.

Skeletal Muscle Physiology: Frogs and Human Subjects

MATERIALS

☐ ATP muscle kits (glycerinated rabbit psoas muscle;* ATP and salt solutions obtainable from Carolina Biological Supply)
☐ Petri dishes
☐ Microscope slides
☐ Coverslips
☐ Millimeter ruler
☐ Compound microscope
☐ Stereomicroscope
☐ Pointed glass probes (teasing needles)
☐ Small beakers (50 ml)
☐ Distilled water
☐ Glass-marking pencil
☐ Textbooks or other heavy books
☐ Watch or timer
☐ Ringer's solution (frog)
☐ Scissors
☐ Metal needle probes
☐ Medicine dropper
☐ Cotton thread
☐ Forceps
☐ Disposable gloves
☐ Glass or porcelain plate
☐ Pithed bullfrog†

Notes to the Instructor:
*At the beginning of the lab, the muscle bundle should be removed from the test tube and cut into approximately 2-cm lengths. Both the cut muscle segments and the entubed glycerol should be put into a petri dish. One muscle *segment* is sufficient for every two to four students making observations.
†Bullfrogs to be pithed by lab instructor as needed for student experimentation. (If instructor prefers that students pith their own specimens, an instructional sheet on that procedure suitable for copying for student handouts is provided in the Instructor's Guide.)

Text continues on next page.

OBJECTIVES

1. To observe muscle contraction on the microscopic level and describe the role of ATP and various ions in muscle contraction.
2. To define and explain the physiological basis of the following:

   depolarization threshold stimulus
   repolarization maximal stimulus
   action potential wave summation
   absolute and relative refractory tetanus
     periods muscle fatigue
   subthreshold stimulus

3. To trace the events that result from the electrical stimulation of a muscle.
4. To recognize that a graded response of skeletal muscle is a function of the number of muscle fibers stimulated and the frequency of the stimulus.
5. To name and describe the phases of a muscle twitch.
6. To distinguish between a muscle twitch and a sustained (tetanic) contraction and to describe their importance in normal muscle activity.
7. To demonstrate how a computer or physiograph can be used to obtain pertinent and representative recordings of various physiological events of skeletal muscle activity.
8. To explain the significance of muscle tracings obtained during experimentation.

PRE-LAB QUIZ

1. Circle the correct term. The potential difference, or voltage, across the plasma membrane is the result of the difference in membrane permeability to <u>anions</u> / <u>cations,</u> most importantly Na^+ and K^+.
2. Depolarization of skeletal muscle is caused by a(n)
   a. influx of Ca^+ c. influx of Na^+
   b. influx of K^+ d. release of Na^+
3. The _____ wave follows the depolarization wave across the sarcolemma.
   a. hyperpolarization
   b. refraction
   c. repolarization
4. Circle the correct term. Contraction of a skeletal muscle that results from a single stimulus is called <u>twitch</u> / <u>tetanus.</u>
5. Circle True or False. The voltage at which the first noticeable contractile response is obtained is called the threshold stimulus.
6. Circle True or False. A single muscle is made up of many motor units, and the gradual activation of these motor units results in a graded contraction of the whole muscle.
7. A sustained, smooth, muscle contraction that is a result of high-frequency stimulation is
   a. tetanus b. tonus c. twitch

Text continues on next page.

myA&P For practice quizzes on this lab, go to www.myaandp.com.

235

□ Apparatus A or B:‡
A: physiograph, physiograph paper and
ink, force transducer, pin electrodes,
stimulator, stimulator output extension
cable, transducer stand and cable,
straight pins, frog board, laboratory
stand, clamp

BIOPAC B: BIOPAC® MP36 (or MP35/30)
data acquisition unit, PC or Mac
computer, BIOPAC Student Lab
electrode lead set, hand dynamometer,
headphones, metric tape measure,
disposable vinyl electrodes, and
conduction gel

New versions of the BSL software 3.7.5 and
higher for Windows, and 3.7.4 and higher for
Mac) require slightly different channel
settings and collection strategies.
Instructions for using the newer software with
the MP36/35 data acquisition units can be
found on myA&P. In addition, instructions for
use of the new 2-channel data acquisition
unit, the MP45, may also be found on myA&P.

PEx PhysioEx™ 8.0 Computer Simulation
on page PEx-23

‡Additionally, instructions for Activity 3 using
a kymograph can be found in the Instructor
Guide. Instructions for using PowerLab®
equipment can be found on myA&P.

8. Muscle fatigue, the loss of the ability to contract, may be a result of
    a. oxygen debt in the tissue after prolonged activity
    b. potassium buildup in the tissue after prolonged activity
    c. sodium debt in the tissue after prolonged activity
    d. the accumulation of ATP in the tissue after prolonged activity

The contraction of skeletal and cardiac muscle fibers can be considered in terms of three events—electrical excitation of the muscle cell, excitation-contraction coupling, and shortening of the muscle cell due to sliding of the myofilaments within it.

At rest, all cells maintain a potential difference, or voltage, across their plasma membrane; the inner face of the membrane is approximately −60 to −90 millivolts (mV) compared with the cell exterior. This potential difference is a result of differences in membrane permeability to cations, most importantly sodium (Na^+) and potassium (K^+) ions. Intracellular potassium concentration is much greater than its extracellular concentration, and intracellular sodium concentration is considerably less than its extracellular concentration. Hence, steep concentration gradients across the membrane exist for both cations. Because the plasma membrane is more permeable to K^+ than to Na^+, the cell's **resting membrane potential** is more negative inside than outside. The resting membrane potential is of particular interest in excitable cells, like muscle cells and neurons, because changes in that voltage underlie their ability to do work (to contract and/or issue electrical signals).

Action Potential

When a muscle cell is stimulated, the sarcolemma becomes temporarily more permeable to Na^+, which enters the cell. This sudden influx of Na^+ alters the membrane potential. That is, the cell interior becomes less negatively charged at that point, an event called **depolarization.** When depolarization reaches a certain level and the sarcolemma momentarily changes its polarity, a depolarization wave travels along the sarcolemma. Even as the influx of Na^+ occurs, the sarcolemma becomes less permeable to Na^+ and more permeable to K^+. Consequently, K^+ ions move out of the cell, restoring the resting membrane potential (but not the original ionic conditions), an event called **repolarization.** The repolarization wave follows the depolarization wave across the sarcolemma. This rapid depolarization and repolarization of the membrane that is propagated along the entire membrane from the point of stimulation is called the **action potential.**

The **absolute refractory period** is the period of time when Na^+ permeability of the sarcolemma is rapidly changing and maximal, and the following period when Na^+ permeability becomes restricted. During this period there is no possibility of generating another action potential. As Na^+ permeability is gradually restored to resting levels during repolarization, an especially strong stimulus to the muscle cell may provoke another action potential. This period of time is the **relative refractory period.** Repolarization restores the muscle cell's normal excitability. If the muscle cell is stimulated to contract rapidly again and again, the changes in Na^+ and K^+ concentrations near the membrane begin to reduce its ability to respond. Therefore, the sodium-potassium pump, which actively transports K^+ into the cell and Na^+ out of the cell, must be "revved up" (become more active) to reestablish the ionic concentrations of the resting state.

Contraction

Propagation of the action potential along the sarcolemma causes the release of calcium ions (Ca^{2+}) from storage in the sarcoplasmic reticulum within the muscle cell. When the calcium ions bind to regulatory proteins on the actin myofilaments, they act as an ionic trigger that initiates contraction, and the actin and myosin filaments slide past each other. Once the action potential ends, the calcium ions are almost immediately transported back into the sarcoplasmic reticulum. Instantly the muscle cell relaxes.

The events of the contraction process can most simply be summarized as follows: Muscle cell contraction is initiated by generation and transmission of an action potential along the sarcolemma. This electrical event is coupled to the sliding of the myofilaments—contraction—by the release of calcium ions (Ca^{2+}). Keep in mind this sequence of events as you conduct the experiments.

Observing Muscle Fiber Contraction

In this simple observational experiment, you will have the opportunity to review your understanding of muscle cell anatomy and to watch fibers respond to the presence of ATP and/or a solution of K^+ and magnesium ions (Mg^{2+}).

This experiment uses preparations of glycerinated muscle. The glycerination process denatures troponin and tropomyosin. Consequently, calcium, so critical for contraction in vivo, is not necessary here. The role of magnesium and potassium salts as cofactors in the contraction process is not well understood, but magnesium and potassium salts seem to be required for ATPase activity in this system.

1. Talk with other members of your lab group to develop a hypothesis about requirements for muscle fiber contraction for this experiment. The hypothesis should have three parts: (1) salts only, (2) ATP only, and (3) salts and ATP.

2. Obtain the following materials from the supply area: two glass teasing needles; six glass microscope slides and six coverslips; millimeter ruler; dropper bottles containing the following solutions: (a) 0.25% ATP in triply distilled water, (b) 0.25% ATP plus 0.05 M KCl plus 0.001 M $MgCl_2$ in distilled water, and (c) 0.05 M KCl plus 0.001 M $MgCl_2$ in distilled water; a petri dish; a beaker of distilled water; a glass-marking pencil; and a small portion of a previously cut muscle bundle segment. While you are at the supply area, place the muscle fibers in the petri dish and pour a small amount of glycerol (the fluid in the supply petri dish) over your muscle cells. Also obtain both a compound and a stereo microscope and bring them to your laboratory bench.

3. Using clean fine glass needles, tease the muscle segment to separate its fibers. The objective is to isolate *single* muscle cells or fibers for observation. Be patient and work carefully so that the fibers do not get torn during this isolation procedure.

4. Transfer one or more of the fibers (or the thinnest strands you have obtained) onto a clean microscope slide with a glass needle, and cover it with a coverslip. Examine the fiber under the compound microscope at low- and then high-power magnifications to observe the striations and the smoothness of the fibers when they are in the relaxed state.

5. Clean three microscope slides well and rinse in distilled water. Label the slides A, B, and C.

6. Transfer three or four fibers to microscope slide A with a glass needle. Using the needle as a prod, carefully position the fibers so that they are parallel to one another and as straight as possible. Place this slide under a *stereomicroscope* and measure the length of each fiber by holding a millimeter ruler adjacent to it. Alternatively, you can rest the microscope slide *on* the millimeter ruler to make your length determinations. Record the data on the chart below.

7. Flood the fibers (situated under the stereomicroscope) with several drops of the solution containing ATP, K^+, and Mg^{2+}. Watch the reaction of the fibers after adding the solution. After 30 seconds (or slightly longer), remeasure each fiber and record the observed lengths on the chart. Also, observe the fibers to see if any width changes have occurred. Calculate the degree (or percentage) of contraction by using the simple formula on the next page, and record this data on the chart below.

Salts and ATP, slide A	Muscle fiber 1	Muscle fiber 2	Muscle fiber 3	Average
Initial length (mm)				
Contracted length (mm)				
% Contraction				
ATP only, slide B				
Initial length (mm)				
Contracted length (mm)				
% Contraction				
Salts only, slide C				
Initial length (mm)				
Contracted length (mm)				
% Contraction				

$$\frac{Initial}{length\ (mm)} - \frac{contracted}{length\ (mm)} = \frac{degree\ of}{contraction\ (mm)}$$

then:

$$\frac{Degree\ of\ contraction\ (mm)}{initial\ length\ (mm)} \times 100 = \underline{\hspace{1cm}}\%\ contraction$$

8. Carefully transfer one of the contracted fibers to a clean, unmarked microscope slide, cover with a coverslip, and observe with the compound microscope. Mentally compare your initial observations with the view you are observing now. What differences do you see? (Be specific.)

_____

_____

_____

What zones (or bands) have disappeared?

_____

_____

9. Repeat steps 6 through 8 twice more, using clean slides and fresh muscle cells. On slide B use the solution of ATP in distilled water (no salts). Then, on slide C use the solution containing only salts (no ATP) for the third series. Record data on the chart on page 237.

10. Collect the data from all the groups in your laboratory and use these data to prepare a lab report. (See Getting Started, page xv.) Include in your discussion the following questions:

What degree of contraction was observed when ATP was applied in the absence of K^+ and Mg^{2+}?

_____

_____

What degree of contraction was observed when the muscle fibers were flooded with a solution containing K^+ Mg^{2+}, and lacking ATP?

_____

_____

What conclusions can you draw about the importance of ATP, K^+, and Mg^{2+} to the contractile process?

_____

_____

_____

Can you draw exactly the same conclusions from the data provided by each group? List some variables that might have been introduced into the procedure and that might account for any differences.

_____

_____

Demonstrating Muscle Fatigue in Humans

1. Work in small groups. In each group select a subject, a timer, and a recorder.

2. Obtain a copy of the laboratory manual and a copy of the textbook. Weigh each book separately, and then record the weight of each in the chart in step 6.

3. The subject is to extend an upper limb straight out in front of him or her, holding the position until the arm shakes or the muscles begin to ache. Record the time to fatigue on the chart.

4. Allow the subject to rest for several minutes. Now ask the subject to hold the laboratory manual while keeping the arm and forearm in the same position as in step 3 above. Record the time to fatigue on the chart.

5. Allow the subject to rest again for several minutes. Now ask the subject to hold the textbook while keeping the upper limb in the same position as in steps 3 and 4 above. Record the time to fatigue on the chart.

6. Each person in the group should take a turn as the subject, and all data should be recorded in the chart below.

Load	Weight of object	Time elapsed Until fatigue		
		Subject 1	Subject 2	Subject 3
Appendage	N/A			
Lab Manual				
Textbook				

7. What can you conclude about the effect of load on muscle fatigue? Explain.

_____

_____

_____

Inducing Contraction in the Frog Gastrocnemius Muscle

Physiologists have learned a great deal about the way muscles function by isolating muscles from laboratory animals and then stimulating these muscles to observe their responses. Various stimuli—electrical shock, temperature changes, extremes of pH, certain chemicals—elicit muscle activity, but laboratory experiments of this type typically use electrical shock. This is because it is easier to control the onset and cessation of electrical shock, as well as the strength of the stimulus.

Various types of apparatus are used to record muscle contraction. All include a way to mark time intervals, a way to indicate exactly when the stimulus was applied, and a way to

FIGURE 16A.1 Physiograph setup for frog gastrocnemius experiments.

measure the magnitude of the contractile response. Instructions are provided here for setting up a physiograph apparatus (Figure 16A.1). Specific instructions for use of recording apparatus during recording will be provided by your instructor.

Preparing a Muscle for Experimentation

The preparatory work that precedes the recording of muscle activity tends to be quite time-consuming. If you work in teams of two or three, the work can be divided. While one of you is setting up the recording apparatus, one or two students can dissect the frog leg (Figure 16a.2). Experimentation should begin as soon as the dissection is completed.

Materials

Channel amplifier and transducer cable

Stimulator panel and stimulator output extension cable

Force transducer

Transducer tension adjuster

Transducer stand

Two pin electrodes

Frog board and straight pins

Prepared frog (gastrocnemius muscle freed and calcaneal tendon ligated)

Frog Ringer's solution

Procedure

1. Connect transducer to tranducer stand and attach frog board to stand.

2. Attach tranducer cable to transducer and to input connection on channel amplifier.

3. Attach stimulator output extension cable to output on stimulator panel (red to red, black to black).

4. Using clip at opposite end of extension cable, attach cable to bottom of transducer stand adjacent to frog board.

5. Attach two pin electrodes securely to electrodes on clip.

6. Place knee of prepared frog in clip-on frog board and secure by inserting a straight pin through tissues of frog. Keep frog muscle moistened with Ringer's solution.

7. Attach thread from the calcaneal tendon of frog to transducer spring hook.

8. Adjust position of tranducer on stand to produce a constant tension on thread attached to muscle (taut but not tight). Gastrocnemius muscle should hang vertically directly below hook.

9. Insert free ends of pin electrodes into the muscle, one at proximal end and the other at distal end.

FIGURE 16A.2 Preparation of the frog gastrocnemius muscle. Numbers indicate the sequence of manipulation.

  DISSECTION:

Frog Hind Limb

1.   Before beginning the frog dissection, have the following supplies ready at your laboratory bench: a small beaker containing 20 to 30 ml of frog Ringer's solution, scissors, a metal needle probe, a glass probe with a pointed tip, a medicine dropper, cotton thread, forceps, a glass or porcelain plate, and disposable gloves. While these supplies are being accumulated, one member of your team should notify the instructor that you are ready to begin experimentation, so that a frog can be prepared (pithed). Preparation of a frog in this manner renders it unable to feel pain and prevents reflex movements (like hopping) that would interfere with the experiments.

⚠   2.   All students who will be handling the frog should don disposable gloves. Obtain a pithed frog and place

it ventral surface down on the glass plate. Make an incision into the skin approximately midthigh (Figure 16A.2), and then continue the cut completely around the thigh. Grasp the skin with the forceps and strip it from the leg and hindfoot. The skin adheres more at the joints, but a careful, persistent pulling motion—somewhat like pulling off a nylon stocking—will enable you to remove it in one piece. _From this point on, the exposed muscle tissue should be kept moistened with the Ringer's solution_ to prevent spontaneous twitches.

3.   Identify the gastrocnemius muscle (the fleshy muscle of the posterior calf) and the calcaneal (Achilles) tendon that secures it to the heel.

4.   Slip a glass probe under the gastrocnemius muscle and run it along the entire length and under the calcaneal tendon to free them from the underlying tissues.

5.   Cut a piece of thread about 10 inches long and use the glass probe to slide the thread under the calcaneal tendon. Knot the thread firmly around the tendon and then sever the tendon distal to the thread. Alternatively, you can bend a common pin into a Z-shape and insert the pin securely into the tendon. The thread is then attached to the opposite end of the pin. Once the tendon has been tied or pinned, the frog is ready for experimentation (see Figure 16A.2).

Recording Muscle Activity

Skeletal muscles consist of thousands of muscle cells and react to stimuli with graded responses. Thus muscle contractions can be weak or vigorous, depending on the requirements of the task. Graded responses (different degrees of shortening) of a skeletal muscle depend on the number of muscle cells being stimulated. In the intact organism, the number of motor units firing at any one time determines how many muscle cells will be stimulated. In this laboratory, the frequency and strength of an electrical current determines the response.

A single contraction of skeletal muscle is called a **muscle twitch.** A tracing of a muscle twitch (Figure 16A.3) shows three distinct phases: latent, contraction, and relaxation. The **latent phase** is the interval from stimulus application until the muscle begins to shorten. Although no activity is indicated on the tracing during this phase, important electrical and chemical changes are occurring within the muscle. During the **contraction phase,** the muscle fibers shorten; the tracing shows an increasingly higher needle deflection and the tracing peaks. During the **relaxation phase,** represented by a downward curve of the tracing, the muscle fibers relax and lengthen. On a slowly moving recording surface, the single muscle twitch appears as a spike (rather than a bell-shaped curve, as in Figure 16A.3), but on a rapidly moving recording surface, the three distinct phases just described become recognizable.

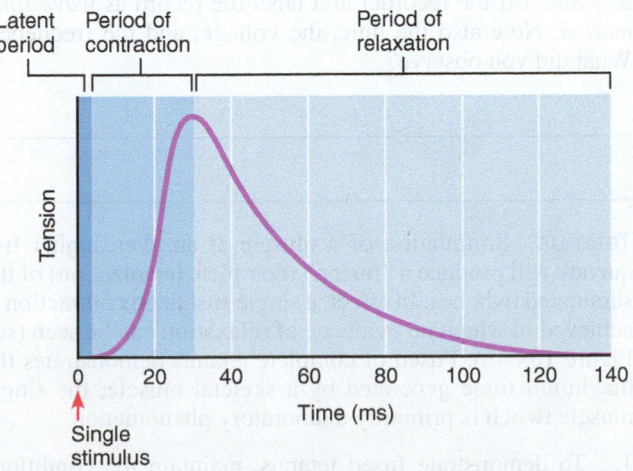

FIGURE 16A.3 Tracing of a muscle twitch.

Determining the Threshold Stimulus

1.   Assuming that you have already set up the recording apparatus, set the time marker to deliver one pulse per second and set the paper speed at a slow rate, approximately 0.1 cm per second.

2.   Set the duration control on the stimulator between 7 and 15 milliseconds (msec), multiplier ×1. Set the voltage control at 0 V, multiplier ×1. Turn the sensitivity control knob of the stimulator fully clockwise (lowest value, greatest sensitivity).

3.   Administer single stimuli to the muscle at 1-minute intervals, beginning with 0.1 V and increasing each successive stimulus by 0.1 V until a contraction is obtained (shown by a spike on the paper).

At what voltage did contraction occur? _____ V

The voltage at which the first perceptible contractile response is obtained is called the **threshold stimulus.** All stimuli applied prior to this point are termed **subthreshold stimuli,** because at those voltages no response was elicited.

4.   Stop the recording and mark the record to indicate the threshold stimulus, voltage, and time. _Do not remove the record from the recording surface;_ continue with the next experiment. _Remember: keep the muscle preparation moistened with Ringer's solution at all times._

Observing Graded Muscle Response to Increased Stimulus Intensity

1.   Follow the previous setup instructions, but set the voltage control at the threshold voltage (as determined in the first experiment).

2.   Deliver single stimuli at 1-minute intervals. Initially increase the voltage between shocks by 0.5 V; then increase the voltage by 1 to 2 V between shocks as the experiment continues, until contraction height increases no further. Stop the recording apparatus.

What voltage produced the highest spike (and thus the maximal strength of contraction)? _____ V

This voltage, called the **maximal stimulus** (for _your_ muscle specimen), is the weakest stimulus at which all muscle cells are being stimulated.

3.   Mark the record _maximal stimulus._ Record the maximal stimulus voltage and the time you completed the experiment.

4.   What is happening to the muscle as the voltage is increased?

_____

_____

What is another name for this phenomenon?

_____

5.   Explain why the strength of contraction does not increase once the maximal stimulus is reached.

_____

_____

Timing the Muscle Twitch

1.   Follow the previous setup directions, but set the voltage for the maximal stimulus (as determined in the preceding experiment) and set the paper advance or recording speed at maximum. Record the paper speed setting:

_____ mm/sec

2.   Determine the time required for the paper to advance 1 mm by using the formula

$$\frac{1 \text{ mm}}{\text{mm/sec (paper speed)}}$$

(Thus, if your paper speed is 25 mm/sec, each mm on the chart equals 0.04 sec.) Record the computed value:

1 mm = _____ sec

3.   Deliver single stimuli at 1-minute intervals to obtain several "twitch" curves. Stop the recording.

4.   Determine the duration of the latent, contraction, and relaxation phases of the twitches and record the data below.

Duration of latent period: _____ sec

Duration of contraction period: _____ sec

Duration of relaxation period: _____ sec

5.   Label the record to indicate the point of stimulus, the beginning of contraction, the end of contraction, and the end of relaxation.

6.   Allow the muscle to rest (but keep it moistened with Ringer's solution) before continuing with the next experiment.

Observing Graded Muscle Response to Increased Stimulus Frequency

Muscles subjected to frequent stimulation, without a chance to relax, exhibit two kinds of responses—wave summation and tetanus—depending on the level of stimulus frequency (Figure 16A.4).

Wave Summation   If a muscle is stimulated with a rapid series of stimuli of the same intensity before it has had a chance to relax completely, the response to the second and subsequent stimuli will be greater than to the first stimulus (see Figure 16A.4a). This phenomenon, called **wave,** or **temporal, summation,** occurs because the muscle is already in a partially contracted state when subsequent stimuli are delivered.

(a)

(b)

FIGURE 16A.4 Muscle response to stimulation. Arrows represent stimuli **(a)** Wave summation at low frequency stimulation. **(b)** Fused tetanus occurs as stimulation rate is increased.

1.   Set up the apparatus as in the previous experiment, setting the voltage to the maximal stimulus as determined earlier and the chart speed to maximum.

2.   With the stimulator in single mode, deliver two successive stimuli as rapidly as possible.

3.   Shut off the recorder and label the record as _wave summation._ Note also the time, the voltage, and the frequency. What did you observe?

_____

_____

Tetanus   Stimulation of a muscle at an even higher frequency will produce a "fusion" (complete tetanization) of the summated twitches. In effect, a single sustained contraction is achieved in which no evidence of relaxation can be seen (see Figure 16A.4b). Fused or complete tetanus demonstrates the maximum force generated by a skeletal muscle; the single muscle twitch is primarily a laboratory phenomenon.

1.   To demonstrate fused tetanus, maintain the conditions used for wave summation except for the frequency of stimulation. Set the stimulator to deliver 60 stimuli per second.

2.   As soon as you obtain a single smooth, sustained contraction (with no evidence of relaxation), discontinue stimulation and shut off the recorder.

3.   Label the tracing with the conditions of experimentation, the time, and the area of *fused* or *complete tetanus*.

Inducing Muscle Fatigue

Muscle fatigue, the loss of the ability to contract, may be a result of the oxygen debt that occurs in the tissue after prolonged activity (through the accumulation of such waste products as lactic acid, as well as the depletion of ATP), depletion of nutrients, ion imbalances, or tissue damage. True muscle fatigue rarely occurs in the body because it is most often preceded by a subjective feeling of fatigue. Furthermore, fatigue of the neuromuscular junctions typically precedes fatigue of the muscle.

1.   To demonstrate muscle fatigue, set up an experiment like the tetanus experiment but continue stimulation until the muscle completely relaxes and the contraction curve returns to the base line.

2.   Measure the time interval between the beginning of complete tetanus and the beginning of fatigue (when the tracing begins its downward curve). Mark the record appropriately.

3.   Determine the time required for complete fatigue to occur (the time interval from the beginning of fatigue until the return of the curve to the base line). Mark the record appropriately.

4.   Allow the muscle to rest (keeping it moistened with Ringer's solution) for 10 minutes, and then repeat the experiment.

What was the effect of the rest period on the fatigued muscle?

_____

_____

_____

What is the physiological basis for this reaction?

_____

_____

_____

Determining the Effect of Load on Skeletal Muscle

When the fibers of a skeletal muscle are slightly stretched by a weight or tension, the muscle responds by contracting more forcibly and thus is capable of doing more work. When the actin and myosin barely overlap, sliding can occur along nearly the entire length of the actin filaments. If the load is increased beyond the optimum, the latent period becomes longer, contractile force decreases, and relaxation (fatigue) occurs more quickly. With excessive stretching, the muscle is unable to develop any active tension and no contraction occurs. Since the filaments no longer overlap at all with this degree of stretching, the sliding force cannot be generated.

If your equipment allows you to add more weights to the muscle specimen or to increase the tension on the muscle, perform the following experiment to determine the effect of loading on skeletal muscle and to develop a work curve for the frog's gastrocnemius muscle.

1.   Set the stimulator to deliver the maximal voltage as previously determined.

2.   Stimulate the unweighted muscle with single shocks at 1- to 2-second intervals to achieve three or four muscle twitches.

3.   Stop the recording apparatus and add 10 g of weight or tension to the muscle. Restart and advance the recording about 1 cm, and then stimulate again to obtain three or four spikes.

4.   Repeat the previous step seven more times, increasing the weight by 10 g each time until the total load on the muscle is 80 g or the muscle fails to respond. If the calcaneal tendon tears, the weight will drop, thus ending the trial. In such cases, you will need to prepare another frog's leg to continue the experiments and the maximal stimulus will have to be determined for the new muscle preparation.

5.   When these "loading" experiments are completed, discontinue recording. Mark the curves on the record to indicate the load (in grams).

6.   Measure the height of contraction (in millimeters) for each sequence of twitches obtained with each load, and insert this information on the chart on page 244.

7.   Compute the work done by the muscle for each twitch (load) sequence.

Weight of load (g) $\times$ distance load lifted (mm) = work done

Enter these calculations into the chart in the column labeled Work done, Trial 1.

8.   Allow the muscle to rest for 5 minutes. Then conduct a second trial in the same manner (i.e., repeat steps 2 through 7). Record this second set of measurements and calculations in the columns labeled Trial 2. Be sure to keep the muscle well moistened with Ringer's solution during the resting interval.

9.   Using two different colors, plot a line graph of work done against the weight on the grid accompanying the chart for each trial. Label each plot appropriately.

10.   Dismantle all apparatus and prepare the equipment for storage. Dispose of the frog remains in the appropriate container. Discard the gloves as instructed and wash and dry your hands.

11.   Inspect your records of the experiments and make sure each is fully labeled with the experimental conditions, the date, and the names of those who conducted the experiments. For future reference, attach a tracing (or a copy of the tracing) for each experiment to this page. ■■

Load (g)	Distance load lifted (mm)		Work done	
	Trial 1	Trial 2	Trial 1	Trial 2
0				
10				
20				
30				
40				
50				
60				
70				
80				

A C T I V I T Y   4

Electromyography in a Human Subject Using BIOPAC®

Part 1: Temporal and Multiple Motor Unit Summation

This activity is an introduction to a procedure known as **electromyography,** the recording of skin-surface voltage manifestations of underlying skeletal muscle contraction. The actual visible recording of the resulting voltage waveforms is called an **electromyogram** (EMG).

A single skeletal muscle consists of numerous elongated *skeletal muscle cells,* also called *skeletal muscle fibers,* as discussed in Exercise 14. These muscle cells are excited by *motor neurons* of the central nervous system whose *axons* terminate at the muscle. An axon of a motor neuron branches profusely at the muscle; each branch produces multiple **axon terminals,** each of which innervates a single fiber. The number of muscle cells controlled by a single motor neuron can vary greatly, from five (for fine control needed in the hand) to 500 (for gross control, such as in the buttocks). The most important organizational concept in the physiology of muscle contraction is the *motor unit,* a single motor neuron and all of the cells within a muscle that it activates (see Figure 14.6 p. 192). Understanding gross muscular contraction depends upon realizing that a single muscle consists of multiple motor units, and that the gradual and coordinated activation of these motor units results in **graded contraction** of the whole muscle.

The nervous system controls muscle contraction by two mechanisms:

1. **Multiple motor unit summation (recruitment):** the gradual activation of more and more motor units

2. **Temporal (wave) summation:** an increase in the *frequency* of nerve impulses for each active motor unit

Thus, increasing the force of contraction of a muscle arises from gradually increasing the number of motor units being activated and increasing the frequency of nerve impulses delivered by those active motor units.

A final phenomenon, which is hardly noticeable except when performing electromyography, is **tonus,** a constant state of slight excitation of a muscle while it is in the relaxed state. Even while "at rest," a small number of motor units to a skeletal muscle remain slightly active to prepare the muscle for possible contraction.

Setting Up the Equipment

1. Connect the BIOPAC® unit to the computer.

2. Turn the computer **ON.**

3. Make sure the BIOPAC® unit is **OFF.**

4. Plug in the equipment as shown in Figure 16A.5.

- Electrode lead set—CH 3

- Headphones—back of unit

5. Turn the BIOPAC® unit **ON.**

6. Attach three electrodes to the subject's dominant forearm as shown in Figure 16A.6 and attach the electrode leads according to the colors indicated.

7. Start the BIOPAC® Student Lab program by double-clicking the icon on the desktop or by following your instructor's guidance.

FIGURE 16A.5 Setting up the BIOPAC® equipment to observe temporal and multiple motor unit summation. Plug the headphones into the back of the data acquisition unit and the electrode lead set into Channel 3.

8.   Select lesson **L01-EMG-1** from the menu and click **OK.**

9.   Type in a filename that will save this subject's data on the computer hard drive. You may want to use the subject's last name followed by EMG-1 (for example, SmithEMG-1). Then click **OK.**

Calibrating the Equipment

1.   With the subject in a still position, click **Calibrate.** This initiates the process by which the computer automatically establishes parameters to record the data properly for the subject.

White lead
(−)

Red lead
(+)

Black lead
(ground)

FIGURE 16A.6 Placement of electrodes and the appropriate attachment of electrode leads by color.

2.   After you click **OK,** have the subject wait for 2 seconds, clench the fist tightly for 2 seconds, then release the fist and relax. The computer then automatically stops the recording.

3.   Observe the recording of the calibration data, which should look like the waveform in Figure 16A.7.

- If the data look very different, click **Redo Calibration** and repeat the steps above.

- If the data look similar, proceed to the next section.

Recording the Data

1.   After you click **Record,** have the subject clench the fist softly for 2 seconds, then relax for 2 seconds, then clench harder for 2 seconds, and relax for 2 seconds, then clench even harder for 2 seconds, and relax for 2 seconds, and finally clench with maximum strength then relax. The result should be a series of four clenches of increasing intensity.

FIGURE 16A.7 Example of waveform during the calibration procedure.

FIGURE 16A.8 Example of waveforms during the recording of data. Note the increased signal strength with the increasing force of the clench.

When the subject is ready to do this, click **Record;** then click **Suspend** when the subject is finished.

2.   Observe the recording of the data, which should look like the waveforms in Figure 16A.8.

● If the data look very different, click **Redo** and repeat the steps above.

● If the data look similar, click **STOP.** Click **YES** in response to the question, "Are you finished with both forearm recordings?"

Optional: Anyone can use the headphones to listen to an "auditory version" of the electrical activity of contraction by clicking **Listen** and having the subject clench and relax. Note that the frequency of the auditory signal corresponds with the frequency of action potentials stimulating the muscles. The signal will continue to run until you click **STOP.**

3.   Click **Done,** and then remove all electrodes from the forearm.

● If you wish to record from another subject, choose the **Record from another subject** option and return to step 6 under Setting Up the Equipment.

● If you are finished recording, choose **Analyze current data file** and click **OK.** Proceed to Data Analysis, step 2.

Data Analysis

1.   If you are just starting the BIOPAC® program to perform data analysis, enter **Review Saved Data** mode and choose the file with the subject's EMG data (for example, SmithEMG-1).

2.   Observe the **Raw EMG** recording and computer-calculated **Integrated EMG.** The raw EMG is the actual recording of the voltage (in mV) at each instant in time, while the integrated EMG reflects the absolute intensity of the voltage from baseline at each instant in time.

FIGURE 16A.9 Using the I-beam cursor to highlight a cluster of data for analysis.

3.   To analyze the data, set up the first four pairs of channel/measurement boxes at the top of the screen by selecting the following channels and measurement types from the drop-down menus (note that Channel 3 contains the raw EMG data and Channel 40 contains the integrated EMG data):

Channel	Measurement
CH 3	min
CH 3	max
CH 3	p-p
CH 40	mean

4.   Use the arrow cursor and click the I-beam cursor box at the lower right of the screen to activate the "area selection" function. Using the activated I-beam cursor, highlight the first EMG cluster, representing the first fist-clenching (Figure 16A.9).

5.   Notice that the computer automatically calculates the **min, max, p-p,** and **mean** for the selected area. These measurements, calculated from the data by the computer, represent the following:

min: Displays the *minimum* value in the selected area

max: Displays the *maximum* value in the selected area

p-p (peak-to-peak): Measures the difference in value between the highest and lowest values in the selected area

mean: Displays the average value in the selected area

6.   Write down the data for clench 1 in the chart on page 247 (round to the nearest 0.01 mV).

7. Using the I-beam cursor, highlight the clusters for clenches 2, 3, and 4, and record the data in the chart below.

	Min	Max	P-P	Mean
Clench 1				
Clench 2				
Clench 3				
Clench 4				

From the data recorded in the chart, what trend do you observe for each of these measurements as the subject gradually increases the force of muscle contraction?

_____

_____

What is the relationship between maximum voltage for each clench and the number of motor units in the forearm that are being activated?

_____

_____

Part 2: Force Measurement and Fatigue

In this set of activities you will be observing graded muscle contractions and fatigue in a subject. **Graded muscle contractions,** which represent increasing levels of force generated by a muscle, depend upon: (1) the gradual activation of more motor units, and (2) increasing the frequency of motor neuron action potentials for each active motor unit. This permits a range of forces to be generated by any given muscle or group of muscles, all the way up to the maximum force.

For example, the biceps muscle will have more active motor units and exert more force when lifting a 10-kg object than when lifting a 2-kg object. In addition, the motor neuron of each active motor unit will increase the frequency of action potentials delivered to the motor units, resulting in tetanus. When all of the motor units of a muscle are activated and in a state of tetanus, the maximum force of that muscle is achieved. Recall that fatigue is a condition in which the muscle gradually loses some or all of its ability to contract after contracting for an extended period of time. **Physiological fatigue** occurs when there is a subsequent decrease in the amount of ATP available for contraction; increased levels of the anaerobic by-product, lactic acid; and ionic imbalances.

In this exercise, you will observe and measure graded contractions of the fist, and then observe fatigue, in both the dominant and nondominant arms. To measure the force generated during fist contraction, you will use a **hand dynamometer** (*dynamo* = force; *meter* = measure). The visual recording of force is called a **dynagram,** and the procedure of measuring the force itself is called **dynamometry.**

You will first record data from the subject's **dominant arm** (forearm 1) indicated by his or her "handedness," then repeat the procedures on the subject's **nondominant arm** (forearm 2) for comparison.

Setting Up the Equipment

1. Connect the BIOPAC® unit to the computer and turn the computer **ON.**

2. Make sure the BIOPAC® unit is **OFF.**

3. Plug in the equipment as shown in Figure 16A.10.

- Hand dynamometer—CH 1

- Electrode lead set—CH 3

- Headphones—back of unit

4. Turn the BIOPAC® unit **ON.**

5. Attach three electrodes to the subject's *dominant* forearm (forearm 1) as shown in Figure 16A.11, and attach the electrode leads according to the colors indicated.

6. Start the BIOPAC® Student Lab program on the computer by double-clicking the icon on the desktop or by following your instructor's guidance.

7. Select lesson **L02-EMG-2** from the menu and click **OK.**

8. Type in a filename that will save this subject's data on the computer hard drive. You may want to use subject's last name followed by EMG-2 (for example, SmithEMG-2). Then click **OK.**

BIOPAC® data
acquisition unit

Headphones (plug into
back of BIOPAC® unit)

Electrode lead set
(plugs into Channel 3)

Hand dynamometer
(plugs into Channel 1)

**FIGURE 16A.10 Setting up the BIOPAC® equipment to observe graded muscle
contractions and muscle fatigue.** Plug the headphones into the back of the data
acquisition unit, the hand dynamometer into Channel 1, and the electrode lead set into
Channel 3.

Calibrating the Equipment

1. With the hand dynamometer at rest on the table, click
Calibrate. This initiates the process by which the computer
automatically establishes parameters to record the data properly for the subject.

2. A pop-up window prompts the subject to remove any
grip force. This is to ensure that the dynamometer has been at
rest on the table and that no force is being applied. When this
is so, click **OK.**

White lead
(−)

Red lead
(+)

Black lead
(ground)

**FIGURE 16A.11 Placement of electrodes and the
appropriate attachment of electrode leads by color.**

3. As instructed by the pop-up window, the subject is to
grasp the hand dynamometer with the dominant hand. With
model SS25L, grasp as close to the crossbar as possible
without actually touching the crossbar, as shown in Figure
16A.12a. The crossbar should be held parallel to the floor, not
at an angle. With model SS25LA, grasp the dynamometer
with the palm of the hand against the short grip bar, as shown
in Figure 16A.12b. Hold model SS25LA vertically. When this
is so, click **OK.** The instructions that follow apply to either
model of dynamometer.

4. As instructed by the next pop-up window, have the subject wait 2 seconds, then squeeze the hand dynamometer as
hard as possible for 2 seconds, and then relax. The computer
will automatically stop the calibration.

5. When the subject is ready to proceed, click **OK** and
follow the instructions in step 4. The calibration will stop
automatically.

6. Observe the recording of the calibration data, which
should look like the waveforms in Figure 16A.13.

- If the data look very different, click **Redo Calibration**
  and repeat the steps above.

- If the data look similar, proceed to the next section.

Recording Incremental Force Data for the Forearm

1. Using the force data from the calibration procedure, estimate the **maximum force** that the subject generated (kg).

2. Divide that maximum force by four. In the next activity,
the subject will gradually increase the force in approximately

Dynagrip crossbar

Hand close to bracket but not touching it

Short grip bar

(b) Model SS25LA

(a) Model SS25L

FIGURE 16A.12 Proper grasp of the hand dynamometer using either model SS25L or model SS25LA.

2.   Divide that maximum force by four. In the next activity, the subject will gradually increase the force in approximately these increments. For example, if the maximum force generated was 20 kg, the increment will be 20/4 = 5 kg. The subject will grip at 5 kg, then 10 kg, then 15 kg, and then 20 kg. The subject should watch the tracing on the computer screen and compare it to the scale on the right to determine each target force.

3.   After you click **Record,** have the subject wait 2 seconds, clench at the first force increment 2 seconds (for example, 5 kg), then relax 2 seconds, clench at the second force increment 2 seconds (10 kg), then relax 2 seconds, clench at the

third force increment 2 seconds (15 kg), then relax 2 seconds, then clench with the maximum force 2 seconds (20 kg), and then relax. When the subject relaxes after the maximum clench, click **Suspend** to stop the recording.

4.   Observe the recording of the data, which should look similar to the data in Figure 16A.14.

• If the data look very different, click **Redo** and repeat the steps above.

• If the data look similar, proceed to observation and recording of muscle fatigue.

FIGURE 16A.13 Example of calibration data. Force is measured in kilograms at the top and electromyography is measured in millivolts at the bottom.

FIGURE 16A.14 Example of incremental force data.

FIGURE 16A.15 Example of muscle fatigue data.

Recording Muscle Fatigue Data for the Forearm

Continuing from the end of the incremental force recording, the subject will next record muscle fatigue.

1. After you click **Resume,** the recording will continue from where it stopped and the subject will clench the dynamometer with maximum force for as long as possible. A triangular "marker" will appear at the top of the data, denoting the beginning of this recording segment. When the subject's clench force falls below 50% of the maximum (for example, below 10 kg for a subject with 20 kg maximum force), click **Suspend.** The subject should not watch the screen during this procedure; those helping can inform the subject when it is time to relax.

2. Observe the recording of the data, which should look similar to the data in Figure 16A.15.

- If the data look very different, click **Redo** and repeat the steps above.

- If the data look similar, click **STOP.**

3. When you click **STOP,** a dialog box comes up asking if you are sure you want to stop recording. Click **NO** to return to the **Resume** or **Stop** options, providing one last chance to redo the fatigue recording. Click **YES** to end the recording session and automatically save your data with an added filename extension (1-L02), which indicates forearm 1 for lesson 2. This extension is appended to the filename you entered previously (for example, SmithEMG-2-1-L02).

Optional: Anyone can use the headphones to listen to an "auditory version" of the electrical activity of contraction by clicking **Listen** and having the subject clench and relax. Note that the frequency of the auditory signal corresponds to the frequency of action potentials stimulating the muscles. The signal will continue to run until you click **STOP.**

4. If you want to proceed with recording data from the nondominant arm (forearm 2), move to the next section. If not, click **Done,** then choose **Analyze current data file** and proceed to Data Analysis, step 2.

5. Remove all electrodes from the arm of the subject.

Recording from the Nondominant Arm

1. Click **Forearm 2.**

2. To record from the nondominant forearm, return to step 5 under Setting Up the Equipment in Part 2, and repeat the entire procedure up to step 5 above. The extension 2-L02 will be added to your filename as described in step 3 above.

Data Analysis

1. In **Review Saved Data** mode, select the file that is to be analyzed (for example, Smith EMG-2-1-L02). If data was collected for both forearms, be sure to select the file with the proper extension (1-L02 dominant; 2-L02 nondominant).

2. Observe the recordings of the clench **Force** (kg), **Raw EMG** (mV), and computer-calculated **Integrated EMG** (mV). The force is the actual measurement of the strength of clench in kilograms at each instant in time. The raw EMG is the actual recording of the voltage (in mV) at each instant in time, and the integrated EMG indicates the absolute intensity of the voltage from baseline at each instant in time.

3. To analyze the data, set up the first three pairs of channel/measurement boxes at the top of the screen. Channel 1 contains the Force data, Channel 3 contains the Raw EMG data, and Channel 40 contains the Integrated EMG data. Select the following channels and measurement types:

Channel	Measurement
CH 1	mean
CH 3	p-p
CH 40	mean

4. Use the arrow cursor and click the I-beam cursor box on the lower right side of the screen to activate the "area selection" function. Using the activated I-beam cursor, highlight the "plateau phase" of the first clench cluster. The plateau

FIGURE 16A.16 Highlighting the "plateau" of clench cluster 1.

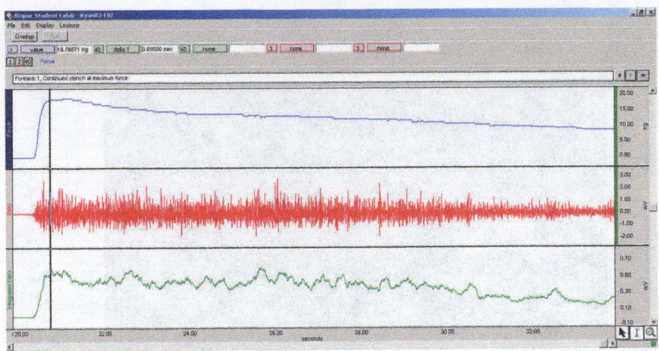

FIGURE 16A.17 Selection of single point of maximum clench.

should be a relatively flat force in the middle of the cluster as shown in Figure 16A.16.

5. Observe that the computer automatically calculates the **p-p** and **mean** values for the selected area. These measurements, calculated from the data by the computer, represent the following:

p-p (peak-to-peak): Measures the difference in value between the highest and lowest values in the selected area

mean: Displays the average value in the selected area

6. In the chart below, record the data for clench 1 (for example, 5-kg clench) to the nearest 0.01.

7. Using the I-beam cursor, highlight the clusters for the subsequent clenches and record the data in the chart.

Dominant Forearm Clench Increments

	Force at plateau Mean (kg)	Raw EMG P-P (msV)	Integrated EMG Mean (mV)
Clench 1			
Clench 2			
Clench 3			
Clench 4			

8. Scroll along the bottom of the data page to the segment that includes the recording of muscle fatigue (it should begin after the "marker" that appears at the top of the data).

9. Change the channel/measurement boxes so that the first two selected appear as follows (the third should be set to "none"):

Channel	Measurement
CH 1	value
CH 40	delta T

value: Measures the highest value in the selected area (CH 1 is force measured in kg)

delta T: Measures the time elapsed in the selected area (CH 40 is time measured in seconds)

10. Use the arrow cursor and click on the I-beam cursor box on the lower right side of the screen to activate the "area selection" function.

11. Using the activated I-beam cursor, select just the single point of maximum clench strength at the start of this data segment, as shown in Figure 16A.17.

12. Note the maximum force measurement for this point (CH 1). Record this data in the next chart.

Dominant Forearm Fatigue Measurement

Maximum clench force (kg)	50% of the maximum clench force (divide maximum clench force by 2)	Time to fatigue (seconds)

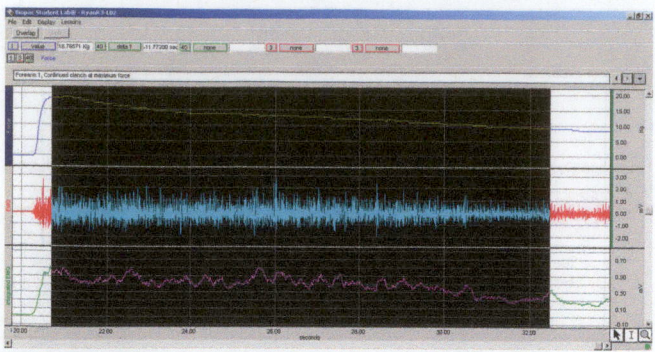

FIGURE 16A.18 Highlighting to measure elapsed time to 50% of the maximum clench force.

13. Calculate the value of 50% of the maximum clench force, and record this in the data chart.

14. Using a metric tape measure, measure the circumference of the subject's dominant forearm at its greatest diameter:

_____ cm

15. Measure the amount of time that elapsed between the initial maximum force and the point at which the subject fatigued to 50% of this level. Using the activated I-beam cursor, highlight the area from the point of 50% clench force back to the point of maximal clench force, as shown in Figure 16A.18.

16. Note the time it took the subject to reach this point of fatigue (CH 40 delta T) and record this data in the Dominant Forearm Fatigue Measurement chart.

Repeat Data Analysis for the Nondominant Forearm

1. Return to step 1 of the Data Analysis section and repeat the same measurements for the nondominant forearm (forearm 2).

2. Record your data in the two charts that follow; this data will be used for comparison.

3. Using a tape measure, measure the circumference of the subject's nondominant forearm at its greatest:

_____ cm

4. When finished, exit the program by going to the **File** menu at the top of the screen and clicking **Quit.**

Is there a difference in maximal force that was generated between the dominant and nondominant forearms? If so, how much?

_____

Calculate the percentage difference in force between the dominant maximal force and nondominant maximal force.

_____

_____

Nondominant Forearm Clench Increments			
	Force at plateau Mean (kg)	Raw EMG P-P (msV)	Integrated EMG Mean (mV)
Clench 1			
Clench 2			
Clench 3			
Clench 4			

Nondominant Forearm Fatigue Measurement		
Maximum Clench Force (kg)	50% of the maximum clench force (divide maximum clench force by 2)	Time to fatigue (seconds)

Is there a difference in the circumference between the dominant and nondominant forearms? If so, how much?

_____

If there is a difference in circumference, is this difference likely to be due to a difference in the *number* of muscle fibers in each forearm or in the *diameter* of each muscle fiber in the forearms? Explain.

_____

_____

Compare the time to fatigue between the two forearms.

_____

_____

Skeletal Muscle Physiology: Frogs and Human Subjects

Muscle Activity

1. The following group of incomplete statements refers to a muscle cell in the resting state just before stimulation. Complete each statement by choosing the correct response from the key items.

Key: a. Na^+ diffuses out of the cell   g.   relative ionic concentrations on the two sides of the membrane
        b. K^+ diffuses out of the cell   h.   electrical conditions
        c. Na^+ diffuses into the cell   i.   activation of the sodium-potassium pump, which moves K^+ into
        d. K^+ diffuses into the cell   the cell and Na^+ out of the cell
        e.   inside the cell   j.   activation of the sodium-potassium pump, which moves Na^+ into
        f.   outside the cell   the cell and K^+ out of the cell

There is a greater concentration of Na^+ _____; there is a greater concentration of K^+ _____. When the

stimulus is delivered, the permeability of the membrane at that point is changed; and _____, initiating the depolariza-

tion of the membrane. Almost as soon as the depolarization wave has begun, a repolarization wave follows it across the mem-

brane. This occurs as _____. Repolarization restores the _____ of the resting cell membrane. The _____

is (are) reestablished by _____.

2. Number the following statements in the proper sequence to describe the contraction mechanism in a skeletal muscle cell. Number 1 has already been designated.

_____1_____ Depolarization occurs, and the action potential is generated.

_____ The muscle cell relaxes and lengthens.

_____ The calcium ion concentrations at the myofilaments increase; the myofilaments slide past one another, and the cell shortens.

_____ The action potential, carried deep into the cell by the T tubules, triggers the release of calcium ions from the sarcoplasmic reticulum.

_____ The concentration of the calcium ions at the myofilaments decreases as they are actively transported into the sarcoplasmic reticulum.

3. Refer to your observations of muscle fiber contraction on page 237–238 to answer the following questions.

a.   Did your data support your hypothesis? _____

b.   *Explain* your observations fully. _____

_____

_____

c. Draw a relaxed and a contracted sarcomere below.

Relaxed   Contracted

Induction of Contraction in the Frog Gastrocnemius Muscle

4. Why is it important to destroy the brain and spinal cord of a frog before conducting physiological experiments on muscle contraction? _____

_____

5. What kind of stimulus (electrical or chemical) travels from the motor neuron to skeletal muscle? _____

What kind of stimulus (electrical or chemical) travels from the axon terminal to the sarcolemma? _____

6. Give the name and duration of each of the three phases of the muscle twitch, and describe what is happening during each phase.

a. _____, _____ msec, _____

_____

b. _____, _____ msec, _____

c. _____, _____ msec, _____

7. Use the items in the key to identify the conditions described.

Key:

a. maximal stimulus
b. multiple motor unit summation
c. subthreshold stimulus

d. tetanus
e. threshold stimulus

f. wave summation

_____ 1. sustained contraction without any evidence of relaxation

_____ 2. stimulus that results in no perceptible contraction

_____ 3. stimulus at which the muscle first contracts perceptibly

_____ 4. increasingly stronger contractions owing to stimulation at a rapid rate

_____ 5. increasingly stronger contractions owing to increased stimulus strength

_____ 6. weakest stimulus at which all muscle cells in the muscle are contracting

8. Complete the following statements by writing the appropriate words on the correspondingly numbered blanks at the right.

When a weak but smooth muscle contraction is desired, a few motor units are stimulated at a __1__ rate. If blue litmus paper is pressed to the cut surface of a fatigued muscle, the paper color changes to red, indicating low pH. This situation is caused by the accumulation of __2__ in the muscle. Within limits, as the load on a muscle is increased, the muscle contracts __3__ (more/less) strongly.

1. _____

2. _____

3. _____

9. During the frog experiment on muscle fatigue, how did the muscle contraction pattern change as the muscle began to fatigue?

_____

_____

How long was stimulation continued before fatigue was apparent? _____

If the sciatic nerve that stimulates the living frog's gastrocnemius muscle had been left attached to the muscle and the stimulus had been applied to the nerve rather than the muscle, would fatigue have become apparent sooner or later?

_____

Explain your answer. _____

_____

10. What will happen to a muscle in the body when its nerve supply is destroyed or badly damaged?

_____

_____

11. Explain the relationship between the load on a muscle and its strength of contraction. _____

_____

_____

12. The skeletal muscles are maintained in a slightly stretched condition for optimal contraction. How is this accomplished?

_____

Why does stretching a muscle beyond its optimal length reduce its ability to contract? (Include an explanation of the

events at the level of the myofilaments.) _____

_____

_____

13. If the length but not the tension of a muscle is changed, the contraction is called an isotonic contraction. In an isometric contraction, the tension is increased but the muscle does not shorten. Which type of contraction did you observe most often during the laboratory experiments? _____

Electromyography in a Human Subject Using BIOPAC®

14. If you were a physical therapist applying a constant voltage to the forearm, what might you observe if you gradually increased the *frequency* of stimulatory impulses, keeping the voltage constant each time?

_____

_____

15. Describe what is meant by the term *motor unit recruitment*. _____

_____

16. Describe the physiological processes occurring in the muscle cells that account for the gradual onset of muscle fatigue.

_____

_____

17. Most subjects use their dominant forearm far more than their nondominant forearm. What does this indicate about degree of activation of motor units and these factors: muscle fiber diameter, maximum muscle fiber force, and time to muscle fatigue? (You may need to use your textbook for help with this one.)

_____

_____

_____

_____

18. Define *dynamometry*. _____

_____

19. How might dynamometry be used to assess patients in a clinical setting? _____

_____

_____

17

Histology of Nervous Tissue

MATERIALS

- ☐ Model of a "typical" neuron (if available)
- ☐ Compound microscope
- ☐ Immersion oil
- ☐ Prepared slides of an ox spinal cord smear and teased myelinated nerve fibers
- ☐ Prepared slides of Purkinje cells (cerebellum), pyramidal cells (cerebrum), and a dorsal root ganglion
- ☐ Prepared slide of a nerve (x.s.)

OBJECTIVES

1. To differentiate between the functions of neurons and neuroglia.
2. To list six types of neuroglia cells and indicate nervous system location of each.
3. To identify the important anatomical characteristics of a neuron on an appropriate diagram or projected slide.
4. To state the functions of axons, dendrites, axon terminals, neurofibrils, and myelin sheaths.
5. To explain how a nerve impulse is transmitted from one neuron to another.
6. To explain the role of Schwann cells in the formation of the myelin sheath.
7. To classify neurons according to structure and function.
8. To distinguish between a nerve and a tract and between a ganglion and a nucleus.
9. To describe the structure of a nerve, identifying the connective tissue coverings (endoneurium, perineurium, and epineurium) and citing their functions.

PRE-LAB QUIZ

1. Circle the correct term. Nervous tissue is made up of <u>two</u> / <u>three</u> principal cell populations.
2. Neuroglia of the peripheral nervous system include
   a. ependymal cells and satellite cells
   b. oligodendrocytes and astrocytes
   c. satellite cells and Schwann cells
3. _____ are the basic functional units of nervous tissue.
4. These branching neuron processes serve as receptive regions and transmit electrical signals toward the cell body. They are:
   a. axons   c. dendrites
   b. collaterals   d. neuroglia
5. Circle True or False. Axons are the neuron processes that generate and conduct nerve impulses.
6. Most axons are covered with a fatty material called _____, which insulates the fibers and increases the speed of neurotransmission.
7. Circle the correct term. Neuron fibers (axons) running through the central nervous system form <u>tracts</u> / <u>nerves</u> of white matter.
8. Neurons can be classified according to structure. _____ neurons have many processes that issue from the cell body.
   a. Bipolar   b. Multipolar   c. Unipolar
9. Circle the correct term. Neurons can be classified according to function. <u>Afferent</u> / <u>Efferent</u> or motor neurons carry activating impulses from the central nervous system primarily to body muscles or glands.
10. Within a nerve, each fiber is surrounded by a delicate connective tissue sheath called the:
    a. endoneurium   b. epineurium   c. perineurium

myA&P *For practice quizzes on this lab, go to www.myaandp.com.*

PAL *For access to anatomical models and more, check out Practice Anatomy Lab.*

The nervous system is the master integrating and coordinating system, continuously monitoring and processing sensory information both from the external environment and from within the body. Every thought, action, and sensation is a reflection of its activity. Like a computer, it processes and integrates new "inputs" with information previously fed into it ("programmed") to produce an appropriate response ("readout"). However, no computer can possibly compare in complexity and scope to the human nervous system.

Despite its complexity, nervous tissue is made up of just two principal cell populations: neurons and supporting cells referred to as **neuroglia** ("nerve glue"), or **glial cells.** The neuroglia in the central nervous system (CNS: brain and spinal cord) include *astrocytes, oligodendrocytes, microglia,* and *ependymal cells* (Figure 17.1). The most important glial cells in the peripheral nervous system (PNS), that is, in the neural structures outside the CNS, are *Schwann cells* and *satellite cells.*

Neuroglia serve the needs of the delicate neurons by bracing and protecting them. In addition, they act as phagocytes (microglia), myelinate the cytoplasmic extensions of the neurons (oligodendrocytes and Schwann cells), play a role in capillary-neuron exchanges, and control the chemical environment around neurons (astrocytes). Although neuroglia resemble neurons in some ways (they have fibrous cellular extensions), they are not capable of generating and transmitting nerve impulses, a capability that is highly developed in neurons. Our focus in this exercise is the highly excitable neurons.

Neuron Anatomy

Neurons are the basic functional units of nervous tissue. They are highly specialized to transmit messages (nerve impulses) from one part of the body to another. Although neurons differ structurally, they have many identifiable features in common (Figure 17.2a and c). All have a **cell body** from which slender processes extend. Although neuron cell bodies are typically found in the CNS in clusters called **nuclei,** occasionally they reside in **ganglia** (collections of neuron cell bodies outside the CNS). They make up the gray matter of the nervous system. Neuron fibers running through the CNS form **tracts** of white matter; in the PNS they form the peripheral **nerves.**

The neuron cell body contains a large round nucleus surrounded by cytoplasm (*neuroplasm*). The cytoplasm is riddled with neurofibrils and with darkly staining structures called Nissl bodies. **Neurofibrils,** the cytoskeletal elements of the neuron, have a support and intracellular transport function. **Nissl** (chromatophilic) **bodies,** an elaborate type of rough endoplasmic reticulum, are involved in the metabolic activities of the cell.

There are two types of neuron processes. **Dendrites** are *receptive regions* (they bear receptors for neurotransmitters released by other neurons) and **axons,** also called *nerve fibers,* generate and conduct *nerve impulses.* Neurons have only one axon (which may branch into **collaterals**) but may have many dendrites, depending on the neuron type.

FIGURE 17.1 Neuroglia. (a–d) Supporting cells of the central nervous system. **(e)** Supporting cells of the peripheral nervous system.

(a) Astrocytes are the most abundant CNS neuroglia.

Capillary
Neuron
Astrocyte

(b) Microglial cells are defensive cells in the CNS.

Neuron
Microglial cell

Fluid-filled cavity
Ependymal cells
Brain or spinal cord tissue

(c) Ependymal cells line cerebrospinal fluid–filled cavities.

Myelin sheath
Process of oligodendrocyte
Nerve fibers

(d) Oligodendrocytes have processes that form myelin sheaths around CNS nerve fibers.

Satellite cells
Cell body of neuron
Schwann cells (forming myelin sheath)
Nerve fiber

(e) Satellite cells and Schwann cells (which form myelin) surround neurons in the PNS.

FIGURE 17.2 Structure of a typical motor neuron. (a) Diagrammatic view. **(b)** An enlarged synapse. **(c)** Photomicrograph (250×).

In general, a neuron is excited by other neurons when their axons release neurotransmitters close to its dendrites or cell body. The electrical current produced travels across the cell body and if it is great enough, it elicits a regenerative electrical signal, an *impulse* or *action potential*, that travels down the axon. As Figure 17.2a shows, the axon (in motor neurons) begins just distal to a slightly enlarged cell body structure called the **axon hillock.** The point at which the axon hillock narrows to axon diameter is referred to as the *initial segment*. The axon ends in many small structures called **axon**

terminals, or *synaptic knobs*, which form **synapses** or junctions with neurons or effector cells. These terminals store the neurotransmitter chemical in tiny vesicles. Each axon terminal is separated from the cell body or dendrites of the next (postsynaptic) neuron by a tiny gap called the **synaptic cleft** (Figure 17.2b). Thus, although they are close, there is no actual physical contact between neurons. When an impulse reaches the axon terminals, some of the *synaptic vesicles* rupture and release neurotransmitter into the synaptic cleft. The neurotransmitter then diffuses across the synaptic cleft to

FIGURE 17.3 Myelination of neuron processes by individual Schwann cells.
(a) A Schwann cell becomes apposed to an axon and envelops it in a trough. It then begins to rotate around the axon, wrapping it loosely in successive layers of its plasma membrane. Eventually, the Schwann cell cytoplasm is forced from between the membranes and comes to lie peripherally just beneath the exposed portion of the Schwann cell membrane. The tight membrane wrappings surrounding the axon form the myelin sheath. The area of Schwann cell cytoplasm and its exposed membrane are referred to as the neurilemma, or sheath of Schwann. **(b)** Longitudinal view of myelinated axon showing portions of adjacent Schwann cells and the node of Ranvier between them. **(c)** Electron micrograph of cross section through a myelinated axon (8,000×).

bind to membrane receptors on the next neuron, initiating an electrical current or *synaptic potential*. Specialized synapses between neurons and skeletal muscles are called neuromuscular junctions. They are discussed in Exercise 14.

Most long nerve fibers are covered with a fatty material called *myelin*, and such fibers are referred to as **myelinated fibers.** Axons in the peripheral nervous system are typically heavily myelinated by special supporting cells called **Schwann cells,** which wrap themselves tightly around the axon in jellyroll fashion (Figure 17.3). During the wrapping process, the cytoplasm is squeezed from between adjacent layers of the Schwann cell membranes, so that when the process is completed a tight core of plasma membrane material (protein-lipid material) encompasses the axon. This wrapping is the **myelin sheath.** The Schwann cell nucleus and the bulk of its cytoplasm end up just beneath the outermost portion of its plasma membrane. This peripheral part of the Schwann cell and its exposed plasma membrane is referred to as the **neurilemma,** or *sheath of Schwann*. Since the myelin sheath is formed by many individual Schwann cells, it is a discontinuous sheath. The gaps or indentations in the sheath are called **nodes of Ranvier** (see Figures 17.2 and 17.3).

Within the CNS, myelination is accomplished by glial cells called **oligodendrocytes** (see Figure 17.1d). These CNS sheaths do not exhibit the neurilemma seen in fibers myelinated by Schwann cells. Because of its chemical composition, myelin insulates the fibers and greatly increases the speed of neurotransmission by neuron fibers.

Node of Ranvier

Axon

Myelin

Schwann cell nucleus

FIGURE 17.4 Photomicrograph of a small portion of a peripheral nerve in longitudinal section (220×).

ACTIVITY 1

Identifying Parts of a Neuron

1. Study the typical motor neuron shown in Figure 17.2, noting the structural details described above, and then identify these structures on a neuron model.

2. Obtain a prepared slide of the ox spinal cord smear, which has large, easily identifiable neurons. Study one representative neuron under oil immersion and identify the cell body; the nucleus; the large, prominent "owl's eye" nucleolus; and the granular Nissl bodies. If possible, distinguish the axon from the many dendrites.

Sketch the cell in the space provided below, and label the important anatomical details you have observed. Compare your sketch to Figure 17.2c.

3. Obtain a prepared slide of teased myelinated nerve fibers. Using Figure 17.4 as a guide, identify the following: nodes of Ranvier, axon, Schwann cell nuclei, and myelin sheath.

Sketch a portion of a myelinated nerve fiber in the space provided below, illustrating a node of Ranvier. Label the axon, myelin sheath, node, and neurilemma.

Do the nodes seem to occur at consistent intervals, or are they irregularly distributed? _____

Explain the functional significance of this finding: _____

_____

_____

Neuron Classification

Neurons may be classified on the basis of structure or of function.

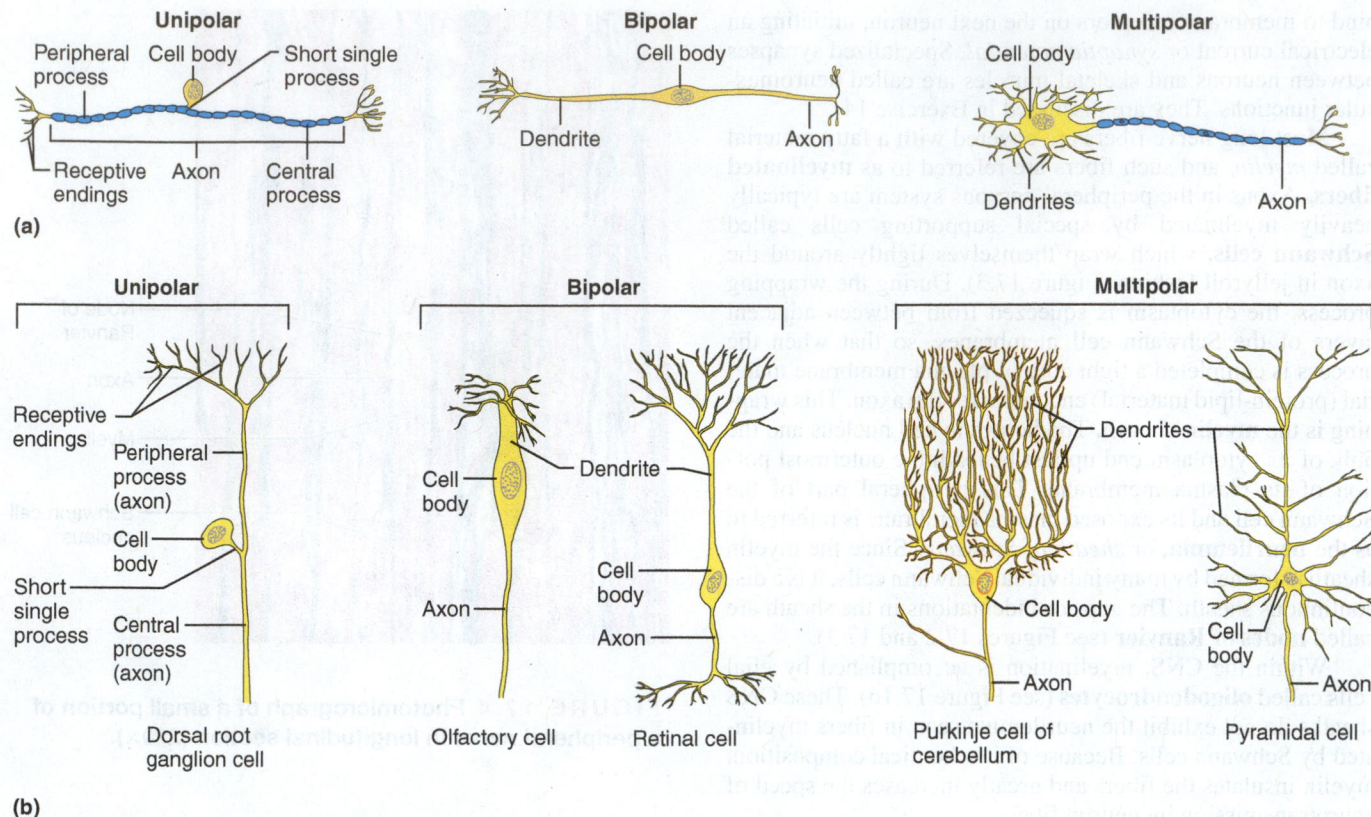

FIGURE 17.5 Classification of neurons according to structure. (a) Classification of neurons based on structure (number of processes extending from the cell body). **(b)** Structural variations within the classes.

Classification by Structure

Structurally, neurons may be differentiated according to the number of processes attached to the cell body (Figure 17.5a). In **unipolar neurons,** one very short process, which divides into *peripheral* and *central processes,* extends from the cell body. Functionally, only the most distal portions of the peripheral process act as receptive endings; the rest acts as an axon along with the central process. Nearly all neurons that conduct impulses toward the CNS are unipolar.

Bipolar neurons have two processes attached to the cell body. This neuron type is quite rare, typically found only as part of the receptor apparatus of the eye, ear, and olfactory mucosa.

Many processes issue from the cell body of **multipolar neurons,** all classified as dendrites except for a single axon. Most neurons in the brain and spinal cord (CNS neurons) and those whose axons carry impulses away from the CNS fall into this last category.

ACTIVITY 2

Studying the Microscopic Structure of Selected Neurons

Obtain prepared slides of pyramidal cells of the cerebral cortex, Purkinje cells of the cerebellar cortex, and a dorsal root

ganglion. As you observe them under the microscope, try to pick out the anatomical details depicted in Figure 17.5b and Figure 17.6. Notice that the neurons of the cerebral and cerebellar tissues (both brain tissues) are extensively branched; in contrast, the neurons of the dorsal root ganglion are more rounded. The many small nuclei visible surrounding the neurons are those of abutting glial cells.

Which of these neuron types would be classified as multipolar neurons?

_____

Which as unipolar?_____ ▆

Classification by Function

In general, neurons carrying impulses from sensory receptors in the internal organs (viscera), the skin, skeletal muscles, joints, or special sensory organs are termed **sensory,** or **afferent, neurons** (see Figure 17.7). The receptive endings of sensory neurons are often equipped with specialized receptors that are stimulated by specific changes in their immediate environment. The structure and function of these receptors arel considered separately in Exercise 23 (General Sensation). The cell bodies of sensory neurons are always found in

(a)

FIGURE 17.6 Photomicrographs of neurons.
(a) Pyramidal neuron from cerebral cortex (200×).
(b) Purkinje cell from the cerebellar cortex (150×).
(c) Dorsal root ganglion cells (130×).

(b)

(c)

Nucleus

Dendrites

Dendrites

Cell body

Nerve fibers

Satellite cells

Cell bodies

Ganglion — Cell body

Sensory neuron

Central process (axon)

Spinal nerve

Peripheral process (axon)

Afferent transmission

Interneuron

White matter

Gray matter

Receptive endings

Efferent transmission

Motor neuron

Spinal cord (central nervous system)

To effectors (muscles)

FIGURE 17.7 Classification of neurons on the basis of function. Sensory (afferent) neurons conduct impulses from the body's sensory receptors to the central nervous system; most are unipolar neurons with their nerve cell bodies in ganglia in the peripheral nervous system (PNS). Motor (efferent) neurons transmit impulses from the CNS to effectors (muscles). Interneurons (association neurons) complete the communication line between sensory and motor neurons. They are typically multipolar, and their cell bodies reside in the CNS.

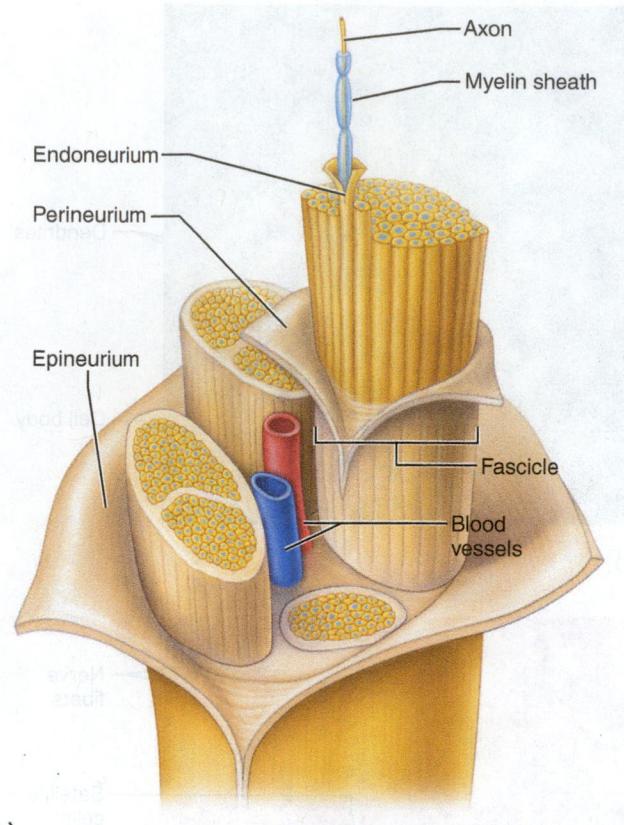

- Axon
- Myelin sheath
- Endoneurium
- Perineurium
- Epineurium
- Fascicle
- Blood vessels

(a)

- Myelin sheath
- Nonmyelinated axon
- Endoneurium
- Heavily myelinated axons
- Perineurium
- Epineurium

(b)

FIGURE 17.8 Structure of a nerve showing connective tissue wrappings. **(a)** Three-dimensional view of a portion of a nerve. **(b)** Photomicrograph of a cross-sectional view of part of a peripheral nerve (330×).

a ganglion outside the CNS, and these neurons are typically unipolar.

Neurons carrying impulses from the CNS to the viscera and/or body muscles and glands are termed **motor,** or **efferent, neurons.** Motor neurons are most often multipolar, and their cell bodies are almost always located in the CNS.

The third functional category of neurons is **interneurons** or *association neurons,* which are situated between and contribute to pathways that connect sensory and motor neurons. Their cell bodies are always located within the CNS, and they are multipolar neurons structurally.

Structure of a Nerve

A nerve is a bundle of neuron fibers (axons) wrapped in connective tissue coverings that extends to and/or from the CNS and visceral organs or structures of the body periphery (such as skeletal muscles, glands, and skin).

Like neurons, nerves are classified according to the direction in which they transmit impulses. Nerves that carry only sensory processes and conduct impulses only toward the CNS are referred to as **sensory, or afferent, nerves.** A few of the cranial nerves are pure sensory nerves. The ventral roots of the spinal cord, which carry only motor fibers, can be considered **motor, or efferent, nerves.** Nerves carrying both sensory (afferent) and motor (efferent) fibers are called **mixed nerves;** most nerves of the body, including all spinal nerves, are mixed nerves.

Within a nerve, each fiber is surrounded by a delicate connective tissue sheath called an **endoneurium,** which insulates it from the other neuron processes adjacent to it. The endoneurium is often mistaken for the myelin sheath; it is instead an additional sheath that surrounds the myelin sheath. Groups of fibers are bound by a coarser connective tissue, called the **perineurium,** to form bundles of fibers called **fascicles.** Finally, all the fascicles are bound together by a white, fibrous connective tissue sheath called the **epineurium,** forming the cordlike nerve (Figure 17.8). In addition to the connective tissue wrappings, blood vessels and lymphatic vessels serving the fibers also travel within a nerve.

ACTIVITY 3

Examining the Microscopic Structure of a Nerve

Use the compound microscope to examine a prepared cross section of a peripheral nerve. Using Figure 17.8b as an aid, identify nerve fibers, myelin sheaths, fascicles, and endoneurium, perineurium, and epineurium sheaths. If desired, sketch the nerve in the space below. ◼

NAME _____

LAB TIME/DATE _____

Histology of Nervous Tissue

1. The basic functional unit of the nervous system is the neuron. What is the major function of this cell type?

_____

2. Name four types of neuroglia in the CNS, and list a function for each of these cells. (You will need to consult your textbook for this.)

Types

a. _____

b. _____

c. _____

d. _____

Functions

a. _____

_____

b. _____

_____

c. _____

_____

d. _____

_____

Name the PNS glial cell that forms myelin. _____

Name the PNS glial cell that surrounds dorsal root ganglion neurons. _____

3. Match each statement with a response chosen from the key.

Key: a. afferent neuron
    b. central nervous system
    c. efferent neuron
    d. ganglion

e. interneuron
f. neuroglia
g. neurotransmitters
h. nerve

i. nuclei
j. peripheral nervous system
k. synapse
l. tract

_____ 1. the brain and spinal cord collectively

_____ 2. specialized supporting cells in the CNS

_____ 3. junction or point of close contact between neurons

_____ 4. a bundle of nerve processes inside the CNS

_____ 5. neuron serving as part of the conduction pathway between sensory and motor neurons

_____ 6. ganglia and spinal and cranial nerves

_____ 7. collection of nerve cell bodies found outside the CNS

_____ 8. neuron that conducts impulses away from the CNS to muscles and glands

_____ 9. neuron that conducts impulses toward the CNS from the body periphery

_____ 10. chemicals released by neurons that stimulate or inhibit other neurons or effectors

Neuron Anatomy

4. Match the following anatomical terms (column B) with the appropriate description or function (column A).

Column A

_____ 1. region of the cell body from which the axon originates

_____ 2. secretes neurotransmitters

_____ 3. receptive region of a neuron

_____ 4. insulates the nerve fibers

_____ 5. site of the nucleus and most important metabolic area

_____ 6. may be involved in the transport of substances within the neuron

_____ 7. essentially rough endoplasmic reticulum, important metabolically

_____ 8. impulse generator and transmitter

Column B

a.   axon

b.   axon terminal

c.   axon hillock

d.   dendrite

e.   myelin sheath

f.   neurofibril

g.   neuronal cell body

h.   Nissl bodies

5. Draw a "typical" multipolar neuron in the space below. Include and label the following structures on your diagram: cell body, nucleus, nucleolus, Nissl bodies, dendrites, axon, axon collateral branch, myelin sheath, nodes of Ranvier, axon terminals, and neurofibrils.

6. What substance is found in synaptic vesicles of the axon terminal? _____

What role does this substance play in neurotransmission? _____

_____

_____

7. What anatomical characteristic determines whether a particular neuron is classified as unipolar, bipolar, or multipolar?

_____

Make a simple line drawing of each type here.

       Unipolar neuron   **Bipolar neuron**   **Multipolar neuron**

8. Correctly identify the sensory (afferent) neuron, interneuron (association neuron), and motor (efferent) neuron in the figure below.

Which of these neuron types is/are unipolar? _____

Which is/are most likely multipolar? _____

Receptors (thermal and pain in the skin)

Effector (biceps brachii muscle)

9. Describe how the Schwann cells form the myelin sheath and the neurilemma encasing the nerve processes.

_____

_____

Structure of a Nerve

10. What is a nerve? _____

_____

11. State the location of each of the following connective tissue coverings.

endoneurium: _____

perineurium: _____

epineurium: _____

12. What is the function of the connective tissue wrappings found in a nerve? _____

_____

13. Define *mixed nerve.* _____

_____

14. Identify all indicated parts of the nerve section.

Neurophysiology of Nerve Impulses: Wet Lab

MATERIALS

- ☐ *Rana pipiens**
- ☐ Dissecting instruments and tray
- ☐ Disposable gloves
- ☐ Ringer's solution (frog) in dropper bottles, some at room temperature and some in an ice bath
- ☐ Thread
- ☐ Glass rods or probes
- ☐ Glass plates or slides
- ☐ Ring stand and clamp
- ☐ Stimulator; platinum electrodes
- ☐ Forceps
- ☐ Filter paper
- ☐ 0.01% hydrochloric acid (HCl) solution
- ☐ Sodium chloride (NaCl) crystals
- ☐ Heat-resistant mitts
- ☐ Bunsen burner
- ☐ Safety goggles
- ☐ Absorbent cotton
- ☐ Ether
- ☐ Pipettes
- ☐ 1-cc syringe with small-gauge needle
- ☐ 0.5% tubocurarine solution
- ☐ Frog board
- ☐ Oscilloscope
- ☐ Nerve chamber

 PhysioEx™ 8.0 Computer Simulation on page PEx-37

*Instructor to provide freshly pithed frogs (*Rana pipiens*) for student experimentation.

OBJECTIVES

1. To list the two major physiological properties of neurons.
2. To describe the polarized and depolarized states of the nerve cell membrane and to describe the events that lead to generation and conduction of a nerve impulse.
3. To explain how a nerve impulse is transmitted from one neuron to another.
4. To define *action potential, depolarization, repolarization, relative refractory period,* and *absolute refractory period.*
5. To list various substances and factors that can stimulate neurons.
6. To recognize that neurotransmitters may be either stimulatory or inhibitory in nature.
7. To state the site of action of the blocking agents ether and curare.

PRE-LAB QUIZ

1. Circle the correct term. <u>Excitability</u> / <u>Conductivity</u> is the ability to transmit nerve impulses to other neurons.
2. When a neuron is stimulated, the membrane becomes more permeable to Na$^+$ ions, which diffuse into the cell causing
   a. depolarization
   b. hyperpolarization
   c. repolarization
3. As an action potential progresses, the permeability to Na$^+$ decreases and the permeability to this ion increases:
   a. Ca^{2+}
   b. K$^+$
   c. Na$^+$
4. The period of time when the neuron is totally insensitive to further stimulation and cannot generate another action potential is
   a. absolute refractory period
   b. membrane potential
   c. repolarization
   d. threshold
5. What muscle and nerve will you need to isolate to study the physiology of nerve fibers?
   a. gastrocnemius and sciatic
   b. sartorius and femoral
   c. triceps brachii and radial
6. Circle True or False. Today you will use *alcohol* to inhibit the nerve impulse in your animal.
7. Circle the correct term. In the last portion of this experiment, you will electrically stimulate the frog's nerve and observe the compound action potential on a(n) <u>oscilloscope</u> / <u>dissecting microscope.</u>

myA&P For practice quizzes on this lab, go to www.myaandp.com.

FIGURE 18A.1 The nerve impulse. (a) Resting membrane potential. There is an excess of positive ions at the external cell surface, with Na$^+$ the predominant extracellular fluid ion and K$^+$ the predominant intracellular ion. The plasma membrane has a low permeability to Na$^+$. **(b)** Depolarization—reversal of the resting potential. Application of a stimulus changes the membrane permeability, and Na$^+$ ions are allowed to diffuse rapidly into the cell. **(c)** Generation of the action potential or nerve impulse. If the stimulus is of adequate intensity, the depolarization wave spreads rapidly along the entire length of the membrane. **(d)** Repolarization—reestablishment of the resting potential. The negative charge on the internal plasma membrane surface and the positive charge on its external surface are reestablished by diffusion of K$^+$ ions out of the cell, proceeding in the same direction as in depolarization. **(e)** In the resting state, Na$^+$ ions leak into the cell and K$^+$ ions leak out. The resting membrane potential is maintained by the active sodium-potassium pump. **(f)** The action potential is caused by permeability changes in the plasma membrane.

Neurons are **excitable;** they respond to stimuli by producing an elecrical signal. Excited neurons communicate—they transmit electrical signals to neurons, muscles, glands and other tissues of the body, a property called **conductivity.** In a resting neuron, the interior of the cell membrane is slightly more negatively charged than the exterior surface as illustrated in Figure 18A.1a. The difference in electrical charge produces a **resting membrane potential** across the membrane that is measured in millivolts. As in most cells, the predominant intracellular cation is K$^+$, and Na$^+$ is the predom-inant cation in the extracellular fluid. In a resting neuron, Na$^+$ leaks into the cell and K$^+$ leaks out. The resting membrane potential is maintained by the sodium-potassium pump, which transports Na$^+$ back out of the cell and K$^+$ back into the cell.

The Nerve Impulse

When a neuron receives an excitatory stimulus, the membrane becomes more permeable to sodium ions, and Na$^+$ diffuses down its electrochemical gradient into the cell. As a result, the interior of the membrane becomes less negative (Figure 18A.1b), an event is called **depolarization.** If the stimulus is great enough to depolarize the initial segment of the axon to **threshold,** a **nerve impulse** or **action potential** is generated. The initial segment of the axon in multipolar neurons is at the axon hillock of the cell body. In peripheral sensory neurons, the initial segment is just proximal to the sensory receptor far from the cell body located in the dorsal root ganglion.

When the threshold voltage is reached, the membrane permeability to Na^+ increases rapidly (Figure 18A.1f). As the neuron depolarizes, the polarity of the membrane reverses with the interior surface now becoming more positive than the exterior (Figure 18A.1c). As the membrane permeability to Na^+ falls, the permeability to K^+ increases, and K^+ diffuses down its electrochemical gradient and out of the cell (Figure 18A.1d). Once again the interior of the membrane becomes more negative than the exterior. This event is called **repolarization.**

The period of time when Na^+ permeability is rapidly changing and maximal, and the period immediately following when Na^+ permeability becomes restricted, together correspond to a time when the neuron is insensitive to further stimulation and cannot generate another action potential. This period is called the **absolute refractory period.** As Na^+ permeability is gradually restored to resting levels during repolarization, an especially strong stimulus to the neuron may provoke another action potential. This period of time is the **relative refractory period.** Restoration of the resting membrane potential restores the neuron's normal excitability.

Once generated, the action potential propagates along the entire length of the axon. It is never partially transmitted. Furthermore, it retains a constant amplitude and duration; the action potential is not small when a stimulus is small and large when a stimulus is large. Since the action potential of a given neuron is always the same, it is said to be an all-or-none response. When an action potential reaches the axon terminals, it causes neurotransmitter to be released. The neurotransmitter may be excitatory or inhibitory to the next cell in the transmission chain, depending on the receptor types on that cell. (The experiments in this exercise consider only excitatory neurotransmitters.)

The concentration of Na^+ and K^+ both inside and outside an active neuron change very little during a single action potential. Even when many action potentials are generated in a given area, the sodium-potassium pumps maintain the concentration differences across the membrane that are needed for the normal function of these excitable cells (Figure 18A.1e).

Physiology of Nerve Fibers

The sciatic nerve is a bundle of axons that vary in diameter. An electrical signal recorded from a nerve represents the summed electrical activity of all the nerve fibers. This summed activity is called a **compound action potential**. Unlike an action potential in a single nerve fiber, the compound action potential varies in shape according to which fibers are producing action potentials. When a nerve is stimulated by external electrodes, as in our experiments, the largest fibers reach threshold first and generate action potentials. Higher-intensity stimuli are required to produce action potentials in smaller fibers.

In this laboratory session, you will investigate the functioning of nerve fibers by subjecting the sciatic nerve of a frog to various types of stimuli and blocking agents. Work in groups of two to four to lighten the workload.

FIGURE 18A.2 Removal of the sciatic nerve and gastrocnemius muscle. (1) Cut through the frog's skin around the circumference of the trunk. **(2)** Pull the skin down over the trunk and legs. **(3)** Make a longitudinal cut through the abdominal musculature and expose the roots of the sciatic nerve (arising from spinal nerves 7–9). Ligate the nerve and cut the roots proximal to the ligature. **(4)** Use a glass probe to expose the sciatic nerve beneath the posterior thigh muscles. **(5)** Ligate the calcaneal (Achilles) tendon and cut it free distal to the ligature. Release the gastrocnemius muscle from the connective tissue of the knee region.

DISSECTION:
Isolating the Gastrocnemius Muscle and Sciatic Nerve

1. Don gloves to protect yourself from any parasites the frogs might have. Obtain a pithed frog from your instructor, and bring it to your laboratory bench. Also obtain dissecting instruments, a tray, thread, two glass rods or probes, and frog Ringer's solution at room temperature from the supply area.

2. Prepare the sciatic nerve as illustrated in Figure 18A.2. Place the pithed frog on the dissecting tray, dorsal side down. Make a cut through the skin around the circumference of the frog approximately halfway down the trunk, and then pull the skin down over the muscles of the legs. Open the abdominal cavity and push the abdominal organs to one side to expose the origin of the glistening white sciatic nerve, which arises from the last three spinal nerves. _Once the sciatic nerve has been exposed, it should be kept continually moist with room temperature Ringer's solution._

3. Using a glass probe, slip a piece of thread moistened with Ringer's solution under the sciatic nerve close to its origin at the vertebral column. Make a single ligature (tie it firmly with

the thread), and then cut through the nerve roots to free the proximal end of the sciatic nerve from its attachments. Using a glass rod or probe, carefully separate the posterior thigh muscles to locate and then free the sciatic nerve, which runs down the posterior aspect of the thigh.

4.   Tie a piece of thread around the calcaneal (Achilles) tendon of the gastrocnemius muscle, and then cut through the tendon distal to the ligature to free the gastrocnemius muscle from the heel. Using a scalpel, carefully release the gastrocnemius muscle from the connective tissue in the knee region. At this point you should have completely freed both the gastrocnemius muscle and the sciatic nerve, which innervates it.

ACTIVITY 1

Eliciting a Nerve Impulse

In this first set of experiments, stimulation of the nerve and generation of the compound action potential will be indicated by contraction of the gastrocnemius muscle. Because you will make no mechanical recording (unless your instructor asks you to), you must keep complete and accurate records of all experimental procedures and results.

1.   Obtain a glass slide or plate, ring stand and clamp, stimulator, electrodes, salt (NaCl), forceps, filter paper, 0.01% hydrochloric acid (HCl) solution, Bunsen burner, and heat-resistant mitts. With glass rods, transfer the isolated muscle-nerve preparation to a glass plate or slide, and then attach the slide to a ring stand with a clamp. Allow the end of the sciatic nerve to hang over the free edge of the glass slide, so that it is easily accessible for stimulation. *Remember to keep the nerve moist at all times.*

2.   You are now ready to investigate the response of the sciatic nerve to various stimuli, beginning with electrical stimulation. Using the stimulator and platinum electrodes, stimulate the sciatic nerve with single shocks, gradually increasing the intensity of the stimulus until the threshold stimulus is determined.

(The muscle as a whole will just barely contract at the threshold stimulus.) Record the voltage of this stimulus:

Threshold stimulus: _____ V

Continue to increase the voltage until you find the point beyond which no further increase occurs in the strength of muscle contraction—that is, the point at which the maximal contraction of the muscle is obtained. Record this voltage below.

Maximal stimulus: _____ V

Delivering multiple or repeated shocks to the sciatic nerve causes volleys of impulses in the nerve. Shock the nerve with multiple stimuli. Observe the response of the muscle. How does this response compare with the response to the single electrical shocks?

_____

_____

3.   To investigate mechanical stimulation, pinch the free end of the nerve by firmly pressing it between two glass rods or by pinching it with forceps. What is the result?

_____

4.   Chemical stimulation can be tested by applying a small piece of filter paper saturated with HCl solution (from the supply area) to the free end of the nerve. What is the result?

_____

Drop a few grains of salt (NaCl) on the free end of the nerve. What is the result?

_____

5.   Now test thermal stimulation. Wearing the heat-resistant mitts, heat a glass rod for a few moments over a Bunsen burner. Then touch the rod to the free end of the nerve. What is the result?

_____

What do these muscle reactions say about the irritability and conductivity of neurons?

_____

_____

Although most neurons within the body are stimulated to the greatest degree by a particular stimulus (in many cases, a chemical neurotransmitter), a variety of other stimuli may trigger nerve impulses, as illustrated by the experimental series just conducted. Generally, no matter what type of stimulus is present, if the affected part responds by becoming activated, it will always react in the same way. Familiar examples are the well-known phenomenon of "seeing stars" when you receive a blow to the head or press on your eyeball (try it), both of which trigger impulses in your optic nerves.

ACTIVITY 2

Inhibiting the Nerve Impulse

Numerous physical factors and chemical agents can impair the ability of nerve fibers to function. For example, deep pressure and cold temperature both block nerve impulse transmission by preventing the local blood supply from reaching the nerve fibers. Local anesthetics, alcohol, and numerous other chemicals are also very effective at blocking nerve transmission. Ether, one such chemical blocking agent, will be investigated first.

⚠️   Since ether is extremely volatile and explosive, perform this experiment in a vented hood. *Don safety goggles before beginning this procedure.*

1.   Obtain another glass slide or plate, absorbent cotton, ether, and a pipette. Clamp the new glass slide to the ring stand slightly below the first slide of the apparatus setup for the previous experiment. With glass rods, gently position the sciatic nerve on this second slide, allowing a small portion of the nerve's distal end to extend over the edge. Place a piece of absorbent cotton soaked with ether under the midsection of the nerve on the slide, prodding it into position with a glass rod. Using a voltage slightly above the threshold stimulus, stimulate the distal end of the nerve at 2-minute intervals until the muscle fails to respond. (If the cotton dries before this, re-wet it with ether using a pipette.) How long did it take for anesthesia to occur?

_____ sec

2.   Once anesthesia has occurred, stimulate the nerve beyond the anesthetized area, between the ether-soaked pad and the muscle. What is the result?

_____

3.   Remove the ether-soaked pad and flush the nerve fibers with Ringer's solution. Again stimulate the nerve at its distal end at 2-minute intervals. How long does it take for recovery?

_____

Does ether exert its blocking effect on the nerve fibers *or* on the muscle cells?

_____ Explain your reasoning.

_____

_____

_____

If sufficient frogs are available and time allows, you may do the following classic experiment. In the 1800s Claude Bernard described an investigation into the effect of curare on nerve-muscle interaction. *Curare* was used by some South American Indian tribes to tip their arrows. Victims struck with these arrows were paralyzed, but the paralysis was not accompanied by loss of sensation.

1.   Prepare another frog as described in steps 1 through 3 of the dissection instructions. However, in this case position the frog ventral side down on a frog board. In exposing the sciatic nerve, take care not to damage the blood vessels in the thigh region, as the success of the experiment depends on maintaining the blood supply to the muscles of the leg.

2.   Expose and gently tie the left sciatic nerve so that it can be lifted away from the muscles of the leg for stimulation. Slip another length of thread under the nerve, and then tie the thread tightly around the thigh muscles to cut off circulation to the leg. The sciatic nerve should be above the thread and *not in* the ligated tissue. Expose and ligate the sciatic nerve of the *right* leg in the same manner, but this time do *not* ligate the thigh muscles.

⚠ 3.   Obtain a syringe and needle, and a vial of 0.5% tubocurarine. Slowly and carefully inject 1 cc of the tubocurarine into the dorsal lymph sac of the frog.* The dorsal lymph sacs are located dorsally at the level of the scapulae, so introduce the needle of the syringe just beneath the skin between the scapulae and toward one side of the spinal column. <u>*Handle the tubocurarine very carefully, because it is extremely poisonous.*</u> <u>Do not get any on your skin.</u>

4.   Wait 15 minutes after injection of the tubocurarine to allow it to be distributed throughout the body in the blood and lymphatic stream. Then electrically stimulate the left sciatic nerve. Be careful not to touch any of the other tissues with the electrode. Gradually increasing the voltage, deliver single shocks until the threshold stimulus is determined for this specimen.

Threshold stimulus: _____ V

Now stimulate the right sciatic nerve with the same voltage intensity. Is there any difference in the reaction of the two muscles?

_____ If so, explain. _____

_____

If you did not find any difference, wait an additional 10 to 15 minutes and restimulate both sciatic nerves.

What is the result? _____

_____

5.   To determine the site at which tubocurarine acts, directly stimulate each gastrocnemius muscle. What is the result?

_____

_____

_____

Explain the difference between the responses of the right and left sciatic nerves.

_____

_____

_____

*To obtain 1 cc of the tubocurarine, inject 1 cc of air into the vial through the rubber membrane, and then draw up 1 cc of the chemical into the syringe.

(a)

(b)

(c)

(d)

FIGURE 18A.3 Recordings of the compound action potential from the sciatic nerve. The first compound action potential in each scan is circled. **(a)** Stimulus artifacts only **(b)**–**(d)** Increasing stimulas strengths reveal the graded nature of the compound action potential.

Explain the results when the muscles were stimulated directly.

_____

_____

_____

At what site does tubocurarine (or curare) act?

_____

The Oscilloscope: An Experimental Tool

In this exercise, a frog's sciatic nerve will be electrically stimulated, and the compound action potential generated will be observed on the oscilloscope. The **oscilloscope** is an instrument that visually displays the rapid changes in voltage that occur during an action potential. The dissected nerve will be placed in contact with two pairs of electrodes—*stimulating* and *recording*. The stimulating electrodes will be used to deliver a pulse of electricity to a point on the sciatic nerve. At another point on the nerve, a pair of recording electrodes connected to the oscilloscope will deliver the current to the oscilloscope, and the electrical pulse will be visible on the screen as a vertical deflection, or a *stimulus artifact*

(Figure 18A.3a). As the nerve is stimulated with increasingly higher voltage, the stimulus artifact increases in amplitude as well. When the stimulus voltage reaches a high enough level (threshold), a compound action potential will be generated by the nerve, and a *second* vertical deflection will appear on the screen, approximately 2 milliseconds after the stimulus artifact (Figure 18A.3b–d). This second deflection reports the potential difference between the two recording electrodes— that is, between the first recording electrode that has already depolarized (and is in the process of repolarizing as the compound action potential travels along the nerve) and the second recording electrode.

ACTIVITY 3

Visualizing the Action Potential with an Oscilloscope

1. Obtain a nerve chamber, an oscilloscope, a stimulator, frog Ringer's solution (room temperature), a dissecting needle, and glass probes. Set up the experimental apparatus as illustrated in Figure 18A.4. Connect the two stimulating electrodes to the output terminals of the stimulator and the two recording electrodes to the preamplifier of the oscilloscope.

2. Obtain another pithed frog, and prepare one of its sciatic nerves for experimentation as indicated on page 271 in steps 1 through 3 in the dissection instructions. While working, be careful not to touch the nerve with your fingers, and do not allow the nerve to touch the frog's skin.

3. When you have freed the sciatic nerve to the knee region with the glass probe, slip another thread length beneath that end of the nerve and make a ligature. Cut the nerve distal to this tied thread and then carefully lift the cut nerve away from the thigh of the frog by holding the threads at the nerve's proximal and distal ends. Place the nerve in the nerve chamber so that it rests across all four electrodes (the two stimulating and two recording electrodes) as shown in Figure 18A.4. Flush the nerve with room temperature frog Ringer's solution.

4. Adjust the horizontal sweep according to the instructions given in the manual or by your instructor, and set the stimulator duration, frequency, and amplitude to their lowest settings.

5. Begin to stimulate the nerve with single stimuli, slowly increasing the voltage until a threshold stimulus is achieved. The compound action potential will appear as a small rounded "hump" immediately following the stimulus artifact. Record the voltage of the threshold stimulus:

Threshold stimulus: _____ V

6. Flush the nerve with the Ringer's solution and continue to increase the voltage, watching as the vertical deflections produced by the compound action potential become diphasic (show both upward and downward vertical deflections). Record the voltage at which the compound action potential reaches its maximal amplitude; this is the maximal stimulus.

Maximal stimulus: _____ V

FIGURE 18A.4 Setup for oscilloscope visualization of action potentials in a nerve.

7. Set the stimulus voltage at a level just slightly lower than the maximal stimulus and gradually increase the frequency of stimulation. What is the effect on the size (amplitude) of the compound action potential?

_____

8. Flush the nerve with room temperature Ringer's solution once again, and allow the nerve to sit for a few minutes while you obtain a bottle of Ringer's solution from the ice bath. Repeat steps 5 and 6 while your partner continues to flush the nerve preparation with the cold saline. Record the threshold and maximal stimuli, and watch the oscilloscope pattern carefully to detect any differences in the velocity or speed of conduction from what was seen previously.

Threshold stimulus: _____ V

Maximal stimulus: _____ V

9. Flush the nerve preparation with room temperature Ringer's solution again and then gently lift the nerve by its attached threads. Then turn the nerve around so that the end formerly resting on the stimulating electrodes now rests on the recording electrodes and vice versa. Stimulate the nerve. Is the impulse conducted in the opposite direction?

_____

10. Dispose of the frog remains and gloves in the appropriate containers, clean the lab bench and equipment, and return your equipment to the proper supply area. ■

FIGURE 18A.4 Setup for oscilloscope visualization of action potentials in a nerve.

NAME_____

LAB TIME/DATE _____

Neurophysiology of Nerve Impulses: Wet Lab

The Nerve Impulse

1. Match the terms in column B to the appropriate definition in column A.

Column A

_____ 1. period of depolarization of the neuron membrane during which it cannot respond to a second stimulus

_____ 2. reversal of the resting potential due to an influx of sodium ions

_____ 3. period during which potassium ions diffuse out of the neuron because of a change in membrane permeability

_____ 4. period of repolarization when only a strong stimulus will elicit an action potential

_____ 5. mechanism in which ATP is used to move sodium out of the cell and potassium into the cell; restores the resting membrane voltage and intracellular ionic concentrations

Column B

a. absolute refractory period

b. action potential

c. depolarization

d. relative refractory period

e. repolarization

f. sodium-potassium pump

2. Define the term *depolarization*. _____

_____

How does an action potential differ from simple depolarization? _____

_____

3. Would a substance that decreases membrane permeability to sodium increase or decrease the probability of generating an action potential? Why?

_____

_____

4. The diagram here represents a section of an axon. Complete the figure by illustrating an area of resting membrane potential, an area of depolarization, and local current flow. Indicate the direction of the depolarization wave.

$[Na^+]$ $[K^+]$

$[Na^+]$ $[K^+]$

Physiology of Nerve Fibers: Eliciting and Inhibiting the Nerve Impulse

5. Respond appropriately to each question posed below. Insert your responses in the corresponding numbered blanks to the right.

1–3. Name three types of stimuli that resulted in action potential generation in the sciatic nerve of the frog.

4. Which of the stimuli resulted in the most effective nerve stimulation?

5. Which of the stimuli employed in that experiment might represent types of stimuli to which nerves in the human body are subjected?

6. What is the usual mode of stimulus transfer in neuron-to-neuron interactions?

7. Since the action potentials themselves were not visualized with an oscilloscope during this initial set of experiments, how did you recognize that impulses were being transmitted?

1. _____

2. _____

3. _____

4. _____

5. _____

6. _____

7. _____

6. How did the site of action of ether and tubocurarine differ? _____

_____

In the curare experiment, why was one of the frog's legs ligated? _____

_____

Visualizing the Action Potential with an Oscilloscope

7. Explain why the amplitude of the compound action potential recorded from the frog sciatic nerve increased when the

voltage of the stimulus was increased above the threshold value. _____

_____

8. What was the effect of cold temperature (flooding the nerve with iced Ringer's solution) on the functioning of the sciatic

nerve tested? _____

_____

9. When the nerve was reversed in position, was the impulse conducted in the opposite direction? _____

How can this result be reconciled with the concept of one-way conduction in neurons? _____

_____

_____

_____

Gross Anatomy of the Brain and Cranial Nerves

MATERIALS

- ☐ Human brain model (dissectible)
- ☐ Preserved human brain (if available)
- ☐ Three-dimensional model of ventricles
- ☐ Coronally sectioned human brain slice (if available)
- ☐ Materials as needed for cranial nerve testing (see Table 19.1): aromatic oils (e.g., vanilla and cloves); eye chart; ophthalmoscope penlight; safety pin; blunt probe (hot and cold); cotton; solutions of sugar, salt, vinegar, and quinine; ammonia; tuning fork; and tongue depressor
- ☐ Preserved sheep brain (meninges and cranial nerves intact)
- ☐ Dissecting instruments and tray
- ☐ Disposable gloves
- ☐ *The Human Nervous System: The Brain and Cranial Nerves* videotape

OBJECTIVES

1. To identify the following brain structures on a dissected specimen (or slices), human brain model, or appropriate diagram, and to state their functions:
   - *Cerebral hemisphere structures:* lobes, important fissures, lateral ventricles, basal ganglia, corpus callosum, fornix, septum pellucidum
   - *Diencephalon structures:* thalamus, intermediate mass, hypothalamus, optic chiasma, pituitary gland, mammillary bodies, pineal body, choroid plexus of the third ventricle, interventricular foramen
   - *Brain stem structures:* corpora quadrigemina, cerebral aqueduct, cerebral peduncles of the midbrain, pons, medulla, fourth ventricle
   - *Cerebellum structures:* cerebellar hemispheres, vermis, arbor vitae
2. To describe the composition of gray and white matter.
3. To locate the well-recognized functional areas of the human cerebral hemispheres.
4. To define *gyri, fissures,* and *sulci.*
5. To identify the three meningeal layers and state their function, and to locate the falx cerebri, falx cerebelli, and tentorium cerebelli.
6. To state the function of the arachnoid villi and dural sinuses.
7. To discuss the formation, circulation, and drainage of cerebrospinal fluid.
8. To identify at least four pertinent anatomical differences between the human brain and that of the sheep (or other mammal).
9. To identify the cranial nerves by number and name on a model or diagram, stating the origin and function of each.

PRE-LAB QUIZ

1. Circle the correct term. The <u>central nervous system</u> / <u>peripheral nervous system</u> consists of the brain and spinal cord.
2. Circle the correct term. The most superior portion of the brain is the <u>cerebral hemispheres</u> / <u>brain stem.</u>
3. Circle True or False. Deep grooves within the cerebral hemispheres are known as gyri.
4. On the ventral surface of the brain, you can observe the optic nerves and chiasma, the pituitary gland, and the mammillary bodies. These externally visible structures form the floor of the
   a. brain stem
   b. diencephalon
   c. frontal lobe
   d. occipital lobe
5. Circle the correct term. The lowest region of the brain stem, the <u>medulla oblongata</u> / <u>cerebellum</u> houses many vital autonomic centers involved in the control of heart rate, respiratory rhythm, and blood pressure.
6. Directly under the occipital lobes of the cerebrum is a large cauliflower-like structure known as the _____.
   a. brain stem
   b. cerebellum
   c. diencephalon

Text continues on next page.

myA&P *For practice quizzes on this lab, go to www.myaandp.com.*

PAL *For access to anatomical models and more, check out Practice Anatomy Lab.*

7. Circle the correct term. The outer cortex of the brain contains the cell bodies of cerebral neurons and is known as <u>white matter</u> / <u>gray matter.</u>

8. The brain and spinal cord are covered and protected by three connective tissue layers called
   a. lobes   c. sulci
   b. meninges   d. ventricles

9. Circle True or False. Cerebrospinal fluid is produced by the frontal lobe of the cerebrum and is unlike any other body fluid.

10. How many pairs of cranial nerves are there?
   _____

When viewed alongside all nature's animals, humans are indeed unique, and the key to their uniqueness is found in the brain. Each of us is a composite reflection of our brain's experience. If all past sensory input could mysteriously and suddenly be "erased," we would be unable to walk, talk, or communicate in any manner. Spontaneous movement would occur, as in a fetus, but no voluntary integrated function of any type would be possible. Clearly we would cease to be the same individuals.

Because of the complexity of the nervous system, its anatomical structures are usually considered in terms of two principal divisions: the central nervous system and the peripheral nervous system. The **central nervous system (CNS)** consists of the brain and spinal cord, which primarily interpret incoming sensory information and issue instructions based on that information and on past experience. The **peripheral nervous system (PNS)** consists of the cranial and spinal nerves, ganglia, and sensory receptors. These structures serve as communication lines as they carry impulses—from the sensory receptors to the CNS and from the CNS to the appropriate glands, muscles, or other effector organs.

The PNS has two major subdivisions: the **sensory portion,** which consists of nerve fibers that conduct impulses toward the CNS, and the **motor portion,** which contains nerve fibers that conduct impulses away from the CNS. The motor portion, in turn, consists of the **somatic division** (sometimes called the *voluntary system*), which controls the skeletal muscles, and the **autonomic nervous system (ANS),** which controls smooth and cardiac muscles and glands. The ANS is often referred to as the *involuntary nervous system*. Its sympathetic and parasympathetic branches play a major role in maintaining homeostasis.

In this exercise both the brain (CNS) and cranial nerves (PNS) will be studied because of their close anatomical relationship.

The Human Brain

During embryonic development of all vertebrates, the CNS first makes its appearance as a simple tubelike structure, the **neural tube,** that extends down the dorsal median plane. By the fourth week, the human brain begins to form as an expansion of the anterior or rostral end of the neural tube (the end toward the head). Shortly thereafter, constrictions appear, dividing the developing brain into three major regions—**forebrain, midbrain,** and **hindbrain** (Figure 19.1). The remainder of the neural tube becomes the spinal cord.

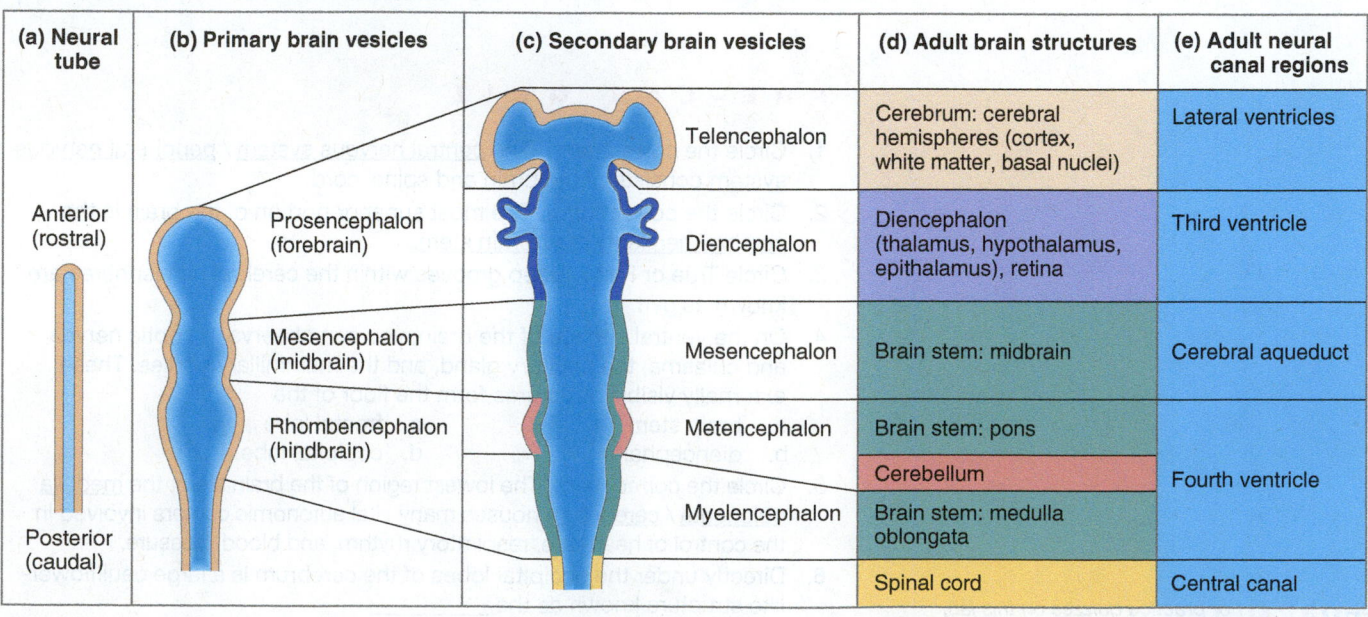

FIGURE 19.1 Embryonic development of the human brain. (a) The neural tube subdivides into **(b)** the primary brain vesicles, which subsequently form **(c)** the secondary brain vesicles, which differentiate into **(d)** the adult brain structures. **(e)** The adult structures derived from the neural canal.

During fetal development, two anterior outpocketings extend from the forebrain and grow rapidly to form the cerebral hemispheres. Because of space restrictions imposed by the skull, the cerebral hemispheres are forced to grow posteriorly and inferiorly, and finally end up enveloping and obscuring the rest of the forebrain and most midbrain structures. Somewhat later in development, the dorsal hindbrain also enlarges to produce the cerebellum. The central canal of the neural tube, which remains continuous throughout the brain and cord, enlarges in four regions of the brain, forming chambers called **ventricles** (see Figure 19.8a and b, page 288).

ACTIVITY 1

Identifying External Brain Structures

Identify external brain structures using the figures cited. Also use a model of the human brain and other learning aids as they are mentioned.

Generally, the brain is studied in terms of four major regions: the cerebral hemispheres, diencephalon, brain stem, and cerebellum. The relationship between these four anatomical regions and the structures of the forebrain, midbrain, and hindbrain is also outlined in Figure 19.1.

Cerebral Hemispheres

The **cerebral hemispheres** are the most superior portion of the brain (Figure 19.2). Their entire surface is thrown into elevated ridges of tissue called **gyri** that are separated by shallow grooves called **sulci** or deeper grooves called **fissures.** Many of the fissures and gyri are important anatomical landmarks.

The cerebral hemispheres are divided by a single deep fissure, the **longitudinal fissure.** The **central sulcus** divides the **frontal lobe** from the **parietal lobe,** and the **lateral sulcus** separates the **temporal lobe** from the parietal lobe. The **parieto-occipital sulcus** on the medial surface of each hemisphere divides the **occipital lobe** from the parietal lobe. It is not visible externally. A fifth lobe of each cerebral hemisphere, the **insula,** is buried deep within the lateral sulcus, and is covered by portions of the temporal, parietal, and frontal lobes. Notice that most cerebral hemisphere lobes are named for the cranial bones that lie over them.

Some important functional areas of the cerebral hemispheres have also been located (Figure 19.2d). The **primary somatosensory cortex** is located in the **postcentral gyrus** of the parietal lobe. Impulses traveling from the body's sensory receptors (such as those for pressure, pain, and temperature) are localized in this area of the brain. ("This information is from

Motor Areas:
- Primary motor area
- Premotor cortex
- Frontal eye field

Prefrontal Cortex:
- Working memory for spatial tasks
- Executive area for task management
- Broca's area
- Working memory for object-recall tasks
- Solving complex, multitask problems

Central sulcus

Sensory Areas and Related Association Areas:
- Primary somatosensory cortex — Somatic sensation
- Somatosensory association area
- Gustatory cortex (in insula) — Taste
- Wernicke's area (outlined by dashes)
- General interpretation area (outlined by dots)
- Primary visual cortex — Vision
- Visual association area
- Auditory association area — Hearing
- Primary auditory cortex

(d)

FIGURE 19.2 *(continued)* **External structure of the cerebral hemispheres. (d)** Functional areas of the left cerebral cortex. The olfactory area, which is deep to the temporal lobe on the medial hemispheric surface, is not identified. Numbers indicate brain regions plotted by the Brodmann system.

my big toe.") Immediately posterior to the primary somatosensory area is the **somatosensory association area,** in which the meaning of incoming stimuli is analyzed. ("Ouch! I have a *pain* there.") Thus, the somatosensory association area allows you to become aware of pain, coldness, a light touch, and the like.

Impulses from the special sense organs are interpreted in other specific areas also noted in Figure 19.2d. For example, the visual areas are in the posterior portion of the occipital lobe, and the auditory area is located in the temporal lobe in the gyrus bordering the lateral sulcus. The olfactory area is deep within the temporal lobe along its medial surface, in a region called the **uncus** (see Figure 19.4a, page 284).

The **primary motor area,** which is responsible for conscious or voluntary movement of the skeletal muscles, is located in the **precentral gyrus** of the frontal lobe. A specialized motor speech area called **Broca's area** is found at the base of the precentral gyrus just above the lateral sulcus. Damage to this area (which is located in only one cerebral hemisphere, usually the left) reduces or eliminates the ability to articulate words. Many areas involved in intellect, complex reasoning, and personality lie in the anterior portions of the frontal lobes, in a region called the **prefrontal cortex.**

A rather poorly defined region at the junction of the parietal and temporal lobes is **Wernicke's area,** an area in which unfamiliar words are sounded out. Like Broca's area, Wernicke's area is located in one cerebral hemisphere only, typically the left.

Although there are many similar functional areas in both cerebral hemispheres, each hemisphere is also a "specialist" in certain ways. For example, the left hemisphere is the "language brain" in most of us, because it houses centers associated with language skills and speech. The right hemisphere is more concerned with abstract, conceptual, or spatial processes—skills associated with artistic or creative pursuits.

The cell bodies of cerebral neurons involved in these functions are found only in the outermost gray matter of the cerebrum, the **cerebral cortex.** Most of the balance of cerebral tissue—the deeper **cerebral white matter**—is composed of fiber tracts carrying impulses to or from the cortex.

Using a model of the human brain (and a preserved human brain, if available), identify the areas and structures of the cerebral hemispheres described above.

Then continue using the model and preserved brain along with the figures as you read about other structures.

Diencephalon

The **diencephalon,** sometimes considered the most superior portion of the brain stem, is embryologically part of the forebrain, along with the cerebral hemispheres.

Turn the brain model so the ventral surface of the brain can be viewed. Using Figure 19.3 as a guide, start superiorly and identify the externally visible structures that mark the position of the floor of the diencephalon. These are the **olfactory bulbs** (synapse point of cranial nerve I) and **tracts, optic nerves** (cranial nerve II), **optic chiasma** (where the fibers of the optic nerves partially cross over), **optic tracts, pituitary gland,** and **mammillary bodies.**

Brain Stem

Continue inferiorly to identify the **brain stem** structures—the **cerebral peduncles** (fiber tracts in the **midbrain** connecting the pons below with cerebrum above), the pons, and the medulla oblongata. *Pons* means "bridge," and the **pons** consists primarily of motor and sensory fiber tracts connecting the brain with lower CNS centers. The lowest brain stem region, the **medulla oblongata,** is also composed primarily of fiber tracts. You can see the **decussation of pyramids,** a crossover point for the major motor tracts (pyramidal tracts) descending from the motor areas of the cerebrum to the cord, on the medulla's surface. The medulla also houses many vital autonomic centers involved in the control of heart rate, respiratory rhythm, and blood pressure as well as involuntary centers involved in vomiting, swallowing, and so on.

Frontal lobe
Olfactory bulb (synapse point of cranial nerve I)
Optic chiasma
Optic nerve (II)
Optic tract
Mammillary body
Midbrain
Pons
Temporal lobe
Medulla oblongata
Cerebellum
Spinal cord
Pituitary gland
Cerebral peduncle of midbrain
Decussation of pyramids

FIGURE 19.3 Ventral (inferior) aspect of the human brain, showing the three regions of the brain stem. Only a small portion of the midbrain can be seen; the rest is surrounded by other brain regions.

Cerebellum

1. Turn the brain model so you can see the dorsal aspect. Identify the large cauliflower-like **cerebellum,** which projects dorsally from under the occipital lobes of the cerebrum. Notice that, like the cerebrum, the cerebellum has two major hemispheres and a convoluted surface (see Figure 19.6). It also has an outer cortex made up of gray matter with an inner region of white matter.

2. Remove the cerebellum to view the **corpora quadrigemina** (Figure 19.4), located on the posterior aspect of the midbrain, a brain stem structure. The two superior prominences are the **superior colliculi** (visual reflex centers); the two smaller inferior prominences are the **inferior colliculi** (auditory reflex centers). ▪

ACTIVITY 2

Identifying Internal Brain Structures

The deeper structures of the brain have also been well mapped. Like the external structures, these can be studied in terms of the four major regions. As the internal brain areas are described, identify them on the figures cited. Also, use the brain model as indicated to help you in this study.

Cerebral Hemispheres

1. Take the brain model apart so you can see a median sagittal view of the internal brain structures (see Figure 19.4). Observe the model closely to see the extent of the outer cortex (gray matter), which contains the cell bodies of cerebral neu-

rons. The pyramidal cells of the cerebral motor cortex (studied in Exercise 17, page 257) are representative of the neurons seen in the precentral gyrus.

2. Observe the deeper area of white matter, which is composed of fiber tracts. The fiber tracts found in the cerebral hemisphere white matter are called *association tracts* if they connect two portions of the same hemisphere, *projection tracts* if they run between the cerebral cortex and lower brain structures or spinal cord, and *commissures* if they run from one hemisphere to another. Observe the large **corpus callosum,** the major commissure connecting the cerebral hemispheres. The corpus callosum arches above the structures of the diencephalon and roofs over the lateral ventricles. Notice also the **fornix,** a bandlike fiber tract concerned with olfaction as well as limbic system functions, and the membranous **septum pellucidum,** which separates the lateral ventricles of the cerebral hemispheres.

3. In addition to the gray matter of the cerebral cortex, there are several "islands" of gray matter (clusters of neuron cell bodies) called **nuclei** buried deep within the white matter of the cerebral hemispheres. One important group of cerebral nuclei, called the **basal ganglia,** * flank the lateral and third ventricles. You can see these nuclei if you have a dissectible

---

*The historical term for these nuclei, *basal ganglia,* is a misleading term because ganglia are PNS structures. However, the name has been retained to differentiate these nuclei from the basal nuclei of the forebrain in the cerebrum.

Frontal lobe of cerebral hemisphere — Fornix

— Central sulcus

Lateral ventricle —

— Parietal lobe of cerebral hemisphere

Corpus callosum —

— Parieto-occipital sulcus

Anterior commissure —

— Pineal gland

Superior colliculi
Inferior colliculi } Corpora quadrigemina

Hypothalamus —

Optic nerve and chiasma —

— Arbor vitae

Mammillary body —

— Cerebellum

Uncus —

— Fourth ventricle

Thalamus —

— Medulla oblongata

Pons —

(a)

Septum pellucidum —

— Parietal lobe of cerebral hemisphere

Interthalamic adhesion (intermediate mass of thalamus) —

— Corpus callosum

— Fornix

— Choroid plexus

Frontal lobe of cerebral hemisphere —

— Occipital lobe of cerebral hemisphere

— **Thalamus** (encloses third ventricle)

Interventricular foramen —

— Posterior commissure

Anterior commissure —

— **Pineal gland** (part of epithalamus)

Hypothalamus —

Corpora quadrigemina

Optic chiasma —

Cerebral aqueduct } **Midbrain**

Pituitary gland —

Temporal lobe of cerebral hemisphere —

— Arbor vitae

Mammillary body —

— Fourth ventricle

Pons —

— Choroid plexus

Medulla oblongata —

— Cerebellum

Spinal cord —

(b)

FIGURE 19.4 Diencephalon and brain stem structures as seen in a midsagittal section of the brain. (a) Photograph. **(b)** Diagrammatic view.

model or a coronally or cross-sectioned human brain slice. Otherwise, Figure 19.5 will suffice.

The basal ganglia, which are important subcortical motor nuclei (and part of the so-called *extrapyramidal system*), are involved in regulating voluntary motor activities. The most important of them are the arching, comma-shaped **caudate nucleus,** and the **lentiform nucleus,** which is composed of

the **putamen** and **globus pallidus nuclei.** The closely associated *amygdaloid nucleus* (located at the tip of the caudate nucleus) is part of the *limbic system.*

The **corona radiata,** a spray of projection fibers coursing down from the precentral (motor) gyrus, combines with sensory fibers traveling to the sensory cortex to form a broad band of fibrous material called the **internal capsule.** The

Fibers of
corona radiata

**Caudate
nucleus**

Corpus striatum

**Lentiform
nucleus**
• **Putamen**
• **Globus pallidus**
(deep to putamen)

Projection fibers

Thalamus

Tail of caudate
nucleus

(a)

Anterior

Cerebral
cortex

Cerebral
white matter

Corpus
callosum

Anterior horn of
lateral ventricle

**Caudate
nucleus**

Putamen

**Globus
pallidus**

**Lentiform
nucleus**

Internal
capsule

Thalamus

Tail of
caudate
nucleus

Third ventricle

Inferior horn
of lateral ventricle

Posterior

(b)

FIGURE 19.5 Basal ganglia. (a) Three-dimensional view of the basal ganglia
showing their positions within the cerebrum. **(b)** A transverse section of the cerebrum and
diencephalon showing the relationship of the basal ganglia to the thalamus and the lateral
and third ventricles.

internal capsule passes between the diencephalon and the basal
ganglia and through parts of the basal ganglia, giving them a
striped appearance. This is why the caudate nucleus and the
lentiform nucleus are sometimes referred to collectively as the
corpus striatum, or "striped body" (Figure 19.5a).

4.   Examine the relationship of the lateral ventricles and corpus callosum to the diencephalon structures; that is, thalamus

and third ventricle—from the cross-sectional viewpoint (see
Figure 19.5b).

Diencephalon

1.   The major internal structures of the diencephalon are the
thalamus, hypothalamus, and epithalamus (see Figure 19.4). The
thalamus consists of two large lobes of gray matter that laterally

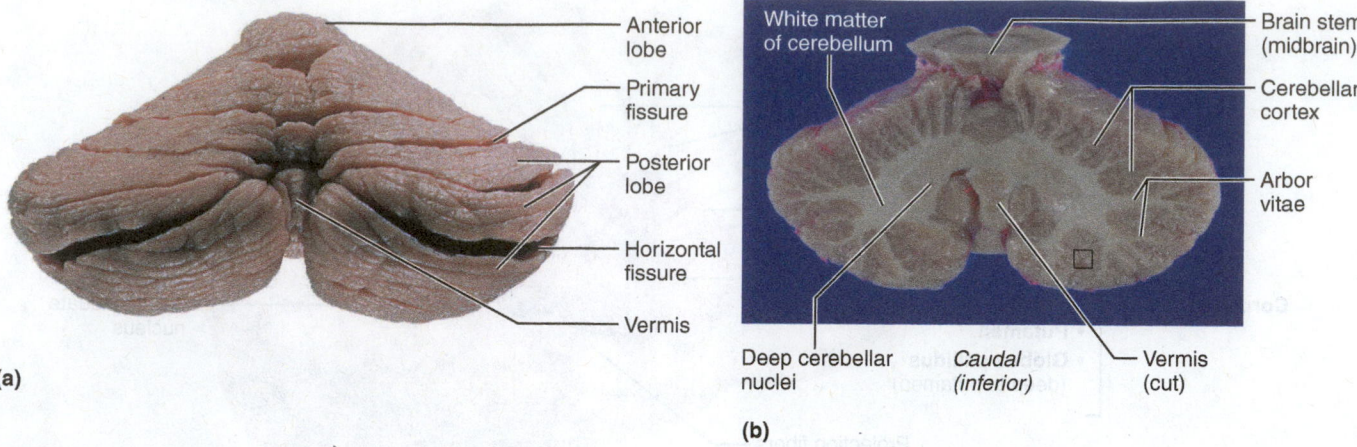

FIGURE 19.6 Cerebellum. (a) Posterior (dorsal) view. **(b)** The cerebellum, sectioned to reveal its cortex and medullary regions. (The cerebellum is sectioned frontally and the brain stem is sectioned horizontally in this posterior view.)

enclose the shallow third ventricle of the brain. A slender stalk of thalamic tissue, the **interthalamic adhesion,** or **intermediate mass,** connects the two thalamic lobes and bridges the ventricle. The thalamus is a major integrating and relay station for sensory impulses passing upward to the cortical sensory areas for localization and interpretation. Locate also the **interventricular foramen** (*foramen of Monro*), a tiny orifice connecting the third ventricle with the lateral ventricle on the same side.

2. The **hypothalamus** makes up the floor and the inferolateral walls of the third ventricle. It is an important autonomic center involved in regulation of body temperature, water balance, and fat and carbohydrate metabolism as well as in many other activities and drives (sex, hunger, thirst). Locate again the pituitary gland, which hangs from the anterior floor of the hypothalamus by a slender stalk, the **infundibulum.** (The pituitary gland is usually not present in preserved brain specimens.) In life, the pituitary rests in the hypophyseal fossa of the sella turcica of the sphenoid bone. Its function is discussed in Exercise 27.

Anterior to the pituitary, identify the optic chiasma portion of the optic pathway to the brain. The **mammillary bodies,** relay stations for olfaction, bulge exteriorly from the floor of the hypothalamus just posterior to the pituitary gland.

3. The **epithalamus** forms the roof of the third ventricle and is the most dorsal portion of the diencephalon. Important structures in the epithalamus are the **pineal gland** (a neuroendocrine structure), and the **choroid plexus** of the third ventricle. The choroid plexuses, knotlike collections of capillaries within each ventricle, form the cerebrospinal fluid.

Brain Stem

1. Now trace the short midbrain from the mammillary bodies to the rounded pons below. Continue to refer to Figure 19.4. The **cerebral aqueduct** is a slender canal traveling through the midbrain; it connects the third ventricle to the fourth ventricle in the hindbrain below. The cerebral peduncles and the rounded corpora quadrigemina make up the midbrain tissue anterior and posterior (respectively) to the cerebral aqueduct.

2. Locate the hindbrain structures. Trace the rounded pons to the medulla oblongata below, and identify the fourth ventricle posterior to these structures. Attempt to identify the sin-

gle median aperture and the two lateral apertures, three orifices found in the walls of the fourth ventricle. These apertures serve as conduits for cerebrospinal fluid to circulate into the subarachnoid space from the fourth ventricle.

Cerebellum

Examine the cerebellum. Notice that it is composed of two lateral hemispheres each with three lobes (*anterior, posterior,* and a deep *flocculonodular*) connected by a midline lobe called the **vermis** (Figure 19.6). As in the cerebral hemispheres, the cerebellum has an outer cortical area of gray matter and an inner area of white matter. The treelike branching of the cerebellar white matter is referred to as the **arbor vitae,** or "tree of life." The cerebellum is concerned with unconscious coordination of skeletal muscle activity and control of balance and equilibrium. Fibers converge on the cerebellum from the equilibrium apparatus of the inner ear, visual pathways, proprioceptors of tendons and skeletal muscles, and from many other areas. Thus the cerebellum remains constantly aware of the position and state of tension of the various body parts. ▬

Meninges of the Brain

The brain (and spinal cord) are covered and protected by three connective tissue membranes called **meninges** (Figure 19.7). The outermost meninx is the leathery **dura mater,** a double-layered membrane. One of its layers (the *periosteal layer*) is attached to the inner surface of the skull, forming the periosteum. The other (the *meningeal layer*) forms the outermost brain covering and is continuous with the dura mater of the spinal cord.

The dural layers are fused together except in three places where the inner membrane extends inward to form a septum that secures the brain to structures inside the cranial cavity. One such extension, the **falx cerebri,** dips into the longitudinal fissure between the cerebral hemispheres to attach to the crista galli of the ethmoid bone of the skull (Figure 19.7a). The cavity created at this point is the large **superior sagittal sinus,** which collects blood draining from the brain tissue. The **falx cerebelli,** separating the two cerebellar hemispheres, and the **tentorium cerebelli,** separating the cerebrum from the cerebellum below, are two other important inward folds of the inner dural membrane.

(a)

(b)

(c)

FIGURE 19.7 Meninges of the brain. (a) Three-dimensional frontal section showing the relationship of the dura mater, arachnoid mater, and pia mater. The meningeal dura forms the falx cerebri fold, which extends into the longitudinal fissure and attaches the brain to the ethmoid bone of the skull. A dural sinus, the superior sagittal sinus, is enclosed by the dural membranes superiorly. Arachnoid villi, which return cerebrospinal fluid to the dural sinus, are also shown. **(b)** Position of the dural folds: the falx cerebri, tentorium cerebelli, and falx cerebelli. **(c)** Posterior view of the brain in place, surrounded by the dura mater. Sinuses between periosteal and meningeal dura contain venous blood.

The middle meninx, the weblike **arachnoid mater,** underlies the dura mater and is partially separated from it by the **subdural space.** Threadlike projections bridge the **subarachnoid space** to attach the arachnoid to the innermost meninx, the **pia mater.** The delicate pia mater is highly vascular and clings tenaciously to the surface of the brain, following its convolutions.

In life, the subarachnoid space is filled with cerebrospinal fluid. Specialized projections of the arachnoid tissue called **arachnoid villi** protrude through the dura mater to allow the cerebrospinal fluid to drain back into the venous circulation via the superior sagittal sinus and other dural sinuses.

Meningitis, inflammation of the meninges, is a serious threat to the brain because of the intimate association between the brain and meninges. Should infection spread to the neural tissue of the brain itself, life-threatening **encephalitis** may occur. Meningitis is often diagnosed by taking a sample of cerebrospinal fluid from the subarachnoid space. ■

Cerebrospinal Fluid

The cerebrospinal fluid, much like plasma in composition, is continually formed by the **choroid plexuses,** small capillary knots hanging from the roof of the ventricles of the brain. The

(a) Anterior view

Lateral ventricle

Anterior horn

Septum pellucidum

Interventricular foramen

Inferior horn

Third ventricle

Lateral aperture

Cerebral aqueduct

Fourth ventricle

Central canal

(b) Left lateral view

Posterior horn

Inferior horn

Median aperture

Lateral aperture

Superior sagittal sinus

Choroid plexus

Interventricular foramen

Third ventricle

Cerebral aqueduct

Lateral aperture

Fourth ventricle

Median aperture

Spinal dura mater

Central canal of spinal cord

Arachnoid villus

Subarachnoid space

Arachnoid mater

Meningeal dura mater

Periosteal dura mater

Right lateral ventricle (deep to cut)

Tentorium cerebelli

Choroid plexus of fourth ventricle

Inferior end of spinal cord

FIGURE 19.8 Location and circulatory pattern of cerebrospinal fluid. (a) Anterior view and **(b)** lateral view of brain ventricles. Different regions of the large lateral ventricles are indicated by the terms *anterior horn*, *posterior horn*, and *inferior horn*. **(c)** Cerebrospinal fluid (CSF) flows from the lateral ventricles, through the interventricular foramina into the third ventricle, and then into the fourth ventricle via the cerebral aqueduct. Most of the CSF circulates in the subarachnoid space and returns to the blood through arachnoid villi.

(c)

cerebrospinal fluid in and around the brain forms a watery cushion that protects the delicate brain tissue against blows to the head.

Within the brain, the cerebrospinal fluid circulates from the two lateral ventricles (in the cerebral hemispheres) into the third ventricle via the **interventricular foramina,** and then through the cerebral aqueduct of the midbrain into the fourth ventricle in the hindbrain (Figure 19.8). Some of the fluid reaching the fourth ventricle continues down the central canal of the spinal cord, but the bulk of it circulates into the subarachnoid space, exiting through the three foramina in the walls of the fourth ventricle (the two lateral and the single median apertures). The fluid returns to the blood in the dural sinuses via the arachnoid villi.

Ordinarily, cerebrospinal fluid forms and drains at a constant rate. However, under certain conditions—for example, obstructed drainage or circulation resulting from tumors or anatomical deviations—cerebrospinal fluid accumulates and exerts increasing pressure on the brain which, uncorrected, causes neurological damage in adults. In infants, **hydrocephalus** (literally, "water on the brain") is indicated by a gradually enlarging head. The infant's skull is still flexible and contains fontanels, so it can expand to accommodate the increasing size of the brain. ∎

Cranial Nerves

The **cranial nerves** are part of the peripheral nervous system and not part of the brain proper, but they are most appropriately identified while studying brain anatomy. The 12 pairs of cranial nerves primarily serve the head and neck. Only one

pair, the vagus nerves, extends into the thoracic and abdominal cavities. All but the first two pairs (olfactory and optic nerves) arise from the brain stem and pass through foramina in the base of the skull to reach their destination.

The cranial nerves are numbered consecutively, and in most cases their names reflect the major structures they control. The cranial nerves are described by name, number (Roman numeral), origin, course, and function in Table 19.1. This information should be committed to memory. A mnemonic device that might be helpful for remembering the cranial nerves in order is "*On occasion, our trusty truck acts funny—very good vehicle anyhow.*" The first letter of each word and the "a" and "h" of the final word "anyhow" will remind you of the first letter of the cranial nerve name.

Most cranial nerves are mixed nerves (containing both motor and sensory fibers). But close scrutiny of Table 19.1 will reveal that three pairs of cranial nerves (optic, olfactory, and vestibulocochlear) are purely sensory in function.

You may recall that the cell bodies of neurons are always located within the central nervous system (cortex or nuclei) or in specialized collections of cell bodies (ganglia) outside the CNS. Neuron cell bodies of the sensory cranial nerves are located in ganglia; those of the mixed cranial nerves are found both within the brain and in peripheral ganglia.

> ### ACTIVITY 3
>
> ## Identifying and Testing the Cranial Nerves
>
> 1. Observe the ventral surface of the brain model to identify the cranial nerves. Figure 19.9 may also aid you in this

Text continues on page 291.

Frontal lobe

Temporal lobe

Infundibulum

Facial nerve (VII)

Vestibulocochlear nerve (VIII)

Glossopharyngeal nerve (IX)

Vagus nerve (X)

Accessory nerve (XI)

Hypoglossal nerve (XII)

Filaments of olfactory nerve (I)

Olfactory bulb

Olfactory tract

Optic nerve (II)

Optic chiasma

Optic tract

Oculomotor nerve (III)

Trochlear nerve (IV)

Trigeminal nerve (V)

Abducens nerve (VI)

Cerebellum

Medulla oblongata

FIGURE 19.9 Ventral aspect of the human brain, showing the cranial nerves. (See also Figure 19.3.)

TABLE 19.1	The Cranial Nerves (see Figure 19.9)		
Number and name	**Origin and course**	**Function***	**Testing**
I. Olfactory	Fibers arise from olfactory epithelium and run through cribriform plate of ethmoid bone to synapse in olfactory bulbs.	Purely sensory—carries afferent impulses associated with sense of smell.	Person is asked to sniff aromatic substances, such as oil of cloves and vanilla, and to identify each.
II. Optic	Fibers arise from retina of eye to form the optic nerve and pass through optic canal of orbit. Fibers partially cross over at the optic chiasma and continue on to the thalamus as the optic tracts. Final fibers of this pathway travel from the thalamus to the visual cortex as the optic radiation.	Purely sensory—carries afferent impulses associated with vision.	Vision and visual field are determined with eye chart and by testing the point at which the person first sees an object (finger) moving into the visual field. Fundus of eye viewed with ophthalmoscope to detect papilledema (swelling of optic disc, or point at which optic nerve leaves the eye) and to observe blood vessels.
III. Oculomotor	Fibers emerge from dorsal midbrain and course ventrally to enter the orbit. They exit from skull via superior orbital fissure.	Primarily motor—somatic motor fibers to inferior oblique and superior, inferior, and medial rectus muscles, which direct eyeball, and to levator palpebrae muscles of the superior eyelid; parasympathetic fibers to iris and smooth muscle controlling lens shape (reflex responses to varying light intensity and focusing of eye for near vision).	Pupils are examined for size, shape, and equality. Pupillary reflex is tested with penlight (pupils should constrict when illuminated). Convergence for near vision is tested, as is subject's ability to follow objects with the eyes.
IV. Trochlear	Fibers emerge from midbrain and exit from skull via superior orbital fissure.	Primarily motor—provides somatic motor fibers to superior oblique muscle that moves the eyeball.	Tested in common with cranial nerve III.
V. Trigeminal	Fibers emerge from pons and form three divisions, which exit separately from skull: mandibular division through foramen ovale in sphenoid bone, maxillary division via foramen rotundum in sphenoid bone, and ophthalmic division through superior orbital fissure of eye socket.	Mixed—major sensory nerve of face; conducts sensory impulses from skin of face and anterior scalp, from mucosae of mouth and nose, and from surface of eyes; mandibular division also contains motor fibers that innervate muscles of mastication and muscles of floor of mouth.	Sensations of pain, touch, and temperature are tested with safety pin and hot and cold objects. Corneal reflex tested with wisp of cotton. Motor branch assessed by asking person to clench his teeth, open mouth against resistance, and move jaw side to side.
VI. Abducens	Fibers leave inferior pons and exit from skull via superior orbital fissure to run to eye.	Carries somatic motor fibers to lateral rectus muscle that moves the eyeball.	Tested in common with cranial nerve III.
VII. Facial	Fibers leave pons and travel through temporal bone via internal acoustic meatus, exiting via stylomastoid foramen to reach the face.	Mixed—supplies somatic motor fibers to muscles of facial expression and parasympathetic motor fibers to lacrimal and salivary glands; carries sensory fibers from taste receptors of anterior portion of tongue.	Anterior two-thirds of tongue is tested for ability to taste sweet (sugar), salty, sour (vinegar), and bitter (quinine) substances. Symmetry of face is checked. Subject is asked to close eyes, smile, whistle, and so on. Tearing is assessed with ammonia fumes.

*Does not include sensory impulses from proprioceptors.

TABLE 19.1	*(continued)*		
Number and name	**Origin and course**	**Function***	**Testing**
VIII. Vestibulocochlear	Fibers run from inner-ear equilibrium and hearing apparatus, housed in temporal bone, through internal acoustic meatus to enter pons.	Purely sensory—vestibular branch transmits impulses associated with sense of equilibrium from vestibular apparatus and semicircular canals; cochlear branch transmits impulses associated with hearing from cochlea.	Hearing is checked by air and bone conduction using tuning fork.
IX. Glossopharyngeal	Fibers emerge from medulla and leave skull via jugular foramen to run to throat.	Mixed—somatic motor fibers serve pharyngeal muscles, and parasympathetic motor fibers serve salivary glands; sensory fibers carry impulses from pharynx, tonsils, posterior tongue (taste buds), and from chemoreceptors and pressure receptors of carotid artery.	A tongue depressor is used to check the position of the uvula. Gag and swallowing reflexes are checked. Subject is asked to speak and cough. Posterior third of tongue may be tested for taste.
X. Vagus	Fibers emerge from medulla and pass through jugular foramen and descend through neck region into thorax and abdomen.	Mixed—fibers carry somatic motor impulses to pharynx and larynx and sensory fibers from same structures; very large portion is composed of parasympathetic motor fibers, which supply heart and smooth muscles of abdominal visceral organs; transmits sensory impulses from viscera.	As for cranial nerve IX (IX and X are tested in common, since they both innervate muscles of throat and mouth).
XI. Accessory	Fibers arise from the superior aspect of spinal cord, enter the skull, and then travel through jugular foramen to reach muscles of neck and back.	Mixed (but primarily motor in function)—provides somatic motor fibers to sternocleidomastoid and trapezius muscles and to muscles of soft palate, pharynx, and larynx (spinal and medullary fibers respectively).	Sternocleidomastoid and trapezius muscles are checked for strength by asking person to rotate head and shrug shoulders against resistance.
XII. Hypoglossal	Fibers arise from medulla and exit from skull via hypoglossal canal to travel to tongue.	Mixed (but primarily motor in function)—carries somatic motor fibers to muscles of tongue.	Person is asked to protrude and retract tongue. Any deviations in position are noted.

*Does not include sensory impulses from proprioceptors.

study. Notice that the first (olfactory) cranial nerves are not visible on the model because they consist only of short axons that run from the nasal mucosa through the cribriform plate of the ethmoid bone. (However, the synapse points of the first cranial nerves, the *olfactory bulbs,* are visible on the model.)

2.   The last column of Table 19.1 describes techniques for testing cranial nerves, which is an important part of any neurological examination. This information may help you understand cranial nerve function, especially as it pertains to some aspects of brain function. Conduct tests of cranial nerve function following directions given in the "testing" column of the table.

3.   Several cranial nerve ganglia are named in the chart here. *Using your textbook or an appropriate reference,* fill in the chart by naming the cranial nerve the ganglion is associated with and stating its location. ▪▪

Cranial nerve ganglion	Cranial nerve	Site of ganglion
Trigeminal		
Geniculate		
Inferior		
Superior		
Spiral		
Vestibular		

DISSECTION:
The Sheep Brain

The sheep brain is enough like the human brain to warrant comparison. Obtain a sheep brain, disposable gloves, dissecting tray, and instruments, and bring them to your laboratory bench.

1. Before beginning the dissection, turn your sheep brain so that you are viewing its left lateral aspect. Compare the various areas of the sheep brain (cerebrum, brain stem, cerebellum) to the photo of the human brain in Figure 19.10. Relatively speaking, which of these structures is obviously much larger in the human brain?

_____

2. Place the intact sheep brain ventral surface down on the dissecting pan, and observe the dura mater. Feel its consistency and note its toughness. Cut through the dura mater along the line of the longitudinal fissure (which separates the cerebral hemispheres) to enter the superior sagittal sinus. Gently force the cerebral hemispheres apart laterally to expose the corpus callosum deep to the longitudinal fissure.

3. Carefully remove the dura mater and examine the superior surface of the brain. Notice that its surface, like that of the human brain, is thrown into convolutions (fissures and gyri). Locate the arachnoid mater, which appears on the brain surface as a delicate "cottony" material spanning the fissures. In contrast, the innermost meninx, the pia mater, closely follows the cerebral contours.

Ventral Structures

Figure 19.11a and b shows the important features of the ventral surface of the brain. Turn the brain so that its ventral surface is uppermost.

1. Look for the clublike olfactory bulbs anteriorly, on the inferior surface of the frontal lobes of the cerebral hemispheres. Axons of olfactory neurons run from the nasal mu-

FIGURE 19.11 Intact sheep brain. (a) Photograph of ventral view.

cosa through the perforated cribriform plate of the ethmoid bone to synapse with the olfactory bulbs.

How does the size of these olfactory bulbs compare with those of humans?

_____

Is the sense of smell more important as a protective and a food-getting sense in sheep or in humans?

_____

2. The optic nerve (II) carries sensory impulses from the retina of the eye. Thus this cranial nerve is involved in the sense of vision. Identify the optic nerves, optic chiasma, and optic tracts.

3. Posterior to the optic chiasma, two structures protrude from the ventral aspect of the hypothalamus—the infundibulum (stalk of the pituitary gland) immediately posterior to the optic chiasma and the mammillary body. Notice that the sheep's mammillary body is a single rounded eminence. In humans it is a double structure.

4. Identify the cerebral peduncles on the ventral aspect of the midbrain, just posterior to the mammillary body of the hypothalamus. The cerebral peduncles are fiber tracts connecting the cerebrum and medulla oblongata. Identify the large oculomotor nerves (III), which arise from the ventral midbrain surface, and

FIGURE 19.10 Photo of lateral aspect of the human brain.

Labels in Figure 19.11: Ventral; Olfactory bulb; Optic nerve (II); Infundibulum; Mammillary body; Cerebral peduncle; Pons; Trigeminal nerve (V); Abducens nerve (VI); Medulla oblongata; (a)

Labels in Figure 19.10: Left cerebral hemisphere; Brain stem; Transverse cerebral fissure; Cerebellum

Olfactory bulb
Olfactory tract
Infundibulum (stalk of pituitary gland)
Mammillary body
Cerebral peduncle
Trigeminal nerve (V)
Pons
Cerebellum
Glossopharyngeal nerve (IX)
Vagus nerve (X)
Spinal root of the accessory nerve (XI)

Cerebrum
Optic nerve (II)
Optic chiasma
Optic tract
Oculomotor nerve (III)
Trochlear nerve (IV)
Abducens nerve (VI)
Facial nerve (VII)
Vestibulocochlear nerve (VIII)
Hypoglossal nerve (XII)
Medulla oblongata

(b)

FIGURE 19.11 (*continued*) Intact sheep brain. (b) Diagrammatic ventral view.

the tiny trochlear nerves (IV), which can be seen at the junction of the midbrain and pons. Both of these cranial nerves provide motor fibers to extrinsic muscles of the eyeball.

5.   Move posteriorly from the midbrain to identify first the pons and then the medulla oblongata, both hindbrain structures composed primarily of ascending and descending fiber tracts.

6.   Return to the junction of the pons and midbrain, and proceed posteriorly to identify the following cranial nerves, all arising from the pons:

- Trigeminal nerves (V), which are involved in chewing and sensations of the head and face.

- Abducens nerves (VI), which abduct the eye (and thus work in conjunction with cranial nerves III and IV)

- Facial nerves (VII), large nerves involved in taste sensation, gland function (salivary and lacrimal glands), and facial expression.

7.   Continue posteriorly to identify:

- Vestibulocochlear nerves (VIII), purely sensory nerves that are involved with hearing and equilibrium.

- Glossopharyngeal nerves (IX), which contain motor fibers innervating throat structures and sensory fibers transmitting taste stimuli (in conjunction with cranial nerve VII).

- Vagus nerves (X), often called "wanderers," which serve many organs of the head, thorax, and abdominal cavity.

- Accessory nerves (XI), which serve muscles of the neck, larynx, and shoulder; actually arise from the spinal cord (C_1 through C_5) and travel superiorly to enter the skull before running to the muscles that they serve.

- Hypoglossal nerves (XII), which stimulate tongue and neck muscles.

It is likely that some of the cranial nerves will have been broken off during brain removal. If so, observe sheep brains of other students to identify those missing from your specimen.

Olfactory bulb

Cerebrum

Cerebellum

Medulla oblongata

Spinal cord

(c)

Dorsal

Cerebrum

Cerebellum

(d)

FIGURE 19.11 *(continued)* **Intact sheep brain. (c** and **d)** Diagrammatic and photographic views of the dorsal view, respectively.

Occipital lobe of cerebral hemisphere

Pineal body

Superior colliculi of corpora quadrigemina

Inferior colliculi of corpora quadrigemina

Cerebellum

FIGURE 19.12 **Means of exposing the dorsal midbrain structures of the sheep brain.**

Dorsal Structures

1. Refer to Figure 19.11c and d as a guide in identifying the following structures. Reidentify the now exposed cerebral hemispheres. How does the depth of the fissures in the sheep's cerebral hemispheres compare to that of the fissures in the human brain?

_____

2. Examine the cerebellum. Notice that, in contrast to the human cerebellum, it is not divided longitudinally, and that its fissures are oriented differently. What dural falx (falx cerebri or falx cerebelli) is missing that is present in humans?

_____

3. Locate the three pairs of cerebellar peduncles, fiber tracts that connect the cerebellum to other brain structures, by lifting the cerebellum dorsally away from the brain stem. The most posterior pair, the inferior cerebellar peduncles, connect the cerebellum to the medulla. The middle cerebellar peduncles attach the cerebellum to the pons, and the superior cerebellar peduncles run from the cerebellum to the midbrain.

4. To expose the dorsal surface of the midbrain, gently separate the cerebrum and cerebellum as shown in Figure 19.12. Identify the corpora quadrigemina, which appear as four rounded prominences on the dorsal midbrain surface.

What is the function of the corpora quadrigemina?

_____

_____

Also locate the pineal gland, which appears as a small oval protrusion in the midline just anterior to the corpora quadrigemina.

Internal Structures

1. The internal structure of the brain can be examined only after further dissection. Place the brain ventral side down on the dissecting tray and make a cut completely through it in a superior to inferior direction. Cut through the longitudinal fissure, corpus callosum, and midline of the cerebellum. Refer to Figure 19.13 as you work.

2. A thin nervous tissue membrane immediately ventral to the corpus callosum that separates the lateral ventricles is the septum pellucidum. If it is still intact, pierce this membrane and probe the lateral ventricle cavity. The fiber tract ventral to the septum pellucidum and anterior to the third ventricle is the fornix.

How does the size of the fornix in this brain compare with the size of the human fornix?

_____

_____

Cerebral hemisphere
Corpus callosum
Frontal lobe of cerebrum
Fornix
Intermediate mass of thalamus
Cerebral peduncle
Optic chiasma

Parietal lobe
Cerebellum
Pineal gland
Arbor vitae
Corpora quadrigemina
Fourth ventricle
Medulla oblongata
Pons

FIGURE 19.13 Photograph of sagittal section of the sheep brain showing internal structures.

FIGURE 19.14 Frontal section of a sheep brain. Major structures include the thalamus, hypothalamus, and lateral and third ventricles.

Why do you suppose this is so? (Hint: What is the function of this band of fibers?)

_____

3. Identify the thalamus, which forms the walls of the third ventricle and is located posterior and ventral to the fornix. The intermediate mass spanning the ventricular cavity appears as an oval protrusion of the thalamic wall. Anterior to the intermediate mass, locate the interventricular foramen, a canal connecting the lateral ventricle on the same side with the third ventricle.

4. The hypothalamus forms the floor of the third ventricle. Identify the optic chiasma, infundibulum, and mammillary body on its exterior surface. You can see the pineal gland at the superoposterior end of the third ventricle, just beneath the junction of the corpus callosum and fornix.

5. Locate the midbrain by identifying the corpora quadrigemina that form its dorsal roof. Follow the cerebral aqueduct (the narrow canal connecting the third and fourth ventricles) through the midbrain tissue to the fourth ventricle. Identify the cerebral peduncles, which form its anterior walls.

6. Identify the pons and medulla oblongata, which lie anterior to the fourth ventricle. The medulla continues into the spinal cord without any obvious anatomical change, but the point at which the fourth ventricle narrows to a small canal is generally accepted as the beginning of the spinal cord.

7. Identify the cerebellum posterior to the fourth ventricle. Notice its internal treelike arrangement of white matter, the arbor vitae.

8. If time allows, obtain another sheep brain and section it along the frontal plane so that the cut passes through the infundibulum. Compare your specimen with the photograph in Figure 19.14, and attempt to identify all the structures shown in the figure.

9. Check with your instructor to determine if cow spinal cord sections (preserved) are available for the spinal cord studies in Exercise 21. If not, save the small portion of the spinal cord from your brain specimen. Otherwise, dispose of all the organic debris in the appropriate laboratory containers and clean the laboratory bench, the dissection instruments, and the tray before leaving the laboratory. ▬

NAME _____

LAB TIME/DATE _____

Gross Anatomy of the Brain and Cranial Nerves

The Human Brain

1. Match the letters on the diagram of the human brain (right lateral view) to the appropriate terms listed at the left.

_____ 1. frontal lobe

_____ 2. parietal lobe

_____ 3. temporal lobe

_____ 4. precentral gyrus

_____ 5. parieto-occipital sulcus

_____ 6. postcentral gyrus

_____ 7. lateral sulcus

_____ 8. central sulcus

_____ 9. cerebellum

_____ 10. medulla

_____ 11. occipital lobe

_____ 12. pons

2. In which of the cerebral lobes are the following functional areas found?

auditory cortex: _____   olfactory cortex: _____

primary motor cortex: _____   visual cortex: _____

primary sensory cortex: _____   Broca's area: _____

3. Which of the following structures are not part of the brain stem? (Circle the appropriate response or responses.)

cerebral hemispheres   pons   midbrain   cerebellum   medulla   diencephalon

4. Complete the following statements by writing the proper word or phrase on the corresponding blanks at the right.

A(n) _1_ is an elevated ridge of cerebral tissue. The convolutions seen in the cerebrum are important because they increase the _2_. Gray matter is composed of _3_. White matter is composed of _4_. A fiber tract that provides for communication between different parts of the same cerebral hemisphere is called a(n) _5_, whereas one that carries impulses from the cerebrum to lower CNS areas is called a(n) _6_ tract. The lentiform nucleus along with the caudate nuclei are collectively called the _7_.

1. _____

2. _____

3. _____

4. _____

5. _____

6. _____

7. _____

297

5. Identify the structures on the following sagittal view of the human brain stem and diencephalon by matching the numbered areas to the proper terms in the list.

_____ a. cerebellum

_____ b. cerebral aqueduct

_____ c. (small part of) cerebral hemisphere

_____ d. cerebral peduncle

_____ e. choroid plexus

_____ f. corpora quadrigemina

_____ g. corpus callosum

_____ h. fornix

_____ i. fourth ventricle

_____ j. hypothalamus

_____ k. intermediate mass

_____ l. mammillary bodies

_____ m. medulla oblongata

_____ n. optic chiasma

_____ o. pineal gland

_____ p. pituitary gland

_____ q. pons

_____ r. septum pellucidum

_____ s. thalamus

6. Using the terms from question 5, match the appropriate structures with the descriptions given below.

_____ 1. site of regulation of body temperature and water balance; most important autonomic center

_____ 2. consciousness depends on the function of this part of the brain

_____ 3. located in the midbrain; contains reflex centers for vision and audition

_____ 4. responsible for regulation of posture and coordination of complex muscular movements

_____ 5. important synapse site for afferent fibers traveling to the sensory cortex

_____ 6. contains autonomic centers regulating blood pressure, heart rate, and respiratory rhythm, as well as coughing, sneezing, and swallowing centers

_____ 7. large commissure connecting the cerebral hemispheres

_____ 8. fiber tract involved with olfaction

_____ 9. connects the third and fourth ventricles

_____ 10. encloses the third ventricle

7. Embryologically, the brain arises from the rostral end of a tubelike structure that quickly becomes divided into three major regions. Groups of structures that develop from the embryonic brain are listed below. Designate the embryonic origin of each group as the hindbrain, midbrain, or forebrain.

_____ 1.   the diencephalon, including the thalamus, optic chiasma, and hypothalamus

_____ 2.   the medulla, pons, and cerebellum

_____ 3.   the cerebral hemispheres

8. What is the function of the basal ganglia? _____

_____

9. What is the corpus striatum, and how is it related to the fibers of the internal capsule? _____

_____

_____

10. A brain hemorrhage within the region of the right internal capsule results in paralysis of the left side of the body.

Explain why the left side (rather than the right side) is affected. _____

_____

11. Explain why trauma to the base of the brain is often much more dangerous than trauma to the frontal lobes. (Hint: Think about the relative functioning of the cerebral hemispheres and the brain stem structures. Which contain centers more vital to life?)

_____

_____

_____

_____

12. In "split brain" experiments, the main commissure connecting the cerebral hemispheres is cut. First, name this commissure.

_____

Then, describe what results (in terms of behavior) can be anticipated in such experiments. (Use an appropriate reference if you need help with this one!)

_____

_____

_____

_____

Meninges of the Brain

13. Identify the meningeal (or associated) structures described below:

_____ 1. outermost meninx covering the brain; composed of tough fibrous connective tissue

_____ 2. innermost meninx covering the brain; delicate and highly vascular

_____ 3. structures instrumental in returning cerebrospinal fluid to the venous blood in the dural sinuses

_____ 4. structure that forms the cerebrospinal fluid

_____ 5. middle meninx; like a cobweb in structure

_____ 6. its outer layer forms the periosteum of the skull

_____ 7. a dural fold that attaches the cerebrum to the crista galli of the skull

_____ 8. a dural fold separating the cerebrum from the cerebellum

Cerebrospinal Fluid

14. Label the structures involved with circulation of cerebrospinal fluid on the accompanying diagram.

Add arrows to the figure above to indicate the flow of cerebrospinal fluid from its formation in the lateral ventricles to the site of its exit from the fourth ventricle. Then fill in the blanks in the following paragraph.

Cerebrospinal fluid flows from the fourth ventricle into the central canal of the spinal cord and the __1__ space surrounding the brain and spinal cord. From this space it drains through the __2__ into the __3__.

2. _____

3. _____

1. _____

Cranial Nerves

15. Using the terms below, correctly identify all structures indicated by leader lines on the diagram.

a. abducens nerve (VI)

b. accessory nerve (XI)

c. cerebellum

d. cerebral peduncle

e. decussation of the pyramids

f. facial nerve (VII)

g. frontal lobe of cerebral hemisphere

h. glossopharyngeal nerve (IX)

i. hypoglossal nerve (XII)

j. longitudinal fissure

k. mammillary body

l. medulla oblongata

m. oculomotor nerve (III)

n. olfactory bulb

o. olfactory tract

p. optic chiasma

q. optic nerve (II)

r. optic tract

s. pituitary gland

t. pons

u. spinal cord

v. temporal lobe of cerebral hemisphere

w. trigeminal nerve (V)

x. trochlear nerve (IV)

y. vagus nerve (X)

z. vestibulocochlear nerve (VIII)

16. Provide the name and number of the cranial nerves involved in each of the following activities, sensations, or disorders.

_____ 1. rotating the head

_____ 2. smelling a flower

_____ 3. raising the eyelids; pupillary constriction

_____ 4. slowing the heart; increasing motility of the digestive tract

_____ 5. involved in Bell's palsy (facial paralysis)

_____ 6. chewing food

_____ 7. listening to music; seasickness

_____ 8. secretion of saliva; tasting well-seasoned food

_____ 9. involved in "rolling" the eyes (three nerves—provide numbers only)

_____ 10. feeling a toothache

_____ 11. reading the newspaper

_____ 12. purely sensory in function (three nerves—provide numbers only)

Dissection of the Sheep Brain

17. In your own words, describe the firmness and texture of the sheep brain tissue as observed when cutting into it.

_____

Because formalin hardens all tissue, what conclusions might you draw about the firmness and texture of living brain tissue?

_____

18. When comparing human and sheep brains, you observe some profound differences between them. Record your observations in the chart below.

Structure	Human	Sheep
Olfactory bulb		
Pons/medulla relationship		
Location of cranial nerve III		
Mammillary body		
Corpus callosum		
Intermediate mass of thalamus		
Relative size of superior and inferior colliculi		
Pineal gland		

Electroencephalography

MATERIALS

- ☐ Oscilloscope and EEG lead-selector box or physiograph and high-gain preamplifier
- ☐ Cot (if available) or pillow
- ☐ Electrode gel
- ☐ EEG electrodes and leads
- ☐ Collodion gel or long elastic EEG straps
- ☐ **BIOPAC®** BIOPAC® MP36 (or MP35/30) data acquisition unit, PC or Mac computer, BIOPAC® Student Lab Software, electrode lead set, disposable vinyl electrodes, Lycra® swim cap (such as Speedo® brand) or supportive wrap (such as 3M Coban™ Self-adhering Support Wrap) to press electrodes against head for improved contact, and a cot or lab bench and pillow.

New versions of the BSL software (3.7.5 and higher for Windows, and 3.7.4 and higher for Mac) require slightly different channel settings and collection strategies. Instructions for using the newer software with the MP36/35 data acquisition units can be found on myA&P. In addition, instructions for use of the **NEW** 2-channel data acquisition unit, the MP45, may also be found on myA&P.

OBJECTIVES

1. To define *electroencephalogram,* and to discuss its clinical significance.
2. To describe or recognize typical tracings of the most common brain wave patterns (alpha, beta, theta, and delta waves), and to indicate the conditions under which each is most likely to be predominant.
3. To indicate the source of brain waves.
4. To define *alpha block.*
5. To monitor electroencephalography and recognize alpha rhythm.
6. To describe the effect of a sudden sound, mental concentration, and alkalosis on brain wave patterns.

PRE-LAB QUIZ

1. What does an electroencephalogram (EEG) actually measure?
   a. electrical activity of the brain
   b. electrical activity of the heart
   c. emotions
   d. physical activity of the subject
2. Circle the correct term. <u>Alpha waves / Beta waves</u> are typical of the attentive or awake state.
3. Circle True or False. Brain waves can change with age, sensory stimuli, and the chemical state of the body.
4. Where will you place the indifferent (ground) electrode on your subject?
   a. the earlobe
   b. the forehead
   c. over the occipital lobe
   d. over the temporal bone
5. During today's activity, students will instruct subjects to *hyperventilate.* What should the subjects do?
   a. breathe in a normal manner
   b. breathe rapidly
   c. breathe very slowly
   d. hold their breath until they almost pass out

Any physiological investigation of the brain can emphasize and expose only a very minute portion of its activity. Higher brain functions, such as consciousness and logical reasoning, are extremely difficult to investigate. It is obviously much easier to do experiments on the brain's input-output functions, some of which can be detected with appropriate recording equipment. Still, the ability to record brain activity does not necessarily guarantee an understanding of the brain.

myA&P *For practice quizzes on this lab, go to www.myaandp.com.*

(a)

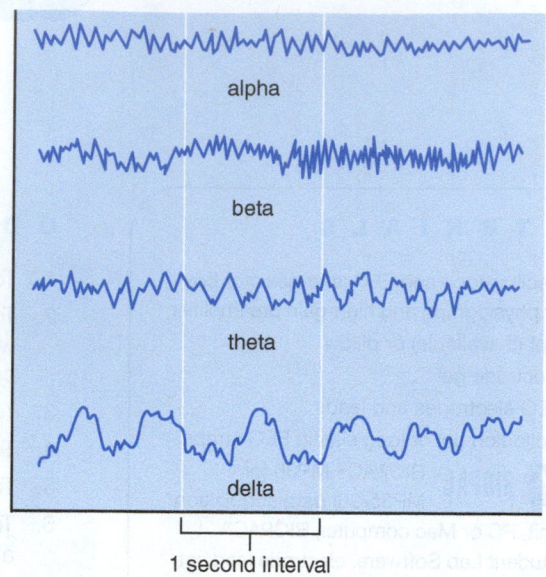

(b)

1 second interval

FIGURE 20.1 **Electroencephalography and brain waves. (a)** To obtain a recording of brain wave activity (an EEG), electrodes are positioned on the patient's scalp and attached to a recording device called an electroencephalograph. **(b)** Typical EEGs. Alpha waves are typical of the awake but relaxed state; beta waves occur in the awake, alert state; theta waves are common in children but not in normal awake adults; delta waves occur during deep sleep.

Brain Wave Patterns and the Electroencephalogram

The **electroencephalogram (EEG),** a record of the electrical activity of the brain, can be obtained through electrodes placed at various points on the skin or scalp of the head. This electrical activity, which is recorded as waves (Figure 20.1), represents the summed synaptic activity of many neurons.

Certain characteristics of brain waves are known. They have a frequency of 1 to 30 hertz (Hz) or cycles per second, a dominant rhythm of 10 Hz, and an average amplitude (voltage) of 20 to 100 microvolts (μV). They vary in frequency in different brain areas, occipital waves having a lower frequency than those associated with the frontal and parietal lobes.

The first of the brain waves to be described by scientists were the alpha waves (or alpha rhythm). **Alpha waves** have an average frequency range of 8 to 13 Hz and are produced when the individual is in a relaxed state with the eyes closed. **Alpha block,** suppression of the alpha rhythm, occurs if the eyes are opened or if the individual begins to concentrate on some mental problem or visual stimulus. Under these conditions, the waves decrease in amplitude but increase in frequency. Under conditions of fright or excitement, the frequency increases still more.

Beta waves, closely related to alpha waves, are faster (14 to 30 Hz) and have a lower amplitude. They are typical of the attentive or alert state.

Very large (high-amplitude) waves with a frequency of 4 Hz or less that are seen in deep sleep are **delta waves. Theta waves** are large, abnormally contoured waves with a frequency of 4 to 7 Hz. Although theta waves are normal in children, they are abnormal in awake adults.

Brain waves change with age, sensory stimuli, brain pathology, and the chemical state of the body. (Glucose deprivation, oxygen poisoning, and sedatives all interfere with the rhythmic activity of brain output by disturbing the metabolism of neurons.) Sleeping individuals and patients in a coma have EEGs that are slower (lower frequency) than the alpha rhythm of normal adults. Fright, epileptic seizures, and various types of drug intoxication can be associated with comparatively faster cortical activity. Thus impairment of cortical function is indicated by neuronal activity that is either too fast or too slow; unconsciousness occurs at both extremes of the frequency range.

Because spontaneous brain waves are always present, even during unconsciousness and coma, the absence of brain waves (a "flat" EEG) is taken as clinical evidence of death. The EEG is used clinically to diagnose and localize many types of brain lesions, including epileptic foci, infections, abscesses, and tumors. ■

ACTIVITY 1

Observing Brain Wave Patterns Using an Oscilloscope or Physiograph

If one electrode (the *active electrode*) is placed over a particular cortical area and another (the *indifferent electrode*) is placed over an inactive part of the head, such as the earlobe, all of the activity of the cortex underlying the active electrode will, theoretically, be recorded. The inactive area provides a zero reference point, or a baseline, and the EEG represents the difference between "activities" occurring under the two electrodes.

1. Connect the EEG lead-selector box to the oscilloscope preamplifier, or connect the high-gain preamplifier to the physiograph channel amplifier. Adjust the horizontal sweep and sensitivity according to the directions given in the instrument manual or by your instructor.

2. Prepare the subject. The subject should lie undisturbed on a cot or on the lab bench with eyes closed in a quiet, dimly lit area.

(Someone who is able to relax easily makes a good subject.) Apply a small amount of electrode gel to the subject's forehead above the left eye and on the left earlobe. Press an electrode to each prepared area and secure each by (1) applying a film of collodion gel to the electrode surface and the adjacent skin or (2) using a long elastic EEG strap (knot tied at the back of the head). If collodion gel is used, allow it to dry before you continue.

3.   Connect the active frontal lead (forehead) to the EEG lead-selector box outlet marked "L Frontal." Connect the lead from the indifferent electrode (earlobe) to the ground outlet (or to the appropriate input terminal on the high-gain preamplifier).

4.   Turn the oscilloscope or physiograph on, and observe the EEG pattern of the relaxed subject for a period of 5 minutes. If the subject is truly relaxed, you should see a typical alpha-wave pattern. (If the subject is unable to relax and the alpha-wave pattern does not appear in this time interval, test another subject.) Discourage all muscle movement during the monitoring period.*

5.   Abruptly and loudly clap your hands. The subject's eyes should open, and alpha block should occur. Observe the immediate brain wave pattern. How do the frequency and amplitude of the brain waves change?

_____

_____

Would you characterize this as beta rhythm? _____

Why? _____

_____

6.   Allow the subject about 5 minutes to achieve complete relaxation once again, then ask him or her to compute a number problem that requires concentration (for example, add 3 and 36, subtract 7, multiply by 2, add 50, etc.). Observe the brain wave pattern during the period of mental computation.

Observations: _____

_____

_____

7.   Once again allow the subject to relax until alpha rhythm resumes. Then, instruct him or her to hyperventilate for 3 minutes. *Be sure to tell the subject when to stop hyperventilating.* Hyperventilation rapidly flushes carbon dioxide out of the lungs, decreasing carbon dioxide levels in the blood and producing respiratory alkalosis.

Observe the changes in the rhythm and amplitude of the brain waves occurring during the period of hyperventilation.

*Note that 60-cycle "noise" (appearing as fast, regular, low amplitude waves superimposed on the more irregular brain waves) may interfere with the tracings being made, particularly if the laboratory has a lot of electrical equipment.

Observations: _____

_____

_____

8.   Think of other stimuli that might affect brain wave patterns. Test your hypotheses. Describe what stimuli you tested and what responses you observed.

_____

_____

_____

_____ ▬

ACTIVITY 2

Electroencephalography Using Biopac®

In this activity, the EEG of the subject will be recorded during a relaxed state, first with the eyes closed, then with the eyes open while silently counting to ten, and finally with the eyes closed again.

Setting Up the Equipment

1.   Connect the BIOPAC® unit to the computer and turn the computer **ON.**

2.   Make sure the BIOPAC® unit is **OFF.**

3.   Plug in the equipment as shown in Figure 20.2.

•   Electrode lead set—CH 1

4.   Turn the BIOPAC® unit **ON.**

5.   Attach three electrodes to the subject's scalp and ear as shown in Figure 20.3. Follow these important guidelines to assist in effective electrode placement:

•   Select subjects with the easiest access to the scalp.

•   Move as much hair out of the way as possible.

•   Apply a dab of electrode gel to the spots where the electrodes will be attached.

•   Apply pressure to the electrodes for 1 minute to ensure attachment.

•   Use a swimcap or supportive wrap to maintain attachment.

•   Do not touch the electrodes while recording.

•   The earlobe electrode may be folded under the lobe itself.

6.   When the electrodes are attached, the subject should lie down and relax with eyes closed for 5 minutes before recording.

7.   Start the BIOPAC® Student Lab program on the computer by double-clicking the icon on the desktop or by following your instructor's guidance.

8.   Select lesson **L03-EEG-1** from the menu, and click **OK.**

9.   Type in a filename that will save this subject's data on the computer hard drive. You may want to use the subject's last name followed by EEG-1 (for example, SmithEEG-1), then click **OK.**

FIGURE 20.2 **FIGURE 20.2 Setting up the BIOPAC®
equipment.** Plug the electrode set into Channel 1.

BIOPAC® data
acquisition unit

Electrode lead set
(plugs into Channel 1)

10. During this preparation, the subject should be very still
and in a relaxed state with eyes closed. Allow the subject to
relax with minimal stimuli.

Calibrating the Equipment

1. Make sure that the electrodes remain firmly attached to the
surface of the scalp and earlobe. The subject should remain absolutely still and try to avoid movement of the body or face.

2. With the subject in a relaxed position, click **Calibrate.**

3. You will be prompted to check electrode attachment one
final time. When ready, click **OK;** the computer will record
for 15 seconds and stop automatically.

4. Observe the recording of the calibration data, which
should look like Figure 20.4.

- If the data look very different, click **Redo Calibration**
and repeat the steps above.

- If the data look similar, proceed to the next section.

Recording the Data

1. The subject should remain relaxed with eyes closed.

2. After clicking **Record,** the "director" will instruct the
subject to keep his or her eyes closed for the first 10 seconds
of recording, then open the eyes and *mentally* (not verbally)
count to ten, then close the eyes again and relax for 10 seconds. The director will insert a marker by pressing the **F9** key
(PC) or **ESC** key (Mac) when the command to open eyes is
given, and another marker when the subject reaches the count
of ten and closes the eyes. Click **Stop** 10 seconds after the
subject recloses the eyes.

3. Observe the recording of the data, which should look
similar to the data in Figure 20.5.

- If the data look very different, click **Redo** and repeat the
steps above. If the subject moved too much during the
recording, it is likely that artifact spikes will appear in
the data.

- If the data look similar, proceed to the next step.

4. Click the buttons for each of the different EEG rhythms at
the top of the data in the following order: **alpha, beta, delta,**
and **theta.** When you click each button, the software will extract
and display each of the specific frequency bands.

Red lead
(+)

White lead
(−)

Black lead
(Ground)

**FIGURE 20.3 Placement of electrodes and the
appropriate attachment of electrode leads by color.**

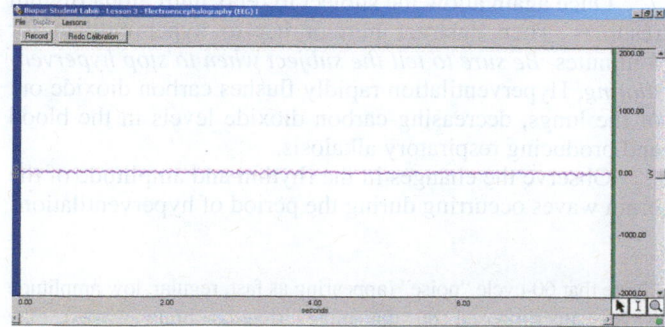

FIGURE 20.4 Example of calibration data.

FIGURE 20.5 Example of EEG data.

FIGURE 20.6 Highlighting the first data segment.

- To properly view each of the waveforms, you may have to click the **Display** menu and select **Autoscale Waveforms.** This function rescales the data for the rhythm band that is selected.

5. Observe the **alpha rhythm** band of data. The intensity of the alpha signal should decrease during the "eyes open" phase of the recording.

- If the data do not demonstrate this change, it is possible that the electrodes were not properly attached. You should redo the recording.

6. When finished, click **Done.** If you are certain you want to stop recording, click **YES.** Remove the electrodes from the subject's scalp.

7. A pop-up window will appear. To record from another subject select **Record from another subject** and return to step 5 under Setting Up the Equipment. If continuing to the Data Analysis section, select **Analyze current data file** and proceed to step 2.

Data Analysis

1. If just starting the BIOPAC® program to perform data analysis, enter **Review Saved Data** mode and choose the file with the subject's EEG data (for example, SmithEEG-1).

2. Observe the way the channel numbers are designated: CH 1—**raw EEG;** CH 2—**alpha;** CH 3—**beta;** CH 4—**delta;** and CH 5—**theta.**

3. To set up the display for optimal viewing, hide Channel 1. To do this, hold down the Ctrl key (PC) or Option key (Mac) while using the cursor to click channel box 1 (the small box with a 1 at the upper left of the screen).

4. To analyze the data, set up the first four pairs of channel/measurement boxes at the top of the screen by selecting the following channels and measurement types from the drop-down menus:

Channel	Measurement
CH 2	stdev
CH 3	stdev
CH 4	stdev
CH 5	stdev

stdev (standard deviation): This is a statistical calculation that estimates the variability of the data in the area highlighted by the I-beam cursor. This function minimizes the effects of extreme values and electrical artifacts that may unduly influence interpretation of the data.

5. Use the arrow cursor and click the I-beam cursor box at the lower right of the screen to activate the "area selection" function. Using the activated I-beam cursor, highlight the first 10-second segment of EEG data, which represents the subject at rest with eyes closed (Figure 20.6).

6. Observe that the computer automatically calculates the stdev for each of the channels of data (alpha, beta, delta, and theta).

7. Record the data for each rhythm in the chart below, rounding to the nearest 0.01 µV.

		Standard Deviations (stdev) of Signals in Each Segment		
Rhythm	**Channel**	**Eyes closed Segment 1 Seconds 0–10**	**Eyes open Segment 2 Seconds 10–20**	**Eyes reclosed Segment 3 Seconds 20–30**
Alpha	CH 2			
Beta	CH 3			
Delta	CH 4			
Theta	CH 5			

8. Repeat steps 5–7 to analyze and record the data for the next two segments of data, with eyes open, and with eyes reclosed. The triangular markers inserted at the top of the data should provide guidance for highlighting.

9. To continue the analysis, change the settings in the first four pairs of channel/measurement boxes. Select the following channels and measurement types:

Channel	Measurement
CH 2	Freq
CH 3	Freq
CH 4	Freq
CH 5	Freq

Freq (frequency): This gives the frequency in hertz (Hz) of an individual wave that is highlighted by the I-beam cursor.

10. To view an individual wave from among the high-frequency waveforms, you must use the zoom function. To activate the zoom function, use the cursor to click the magnifying glass at the lower-right corner of the screen (near the I-beam cursor box). The cursor will become a magnifying glass.

11. To examine individual waves within the **alpha** data, click that band with the magnifying glass until it is possible to observe the peaks and troughs of individual waves within **Segment 1.**

• To properly view each of the waveforms, you may have to click the **Display** menu and select **Autoscale Waveforms.** This function rescales the data for the rhythm band that is selected.

12. At this time, focus on alpha waves only. Reactivate the I-beam cursor by clicking its box in the lower-right corner. Highlight a *single* alpha wave from peak to peak as shown in Figure 20.7.

13. Read the calculated frequency (in Hz) in the measurement box for CH 2, and record this as the frequency of Wave 1 for alpha rhythm in the chart below.

FIGURE 20.7 Highlighting a single alpha wave from peak to peak.

14. Use the I-beam cursor to select two more individual **alpha** waves and record their frequencies in the chart.

15. You will now perform the same frequency measurements for three waves in each of the **beta** (CH 3), **delta** (CH 4), and **theta** (CH 5) data sets. Record these measurements in the chart.

16. Calculate the average of the three waves measured for each of the brain rhythms, and record the average in the chart.

17. When finished, answer the following questions and then exit the program by going to the **File** menu at the top of the page and clicking **Quit.**

Look at the waveforms you recorded and carefully examine all three segments of the alpha rhythm record. Is there a difference in electrical activity in this frequency range when the eyes are open versus closed? Describe your observations.

_____

_____

_____

Carefully examine all three segments of the beta rhythm record. Is there a difference in electrical activity in this

Frequencies of Waves for Each Rhythm (Hz)					
Rhythm	Channel	Wave 1	Wave 2	Wave 3	Average
Alpha	CH 2				
Beta	CH 3				
Delta	CH 4				
Theta	CH 5				

frequency range when the eyes are open versus closed? Describe what you observe.

_____

_____

_____

This time, compare the intensity (height) of the alpha and beta waveforms throughout all three segments. Does the intensity of one signal appear more varied than the other in the record? Describe your observations.

_____

_____

_____

Examine the data for the delta and theta rhythms. Is there any change in the waveform as the subject changes states? If so, describe the change observed.

_____

_____

_____

The degree of variation in the intensity of the signal was estimated by calculating the standard deviation of the waves in each segment of data. In which time segment (eyes open, eyes closed, or eyes reclosed) is the difference in the standard deviations the greatest?

_____

NAME_____

LAB TIME/DATE_____

Electroencephalography

Brain Wave Patterns and the Electroencephalogram

1. Define *EEG*. _____

2. Identify the type of brain wave pattern described in each statement below.

    _____ below 4 Hz; slow, large waves; normally seen during deep sleep

    _____ rhythm generally apparent when an individual is in a relaxed, nonattentive state with the eyes closed

    _____ correlated to the alert state; usually about 15 to 30 Hz

3. What is meant by the term *alpha block*? _____

   _____

4. List at least four types of brain lesions that may be determined by EEG studies. _____

   _____

5. What is the common result of hypoactivity or hyperactivity of the brain neurons? _____

Observing Brain Wave Patterns

6. How was alpha block demonstrated in the laboratory experiment? _____

   _____

7. What was the effect of mental concentration on the brain wave pattern? _____

   _____

   _____

8. What effect on the brain wave pattern did hyperventilation have? _____

Electroencephalography Using BIOPAC®

9. Observe the average frequency of the waves you measured for each rhythm. Did the calculated average for each fall within the specified range indicated in the introduction to encephalograms?

_____

_____

10. Suggest the possible advantages and disadvantages of using electroencephalography in a clinical setting.

_____

_____

_____

21

Spinal Cord, Spinal Nerves, and the Autonomic Nervous System

M A T E R I A L S

- ☐ Spinal cord model (cross section)
- ☐ Three-dimensional laboratory charts or models of the spinal cord, spinal nerves, and sympathetic chain
- ☐ Red and blue pencils
- ☐ Preserved cow spinal cord sections with meninges and nerve roots intact (or spinal cord segment saved from the brain dissection in Exercise 19)
- ☐ Dissecting instruments and tray
- ☐ Disposable gloves
- ☐ Stereomicroscope
- ☐ Prepared slide of spinal cord (x.s.)
- ☐ Compound microscope
- ☐ **BIOPAC®** BIOPAC® MP36 (MP35/30) data acquisition unit, PC or Mac computer. BIOPAC® Student Lab Software, respiratory transducer belt, GSR finger leads, electrode lead set, disposable vinyl electrodes, conduction gel, and nine 8½ × 11 inch sheets of paper of different colors (white, black, red, blue, green, yellow, orange, brown, and purple) to be viewed in this sequence. New versions of the BSL software (3.7.5 and higher for Windows, and 3.7.4 and higher for Mac) require slightly different channel settings and collection strategies. Instructions for using the newer software with the MP36/35 data acquisition units can be found on myA&P. In addition, instructions for use of the **NEW** 2-channel data acquisition unit, the MP45, may also be found on myA&P.
- ☐ *The Human Nervous System: The Spinal Cord and Spinal Nerves* videotape

🖊 For instructions on animal dissections, see the dissection exercises starting on p. 697 in the cat, fetal pig, and rat editions of this manual.

O B J E C T I V E S

1. To identify important anatomical areas on a model or appropriate diagram of the spinal cord, and to name the neuron type found in these areas (where applicable).
2. To indicate two major areas where the spinal cord is enlarged, and to explain the reasons for the enlargement.
3. To define *conus medullaris, cauda equina,* and *filum terminale.*
4. To locate on a diagram the fiber tracts in the spinal cord, and to state their functional importance.
5. To list two major functions of the spinal cord.
6. To name the meningeal coverings of the spinal cord, and to state their function.
7. To describe the origin, fiber composition, and distribution of the spinal nerves, differentiating between roots, the spinal nerve proper, and rami, and to discuss the result of transecting these structures.
8. To discuss the distribution of the dorsal rami and ventral rami of the spinal nerves.
9. To identify the four major nerve plexuses, the major nerves of each, and their distribution.
10. To identify the site of origin and the function of the sympathetic and parasympathetic divisions of the autonomic nervous system, and to state how the autonomic nervous system differs from the somatic nervous system.
11. To record and analyze data associated with the galvanic skin response, a measure of changes that occur in the skin due to changes in autonomic stimulation.

P R E - L A B   Q U I Z

1. The spinal cord extends from the foramen magnum of the skull to the first or second lumbar vertebrae, where it terminates in the
   a. conus medullaris
   b. denticulate ligament
   c. filum terminale
   d. gray matter
2. How many pairs of spinal nerves do humans have?
   a. 10   c. 31
   b. 12   d. 47
3. Circle the correct term. In cross section, the gray / white matter of the spinal cord looks like a butterfly or the letter H.
4. Circle True or False. The cell bodies of sensory neurons are found in an enlarged area of the dorsal root called the gray commissure.

Text continues on next page.

5. Circle the correct term. Fiber tracts conducting impulses to the brain are called ascending or <u>sensory</u> / <u>motor</u> tracts.

6. Circle True or False. Because the spinal nerves arise from fusion of the ventral and dorsal roots of the spinal cord, and contain motor and sensory fibers, all spinal nerves are considered mixed nerves.

7. The ventral rami of all spinal nerves except for T_2 through T_{12} form complex networks of nerves known as _____.
   a. fissures
   b. ganglia
   c. plexuses
   d. sulci

8. Severe injuries to the _____ plexus cause weakness or paralysis of the entire upper limb.
   a. brachial
   b. cervical
   c. lumbar
   d. sacral

9. The _____ nervous system is the subdivision of the peripheral nervous system that regulates body activities that are generally not under conscious control.
   a. autonomic
   b. peripheral
   c. somatic
   d. vascular

10. The _____ division of the autonomic nervous system is responsible for the "fight-or-flight" response that readies the body to cope with situations that threaten homeostasis.
   a. parasympathetic
   b. peripheral
   c. somatic
   d. sympathetic

The cylindrical **spinal cord,** a continuation of the brain stem, is an association and communication center. It plays a major role in spinal reflex activity and provides neural pathways to and from higher nervous centers.

Anatomy of the Spinal Cord

Enclosed within the vertebral canal of the spinal column, the spinal cord extends from the foramen magnum of the skull to the first or second lumbar vertebra, where it terminates in the cone-shaped **conus medullaris** (Figure 21.1). Like the brain, the cord is cushioned and protected by meninges. The dura mater and arachnoid meningeal coverings extend beyond the conus medullaris, approximately to the level of S_2, and the **filum terminale,** a fibrous extension of the pia mater, extends even farther (into the coccygeal canal) to attach to the posterior coccyx. **Denticulate ligaments,** saw-toothed shelves of pia mater, secure the spinal cord to the bony wall of the vertebral column all along its length (see Figure 21.1c).

The cerebrospinal fluid-filled meninges extend well beyond the end of the spinal cord, providing an excellent site for removing cerebrospinal fluid for analysis (as when bacterial or viral infections of the spinal cord or the meninges are suspected) without endangering the delicate spinal cord. This procedure, called a *lumbar tap,* is usually performed below L_3. Additionally, "saddle block," or caudal anesthesia for childbirth, is normally administered (injected) between L_3 and L_5.

In humans, 31 pairs of spinal nerves arise from the spinal cord and pass through intervertebral foramina to serve the body area at their approximate level of emergence. The cord is about the size of a finger in circumference for most of its length, but there are obvious enlargements in the *cervical* and *lumbar* areas where the nerves serving the upper and lower limbs issue from the cord.

Because the spinal cord does not extend to the end of the vertebral column, the spinal nerves emerging from the inferior end of the cord must travel through the vertebral canal for some distance before exiting at the appropriate intervertebral foramina. This collection of spinal nerves traversing the inferior end of the vertebral canal is called the **cauda equina** (Figure 21.1a and d) because of its similarity to a horse's tail (the literal translation of *cauda equina*).

ACTIVITY 1

Identifying Structures of the Spinal Cord

Obtain a three-dimensional model or laboratory chart of a cross section of a spinal cord and identify its structures as they are described next. ■

Gray Matter

In cross section, the **gray matter** of the spinal cord looks like a butterfly or the letter H (Figure 21.2). The two dorsal projections are called the **dorsal (posterior) horns.** The two ventral projections are the **ventral (anterior) horns.** The tips of the ventral horns are broader and less tapered than those of the dorsal horns. In the thoracic and lumbar regions of the cord, there is also a lateral outpocketing of gray matter on each side referred to as the **lateral horn.** The central area of gray matter connecting the two vertical regions is the **gray commissure.** The gray commissure surrounds the **central canal** of the cord, which contains cerebrospinal fluid.

Neurons with specific functions can be localized in the gray matter. The dorsal horns contain interneurons and sensory fibers that enter the cord from the body periphery via the **dorsal root.** The cell bodies of these sensory neurons are found in an enlarged area of the dorsal root called the **dorsal root ganglion.** The ventral horns mainly contain cell bodies of motor neurons of the somatic nervous system (voluntary system), which send their axons out via the **ventral root** of the cord to enter the adjacent spinal nerve. Since they are formed by the fusion of the dorsal and ventral roots, all **spinal nerves** are **mixed nerves** containing both sensory and motor fibers. The lateral horns, where present, contain nerve cell bodies of motor neurons of the autonomic nervous system (sympathetic division). Their axons also leave the cord via the ventral roots, along with those of the motor neurons of the ventral horns.

White Matter

The **white matter** of the spinal cord is nearly bisected by fissures (see Figure 21.2). The more open ventral fissure is the **ventral median fissure,** and the dorsal one is the shallow **dorsal median sulcus.** The white matter is composed of myelinated fibers—some running to higher centers, some

Cranial dura mater

Terminus of medulla oblongata of brain

Spinal nerve rootlets

Dorsal median sulcus of spinal cord

Sectioned pedicles of cervical vertebrae

(b) Cervical spinal cord.

Cervical spinal nerves

Cervical enlargement

Dura and arachnoid mater

Thoracic spinal nerves

Lumbar enlargement

Conus medullaris

Cauda equina

Filum terminale

Lumbar spinal nerves

Sacral spinal nerves

(a) The spinal cord and its nerve roots, with the bony vertebral arches removed. The dura mater and arachnoid mater are cut open and reflected laterally.

Spinal cord

Denticulate ligament

Arachnoid mater

Vertebral arch

Denticulate ligament

Dorsal median sulcus

Dorsal root

Spinal dura mater

(c) Thoracic spinal cord, showing denticulate ligaments.

Spinal cord

First lumbar vertebral arch (cut across)

Spinous process of second lumbar vertebra

Cauda equina

Conus medullaris

Filum terminale

(d) Inferior end of spinal cord, showing conus medullaris, cauda equina, and filum terminale.

FIGURE 21.1 Gross structure of the spinal cord, dorsal view.

Epidural space (contains fat)

Subdural space

Subarachnoid space (contains CSF)

Spinal nerve

Pia mater
Arachnoid mater — Spinal meninges
Dura mater

Bone of vertebra

Dorsal root ganglion

Body of vertebra

(a)

Dorsal funiculus
Ventral funiculus
Lateral funiculus

White columns

Dorsal root ganglion

Spinal nerve

Dorsal root (fans out into dorsal rootlets)

Ventral root (derived from several ventral rootlets)

Dorsal median sulcus
Gray commissure
Dorsal horn
Ventral horn — Gray matter
Lateral horn

Central canal

Ventral median fissure

Pia mater

Arachnoid mater

Spinal dura mater

(b)

FIGURE 21.2 Anatomy of the human spinal cord. (a) Cross section through the spinal cord illustrating its relationship to the surrounding vertebra. **(b)** Anterior view of the spinal cord and its meningeal coverings.

traveling from the brain to the cord, and some conducting impulses from one side of the cord to the other.

Because of the irregular shape of the gray matter, the white matter on each side of the cord can be divided into three primary regions or **white columns**: the **dorsal (pos-**

terior), lateral, and **ventral (anterior) funiculi.** Each funiculus contains a number of fiber **tracts** composed of axons with the same origin, terminus, and function. Tracts conducting sensory impulses to the brain are called *ascending,* or *sensory, tracts;* those carrying impulses

Ascending tracts   Descending tracts

FIGURE 21.3 Cross section of the spinal cord showing the relative positioning of its major tracts.

from the brain to the skeletal muscles are *descending, or motor, tracts.*

Because it serves as the transmission pathway between the brain and the body periphery, the spinal cord is an extremely important functional area. Even though it is protected by meninges and cerebrospinal fluid in the vertebral canal, it is highly vulnerable to traumatic injuries, such as might occur in an automobile accident.

When the cord is transected (or severely traumatized), both motor and sensory functions are lost in body areas normally served by that (and lower) regions of the spinal cord. Injury to certain spinal cord areas may even result in a permanent flaccid paralysis of both legs (**paraplegia**) or of all four limbs (**quadriplegia**). ■

ACTIVITY 2

Identifying Spinal Cord Tracts

With the help of your textbook, label Figure 21.3 with the tract names that follow. Each tract is represented on both sides of the cord, but for clarity, label the motor tracts on the right side of the diagram and the sensory tracts on the left side of the diagram. *Color ascending tracts blue and descending tracts red.* Then fill in the functional importance of each tract beside its name below. As you work, try to be aware of how the naming of the tracts is related to their anatomical distribution.

Dorsal columns

   Fasciculus gracilis _____

   Fasciculus cuneatus _____

Dorsal spinocerebellar _____

Ventral spinocerebellar _____

Lateral spinothalamic _____

Ventral spinothalamic _____

Lateral corticospinal _____

Ventral corticospinal _____

Rubrospinal _____

Tectospinal _____

Vestibulospinal _____

Medial reticulospinal _____

Lateral reticulospinal _____ ■

DISSECTION:

Spinal Cord

1.   Obtain a dissecting tray and instruments, disposable gloves, and a segment of preserved spinal cord (from a cow or saved from the brain specimen used in Exercise 19). Identify the tough outer meninx (dura mater) and the weblike arachnoid mater.

What name is given to the third meninx, and where is it found?

_____

_____

Peel back the dura mater and observe the fibers making up the dorsal and ventral roots. If possible, identify a dorsal root ganglion.

2.   Cut a thin cross section of the cord and identify the ventral and dorsal horns of the gray matter with the naked eye or with the aid of a dissecting microscope.

Dorsal median sulcus

Dorsal funiculus

Dorsal (posterior) horn

Lateral funiculus

Ventral (anterior) horn

Ventral funiculus

Ventral median fissure

FIGURE 21.4 Cross section of the spinal cord (10×).

How can you be certain that you are correctly identifying the ventral and dorsal horns?

_____

_____

Also identify the central canal, white matter, ventral median fissure, dorsal median sulcus, and dorsal, ventral, and lateral funiculi.

3.   Obtain a prepared slide of the spinal cord (cross section) and a compound microscope. Refer to Figure 21.4 as you examine the slide carefully under low power. Observe the shape of the central canal.

Is it basically circular or oval? _____

Name the glial cell type that lines this canal. _____

What would you expect to find in this canal in the living animal?

_____

Can any neuron cell bodies be seen? _____

Where? _____

_____

What type of neurons would these most likely be—motor, sensory, or interneuron?

_____

Spinal Nerves and Nerve Plexuses

The 31 pairs of human spinal nerves arise from the fusions of the ventral and dorsal roots of the spinal cord (see Figure 21.2a). There are 8 pairs of cervical nerves (C_1-C_8), 12 pairs of thoracic nerves (T_1-T_{12}), 5 pairs of lumbar nerves (L_1-L_5), 5 pairs of sacral nerves (S_1-S_5), and 1 pair of coccygeal nerves (Co_1) (see Figure 21.5a, but note that the tiny S_5 and Co_1 nerves are not shown). The first pair of spinal nerves leaves the vertebral canal between the base of the occiput and the atlas, but all the rest exit via the intervertebral foramina. The first through seventh pairs of cervical nerves emerge *above* the vertebra for which they are named; C_8 emerges between C_7 and T_1. (Notice that there are seven cervical vertebrae, but eight pairs of cervical nerves.) The remaining spinal nerve pairs emerge from the spinal cord *below* the same-numbered vertebra.

Almost immediately after emerging, each nerve divides into **dorsal** and **ventral rami.** (Thus each spinal nerve is only about 1 or 2 cm long.) The rami, like the spinal nerves, contain both motor and sensory fibers. The smaller dorsal rami serve the skin and musculature of the posterior body trunk at their approximate level of emergence. The ventral rami of spinal nerves T_2 through T_{12} pass anteriorly as the **intercostal nerves** to supply the muscles of intercostal spaces, and the skin and muscles of the anterior and lateral trunk. The ventral rami of all other spinal nerves form complex networks of nerves called **plexuses.** These plexuses serve the motor and sensory needs of the muscles of the anterior and lateral trunk (see Figure 21.5b). The ventral rami of all other spinal nerves form complex networks called **nerve plexuses**. These plexuses primarily serve the muscles and skin of the limbs. The four major nerve plexuses and their chief peripheral nerves are described in Tables 21.1–21.4 and

FIGURE 21.5 Human spinal nerves.
(a) Relationship of spinal nerves to vertebrae (areas of plexuses formed by the ventral rami are indicated). **(b)** Relative distribution of the ventral and dorsal rami of a spinal nerve (cross section of left trunk).

Cervical nerves

Thoracic nerves

Lumbar nerves

Sacral nerves

Ventral rami form cervical plexus

Ventral rami form brachial plexus

No plexus formed (intercostal nerves)

Ventral rami form lumbar plexus

Ventral rami form sacral plexus

(a)

Dorsal ramus

Ventral ramus

Intercostal nerve

Spinal nerve

Rami communicantes

Dorsal root ganglion

Sympathetic chain ganglion

Ventral root

Dorsal root

Branches of intercostal nerve

Lateral cutaneous

Anterior cutaneous

Thoracic cavity

Sternum

(b)

Ventral rami

Hypoglossal nerve (XII)

Lesser occipital nerve

Greater auricular nerve

Transverse cervical nerve

Ansa cervicalis

Accessory nerve (XI)

Phrenic nerve

Supraclavicular nerves

Segmental branches

Ventral rami:

C_1

C_2

C_3

C_4

C_5

FIGURE 21.6 The cervical plexus. The nerves colored gray connect to the plexus but do not belong to it. (See Table 21.1.)

illustrated in Figures 21.6–21.9. Their names and site of origin should be committed to memory. The tiny S_5 and Co_1 spinal nerves contribute to a small plexus that serves part of the pelvic floor.

Cervical Plexus and the Neck

The **cervical plexus** (Figure 21.6 and Table 21.1) arises from the ventral rami of C_1 through C_5 to supply muscles of the shoulder and neck. The major motor branch of this plexus is the **phrenic nerve,** which arises from C_3 through C_4 (plus some fibers from C_5) and passes into the thoracic cavity in front of the first rib to innervate the diaphragm. The primary danger of a broken neck is that the phrenic nerve may be severed, leading to paralysis of the diaphragm and cessation of breathing. A jingle to help you remember the rami (roots) forming the phrenic nerves is "C_3, C_4, C_5 keep the diaphragm alive."

Brachial Plexus and the Upper Limb

The **brachial plexus** is large and complex, arising from the ventral rami of C_5 through C_8 and T_1 (Table 21.2). The plexus, after being rearranged consecutively into *trunks, divisions,* and *cords,* finally becomes subdivided into five major *peripheral nerves* (Figure 21.7).

The **axillary nerve,** which serves the muscles and skin of the shoulder, has the most limited distribution. The large **radial nerve** passes down the posterolateral surface of the arm and forearm, supplying all the extensor muscles of the arm, forearm, and hand and the skin along its course. The radial nerve is often injured in the axillary region by the pressure of a crutch or by hanging one's arm over the back of a chair. The **median nerve** passes down the anteromedial surface of the arm to supply most of the flexor muscles in the forearm and several muscles in the hand (plus the skin of the lateral surface of the palm of the hand).

• Hyperextend your wrist to identify the long, obvious tendon of your palmaris longus muscle, which crosses the exact midline of the anterior wrist. Your median nerve lies immediately deep to that tendon, and the radial nerve lies just *lateral* to it.

The **musculocutaneous nerve** supplies the arm muscles that flex the forearm and the skin of the lateral surface of the forearm. The **ulnar nerve** travels down the posteromedial surface of the arm. It courses around the medial epicondyle of the humerus to supply the flexor carpi ulnaris, the ulnar head of

TABLE 21.1	Branches of the Cervical Plexus (See Figure 21.6)	
Nerves	**Spinal roots (ventral rami)**	**Structures served**
Cutaneous Branches (Superficial)		
Lesser occipital	C_2 (C_3)	Skin on posterolateral aspect of neck
Greater auricular	C_2, C_3	Skin of ear, skin over parotid gland
Transverse cutaneous (cervical)	C_2, C_3	Skin on anterior and lateral aspect of neck
Supraclavicular (medial, intermediate, and lateral)	C_3, C_4	Skin of shoulder and anterior aspect of chest
Motor Branches (Deep)		
Ansa cervicalis (superior and inferior roots)	C_1–C_3	Infrahyoid muscles of neck (omohyoid, sternohyoid, and sternothyroid)
Segmental and other muscular branches	C_1–C_5	Deep muscles of neck (geniohyoid and thyrohyoid) and portions of scalenes, levator scapulae, trapezius, and sternocleidomastoid muscles
Phrenic	C_3–C_5	Diaphragm (sole motor nerve supply)

Anterior divisions | Posterior divisions | Trunks | Roots

Roots (ventral rami):

Dorsal scapular
Nerve to subclavius
Suprascapular

C₄
C₅
C₆
C₇
C₈
T₁

Upper
Middle — **Trunks**
Lower

Posterior divisions

Cords
— Lateral
— Posterior
— Medial

Axillary
Musculo- cutaneous
Radial
Median
Ulnar

Long thoracic
Medial pectoral
Lateral pectoral
Upper subscapular
Lower subscapular
Thoracodorsal
Medial cutaneous nerves of the arm and forearm

(a) Roots (rami C₅–T₁), trunks, divisions, and cords

Axillary nerve

Humerus

Radial nerve

Musculo- cutaneous nerve

Ulna
Radius

Ulnar nerve

Median nerve

Radial nerve (superficial branch)

Dorsal branch of ulnar nerve
Superficial branch of ulnar nerve
Digital branch of ulnar nerve

Muscular branch
Digital branch — Median nerve

(c) The major nerves of the upper limb

Musculocutaneous nerve
Axillary nerve
Biceps brachii
Coracobrachialis
Median nerve
Radial nerve branches to triceps

Lateral cord
Posterior cord
Medial cord
Radial nerve
Ulnar nerve

(b) Cadaver photo

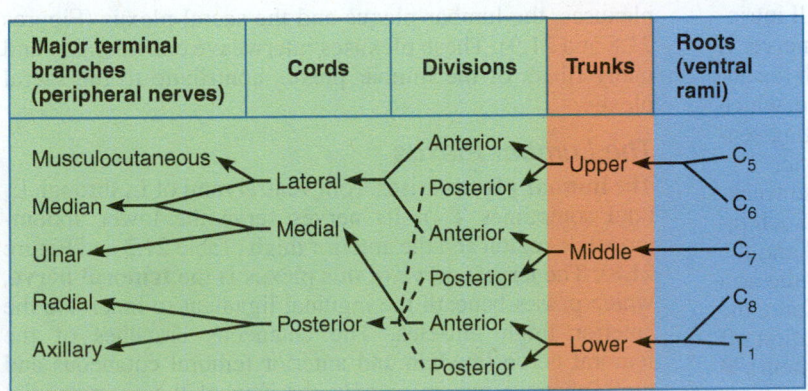

Major terminal branches (peripheral nerves)	Cords	Divisions	Trunks	Roots (ventral rami)
Musculocutaneous	Lateral	Anterior	Upper	C₅
Median		Posterior		C₆
Ulnar	Medial	Anterior	Middle	C₇
Radial		Posterior		C₈
Axillary	Posterior	Anterior	Lower	T₁
		Posterior		

(d) Flowchart summarizing relationships within the brachial plexus

FIGURE 21.7 The brachial plexus. (See Table 21.2.)

TABLE 21.2	Branches of the Brachial Plexus (See Figure 21.7)	
Nerves	**Cord and spinal roots (ventral rami)**	**Structures served**
Axillary	Posterior cord (C_5, C_6)	Muscular branches: deltoid and teres minor muscles Cutaneous branches: some skin of shoulder region
Musculocutaneous	Lateral cord (C_5–C_7)	Muscular branches: flexor muscles in anterior arm (biceps brachii, brachialis, coracobrachialis) Cutaneous branches: skin on anterolateral forearm (extremely variable)
Median	By two branches, one from medial cord (C_8, T_1) and one from the lateral cord (C_5–C_7)	Muscular branches to flexor group of anterior forearm (palmaris longus, flexor carpi radialis, flexor digitorum superficialis, flexor pollicis longus, lateral half of flexor digitorum profundus, and pronator muscles); intrinsic muscles of lateral palm and digital branches to the fingers Cutaneous branches: skin of lateral two-thirds of hand, palm side and dorsum of fingers 2 and 3
Ulnar	Medial cord (C_8, T_1)	Muscular branches: flexor muscles in anterior forearm (flexor carpi ulnaris and medial half of flexor digitorum profundus); most intrinsic muscles of hand Cutaneous branches: skin of medial third of hand, both anterior and posterior aspects
Radial	Posterior cord (C_5–C_8, T_1)	Muscular branches: posterior muscles of arm, forearm, and hand (triceps brachii, anconeus, supinator, brachioradialis, extensors carpi radialis longus and brevis, extensor carpi ulnaris, and several muscles that extend the fingers) Cutaneous branches: skin of posterolateral surface of entire limb (except dorsum of fingers 2 and 3)
Dorsal scapular	Branches of C_5 rami	Rhomboid muscles and levator scapulae
Long thoracic	Branches of C_5–C_7 rami	Serratus anterior muscle
Subscapular	Posterior cord; branches of C_5 and C_6 rami	Teres major and subscapular muscles
Suprascapular	Upper trunk (C_5, C_6)	Shoulder joint; supraspinatus and infraspinatus muscles
Pectoral (lateral and medial)	Branches of lateral and medial cords (C_5–T_1)	Pectoralis major and minor muscles

the flexor digitorum profundus of the forearm, and all intrinsic muscles of the hand not served by the median nerve. It supplies the skin of the medial third of the hand, both the anterior and posterior surfaces. Trauma to the ulnar nerve, which often occurs when the elbow is hit, produces a smarting sensation commonly referred to as "hitting the funny bone."

Severe injuries to the brachial plexus cause weakness or paralysis of the entire upper limb. Such injuries may occur when the upper limb is pulled hard and the plexus is stretched (as when a football tackler yanks the arm of the halfback), and by blows to the shoulder that force the humerus inferiorly (as when a cyclist is pitched headfirst off his motorcycle and grinds his shoulder into the pavement). ■

Lumbosacral Plexus and the Lower Limb

The **lumbosacral plexus,** which serves the pelvic region of the trunk and the lower limbs, is actually a complex of two plexuses, the lumbar plexus and the sacral plexus (Figures 21.8 and 21.9). These plexuses interweave considerably and many fibers of the lumbar plexus contribute to the sacral plexus.

The Lumbar Plexus

The **lumbar plexus** arises from ventral rami of L_1 through L_4 (and sometimes T_{12}). Its nerves serve the lower abdominopelvic region and the anterior thigh (Table 21.3 and Figure 21.8). The largest nerve of this plexus is the **femoral nerve,** which passes beneath the inguinal ligament to innervate the anterior thigh muscles. The cutaneous branches of the femoral nerve (median and anterior femoral cutaneous and the saphenous nerves) supply the skin of the anteromedial surface of the entire lower limb.

TABLE 21.3	**Branches of the Lumbar Plexus (See Figure 21.8)**	
Nerves	Spinal roots (ventral rami)	Structures served
Femoral	L_2–L_4	Skin of anterior and medial thigh via *anterior femoral cutaneous* branch; skin of medial leg and foot, hip and knee joints via *saphenous* branch; motor to anterior muscles (quadriceps and sartorius) of thigh; pectineus, iliacus
Obturator	L_2–L_4	Motor to adductor magnus (part), longus, and brevis muscles, gracilis muscle of medial thigh, obturator externus; sensory for skin of medial thigh and for hip and knee joints
Lateral femoral cutaneous	L_2, L_3	Skin of lateral thigh; some sensory branches to peritoneum
Iliohypogastric	L_1	Skin of lower abdomen, lower back, and hip; muscles of anterolateral abdominal wall (obliques and transversus) and pubic region
Ilioinguinal	L_1	Skin of external genitalia and proximal medial aspect of the thigh; inferior abdominal muscles
Genitofemoral	L_1, L_2	Skin of scrotum in males, of labia majora in females, and of anterior thigh inferior to middle portion of inguinal region; cremaster muscle in males

FIGURE 21.8 The lumbar plexus (anterior view.)
(a) Spinal roots (ventral rami) and major branches of the lumbar plexus. **(b)** Distribution of the major peripheral nerves of the lumbar plexus in the lower limb. (See Table 21.3.)

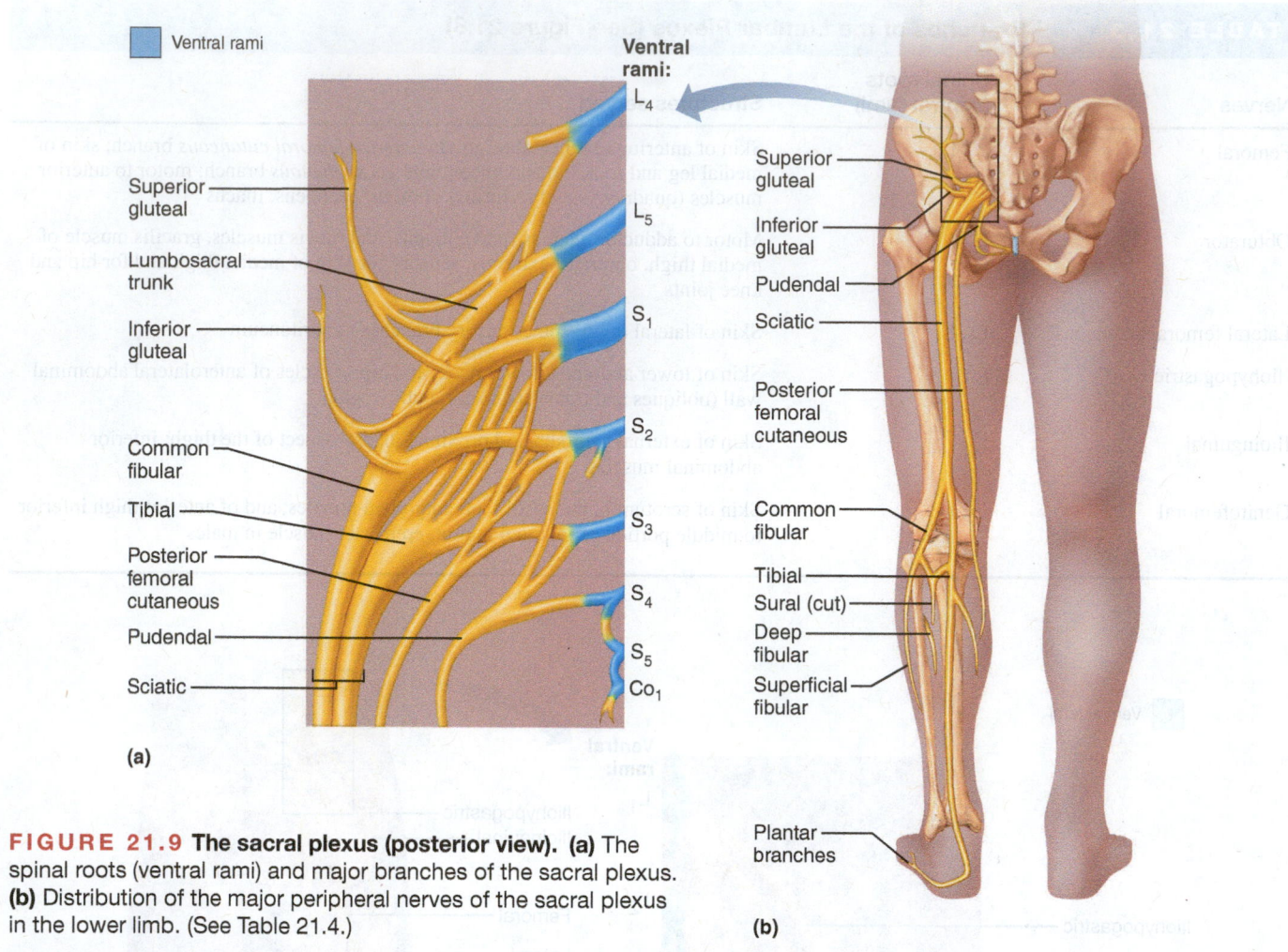

FIGURE 21.9 The sacral plexus (posterior view). (a) The spinal roots (ventral rami) and major branches of the sacral plexus. **(b)** Distribution of the major peripheral nerves of the sacral plexus in the lower limb. (See Table 21.4.)

TABLE 21.4	Branches of the Sacral Plexus (See Figure 21.9)	
Nerves	**Spinal roots (ventral rami)**	**Structures served**
Sciatic nerve	L_4–S_3	Composed of two nerves (tibial and common fibular) in a common sheath that diverge just proximal to the knee
Tibial (including sural, medial and lateral plantar, and medial calcaneal branches)	L_4–S_3	Cutaneous branches: to skin of posterior surface of leg and sole of foot. Motor branches: to muscles of back of thigh, leg, and foot (hamstrings [except short head of biceps femoris], posterior part of adductor magnus, triceps surae, tibialis posterior, popliteus, flexor digitorum longus, flexor hallucis longus, and intrinsic muscles of foot)
Common fibular (superficial and deep branches)	L_4–S_2	Cutaneous branches: to skin of anterior surface of leg and dorsum of foot. Motor branches: to short head of biceps femoris of thigh, fibularis muscles of lateral compartment of leg, tibialis anterior, and extensor muscles of toes (extensor hallucis longus, extensors digitorum longus and brevis)
Superior gluteal	L_4–S_1	Motor branches: to gluteus medius and minimus and tensor fasciae latae
Inferior gluteal	L_5–S_2	Motor branches: to gluteus maximus
Posterior femoral cutaneous	S_1–S_3	Skin of buttock, posterior thigh, and popliteal region; length variable; may also innervate part of skin of calf and heel
Pudendal	S_2–S_4	Supplies most of skin and muscles of perineum (region encompassing external genitalia and anus and including clitoris, labia, and vaginal mucosa in females, and scrotum and penis in males); external anal sphincter

The Sacral Plexus

Arising from L_4 through S_4, the nerves of the **sacral plexus** supply the buttock, the posterior surface of the thigh, and virtually all sensory and motor fibers of the leg and foot (Table 21.4 and Figure 21.9). The major peripheral nerve of this plexus is the **sciatic nerve,** the largest nerve in the body. The sciatic nerve leaves the pelvis through the greater sciatic notch and travels down the posterior thigh, serving its flexor muscles and skin. In the popliteal region, the sciatic nerve divides into the **common fibular nerve** and the **tibial nerve,** which together supply the balance of the leg muscles and skin, both directly and via several branches.

Injury to the proximal part of the sciatic nerve, as might follow a fall or disc herniation, results in a number of lower limb impairments. **Sciatica** (si-at'ĭ-kah), characterized by stabbing pain radiating over the course of the sciatic nerve, is common. When the sciatic nerve is completely severed, the leg is nearly useless. The leg cannot be flexed and the foot drops into plantar flexion (dangles), a condition called **footdrop.** ■

ACTIVITY 3

Identifying the Major Nerve Plexuses and Peripheral Nerves

Identify each of the four major nerve plexuses (and its major nerves) shown in Figures 21.6 to 21.9 on a large laboratory chart or model. Trace the courses of the nerves and relate those observations to the information provided in Tables 21.1 to 21.4. ▬

The Autonomic Nervous System

The **autonomic nervous system (ANS)** is the subdivision of the peripheral nervous system (PNS) that regulates body activities that are generally not under conscious control. It is composed of a special group of motor neurons serving cardiac muscle (the heart), smooth muscle (found in the walls of the visceral organs and blood vessels), and internal glands. Because these structures typically function without conscious control, this system is often referred to as the *involuntary nervous system*.

There is a basic anatomical difference between the motor pathways of the **somatic** (voluntary) **nervous system,** which innervates the skeletal muscles, and those of the autonomic nervous system. In the somatic division, the cell bodies of the motor neurons reside in the CNS (brain stem or ventral horns of the spinal cord), and their axons, sheathed in cranial or spinal nerves, extend directly to the skeletal muscles they serve. However, the autonomic nervous system consists of chains of two motor neurons. The first motor neuron of each pair, called the *preganglionic neuron,* resides in the brain stem or lateral horn of the spinal cord. Its axon leaves the CNS to synapse with the second motor neuron *(ganglionic neuron),* whose cell body is located in a ganglion outside the CNS. The axon of the ganglionic neuron then extends to the organ it serves.

The autonomic nervous system has two major functional subdivisions (Figure 21.10). These, the sympathetic and

FIGURE 21.10 Overview of the subdivisions of the autonomic nervous system. The parasympathetic and sympathetic divisions differ anatomically in (1) the sites of origin of their nerves, (2) the relative lengths of preganglionic and postganglionic fibers, and (3) the locations of their ganglia (synapse sites). Although sympathetic innervation to the skin[*] is shown only for the cervical area, all nerves to the periphery carry postganglionic sympathetic fibers.

parasympathetic divisions, serve most of the same organs but generally cause opposing or antagonistic effects.

Parasympathetic Division

The preganglionic neurons of the **parasympathetic,** or **craniosacral,** division are located in brain stem nuclei of cranial nerves III, VII, IX, X and in the S_2 through S_4 level of the spinal cord. The axons of the preganglionic neurons of the cranial region travel in their respective cranial nerves to the *immediate area* of the head and neck organs to be stimulated. There they synapse with the ganglionic neuron in a **terminal,** or **intramural** (literally, "within the walls"), **ganglion.** The ganglionic neuron then sends out a very short axon (postganglionic axon) to the organ it serves. In the sacral region, the preganglionic axons leave the ventral roots of the spinal cord and collectively form the **pelvic splanchnic nerves,** which travel to the pelvic cavity. In the pelvic cavity, the preganglionic axons synapse with the ganglionic neurons in ganglia located on or close to the organs served.

(a) Location of the sympathetic trunk

Spinal cord
Dorsal root ganglion
Ventral root
Rib
Sympathetic trunk ganglion
Sympathetic trunk
Ventral ramus of spinal nerve
Gray ramus communicans
White ramus communicans
Thoracic splanchnic nerves

Skin (arrector pili muscles and sweat glands)
To effector
Blood vessels

Dorsal root
Dorsal root ganglion
Dorsal ramus of spinal nerve
Ventral ramus of spinal nerve
Gray ramus communicans
White ramus communicans

Lateral horn (visceral motor zone)
Ventral root
Sympathetic trunk ganglion
Sympathetic trunk

① Synapse at the same level

② Synapse at a higher or lower level

Splanchnic nerve
Collateral ganglion (such as the celiac)
Target organ in abdomen (e.g., intestine)

③ Synapse in a distant collateral ganglion anterior to the vertebral column

(b) Three pathways of sympathetic innervation

FIGURE 21.11 Sympathetic trunks and pathways. (a) Diagram of the sympathetic trunk in the posterior thorax, along the side of the vertebral column. **(b)** Synapses between preganglionic and ganglionic neurons can occur at three different locations—either in a sympathetic trunk ganglion at the same or a different level, or in a collateral ganglion.

Sympathetic Division

The preganglionic neurons of the **sympathetic,** or **thoracolumbar,** division are in the lateral horns of the gray matter of the spinal cord from T_1 through L_2. The preganglionic axons leave the cord via the ventral root (in conjunction with the axons of the somatic motor neurons), enter the spinal nerve, and then travel briefly in the ventral ramus (Figure 21.11). From the ventral ramus, they pass through a small branch called the **white ramus communicans** to enter a **sympathetic trunk ganglion.** These two trunks **(chains)** lie alongside the vertebral column and are also called *paravertebral ganglia.*

Having reached the ganglion, a preganglionic axon may take one of three main courses (see Figure 21.11b). First, it may synapse with a ganglionic neuron in the sympathetic chain at that level. Second, the axon may travel upward or downward through the sympathetic chain to synapse with a ganglionic neuron at another level. In either of these two instances, the postganglionic axons then reenter the spinal nerve via a **gray ramus communicans** and travel in branches of a dorsal or ventral ramus to innervate skin structures (sweat glands, arrector pili muscles attached to hair follicles, and the smooth muscles of blood vessel walls) and thoracic organs. Third, the axon may pass through the ganglion without synapsing and form part of the **splanchnic nerves,** which travel to the viscera to synapse with a ganglionic neuron in a **collateral,** or **prevertebral, ganglion.** The major collateral ganglia—the *celiac, superior mesenteric, inferior mesenteric,* and *inferior hypogastric ganglia*—supply the abdominal and pelvic visceral organs. The postganglionic axon then leaves the ganglion and travels to a nearby visceral organ which it innervates.

ACTIVITY 4

Locating the Sympathetic Chain

Locate the sympathetic chain on the spinal nerve chart. ▬

Autonomic Functioning

As noted earlier, most body organs served by the autonomic nervous system receive fibers from both the sympathetic and parasympathetic divisions. The only exceptions are the structures of the skin (sweat glands and arrector pili muscles attached to the hair follicles), the adrenal medulla, and essentially all blood vessels except those of the external genitalia, all of which receive sympathetic innervation only. When both divisions serve an organ, they have antagonistic effects. This is because their postganglionic axons release different neurotransmitters. The parasympathetic fibers, called **cholinergic fibers,** release acetylcholine; the sympathetic postganglionic fibers, called **adrenergic fibers,** release norepinephrine. (However, there are isolated examples of postganglionic sympathetic fibers, such as those serving sweat glands and some blood vessels that release acetylcholine.) The preganglionic fibers of both divisions release acetylcholine.

The parasympathetic division is often referred to as the housekeeping, or "resting and digesting," system because it maintains the visceral organs in a state most suitable for normal functions and internal homeostasis; that is, it promotes normal digestion and elimination. In contrast, activation of the sympathetic division is referred to as the "fight-or-flight" response because it readies the body to cope with situations that threaten homeostasis. Under such emergency conditions, the sympathetic nervous system induces an increase in heart rate and blood pressure, dilates the bronchioles of the lungs, increases blood sugar levels, and promotes many other effects that help the individual cope with a stressor.

Organ or function	Parasympathetic effect	Sympathetic effect
Heart		
Bronchioles of lungs		
Digestive tract activity		
Urinary bladder		
Iris of the eye		
Blood vessels (most)		
Penis/clitoris		
Sweat glands		
Adrenal medulla		
Pancreas		

BIOPAC® data
acquisition unit

GSR finger leads
(plug into Channel 3)

Respiratory transducer belt
(plugs into Channel 1)

Electrode lead set
(plugs into Channel 2)

FIGURE 21.12 Setting up the BIOPAC® equipment. Plug the respiratory transducer belt into Channel 1, the electrode lead set into Channel 2, and the GSR finger leads into Channel 3.

As we grow older, our sympathetic nervous system gradually becomes less and less efficient, particularly in causing vasoconstriction of blood vessels. When elderly people stand up quickly after sitting or lying down, they often become light-headed or faint. This is because the sympathetic nervous system is not able to react quickly enough to counteract the pull of gravity by activating the vasoconstrictor fibers. So, blood pools in the feet. This condition, **orthostatic hypotension,** is a type of low blood pressure resulting from changes in body position as described. Orthostatic hypotension can be prevented to some degree if *slow* changes in position are made. This gives the sympathetic nervous system a little more time to react and adjust. ■

ACTIVITY 5

Comparing Sympathetic and Parasympathetic Effects

Several body organs are listed in the chart on the previous page. Using your textbook as a reference, list the effect of the sympathetic and parasympathetic divisions on each. ▬

ACTIVITY 6

Exploring the Galvanic Skin Response within a Polygraph Using BIOPAC®

The autonomic nervous system is intimately integrated with the emotions, or affect, of an individual. A sad event, sharp pain, or simple stress can elicit measurable changes in autonomic regulation of heart rate, respiration, and blood pressure. In addition to these obvious physiological phenomena, more subtle autonomic changes can occur in the skin. Specifically, changes in autonomic tone in response to

external circumstances can influence the rate of sweat gland secretion and blood flow to the skin that may not be overtly observable but nonetheless can be measured. The **galvanic skin response** is an electrophysiological measurement of changes that occur in the skin due to changes in autonomic stimulation.

The galvanic skin response is measured by recording the changes in **galvanic skin resistance (GSR)** and **galvanic skin potential (GSP).** Resistance, recorded in *ohms* (Ω), is a measure of the opposition of the flow of current from one electrode to another. Increasing resistance results in decreased current. Potential, measured in *volts* (V), is a measure of the amount of charge separation between two points. Increased sympathetic stimulation of sweat glands, in response to change in affect, decreases resistance on the skin because of increased water and electrolytes on the skin surface.

In this experiment you will record heart rate, respiration, and GSR while the subject is exposed to various conditions. Because "many" variables will be "recorded," this process is often referred to as a **polygraph.** The goal of this exercise is to record and analyze data to observe how this process works. This is not a "lie detector test," as its failure rate is far too high to provide true scientific or legal certainty. However, the polygraph can be used as an investigative tool.

Setting Up the Equipment

1. Connect the BIOPAC® unit to the computer and turn the computer **ON.**

2. Make sure the BIOPAC® unit is **OFF.**

3. Plug in the equipment as shown in Figure 21.12.

• Respiratory transducer belt—CH 1

• Electrode lead set—CH 2

• GSR finger leads—CH 3

FIGURE 21.13 **Proper placement of the respiratory transducer belt around the subject's thorax.**

4. Turn the BIOPAC unit **ON.**

5. Attach the respiratory transducer belt to the subject as shown in Figure 21.13. It should be fastened so that it is slightly tight even at the point of maximal expiration.

6. Fill both cavities of the GSR transducer with conduction gel, and attach the sensors to the subject's fingers as shown in Figure 21.14. The electrodes should be placed on

FIGURE 21.14 **Placement of the GSR finger leads to the fingers.**

FIGURE 21.15 **Placement of electrodes and the appropriate attachment of electrode leads by color.**

the middle and index fingers with the sensors on the skin, not the fingernail. They should fit snugly but not be so tight as to cut off circulation. To pick up a good GSR signal, it is important that the subject's hand have enough sweat (as it normally would). *The subject should not have freshly washed or cold hands.*

7. In order to record the heart rate, place the electrodes on the subject as shown in Figure 21.15. Place an electrode on the medial surface of each leg, just above the ankle. Place another electrode on the right anterior forearm just above the wrist.

8. Attach the electrode lead set to the electrodes according to the colors shown in Figure 21.15. Wait 5 minutes before starting the calibration procedure.

9. Start the BIOPAC® Student Lab program on the computer by double-clicking the icon on the desktop or by following your instructor's guidance.

10. Select lesson **L09-Poly-1** from the menu and click **OK.**

11. Type in a filename that will save this subject's data on the computer hard drive. You may want to use the subject's last name followed by Poly-1 (for example, SmithPoly-1), then click **OK.**

Calibrating the Equipment

1. Have the subject sit facing the director, but do not allow the subject to see the computer screen. The subject should remain immobile but be relaxed with legs and arms in a comfortable position.

2. When the subject is ready, click **Calibrate.** After 3 seconds, the subject will hear a beep and should inhale and exhale deeply for one breath.

3. Wait for the calibration to stop automatically after 10 seconds.

FIGURE 21.16 Example of waveforms during the calibration procedure.

4. Observe the data, which should look similar to that in Figure 21.16.

• If the data look very different, click **Redo Calibration** and repeat the steps above.

• If the data look similar, proceed to the next section.

Recording the Data

Hints to obtaining the best data:

• Do not let the subject see the data as it is being recorded.

• Conduct the exam in a quiet setting.

• Keep the subject as still as possible.

• Take care to have the subject move the mouth as little as possible when responding to questions.

• Make sure the subject is relaxed at resting heart rate before the exam begins.

The data will be recorded in three segments. The director must read through the directions for the entire segment before proceeding so that the subject can be prompted and questioned appropriately.

Segment 1: Baseline Data

1. When the subject and director are ready, click **Record.**

2. After waiting 5 seconds, the director will ask the subject to respond to the following questions and should remind the subject to minimize mouth movements when answering. Use the **F9** key (PC) or **ESC** key (Mac) to insert a marker after each response. Wait about 5 seconds between each answer.

• Quietly state your name.

• Slowly count down from ten to zero.

• Count backward from 30 by increasing odd numbers (subtract 1, then 3, then 5, etc.).

• Finally, the director lightly touches the subject on the cheek.

3. After the final, cheek-touching test, click **Suspend.**

FIGURE 21.17 Example of Segment 1 data.

4. Observe the data, which should look similar to the data in Figure 21.17.

• If the data look very different, click **Redo** and repeat the steps above.

• If the data look similar, proceed to record Segment 2.

Segment 2: Response to Different Colors

1. When the subject and director are ready, click **Resume.**

2. The director will sequentially hold up nine differently colored paper squares about 2 feet in front of the subject's face. He or she will ask the subject to focus on the particular color for 10 seconds before moving to the next color in the sequence. The director will display the colors and insert a marker in the following order: white, black, red, blue, green, yellow, orange, brown, and purple. The director or assistant will use the **F9** key (PC) or **ESC** key (Mac) to insert a marker at the start of each color.

3. The subject will be asked to view the complete set of colors. After the color purple, click **Suspend.**

4. Observe the data, which should look similar to the data in Figure 21.18.

• If the data look very different, click **Redo** and repeat the steps above.

• If the data look similar, proceed to record Segment 3.

FIGURE 21.18 Example of Segment 2 data.

FIGURE 21.19 Example of Segment 3 data.

FIGURE 21.20 Example of polygraph recording with GSR, respiration, and heart rate.

Segment 3: Response to Different Questions

1. When the subject and director are ready, click **Resume**.

2. The director will ask the subject the ten questions in step 3 and note if the answer is Yes or No. In this segment, the recorder will use the **F9** key (PC) or **ESC** key (Mac) to insert a marker at the end of each question and the end of each answer. The director will circle the Yes or No response of the subject in the "Response" column of the Segment 3 Measurements chart on page 333.

3. The following questions are to be asked and answered either Yes or No:

- Are you currently a student?
- Are your eyes blue?
- Do you have any brothers?
- Did you earn an "A" on the last exam?
- Do you drive a motorcycle?
- Are you less than 25 years old?
- Have you ever traveled to another planet?
- Have aliens from another planet ever visited you?
- Do you watch *Sesame Street*?
- Have you answered all of the preceding questions truthfully?

4. After the last question is answered, click **Suspend**.

5. Observe the data, which should look similar to the data in Figure 21.19.

- If the data look very different, click **Redo** and repeat the steps above.
- If the data look similar, click **Done**.

6. Without recording, simply ask the subject to respond once again to all of the questions as honestly as possible. The director circles the Yes or No response of the subject in the "Truth" column of the Segment 3 Measurements chart on page 333.

7. Remove all of the sensors and equipment from the subject, and continue to Data Analysis.

Data Analysis

1. If just starting the BIOPAC® program to perform data analysis, enter **Review Saved Data** mode and choose the file with the subject's GSR data (for example, SmithPoly-1).

2. Observe how the channel numbers are designated, as shown in Figure 21.20: CH 3—**GSR;** CH 40—**Respiration;** CH 41—**Heart Rate.**

3. You may need to use the following tools to adjust the data in order to clearly view and analyze the first 5 seconds of the recording.

- Click the magnifying glass in the lower right corner of the screen (near the I-beam box) to activate the **zoom** function. Use the magnifying glass cursor to click on the very first waveforms until the first 5 seconds of data are represented (see horizontal time scale at the bottom of the screen).
- Select the **Display** menu at the top of the screen and click **Autoscale Waveforms** in the drop-down menu. This function will adjust the data for better viewing.

4. To analyze the data, set up the first three pairs of channel/measurement boxes at the top of the screen. (Each box activates a drop-down menu when you click it.) Select the following channels and measurement types:

Channel	Measurement
CH 41	value
CH 40	BPM
CH 3	value

Value: Displays the value of the measurement (for example, heart rate or GSR) at the point in time that is selected.

BPM: In this analysis, the BPM calculates breaths per minute when the area that is highlighted starts at the beginning of one inhalation and ends at the beginning of the next inhalation.

FIGURE 21.21 Selecting the two-second point for data analysis.

FIGURE 21.22 Highlighting the waveforms from the start of one inhalation to the start of the next.

5. Use the arrow cursor and click the I-beam cursor box at the lower right side of the screen to activate the "area selection" function. Using the activated I-beam cursor, select the 2-second point on the data as shown in Figure 21.21. Record the heart rate and GSR values for Segment 1 data in the chart below. This point represents the resting or baseline data.

6. Using data from the first 6 seconds, use the I-beam cursor tool to highlight an area from the start of one inhalation to the start of the next inhalation, as shown in Figure 21.22. The start of an inhalation is indicated by the beginning of the ascension of the waveform. Record this as the baseline respiratory rate in the chart below showing measurements for Segment 1.

7. Using the markers as guides, scroll along the bottom scroll bar until the data from Segment 1 appears.

8. Analyze all parts of Segment 1. Using the tools described in steps 5 and 6, acquire the measurements for the heart rate, GSR, and respiration rate soon after each subject response. Use the maximum GSR value in that time frame as the point of measurement for GSR and heart rate. Use the beginning of two consecutive inhalations in that same time frame to measure respiration rate. Record these data in the chart showing measurements for Segment 1.

9. Repeat these same procedures to measure GSR, heart rate, and respiration rate for each color in Segment 2. Record these data in the chart of measurements for Segment 2.

Segment 1 Measurements			
Procedure	Heart rate [CH 41 value]	Respiratory rate [CH 40 BPM]	GSR [CH 3 value]
Baseline			
Quietly say name			
Count from 10			
Count from 30			
Face is touched			

Segment 2 Measurements

Color	Heart rate [CH 41 value]	Respiratory rate [CH 40 BPM]	GSR [CH 3 value]
White			
Black			
Red			
Blue			
Green			
Yellow			
Orange			
Brown			
Purple			

Segment 3 Measurements

Question	Response		Truth		Heart rate [CH 41 value]	Resp. rate [CH 40 BPM]	GSR [CH 3 value]
Student?	Y	N	Y	N			
Blue eyes?	Y	N	Y	N			
Brothers?	Y	N	Y	N			
Earn "A"?	Y	N	Y	N			
Motorcycle?	Y	N	Y	N			
Under 25?	Y	N	Y	N			
Planet?	Y	N	Y	N			
Aliens?	Y	N	Y	N			
Sesame?	Y	N	Y	N			
Truthful?	Y	N	Y	N			

10. Repeat these same procedures to measure GSR, heart rate, and respiration rate for responses to each question in Segment 3. Record these data in the chart of measurements for Segment 3.

11. Examine GSR, heart rate, and respiration rate of the baseline data in the chart showing measurements for Segment 1.

12. For every condition to which the subject was exposed, write **H** if that value is higher than baseline, write **L** if the value is lower, and write **NC** if there is no significant change. Repeat this analysis for Segments 2 and 3.

Examine the data in the chart showing measurements for Segment 1. Is there any noticeable difference between the baseline GSR, heart rate, and respiration rate after each prompt? Under which prompts is the most significant change noted?

_____

_____

_____

Examine the data in the chart showing measurements for Segment 2. Is there any noticeable difference between the baseline GSR, heart rate, and respiration rate after each color presentation? Under which colors is the most significant change noted?

_____

_____

Examine the data in the chart showing measurements for Segment 3. Is there any noticeable difference between the baseline GSR, heart rate, and respiration rate after each question? After which is the most significant change noted?

_____

_____

_____

Speculate as to the reasons why a subject may demonstrate a change in GSR from baseline under different color conditions.

_____

_____

_____

Speculate as to the reasons why a subject may demonstrate a change in GSR from baseline when a particular question is asked.

_____

_____

NAME_____

LAB TIME/DATE_____

Spinal Cord, Spinal Nerves, and the Autonomic Nervous System

Anatomy of the Spinal Cord

1. Match each anatomical term in the key to the descriptions given below.

Key: a. cauda equina   b. conus medullaris   c. filum terminale   d. foramen magnum

_____ 1. most superior boundary of the spinal cord

_____ 2. meningeal extension beyond the spinal cord terminus

_____ 3. spinal cord terminus

_____ 4. collection of spinal nerves traveling in the vertebral canal below the terminus of the spinal cord

2. Match the key letters on the diagram with the following terms.

_____ 1. arachnoid mater

_____ 2. central canal

_____ 3. dorsal horn

_____ 4. dorsal ramus of spinal nerve

_____ 5. dorsal root ganglion

_____ 6. dorsal root of spinal nerve

_____ 7. dura mater

_____ 8. gray commissure

_____ 9. lateral horn

_____ 10. pia mater

_____ 11. spinal nerve

_____ 12. ventral horn

_____ 13. ventral ramus of spinal nerve

_____ 14. ventral root of spinal nerve

_____ 15. white matter

3. Choose the proper answer from the following key to respond to the descriptions relating to spinal cord anatomy.

Key: a.   sensory   b.   motor   c.   both sensory and motor   d.   interneurons

_____ 1.   neuron type found in dorsal horn   _____ 4.   fiber type in ventral root

_____ 2.   neuron type found in ventral horn   _____ 5.   fiber type in dorsal root

_____ 3.   neuron type in dorsal root ganglion   _____ 6.   fiber type in spinal nerve

4. Where in the vertebral column is a lumbar puncture generally done? _____

Why is this the site of choice? _____

_____

5. The spinal cord is enlarged in two regions, the _____ and the _____ regions.

What is the significance of these enlargements? _____

_____

6. How does the position of the gray and white matter differ in the spinal cord and the cerebral hemispheres?

_____

_____

7. From the key, choose the name of the tract that might be damaged when the following conditions are observed. (More than one choice may apply.)

_____ 1.   uncoordinated movement   Key: a.   dorsal columns (fasciculus cuneatus
                                                                      and fasciculus gracilis)
_____ 2.   lack of voluntary movement   b.   lateral corticospinal tract
                                                                      c.   ventral corticospinal tract
_____ 3.   tremors, jerky movements   d.   tectospinal tract
                                                                      e.   rubrospinal tract
_____ 4.   diminished pain perception   f.   vestibulospinal tract
                                                                      g.   lateral spinothalamic tract
_____ 5.   diminished sense of touch   h.   ventral spinothalamic tract
                                                                      i.   dorsal spinocerebellar tract
                                                                      j.   ventral spinocerebellar tract

Dissection of the Spinal Cord

8. Compare and contrast the meninges of the spinal cord and the brain. _____

_____

9. How can you distinguish between the dorsal and ventral horns? _____

_____

Spinal Nerves and Nerve Plexuses

10. In the human, there are 31 pairs of spinal nerves, named according to the region of the vertebral column from which they issue. The spinal nerves are named below. Indicate how they are numbered.

cervical nerves _____   sacral nerves _____

lumbar nerves _____   thoracic nerves _____

11. The ventral rami of spinal nerves C_1 through T_1 and T_{12} through S_4 take part in forming _____,

which serve the _____ of the body. The ventral rami of T_2 through T_{12} run

between the ribs to serve the _____. The dorsal rami of the spinal nerves

serve _____.

12. What would happen if the following structures were damaged or transected? (Use the key choices for responses.)

Key: a.   loss of motor function   b.   loss of sensory function   c.   loss of both motor and sensory function

_____   1.   dorsal root of a spinal nerve   _____   3.   ventral ramus of a spinal nerve

_____   2.   ventral root of a spinal nerve

13. Define *plexus.* _____

_____

14. Name the major nerves that serve the following body areas.

_____   1.   head, neck, shoulders (name plexus only)

_____   2.   diaphragm

_____   3.   posterior thigh

_____   4.   leg and foot (name two)

_____   5.   anterior forearm muscles (name two)

_____   6.   arm muscles (name two)

_____   7.   abdominal wall (name plexus only)

_____   8.   anterior thigh

_____   9.   medial side of the hand

The Autonomic Nervous System

15. For the most part, sympathetic and parasympathetic fibers serve the same organs and structures. How can they exert antagonistic effects? (After all, nerve impulses are nerve impulses—aren't they?)

_____

16. Name three structures that receive sympathetic but not parasympathetic innervation.

_____

17. A pelvic splanchnic nerve contains (circle one):

    a. preganglionic sympathetic fibers   c. preganglionic parasympathetic fibers

    b. postganglionic sympathetic fibers   d. postganglionic parasympathetic fibers

18. The following chart states a number of conditions. Use a check mark to show which division of the autonomic nervous system is involved in each.

Sympathetic division	Condition	Parasympathetic division
	Secretes norepinephrine; adrenergic fibers	
	Secretes acetylcholine; cholinergic fibers	
	Long preganglionic axon; short postganglionic axon	
	Short preganglionic axon; long postganglionic axon	
	Arises from cranial and sacral nerves	
	Arises from spinal nerves T_1 through L_3	
	Normally in control	
	"Fight-or-flight" system	
	Has more specific control (Look it up!)	

Galvanic Skin Response Using BIOPAC®

19. Describe exactly how, from a physiological standpoint, GSR can be correlated with activity of the autonomic nervous system.

_____

_____

_____

20. Based on this brief and unprofessional exposure to a polygraph, explain why this might not be an exact tool for testing the sincerity and honesty of a subject.

_____

_____

_____

Human Reflex Physiology

MATERIALS

- ☐ Reflex hammer
- ☐ Sharp pencils
- ☐ Cot (if available)
- ☐ Absorbent cotton (sterile)
- ☐ Tongue depressor
- ☐ Metric ruler
- ☐ Flashlight
- ☐ 100- or 250-ml beaker
- ☐ 10- or 25-ml graduated cylinder
- ☐ Lemon juice in dropper bottle
- ☐ Wide-range pH paper
- ☐ Large laboratory bucket containing freshly prepared 10% household bleach solution for saliva-soiled glassware
- ☐ Disposable autoclave bag
- ☐ Wash bottle containing 10% bleach solution
- ☐ Reaction time ruler (if available)

BIOPAC® BIOPAC® MP36 (MP35/30) data acquisition unit, PC or Mac computer. BIOPAC® Student Lab Software, hand switch, and headphones. New versions of the BSL software (3.7.5 and higher for Windows, and 3.7.4 and higher for Mac) require slightly different channel settings and collection strategies. Instructions for using the newer software with the MP36/35 data acquisition units can be found on myA&P. In addition, instructions for use of the **NEW** 2-channel data acquisition unit, the MP45, may also be found on myA&P.

Note: Instructions for using PowerLab® equipment can be found on myA&P.

myA&P For practice quizzes on this lab, go to www.myaandp.com.

OBJECTIVES

1. To define *reflex* and *reflex arc*.
2. To name, identify, and describe the function of each element of a reflex arc.
3. To explain why reflex testing is an important part of every physical examination.
4. To describe and discuss several types of reflex activities as observed in the laboratory; to indicate the functional or clinical importance of each; and to categorize each as a somatic or autonomic reflex action.
5. To explain why cord-mediated reflexes are generally much faster than those involving input from the higher brain centers.
6. To investigate differences in reaction time of reflexes and learned responses.

PRE-LAB QUIZ

1. Define *reflex*. _____
_____
2. Circle the correct term. <u>Autonomic</u> / <u>Somatic</u> reflexes include all those reflexes that involve stimulation of skeletal muscles.
3. In a reflex arc, the _____ transmits afferent impulses to the central nervous system.
   a. integration center
   b. motor neuron
   c. receptor
   d. sensory neuron
4. Circle True or False. Most reflexes are simple, two-neuron, monosynaptic reflex arcs.
5. Stretch reflexes are initiated by tapping a _____ which stretches the associated muscle.
   a. bone
   b. ligament
   c. tendon
6. An example of an autonomic reflex that you will be studying in today's lab is the _____ reflex.
   a. crossed-extensor   c. plantar
   b. gag   d. salivary
7. Name one of the pupillary reflexes you will be examining today.
   _____
8. Circle the correct term. The effectors of the salivary reflex are <u>muscles / glands.</u>
9. Circle True or False. Learned reflexes involve far fewer neural pathways and fewer types of higher intellectual activities, which shortens their response time.

Reflexes are rapid, predictable, involuntary motor responses to stimuli; they are mediated over neural pathways called reflex arcs.

Reflexes can be categorized into one of two large groups: autonomic reflexes and somatic reflexes. **Autonomic** (or visceral) **reflexes** are mediated through the autonomic nervous system, and we are not usually aware of them. These reflexes activate smooth muscles, cardiac muscle, and the glands of the body, and they regulate body functions such as digestion, elimination, blood pressure, salivation, and sweating. **Somatic reflexes** include all those reflexes that involve stimulation of skeletal muscles by the somatic division of the nervous system. An example of such a reflex is the rapid withdrawal of a hand from a hot object.

Reflex testing is an important diagnostic tool for assessing the condition of the nervous system. Distorted, exaggerated, or absent reflex responses may indicate degeneration or pathology of portions of the nervous system, often before other signs are apparent.

If the spinal cord is damaged, the easily performed reflex tests can help pinpoint the area (level) of spinal cord injury. Motor nerves above the injured area may be unaffected, whereas those at or below the lesion site may be unable to participate in normal reflex activity. ■

Components of a Reflex Arc

Reflex arcs have five basic components (Figure 22.1):

1. The *receptor* is the site of stimulus action.

2. The *sensory neuron* transmits afferent impulses to the CNS.

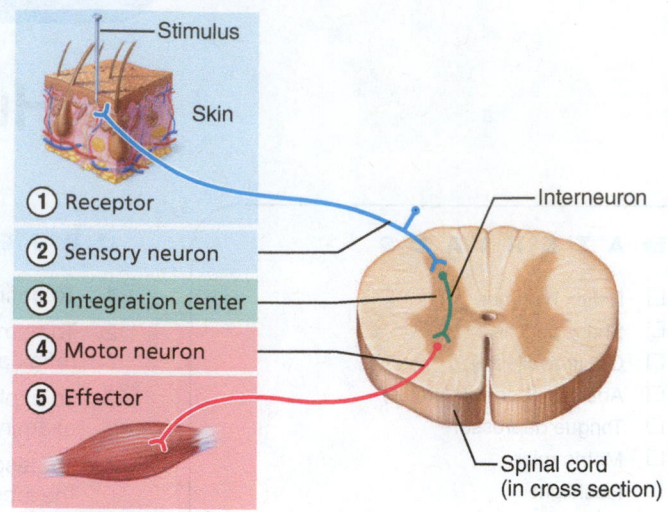

FIGURE 22.1 The five basic components of reflex arcs. The reflex illustrated is polysynaptic.

3. The *integration center* consists of one or more neurons in the CNS.

4. The *motor neuron* conducts efferent impulses from the integration center to an effector organ.

5. The *effector,* muscle fibers or glands, responds to efferent impulses characteristically (by contracting or secreting, respectively).

The simple patellar or knee-jerk reflex shown in Figure 22.2a is an example of a simple, two-neuron, *monosynaptic*

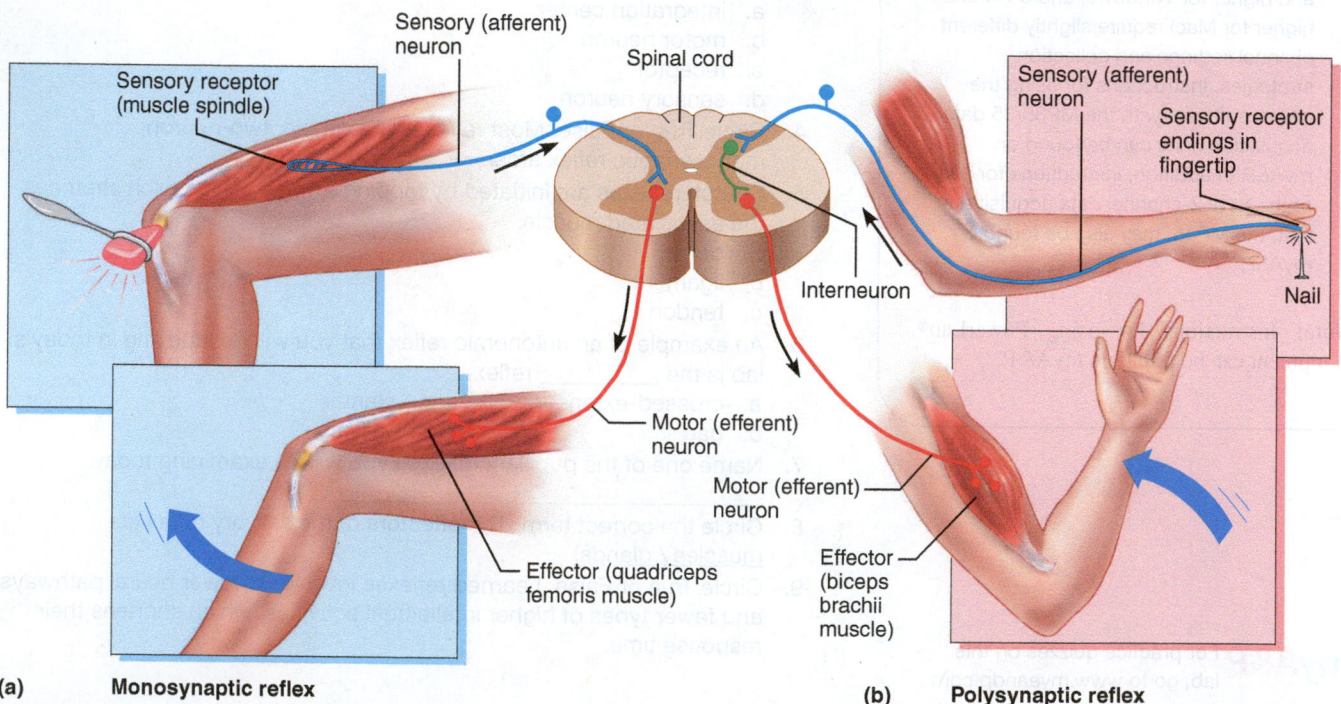

(a)   **Monosynaptic reflex**

(b)   **Polysynaptic reflex**

FIGURE 22.2 Monosynaptic and polysynaptic reflex arcs. The integration center is in the spinal cord, and in each example the receptor and effector are in the same limb. **(a)** The patellar reflex, a two-neuron monosynaptic reflex. **(b)** A flexor reflex, an example of a polysynaptic reflex.

① Tapping the patellar ligament excites muscle spindles in the quadriceps.

② Afferent impulses (blue) travel to the spinal cord, where synapses occur with motor neurons and interneurons.

③a The motor nuerons (red) send activating impulses to the quadriceps causing it to contract, extending the knee.

③b The interneurons (green) make inhibitory synapses with ventral horn neurons (purple) that prevent the antagonist muscles (hamstrings) from resisting the contraction of the quadriceps.

FIGURE 22.3 **The patellar (knee-jerk) reflex—a specific example of a stretch reflex.**

(literally, "one synapse") reflex arc. It will be demonstrated in the laboratory. However, most reflexes are more complex and *polysynaptic,* involving the participation of one or more interneurons (association neurons) in the reflex arc pathway. A three-neuron reflex arc (flexor reflex) is diagrammed in Figure 22.2b. Since delay or inhibition of the reflex may occur at the synapses, the more synapses encountered in a reflex pathway, the more time is required to effect the reflex.

Reflexes of many types may be considered programmed into the neural anatomy. Many *spinal reflexes,* reflexes that are initiated and completed at the spinal cord level, occur without the involvement of higher brain centers. Generally these reflexes are present in animals whose brains have been destroyed, as long as the spinal cord is functional. Conversely, other reflexes require the involvement of the brain, since many different inputs must be evaluated before the appropriate reflex is determined. Superficial cord reflexes and pupillary responses to light are in this category. In addition, although many spinal reflexes do not require the involvement of higher centers, the brain is "advised" of spinal cord reflex activity and may alter it by facilitating or inhibiting the reflexes.

Somatic Reflexes

There are several types of somatic reflexes, including several that you will be eliciting during this laboratory session—the

stretch, crossed extensor, superficial cord, corneal, and gag reflexes. Some require only spinal cord activity; others require brain involvement as well.

Spinal Reflexes

Stretch Reflexes

Stretch reflexes are important postural reflexes, normally acting to maintain posture, balance, and locomotion. Stretch reflexes are initiated by tapping a tendon, which stretches the muscle the tendon is attached to (Figure 22.3). This stimulates the muscle spindles and causes reflex contraction of the stretched muscle or muscles. Branches of the afferent fibers from the muscle spindles also synapse with interneurons controlling the antagonist muscles. The inhibition of those interneurons and the antagonist muscles that follows, called *reciprocal inhibition,* causes them to relax and prevents them from resisting (or reversing) the contraction of the stretched muscle. Additionally, impulses are relayed to higher brain centers (largely via the dorsal white columns) to advise of muscle length, speed of shortening, and the like—information needed to maintain muscle tone and posture. Stretch reflexes tend to be hypoactive or absent in cases of peripheral nerve damage or ventral horn disease and hyperactive in corticospinal tract lesions. They are absent in deep sedation and coma.

FIGURE 22.4 Testing the patellar reflex. The examiner supports the subject's knee so that the subject's muscles are relaxed, and then strikes the patellar ligament with the reflex hammer. The proper location may be ascertained by palpation of the patella.

ACTIVITY 1

Initiating Stretch Reflexes

1. Test the **patellar,** or knee-jerk, **reflex** by seating a subject on the laboratory bench with legs hanging free (or with knees crossed). Tap the patellar ligament sharply with the reflex hammer just below the knee between the patella and the tibial tuberosity as shown in Figure 22.4. The knee-jerk response assesses the L_2–L_4 level of the spinal cord. Test both knees and record your observations. (Sometimes a reflex can be altered by your actions. If you encounter difficulty, consult your instructor for helpful hints.)

_____

_____

Which muscles contracted? _____

_____

What nerve is carrying the afferent and efferent impulses?

_____

2. Test the effect of mental distraction on the patellar reflex by having the subject add a column of three-digit numbers while you test the reflex again. Is the response more *or* less vigorous than the first response?

_____

What are your conclusions about the effect of mental distraction on reflex activity?

_____

_____

3. Now test the effect of muscular activity occurring simultaneously in other areas of the body. Have the subject clasp

FIGURE 22.5 Testing the Achilles reflex. The examiner slightly dorsiflexes the subject's ankle by supporting the foot lightly in the hand, and then taps the Achilles tendon just above the ankle.

the edge of the laboratory bench and vigorously attempt to pull it upward with both hands. At the same time, test the patellar reflex again. Is the response more or less vigorous than the first response?

_____

4. Fatigue also influences the reflex response. The subject should jog in position until she or he is very fatigued (*really fatigued*—no slackers). Test the patellar reflex again, and record whether it is more or less vigorous than the first response.

_____

Would you say that nervous system activity *or* muscle function is responsible for the changes you have just observed?

Explain your reasoning. _____

_____

_____

_____

5. The **Achilles,** or ankle-jerk, **reflex** assesses the first two sacral segments of the spinal cord. With your shoe removed and your foot dorsiflexed slightly to increase the tension of the gastrocnemius muscle, have your partner sharply tap your calcaneal (Achilles) tendon with the broad side of the reflex hammer (Figure 22.5).

What is the result? _____

_____

During walking, what is the action of the gastrocnemius at the ankle?

_____

Crossed-Extensor Reflex

The **crossed-extensor reflex** is more complex than the stretch reflex. It consists of a flexor, or withdrawal, reflex followed by extension of the opposite limb.

This reflex is quite obvious when, for example, a stranger suddenly and strongly grips one's arm. The immediate response is to withdraw the clutched arm and push the intruder away with the other arm. The reflex is more difficult to demonstrate in a laboratory because it is anticipated, and under these conditions the extensor part of the reflex may be inhibited.

ACTIVITY 2

Initiating the Crossed-Extensor Reflex

The subject should sit with eyes closed and with the dorsum of one hand resting on the laboratory bench. Obtain a sharp pencil, and suddenly prick the subject's index finger. What are the results?

_____

_____

_____

Did the extensor part of this reflex occur simultaneously or more slowly than the other reflexes you have observed?

_____

What are the reasons for this? _____

_____

_____

The reflexes that have been demonstrated so far—the stretch and crossed-extensor reflexes—are examples of reflexes in which the reflex pathway is initiated and completed at the spinal cord level.

Superficial Cord Reflexes

The **superficial cord reflexes** (abdominal, cremaster, and plantar reflexes) result from pain and temperature changes. They are initiated by stimulation of receptors in the skin and mucosae. The superficial cord reflexes depend _both_ on functional upper-motor pathways and on the cord-level reflex arc. Since only the plantar reflex can be tested conveniently in a laboratory setting, we will use this as our example.

The **plantar reflex,** an important neurological test, is elicited by stimulating the cutaneous receptors in the sole of the foot. In adults, stimulation of these receptors causes the toes to flex and move closer together. Damage to the pyramidal (or corticospinal) tract, however, produces _Babinski's sign_, an abnormal response in which the toes flare and the great toe moves in an upward direction. (In newborn infants, it is normal to see Babinski's sign due to incomplete myelination of the nervous system.)

FIGURE 22.6 Testing the plantar reflex. Using a moderately sharp object, the examiner strokes the lateral border of the subject's sole, starting at the heel and continuing toward the big toe across the ball of the foot.

ACTIVITY 3

Initiating the Plantar Reflex

Have the subject remove a shoe and lie on the cot or laboratory bench with knees slightly bent and thighs rotated so that the posterolateral side of the foot rests on the cot. Alternatively, the subject may sit up and rest the lateral surface of the foot on a chair. Draw the handle of the reflex hammer firmly along the lateral side of the exposed sole from the heel to the base of the great toe (Figure 22.6).

What is the response? _____

_____

Is this a normal plantar reflex or a Babinski's sign?

_____

Cranial Nerve Reflex Tests

In these experiments, you will be working with your lab partner to illustrate two somatic reflexes mediated by cranial nerves.

Corneal Reflex

The **corneal reflex** is mediated through the trigeminal nerve (cranial nerve V). The absence of this reflex is an ominous sign because it often indicates damage to the brain stem resulting from compression of the brain or other trauma.

ACTIVITY 4

Initiating the Corneal Reflex

Stand to one side of the subject; the subject should look away from you toward the opposite wall. Wait a few seconds and then quickly, _but gently_, touch the subject's cornea (on the side toward you) with a wisp of absorbent cotton. What reflexive reaction occurs when something touches the cornea?

_____

What is the function of this reflex?

_____

_____

_____ ▬

Gag Reflex

The **gag reflex** tests the somatic motor responses of cranial nerves IX and X. When the oral mucosa on the side of the uvula is stroked, each side of the mucosa should rise, and the amount of elevation should be equal.*

ACTIVITY 5

Initiating the Gag Reflex

For this experiment, select a subject who does not have a queasy stomach, because regurgitation is a possibility. Gently stroke the oral mucosa on each side of the subject's uvula with a tongue depressor. What happens?

_____

_____

⚠ Discard the used tongue depressor in the disposable autoclave bag before continuing. *Do not* lay it on the laboratory bench at any time. ▬

Autonomic Reflexes

The autonomic reflexes include the pupillary, ciliospinal, and salivary reflexes, as well as a multitude of other reflexes. Work with your partner to demonstrate the four autonomic reflexes described next.

Pupillary Reflexes

There are several types of pupillary reflexes. The **pupillary light reflex** and the **consensual reflex** will be examined here. In both of these pupillary reflexes, the retina of the eye is the receptor, the optic nerve (cranial nerve II) contains the afferent fibers, the oculomotor nerve (cranial nerve III) is responsible for conducting efferent impulses to the eye, and the smooth muscle of the iris is the effector. Many central nervous system centers are involved in the integration of these responses. Absence of normal pupillary reflexes is generally a late indication of severe trauma or deterioration of the vital brain stem tissue due to metabolic imbalance.

ACTIVITY 6

Initiating Pupillary Reflexes

1.   Conduct the reflex testing in an area where the lighting is relatively dim. Before beginning, obtain a metric ruler and

*The uvula is the fleshy tab hanging from the roof of the mouth just above the root of the tongue.

a flashlight. Measure and record the size of the subject's pupils as best you can.

Right pupil: _____ mm   Left pupil: _____ mm

2.   Stand to the left of the subject to conduct the testing. The subject should shield his or her right eye by holding a hand vertically between the eye and the right side of the nose.

3.   Shine a flashlight into the subject's left eye. What is the pupillary response?

_____

Measure the size of the left pupil: _____ mm

4.   Without moving the flashlight, observe the right pupil. Has the same type of change (called a *consensual response*) occurred in the right eye?

_____

Measure the size of the right pupil: _____ mm

The consensual response, or any reflex observed on one side of the body when the other side has been stimulated, is called a **contralateral response.** The pupillary light response, or any reflex occurring on the same side stimulated, is referred to as an **ipsilateral response.**

What does the occurrence of a contralateral response indicate about the pathways involved?

_____

_____

Was the sympathetic *or* the parasympathetic division of the autonomic nervous system active during the testing of these reflexes?

_____

What is the function of these pupillary responses?

_____

_____ ▬

Ciliospinal Reflex

The **ciliospinal reflex** is another example of reflex activity in which pupillary responses can be observed. This response may initially seem a little bizarre, especially in view of the consensual reflex just demonstrated.

Initiating the Ciliospinal Reflex

1. While observing the subject's eyes, gently stroke the skin (or just the hairs) on the left side of the back of the subject's neck, close to the hairline.

What is the reaction of the left pupil? _____

The reaction of the right pupil? _____

2. If you see no reaction, repeat the test using a gentle pinch in the same area.

The response you should have noted—pupillary dilation—is consistent with the pupillary changes occurring when the sympathetic nervous system is stimulated. Such a response may also be elicited in a single pupil when more impulses from the sympathetic nervous system reach it for any reason. For example, when the left side of the subject's neck was stimulated, sympathetic impulses to the left iris increased, resulting in the ipsilateral reaction of the left pupil.

On the basis of your observations, would you say that the sympathetic innervation of the two irises is closely integrated?

_____ Why or why not? _____

_____

Salivary Reflex

Unlike the other reflexes, in which the effectors were smooth or skeletal muscles, the effectors of the **salivary reflex** are glands. The salivary glands secrete varying amounts of saliva in response to reflex activation.

Initiating the Salivary Reflex

1. Obtain a small beaker, a graduated cylinder, lemon juice, and wide-range pH paper. After refraining from swallowing for 2 minutes, the subject is to expectorate (spit) the accumulated saliva into a small beaker. Using the graduated cylinder, measure the volume of the expectorated saliva and determine its pH.

Volume: _____ cc   pH: _____

2. Now place 2 or 3 drops of lemon juice on the subject's tongue. Allow the lemon juice to mix with the saliva for 5 to 10 seconds, and then determine the pH of the subject's saliva by touching a piece of pH paper to the tip of the tongue.

pH: _____

As before, the subject is to refrain from swallowing for 2 minutes. After the 2 minutes is up, again collect and measure the volume of the saliva and determine its pH.

Volume: _____ cc   pH: _____

3. How does the volume of saliva collected after the application of the lemon juice compare with the volume of the first saliva sample?

_____

How does the final saliva pH reading compare to the initial reading?

_____

How does the final saliva pH reading compare to that obtained 10 seconds after the application of lemon juice?

_____

What division of the autonomic nervous system mediates the reflex release of saliva?

_____

_____

⚠️ Dispose of the saliva-containing beakers and the graduated cylinders in the laboratory bucket that contains bleach and put the used pH paper into the disposable autoclave bag. Wash the bench down with 10% bleach solution before continuing. ▪

Reaction Time of Basic and Learned or Acquired Reflexes

The time required for reaction to a stimulus depends on many factors—sensitivity of the receptors, velocity of nerve conduction, the number of neurons and synapses involved, and the speed of effector activation, to name just a few. Some reflexes are *basic,* or inborn; others are *learned,* or *acquired,* reflexes resulting from practice or repetition. There is no clear-cut distinction between basic and learned reflexes, as most reflex actions are subject to modification by learning or conscious effort. In general, however, if the response involves a specific reflex arc, the synapses are facilitated and the response time is short. Learned reflexes involve a far larger number of neural pathways and many types of higher intellectual activities, including choice and decision making, which lengthens the response time.

There are various ways of testing reaction time of reflexes. The tests range from simple to ultrasophisticated. The following activities provide an opportunity to demonstrate the major time difference between simple and learned reflexes and to measure response time under various conditions.

Testing Reaction Time for Basic and Acquired Reflexes

1. Using a reflex hammer, elicit the patellar reflex in your partner. Note the relative reaction time needed for this basic reflex to occur.

2. Now test the reaction time for learned reflexes. The subject should hold a hand out, with the thumb and index finger extended. Hold a metric ruler so that its end is exactly 3 cm above the subject's outstretched hand. The ruler should be in the vertical position with the numbers reading from the bottom up. When the ruler is dropped, the subject should be able to grasp it between thumb and index finger as it passes, without having to change position. Have the subject catch the ruler five times, varying the time between trials. The relative speed of reaction can be determined by reading the number on the ruler at the point of the subject's fingertips.* (Thus if the number at the fingertips is 15 cm, the subject was unable to catch the ruler until 18 cm of length had passed through his or her fingers; 15 cm of ruler length plus 3 cm to account for the distance of the ruler above the hand.)† Record the number of centimeters that pass through the subject's fingertips (or the number of seconds required for reaction) for each trial:

Trial 1: _____ cm   Trial 4: _____ cm
        _____ sec   _____ sec
Trial 2: _____ cm   Trial 5: _____ cm
        _____ sec   _____ sec
Trial 3: _____ cm
        _____ sec

3. Perform the test again, but this time say a simple word each time you release the ruler. Designate a specific word as a signal for the subject to catch the ruler. On all other words, the subject is to allow the ruler to pass through his fingers. Trials in which the subject erroneously catches the ruler are to be disregarded. Record the distance the ruler travels (or the number of seconds required for reaction) in five *successful* trials:

Trial 1: _____ cm   Trial 4: _____ cm
        _____ sec   _____ sec
Trial 2: _____ cm   Trial 5: _____ cm
        _____ sec   _____ sec
Trial 3: _____ cm
        _____ sec

Did the addition of a specific word to the stimulus increase or decrease the reaction time?

_____

4. Perform the testing once again to investigate the subject's reaction to word association. As you drop the ruler, say a word—for example, *hot*. The subject is to respond with a word he or she associates with the stimulus word—for example, *cold*—catching the ruler while responding. If unable to make a word association, the subject must allow the ruler to pass through his or her fingers. Record the distance the ruler

*Distance (*d*) can be converted to time (*t*) using the simple formula:

$$d \text{ (in cm)} = (1/2)(980 \text{ cm/sec}^2)t^2$$
$$t^2 = (d/490 \text{ cm/sec}^2)$$
$$t = \sqrt{(d/(490 \text{ cm/sec}^2)}$$

†An alternative would be to use a reaction time ruler, which converts distance to time (seconds).

travels (or the number of seconds required for reaction) in five successful trials, as well as the number of times the ruler is not caught by the subject.

Trial 1: _____ cm   Trial 4: _____ cm
        _____ sec   _____ sec
Trial 2: _____ cm   Trial 5: _____ cm
        _____ sec   _____ sec
Trial 3: _____ cm
        _____ sec

Number of times the subject did not catch the ruler:

_____

You should have noticed quite a large variation in reaction time in this series of trials. Why is this so?

_____

_____

_____

_____

ACTIVITY 10

Measuring Reaction Time Using BIOPAC®

Setting Up the Equipment

1. Connect the BIOPAC® unit to the computer and turn the computer **ON**.

2. Make sure the BIOPAC® unit is **OFF**.

3. Plug in the equipment as shown in Figure 22.7.

• Hand switch—CH1

• Headphones—back of unit

4. Turn the BIOPAC® unit **ON**.

5. Start the BIOPAC® Student Lab program on the computer by double-clicking the icon on the desktop or by following your instructor's guidance.

6. Select lesson **L11-React-1** from the menu and click **OK**.

7. Type in a filename that will save this subject's data on the computer hard drive. You may want to use the subject's last name followed by React-1 (for example, SmithReact-1), then click **OK**.

Calibrating the Equipment

1. Seat the subject comfortably so that he or she cannot see the computer screen and keyboard.

2. Put the headphones on the subject and give the subject the hand switch to hold.

3. Inform the subject to push the hand switch button when a "click" is heard.

4. Click **Calibrate**, and then click **OK** when the subject is ready.

BIOPAC® data
acquisition unit

Headphones (plug into
back of BIOPAC® unit)

Hand switch (plugs
into Channel 1)

FIGURE 22.7 Setting up the BIOPAC® equipment. Plug the headphones into the
back of the unit and the hand switch into Channel 1.

5. Observe the recording of the calibration data, which should look like the waveforms in Figure 22.8.

- If the data look very different, click **Redo Calibration** and repeat the steps above.
- If the data look similar, proceed to the next section.

Recording the Data

In this experiment, you will record four different segments of data. In Segments 1 and 2, the subject will respond to random click stimuli. In Segments 3 and 4, the subject will respond to click stimuli at fixed intervals (about 4 seconds). The director will click **Record** to initiate the Segment 1 recording, and **Resume** to initiate Segments 2, 3, and 4. The subject should focus only on responding to the sound.

Segment 1: Random Trial 1

1. Each time a sound is heard, the subject should respond by pressing the button on the hand switch as quickly as possible.

2. When the subject is ready, the director should click **Record** to begin the stimulus-response sequence. The recording will stop automatically after ten clicks.

- A triangular marker will be inserted above the data each time a "click" stimulus occurs.
- An upward-pointing "pulse" will be inserted each time the subject responds to the stimulus.

3. Observe the recording of the data, which should look similar to the data in Figure 22.9.

- If the data look very different, click **Redo** and repeat the steps above.
- If the data look similar, move on to recording the next segment.

Segment 2: Random Trial 2

1. Each time a sound is heard, the subject should respond by pressing the button on the hand switch as quickly as possible.

FIGURE 22.8 Example of waveforms during the calibration procedure.

FIGURE 22.9 Example of waveforms during the recording of data.

2. When the subject is ready, the director should click **Resume** to begin the stimulus-response sequence. The recording will stop automatically after ten clicks.

3. Observe the recording of the data, which should again look similar to the data in Figure 22.9.

- If the data look very different, click **Redo** and repeat the steps above.
- If the data look similar, move on to recording the next segment.

Segment 3: Fixed Interval Trial 3

Repeat the steps for Segment 2 above.

Segment 4: Fixed Interval Trial 4

1. Repeat the steps for Segment 2 above.

2. If the data after this final segment is fine, click **Done.** A pop-up window will appear; to record from another subject select **Record from another subject,** and return to step 7 under Setting Up the Equipment. If continuing to the Data Analysis section, select **Analyze current data file** and proceed to step 2 in the Data Analysis section.

Data Analysis

1. If just starting the BIOPAC® program to perform data analysis, enter **Review Saved Data** mode and choose the file with the subject's reaction data (for example, SmithReact-1).

2. Observe that all ten reaction times are automatically calculated for each segment and are placed in the journal at the bottom of the computer screen.

3. Record the ten reaction times for each segment in the chart below.

4. Delete the highest and lowest values of each segment, then calculate and record the average for the remaining eight data points.

5. When finished, exit the program by going to the **File** menu at the top of the page and clicking **Quit.**

Do you observe a significant difference between the average response times of Segment 1 and Segment 2? If so, what might account for the difference, even though they are both random trials?

_____

_____

Likewise, do you observe a significant difference between the average response times of Segment 3 and Segment 4? If so, what might account for the difference, even though they are both fixed interval trials?

_____

Optional Activity with BIOPAC® Reaction Time Measurement

To expand the experiment, choose another variable to test. Response to visual cues may be tested, or you may have the subject change the hand used when clicking the hand switch button. Devise the experiment, conduct the test, then record and analyze the data as described above.

	Reaction Times (seconds)				
	Random			**Fixed Interval**	
Stimulus #	Segment 1	Segment 2	Segment 3	Segment 4	
1					
2					
3					
4					
5					
6					
7					
8					
9					
10					
Average					

Human Reflex Physiology

The Reflex Arc

1. Define *reflex.* _____

_____

2. Name five essential components of a reflex arc: _____ , _____ ,

_____ , _____ , and _____

3. In general, what is the importance of reflex testing in a routine physical examination? _____

_____

_____

Somatic and Autonomic Reflexes

4. Use the key terms to complete the statements given below.

Key: a. abdominal reflex   d. corneal reflex   g. patellar reflex
       b. Achilles reflex   e. crossed-extensor reflex   h. plantar reflex
       c. ciliospinal reflex   f. gag reflex   i. pupillary light reflex

Reflexes classified as somatic reflexes include a _____ , _____ , _____ , _____ , _____ , _____ , and _____ .

Of these, the simple stretch reflexes are _____ and _____ , and the superficial cord reflexes are _____ and _____ .

Reflexes classified as autonomic reflexes include _____ and _____ .

5. Name two cord-mediated reflexes. _____ and _____

_____

Name two somatic reflexes in which the higher brain centers participate. _____

and _____

6. Can the stretch reflex be elicited in a pithed animal (that is, an animal in which the brain has been destroyed)? _____

Explain your answer. _____

_____

7. Trace the reflex arc, naming efferent and afferent nerves, receptors, effectors, and integration centers, for the two reflexes listed. (Hint: Remember which nerve innervates the anterior thigh, and which nerve innervates the posterior thigh.)

   patellar reflex: _____

   _____

   _____

   Achilles reflex: _____

   _____

   _____

8. Three factors that influence the rapidity and effectiveness of reflex arcs were investigated in conjunction with patellar reflex testing—mental distraction, effect of simultaneous muscle activity in another body area, and fatigue.

   Which of these factors increases the excitatory level of the spinal cord? _____

   Which factor decreases the excitatory level of the muscles? _____

   When the subject was concentrating on an arithmetic problem, did the change noted in the patellar reflex indicate that brain

   activity is necessary for the patellar reflex or only that it may modify it? _____

   _____

9. Name the division of the autonomic nervous system responsible for each of the reflexes listed.

   ciliospinal reflex: _____ salivary reflex: _____

   pupillary light reflex: _____

10. The pupillary light reflex, the crossed-extensor reflex, and the corneal reflex illustrate the purposeful nature of reflex activity. Describe the protective aspect of each.

    pupillary light reflex: _____

    corneal reflex: _____

    crossed-extensor reflex: _____

    _____

    _____

11. Was the pupillary consensual response contralateral or ipsilateral? _____

    Why would such a response be of significant value in this particular reflex? _____

    _____

12. Differentiate between the types of activities accomplished by somatic and autonomic reflexes. _____

_____

_____

_____

13. Several types of reflex activity were not investigated in this exercise. The most important of these are autonomic reflexes, which are difficult to illustrate in a laboratory situation. To rectify this omission, complete the following chart, using references as necessary.

Reflex	Organ involved	Receptors stimulated	Action
Micturition (urination)			
Hering-Breuer			
Defecation			
Carotid sinus			

Reaction Time of Basic and Learned or Acquired Reflexes

14. How do basic and learned or acquired reflexes differ? _____

_____

15. Name at least three factors that may modify reaction time to a stimulus. _____

16. In general, how did the response time for the learned activity performed in the laboratory compare to that for the simple

patelar reflex? _____

17. Did the response time without verbal stimuli decrease with practice? _____ Explain the reason for this.

_____

18. Explain, in detail, why response time increased when the subject had to react to a word stimulus.

_____

_____

19. When measuring reaction time in the BIOPAC® activity, was there a difference in reaction time when the stimulus was predictable versus unpredictable? Explain your answer.

_____

_____

General Sensation

MATERIALS

- ☐ Compound microscope
- ☐ Immersion oil
- ☐ Prepared slides (longitudinal sections) of Pacinian corpuscles, Meissner's corpuscles, Golgi tendon organs, and muscle spindles
- ☐ Calipers or esthesiometer
- ☐ Small metric ruler
- ☐ Fine-point, felt-tipped markers (black, red, and blue)
- ☐ Blunt probes (obtainable from Carolina Biological Supply)
- ☐ Von Frey's hairs (or 1-in. lengths of horsehair glued to a matchstick) or sharp pencil
- ☐ Large beaker of ice water; chipped ice
- ☐ Hot water bath set at 45°C; laboratory thermometer
- ☐ Towel
- ☐ Four coins (nickels or quarters)
- ☐ Three large finger bowls or 1000-ml beakers

OBJECTIVES

1. To recognize various types of general sensory receptors as studied in the laboratory, and to describe the function and location of each type.
2. To define *exteroceptor, interoceptor,* and *proprioceptor.*
3. To explain the tactile two-point discrimination test, and to state its anatomical basis.
4. To define *tactile localization,* and to describe how this ability varies in different areas of the body.
5. To demonstrate and relate differences in relative density and distribution of tactile and thermoreceptors in the skin.
6. To define *adaptation* and *negative afterimage.*
7. To define *referred pain* and *projection.*

PRE-LAB QUIZ

1. Name one of the special senses. _____
2. Sensory receptors can be classified according to their source of stimulus. _____ are found close to the body surface and react to stimuli in the external environment.
   a. Exteroceptors   c. Proprioceptors
   b. Interoceptors   d. Visceroceptors
3. Circle True or False. General sensory receptors are widely distributed throughout the body and respond to, among other things, touch, pain, stretch, and changes in position.
4. Meissner's corpuscles respond to light touch. Where would you expect to find Meissner's corpuscles?
   a. deep within the dermal layer of hairy skin
   b. in the dermal papillae of hairless skin
   c. in the hypodermis of hairless skin
   d. in the uppermost portion of the epidermis
5. Pacinian corpuscles respond to
   a. deep pressure and vibrations   c. pain and temperature
   b. light touch
6. Circle True or False. A map of the sensory receptors for touch, heat, cold, and pain shows that they are not evenly distributed throughout the body.
7. Circle the correct term. Two-point threshold / Tactile localization is the ability to determine which portion of the skin has been touched.
8. When a stimulus is applied for a prolonged period, the rate of receptor discharge slows, and conscious awareness of the stimulus declines. This phenomenon is known as
   a. accommodation   c. adjustment
   b. adaptation   d. discernment
9. You will test referred pain in this activity by immersing the subject's
   a. face in ice water to test the cranial nerve response
   b. elbow in ice water to test the ulnar nerve response
   c. hand in ice water to test the axillary nerve response
   d. leg in ice water to test the sciatic nerve response

People are irritable creatures. Hold a sizzling steak before them and their mouths water. Flash your high beams in their eyes on the highway and they cuss. Tickle them and they giggle. These "irritants" (the steak, the light, and the tickle) and many others are stimuli that continually assault us.

The body's **sensory receptors** react to stimuli or changes within the body and in the external environment. The tiny sensory receptors of the **general senses** react to touch, pressure, pain, heat, cold, stretch, vibration, and changes in position and are distributed throughout the body. In contrast to these widely distributed *general sensory receptors,* the receptors of the special senses are large, complex *sense organs* or small, localized groups of receptors. The **special senses** include sight, hearing, equilibrium, smell, and taste.

Sensory receptors may be classified according to the source of their stimulus. **Exteroceptors** react to stimuli in the external environment, and typically they are found close to the body surface. Exteroceptors include the simple cutaneous receptors in the skin and the highly specialized receptor structures of the special senses (the vision apparatus of the eye, and the hearing and equilibrium receptors of the ear, for example). **Interoceptors** or **visceroceptors** respond to stimuli arising within the body. Interoceptors are found in the internal visceral organs and include stretch receptors (in walls of hollow organs), chemoreceptors,

and others. **Proprioceptors,** like interoceptors, respond to internal stimuli but are restricted to skeletal muscles, tendons, joints, ligaments, and connective tissue coverings of bones and muscles. They provide information on the position and degree of stretch of those structures.

The receptors of the special sense organs are complex and deserve considerable study. Thus the special senses (vision, hearing, equilibrium, taste, and smell) are covered separately in Exercises 24 through 26. Only the anatomically simpler **general sensory receptors**—cutaneous receptors and proprioceptors—will be studied in this exercise.

Structure of General Sensory Receptors

You cannot become aware of changes in the environment unless your sensory neurons and their receptors are operating properly. Sensory receptors are modified dendritic endings (or specialized cells associated with the dendrites) that are sensitive to specific environmental stimuli. They react to such stimuli by initiating a nerve impulse. Several histologically distinct types of general sensory receptors have been identified in the skin. Their structures are depicted in Figure 23.1.

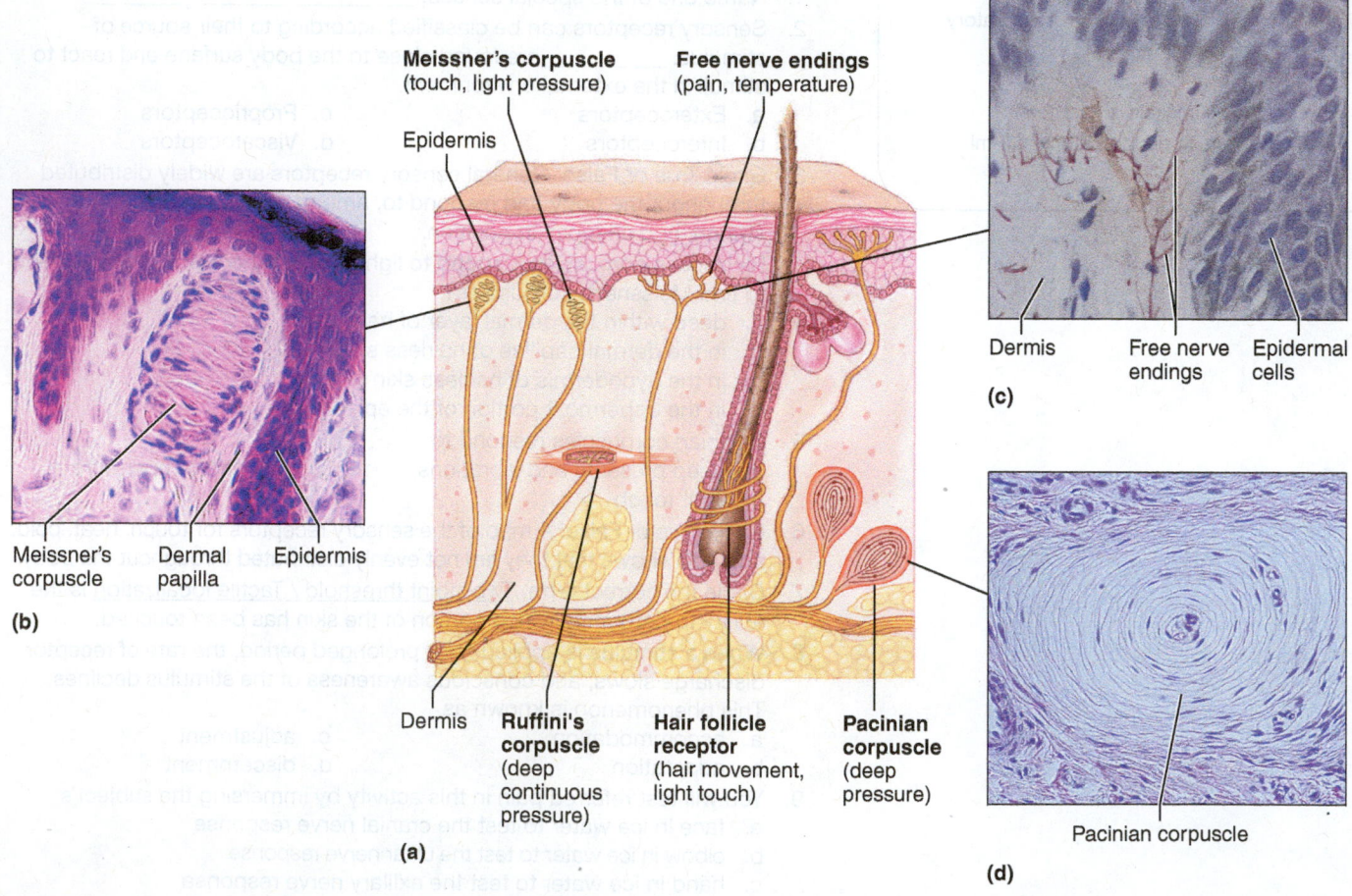

FIGURE 23.1 Examples of cutaneous receptors. Drawing **(a)** and photomicrographs **(b–d).**
(a) Free nerve endings, hair follicle receptor, Meissner's corpuscles, Pacinian corpuscles, and Ruffini's corpuscle. Tactile (Merkel) discs are not illustrated. **(b)** Meissner's corpuscle in a dermal papilla (145×). **(c)** Free nerve endings at dermal-epidermal junction (185×). **(d)** Cross section of a Pacinian corpuscle in the dermis (100×).

FIGURE 23.2 Proprioceptors. (a) Diagrammatic view of a muscle spindle and Golgi tendon organ. Myelin has been omitted from all nerve fibers for clarity. **(b)** Photomicrograph of a muscle spindle (100×).

Many references link each type of receptor to specific stimuli, but there is still considerable controversy about the precise qualitative function of each receptor. Responses of all these receptors probably overlap considerably. Certainly, intense stimulation of any of them is always interpreted as pain.

The least specialized of the cutaneous receptors are the **free,** or **naked, nerve endings** of sensory neurons (Figure 23.1c), which respond chiefly to pain and temperature. The pain receptors are widespread in the skin and make up a sizable portion of the visceral interoceptors. Certain free nerve endings associate with specific epidermal cells to form **tactile (Merkel) discs,** or entwine in hair follicles to form **hair follicle receptors.** Both tactile discs and hair follicle receptors function as light touch receptors.

The other cutaneous receptors are a bit more complex, and the nerve endings are *encapsulated* by connective tissue cells. **Meissner's corpuscles,** also called **tactile corpuscles** because they respond to light touch, are located in the dermal papillae of hairless (glabrous) skin only (Figure 23.1b). **Ruffini's corpuscles** appear to respond to deep pressure and stretch stimuli. **Pacinian corpuscles,** also called **lamellated corpusles,** are anatomically more distinctive and lie deepest in the dermis (Figure 23.1c). Pacinian corpuscles respond only when deep pressure is first applied. They are best suited to monitor high-frequency vibrations.

Studying the Structure of Selected Sensory Receptors

1.   Obtain a compound microscope and histologic slides of Pacinian and Meissner's corpuscles. Locate, under low power, a Meissner's corpuscle in the dermal layer of the skin.

As mentioned above, these are usually found in the dermal papillae. Then switch to the oil immersion lens for a detailed study. Notice that the naked nerve fibers within the capsule are aligned parallel to the skin surface. Compare your observations to Figure 23.1b.

2.   Next observe a Pacinian corpuscle located much deeper in the dermis. Try to identify the slender naked nerve ending in the center of the receptor and the heavy capsule of connective tissue surrounding it (which looks rather like an onion cut lengthwise). Also, notice how much larger the Pacinian corpuscles are than the Meissner's corpuscles. Compare your observations to Figure 23.1d.

3.   Obtain slides of muscle spindles and Golgi tendon organs, the two major types of proprioceptors (Figure 23.2). In the slide of **muscle spindles,** note that minute extensions of the nerve endings of the sensory neurons coil around specialized slender skeletal muscle cells called **intrafusal cells,** or **fibers.** The **Golgi tendon organs** are composed of nerve endings that ramify through the tendon tissue close to the attachment between muscle and tendon. Stretching of muscles or tendons excites these receptors, which then transmit impulses that ultimately reach the cerebellum for interpretation. Compare your observations to Figure 23.2. ▪

Receptor Physiology

Sensory receptors act as **transducers,** changing environmental stimuli into afferent nerve impulses. Since the action potential generated in all nerve fibers is essentially identical, the stimulus is identified entirely by the area of the brain's sensory cortex that is stimulated (which, of course, differs for the various afferent nerves).

Four qualities of cutaneous sensations have traditionally been recognized: tactile (touch), heat, cold, and pain. Mapping these sensations on the skin has revealed that the sensory receptors for these qualities are not distributed uniformly. Instead, they have discrete locations and are characterized by clustering at certain points—**punctate distribution.**

The simple pain receptors, extremely important in protecting the body, are the most numerous. Touch receptors cluster where greater sensitivity is desirable, as on the hands and face. It may be surprising to learn that rather large areas of the skin are quite insensitive to touch because of a relative lack of touch receptors.

There are several simple experiments you can conduct to investigate the location and physiology of cutaneous receptors. In each of the following activities, work in pairs with one person as the subject and the other as the experimenter. After you have completed an experiment, switch roles and go through the procedures again so that all class members obtain individual results. Keep an accurate account of each test that you perform.

Two-Point Discrimination Test

As noted, the density of the touch receptors varies significantly in different areas of the body. In general, areas that have the greatest density of tactile receptors have a heightened ability to "feel." These areas correspond to areas that receive the greatest motor innervation; thus they are also typically areas of fine motor control.

On the basis of this information, which areas of the body do you *predict* will have the greatest density of touch receptors?

_____

_____

ACTIVITY 2

Determining the Two-Point Threshold

1.   Using calipers or an esthesiometer and a metric ruler, test the ability of the subject to differentiate two distinct sensations when the skin is touched simultaneously at two points. Beginning with the face, start with the caliper arms completely together. Gradually increase the distance between the arms, testing the subject's skin after each adjustment. Continue with this testing procedure until the subject reports that *two points* of contact can be felt. This measurement, the smallest distance at which two points of contact can be felt, is the **two-point threshold.**

2.   Repeat this procedure on the back and palm of the hand, fingertips, lips, back of the neck, and ventral forearm. Record your results in the chart, Determining Two-Point Threshold.

3.   Which area has the smallest two-point threshold?

_____

Tactile Localization

Tactile localization is the ability to determine which portion of the skin has been touched. The tactile receptor field of the body periphery has a corresponding "touch" field in the brain's somatosensory cortex. Some body areas are well represented with touch receptors, allowing tactile stimuli to be

Determining Two-Point Threshold	
Body area tested	Two-point threshold (mm)
Face	
Back of hand	
Palm of hand	
Fingertip	
Lips	
Back of neck	
Ventral forearm	

localized with great accuracy, but touch-receptor density in other body areas allows only crude discrimination.

ACTIVITY 3

Testing Tactile Localization

1.   The subject's eyes should be closed during the testing. The experimenter touches the palm of the subject's hand with a pointed black felt-tipped marker. The subject should then try to touch the exact point with his or her own marker, which should be of a different color. Measure the error of localization in millimeters.

2.   Repeat the test in the same spot twice more, recording the error of localization for each test. Average the results of the three determinations, and record it in the chart Testing Tactile Location.

Testing Tactile Localization	
Body area tested	Average error (mm)
Palm of hand	
Fingertip	
Ventral forearm	
Back of hand	
Back of neck	

Does the ability to localize the stimulus improve the second time? _____ _____ The third time? _____

Explain. _____

_____

3. Repeat the preceding procedure on a fingertip, the ventral forearm, the back of a hand, and the back of the neck. Record the averaged results in the chart on the previous page.

4. Which area has the smallest error of localization?

_____

Density and Location of Touch and Temperature Receptors

Plotting the Relative Density and Location of Touch and Temperature Receptors

1. Obtain two blunt probes, metric ruler, Von Frey's hair (or a sharp pencil), a towel, and black, red, and blue felt-tipped markers and bring them to your laboratory bench.

2. Place one blunt probe in a beaker of ice water and the other in a water bath controlled at 45°C. With a felt marker, draw a square (2 cm on each side) on the ventral surface of the subject's forearm. The square should not contain dots made previously. During the following tests, the subject's eyes are to remain closed. The subject should tell the examiner when a stimulus is detected.

3. Working in a systematic manner from one side of the marked square to the other, gently touch the Von Frey's hair or a sharp pencil tip to different points within the square. The *hairs* should be applied with a pressure that just causes them to bend; use the same pressure for each contact. Do not apply deep pressure. The goal is to stimulate only the more superficially located Meissner's corpuscles (as opposed to the Pacinian corpuscles located in the subcutaneous tissue). Mark with a *black dot* all points at which the touch is perceived.

4. Go to the area where the ice bath and 45°C water bath are set up. Remove the blunt probe from the ice water and, using a towel, quickly wipe it dry. Repeat the procedure outlined above, noting all points of cold perception with a *blue dot*.* Perception should be for temperature, not simply touch.

5. Remove the second blunt probe from the 45°C water bath and repeat the procedure once again, marking all points of heat perception with a *red dot*.*

6. After each student has acted as the subject, draw a "map" of your own and your partner's receptor areas in the squares provided here. Use the same color codes as on the skin.

*The blunt probes will have to be returned to the water baths approximately every 2 minutes to maintain the desired testing temperatures.

Student 1: _____   Student 2: _____

2 cm   2 cm

How does the density of the heat receptors correspond to that of the touch receptors?

_____

To that of the cold receptors?_____

On the basis of your observations, which of these three types of receptors appears to be most abundant (at least in the area tested)?

_____

Adaptation of Sensory Receptors

The number of impulses transmitted by sensory receptors often changes both with the intensity of the stimulus and with the length of time the stimulus is applied. In many cases, when a stimulus is applied for a prolonged period, the rate of receptor discharge slows and conscious awareness of the stimulus declines or is lost until some type of stimulus change occurs. This phenomenon is referred to as **adaptation.** The touch receptors adapt particularly rapidly, which is highly desirable. Who, for instance, would want to be continually aware of the pressure of clothing on their skin? The simple experiments to be conducted next allow you to investigate the phenomenon of adaptation.

Demonstrating Adaptation of Touch Receptors

1. The subject's eyes should be closed. Obtain four coins. Place one coin on the anterior surface of the subject's forearm, and determine how long the sensation persists for the subject. Duration of the sensation:

_____ sec

2. Repeat the test, placing the coin at a different forearm location. How long does the sensation persist at the second location?

_____ sec

3. After awareness of the sensation has been lost at the second site, stack three more coins atop the first one.

Does the pressure sensation return? _____

If so, for how long is the subject aware of the pressure in this instance?

_____ sec

Are the same receptors being stimulated when the four coins, rather than the one coin, are used? _____

Explain. _____

_____

4.   To further illustrate the adaptation of touch receptors— in this case, the hair follicle receptors—gently and slowly bend one hair shaft with a pen or pencil until it springs back (away from the pencil) to its original position. Is the tactile sensation greater when the hair is being slowly bent or when it springs back?

_____

Why is the adaptation of the touch receptors in the hair follicles particularly important to a woman who wears her hair in a ponytail? If the answer is not immediately apparent, consider the opposite phenomenon: what would happen, in terms of sensory input from her hair follicles, if these receptors did not exhibit adaptation?

_____

_____

A C T I V I T Y   6

Demonstrating Adaptation of Temperature Receptors

Adaptation of the temperature receptors can be tested using some very unsophisticated methods.

1.   Obtain three large finger bowls or 1000-ml beakers and fill the first with 45°C water. Have the subject immerse her or his left hand in the water and report the sensation. Keep the left hand immersed for 1 minute and then also immerse the right hand in the same bowl.

What is the sensation of the left hand when it is first immersed?

_____

What is the sensation of the left hand after 1 minute as compared to the sensation in the right hand just immersed?

_____

Had adaptation occurred in the left hand? _____

2.   Rinse both hands in tap water, dry them, and wait 5 minutes before conducting the next test. Just before beginning the

test, refill the finger bowl with fresh 45°C water, fill a second with ice water, and fill a third with water at room temperature.

3.   Place the *left* hand in the ice water and the *right* hand in the 45°C water. What is the sensation in each hand after 2 minutes as compared to the sensation perceived when the hands were first immersed?

_____

Which hand seemed to adapt more quickly?

_____

4.   After reporting these observations, the subject should then place both hands simultaneously into the finger bowl containing the water at room temperature. Record the sensa-

tion in the left hand: _____

The right hand: _____

The sensations that the subject experiences when both hands were put into room-temperature water are called **negative afterimages.** They are explained by the fact that sensations of heat and cold depend on the rapidity of heat loss or gain by the skin and differences in the temperature gradient. ■

Referred Pain

Experiments on pain receptor localization and adaptation are commonly conducted in the laboratory. However, there are certain problems with such experiments. Pain receptors are densely distributed in the skin, and they adapt very little, if at all. (This lack of adaptability is due to the protective function of the receptors. The sensation of pain often indicates tissue damage or trauma to body structures.) Thus no attempt will be made in this exercise to localize the pain receptors or to prove their nonadaptability, since both would cause needless discomfort to those of you acting as subjects and would not add any additional insight.

However, the phenomenon of referred pain is easily demonstrated in the laboratory, and such experiments provide information that may be useful in explaining common examples of this phenomenon. **Referred pain** is a sensory experience in which pain is perceived as arising in one area of the body when in fact another, often quite remote area is receiving the painful stimulus. Thus the pain is said to be "referred" to a different area. The phenomenon of **projection,** the process by which the brain refers sensations to their *usual* point of stimulation, provides the most simple explanation of such experiences. Many of us have experienced referred pain as a radiating pain in the forehead after quickly swallowing an ice-cold drink. Referred pain is important in many types of clinical diagnosis because damage to many visceral organs results in this phenomenon. For example, inadequate oxygenation of the heart muscle often results in pain being referred to the chest wall and left shoulder (*angina pectoris*), and the reflux of gastric juice into the esophagus causes a sensation of intense discomfort in the thorax referred to as *heartburn*.

ACTIVITY 7

Demonstrating the Phenomenon of Referred Pain

Immerse the subject's elbow in a finger bowl containing ice water. In the chart below, record the quality (such as discomfort, tingling, or pain) and the quality progression of the sensations he or she reports for the intervals indicated. The elbow should be removed from ice water after the 2-minute reading.

The last recording is to occur 3 minutes after removal of the subject's elbow from the ice water.

Also record the location of the perceived sensations. The ulnar nerve, which serves the medial third of the hand, is involved in the phenomenon of referred pain experienced during this test. How does the localization of this referred pain correspond to the areas served by the ulnar nerve?

_____

Demonstrating Referred Pain		
Time of observation	Quality of sensation	Localization of sensation
On immersion		
After 1 min		
After 2 min		
3 min after removal		

General Sensation

Structure of General Sensory Receptors

1. Differentiate between interoceptors and exteroceptors relative to location and stimulus source.

interoceptor: _____

exteroceptor: _____

2. A number of activities and sensations are listed in the chart below. For each, check whether the receptors would be exteroceptors or interoceptors; and then name the specific receptor types. (Because visceral receptors were not described in detail in this exercise, you need only indicate that the receptor is a visceral receptor if it falls into that category.)

Activity or sensation	Exteroceptor	Interoceptor	Specific receptor type
Backing into a sun-heated iron railing			
Someone steps on your foot			
Reading a book			
Leaning on your elbows			
Doing sit-ups			
The "too full" sensation			
Seasickness			

Receptor Physiology

3. Explain how the sensory receptors act as transducers. _____

_____

4. Define *stimulus*. _____

5. What was demonstrated by the two-point discrimination test? _____

_____

How well did your results correspond to your predictions? _____

_____

What is the relationship between the accuracy of the subject's tactile localization and the results of the two-point discrimination

test? _____

6. Define *punctate distribution.* _____

_____

7. Several questions regarding general sensation are posed below. Answer each by placing your response in the appropriately numbered blanks to the right.

   1. Which cutaneous receptors are the most numerous?

   2–3. Which two body areas tested were most sensitive to touch?

   4–5. Which two body areas tested were least sensitive to touch?

   6. Which appear to be more numerous—receptors that respond to cold or to heat?

   7–9. Where would referred pain appear if the following organs were receiving painful stimuli—(7) gallbladder, (8) kidneys, and (9) appendix? (Use your textbook if necessary.)

   10. Where was referred pain felt when the elbow was immersed in ice water during the laboratory experiment?

   11. What region of the cerebrum interprets the kind and intensity of stimuli that cause cutaneous sensations?

1. _____

2. _____

3. _____

4. _____

5. _____

6. _____

7. _____

8. _____

9. _____

10. _____

11. _____

8. Define *adaptation of sensory receptors.* _____

_____

9. Why is it advantageous to have pain receptors that are sensitive to all vigorous stimuli, whether heat, cold, or pressure? _____

Why is the nonadaptability of pain receptors important? _____

_____

10. Imagine yourself without any cutaneous sense organs. Why might this be very dangerous? _____

_____

_____

11. Define *referred pain.* _____

_____

What is the probable explanation for referred pain? (Consult your textbook or an appropriate reference if necessary.)

_____

_____

MATERIALS

- ☐ Chart of eye anatomy
- ☐ Dissectible eye model
- ☐ Prepared slide of longitudinal section of an eye showing retinal layers
- ☐ Compound microscope
- ☐ Preserved cow or sheep eye
- ☐ Dissecting instruments and tray
- ☐ Disposable gloves
- ☐ Metric ruler; meter stick
- ☐ Common (straight) pins
- ☐ Snellen eye chart (floor marked with chalk to indicate 20-ft. distance from posted Snellen chart)
- ☐ Ishihara's color plates
- ☐ Two pencils
- ☐ Test tubes
- ☐ Laboratory lamp or penlight
- ☐ Ophthalmoscope (if available)

OBJECTIVES

1. To describe the structure and function of the accessory visual structures.
2. To identify the structural components of the eye when provided with a model, an appropriate diagram, or a preserved sheep or cow eye, and to list the function(s) of each.
3. To describe the cellular makeup of the retina.
4. To discuss the mechanism of image formation on the retina.
5. To trace the visual pathway to the visual cortex, and to indicate the effects of damage to various parts of this pathway.
6. To define the following terms:

   accommodation   convergence   hyperopia
   astigmatism   emmetropia   myopia
   cataract   glaucoma   refraction
   conjunctivitis

7. To discuss the importance of the pupillary and convergence reflexes.
8. To explain the difference between rods and cones with respect to visual perception and retinal localization.
9. To state the importance of an ophthalmoscopic examination.

PRE-LAB QUIZ

1. The anterior surface of each eye is protected by eyelids or _____.
   a. ducts
   b. lacrimal glands
   c. palpebrae
2. Name the mucous membrane that lines the internal surface of the eyelids and continues over the anterior surface of the eyeball.

   _____

3. How many extrinsic eye muscles are attached to the exterior surface of each eyeball?
   a. three   c. five
   b. four   d. six
4. The wall of the eye has three layers. The outermost fibrous layer is composed of the opaque, white sclera and the transparent _____.
   a. choroid   c. cornea
   b. ciliary gland   d. lacrima
5. Circle the correct term. Photoreceptor cells are distributed over the entire neural retina, except where the optic nerve leaves the eyeball. This site is called the <u>macula lutea / optic disc.</u>
6. Circle the correct term. The <u>aqueous humor / vitreous humor</u> is a clear, watery fluid that helps to maintain the intraocular pressure of the eye and provides nutrients for the avascular lens and cornea.
7. Photoreceptors of the eye include rods and cones. Which one is responsible for interpreting color, but can function only under conditions of high light intensity? _____

Text continues on next page.

myA&P For practice quizzes on this lab, go to www.myaandp.com.

PAL For access to anatomical models and more, check out Practice Anatomy Lab.

8. Photoreceptors stimulate _____ neurons, which in turn stimulate ganglion cells.
    a. unipolar   b. bipolar
    c. multipolar
9. Circle True or False. At the optic chiasma, the fibers from the medial side of each eye cross over to the opposite side.

10. The ability of the eye to focus differentially for objects of near vision is called
    a. accommodation
    b. adaptation
    c. astigmatism
    d. refraction

Anatomy of the Eye

External Anatomy and Accessory Structures

The adult human eye is a sphere measuring about 2.5 cm (1 inch) in diameter. Only about one-sixth of the eye's anterior surface is observable (Figure 24.1); the remainder is enclosed and protected by a cushion of fat and the walls of the bony orbit.

The **lacrimal apparatus** consists of the lacrimal gland, lacrimal canaliculi, lacrimal sac, and the nasolacrimal duct. The **lacrimal glands** are situated superior to the lateral aspect of each eye. They continually liberate a dilute salt solution (tears) that flows onto the anterior surface of the eyeball through several small ducts. The tears flush across the eyeball and through the **lacrimal puncta,** the tiny openings of the

lacrimal canaliculi medially, then into the **lacrimal sac,** and finally into the **nasolacrimal duct,** which empties into the nasal cavity. The lacrimal secretion also contains **lysozyme,** an antibacterial enzyme. Because it constantly flushes the eyeball, the lacrimal fluid cleanses and protects the eye surface as it moistens and lubricates it. As we age, our eyes tend to become dry due to decreased lacrimation, and thus are more vulnerable to bacterial invasion and irritation.

The anterior surface of each eye is protected by the **eyelids,** or **palpebrae.** (See Figure 24.1.) The medial and lateral junctions of the upper and lower eyelids are referred to as the **medial** and **lateral commissures** (*canthi*), respectively. The **lacrimal caruncle,** a fleshy elevation at the medial commissure, produces a whitish oily secretion. A mucous membrane, the **conjunctiva,** lines the internal surface of the eyelids (as the *palpebral conjunctiva*) and continues over the anterior surface of the eyeball to its junction with the corneal

Levator palpebrae superioris muscle
Orbicularis oculi muscle
Eyebrow
Tarsal plate
Palpebral conjunctiva
Tarsal glands
Cornea
Palpebral fissure
Eyelashes
Bulbar conjunctiva
Conjunctival sac
Orbicularis oculi muscle

(a)

Lacrimal sac
Medial commissure (canthus)
Lacrimal caruncle
Upper eyelid
Lacrimal gland
Excretory ducts of lacrimal glands
Lateral commissure (canthus)
Lower eyelid
Lacrimal punctum
Lacrimal canaliculus
Nasolacrimal duct
Inferior meatus of nasal cavity
Nostril

(b)

FIGURE 24.1 External anatomy of the eye and accessory structures. (a) Lateral view; some structures shown in sagittal section. **(b)** Anterior view with lacrimal apparatus.

FIGURE 24.2 Extrinsic muscles of the eye. (a) Lateral view of the right eye.
(b) Superior view of the right eye. **(c)** Summary of actions of the extrinsic eye muscles
and cranial nerves that control them.

epithelium (as the *bulbar conjunctiva*). The conjunctiva se-cretes mucus, which aids in lubricating the eyeball. Inflam-mation of the conjunctiva, often accompanied by redness of the eye, is called **conjunctivitis.**

Projecting from the border of each eyelid is a row of short hairs, the **eyelashes.** The **ciliary glands,** modified sweat glands, lie between the eyelash hair follicles and help lubri-cate the eyeball. Small sebaceous glands associated with the hair follicles and the larger **tarsal** *(meibomian)* **glands,** lo-cated posterior to the eyelashes, secrete an oily substance. An inflammation of one of the ciliary glands or a small oil gland is called a **sty.**

Six **extrinsic eye muscles** attached to the exterior surface of each eyeball control eye movement and make it possible for the eye to follow a moving object. The names and positioning of these extrinsic muscles are noted in Figure 24.2. Their ac-tions are given in the chart accompanying that figure.

Identifying Accessory Eye Structures

Using Figure 24.1 or a chart of eye anatomy, observe the eyes of another student, and identify as many of the accessory structures as possible. Ask the student to look to the left. What extrinsic eye muscles are responsible for this action?

Right eye: _____

Left eye: _____

Internal Anatomy of the Eye

Anatomically, the wall of the eye is constructed of three lay-ers (Figure 24.3). The outermost **fibrous layer** is a protective layer composed of dense avascular connective tissue. It has

FIGURE 24.3 Internal anatomy of the eye. (a) Diagrammatic view of sagittal section of the eye. The vitreous humor is illustrated only in the bottom half of the eyeball. **(b)** Photograph of the human eye. **(c)** Posterior view of anterior half of the eye.

two obviously different regions: The opaque white **sclera** forms the bulk of the fibrous layer and is observable anteriorly as the "white of the eye." Its anteriormost portion is modified structurally to form the transparent **cornea,** through which light enters the eye.

The middle layer, called the **uvea,** is the **vascular layer.** Its posteriormost part, the **choroid,** is a blood-rich nutritive region containing a dark pigment that prevents light scattering within the eye. Anteriorly, the choroid is modified to form the **ciliary body,** which is chiefly composed of *ciliary* *muscles,* important in controlling lens shape, and *ciliary processes.* The ciliary processes secrete aqueous humor. The most anterior part of the uvea is the pigmented **iris.** The iris is incomplete, resulting in a rounded opening, the **pupil,** through which light passes.

The iris is composed of circularly and radially arranged smooth muscle fibers and acts as a reflexively activated diaphragm to regulate the amount of light entering the eye. In close vision and bright light, the circular muscles of the iris contract, and the pupil constricts. In distant vision and in dim light, the radial fibers contract, enlarging (dilating) the pupil and allowing more light to enter the eye.

The innermost **sensory layer** of the eye is the delicate, two-layered **retina** (Figures 24.3 and 24.4 on pages 366 and 368). The outer **pigmented epithelium** abuts the choroid and extends anteriorly to cover the ciliary body and the posterior side of the iris. The transparent inner **neural layer** extends anteriorly only to the ciliary body. It contains the photoreceptors, **rods** and **cones,** which begin the chain of electrical events that ultimately result in the transduction of light energy into nerve impulses that are transmitted to the optic cortex of the brain. Vision is the result. The photoreceptor cells are distributed over the entire neural retina, except where the optic nerve leaves the eyeball. This site is called the **optic disc,** or *blind spot.* Lateral to each blind spot, and directly posterior to the lens, is an area called the **macula lutea** ("yellow spot"), an area of high cone density. In its center is the **fovea centralis,** a minute pit about 0.4 mm in diameter, which contains mostly cones and is the area of greatest visual acuity. Focusing for discriminative vision occurs in the fovea centralis.

Light entering the eye is focused on the retina by the **lens,** a flexible crystalline structure held vertically in the eye's interior by the **suspensory ligament,** more specifically called the **ciliary zonule,** attached to the ciliary body. Activity of the ciliary muscle, which accounts for the bulk of ciliary body tissue, changes lens thickness to allow light to be properly focused on the retina.

In the elderly the lens becomes increasingly hard and opaque. **Cataracts,** which often result from this process, cause vision to become hazy or entirely obstructed. ■

The lens divides the eye into two segments: the **anterior segment** anterior to the lens, which contains a clear watery fluid called the **aqueous humor,** and the **posterior segment** behind the lens, filled with a gel-like substance, the **vitreous humor,** or **vitreous body.** The anterior segment is further divided into **anterior** and **posterior chambers,** located before and after the iris, respectively. The aqueous humor is continually formed by the capillaries of the **ciliary processes** of the ciliary body. It helps to maintain the intraocular pressure of the eye and provides nutrients for the avascular lens and cornea. The aqueous humor is reabsorbed into the **scleral venous sinus** (*canal of Schlemm*). The vitreous humor provides the major internal reinforcement of the posterior part of the eyeball, and helps to keep the retina pressed firmly against the wall of the eyeball. It is formed *only* before birth.

Anything that interferes with drainage of the aqueous fluid increases intraocular pressure. When intraocular pressure reaches dangerously high levels, the retina and optic nerve are compressed, resulting in pain and possible blindness, a condition called **glaucoma.** ■

ACTIVITY 2

Identifying Internal Structures of the Eye

Obtain a dissectible eye model and identify its internal structures described above. As you work, also refer to Figure 24.3. ■

Microscopic Anatomy of the Retina

As described above, the retina consists of two main types of cells: a pigmented *epithelium,* which abuts the choroid, and an inner cell layer composed of *neurons,* which is in contact with the vitreous humor (see Figure 24.4). The inner neural layer is composed of three major populations of cells. These are, from outer to inner aspect, the **photoreceptors** (rods and cones), the **bipolar cells,** and the **ganglion cells.**

The **rods** are the specialized receptors for dim light. Visual interpretation of their activity is in gray tones. The **cones** are color receptors that permit high levels of visual acuity, but they function only under conditions of high light intensity; thus, for example, no color vision is possible in moonlight. Mostly cones are found in the fovea centralis, and their number decreases as the retinal periphery is approached. By contrast, rods are most numerous in the periphery, and their density decreases as the macula is approached.

Light must pass through the ganglion cell layer and the bipolar neuron layer to reach and excite the rods and cones. As a result of a light stimulus, the photoreceptors undergo changes in their membrane potential that influence the bipolar neurons. These in turn stimulate the ganglion cells, whose axons leave the retina in the tight bundle of fibers known as the **optic nerve** (Figure 24.3). The retinal layer is thickest where the optic nerve attaches to the eyeball because an increasing number of ganglion cell axons converge at this point. It thins as it approaches the ciliary body. In addition to these three major cell types, the retina also contains horizontal cells and amacrine cells, which play a role in visual processing.

ACTIVITY 3

Studying the Microscopic Anatomy of the Retina

Use a compound microscope to examine a histologic slide of a longitudinal section of the eye. Identify the retinal layers by comparing your view to Figure 24.4. ■

Pathway of light

FIGURE 24.4 Microscopic anatomy of the retina. (a) Diagrammatic view of cells of the neural retina. Note the pathway of light through the retina. Neural signals (output of the retina) flow in the opposite direction. **(b)** Photomicrograph of the retina (150×).

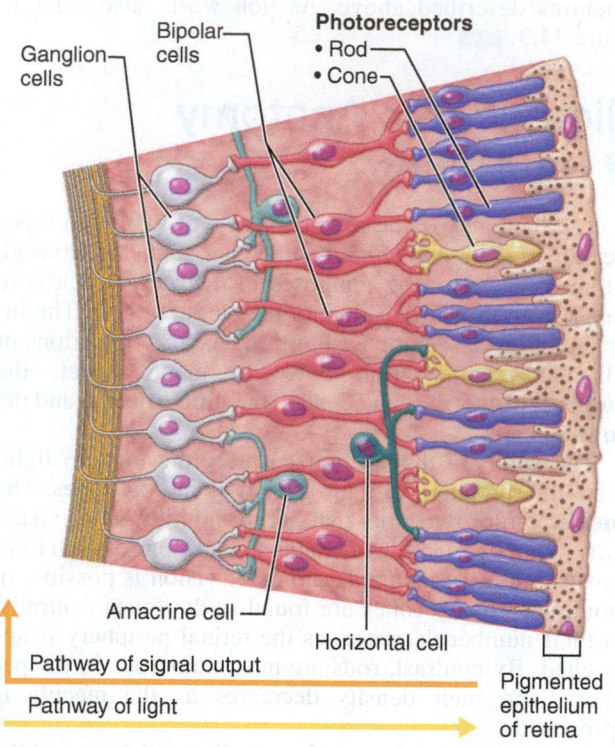

Ganglion cells

Bipolar cells

Photoreceptors
• Rod
• Cone

Amacrine cell

Horizontal cell

Pathway of signal output

Pathway of light

Pigmented epithelium of retina

(a)

Nuclei of ganglion cells

Outer segments of rods and cones

Choroid

Axons of ganglion cells

Nuclei of bipolar cells

Nuclei of rods and cones

Pigmented epithelium of retina

(b)

DISSECTION:
The Cow (Sheep) Eye

1.   Obtain a preserved cow or sheep eye, dissecting instruments, and a dissecting tray. Don disposable gloves.

2.   Examine the external surface of the eye, noting the thick cushion of adipose tissue. Identify the optic nerve (cranial nerve II) as it leaves the eyeball, the remnants of the extrinsic eye muscles, the conjunctiva, the sclera, and the cornea. The normally transparent cornea is opalescent or opaque if the eye has been preserved. Refer to Figure 24.5 as you work.

3.   Trim away most of the fat and connective tissue, but leave the optic nerve intact. Holding the eye with the cornea facing downward, carefully make an incision with a sharp scalpel into the sclera about 6 mm (¼ inch) above the cornea. (The sclera of the preserved eyeball is *very* tough, so you will have to apply substantial pressure to penetrate it.) Using scissors, complete the incision around the circumference of the eyeball paralleling the corneal edge.

4.   Carefully lift the anterior part of the eyeball away from the posterior portion. Conditions being proper, the vitreous body should remain with the posterior part of the eyeball.

5.   Examine the anterior part of the eye, and identify the following structures:

Ciliary body: Black pigmented body that appears to be a halo encircling the lens.

Lens: Biconvex structure that is opaque in preserved specimens.

Carefully remove the lens and identify the adjacent structures:

Iris: Anterior continuation of the ciliary body penetrated by the pupil.

Cornea: More convex anteriormost portion of the sclera; normally transparent but cloudy in preserved specimens.

6.   Examine the posterior portion of the eyeball. Carefully remove the vitreous humor, and identify the following structures:

Adipose (fatty) cushion

(a)

Cornea

Sclera

Optic nerve

Extrinsic muscle attachments

(b)

Ciliary body

Lens

(c)

Optic disc

Sclera

Retina (delicate white membrane overlying the darkly pigmented choroid coat)

Anterior portion

Posterior portion (concavity filled with vitreous humor)

FIGURE 24.5 Anatomy of the cow eye. (a) Cow eye (entire) removed from orbit (notice the large amount of fat cushioning the eyeball). **(b)** Cow eye (entire) with fat removed to show the extrinsic muscle attachments and optic nerve. **(c)** Cow eye cut along the frontal plane to reveal internal structures.

Retina: The neural layer of the retina appears as a delicate tan, probably crumpled membrane that separates easily from the pigmented choroid.

Note its point of attachment. What is this point called?

Pigmented choroid coat: Appears iridescent in the cow or sheep eye owing to a special reflecting surface called the **tapetum lucidum.** This specialized surface reflects the light within the eye and is found in the eyes of animals that live under conditions of low-intensity light. It is not found in humans. ■

FIGURE 24.6 **Inferior views of the visual pathway to the brain.** **(a)** Diagram. Note that fibers from the lateral portion of each retinal field do not cross at the optic chiasma. **(b)** Photograph. Right side is dissected to reveal internal structures.

Visual Pathways to the Brain

The axons of the ganglion cells of the retina converge at the posterior aspect of the eyeball and exit from the eye as the optic nerve. At the **optic chiasma,** the fibers from the medial side of each eye cross over to the opposite side (Figure 24.6). The fiber tracts thus formed are called the **optic tracts.** Each optic tract contains fibers from the lateral side of the eye on the same side and from the medial side of the opposite eye.

The optic tract fibers synapse with neurons in the **lateral geniculate body** of the thalamus, whose axons form the **optic radiation,** terminating in the **visual cortex** in the occipital lobe of the brain. Here they synapse with the cortical neurons, and visual interpretation occurs.

ACTIVITY 4

Predicting the Effects of Visual Pathway Lesions

After examining Figure 24.6, determine what effects lesions in the following areas would have on vision:

In the right optic nerve: _____

_____

Through the optic chiasma: _____

_____

In the left optic tract: _____

_____

FIGURE 24.7 Blind spot test figure.

In the right cerebral cortex (visual area): _____

_____

Visual Tests and Experiments

The Blind Spot

A C T I V I T Y   5

Demonstrating the Blind Spot

1.   Hold Figure 24.7 about 46 cm (18 inches) from your eyes. Close your left eye, and focus your right eye on the X, which should be positioned so that it is directly in line with your right eye. Move the figure slowly toward your face- keeping your right eye focused on the X. When the dot focuses on the blind spot, which lacks photoreceptors, it will disappear.

2.   Have your laboratory partner record in metric units the distance at which this occurs. The dot will reappear as the figure is moved closer. Distance at which the dot disappears:

Right eye _____

Repeat the test for the left eye, this time closing the right eye and focusing the left eye on the dot. Record the distance at which the X disappears:

Left eye _____

Refraction, Visual Acuity, and Astigmatism

When light rays pass from one medium to another, their velocity, or speed of transmission, changes, and the rays are bent, or **refracted.** Thus the light rays in the visual field are refracted as they encounter the cornea, lens, and vitreous humor of the eye.

The refractive index (bending power) of the cornea and vitreous humor are constant. But the lens's refractive index can be varied by changing the lens's shape—that is, by making it more or less convex so that the light is properly converged and focused on the retina. The greater the lens convexity, or bulge, the more the light will be bent and the stronger the lens. Conversely, the less the lens convexity (the flatter it is), the less it bends the light.

Nearly parallel rays
from distant object

Lens

FIGURE 24.8 Refraction and real images. The refraction of light in the eye produces a real image (reversed, inverted, and reduced) on the retina.

In general, light from a distant source (over 6 m, or 20 feet) approaches the eye as parallel rays, and no change in lens convexity is necessary for it to focus properly on the retina. However, light from a close source tends to diverge, and the convexity of the lens must increase to make close vision possible. To achieve this, the ciliary muscle contracts, decreasing the tension on the suspensory ligament attached to the lens and allowing the elastic lens to "round up." Thus, a lens capable of bringing a *close* object into sharp focus is stronger (more convex) than a lens focusing on a more distant object. The ability of the eye to focus differentially for objects of near vision (less than 6 m, or 20 feet) is called **accommodation.** It should be noted that the image formed on the retina as a result of the refractory activity of the lens (Figure 24.8) is a **real image** (reversed from left to right, inverted, and smaller than the object).

The normal, or **emmetropic, eye** is able to accommodate properly (Figure 24.9a). However, visual problems may result (1) from lenses that are too strong or too "lazy" (overconverging and underconverging, respectively), (2) from structural problems such as an eyeball that is too long or too short to provide for proper focusing by the lens, or (3) from a cornea or lens with improper curvatures.

Individuals in whom the image normally focuses in front of the retina are said to have **myopia,** or nearsightedness (Figure 24.9b); they can see close objects without difficulty, but distant objects are blurred or seen indistinctly. Correction requires a concave lens, which causes the light reaching the eye to diverge.

If the image focuses behind the retina, the individual is said to have **hyperopia,** or farsightedness. Such persons have no problems with distant vision but need glasses with convex lenses to augment the converging power of the lens for close vision (Figure 24.9c).

Irregularities in the curvatures of the lens and/or the cornea lead to a blurred vision problem called **astigmatism.** Cylindrically ground lenses, which compensate for inequalities in the curvatures of the refracting surfaces, are prescribed to correct the condition. ■

Near-Point Accommodation

The elasticity of the lens decreases dramatically with age, resulting in difficulty in focusing for near or close vision. This condition is called **presbyopia**—literally, old vision. Lens elasticity can be tested by measuring the **near point of accommodation.** The near point of vision is about 10 cm from the eye in young adults. It is closer in children and farther in old age.

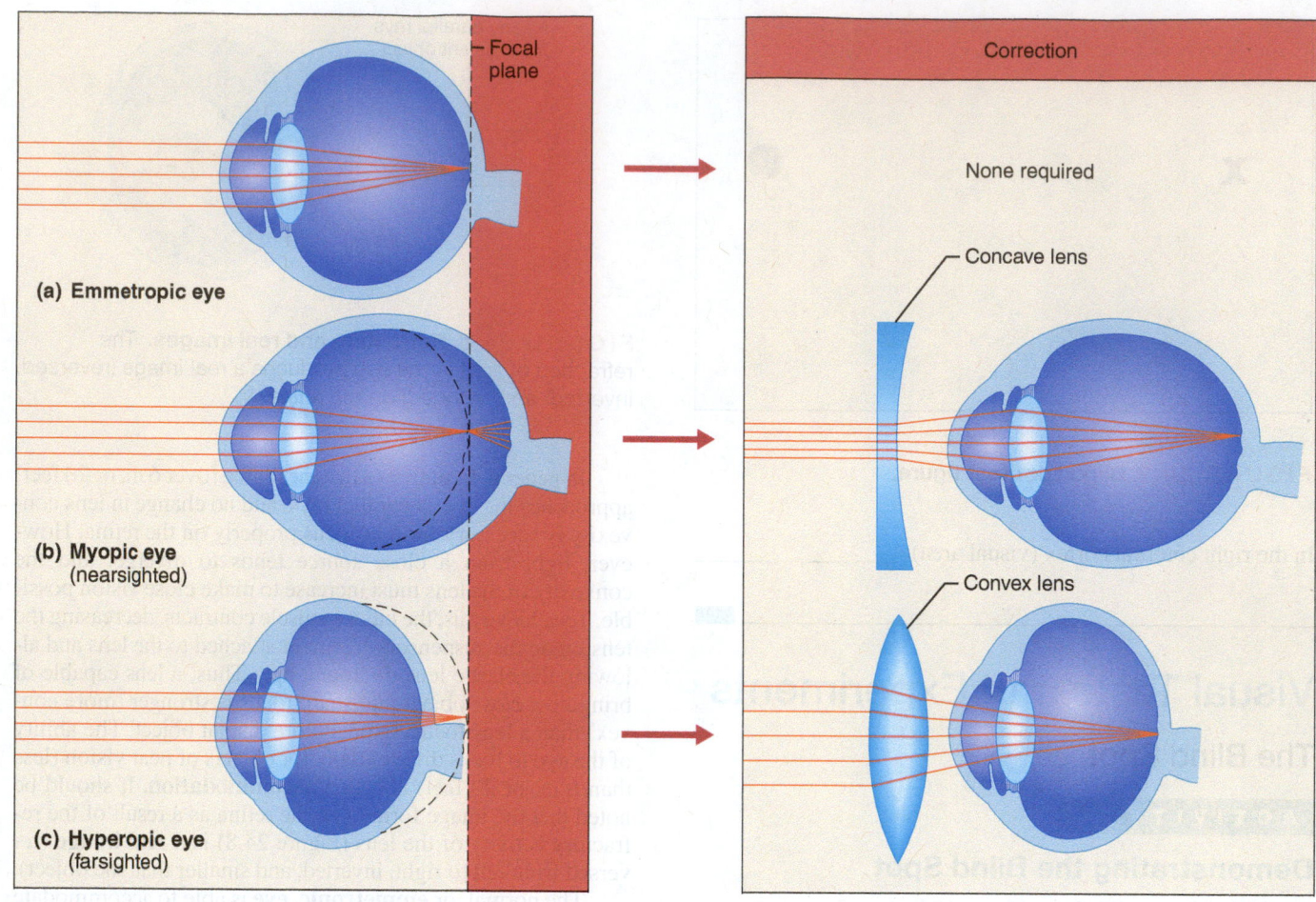

FIGURE 24.9 Problems of refraction. (a) In the emmetropic (normal) eye, light from both near and far objects is focused properly on the retina. **(b)** In a myopic eye, light from distant objects is brought to a focal point before reaching the retina. It then diverges. Applying a concave lens focuses objects properly on the retina. **(c)** In the hyperopic eye, light from a near object is brought to a focal point behind (past) the retina. Applying a convex lens focuses objects properly on the retina. The refractory effect of the cornea is ignored here.

ACTIVITY 6

Determining Near Point of Accommodation

To determine your near point of accommodation, hold a common straight pin at arm's length in front of one eye. (If desired, the text in the lab manual can be used rather than a pin.) Slowly move the pin toward that eye until the pin image becomes distorted. Have your lab partner use a metric ruler to measure the distance from your eye to the pin at this point, and record the distance below. Repeat the procedure for the other eye.

Near point for right eye: _____

Near point for left eye: _____

Visual Acuity

Visual acuity, or sharpness of vision, is generally tested with a Snellen eye chart, which consists of letters of various sizes printed on a white card. This test is based on the fact that let-

ters of a certain size can be seen clearly by eyes with normal vision at a specific distance. The distance at which the normal, or emmetropic, eye can read a line of letters is printed at the end of that line.

ACTIVITY 7

Testing Visual Acuity

1.   Have your partner stand 6 m (20 feet) from the posted Snellen eye chart and cover one eye with a card or hand. As your partner reads each consecutive line aloud, check for accuracy. If this individual wears glasses, give the test twice—first with glasses off and then with glasses on. *Do not remove contact lenses, but note that they were in place during the test.*

2.   Record the number of the line with the smallest-sized letters read. If it is 20/20, the person's vision for that eye is normal. If it is 20/40, or any ratio with a value less than one, he or she has less than the normal visual acuity. (Such an individual is myopic.) If the visual acuity is 20/15, vision is better than normal, because this person can stand at 6 m (20 feet) from the

FIGURE 24.10 Astigmatism testing chart.

chart and read letters that are discernible by the normal eye only at 4.5 m (15 feet). Give your partner the number of the line corresponding to the smallest letters read, to record in step 4.

3. Repeat the process for the other eye.

4. Have your partner test and record your visual acuity. If you wear glasses, the test results *without* glasses should be recorded first.

Visual acuity, right eye without glasses: _____

Visual acuity, right eye with glasses: _____

Visual acuity, left eye without glasses: _____

Visual acuity, left eye with glasses: _____ ▮

ACTIVITY 8

Testing for Astigmatism

The astigmatism chart (Figure 24.10) is designed to test for defects in the refracting surface of the lens and/or cornea.

View the chart first with one eye and then with the other, focusing on the center of the chart. If all the radiating lines appear equally dark and distinct, there is no distortion of your refracting surfaces. If some of the lines are blurred or appear less dark than others, at least some degree of astigmatism is present.

Is astigmatism present in your left eye? _____

Right eye? _____ ▮

Color Blindness

Ishihara's color plates are designed to test for deficiencies in the cones or color photoreceptor cells. There are three cone types, each containing a different light-absorbing pigment. One type primarily absorbs the red wavelengths of the visible light spectrum, another the blue wavelengths, and a third the green wavelengths. Nerve impulses reaching the brain from these different photoreceptor types are then interpreted (seen) as red, blue, and green, respectively. Interpretation of the intermediate colors of the visible light spectrum is a result of overlapping input from more than one cone type.

ACTIVITY 9

Testing for Color Blindness

1. Find the interpretation table that accompanies the Ishihara color plates, and prepare a sheet to record data for the test. Note which plates are patterns rather than numbers.

2. View the color plates in bright light or sunlight while holding them about 0.8 m (30 inches) away and at right angles to your line of vision. Report to your laboratory partner what you see in each plate. Take no more than 3 seconds for each decision.

3. Your partner should record your responses and then check their accuracy with the correct answers provided in the color plate book. Is there any indication that you have some degree of color blindness? _____ If so, what type?

_____

_____

Repeat the procedure to test your partner's color vision. ▮

Binocular Vision

Humans, cats, predatory birds, and most primates are endowed with **binocular** (two-eyed) **vision.** Although both eyes look in approximately the same direction, they see slightly different views. Their visual fields, each about 170 degrees, overlap to a considerable extent; thus there is two-eyed vision at the overlap area (Figure 24.11).

In contrast, the eyes of many animals (rabbits, pigeons, and others) are more on the sides of their head. Such animals see in two different directions and thus have a panoramic field of view and **panoramic vision.** A mnemonic device to keep these straight is "Eyes in the front—likes to hunt. Eyes on the side—likes to hide."

Although both types of vision have their good points, binocular vision provides three-dimensional vision and an accurate means of locating objects in space. The slight differences

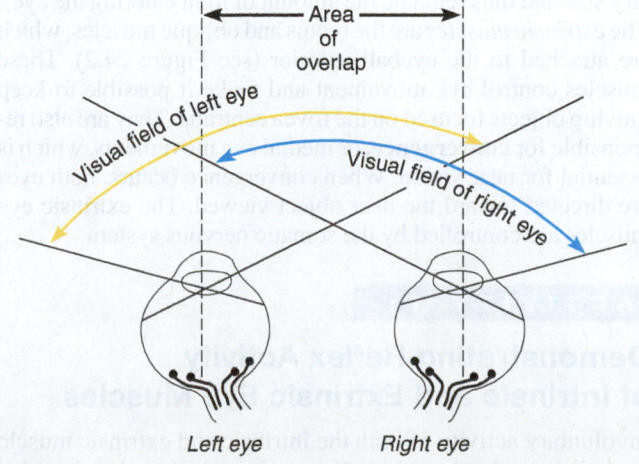

FIGURE 24.11 Overlapping of the visual fields.

between the views seen by the two eyes are fused by the higher centers of the visual cortex to give us *depth perception.* Because of the manner in which the visual cortex resolves these two different views into a single image, it is sometimes referred to as the "cyclopean eye of the binocular animal."

Testing for Binocular Vision

1. To demonstrate that a slightly different view is seen by each eye, perform the following simple experiment.

Close your left eye. Hold a pencil at arm's length directly in front of your right eye. Position another pencil directly beneath it and then move the lower pencil about half the distance toward you. As you move the lower pencil, make sure it remains in the *same plane* as the stationary pencil, so that the two pencils continually form a straight line. Then, without moving the pencils, close your right eye and open your left eye. Notice that with only the right eye open, the moving pencil stays in the same plane as the fixed pencil, but that when viewed with the left eye, the moving pencil is displaced laterally away from the plane of the fixed pencil.

2. To demonstrate the importance of two-eyed binocular vision for depth perception, perform this second simple experiment.

Have your laboratory partner hold a test tube erect about arm's length in front of you. With both eyes open, quickly insert a pencil into the test tube. Remove the pencil, bring it back close to your body, close one eye, and quickly and without hesitation insert the pencil into the test tube. (*Do not feel for the test tube with the pencil!*) Repeat with the other eye closed.

Was it as easy to dunk the pencil with one eye closed as with both eyes open?

_____

Eye Reflexes

Both intrinsic (internal) and extrinsic (external) muscles are necessary for proper eye functioning. The *intrinsic muscles,* controlled by the autonomic nervous system, are those of the ciliary body (which alters the lens curvature in focusing) and the radial and circular muscles of the iris (which control pupillary size and thus regulate the amount of light entering the eye). The *extrinsic muscles* are the rectus and oblique muscles, which are attached to the eyeball exterior (see Figure 24.2). These muscles control eye movement and make it possible to keep moving objects focused on the fovea centralis. They are also responsible for **convergence,** or medial eye movements, which is essential for near vision. When convergence occurs, both eyes are directed toward the near object viewed. The extrinsic eye muscles are controlled by the somatic nervous system.

Demonstrating Reflex Activity of Intrinsic and Extrinsic Eye Muscles

Involuntary activity of both the intrinsic and extrinsic muscle types is brought about by reflex actions that can be observed in the following experiments.

Photopupillary Reflex

Sudden illumination of the retina by a bright light causes the pupil to constrict reflexively in direct proportion to the light intensity. This protective response prevents damage to the delicate photoreceptor cells.

Obtain a laboratory lamp or penlight. Have your laboratory partner sit with eyes closed and hands over his or her eyes. Turn on the light and position it so that it shines on the subject's right hand. After 1 minute, ask your partner to uncover and open the right eye. Quickly observe the pupil of that eye. What happens to the pupil?

_____

Shut off the light and ask your partner to uncover and open the opposite eye. What are your observations of the pupil?

_____

_____

Accommodation Pupillary Reflex

Have your partner gaze for approximately 1 minute at a distant object in the lab—*not* toward the windows or another light source. Observe your partner's pupils. Then hold some printed material 15 to 25 cm (6 to 10 inches) from his or her face, and direct him or her to focus on it.

How does pupil size change as your partner focuses on the printed material?

_____

Explain the value of this reflex. _____

_____

_____

_____

Convergence Reflex

Repeat the previous experiment, this time using a pen or pencil as the close object to be focused on. Note the position of your partner's eyeballs while he or she gazes at the distant object, and then at the close object. Do they change position as the object of focus is changed?

_____ In what way? _____

_____

_____

(a)

Viewing window
(look at eye interior
through this)

Filter switch

Lens
selection disc
(rotate to change lens in use)

Aperture
selection dial

Rheostat control
(rotate to control light intensity)

Rheostat lock
(on-off switch)

Handle

(b)

FIGURE 24.12 Structure and use of an ophthalmoscope. (a) Structure of an ophthalmoscope. **(b)** Proper position for beginning to examine the right eye with an ophthalmoscope.

Explain the importance of the convergence reflex.

_____

_____

_____

Ophthalmoscopic Examination of the Eye (Optional)

The ophthalmoscope is an instrument used to examine the *fundus,* or eyeball interior, to determine visually the condition of the retina, optic disc, and internal blood vessels. Certain pathologic conditions such as diabetes mellitus, arteriosclerosis, and degenerative changes of the optic nerve and retina can be detected by such an examination. The ophthalmoscope consists of a set of lenses mounted on a rotating disc (the **lens selection disc**), a light source regulated by a **rheostat control,** and a mirror that reflects the light so that the eye interior can be illuminated (Figure 24.12a).

The lens selection disc is positioned in a small slit in the mirror, and the examiner views the eye interior through this slit, appropriately called the **viewing window.** The focal length of each lens is indicated in diopters preceded by a plus

(+) sign if the lens is convex and by a negative (−) sign if the lens is concave. When the zero (0) is seen in the **diopter window,** on the examiner side of the instrument, there is no lens positioned in the slit. The depth of focus for viewing the eye interior is changed by changing the lens.

The light is turned on by depressing the red **rheostat lock button** and then rotating the rheostat control in the clockwise direction. The **aperture selection dial** on the front of the instrument allows the nature of the light beam to be altered. The **filter switch,** also on the front, allows the choice of a green, unfiltered, or polarized light beam. Generally, green light allows for clearest viewing of the blood vessels in the eye interior and is most comfortable for the subject.

Once you have examined the ophthalmoscope and have become familiar with it, you are ready to conduct an eye examination.

Conducting an Ophthalmoscopic Examination

1.   Conduct the examination in a dimly lit or darkened room with the subject comfortably seated and gazing straight ahead. To examine the right eye, sit face-to-face with the subject, hold

the instrument in your right hand, and use your right eye to view the eye interior (Figure 24.12b). You may want to steady yourself by resting your left hand on the subject's shoulder. To view the left eye, use your left eye, hold the instrument in your left hand, and steady yourself with your right hand.

2.   Begin the examination with the 0 (no lens) in position. Grasp the instrument so that the lens disc may be rotated with the index finger. Holding the ophthalmoscope about 15 cm (6 inches) from the subject's eye, direct the light into the pupil at a slight angle—through the pupil edge rather than directly through its center. You will see a red circular area that is the illuminated eye interior.

3.   Move in as close as possible to the subject's cornea (to within 5 cm, or 2 inches) as you continue to observe the area. Steady your instrument-holding hand on the subject's cheek if necessary. If both your eye and that of the subject are normal, the fundus can be viewed clearly without further adjustment of the ophthalmoscope. If the fundus cannot be focused, slowly rotate the lens disc counterclockwise until the fundus can be clearly seen. When the ophthalmoscope is correctly set, the fundus of the right eye should appear as shown in Figure 24.13. (**Note:** If a positive [convex] lens is required and your eyes are normal, the subject has hyperopia. If a negative [concave] lens is necessary to view the fundus and your eyes are normal, the subject is myopic.)

When the examination is proceeding correctly, the subject can often see images of retinal vessels in his own eye that appear rather like cracked glass. If you are unable to achieve a sharp focus or to see the optic disc, move medially or laterally and begin again.

4.   Examine the optic disc for color, elevation, and sharpness of outline, and observe the blood vessels radiating from near

FIGURE 24.13 Posterior portion of right retina.

its center. Locate the macula, lateral to the optic disc. It is a darker area in which blood vessels are absent, and the fovea appears to be a slightly lighter area in its center. The macula is most easily seen when the subject looks directly into the light of the ophthalmoscope.

 Do not examine the macula for longer than 1 second at a time.

5.   When you have finished examining your partner's retina, shut off the ophthalmoscope. Change places with your partner (become the subject) and repeat steps 1–4. ▅

NAME _____

LAB TIME/DATE _____

Special Senses: Vision

Anatomy of the Eye

1. Name five accessory eye structures that contribute to the formation of tears and/or aid in lubrication of the eyeball, and then name the major secretory product of each. Indicate which has antibacterial properties by circling the correct secretory product.

Accessory structures	Product

2. The eyeball is wrapped in adipose tissue within the orbit. What is the function of the adipose tissue?

_____

3. Why does one often have to blow one's nose after crying? _____

_____

4. Identify the extrinsic eye muscle predominantly responsible for each action described below.

_____ 1. turns the eye laterally

_____ 2. turns the eye medially

_____ 3. turns the eye up and laterally

_____ 4. turns the eye inferiorly and medially

_____ 5. turns the eye superiorly and medially

_____ 6. turns the eye down and laterally

5. What is a sty? _____

_____

Conjunctivitis? _____

6. Correctly identify each lettered structure in the diagram by writing the letter next to its name in the numbered list.

_____ 1. anterior chamber

_____ 2. anterior segment

_____ 3. bipolar neurons

_____ 4. choroid

_____ 5. ciliary body and processes

_____ 6. ciliary muscle

_____ 7. cornea

_____ 8. dura mater

_____ 9. fovea centralis

_____ 10. ganglion cells

_____ 11. iris

_____ 12. lens

_____ 13. optic disc

_____ 14. optic nerve

_____ 15. photoreceptors

_____ 16. posterior chamber

_____ 17. retina

_____ 18. sclera

_____ 19. scleral venous sinus

_____ 20. suspensory ligaments (ciliary zonule)

_____ 21. posterior segment

Notice the arrows drawn close to the left side of the iris in the diagram above. What do they indicate?

_____

7. The iris is composed primarily of two smooth muscle layers, one arranged radially and the other circularly.

Which of these dilates the pupil? _____

8. You would expect the pupil to be dilated in which of the following circumstances? Circle the correct response(s).

a. in bright light　　　b. in dim light　　　c. focusing for near vision　　　d. observing distant objects

9. The intrinsic eye muscles are controlled by (circle the correct response):

autonomic nervous system　　　somatic nervous system

10. Match the key responses with the descriptive statements that follow.

Key: a. *aqueous humor*　　　e. cornea　　　　　　j. retina
　　 b. choroid　　　　　　　f. fovea centralis　　　k. sclera
　　 c. ciliary body　　　　　g. iris　　　　　　　 l. scleral venous sinus
　　 d. ciliary processes of　 h. lens　　　　　　　 m. vitreous humor
　　　　the ciliary body　　　i. optic disc

_____ 1. fluid filling the anterior segment of the eye

_____ 2. the "white" of the eye

_____ 3. part of the retina that lacks photoreceptors

_____ 4. modification of the choroid that controls the shape of the crystalline lens
　　　　　　　　　　　　　　　　　and contains the ciliary muscle

_____ 5. drains the aqueous humor from the eye

_____ 6. layer containing the rods and cones

_____ 7. substance occupying the posterior segment of the eyeball

_____ 8. forms the bulk of the heavily pigmented vascular layer

_____, _____ 9. smooth muscle structures (2)

_____ 10. area of critical focusing and discriminatory vision

_____ 11. form (by filtration) the aqueous humor

_____, _____ 12. light-bending media of the eye (4)

_____, _____

_____ 13. anterior continuation of the sclera—your "window on the world"

_____ 14. composed of tough, white, opaque, fibrous connective tissue

Microscopic Anatomy of the Retina

11. The two major layers of the retina are the epithelial and neural layers. In the neural layer, the neuron populations are arranged as follows from the pigmented epithelial layer to the vitreous humor. (Circle the proper response.)

bipolar cells, ganglion cells, photoreceptors　　　　　photoreceptors, ganglion cells, bipolar cells

ganglion cells, bipolar cells, photoreceptors　　　　　photoreceptors, bipolar cells, ganglion cells

12. The axons of the _____ cells form the optic nerve, which exits from the eyeball.

13. Complete the following statements by writing either *rods* or *cones* on each blank.

The dim light receptors are the _____. Only _____ are found in the fovea centralis, whereas

mostly _____ are found in the periphery of the retina. _____ are the photoreceptors that operate best

in bright light and allow for color vision.

Dissection of the Cow (Sheep) Eye

14. What modification of the choroid that is not present in humans is found in the cow eye? _____

What is its function? _____

_____

15. What does the retina look like? _____

At what point is it attached to the posterior aspect of the eyeball? _____

Visual Pathways to the Brain

16. The visual pathway to the occipital lobe of the brain consists most simply of a chain of five cells. Beginning with the photoreceptor cell of the retina, name them and note their location in the pathway.

1. _____   4. _____

2. _____   5. _____

3. _____

17. Visual field tests are done to reveal destruction along the visual pathway from the retina to the optic region of the brain. Note where the lesion is likely to be in the following cases.

Normal vision in left eye visual field; absence of vision in right eye visual field: _____

Normal vision in both eyes for right half of the visual field; absence of vision in both eyes for left half of the visual field:

_____

18. How is the right optic *tract* anatomically different from the right optic *nerve*? _____

_____

_____

Visual Tests and Experiments

19. Match the terms in column B with the descriptions in column A.

Column A		Column B
_____ 1. light bending		a. accommodation
_____ 2. ability to focus for close (less than 20 feet) vision		b. astigmatism
_____ 3. normal vision		c. convergence
_____ 4. inability to focus well on close objects (farsightedness)		d. emmetropia
_____ 5. nearsightedness		e. hyperopia
_____ 6. blurred vision due to unequal curvatures of the lens or cornea		f. myopia
_____ 7. medial movement of the eyes during focusing on close objects		g. refraction

20. Complete the following statements:

In farsightedness, the light is focused __1__ the retina. The lens required to treat myopia is a __2__ lens. The "near point" increases with age because the __3__ of the lens decreases as we get older. A convex lens, like that of the eye, produces an image that is upside down and reversed from left to right. Such an image is called a __4__ image.

1. _____

2. _____

3. _____

4. _____

21. Use terms from the key to complete the statements concerning near and distance vision.

Key: a.   *contracted*   b.   *decreased*   c.   *increased*   d.   *relaxed*   e.   *taut*

During distance vision, the ciliary muscle is _____, the suspensory ligament is _____, the convexity of the lens

is _____, and light refraction is _____. During close vision, the ciliary muscle is _____, the suspensory ligament is

_____, lens convexity is _____, and light refraction is _____.

22. Explain why vision is lost when light hits the blind spot. _____

23. Using your Snellen eye test results, answer the following questions.

Is your visual acuity normal, less than normal, or better than normal? _____

Explain your answer. _____

_____

Explain why each eye is tested separately when using the Snellen eye chart. _____

_____

Explain 20/40 vision. _____

_____

Explain 20/10 vision. _____

_____

24. Define *astigmatism.* _____

_____

How can it be corrected? _____

25. Define *presbyopia.* _____

_____

What causes it? _____

26. To which wavelengths of light do the three cone types of the retina respond maximally?

_____, _____, and _____

27. How can you explain the fact that we see a great range of colors even though only three cone types exist?

_____

_____

28. Explain the difference between binocular and panoramic vision. _____

_____

What is the advantage of binocular vision? _____

What factor(s) are responsible for binocular vision? _____

_____

29. In the experiment on the convergence reflex, what happened to the position of the eyeballs as the object was moved closer

to the subject's eyes? _____

What extrinsic eye muscles control the movement of the eyes during this reflex? _____

What is the value of this reflex? _____

_____

30. In the experiment on the photopupillary reflex, what happened to the pupil of the eye exposed to light?

_____ What happened to the pupil of the nonilluminated eye? _____

Explanation? _____

_____

31. Why is the ophthalmoscopic examination an important diagnostic tool? _____

_____

32. Many college students struggling through mountainous reading assignments are told that they need glasses for "eyestrain." Why is it more of a strain on the extrinsic and intrinsic eye muscles to look at close objects than at far objects?

_____

_____

Special Senses: Hearing and Equilibrium

M A T E R I A L S

- ☐ Three-dimensional dissectible ear model and/or chart of ear anatomy
- ☐ Otoscope (if available)
- ☐ Disposable otoscope tips (if available) and autoclave bag
- ☐ Alcohol swabs
- ☐ Compound microscope
- ☐ Prepared slides of the cochlea of the ear
- ☐ Absorbent cotton
- ☐ Pocket watch or clock that ticks
- ☐ Metric ruler
- ☐ Tuning forks (range of frequencies)
- ☐ Rubber mallet
- ☐ Audiometer
- ☐ Red and blue pencils
- ☐ Demonstration: Microscope focused on a slide of a crista ampullaris receptor of a semicircular canal
- ☐ Three coins of different sizes
- ☐ Rotating chair or stool
- ☐ Blackboard and chalk

O B J E C T I V E S

1. To identify, by appropriately labeling a diagram, the anatomical structures of the external, middle, and internal ear, and to explain their functions.
2. To describe the anatomy of the organ of hearing (spiral organ of Corti in the cochlea), and to explain its function in sound reception.
3. To describe the anatomy of the equilibrium organs of the internal ear (cristae ampullares and maculae), and to explain their relative function in maintaining equilibrium.
4. To explain how one is able to localize the source of sounds.
5. To define or explain *sensorineural deafness, conduction deafness,* and *nystagmus.*
6. To state the purpose of the Weber, Rinne, balance, Barany, and Romberg tests.
7. To describe the effects of acceleration on the semicircular canals.
8. To explain the role of vision in maintaining equilibrium.

P R E - L A B   Q U I Z

1. Circle the correct term. The ear is divided into <u>three / four</u> major areas.
2. The external ear is composed primarily of the _____ and the external acoustic meatus.
   - a. auricle
   - b. cochlea
   - c. eardrum
   - d. stapes
3. Circle the correct term. Sound waves that enter the external acoustic meatus eventually encounter the <u>tympanic membrane / oval window</u>, which then vibrates at the same frequency as the sound waves hitting it.
4. Three small bones found within the middle ear are the malleus, incus, and _____.
   - a. auricle
   - b. cochlea
   - c. eardrum
   - d. stapes
5. The snail-like _____, found in the inner ear, contains sensory receptors for hearing.
   - a. cochlea
   - b. lobule
   - c. semicircular canals
   - d. vestibule
6. Circle the correct term. Today you will use an <u>ophthalmoscope / otoscope</u> to examine the ear.
7. The _____ test is used for comparing bone and air-conduction hearing.
   - a. Barany
   - b. Rinne
   - c. Weber
8. The equilibrium apparatus of the ear, the vestibular apparatus, is found in the
   - a. external ear
   - b. inner ear
   - c. middle ear

Text continues on next page.

myA&P *For practice quizzes on this lab, go to www.myaandp.com.*

PAL *For access to anatomical models and more, check out Practice Anatomy Lab.*

9. Circle the correct terms. The <u>crista ampullaris / macula</u> located in the <u>semicircular duct / vestibule</u> is essential for detecting static equilibrium.

10. Nystagmus is
    a. ability to hear only high frequency tones
    b. ability to hear only low frequency tones
    c. involuntary trailing of eyes in one direction, then rapid movement in the other
    d. sensation of dizziness

The ear is a complex structure containing sensory receptors for hearing and equilibrium. The ear is divided into three major areas: the *external ear,* the *middle ear,* and the *internal ear* (Figure 25.1). The external and middle ear structures serve the needs of the sense of hearing *only,* whereas internal ear structures function both in equilibrium and hearing reception.

Anatomy of the Ear

Gross Anatomy

ACTIVITY 1

Identifying Structures of the Ear

Obtain a dissectible ear model or chart of ear anatomy and identify the structures described below. Refer to Figure 25.1 as you work. ■

The **external,** or **outer, ear** is composed primarily of the auricle and the external acoustic meatus. The **auricle,** or **pinna,*** is the skin-covered cartilaginous structure encircling

*Although the preferred anatomical terms for *pinna* and *external auditory canal* are *auricle* and *external acoustic meatus,* "pinna" and "external auditory canal" are heard often in clinical situations and will continue to be used here.

the auditory canal opening. In many animals, it collects and directs sound waves into the external auditory canal. In humans this function of the pinna is largely lost. The portion of the pinna lying inferior to the external auditory canal is the **lobule.**

The **external acoustic meatus,** or **external auditory canal,*** is a short, narrow (about 2.5 cm long by 0.6 cm wide) chamber carved into the temporal bone. In its skin-lined walls are wax-secreting glands called **ceruminous glands.** Sound waves that enter the external auditory meatus eventually encounter the **tympanic membrane,** or **eardrum,** which vibrates at exactly the same frequency as the sound wave(s) hitting it. The membranous eardrum separates the external from the middle ear.

The **middle ear** is essentially a small chamber—the **tympanic cavity**—found within the temporal bone. The cavity is spanned by three small bones, collectively called the **auditory ossicles** (**malleus, incus,** and **stapes**), which articulate to form a lever system that amplifies and transmits the vibratory motion of the eardrum to the fluids of the inner ear via the **oval window.** The ossicles are often referred to by their common names, that is, hammer, anvil, and stirrup, respectively.

Connecting the middle ear chamber with the nasopharynx is the **pharyngotympanic,** or **auditory, tube** (formerly known as the eustachian tube). Normally this tube is flattened and closed, but swallowing or yawning can cause it to open temporarily to equalize the pressure of the middle ear cavity

FIGURE 25.1 Anatomy of the ear.

External ear   Middle ear   Internal ear (labyrinth)

Auricle (pinna)

Helix

Lobule

External acoustic meatus

Tympanic membrane

Pharyngotympanic (auditory) tube

Malleus (hammer)

Incus (anvil)

Stapes (stirrup)

Auditory ossicles

**Semicircular ducts in
semicircular canals**
Anterior
Posterior
Lateral

Cristae ampullares
in the membranous
ampullae

Utricle in vestibule

Saccule in vestibule

Stapes in
oval window

*Temporal
bone*

Facial nerve
Vestibular nerve
Superior vestibular ganglion
Inferior vestibular ganglion
Cochlear nerve
Maculae
Spiral organ (of Corti)
Cochlear duct in cochlea

Round window

FIGURE 25.2 Internal ear. Right membranous labyrinth (blue) shown within the bony labyrinth (tan). The locations of sensory organs for hearing and equilibrium are shown in purple.

with external air pressure. This is an important function. The eardrum does not vibrate properly unless the pressure on both of its surfaces is the same.

Because the mucosal membranes of the middle ear cavity and nasopharynx are continuous through the pharyngotympanic tube, **otitis media,** or inflammation of the middle ear, is a fairly common condition, especially among youngsters prone to sore throats. In cases where large amounts of fluid or pus accumulate in the middle ear cavity, an emergency myringotomy (lancing of the eardrum) may be necessary to relieve the pressure. Frequently, tiny ventilating tubes are put in during the procedure. ■

The **internal,** or **inner, ear** consists of a system of bony and rather tortuous chambers called the **osseous,** or **bony, labyrinth,** which is filled with an aqueous fluid called **perilymph** (Figure 25.2). Suspended in the perilymph is the **membranous labyrinth,** a system that mostly follows the contours of the osseous labyrinth. The membranous labyrinth is filled with a more viscous fluid called **endolymph.** The three subdivisions of the bony labyrinth are the cochlea, the vestibule, and the semicircular canals, with the vestibule situated between the cochlea and semicircular canals. The **vestibule** and the **semicircular canals** are involved with equilibrium.

The snail-like **cochlea** (see Figures 25.2 and 25.3) contains the sensory receptors for hearing. The cochlear membranous labyrinth, the **cochlear duct,** is a soft wormlike tube about 3.8 cm long. It winds through the full two and three-quarter turns of the cochlea and separates the perilymph—containing cochlear cavity into upper and lower chambers, the **scala vestibuli** and **scala tympani** (the vestibular and tympanic ducts), respectively. The scala vestibuli terminates at the oval window, which "seats" the foot plate of the stirrup located laterally in the tympanic cavity. The scala tympani is bounded by a membranous area called the **round window.** The cochlear duct, itself filled with endolymph, supports the **spiral organ (of**

Corti), which contains the receptors for hearing—the sensory hair cells and nerve endings of the **cochlear nerve,** a division of the vestibulocochlear nerve (VIII).

ACTIVITY 2

Examining the Ear
with an Otoscope (Optional)

1. Obtain an otoscope and two alcohol swabs. Inspect your partner's external ear canal and then select the largest—*diameter* (not length!) speculum that will fit comfortably into his or her ear to permit full visibility. Clean the speculum thoroughly with an alcohol swab, and then attach the speculum to the battery-containing otoscope handle. Before beginning, check that the otoscope light beam is strong. (If not, obtain another otoscope or new batteries.) Some otoscopes come with disposable tips. Be sure to use a new tip for each ear examined. Dispose of these tips in an autoclave bag after use.

2. When you are ready to begin the examination, hold the lighted otoscope securely between your thumb and forefinger (like a pencil), and rest the little finger of the otoscope-holding hand against your partner's head. This maneuver forms a brace that allows the speculum to move as your partner moves and prevents the speculum from penetrating too deeply into the ear canal during unexpected movements.

3. Grasp the ear pinna firmly and pull it up, back, and slightly laterally. If your partner experiences pain or discomfort when the pinna is manipulated, an inflammation or infection of the external ear may be present. If this occurs, do not attempt to examine the ear canal.

4. Carefully insert the speculum of the otoscope into the external auditory canal in a downward and forward direction only far enough to permit examination of the tympanic membrane, or

(a)

(b)

FIGURE 25.3 Anatomy of the cochlea. (a) Magnified cross-sectional view of one turn of the cochlea, showing the relationship of the three scalae. The scalae vestibuli and tympani contain perilymph; the cochlear duct (scala media) contains endolymph. **(b)** Detailed structure of the spiral organ (of Corti).

eardrum. Note its shape, color, and vascular network. The healthy tympanic membrane is pearly white. During the examination, notice if there is any discharge or redness in the canal and identify earwax.

5.   After the examination, thoroughly clean the speculum with the second alcohol swab before returning the otoscope to the supply area. ▮

Microscopic Anatomy of the Spiral Organ of Corti and the Mechanism of Hearing

The anatomical details of the spiral organ (of Corti) are shown in Figure 25.3. The hair (auditory receptor) cells rest on the **basilar membrane,** which forms the floor of the cochlear duct, and their "hairs" (stereocilia) project into a gelatinous membrane, the **tectorial membrane,** that overlies them. The roof of the cochlear duct is called the **vestibular membrane.** The endolymph-filled chamber of the cochlear duct is the **scala media.**

ACTIVITY 3

Examining the Microscopic Structure of the Cochlea

Obtain a compound microscope and a prepared microscope slide of the cochlea and identify the areas shown in Figure 25.4. ▮

The mechanism of hearing begins as sound waves pass through the external auditory canal and through the middle ear into the internal ear, where the vibration eventually reaches the spiral organ (of Corti), which contains the receptors for hearing.

The popular "traveling wave" hypothesis of von Békésy suggests that vibration of the stirrup at the oval window initiates

FIGURE 25.4 Histological image of the spiral organ (of Corti) (80×).

traveling waves that cause maximal displacements of the basilar membrane where they peak and stimulate the hair cells of the spiral organ in that region. Since the area at which the traveling waves peak is a high-pressure area, the vestibular membrane is compressed at this point and, in turn, compresses the endolymph and the basilar membrane of the cochlear duct. The resulting pressure on the perilymph in the scala tympani causes the membrane of the round window to bulge outward into the middle ear chamber, thus acting as a relief valve for the compressional wave. Georg von Békésy found that high-frequency waves (high-pitched sounds) peaked close to the oval window and that low-frequency waves (low-pitched sounds) peaked farther up the basilar membrane near the apex of the cochlea. The mechanism of sound reception by the spiral organ (of Corti) is complex. We do know that hair cells on the basilar membrane are

(a)

Relative lengths of basilar fibers within different regions of basilar membrane

Base			Apex
Hz 20,000 (High notes)	Hz 2000	Hz 200	Hz 20 (Low notes)

(b)

Basilar membrane — 500 Hz

— 4000 Hz

— 20,000 Hz

(c)

FIGURE 25.5 Resonance of the basilar membrane. The cochlea is depicted as if it has been uncoiled. **(a)** Fluid movement in the cochlea following the stirrup thrust at the oval window. Compressional wave thus created causes the round window to bulge into the middle ear. Pressure waves set up vibrations in the basilar membrane. **(b)** Fibers span the basilar membrane. The length of the fibers "tunes" specific regions to vibrate at specific frequencies. **(c)** Different frequencies of pressure waves in the cochlea stimulate particular hair cells and neurons.

uniquely stimulated by sounds of various frequencies and amplitude and once stimulated they depolarize and begin the chain of nervous impulses via the cochlear nerve to the auditory centers of the temporal lobe cortex. This series of events results in the phenomenon we call hearing (Figure 25.5).

By the time most people are in their sixties, a gradual deterioration and atrophy of the spiral organ of Corti begins and leads to a loss in the ability to hear high tones and speech sounds. This condition, **presbycusis,** is a type of sensorineural deafness. Because many elderly people refuse to accept their hearing loss and resist using hearing aids, they begin to rely more and more on their vision for clues as to what is going on around them and may be accused of ignoring people.

Although presbycusis is considered to be a disability of old age, it is becoming much more common in younger people as our world grows noisier. The damage (breakage of the "hairs" of the hair cells) caused by excessively loud sounds is progressive and cumulative. Each assault causes a bit more damage. Music played and listened to at deafening levels definitely contributes to the deterioration of hearing receptors. ■

ACTIVITY 4

Conducting Laboratory Tests of Hearing

Perform the following hearing tests in a quiet area. Test both the right and left ears.

Acuity Test

Have your lab partner pack one ear with cotton and sit quietly with eyes closed. Obtain a ticking clock or pocket watch and hold it very close to his or her *unpacked* ear. Then slowly move it away from the ear until your partner signals that the ticking is no longer audible. Record the distance in centimeters at which ticking is inaudible and then remove the cotton from the packed ear.

Right ear: _____ Left ear: _____

Is the threshold of audibility sharp or indefinite?

_____

Sound Localization

Ask your partner to close both eyes. Hold the pocket watch at an audible distance (about 15 cm) from his or her ear, and move it to various locations (front, back, sides, and above his or her head). Have your partner locate the position by pointing in each instance. Can the sound be localized equally well at all positions?

_____

If not, at what position(s) was the sound less easily located?

_____

_____

The ability to localize the source of a sound depends on two factors—the difference in the loudness of the sound reaching each ear and the time of arrival of the sound at each ear. How does this information help to explain your findings?

_____

_____

(a)

(b)

(c)

FIGURE 25.6 The Weber and Rinne tuning fork tests. (a) The Weber test to evaluate whether the sound remains centralized (normal) or lateralizes to one side or the other (indicative of some degree of conduction or sensorineural deafness). **(b and c)** The Rinne test to compare bone conduction and air conduction.

Frequency Range of Hearing

Obtain three tuning forks: one with a low frequency (75 to 100 Hz [cps]), one with a frequency of approximately 1000 Hz, and one with a frequency of 4000 to 5000 Hz. Strike the lowest-frequency fork on the heel of your hand or with a rubber mallet, and hold it close to your partner's ear. Repeat with the other two forks.

Which fork was heard most clearly and comfortably?

_____ Hz

Which was heard least well? _____ Hz

Weber Test to Determine Conduction and Sensorineural Deafness

Strike a tuning fork and place the handle of the tuning fork medially on your partner's head (see Figure 25.6a). Is the tone equally loud in both ears, or is it louder in one ear?

_____

If it is equally loud in both ears, you have equal hearing or equal loss of hearing in both ears. If sensorineural deafness is present in one ear, the tone will be heard in the unaffected ear but not in the ear with sensorineural deafness. If conduction deafness is present, the sound will be heard more strongly in the ear in which there is a hearing loss due to sound conduction by the bone of the skull. Conduction deafness can be simulated by plugging one ear with cotton to interfere with the conduction of sound to the inner ear.

Rinne Test for Comparing Bone- and Air-Conduction Hearing

1. Strike the tuning fork, and place its handle on your partner's mastoid process (Figure 25.6b).

2. When your partner indicates that the sound is no longer audible, hold the still-vibrating prongs close to his auditory canal (Figure 25.6c). If your partner hears the fork again (by air conduction) when it is moved to that position, hearing is not impaired and the test result is to be recorded as positive (+). (Record below step 5.)

3. Repeat the test on the same ear, but this time test air-conduction hearing first.

4. After the tone is no longer heard by air conduction, hold the handle of the tuning fork on the bony mastoid process. If the subject hears the tone again by bone conduction after hearing by air conduction is lost, there is some conduction deafness and the result is recorded as negative (−).

5. Repeat the sequence for the opposite ear.

Right ear: _____ Left ear: _____

Does the subject hear better by bone or by air conduction?

_____

Audiometry

When the simple tuning fork tests reveal a problem in hearing, audiometer testing is usually prescribed to determine the precise nature of the hearing deficit. An *audiometer* is an instrument (specifically, an electronic oscillator with earphones) used to determine hearing acuity by exposing each ear to sound stimuli of differing *frequencies* and *intensities*. The hearing range of human beings during youth is from 20 to 20,000 Hz, but hearing acuity declines with age, with reception for the high-frequency sounds lost first. Though this loss represents a major problem for some people, such as musicians, most of us tend to be fairly unconcerned until we begin to have problems hearing sounds in the range of 125 to 8000 Hz, the normal frequency range of speech.

The basic procedure of audiometry is to initially deliver tones of different frequencies to one ear of the subject at an intensity of 0 decibels (dB). (Zero decibels is not the complete absence of sound, but rather the softest sound intensity that can be heard by a person of normal hearing at each frequency.) If the subject cannot hear a particular frequency stimulus of 0 dB, the hearing threshold level control is adjusted until the subject reports that he or she can hear the tone. The number of decibels of intensity required above 0 dB is recorded as the hearing loss. For example, if the subject cannot hear a particular frequency tone until it is delivered at 30 dB intensity, then he or she has a hearing loss of 30 dB for that frequency.

ACTIVITY 5
Audiometry Testing

1.   Obtain an audiometer and earphones, and a red and a blue pencil. Before beginning the tests, examine the audiometer to identify the two tone controls: one to regulate frequency and a second to regulate the intensity (loudness) of the sound stimulus. Identify the two output control switches that regulate the delivery of sound to one ear or the other (*red* to the right ear, *blue* to the left ear). Also find the *hearing threshold level control,* which is calibrated to deliver a basal tone of 0 dB to the subject's ears.

2.   Place the earphones on the subject's head so that the red cord or ear-cushion is over the right ear and the blue cord or ear-cushion is over the left ear. Instruct the subject to raise one hand when he or she hears a tone.

3.   Set the frequency control at 125 Hz and the intensity control at 0 dB. Press the red output switch to deliver a tone to the subject's right ear. If the subject does not respond, raise the

sound intensity slowly by rotating the hearing level control counterclockwise until the subject reports (by raising a hand) that a tone is heard. Repeat this procedure for frequencies of 250, 500, 1000, 2000, 4000, and 8000.

4.   Record the results in the grid above by marking a small red circle on the grid at each frequency-dB junction at which a tone was heard. Then connect the circles with a red line to produce a hearing acuity graph for the right ear.

5.   Repeat steps 3 and 4 for the left (blue) ear, and record the results with blue circles and connecting lines on the grid. ■

Microscopic Anatomy of the Equilibrium Apparatus and Mechanisms of Equilibrium

The equilibrium apparatus of the inner ear, the **vestibular apparatus,** is in the vestibule and semicircular canals of the bony labyrinth. Their chambers are filled with perilymph, in which membranous labyrinth structures are suspended. The vestibule contains the saclike **utricle** and **saccule,** and the semicircular chambers contain **membranous semicircular ducts.** Like the cochlear duct, these membranes are filled with endolymph and contain receptor cells that are activated by the bending of their cilia.

Semicircular Canals

The semicircular canals are centrally involved in the **mechanism of dynamic equilibrium.** They are 1.2 cm in circumference and are oriented in three planes—horizontal, frontal, and sagittal. At the base of each semicircular duct is an enlarged region, the **ampulla,** which communicates with the utricle of the vestibule. Within each ampulla is a receptor region called a **crista ampullaris,** which consists of a tuft of hair cells covered

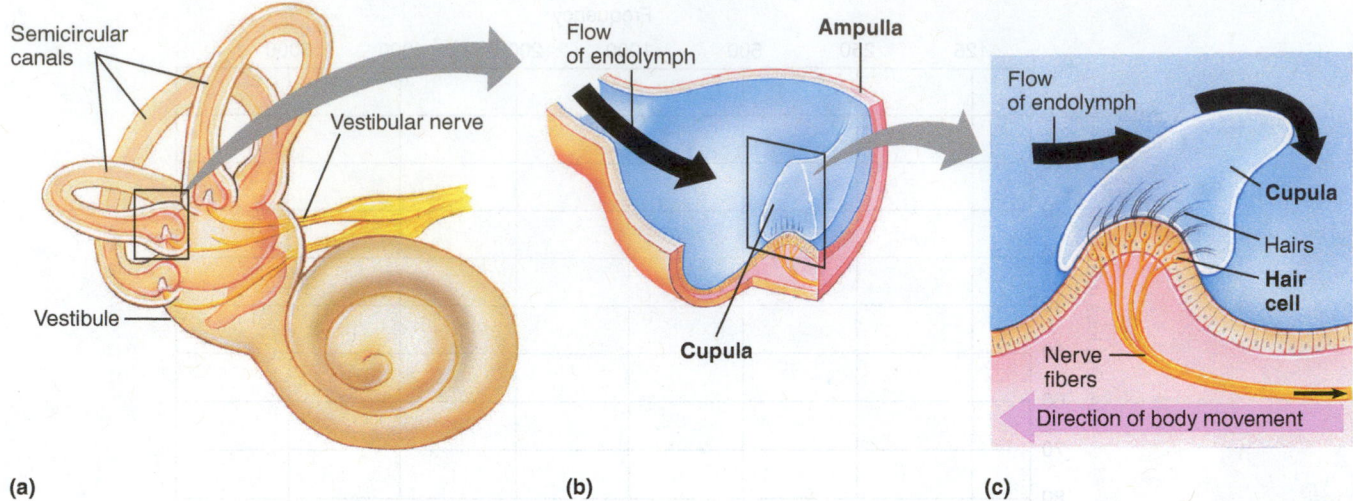

(a)   **(b)**   **(c)**

FIGURE 25.7 Structure and function of the crista ampullaris. (a) Arranged in the three spatial planes, the semicircular ducts in the semicircular canals each have a swelling called an ampulla at their base. **(b)** Each ampulla contains a crista ampullaris, a receptor that is essentially a cluster of hair cells with hairs projecting into a gelatinous cap called the cupula. **(c)** When the rate of rotation changes, inertia prevents the endolymph in the semicircular canals from moving with the head, so the fluid presses against the cupula, bending the hair cells in the opposite direction. The bending increases the frequency of action potentials in the sensory neurons in direct proportion to the amount of rotational acceleration. The mechanism adjusts quickly if rotation continues at a constant speed.

with a gelatinous cap, or **cupula** (Figure 25.7). When your head position changes in an angular direction, as when twirling on the dance floor or when taking a rough boat ride, the endolymph in the canal lags behind, pushing the cupula—like a swinging door—in a direction opposite to that of the angular motion (Figure 25.7c). This movement depolarizes the hair cells, resulting in enhanced impulse transmission up the vestibular division of the eighth cranial nerve to the brain. Likewise, when the angular motion stops suddenly, the inertia of the endolymph causes it to continue to move, pushing the cupula in the same direction as the previous body motion. This movement again initiates electrical changes in the hair cells (in this case, it hyperpolarizes them). (This phenomenon accounts for the reversed motion sensation you feel when you stop suddenly after twirling.) When you move at a constant rate of motion, the endolymph eventually comes to rest and the cupula gradually returns to its original position. The hair cells, no longer bent, send no new signals, and you lose the sensation of spinning. Thus the response of these dynamic equilibrium receptors is a reaction to *changes* in angular motion rather than to motion itself.

ACTIVITY 6

Examining the Microscopic Structure of the Crista Ampullaris

Go to the demonstration area and examine the slide of a crista ampullaris. Identify the areas depicted in Figure 25.8 and Figure 25.7b and c. ■

Maculae

Maculae in the vestibule contain the **hair cells,** receptors that are essential to the **mechanism of static equilibrium.** The maculae respond to gravitational pull, thus providing information on which way is up or down, and to linear or straightforward

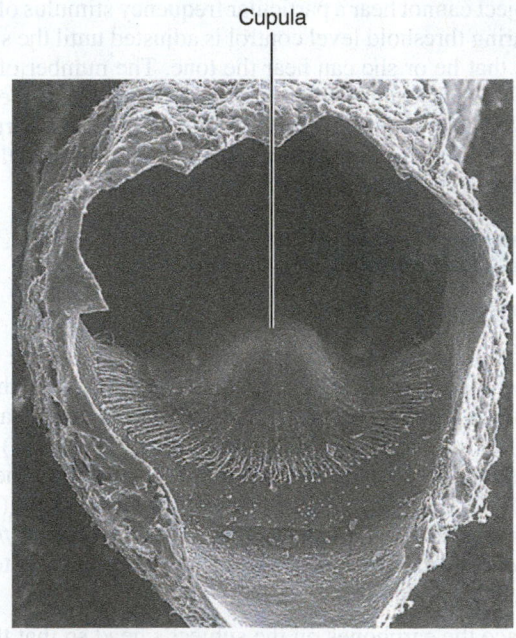

FIGURE 25.8 Scanning electron micrograph of a crista ampullaris (290×).

changes in speed. They are located on the walls of the saccule and utricle. The hair cells in each macula are embedded in the **otolithic membrane,** a gelatinous material containing small grains of calcium carbonate **(otoliths).** When the head moves, the otoliths move in response to variations in gravitational pull. As they deflect different hair cells, they trigger hyperpolarization or depolarization of the hair cells and modify the rate of impulse transmission along the vestibular nerve (Figure 25.9).

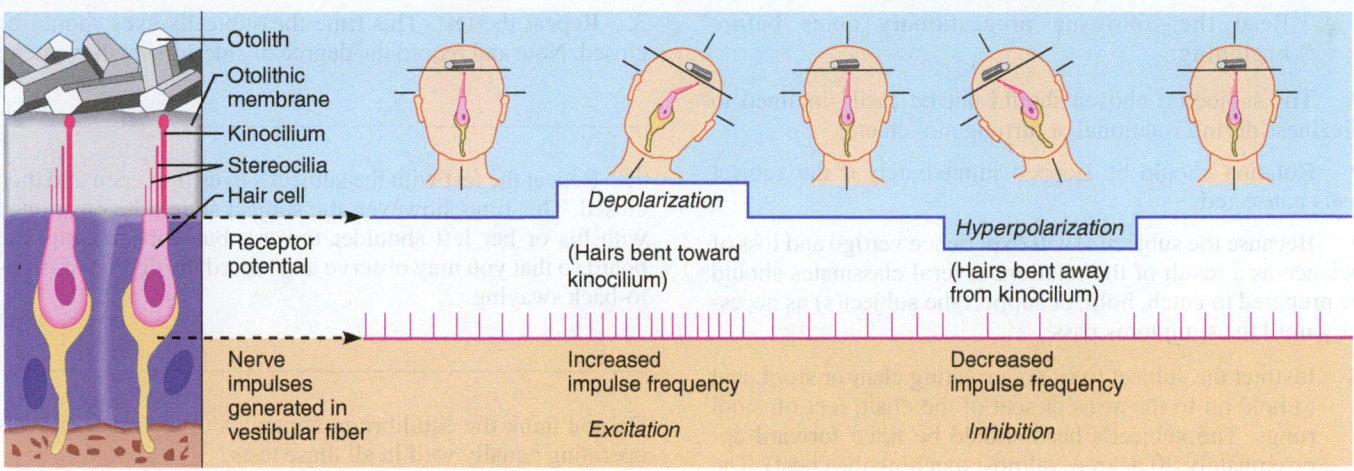

FIGURE 25.9 The effect of gravitational pull on a macula receptor in the utricle. When movement of the otolithic membrane bends the hair cells in the direction of the kinocilium, the vestibular fibers depolarize and generate action potentials more rapidly. When the hairs are bent in the direction away from the kinocilium, the hair cells become hyperpolarized, and the nerve fibers send impulses at a reduced rate (i.e., below the resting rate of discharge).

Although the receptors of the semicircular canals and the vestibule are responsible for dynamic and static equilibrium respectively, they rarely act independently. Complex interaction of many of the receptors is the rule. Processing is also complex and involves the brain stem and cerebellum as well as input from proprioceptors and the eyes.

ACTIVITY 7

Conducting Laboratory Tests on Equilibrium

The function of the semicircular canals and vestibule are not routinely tested in the laboratory, but the following simple tests illustrate normal equilibrium apparatus function as well as some of the complex processing interactions.

In the first balance test and the Barany test, you will look for **nystagmus,** which is the involuntary rolling of the eyes in any direction or the trailing of the eyes slowly in one direction, followed by their rapid movement in the opposite direction. It is normal during and after rotation; abnormal otherwise. The direction of nystagmus is that of its quick phase on acceleration.

Balance Tests

1. Have your partner walk a straight line, placing one foot directly in front of the other.

Is he or she able to walk without undue wobbling from side to

side? _____

Did he or she experience any dizziness? _____

The ability to walk with balance and without dizziness, unless subject to rotational forces, indicates normal function of the equilibrium apparatus.

Was nystagmus present? _____

2. Place three coins of different sizes on the floor. Ask your lab partner to pick up the coins, and carefully observe his or her muscle activity and coordination.

Did your lab partner have any difficulty locating and picking

up the coins? _____

Describe your observations and your lab partner's observations during the test.

_____

_____

_____

What kinds of interactions involving balance and coordination must occur for a person to move fluidly during this test?

_____

_____

_____

3. If a person has a depressed nervous system, mental concentration may result in a loss of balance. Ask your lab partner to stand up and count backward from ten as rapidly as possible.

Did your lab partner lose balance? _____

Barany Test (Induction of Nystagmus and Vertigo*)

This experiment evaluates the semicircular canals and should be conducted as a group effort to protect the test subject(s) from possible injury.

*Vertigo** is a sensation of dizziness and rotational movement when such movement is not occurring or has ceased.

Read the following precautionary notes before beginning:

- The subject(s) chosen should not be easily inclined to dizziness during rotational or turning movements.

- Rotation should be stopped immediately if the subject feels nauseated.

- Because the subject(s) will experience vertigo and loss of balance as a result of the rotation, several classmates should be prepared to catch, hold, or support the subject(s) as necessary until the symptoms pass.

1. Instruct the subject to sit on a rotating chair or stool, and to hold on to the arms or seat of the chair, feet on stool rungs. The subject's head should be tilted forward approximately 30 degrees (almost touching the chest). The horizontal (lateral) semicircular canal is stimulated when the head is in this position. The subject's eyes are to remain *open* during the test.

2. Four classmates should position themselves so that the subject is surrounded on all sides. The classmate posterior to the subject will rotate the chair.

3. Rotate the chair to the subject's right approximately 10 revolutions in 10 seconds, then suddenly stop the rotation.

4. Immediately note the direction of the subject's resultant nystagmus; and ask him or her to describe the feelings of movement, indicating speed and direction sensation. Record this information below.

_____

_____

_____

If the semicircular canals are operating normally, the subject will experience a sensation that the stool is still rotating immediately after it has stopped and *will* demonstrate nystagmus.

When the subject is rotated to the right, the cupula will be bent to the left, causing nystagmus during rotation in which the eyes initially move slowly to the left and then quickly to the right. Nystagmus will continue until the cupula has returned to its initial position. Then, when rotation is stopped abruptly, the cupula will be bent to the right, producing nystagmus with its slow phase to the right and its rapid phase to the left. In many subjects, this will be accompanied by a feeling of vertigo and a tendency to fall to the right.

Romberg Test

The Romberg test determines the integrity of the dorsal white column of the spinal cord, which transmits impulses to the brain from the proprioceptors involved with posture.

1. Have your partner stand with his or her back to the blackboard.

2. Draw one line parallel to each side of your partner's body. He or she should stand erect, with eyes open and staring straight ahead for 2 minutes while you observe any movements. Did you see any gross swaying movements?

_____

3. Repeat the test. This time the subject's eyes should be closed. Note and record the degree of side-to-side movement.

_____

4. Repeat the test with the subject's eyes first open and then closed. This time, however, the subject should be positioned with his or her left shoulder toward, but not touching, the board so that you may observe and record the degree of front-to-back swaying.

_____

Do you think the equilibrium apparatus of the inner ear was operating equally well in all these tests?

_____

The proprioceptors? _____

Why was the observed degree of swaying greater when the eyes were closed?

_____

_____

What conclusions can you draw regarding the factors necessary for maintaining body equilibrium and balance?

_____

_____

Role of Vision in Maintaining Equilibrium

To further demonstrate the role of vision in maintaining equilibrium, perform the following experiment. (Ask your lab partner to record observations and act as a "spotter.") Stand erect, with your eyes open. Raise your left foot approximately 30 cm off the floor, and hold it there for 1 minute.

Record the observations: _____

_____

_____

Rest for 1 or 2 minutes; and then repeat the experiment with the same foot raised but with your eyes closed. Record the observations:

_____

_____

Special Senses: Hearing and Equilibrium

Anatomy of the Ear

1. Select the terms from column B that apply to the column A descriptions. Some terms are used more than once.

Column A

_____, _____, _____, 1. structure composing the external ear

_____, _____, _____, 2. structures composing the internal ear

_____, _____, _____, 3. collectively called the ossicles

_____ 4. involved in equalizing the pressure in the middle ear with atmospheric pressure

_____ 5. vibrates at the same frequency as sound waves hitting it; transmits the vibrations to the ossicles

_____, _____ 6. contain receptors for the sense of balance

_____ 7. transmits the vibratory motion of the stirrup to the fluid in the scala vestibuli of the inner ear

_____ 8. acts as a pressure relief valve for the increased fluid pressure in the scala tympani; bulges into the tympanic cavity

_____ 9. passage between the throat and the tympanic cavity

_____ 10. fluid contained within the membranous labyrinth

_____ 11. fluid contained within the osseous labyrinth and bathing the membranous labyrinth

Column B

a. pharyngotympanic (auditory) tube

b. cochlea

c. endolymph

d. external auditory canal

e. incus (anvil)

f. malleus (hammer)

g. oval window

h. perilymph

i. pinna (auricle)

j. round window

k. semicircular canals

l. stapes (stirrup)

m. tympanic membrane

n. vestibule

2. Identify all indicated structures and ear regions in the following diagram.

3. Match the membranous labyrinth structures listed in column B with the descriptive statements in column A.

Column A

_____, _____ 1. sacs found within the vestibule

_____ 2. contains the spiral organ (of Corti)

_____, _____ 3. sites of the maculae

_____ 4. positioned in all spatial planes

_____ 5. hair cells of spiral organ (of Corti) rest on this membrane

_____ 6. gelatinous membrane overlying the hair cells of the spiral organ (of Corti)

_____ 7. contains the crista ampullaris

_____, _____, _____, _____ 8. function in static equilibrium

_____, _____, _____, _____ 9. function in dynamic equilibrium

_____ 10. carries auditory information to the brain

_____ 11. gelatinous cap overlying hair cells of the crista ampullaris

_____ 12. grains of calcium carbonate in the maculae

Column B

a. ampulla

b. basilar membrane

c. cochlear duct

d. cochlear nerve

e. cupula

f. otoliths

g. saccule

h. semicircular ducts

i. tectorial membrane

j. utricle

k. vestibular nerve

4. Sound waves hitting the tympanic membrane (eardrum) initiate its vibratory motion. Trace the pathway through which vibrations and fluid currents are transmitted to finally stimulate the hair cells in the spiral organ (of Corti). (Name the appropriate ear structures in their correct sequence.)

Tympanic membrane → _____

_____

_____

5. Describe how sounds of different frequency (pitch) are differentiated in the cochlea. _____

_____

_____

_____

6. Explain the role of the endolymph of the semicircular canals in activating the receptors during angular motion.

_____

_____

_____

7. Explain the role of the otoliths in perception of static equilibrium (head position). _____

_____

_____

_____

Laboratory Tests

8. Was the auditory acuity measurement made during the experiment on page 387 the same or different for both ears?

_____ What factors might account for a difference in the acuity of the two ears?

_____

_____

9. During the sound localization experiment on page 387, note the position(s) in which the sound was least easily located.

How can this phenomenon be explained? _____

_____

10. In the frequency experiment on page 388, note which tuning fork was the most difficult to hear. _____

What conclusion can you draw? _____

_____

11. When the tuning fork handle was pressed to your forehead during the Weber test, where did the sound seem to originate?

_____

Where did it seem to originate when one ear was plugged with cotton? _____

How do sound waves reach the cochlea when conduction deafness is present? _____

_____

12. Indicate whether the following conditions relate to conduction deafness (C) or sensorineural deafness (S).

_____ 1. can result from the fusion of the ossicles

_____ 2. can result from a lesion on the cochlear nerve

_____ 3. sound heard in one ear but not in the other during bone and air conduction

_____ 4. can result from otitis media

_____ 5. can result from impacted cerumen or a perforated eardrum

_____ 6. can result from a blood clot in the auditory cortex

13. The Rinne test evaluates an individual's ability to hear sounds conducted by air or bone. Which is more indicative of normal

hearing? _____

14. Define *nystagmus.* _____

_____

Define *vertigo.* _____

_____

15. The Barany test investigated the effect that rotatory acceleration had on the semicircular canals. Explain *why* the subject still

had the sensation of rotation immediately after being stopped. _____

_____

16. What is the usual reason for conducting the Romberg test? _____

_____

Was the degree of sway greater with the eyes open or closed? Why? _____

_____

17. Normal balance, or equilibrium, depends on input from a number of sensory receptors. Name them.

_____

18. What effect does alcohol consumption have on balance and equilibrium? Explain. _____

_____

Special Senses: Olfaction and Taste

MATERIALS

- ☐ Prepared slides: nasal olfactory epithelium (l.s.); the tongue showing taste buds (x.s.)
- ☐ Compound microscope
- ☐ Small mirror
- ☐ Paper towels
- ☐ Packets of granulated sugar
- ☐ Disposable autoclave bag
- ☐ Paper plates
- ☐ Equal-size food cubes of cheese, apple, raw potato, dried prunes, banana, raw carrot, and hard-cooked egg white (These prepared foods should be in an opaque container; a foil-lined egg carton would work well.)
- ☐ Toothpicks
- ☐ Disposable gloves
- ☐ Cotton-tipped swabs
- ☐ Paper cups
- ☐ Flask of distilled or tap water
- ☐ Prepared vials of oil of cloves, oil of peppermint, and oil of wintergreen or corresponding flavors found in the condiment section of a supermarket
- ☐ Chipped ice
- ☐ Five numbered vials containing common household substances with strong odors (herbs, spices, etc.)
- ☐ Nose clips
- ☐ Absorbent cotton

OBJECTIVES

1. To describe the location and cellular composition of the olfactory epithelium.
2. To describe the structure and function of the taste receptors.
3. To name the five basic qualities of taste sensation, and to list the chemical substances that elicit them.
4. To explain the interdependence between the senses of smell and taste.
5. To name two factors other than olfaction that influence taste appreciation of foods.
6. To define *olfactory adaptation*.

PRE-LAB QUIZ

1. Circle True or False. Receptors for olfaction and taste are classified as chemoreceptors because they respond to chemicals in solution.
2. The organ of smell is the _____, located in the roof of the nasal cavity.
   a. nares
   b. nostrils
   c. olfactory epithelium
   d. olfactory nerve
3. Circle the correct term. Olfactory receptor cells are bipolar / unipolar neurons whose olfactory cilia extend outward from the epithelium.
4. Most taste buds are located in _____, peglike projections of the tongue mucosa.
   a. cilia
   b. concha
   c. papillae
   d. supporting cells
5. Circle the correct term. Most taste buds are made of two / three types of modified epithelial cells.
6. There are five basic taste sensations. Name one. _____
7. Circle True or False. Texture, temperature, and smell have little or no effect on the sensation of taste.
8. You will use absorbent cotton and oil of wintergreen, peppermint, or cloves to test for olfactory
   a. accommodation
   b. adaptation
   c. identification
   d. recognition

The receptors for olfaction and taste are classified as **chemoreceptors** because they respond to chemicals in solution. Although five relatively specific types of taste receptors have been identified, the olfactory receptors are considered sensitive to a much wider range of chemical sensations. The sense of smell is the least understood of the special senses.

Location and Anatomy of the Olfactory Receptors

The **olfactory epithelium** (organ of smell) occupies an area of about 5 cm² in the roof of the nasal cavity (Figure 26.1a). Since the air entering the human nasal cavity must make a hairpin turn to enter the respiratory passages below, the nasal epithelium is in a rather poor position for performing its function. This is why sniffing, which brings more air into contact with the receptors, intensifies the sense of smell.

The specialized receptor cells in the olfactory epithelium are surrounded by **supporting cells,** non-sensory epithelial cells. The **olfactory receptor cells** are bipolar neurons whose **olfactory cilia** extend outward from the epithelium. Axonal nerve filaments emerging from their basal ends penetrate the cribriform plate of the ethmoid bone and proceed as the *olfactory nerves* to synapse in the olfactory bulbs lying on either side of the crista galli of the ethmoid bone. Impulses from neurons of the olfactory bulbs are then conveyed to the olfactory portion of the cortex (uncus) without synapsing in the thalamus.

(a)

(b)

FIGURE 26.1 Location and cellular composition of olfactory epithelium. (a) Diagrammatic representation of olfactory epithelium. Enlarged view shows the course of the olfactory nerve filaments. **(b)** Histological image of the olfactory epithelium (220×).

Microscopic Examination of the Olfactory Epithelium

Obtain a longitudinal section of olfactory epithelium. Examine it closely using a compound microscope, comparing it to Figure 26.1b. ▇

Location and Anatomy of Taste Buds

The **taste buds,** specific receptors for the sense of taste, are widely but not uniformly distributed in the oral cavity. Most are located in **papillae,** peglike projections of the mucosa, on the dorsal surface of the tongue (as described next). A few are found on the soft palate, epiglottis, pharynx, and inner surface of the cheeks.

Taste buds are located primarily on the sides of the large round **circumvallate papillae** (arranged in a V formation on the posterior surface of the tongue); in the side walls of the **foliate papillae;** and on the tops of the more numerous, mushroom-shaped **fungiform papillae.** (See Figure 26.2.)

• Use a mirror to examine your tongue. Which of the various papillae types can you pick out? _____

_____

Each taste bud consists largely of a globular arrangement of two types of modified epithelial cells: the **gustatory,** or **taste cells,** which are the actual receptor cells, and basal cells. Several nerve fibers enter each taste bud and supply sensory nerve endings to each of the taste cells. The long microvilli of the receptor cells penetrate the epithelial surface through an opening called the **taste pore.** When these microvilli, called **gustatory hairs,** contact specific chemicals in the solution, the taste cells depolarize. The afferent fibers from the taste buds to the sensory cortex in the postcentral gyrus of the brain are carried in three cranial nerves: the *facial nerve (VII)* serves the anterior two-thirds of the tongue; the *glossopharyngeal nerve (IX)* serves the posterior third of the tongue; and the *vagus nerve (X)* carries a few fibers from the pharyngeal region.

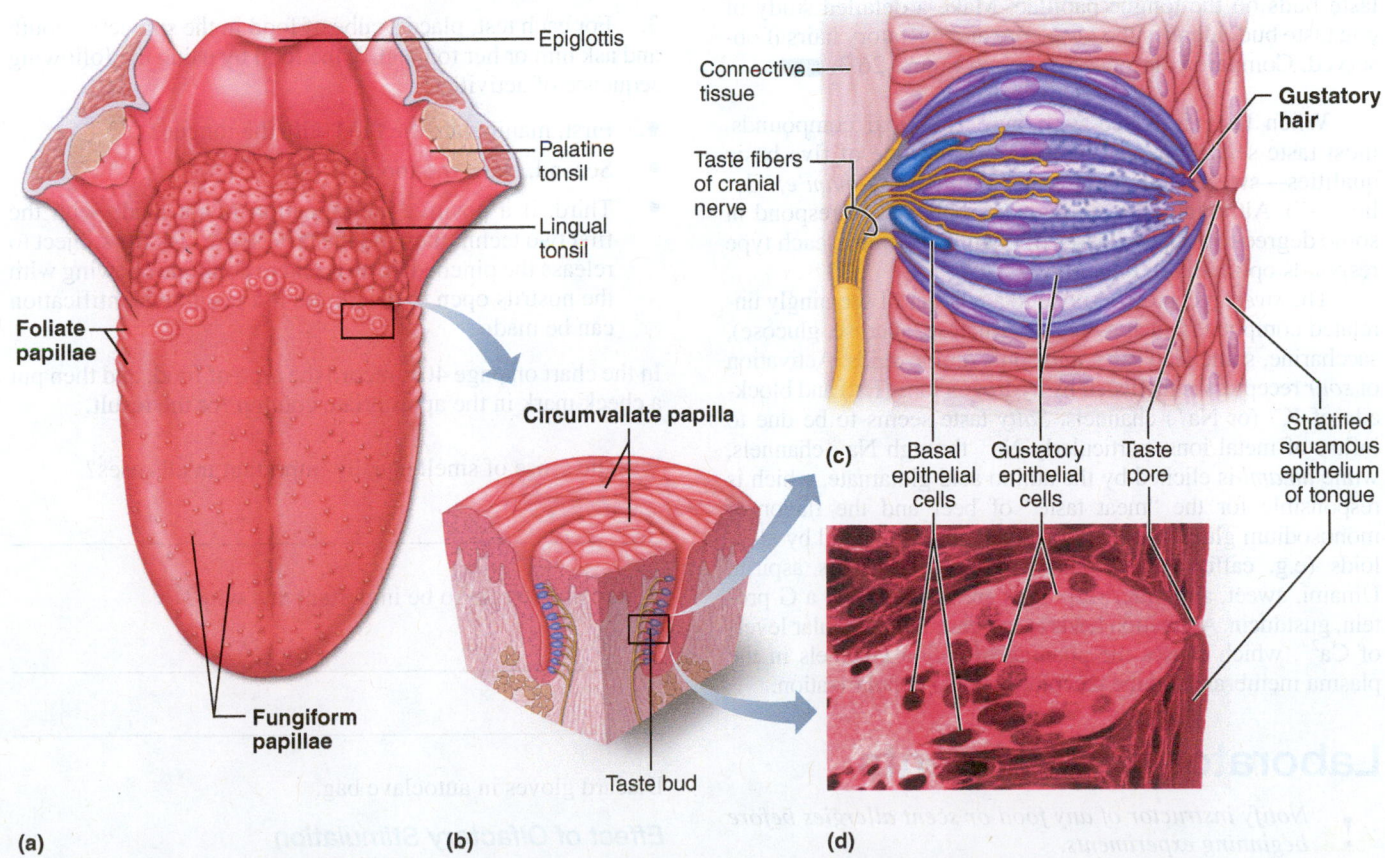

FIGURE 26.2 Location and structure of taste buds. (a) Taste buds on the tongue are associated with papillae, projections of the tongue mucosa. **(b)** A sectioned circumvallate papilla shows the position of the taste buds in its lateral walls. **(c)** An enlarged view of a taste bud. **(d)** Photomicrograph of a taste bud (210×).

FIGURE 26.3 Taste buds on the lateral aspects of foliate papillae of the tongue (100×).

Microscopic Examination of Taste Buds

Obtain a microscope and a prepared slide of a tongue cross section. Use Figure 26.2b as a guide to aid you in locating the taste buds on the tongue papillae. Make a detailed study of one taste bud. Identify the taste pore and gustatory hairs if observed. Compare your observations to Figure 26.3. ▇

When taste is tested with pure chemical compounds, most taste sensations can be grouped into one of five basic qualities—sweet, sour, bitter, salty, or umami (*u-mam'e*; "delicious"). Although all taste buds are believed to respond in some degree to all five classes of chemical stimuli, each type responds optimally to only one.

The *sweet* receptors respond to a number of seemingly unrelated compounds such as sugars (fructose, sucrose, glucose), saccharine, some lead salts, and some amino acids. Activation of *sour* receptors is mediated by hydrogen ions (H^+) and blockade of K^+ (or Na^+) channels. *Salty* taste seems to be due to influx of metal ions, particularly Na^+ through Na^+ channels, while *umami* is elicited by the amino acid glutamate, which is responsible for the "meat taste" of beef and the flavor of monosodium glutamate (MSG). *Bitter* taste is elicited by alkaloids (e.g. caffeine) and other substances such as aspirin. Umami, sweet, and bitter responses are mediated by a G protein, gustducin. Activation leads to increased intracellular levels of Ca^{2+}, which causes the opening of cation channels in the plasma membrane of the receptor cell and depolarization.

Laboratory Experiments

 Notify instructor of any food or scent allergies before beginning experiments.

Stimulating Taste Buds

1.   Obtain several paper towels, a sugar packet, and a disposable autoclave bag and bring them to your bench.

2.   With a paper towel, dry the dorsal surface of your tongue.

⚠ Immediately dispose of the paper towel in the autoclave bag.

3.   Tear off a corner of the sugar packet and shake a few sugar crystals on your dried tongue. Do *not* close your mouth.

Time how long it takes to taste the sugar. _____ sec

Why couldn't you taste the sugar immediately?

_____

Examining the Combined Effects of Smell, Texture, and Temperature on Taste

Effects of Smell and Texture

1.   Ask the subject to sit with eyes closed and to pinch his or her nostrils shut.

2.   Using a paper plate, obtain samples of the food items provided by your laboratory instructor. At no time should the subject be allowed to see the foods being tested. Wear plastic gloves and use toothpicks to handle food.

3.   For each test, place a cube of food in the subject's mouth and ask him or her to identify the food by using the following sequence of activities:

• First, manipulate the food with the tongue.

• Second, chew the food.

• Third, if a positive identification is not made with the first two techniques and the taste sense, ask the subject to release the pinched nostrils and to continue chewing with the nostrils open to determine if a positive identification can be made.

In the chart on page 401, record the type of food, and then put a check mark in the appropriate column for the result.

Was the sense of smell equally important in all cases?

_____

Where did it seem to be important and why?

_____

_____

Discard gloves in autoclave bag.

Effect of Olfactory Stimulation

There is no question that what is commonly referred to as taste depends heavily on stimulation of the olfactory receptors, particularly in the case of strongly odoriferous substances. The following experiment should illustrate this fact.

1.   Obtain vials of oil of wintergreen, peppermint, and cloves, paper cup, flask of water, paper towels, and some

Identification by Texture and Smell				
Food tested	Texture only	Chewing with nostrils pinched	Chewing with nostrils open	Identification not made

fresh cotton-tipped swabs. Ask the subject to sit so that he or she cannot see which vial is being used, and to dry the tongue and close the nostrils.

2.   Use a cotton swab to apply a drop of one of the oils to the subject's tongue. Can he or she distinguish the flavor?

_____

   Put the used swab in the autoclave bag. *Do not redip the swab into the oil.*

3.   Have the subject open the nostrils, and record the change in sensation he or she reports.

_____

4.   Have the subject rinse the mouth well and dry the tongue.

5.   Prepare two swabs, each with one of the two remaining oils.

6.   Hold one swab under the subject's open nostrils, while touching the second swab to the tongue.

Record the reported sensations. _____

_____

_____

   7.   Dispose of the used swabs and paper towels in the autoclave bag before continuing.

Which sense, taste or smell, appears to be more important in the proper identification of a strongly flavored volatile substance?

_____

Effect of Temperature

In addition to the effect that olfaction and food texture play in determining our taste sensations, the temperature of foods also helps determine if the food is appreciated or even tasted. To illustrate this, have your partner hold some chipped ice on the tongue for approximately a minute and then close his or her eyes. Immediately place any of the foods previously identified in his or her mouth and ask for an identification.

Results? _____

_____

_____ ▬

Identification by Mouth and Nasal Inhalation			
Vial number	Identification with nose clips	Identification without nose clips	Other observations
1			
2			
3			
4			
5			

ACTIVITY 5

Assessing the Importance of Taste and Olfaction in Odor Identification

1. Go to the designated testing area. Close your nostrils with a nose clip, and breathe through your mouth. Breathing through your mouth only, attempt to identify the odors of common substances in the numbered vials at the testing area. Do not look at the substance in the container. Record your responses on the chart above.

2. Remove the nose clips, and repeat the tests using your nose to sniff the odors. Record your responses on the chart above.

3. Record any other observations you make as you conduct the tests.

4. Which method gave the best identification results?

_____

What can you conclude about the effectiveness of the senses of taste and olfaction in identifying odors?

_____

ACTIVITY 6

Demonstrating Olfactory Adaptation

Obtain some absorbent cotton and two of the following oils (oil of wintergreen, peppermint, or cloves). Place several drops of oil on the absorbent cotton. Press one nostril shut. Hold the cotton under the open nostril and exhale through the mouth. Record the time required for the odor to disappear (for olfactory adaptation to occur).

_____ sec

Repeat the procedure with the other nostril.

_____ sec

Immediately test another oil with the nostril that has just experienced olfactory adaptation. What are the results?

_____

What conclusions can you draw? _____

_____

NAME _____

LAB TIME/DATE _____

Special Senses: Olfaction and Taste

Location and Anatomy of the Olfactory Receptors

1. Describe the location and cellular composition of the olfactory epithelium. _____

   _____

   _____

2. How and why does sniffing improve your sense of smell? _____

   _____

Location and Anatomy of Taste Buds

3. Name five sites where receptors for taste are found, and circle the predominant site.

   _____, _____, _____,

   _____, and _____

4. Describe the cellular makeup and arrangement of a taste bud. (Use a diagram, if helpful.) _____

   _____

Laboratory Experiments

5. Taste and smell receptors are both classified as _____, because they both

   respond to _____

6. Why is it impossible to taste substances with a dry tongue? _____

   _____

7. The basic taste sensations are mediated by specific chemical substances or groups. Name them for the following taste modalities.

   salt: _____   sour: _____   umami: _____

   bitter: _____   sweet: _____

8. Name three factors that influence our appreciation of foods. Substantiate each choice with an example from the laboratory experience.

1. _____ Substantiation: _____

_____

2. _____ Substantiation: _____

_____

3. _____ Substantiation: _____

_____

Which of the factors chosen is most important? _____ Substantiate your choice with an example from

everyday life. _____

_____

Expand on your explanation and choices by explaining why a cold, greasy hamburger is unappetizing to most people.

_____

_____

9. How palatable is food when you have a cold? _____ Explain your answer. _____

_____

10. In your opinion, is olfactory adaptation desirable? _____ Explain your answer.

_____

27

Functional Anatomy of the Endocrine Glands

MATERIALS

- ☐ Human torso model
- ☐ Anatomical chart of the human endocrine system
- ☐ Compound microscope
- ☐ Prepared slides of the anterior pituitary,* posterior pituitary, thyroid gland, parathyroid glands, adrenal gland, and pancreas*

For instructions on animal dissections, see the dissection exercises starting on page 697 in the cat, fetal pig, and rat editions of this manual.

*With differential staining if possible

OBJECTIVES

1. To identify and name the major endocrine glands and tissues of the body when provided with an appropriate diagram.
2. To list the hormones produced by the endocrine glands and discuss the general function of each.
3. To indicate the means by which hormones contribute to body homeostasis by giving appropriate examples of hormonal actions.
4. To cite mechanisms by which the endocrine glands are stimulated to release their hormones.
5. To describe the structural and functional relationship between the hypothalamus and the pituitary.
6. To describe a major pathological consequence of hypersecretion and hyposecretion of several of the hormones considered.
7. To correctly identify the histologic structure of the thyroid, parathyroid, pancreas, anterior and posterior pituitary, adrenal cortex, and adrenal medulla by microscopic inspection or when presented with an appropriate photomicrograph or diagram.
8. To name and point out the specialized hormone-secreting cells in the above tissues as studied in the laboratory.

PRE-LAB QUIZ

1. Define *hormone*. _____
2. Circle the correct term. An <u>endocrine</u> / <u>exocrine</u> gland is a ductless gland that empties its hormone into the extracellular fluid, from which it enters the blood.
3. The pituitary gland, also known as the _____, is located in the sella turcica of the sphenoid bone.
   a. hypophysis
   b. hypothalamus
   c. thalamus
4. Circle True or False. The anterior pituitary gland is also referred to as the master endocrine gland because it controls the activity of many other endocrine glands.
5. The _____ gland composed of two lobes, is located in the throat, just inferior to the larynx.
   a. pancreas   c. thymus
   b. posterior pituitary d. thyroid
6. The pancreas produces two hormones that are responsible for regulating blood sugar levels. Name the hormone that increases blood glucose levels. _____
7. Circle True or False. The gonads are considered to be both endocrine and exocrine glands.

Text continues on next page.

myA&P For practice quizzes on this lab, go to www.myaandp.com.

PAL For access to anatomical models and more, check out Practice Anatomy Lab.

8. This gland is rather large in an infant, but begins to atrophy at puberty and is relatively inconspicuous by old age. It produces hormones that direct the maturation of T cells. It is the _____ gland.
   a. pineal
   b. testes
   c. thymus
   d. thyroid

9. Circle the correct term. Islets of <u>Pancreatic islets / Acinar cells</u> form the endocrine portion of the pancreas.

10. The outer cortex of the adrenal gland is divided into three zones (zonas). Which one produces aldosterone?
    a. zona fasciculata
    b. zona glomerulosa
    c. zona reticularis

The **endocrine system** is the second major control system of the body. Acting with the nervous system, it helps coordinate and integrate the activity of the body's cells. However, the nervous system employs electrochemical impulses to bring about rapid control, whereas the more slowly acting endocrine system employs chemical "messengers," or **hormones,** which are released into the blood to be transported throughout the body.

The term *hormone* comes from a Greek word meaning "to arouse." The body's hormones, which are steroids or amino acid–based molecules, arouse the body's tissues and cells by stimulating changes in their metabolic activity. These changes lead to growth and development and to the physiological homeostasis of many body systems. Although all hormones are bloodborne, a given hormone affects only the biochemical activity of a specific organ or organs. Organs that respond to a particular hormone are referred to as the **target organs** of that hormone. The ability of the target tissue to respond seems to depend on the ability of the hormone to bind with specific receptors (proteins) occurring on the cells' plasma membrane or within the cells.

Although the function of some hormone-producing glands (the anterior pituitary, thyroid, adrenals, parathyroids) is purely endocrine, the function of others (the pancreas and gonads) is mixed—both endocrine and exocrine. Both types of glands are derived from epithelium, but the endocrine, or ductless, glands release their product (always hormonal) directly into the extracellular fluid from which it enters blood or lymph. The exocrine glands release their products at the body's surface or upon an epithelial membrane via ducts. In addition, there are hormone-producing cells in the heart, the gastrointestinal tract, kidney, skin, adipose tissue, skeleton, and placenta, organs whose functions are primarily nonendocrine. Only the major endocrine organs, plus the pineal gland and the thymus, are considered here.

Gross Anatomy and Basic Function of the Endocrine Glands

Pituitary Gland (Hypophysis)

The *pituitary gland,* or *hypophysis,* is located in the hypophyseal fossa of the sella turcica of the sphenoid bone. It consists largely of two functional *lobes,* the **adenohypophysis,** or **anterior pituitary,** and the **neurohypophysis,** consisting mainly of the **posterior pituitary** (Figure 27.1). The pituitary gland is attached to the hypothalamus by a stalk called the **infundibulum.**

Anterior Pituitary Hormones

The anterior pituitary (lobe) secretes a number of hormones. Four of these are **tropic hormones.** A tropic hormone stimulates its target organ, which is also an endocrine gland, to secrete its hormones. Target organ hormones then exert their effects on other body organs and tissues. The anterior pituitary tropic hormones include:

- **Gonadotropins–follicle-stimulating hormone (FSH)** and **luteinizing hormone (LH)**—regulate gamete production and hormonal activity of the gonads (ovaries and testes). The precise roles of the gonadotropins are described in Exercise 43 along with other considerations of reproductive system physiology.

- **Adrenocorticotropic hormone (ACTH)** regulates the endocrine activity of the cortex portion of the adrenal gland.

- **Thyroid-stimulating hormone (TSH),** or **thyrotropin,** influences the growth and activity of the thyroid gland.

The two other important hormones produced by the anterior pituitary are not directly involved in the regulation of other endocrine glands of the body.

- **Growth hormone (GH)** is a general metabolic hormone that plays an important role in determining body size. It affects many tissues of the body; however, its major effects are exerted on the growth of muscle and the long bones of the body. Hyposecretion results in pituitary dwarfism in children. Hypersecretion causes gigantism in children and **acromegaly** (overgrowth of bones in hands, feet, and face) in adults. ■

- **Prolactin (PRL)** stimulates breast development and promotes and maintains lactation by the mammary glands after childbirth. It may stimulate testosterone production in males.

A less important secretory product of the anterior pituitary is pro-opiomelanocortin (POMC), a prohormone. POMC is split by enzymes into ACTH, enkephalin and beta endorphin (natural opiates), and melanocyte-stimulating hormone (MSH).

The anterior pituitary controls the activity of so many other endocrine glands that it has often been called the *master endocrine gland*. However, the anterior pituitary is controlled by neurosecretions, *releasing* or *inhibiting hormones,* produced by neurons of the ventral hypothalamus. These hypothalamic hormones are liberated into the **hypophyseal portal system** (Figure 27.1), and carried to cells of the anterior pituitary where they control release of anterior pituitary hormones.

Posterior Pituitary Hormones

The posterior pituitary (lobe) is not an endocrine gland in a strict sense because it

Hypothalamic neurons in the paraventricular nuclei

Neurons in the ventral hypothalamus

Hypothalamic neurons in the supraoptic nuclei

Superior hypophyseal artery

Infundibulum (connecting stalk)

Hypothalamic-hypophyseal tract

Hypophyseal portal system

Inferior hypophyseal artery

• Primary capillary plexus

Neurohypophysis (storage area for hypothalamic hormones)

• Hypophyseal portal veins

• Secondary capillary plexus

Posterior pituitary

Anterior pituitary

Secretory cells of adenohypophysis

TSH, FSH, LH, ACTH, GH, PRL

Oxytocin ADH

Venule

Venule

FIGURE 27.1 **Hypothalamus and pituitary gland.** Neural and vascular relationships between the hypothalamus and the anterior and posterior lobes of the pituitary are depicted.

does not synthesize the hormones it releases. Instead, it acts as a storage area for two hormones transported to it via the axons of neurons in the paraventricular and supraoptic nuclei of the hypothalamus. The hormones are released in response to nerve impulses from these neurons. The first of these hormones is **oxytocin,** which stimulates powerful uterine contractions during birth and coitus and also causes milk ejection in the lactating mother. The second, **antidiuretic hormone (ADH),** causes the distal and collecting tubules of the kidneys to reabsorb more water from the urinary filtrate, thereby reducing urine output and conserving body water.

Hyposecretion of ADH results in dehydration from excessive urine output, a condition called **diabetes insipidus.** Individuals with this condition experience an insatiable thirst. Hypersecretion results in edema, headache, and disorientation. ■

Pineal Gland

The *pineal gland* is a small cone-shaped gland located in the roof of the third ventricle of the brain. Its major endocrine product is **melatonin,** which exhibits a diurnal (daily) cycle. It peaks at night, making us drowsy, and is lowest around noon.

The endocrine role of the pineal body in humans is still controversial, but it is known to play a role in the biological rhythms (particularly mating and migratory behavior) of other animals. In humans, melatonin appears to exert some in-

hibitory effect on the reproductive system that prevents precocious sexual maturation.

Thyroid Gland

The *thyroid gland* is composed of two lobes joined by a central mass, or isthmus. It is located in the throat, just inferior to the larynx. It produces two major hormones, thyroid hormone and calcitonin.

Thyroid hormone (TH) is actually two physiologically active hormones known as T_4 **(thyroxine)** and T_3 **(triiodothyronine).** Because its primary function is to control the rate of body metabolism and cellular oxidation, TH affects virtually every cell in the body.

Hyposecretion of thyroxine leads to a condition of mental and physical sluggishness, which is called **myxedema** in the adult. Hypersecretion causes elevated metabolic rate, nervousness, weight loss, sweating, and irregular heartbeat. ■

Calcitonin decreases blood calcium levels by stimulating calcium salt deposit in the bones. Although it acts antagonistically to parathyroid hormone, the hormonal product of the parathyroid glands, calcitonin is not involved in day-to-day control of calcium homeostasis.

Parathyroid Glands

The *parathyroid glands* are found embedded in the posterior surface of the thyroid gland. Typically, there are two

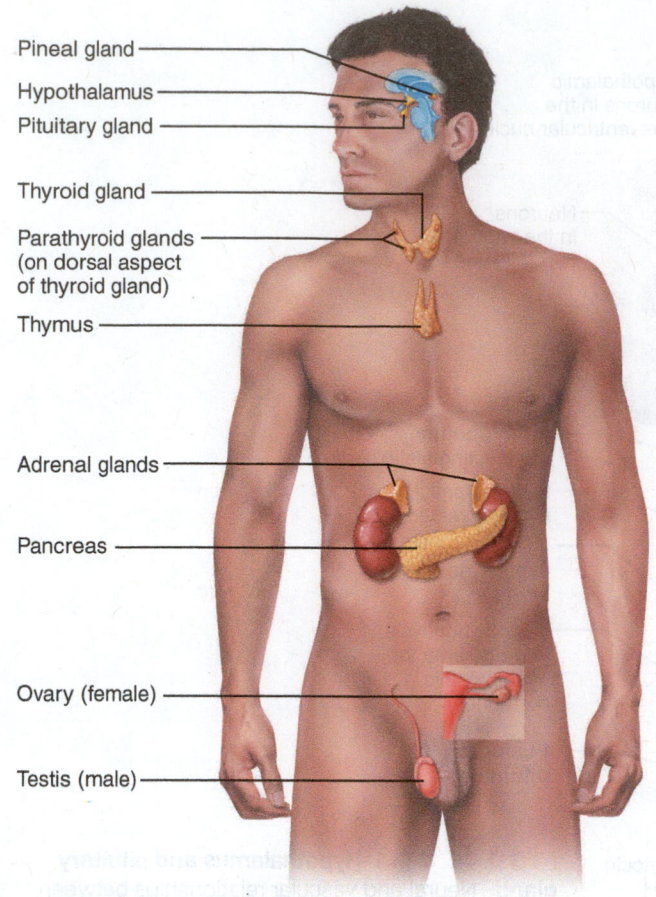

Pineal gland

Hypothalamus

Pituitary gland

Thyroid gland

Parathyroid glands
(on dorsal aspect
of thyroid gland)

Thymus

Adrenal glands

Pancreas

Ovary (female)

Testis (male)

FIGURE 27.2 Human endocrine organs.

small oval glands on each lobe, but there may be more and some may be located in other regions of the neck. They secrete **parathyroid hormone (PTH),** the most important regulator of calcium balance of the blood. When blood calcium levels decrease below a certain critical level, the parathyroids release PTH, which causes release of calcium from bone matrix and prods the kidney to reabsorb more calcium and less phosphate from the filtrate. PTH also stimulates the kidneys to convert vitamin D to its active D_3 form, *calcitriol.*

Hyposecretion increases neural excitability and may lead to **tetany,** prolonged muscle spasms that can result in respiratory paralysis and death. Hypersecretion of PTH results in loss of calcium from bones, causing deformation, softening, and spontaneous fractures. ■

Thymus

The *thymus* is a bilobed gland situated in the superior thorax, posterior to the sternum and anterior to the heart and lungs. Conspicuous in the infant, it begins to atrophy at puberty, and by old age it is relatively inconspicuous. The thymus produces several different families of hormones including **thymulin, thymosins,** and **thymopoietins.** These hormones are thought to be involved in the development of T lymphocytes and the immune response. Their role is poorly understood; they appear to act mainly locally as paracrines.

Adrenal Glands

The two *adrenal,* or *suprarenal, glands* are located atop or close to the kidneys. Anatomically, the **adrenal medulla** develops from neural crest tissue, and it is directly controlled by the sympathetic nervous system. The medullary cells respond to this stimulation by releasing **epinephrine** (80%) or **norepinephrine** (20%), which act in conjunction with the sympathetic nervous system to elicit the fight-or-flight response to stressors.

The **adrenal cortex** produces three major groups of steroid hormones, collectively called **corticosteroids.** The **mineralocorticoids,** chiefly *aldosterone,* regulate water and electrolyte balance in the extracellular fluids, mainly by regulating sodium ion reabsorption by kidney tubules. The **glucocorticoids** (*cortisol* [*hydrocortisone*], *cortisone,* and *corticosterone*) enable the body to resist long-term stressors, primarily by increasing blood glucose levels. The **gonadocorticoids,** or **sex hormones,** produced by the adrenal cortex are chiefly *androgens* (male sex hormones), but some *estrogens* (female sex hormones) are formed.

The gonadocorticoids are produced throughout life in relatively insignificant amounts; however, hypersecretion of these hormones produces abnormal hairiness (**hirsutism**), and masculinization occurs. ■

Pancreas

The *pancreas,* located partially behind the stomach in the abdomen, functions as both an endocrine and exocrine gland. It produces digestive enzymes as well as insulin and glucagon, important hormones concerned with the regulation of blood sugar levels.

Elevated blood glucose levels stimulate release of **insulin,** which decreases blood sugar levels, primarily by accelerating the transport of glucose into the body cells, where it is oxidized for energy or converted to glycogen or fat for storage.

Hyposecretion of insulin or some deficiency in the insulin receptors leads to **diabetes mellitus,** which is characterized by the inability of body cells to utilize glucose and the subsequent loss of glucose in the urine. Alterations of protein and fat metabolism also occur secondary to derangements in carbohydrate metabolism. Hypersecretion causes low blood sugar, or **hypoglycemia.** Symptoms include anxiety, nervousness, tremors, and weakness. ■

Glucagon acts antagonistically to insulin. When blood glucose levels are low, it stimulates the liver, its primary target organ, to break down glycogen stores to glucose and subsequently to release the glucose to the blood.

The Gonads

The *female gonads,* or *ovaries,* are paired, almond-sized organs located in the pelvic cavity. In addition to producing the female sex cells (ova), the ovaries produce two steroid hormone groups, the estrogens and progesterone. The endocrine and exocrine functions of the ovaries do not begin until the onset of puberty. The **estrogens** are responsible for the development of the secondary sex characteristics of the female at puberty (primarily maturation of the reproductive organs and development of the breasts) and act with progesterone to bring about cyclic changes of the uterine lining that occur during the menstrual cycle. The estrogens also help prepare the mammary glands for lactation. During pregnancy progesterone maintains the uterine musculature in a quiescent state and helps to prepare the breast tissue for lactation.

The paired oval *testes* of the male are suspended in a pouchlike sac, the scrotum, outside the pelvic cavity. In addition to the male sex cells (sperm), the testes produce the male sex hormone, **testosterone.** Testosterone promotes the maturation of the reproductive system accessory structures, brings about the development of the male secondary sex characteristics, and is responsible for sexual drive, or libido. Both the endocrine and exocrine functions of the testes begin at puberty. For a more detailed discussion of the function and histology of the ovaries and testes, see Exercises 42 and 43.

ACTIVITY 1

Identifying the Endocrine Organs

Locate the endocrine organs on Figure 27.2. Also locate these organs on the anatomical charts or torso.

Microscopic Anatomy of Selected Endocrine Glands

ACTIVITY 2

Examining the Microscopic Structure of Endocrine Glands

Obtain a microscope and one of each slide on the materials list. We will study only organs in which it is possible to identify the endocrine-producing cells. Compare your observations with the histology images in Figure 27.3a–f.

Thyroid Gland

1. Scan the thyroid under low power, noting the **follicles,** spherical sacs containing a pink-stained material *(colloid).* Stored T_3 and T_4 are attached to the protein colloidal material stored in the follicles as **thyroglobulin** and are released gradually to the blood. Compare the tissue viewed to Figure 27.3a.

2. Observe the tissue under high power. Notice that the walls of the follicles are formed by simple cuboidal or squamous epithelial cells that synthesize the follicular products. The **parafollicular,** or **C, cells** you see between the follicles are responsible for calcitonin production.

When the thyroid gland is actively secreting, the follicles appear small, and the colloidal material has a ruffled border. When the thyroid is hypoactive or inactive, the follicles are large and plump, and the follicular epithelium appears to be squamouslike.

Parathyroid Glands

Observe the parathyroid tissue under low power to view its two major cell types, the chief cells and the oxyphil cells. Compare your observations to Figure 27.3b. The **chief cells,** which synthesize parathyroid hormone (PTH), are small and abundant, and arranged in thick branching cords. The function of the scattered, much larger **oxyphil cells** is unknown.

(a) Thyroid gland (330×)

(b) Parathyroid gland (330×)

(c) Pancreatic islet

FIGURE 27.3 Microscopic anatomy of selected endocrine organs.

Pancreas

1. Observe pancreas tissue under low power to identify the roughly circular **pancreatic islets (islets of Langerhans),** the endocrine portions of the pancreas. The islets are scattered

(d) Anterior pituitary (280×)

- Acidophils
- Chromophobe
- Basophil

(e) Posterior pituitary (465×)

- Pituicytes
- Nerve fibers

(f) Adrenal gland (110×)

- Zona glomerulosa
- Zona fasciculata
- Zona reticularis
- Medulla cells

FIGURE 27.3 (continued) Microscopic anatomy of selected endocrine organs.

amid the more numerous **acinar cells** and stain differently (usually lighter), which makes their identification possible. The deeper-staining acinar cells form the major portion of the pancreatic tissue. Acinar cells produce the exocrine secretion of hydrolytic enzymes that is released into the duodenum through the pancreatic duct. Alkaline fluid produced by duct cells accompanies the hydrolytic enzymes. See Figure 27.3c.

2. Focus on islet cells under high power. Notice that they are densely packed and have no definite arrangement. In contrast, the cuboidal acinar cells are arranged around secretory ducts. If special stains are used, it will be possible to distinguish the **alpha cells,** which tend to cluster at the periphery of the islets and produce glucagon, from the **beta cells,** which synthesize insulin. With these specific stains, the beta cells are larger and stain gray-blue, and the alpha cells are smaller and appear bright pink, as shown in Figure 27.3c.

Pituitary Gland

1. Observe the general structure of the pituitary gland under low power to differentiate between the glandular anterior pituitary and the neural posterior pituitary.

2. Using the high-power lens, focus on the nests of cells of the anterior pituitary. When differential stains are used it is possible to identify the specialized cell types that secrete the specific hormones. Using the photomicrograph in Figure 27.3d as a guide, locate the reddish brown–stained **acidophil cells,** which produce growth hormone and prolactin, and the **basophil cells,** whose deep-blue granules are responsible for the production of the tropic hormones (TSH, ACTH, FSH, and LH). **Chromophobes,** the third cellular population, do not take up the stain and appear rather dull and colorless. The role of the chromophobes is controversial, but they apparently are not directly involved in hormone production.

3. Switch your focus to the posterior pituitary where two hormones (oxytocin and antidiuretic hormone) synthesized by hypothalamic neurons are stored. Observe the axons of hypothalamic neurons that compose most of this portion of the pituitary. Also note the glial cells, or **pituicytes** (Figure 27.3e).

Adrenal Gland

1. Hold the slide of the adrenal gland up to the light to distinguish the outer cortex and inner medulla areas. Then scan the cortex under low power to distinguish the differences in cell appearance and arrangement in the three cortical areas. Refer to Figure 27.3f as you work. In the outermost **zona glomerulosa,** where most mineralocorticoid production occurs, the tightly packed cells are arranged in spherical clusters. The deeper intermediate **zona fasciculata** produces glucocorticoids. This is the thickest part of the cortex. Its cells are arranged in parallel cords. The innermost cortical zone, the **zona reticularis** produces sex hormones and some glucocorticoids. The cells here stain intensely and form a branching network.

2. Switch to higher power to view the large, lightly stained cells of the adrenal medulla, which produce epinephrine and norepinephrine. Notice their clumped arrangement. ■

Functional Anatomy of the Endocrine Glands

Gross Anatomy and Basic Function of the Endocrine Glands

1. Both the endocrine and nervous systems are major regulating systems of the body; however, the nervous system has been compared to an airmail delivery system and the endocrine system to the Pony Express. Briefly explain this comparison.

_____

_____

_____

2. Define *hormone.* _____

_____

3. Chemically, hormones belong chiefly to two molecular groups, the _____

and the _____.

4. Define *target organ.* _____

_____

5. If hormones travel in the bloodstream, why don't all tissues respond to all hormones? _____

_____

6. Identify the endocrine organ described by each of the following statements.

_____ 1. located in the throat; bilobed gland connected by an isthmus

_____ 2. found close to the kidney

_____ 3. a mixed gland, located close to the stomach and small intestine

_____ 4. paired glands suspended in the scrotum

_____ 5. ride "horseback" on the thyroid gland

_____ 6. found in the pelvic cavity of the female, concerned with ova and female hormone production

_____ 7. found in the upper thorax overlying the heart; large during youth

_____ 8. found in the roof of the third ventricle

7. The table below lists the functions of many of the hormones you have studied. From the keys below, fill in the hormones responsible for each function, and the endocrine glands that produce each hormone. Glands may be used more than once.

Hormones Key:

ACTH	estrogens	progesterone
ADH	FSH	prolactin
aldosterone	glucagon	PTH
calcitonin	insulin	T_3/T_4
cortisol	LH	testosterone
epinephrine	oxytocin	TSH

Glands Key:

adrenal cortex	pancreas
adrenal medulla	parathyroid glands
anterior pituitary	posterior pituitary
hypothalamus	testes
ovaries	thyroid gland

Function	Hormone(s)	Gland(s)
Regulate the function of another endocrine gland	1.	
	2.	
	3.	
	4.	
Maintenance of salt and water balance in the extracellular fluid	1.	
	2.	
Directly involved in milk production and ejection	1.	
	2.	
Controls the rate of body metabolism and cellular oxidation	1.	
Regulate blood calcium levels	1.	
	2.	
Regulate blood glucose levels; produced by the same "mixed" gland	1.	
	2.	
Released in response to stressors	1.	
	2.	
Drive development of secondary sex characteristics in males	1.	
Directly responsible for regulation of the menstrual cycle	1.	
	2.	

8. Although the pituitary gland is often referred to as the master gland of the body, the hypothalamus exerts some control over the pituitary gland. How does the hypothalamus control both anterior and posterior pituitary functioning?

_____

_____

9. Indicate whether the release of the hormones listed below is stimulated by (A) another hormone; (B) the nervous system (neurotransmitters, or neurosecretions); or (C) humoral factors (the concentration of specific nonhormonal substances in the blood or extracellular fluid). (Use your textbook as necessary.)

_____ 1. ACTH   _____ 4. insulin   _____ 7. T_4/T_3

_____ 2. calcitonin   _____ 5. norepinephrine   _____ 8. testosterone

_____ 3. estrogens   _____ 6. parathyroid hormone   _____ 9. TSH, FSH

10. Name the hormone(s) produced in _inadequate_ amounts that directly result in the following conditions.

_____ 1. tetany

_____ 2. excessive diuresis without high blood glucose levels

_____ 3. loss of glucose in the urine

_____ 4. abnormally small stature, normal proportions

_____ 5. low BMR, mental and physical sluggishness

11. Name the hormone(s) produced in _excessive_ amounts that directly result in the following conditions.

_____ 1. large hands and feet in the adult, large facial bones

_____ 2. nervousness, irregular pulse rate, sweating

_____ 3. demineralization of bones, spontaneous fractures

Microscopic Anatomy of Selected Endocrine Glands

12. Choose a response from the key below to name the hormone(s) produced by the cell types listed.

Key: a. _calcitonin_   d. glucocorticoids   g. PTH
      b. GH, prolactin   e. insulin   h. T_4/T_3
      c. glucagon   f. mineralocorticoids   i. TSH, ACTH, FSH, LH

_____ 1. parafollicular cells of the thyroid   _____ 6. zona fasciculata cells

_____ 2. follicular epithelial cells of the thyroid _____ 7. zona glomerulosa cells

_____ 3. beta cells of the pancreatic islets (islets _____ 8. chief cells of the parathyroid
            of Langerhans)

                                                        _____ 9. acidophil cells of the anterior pituitary
_____ 4. alpha cells of the pancreatic islets (islets
            of Langerhans)

_____ 5. basophil cells of the anterior pituitary

13. Six diagrams of the microscopic structures of the endocrine glands are presented here. Identify each and name all structures indicated by a leader line or bracket.

(a) _____

(b) _____

(c) _____

(d) _____

(e) _____

(f) _____

28A

Role of Thyroid Hormone, Pituitary Hormone, Insulin, and Epinephrine: Wet Lab

MATERIALS

Activity 1: Thyroid hormone and metabolic rate

- ☐ Glass desiccator, manometer, 20-ml glass syringe, two-hole rubber stopper, and T-valve (1 for every 3–4 students)
- ☐ Soda lime (desiccant)
- ☐ Hardware cloth squares
- ☐ Petrolatum
- ☐ Rubber tubing; tubing clamp; scissors
- ☐ 7.6-cm (3-in.) pieces of glass tubing
- ☐ Animal balances
- ☐ Heavy animal-handling gloves
- ☐ Young rats of the same sex, obtained 2 weeks prior to the laboratory session and treated as follows for 14 days:

  Group 1: control group—fed normal rat chow and water

  Group 2: experimental group A—fed normal rat chow and drinking water containing 0.02% propylthiouracil*

  Group 3: experimental group B—fed rat chow containing desiccated thyroid (2% by weight) and given normal drinking water

- ☐ Chart set up on chalkboard so that each student group can record its computed metabolic rate figures under the appropriate headings

*Note to the Instructor: propylthiouracil (PTU) is degraded by light and should be stored in light-resistant containers or in the dark.

Text continues on next page.

myA&P For practice quizzes on this lab, go to www.myaandp.com.

OBJECTIVES

1. To understand the physiological (and clinical) importance of metabolic rate measurement.
2. To investigate the effect of hypo-, hyper-, and euthyroid conditions on oxygen consumption and metabolic rate.
3. To assemble the necessary apparatus and properly use a manometer to obtain experimental results.
4. To calculate metabolic rate in terms of O_2 consumption.
5. To describe and explain the effect of pituitary hormones on the ovary.
6. To describe and explain the effects of hyperinsulinism.
7. To describe and explain the effect of epinephrine on the heart.

PRE-LAB QUIZ

1. Define *metabolism*. _____
   _____
2. Circle the correct term. <u>Catabolism / Anabolism</u> is the process by which substances are broken down into simpler substances.
3. _____ is the single most important hormone responsible for influencing the rate of cellular metabolism and body heat production.
   a. Calcitonin   c. Insulin
   b. Estrogen   d. Thyroid hormone
4. Circle the correct term. <u>Control / Experimental group B</u> animals are assumed to have normal thyroid function and metabolic rate.
5. Basal metabolic rate (BMR) is:
   a. decreased in individuals with hyperthyroidism
   b. increased in individuals with hyperthyroidism
   c. increased in obese individuals
6. In this activity, _____ consumption will be measured with a respirator-manometer device.
   a. carbon dioxide   c. oxygen
   b. food   d. water
7. Circle True or False. Gonadotropins are produced by the anterior pituitary gland.
8. Circle the correct term. Many people with diabetes mellitus need injections of <u>insulin / glucagon</u> to maintain homeostasis.
9. What experiment will you do to observe the effects of epinephrine?
   a. Flush the heart of a dissected frog with epinephrine.
   b. Flush the heart of a dissected frog with insulin.
   c. Inject a rat with epinephrine.
   d. Inject a rat with follicle-stimulating hormone and epinephrine.

Activity 2: Pituitary hormone and ovary†

- ☐ Female frogs (*Rana pipiens*)
- ☐ Disposable gloves
- ☐ Battery jars
- ☐ Syringe (2-ml capacity)
- ☐ 20- to 25-gauge needle
- ☐ Frog pituitary extract
- ☐ Physiological saline
- ☐ Spring or pond water
- ☐ Wax marking pencils

Activity 3: Hyperinsulinism†

- ☐ 500- or 600-ml beakers

- ☐ 20% glucose solution
- ☐ Commercial insulin solution (400 Immunizing units [IU] per 100 ml of H₂O)
- ☐ Finger bowls
- ☐ Small (4–5 cm, or 1½–2 in.) freshwater fish (guppy, bluegill, or sunfish—listed in order of preference)
- ☐ Wax marking pencils

Activity 4: Epinephrine and heart†

- ☐ Frog (*Rana pipiens*)
- ☐ Dissecting instruments, tray, and pins

- ☐ Frog Ringer's solution in dropper bottle
- ☐ 1:1000 epinephrine (Adrenalin) solution in dropper bottles
- ☐ Disposable gloves

PEx   PhysioEx™ 8.0 Computer Simulation on page PEx-49

†*The Selected Actions of Hormones and Other Chemical Messengers* videotape (available to qualified adopters from Pearson Education) may be used in lieu of student participation in Activities 2–4 of Exercise 28A.

The endocrine system exerts many complex and interrelated effects on the body as a whole, as well as on specific organs and tissues. Most scientific knowledge about this system is contemporary, and new information is constantly being presented. Many experiments on the endocrine system require relatively large laboratory animals; are time-consuming (requiring days to weeks of observation); and often involve technically difficult surgical procedures to remove the glands or parts of them, all of which makes it difficult to conduct more general types of laboratory experiments. Nevertheless, the four technically unsophisticated experiments presented here should illustrate how dramatically hormones affect body functioning.

To conserve laboratory specimens, experiments can be conducted by groups of four students. The use of larger working groups should not detract from benefits gained, since the major value of these experiments lies in observation.

Determining the Effect of Thyroid Hormone on Metabolic Rate

Metabolism is a broad term referring to all chemical reactions that are necessary to maintain life. It involves both *catabolism,* enzymatically controlled processes in which substances are broken down to simpler substances, and *anabolism,* processes in which larger molecules or structures are built from smaller ones. Most catabolic reactions in the body are accompanied by a net release of energy. Some of the liberated energy is captured to make ATP, the energy-rich molecule used by body cells to energize all their activities; the balance is lost in the form of thermal energy or heat. Maintaining body temperature is critically related to the heat-liberating aspects of metabolism.

Various foodstuffs make different contributions to the process of metabolism. For example, carbohydrates, particularly glucose, are generally broken down or oxidized to make ATP, whereas fats are utilized to form cell membranes and myelin sheaths, and to insulate the body with a fatty cushion. Fats are used secondarily for producing ATP, particularly when the diet is inadequate in carbohydrates. Proteins and amino acids tend to be conserved by body cells, and understandably so, since most structural elements of the body are proteinaceous in nature.

Thyroid hormone (collectively T_3 and T_4), produced by the thyroid gland, is the single most important hormone influencing the rate of cellular metabolism and body heat production. Under conditions of excess thyroid hormone production (hyperthyroidism), an individual's basal metabolic rate (BMR), heat production, and oxygen consumption increase, and the individual tends to lose weight and become heat-intolerant and irritable. Conversely, hypothyroid individuals become mentally and physically sluggish and obese, and are cold-intolerant because of their low BMR. ■

Many factors other than thyroid hormone levels contribute to metabolic rate (for example, body size and weight, age, and activity level), but the focus of the following experiment is to investigate how differences in thyroid hormone concentration affect metabolism.

Three groups of laboratory rats will be used. *Control group* animals are assumed to have normal thyroid function (to be euthyroid) and to have normal metabolic rates for their relative body weights. *Experimental group A* animals have received water containing the chemical propylthiouracil, which counteracts or antagonizes the effects of thyroid hormone in the body. *Experimental group B* animals have been fed rat chow containing dried thyroid tissue, which contains thyroid hormone. The rates of oxygen consumption (an indirect means of determining metabolic rate) in the animals of the three groups will be measured and compared to investigate the effects of hyperthyroid, hypothyroid, and euthyroid conditions.

Oxygen consumption will be measured with a simple respirometer-manometer apparatus. Each animal will be placed in a closed chamber containing soda lime. As carbon dioxide is evolved and expired, it will be absorbed by the soda lime; therefore, the pressure changes observed will indicate the volume of oxygen consumed by the animal during the testing interval. Students will work in groups of three to four to assemble the apparatus, make preliminary weight measurements on the animals, and record the data.

Preparing the Respirometer-Manometer Apparatus

1. Obtain a desiccator, a two-hole rubber stopper, a 20-ml glass syringe, a hardware cloth square, a T-valve, scissors, rubber tubing, two short pieces of glass tubing, soda lime, a manometer, a clamp, and petrolatum, and bring them to your laboratory bench. The apparatus will be assembled as illustrated in Figure 28A.1.

- Clamp
- Rubber tubing
- Glass tubing
- Rubber stopper
- Rat
- Hardware cloth
- Soda lime
- T-valve
- Rubber tubing
- Desiccator with cover
- Manometer with fluid
- 20-ml syringe

FIGURE 28A.1 Respirometer-manometer apparatus.

2. Shake soda lime into the bottom of the desiccator to thoroughly cover the glass bottom. Then place the hardware cloth on the ledge of the desiccator over the soda lime. The hardware cloth should be well above the soda lime, so that the animal will not be able to touch it. Soda lime is quite caustic and can cause chemical burns.

3. Lubricate the ends of the two pieces of glass tubing with petrolatum, and twist them into the holes in the rubber stopper until their distal ends protrude from the opposite side. *Do not plug the tubing with petrolatum*. Place the stopper into the desiccator cover, and set the cover on the desiccator temporarily.

4. Cut off a short (7.6-cm, or 3-in.) piece of rubber tubing, and attach it to the top of one piece of glass tubing extending from the stopper. Cut and attach a 30- to 35-cm (12- to 14-in.) piece of rubber tubing to the other glass tubing. Insert the T-valve stem into the distal end of the longer-length tubing.

5. Cut another short piece of rubber tubing; attach one end to the T-valve and the other to the nib of the 20-ml syringe. Remove the plunger of the syringe and grease its sides generously with petrolatum. Insert the plunger back into the syringe barrel and work it up and down to evenly disperse the petrolatum on the inner walls of the syringe, then pull the plunger out to the 20-ml marking.

6. Cut a piece of rubber tubing long enough to reach from the third arm of the T-valve to one arm of the manometer. (The manometer should be partially filled with water so that a U-shaped water column is seen.) Attach the tubing to the T-valve and the manometer arm.

7. Remove the desiccator cover and generously grease the cover's bottom edge with petrolatum. Place the cover back on

the desiccator and firmly move it from side to side to spread the lubricant evenly.

8. Test the system for leaks as follows: Firmly clamp the *short* length of rubber tubing extending from the stopper. Now gently push in on the plunger of the syringe. If the system is properly sealed, the fluid in the manometer will move away from the rubber tubing attached to its arm. If there is an air leak, the manometer fluid level will not change, or it will change and then quickly return to its original level. If either of these events occurs, check all glass-to-glass or glass-to-rubber tubing connections. Smear additional petrolatum on suspect areas and test again. The apparatus must be airtight before experimentation can begin.

9. After ensuring that there are no leaks in the system, unclamp the short rubber tubing, and remove the desiccator cover.

Preparing the Animal

⚠ 1. Put on the heavy animal-handling gloves, and obtain one of the animals as directed by your instructor. Handling it gently, weigh the animal to the nearest 0.1 g on the animal balance.

2. Carefully place the animal on the hardware cloth in the desiccator. The objective is to measure oxygen usage at basal levels, so you do not want to prod the rat into high levels of activity, which would produce errors in your measurements.

3. Record the animal's group (control or experimental group A or B) and its weight in kilograms (that is, weight in grams/1000) on the data sheet on page 418.

Metabolic Rate Data Sheet

Animal used from group: _____

14-day prior treatment of animal: _____

Body weight in grams: _____ /1000 = body weight in kg: _____

O_2 consumption/min: Test 1   **O_2 consumption/min: Test 2**

Beginning syringe reading _____ ml   Beginning syringe reading _____ ml

min 1 _____	min 6 _____	min 1 _____	min 6 _____
min 2 _____	min 7 _____	min 2 _____	min 7 _____
min 3 _____	min 8 _____	min 3 _____	min 8 _____
min 4 _____	min 9 _____	min 4 _____	min 9 _____
min 5 _____	min 10 _____	min 5 _____	min 10 _____

_____ Total O_2/10 min   _____ Total O_2/10 min

Average ml O_2 consumed/10 min: _____

Milliliters O_2 consumed/hr: _____

Metabolic rate: _____ ml O_2/kg/hr

Averaged class results:

Metabolic rate of control animals: _____ ml O_2/kg/hr

Metabolic rate of experimental group A animals (PTU-treated): _____ ml O_2/kg/hr

Metabolic rate of experimental group B animals (desiccated thyroid-treated): _____ ml O_2/kg/hr

Equilibrating the Chamber

1. Place the lid on the desiccator, and move it slightly from side to side to seal it firmly.

2. Leave the short tubing unclamped for 7 to 10 minutes to allow temperature equilibration in the chamber. (Since the animal's body heat will warm the air in the container, the air will expand initially. This must be allowed to occur before any measurements of oxygen consumption are taken. Otherwise, it would appear that the animal is generating oxygen rather than consuming it.)

Determining Oxygen Consumption of the Animal

1. Once again clamp the short rubber tubing extending from the desiccator lid stopper.

2. Check the manometer to make sure that the fluid level is the same in both arms. (If not, manipulate the syringe plunger

to make the fluid levels even.) Record the time and the position of the bottom of the plunger (use ml marking) in the syringe.

3. Observe the manometer fluid levels at 1-minute intervals. Each time make the necessary adjustment to bring the fluid levels even in the manometer by carefully pushing the syringe plunger further into the barrel. Determine the amount of oxygen used per minute in each interval by computing the difference in air volumes within the syringe. For example, if after the first minute, you push the plunger from the 20- to the 17-ml marking, the oxygen consumption would be 3 ml/min. Then, if the plunger is pushed from 17 ml to 15 ml at the second minute reading, the oxygen usage during minute 2 would be 2 ml, and so on.

4. Continue taking readings (and recording oxygen consumption per minute interval on the data sheet) for 10 consecutive minutes or until the syringe plunger has been pushed nearly to the 0-ml mark. Then unclamp the short rubber

tubing, remove the desiccator cover, and allow the apparatus to stand open for 2 to 3 minutes to flush out the stale air.

5. Repeat the recording procedures for another 10-minute interval. _Make sure that you equilibrate the temperature within the chamber before beginning this second recording series._

6. After you have recorded the animal's oxygen consumption for two 10-minute intervals, unclamp the short rubber tubing, remove the desiccator lid, and carefully return the rat to its cage.

Computing Metabolic Rate

Metabolic rate calculations are generally reported in terms of kcal/m²/hr and require that corrections be made to present the data in terms of standardized pressure and temperature conditions. These more complex calculations will not be used here, since the object is simply to arrive at some generalized conclusions concerning the effect of thyroid hormone on metabolic rate.

1. Obtain the average figure for milliliters of oxygen consumed per 10-minute interval by adding up the minute-interval consumption figures for each 10-minute testing series and dividing the total by 2.

$$\frac{\text{Total ml O}_2 \text{ in test series 1 } + \text{ total ml O}_2 \text{ in test series 2}}{2}$$

2. Determine oxygen consumption per hour using the following formula, and record the figure on the data sheet:

$$\frac{\text{Average ml O}_2 \text{ consumed}}{10 \text{ min}} \times \frac{60 \text{ min}}{\text{hr}} = \text{ml O}_2/\text{hr}$$

3. To determine the metabolic rate in milliliters of oxygen consumed per kilogram of body weight per hour so that the results of all experiments can be compared, divide the figure just obtained in step 2 by the animal's weight in kilograms (kg = lb ÷ 2.2).

$$\text{Metabolic rate} = \frac{\text{ml O}_2/\text{hr}}{\text{weight (kg)}} = \underline{\hspace{2cm}} \text{ml O}_2/\text{kg/hr}$$

Record the metabolic rate on the data sheet and also in the appropriate space on the chart on the chalkboard.

4. Once all groups have recorded their final metabolic rate figures on the chalkboard, average the results of each animal grouping to obtain the mean for each experimental group. Also record this information on the data sheet. ▬

ACTIVITY 2

Determining the Effect of Pituitary Hormones on the Ovary

As indicated in Exercise 43, anterior pituitary hormones called _gonadotropins,_ specifically follicle-stimulating hormone (FSH) and luteinizing hormone (LH), regulate the ovarian cycles of the female. Although amphibians normally ovulate seasonally, many can be stimulated to ovulate "on demand" by injecting an extract of pituitary hormones.

⚠ 1. Don disposable gloves, and obtain two frogs. Place them in separate battery jars to bring them to your laboratory bench. Also bring back a syringe and needle,

a wax marking pencil, pond or spring water, and containers of pituitary extract and physiological saline.

2. Before beginning, examine each frog for the presence of eggs. Hold the frog firmly with one hand and exert pressure on its abdomen toward the cloaca (in the direction of the legs). If ovulation has occurred, any eggs present in the oviduct will be forced out and will appear at the cloacal opening. If no eggs are present, continue with step 3.

If eggs are expressed, return the animal to your instructor and obtain another frog for experimentation. Repeat the procedure for determining if eggs are present until two frogs that lack eggs have been obtained.

3. Aspirate 1 to 2 ml of the pituitary extract into a syringe. Inject the extract subcutaneously into the anterior abdominal (peritoneal) cavity of the frog you have selected to be the experimental animal. To inject into the peritoneal cavity, hold the frog with its ventral surface superiorly. Insert the needle through the skin and muscles of the abdominal wall in the lower quarter of the abdomen. Do not insert the needle far enough to damage any of the vital organs. With a wax marker, label its large battery jar "experimental," and place the frog in it. Add a small amount of pond water to the battery jar before continuing.

4. Aspirate 1 to 2 ml of physiological saline into a syringe and inject it into the peritoneal cavity of the second frog—this will be the control animal. (Make sure you inject the same volume of fluid into both frogs.) Place this frog into the second battery jar, marked "control." Allow the animals to remain undisturbed for 24 hours.

5. After 24 hours,* again check each frog for the presence of eggs in the cloaca. (See step 2.) If no eggs are present, make arrangements with your laboratory instructor to return to the lab on the next day (at 48 hours after injection) to check your frogs for the presence of eggs.

6. Return the frogs to the terrarium before leaving or continuing with the lab.

In which of the prepared frogs was ovulation induced?

_____

Specifically, what hormone in the pituitary extract causes ovulation to occur?

_____ ▬

ACTIVITY 3

Observing the Effects of Hyperinsulinism

Many people with diabetes mellitus need injections of insulin to maintain blood sugar (glucose) homeostasis. Adequate levels of blood glucose are essential for proper functioning of the nervous system; thus, the administration of insulin must be carefully controlled. If blood glucose levels fall precipitously, the patient will go into insulin shock.

*The student needs to inject the frog the day before the lab session or return to check results the day after the scheduled lab session.

A small fish will be used to demonstrate the effects of hyperinsulinism. Since the action of insulin on the fish parallels that in the human, this experiment should provide valid information concerning its administration to humans.

1. Prepare two finger bowls. Using a wax marking pencil, mark one A and the other B. To finger bowl A, add 100 ml of the commercial insulin solution. To finger bowl B, add 200 ml of 20% glucose solution.

2. Place a small fish in finger bowl A and observe its actions carefully as the insulin diffuses into its bloodstream through the capillary circulation of its gills.

Approximately how long did it take for the fish to become comatose?

_____

What types of activity did you observe in the fish before it became comatose?

_____

_____

_____

3. When the fish is comatose, carefully transfer it to finger bowl B and observe its actions. What happens to the fish after it is transferred?

_____

_____

_____

_____

Approximately how long did it take for this recovery?

_____

4. After all observations have been made and recorded, carefully return the fish to the aquarium. ■

Testing the Effect of Epinephrine on the Heart

As noted in Exercise 27, the adrenal medulla and the sympathetic nervous system are closely interrelated, specifically because the cells of the adrenal medulla and the postganglionic axons of the sympathetic nervous system both release catecholamines. This experiment demonstrates the effects of epinephrine on the frog heart.

⚠ 1. Obtain a frog, dissecting instruments and tray, disposable gloves, frog Ringer's solution, and dropper bottle of 1:1000 epinephrine solution. Bring them to your laboratory bench and don the gloves before beginning step 2.

2. Destroy the nervous system of the frog. (A frog used in the experiment on pituitary hormone effects may be used if your test results have already been obtained and are positive. Otherwise, obtain another frog.) Insert one blade of a scissors into its mouth as far as possible and quickly cut off the top of its head, posterior to the eyes. Then identify the spinal cavity and insert a dissecting needle into it to destroy the spinal cord.

3. Place the frog dorsal side down on a dissecting tray, and carefully open its ventral body cavity by making a vertical incision with the scissors.

4. Identify the beating heart, and carefully cut through the saclike pericardium to expose the heart tissue.

5. Visually count the heart rate for 1 minute, and record below. Keep the heart moistened with frog Ringer's solution during this interval.

Beats per minute: _____

6. Flush the heart with epinephrine solution. Record the heartbeat rate per minute for 5 consecutive minutes.

minute 1 _____   minute 4 _____

minute 2 _____   minute 5 _____

minute 3 _____

What was the effect of epinephrine on the heart rate?

_____

Was the effect long-lived? _____

7. Dispose of the frog in an appropriate container, and clean the dissecting tray and instruments before returning them to the supply area. ■

NAME _____

LAB TIME/DATE _____

Role of Thyroid Hormone, Pituitary Hormone, Insulin, and Epinephrine: Wet Lab

Determining the Effect of Thyroid Hormone on Metabolic Rate

1. In the measurement of oxygen consumption in rats, which group had the highest metabolic rate? _____

   _____ Which group had the lowest metabolic rate? _____

   Correlate these observations with the pretreatment these animals received. _____

   _____

   _____

   Which group of rats was hyperthyroid? _____

   Which euthyroid? _____ Which hypothyroid? _____

2. Since oxygen used = carbon dioxide generated, how do you know that what you measured was oxygen consumption?

   _____

   _____

3. What did changes in the fluid levels in the manometer arms indicate? _____

   _____

4. The techniques used in this set of laboratory experiments probably permitted several inaccuracies. One was the inability to control the activity of the rats. How would changes in their activity levels affect the results observed?

   _____

   _____

   Another possible source of error was the lack of control over the amount of food consumed by the rats in the 14-day period preceding the laboratory session. If each of the rats had been force-fed equivalent amounts of food in that 14-day period, which group (do you think) would have gained the most weight?

   _____ Which the least? _____

   Explain your answers. _____

   _____

   _____

5. TSH, produced by the anterior pituitary, causes the thyroid gland to release thyroid hormone to the blood. Which group of

rats can be assumed to have the *highest* blood levels of TSH? _____ Which the lowest? _____

Explain your reasoning. _____

_____

6. Use an appropriate reference to determine how each of the following factors modifies metabolic rate. Indicate increase by
   ↑ and decrease by ↓.

increased exercise _____   aging _____   infection/fever _____

small/slight stature _____   obesity _____   sex (♂ or ♀) _____

Determining the Effect of Pituitary Hormones on the Ovary

7. In the experiment on the effects of pituitary hormones, two anterior pituitary hormones caused ovulation to occur in the experimental animal. Which of these actually triggered ovulation or egg expulsion?

_____ The normal function of the second hormone involved, _____,

is to _____.

8. Why was a second frog injected with saline? _____

Observing the Effects of Hyperinsulinism

9. Briefly explain what was happening within the fish's system when the fish was immersed in the insulin solution. _____

_____

_____

10. What is the mechanism of the recovery process observed? _____

_____

11. What would you do to help a friend who had inadvertently taken an overdose of insulin? _____

_____ Why? _____

_____

Testing the Effect of Epinephrine on the Heart

12. Based on your observations, what is the effect of epinephrine on the heart rate?

_____

13. What is the role of this effect in the "fight-or-flight" response?

_____

Blood

MATERIALS

General supply area:*

- ☐ Disposable gloves
- ☐ Safety glasses (student-provided)
- ☐ Bucket or large beaker containing 10% household bleach solution for slide and glassware disposal
- ☐ Spray bottles containing 10% bleach solution
- ☐ Autoclave bag
- ☐ Designated lancet (sharps) disposal container
- ☐ Plasma (obtained from an animal hospital or prepared by centrifuging animal [for example, cattle or sheep] blood obtained from a biological supply house)
- ☐ Test tubes and test tube racks
- ☐ Wide-range pH paper
- ☐ Stained smears of human blood from a biological supply house or, if desired by the instructor, heparinized animal blood obtained from a biological supply house or an animal hospital (for example, dog blood), or EDTA-treated red cells (reference cells†) with blood type labels obscured (available from Immucor, Inc.)
- ☐ Clean microscope slides
- ☐ Glass stirring rods

*Note to the Instructor: See directions for handling of soiled glassware and disposable items on page 424.

†The blood in these kits (each containing four blood cell types—A1, A2, B, and O—individually supplied in 10-ml vials) is used to calibrate cell counters and other automated clinical laboratory equipment. This blood has been carefully screened and can be safely used by students for blood typing and determining hematocrits. It is not usable for hemoglobin determinations or coagulation studies.

Text continues on next page.

myA&P For practice quizzes on this lab, go to www.myaandp.com.

PAL For access to anatomical models and more, check out Practice Anatomy Lab.

OBJECTIVES

1. To name the two major components of blood, and to state their average percentages in whole blood.
2. To describe the composition and functional importance of plasma.
3. To define *formed elements* and list the cell types composing them, cite their relative percentages, and describe their major functions.
4. To identify red blood cells, basophils, eosinophils, monocytes, lymphocytes, and neutrophils when provided with a microscopic preparation or appropriate diagram.
5. To provide the normal values for a total white blood cell count and a total red blood cell count, and to state the importance of these tests.
6. To conduct the following blood tests in the laboratory, and to state their norms and the importance of each.

    differential white blood cell count
    hematocrit
    hemoglobin determination
    clotting time
    ABO and Rh blood typing
    plasma cholesterol concentration
7. To discuss the reason for transfusion reactions resulting from the administration of mismatched blood.
8. To define *leukocytosis, leukopenia, leukemia, polycythemia,* and *anemia* and to cite a possible reason for each condition.

PRE-LAB QUIZ

1. Circle True or False. There are no special precautions that I need to observe when performing today's lab.
2. Three types of formed elements found in blood include erythrocytes, leucocytes, and _____.
   a. electrolytes
   b. fibers
   c. platelets
   d. sodium salts
3. Circle the correct term. Mature <u>erythrocytes / leucocytes</u> are the most numerous blood cells and do not have a nucleus.
4. The least numerous but largest of all agranulocytes is the
   a. basophil
   b. lymphocyte
   c. monocyte
   d. neutrophil
5. _____ are the leukocytes responsible for releasing histamine and other mediators of inflammation.
   a. Basophils
   b. Eosinophils
   c. Monocytes
   d. Neutrophils
6. Circle the correct term. When determining the <u>hematocrit / hemoglobin</u>, you will centrifuge whole blood in order to allow the formed elements to sink to the bottom of the sample.
7. Circle the correct term. Blood typing is based on the presence of proteins known as <u>antigens / antibodies</u> on the outer surface of the red blood cell plasma membrane.
8. Circle True or False. If an individual is transfused with the wrong type blood, the recipient's antibodies react with the donor's antigens, eventually clumping and hemolyzing the donated RBCs.

- ☐ Wright's stain in a dropper bottle
- ☐ Distilled water in a dropper bottle
- ☐ Sterile lancets
- ☐ Absorbent cotton balls
- ☐ Alcohol swabs (wipes)
- ☐ Paper towels
- ☐ Compound microscope
- ☐ Immersion oil
- ☐ Three-dimensional models (if available) and charts of blood cells
- ☐ Assorted slides of white blood count pathologies labeled "Unknown Sample _____"
- ☐ Timer

Because many blood tests are to be conducted in this exercise, it is advisable to set up a number of appropriately labeled supply areas for the various tests, as designated below. Some needed supplies are located in the general supply area.

Note: Artificial blood prepared by Ward's Natural Science can be used for differential counts, hematocrit, and blood typing.

Activity 4: Hematocrit

- ☐ Heparinized capillary tubes
- ☐ Microhematocrit centrifuge and reading gauge (if the reading gauge is not available, a millimeter ruler may be used)
- ☐ Capillary tube sealer or modeling clay

Activity 5: Hemoglobin determination

- ☐ Hemoglobinometer, hemolysis applicator, and lens paper; or Tallquist hemoglobin scale and test paper

Activity 6: Coagulation time

- ☐ Capillary tubes (nonheparinized)
- ☐ Fine triangular file

Activity 7: Blood typing

- ☐ Blood typing sera (anti-A, anti-B, and anti-Rh [anti-D])

- ☐ Rh typing box
- ☐ Wax marking pencil
- ☐ Toothpicks
- ☐ Medicine dropper
- ☐ Blood test cards or microscope slides

Activity 8: Demonstration

- ☐ Microscopes set up with prepared slides demonstrating the following bone (or bone marrow) conditions: macrocytic hypochromic anemia, microcytic hypochromic anemia, sickle cell anemia, lymphocytic leukemia (chronic), and eosinophilia

Activity 9: Cholesterol measurement

- ☐ Cholesterol test cards and color scale

PEx PhysioEx™ 8.0 Computer Simulation on page PEx-69

In this exercise you will study plasma and formed elements of blood and conduct various hematologic tests. These tests are useful diagnostic tools for the physician because blood composition (number and types of blood cells, and chemical composition) reflects the status of many body functions and malfunctions.

⚠️ **ALERT: Special precautions when handling blood.** This exercise provides information on blood from several sources: human, animal, human treated, and artificial blood. The decision to use animal blood for testing or to have students test their own blood will be made by the instructor in accordance with the educational goals of the student group. For example, for students in the nursing or laboratory technician curricula, learning how to safely handle human blood or other human wastes is essential. Whenever blood is being handled, special attention must be paid to safety precautions. Instructors who opt to use human blood are responsible for its safe handling. Precautions should be used regardless of the source of the blood. This will both teach good technique and ensure the safety of the students.

Follow exactly the safety precautions listed below.

1. Wear safety gloves at all times. Discard appropriately.

2. Wear safety glasses throughout the exercise.

3. Handle only your own, freshly let (human) blood.

4. Be sure you understand the instructions and have all supplies on hand before you begin any part of the exercise.

5. Do not reuse supplies and equipment once they have been exposed to blood.

6. Keep the lab area clean. Do not let anything that has come in contact with blood touch surfaces or other individuals in the lab. Pay attention to the location of any supplies and equipment that come into contact with blood.

7. Dispose of lancets immediately after use in a designated disposal container. Do not put them down on the lab bench, even temporarily.

8. Dispose of all used cotton balls, alcohol swabs, blotting paper, and so forth in autoclave bags and place all soiled glassware in containers of 10% bleach solution.

9. Wipe down the lab bench with 10% bleach solution when you finish.

Composition of Blood

Circulating blood is a rather viscous substance that varies from bright scarlet to a dull brick red, depending on the amount of oxygen it is carrying. The average volume of blood in the body is about 5–6 L in adult males and 4–5 L in adult females.

Blood is classified as a type of connective tissue because it consists of a nonliving fluid matrix (the **plasma**) in which living cells (**formed elements**) are suspended. The fibers typical of a connective tissue matrix become visible in blood only when clotting occurs. They then appear as fibrin threads, which form the structural basis for clot formation.

More than 100 different substances are dissolved or suspended in plasma (Figure 29A.1), which is over 90% water. These include nutrients, gases, hormones, various wastes and metabolites, many types of proteins, and electrolytes. The composition of plasma varies continuously as cells remove or add substances to the blood.

Three types of formed elements are present in blood (Table 29A.1). Most numerous are **erythrocytes,** or **red blood cells (RBCs),** which are literally sacs of hemoglobin

Plasma 55%

Constituent	Major Functions
Water	Solvent for carrying other substances; absorbs heat
Salts (electrolytes) Sodium Potassium Calcium Magnesium Chloride Bicarbonate	Osmotic balance, pH buffering, regulation of membrane permeability
Plasma proteins Albumin	Osmotic balance, pH buffering
Fibrinogen	Clotting of blood
Globulins	Defense (antibodies) and lipid transport
Substances transported by blood Nutrients (glucose, fatty acids, amino acids, vitamins) Waste products of metabolism (urea, uric acid) Respiratory gases (O_2 and CO_2) Hormones	

Formed elements (cells) 45%

Cell Type	Number (per mm^3 of blood)	Functions
Erythrocytes (red blood cells)	4 – 6 million	Transport oxygen and help transport carbon dioxide
Leukocytes (white blood cells)	4800 – 10,800	Defense and immunity
Basophil		
Eosinophil		Lymphocyte
Neutrophil		Monocyte
Platelets	150,000 – 400,000	Blood clotting

FIGURE 29A.1 **The composition of blood.**

molecules that transport the bulk of the oxygen carried in the blood (and a small percentage of the carbon dioxide). **Leukocytes,** or **white blood cells (WBCs),** are part of the body's nonspecific defenses and the immune system, and **platelets** function in hemostasis (blood clot formation). Formed elements normally constitute 45% of whole blood; plasma accounts for the remaining 55%.

ACTIVITY 1

Determining the Physical Characteristics of Plasma

Go to the general supply area and carefully pour a few milliliters of plasma into a test tube. Also obtain some wide-range pH paper, and then return to your laboratory bench to make the following simple observations.

pH of Plasma

Test the pH of the plasma with wide-range pH paper. Record the pH observed. _____

Color and Clarity of Plasma

Hold the test tube up to a source of natural light. Note and record its color and degree of transparency. Is it clear, translucent, or opaque?

Color _____

Degree of transparency _____

TABLE 29A.1		Summary of Formed Elements of the Blood			

Cell type	Illustration	Description*	Cells/mm³ (µl) of blood	Duration of development (D) and life span (LS)	Function
Erythrocytes (red blood cells, RBCs)		Biconcave, anucleate disc; salmon-colored; diameter 7–8 µm	4–6 million	D: about 15 days LS: 100–120 days	Transport oxygen and carbon dioxide
Leukocytes (white blood cells, WBCs)		Spherical, nucleated cells	4800–10,800		
Granulocytes Neutrophil		Nucleus multilobed; inconspicuous cytoplasmic granules; diameter 10–12 µm	3000–7000	D: about 14 days LS: 6 hours to a few days	Phagocytize bacteria
Eosinophil		Nucleus bilobed; red cytoplasmic granules; diameter 10–14 µm	100–400	D: about 14 days LS: 8–12 days	Kill parasitic worms; complex role in allergy and asthma
Basophil		Nucleus lobed; large blue-purple cytoplasmic granules; diameter 10–14 µm	20–50	D: 1–7 days LS: ? (a few hours to a few days)	Release histamine and other mediators of in-flammation; contain heparin, an anticoagulant
Agranulocytes Lymphocyte		Nucleus spherical or indented; pale blue cytoplasm; diameter 5–17 µm	1500–3000	D: days to weeks LS: hours to years	Mount immune response by direct cell attack or via antibodies
Monocyte		Nucleus U- or kidney-shaped; gray-blue cytoplasm; diameter 14–24 µm	100–700	D: 2–3 days LS: months	Phagocytosis; develop into macrophages in tissues
Platelets		Discoid cytoplasmic fragments containing granules; stain deep purple; diameter 2–4 µm	150,000–400,000	D: 4–5 days LS: 5–10 days	Seal small tears in blood vessels; instrumental in blood clotting

*Appearance when stained with Wright's stain.

Consistency

While wearing gloves, dip your finger and thumb into plasma and then press them firmly together for a few seconds. Gently pull them apart. How would you describe the consistency of plasma (slippery, watery, sticky, granular)? Record your observations.

ACTIVITY 2

Examining the Formed Elements of Blood Microscopically

In this section, you will observe blood cells on an already prepared (purchased) blood slide or on a slide prepared from your own blood or blood provided by your instructor.

• Those using the purchased blood slide are to obtain a slide and begin their observations at step 6.

• Those testing blood provided by a biological supply source or an animal hospital are to obtain a tube of the supplied blood, disposable gloves, and the supplies listed in

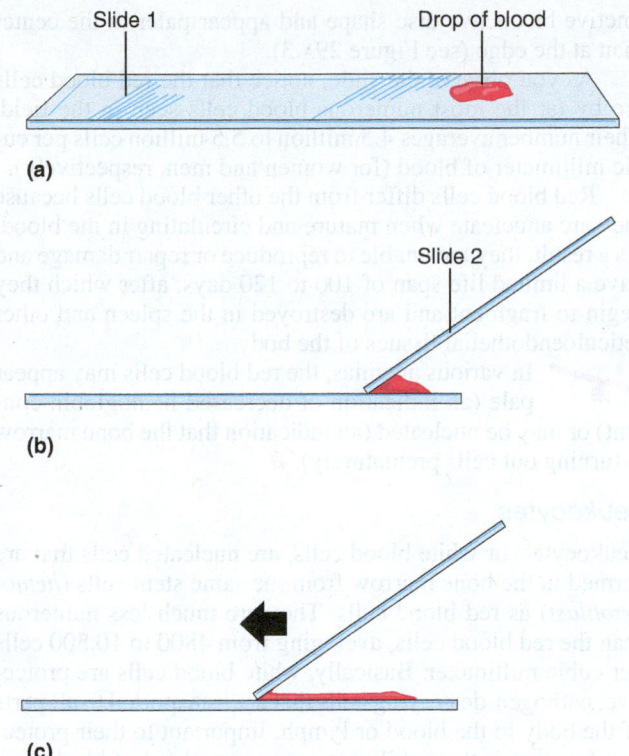

(a) Slide 1   Drop of blood

(b) Slide 2

(c)

FIGURE 29A.2 Procedure for making a blood smear. (a) Place a drop of blood on slide 1 approximately ½ inch from one end. **(b)** Hold slide 2 at a 30° to 40° angle to slide 1 (it should touch the drop of blood) and allow blood to spread along entire bottom edge of angled slide. **(c)** Smoothly advance slide 2 to end of slide 1 (blood should run out before reaching the end of slide 1). Then lift slide 2 away from slide 1 and place it on a paper towel.

step 1, except for the lancets and alcohol swabs. After donning gloves, those students will go to step 3b to begin their observations.

- If you are examining your own blood, you will perform all the steps described below *except* step 3b.

1. Obtain two glass slides, a glass stirring rod, dropper bottles of Wright's stain and distilled water, two or three lancets, cotton balls, and alcohol swabs. Bring this equipment to the laboratory bench. Clean the slides thoroughly and dry them.

2. Open the alcohol swab packet and scrub your third or fourth finger with the swab. (Because the pricked finger may be a little sore later, it is better to prepare a finger on the nondominant hand.) Circumduct your hand (swing it in a cone-shaped path) for 10 to 15 seconds. This will dry the alcohol and cause your fingers to become engorged with blood. Then, open the lancet packet and grasp the lancet by its blunt end. Quickly jab the pointed end into the prepared finger to produce a free flow of blood. It is *not* a good idea to squeeze or "milk" the finger, as this forces out tissue fluid as well as blood. If the blood is not flowing freely, another puncture should be made.

⚠ <u>*Under no circumstances is a lancet to be used for more than one puncture.*</u> Dispose of the lancets in the designated disposal container immediately after use.

3a. With a cotton ball, wipe away the first drop of blood; then allow another large drop of blood to form. Touch the blood to one of the cleaned slides approximately 1.3 cm, or ½ inch, from the end. Then quickly (to prevent clotting) use the second slide to form a blood smear as shown in Figure 29A.2. When properly prepared, the blood smear is uniformly thin. If the blood smear appears streaked, the blood probably began to clot or coagulate before the smear was made, and another slide should be prepared. Continue at step 4.

3b. Dip a glass rod in the blood provided, and transfer a generous drop of blood to the end of a cleaned microscope slide. For the time being, lay the glass rod on a paper towel on the bench. Then, as described in step 3a and Figure 29A.2, use the second slide to make your blood smear.

4. Dry the slide by waving it in the air. When it is completely dry, it will look dull. Place it on a paper towel, and flood it with Wright's stain. Count the number of drops of stain used. Allow the stain to remain on the slide for 3 to 4 minutes, and then flood the slide with an equal number of drops of distilled water. Allow the water and Wright's stain mixture to remain on the slide for 4 or 5 minutes or until a metallic green film or scum is apparent on the fluid surface. Blow on the slide gently every minute or so to keep the water and stain mixed during this interval.

5. Rinse the slide with a stream of distilled water. Then flood it with distilled water, and allow it to lie flat until the slide becomes translucent and takes on a pink cast. Then stand the slide on its long edge on the paper towel, and allow it to dry completely. Once the slide is dry, you can begin your observations.

6. Obtain a microscope and scan the slide under low power to find the area where the blood smear is the thinnest. After scanning the slide in low power to find the areas with the largest numbers of nucleated WBCs, read the following descriptions of cell types, and find each one on Figure 29A.1 and Table 29A.1. (The formed elements are also shown in Figure 29A.3 and Figure 29A.4.) Then, switch to

Platelets Erythrocytes Monocyte
Neutrophils Lymphocyte

FIGURE 29A.3 Photomicrograph of a human blood smear stained with Wright's stain (610×).

(a) Neutrophil; multilobed nucleus

(b) Eosinophil; bilobed nucleus, red cytoplasmic granules

(c) Basophil; bilobed nucleus, purplish-black cytoplasmic granules

(d) Small lymphocyte; large spherical nucleus

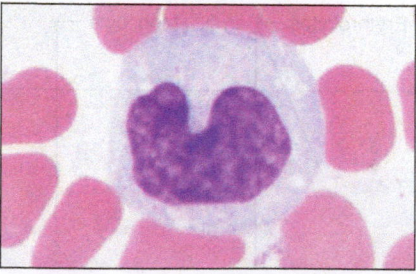

(e) Monocyte; kidney-shaped nucleus

FIGURE 29A.4 Leukocytes. In each case the leukocytes are surrounded by erythrocytes (1850×, Wright's stain).

the oil immersion lens, and observe the slide carefully to identify each cell type.

7. Set your prepared slide aside for use in Activity 3.

Erythrocytes

Erythrocytes, or red blood cells, which average 7.5 μm in diameter, vary in color from a salmon red color to pale pink, depending on the effectiveness of the stain. They have a dis-

tinctive biconcave disc shape and appear paler in the center than at the edge (see Figure 29A.3).

As you observe the slide, notice that the red blood cells are by far the most numerous blood cells seen in the field. Their number averages 4.5 million to 5.5 million cells per cubic millimeter of blood (for women and men, respectively).

Red blood cells differ from the other blood cells because they are anucleate when mature and circulating in the blood. As a result, they are unable to reproduce or repair damage and have a limited life span of 100 to 120 days, after which they begin to fragment and are destroyed in the spleen and other reticuloendothelial tissues of the body.

In various anemias, the red blood cells may appear pale (an indication of decreased hemoglobin content) or may be nucleated (an indication that the bone marrow is turning out cells prematurely). ∎

Leukocytes

Leukocytes, or white blood cells, are nucleated cells that are formed in the bone marrow from the same stem cells (*hemocytoblast*) as red blood cells. They are much less numerous than the red blood cells, averaging from 4800 to 10,800 cells per cubic millimeter. Basically, white blood cells are protective, pathogen-destroying cells that are transported to all parts of the body in the blood or lymph. Important to their protective function is their ability to move in and out of blood vessels, a process called **diapedesis,** and to wander through body tissues by **amoeboid motion** to reach sites of inflammation or tissue destruction. They are classified into two major groups, depending on whether or not they contain conspicuous granules in their cytoplasm.

Granulocytes make up the first group. The granules in their cytoplasm stain differentially with Wright's stain, and they have peculiarly lobed nuclei, which often consist of expanded nuclear regions connected by thin strands of nucleoplasm. There are three types of granulocytes:

Neutrophil: The most abundant of the white blood cells (50% to 70% of the leukocyte population); nucleus consists of 3 to 6 lobes and the pale lilac cytoplasm contains fine cytoplasmic granules, which are generally indistinguishable and take up both the acidic (red) and basic (blue) dyes (*neutrophil* = neutral loving); functions as an active phagocyte. The number of neutrophils increases exponentially during acute infections. (See Figure 29A.4a.)

Eosinophil: Represents 2% to 4% of the leukocyte population; nucleus is generally figure-8 or bilobed in shape; contains large cytoplasmic granules (elaborate lysosomes) that stain red-orange with the acid dyes in Wright's stain (see Figure 29A.4b). Eosinophils are about the size of neutrophils and play a role in counterattacking parasitic worms. Eosinophils have complex roles in many other diseases, especially in allergy and asthma.

Basophil: Least abundant leukocyte type representing less than 1% of the population; large U- or S-shaped nucleus with two or more indentations. Cytoplasm contains coarse, sparse granules that are stained deep purple by the basic dyes in Wright's stain (see Figure 29A.4c). The granules contain several chemicals, including histamine, a vasodilator that is discharged on exposure to antigens and helps mediate the inflammatory response. Basophils are about the size of neutrophils.

The second group, **agranulocytes,** or **agranular leukocytes,** contains no *visible* cytoplasmic granules. Although found in the bloodstream, they are much more abundant in lymphoid tissues. Their nuclei tend to be closer to the norm, that is, spherical, oval, or kidney-shaped. Specific characteristics of the two types of agranulocytes are listed below.

Lymphocyte: The smallest of the leukocytes, approximately the size of a red blood cell (see Figure 29A.4d). The nucleus stains dark blue to purple, is generally spherical or slightly indented, and accounts for most of the cell mass. Sparse cytoplasm appears as a thin blue rim around the nucleus. Concerned with immunologic responses in the body; one population, the *B lymphocytes,* gives rise to *plasma cells* that produce antibodies released to blood. The second population, *T lymphocytes,* plays a regulatory role and destroys grafts, tumors, and virus-infected cells. Represents 25% or more of the WBC population.

Monocyte: The largest of the leukocytes; approximately twice the size of red blood cells (see Figure 29A.4e). Represents 3% to 8% of the leukocyte population. Dark blue nucleus is generally kidney-shaped; abundant cytoplasm stains gray-blue. Once in the tissues, monocytes convert to macrophages, active phagocytes (the "long-term cleanup team"), increasing dramatically in number during chronic infections such as tuberculosis.

Students are often asked to list the leukocytes in order from the most abundant to the least abundant. The following silly phrase may help you with this task: *Never let monkeys eat bananas* (neutrophils, lymphocytes, monocytes, eosinophils, basophils).

Platelets

Platelets are cell fragments of large multinucleate cells (**megakaryocytes**) formed in the bone marrow. They appear as darkly staining, irregularly shaped bodies interspersed among the blood cells (see Figure 29A.3). The normal platelet count in blood ranges from 150,000 to 400,000 per cubic millimeter. Platelets are instrumental in the clotting process that occurs in plasma when blood vessels are ruptured.

After you have identified these cell types on your slide, observe charts and three-dimensional models of blood cells if these are available. Do not dispose of your slide, as you will use it later for the differential white blood cell count. ▬

Hematologic Tests

When someone enters a hospital as a patient, several hematologic tests are routinely done to determine general level of health as well as the presence of pathologic conditions. You will be conducting the most common of these tests in this exercise.

⚠ Materials such as cotton balls, lancets, and alcohol swabs are used in nearly all of the following diagnostic tests. These supplies are at the general supply area and should be properly disposed of (glassware to the bleach bucket, lancets in a designated disposal container, and disposable items to the autoclave bag) immediately after use.

Other necessary supplies and equipment are at specific supply areas marked according to the test with which they are used. Since nearly all of the tests require a finger stab, if you will be using your own blood it might be wise to quickly read through the tests to determine in which instances more than one preparation can be done from the same finger stab. A little planning will save you the discomfort of a multiple-punctured finger.

An alternative to using blood obtained from the finger stab technique is using heparinized blood samples supplied by your instructor. The purpose of using heparinized tubes is to prevent the blood from clotting. Thus blood collected and stored in such tubes will be suitable for all tests except coagulation time testing.

Total White and Red Blood Cell Counts

A **total WBC count** or **total RBC count** determines the total number of that cell type per unit volume of blood. Total WBC and RBC counts are a routine part of any physical exam. Most clinical agencies use computers to conduct these counts. Since the hand counting technique typically done in college labs is rather outdated, total RBC and WBC counts will not be done here, but the importance of such counts (both normal and abnormal values) is briefly described below.

Total White Blood Cell Count

Since white blood cells are an important part of the body's defense system, it is essential to note any abnormalities in them. **Leukocytosis,** an abnormally high WBC count, may indicate bacterial or viral infection, metabolic disease, hemorrhage, or poisoning by drugs or chemicals. A decrease in the white cell number below 4000/mm³ (**leukopenia**) may indicate typhoid fever, measles, infectious hepatitis or cirrhosis, tuberculosis, or excessive antibiotic or X-ray therapy. A person with leukopenia lacks the usual protective mechanisms. **Leukemia,** a malignant disorder of the lymphoid tissues characterized by uncontrolled proliferation of abnormal WBCs accompanied by a reduction in the number of RBCs and platelets, is detectable not only by a total WBC count but also by a differential WBC count. ■

Total Red Blood Cell Count

Since RBCs are absolutely necessary for oxygen transport, a doctor typically investigates any excessive change in their number immediately. An increase in the number of RBCs (**polycythemia**) may result from bone marrow cancer or from living at high altitudes where less oxygen is available. A decrease in the number of RBCs results in anemia. (The term **anemia** simply indicates a decreased oxygen-carrying capacity of blood that may result from a decrease in RBC number or size or a decreased hemoglobin content of the RBCs.) A decrease in RBCs may result suddenly from hemorrhage or more gradually from conditions that destroy RBCs or hinder RBC production. ■

Differential White Blood Cell Count

To make a **differential white blood cell count,** 100 WBCs are counted and classified according to type. Such a count is routine in a physical examination and in diagnosing illness, since any abnormality or significant elevation in percentages of WBC types may indicate a problem or the source of pathology.

ACTIVITY 3

Conducting a Differential WBC Count

1. Use the slide prepared for the identification of the blood cells in Activity 2. Begin at the edge of the smear and move the slide in a systematic manner on the microscope stage—either up and down or from side to side as indicated in Figure 29A.5.

FIGURE 29A.5 Alternative methods of moving the slide for a differential WBC count.

2. Record each type of white blood cell you observe by making a count in the first blank column of the chart below (for example, ⅠⅠⅠ ⅠⅠ = 7 cells) until you have observed and recorded a total of 100 WBCs. Using the following equation, compute the percentage of each WBC type counted, and record the percentages on the Hematologic Test Data Sheet on page 436.

$$\text{Percent (\%)} = \frac{\text{\# observed}}{\text{Total \# counted (100)}} \times 100$$

3. Select a slide marked "Unknown sample," record the slide number, and use the count chart below to conduct a differential count. Record the percentages on the data sheet on page 436.

How does the differential count from the unknown sample slide compare to a normal count?

_____

_____

Count of 100 WBCs		
	Number observed	
Cell type	**Student blood smear**	**Unknown sample # ___**
Neutrophils		
Eosinophils		
Basophils		
Lymphocytes		
Monocytes		

Using the text and other references, try to determine the blood pathology on the unknown slide. Defend your answer.

_____

_____

4. How does your differential white blood cell count correlate with the percentages given for each type on pages 428–429?

_____

_____

Hematocrit

The **hematocrit,** or **packed cell volume (PCV),** is routinely determined when anemia is suspected. Centrifuging whole blood spins the formed elements to the bottom of the tube, with plasma forming the top layer (see Figure 29A.1). Since the blood cell population is primarily RBCs, the PCV is generally considered equivalent to the RBC volume, and this is the only value reported. However, the relative percentage of WBCs can be differentiated, and both WBC and plasma volume will be reported here. Normal hematocrit values for the male and female, respectively, are 47.0 ± 7 and 42.0 ± 5.

ACTIVITY 4

Determining the Hematocrit

The hematocrit is determined by the micromethod, so only a drop of blood is needed. If possible (and the centrifuge allows), all members of the class should prepare their capillary tubes at the same time so the centrifuge can be run only once.

1. Obtain two heparinized capillary tubes, capillary tube sealer or modeling clay, a lancet, alcohol swabs, and some cotton balls.

2. If you are using your own blood, cleanse a finger, and allow the blood to flow freely. Wipe away the first few drops and, holding the red-line-marked end of the capillary tube to the blood drop, allow the tube to fill at least three-fourths full by capillary action (Figure 29A.6a). If the blood is not flowing freely, the end of the capillary tube will not be completely submerged in the blood during filling, air will enter, and you will have to prepare another sample.

   If you are using instructor-provided blood, simply immerse the red-marked end of the capillary tube in the blood sample and fill it three-quarters full as just described.

3. Plug the blood-containing end by pressing it into the capillary tube sealer or clay (Figure 29A.6b). Prepare a second tube in the same manner.

4. Place the prepared tubes opposite one another in the radial grooves of the microhematocrit centrifuge with the sealed ends abutting the rubber gasket at the centrifuge periphery (Figure 29A.6c). This loading procedure balances the centrifuge and prevents blood from spraying everywhere by centrifugal force. *Make a note of the numbers of the grooves your tubes are in.* When all the tubes have been loaded, make sure the centrifuge is properly balanced, and secure the centrifuge cover. Turn the centrifuge on, and set the timer for 4 or 5 minutes.

(a)

(b)

(c)

FIGURE 29A.6 Steps in a hematocrit determination.
(a) Load a heparinized capillary tube with blood. **(b)** Plug the
blood-containing end of the tube with clay. **(c)** Place the
tube in a microhematocrit centrifuge. (Centrifuge must be
balanced.)

5.   Determine the percentage of RBCs, WBCs, and plasma
by using the microhematocrit reader. The RBCs are the bottom layer, the plasma is the top layer, and the WBCs are the
buff-colored layer between the two. If the reader is not available, use a millimeter ruler to measure the length of the filled

capillary tube occupied by each element, and compute its percentage by using the following formula:

$$\frac{\text{Height of the column composed of the element (mm)}}{\text{Height of the original column of whole blood (mm)}} \times 100$$

Record your calculations below and on the data sheet on
page 436.

% RBC _____ % WBC _____ % plasma _____

Usually WBCs constitute 1% of the total blood volume. How
do your blood values compare to this figure and to the normal
percentages for RBCs and plasma? (See page 425.)

_____

As a rule, a hematocrit is considered a more accurate test than
the total RBC count for determining the RBC composition of
the blood. A hematocrit within the normal range generally indicates a normal RBC number, whereas an abnormally high
or low hematocrit is cause for concern. ■

Hemoglobin Concentration

As noted earlier, a person can be anemic even with a normal
RBC count. Since hemoglobin (Hb) is the RBC protein responsible for oxygen transport, perhaps the most accurate way
of measuring the oxygen-carrying capacity of the blood is to
determine its hemoglobin content. Oxygen, which combines
reversibly with the heme (iron-containing portion) of the hemoglobin molecule, is picked up by the blood cells in the lungs
and unloaded in the tissues. Thus, the more hemoglobin molecules the RBCs contain, the more oxygen they will be able to
transport. Normal blood contains 12 to 18 g of hemoglobin per
100 ml of blood. Hemoglobin content in men is slightly higher
(13 to 18 g) than in women (12 to 16 g).

(a) A drop of blood is added to the moat plate of the blood chamber. The blood must flow freely.

(b) The blood sample is hemolyzed with a wooden hemolysis applicator. Complete hemolysis requires 35 to 45 seconds.

(c) The charged blood chamber is inserted into the slot on the side of the hemoglobinometer.

(d) The colors of the green split screen are found by moving the slide with the right index finger. When the two colors match in density, the grams/100 ml and % Hb are read on the scale.

FIGURE 29A.7 **Hemoglobin determination using a hemoglobinometer.**

ACTIVITY 5

Determining Hemoglobin Concentration

Several techniques have been developed to estimate the hemoglobin content of blood, ranging from the old, rather inaccurate Tallquist method to expensive colorimeters, which are precisely calibrated and yield highly accurate results. Directions for both the Tallquist method and a hemoglobinometer are provided here.

Tallquist Method

1. Obtain a Tallquist hemoglobin scale, test paper, lancets, alcohol swabs, and cotton balls.

2. Use instructor-provided blood or prepare the finger as previously described. (For best results, make sure the alcohol evaporates before puncturing your finger.) Place one good-sized drop of blood on the special absorbent paper provided with the color scale. The blood stain should be larger than the holes on the color scale.

3. As soon as the blood has dried and loses its glossy appearance, match its color, under natural light, with the color standards by moving the specimen under the comparison scale so that the blood stain appears at all the various apertures. (The blood should not be allowed to dry to a brown color, as this will result in an inaccurate reading.) Because the colors on the scale represent 1% variations in hemoglobin content, it may be necessary to estimate the percentage if the color of your blood sample is intermediate between two color standards.

4. On the data sheet on page 436, record your results as the percentage of hemoglobin concentration and as grams per 100 ml of blood.

Hemoglobinometer Determination

1. Obtain a hemoglobinometer, hemolysis applicator, alcohol swab, and lens paper, and bring them to your bench. Test the hemoglobinometer light source to make sure it is working; if not, request new batteries before proceeding and test it again.

2. Remove the blood chamber from the slot in the side of the hemoglobinometer and disassemble the blood chamber by separating the glass plates from the metal clip. Notice as you do this that the larger glass plate has an H-shaped depression cut into it that acts as a moat to hold the blood, whereas the smaller glass piece is flat and serves as a coverslip.

3. Clean the glass plates with an alcohol swab, and then wipe them dry with lens paper. Hold the plates by their sides to prevent smearing during the wiping process.

4. Reassemble the blood chamber (remember: larger glass piece on the bottom with the moat up), but leave the moat plate about halfway out to provide adequate exposed surface to charge it with blood.

5. Obtain a drop of blood (from the provided sample or from your fingertip as before), and place it on the depressed area of the moat plate that is closest to you (Figure 29A.7a).

6. Using the wooden hemolysis applicator, stir or agitate the blood to rupture (lyse) the RBCs (Figure 29A.7b). This usually takes 35 to 45 seconds. Hemolysis is complete when the blood appears transparent rather than cloudy.

7. Push the blood-containing glass plate all the way into the metal clip and then firmly insert the charged blood chamber back into the slot on the side of the instrument (Figure 29A.7c).

8. Hold the hemoglobinometer in your left hand with your left thumb resting on the light switch located on the underside of the instrument. Look into the eyepiece and notice that there is a green area divided into two halves (a split field).

9. With the index finger of your right hand, slowly move the slide on the right side of the hemoglobinometer back and forth until the two halves of the green field match (Figure 29A.7d).

10. Note and record on the data sheet on page 436 the grams of Hb (hemoglobin)/100 ml of blood indicated on the uppermost scale by the index mark on the slide. Also record % Hb, indicated by one of the lower scales.

11. Disassemble the blood chamber once again, and carefully place its parts (glass plates and clip) into a bleach-containing beaker.

Generally speaking, the relationship between the PCV and grams of hemoglobin per 100 ml of blood is 3:1—for example, a PCV of 36 with 12 g of Hb per 100 ml of blood is a ratio of 3:1. How do your values compare?

_____

Record on the data sheet (page 436) the value obtained from your data. ■

Bleeding Time

Normally a sharp prick of the finger or earlobe results in bleeding that lasts from 2 to 7 minutes (Ivy method) or 0 to 5 minutes (Duke method), although other factors such as altitude affect the time. How long the bleeding lasts is referred to as **bleeding time** and tests the ability of platelets to stop bleeding in capillaries and small vessels. Absence of some clotting factors may affect bleeding time, but prolonged bleeding time is most often associated with deficient or abnormal platelets.

Coagulation Time

Blood clotting, or **coagulation,** is a protective mechanism that minimizes blood loss when blood vessels are ruptured. This process requires the interaction of many substances normally present in the plasma (clotting factors, or procoagulants) as well as some released by platelets and injured tissues. Basically hemostasis proceeds as follows (Figure 29A.8a): The injured tissues and platelets release **tissue factor (TF)** and PF_3 respectively, which trigger the clotting mechanism, or cascade. Tissue factor and PF_3 interact with other blood protein clotting factors and calcium ions to form **prothrombin activator,** which in turn converts **prothrombin** (present in plasma) to **thrombin.** Thrombin then acts enzymatically to polymerize the soluble **fibrinogen** proteins (present in plasma) into insoluble **fibrin,** which forms a meshwork of strands that traps the RBCs and forms the basis of the clot (Figure 29A.8b). Normally, blood removed from the body clots within 2 to 6 minutes.

ACTIVITY 6

Determining Coagulation Time

1. Obtain a *nonheparinized* capillary tube, a timer (or watch), a lancet, cotton balls, a triangular file, and alcohol swabs.

2. Clean and prick the finger to produce a free flow of blood. Discard the lancet in the disposal container.

3. Place one end of the capillary tube in the blood drop, and hold the opposite end at a lower level to collect the sample.

4. Lay the capillary tube on a paper towel.

Record the time. _____

5. At 30-second intervals, make a small nick on the tube close to one end with the triangular file, and then carefully break the tube. Slowly separate the ends to see if a gel-like thread of fibrin spans the gap. When this occurs, record below and on the data sheet on page 436 the time for coagulation to occur. Are your results within the normal time range?

_____

6. Put used supplies in the autoclave bag and broken capillary tubes into the sharps container. ■

Blood Typing

Blood typing is a system of blood classification based on the presence of specific glycoproteins on the outer surface of the RBC plasma membrane. Such proteins are called **antigens,** or **agglutinogens,** and are genetically determined. In many cases, these antigens are accompanied by plasma proteins, **antibodies** or **agglutinins,** that react with RBCs bearing different antigens, causing them to be clumped, agglutinated, and eventually hemolyzed. It is because of this phenomenon that a person's blood must be carefully typed before a whole blood or packed cell transfusion.

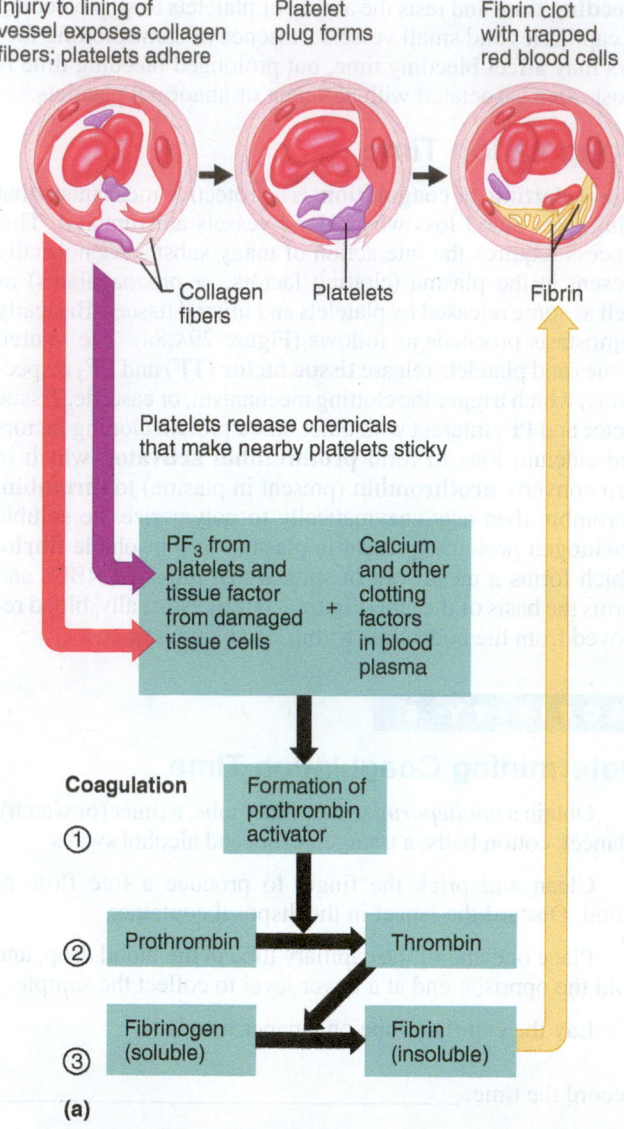

Injury to lining of vessel exposes collagen fibers; platelets adhere

Platelet plug forms

Fibrin clot with trapped red blood cells

Collagen fibers

Platelets

Fibrin

Platelets release chemicals that make nearby platelets sticky

| PF₃ from platelets and tissue factor from damaged tissue cells | + | Calcium and other clotting factors in blood plasma |

Coagulation

① Formation of prothrombin activator

② Prothrombin → Thrombin

③ Fibrinogen (soluble) → Fibrin (insoluble)

(a)

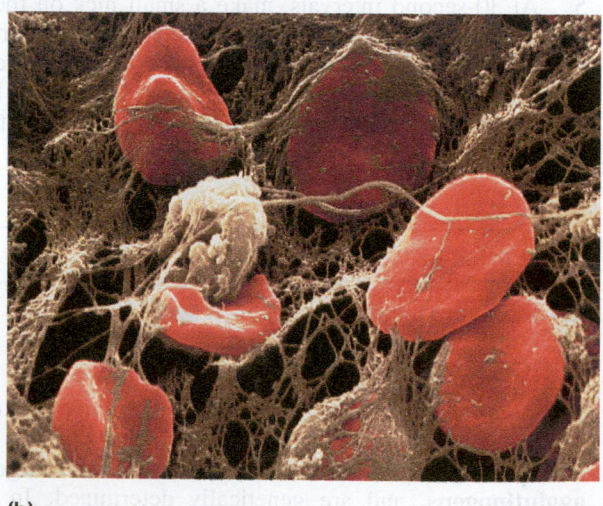

(b)

FIGURE 29A.8 Events of hemostasis and blood clotting.
(a) Simple schematic of events. Steps numbered 1–3 represent the major events of coagulation. **(b)** Photomicrograph of RBCs trapped in a fibrin mesh (2700×).

Several blood typing systems exist, based on the various possible antigens, but the factors routinely typed for are antigens of the ABO and Rh blood groups which are most commonly involved in transfusion reactions. Other blood factors, such as Kell, Lewis, M, and N, are not routinely typed for unless the individual will require multiple transfusions. The basis of the ABO typing is shown in Table 29A.2.

Individuals whose red blood cells carry the Rh antigen are Rh positive (approximately 85% of the U.S. population); those lacking the antigen are Rh negative. Unlike ABO blood groups, neither the blood of the Rh-positive (Rh⁺) nor Rh-negative (Rh⁻) individuals carries preformed anti-Rh antibodies. This is understandable in the case of the Rh-positive individual. However, Rh-negative persons who receive transfusions of Rh-positive blood become sensitized by the Rh antigens of the donor RBCs, and their systems begin to produce anti-Rh antibodies. On subsequent exposures to Rh-positive blood, typical transfusion reactions occur, resulting in the clumping and hemolysis of the donor blood cells.

Although the blood of dogs and other mammals does react with some of the human agglutinins (present in the antisera), the reaction is not as pronounced and varies with the animal blood used. Hence, the most accurate and predictable blood typing results are obtained with human blood. The artificial blood kit does not use any body fluids and produces results similar to but not identical to results for human blood.

ACTIVITY 7

Typing for ABO and Rh Blood Groups

Blood may be typed on glass slides or using blood test cards. Each method is described in this activity.

Typing Blood Using Glass Slides

1. Obtain two clean microscope slides, a wax marking pencil, anti-A, anti-B, and anti-Rh typing sera, toothpicks, lancets, alcohol swabs, medicine dropper, and the Rh typing box.

2. Divide slide 1 into halves with the wax marking pencil. Label the lower left-hand corner "anti-A" and the lower right-hand corner "anti-B." Mark the bottom of slide 2 "anti-Rh."

3. Place one drop of anti-A serum on the *left* side of slide 1. Place one drop of anti-B serum on the *right* side of slide 1. Place one drop of anti-Rh serum in the center of slide 2.

4. If you are using your own blood, cleanse your finger with an alcohol swab, pierce the finger with a lancet, and wipe away the first drop of blood. Obtain 3 drops of freely flowing blood, placing one drop on each side of slide 1 and a drop on slide 2. Immediately dispose of the lancet in a designated disposal container.

If using instructor-provided animal blood or EDTA-treated red cells, use a medicine dropper to place one drop of blood on each side of slide 1 and a drop of blood on slide 2.

⚠ 5. Quickly mix each blood-antiserum sample with a *fresh* toothpick. Then dispose of the toothpicks and used alcohol swab in the autoclave bag.

6. Place slide 2 on the Rh typing box and rock gently back and forth. (A slightly higher temperature is required for precise Rh typing than for ABO typing.)

TABLE 29A.2	ABO Blood Typing		% of U.S. population		
ABO blood type	Antigens present on RBC membranes	Antibodies present in plasma	White	Black	Asian
A	A	Anti-B	40	27	28
B	B	Anti-A	11	20	27
AB	A and B	None	4	4	5
O	Neither	Anti-A and anti-B	45	49	40

7. After 2 minutes, observe all three blood samples for evidence of clumping. The agglutination that occurs in the positive test for the Rh factor is very fine and difficult to perceive; thus if there is any question, observe the slide under the microscope. Record your observations in the Blood Typing chart.

8. Interpret your ABO results in light of the information in Figure 29A.9. If clumping was observed on slide 2, you are Rh positive. If not, you are Rh negative.

Blood Typing		
Result	Observed (+)	Not observed (−)
Presence of clumping with anti-A		
Presence of clumping with anti-B		
Presence of clumping with anti-Rh		

FIGURE 29A.9 Blood typing of ABO blood types. When serum containing anti-A or anti-B antibodies (agglutinins) is added to a blood sample, agglutination will occur between the antibody and the corresponding antigen (agglutinogen A or B). As illustrated, agglutination occurs with both sera in blood group AB, with anti-B serum in blood group B, with anti-A serum in blood group A, and with neither serum in blood group O.

9. Record your blood type on the data sheet on page 436.

10. Put the used slides in the bleach-containing bucket at the general supply area; put disposable supplies in the autoclave bag.

Using Blood Typing Cards

1. Obtain a blood typing card marked A, B, and Rh, dropper bottles of anti-A serum, anti-B serum, and anti-Rh serum, toothpicks, lancets, and alcohol swabs.

2. Place a drop of anti-A serum in the spot marked anti-A, place a drop of anti-B serum on the spot marked anti-B, and place a drop of anti-Rh serum on the spot marked anti-Rh (or anti-D).

3. Carefully add a drop of blood to each of the spots marked "Blood" on the card. If you are using your own blood, refer to step 4 in the Activity 7 section Typing Blood Using Glass Slides. Immediately discard the lancet in the designated disposal container.

4. Using a new toothpick for each test, mix the blood sample with the antibody. Dispose of the toothpicks appropriately.

5. Gently rock the card to allow the blood and antibodies to mix.

6. After 2 minutes, observe the card for evidence of clumping. The Rh clumping is very fine and may be difficult to observe. Record your observations in the Blood Typing chart. Use Figure 29A.9 to interpret your results.

7. Record your blood type on the chart on page 436, and discard the card in an autoclave bag. ▬

Hematologic Test Data Sheet

Differential WBC count:

WBC	Student blood smear	Unknown sample # ___
% neutrophils	_____	_____
% eosinophils	_____	_____
% basophils	_____	_____
% monocytes	_____	_____
% lymphocytes	_____	_____

Hematocrit (PCV):

RBC _____ % of blood volume

WBC _____ % of blood volume   not generally reported

Plasma _____ % of blood

Hemoglobin (Hb) content:

Tallquist method: _____ g/100 ml of blood; _____ % Hb

Hemoglobinometer (type: _____)

_____ g/100 ml of blood; _____ %Hb

Ratio (PCV to grams of Hb per 100 ml of blood): _____

Coagulation time _____

Blood typing:

ABO group _____   Rh factor _____

Cholesterol concentration _____ mg/dl of blood

Observing Demonstration Slides

Before continuing on to the cholesterol determination, take the time to look at the slides of *macrocytic hypochromic anemia, microcytic hypochromic anemia, sickle cell anemia, lymphocytic leukemia* (chronic), and *eosinophilia* that have been put on demonstration by your instructor. Record your observations in the appropriate section of the Exercise 29A Review Sheet. You can refer to your notes, the text, and other references later to respond to questions about the blood pathologies represented on the slides. ■

Cholesterol Concentration in Plasma

Atherosclerosis is the disease process in which the body's blood vessels become increasingly occluded by plaques. Because the plaques narrow the arteries, they can contribute to hypertensive heart disease. They also serve as focal points for the formation of blood clots (thrombi), which may break away and block smaller vessels farther downstream in the circulatory pathway and cause heart attacks or strokes.

Ever since medical clinicians discovered that cholesterol is a major component of the smooth muscle plaques formed during atherosclerosis, it has had a bad press. Today, virtually no physical examination of an adult is considered complete until cholesterol levels are assessed along with other lifestyle risk factors. A normal value for plasma cholesterol in adults ranges from 130 to 200 mg per 100 ml of plasma; you will use blood to make such a determination.

Although the total plasma cholesterol concentration is valuable information, it may be misleading, particularly if a person's high-density lipoprotein (HDL) level is high and

low-density lipoprotein (LDL) level is relatively low. Cholesterol, being water insoluble, is transported in the blood complexed to lipoproteins. In general, cholesterol bound into HDLs is destined to be degraded by the liver and then eliminated from the body, whereas that forming part of the LDLs is "traveling" to the body's tissue cells. When LDL levels are excessive, cholesterol is deposited in the blood vessel walls; hence, LDLs are considered to carry the "bad" cholesterol.

Measuring Plasma Cholesterol Concentration

1. Go to the appropriate supply area, and obtain a cholesterol test card and color scale, lancet, and alcohol swab.

2. Clean your fingertip with the alcohol swab, allow it to dry, then prick it with a lancet. Place a drop of blood on the test area of the card. Put the lancet in the designated disposal container.

3. After 3 minutes, remove the blood sample strip from the card and discard in the autoclave bag.

4. Analyze the underlying test spot, using the included color scale. Record the cholesterol level below and on the data sheet above.

Cholesterol level _____ mg/dl

⚠ 5. Before leaving the laboratory, use the spray bottle of bleach solution and saturate a paper towel to thoroughly wash down your laboratory bench. ■

NAME _____

LAB TIME/DATE _____

Blood

Composition of Blood

1. What is the blood volume of an average-size adult male? _____ liters An average adult female? _____ liters

2. What determines whether blood is bright red or a dull brick-red? _____

_____

3. Use the key to identify the cell type(s) or blood elements that fit the following descriptive statements.

Key: a.   red blood cell   d.   basophil   g.   lymphocyte
         b.   megakaryocyte   e.   monocyte   h.   formed elements
         c.   eosinophil   f.   neutrophil   i.   plasma

_____   1.   most numerous leukocyte

_____, _____, and _____   2.   granulocytes (3)

_____   3.   also called an erythrocyte; anucleate formed element

_____, _____   4.   actively phagocytic leukocytes

_____, _____   5.   agranulocytes

_____   6.   ancestral cell of platelets

_____   7.   (a) through (g) are all examples of these

_____   8.   number rises during parasite infections

_____   9.   releases histamine; promotes inflammation

_____   10.   many formed in lymphoid tissue

_____   11.   transports oxygen

_____   12.   primarily water, noncellular; the fluid matrix of blood

_____   13.   increases in number during prolonged infections

_____, _____, _____,

_____, _____   14.   the five types of white blood cells

4. List four classes of nutrients normally found in plasma. _____ ,

_____ , _____ , and _____

Name two gases. _____ and _____

Name three ions. _____ , _____ , and _____

5. Describe the consistency and color of the plasma you observed in the laboratory. _____

_____

6. What is the average life span of a red blood cell? How does its anucleate condition affect this life span?

_____

_____

_____

7. From memory, describe the structural characteristics of each of the following blood cell types as accurately as possible, and note the percentage of each in the total white blood cell population.

eosinophils: _____

_____

neutrophils: _____

_____

lymphocytes: _____

_____

basophils: _____

_____

monocytes: _____

_____

8. Correctly identify the blood pathologies described in column A by matching them with selections from column B:

Column A   **Column B**

_____ 1. abnormal increase in the number of WBCs   a. anemia

_____ 2. abnormal increase in the number of RBCs   b. leukocytosis

_____ 3. condition of too few RBCs or of RBCs with   c. leukopenia
                              hemoglobin deficiencies

                                                                                                          d. polycythemia

_____ 4. abnormal decrease in the number of WBCs

Hematologic Tests

9. Broadly speaking, why are hematologic studies of blood so important in the diagnosis of disease?

_____

_____

10. In the chart below, record information from the blood tests you read about or conducted. Complete the chart by recording values for healthy male adults and indicating the significance of high or low values for each test.

Test	Student test results	Normal values (healthy male adults)	Significance	
			High values	Low values
Total WBC count	No data			
Total RBC count	No data			
Hematocrit				
Hemoglobin determination				
Bleeding time	No data			
Coagulation time				

11. Why is a differential WBC count more valuable than a total WBC count when trying to pin down the specific source of

pathology? _____

_____

_____

12. What name is given to the process of RBC production? _____

What hormone acts as a stimulus for this process? _____

Why might patients with kidney disease suffer from anemia? _____

_____

How can such patients be treated? _____

13. Discuss the effect of each of the following factors on RBC count. Consult an appropriate reference as necessary, and explain your reasoning.

long-term effect of athletic training (for example, running 4 to 5 miles per day over a period of six to nine months):

_____

_____

a permanent move from sea level to a high-altitude area: _____

_____

_____

14. Define *hematocrit*. _____

15. If you had a high hematocrit, would you expect your hemoglobin determination to be high or low? _____

Why? _____

_____

16. What is an anticoagulant? _____

Name two anticoagulants used in conducting the hematologic tests. _____

and _____

What is the body's natural anticoagulant? _____

17. If your blood clumped with both anti-A and anti-B sera, your ABO blood type would be _____

To what ABO blood groups could you give blood? _____

From which ABO donor types could you receive blood? _____

Which ABO blood type is most common? _____ Least common? _____

18. What blood type is theoretically considered the universal donor? _____ Why? _____

_____

19. Assume the blood of two patients has been typed for ABO blood type.

Typing results
Mr. Adams:

Blood drop and   Blood drop and
anti-A serum   anti-B serum

Typing results
Mr. Calhoon:

Blood drop and   Blood drop and
anti-A serum   anti-B serum

On the basis of these results, Mr. Adams has type _____ blood, and Mr. Calhoon has type _____ blood.

20. Explain why an Rh-negative person does not have a transfusion reaction on the first exposure to Rh-positive blood but *does*

have a reaction on the second exposure. _____

_____

What happens when an ABO blood type is mismatched for the first time? _____

_____

21. Record your observations of the five demonstration slides viewed.

a.   Macrocytic hypochromic anemia: _____

b.   Microcytic hypochromic anemia: _____

_____

c.   Sickle cell anemia: _____

d.   Lymphocytic leukemia (chronic): _____

_____

e.   Eosinophilia: _____

Which of the slides above (a through e) corresponds with the following conditions?

_____ 1.   iron-deficient diet   _____ 4.   lack of vitamin B_{12}

_____ 2.   a type of bone marrow cancer   _____ 5.   a tapeworm infestation in the body

_____ 3.   genetic defect that causes hemoglobin   _____ 6.   a bleeding ulcer
                  to become sharp/spiky

22. Provide the normal, or at least "desirable," range for plasma cholesterol concentration.

_____ mg/100 ml

23. Describe the relationship between high blood cholesterol levels and cardiovascular diseases such as hypertension, heart attacks, and strokes.

_____

_____

_____

_____

_____

Anatomy of the Heart

M A T E R I A L S

- ☐ X ray of the human thorax for observation of the position of the heart in situ; X-ray viewing box
- ☐ Three-dimensional heart model and torso model or laboratory chart showing heart anatomy
- ☐ Red and blue pencils
- ☐ Highlighter
- ☐ Three-dimensional models of cardiac and skeletal muscle
- ☐ Compound microscope
- ☐ Prepared slides of cardiac muscle (l.s.)
- ☐ Preserved sheep heart, pericardial sacs intact (if possible)
- ☐ Dissecting instruments and tray
- ☐ Pointed glass rods or blunt probes
- ☐ Plastic rulers
- ☐ Disposable gloves
- ☐ Container for disposal of organic debris
- ☐ Laboratory detergent
- ☐ Spray bottle with 10% household bleach solution
- ☐ *Human Cardiovascular System: The Heart* videotape

O B J E C T I V E S

1. To describe the location of the heart.
2. To name and locate the major anatomical areas and structures of the heart when provided with an appropriate model, diagram, or dissected sheep heart, and to explain the function of each.
3. To trace the pathway of blood through the heart.
4. To explain why the heart is called a double pump, and to compare the pulmonary and systemic circuits.
5. To explain the operation of the atrioventricular and semilunar valves.
6. To trace the functional blood supply of the heart and name the associated blood vessels.
7. To describe the histology of cardiac muscle, and to note the importance of its intercalated discs and the spiral arrangement of its cells.

P R E - L A B   Q U I Z

1. The heart is enclosed in a double-walled sac called the
   a. apex
   b. mediastinum
   c. pericardium
   d. thorax
2. The heart is divided into _____ chambers.
   a. two
   b. three
   c. four
   d. five
3. What is the name of the two receiving chambers of the heart?
   _____
4. The left ventricle discharges blood into the _____, from which all systemic arteries of the body diverge to supply the body tissues.
   a. aorta
   b. pulmonary artery
   c. pulmonary vein
   d. vena cava
5. Circle True or False. Blood flows through the heart in one direction—from the atria to the ventricles.
6. Circle the correct term. The right atrioventricular valve, or tricuspid / mitral, prevents backflow into the right atrium when the right ventricle is contracting.
7. Circle the correct term. The heart serves as a double pump. The right / left side serves as the pulmonary circulation pump, shunting carbon dioxide–rich blood to the lungs.
8. The functional blood supply of the heart itself is provided by the
   a. aorta
   b. carotid arteries
   c. coronary arteries
   d. pulmonary trunk
9. Two microscopic features of cardiac cells that help distinguish them from other types of muscle cells are branching and
   a. intercalated discs
   b. myosin fibers
   c. sarcolemma
   d. striations
10. Circle the correct term. In the heart, the left / right ventricle has thicker walls and a basically circular cavity shape.

my A&P *For practice quizzes on this lab, go to www.myaandp.com.*

PAL *For access to anatomical models and more, check out Practice Anatomy Lab.*

The major function of the **cardiovascular system** is transportation. Using blood as the transport vehicle, the system carries oxygen, digested foods, cell wastes, electrolytes, and many other substances vital to the body's homeostasis to and from the body cells. The system's propulsive force is the contracting heart, which can be compared to a muscular pump equipped with one-way valves. As the heart contracts, it forces blood into a closed system of large and small plumbing tubes (blood vessels) within which the blood is confined and circulated. This exercise deals with the structure of the heart, or circulatory pump. The anatomy of the blood vessels is considered separately in Exercise 32.

Gross Anatomy of the Human Heart

The **heart,** a cone-shaped organ approximately the size of a fist, is located within the mediastinum, or medial cavity, of the thorax. It is flanked laterally by the lungs, posteriorly by the vertebral column, and anteriorly by the sternum (Figure 30.1). Its more pointed **apex** extends slightly to the left and rests on the diaphragm, approximately at the level of the fifth intercostal space. Its broader **base,** from which the great vessels emerge, lies beneath the second rib and points toward the right shoulder. In situ, the right ventricle of the heart forms most of its anterior surface.

The apical pulse may be heard in the 5th intercostal space at the point of maximal intensity (PMI).

• If an X ray of a human thorax is available, verify the relationships described above; otherwise, Figure 30.1 should suffice.

The heart is enclosed within a double-walled fibroserous sac called the pericardium. The thin **epicardium,** or **visceral pericardium,** is closely applied to the heart muscle. It reflects downward at the base of the heart to form its companion serous membrane, the outer, loosely applied **parietal pericardium,** which is attached at the heart apex to the diaphragm. Serous fluid produced by these membranes allows the heart to beat in a relatively frictionless environment. The serous parietal pericardium, in turn, lines the loosely fitting superficial **fibrous pericardium** composed of dense connective tissue.

Inflammation of the pericardium, **pericarditis,** causes painful adhesions between the serous pericardial layers. These adhesions interfere with heart movements. ■

The walls of the heart are composed primarily of cardiac muscle—the **myocardium**—which is reinforced internally by a dense fibrous connective tissue network. This network—the *fibrous skeleton of the heart*—is more elaborate and thicker in certain areas, for example, around the valves and at the base of the great vessels leaving the heart.

Figure 30.2 shows three views of the heart—external anterior and posterior views and a frontal section. As its anatomical areas are described in the text, consult the figure.

Heart Chambers

The heart is divided into four chambers: two superior **atria** (singular: *atrium*) and two inferior **ventricles,** each lined by thin serous endothelium called the **endocardium.** The septum that divides the heart longitudinally is referred to as the **interatrial** or **interventricular septum,** depending on which chambers it partitions. Functionally, the atria are receiving chambers and are relatively ineffective as pumps. Blood flows into the atria under low pressure from the veins of the body. The right atrium receives relatively oxygen-poor blood from the body via the **superior** and **inferior venae cavae** and the coronary sinus. Four **pulmonary veins** deliver oxygen-rich blood from the lungs to the left atrium.

The inferior thick-walled ventricles, which form the bulk of the heart, are the discharging chambers. They force blood out of the heart into the large arteries that emerge from its base. The right ventricle pumps blood into the **pulmonary trunk,** which routes blood to the lungs to be oxygenated. The left ventricle discharges blood into the **aorta,** from which all systemic arteries of the body diverge to supply the body tissues. Discussions of the heart's pumping action usually refer to ventricular activity.

Heart Valves

Four valves enforce a one-way blood flow through the heart chambers. The **atrioventricular (AV) valves,** located between the atrial and ventricular chambers on each side, prevent backflow into the atria when the ventricles are contracting. The left atrioventricular valve, also called the **mitral** or *bicuspid valve,* consists of two cusps, or flaps, of endocardium. The right atrioventricular valve, the **tricuspid valve,** has three cusps (Figure 30.3). Tiny white collagenic cords called the **chordae tendineae** (literally, heart strings) anchor the cusps to the ventricular walls. The chordae tendineae originate from small bundles of cardiac muscle, called **papillary muscles,** that project from the myocardial wall (see Figure 30.2b).

When blood is flowing passively into the atria and then into the ventricles during **diastole** (the period of ventricular filling), the AV valve flaps hang limply into the ventricular chambers and then are carried passively toward the atria by the accumulating blood. When the ventricles contract **(systole)** and compress the blood in their chambers, the intraventricular blood pressure rises, causing the valve flaps to be reflected superiorly, which closes the AV valves. The chordae tendineae, pulled taut by the contracting papillary muscles, anchor the flaps in a closed position that prevents backflow into the atria during ventricular contraction. If unanchored,

Midsternal line ——————

2nd rib ——————

Diaphragm ——————

—— Sternum

—— Point of maximal intensity (PMI)

FIGURE 30.1 Location of the heart in the thorax.

(a)

Brachiocephalic trunk

Superior vena cava

Right pulmonary artery

Ascending aorta

Pulmonary trunk

Right pulmonary veins

Right atrium

Right coronary artery (in coronary sulcus)

Anterior cardiac vein

Right ventricle

Right marginal artery

Small cardiac vein

Inferior vena cava

Left common carotid artery

Left subclavian artery

Aortic arch

Ligamentum arteriosum

Left pulmonary artery

Left pulmonary veins

Auricle of left atrium

Circumflex artery

Left coronary artery (in coronary sulcus)

Left ventricle

Great cardiac vein

Anterior interventricular artery (in anterior interventricular sulcus)

Apex

(b)

Superior vena cava

Right pulmonary artery

Pulmonary trunk

Right atrium

Right pulmonary veins

Fossa ovalis

Pectinate muscles

Tricuspid valve

Right ventricle

Chordae tendineae

Trabeculae carneae

Inferior vena cava

Aorta

Left pulmonary artery

Left atrium

Left pulmonary veins

Mitral (bicuspid) valve

Aortic valve

Pulmonary valve

Left ventricle

Papillary muscle

Interventricular septum

Epicardium

Myocardium

Endocardium

FIGURE 30.2 Gross anatomy of the human heart. (a) External anterior view. (b) Frontal section.

Aorta

Left pulmonary artery

Left pulmonary veins

Auricle of left atrium

Left atrium

Great cardiac vein

Posterior vein of left ventricle

Left ventricle

Apex

Superior vena cava

Right pulmonary artery

Right pulmonary veins

Right atrium

Inferior vena cava

Coronary sinus

Right coronary artery
(in coronary sulcus)

Posterior interventricular
artery (in posterior
interventricular sulcus)

Middle cardiac vein

Right ventricle

(c)

FIGURE 30.2 *(continued)* Gross anatomy of the human heart. (c) Exterior posterior view.

the flaps would blow upward into the atria rather like an umbrella being turned inside out by a strong wind.

The second set of valves, the **pulmonary** and **aortic (semilunar, SL) valves,** each composed of three pocketlike cusps, guards the bases of the two large arteries leaving the ventricular chambers. The valve cusps are forced open and flatten against the walls of the artery as the ventricles discharge their blood into the large arteries during systole. However, when the ventricles relax, blood flows backward toward the heart and the cusps fill with blood, closing the semilunar valves and preventing arterial blood from reentering the heart.

ACTIVITY 1

Using the Heart Model to Study Heart Anatomy

When you have located in Figure 30.2 all the structures described above, observe the human heart model and laboratory charts and reidentify the same structures without referring to the figure. ▪

Pulmonary, Systemic, and Cardiac Circulations

Pulmonary and Systemic Circulations

The heart functions as a double pump. The right side serves as the **pulmonary circulation** pump, shunting the carbon dioxide–rich blood entering its chambers to the lungs to unload carbon dioxide and pick up oxygen, and then back to the left side of the heart (Figure 30.4). The function of this circuit is strictly to provide for gas exchange. The second circuit, which carries oxygen-rich blood from the left heart through the body tissues and back to the right side of the heart, is called the **systemic circulation.** It provides the functional blood supply to all body tissues.

ACTIVITY 2

Tracing the Path of Blood Through the Heart

Use colored pencils to trace the pathway of a red blood cell through the heart by adding arrows to the frontal section diagram (Figure 30.2b). Use red arrows for the oxygen-rich blood and blue arrows for the less oxygen-rich blood. ▪

Pulmonary valve
Aortic valve
Area of cutaway
Mitral valve
Tricuspid valve

FIGURE 30.3 Heart valves. (a) Superior view of the two sets of heart valves (atria removed). **(b)** Photograph of the heart valves, superior view. **(c)** Photograph of the right AV valve. View begins in the right ventricle, looking toward the right atrium. **(d)** Coronal section of the heart.

Myocardium

Tricuspid (right atrioventricular) valve

Mitral (left atrioventricular) valve

Aortic valve

Pulmonary valve

Fibrous skeleton

Anterior

(a)

(b)

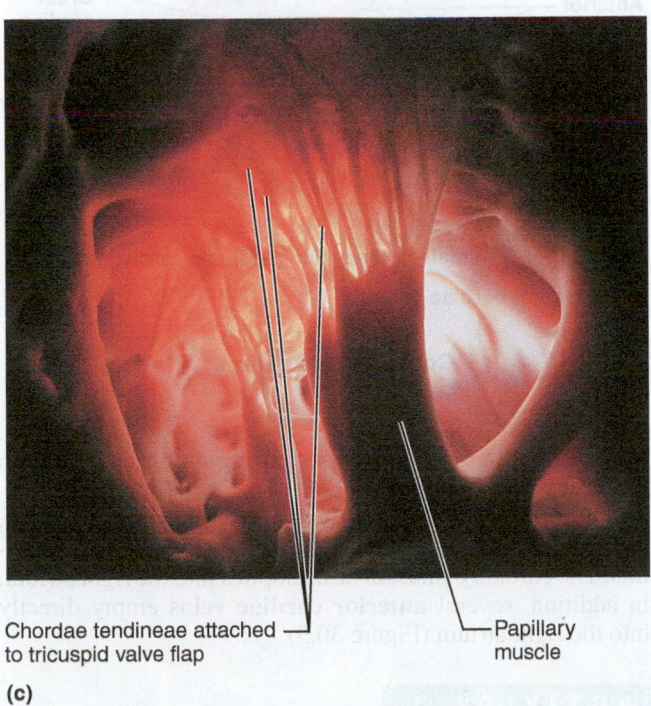

Chordae tendineae attached to tricuspid valve flap

Papillary muscle

(c)

Opening of inferior vena cava

Tricuspid valve

Myocardium of right ventricle

Papillary muscles

Mitral valve

Chordae tendineae

Interventricular septum

Myocardium of left ventricle

(d)

Coronary Circulation

Even though the heart chambers are almost continually bathed with blood, this contained blood does not nourish the myocardium. The functional blood supply of the heart is provided by the coronary arteries (see Figures 30.2 and 30.5). The **right**

and **left coronary arteries** issue from the base of the aorta just above the aortic semilunar valve and encircle the heart in the **coronary sulcus** at the junction of the atria and ventricles. They then ramify over the heart's surface, the right coronary artery supplying the posterior surface of the ventricles and the lateral aspect of the right side of the heart, largely through

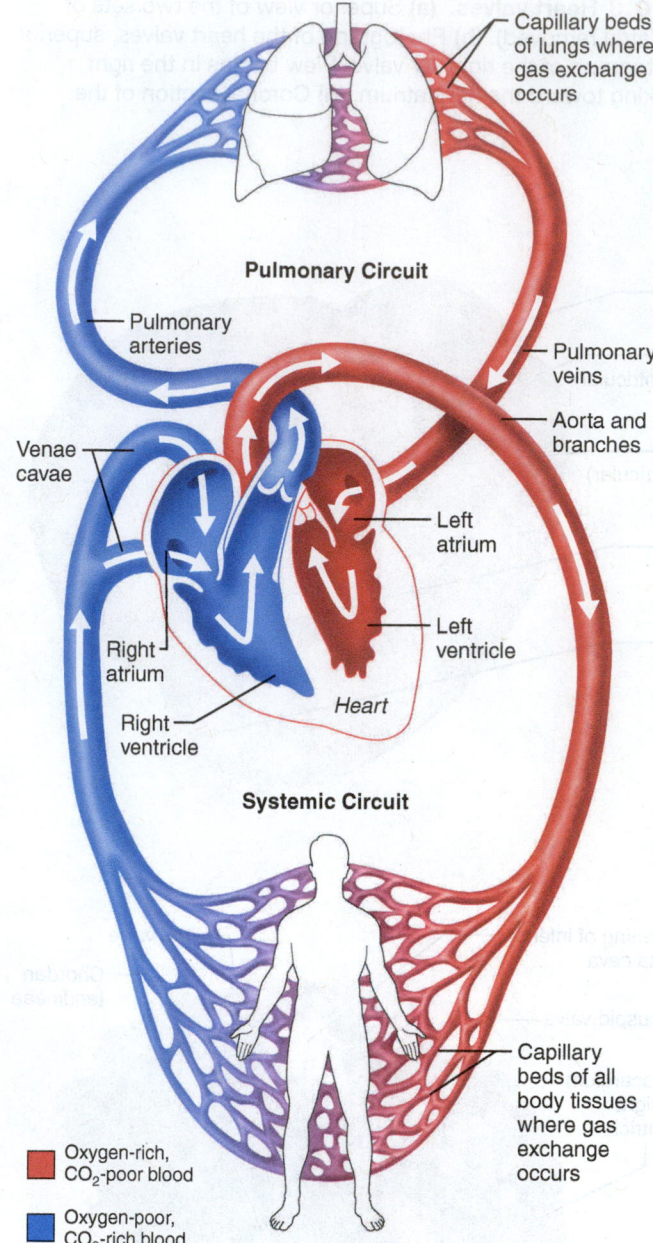

Pulmonary Circuit

Capillary beds of lungs where gas exchange occurs

Pulmonary arteries

Pulmonary veins

Aorta and branches

Venae cavae

Left atrium

Left ventricle

Right atrium

Heart

Right ventricle

Systemic Circuit

Capillary beds of all body tissues where gas exchange occurs

Oxygen-rich, CO_2-poor blood

Oxygen-poor, CO_2-rich blood

FIGURE 30.4 **The systemic and pulmonary circuits.** The heart is a double pump that serves two circulations. The right side of the heart pumps blood through the pulmonary circuit to the lungs and back to the left heart. (For simplicity, the actual number of two pulmonary arteries and four pulmonary veins has been reduced to one each.) The left side of the heart pumps blood via the systemic circuit to all body tissues and back to the right heart. Notice that blood flowing through the pulmonary circuit gains oxygen (O_2) and loses carbon dioxide (CO_2) as depicted by the color change from blue to red. Blood flowing through the systemic circuit loses oxygen and picks up carbon dioxide (red to blue color change).

its **posterior interventricular** and **right marginal artery** branches. The left coronary artery supplies the anterior ventricular walls and the laterodorsal part of the left side of the heart via its two major branches, the **anterior interventricular artery** and the **circumflex artery.** The coronary arteries

Aorta

Superior vena cava

Pulmonary trunk

Left atrium

Anastomosis (junction of vessels)

Left coronary artery

Right atrium

Circumflex artery

Right coronary artery

Left ventricle

Right ventricle

Right marginal artery

Posterior interventricular artery

Anterior interventricular artery

(a) The major coronary arteries

Superior vena cava

Anterior cardiac veins

Great cardiac vein

Coronary sinus

Small cardiac vein   **Middle cardiac vein**

(b) The major cardiac veins

FIGURE 30.5 Coronary circulation.

and their branches are compressed during systole and fill when the heart is relaxed.

The myocardium is largely drained by the **great, middle, and small cardiac veins,** which empty into the **coronary sinus.** The coronary sinus, in turn, empties into the right atrium. In addition, several **anterior cardiac veins** empty directly into the right atrium (Figure 30.5).

ACTIVITY 3

Using the Heart Model to Study Cardiac Circulation

1.   Obtain a highlighter and highlight all the cardiac blood vessels in Figure 30.2a and c. Note how arteries and veins travel together.

FIGURE 30.6 The circular and spiral arrangement of cardiac muscle bundles in the myocardium.

FIGURE 30.7 Photomicrograph of cardiac muscle (570×).

2.   On a model of the heart, locate all the cardiac blood vessels shown in Figure 30.5. Use your finger to trace the pathway of blood from the right coronary artery to the lateral aspect of the right side of the heart and back to the right atrium. Name the arteries and veins along the pathway. Trace the pathway of blood from the left coronary artery to the anterior ventricular walls and back to the right atrium. Name the arteries and veins along the pathway. Note that there are multiple different pathways to distribute blood to these parts of the heart. ▬

Microscopic Anatomy of Cardiac Muscle

Cardiac muscle is found in only one place—the heart. The heart acts as a vascular pump, propelling blood to all tissues of the body; cardiac muscle is thus very important to life. Cardiac muscle is involuntary, ensuring a constant blood supply.

The cardiac cells, only sparingly invested in connective tissue, are arranged in spiral or figure-8-shaped bundles (Figure 30.6). When the heart contracts, its internal chambers become smaller (or are temporarily obliterated), forcing the blood into the large arteries leaving the heart.

Examining Cardiac Muscle Tissue Anatomy

1.   Observe the three-dimensional model of cardiac muscle, examining its branching cells and the areas where the cells interdigitate, the **intercalated discs.** These two structural features provide a continuity to cardiac muscle not seen in other muscle tissues and allow close coordination of heart activity.

2.   Compare the model of cardiac muscle to the model of skeletal muscle. Note the similarities and differences between the two kinds of muscle tissue.

3.   Obtain and observe a longitudinal section of cardiac muscle under high power. Identify the nucleus, striations, intercalated discs, and sarcolemma of the individual cells and then compare your observations to the view seen in Figure 30.7. ▬

DISSECTION: The Sheep Heart

Dissection of a sheep heart is valuable because it is similar in size and structure to the human heart. Also, a dissection experience allows you to view structures in a way not possible with models and diagrams. Refer to Figure 30.8 as you proceed with the dissection.

1.   Obtain a preserved sheep heart, a dissecting tray, dissecting instruments, a glass probe, a plastic ruler, and gloves. Rinse the sheep heart in cold water to remove excessive preservatives and to flush out any trapped blood clots. Now you are ready to make your observations.

2.   Observe the texture of the pericardium. Also, note its point of attachment to the heart. Where is it attached?

_____

3.   If the serous pericardial sac is still intact, slit open the parietal pericardium and cut it from its attachments. Observe the visceral pericardium (epicardium). Using a sharp scalpel, carefully pull a little of this serous membrane away from the myocardium. How do its position, thickness, and apposition to the heart differ from those of the parietal pericardium?

_____

_____

_____

FIGURE 30.8 Anatomy of the sheep heart. (a) Anterior view. (b) Posterior view. Diagrammatic views at top; photographs at bottom.

4. Examine the external surface of the heart. Notice the accumulation of adipose tissue, which in many cases marks the separation of the chambers and the location of the coronary arteries that nourish the myocardium. Carefully scrape away some of the fat with a scalpel to expose the coronary blood vessels.

5. Identify the base and apex of the heart, and then identify the two wrinkled **auricles,** earlike flaps of tissue projecting from the atrial chambers. The balance of the heart muscle is ventricular tissue. To identify the left ventricle, compress the ventricular chambers on each side of the longitudinal fissures carrying the coronary blood vessels. The side that feels

thicker and more solid is the left ventricle. The right ventricle feels much thinner and somewhat flabby when compressed. This difference reflects the greater demand placed on the left ventricle, which must pump blood through the much longer systemic circulation, a pathway with much higher resistance than the pulmonary circulation served by the right ventricle. Hold the heart in its anatomical position (Figure 30.8a), with the anterior surface uppermost. In this position the left ventricle composes the entire apex and the left side of the heart.

6. Identify the pulmonary trunk and the aorta extending from the superior aspect of the heart. The pulmonary trunk is more anterior, and you may see its division into the right and left pulmonary arteries if it has not been cut too closely to the heart. The thicker-walled aorta, which branches almost immediately, is located just beneath the pulmonary trunk. The first observable branch of the sheep aorta, the **brachiocephalic artery,** is identifiable unless the aorta has been cut immediately as it leaves the heart. The brachiocephalic artery splits to form the right carotid and subclavian arteries, which supply the right side of the head and right forelimb, respectively.

Gently pull on the aorta with your gloved fingers or forceps to stretch it. Repeat with the vena cava.

Which vessel is easier to stretch? _____

How does the elasticity of each vessel relate to its ability to withstand pressure?

_____

Carefully clear away some of the fat between the pulmonary trunk and the aorta to expose the **ligamentum arteriosum,** a cordlike remnant of the **ductus arteriosus.** (In the fetus, the ductus arteriosus allows blood to pass directly from the pulmonary trunk to the aorta, thus bypassing the nonfunctional fetal lungs.)

7. Cut through the wall of the aorta until you see the aortic (semilunar) valve. Identify the two openings to the coronary arteries just above the valve. Insert a probe into one of these holes to see if you can follow the course of a coronary artery across the heart.

8. Turn the heart to view its posterior surface. The heart will appear as shown in Figure 30.8b. Notice that the right and left ventricles appear equal-sized in this view. Try to identify the four thin-walled pulmonary veins entering the left atrium. Identify the superior and inferior venae cavae entering the right atrium. Because of the way the heart is trimmed, the pulmonary veins and superior vena cava may be very short or missing. If possible, compare the approximate diameter of the superior vena cava with the diameter of the aorta.

Which is larger? _____

Which has thicker walls? _____

Why do you suppose these differences exist?

_____

_____

_____

9. Insert a probe into the superior vena cava, through the right atrium, and out the inferior vena cava. Use scissors to cut along the probe so that you can view the interior of the right atrium. Observe the tricuspid valve.

How many flaps does it have? _____

Pour some water into the right atrium and allow it to flow into the ventricle. *Slowly and gently* squeeze the right ventricle to watch the closing action of this valve. (If you squeeze too vigorously, you'll get a face full of water!) Drain the water from the heart before continuing.

10. Return to the pulmonary trunk and cut through its anterior wall until you can see the pulmonary (semilunar) valve (Figure 30.9). Pour some water into the base of the pulmonary trunk to observe the closing action of this valve. How does its action differ from that of the tricuspid valve?

_____

_____

_____

After observing pulmonary valve action, drain the heart once again. Extend the cut through the pulmonary trunk into the right ventricle. Cut down, around, and up through the tricuspid valve to make the cut continuous with the cut across the right atrium (see Figure 30.9).

11. Reflect the cut edges of the superior vena cava, right atrium, and right ventricle to obtain the view seen in Figure 30.9. Observe the comblike ridges of muscle throughout most of the right atrium. This is called **pectinate muscle** (*pectin* = comb). Identify, on the ventral atrial wall, the large opening of the inferior vena cava and follow it to its external opening with a probe. Notice that the atrial walls in the vicinity of the venae cavae are smooth and lack the roughened appearance (pectinate musculature) of the other regions of the atrial walls. Just below the inferior vena caval opening, identify the opening of the **coronary sinus,** which returns venous blood of the coronary circulation to the right atrium. Nearby, locate an oval depression, the **fossa ovalis,** in the interatrial septum. This depression marks the site of an opening in the fetal heart, the **foramen ovale,** which allows blood to pass from the right to the left atrium, thus bypassing the fetal lungs.

12. Identify the papillary muscles in the right ventricle, and follow their attached chordae tendineae to the flaps of the tricuspid valve. Notice the pitted and ridged appearance (**trabeculae carneae**) of the inner ventricular muscle.

13. Identify the **moderator band** (septomarginal band), a bundle of cardiac muscle fibers connecting the interventricular septum to anterior papillary muscles. It contains a branch of the atrioventricular bundle and helps coordinate contraction of the ventricle.

14. Make a longitudinal incision through the left atrium and continue it into the left ventricle. Notice how much thicker the myocardium of the left ventricle is than that of the right

Entrance of inferior vena cava

Fossa ovalis

Peg in opening of **coronary sinus**

Chordae tendineae

Papillary muscle

Wall of right ventricle (reflected)

Heart apex

Cut surface of wall of right ventricle

Flap of pulmonary valve

Flap of tricuspid valve

Moderator band

FIGURE 30.9 Right side of the sheep heart opened and reflected to reveal internal structures.

ventricle. Measure the thickness of right and left ventricular walls and record the numbers.

_____

How do your numbers compare with those of your classmates?

_____

Compare the *shape* of the left ventricular cavity to the shape of the right ventricular cavity. (See Figure 30.10.)

_____

_____

Are the papillary muscles and chordae tendineae observed in

the right ventricle also present in the left ventricle? _____

Count the number of cusps in the mitral valve. How does this compare with the number seen in the tricuspid valve?

_____

_____

How do the sheep valves compare with their human counterparts?

_____

15. Reflect the cut edges of the atrial wall, and attempt to locate the entry points of the pulmonary veins into the left

atrium. Follow the pulmonary veins, if present, to the heart exterior with a probe. Notice how thin-walled these vessels are.

16. Dispose of the organic debris in the designated container, clean the dissecting tray and instruments with detergent and water, and wash the lab bench with bleach solution before leaving the laboratory. ▬

Left ventricle

Right ventricle

Interventricular septum

FIGURE 30.10 Anatomical differences between the right and left ventricles. The left ventricle has thicker walls, and its cavity is basically circular; by contrast, the right ventricle cavity is crescent-shaped and wraps around the left ventricle.

Anatomy of the Heart

Gross Anatomy of the Human Heart

1. An anterior view of the heart is shown here. Match each structure listed on the left with the correct letter in the figure.

_____ 1. right atrium

_____ 2. right ventricle

_____ 3. left atrium

_____ 4. left ventricle

_____ 5. superior vena cava

_____ 6. inferior vena cava

_____ 7. ascending aorta

_____ 8. aortic arch

_____ 9. brachiocephalic artery

_____ 10. left common carotid artery

_____ 11. left subclavian artery

_____ 12. pulmonary trunk

_____ 13. right pulmonary artery

_____ 14. left pulmonary artery

_____ 15. ligamentum arteriosum

_____ 16. right pulmonary veins

_____ 17. left pulmonary veins

_____ 18. right coronary artery

_____ 19. anterior cardiac vein

_____ 20. left coronary artery

_____ 21. circumflex artery

_____ 22. anterior interventricular artery

_____ 23. apex of heart

_____ 24. great cardiac vein

2. What is the function of the fluid that fills the pericardial sac? _____

_____

3. Match the terms in the key to the descriptions provided below.

    Key:

_____ 1. location of the heart in the thorax

_____ 2. superior heart chambers

_____ 3. inferior heart chambers

_____ 4. visceral pericardium

_____ 5. "anterooms" of the heart

_____ 6. equals cardiac muscle

_____ 7. provide nutrient blood to the heart muscle

_____ 8. lining of the heart chambers

_____ 9. actual "pumps" of the heart

_____ 10. drains blood into the right atrium

Key:

a. atria

b. coronary arteries

c. coronary sinus

d. endocardium

e. epicardium

f. mediastinum

g. myocardium

h. ventricles

4. What is the function of the valves found in the heart? _____

_____

5. What is the role of the chordae tendineae? _____

_____

Pulmonary, Systemic, and Cardiac Circulations

6. A simple schematic of general circulation is shown below. What part of the circulation is missing from this diagram?

_____ Add to the diagram as best you can to make it depict a complete systemic/pulmonary circulation. Label the systemic and pulmonary circulations.

Heart   Systemic arteries   Systemic capillaries   Systemic veins

_____   _____

7. Differentiate clearly between the roles of the pulmonary and systemic circulations. _____

_____

_____

8. Complete the following scheme of circulation of a red blood cell in the human body.

Right atrium through the tricuspid valve to the _____, through the _____

valve to the pulmonary trunk, to the _____, to the capillary beds of the lungs, to the _____,

to the _____ of the heart, through the _____ valve to the _____,

through the _____ valve to the _____, to the systemic arteries, to the

_____ of the tissues, to the systemic veins, to the _____, _____,

and _____ entering the right atrium of the heart.

9. If the mitral valve does not close properly, which circulation is affected? _____

10. Why might a thrombus (blood clot) in the anterior descending branch of the left coronary artery cause sudden death?

_____

Microscopic Anatomy of Cardiac Muscle

11. How would you distinguish the structure of cardiac muscle from that of skeletal muscle? _____

_____

_____

12. Add the following terms to the photograph of cardiac muscle below.

  a. intercalated disc   b. nucleus of cardiac fiber   c. striations   d. cardiac muscle fiber

Describe the unique anatomical features of cardiac muscle. What role does the unique structure of cardiac muscle play in its function?

_____

_____

_____

_____

_____

_____

Dissection of the Sheep Heart

13. During the sheep heart dissection, you were asked initially to identify the right and left ventricles without cutting into the heart. During this procedure, what differences did you observe between the two chambers?

_____

_____

When you measured thickness of ventricular walls, was the right or left ventricle thicker? _____

Knowing that structure and function are related, how would you say this structural difference reflects the relative functions

of these two heart chambers? _____

_____

14. Semilunar valves prevent backflow into the _____; mitral and tricuspid valves prevent back-

flow into the _____. Using your own observations, explain how the operation of the semilu-

nar valves differs from that of the mitral and tricuspid valves. _____

_____

_____

_____

15. Compare and contrast the structure of the mitral and tricuspid valves. _____

_____

16. Two remnants of fetal structures are observable in the heart—the ligamentum arteriosum and the fossa ovalis. What were they called in the fetal heart, where was each located, and what common purpose did they serve as functioning fetal structures?

_____

_____

_____

Conduction System of the Heart and Electrocardiography

MATERIALS

☐ Apparatus A or B:*

A: ECG recording apparatus, electrode paste, alcohol swabs, rubber straps or disposable electrodes

BIOPAC® B: BIOPAC® MP36 (or MP35/30) data acquisition unit, PC or Mac computer BIOPAC® Student Lab Software, electrode lead set, disposable vinyl electrodes

New versions of the BSL software (3.7.5 and higher for Windows, and 3.7.4 and higher for Mac) require slightly different channel settings and collection strategies. Instructions for using the newer software with the MP36/35 data acquisition units can be found on myA&P. In addition, instructions for use of the NEW 2-channel data acquisition unit, the MP45, may also be found on myA&P.

☐ Cot or lab table; pillow (optional)

☐ Millimeter ruler

*Note: Instructions for using PowerLab® equipment can be found on myA&P.

OBJECTIVES

1. To list and localize the elements of the intrinsic conduction, or nodal, system of the heart, and to describe how impulses are initiated and conducted through this system and the myocardium.

2. To interpret the ECG in terms of depolarization and repolarization events occurring in the myocardium; and to identify the P, QRS, and T waves on an ECG recording using an ECG recorder or BIOPAC®.

3. To calculate the heart rate, QRS interval, P–R interval, and Q–T interval from an ECG obtained during the laboratory period.

4. To define *tachycardia, bradycardia,* and *fibrillation.*

PRE-LAB QUIZ

1. Circle True or False. Cardiac muscle cells are electrically connected by gap junctions and behave as a single unit.

2. Because it sets the rate of depolarization for the normal heart, the _____ node is known as the pacemaker of the heart.
   a. atrioventricular
   b. Purkinje
   c. sinoatrial

3. Circle True or False. Activity of the nerves of the autonomic nervous system is essential for cardiac muscle to contract.

4. Today you will create a graphic recording of the electrical changes that occur during a cardiac cycle. This is known as an
   a. electrocardiogram
   b. electroencephalogram
   c. electromyogram

5. Circle the correct term. The typical ECG has <u>three / six</u> normally recognizable deflection waves.

6. In a typical ECG, the _____ wave signals the depolarization of the atria immediately before they contract.
   a. P   c. R
   b. Q   d. T

7. Circle True or False. The repolarization of the atria is usually masked by the large QRS complex.

8. Circle the correct term. A heart rate over 100 beats/minute is known as <u>tachycardia / bradycardia.</u>

9. How many electrodes will you place on your subject for today's activity if using a standard ECG apparatus?
   a. 3   c. 10
   b. 4   d. 12

10. Circle True or False. Electrical activity recorded by any lead depends on the location and orientation of the recording electrodes.

myA&P *For practice quizzes on this lab, go to www.myaandp.com.*

FIGURE 31.1 The intrinsic conduction system of the heart. Dashed-line arrows indicate transmission of the impulse from the SA node through the atria. Solid yellow arrow indicates transmission of the impulse from the SA node to the AV node via the internodal pathway.

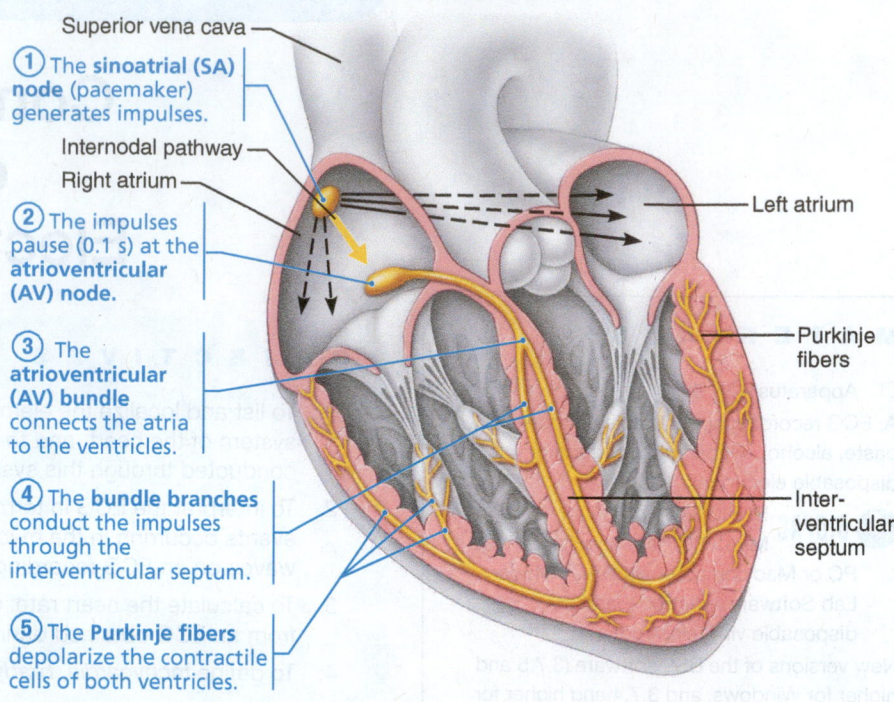

Superior vena cava

① The **sinoatrial (SA) node** (pacemaker) generates impulses.

Internodal pathway

Right atrium

② The impulses pause (0.1 s) at the **atrioventricular (AV) node.**

③ The **atrioventricular (AV) bundle** connects the atria to the ventricles.

④ The **bundle branches** conduct the impulses through the interventricular septum.

⑤ The **Purkinje fibers** depolarize the contractile cells of both ventricles.

Left atrium

Purkinje fibers

Interventricular septum

Heart contraction results from a series of electrical potential changes (depolarization waves) that travel through the heart preliminary to each beat. Because cardiac muscle cells are electrically connected by gap junctions, the entire myocardium behaves like a single unit, a **functional syncytium** (sin-sih'shum).

The Intrinsic Conduction System

The ability of cardiac muscle to beat is intrinsic—it does not depend on impulses from the nervous system to initiate its contraction and will continue to contract rhythmically even if all nerve connections are severed. However, two types of controlling systems exert their effects on heart activity. One of these involves nerves of the autonomic nervous system, which accelerate or decelerate the heartbeat rate depending on which division is activated. The second system is the **intrinsic conduction system,** or **nodal system,** of the heart, consisting of specialized noncontractile myocardial tissue. The intrinsic conduction system ensures that heart muscle depolarizes in an orderly and sequential manner (from atria to ventricles) and that the heart beats as a coordinated unit.

The components of the intrinsic conduction system include the **sinoatrial (SA) node,** located in the right atrium just inferior to the entrance to the superior vena cava; the **atrioventricular (AV) node** in the lower atrial septum at the junction of the atria and ventricles; the **AV bundle (bundle of His)** and right and left **bundle branches,** located in the interventricular septum; and the **Purkinje fibers,** essentially long strands of barrel-shaped cells called *Purkinje myocytes,* which ramify within the muscle bundles of the ventricular

walls. The Purkinje fiber network is much denser and more elaborate in the left ventricle because of the larger size of this chamber (Figure 31.1).

The SA node, which has the highest rate of discharge, provides the stimulus for contraction. Because it sets the rate of depolarization for the heart as a whole, the SA node is often referred to as the *pacemaker.* From the SA node, the impulse spreads throughout the atria and to the AV node. This electrical wave is immediately followed by atrial contraction. At the AV node, the impulse is momentarily delayed (approximately 0.1 sec), allowing the atria to complete their contraction. It then passes through the AV bundle, the right and left bundle branches, and the Purkinje fibers, finally resulting in ventricular contraction. Note that the atria and ventricles are separated from one another by a region of electrically inert connective tissue, so the depolarization wave can be transmitted to the ventricles only via the tract between the AV node and AV bundle. Thus, any damage to the AV node-bundle pathway partially or totally insulates the ventricles from the influence of the SA node. Although autorhythmic cells are found throughout the heart, their rates of spontaneous depolarization differ. The nodal system increases the rate of heart depolarization and synchronizes heart activity.

Electrocardiography

The conduction of impulses through the heart generates electrical currents that eventually spread throughout the body. These impulses can be detected on the body's surface and recorded with an instrument called an *electrocardiograph.* The graphic recording of the electrical changes (depolarization followed by repolarization) occurring during the cardiac cycle is called an **electrocardiogram (ECG or EKG)** (Figure 31.2). For analysis, the ECG is divided into segments and intervals,

(a)

QRS complex

Time Scale:
small squares = 0.04 sec
1 large square = 0.20 sec
5 large squares = 1.00 sec

R

P

T

PR
interval

ST segment

Q   S

QT
interval

(b)

FIGURE 31.2 The normal electrocardiogram.
(a) Regular sinus rhythm. **(b)** Waves, segments, and intervals of a normal ECG.

which are defined in Table 31.1. The relationship between the deflection waves of an ECG and sequential excitation of the heart is shown in Figure 31.3.

TABLE 31.1	Boundaries of Each ECG Component
Feature	**Boundaries**
P wave	Start of P deflection to return to isoelectric line
P–R interval	Start of P deflection to start of Q deflection
P–R segment	End of P wave to start of Q deflection
QRS complex	Start of Q deflection to S return to isoelectric line
S–T segment	End of S deflection to start of T wave
Q–T interval	Start of Q deflection to end of T wave
T wave	Start of T deflection to return to isoelectric line
End T to next R	End of T wave to next R spike

It is important to understand what an ECG does *and does not* show: First, an ECG is a record of voltage and time—nothing else. Although we can and do infer that muscle contraction follows its excitation, sometimes it does not. Second, an ECG records electrical events occurring in relatively large amounts of muscle tissue (i.e., the bulk of the heart muscle), *not* the activity of nodal tissue which, like muscle contraction, can only be inferred. Nonetheless, abnormalities of the deflection waves and changes in the time intervals of the ECG are useful in detecting myocardial infarcts or problems with the conduction system of the heart. The P–R interval represents the time between the beginning of atrial depolarization and ventricular depolarization. Thus, it typically includes the period during which the depolarization wave passes to the AV node, atrial systole, and

SA node generates impulse;
atrial depolarization begins

SA node

Impulse delayed
at AV node

AV node

Impulse passes to
heart apex; ventricular
depolarization begins

Bundle
branches

Ventricular depolarization
complete

Purkinje
fibers

R   R   R   R

P   T   P   T   P   T   P   T

Q S   Q S   Q S   Q S

FIGURE 31.3 The sequence of excitation of the heart related to the deflection waves of an ECG tracing.

the passage of the excitation wave to the balance of the conducting system. Generally, the P–R interval is about 0.16 to 0.18 sec. A longer interval may suggest a partial AV heart block caused by damage to the AV node. In total heart block, no impulses are transmitted through the AV node, and the atria and ventricles beat independently of one another—the atria at the SA node rate and the ventricles at their intrinsic rate, which is considerably slower.

A prolonged QRS complex (normally 0.08 sec) may indicate a right or left bundle branch block in which one ventricle is contracting later than the other. The Q–T interval is the period from the beginning of ventricular depolarization through repolarization and includes the time of ventricular contraction (the S–T segment). With a heart rate of 70 beats/min, this interval is normally 0.31 to 0.41 sec. As the rate increases, this interval becomes shorter; conversely, when the heart rate drops, the interval is longer. The repolarization of the atria, which occurs during the QRS interval, is generally obscured by the large QRS complex.

A heart rate over 100 beats/min is referred to as **tachycardia;** a rate below 60 beats/min is **bradycardia.** Although neither condition is pathological, prolonged tachycardia may progress to **fibrillation,** a condition of rapid uncoordinated heart contractions which makes the heart useless as a pump. Bradycardia in athletes is a positive finding; that is, it indicates an increased efficiency of cardiac functioning. Because *stroke volume* (the amount of blood ejected by a ventricle with each contraction) increases with physical conditioning, the heart can contract more slowly and still meet circulatory demands.

Twelve standard leads are used to record an ECG for diagnostic purposes. Three of these are bipolar leads that measure the voltage difference between the arms, or an arm and a leg, and nine are unipolar leads. Together the 12 leads provide a fairly comprehensive picture of the electrical activity of the heart.

For this investigation, four electrodes are used (Figure 31.4), and results are obtained from the three *standard limb leads* (also shown in Figure 31.4). Several types of physiographs or ECG recorders are available. Your instructor will provide specific directions on how to set up and use the available apparatus if standard ECG apparatus is used (Activity 1a). Instructions for use of BIOPAC® apparatus (Activity 1b) are provided on pages 462–466.

Understanding the Standard Limb Leads

As you might expect, electrical activity recorded by any lead depends on the location and orientation of the recording electrodes. Clinically, it is assumed that the heart lies in the center of a triangle with sides of equal lengths *(Einthoven's triangle)* and that the recording connections are made at the vertices (corners) of that triangle. But in practice, the electrodes connected to each arm and to the left leg are considered to connect to the triangle vertices. The standard limb leads record the voltages generated in the extracellular fluids surrounding the heart by the ion flows occurring simultaneously in many cells between any two of the connections. A recording using lead I (RA–LA), which connects the right arm (RA) and the left arm (LA), is most sensitive to electrical activity spreading horizontally across the heart. Lead II (RA–LL) and lead III (LA–LL) record activity along the vertical axis (from the base of the heart to its apex) but from different orientations. The significance of Einthoven's triangle is that the sum of the voltages of leads I and III equals that in lead II (Einthoven's law). Hence, if the voltages of two of the standard leads are recorded, that of the third lead can be determined mathematically.

Once the subject is prepared, the ECG will be recorded first under baseline (resting) conditions and then under condi-

FIGURE 31.4 **ECG recording positions for the standard limb leads.**

tions of fairly strenuous activity. Finally, recordings will be made while the subject holds his or her breath or carries out deep breathing. The activity recordings and those involving changes in respiratory rate or depth will be compared to the baseline recordings, and you will be asked to determine the reasons for the observed differences in the recordings.

ACTIVITY 1A

Recording ECGs Using a Standard ECG Apparatus

Preparing the Subject

1.   If using electrodes that require paste, place electrode paste on four electrode plates and position each electrode as follows after scrubbing the skin at the attachment site with an alcohol swab. Attach an electrode to the anterior surface of each forearm, about 5 to 8 cm (2 to 3 in.) above the wrist, and secure them with rubber straps. In the same manner, attach an electrode to each leg, approximately 5 to 8 cm above the medial malleolus (inner aspect of the ankle). Disposable electrodes may be placed directly on the subject in the same areas.

2.   Attach the appropriate tips of the patient cable to the electrodes. The cable leads are marked RA (right arm), LA (left arm), LL (left leg), and RL (right leg, the ground).

Making a Baseline Recording

1.   Position the subject comfortably in a supine position on a cot (if available), or sitting relaxed on a laboratory chair.

2.   Turn on the power switch and adjust the sensitivity knob to 1. Set the paper speed to 25 mm/sec and the lead selector to the position corresponding to recording from lead I (RA–LA).

3.   Set the control knob at the **RUN** position and record the subject's at-rest ECG from lead I for 2 to 3 minutes or until the recording stabilizes. (You will need a tracing long enough to provide each student in your group with a representative segment.) The subject should try to relax and not move unnecessarily, because the skeletal muscle action potentials will also be picked up and recorded.

4.   Stop the recording and mark it "lead I."

5.   Repeat the recording procedure for leads II (RA–LL) and III (LA–LL).

6.   Each student should take a representative segment of one of the lead recordings and label the record with the name of the subject and the lead used. Identify and label the P, QRS, and T waves. The calculations you perform for your recording should be based on the following information: Because the paper speed was 25 mm/sec, each millimeter of paper corresponds to a time interval of 0.04 sec. Thus, if an interval requires 4 mm of paper, its duration is 4 mm × 0.04 sec/mm = 0.16 sec.

7.   Compute the heart rate. Obtain a millimeter ruler and measure the distance from the beginning of one QRS complex to the beginning of the next QRS complex. Enter this value into the following equation to find the time for one heartbeat.

_____ mm/beat × 0.04 sec/mm = _____ sec/beat

Now find the beats per minute, or heart rate, by using the figure just computed for seconds per beat in the following equation:

$$\frac{1}{\text{\_\_\_\_\_ sec/beat}} \times 60 \text{ sec/min} = \text{_____ beats/min}$$

Is the obtained value within normal limits?_____

Measure the QRS complex, and compute its duration.

_____

Measure the Q–T interval, and compute its duration.

_____

Measure the P–R interval, and compute its duration.

_____

Are the computed values within normal limits?

_____

8.   At the bottom of this page, attach segments of the ECG recordings from leads I through III. Make sure you indicate the paper speed, lead, and subject's name on each tracing. To the recording on which you based your previous computations, add your calculations for the duration of the QRS complex and the P–R and Q–T intervals above the respective area of tracing. Also record the heart rate on that tracing.

Recording the ECG for Running in Place

1.   Make sure the electrodes are securely attached to prevent electrode movement while recording the ECG.

2.   Set the paper speed to 25 mm/sec, and prepare to make the recording using lead I.

3.   Record the ECG while the subject is running in place for 3 minutes. Then have the subject sit down, but continue to record the ECG for an additional 4 minutes. *Mark the recording* at the end of the 3 minutes of running and at 1 minute after cessation of activity.

4.   Stop the recording. Compute the beats/min during the third minute of running, at 1 minute after exercise, and at 4 minutes after exercise. Record below:

_____ beats/min while running in place

_____ beats/min at 1 minute after exercise

_____ beats/min at 4 minutes after exercise

5.   Compare this recording with the previous recording from lead I. Which intervals are shorter in the "running" recording?

_____

Does the subject's heart rate return to resting level by 4 minutes after exercise?

_____

Recording the ECG During Breath Holding

1.   Position the subject comfortably in the sitting position.

2.   Using lead I and a paper speed of 25 mm/sec, begin the recording. After approximately 10 seconds, instruct the subject to begin breath holding and mark the record to indicate the onset of the 1-minute breath-holding interval.

3.   Stop the recording after 1 minute and remind the subject to breathe. Compute the beats/minute during the 1-minute experimental (breath-holding) period.

Beats/min during breath holding: _____

4.   Compare this recording with the lead I recording obtained under resting conditions.

What differences are seen? _____

Attempt to explain the physiological reason for the differences you have seen. (Hint: A good place to start might be to check hypoventilation or the role of the respiratory system in acid-base balance of the blood.)

_____

_____

_____

FIGURE 31.5 **Setting up the BIOPAC® unit.** Plug the electrode lead set into Channel 2.

BIOPAC® data acquisition unit

Electrode lead set (plugs into Channel 2)

ACTIVITY 1B

Electrocardiography Using BIOPAC®

In this activity, you will record the electrical activity of the heart under three different conditions: (1) while the subject is lying down, (2) after the subject sits up and breathes normally, and (3) after the subject has exercised and is breathing deeply.

Since the electrodes are not placed directly over the heart, artifacts can result from the recording of unwanted skeletal muscle activity. In order to obtain a clear ECG, it is important that the subject:

- Remain still during the recording.
- Refrain from laughing or talking during the recording.
- When in the sitting position, keep arms and legs steady and relaxed.

Setting Up the Equipment

1. Connect the BIOPAC® unit to the computer and turn the computer **ON.**

2. Make sure the BIOPAC® unit is **OFF.**

3. Plug in the equipment as shown in Figure 31.5:

- Electrode lead set—CH 2

4. Turn the BIOPAC® unit **ON.**

5. Place the three electrodes on the subject as shown in Figure 31.6, and attach the electrode leads according to the colors indicated. The electrodes should be placed on the medial surface of each leg, 5 to 8 cm (2 to 3 in.) superior to the ankle. The other electrode should be placed on the right anterior forearm 5 to 8 cm above the wrist.

6. The subject should lie down and relax in a comfortable position. A chair or place to sit up should be available nearby.

7. Start the BIOPAC® Student Lab program on the computer by double-clicking the icon on the desktop or by following your instructor's guidance.

8. Select lesson **L05-ECG-1** from the menu, and click **OK.**

9. Type in a filename that will save this subject's data on the computer hard drive. You may want to use the subject's last name followed by ECG-1 (for example, SmithECG-1), then click **OK.**

Calibrating the Equipment

- Examine the electrodes and the electrode leads to be certain they are properly attached.

1. The subject must remain still and relaxed. With the subject in a still position, click **Calibrate.** This will initiate the process whereby the computer will automatically establish parameters to record the data.

2. The calibration procedure will stop automatically after 8 seconds.

3. Observe the recording of the calibration data, which should look similar to the data in Figure 31.7.

White lead (right forearm)

Black lead (ground) (right leg)

Red lead (left leg)

FIGURE 31.6 **Placement of electrodes and the appropriate attachment of electrode leads by color.**

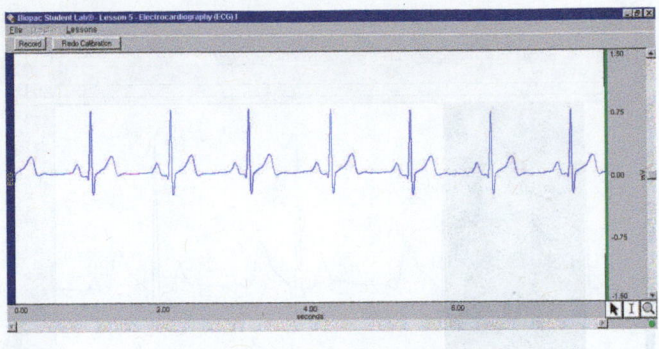

FIGURE 31.7 Example of calibration data.

FIGURE 31.9 Example of ECG data after the subject sits up and breathes normally.

- If the data look very different, click **Redo Calibration** and repeat the steps above.

- If the data look similar, proceed to the next section.

Recording Segment 1: Subject Lying Down

1. To prepare for the recording, remind the subject to remain still and relaxed while lying down.

2. When prepared, click **Record** and gather data for 20 seconds. At the end of 20 seconds, click **Suspend.**

3. Observe the data, which should look similar to the data in Figure 31.8.

- If the data look very different, click **Redo** and repeat the steps above. Be certain to check attachment of the electrodes and leads, and remind the subject not to move, talk, or laugh.

- If the data look similar, move on to the next recording segment.

Recording Segment 2: After Subject Sits Up, With Normal Breathing

1. Tell the subject to be ready to sit up in the designated location. With the exception of breathing, the subject should try to remain motionless after assuming the seated position. *If the subject moves too much during recording after sitting up, unwanted skeletal muscle artifacts will affect the recording.*

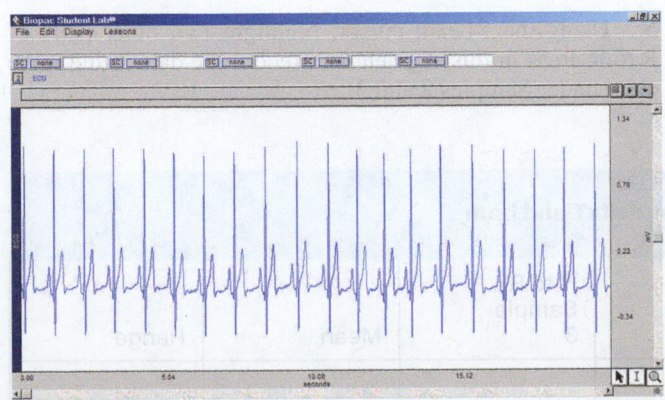

FIGURE 31.8 Example of ECG data while the subject is lying down.

2. When prepared, instruct the subject to sit up. Immediately after the subject assumes a motionless state, click **Resume,** and the data will begin recording.

3. At the end of 20 seconds, click **Suspend** to stop recording.

4. Observe the data, which should look similar to the data in Figure 31.9.

- If the data look very different, click **Redo** and repeat the steps above. Be certain to check attachment of the electrodes, and do not click **Resume** until the subject is motionless.

- If the data look similar, move on to the next recording segment. *Note: For start of next segment, ignore the program instructions at the bottom of the computer screen.*

Recording Segment 3: After Subject Exercises, With Deep Breathing

1. Remove the electrode pinch connectors from the electrodes on the subject.

2. Have the subject do a brief round of exercise, such as jumping jacks or running in place for 1 minute, in order to elevate the heart rate.

3. As quickly as possible after the exercise, have the subject resume a motionless, seated position and reattach the pinch connectors. Once again, if the subject moves too much during recording, unwanted skeletal muscle artifacts will affect the data. After exercise, the subject is likely to be breathing deeply, but otherwise should remain as still as possible.

4. Immediately after the subject assumes a motionless, seated state, click **Resume,** and the data will begin recording. Record the ECG for 60 seconds in order to observe postexercise recovery.

5. After 60 seconds, click **Suspend** to stop recording.

6. Observe the data, which should look similar to the data in Figure 31.10.

- If the data look very different, click **Redo** and repeat the steps above. Be certain to check attachment of the electrodes and leads, and remember not to click **Resume** until the subject is motionless.

7. When finished, click **Done.** Remove the electrodes from the subject.

FIGURE 31.10 Example of ECG data after the subject exercises.

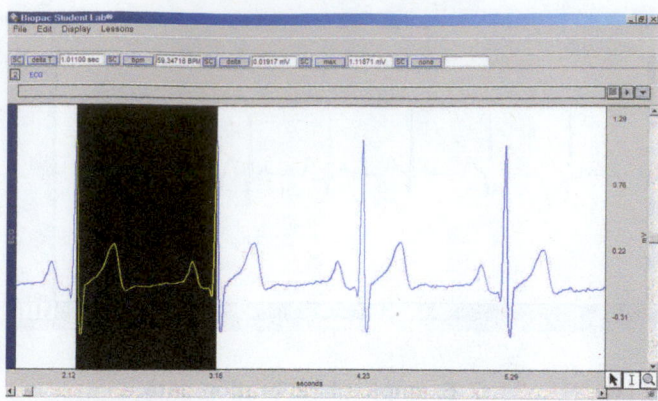

FIGURE 31.11 Example of highlighting from R-wave to R-wave.

8. A pop-up window will appear. To record from another subject, select **Record data from another subject** and return to step 5 under Setting Up the Equipment. If continuing to the Data Analysis section, select **Analyze current data file** and proceed to step 2 of the Data Analysis section.

Data Analysis

1. If just starting the BIOPAC® program to perform data analysis, enter **Review Saved Data** mode and choose the file with the subject's ECG data (for example, SmithECG-1).

2. Use the following tools to adjust the data in order to clearly view and analyze four consecutive cardiac cycles:

- Click the magnifying glass in the lower right corner of the screen (near the I-beam cursor box) to activate the **zoom** function. Use the magnifying glass cursor to click on the very first waveforms until there are about 4 seconds of data represented (see horizontal time scale at the bottom of the screen).

- Select the **Display** menu at the top of the screen, and click **Autoscale Waveforms.** This function will adjust the data for better viewing.

- Click the **Adjust Baseline** button. Two new buttons will appear; simply click these buttons to move the waveforms **Up** or **Down** so they appear clearly in the center of the screen. Once they are centered, click **Exit.**

3. Set up the first two pairs of channel/measurement boxes at the top of the screen by selecting the following channels and measurement types from the drop-down menus (note that Channel 2 contains the ECG data):

Channel	Measurement
CH 2	deltaT
CH 2	bpm

Analysis of Segment 1: Subject Lying Down

1. Use the arrow cursor and click the I-beam cursor box on the lower right side of the screen to activate the "area selection" function.

2. First measure **deltaT** and **bpm** in Segment 1 (approximately seconds 0–20). Using the I-beam cursor, highlight from the peak of one R-wave to the peak of the next R-wave, as shown in Figure 31.11.

3. Observe that the computer automatically calculates the **deltaT** and **bpm** for the selected area. These measurements represent the following:

deltaT (difference in time): Computes the elapsed time between the beginning and end of the highlighted area

bpm (beats per minute): Computes the beats per minute when highlighting from the R-wave of one cycle to the R-wave of another cycle

4. Record this data in the Segment 1 Samples chart below under R to R Sample 1 (round to the nearest 0.01 second and 0.1 beat per minute).

5. Using the I-beam cursor, highlight two other pairs of R to R areas in this segment and record the data in the same chart under Samples 2 and 3.

Segment 1 Samples for deltaT and bpm						
Measure	Channel	R to R Sample 1	R to R Sample 2	R to R Sample 3	Mean	Range
deltaT	CH 2					
bpm	CH 2					

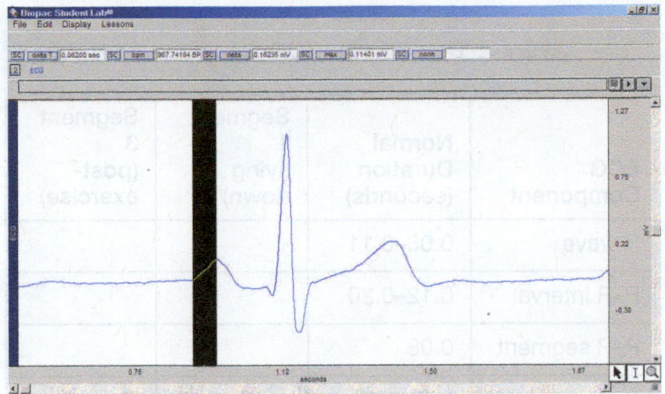

FIGURE 31.12 Example of a single ECG waveform with the first part of the P wave highlighted.

6. Calculate the means and ranges of the data in this chart.

7. Next, use the **zoom, Autoscale Waveforms,** and **Adjust Baseline** tools described above to focus in on one ECG waveform within Segment 1. See the example in Figure 31.12.

8. Once a single ECG waveform is centered for analysis, click the I-beam cursor box on the lower right side of the screen to activate the "area selection" function.

9. Using the highlighting function and **deltaT** computation, measure the duration of every component of the ECG waveform. Refer to Figure 31.2b and Table 31.1 for guidance in highlighting each component.

10. Highlight each component of one cycle. Observe the elapsed time, and record this data under Cycle 1 in the Segment 1 Elapsed Time chart.

11. Scroll along the horizontal axis at the bottom of the data to view and analyze two additional cycles in Segment 1. Record the elapsed time for every component of Cycle 2 and Cycle 3 in the Segment 1 Elapsed Time chart.

12. In the same chart, calculate the means for the three cycles of data and record.

Segment 1 Elapsed Time for ECG Components (seconds)				
Component	Cycle 1	Cycle 2	Cycle 3	Mean
P wave				
P–R interval				
P–R segment				
QRS complex				
S–T segment				
Q–T interval				
T wave				
End T to next R				

Analysis of Segment 2: Subject Sitting Up and Breathing Normally

1. Scroll along the horizontal time bar until you reach the data for Segment 2 (approximately seconds 20–40). A marker with "After sitting up" should denote the beginning of this data.

2. As in the analysis of Segment 1, use the I-beam tool to highlight and measure the **deltaT** and **bpm** between three different pairs of R-waves in this segment, and record the data in the Segment 2 Samples chart below.

Analysis of Segment 3: After Exercise with Deep Breathing

1. Scroll along the horizontal time bar until you reach the data for Segment 3 (approximately seconds 40–60). A marker with "After exercise" should denote the beginning of this data.

Segment 2 Samples for deltaT and bpm						
Measure	Channel	R to R Sample 1	R to R Sample 2	R to R Sample 3	Mean	Range
deltaT	CH 2					
bpm	CH 2					

Segment 3 Samples for deltaT and bpm						
Measure	Channel	R to R Sample 1	R to R Sample 2	R to R Sample 3	Mean	Range
deltaT	CH 2					
bpm	CH 2					

Segment 3 Elapsed Time for ECG Components (seconds)				
Component	Cycle 1	Cycle 2	Cycle 3	Mean
P wave				
P–R interval				
P–R segment				
QRS complex				
S–T segment				
Q–T interval				
T wave				
End T to next R				

Average Duration for ECG Components			
ECG Component	Normal Duration (seconds)	Segment 1 (lying down)	Segment 3 (post-exercise)
P wave	0.06–0.11		
P–R interval	0.12–0.20		
P–R segment	0.08		
QRS complex	Less than 0.12		
S–T segment	0.12		
Q–T interval	0.31–0.41		
T wave	0.16		
End T to next R	varies		

2.   As before, use the I-beam tool to highlight and measure the **deltaT** and **bpm** between three pairs of R-waves in this segment, and record the data in the Segment 3 Samples chart on the previous page.

3.   Using the instructions for steps 8 and 9 in the section Analysis of Segment 1, highlight and observe the elapsed time for each component of one cycle, and record these data under Cycle 1 in the Segment 3 Elapsed Time chart above.

4.   Scroll along the horizontal axis at the bottom of the data to view and analyze two other cycles in Segment 3. Record the elapsed time for each component of Cycle 2 and Cycle 3 in the Segment 3 Elapsed Time chart above.

5.   In the same chart, calculate the means for each component in Segment 3.

6.   When finished, **Exit** the program.

Compare the average **deltaT** times and average **bpm** between the data in Segment 1 (lying down) and the data in Segment 3 (after exercise). Which is greater in each case?

_____

_____

What is the relationship between elapsed time (**deltaT**) between R-waves and the heart rate?

_____

_____

Is there a change in heart rate when the subject makes the transition from lying down (Segment 1) to a sitting position (Segment 2)?

_____

_____

Examine the average duration of each of the ECG components in Segment 1 and Segment 3. In the chart that follows, record the average values of each component. Draw a circle around those measures that fit within the normal range.

Compare the Q–T intervals in the data while the subject is at rest versus after exercise; this interval corresponds closely to the duration of contraction of the ventricles. Describe and explain any difference.

_____

_____

_____

Compare the duration in the period from the end of each T wave to the next R-spike while the subject is at rest versus after exercise. This interval corresponds closely to the duration of relaxation of the ventricles. Describe and explain any difference.

_____

_____

Which, if any, of the components in the Average Duration chart above demonstrates a significant difference from the normal value? Based on the events of the cardiac cycle and their representation in an ECG, what abnormality might the data suggest?

_____

_____

Conduction System of the Heart and Electrocardiography

The Intrinsic Conduction System

1. List the elements of the intrinsic conduction system in order, starting from the SA node.

   SA node → _____ → _____ →

   _____ → _____

   At what structure in the transmission sequence is the impulse temporarily delayed? _____

   Why? _____

   _____

2. Even though cardiac muscle has an inherent ability to beat, the nodal system plays a critical role in heart physiology. What

   is that role? _____

   _____

Electrocardiography

3. Define *ECG*. _____

   _____

4. Draw an ECG wave form representing one heartbeat. Label the P, QRS, and T waves; the P–R interval; the S–T segment, and the Q–T interval.

5. Why does heart rate increase during running? _____

   _____

   _____

6. Describe what happens in the cardiac cycle in the following situations.

   1.   immediately before the P wave: _____

   2.   during the P wave: _____

   3.   immediately after the P wave (P–R segment): _____

   4.   during the QRS wave: _____

   5.   immediately after the QRS wave (S–T interval): _____

   6.   during the T wave: _____

7. Define the following terms.

   1.   *tachycardia:* _____

   2.   *bradycardia:* _____

   3.   *fibrillation:* _____

8. Which would be more serious, atrial or ventricular fibrillation? _____

   Why? _____

   _____

9. Abnormalities of heart valves can be detected more accurately by auscultation than by electrocardiography. Why is this so?

   _____

   _____

   _____

Anatomy of Blood Vessels

MATERIALS

- ☐ Compound microscope
- ☐ Prepared microscope slides showing cross sections of an artery and vein
- ☐ Anatomical charts of human arteries and veins (or a three-dimensional model of the human circulatory system)
- ☐ Anatomical charts of the following specialized circulations: pulmonary circulation, hepatic portal circulation, fetal circulation, arterial supply of the brain (or a brain model showing this circulation)
- ☐ *Human Cardiovascular System: The Blood Vessels* videotape

📖 For instructions on animal dissections, see the dissection exercises starting on page 697 in the cat, fetal pig, and rat editions of this manual.

OBJECTIVES

1. To describe the tunics of blood vessel walls, and to state the function of each layer.
2. To correlate differences in artery, vein, and capillary structure with the functions of these vessels.
3. To recognize a cross-sectional view of an artery and vein when provided with a microscopic view or appropriate diagram.
4. To list and/or identify the major arteries arising from the aorta, and to indicate the body region supplied by each.
5. To list and/or identify the major veins draining into the superior and inferior venae cavae, and to indicate the body regions drained.
6. To point out and/or discuss the unique features of special circulations (pulmonary circulation, hepatic portal system, fetal circulation, cerebral arterial circle [circle of Willis]) in the body.

PRE-LAB QUIZ

1. Circle the correct term. <u>Arteries / Veins</u> drain tissues and return blood to the heart.
2. Circle True or False. It is through the walls of capillaries that actual gas exchange takes place between tissue cells and blood.
3. The _____ is the largest artery of the body.
   - a. aorta
   - b. carotid artery
   - c. femoral artery
   - d. subclavian artery
4. Circle the correct term. The largest branch of the abdominal aorta, the <u>renal / superior mesenteric</u> artery, supplies most of the small intestine and the first half of the large intestine.
5. The anterior tibial artery terminates with the _____ artery, which is often palpated in patients with circulatory problems to determine the circulatory efficiency of the lower limb.
   - a. dorsalis pedis
   - b. external iliac
   - c. obturator
   - d. tibial
6. Circle the correct term. Veins draining the head and upper extremities empty into the <u>superior / inferior</u> vena cava.
7. Located in the lower limb, the _____ is the longest vein in the body.
   - a. external iliac
   - b. fibular
   - c. great saphenous
   - d. internal iliac
8. Circle the correct term. The <u>renal / hepatic</u> veins drain the liver.
9. The function of the _____ is to drain the digestive viscera and carry dissolved nutrients to the liver for processing.
   - a. fetal circulation
   - b. hepatic portal circulation
   - c. pulmonary circulation system
10. Circle the correct term. In the developing fetus, the umbilical <u>artery / vein</u> carries blood rich in nutrients and oxygen to the fetus.

myA&P For practice quizzes on this lab, go to www.myaandp.com.

PAL For access to anatomical models and more, check out Practice Anatomy Lab.

The blood vessels constitute a closed transport system. As the heart contracts, blood is propelled into the large arteries leaving the heart. It moves into successively smaller arteries and then to the arterioles, which feed the capillary beds in the tissues. Capillary beds are drained by the venules, which in turn empty into veins that ultimately converge on the great veins entering the heart.

Arteries, carrying blood away from the heart, and veins, which drain the tissues and return blood to the heart, function simply as conducting vessels or conduits. Only the tiny capillaries that connect the arterioles and venules and ramify throughout the tissues directly serve the needs of the body's cells. It is through the capillary walls that exchanges are made between tissue cells and blood. Respiratory gases, nutrients, and wastes move along diffusion gradients. Thus, oxygen and nutrients diffuse from the blood to the tissue cells, and carbon dioxide and metabolic wastes move from the cells to the blood.

In this exercise you will examine the microscopic structure of blood vessels and identify the major arteries and veins of the systemic circulation and other special circulations.

Microscopic Structure of the Blood Vessels

Except for the microscopic capillaries, the walls of blood vessels are constructed of three coats, or *tunics* (Figure 32.1).

FIGURE 32.1 Generalized structure of arteries, veins, and capillaries. (a) Light photomicrograph of a muscular artery and the corresponding vein in cross section (30×). **(b)** Comparison of wall structure of arteries, veins, and capillaries. Note that the tunica media is thick in arteries and thin in veins, while the tunica externa is thin in arteries and relatively thicker in veins. Capillaries have only endothelium and a sparse basal lamina.

Artery

Vein

(a)

Tunica intima
• Endothelium
• Subendothelial layer
Internal elastic lamina

Tunica media
(smooth muscle and elastic fibers)

External elastic lamina

Tunica externa
(collagen fibers)

Lumen

Artery

Capillary network

Valve

Lumen

Vein

Basement membrane
Endothelial cells

Capillary

(b)

FIGURE 32.2 Schematic of the systemic arterial circulation. (R. = right, L. = left)

The **tunica intima,** or **interna,** which lines the lumen of a vessel, is a single thin layer of *endothelium* (squamous cells underlain by a scant basal lamina) that is continuous with the endocardium of the heart. Its cells fit closely together, forming an extremely smooth blood vessel lining that helps decrease resistance to blood flow.

The **tunica media** is the more bulky middle coat and is composed primarily of smooth muscle and elastin. The smooth muscle, under the control of the sympathetic nervous system, plays an active role in regulating the diameter of blood vessels, which in turn alters peripheral resistance and blood pressure.

The **tunica externa,** or **adventitia,** the outermost tunic, is composed of areolar or fibrous connective tissue. Its function is basically supportive and protective.

In general, the walls of arteries are thicker than those of veins. The tunica media in particular tends to be much heavier and contains substantially more smooth muscle and elastic tissue. This anatomical difference reflects a functional difference in the two types of vessels. Arteries, which are closer to the pumping action of the heart, must be able to expand as an increased volume of blood is propelled into them during systole and then recoil passively as the blood flows off into the circulation during diastole. Their walls must be sufficiently strong and resilient to withstand such pressure fluctuations. Since these larger arteries have such large amounts of elastic tissue in their media, they are often referred to as *elastic arteries.* Smaller arteries, further along in the circulatory pathway, are exposed to less extreme pressure fluctuations. They have less elastic tissue but still have substantial amounts of smooth muscle in their media. For this reason, they are called *muscular arteries.* A schematic of the systemic arteries is provided in Figure 32.2.

By contrast, veins, which are far removed from the heart in the circulatory pathway, are not subjected to such pressure fluctuations and are essentially low-pressure vessels. Thus, veins may be thinner-walled without jeopardy. However, the low-pressure condition itself and the fact that blood returning to the heart often flows against gravity require structural modifications to ensure that venous return equals cardiac output. Thus, the lumens of veins tend to be substantially larger than those of corresponding arteries, and valves in larger veins act to prevent backflow of blood in much the same manner as the semilunar valves of the heart. The skeletal muscle "pump" also promotes venous return; as the skeletal muscles surrounding the veins contract and relax, the blood is milked through the veins toward the heart. (Anyone who has been standing relatively still for an extended time has experienced swelling in the ankles, caused by blood pooling in their feet during the period of muscle inactivity.) Pressure changes that occur in the thorax during breathing also aid the return of blood to the heart.

•   To demonstrate how efficiently venous valves prevent backflow of blood, perform the following simple experiment. Allow one hand to hang by your side until the blood vessels on the dorsal aspect become distended. Place two fingertips against one of the distended veins and, pressing firmly, move the superior finger proximally along the vein and then release this finger. The vein will remain flattened and collapsed despite gravity. Then remove the distal fingertip and observe the rapid filling of the vein.

The transparent walls of the tiny capillaries are only one cell layer thick, consisting of just the endothelium underlain by a basal lamina, that is, the tunica intima. Because of this exceptional thinness, exchanges are easily made between the blood and tissue cells.

A C T I V I T Y   1

Examining the Microscopic Structure of Arteries and Veins

1.   Obtain a slide showing a cross-sectional view of blood vessels and a microscope.

2.   Using Figure 32.1 as a guide, scan the section to identify a thick-walled artery. Very often, but not always, its lumen will appear scalloped due to the constriction of its walls by the elastic tissue of the media.

3.   Identify a vein. Its lumen may be elongated or irregularly shaped and collapsed, and its walls will be considerably thinner. Notice the difference in the relative amount of elastic fibers in the media of the two vessels. Also, note the thinness of the intima layer, which is composed of flat squamous-type cells. ▬

Major Systemic Arteries of the Body

The **aorta** is the largest artery of the body. Extending upward as the ascending aorta from the left ventricle, it arches posteriorly and to the left (aortic arch) and then courses downward as the descending aorta through the thoracic cavity. It pene-

trates the diaphragm to enter the abdominal cavity just anterior to the vertebral column.

Figure 32.2 depicts the relationship of the aorta and its major branches. As you locate the arteries on the figure and other anatomical charts and models, be aware of ways in which you can make your memorization task easier. In many cases the name of the artery reflects the body region traversed (axillary, subclavian, brachial, popliteal), the organ served (renal, hepatic), or the bone followed (tibial, femoral, radial, ulnar).

Ascending Aorta

The only branches of the ascending aorta are the **right** and the **left coronary arteries,** which supply the myocardium. The coronary arteries are described in Exercise 30 in conjunction with heart anatomy.

Aortic Arch and Thoracic Aorta

The **brachiocephalic** (literally, "arm-head") **trunk** is the first branch of the aortic arch (Figure 32.3). The other two major arteries branching off the aortic arch are the **left common carotid artery** and the **left subclavian artery.** The brachiocephalic artery persists briefly before dividing into the **right common carotid artery** and the **right subclavian artery.**

Arteries Serving the Head and Neck

The common carotid artery on each side divides to form an **internal** and an external **carotid artery**. The **internal carotid artery** serves the brain and gives rise to the **ophthalmic artery** that supplies orbital structures. The **external carotid artery** supplies the extracranial tissues of the neck and head, largely via its **superficial temporal, maxillary, facial,** and **occipital** arterial branches. (Notice that several arteries are shown in the figure that are not described here. Ask your instructor which arteries you are required to identify.)

The right and left subclavian arteries each give off several branches to the head and neck. The first of these is the **vertebral artery,** which runs up the posterior neck to supply the cerebellum, part of the brain stem, and the posterior cerebral hemispheres. Issuing just lateral to the vertebral artery are the **thyrocervical trunk,** which mainly serves the thyroid gland and some scapular muscles, and the **costocervical trunk,** which supplies deep neck muscles and some of the upper intercostal muscles. In the armpit, the subclavian artery becomes the axillary artery, which serves the upper limb.

Arteries Serving the Brain

A continuous blood supply to the brain is crucial because oxygen deprivation for even a few minutes causes irreparable damage to the delicate brain tissue. The brain is supplied by two pairs of arteries arising from the region of the aortic arch—the internal carotid arteries and the vertebral arteries. Figure 32.3a is a diagram of the brain's arterial supply.

Within the cranium, each internal carotid artery divides into **anterior** and **middle cerebral arteries,** which supply the bulk of the cerebrum. The right and left anterior cerebral arteries are connected by a short shunt called the **anterior communicating artery.** This shunt, along with shunts from each of the middle cerebral arteries, called the **posterior communicating arteries,** contribute to the formation of the **cerebral arterial circle (circle of Willis),** an arterial anastomosis at the base of the brain surrounding the pituitary gland and the optic chiasma.

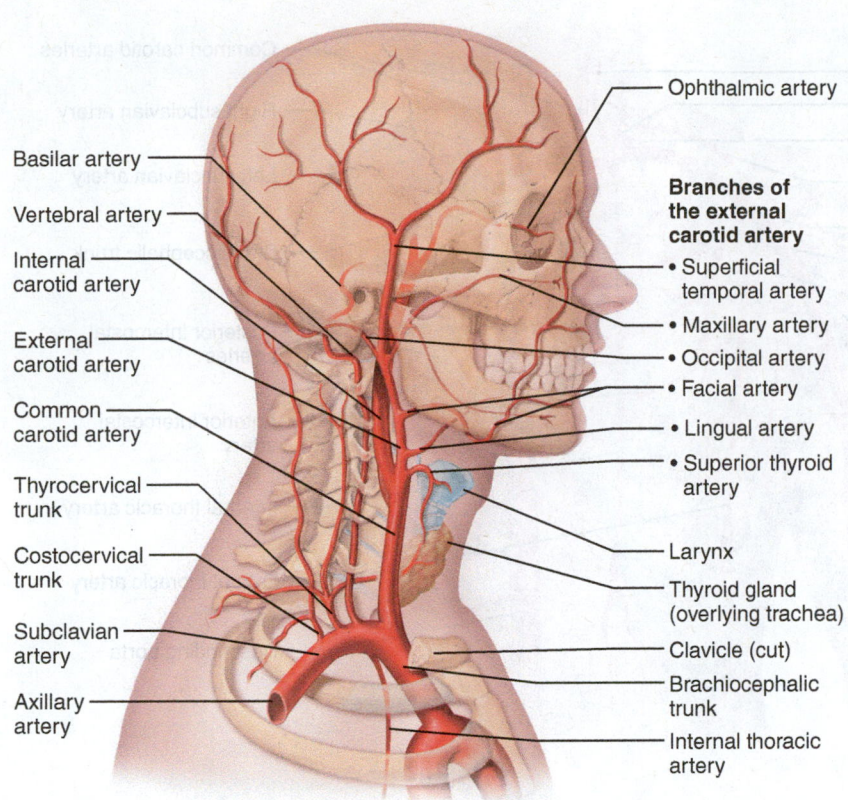

Ophthalmic artery

Basilar artery

Vertebral artery

Internal
carotid artery

External
carotid artery

Common
carotid artery

Thyrocervical
trunk

Costocervical
trunk

Subclavian
artery

Axillary
artery

**Branches of
the external
carotid artery**

• Superficial
  temporal artery

• Maxillary artery

• Occipital artery

• Facial artery

• Lingual artery

• Superior thyroid
  artery

Larynx

Thyroid gland
(overlying trachea)

Clavicle (cut)

Brachiocephalic
trunk

Internal thoracic
artery

(a)

**FIGURE 32.3 Arteries of the head, neck,
and brain.** **(a)** Right aspect. **(b)** Drawing of
the cerebral arteries. Cerebellum is not shown
on the left side of the figure. **(c)** Cerebral
arterial circle (circle of Willis) in a human brain.

Anterior

Frontal lobe

Olfactory bulb

Optic chiasma

Middle
cerebral
artery

Internal
carotid
artery

Pituitary
gland

Temporal
lobe

Pons

Occipital
lobe

Vertebral artery

Posterior

(b)

**Cerebral arterial
circle (circle
of Willis)**

• Anterior
  communicating
  artery

• Anterior
  cerebral artery

• Posterior
  communicating
  artery

• Posterior
  cerebral
  artery

• Basilar artery

Cerebellum

(c)

The paired **vertebral arteries** diverge from the subclavian arteries and pass superiorly through the foramina of the transverse process of the cervical vertebrae to enter the skull through the foramen magnum. Within the skull, the vertebral arteries unite to form a single **basilar artery,** which continues superiorly along the ventral aspect of the brain stem, giving off branches to the pons, cerebellum, and inner ear. At the

base of the cerebrum, the basilar artery divides to form the posterior cerebral arteries. These supply portions of the temporal and occipital lobes of the cerebrum and complete the cerebral arterial circle posteriorly.

The uniting of the blood supply of the internal carotid arteries and the vertebral arteries via the cerebral arterial circle is a protective device that theoretically provides an alternative

Vertebral artery
Thyrocervical trunk
Costocervical trunk
Suprascapular artery
Thoracoacromial artery
Axillary artery
Subscapular artery
Posterior circumflex humeral artery
Anterior circumflex humeral artery
Brachial artery
Deep artery of arm
Common interosseous artery
Radial artery
Ulnar artery

Common carotid arteries
Right subclavian artery
Left subclavian artery
Brachiocephalic trunk
Posterior intercostal arteries
Anterior intercostal artery
Internal thoracic artery
Lateral thoracic artery
Descending aorta

Deep palmar arch
Superficial palmar arch
Digital arteries

FIGURE 32.4 Arteries of the right upper limb and thorax.

set of pathways for blood to reach the brain tissue in the case of arterial occlusion or impaired blood flow anywhere in the system. In actuality, the communicating arteries are tiny, and in many cases the communicating system is defective.

Arteries Serving the Thorax and Upper Limbs

As the **axillary artery** runs through the axilla, it gives off several branches to the chest wall and shoulder girdle (Figure 32.4). These include the **thoracoacromial artery** (to shoulder and pectoral region), the **lateral thoracic artery** (lateral chest wall), the **subscapular artery** (to scapula and dorsal thorax), and the **anterior** and **posterior circumflex humeral arteries** (to the shoulder and the deltoid muscle). At the inferior edge of the teres major muscle, the

axillary artery becomes the **brachial artery** as it enters the arm. The brachial artery gives off a major branch, the **deep artery of the arm,** and as it nears the elbow it gives off several small branches. At the elbow, the brachial artery divides into the **radial** and **ulnar arteries,** which follow the same-named bones to supply the forearm and hand.

The **internal thoracic arteries** that arise from the subclavian arteries supply the mammary glands, most of the thorax wall, and anterior intercostal structures via their **anterior intercostal artery** branches. The first two pairs of **posterior intercostal arteries** arise from the costocervical trunk, noted above. The more inferior pairs arise from the thoracic aorta. Not shown in Figure 32.4 are the small arteries that serve the diaphragm (*phrenic arteries*), esophagus (*esophageal arteries*), bronchi (*bronchial arteries*), and other structures of the mediastinum (*mediastinal and pericardial arteries*).

Abdominal Aorta

Although several small branches of the descending aorta serve the thorax (see the previous section), the more major branches of the descending aorta are those serving the abdominal organs and ultimately the lower limbs (Figure 32.5).

Arteries Serving Abdominal Organs

The **celiac trunk** (Figure 32.5a) is an unpaired artery that subdivides almost immediately into three branches: the **left gastric artery** supplying the stomach, the **splenic artery** supplying the spleen, and the **common hepatic artery,** which runs superiorly and gives off branches to the stomach (**right gastric artery**), duodenum, and pancreas. Where the **gastroduodenal artery** branches off, the common hepatic artery becomes the **hepatic artery proper,** which serves the liver. The **right** and **left gastroepiploic arteries,** branches of

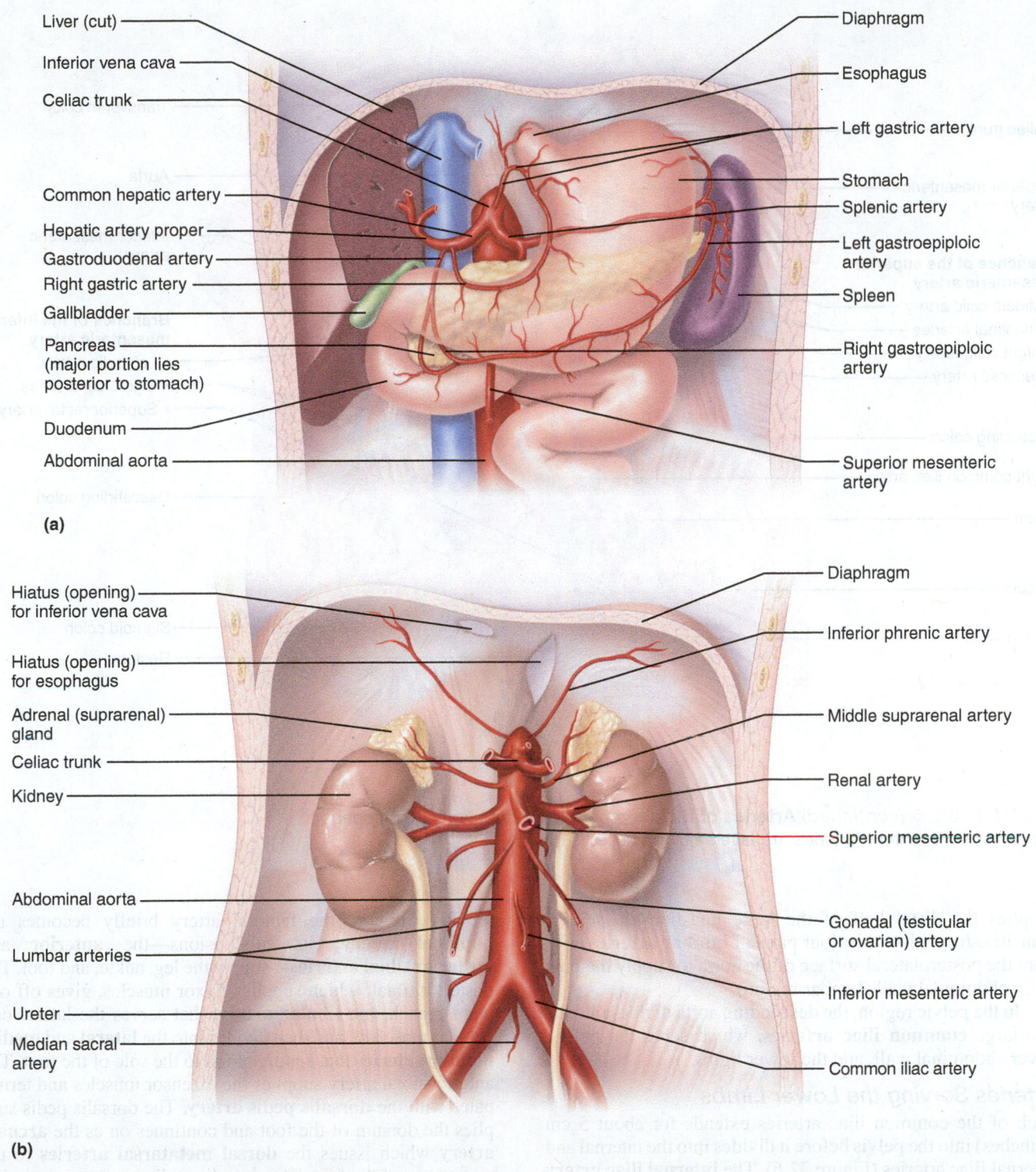

FIGURE 32.5 Arteries of the abdomen. (a) The celiac trunk and its major branches. **(b)** Major branches of the abdominal aorta.

the gastroduodenal and splenic arteries respectively, serve the left (greater) curvature of the stomach.

The largest branch of the abdominal aorta, the **superior mesenteric artery** (Figure 32.5b and 32.5c), supplies most of the small intestine (via the intestinal arteries) and the first half of the large intestine (via the ileocolic and colic arteries). Flanking the superior mesenteric artery on the left and right are the **middle suprarenal arteries** serving the adrenal glands that sit atop the kidneys.

The paired **renal arteries** (Figure 32.5b) supply the kidneys, and the **gonadal arteries,** arising from the ventral aortic surface just below the renal arteries, run inferiorly to serve the gonads. They are called **ovarian arteries** in the female and **testicular arteries** in the male. Since these vessels must travel through the inguinal canal to supply the testes, they are considerably longer in the male than the female.

The final major branch of the abdominal aorta is the **inferior mesenteric artery** (Figure 32.5b and 32.5c), which

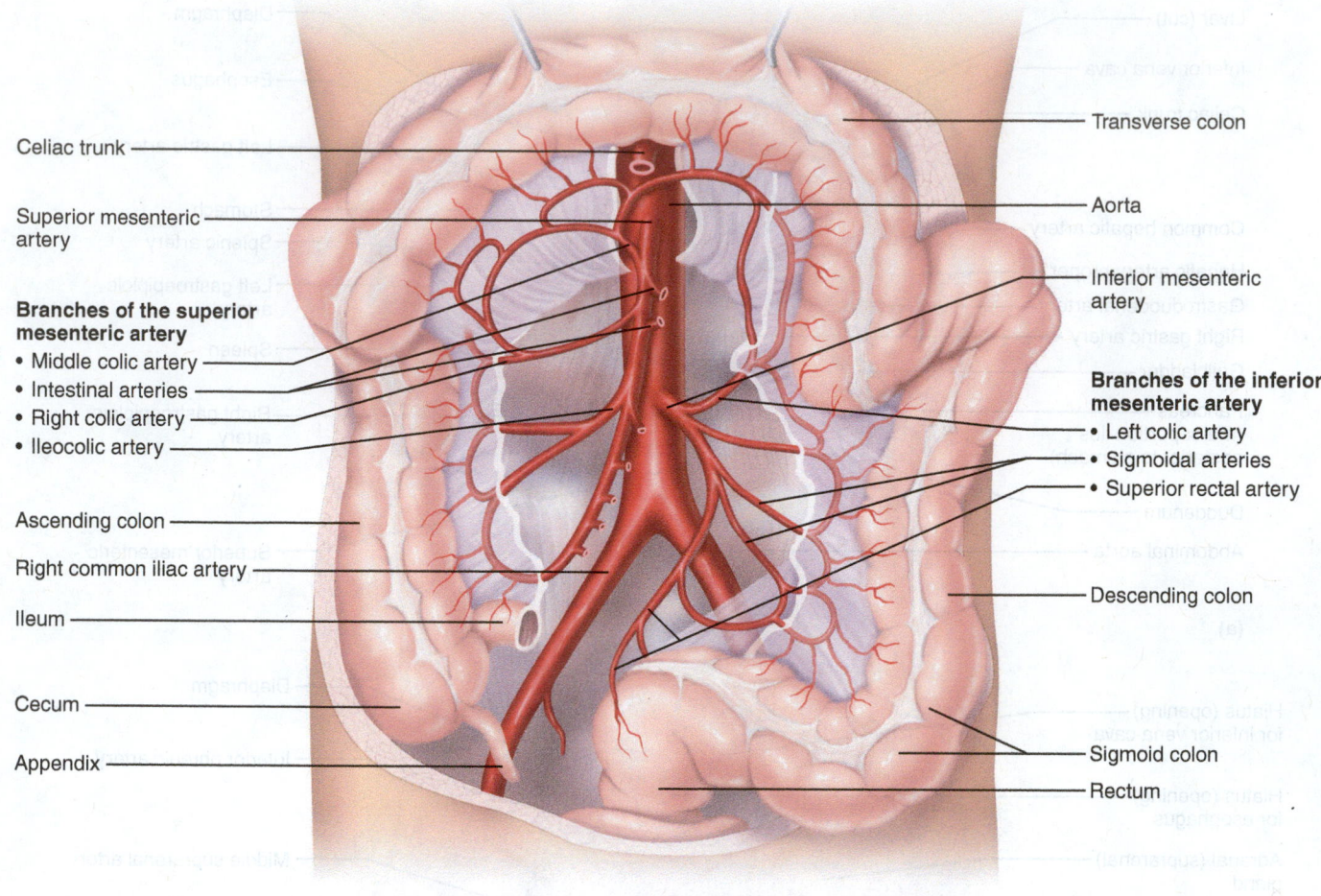

Celiac trunk

Superior mesenteric artery

Branches of the superior mesenteric artery
- Middle colic artery
- Intestinal arteries
- Right colic artery
- Ileocolic artery

Ascending colon

Right common iliac artery

Ileum

Cecum

Appendix

Transverse colon

Aorta

Inferior mesenteric artery

Branches of the inferior mesenteric artery
- Left colic artery
- Sigmoidal arteries
- Superior rectal artery

Descending colon

Sigmoid colon

Rectum

(c)

FIGURE 32.5 *(continued)* **Arteries of the abdomen. (c)** Distribution of the superior and inferior mesenteric arteries, transverse colon pulled superiorly.

supplies the distal half of the large intestine via several branches. Just below this, four pairs of **lumbar arteries** arise from the posterolateral surface of the aorta to supply the posterior abdominal wall (lumbar region).

In the pelvic region, the descending aorta divides into the two large **common iliac arteries,** which serve the pelvis, lower abdominal wall, and the lower limbs.

Arteries Serving the Lower Limbs

Each of the common iliac arteries extends for about 5 cm (2 inches) into the pelvis before it divides into the internal and external iliac arteries (Figure 32.6). The **internal iliac artery** supplies the gluteal muscles via the **superior** and **inferior gluteal arteries** and the adductor muscles of the medial thigh via the **obturator artery,** as well as the external genitalia and perineum (via the *internal pudendal artery,* not illustrated).

The **external iliac artery** supplies the anterior abdominal wall and the lower limb. As it continues into the thigh, its name changes to **femoral artery.** Proximal branches of the femoral artery, the **circumflex femoral arteries,** supply the head and neck of the femur and the hamstring muscles. The femoral artery gives off a deep branch, the **deep artery of the thigh** (also called the **deep femoral artery**), which is the main supply to the thigh muscles (hamstrings, quadriceps, and adductors). In

the knee region, the femoral artery briefly becomes the **popliteal artery;** its subdivisions—the **anterior** and **posterior tibial arteries**—supply the leg, ankle, and foot. The posterior tibial, which supplies flexor muscles, gives off one main branch, the **fibular artery,** that serves the lateral calf (fibular muscles), and then divides into the **lateral** and **medial plantar arteries** that supply blood to the sole of the foot. The anterior tibial artery supplies the extensor muscles and terminates with the **dorsalis pedis artery.** The dorsalis pedis supplies the dorsum of the foot and continues on as the **arcuate artery** which issues the **dorsal metatarsal arteries** to the metatarsus of the foot. The dorsalis pedis is often palpated in patients with circulation problems of the leg to determine the circulatory efficiency to the limb as a whole.

- Palpate your own dorsalis pedis artery.

ACTIVITY 2

Locating Arteries on an Anatomical Chart or Model

Now that you have identified the arteries on Figures 32.2–32.6, attempt to locate and name them (without a reference) on a

- Common iliac artery
- Internal iliac artery
- Superior gluteal artery
- External iliac artery
- Deep artery of thigh
- Obturator artery
- Medial circumflex femoral artery
- Lateral circumflex femoral artery
- Femoral artery
- Adductor hiatus
- Popliteal artery
- Anterior tibial artery
- Posterior tibial artery
- Fibular artery
- Dorsalis pedis artery
- Arcuate artery
- Dorsal metatarsal arteries

- Popliteal artery
- Anterior tibial artery
- Fibular artery
- Posterior tibial artery
- Lateral plantar artery
- Medial plantar artery
- Dorsalis pedis artery (from top of foot)
- Plantar arch

(a)   **(b)**

FIGURE 32.6 Arteries of the right pelvis and lower limb. (a) Anterior view. **(b)** Posterior view.

large anatomical chart or three-dimensional model of the vascular system. ▬

Major Systemic Veins of the Body

Arteries are generally located in deep, well-protected body areas. However, many veins follow a more superficial course and are often easily seen and palpated on the body surface. Most deep veins parallel the course of the major arteries, and in many cases the naming of the veins and arteries is identical except for the designation of the vessels as veins. Whereas the major systemic arteries branch off the aorta, the veins tend to converge on the venae cavae, which enter the right atrium of the heart. Veins draining the head and upper extremities empty into the **superior vena cava,** and those draining the lower body empty into the **inferior vena cava.** Figure 32.7 is a schematic of the systemic veins and their relationship to the venae cavae to get you started.

Veins Draining into the Inferior Vena Cava

The inferior vena cava, a much longer vessel than the superior vena cava, returns blood to the heart from all body regions below the diaphragm (see Figure 32.7). It begins in the lower abdominal region with the union of the paired **common iliac veins,** which drain venous blood from the legs and pelvis.

Veins of the Lower Limbs

Each common iliac vein is formed by the union of the **internal iliac vein,** draining the pelvis, and the **external iliac vein,** which receives venous blood from the lower limb (Figure 32.8). Veins of the leg include the **anterior** and **posterior tibial veins,** which serve the calf and foot. The anterior tibial vein is a superior continuation of the **dorsalis pedis vein** of the foot. The posterior tibial vein is formed by the union of the **medial** and **lateral plantar veins,** and ascends deep in the calf muscles. It receives the **fibular vein** in the calf and then joins with the anterior tibial vein at the knee to produce the **popliteal vein,** which crosses the back of the knee. The popliteal vein becomes the **femoral vein** in the thigh; the femoral vein in turn becomes the external iliac vein in the inguinal region.

The **great saphenous vein,** a superficial vein, is the longest vein in the body. Beginning in common with the **small saphenous vein** from the **dorsal venous arch,** it extends up the medial side of the leg, knee, and thigh to empty into the femoral vein. The small saphenous vein runs along the lateral aspect of the foot and through the calf muscle, which it drains, and then empties into the popliteal vein at the knee (Figure 32.8b).

Veins of the Abdomen

Moving superiorly in the abdominal cavity (Figure 32.9), the inferior vena cava receives blood from the posterior abdominal wall via several pairs of **lumbar veins,** and from the right ovary or testis via the **right gonadal vein.** (The **left gonadal [ovarian or testicular] vein** drains into the left renal vein superiorly.) The paired **renal veins** drain the kidneys. Just above the right renal vein, the **right suprarenal vein** (receiving blood from the adrenal gland on the same side) drains into the inferior vena cava, but its partner, the **left suprarenal**

FIGURE 32.7 Schematic of systemic venous circulation.

vein, empties into the left renal vein inferiorly. The **hepatic veins** drain the liver. The unpaired veins draining the digestive tract organs empty into a special vessel, the hepatic portal vein, which carries blood to the liver to be processed before it enters the systemic venous system. (The hepatic portal system is discussed separately on page 484.)

Veins Draining into the Superior Vena Cava

Veins draining into the superior vena cava are named from the superior vena cava distally, _but remember that the flow of blood is in the opposite direction_.

Veins of the Head and Neck

The **right** and **left brachiocephalic veins** drain the head, neck, and upper extremities and unite to form the superior vena cava (Figure 32.10). Notice that although there is only one brachiocephalic artery, there are two brachiocephalic veins.

Branches of the brachiocephalic veins include the internal jugular, vertebral, and subclavian veins. The **internal jugular veins** are large veins that drain the superior sagittal sinus and other **dural sinuses** of the brain. As they run inferiorly, they receive blood from the head and neck via the **superficial temporal** and **facial veins.** The **vertebral veins** drain the posterior aspect of the head including the cervical vertebrae and spinal cord. The **subclavian veins** receive venous blood from the upper extremity. The **external jugular vein** joins the subclavian vein near its origin to return the venous drainage of the extracranial (superficial) tissues of the head and neck.

Veins of the Upper Limb and Thorax

As the subclavian vein traverses the axilla, it becomes the **axillary vein** and then the **brachial vein** as it courses along the posterior aspect of the humerus (Figure 32.11). The brachial vein is formed by the union of the deep **radial** and **ulnar veins** of the forearm. The superficial venous drainage of the arm includes the **cephalic vein,** which courses along the lateral aspect of the arm and empties into the axillary vein; the **basilic vein,** found on the medial aspect of the arm and entering the brachial vein; and the **median cubital vein,** which runs between the cephalic and basilic veins in the anterior aspect of the elbow (this vein is often the site of choice for removing blood for testing purposes). The **median antebrachial vein** lies between the radial and ulnar veins, and terminates variably by entering the cephalic or basilic vein at the elbow.

The **azygos system** (Figure 32.11) drains the intercostal muscles of the thorax and provides an accessory venous system to drain the abdominal wall. The **azygos vein,** which drains the right side of the thorax, enters the dorsal aspect of the superior vena cava immediately before that vessel enters the right atrium. Also part of the azygos system are the **hemiazygos** (a continuation of the **left ascending lumbar vein** of the abdomen) and the **accessory hemiazygos veins,** which together drain the left side of the thorax and empty into the azygos vein.

Identifying the Systemic Veins

Identify the important veins of the systemic circulation on the large anatomical chart or model without referring to the figures. ▬

Special Circulations

Pulmonary Circulation

The pulmonary circulation (discussed previously in relation to heart anatomy on page 446) differs in many ways from systemic circulation because it does not serve the metabolic needs of the body tissues with which it is associated (in this case, lung

Common iliac vein
Internal iliac vein
External iliac vein
Inguinal ligament
Femoral vein
Great saphenous vein (superficial)
Great saphenous vein
Popliteal vein
Popliteal vein
Small saphenous vein
Anterior tibial vein
Fibular vein
Fibular vein
Anterior tibial vein
Small saphenous vein (superficial)
Dorsalis pedis vein
Posterior tibial vein
Dorsal venous arch
Plantar veins
Dorsal metatarsal veins
Deep plantar arch
Digital veins

(a) Anterior view   **(b) Posterior view**

FIGURE 32.8 Veins of the right pelvis and lower limb.
(a) Anterior view. **(b)** Posterior view.

tissue). It functions instead to bring the blood into close contact with the alveoli of the lungs to permit gas exchanges that rid the blood of excess carbon dioxide and replenish its supply of vital oxygen. The arteries of the pulmonary circulation are structurally much like veins, and they create a low-pressure bed in the lungs. (If the arterial pressure in the systemic circulation is 120/80, the pressure in the pulmonary artery is likely to be approximately 24/8.) The functional blood supply of the lungs is provided by the **bronchial arteries** (not shown), which diverge from the thoracic portion of the descending aorta.

Hepatic veins

Inferior vena cava

Right suprarenal vein

Right gonadal vein

External iliac vein

Inferior phrenic vein

Left suprarenal vein

Renal veins

Left ascending lumbar vein

Lumbar veins

Left gonadal vein

Common iliac vein

Internal iliac vein

FIGURE 32.9 Venous drainage of abdominal organs not drained by the hepatic portal vein.

Ophthalmic vein

Superficial temporal vein

Facial vein

Occipital vein

Posterior auricular vein

External jugular vein

Vertebral vein

Internal jugular vein

Superior and middle thyroid veins

Brachiocephalic vein

Subclavian vein

Superior vena cava

(a)

Superior sagittal sinus

Falx cerebri

Inferior sagittal sinus

Straight sinus

Cavernous sinus

Confluence of sinuses

Transverse sinuses

Sigmoid sinus

Jugular foramen

Right internal jugular vein

(b)

FIGURE 32.10 Venous drainage of the head, neck, and brain. (a) Veins of the head and neck, right superficial aspect. (b) Dural sinuses of the brain, right aspect.

Brachiocephalic veins

Right subclavian vein

Axillary vein

Brachial vein

Cephalic vein

Basilic vein

Median cubital vein

Median antebrachial vein

Cephalic vein

Radial vein

Internal jugular vein

External jugular vein

Left subclavian vein

Superior vena cava

Azygos vein

Accessory hemiazygos vein

Hemiazygos vein

Posterior intercostals

Inferior vena cava

Ascending lumbar vein

Basilic vein

Ulnar vein

Deep palmar venous arch

Superficial palmar venous arch

Digital veins

FIGURE 32.11 Veins of the thorax and right upper limb. For clarity, the abundant branching and anastomoses of these vessels are not shown.

Pulmonary circulation begins with the large **pulmonary trunk,** which leaves the right ventricle and divides into the **right** and **left pulmonary arteries** about 5 cm (2 inches) above its origin. The right and left pulmonary arteries plunge into the lungs, where they subdivide into **lobar arteries** (three on the right and two on the left). The lobar arteries accompany the main bronchi into the lobes of the lungs and branch extensively within the lungs to form arterioles, which finally terminate in the capillary networks surrounding the alveolar sacs of the lungs. Diffusion of the respiratory gases occurs across the walls of the alveoli and **pulmonary capillaries.** The pulmonary capillary beds are drained by venules, which converge to form sequentially larger veins and finally the four **pulmonary veins** (two leaving each lung), which return the blood to the left atrium of the heart.

ACTIVITY 4

Identifying Vessels of the Pulmonary Circulation

As you read the descriptions below, find the vessels of the pulmonary circulation on Figure 32.12 and on an anatomical chart (if one is available).

Left pulmonary artery

Aortic arch

Pulmonary trunk

Right pulmonary artery

Three lobar arteries to right lung

Right pulmonary veins

Right atrium

Right ventricle

Left ventricle

Two lobar arteries to left lung

Left pulmonary veins

Left atrium

FIGURE 32.12 The pulmonary circulation. The pulmonary arterial system is shown in blue to indicate that the blood carried is oxygen-poor. The pulmonary venous drainage is shown in red to indicate that the blood transported is oxygen-rich.

Fetal Circulation

In a developing fetus, the lungs and digestive system are not yet functional, and all nutrient, excretory, and gaseous exchanges occur through the placenta (see Figure 32.14a). Nutrients and oxygen move across placental barriers from the mother's blood into fetal blood, and carbon dioxide and other metabolic wastes move from the fetal blood supply to the mother's blood.

ACTIVITY 5

Tracing the Pathway of Fetal Blood Flow

Use Figure 32.13a and an anatomical chart (if available) to trace the pathway of fetal blood flow. Locate all the named vessels. Use Figure 32.13b to identify the named remnants of the foramen ovale and fetal vessels. ▮▮▮

Fetal blood travels through the umbilical cord, which contains three blood vessels: two smaller umbilical arteries and one large umbilical vein. The **umbilical vein** carries blood rich in nutrients and oxygen to the fetus; the **umbilical arteries** carry carbon dioxide and waste-laden blood from the fetus to the placenta. The umbilical arteries, which transport blood away from the fetal heart, meet the umbilical vein at the *umbilicus* (navel, or belly button) and wrap around the vein within the cord en route to their placental attachments. Newly oxygenated blood flows in the umbilical vein superiorly toward the fetal heart.

Some of this blood perfuses the liver, but the larger proportion is ducted through the relatively nonfunctional liver to the inferior vena cava via a shunt vessel called the **ductus venosus,** which carries the blood to the right atrium of the heart.

Because fetal lungs are nonfunctional and collapsed, two shunting mechanisms ensure that blood almost entirely bypasses the lungs. Much of the blood entering the right atrium is shunted into the left atrium through the **foramen ovale,** a flaplike opening in the interatrial septum. The left ventricle then pumps the blood out the aorta to the systemic circulation. Blood that does enter the right ventricle and is pumped out of the pulmonary trunk encounters a second shunt, the **ductus arteriosus,** a short vessel connecting the pulmonary trunk and the aorta. Because the collapsed lungs present an extremely high-resistance pathway, blood more readily enters the systemic circulation through the ductus arteriosus.

The aorta carries blood to the tissues of the body; this blood ultimately finds its way back to the placenta via the umbilical arteries. The only fetal vessel that carries highly oxygenated blood is the umbilical vein. All other vessels contain varying degrees of oxygenated and deoxygenated blood.

At birth, or shortly after, the foramen ovale closes and becomes the **fossa ovalis,** and the ductus arteriosus collapses and is converted to the fibrous **ligamentum arteriosum** (Figure 32.13b). Lack of blood flow through the umbilical vessels leads to their eventual obliteration, and the circulatory pattern becomes that of the adult. Remnants of the umbilical

Fetus

Newborn

Aortic arch

Superior vena cava

Ductus arteriosus
↓
Ligamentum arteriosum

Pulmonary artery

Pulmonary veins

Heart

Lung

Foramen ovale
↓
Fossa ovalis

Liver

Ductus venosus
↓
Ligamentum venosum

Hepatic portal vein

Umbilical vein
↓
Ligamentum teres

Inferior vena cava

Umbilicus

Abdominal aorta

Common iliac artery

Umbilical arteries
↓
Medial umbilical ligaments

Urinary bladder

Umbilical cord

Placenta

High oxygenation
Moderate oxygenation
Low oxygenation
Very low oxygenation

(a)

(b)

FIGURE 32.13 Circulation in fetus and newborn. Arrows indicate direction of blood flow. Arrows in the blue boxes go from the fetal structure to what it becomes after birth. **(a)** Special adaptations for embryonic and fetal life. The umbilical vein (red) carries oxygen- and nutrient-rich blood from the placenta to the fetus. The umbilical arteries (pink) carry waste-laden blood from the fetus to the placenta. **(b)** Changes in the cardiovascular system at birth. The umbilical vessels are occluded, as are the liver and lung bypasses (ductus venosus and arteriosus, and the foramen ovale).

Hepatic veins

Liver

Hepatic portal vein

Small intestine

Rectum

Inferior vena cava
(not part of hepatic
portal system)

Gastric veins

Spleen

Splenic vein

Right
gastroepiploic vein

Inferior
mesenteric vein

Superior
mesenteric vein

Large intestine

FIGURE 32.14 Hepatic portal circulation.

arteries persist as the **medial umbilical ligaments** on the inner surface of the anterior abdominal wall, of the umbilical vein as the **ligamentum teres** (or **round ligament**) of the liver, and of the ductus venosus as a fibrous band called the **ligamentum venosum** on the inferior surface of the liver.

Hepatic Portal Circulation

Blood vessels of the hepatic portal circulation drain the digestive viscera, spleen, and pancreas and deliver this blood to the liver for processing via the **hepatic portal vein.** If a meal has recently been eaten, the hepatic portal blood will be nutrient rich. The liver is the key body organ involved in maintaining proper sugar, fatty acid, and amino acid concentrations in the blood, and this system ensures that these substances pass through the liver before entering the systemic circulation. As blood percolates through the liver sinusoids, some of the nutrients are removed to be stored or processed in various ways for release to the general circulation. At the same time, the hepatocytes are detoxifying alcohol and other possibly harmful chemicals present in the blood, and the liver's macrophages are removing bacteria and other debris from the passing blood. The liver in

turn is drained by the hepatic veins that enter the inferior vena cava.

ACTIVITY 6

Tracing the Hepatic Portal Circulation

Locate on Figure 32.14, and on an anatomical chart of the hepatic portal circulation (if available), the vessels named below. ■

The **inferior mesenteric vein,** draining the distal portions of the large intestine, joins the **splenic vein,** which drains the spleen and part of the pancreas and stomach. The splenic vein and the **superior mesenteric vein,** which receives blood from the small intestine and the ascending and transverse colon, unite to form the hepatic portal vein. The **left gastric vein,** which drains the lesser curvature of the stomach, drains directly into the hepatic portal vein.

For instructions on animal dissections, see the dissection exercises starting on page 697 in the cat, rat, and pig editions of this manual.

Anatomy of Blood Vessels

Microscopic Structure of the Blood Vessels

1. Cross-sectional views of an artery and of a vein are shown here. Identify each; on the lines to the sides, note the structural details that enabled you to make these identifications:

(vessel type) _____

_____
(a)

_____
(b)

(vessel type) _____

_____
(a)

_____
(b)

Now describe each tunic more fully by selecting its characteristics from the key below and placing the appropriate key letters on the answer lines.

Tunica intima _____   Tunica media _____   Tunica externa _____

Key:

a. innermost tunic
b. most superficial tunic
c. thin tunic of capillaries

d. especially thick in elastic arteries
e. contains smooth muscle and elastin
f. has a smooth surface to decrease resistance to blood flow

2. Why are valves present in veins but not in arteries? _____

_____

_____

3. Name two events *occurring within the body* that aid in venous return.

_____ and _____

4. Why are the walls of arteries proportionately thicker than those of the corresponding veins? _____

_____

_____

Major Systemic Arteries and Veins of the Body

5. Use the key on the right to identify the arteries or veins described on the left.

Key: a. anterior tibial

_____ 1. the arterial system has one of these; the venous system has two

b. basilic

_____ 2. these arteries supply the myocardium

c. brachial

_____, _____ 3. two paired arteries serving the brain

d. brachiocephalic

_____ 4. longest vein in the lower limb

e. celiac trunk

f. cephalic

_____ 5. artery on the dorsum of the foot checked after leg surgery

g. common carotid

_____ 6. serves the posterior thigh

h. common iliac

_____ 7. supplies the diaphragm

i. coronary

_____ 8. formed by the union of the radial and ulnar veins

j. deep artery of the thigh

_____, _____ 9. two superficial veins of the arm

k. dorsalis pedis

_____ 10. artery serving the kidney

l. external carotid

_____ 11. veins draining the liver

m. femoral

_____ 12. artery that supplies the distal half of the large intestine

n. fibular

_____ 13. drains the pelvic organs

o. great saphenous

_____ 14. what the external iliac artery becomes on entry into the thigh

p. hepatic

q. inferior mesenteric

_____ 15. major artery serving the arm

r. internal carotid

_____ 16. supplies most of the small intestine

s. internal iliac

_____ 17. join to form the inferior vena cava

t. phrenic

_____ 18. an arterial trunk that has three major branches, which run to the liver, spleen, and stomach

u. posterior tibial

v. radial

_____ 19. major artery serving the tissues external to the skull

w. renal

_____, _____, _____ 20. three veins serving the leg

x. subclavian

_____ 21. artery generally used to take the pulse at the wrist

y. superior mesenteric

6. What is the function of the cerebral arterial circle (circle of Willis)?

z. vertebral

_____

7. The anterior and middle cerebral arteries arise from the _____ artery.

They serve the _____ of the brain.

8. Trace the pathway of a drop of blood from the aorta to the left occipital lobe of the brain, noting all structures through which it flows. _____

_____

9. The human arterial and venous systems are diagrammed on this page and the next. Identify all indicated blood vessels.

Arteries

Veins

10. Trace the blood flow for each of the following situations.

a. from the capillary beds of the left thumb to the capillary beds of the right thumb: _____

_____

_____

b. from the mitral valve to the tricuspid valve by way of the great toe:

_____

_____

Pulmonary Circulation

11. Trace the pathway of a carbon dioxide gas molecule in the blood from the inferior vena cava until it leaves the bloodstream. Name all structures (vessels, heart chambers, and others) passed through en route.

_____

_____

12. Trace the pathway of oxygen gas molecules from an alveolus of the lung to the right ventricle of the heart. Name all structures

through which it passes. Circle the areas of gas exchange. _____

_____

13. Most arteries of the adult body carry oxygen-rich blood, and the veins carry carbon dioxide–rich blood.

How does this differ in the pulmonary arteries and veins? _____

_____

14. How do the arteries of the pulmonary circulation differ structurally from the systemic arteries? What condition is indicated

by this anatomical difference? _____

_____

Hepatic Portal Circulation

15. What is the source of blood in the hepatic portal system? _____

_____

16. Why is this blood carried to the liver before it enters the systemic circulation? _____

_____

17. The hepatic portal vein is formed by the union of (a) _____, which drains the _____,

_____, _____, _____, and (b) _____, which

drains the _____ and _____. The _____ vein, which drains the lesser

curvature of the stomach, empties directly into the hepatic portal vein.

18. Trace the flow of a drop of blood from the small intestine to the right atrium of the heart, noting all structures encountered

or passed through on the way. _____

_____

Fetal Circulation

19. For each of the following structures, first indicate its function in the fetus; and then note its fate (what happens to it or what
it is converted to after birth). Circle the blood vessel that carries the most oxygen-rich blood.

Structure	Function in fetus	Fate
Umbilical artery		
Umbilical vein		
Ductus venosus		
Ductus arteriosus		
Foramen ovale		

20. What organ serves as a respiratory/digestive/excretory organ for the fetus? _____

33A

Human Cardiovascular Physiology: Blood Pressure and Pulse Determinations

MATERIALS

- ☐ Recording of "Interpreting Heart Sounds" (if available on free loan from the local chapters of the American Heart Association) or any of the suitable Internet sites on heart sounds
- ☐ Stethoscope
- ☐ Alcohol swabs
- ☐ Watch (or clock) with second hand

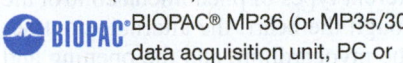 BIOPAC® MP36 (or MP35/30) data acquisition unit, PC or Mac computer, BIOPAC® Student Lab Software, BIOPAC® pulse plethysmograph

New versions of the BSL software (3.7.5 and higher for Windows, and 3.7.4 and higher for Mac) require slightly different channel settings and collection strategies. Instructions for using the newer software with the MP36/35 data acquisition units can be found on myA&P. In addition, instructions for use of the NEW 2-channel data acquisition unit, the MP45, may also be found on myA&P.

- ☐ Sphygmomanometer
- ☐ Felt marker
- ☐ Meter stick
- ☐ Cot (if available)
- ☐ Step stools (0.4 m [16 in.] and 0.5 m [20 in.] in height)
- ☐ Small basin suitable for the immersion of one hand
- ☐ Ice
- ☐ Laboratory thermometer

PEx PhysioEx™ 8.0 Computer Simulation on page PEx-87

Note: Instructions for using PowerLab® equipment can be found on myA&P.

 For practice quizzes on this lab, go to www.myaandp.com.

OBJECTIVES

1. To define *systole, diastole,* and *cardiac cycle.*
2. To indicate the normal length of the cardiac cycle, the relative pressure changes occurring within the atria and ventricles during the cycle, and the timing of valve closure.
3. To use the stethoscope to auscultate heart sounds, and to relate heart sounds to cardiac cycle events.
4. To describe the clinical significance of heart sounds and heart murmurs.
5. To demonstrate thoracic locations where the first and second heart sounds are most accurately auscultated.
6. To define *pulse, pulse deficit, blood pressure,* and *sounds of Korotkoff.*
7. To accurately determine a subject's apical and radial pulse.
8. To accurately determine a subject's blood pressure with a sphygmomanometer, and to relate systolic and diastolic pressures to events of the cardiac cycle.
9. To investigate the effects of exercise on blood pressure, pulse, and cardiovascular fitness.
10. To indicate factors affecting and/or determining blood flow and skin color.

PRE-LAB QUIZ

1. Circle the correct term. According to general usage, <u>systole / diastole</u> refers to ventricular relaxation.
2. A graph illustrating the pressure and volume changes during one heartbeat is called the
   a. blood pressure
   b. cardiac cycle
   c. conduction system of the heart
   d. electrical events of the heartbeat
3. Circle True or False. When ventricular systole begins, intraventricular pressure increases rapidly, closing the atrioventricular (AV) valves.
4. The average heart beats approximately _____ times per minute.
   a. 50
   b. 75
   c. 100
   d. 125
5. Circle the correct term. Abnormal heart sounds called <u>murmurs / stroke</u> can indicate valvular problems.
6. The term _____ refers to the alternating surges of pressure in an artery that occur with each contraction and relaxation of the left ventricle.
   a. diastole
   b. murmur
   c. pulse
   d. systole

Text continues on next page.

7. Circle the correct term. The pulse is most often taken at the lateral aspect of the wrist, above the thumb, compressing the <u>popliteal / radial</u> artery.

8. What device will you use today to measure your subject's blood pressure?

_____

9. In reporting a blood pressure of 120/90, which number represents the *diastolic* pressure? _____

10. The _____ are characteristic sounds that indicate the resumption of blood flow to the artery being occluded when taking blood pressure.
   a. ectopic heartbeats
   b. heart murmurs
   c. heart rhythms
   d. sounds of Korotkoff

Any comprehensive study of human cardiovascular physiology takes much more time than a single laboratory period. However, it is possible to conduct investigations of a few phenomena such as pulse, heart sounds, and blood pressure, all of which reflect the heart in action and the function of blood vessels. (The electrocardiogram is studied separately in Exercise 31.) A discussion of the cardiac cycle will provide a basis for understanding and interpreting the various physiological measurements taken.

Cardiac Cycle

In a healthy heart, the two atria contract simultaneously. As they begin to relax, the ventricles contract simultaneously. According to general usage, the terms **systole** and **diastole** refer to events of ventricular contraction and relaxation, respectively. The **cardiac cycle** is equivalent to one complete heartbeat—during which both atria and ventricles contract and then relax. It is marked by a succession of changes in blood volume and pressure within the heart.

Figure 33A.1 is a graphic representation of the events of the cardiac cycle for the left side of the heart. Although pressure changes in the right side are less dramatic than those in the left, the same relationships apply.

We will begin the discussion of the cardiac cycle with the heart in complete relaxation (diastole). At this point, pressure in the heart is very low, blood is flowing passively from the pulmonary and systemic circulations into the atria and on through to the ventricles; the semilunar valves are closed, and the AV valves are open. Shortly, atrial contraction occurs and atrial pressure increases, forcing residual blood into the ventricles. Then ventricular systole begins and intraventricular pressure increases rapidly, closing the AV valves. When ventricular pressure exceeds that of the large arteries leaving the heart, the semilunar valves are forced open, and the blood in the ventricular chambers is expelled through the valves. During this phase, the aortic pressure reaches approximately 120 mm Hg in a healthy young adult. During ventricular systole, the atria relax and their chambers fill with blood, which results in gradually increasing atrial pressure. At the end of ventricular systole, the ventricles relax; the semilunar valves snap shut, preventing backflow, and momentarily, the ventricles are closed chambers. When the aortic semilunar valve snaps shut, a momentary increase in the aortic pressure results from the elastic recoil of the aorta after valve closure. This event results in the pressure fluctuation called the *dicrotic notch* (see Figure 33A.1a). As the ventricles relax, the pressure within them begins to drop. When intraventricular pressure is again less than atrial pressure, the AV valves are forced open, and the ventricles again begin to fill with blood. Atrial and aortic pressures decrease, and the ventricles rapidly refill, completing the cycle.

The average heart beats approximately 75 beats per minute, and so the length of the cardiac cycle is about 0.8 second. Of this time period, atrial contraction occupies the first 0.1 second, which is followed by atrial relaxation and ventricular contraction for the next 0.3 second. The remaining 0.4 second is the quiescent, or ventricular relaxation, period. When the heart beats at a more rapid pace than normal, this last period decreases.

Notice that two different types of phenomena control the movement of blood through the heart: the alternate contraction and relaxation of the myocardium, and the opening and closing of valves, which is entirely dependent on the pressure changes within the heart chambers.

Study Figure 33A.1 carefully to make sure you understand what has been discussed before continuing with the next portion of the exercise.

Heart Sounds

Sounds heard in the cardiovascular system result from turbulent blood flow. Two distinct sounds can be heard during each cardiac cycle. These heart sounds are commonly described by the monosyllables "lub" and "dup"; and the sequence is designated lub-dup, pause, lub-dup, pause, and so on. The first heart sound (lub) is referred to as S_1 and is associated with closure of the AV valves at the beginning of ventricular systole. The second heart sound (dup), called S_2, occurs as the semilunar valves close and corresponds with the end of systole. Figure 33A.1a indicates the correlation of heart sounds with events of the cardiac cycle.

• Listen to the recording "Interpreting Heart Sounds" or another suitable recording so that you may hear both normal and abnormal heart sounds.

Abnormal heart sounds are called **murmurs** and often indicate valvular problems. In valves that do not close tightly, closure is followed by a swishing sound due to the backflow of blood (regurgitation). Distinct sounds, often described as high-pitched screeching, are associated with the tortuous flow of blood through constricted, or stenosed, valves. ■

ACTIVITY 1

Auscultating Heart Sounds

In the following procedure, you will auscultate your partner's heart sounds with an ordinary stethoscope. A number of more sophisticated heart-sound amplification systems are on the market, and your instructor may prefer to use one if it is available. If so, directions for the use of this apparatus will be provided by the instructor.

FIGURE 33A.1 Summary of events occurring in the heart during the cardiac cycle. (a) An ECG tracing is superimposed on the graph (top) so that electrical events can be related to pressure and volume changes (center) in the left side of the heart. Pressures are lower in the right side of the heart. Time occurrence of heart sounds is also indicated. (EDV = end diastolic volume, SV = stroke volume, ESV = end systolic volume) **(b)** Events of phases 1 through 3 of the cardiac cycle are depicted in diagrammatic views of the heart.

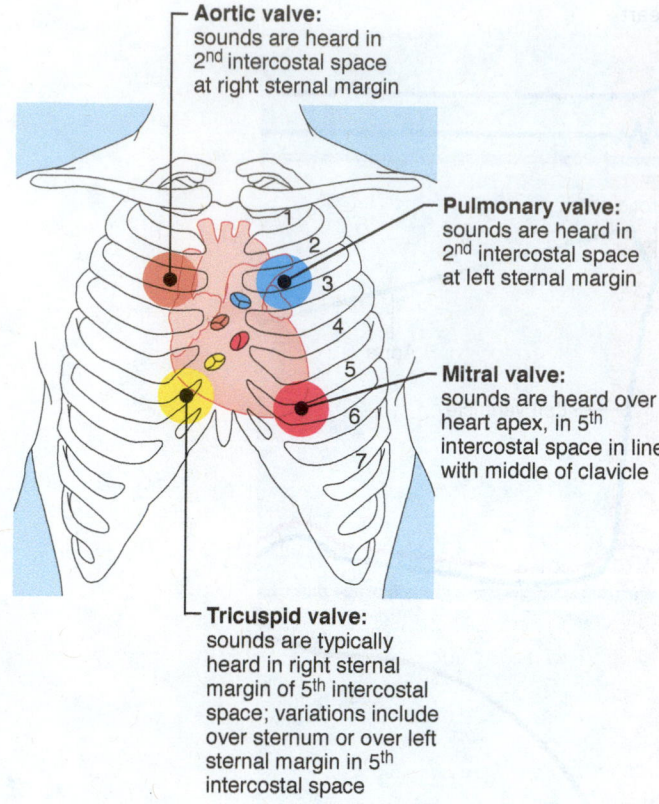

Aortic valve: sounds are heard in 2nd intercostal space at right sternal margin

Pulmonary valve: sounds are heard in 2nd intercostal space at left sternal margin

Mitral valve: sounds are heard over heart apex, in 5th intercostal space in line with middle of clavicle

Tricuspid valve: sounds are typically heard in right sternal margin of 5th intercostal space; variations include over sternum or over left sternal margin in 5th intercostal space

FIGURE 33A.2 Areas of the thorax where heart sounds can best be detected.

1. Obtain a stethoscope and some alcohol swabs. Heart sounds are best auscultated (listened to) if the subject's outer clothing is removed, so a male subject is preferable.

2. With an alcohol swab, clean the earpieces of the stethoscope. Allow the alcohol to dry. Notice that the earpieces are angled. For comfort and best auscultation, the earpieces should be angled in a *forward* direction when placed into the ears.

3. Don the stethoscope. Place the diaphragm of the stethoscope on your partner's thorax, just to the sternal side of the left nipple at the fifth intercostal space, and listen carefully for heart sounds. The first sound will be a longer, louder (more booming) sound than the second, which is short and sharp. After listening for a couple of minutes, try to time the pause between the second sound of one heartbeat and the first sound of the subsequent heartbeat.

How long is this interval? _____ sec

How does it compare to the interval between the first and second sounds of a single heartbeat?

_____

4. To differentiate individual valve sounds somewhat more precisely, auscultate the heart sounds over specific thoracic regions. Refer to Figure 33A.2 for the positioning of the stethoscope.

Auscultation of AV Valves

As a rule, the mitral valve closes slightly before the tricuspid valve. You can hear the mitral valve more clearly if you place the stethoscope over the apex of the heart, which is at the fifth intercostal space, approximately in line with the middle region of the left clavicle. Listen to the heart sounds at this region; then move the stethoscope medially to the right margin of the sternum to auscultate the tricuspid valve. Can you detect the slight lag between the closure of the mitral and tricuspid valves?

_____

There are normal variations in the site for "best" auscultation of the tricuspid valve. These range from the site depicted in Figure 33A.2 (right sternal margin over fifth intercostal space) to over the sternal body in the same plane, to the left sternal margin over the fifth intercostal space. If you have difficulty hearing closure of the tricuspid valve, try one of these other locations.

Auscultation of Semilunar Valves

Again there is a slight dissynchrony of valve closure; the aortic semilunar valve normally snaps shut just ahead of the pulmonary semilunar valve. If the subject inhales deeply but gently, filling of the right ventricle (due to decreased intrapulmonary pressure) and closure of the pulmonary valve will be delayed slightly. The two sounds can therefore be heard more distinctly.

Position the stethoscope over the second intercostal space, just to the *right* of the sternum. The aortic valve is best heard at this position. As you listen, have your partner take a deep breath. Then move the stethoscope to the *left* side of the sternum in the same line, and auscultate the pulmonary valve. Listen carefully; try to hear the "split" between the closure of these two valves in the second heart sound.

Although at first it may seem a bit odd that the pulmonary valve issuing from the *right* heart is heard most clearly to the *left* of the sternum and the aortic valve of the left heart is best heard at the right sternal border, this is easily explained by reviewing heart anatomy. Because the heart is twisted, with the right ventricle forming most of the anterior ventricular surface, the pulmonary trunk actually crosses to the left as it issues from the right ventricle. Similarly, the aorta issues from the left ventricle at the left side of the pulmonary trunk before arching up and over that vessel. ▮

The Pulse

The term **pulse** refers to the alternating surges of pressure (expansion and then recoil) in an artery that occur with each contraction and relaxation of the left ventricle. This difference between systolic and diastolic pressure is called the **pulse pressure**. (See page 498.) Normally the pulse rate (pressure surges per minute) equals the heart rate (beats per minute), and the pulse averages 70 to 76 beats per minute in the resting state.

Parameters other than pulse rate are also useful clinically. You may also assess the regularity (or rhythmicity) of the pulse, and its amplitude and/or tension—does the blood vessel expand and recoil (sometimes visibly) with the pressure waves? Can you feel it strongly, or is it difficult to detect? Is it regular like the ticking of a clock, or does it seem to skip beats?

ACTIVITY 2

Palpating Superficial Pulse Points

The pulse may be felt easily on any superficial artery when the artery is compressed over a bone or firm tissue. Palpate the following pulse or pressure points on your partner by placing the fingertips of the first two or three fingers of one hand over the artery. It helps to compress the artery firmly as you begin your palpation and then immediately ease up on the pressure slightly. In each case, notice the regularity of the pulse, and assess the degree of tension or amplitude. Figure 33A.3 illustrates the superficial pulse points to be palpated.

Superficial temporal artery: Anterior to the ear, in the temple region.

Facial artery: Clench the teeth, and palpate the pulse just anterior to the masseter muscle on the mandible (in line with the corner of the mouth).

Common carotid artery: At the side of the neck.

Brachial artery: In the antecubital fossa, at the point where it bifurcates into the radial and ulnar arteries.

Radial artery: At the lateral aspect of the wrist, above the thumb.

Femoral artery: In the groin.

Popliteal artery: At the back of the knee.

Posterior tibial artery: Just above the medial malleolus.

Dorsalis pedis artery: On the dorsum of the foot.

Which pulse point had the greatest amplitude?

_____

Which had the least? _____

Can you offer any explanation for this? _____

_____

_____

_____

Because of its easy accessibility, the pulse is most often taken on the radial artery. With your partner sitting quietly, practice counting the radial pulse for 1 minute. Make three counts and average the results.

count 1 _____   count 2 _____

count 3 _____   average _____ ▇

Due to the elasticity of the arteries, blood pressure decreases and smooths out as blood moves farther away from the heart. A pulse, however, can still be felt in the fingers. A device called a plethysmograph or a piezoelectric pulse transducer can measure this pulse.

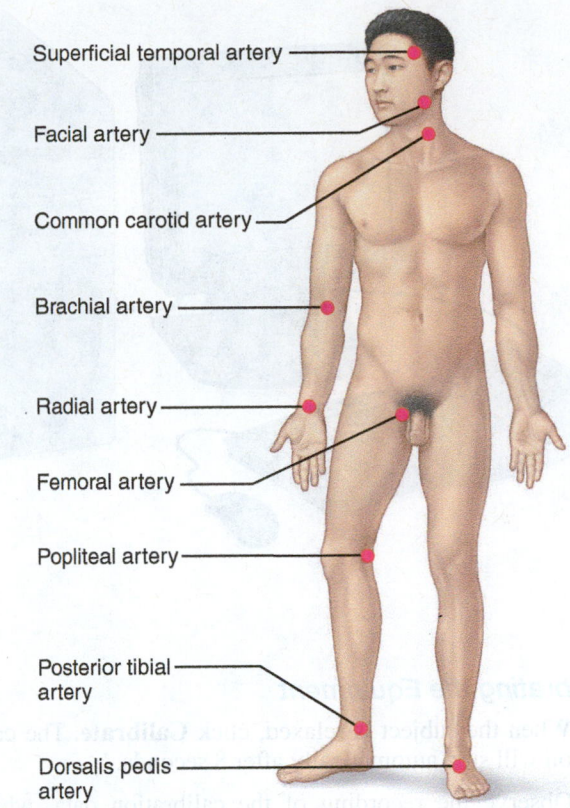

FIGURE 33A.3 Body sites where the pulse is most easily palpated.

ACTIVITY 3

Measuring Pulse Using BIOPAC®

Setting Up the Equipment

1. Connect the BIOPAC® apparatus to the computer and turn the computer **ON.**

2. Make sure the BIOPAC® unit is **OFF.**

3. Plug in the equipment as shown in Figure 33A.4:

• Pulse transducer (plethysmograph)—CH 2

4. Turn the BIOPAC® unit **ON.**

5. Wrap the pulse transducer around the tip of the index finger as shown in Figure 33A.5. Wrap the Velcro® around the finger gently (if wrapped too tight, it will reduce circulation to the finger and obscure the recording). *Do not wiggle the finger or move the plethysmograph cord during recording.*

6. Have the subject sit down with the forearms supported and relaxed.

7. Start the BIOPAC® Student Lab program on the computer by double-clicking the icon on the desktop or by following your instructor's guidance.

8. Select lesson **L07-ECG&P-1** from the menu, and click **OK.**

9. Type in a filename that will save this subject's data on the computer hard drive. You may want to use the subject's last name followed by Pulse (for example, SmithPulse-1), then click OK.

FIGURE 33A.4 Setting up the BIOPAC® equipment. Plug the pulse tranducer into Channel 2.

BIOPAC® data acquisition unit

Pulse transducer
(plugs into Channel 2)

Calibrating the Equipment

1. When the subject is relaxed, click **Calibrate.** The calibration will stop automatically after 8 seconds.

2. Observe the recording of the calibration data, which should look like the waveforms in Figure 33A.6.

- If the data look very different, click **Redo Calibration** and repeat the steps above. If there is no signal, you may need to loosen the Velcro® on the finger and check all attachments.

- If the data look similar, proceed to the next section.

Recording the Data

1. When the subject is ready, click **Record** to begin recording the pulse. After 30 seconds, click **Suspend.**

2. Observe the data, which should look similar to the pulse data in Figure 33A.7.

- If the data look very different, click **Redo** and repeat the steps above.

- If the data look similar, go to the next step.

3. When you are finished, click **Done.** A pop-up window will appear; to record from another subject select **Record from another subject** and return to step 5 under Setting Up the Equipment. If continuing to the Data Analysis section, select **Analyze current data file** and proceed to step 2 in the Data Analysis section.

Data Analysis

1. If just starting the BIOPAC® program to perform data analysis, enter **Review Saved Data** mode and choose the file with the subject's pulse data (for example, SmithPulse-1).

2. Observe that pulse data is in the lower scale (ECG data was not recorded in this activity and will not be used for analysis).

Sensor attaches to
bottom of fingertip

Velcro® strap
wraps around
finger

FIGURE 33A.5 Placement of the pulse transducer around the tip of the index finger.

FIGURE 33A.6 Example of waveforms during the calibration procedure.

FIGURE 33A.7 Example of waveforms during the recording of data.

FIGURE 33A.8 Using the I-beam cursor to highlight data for analysis.

3. To analyze the data, set up the first channel/measurement boxes at the top of the screen. Channel 40 contains the pulse data.

Channel	Measurement
CH 40	deltaT

deltaT: Measures the time elapsed in the selected area

4. Use the arrow cursor and click the I-beam cursor box on the lower right side of the screen to activate the "area selection" function. Using the activated I-beam cursor, highlight from the peak of one pulse to the peak of the next pulse as shown in Figure 33A.8.

Observe the elapsed time between heartbeats and record here

(to the nearest 0.01 second): _____.

5. Calculate the beats per minute by inserting the elapsed time into this formula:

(1 beat/ _____ sec) × (60 sec/min)

= _____ beats/min

Optional Activity with BIOPAC® Pulse Measurement

To expand the experiment, you can measure the effects of heat and cold on pulse rate. To do this, you can submerge the subject's hand (the hand without the plethysmograph!) in hot and/or ice water for 2 minutes, and then record the pulse. Alternatively, you can investigate change in pulse rate after brief exercise such as jogging in place. ■

Apical-Radial Pulse

The correlation between the apical and radial pulse rates can be determined by simultaneously counting them. The **apical pulse** (actually the counting of heartbeats) may be slightly faster than the radial because of a slight lag in time as the blood rushes from the heart into the large arteries where it can be palpated. However, any *large* difference between the values observed, referred to as a **pulse deficit,** may indicate cardiac impairment (a weakened heart that is unable to pump blood into the arterial tree to a normal extent), low cardiac output, or abnormal heart

rhythms. In the case of atrial fibrillation or ectopic heartbeats, for instance, the second beat may follow the first so quickly that no second pulse is felt even though the apical pulse can still be heard (auscultated). Apical pulse counts are routinely ordered for those with cardiac decompensation.

ACTIVITY 4

Taking an Apical Pulse

With the subject sitting quietly, one student, using a stethoscope, should determine the apical pulse rate while another simultaneously counts the radial pulse rate. The stethoscope should be positioned over the fifth left intercostal space. The person taking the radial pulse should determine the starting point for the count and give the stop-count signal exactly 1 minute later. Record your values below.

apical count _____ beats/min

radial count _____ pulses/min

pulse deficit _____ pulses/min ■

Blood Pressure Determinations

Blood pressure (BP) is defined as the pressure the blood exerts against any unit area of the blood vessel walls, and it is generally measured in the arteries. Because the heart alternately contracts and relaxes, the resulting rhythmic flow of blood into the arteries causes the blood pressure to rise and fall during each beat. Thus you must take two blood pressure readings: the **systolic pressure,** which is the pressure in the arteries at the peak of ventricular ejection, and the **diastolic pressure,** which reflects the pressure during ventricular relaxation. Blood pressures are reported in millimeters of mercury (mm Hg), with the systolic pressure appearing first; 120/80 translates to 120 over 80, or a systolic pressure of 120 mm Hg and a diastolic pressure of 80 mm Hg. Normal blood pressure varies considerably from one person to another.

FIGURE 33A.9 Procedure for measuring blood pressure. (a) The course of the brachial artery of the arm. Assume a blood pressure of 120/70. **(b)** The blood pressure cuff is wrapped snugly around the arm just above the elbow and inflated until blood flow into the forearm is stopped and no brachial pulse can be felt or heard. **(c)** Pressure in the cuff is gradually reduced while the examiner listens (auscultates) for sounds (of Korotkoff) in the brachial artery with a stethoscope. The pressure, read as the first soft tapping sounds are heard (the first point at which a small amount of blood is spurting through the constricted artery), is recorded as the systolic pressure. **(d)** As the pressure is reduced still further, the sounds become louder and more distinct, but when the artery is no longer restricted and blood flows freely, the sounds can no longer be heard. The pressure at which the sounds disappear is routinely recorded as the diastolic pressure.

In this procedure, you will measure arterial pressure by indirect means and under various conditions. You will investigate and demonstrate factors affecting blood pressure, and the rapidity of blood pressure changes.

ACTIVITY 5

Using a Sphygmomanometer to Measure Arterial Blood Pressure Indirectly

The **sphygmomanometer,** commonly called a *blood pressure cuff,* is an instrument used to obtain blood pressure readings by the auscultatory method (Figure 33A.9). It consists of an inflatable cuff with an attached pressure gauge. The cuff is placed around the arm and inflated to a pressure higher than systolic pressure to occlude circulation to the forearm. As cuff pressure is gradually released, the examiner listens with a stethoscope for characteristic sounds called the **sounds of Korotkoff,** which indicate the resumption of blood flow into the forearm. The pressure at which the first soft tapping sounds can be detected is recorded as the systolic pressure. As the pressure is reduced further, blood flow becomes more turbulent, and the sounds become louder. As the pressure is reduced still further, below the diastolic pressure, the artery is no longer compressed; and blood flows freely and without turbulence. At this point, the sounds of Korotkoff can no longer be detected. The pressure at which the sounds disappear is recorded as the diastolic pressure.

1. Work in pairs to obtain radial artery blood pressure readings. Obtain a felt marker, stethoscope, alcohol swabs, and a sphygmomanometer. Clean the earpieces of the stethoscope with the alcohol swabs, and check the cuff for the presence of trapped air by compressing it against the laboratory table. (A partially inflated cuff will produce erroneous measurements.)

2. The subject should sit in a comfortable position with one arm resting on the laboratory table (approximately at heart level if possible). Wrap the cuff around the subject's arm, just above the elbow, with the inflatable area on the medial arm surface. The cuff may be marked with an arrow; if so, the arrow should be positioned over the brachial artery (Figure 33A.9). Secure the cuff by tucking the distal end under the wrapped portion or by bringing the Velcro® areas together.

3. Palpate the brachial pulse, and lightly mark its position with a felt pen. Don the stethoscope, and place its diaphragm over the pulse point.

⚠️ *The cuff should not be kept inflated for more than 1 minute.* If you have any trouble obtaining a reading within this time, deflate the cuff, wait 1 or 2 minutes, and try again. (A prolonged interference with BP homeostasis can lead to fainting.)

4. Inflate the cuff to approximately 160 mm Hg pressure, and slowly release the pressure valve. Watch the pressure gauge as you listen carefully for the first soft thudding

sounds of the blood spurting through the partially occluded artery. Mentally note this pressure (systolic pressure), and continue to release the cuff pressure. You will notice first an increase, then a muffling, of the sound. For the diastolic pressure, note the pressure at which the sound becomes muffled or disappears. Controversy exists over which of the two points should be recorded as the diastolic pressure; so in some cases you may see readings such as 120/80/78, which indicates the systolic pressure followed by the *first* and *second diastolic end points*. The first diastolic end point is the pressure at which the sound muffles; the second is the pressure at which the sound disappears. It makes little difference here which of the two diastolic pressures is recorded, but be consistent. Make two blood pressure determinations, and record your results below.

First trial: **Second trial:**

systolic pressure _____   systolic pressure _____

diastolic pressure _____   diastolic pressure _____

5.   Compute the **pulse pressure** for each trial. The pulse pressure is the difference between the systolic and diastolic pressures, and it indicates the amount of blood forced from the heart during systole, or the actual "working" pressure. A narrowed pulse pressure (less than 30 mm Hg) may be a signal of severe aortic stenosis, constrictive pericarditis, or tachycardia. A widened pulse pressure (over 40 mm Hg) is common in hypertensive individuals.

Pulse pressure:

first trial _____   second trial _____

6.   Compute the **mean arterial pressure (MAP)** for each trial using the following equation:

$$MAP = \text{diastolic pressure} + \frac{\text{pulse pressure}}{3}$$

first trial _____   second trial _____

ACTIVITY 6

Estimating Venous Pressure

It is not possible to measure venous pressure with the sphygmomanometer. The methods available for measuring it produce estimates at best, because venous pressures are so much lower than arterial pressures. The difference in pressure becomes obvious when these vessels are cut. If a vein is cut, the blood flows evenly from the cut. A lacerated artery produces rapid spurts of blood. In this activity, you will estimate venous pressures.

1.   Obtain a meter stick, and ask your lab partner to stand with his or her right side toward the blackboard, arms hanging freely at the sides. On the board, mark the approximate level of the right atrium. (This will be just slightly higher than the point at which you auscultated the apical pulse.)

2.   Observe the superficial veins on the dorsum of the right hand as the subject alternately raises and lowers it. Notice the collapsing and filling of the veins as internal pressures change. Have the subject repeat this action until you can determine the point at which the veins have just collapsed. Mark this hand level on the board. Then measure, in millimeters, the distance in the vertical plane from this point to the level of the right atrium (previously marked). Record this value. Distance of right arm from right atrium at point of venous collapse:

_____ mm

3.   Compute the venous pressure (P_v), in millimeters of mercury, with the following formula:

$$P_v = \frac{1.056 \text{ (specific gravity of blood)} \times \text{mm (measured)}}{13.6 \text{ (specific gravity of Hg)}}$$

Venous pressure computed:_____ mm Hg

Normal venous pressure varies from approximately 30 to 90 mm Hg. That of the hand ranges between 30 and 40 mm Hg. How does your computed value compare?

_____

4.   Because venous walls are so thin, pressure within them is readily affected by external factors such as muscle activity, deep pressure, and pressure changes occurring in the thorax during breathing. The Valsalva maneuver, which increases intrathoracic pressure, is used to demonstrate the effect of thoracic pressure changes on venous pressure.

To perform this maneuver take a deep breath, and then mimic the motions of exhaling forcibly, but without actually exhaling. In reaction to this, the glottis will close; and intrathoracic pressure will increase. (Most of us have performed this maneuver unknowingly in acts of defecation in which there is "straining at stool.") Have the same subject again stand next to the blackboard mark for the level of his or her right atrium. While the subject performs the Valsalva maneuver and raises and lowers one hand, determine the point of venous collapse and mark it on the board. Measure the distance of that mark from the right atrium level and record it below. Then compute the venous pressure and record it.

_____ mm   Venous pressure: _____ mm Hg

How does this value compare with the venous pressure measurement computed for the relaxed state?

_____

Explain: _____

_____

_____

Posture				
	Trial 1		Trial 2	
	BP	Pulse	BP	Pulse
Sitting quietly				
Reclining (after 2 to 3 min)				
Immediately on standing from the reclining position ("at attention" stance)				
After standing for 3 min				

ACTIVITY 7

Observing the Effect of Various Factors on Blood Pressure and Heart Rate

Arterial blood pressure is directly proportional to cardiac output (CO, amount of blood pumped out of the left ventricle per unit time) and peripheral resistance (PR) to blood flow, that is

$$BP = CO \times PR$$

Peripheral resistance is increased by blood vessel constriction (most importantly the arterioles), by an increase in blood viscosity, and by a loss of elasticity of the arteries (seen in arteriosclerosis). Any factor that increases either the cardiac output or the peripheral resistance causes an almost immediate reflex rise in blood pressure. A close examination of these relationships reveals that many factors—age, weight, time of day, exercise, body position, emotional state, and various drugs, for example—alter blood pressure. The influence of a few of these factors is investigated here.

The following tests are done most efficiently if one student acts as the subject; two are examiners (one taking the radial pulse and the other auscultating the brachial blood pressure); and a fourth student collects and records data. The sphygmomanometer cuff should be left on the subject's arm throughout the experiments (in a deflated state, of course) so that, at the proper times, the blood pressure can be taken quickly. In each case, take the measurements at least twice. For each of the following tests, students should formulate hypotheses, collect data, and write lab reports. (See Getting Started, page xiv.) Conclusions should be shared with the class.

Posture

To monitor circulatory adjustments to changes in position, take blood pressure and pulse measurements under the conditions noted in the Posture chart above. Record your results on the chart.

Exercise

Blood pressure and pulse changes during and after exercise provide a good yardstick for measuring one's overall cardiovascular fitness. Although there are more sophisticated and more accurate tests that evaluate fitness according to a specific point system, the *Harvard step test* described here is a quick way to compare the relative fitness level of a group of people.

You will be working in groups of four, duties assigned as indicated above, except that student 4, in addition to recording the data, will act as the timer and call the cadence.

 Any student with a known heart problem should refuse to participate as the subject.

All four students may participate as the subject in turn, if desired, but the bench stepping is to be performed *at least twice* in each group—once with a well-conditioned person acting as the subject, and once with a poorly conditioned subject.

Bench stepping is the following series of movements repeated sequentially:

1.   Place one foot on the step.

2.   Step up with the other foot so that both feet are on the platform. Straighten the legs and the back.

3.   Step down with one foot.

4.   Bring the other foot down.

The pace for the stepping will be set by the "timer" (student 4), who will repeat "Up-2-3-4, up-2-3-4" at such a pace that each "up-2-3-4" sequence takes 2 sec (30 cycles/min).

1.   Student 4 should obtain the step (0.5 m [20-in.] height for male subject or 0.4 m [16-in.] for a female subject) while baseline measurements are being obtained on the subject.

Harvard step test for 5 min at 30/min	Baseline		Interval Following Test							
			Immediately		1 min		2 min		3 min	
	BP	P	BP	P	BP	P	BP	P	BP	P
Well-conditioned individual	___	___	___	___	___	___	___	___	___	___
Poorly conditioned individual	___	___	___	___	___	___	___	___	___	___

(Table header spanning "Exercise")

2. Once the baseline pulse and blood pressure measurements have been recorded on the Exercise chart above, the subject is to stand quietly at attention for 2 minutes to allow his or her blood pressure to stabilize before beginning to step.

3. The subject is to perform the bench stepping for as long as possible, up to a maximum of 5 minutes, according to the cadence called by the timer. The subject is to be watched for and warned against crouching (posture must remain erect). If he or she is unable to keep the pace for a span of 15 seconds, the test is to be terminated.

4. When the subject is stopped by the pacer for crouching, stops voluntarily because he or she is unable to continue, or has completed 5 minutes of bench stepping, he or she is to sit down. The duration of exercise (in seconds) is to be recorded, and the blood pressure and pulse are to be measured immediately and thereafter at 1-minute intervals for 3 minutes post-exercise.

Duration of exercise: _____ sec

5. The subject's *index of physical fitness* is to be calculated using the following formula:

$$\text{Index} = \frac{\text{duration of exercise in seconds} \times 100}{2 \times \text{sum of the three pulse counts in recovery}}$$

Scores are interpreted according to the following scale:

below 55	poor physical condition
55 to 62	low average
63 to 71	average
72 to 79	high average
80 to 89	good
90 and over	excellent

6. Record the test values on the Exercise chart above, and repeat the testing and recording procedure with the second subject.

When did you notice a greater elevation of blood pressure and pulse?

_____

Explain:_____

_____

_____

Was there a sizable difference between the after-exercise values for well-conditioned and poorly conditioned individuals?

_____ Explain:_____

_____

Did the diastolic pressure also increase?_____

Explain:_____

_____

A Noxious Sensory Stimulus (Cold)

There is little question that blood pressure is affected by emotions and pain. This lability of blood pressure will be investigated through use of the **cold pressor test,** in which one hand will be immersed in unpleasantly (even painfully) cold water.

1. Measure the blood pressure and pulse of the subject as he or she sits quietly. Record these as the baseline values on the Noxious Sensory Stimulus chart (next page).

2. Obtain a basin and thermometer, fill the basin with ice cubes, and add water. When the temperature of the ice bath has reached 5°C, immerse the subject's other hand (the non-cuffed limb) in the ice water. With the hand still immersed, take blood pressure and pulse readings at 1-minute intervals for a period of 3 minutes, and record the values on the chart.

A Noxious Sensory Stimulus (Cold)							
Baseline		1 min		2 min		3 min	
BP	P	BP	P	BP	P	BP	P

How did the blood pressure change during cold exposure?

_____

_____

Was there any change in pulse?_____

3.   Subtract the respective baseline readings of systolic and diastolic blood pressure from the highest single reading of systolic and diastolic pressure obtained during cold immersion. (For example, if the highest experimental reading is 140/88 and the baseline reading is 120/70, then the differences in blood pressure would be systolic pressure, 20 mm Hg, and diastolic pressure, 18 mm Hg.) These differences are called the index of response. According to their index of response, subjects can be classified as follows:

Hyporeactors (stable blood pressure): Exhibit a rise of diastolic and/or systolic pressure ranging from 0 to 22 mm Hg or a drop in pressures

Hyperreactors (labile blood pressure): Exhibit a rise of 23 mm Hg or more in the diastolic and/or systolic blood pressure

Is the subject tested a hypo- or hyperreactor?

_____

Skin Color as an Indicator of Local Circulatory Dynamics

Skin color reveals with surprising accuracy the state of the local circulation, and allows inferences concerning the larger blood vessels and the circulation as a whole. The Activity 8 experiments on local circulation illustrate a number of factors that affect blood flow to the tissues.

Clinical expertise often depends upon good observation skills, accurate recording of data, and logical interpretation of the findings. A single example will be given to demonstrate this statement: A massive hemorrhage may be internal and hidden (thus, not obvious) but will still threaten the blood delivery to the brain and other vital organs. One of the earliest compensatory responses of the body to such a threat is constriction of cutaneous blood vessels, which reduces blood

flow to the skin and diverts it into the circulatory mainstream to serve other, more vital tissues. As a result, the skin of the face and particularly of the extremities becomes pale, cold, and eventually moist with perspiration. Therefore, pale, cold, clammy skin should immediately lead the careful diagnostician to suspect that the circulation is dangerously inefficient. Other conditions, such as local arterial obstruction and venous congestion, as well as certain pathologies of the heart and lungs, also alter skin texture, color, and circulation in characteristic ways.

ACTIVITY 8

Examining the Effect of Local Chemical and Physical Factors on Skin Color

The local blood supply to the skin (indeed, to any tissue) is influenced by (1) local metabolites, (2) oxygen supply, (3) local temperature, (4) autonomic nervous system impulses, (5) local vascular reflexes, (6) certain hormones, and (7) substances released by injured tissues. A number of these factors are examined in the simple experiments that follow. Each experiment should be conducted by students in groups of three or four. One student will act as the subject; the others will conduct the tests and make and record observations.

Vasodilation and Flushing of the Skin Due to Local Metabolites

1.   Obtain a sphygmomanometer (blood pressure cuff) and stethoscope. You will also need a watch or clock with a second hand.

2.   The subject should bare both arms by rolling up the sleeves as high as possible and then lay the forearms side by side on the bench top.

3.   Observe the general color of the subject's forearm skin, and the normal contour and size of the veins. Notice whether skin color is bilaterally similar. Record your observations:

_____

_____

_____

4. Apply the blood pressure cuff to one arm, and inflate it to 250 mm Hg. Keep it inflated for 1 minute. During this period, repeat the observations made above, and record the results:

_____

_____

_____

5. Release the pressure in the cuff (leaving the deflated cuff in position), and again record the forearm skin color and the condition of the forearm veins. Make this observation immediately after deflation and then again 30 seconds later.

Immediately after deflation:_____

_____

30 sec after deflation:_____

   The above observations constitute your baseline information. Now conduct the following tests.

6. Instruct the subject to raise the cuffed arm above his or her head and to clench the fist as tightly as possible. While the hand and forearm muscles are tightly contracted, rapidly inflate the cuff to 240 mm Hg or more. This maneuver partially empties the hand and forearm of blood and stops most blood flow to the hand and forearm. Once the cuff has been inflated, the subject is to relax the fist and return the forearm to the bench top so that it can be compared to the other forearm.

7. Leave the cuff inflated for exactly 1 minute. During this interval, compare the skin color in the "ischemic" (blood-deprived) hand to that of the "normal" (non-cuffed-limb) hand. Quickly release the pressure immediately after 1 minute.

What are the subjective effects* of stopping blood flow to the arm and hand for 1 minute?

_____

_____

What are the objective effects (color of skin and condition of veins)?

_____

_____

How long does it take for the subject's ischemic hand to regain its normal color?

_____

Effects of Venous Congestion

1. Again, but with a different subject, observe and record the appearance of the skin and veins on the forearms resting on the bench top. This time, pay particular attention to the color of the fingers, particularly the distal phalanges, and the nail beds. Record this information:

_____

_____

2. Wrap the blood pressure cuff around one of the subject's arms, and inflate it to 40 mm Hg. Maintain this pressure for 5 minutes. Make a record of the subjective and objective findings just before the 5 minutes are up, and then again immediately after release of the pressure at the end of 5 minutes.

Subjective (arm cuffed):_____

_____

Objective (arm cuffed):_____

_____

Subjective (pressure released):_____

_____

Objective (pressure released):_____

_____

3. With still another subject, conduct the following simple experiment: Raise one arm above the head, and let the other hang by the side for 1 minute. After 1 minute, quickly lay both arms on the bench top, and compare their color.

Color of raised arm:_____

Color of dependent arm:_____

From this and the two preceding observations, analyze the factors that determine tint of color (pink or blue) and intensity of skin color (deep pink or blue as opposed to light pink or blue). Record your conclusions.

_____

_____

_____

_____

*Subjective effects are sensations—such as pain, coldness, warmth, tingling, and weakness—experienced by the subject. They are "symptoms" of a change in function.

Collateral Blood Flow

In some diseases, blood flow to an organ through one or more arteries may be completely and irreversibly obstructed. Fortunately, in most cases a given body area is supplied both by one main artery and by anastomosing channels connecting the main artery with one or more neighboring blood vessels. Consequently, an organ may remain viable even though its main arterial supply is occluded, as long as the **collateral vessels** are still functional.

The effectiveness of collateral blood flow in preventing ischemia can be easily demonstrated.

1.   Check the subject's hands to be sure they are *warm* to the touch. If not, choose another subject, or warm the subject's hands in 35°C water for 10 minutes before beginning.

2.   Palpate the subject's radial and ulnar arteries approximately 2.5 cm (1 in.) above the wrist flexure, and mark their locations with a felt marker.

3.   Instruct the subject to supinate one forearm and to hold it in a partially flexed (about a 30° angle) position, with the elbow resting on the bench top.

4.   Face the subject and grasp his or her forearm with both of your hands, the thumb and fingers of one hand compressing the marked radial artery and the thumb and fingers of the other hand compressing the ulnar artery. Maintain the pressure for 5 minutes, noticing the progression of the subject's hand to total ischemia.

5.   At the end of 5 minutes, release the pressure abruptly. Record the subject's sensations, as well as the intensity and duration of the flush in the previously occluded hand. (Use the other hand as a baseline for comparison.)

_____

_____

_____

6.   Allow the subject to relax for 5 minutes; then repeat the maneuver, but this time *compress only the radial artery.* Record your observations.

_____

_____

How do the results of the first test differ from those of the second test with respect to color changes during compression

and to the intensity and duration of reactive hyperemia (redness of the skin)?

_____

_____

_____

_____

7.   Once again allow the subject to relax for 5 minutes. Then repeat the maneuver, *with only the ulnar artery compressed.* Record your observations:

_____

_____

_____

What can you conclude about the relative sizes of, and hand areas served by, the radial and ulnar arteries?

_____

_____

Effect of Mechanical Stimulation of Blood Vessels of the Skin

With moderate pressure, draw the blunt end of your pen across the skin of a subject's forearm. Wait 3 minutes to observe the effects, and then repeat with firmer pressure.

What changes in skin color do you observe with light-to-moderate pressure?

_____

With heavy pressure? _____

The redness, or *flare,* observed after mechanical stimulation of the skin results from a local inflammatory response promoted by chemical mediators released by injured tissues. These mediators stimulate increased blood flow into the area and leaking of fluid (from the capillaries) into the local tissues. (**Note:** People differ considerably in skin sensitivity. Those most sensitive will show **dermatographism,** a condition in which the direct line of stimulation will swell quite obviously. This excessively swollen area is called a *wheal.*) ▬▬

Human Cardiovascular Physiology: Blood Pressure and Pulse Determinations

NAME _____

LAB TIME/DATE _____

Cardiac Cycle

1. Using the grouped sets of terms to the right of the diagram, correctly identify each trace, valve closings and openings, and each time period of the cardiac cycle.

_____ 1. aortic pressure

_____ 2. atrial pressure

_____ 3. ECG

_____ 4. first heart sound

_____ 5. second heart sound

_____ 6. ventricular pressure

_____ 7. ventricular volume

_____ 8. aortic semilunar valve closes

_____ 9. aortic semilunar valve opens

_____ 10. AV and semilunar valves closed

_____ 11. AV valve closes

_____ 12. AV valve opens

_____ 13. ventricular diastole

_____ 14. ventricular systole

2. Define the following terms.

*systole:*_____

*diastole:*_____

*cardiac cycle:*_____

3. Answer the following questions concerning events of the cardiac cycle.

When are the AV valves closed?_____

What event within the heart causes the AV valves to open?_____

When are the semilunar valves closed?_____

What event causes the semilunar valves to open?_____

Are both sets of valves closed during any part of the cycle?_____

If so, when?_____

Are both sets of valves open during any part of the cycle?_____

At what point in the cardiac cycle is the pressure in the heart highest?_____

Lowest_____

_____

What event results in the pressure deflection called the dicrotic notch?_____

_____

4. Using the key below, indicate the time interval occupied by the following events of the cardiac cycle.

Key: a.   *0.8 sec*   b.   *0.4 sec*   c.   *0.3 sec*   d.   *0.1 sec*

_____ 1.   the length of the normal cardiac cycle   _____ 3.   the quiescent period, or pause

_____ 2.   the time interval of atrial systole   _____ 4.   the ventricular contraction period

5. If an individual's heart rate is 80 beats/min, what is the length of the cardiac cycle? _____ What portion of

the cardiac cycle is shortened by this more rapid heart rate? _____

_____

6. What two factors promote the movement of blood through the heart?_____

_____ and _____

_____

Heart Sounds

7. Complete the following statements.

    The monosyllables describing the heart sounds are __1__. The first heart sound is a result of closure of the __2__ valves, whereas the second is a result of closure of the __3__ valves. The heart chambers that have just been filled when you hear the first heart sound are the __4__, and the chambers that have just emptied are the __5__. Immediately after the second heart sound, both the __6__ and __7__ are filling with blood.

1. _____

2. _____

3. _____

4. _____

5. _____

6. _____

7. _____

8. As you listened to the heart sounds during the laboratory session, what differences in pitch, length, and amplitude (loudness)

of the two sounds did you observe?_____

_____

_____

9. In order to auscultate most accurately, indicate where you would place your stethoscope for the following sounds:

closure of the tricuspid valve:_____

closure of the aortic semilunar valve:_____

apical heartbeat:_____

Which valve is heard most clearly when the apical heartbeat is auscultated?_____

10. No one expects you to be a full-fledged physician on such short notice; but on the basis of what you have learned about heart sounds, how might abnormal sounds be used to diagnose heart problems?

_____

_____

_____

The Pulse

11. Define *pulse.*_____

12. Describe the procedure used to take the pulse._____

_____

_____

13. Identify the artery palpated at each of the pressure points listed.

at the wrist:_____   on the dorsum of the foot:_____

in front of the ear:_____   at the side of the neck:_____

14. When you were palpating the various pulse or pressure points, which appeared to have the greatest amplitude or tension?

_____ Why do you think this was so?_____

_____

15. Assume someone has been injured in an auto accident and is hemorrhaging badly. What pressure point would you compress to help stop bleeding from each of the following areas?

the thigh:_____   the calf:_____

the forearm:_____   the thumb:_____

16. How could you tell by simple observation whether bleeding is arterial or venous?_____

_____

17. You may sometimes observe a slight difference between the value obtained from an apical pulse (beats/min) and that from an arterial pulse taken elsewhere on the body. What is this difference called?

_____

Blood Pressure Determinations

18. Define *blood pressure*._____

19. Identify the phase of the cardiac cycle to which each of the following apply.

systolic pressure:_____ diastolic pressure:_____

20. What is the name of the instrument used to compress the artery and record pressures in the auscultatory method of determining

blood pressure?_____

21. What are the sounds of Korotkoff?_____

_____

What causes the systolic sound?_____

_____

What causes the disappearance of the sound?_____

22. Interpret 145/85/82._____

_____

_____

23. Assume the following BP measurement was recorded for an elderly patient with severe arteriosclerosis:170/110/–. Explain the inability to obtain the third reading.

_____

_____

24. Define *pulse pressure.*_____

    Why is this measurement important?_____

    _____

25. How do venous pressures compare to arterial pressures?_____

    Why?_____

26. What maneuver to increase the thoracic pressure illustrates the effect of external factors on venous pressure?_____

    How is it performed?_____

    _____

27. What might an abnormal increase in venous pressure indicate? (Think!)_____

    _____

Observing the Effect of Various Factors on Blood Pressure and Heart Rate

28. What effect do the following have on blood pressure? (Indicate increase by ↑ and decrease by ↓.)

    _____ 1. increased diameter of the arterioles   _____ 4. hemorrhage

    _____ 2. increased blood viscosity   _____ 5. arteriosclerosis

    _____ 3. increased cardiac output   _____ 6. increased pulse rate

29. In which position (sitting, reclining, or standing) is the blood pressure normally the highest?

    _____ The lowest?_____

    What immediate changes in blood pressure did you observe when the subject stood up after being in the sitting or reclining

    position?_____

    _____

    What changes in the blood vessels might account for the change?_____

    _____

    _____

    After the subject stood for 3 minutes, what changes in blood pressure were observed?_____

    _____

    How do you account for this change?_____

30. What was the effect of exercise on blood pressure?_____

On pulse rate?_____ Do you think these effects reflect changes in cardiac output *or* in

peripheral resistance?_____

Why are there normally no significant increases in diastolic pressure after exercise?_____

_____

31. What effects of the following did you observe on blood pressure in the laboratory?

cold temperature:_____

What do you think the effect of heat would be?_____

Why?_____

32. Differentiate between a hypo- and a hyperreactor relative to the cold pressor test._____

_____

Skin Color as an Indicator of Local Circulatory Dynamics

33. Describe normal skin color and the appearance of the veins in the subject's forearm before any testing was conducted.

_____

34. What changes occurred when the subject emptied the forearm of blood (by raising the arm and making a fist) and the flow

was occluded with the cuff?_____

What changes occurred during venous congestion?_____

_____

35. What is the importance of collateral blood supplies?_____

_____

36. Explain the mechanism by which mechanical stimulation of the skin produced a flare._____

_____

Frog Cardiovascular Physiology: Wet Lab

MATERIALS

- ☐ Dissecting instruments and tray
- ☐ Disposable gloves
- ☐ Petri dishes
- ☐ Medicine dropper
- ☐ Millimeter ruler
- ☐ Disposal container for organic debris
- ☐ Frog Ringer's solutions (at room temperature, 5°C, and 32°C)
- ☐ Frogs*
- ☐ Thread
- ☐ Large rubber bands
- ☐ Fine common pins
- ☐ Frog board
- ☐ Cotton balls
- ☐ Apparatus A or B:[†]

  A: Physiograph (polygraph), physiograph paper and ink, force transducer, transducer cable, transducer stand, stimulator output extension cable, electrodes

  🔺 BIOPAC® B: BIOPAC® MP36 (or MP35/30) data acquisition unit, PC or Mac computer BIOPAC® BSL *PRO* Software, BIOPAC® HDW100A tension adjuster (or equivalent), BIOPAC® SS12LA force transducer with S-hook, small hook with thread, and transducer (or ring) stand

*Instructor will double-pith frogs as required for student experimentation.
[†]**Note:** Instructions for using PowerLab® equipment can be found on myA&P.

Text continues on next page.

OBJECTIVES

1. To list the properties of cardiac muscle as automaticity and rhythmicity, and define each property.
2. To explain the statement "Cardiac muscle has an intrinsic ability to beat."
3. To compare the intrinsic rate of contraction of the "pacemaker" of the frog heart (sinus venosus) to that of the atria and ventricle.
4. To compare the relative length of the refractory period of cardiac muscle with that of skeletal muscle, and to explain why it is not possible to tetanize cardiac muscle.
5. To define *extrasystole,* and to explain at what point in the cardiac cycle (and on an ECG tracing) an extrasystole can be induced.
6. To describe the effect of the following on heart rate: cold, heat, vagal stimulation, pilocarpine, atropine sulfate, epinephrine, digitalis, and potassium, sodium, and calcium ions.
7. To define *vagal escape* and discuss its value.
8. To define *ectopic pacemaker.*
9. To define *partial* and *total heart block.*
10. To describe how heart block was induced in the laboratory and explain the results, and to explain how heart block might occur in the human body.
11. To list the components of the microcirculatory system.
12. To identify an arteriole, venule, and capillaries in a frog's web, and to cite differences between relative size, rate of blood flow, and regulation of blood flow in these vessels.
13. To describe the effect of heat, cold, local irritation, and histamine on the rate of blood flow in the microcirculation, and to explain how these responses help maintain homeostasis.

PRE-LAB QUIZ

1. Circle True or False. Heart muscle can depolarize spontaneously in the absence of any external stimulation.
2. Spontaneous depolarization-repolarization events occur in a regular and continuous manner in cardiac muscle, a property known as
   a. automaticity   b. rhythmicity   c. synchronicity
3. How many chambers does the frog heart have?
   a. two   b. three   c. four
4. Circle True or False. Heart rate can be modified by extrinsic impulses from the autonomic nerves.
5. What is an extrasystole? _____
   _____
6. Which chemical agent will you use to modify the frog heart rate?
   a. caffeine   c. magnesium solution
   b. digitalis   d. Ringer's solution

Text continues on next page.

New versions of the BSL software (3.7.5 and higher for Windows, and 3.7.4 and higher for Mac) require slightly different channel settings and collection strategies. Instructions for using the newer software with the MP36/35 data acquisition units can be found on myA&P. In addition, instructions for use of the (NEW) 2-channel data acquisition unit, the MP45, may also be found on myA&P.

☐ Dropper bottles of freshly prepared solutions (using frog Ringer's solution as the solvent) of the following:

2.5% pilocarpine

5% atropine sulfate

1% epinephrine

2% digitalis

2% calcium chloride ($CaCl_2$)

0.7% sodium chloride (NaCl)

5% potassium chloride (KCl)

0.01% histamine

0.01 N HCl

☐ Dissecting pins

☐ Paper towels

☐ Compound microscope

 PhysioEx 8.0™ Computer Simulation on page 101

7. The _____ nerve carries parasympathetic impulses to the heart.
   a. cardiac   b. olfactory   c. phrenic   d. vagus

8. Circle the correct term. The phenomenon of vagal escape / heart block occurs when the heart stops momentarily then begins to beat again.

9. Circle True or False. The flow of blood through capillary beds is slow and intermittent.

10. _____ causes extensive vasodilation when applied to the frog web.
    a. Calcium   c. Histamine
    b. Epinephrine   d. Ringer's solution

Investigations of human cardiovascular physiology are very interesting, but many areas obviously do not lend themselves to experimentation. It would be tantamount to murder to inject a human subject with various drugs to observe their effects on heart activity or to expose the human heart in order to study the length of its refractory period. However, this type of investigation can be done on frogs or small laboratory animals and provides valuable data because the physiological mechanisms in these animals are similar, if not identical, to those in humans.

In this exercise, you will conduct the cardiac investigations just mentioned and others. In addition, you will observe the microcirculation in a frog's web and subject it to various chemical and thermal agents to demonstrate their influence on local blood flow.

Special Electrical Properties of Cardiac Muscle: Automaticity and Rhythmicity

Cardiac muscle differs from skeletal muscle both functionally and in its fine structure. Skeletal muscle must be electrically stimulated to contract. In contrast, heart muscle can and does depolarize spontaneously in the absence of external stimulation. This property, called **automaticity,** is due to plasma membranes that have reduced permeability to potassium ions but still allow sodium ions to slowly leak into the cells. This leakage causes the muscle cells to gradually depolarize until the action potential threshold is reached and *fast calcium channels* open, allowing Ca^{2+} entry from the extracellular fluid. Shortly thereafter, contraction occurs. Also, the spontaneous depolarization-repolarization events occur in a regular, continuous manner in cardiac muscle, a property called **rhythmicity.**

In the following experiment, you will observe these properties of cardiac muscle in vitro (that is, removed from the body). Work together in groups of three or four. (The instructor may choose to demonstrate this procedure if time or frogs are at a premium.)

ACTIVITY 1

Investigating the Automaticity and Rhythmicity of Heart Muscle

1. Obtain a dissecting tray and instruments, disposable gloves, two petri dishes, frog Ringer's solution, a metric ruler, and a medicine dropper, and bring them to your laboratory bench.

2. Don the gloves, and then request and obtain a doubly pithed frog from your instructor. Quickly open the thoracic cavity and observe the heart rate in situ (at the site or within the body).

Record the heart rate: _____ beats/min

3. Dissect out the heart and the gastrocnemius muscle of the calf and place the removed organs in separate petri dishes containing frog Ringer's solution. (**Note:** Just in case you don't remember, the procedure for removing the gastrocnemius

muscle is provided on pages 240–241 in Exercise 16A. The extreme care used in that procedure for the removal of the gastrocnemius muscle need not be exercised here.)

4. Observe the activity of the two organs for a few seconds.

Which is contracting? _____

At what rate? _____ beats/min

Is the contraction rhythmic? _____

5. Sever the sinus venosus from the heart (see Figure 34A.1). The **sinus venosus** of the frog's heart corresponds to the SA node of the human heart.

Does the sinus venosus continue to beat? _____

If not, lightly touch it with a probe to stimulate it. Record its rate of contraction.

Rate: _____ beats/min

6. Sever the right atrium from the heart; then remove the left atrium. Does each atrium continue to beat?

_____ Rate: _____ beats/min

Does the ventricle continue to beat? _____

Rate: _____ beats/min

7. Notice in Figure 34A.1 that frogs have a single ventricle. Fragment the ventricle to determine how small the ventricular fragments must be before the automaticity of ventricular muscle is abolished. Measure these fragments and record their approximate size.

_____ mm × _____ mm × _____ mm

Which portion of the heart exhibited the most marked automaticity?

_____

Which showed the least? _____

8. Properly dispose of the frog and heart fragments in the organic debris container before continuing. ▬

(a)

(b)

(c)

FIGURE 34A.1 Anatomy of the frog heart. (a) Ventral view showing the single truncus arteriosus leaving the undivided ventricle. **(b)** Longitudinal section showing the two atrial and single ventricular chambers. **(c)** Dorsal view showing the sinus venosus (pacemaker).

Baseline Frog Heart Activity

The heart's effectiveness as a pump is dependent both on intrinsic (within the heart) and extrinsic (external to the heart) controls. In this activity, you will investigate some of these factors.

The nodal system, in which the "pacemaker" imposes its depolarization rate on the rest of the heart, is one intrinsic factor that influences the heart's pumping action. If its impulses fail to reach the ventricles (as in heart block), the ventricles continue to beat but at their own inherent rate, which is much slower than that usually imposed on them. Although heart contraction does not depend on nerve impulses, its rate can be modified by extrinsic impulses reaching it through the autonomic nerves. Additionally, cardiac activity is modified by various chemicals, hormones, ions, and metabolites. The effects of several of these chemical factors are examined in the next experimental series.

The frog heart has two atria and a single, incompletely divided ventricle (see Figure 34A.1). The pacemaker is

FIGURE 34A.2 Physiograph setup for recording the activity of the frog heart.

located in the sinus venosus, an enlarged region between the venae cavae and the right atrium. The SA node of mammals may have evolved from the sinus venosus.

ACTIVITY 2

Recording Baseline Frog Heart Activity

To record baseline frog heart activity, work in groups of four—two students handling the equipment setup and two preparing the frog for experimentation. Two sets of instructions are provided for apparatus setup—one for the physiograph (Figure 34A.2), the other for BIOPAC® (Figure 34A.3). Follow the procedure outlined for the apparatus you will be using.

Apparatus Setups

Physiograph Apparatus Setup

1. Obtain a force transducer, transducer cable, and transducer stand, and bring them to the recording site.

2. Attach the force transducer to the transducer stand as shown in Figure 34A.2.

3. Then attach the transducer cable to the transducer coupler (input) on the channel amplifier of the physiograph and to the force transducer.

4. Attach the stimulator output extension cable to output on the stimulator panel (red to red, black to black).

BIOPAC® Apparatus Setup

1. Connect the BIOPAC® apparatus to the computer and turn the computer **ON.**

2. Make sure the BIOPAC® unit is **OFF.**

3. Set up the equipment as shown in Figure 34A.3.

4. Turn the BIOPAC® unit **ON.**

5. Launch the BIOPAC® BSL *PRO* software by clicking the icon on the desktop or by following your instructor's guidance.

6. Open the Frog Heart template by going to the **File** menu at the top of the screen and choosing **Open > Files of Type = Graph Template (GTL) > FrogHeart.gtl.**

7. Put the tension adjuster (BIOPAC® HDW100A, or equivalent) on the transducer stand, and attach the BIOPAC® SS12LA force transducer with the hook holes pointing down. Level the force transducer both horizontally and vertically.

8. Set the tension adjuster to approximately one quarter of its full range. (***Note:*** *Do not firmly tighten any of the thumbscrews at this stage.*) Select a force range of 0 to 50 grams for this experiment.

9. Select and attach the small S-hook to the force transducer.

FIGURE 34A.3 BIOPAC® setup for recording the activity of the frog heart.

Preparation of the Frog

1. Obtain room-temperature frog Ringer's solution, a medicine dropper, dissecting instruments and tray, disposable gloves, fine common pins (physiograph) or small hook (BIOPAC®), cotton ball, frog board, large rubber bands, and some thread, and bring them to your bench.

⚠ 2. Don the gloves, and obtain a doubly pithed frog from your instructor.

3. Make a longitudinal incision through the abdominal and thoracic walls with scissors, and then cut through the sternum to expose the heart.

4. Grasp the pericardial sac with forceps, and cut it open so that the beating heart can be observed.

Is the sequence an atrial-ventricular one? _____

5. Locate the vagus nerve, which runs down the lateral aspect of the neck and parallels the trachea and carotid artery. (In good light, it appears to be striated.) Slip an 18-inch length of thread under the vagus nerve so that it can later be lifted away from the surrounding tissues by the thread. Then place a Ringer's solution–soaked cotton ball over the nerve to keep it moistened until you are ready to stimulate it later in the procedure.

6. Using a medicine dropper, flush the heart with Ringer's solution. *From this point on the heart must be kept continually moistened with room-temperature Ringer's solution unless other solutions are being used for the experimentation.*

7. Attach the frog to the frog board using large rubber bands.

Physiograph Frog Heart Preparation

1. Bend a common pin to a 90° angle, and tie to its head a thread 0.46–0.5 m (18–20 inches) long. Force the pin through the apex of the heart (but do not penetrate the ventricular chamber) until the apex is well secured in the angle of the pin.

2. Tie the thread from the heart to the hook on the force transducer. Do not pull the thread too tightly. It should be taut enough to lift the heart apex upward, away from the thorax, but should *not* stretch the heart. Adjust the force transducer as necessary. (See Figure 34A.2.)

BIOPAC® Frog Heart Preparation

1. Attach a small hook tied with thread to the frog heart, following the instructions in step 1 of the physiograph instructions above to insert it through the apex of the heart. Confirm that the prepared frog is firmly attached to the frog board, positioned below the ring stand with the line running vertically from the frog heart to the transducer.

2. Slide the tension adjuster/force transducer assembly down the ring stand until you can hang the loop loosely from the S-hook, then slide it back up until the line is taut but the heart muscle is not stretched (be careful not to tear the heart).

3. Position the tension adjuster and/or force transducer so that the top is level, with approximately 10 cm (4 inches) of line from the heart tendon to the S-hook. Adjust the assembly so that the thread line runs vertically; for a true reflection of the muscle's contractile force, the muscle must not be pulled at an angle.

4. Use the tension adjuster knob to make the line taut and tighten all thumbscrews to secure positioning of the assembly. Let the setup sit for a minute, then recheck the tension to make sure nothing has slipped or stretched.

5. Data may be distorted if the transducer line is not pulling directly vertical from the frog heart to the S-hook. Once again, align the frog as described above and make sure that the heart is not twisting the thread. If it is twisting, you will need to *carefully* remove the hook and repeat the setup.

6. BIOPAC® calculates *rate* data, which always trails the actual rate by one cycle. Data collection is a sensitive process and may display artifacts from table movement, heart movement (for instance, from breathing on the heart), and chemicals

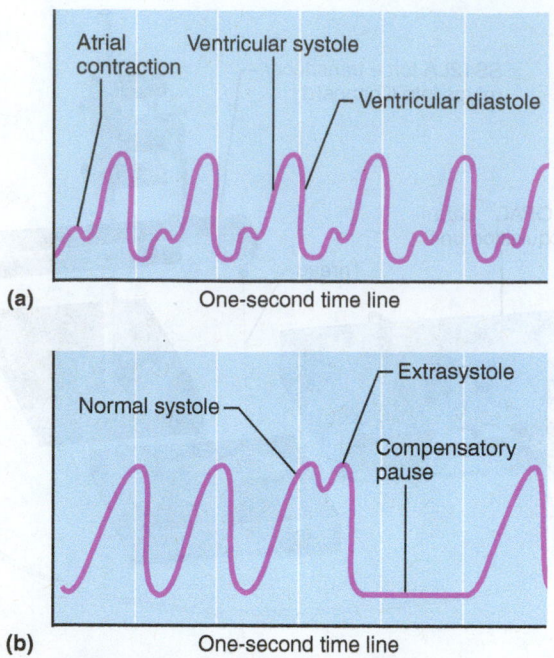

FIGURE 34A.4 Physiograph recording of contractile activity of a frog heart. (a) Normal heartbeat. **(b)** Induction of an extrasystole.

touching the heart. To get the best data, keep the experimental area stable, clean, and clear of obstructions. Hints for obtaining best data:

- The SS12LA force transducer must be level on the horizontal and vertical planes.

- Set up the tension adjuster and force transducer in positions that minimize their movement when tension is applied. Keep the point of S-hook attachment as close as possible to the ring stand support.

- Position the tension adjuster so that you will not bump the cables or frog board when using the adjustment knob.

- Position and/or tape the force transducer cables where they will not be pulled or bumped easily.

- Make sure the frog board is on a stable surface.

- Make sure the frog is firmly attached to the frog board so it will not rise up when tension is applied.

Making the Baseline Recording

Using the Physiograph

1. Turn the amplifier on and balance the apparatus according to instructions provided by your instructor. Set the paper speed at 0.5 cm/sec. Press the record and paper advance buttons.

2. Set the signal magnet or time marker at 1/sec.

3. Record 12 to 15 normal heartbeats. Be sure you can distinguish atrial and ventricular contractions (see Figure 34A.4). Then adjust the paper or scroll speed so that the peaks of ventricular contractions are approximately 2 cm apart. (Peaks indicate systole; troughs indicate diastole.) Pay attention to the relative force of heart contractions while recording.

FIGURE 34A.5 Example of baseline frog heart rate data.

Using BIOPAC®

1. Click **Start** to begin recording.

2. Observe at least 5 heart rate cycles, then click **Stop** to stop recording. Your data should look like that in Figure 34A.5.

3. Choose **Save** from the File menu, and type in a file-name to save the recorded data. You may want to save by your team's name followed by FrogHeart-1 (for example, Smith-FrogHeart-1).

Analyzing the Baseline Data

Count the number of ventricular contractions per minute from your physiograph or BIOPAC® data, and record:

_____ beats/min

Compute the A–V interval (period from the beginning of atrial contraction to the beginning of ventricular contraction).

_____ sec

How do the two tracings compare in time?

_____

_____

_____

Mark the atrial and ventricular systoles on the record. *Remember to keep the heart moistened with Ringer's solution.*

Investigating the Refractory Period of Cardiac Muscle Using the Physiograph

In conducting Exercise 16A, you saw that repeated rapid stimuli could cause skeletal muscle to remain in a contracted state. In other words, the muscle could be tetanized. This was possible because of the relatively short refractory period of skeletal muscle. In this experiment, you will use the physiograph to investigate the refractory period of cardiac muscle and its response to stimulation.* During the procedure, one student should keep the stimulating electrodes in constant contact with the frog heart ventricle while another student operates the stimulator panel.

1.   Using the physiograph, set the stimulator to deliver 20-V shocks of 2-msec duration, and begin recording.

2.   Deliver single shocks at the beginning of ventricular contraction, the peak of ventricular contraction, and then later and later in the cardiac cycle.

3.   Observe the recording for **extrasystoles,** which are extra beats that show up riding on the ventricular contraction peak. Also note the **compensatory pause,** which allows the heart to get back on schedule after an extrasystole. (See Figure 34A.4b.)

During which portion of the cardiac cycle was it possible to induce an extrasystole?

_____

_____

4.   Attempt to tetanize the heart by stimulating it at the rate of 20 to 30 impulses per second. What is the result?

_____

_____

Considering the function of the heart, why is it important that heart muscle cannot be tetanized?

_____

_____

Assessing Physical and Chemical Modifiers of Heart Rate

Now that you have observed normal frog heart activity, you will have an opportunity to investigate the effects of various factors that modify heart activity. In each case, record a few normal heartbeats before introducing the modifying factor. After removing the agent, allow the heart to return to its normal rate before continuing with the testing. On each record, indicate the point of introduction and removal of the modifying agent.

*BIOPAC® users may investigate the refractory period of cardiac muscle by using PhysioEx Exercise 34B.

For each physical agent or solution that is applied:
If using the physiograph, increase the scroll or paper speed so that heartbeats appear as spikes 4 to 5 mm apart.
If using BIOPAC®, after applying each solution, click the **Start** button. When the effect is observed, record the effect for five cycles, then click **Stop.** Choose **Save** from the File menu to save your data.

(**Note:** Repeat these steps for each physical agent or chemical solution that is being applied.)

Temperature

1.   Obtain 5°C and 32°C frog Ringer's solutions and medicine droppers.

2.   Bathe the heart with 5°C Ringer's solution, and continue to record until the recording indicates a change in cardiac activity and five cardiac cycles have been recorded.

3.   Stop recording, pipette off the cold Ringer's solution (remove the fluid by sucking it into the barrel of a medicine dropper), and flood the heart with room-temperature Ringer's solution.

4.   Start recording again to determine the resumption of the normal heart rate. When this has been achieved, flood the heart with 32°C Ringer's solution, and again record five cardiac cycles after a change is noted.

5.   Stop the recording, pipette off the warm Ringer's solution, and bathe the heart with room-temperature Ringer's solution once again.

What change occurred with the cold (5°C) Ringer's solution?

_____

_____

What change occurred with the warm (32°C) Ringer's solution?

_____

_____

6.   Count the heart rate at the two temperatures, and record the data below.

_____ beats/min at 5°C; _____ beats/min at 32°C

Chemical Agents

Pilocarpine   Flood the heart with a 2.5% solution of pilocarpine. Record until a change in the pattern of the ECG is noticed. Pipette off the excess pilocarpine solution, and proceed immediately to the next test, which uses atropine as the testing solution. What happened when the heart was bathed in the pilocarpine solution?

_____

_____

Pilocarpine simulates the effect of parasympathetic (vagal) nerve stimulation by enhancing acetylcholine release; such drugs are called parasympathomimetic drugs.

Is pilocarpine an agonist or an antagonist of acetylcholine?

_____

Atropine Sulfate   Apply a few drops of atropine sulfate to the frog's heart, and observe the recording. If no changes are observed within 2 minutes, apply a few more drops. When you observe a response, pipette off the excess atropine sulfate and flood the heart with room-temperature Ringer's solution. What happens when the atropine sulfate is added?

_____

_____

Atropine is a drug that blocks the effect of the neurotransmitter acetylcholine, which is liberated by the parasympathetic nerve endings. Do your results accurately reflect this effect of atropine?

_____

_____

Is atropine an agonist or an antagonist of acetylcholine?

_____

_____

Epinephrine   Flood the frog heart with epinephrine solution, and continue to record until a change in heart activity is noted.

What are the results? _____

_____

_____

Which division of the autonomic nervous system does its effect mimic?

_____

_____

Digitalis   Pipette off the excess epinephrine solution, and rinse the heart with room-temperature Ringer's solution. Continue recording, and when the heart rate returns to baseline values, bathe it in digitalis solution. What is the effect of digitalis on the heart?

_____

_____

_____

Digitalis is a drug commonly prescribed for heart patients with congestive heart failure. It slows heart rate, providing more time for venous return and decreasing the work of the weakened heart. These effects are thought to be due to inhibition of the sodium-potassium pump and enhancement of Ca^{2+} entry into the myocardial fibers.

Various Ions   To test the effect of various ions on the heart, apply the designated solution until you observe a change in heart rate or in strength of contraction. Pipette off the solution, flush with room-temperature Ringer's solution, and allow the heart to resume its normal rate before continuing. _Do not allow the heart to stop._ If the rate should decrease dramatically, flood the heart with room-temperature Ringer's solution.

Effect of Ca^{2+} (use 2% $CaCl_2$) _____

_____

Effect of Na^+ (use 0.7% NaCl) _____

_____

Effect of K^+ (use 5% KCl) _____

Potassium ion concentration is normally higher within cells than in the extracellular fluid. _Hyperkalemia_ decreases the resting potential of plasma membranes, thus decreasing the force of heart contraction. In some cases, the conduction rate of the heart is so depressed that **ectopic pacemakers** (pacemakers appearing erratically and at abnormal sites in the heart muscle) appear in the ventricles, and fibrillation may occur. Was there any evidence of premature beats in the

recording of potassium ion effects? _____

Was arrhythmia produced with any of the ions tested?

_____ If so, which? _____

Vagus Nerve Stimulation

The vagus nerve carries parasympathetic impulses to the heart, which modify heart activity. If you are using the physiograph, you can test this by stimulating the vagus nerve.*

1.   Remove the cotton placed over the vagus nerve. Using the previously tied thread, lift the nerve away from the tissues and place the nerve on the stimulating electrodes.

2.   Using a duration of 0.5 msec at a voltage of 1 mV, stimulate the nerve at a rate of 50/sec. Continue stimulation until the heart stops momentarily and then begins to beat again (**vagal escape**). If no effect is observed, increase stimulus intensity and try again. If no effect is observed after a substantial increase in stimulus voltage, reexamine your "vagus nerve" to make sure that it is not simply strands of connective tissue.

3.   Discontinue stimulation after you observe vagal escape, and flush the heart with room-temperature Ringer's solution until the normal heart rate resumes. What is the effect of vagal stimulation on heart rate?

_____

_____

The phenomenon of vagal escape demonstrates that many factors are involved in heart regulation and that any deleterious factor (in this case, excessive vagal stimulation) will be overcome, if possible, by other physiological mechanisms such as activation of the sympathetic division of the autonomic nervous system (ANS).

*BIOPAC® users may observe the effects of vagal stimulation by using PhysioEx Exercise 34B.

Intrinsic Conduction System Disturbance (Heart Block)

1. Moisten a 25-cm (10-inch) length of thread and make a Stannius ligature (loop the thread around the heart at the junction of the atria and ventricle).

2. If using a physiograph, decrease the scroll or paper speed to achieve intervals of approximately 2 cm between the ventricular contractions, and record a few normal heartbeats.

3. Tighten the ligature in a stepwise manner while observing the atrial and ventricular contraction curves. As heart block occurs, the atria and ventricle will no longer show a 1:1 contraction ratio. Record a few beats each time you observe a different degree of heart block—a 2:1 ratio of atrial to ventricular contractions, 3:1, 4:1, and so on. As long as you can continue to count a whole number ratio between the two chamber types, the heart is in **partial heart block.** When you can no longer count a whole number ratio, the heart is in **total,** or **complete, heart block.**

4. When total heart block occurs, release the ligature to see if the normal A–V rhythm is reestablished. What is the result?

_____

_____

5. Attach properly labeled recordings (or copies of the recordings) made during this procedure to the last page of this exercise for future reference.

6. Dispose of the frog remains and gloves in appropriate containers, and dismantle the experimental apparatus before continuing. ▆▆

The Microcirculation and Local Blood Flow

The thin web of a frog's foot provides an excellent opportunity to observe the flow of blood to, from, and within the capillary beds, where the real business of the circulatory system occurs. The collection of vessels involved in the exchange mechanism is referred to as the **microcirculation;** it consists of arterioles, venules, capillaries, and vascular shunts called *metarteriole–thoroughfare channels* (Figure 34A.6).

The total cross-sectional area of the capillaries in the body is much greater than that of the veins and arteries combined. Thus, the velocity of flow through the capillary beds is quite slow. Capillary flow is also intermittent, because if all capillary beds were filled with blood at the same time, there would be no blood at all in the large vessels. The flow of blood into the capillary beds is regulated by the activity of muscular *terminal arterioles,* which feed the beds, and by *precapillary sphincters* at entrances to the true capillaries. The amount of blood flowing into the true capillaries of the bed is regulated most importantly by local chemical controls (local concentrations of carbon dioxide, histamine, pH). Thus a capillary bed may be flooded with blood or almost entirely bypassed depending on what is happening within the body or in a particular body region at any one time. You will investigate some of the local controls in the next group of experiments.

(a) Sphincters open

(b) Sphincters closed

FIGURE 34A.6 Anatomy of a capillary bed. The composite metarteriole–thoroughfare channels act as shunts to bypass the true capillaries when precapillary sphincters controlling blood entry into the true capillaries are constricted.

ACTIVITY 5

Investigating the Effect of Various Factors on the Microcirculation

1. Obtain a frog board (with a hole at one end), dissecting pins, disposable gloves, frog Ringer's solution (room temperature, 5°C, and 32°C), 0.01 N HCl, 0.01% histamine solution, 1% epinephrine solution, a large rubber band, and some paper towels.

2. Put on the gloves and obtain a frog (alive and hopping, *not* pithed). Moisten several paper towels with room-temperature Ringer's solution, and wrap the frog's body securely with them. One hind leg should be left unsecured and extending beyond the paper cocoon.

3. Attach the frog to the frog board (or other supporting structure) with a large rubber band and then carefully spread (but do not stretch) the web of the exposed hindfoot over the hole in the support. Have your partners hold the edges

of the web firmly for viewing. Alternatively, secure the toes to the board with dissecting pins.

4. Obtain a compound microscope, and observe the web under low power to find a capillary bed. Focus on the vessels in high power. Keep the web moistened with Ringer's solution as you work. If the circulation seems to stop during your observations, massage the hind leg of the frog gently to restore blood flow.

5. Observe the red blood cells of the frog. Notice that, unlike human RBCs, they are nucleated. Watch their movement through the smallest vessels—the capillaries. Do they move in single file, or do they flow through two or three cells abreast?

_____

Are they flexible? _____ Explain. _____

Can you see any white blood cells in the capillaries?

_____ If so, which types? _____

6. Notice the relative speed (velocity) of blood flow through the blood vessels. Differentiate between the arterioles, which feed the capillary bed, and the venules, which drain it. This may be tricky, because images are reversed in the microscope. Thus, the vessel that appears to feed into the capillary bed will actually be draining it. You can distinguish between the vessels, however, if you consider that the flow is more pulsating and turbulent in the arterioles and smoother and steadier in the venules. How does the velocity of flow in the arterioles compare with that in the venules?

_____

In the capillaries? _____

What is the relative difference in the diameter of the arterioles and capillaries?

_____

Temperature

1. To investigate the effect of temperature on blood flow, flood the web with 5°C Ringer's solution two or three times to chill the entire area. Is a change in vessel diameter noticeable?

_____ Which vessels are affected? _____

How? _____

2. Blot the web gently with a paper towel, and then bathe the web with warm (32°C) Ringer's solution. Record your observations.

_____

Inflammation

1. Pipette 0.01 N HCl onto the frog's web. Hydrochloric acid will act as an irritant and cause a localized inflammatory response. Is there an increase or decrease in the blood flow into the capillary bed following the application of HCl?

_____

What purpose do these local changes serve during a localized inflammatory response?

_____

_____

2. Flush the web with room-temperature Ringer's solution and blot.

Histamine

1. Histamine, which is released in large amounts during allergic responses, causes extensive vasodilation. Investigate this effect by adding a few drops of histamine solution to the frog web. What happens?

_____

_____

How does this response compare to that produced by HCl?

_____

2. Blot the web and flood with 32°C Ringer's solution as before. Now add a few drops of 1% epinephrine solution, and observe the web. What are epinephrine's effects on the blood vessels?

_____

Epinephrine is used clinically to reverse the vasodilation seen in severe allergic attacks (such as asthma) which are mediated by histamine and other vasoactive molecules.

3. Return the dropper bottles to the supply area and the frog to the terrarium. Properly clean your work area before leaving the lab. ▰

Frog Cardiovascular Physiology: Wet Lab

Special Electrical Properties of Cardiac Muscle: Automaticity and Rhythmicity

1. Define the following terms.

   automaticity: _____

   rhythmicity: _____

2. Discuss the anatomical differences between frog and human hearts. _____

   _____

   _____

3. Which region of the dissected frog heart had the highest intrinsic rate of contraction? _____

   The greatest automaticity? _____

   The greatest regularity or rhythmicity? _____ How do these properties correlate with

   the duties of a pacemaker? _____

   _____

   Is this region the pacemaker of the frog heart? _____

   Which region had the lowest intrinsic rate of contraction? _____

Investigating the Refractory Period of Cardiac Muscle

4. Define *extrasystole.* _____

5. Respond to the following questions if you used a physiograph. _____

   What was the effect of stimulation of the heart during ventricular contraction? _____

   During ventricular relaxation (first portion)? _____

   During the pause interval? _____

   What does this indicate about the refractory period of cardiac muscle? _____

Assessing Physical and Chemical Modifiers of Heart Rate

6. Describe the effect of thermal factors on the frog heart.

cold: _____ heat: _____

7. Once again refer to your recordings. Did the administration of the following produce any changes in force of contraction (shown by peaks of increasing or decreasing height)? If so, explain the mechanism.

epinephrine: _____

_____

acetylcholine: _____

_____

calcium ions: _____

_____

8. Excessive amounts of each of the following ions would most likely interfere with normal heart activity. Note the type of changes caused in each case.

K^+:_____

Ca^{2+}:_____

Na^+:_____

9. Respond to the following questions if you used a physiograph. What was the effect of vagal stimulation on heart rate?

_____

Which of the following factors cause the same (or very similar) heart rate–reducing effects: epinephrine, acetylcholine, atropine sulfate, pilocarpine, sympathetic nervous system activity, digitalis, potassium ions?

_____

Which of the factors listed above would reverse or antagonize vagal effects? _____

_____

10. What is vagal escape? _____

_____

Why is vagal escape valuable in maintaining homeostasis? _____

_____

11. How does the Stannius ligature used in the laboratory produce heart block? _____

_____

_____

12. Define *partial heart block,* and describe how it was recognized in the laboratory. _____

_____

_____

13. Define *total heart block,* and describe how it was recognized in the laboratory. _____

_____

_____

_____

14. What do your heart block experiment results indicate about the spread of impulses from the atria to the ventricles?

_____

_____

Observing the Microcirculation Under Various Conditions

15. In what way are the red blood cells of the frog different from those of the human? _____

_____

On the basis of this one factor, would you expect their life spans to be longer or shorter? _____

16. The following statements refer to your observation of one or more of the vessel types observed in the microcirculation in the frog's web. Characterize each statement by choosing one or more responses from the key.

Key: a.   arteriole   b.   venule   c.   capillary

_____ 1.   smallest vessels observed

_____ 2.   vessel in which blood flow is rapid, pulsating

_____ 3.   vessel in which blood flow is least rapid

_____ 4.   red blood cells pass through these vessels in single file

_____ 5.   blood flow smooth and steady

_____ 6.   most numerous vessels

_____ 7.   vessels that deliver blood to the capillary bed

_____ 8.   vessels that serve the needs of the tissues via exchanges

_____ 9.   vessels that drain the capillary beds

17. Which of the vessel diameters changed most? _____

What division of the nervous system controls the vessels? _____

18. Discuss the effects of the following on blood vessel diameter (state specifically the blood vessels involved) and rate of blood flow. Then explain the importance of the reaction observed to the general well-being of the body.

local application of cold: _____

_____

local application of heat: _____

_____

inflammation (or application of HCl): _____

_____

histamine: _____

_____

The Lymphatic System and Immune Response

MATERIALS

- Large anatomical chart of the human lymphatic system
- Prepared slides of lymph node, spleen, and tonsil
- Compound microscope
- Wax marking pencil
- Petri dish containing simple saline agar
- Medicine dropper
- Dropper bottles of red and green food color
- Dropper bottles of goat antibody to horse serum albumin, goat antibody to bovine serum albumin, goat antibody to swine serum albumin, horse serum albumin diluted to 20% with physiologic saline, unknown albumin sample diluted to 20% (prepared from horse, swine, and/or bovine albumin)
- Colored pencils

 PEx PhysioEx™ 8.0 Computer Simulation at the myA&P Website

 For instructions on animal dissections, see the dissection exercises starting on page 697 in the cat, fetal pig, and rat editions of this manual.

OBJECTIVES

1. To name the components of the lymphatic system.
2. To relate the function of the lymphatic system to that of the blood vascular system.
3. To describe the formation and composition of lymph, and to describe how it is transported through the lymphatic vessels.
4. To relate immunological memory, specificity, and differentiation of self from nonself to immune function.
5. To differentiate between the roles of B cells and T cells in the immune response.
6. To describe the structure and function of lymph nodes, and to indicate the localization of T cells, B cells, and macrophages in a typical lymph node.
7. To describe (or draw) the structure of the immunoglobulin monomer, and to name the five immunoglobulin subclasses.
8. To differentiate between antigen and antibody.
9. To understand the use of antigen-antibody reaction using the Ouchterlony test.

PRE-LAB QUIZ

1. Circle True or False. The lymphatic system protects the body by removing foreign material such as bacteria from the lymphatic stream.
2. Lymph is
   a. excess blood that has escaped from veins
   b. excess tissue fluid that has leaked out of capillaries
   c. excess tissue fluid that has escaped from arteries
3. Circle True or False. Lymphatic vessels have three tunics and are equipped with valves like veins.
4. _____, which serve as filters for the lymphatic system, occur at various points along the lymphatic vessels.
   a. Glands
   b. Lymph nodes
   c. Valves
5. Circle True or False. The immune response is a systemic response that occurs when the body recognizes a substance as foreign and acts to destroy or neutralize it.
6. Three characteristics of the immune response are the ability to distinguish self from nonself, memory, and
   a. autoimmunity
   b. specificity
   c. susceptibility
7. Circle the correct term. B cells / T cells differentiate in the thymus.
8. Circle the correct term. T cells mediate humoral / cellular immunity because they destroy cells infected with viruses and certain bacteria and parasites.
9. Circle True or False. Antibodies are produced by plasma cells in response to antigens and are found in all body secretions.

myA&P For practice quizzes on this lab, go to www.myaandp.com.

PAL For access to anatomical models and more, check out Practice Anatomy Lab.

The overall function of the lymphatic system is twofold: (1) it transports tissue fluid (lymph) to the blood vessels, and (2) it protects the body by removing foreign material such as bacteria from the lymphatic stream and by serving as a site for lymphocyte "policing" of body fluids and lymphocyte multiplication.

The Lymphatic System

The **lymphatic system** consists of a network of lymphatic vessels (lymphatics), lymphatic tissue, lymph nodes, and a number of other lymphoid organs, such as the tonsils, thymus, and spleen. We will focus on the lymphatic vessels and lymph nodes in this section. The white blood cells which are the central actors in body immunity are described later in this exercise.

Distribution and Function of Lymphatic Vessels and Lymph Nodes

As blood circulates through the body, the hydrostatic and osmotic pressures operating at the capillary beds result in fluid outflow at the arterial end of the bed and in its return at the

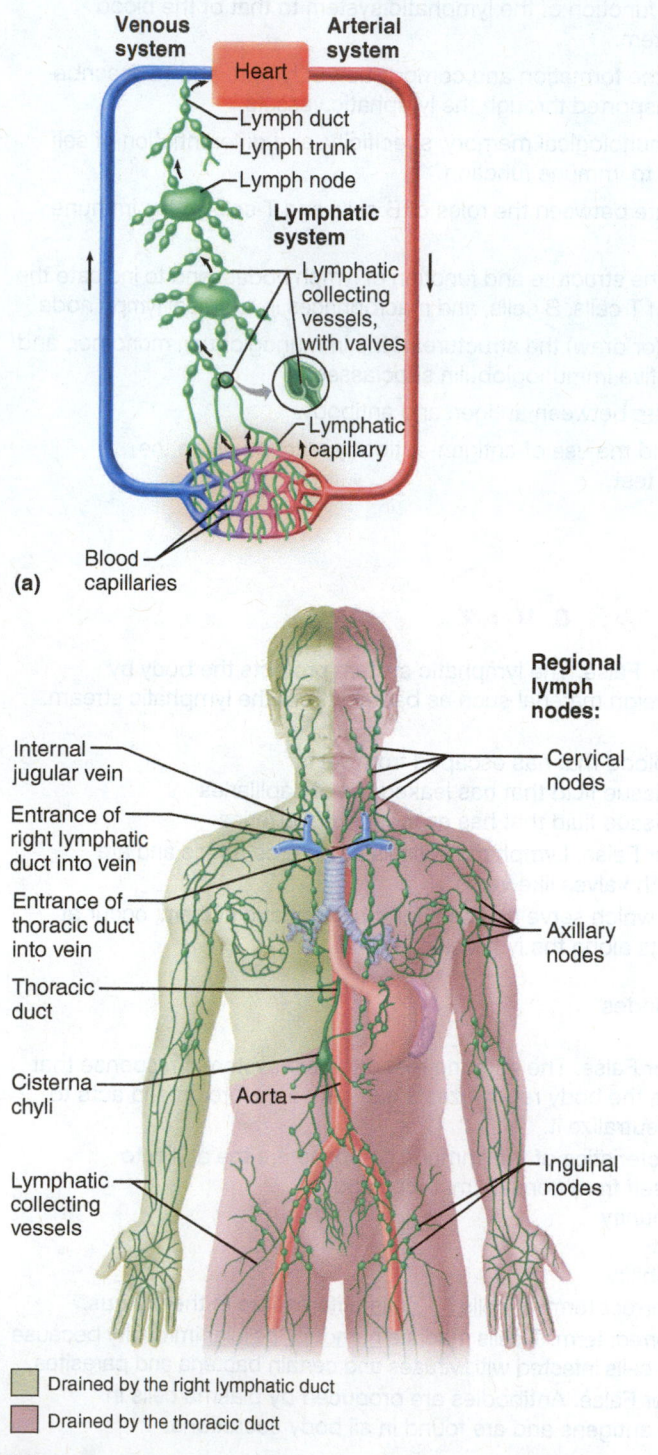

(a)

(b)

Drained by the right lymphatic duct

Drained by the thoracic duct

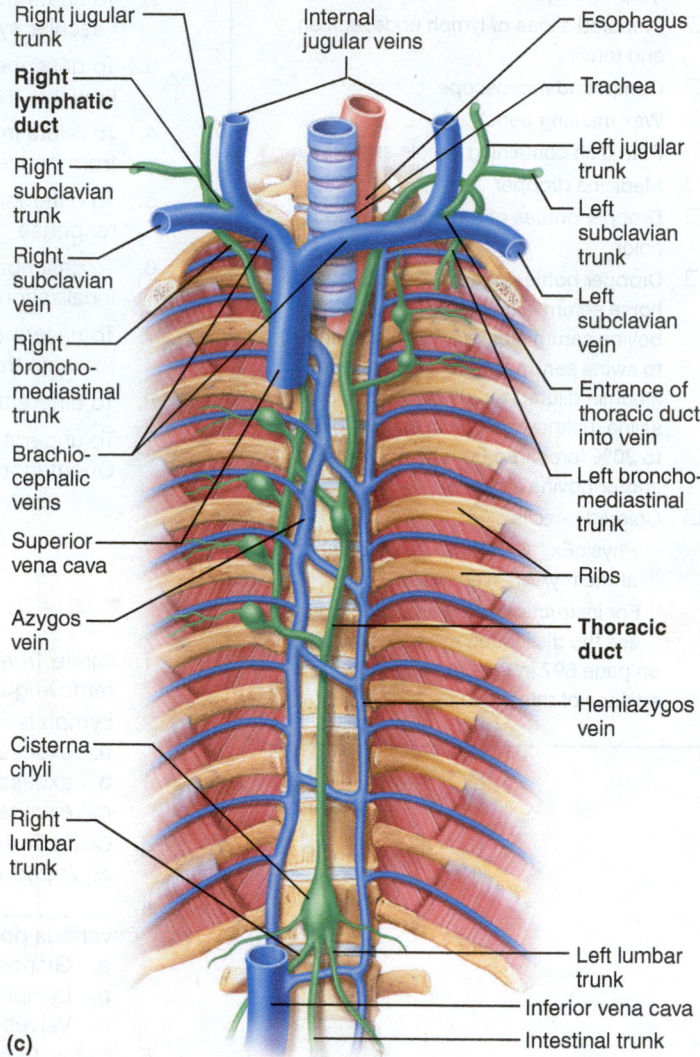

(c)

FIGURE 35A.1 Lymphatic system. (a) Simplified scheme of the relationship of lymphatic vessels to blood vessels of the cardiovascular system. **(b)** Distribution of lymphatic vessels and lymph nodes. The green-shaded area represents body area drained by the right lymphatic duct. **(c)** Major veins in the superior thorax showing entry points of the thoracic and right lymphatic ducts. The major lymphatic trunks are also identified.

FIGURE 35A.2 Lymphatic vessel (550×).

FIGURE 35A.3 Lymphoid organs. Locations of the tonsils, thymus, spleen, appendix, and Peyer's patches.

venous end. However, not all of the lost fluid is returned to the bloodstream by this mechanism, and the fluid that lags behind in the tissue spaces must eventually return to the blood if the vascular system is to operate properly. (If it does not, fluid accumulates in the tissues, producing a condition called *edema.*) It is the microscopic, blind-ended **lymphatic capillaries** (Figure 35A.1a), which ramify through nearly all the tissues of the body, that pick up this leaked fluid (primarily water and a small amount of dissolved proteins) and carry it through successively larger vessels—**lymphatic collecting vessels to lymphatic trunks**—until the lymph finally returns to the blood vascular system through one of the two large ducts in the thoracic region (Figure 35A.1b). The **right lymphatic duct**, present in some but not all individuals, drains lymph from the right upper extremity, head, and thorax delivered by the jugular, subclavian, and bronchomediastinal trunks. In individuals without a right lymphatic duct, those trunks open directly into veins of the neck. The large **thoracic duct** receives lymph from the rest of the body (see Figure 35A.1c). In humans, both ducts empty the lymph into the venous circulation at the junction of the internal jugular vein and the subclavian vein, on their respective sides of the body. Notice that the lymphatic system, lacking both a contractile "heart" and arteries, is a one-way system; it carries lymph only toward the heart.

Like veins of the blood vascular system, the lymphatic collecting vessels have three tunics and are equipped with valves (Figure 35A.2). However, lymphatics tend to be thinner-walled, to have *more* valves, and to anastomose (form branching networks) more than veins. Since the lymphatic system is a pumpless system, lymph transport depends largely on the milking action of the skeletal muscles and on pressure changes within the thorax that occur during breathing.

As lymph is transported, it filters through bean-shaped **lymph nodes,** which cluster along the lymphatic vessels of the body. There are thousands of lymph nodes, but because they are usually embedded in connective tissue, they are not ordinarily seen. Within the lymph nodes are **macrophages,** phagocytes that destroy bacteria, cancer cells, and other foreign matter in the lymphatic stream, thus rendering many harmful substances or cells harmless before the lymph enters the bloodstream. Particularly large collections of lymph nodes are found in the inguinal, axillary, and cervical regions of the body. Although we are not usually aware of the filtering and protective nature of the lymph nodes, most of us have experienced "swollen glands" during an active infection. This swelling is a manifestation of the trapping function of the nodes.

Other lymphoid organs—the tonsils, thymus, and spleen (Figure 35A.3)—resemble the lymph nodes histologically, and house similar cell populations (lymphocytes and macrophages).

ACTIVITY 1

Identifying the Organs of the Lymphatic System

Study the large anatomical chart to observe the general plan of the lymphatic system. Notice the distribution of lymph nodes, various lymphatics, the lymphatic trunks, and the location of the right lymphatic duct and the thoracic duct. Also identify the **cisterna chyli,** the enlarged terminus of the thoracic duct that receives lymph from the digestive viscera. ▪

> For instructions on animal dissections, see the dissection exercises starting on page 697 in the cat, rat, and fetal pig editions of this manual.

The Immune Response

The **adaptive immune system** is a functional system that recognizes something as foreign and acts to destroy or neutralize it. This response is known as the **immune response.** It is a systemic response and is not restricted to the initial infection site. When operating effectively, the immune response protects us from bacterial and viral infections, bacterial toxins, and cancer. When it fails or malfunctions, the body is quickly devastated by pathogens or its own assaults.

FIGURE 35A.4 Structure of lymph node.
(a) Longitudinal view of the internal structure of a lymph node and associated lymphatics. Notice that the afferent vessels outnumber the efferent vessels, which slows the rate of lymph flow. The arrows indicate the direction of the lymph flow. **(b)** Photomicrograph of a part of a lymph node (7×).

Major Characteristics of the Immune Response

The most important characteristics of the immune response are its (1) **memory,** (2) **specificity,** and (3) **ability to differentiate self from nonself.** Not only does the immune system have a "memory" for previously encountered foreign antigens (the chicken pox virus for example), but this memory is also remarkably accurate and highly specific.

An almost limitless variety of macromolecules are *antigenic*—that is, capable of provoking an immune response and reacting with its products. Nearly all foreign proteins, many polysaccharides, and many small molecules (haptens), when linked to our own body proteins, exhibit this capability. The cells that recognize antigens and initiate the immune response are lymphocytes, the second most numerous members of the leukocyte, or white blood cell (WBC), population. Each immunocompetent lymphocyte is virtually monospecific; that is, it has receptors on its surface allowing it to bind with only one or a few very similar antigens.

As a rule, our own proteins are tolerated, a fact that reflects the ability of the immune system to distinguish our own tissues (self) from foreign antigens (nonself). Nevertheless, an inability to recognize self can and does occasionally happen, and our own tissues are attacked by the immune system. This phenomenon is called *autoimmunity.* Autoimmune diseases include multiple sclerosis (MS), myasthenia gravis, Graves' disease, glomerulonephritis, rheumatoid arthritis (RA), and type 1 (or insulin-dependent) diabetes mellitus.

Organs, Cells, and Cell Interactions of the Immune Response

The immune system utilizes as part of its arsenal the **lymphoid organs,** including the thymus, lymph nodes, spleen, tonsils, appendix, and bone marrow. Of these, the thymus and bone marrow are considered to be the *primary lymphoid organs.* The others are *secondary lymphoid areas.*

The stem cells that give rise to the immune system arise in the bone marrow. Their subsequent differentiation into one of the two populations of immunocompetent lymphocytes occurs in the primary lymphoid organs. The **B cells** (B lymphocytes) differentiate in bone marrow, and the **T cells** (T lymphocytes) differentiate in the thymus. While in their "programming organs" the lymphocytes become *immunocompetent,* an event indicated by the appearance of specific cell-surface proteins that enable the lymphocytes to respond (by binding) to a particular antigen.

After differentiation, the B and T cells leave the bone marrow and thymus, respectively; enter the bloodstream; and travel to peripheral (secondary) lymphoid organs, where clonal selection occurs. **Clonal selection** is triggered when an antigen binds to the specific cell-surface receptors of a T or B cell. This event causes the lymphocyte to proliferate rapidly, forming a clone of like cells, all bearing the same antigen-specific receptors. Then, in the presence of certain regulatory signals, the members of the clone specialize, or differentiate—some forming memory cells and others becoming effector or regulatory cells. Upon subsequent meetings with the same antigen, the immune response proceeds considerably faster because the troops are already mobilized and awaiting further orders, so to speak.

(a)

(b)

(c)

In the case of B cell clones, some become **memory B cells;** the others form antibody-producing **plasma cells.** Because the B cells act indirectly through the antibodies that their progeny release into the bloodstream (or other body fluids), they are said to provide **humoral immunity.** T cell clones are more diverse. Although all T cell clones also contain memory cells, some clones contain *cytotoxic T cells* (effector cells that directly attack virus-infected tissue cells). Others contain regulatory cells such as the *helper T cells* (that help activate the B cells and cytotoxic T cells) and still others contain *suppressor T cells* that can inhibit the immune response. Because certain T cells act directly to destroy cells infected with viruses, certain bacteria or parasites, and cancer cells, and to reject foreign grafts, T cells are said to mediate **cellular immunity.**

Absence or failure of thymic differentiation of T lymphocytes results in a marked depression of both antibody and cell-mediated immune functions. Additionally, the observation that the thymus naturally involutes with age has been correlated with the relatively immune-deficient status of elderly individuals. ■

All lymphoid tissues except the thymus and bone marrow contain both T and B cell–dependent regions.

Studying the Microscopic Anatomy of a Lymph Node, the Spleen, and a Tonsil

1. Obtain a compound microscope and prepared slides of a lymph node, spleen, and a tonsil. As you examine the lymph node slide, notice the following anatomical features, depicted in Figure 35A.4. The node is enclosed within a fibrous **capsule,** from which connective tissue septa (**trabeculae**) extend inward to divide the node into several compartments. Very fine strands of reticular connective tissue issue from the trabeculae, forming the stroma of the gland within which cells are found.

In the outer region of the node, the **cortex,** some of the cells are arranged in globular masses, referred to as germinal centers. The **germinal centers** contain rapidly dividing B cells. The rest of the cortical cells are primarily T cells that circulate continuously, moving from the blood into the node and then exiting from the node in the lymphatic stream.

In the internal portion of the gland, the **medulla,** the cells are arranged in cordlike fashion. Most of the medullary cells are macrophages. Macrophages are important not only for their phagocytic function but also because they play an essential role in "presenting" the antigens to the T cells.

Lymph enters the node through a number of *afferent vessels,* circulates through *lymph sinuses* within the node, and leaves the node through *efferent vessels* at the **hilum.** Since each node has fewer efferent than afferent vessels, the lymph flow stagnates somewhat within the node. This allows time for the generation of an immune response and for the macrophages to remove debris from the lymph before it reenters the blood vascular system.

2. As you observe the slide of the spleen, look for the areas of lymphocytes suspended in reticular fibers, the **white pulp,** clustered around central arteries (Figure 35A.5). The remaining tissue in the spleen is the **red pulp,** which is composed of

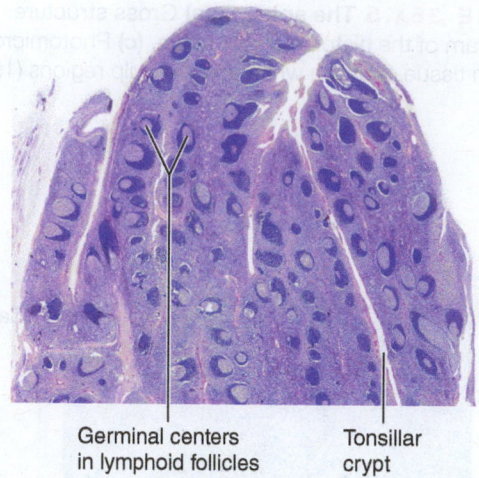

Germinal centers
in lymphoid follicles

Tonsillar
crypt

FIGURE 35A.6 Histology of a palatine tonsil. The luminal surface is covered with epithelium that invaginates deeply to form crypts (10×).

venous sinuses and areas of reticular tissue and macrophages called the **splenic cords.** The white pulp, composed primarily of lymphocytes, is responsible for the immune functions of the spleen. Macrophages remove worn-out red blood cells, debris, bacteria, viruses, and toxins from blood flowing through the sinuses of the red pulp.

3. As you examine the tonsil slide, notice the **follicles** containing **germinal centers** surrounded by scattered lymphocytes. The characteristic **crypts** (invaginations of the mucosal epithelium) of the tonsils trap bacteria and other foreign material (Figure 35A.6). Eventually the bacteria work their way into the lymphoid tissue and are destroyed.

4. Compare and contrast the structure of the lymph node, spleen, and tonsils. ▬

Antibodies and Tests for Their Presence

Antibodies, or **immunoglobulins (Igs),** produced by sensitized B cells and their plasma cell offspring in response to an antigen, are a heterogeneous group of proteins that comprise the general class of plasma proteins called **gamma globulins.** Antibodies are found not only in plasma but also (to greater or lesser extents) in all body secretions. Five major classes of immunoglobulins have been identified: IgM, IgG, IgD, IgA, and IgE. The immunoglobulin classes share a common basic structure but differ functionally and in their localization in the body.

All Igs are composed of one or more monomers (structural units). A monomer consists of four protein chains bound together by disulfide bridges (Figure 35A.7). Two of the chains are quite large and have a high molecular weight; these are the **heavy chains.** The other two chains are only half as long and have a low molecular weight. These are called **light chains.** The two heavy chains have a *constant (C) region,* in which the amino acid sequence is identical in both chains, and a *variable (V) region,* which differs in the Igs formed in response to different antigens. The same is true of the two light chains; each has a constant and a variable region.

The intact Ig molecule has a three-dimensional shape that is generally Y-shaped. Together, the variable regions of the light and heavy chains in each "arm" construct one **antigen-binding site** uniquely shaped to "fit" a specific *antigenic determinant* (portion) of an antigen. Thus, each Ig monomer bears two identical sites that bind to a specific (and the same) antigen. Binding of the immunoglobulins to their complementary antigen(s) effectively immobilizes the antigens until they can be phagocytized or lysed by complement fixation.

Although the role of the immune system is to protect the body, symptoms of certain diseases involve excessively high antibody synthesis (as in multiple myeloma, a cancer of the bone marrow and adjacent bony structures) and/or the production of abnormal antibodies.

FIGURE 35A.7 Antibody structure. (a) Schematic antibody structure consists of two heavy chains and two light chains connected by disulfide bonds. **(b)** Enlargement of an antigen-binding site of an immunoglobulin.

FIGURE 35A.8 Template for well preparation for the Ouchterlony double-gel diffusion experiment.

The antigen-antibody reaction is used diagnostically in a variety of ways. One of the most familiar is blood typing. (See Exercise 29A for instructions on ABO and Rh blood typing.) Pregnancy tests also use the antigen-antibody reaction to test for the presence of human chorionic gonadotropin (hCG), a hormone produced early in pregnancy. Another technique for detecting antigens is the enzyme-linked immunoabsorbent assay (ELISA). Originally designed to measure antibody titer, ELISA has been modified for use in HIV-1 blood screening. The antigen-antibody test that we will use in this laboratory session is the Ouchterlony technique, which is used mainly for rapid screening of suspected antigens.

Ouchterlony Double-Gel Diffusion, an Immunological Technique

The Ouchterlony double-gel diffusion technique was developed in 1948 to detect the presence of particular antigens in sera or extracts. Antigens and antibodies are placed in wells in a gel and allowed to diffuse toward each other. If an antigen reacts with an antibody, a thin white line called a *precipitin line* forms. In the following activity, the double-gel diffusion technique will be used to identify antigens. Work in groups of no more than three.

ACTIVITY 3

Using the Ouchterlony Technique to Identify Antigens

1. Obtain one each of the materials for conducting the Ouchterlony test: petri dish containing saline agar; medicine dropper; wax marking pencil; and dropper bottles of red and

TABLE 35A.1	Section II
Well	Solution
1	Horse serum albumin
2	Goat anti-horse albumin
3	Goat anti-bovine albumin
4	Goat anti-swine albumin

green food dye, horse serum albumin, an unknown serum albumin sample, and antibodies to horse, bovine, and swine albumin. Put your initials and the number of the unknown albumin sample used on the bottom of the petri dish near the edge.

2. Use the wax marking pencil and the template (Figure 35A.8) to divide the dish into three sections, and mark them I, II, and III.

3. Prepare sample wells, again using the template in Figure 35A.8. Squeeze the medicine dropper bulb, and gently touch the tip to the surface of the agar. While releasing the bulb, push the tip down through the agar to the bottom of the dish. Lift the dropper vertically; this should leave a straight-walled well in the agar.

4. Repeat step 3 so that section I has two wells and sections II and III have four wells each.

5. To observe diffusion through the gel, nearly fill one well in section I with red dye and the other well with green dye. Be careful not to overfill the wells. Observe periodically for 30 to 45 minutes as the dyes diffuse through the agar. Draw your results as instructed in the Results section.

6. To demonstrate positive and negative results, fill the wells in section II as listed in Table 35A.1. A precipitin line should form only between wells 1 and 2.

7. To test the unknown sample, fill the wells in section III as listed in Table 35A.2.

8. Replace the cover on the petri dish, and incubate at room temperature for at least 16 hours. Make arrangements to observe the agar for precipitin lines after 16 hours. *The lines may begin to fade after 48 hours.* Draw the results as instructed in the following section, parts 1–3, indicating the location of all precipitin lines that form.

TABLE 35A.2	Section III
Well	Solution
1	Unknown # _____
2	Goat anti-horse albumin
3	Goat anti-bovine albumin
4	Goat anti-swine albumin

Results

1. Demonstration of diffusion using dye. Draw the appearance of section I of your dish after 30 to 45 minutes on Figure 35A.8. Use colored pencils.

2. Draw section II on Figure 35A.8 as it appears after incubation, 16 to 48 hours. Be sure to number the wells.

3. Draw section III on Figure 35A.8 as it appears after incubation, 16 to 48 hours. Be sure to number the wells.

Unknown # _____

4. What evidence for diffusion did you observe in section I?

_____

_____

5. Is there any evidence of a precipitate in section I?

_____

6. Which of the sera functioned as an antigen in section II?

_____

7. Which antibody reacted with the antigen in section II?

_____

How do you know? (Be specific about your observations.)

_____

_____

8. If swine albumin had been placed in well 1, what would you expect to happen? Explain.

_____

_____

9. If chicken albumin had been placed in well 1, what would you expect to happen? Explain.

_____

_____

10. What antigens were present in the unknown solution?

_____

How do you know? (Be specific about your observations.)

_____

NAME _____

LAB TIME/DATE _____

The Lymphatic System and Immune Response

The Lymphatic System

1. Match the terms below with the correct letters on the diagram.

_____ 1. axillary lymph nodes

_____ 2. bone marrow

_____ 3. cervical lymph nodes

_____ 4. cisterna chyli

_____ 5. inguinal lymph nodes

_____ 6. lymphatic vessels

_____ 7. Peyer's patches (in intestine)

_____ 8. right lymphatic duct

_____ 9. spleen

_____ 10. thoracic duct

_____ 11. thymus

_____ 12. tonsils

2. Explain why the lymphatic system is a one-way system, whereas the blood vascular system is a two-way system.

_____

_____

3. How do lymphatic vessels resemble veins? _____

How do lymphatic capillaries differ from blood capillaries? _____

_____

4. What is the function of the lymphatic vessels? _____

_____

5. What is lymph? _____

6. What factors are involved in the flow of lymphatic fluid? _____

_____

7. What name is given to the terminal duct draining most of the body? _____

8. What is the cisterna chyli? _____

_____

How does the composition of lymph in the cisterna chyli differ from that in the general lymphatic stream?

_____

9. Which portion of the body is drained by the right lymphatic duct? _____

10. Note three areas where lymph nodes are densely clustered: _____,

_____, and _____

11. What are the two major functions of the lymph nodes? _____

and _____

12. The radical mastectomy is an operation in which a cancerous breast, surrounding tissues, and the underlying muscles of the anterior thoracic wall, plus the axillary lymph nodes, are removed. After such an operation, the arm usually swells, or becomes edematous, and is very uncomfortable—sometimes for months. Why?

_____

The Immune Response

13. What is the function of B cells in the immune response? _____

_____

14. What is the role of T cells? _____

_____

_____

15. Define the following terms related to the operation of the immune system.

immunological memory: _____

_____

specificity: _____

_____

recognition of self from nonself: _____

_____

autoimmune disease: _____

_____

Studying the Microscopic Anatomy
of a Lymph Node, the Spleen, and a Tonsil

16. In the space below, make a rough drawing of the structure of a lymph node. Identify the cortex area, germinal centers, and medulla. For each identified area, note the cell type (T cell, B cell, or macrophage) most likely to be found there.

17. What structural characteristic ensures a *slow* flow of lymph through a lymph node? _____

_____

Why is this desirable? _____

_____

18. What similarities in structure and function are found in the lymph nodes, spleen, and tonsils? _____

_____

_____

Antibodies and Tests for Their Presence

19. Distinguish between antigen and antibody. _____

_____

20. Describe the structure of the immunoglobulin monomer, and label the diagram with the choices given in the key. _____

_____

Heavy chain
variable region

Heavy chain
constant region

Light chain
variable region

Light chain
constant region

Disulfide bond

Key:

a. antigen-binding site

b. heavy chain

c. hinge region

d. light chain

e. stem region

21. Are the genes coding for one antibody entirely different from those coding for a different antibody? _____

Explain your answer. _____

_____

_____

22. In the Ouchterlony test, what happened when the antibody to horse serum albumin mixed with horse serum albumin?

_____

_____

_____

23. If the unknown antigen contained bovine and swine serum albumin, what would you expect to happen in the Ouchterlony

test, and why? _____

_____

_____

Anatomy of the Respiratory System

MATERIALS

M A T E R I A L S

- ☐ Resin cast of the respiratory tree (if available)
- ☐ Human torso model
- ☐ Respiratory organ system model and/or chart of the respiratory system
- ☐ Larynx model (if available)
- ☐ Preserved inflatable lung preparation (obtained from a biological supply house) or sheep pluck fresh from the slaughterhouse
- ☐ Source of compressed air
- ☐ Dissecting tray
- ☐ Disposable gloves
- ☐ Disposable autoclave bag
- ☐ Prepared slides of the following (if available): trachea (cross section), lung tissue, both normal and pathological specimens (for example, sections taken from lung tissues exhibiting bronchitis, pneumonia, emphysema, or lung cancer)
- ☐ Compound and stereomicroscopes

For instructions on animal dissections, see the dissection exercises starting on page 697 in the cat, fetal pig, and rat editions of this manual.

O B J E C T I V E S

1. To define the following terms: *respiratory system, pulmonary ventilation, external respiration,* and *internal respiration.*
2. To label the major respiratory system structures on a diagram (or identify them on a model), and to describe the function of each.
3. To recognize the histologic structure of the trachea (cross section) and lung tissue on prepared slides, and to describe the functions served by the observed structural modifications.

P R E - L A B   Q U I Z

1. The major role of the respiratory system is to
   a. dispose of waste products in a solid form
   b. permit the flow of nutrients through the body
   c. supply the body with carbon dioxide and dispose of oxygen
   d. supply the body with oxygen and dispose of carbon dioxide
2. Circle True or False. Four processes—pulmonary ventilation, external respiration, transport of respiratory gases, and internal respiration—must all occur in order for the respiratory system to function fully.
3. The upper respiratory structures include the nose, the larynx, and the
   a. epiglottis
   b. lungs
   c. pharynx
   d. trachea
4. Circle the correct term. The <u>thyroid cartilage / oropharynx</u> is the largest and most prominent of the laryngeal cartilages.
5. Circle True or False. The epiglottis forms a lid over the larynx when we swallow food: it closes off the respiratory passageway to incoming food or drink.
6. Air flows from the larynx to the trachea, and then enters the
   a. left and right lungs
   b. left and right main bronchi
   c. pharynx
   d. segmental bronchi
7. Circle the correct term. The lining of the trachea is pseudostratified ciliated <u>columnar epithelium / transitional epithelium,</u> which propels dust particles, bacteria, and other debris away from the lungs.
8. Circle True or False. All but the most minute branches of the respiratory tree have cartilaginous reinforcements in their walls.
9. _____, tiny balloonlike expansions of the alveolar sacs, are composed of a single thin layer of squamous epithelium. They are the main structural and functional units of the lung and the actual sites of gas exchange.
10. Circle the correct term. Fissures divide the lungs into lobes, three on the right and <u>two / three</u> on the left.

Body cells require an abundant and continuous supply of oxygen. As the cells use oxygen, they release carbon dioxide, a waste product that the body must get rid of. These oxygen-using cellular processes, collectively referred to as *cellular respiration,* are more appropriately described in conjunction with the topic of cellular metabolism. The major role of the **respiratory system,** our focus in this exercise, is to supply the body with oxygen and dispose of carbon dioxide. To fulfill this role, at least four distinct processes, collectively referred to as **respiration,** must occur:

(a)

Olfactory epithelium
Mucosa of pharynx
Tubal tonsil
Pharyngotympanic tube
Nasopharynx

Olfactory nerves
Superior nasal concha and superior nasal meatus
Middle nasal concha and middle nasal meatus
Inferior nasal concha and inferior nasal meatus
Hard palate
Soft palate
Uvula

Pharynx
Nasopharynx
Oropharynx
Laryngopharynx

(b)

Cribriform plate of ethmoid bone
Sphenoid sinus
Posterior nasal aperture
Nasopharynx
Pharyngeal tonsil
Opening of pharyngotympanic tube
Uvula
Oropharynx
Palatine tonsil
Isthmus of the fauces
Laryngopharynx
Esophagus
Trachea

Frontal sinus
Nasal cavity
Nasal conchae (superior, middle and inferior)
Nasal meatuses (superior, middle, and inferior)
Nasal vestibule
Nostril
Hard palate
Soft palate
Tongue
Lingual tonsil
Hyoid bone
Larynx
Epiglottis
Vestibular fold
Thyroid cartilage
Vocal fold
Cricoid cartilage
Thyroid gland

(c)

FIGURE 36.1 Structures of the upper respiratory tract (midsagittal section). (a) Photograph. **(b)** Regions of the pharynx. **(c)** Diagrammatic view.

Pulmonary ventilation: The tidelike movement of air into and out of the lungs so that the gases in the alveoli are continuously changed and refreshed. Also more simply called *ventilation,* or *breathing.*

External respiration: The gas exchange between the blood and the air-filled chambers of the lungs (oxygen loading/carbon dioxide unloading).

Transport of respiratory gases: The transport of respiratory gases between the lungs and tissue cells of the body accomplished by the cardiovascular system, using blood as the transport vehicle.

Internal respiration: Exchange of gases between systemic blood and tissue cells (oxygen unloading and carbon dioxide loading).

Only the first two processes are the exclusive province of the respiratory system, but all four must occur for the respiratory system to "do its job." Hence, the respiratory and circulatory systems are irreversibly linked. If either system fails, cells begin to die from oxygen starvation and accumulation of carbon dioxide. Uncorrected, this situation soon causes death of the entire organism.

Upper Respiratory System Structures

The upper respiratory system structures—the nose, pharynx, and larynx—are shown in Figure 36.1 and described below. As you read through the descriptions, identify each structure in the figure.

Air generally passes into the respiratory tract through the **nostrils or nares,** and enters the **nasal cavity** (divided by the **nasal septum**). It then flows posteriorly over three pairs of lobelike structures, the **inferior, superior,** and **middle nasal conchae,** which increase the air turbulence. As the air passes through the nasal cavity, it is also warmed, moistened, and filtered by the nasal mucosa. The air that flows directly beneath the superior part of the nasal cavity may chemically stimulate the olfactory receptors located in the mucosa of that region. The nasal cavity is surrounded by the **paranasal sinuses** in the frontal, sphenoid, ethmoid, and maxillary bones. These sinuses, named for the bones in which they are located, act as resonance chambers in speech. Their mucosae, like that of the nasal cavity, warm and moisten the incoming air.

The nasal passages are separated from the oral cavity below by a partition composed anteriorly of the **hard palate** and posteriorly by the **soft palate.**

The genetic defect called **cleft palate** (failure of the palatine bones and/or the palatine processes of the maxillary bones to fuse medially) causes difficulty in breathing and oral cavity functions such as sucking and, later, mastication and speech. ■

Of course, air may also enter the body via the mouth. From there it passes through the oral cavity to move into the pharynx posteriorly, where the oral and nasal cavities are joined temporarily.

Commonly called the *throat,* the funnel-shaped **pharynx** connects the nasal and oral cavities to the larynx and esophagus inferiorly. It has three named parts (Figure 36.1):

1. The **nasopharynx** lies posterior to the nasal cavity and is continuous with it via the **posterior nasal aperture.** It lies above the soft palate; hence, it serves only as an air passage. High on its posterior wall is the *pharyngeal tonsil,* masses of lymphoid tissue that help to protect the respiratory passages from invading pathogens. The *pharyngotympanic (auditory) tubes,* which allow middle ear pressure to become equalized to atmospheric pressure, drain into the lateral aspects of the nasopharynx. The *tubal tonsils* surround the openings of these tubes into the nasopharynx.

Because of the continuity of the middle ear and nasopharyngeal mucosae, nasal infections may invade the middle ear cavity and cause **otitis media** (middle ear inflammation), which is difficult to treat. ■

2. The **oropharynx** is continuous posteriorly with the oral cavity. Since it extends from the soft palate to the epiglottis of the larynx inferiorly, it serves as a common conduit for food and air. In its lateral walls are the *palatine tonsils.* The *lingual tonsil* covers the base of the tongue.

3. The **laryngopharynx,** like the oropharynx, accommodates both ingested food and air. It lies directly posterior to the upright epiglottis and extends to the larynx, where the common pathway divides into the respiratory and digestive channels. From the laryngopharynx, air enters the lower respiratory passageways by passing through the larynx (voice box) and into the trachea below.

The **larynx** (Figure 36.2) consists of nine cartilages. The two most prominent are the large shield-shaped **thyroid cartilage,** whose anterior medial laryngeal prominence is commonly referred to as *Adam's apple,* and the inferiorly located, ring-shaped **cricoid cartilage,** whose widest dimension faces posteriorly. All the laryngeal cartilages are composed of hyaline cartilage except the flaplike **epiglottis,** a flexible elastic cartilage located superior to the opening of the larynx. The epiglottis, sometimes referred to as the "guardian of the airways," forms a lid over the larynx when we swallow. This closes off the respiratory passageways to incoming food or drink, which is routed into the posterior esophagus, or food chute.

● Palpate your larynx by placing your hand on the anterior neck surface approximately halfway down its length. Swallow. Can you feel the cartilaginous larynx rising?

If anything other than air enters the larynx, a cough reflex attempts to expel the substance. Note that this reflex operates only when a person is conscious. Therefore, you should never try to feed or pour liquids down the throat of an unconscious person.

The mucous membrane of the larynx is thrown into two pairs of folds—the upper **vestibular folds,** also called the **false vocal cords,** and the lower **vocal folds,** or **true vocal cords,** which vibrate with expelled air for speech. The vocal cords are attached posterolaterally to the small triangular **arytenoid cartilages** by the *vocal ligaments.* The slitlike passageway between the folds is called the **glottis.**

Epiglottis

Body of hyoid bone

Thyrohyoid membrane

Thyroid cartilage

Cuneiform cartilage

Laryngeal prominence (Adam's apple)

Corniculate cartilage

Arytenoid cartilage

Cricothyroid ligament

Arytenoid muscles

Cricotracheal ligament

Cricoid cartilage

Tracheal cartilages

Body of hyoid bone

Thyrohyoid membrane

Fatty pad

Vestibular fold (false vocal cord)

Thyroid cartilage

Vocal fold (true vocal cord)

Cricothyroid ligament

Cricotracheal ligament

(a) Anterior superficial view

(b) Sagittal view; anterior surface to the right

FIGURE 36.2 Structure of the larynx.

Lower Respiratory System Structures

Air entering the **trachea,** or windpipe, from the larynx travels down its length (about 11.0 cm or 4 inches) to the level of the *sternal angle* (or the disc between the fourth and fifth thoracic vertebrae). There the passageway divides into the right and left **main (primary) bronchi** (Figure 36.3), which plunge into their respective lungs at an indented area called the **hilum** (see Figure 36.5c). The right main bronchus is wider, shorter, and more vertical than the left, and foreign objects that enter the respiratory passageways are more likely to become lodged in it.

The trachea is lined with a ciliated, mucus-secreting, pseudostratified columnar epithelium, as are many of the other respiratory system passageways. The cilia propel mucus (produced by goblet cells) laden with dust particles, bacteria,

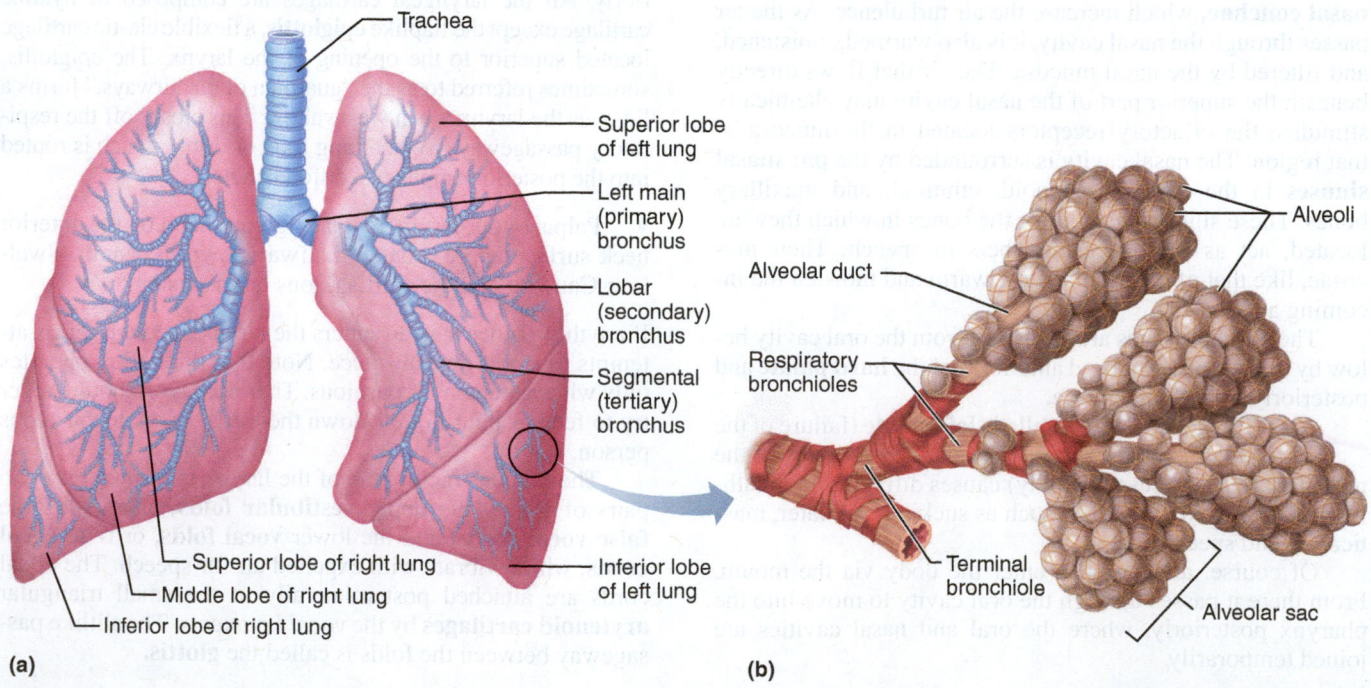

Trachea

Superior lobe of left lung

Left main (primary) bronchus

Lobar (secondary) bronchus

Segmental (tertiary) bronchus

Superior lobe of right lung

Middle lobe of right lung

Inferior lobe of right lung

Inferior lobe of left lung

Alveoli

Alveolar duct

Respiratory bronchioles

Terminal bronchiole

Alveolar sac

(a)

(b)

FIGURE 36.3 Structures of the lower respiratory tract. **(a)** Diagrammatic view. **(b)** Enlarged view of alveoli.

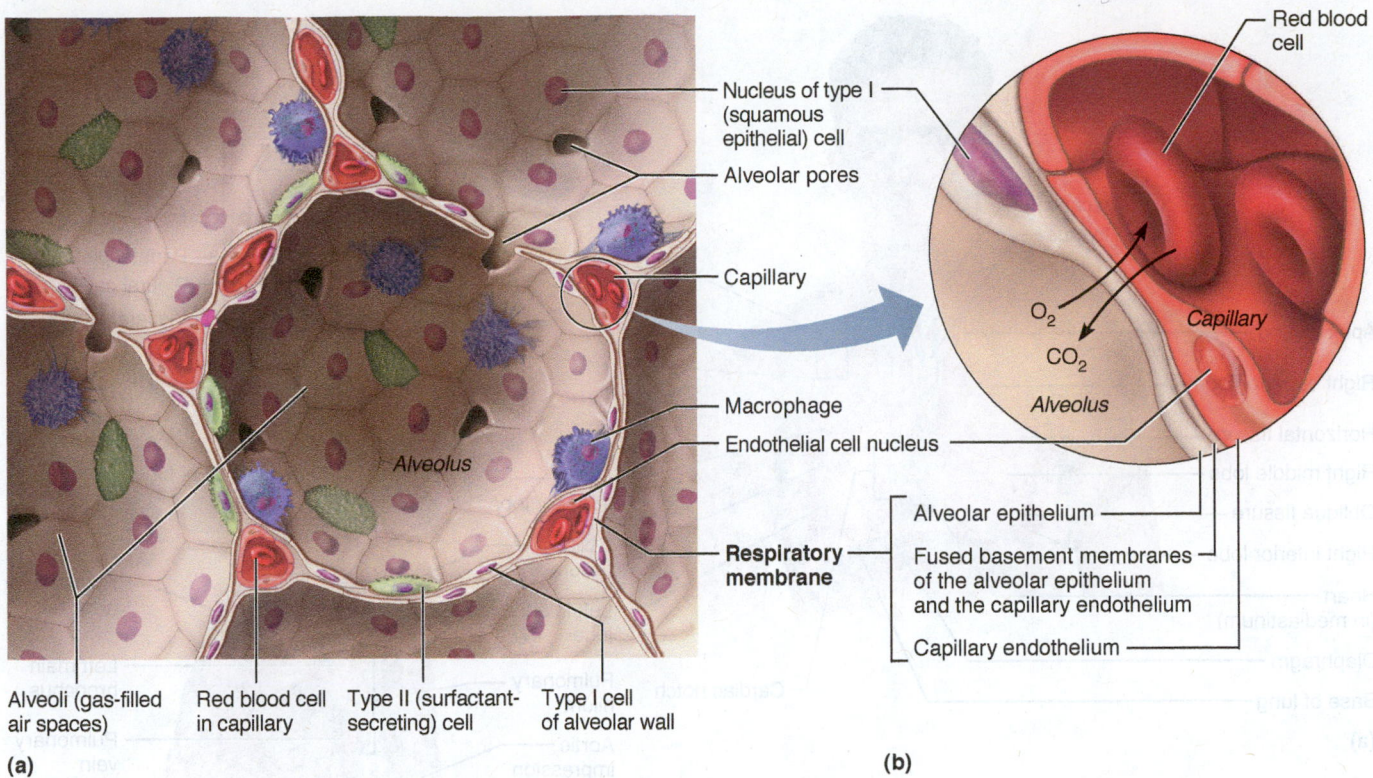

(a)

Nucleus of type I (squamous epithelial) cell

Alveolar pores

Capillary

Macrophage

Endothelial cell nucleus

Respiratory membrane

Alveolus

Alveoli (gas-filled air spaces)

Red blood cell in capillary

Type II (surfactant-secreting) cell

Type I cell of alveolar wall

Red blood cell

O₂

CO₂

Capillary

Alveolus

Alveolar epithelium

Fused basement membranes of the alveolar epithelium and the capillary endothelium

Capillary endothelium

(b)

FIGURE 36.4 Diagrammatic view of the relationship between the alveoli and pulmonary capillaries involved in gas exchange. (a) One alveolus surrounded by capillaries. **(b)** Enlargement of the respiratory membrane.

and other debris away from the lungs and toward the throat, where it can be expectorated or swallowed. The walls of the trachea are reinforced with C-shaped cartilaginous rings, the incomplete portion located posteriorly (see Figure 36.6, page 543). These C-shaped cartilages serve a double function: The incomplete parts allow the esophagus to expand anteriorly when a large food bolus is swallowed. The solid portions reinforce the trachea walls to maintain its open passageway regardless of the pressure changes that occur during breathing.

The primary bronchi further divide into smaller and smaller branches (the secondary, tertiary, on down), finally becoming the **bronchioles,** which have terminal branches called **respiratory bronchioles** (Figure 36.3b). All but the most minute branches have cartilaginous reinforcements in their walls, usually in the form of small plates of hyaline cartilage rather than cartilaginous rings. As the respiratory tubes get smaller and smaller, the relative amount of smooth muscle in their walls increases as the amount of cartilage declines and finally disappears. The complete layer of smooth muscle present in the bronchioles enables them to provide considerable resistance to air flow under certain conditions (asthma, hay fever, etc.). The continuous branching of the respiratory passageways in the lungs is often referred to as the **respiratory tree.** The comparison becomes much more meaningful in a resin cast of the respiratory passages.

• Observe a resin cast of respiratory passages if one is available.

The respiratory bronchioles in turn subdivide into several **alveolar ducts,** which terminate in alveolar sacs that rather resemble clusters of grapes. **Alveoli,** tiny balloonlike expansions along the alveolar sacs and occasionally found protruding from alveolar ducts and respiratory bronchioles, are composed of a single thin layer of squamous epithelium overlying a wispy basal lamina. The external surfaces of the alveoli are densely spiderwebbed with a network of pulmonary capillaries (Figure 36.4). Together, the alveolar and capillary walls and their fused basal laminae form the **respiratory membrane,** also called the *air-blood barrier.*

Because gas exchanges occur by simple diffusion across the respiratory membrane—oxygen passing from the alveolar air to the capillary blood and carbon dioxide leaving the capillary blood to enter the alveolar air—the alveolar sacs, alveolar ducts, and respiratory bronchioles are referred to collectively as **respiratory zone structures.** All other respiratory passageways (from the nasal cavity to the terminal bronchioles) simply serve as access or exit routes to and from these gas exchange chambers and are called **conducting zone structures.** Because the conducting zone structures have no exchange function, they are also referred to as *anatomical dead space.*

The Lungs and Their Pleural Coverings

The paired lungs are soft, spongy organs that occupy the entire thoracic cavity except for the *mediastinum,* which houses the heart, bronchi, esophagus, and other organs (Figure 36.5). Each lung is connected to the mediastinum by a **root** containing its vascular and bronchial attachments. The structures of the root enter (or leave) the lung via a medial indentation called the *hilum.* All structures distal to the primary bronchi are found within the lung substance. A lung's **apex,** the

FIGURE 36.5 Anatomical relationships of organs in the thoracic cavity. (a) Anterior view of the thoracic organs. The lungs flank the central mediastinum. The inset at upper right depicts the pleurae and the pleural cavity. **(b)** Photograph of medial aspect of left lung. **(c)** Transverse section through the superior part of the thorax, showing the lungs and the main organs in the mediastinum.

(a)

Trachea
Thymus
Apex of lung
Right superior lobe
Horizontal fissure
Right middle lobe
Oblique fissure
Right inferior lobe
Heart (in mediastinum)
Diaphragm
Base of lung
Left superior lobe
Oblique fissure
Left inferior lobe
Cardiac notch

Intercostal muscle
Rib
Parietal pleura
Pleural cavity
Visceral pleura
Lung

(b)

Apex of lung
Pulmonary artery
Left main bronchus
Pulmonary vein
Impression of heart
Oblique fissure
Lobules
Pulmonary hilum
Aortic impression

(c)

Posterior
Vertebra
Esophagus (in mediastinum)
Root of lung at hilum
• Left main bronchus
• Left pulmonary artery
• Left pulmonary vein
Left lung
Thoracic wall
Pulmonary trunk
Heart (in mediastinum)
Anterior mediastinum
Right lung
Parietal pleura
Visceral pleura
Pleural cavity
Pericardial membranes
Sternum
Anterior

FIGURE 36.6 Tissue composition of the tracheal wall. (a) Cross-sectional view of the trachea. **(b)** Photomicrograph of a portion of the tracheal wall (110×).

narrower superior aspect, lies just deep to the clavicle, and its **base,** the inferior concave surface, rests on the diaphragm. Anterior, lateral, and posterior lung surfaces are in close contact with the ribs and, hence, are collectively called the **costal surface.** The medial surface of the left lung exhibits a concavity called the **cardiac notch,** which accommodates the heart where it extends left from the body midline. Fissures divide the lungs into a number of **lobes**—two in the left lung and three in the right. Other than the respiratory passageways and air spaces that make up the bulk of their volume, the lungs are mostly elastic connective tissue, which allows them to recoil passively during expiration.

Each lung is enclosed in a double-layered sac of serous membrane called the **pleura.** The outer layer, the **parietal pleura,** is attached to the thoracic walls and the **diaphragm;** the inner layer, covering the lung tissue, is the **visceral pleura.** The two pleural layers are separated by the **pleural cavity,** which is more of a potential space than an actual one. The pleural layers produce lubricating serous fluid that causes them to adhere closely to one another, holding the lungs to the thoracic wall and allowing them to move easily against one another during the movements of breathing.

Identifying Respiratory System Organs

Before proceeding, be sure to locate on the torso model, thoracic cavity structures model, larynx model, or an anatomical chart all the respiratory structures described—both upper and lower respiratory system organs. ▉

For instructions on animal dissections, see the dissection exercises starting on page 697 in the cat, rat, and fetal pig editions of this manual.

ACTIVITY 2

Demonstrating Lung Inflation in a Sheep Pluck

A *sheep pluck* includes the larynx, trachea with attached lungs, the heart and pericardium, and portions of the major blood vessels found in the mediastinum (aorta, pulmonary artery and vein, venae cavae). If a sheep pluck is not available, a good substitute is a preserved inflatable pig lung.

⚠ Don disposable gloves, obtain a dissecting tray and a fresh sheep pluck (or a preserved pluck of another animal), and identify the lower respiratory system organs. Once you have completed your observations, insert a hose from an air compressor (vacuum pump) into the trachea and alternately allow air to flow in and out of the lungs. Notice how the lungs inflate. This observation is educational in a preserved pluck but it is a spectacular sight in a fresh one. Another advantage of using a fresh pluck is that the lung pluck changes color (becomes redder) as hemoglobin in trapped RBCs becomes loaded with oxygen.

⚠ Dispose of the gloves in the autoclave bag immediately after use. ▉

ACTIVITY 3

Examining Prepared Slides of Trachea and Lung Tissue

1. Obtain a compound microscope and a slide of a cross section of the tracheal wall. Identify the smooth muscle layer, the hyaline cartilage supporting rings, and the pseudostratified ciliated epithelium. Use Figure 36.6 as a guide; also try

Pseudostratified epithelium

Smooth muscle

Cartilage plate in the adventitia

Lumen of bronchiole

Lamina propria

(a)

Terminal bronchiole

Respiratory bronchiole

Alveolar duct

Alveolar pores

Alveolar saccule

Alveoli

(b)

FIGURE 36.7 Microscopic structure of a bronchiole and alveoli.
(a) Photomicrograph of a section of a bronchiole (22×). **(b)** Photomicrograph and diagrammatic view of alveoli (70×).

to identify a few goblet cells in the epithelium (see Figure 6A.3c and d on p. 71).

2.   Obtain a slide of lung tissue for examination. The alveolus is the main structural and functional unit of the lung and is the actual site of gas exchange. Identify a bronchiole

(Figure 36.7a) and the thin squamous epithelium of the alveolar walls (Figure 36.7b).

3.   Examine slides of pathological lung tissues, and compare them to the normal lung specimens. Record your observations at the end of the Exercise 36 Review Sheet.

Anatomy of the Respiratory System

Upper and Lower Respiratory System Structures

1. Complete the labeling of the diagram of the upper respiratory structures (sagittal section).

Frontal sinus

Cribriform plate of ethmoid bone

Sphenoidal sinus

Opening of auditory tube

Nasopharynx

Hard palate

Tongue

Hyoid bone

Thyroid cartilage of larynx

Cricoid cartilage

Thyroid gland

2. Two pairs of vocal folds are found in the larynx. Which pair are the true vocal cords (superior or inferior)?

_____

3. Name the specific cartilages in the larynx that correspond to the following descriptions.

forms the Adam's apple:_____   shaped like a signet ring:_____

a "lid" for the larynx:_____   vocal cord attachment:_____

4. What is the significance of the fact that the human trachea is reinforced with cartilaginous rings?

_____

Of the fact that the rings are incomplete posteriorly? _____

_____

5. What is the function of the pleural membranes? _____

_____

_____

6. Name two functions of the nasal cavity mucosa. _____

and _____

7. The following questions refer to the primary bronchi.

Which is longer?_____   Larger in diameter?_____   More horizontal?_____

Which more commonly traps a foreign object that has entered the respiratory passageways?_____

8. Appropriately label all structures provided with leader lines on the diagrams below.

9. Trace a molecule of oxygen from the nostrils to the pulmonary capillaries of the lungs: Nostrils →

_____

_____

_____

10. Match the terms in column B to the descriptions in column A.

Column A

_____ 1. connects the larynx to the primary bronchi

_____ 2. site of tonsils

_____ 3. food passageway posterior to the trachea

_____ 4. covers the glottis during swallowing of food

_____ 5. contains the vocal cords

_____ 6. nerve that activates the diaphragm during inspiration

_____ 7. pleural layer lining the walls of the thorax

_____ 8. site from which oxygen enters the pulmonary blood

_____ 9. connects the middle ear to the nasopharynx

_____ 10. opening between the vocal folds

_____ 11. increases air turbulence in the nasal cavity

_____ 12. separates the oral cavity from the nasal cavity

Column B

a. alveolus

b. bronchiole

c. conchae

d. epiglottis

e. esophagus

f. glottis

g. larynx

h. palate

i. pharyngotympanic tube

j. parietal pleura

k. pharynx

l. phrenic nerve

m. primary bronchi

n. trachea

o. vagus nerve

p. visceral pleura

11. What portions of the respiratory system are referred to as anatomical dead space?_____

_____

_____

Why?_____

12. Define the following terms.

_external respiration:_____

_____

_internal respiration:_____

_____

_cellular respiration:_____

_____

Demonstrating Lung Inflation in a Sheep Pluck

13. Does the lung inflate part by part or as a whole, like a balloon?_____

14. What happened when the pressure was released?_____

15. What type of tissue ensures this phenomenon?_____

Examining Prepared Slides of Trachea and Lung Tissue

16. What structural characteristics of the alveoli make them an ideal site for the diffusion of gases?

_____

Why does oxygen move from the alveoli into the pulmonary capillary blood?_____

_____

_____

17. If you observed pathological lung sections, record your observations. Also record how the tissue differed from normal lung tissue. Complete the table below using your answers.

Slide type	Observations	Comparison to normal lung tissue

Respiratory System Physiology

MATERIALS

- ☐ Model lung (bell jar demonstrator)
- ☐ Tape measure
- ☐ Stethoscope
- ☐ Alcohol swabs
- ☐ Apparatus A or B:

  A: Spirometer, disposable cardboard mouthpieces, nose clips, table (on chalkboard) for recording class data, disposable autoclave bag, battery jar containing 70% ethanol solution

  BIOPAC® B: BIOPAC® MP36 (or MP35/30) data acquisition unit, PC or Mac computer, BIOPAC® Student Lab Software, BIOPAC® airflow transducer, BIOPAC® calibration syringe, disposable mouthpiece, nose clip, bacteriological filter

  New versions of the BSL software (3.7.5 and higher for Windows, and 3.7.4 and higher for Mac) require slightly different channel settings and collection strategies. Instructions for using the newer software with the MP36/35 data acquisition units can be found on myA&P. In addition, instructions for use of the NEW 2-channel data acquisition unit, the MP45, may also be found on myA&P.

- ☐ Physiograph, pneumograph, and recording attachments for physiograph
- ☐ Paper bag
- ☐ 0.05 *M* NaOH
- ☐ Phenol red in a dropper bottle
- ☐ 100-ml beakers
- ☐ Straws

  Text continues on next page.

OBJECTIVES

1. To define the following (and be prepared to provide volume figures if applicable):

   inspiration
   expiration
   tidal volume
   vital capacity

   expiratory reserve volume
   inspiratory reserve volume
   minute respiratory volume

2. To explain the role of muscles and volume changes in the mechanical process of breathing.

3. To describe bronchial and vesicular breathing sounds.

4. To demonstrate proper usage of a spirometer.

5. To explain the relative importance of various mechanical and chemical factors in producing respiratory variations.

6. To explain the importance of the carbonic acid–bicarbonate buffer system in maintaining blood pH.

PRE-LAB QUIZ

1. Circle the correct term. Inspiration / expiration is the phase of pulmonary ventilation when air passes out of the lungs.

2. Which of the following processes does *not* occur during inspiration?
   a. diaphragm moves to a flattened position
   b. gas pressure inside the lungs is lowered
   c. inspiratory muscles relax
   d. size of thoracic cavity increases

3. Circle True or False. Vesicular breathing sounds are produced by air rushing through the trachea and bronchi.

4. During normal quiet breathing, about _____ ml of air moves into and out of the lungs with each breath.
   a. 250
   b. 500
   c. 1000
   d. 2000

5. Circle the correct term. Tidal volume / Vital capacity is the maximum amount of air that can be exhaled after a maximal inspiration.

6. Circle True or False. The neural centers that control respiratory rhythm and maintain a rate of 12–18 respirations per minute are located in the medulla and thalamus.

7. Circle the correct term. Changes in pH and oxygen concentrations in the blood are monitored by chemoreceptor regions in the medulla / aortic and carotid bodies.

8. The carbonic acid–bicarbonate buffer system stabilizes arterial blood pH at:
   a. 2.0 ± 1.00
   b. 6.2 ± 0.07
   c. 7.4 ± 0.02
   d. 9.5 ± 1.15

   Text continues on next page.

- ☐ Concentrated HCl and NaOH in dropper bottles
- ☐ 250- and 50-ml beakers
- ☐ Plastic wash bottles containing distilled water
- ☐ Graduated cylinder (100 ml)
- ☐ Glass stirring rod
- ☐ Animal plasma
- ☐ pH meter (standardized with buffer of pH 7)
- ☐ Buffer solution (pH 7)
- ☐ 0.01 M HCl
- ☐ *Human Respiratory System* videotape

PEx PhysioEx™ 8.0 Computer Simulation on page PEx-113

Note: Instructions for using PowerLab® equipment can be found at myA&P.

9. Circle the correct term. <u>Acids / Bases</u> released into the blood by the body cells tend to lower the pH of the blood and cause it to become acidic.
10. Circle True or False. Rate and depth of breathing, hyperventilation, and hypoventilation should have little or no effect on the acid-base balance of blood.

The body's trillions of cells require O_2 and give off CO_2 as a waste the body must get rid of. The **respiratory system** provides the link with the external environment for both taking in O_2 and eliminating CO_2, but it doesn't work alone. The cardiovascular system via its contained blood provides the watery medium for transporting O_2 and CO_2 in the body. Let's look into how the respiratory system carries out its role.

Mechanics of Respiration

Pulmonary ventilation, or **breathing,** consists of two phases: **inspiration,** during which air is taken into the lungs, and **expiration,** during which air passes out of the lungs. As the inspiratory muscles (external intercostals and diaphragm) contract during inspiration, the size of the thoracic cavity increases. The diaphragm moves from its relaxed dome shape to a flattened position, increasing the superoinferior volume. The external intercostals lift the rib cage, increasing the anteroposterior and lateral dimensions (Figure 37A.1). Because the lungs adhere to the thoracic walls like flypaper owing to the presence of serous fluid in the pleural cavity, the intrapulmonary volume (volume within the lungs) also increases, lowering the air (gas) pressure inside the lungs. The gases then expand to fill the available space, creating a partial vacuum that causes air to flow into the lungs—constituting the act of inspiration. during expiration, the inspiratory muscles relax, and the natural tendency of the elastic lung tissue to recoil acts to decrease the intrathoracic and intrapulmonary volumes. As the gas molecules within the lungs are forced closer together, the intrapulmonary pressure rises to a point higher than atmospheric pressure. This causes gases to flow out of the lungs to equalize the pressure inside and outside the lungs—the act of expiration.

ACTIVITY 1

Operating the Model Lung

Observe the model lung, which demonstrates the principles involved in gas flows into and out of the lungs. It is a simple apparatus with a bottle "thorax," a rubber membrane "diaphragm," and balloon "lungs."

1. Go to the demonstration area and work the model lung by moving the rubber diaphragm up and down. The balloons will not fully inflate or deflate, but notice the *relative* changes in balloon (lung) size as the volume of the thoracic cavity is alternately increased and decreased.

2. Check the appropriate columns in the chart concerning these observations in the Exercise 37A Review Sheet at the end of this exercise.

3. Simulate a pneumothorax. Inflate the balloon lungs by pulling down on the diaphragm. Ask your lab partner to let air into the bottle "thorax" by loosening the rubber stopper.

What happens to the balloon lungs?

_____

4. After observing the operation of the model lung, conduct the following tests on your lab partner. Use the tape measure to determine his or her chest circumference by placing the tape around the chest as high up under the armpits as possible. Record the measurements in inches in the appropriate space for each of the conditions on the following page.

Inspiration

Expiration

Diaphragm

FIGURE 37A.1 Rib cage and diaphragm positions during breathing. (a) At the end of a normal inspiration; chest expanded, diaphragm depressed. **(b)** At the end of a normal expiration; chest depressed, diaphragm elevated.

Trachea

Lung

Diaphragm

(a)   **(b)**

Quiet breathing:

Inspiration _____ Expiration _____

Forced breathing:

Inspiration _____ Expiration _____

Do the results coincide with what you expected on the basis

of what you have learned thus far? _____

How does the structural relationship between the balloon-lungs and bottle-thorax differ from that seen in the human lungs and thorax?

_____

_____

_____

Respiratory Sounds

As air flows in and out of the respiratory tree, it produces two characteristic sounds that can be picked up with a stethoscope (auscultated). The **bronchial sounds** are produced by air rushing through the large respiratory passageways (the trachea and the bronchi). The second sound type, **vesicular breathing sounds,** apparently results from air filling the alveolar sacs and resembles the sound of a rustling or muffled breeze.

ACTIVITY 2

Auscultating Respiratory Sounds

1.   Obtain a stethoscope and clean the earpieces with an alcohol swab. Allow the alcohol to dry before donning the stethoscope.

2.   Place the diaphragm of the stethoscope on the throat of the test subject just below the larynx. Listen for bronchial sounds on inspiration and expiration. Move the stethoscope down toward the bronchi until you can no longer hear sounds.

FIGURE 37A.2 Spirographic record for a healthy young adult male. Comparable values for a healthy young adult female are TV = 500 ml, IRV = 1900 ml, ERV = 700 ml, residual volume (RV) = 1100 ml.

3.   Place the stethoscope over the following chest areas and listen for vesicular sounds during respiration (heard primarily during inspiration).

• At various intercostal spaces

• At the *triangle of auscultation* (a small depressed area of the back where the muscles fail to cover the rib cage; located just medial to the inferior part of the scapula)

• Under the clavicle ▬

⚠ Diseased respiratory tissue, mucus, or pus can produce abnormal chest sounds such as rales (a rasping sound) and wheezing (a whistling sound). ◼

Respiratory Volumes and Capacities—Spirometry

A person's size, sex, age, and physical condition produce variations in respiratory volumes. Normal quiet breathing moves about 500 ml of air in and out of the lungs with each breath. As you have seen in the first activity, a person can usually forcibly inhale or exhale much more air than is exchanged in normal quiet breathing. The terms given to the measurable respiratory volumes are defined next. You should memorize these terms and their normal values for an adult male.

Tidal volume (TV): Amount of air inhaled or exhaled with each breath under resting conditions (500 ml)

Inspiratory reserve volume (IRV): Amount of air that can be forcefully inhaled after a normal tidal volume inhalation (3100 ml)

Expiratory reserve volume (ERV): Amount of air that can be forcefully exhaled after a normal tidal volume exhalation (1200 ml)

Vital capacity (VC): Maximum amount of air that can be exhaled after a maximal inspiration (4800 ml)

$$VC = TV + IRV + ERV$$

An idealized tracing of the various respiratory volumes and their relationships to each other is shown in Figure 37A.2.

Respiratory volumes can be measured, as in Activities 3 and 4, with an apparatus called a **spirometer.** There are two major types of spirometers, which give comparable results—the handheld dry, or wheel, spirometers (such as the Wright spirometer illustrated in Figure 37A.3) and "wet" spirometers, such as the Phipps and Bird spirometer and the Collins spirometer (which is available in both recording and nonrecording varieties). The somewhat more sophisticated wet spirometer consists of a plastic or metal *bell* within a rectangular or cylindrical tank that air can be added to or removed from (Figure 37A.4). The outer tank contains water and has a tube running through it to carry air above the water level. The floating bottomless bell is inverted over the water-containing tank and connected to a volume indicator.

FIGURE 37A.3 The Wright handheld dry spirometer. Reset to zero prior to each test.

Volume indicator scale

Drum retainer

Floating bell

Water tank

Valve assembly

(a)

Reset knob

Drum retainer

Free-breathing valve

Mouthpiece

Floating bell

Flexible arm

Water tank

Kymograph drum with chart paper

Ventilometer pen

Thermometer

Power switch

Oxygen inlet

Speed switch (fast, medium, slow)

(b)

FIGURE 37A.4 Wet spirometers. (a) The Phipps and Bird wet spirometer.
(b) The Collins-9L wet recording spirometer.

In nonrecording spirometers, an indicator moves as air is *exhaled,* and only expired air volumes can be measured directly. By contrast, recording spirometers allow both inspired and expired gas volumes to be measured.

Alternatively, BIOPAC® may be used with an airflow transducer to measure respiratory volumes. Those instructions appear in Activity 5.

ACTIVITY 3

Measuring Respiratory Volumes Using Spirometers

The steps for using a nonrecording spirometer and a wet recording spirometer are given separately below.

Using a Nonrecording Spirometer

1. Before using the spirometer, count and record the subject's normal respiratory rate. The subject should face away from you as you make the count.

Respirations per minute: _____

Now identify the parts of the spirometer you will be using by comparing it to the illustration in Figure 37A.3 or 37A.4a. Examine the spirometer volume indicator *before beginning* to make sure you know how to read the scale. Work in pairs, with one person acting as the subject while the other records the data of the volume determinations. *Reset the indicator to zero before beginning each trial.*

Obtain a disposable cardboard mouthpiece. Insert it in the open end of the valve assembly (attached to the flexible tube) of the wet spirometer or over the fixed stem of the handheld dry spirometer. Before beginning, the subject should practice exhaling through the mouthpiece without exhaling through the nose, or prepare to use the nose clips (clean them first with an alcohol swab). If you are using the handheld spirometer, make sure its dial faces upward so that the volumes can be easily read during the tests.

2. The subject should stand erect during testing. Conduct the test three times for each required measurement. Record the data where indicated in this section, and then find the average volume figure for that respiratory measurement. After you have completed the trials and computed the averages, enter the average values on the table prepared on the chalkboard for tabulation of class data,* and copy all averaged data onto the Exercise 37A Review Sheet.

3. Measuring tidal volume (TV). The TV, or volume of air inhaled and exhaled with each normal respiration, is approximately 500 ml. To conduct the test, inhale a normal breath, and then exhale a normal breath of air into the spirometer mouthpiece. (Do not force the expiration!) Record the volume and repeat the test twice.

*Note to the Instructor: The format of class data tabulation can be similar to that shown here. However, it would be interesting to divide the class into smokers and nonsmokers and then compare the mean average VC and ERV for each group. Such a comparison might help to determine if smokers are handicapped in any way. It also might be a good opportunity for an informal discussion of the early warning signs of bronchitis and emphysema, which are primarily smokers' diseases.

trial 1: _____ ml   trial 2: _____ ml

trial 3: _____ ml   average TV: _____ ml

4. Compute the subject's **minute respiratory volume (MRV)** using the following formula:

$$MRV = TV \times respirations/min = \underline{\qquad} \ ml/min$$

5. Measuring expiratory reserve volume (ERV). The ERV is the volume of air that can be forcibly exhaled after a normal expiration. Normally it ranges between 700 and 1200 ml.

Inhale and exhale normally two or three times, then insert the spirometer mouthpiece and exhale forcibly as much of the additional air as you can. Record your results, and repeat the test twice again.

trial 1: _____ ml   trial 2: _____ ml

trial 3: _____ ml   average ERV: _____ ml

ERV is dramatically reduced in conditions in which the elasticity of the lungs is decreased by a chronic obstructive pulmonary disease (COPD) such as **emphysema.** Since energy must be used to *deflate* the lungs in such conditions, expiration is physically exhausting to individuals suffering from COPD. ■

6. Measuring vital capacity (VC). The VC, or total exchangeable air of the lungs (the sum of TV + IRV + ERV), normally ranges from 3100 ml to 4800 ml.

Breathe in and out normally two or three times, and then bend forward and exhale all the air possible. Then, as you raise yourself to the upright position, inhale as fully as possible. It is important to *strain* to inhale the maximum amount of air that you can. Quickly insert the mouthpiece, and exhale as forcibly as you can. Record your results and repeat the test twice again.

trial 1: _____ ml   trial 2: _____ ml

trial 3: _____ ml   average VC: _____ ml

7. The inspiratory reserve volume (IRV), or volume of air that can be forcibly inhaled following a normal inspiration, can now be computed using the average values obtained for TV, ERV, and VC and plugging them into the equation:

$$IRV = VC - (TV + ERV)$$

Record your average IRV: _____ ml

The normal IRV is substantial, ranging from 1900 to 3100 ml. How does your computed value compare?

_____

Steps 8–10, which provide common directions for use of both nonrecording and recording spirometers, continue on page 556 after the wet recording spirometer directions.

Using a Recording Spirometer

1. In preparation for recording, familiarize yourself with the spirometer by comparing it to the equipment illustrated in Figure 37A.4b.

2. Examine the chart paper, noting that its horizontal lines represent milliliter units. To apply the chart paper to the recording drum, first lift the drum retainer and then remove the kymograph drum. Wrap a sheet of chart paper around the drum, *making sure that the right edge overlaps the left*. Fasten it with tape, and then replace the kymograph drum and lower the drum retainer into its original position in the hole in the top of the drum.

3. Raise and lower the floating bell several times, noting as you do so that the *ventilometer pen* moves up and down on the drum. This pen, which writes in black ink, will be used for recording and should be adjusted so that it records in the approximate middle of the chart paper. This adjustment is made by repositioning the floating bell using the *reset knob* on the metal pulley at the top of the spirometer apparatus. The other pen, the respirometer pen, which records in red ink, will not be used for these tests and should be moved away from the drum's recording surface.

4. Record your normal respiratory rate. Clean the nose clips with an alcohol swab. While you wait for the alcohol to air dry, count and record your normal respiratory rate.

Respirations per minute: _____

5. Recording tidal volume. After the alcohol has air dried, apply the nose clips to your nose. This will enforce mouth breathing.

Open the *free-breathing valve*. Insert a disposable cardboard mouthpiece into the end (valve assembly) of the breathing tube, and then insert the mouthpiece into your mouth. Practice breathing for several breaths to get used to the apparatus. At this time, you are still breathing room air.

Set the spirometer switch to **SLOW** (32 mm/min). Close the free-breathing valve, and breathe in a normal manner for 2 minutes to record your tidal volume—the amount of air inspired or expired with each normal respiratory cycle. This recording should show a regular pattern of inspiration-expiration spikes and should gradually move upward on the chart paper. (A downward slope indicates that there is an air leak somewhere in the system—most likely at the mouthpiece.) Notice that on an apparatus using a counterweighted pen, such as the Collins-9L Ventilometer shown in Figure 37A.4b, inspirations are recorded by upstrokes and expirations are recorded by downstrokes.*

6. Recording vital capacity. To record your vital capacity, take the deepest possible inspiration you can and then exhale to the greatest extent possible—really *push* the air out. The recording obtained should resemble that shown in Figure 37A.5. Repeat the vital capacity measurement twice again. Then turn off the spirometer and remove the chart paper from the kymograph drum.

7. Determine and record your measured, averaged, and corrected respiratory volumes. Because the pressure and tempera-

---

*If a Collins survey spirometer is used, the situation is exactly opposite: Upstrokes are expirations and downstrokes are inspirations.

ture inside the spirometer are influenced by room temperature and differ from those in the body, all measured values are to be multiplied by a **BTPS** (body temperature, atmospheric pressure, and water saturation) **factor.** At room temperature, the BTPS factor is typically 1.1 or very close to that value. Hence, you will multiply your average measured values by 1.1 to obtain your corrected respiratory volume values. Copy the averaged and corrected values onto the Exercise 37A Review Sheet.

- Tidal volume (TV). Select a typical resting tidal breath recording. Subtract the millimeter value of the trough (exhalation) from the millimeter value of the peak (inspiration). Record this value below as *measured TV 1*. Select two other TV tracings to determine the TV values for the TV 2 and TV 3 measurements. Then, determine your average TV and multiply it by 1.1 to obtain the BTPS-corrected average TV value.

measured TV 1: _____ ml   average TV: _____ ml

measured TV 2: _____ ml   corrected average TV:

measured TV 3: _____ ml   _____ ml

Also compute your **minute respiratory volume (MRV)** using the following formula:

MRV = TV × respirations/min = _____ ml/min

- Inspiratory capacity (IC). In the first vital capacity recording, find the expiratory trough immediately preceding the maximal inspiratory peak achieved during vital capacity determination. Subtract the milliliter value of that expiration from the value corresponding to the peak of the maximal inspiration that immediately follows. For example, according to Figure 37A.5, these values would be

$$6600 - 3650 = 2950 \text{ ml}$$

Record your computed value and the results of the two subsequent tests on the appropriate lines below. Then calculate the measured and corrected inspiratory capacity averages and record.

measured IC 1: _____ ml   average IC: _____ ml

measured IC 2: _____ ml   corrected
                              average IC: _____ ml

measured IC 3: _____ ml

- Inspiratory reserve volume (IRV). Subtract the corrected average tidal volume from the corrected average for the inspiratory capacity and record below.

IRV = corrected average IC − corrected average TV

corrected average IRV _____ ml

- Expiratory reserve volume (ERV). Subtract the number of milliliters corresponding to the trough of the maximal expiration obtained during the vital capacity recording from milliliters corresponding to the last *normal* expiration

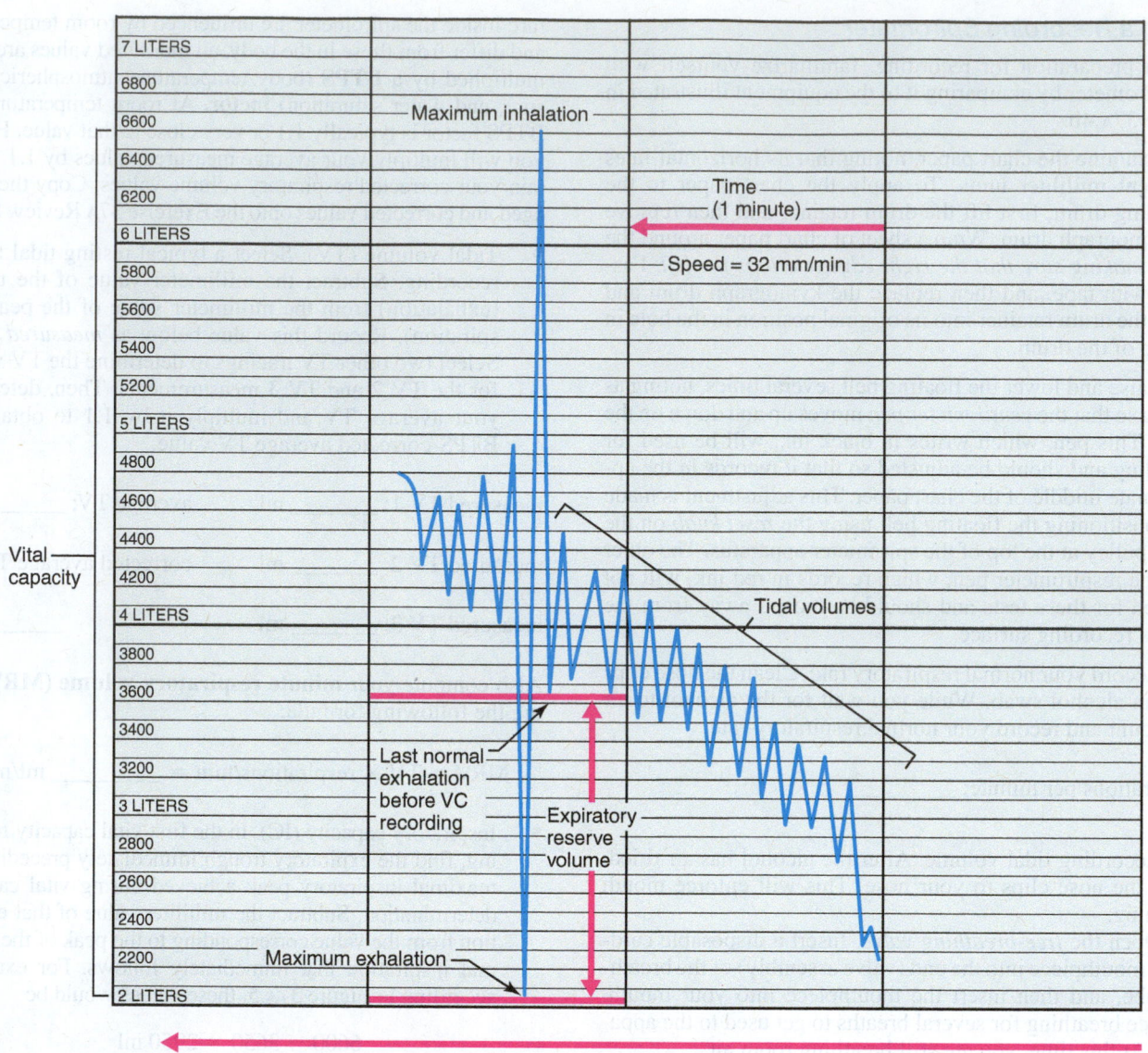

FIGURE 37A.5 A typical spirometry recording of tidal volume, inspiratory capacity, expiratory reserve volume, and vital capacity. At a drum speed of 32 mm/min, each vertical column of the chart represents a time interval of 1 minute. (Note that downstrokes represent exhalations and upstrokes represent inhalations.)

before the VC maneuver is performed. For example, according to Figure 37A.5, these values would be

$$3650 \text{ ml} - 2050 \text{ ml} = 1600 \text{ ml}$$

Record your measured and averaged values (three trials) below.

measured ERV 1: _____ ml   average ERV: _____ ml

measured ERV 2: _____ ml   corrected average ERV:

measured ERV 3: _____ ml   _____ ml

- Vital capacity (VC). Add your corrected values for ERV and IC to obtain the corrected average VC. Record below and on the Exercise 37A Review Sheet.

corrected average VC: _____ ml

Now continue with step 8 (below) whether you are following the procedure for the nonrecording or recording spirometer.

8.   Figure out how closely your measured average vital capacity volume compares with the *predicted values* for someone your age, sex, and height. Obtain the predicted figure either from Table 37A.1 (male values) or Table 37A.2 (female values). Notice that you will have to convert your height in inches to centimeters (cm) to find the corresponding value. This is easily done by multiplying your height in inches by 2.54.

Computed height: _____ cm

Predicted VC value (obtained from the appropriate table):

_____ ml

TABLE 37A.1 Predicted Vital Capacities (ml) for Males

Height in centimeters

Age	146	148	150	152	154	156	158	160	162	164	166	168	170	172	174	176	178	180	182	184	186	188	190	192	194
16	3765	3820	3870	3920	3975	4025	4075	4130	4180	4230	4285	4335	4385	4440	4490	4540	4590	4645	4695	4745	4800	4850	4900	4955	5005
18	3740	3790	3840	3890	3940	3995	4045	4095	4145	4200	4250	4300	4350	4405	4455	4505	4555	4610	4660	4710	4760	4815	4865	4915	4965
20	3710	3760	3810	3860	3910	3960	4015	4065	4115	4165	4215	4265	4320	4370	4420	4470	4520	4570	4625	4675	4725	4775	4825	4875	4930
22	3680	3730	3780	3830	3880	3930	3980	4030	4080	4135	4185	4235	4285	4335	4385	4435	4485	4535	4585	4635	4685	4735	4790	4840	4890
24	3635	3685	3735	3785	3835	3885	3935	3985	4035	4085	4135	4185	4235	4285	4330	4380	4430	4480	4530	4580	4630	4680	4730	4780	4830
26	3605	3655	3705	3755	3805	3855	3905	3955	4000	4050	4100	4150	4200	4250	4300	4350	4395	4445	4495	4545	4595	4645	4695	4740	4790
28	3575	3625	3675	3725	3775	3820	3870	3920	3970	4020	4070	4115	4165	4215	4265	4310	4360	4410	4460	4510	4555	4605	4655	4705	4755
30	3550	3595	3645	3695	3740	3790	3840	3890	3935	3985	4035	4080	4130	4180	4230	4275	4325	4375	4425	4470	4520	4570	4615	4665	4715
32	3520	3565	3615	3665	3710	3760	3810	3855	3905	3950	4000	4050	4095	4145	4195	4240	4290	4340	4385	4435	4485	4530	4580	4625	4675
34	3475	3525	3570	3620	3665	3715	3760	3810	3855	3905	3950	4000	4045	4095	4140	4190	4225	4285	4330	4380	4425	4475	4520	4570	4615
36	3445	3495	3540	3585	3635	3680	3730	3775	3825	3870	3920	3965	4010	4060	4105	4155	4200	4250	4295	4340	4390	4435	4485	4530	4580
38	3415	3465	3510	3555	3605	3650	3695	3745	3790	3840	3885	3930	3980	4025	4070	4120	4165	4210	4260	4305	4350	4400	4445	4495	4540
40	3385	3435	3480	3525	3575	3620	3665	3710	3760	3805	3850	3900	3945	3990	4035	4085	4130	4175	4220	4270	4315	4360	4410	4455	4500
42	3360	3405	3450	3495	3540	3590	3635	3680	3725	3770	3820	3865	3910	3955	4000	4050	4095	4140	4185	4230	4280	4325	4370	4415	4460
44	3315	3360	3405	3450	3495	3540	3585	3630	3675	3725	3770	3815	3860	3905	3950	3995	4040	4085	4130	4175	4220	4270	4315	4360	4405
46	3285	3330	3375	3420	3465	3510	3555	3600	3645	3690	3735	3780	3825	3870	3915	3960	4005	4050	4095	4140	4185	4230	4275	4320	4365
48	3255	3300	3345	3390	3435	3480	3525	3570	3615	3655	3700	3745	3790	3835	3880	3925	3970	4015	4060	4105	4150	4190	4235	4280	4325
50	3210	3255	3300	3345	3390	3430	3475	3520	3565	3610	3650	3695	3740	3785	3830	3870	3915	3960	4005	4050	4090	4135	4180	4225	4270
52	3185	3225	3270	3315	3355	3400	3445	3490	3530	3575	3620	3660	3705	3750	3795	3835	3880	3925	3970	4010	4055	4100	4140	4185	4230
54	3155	3195	3240	3285	3325	3370	3415	3455	3500	3540	3585	3630	3670	3715	3760	3800	3845	3890	3930	3975	4020	4060	4105	4145	4190
56	3125	3165	3210	3255	3295	3340	3380	3425	3465	3510	3550	3595	3640	3680	3725	3765	3810	3850	3895	3940	3980	4025	4065	4110	4150
58	3080	3125	3165	3210	3250	3290	3335	3375	3420	3460	3500	3545	3585	3630	3670	3715	3755	3800	3840	3880	3925	3965	4010	4050	4095
60	3050	3095	3135	3175	3220	3260	3300	3345	3385	3430	3470	3500	3555	3595	3635	3680	3720	3760	3805	3845	3885	3930	3970	4015	4055
62	3020	3060	3110	3150	3190	3230	3270	3310	3350	3390	3440	3480	3520	3560	3600	3640	3680	3730	3770	3810	3850	3890	3930	3970	4020
64	2990	3030	3080	3120	3160	3200	3240	3280	3320	3360	3400	3440	3490	3530	3570	3610	3650	3690	3730	3770	3810	3850	3900	3940	3980
66	2950	2990	3030	3070	3110	3150	3190	3230	3270	3310	3350	3390	3430	3470	3510	3550	3600	3640	3680	3720	3760	3800	3840	3880	3920
68	2920	2960	3000	3040	3080	3120	3160	3200	3240	3280	3320	3360	3400	3440	3480	3520	3560	3600	3640	3680	3720	3760	3800	3840	3880
70	2890	2930	2970	3010	3050	3090	3130	3170	3210	3250	3290	3330	3370	3410	3450	3480	3520	3560	3600	3640	3680	3720	3760	3800	3840
72	2860	2900	2940	2980	3020	3060	3100	3140	3180	3210	3250	3290	3330	3370	3410	3450	3490	3530	3570	3610	3650	3680	3720	3760	3800
74	2820	2860	2900	2930	2970	3010	3050	3090	3130	3170	3200	3240	3280	3320	3360	3400	3440	3470	3510	3550	3590	3630	3670	3710	3740

Courtesy of Warren E. Collins, Inc., Braintree, Mass.

TABLE 37A.2   **Predicted Vital Capacities (ml) for Females**

Height in centimeters

Age	146	148	150	152	154	156	158	160	162	164	166	168	170	172	174	176	178	180	182	184	186	188	190	192	194
16	2950	2990	3030	3070	3110	3150	3190	3230	3270	3310	3350	3390	3430	3470	3510	3550	3590	3630	3670	3715	3755	3800	3840	3880	3920
17	2935	2975	3015	3055	3095	3135	3175	3215	3255	3295	3335	3375	3415	3455	3495	3535	3575	3615	3655	3695	3740	3780	3820	3860	3900
18	2920	2960	3000	3040	3080	3120	3160	3200	3240	3280	3320	3360	3400	3440	3480	3520	3560	3600	3640	3680	3720	3760	3800	3840	3880
20	2890	2930	2970	3010	3050	3090	3130	3170	3210	3250	3290	3330	3370	3410	3450	3490	3525	3565	3605	3645	3695	3720	3760	3800	3840
22	2860	2900	2940	2980	3020	3060	3095	3135	3175	3215	3255	3290	3330	3370	3410	3450	3490	3530	3570	3610	3650	3685	3725	3765	3800
24	2830	2870	2910	2950	2985	3025	3065	3100	3140	3180	3220	3260	3300	3335	3375	3415	3455	3490	3530	3570	3610	3650	3685	3725	3765
26	2800	2840	2880	2920	2960	3000	3035	3070	3110	3150	3190	3230	3265	3300	3340	3380	3420	3455	3495	3530	3570	3610	3650	3685	3725
28	2775	2810	2850	2890	2930	2965	3000	3040	3070	3115	3155	3190	3230	3270	3305	3345	3380	3420	3460	3495	3535	3570	3610	3650	3685
30	2745	2780	2820	2860	2895	2935	2970	3010	3045	3085	3120	3160	3195	3235	3270	3310	3345	3385	3420	3460	3495	3535	3570	3610	3645
32	2715	2750	2790	2825	2865	2900	2940	2975	3015	3050	3090	3125	3160	3200	3235	3275	3310	3350	3385	3425	3460	3495	3535	3570	3610
34	2685	2725	2760	2795	2835	2870	2910	2945	2980	3020	3055	3090	3130	3165	3200	3240	3275	3310	3350	3385	3425	3460	3495	3535	3570
36	2655	2695	2730	2765	2805	2840	2875	2910	2950	2985	3020	3060	3095	3130	3165	3205	3240	3275	3310	3350	3385	3420	3460	3495	3530
38	2630	2665	2700	2735	2770	2810	2845	2880	2915	2950	2990	3025	3060	3095	3130	3170	3205	3240	3275	3310	3350	3385	3420	3455	3490
40	2600	2635	2670	2705	2740	2775	2810	2850	2885	2920	2955	2990	3025	3060	3095	3135	3170	3205	3240	3275	3310	3345	3380	3420	3455
42	2570	2605	2640	2675	2710	2745	2780	2815	2850	2885	2920	2955	2990	3025	3060	3100	3135	3170	3205	3240	3275	3310	3345	3380	3415
44	2540	2575	2610	2645	2680	2715	2750	2785	2820	2855	2890	2925	2960	2995	3030	3060	3095	3130	3165	3200	3235	3270	3305	3340	3375
46	2510	2545	2580	2615	2650	2685	2720	2750	2785	2820	2855	2890	2925	2960	2995	3030	3060	3095	3130	3165	3200	3235	3270	3305	3340
48	2480	2515	2550	2585	2620	2650	2685	2715	2750	2785	2820	2855	2890	2925	2960	2995	3030	3060	3095	3130	3160	3195	3230	3265	3300
50	2455	2485	2520	2555	2590	2625	2655	2690	2720	2755	2785	2820	2855	2890	2925	2955	2990	3025	3060	3090	3125	3155	3190	3225	3260
52	2425	2455	2490	2525	2555	2590	2625	2655	2690	2720	2755	2790	2820	2855	2890	2925	2955	2990	3020	3055	3090	3125	3155	3190	3220
54	2395	2425	2460	2495	2530	2560	2590	2625	2655	2690	2720	2755	2790	2820	2855	2885	2920	2950	2985	3020	3050	3085	3115	3150	3180
56	2365	2400	2430	2460	2495	2525	2560	2590	2625	2655	2690	2720	2755	2790	2820	2855	2885	2920	2950	2980	3015	3045	3080	3110	3145
58	2335	2370	2400	2430	2460	2495	2525	2560	2590	2625	2655	2690	2720	2750	2785	2815	2850	2880	2920	2945	2975	3010	3040	3075	3105
60	2305	2340	2370	2400	2430	2460	2495	2525	2560	2590	2625	2655	2685	2720	2750	2780	2810	2845	2875	2915	2940	2970	3000	3035	3065
62	2280	2310	2340	2370	2405	2435	2465	2495	2525	2560	2590	2620	2655	2685	2715	2745	2775	2810	2840	2870	2900	2935	2965	2995	3025
64	2250	2280	2310	2340	2370	2400	2430	2465	2495	2525	2555	2585	2620	2650	2680	2710	2740	2770	2805	2835	2865	2895	2925	2955	2990
66	2220	2250	2280	2310	2340	2370	2400	2430	2460	2495	2525	2555	2585	2615	2645	2675	2705	2735	2765	2800	2825	2860	2890	2920	2950
68	2190	2220	2250	2280	2310	2340	2370	2400	2430	2460	2490	2520	2550	2580	2610	2640	2670	2700	2730	2760	2795	2820	2850	2880	2910
70	2160	2190	2220	2250	2280	2310	2340	2370	2400	2425	2455	2485	2515	2545	2575	2605	2635	2665	2695	2725	2755	2780	2810	2840	2870
72	2130	2160	2190	2220	2250	2280	2310	2335	2365	2395	2425	2455	2480	2510	2540	2570	2600	2630	2660	2685	2715	2745	2775	2805	2830
74	2100	2130	2160	2190	2220	2245	2275	2305	2335	2360	2390	2420	2450	2475	2505	2535	2565	2590	2620	2650	2680	2710	2740	2765	2795

Courtesy of Warren E. Collins, Inc., Braintree, Mass.

Use the following equation to compute your VC as a percentage of the predicted VC value:

$$\% \text{ of predicted VC} = \frac{\text{average VC}}{\text{predicted value} \times 100}$$

% predicted VC value: _____ %

Figure 37A.2 on page 552 is an idealized tracing of the respiratory volumes described and tested in this exercise. Examine it carefully. How closely do your test results compare to the values in the tracing?

_____

9.   Computing residual volume. A respiratory volume that cannot be experimentally demonstrated here is the residual volume (RV). RV is the amount of air remaining in the lungs after a maximal expiratory effort. The presence of residual air (usually about 1200 ml) that cannot be voluntarily flushed from the lungs is important because it allows gas exchange to go on continuously—even between breaths.

   Although the residual volume cannot be measured directly, it can be approximated by using one of the following factors:

For ages 16–34   Factor = 0.250
For ages 35–49   Factor = 0.305
For ages 50–69   Factor = 0.445

Compute your predicted RV using the following equation:

$$RV = VC \times \text{factor}$$

 10.   Recording is finished for this subject. Before continuing with the next member of your group:

• Dispose of used cardboard mouthpieces in the autoclave bag.

• Swish the valve assembly (if removable) in the 70% ethanol solution, then rinse with tap water.

• Put a fresh mouthpiece into the valve assembly (or on the stem of the handheld spirometer). Using the procedures outlined above, measure and record the respiratory volumes for all members of your group. ■

Forced Expiratory Volume (FEV$_T$) Measurement

While not really diagnostic, pulmonary function tests can help the clinician distinguish between obstructive and restrictive pulmonary diseases. (In obstructive disorders, like chronic bronchitis and asthma, airway resistance is increased, whereas in restrictive diseases, such as polio and tuberculosis, total lung capacity declines.) Two highly useful pulmonary function tests used for this purpose are the FVC and the FEV$_T$ (see Figure 37A.6).

   The **FVC** (forced vital capacity) measures the amount of gas expelled when the subject takes the deepest possible breath and then exhales forcefully and rapidly. This volume is reduced in those with restrictive pulmonary disease. The **FEV$_T$** (forced expiratory volume) involves the same basic testing procedure, but it specifically looks at the percentage of the vital capacity that is exhaled during specific time intervals of the FVC test. FEV$_1$, for instance, is the amount exhaled during the first second. Healthy individuals can expire 75% to 85% of their FVC in the first second. The FEV$_1$ is low in those with obstructive disease.

Measuring the FVC and FEV$_1$

Directions provided here for the FEV$_T$ determination apply only to the recording spirometer.

1.   Prepare to make your recording as described for the recording spirometer, steps 1–5 on page 555.

2.   At a signal agreed upon by you and your lab partner, take the deepest inspiration possible and hold it for 1 to 2 seconds. As the inspiratory peak levels off, your partner is to change the drum speed to **FAST** (1920 mm/min) so that the distance between the vertical lines on the chart represents 1 second.

3.   Once the drum speed is changed, exhale as much air as you can as rapidly and forcibly as possible.

4.   When the tracing plateaus (bottoms out), stop recording and determine your FVC. Subtract the milliliter reading in the expiration trough (the bottom plateau) from the preceding inhalation peak (the top plateau). Record this value.

FVC: _____ ml

5.   Prepare to calculate the FEV$_1$. Draw a vertical line intersecting with the spirogram tracing at the precise point that exhalation began. Identify this line as *line 1*. From line 1, measure 32 mm horizontally to the left, and draw a second vertical line. Label this as *line 2*. The distance between the two lines represents 1 second, and the volume exhaled in the first second is read where line 2 intersects the spirogram tracing. Subtract that milliliter value from the milliliter value of the inhalation peak (at the intersection of line 1), to determine the volume of gas expired in the first second. According to the values given in Figure 37A.6, that figure would be 3400 ml (6800 ml − 3400 ml). Record your measured value below.

Milliliters of gas expired in second 1: _____ ml

6.   To compute the FEV$_1$ use the following equation:

$$FEV_1 = \frac{\text{volume expired in second 1}}{\text{FVC volume}} \times 100\%$$

Record your calculated value below and on the Exercise 37A Review Sheet.

FEV$_1$: _____ % of FVC ■

Measuring Respiratory Volumes Using BIOPAC®

In this activity, you will measure respiratory volumes using the BIOPAC® airflow transducer. An example of these

SURVEY SPIROMETER
CHART PAPER

Speed setting
changed

Interval of
breath
holding at
inhalation
peak

Time
(1 minute)
Speed = 32 mm/min

Time
(1 second)
Speed = 1920 mm/min

Exhalation
trough

Direction of recording

8 LITERS

7800
7600
7400
7200
7 LITERS
6800
6600
6400
6200
6 LITERS
5800
5600
5400
5200
5 LITERS
4800
4600
4400
4200
4 LITERS
3800
3600
3400
3200
3 LITERS
2800
2600
2400
2200
2 LITERS
2000

FIGURE 37A.6 A recording of the forced vital capacity (FVC) and forced expiratory volume (FEV) or timed vital capacity test.

FIGURE 37A.7 Example of a computer-generated spirogram.

volumes is demonstrated in the computer-generated spirogram in Figure 37A.7. Since it is not possible to measure **residual volume (RV)** using the airflow transducer, assume that it is 1.0 liter for each subject, which is a reasonable estimation. It is also important to estimate the **predicted vital capacity** of the subject for comparison to the measured value. A rough estimate of the vital capacity in liters (VC) of a subject can be calculated using the following formulas based on height in centimeters (H) and age in years (A).

Male VC $= (0.052)H - (0.022)A - 3.60$

Female VC $= (0.041)H - (0.018)A - 2.69$

Because many factors besides height and age influence vital capacity, it should be assumed that measured values up to 20% above or below the calculated predicted value are normal.

Setting Up the Equipment

1.   Connect the BIOPAC® unit to the computer and turn the computer **ON.**

2.   Make sure the BIOPAC® unit is **OFF.**

3.   Plug in the equipment as shown in Figure 37A.8.

•   Airflow transducer—CH 1

FIGURE 37A.8 Setting up the BIOPAC® equipment. Plug the airflow transducer into Channel 1.

BIOPAC data acquisition unit

Airflow transducer
(plugs into Channel 1)

FIGURE 37A.9 Placement of the calibration syringe and filter assembly onto the airflow transducer for calibration.

4. Turn the BIOPAC® unit **ON.**

5. Place a *clean* bacteriological filter onto the end of the BIOPAC® calibration syringe as shown in Figure 37A.9. Since the subject will be blowing through a filter, it is necessary to use a filter for calibration also.

6. Insert the calibration syringe and filter assembly into the airflow transducer on the side labeled **Inlet.**

7. Start the BIOPAC® Student Lab program on the computer by double-clicking the icon on the desktop or by following your instructor's guidance.

8. Select lesson **L12-Lung-1** from the menu, and click **OK.**

9. Type in a filename that will save this subject's data on the computer hard drive. You may want to use the subject's last name followed by Lung-1 (for example, SmithLung-1), then click **OK.**

Calibrating the Equipment

Two precautions must be followed:

*   The airflow transducer is sensitive to gravity, so it must be held directly parallel to the ground during calibration and recording.

*   Do not hold onto the airflow transducer when it is attached to the calibration syringe and filter assembly—the syringe tip is likely to break. See Figure 37A.10 for the proper handling of the calibration assembly.

1. Make sure the plunger is pulled all the way out. While the assembly is held in a steady position parallel to the ground,

FIGURE 37A.10 Proper handling of the calibration assembly.

FIGURE 37A.11 Example of calibration data.

click **Calibrate** and then **OK** after you have read the alert box. This part of the calibration will terminate automatically with an alert box ensuring that you have read the onscreen instructions and those indicated in step 2, below.

2. The final part of the calibration involves simulating five breathing cycles using the calibration syringe. A single cycle consists of:

*   Pushing the plunger in (taking 1 second for this stroke)

*   Waiting for 2 seconds

*   Pulling the plunger out (taking 1 second for this stroke)

*   Waiting 2 seconds

Remember to hold the airflow transducer directly parallel to the ground during calibration and recording.

3. When ready to perform this second stage of the calibration, click **Yes.** After you have completed five cycles, click **End Calibration.**

4. Observe the data, which should look similar to that in Figure 37A.11.

*   If the data look very different, click **Redo Calibration** and repeat the steps above.

*   If the data look similar, gently remove the calibration syringe, leaving the air filter attached to the transducer. Proceed to the next section.

Recording the data

Follow these procedures precisely, because the airflow transducer is very sensitive. Hints to obtain the best data:

*   Always insert air filter on, and breathe through, the transducer side labeled **Inlet.**

*   Keep the airflow transducer upright at all times.

*   The subject should not look at the computer screen during the recording of data.

*   The subject must keep a nose clip on throughout the experiment.

1. Insert a clean mouthpiece into the air filter that is already attached to the airflow transducer. *Be sure that the filter is attached to the **Inlet** side of the airflow transducer.*

FIGURE 37A.12 **Proper equipment setup for recording data.**

2. Write the name of the subject on the mouthpiece and air filter. For safety purposes, each subject must use his or her own air filter and mouthpiece.

3. The subject should now place the nose clip on the nose (or hold the nose very tightly with finger pinch), wrap the lips tightly around the mouthpiece, and begin breathing normally through the airflow transducer, as shown in Figure 37A.12.

4. When prepared, the subject will complete the following unbroken series with nose plugged and lips tightly sealed around the mouthpiece:

- Take five normal breaths (1 breath = inhale + exhale).
- Inhale as much air as possible.
- Exhale as much air as possible.
- Take five normal breaths.

5. When the subject is prepared to proceed, click **Record** on the first normal inhalation and proceed. When the subject finishes the last exhalation at the end of the series, click **Stop**.

6. Observe the data, which should look similar to that in Figure 37A.13.

- If the data look very different, click **Redo** and repeat the steps above. Be certain that the lips are sealed around the mouthpiece, the nose is completely plugged, and the transducer is upright.
- If the data look similar, proceed to step 7.

7. When finished, click **Done.** A pop-up window will appear.

- Click **Yes** if you are done and want to stop recording.
- To record from another subject select **Record from another Subject** and return to step 1 under Recording the Data. You will not need to redo the calibration procedure for the second subject.
- If continuing to the data Analysis section, select **Analyze current data file** and proceed to step 2 of the Data Analysis section.

FIGURE 37A.13 **Example of pulmonary data.**

Data Analysis

1. If just starting the BIOPAC® program to perform data analysis, enter **Review Saved Data** mode and choose the file with the subject's Lung data (for example, SmithLung-1).

2. Observe how the channel numbers are designated: CH 1— Airflow; CH 2—Volume.

3. To set up the display for optimal viewing, hide CH 1— Airflow. To do this, hold down the Ctrl key (PC) or Option key (Mac) while using the cursor to click the Channel box 1 (the small box with a 1 at the upper left of the screen).

4. To analyze the data, set up the first pair of channel/measurement boxes at the top of the screen by selecting the following channel and measurement type from the drop-down menu:

Channel	Measurement
CH 2	p-p

5. Take two measures for an averaged TV calculation: Use the arrow cursor and click the I-beam cursor box on the lower right side of the screen to activate the "area selection" function. Using the activated I-beam cursor, highlight the inhalation of cycle 3 as shown in Figure 37A.14.

FIGURE 37A.14 **Highlighting data for the first three breaths.**

6. The computer automatically calculates the **p-p** value for the selected area. This measure is the difference between the highest and lowest values in the selected area. Note the value. Use the I-beam cursor to select the exhalation of cycle 3 and note the **p-p** value.

7. Calculate the average of the two **p-p** values. This represents the **tidal volume** (in liters). Record the value in the Pulmonary Measurements chart below:

Pulmonary Measurements

Volumes	Measurements (liters)
Tidal volume (TV)	
Inspiratory reserve volume (IRV)	
Expiratory reserve volume (ERV)	
Vital capacity (VC)	
Residual volume (RV)	1.00 (assumed)

8. Use the I-beam cursor to measure the IRV: Highlight from the peak of maximum inhalation to the peak of the last normal inhalation just before it (see Figure 37A.7 for an example of IRV). Observe and record the **Δ (delta)** value in the chart (to the nearest 0.01 liter).

9. Use the I-beam cursor to measure the ERV: Highlight from the trough of maximum exhalation to the trough of the last normal exhalation just before it (see Figure 37A.7 for an example of ERV). Observe and record the **Δ (delta)** value in the chart (to the nearest 0.01 liter).

10. Last, use the I-beam cursor to measure the VC: Highlight from the trough of maximum exhalation to the peak of maximum inhalation (see Figure 37A.7 for an example of VC). Observe and record the **p-p** value in the chart (to the nearest 0.01 liter).

11. When finished, **Exit** the program.

Using the measured data, calculate the capacities listed in the Calculated Pulmonary Capacities chart.

Use the formula in the introduction of this activity (page 561) to calculate the predicted vital capacity of the subject based on height and age.

Predicted VC: _____ liters

Calculated Pulmonary Capacities

Capacity	Formula	Calculation (liters)
Inspiratory capacity (IC)	= TV + IRV	
Functional residual capacity (FRC)	= ERV + RV	
Total lung capacity (TLC)	= TV + RV + IRV + ERV	

How does the measured vital capacity compare to the predicted vital capacity?

_____

_____

_____

Describe why height and weight might correspond with a subject's VC.

_____

_____

_____

What other factors might influence the VC of a subject?

_____

_____

Factors Influencing Rate and Depth of Respiration

The neural centers that control respiratory rhythm and maintain a rate of 12 to 18 respirations/min are located in the medulla and pons. On occasion, input from the stretch receptors in the lungs (via the vagus nerve to the medulla) modifies the respiratory rate, as in cases of extreme overinflation of the lungs (Hering-Breuer reflex).

Death occurs when medullary centers are completely suppressed, as from an overdose of sleeping pills or gross overindulgence in alcohol, and respiration ceases completely. ■

Although the nervous system centers initiate the basic rhythm of breathing, there is no question that physical phenomena such as talking, yawning, coughing, and exercise can modify the rate and depth of respiration. So, too, can chemical factors such as changes in oxygen or carbon dioxide concentrations in the blood or fluctuations in blood pH. Changes in carbon dioxide blood levels seem to act directly on the medulla control centers, whereas changes in pH and oxygen concentrations are monitored by chemoreceptor regions in the aortic and carotid bodies, which in turn send input to the medulla. The experimental sequence in Activity 6 is designed to test the relative importance of various physical and chemical factors in the process of respiration.

ACTIVITY 6

Visualizing Respiratory Variations Using the Physiograph-Pneumograph Apparatus*

The **pneumograph,** an apparatus that records variations in breathing patterns, is the best means of observing respiratory variations resulting from physical and chemical factors. The chest pneumograph is a coiled rubber hose that is attached around the thorax. As the subject breathes, chest movements produce pressure changes within the pneumograph that are transmitted to a recorder.

The instructor will demonstrate the method of setting up the recording equipment and discuss the interpretation of the results. Work in pairs so that one person can mark the record to identify the test for later interpretation. Ideally, the student being tested should face away from the recording apparatus to prevent voluntary modification of the record.

1. Attach the pneumograph tubing firmly, but not restrictively, around the thoracic cage at the level of the sixth rib, leaving room for chest expansion during testing. If the subject is female, position the tubing above the breasts to prevent slippage during testing. Set the pneumograph speed at 1 or 2, and the time signal at 10-second intervals. Record quiet breathing for 1 minute with the subject in a sitting position.

Record breaths per minute: _____

2. Make a vital capacity tracing: Record a maximal inhalation followed by a maximal exhalation. This should correlate to the vital capacity measurement obtained earlier and will provide a baseline for comparison during the rest of the pneumograph testing. Stop recording, and mark the graph appropriately to indicate tidal volume, expiratory reserve volume, inspiratory reserve volume, and vital capacity (the total of the three measurements). Also mark, with arrows, the direction the recording stylus moves during inspiration and during expiration.

Measure in mm the height of the vital capacity recording. divide the vital capacity measurement average recorded on the Exercise 37A Review Sheet by the millimeter figure to obtain the volume (in milliliters of air) represented by 1 mm on the recording. For example, if your vital capacity reading is 4000 ml and the vital capacity tracing occupies a vertical distance of 40 mm on the pneumograph recording, then a vertical distance of 1 mm equals 100 ml of air.

Record your computed value: _____ ml of air per mm

3. Record the subject's breathing as he or she performs activities from the following list. Make sure the record is marked accurately to identify each test conducted. Record your results on the Exercise 37A Review Sheet.

talking	swallowing water
yawning	coughing
laughing	lying down
standing	running in place
doing a math problem (concentrating)	

4. Without recording, have the subject breathe normally for 2 minutes, then inhale deeply and hold his or her breath for as long as he or she can.

Time the breath-holding interval: _____ sec

As the subject exhales, turn on the recording apparatus and record the recovery period (time to return to normal breathing—usually slightly over 1 minute):

Time of recovery period: _____ sec

Did the subject have the urge to inspire *or* expire during

breath holding? _____

Without recording, repeat the above experiment, but this time exhale completely and forcefully *after* taking the deep breath.

What was observed this time? _____

_____

Explain the results. (Hint: The vagus nerve is the sensory nerve of the lungs and plays a role here.)

_____

_____

_____

5. Have the subject hyperventilate (breathe deeply and forcefully at the rate of 1 breath/4 sec) for about 30 sec.* Record both during and after hyperventilation. How does the pattern obtained during hyperventilation compare with that recorded during the vital capacity tracing?

_____

Is the respiratory rate after hyperventilation faster *or* slower than during normal quiet breathing?

_____

*Note to the Instructor: This exercise may also be done without using the recording apparatus by simply having the students count the respiratory rate visually.

*A sensation of dizziness may develop. (As the carbon dioxide is washed out of the blood by hyperventilation, the blood pH increases, leading to a decrease in blood pressure and reduced cerebral circulation.) The subject may experience a lack of desire to breathe after forced breathing is stopped. If the period of breathing cessation—apnea—is extended, cyanosis of the lips may occur.

FIGURE 37A.15 Oxygen release and carbon dioxide pickup at the tissues.

6. Repeat the above test, but do not record until after hyperventilating. After hyperventilation, the subject is to hold his or her breath as long as he or she can. Can the breath be held for a longer or shorter time after hyperventilating?

_____

7. Without recording, have the subject breathe into a paper bag for 3 minutes, then record his or her breathing movements.

⚠️ _During the bag-breathing exercise, the subject's partner should watch the subject carefully for any untoward reactions._

Is the breathing rate faster _or_ slower than that recorded during normal quiet breathing?

_____

After hyperventilating? _____

8. Run in place for 2 minutes, and then have your partner determine how long you can hold your breath.

Length of breath holding: _____ sec

9. To prove that respiration has a marked effect on circulation, conduct the following test. Have your lab partner record the rate and relative force of your radial pulse before you begin.

Rate: _____ beats/min   Relative force: _____

Inspire forcibly. Immediately close your mouth and nose to retain the inhaled air, and then make a forceful and prolonged expiration. Your lab partner should observe and record the condition of the blood vessels of your neck and face, and again immediately palpate the radial pulse.

Observations: _____

Radial pulse: _____ beats/min   Relative force: _____

Explain the changes observed. _____

_____

⚠️ Dispose of the paper bag in the autoclave bag. Keep the pneumograph records to interpret results and hand them in if requested by the instructor. Observation of the test results should enable you to determine which chemical factor, carbon dioxide or oxygen, has the greatest effect on modifying the respiratory rate and depth. ▬

Role of the Respiratory System in Acid-Base Balance of Blood

As you have already learned, pulmonary ventilation is necessary for continuous oxygenation of the blood and removal of carbon dioxide (a waste product of cellular respiration) from the blood. Blood pH must be relatively constant for the cells of the body to function optimally. The carbonic acid–bicarbonate buffer system of the blood is extremely important because it helps stabilize arterial blood pH at 7.4 ± 0.02.

When carbon dioxide diffuses into the blood from the tissue cells, much of it enters the red blood cells, where it combines with water to form carbonic acid (Figure 37A.15):

$$H_2O + CO_2 \xrightarrow[\text{enzyme present in RBC}]{\text{carbonic anhydrase}} H_2CO_3$$

Some carbonic acid is also formed in the plasma, but that reaction is very slow because of the lack of the carbonic anhydrase enzyme. Shortly after it forms, carbonic acid dissociates to release bicarbonate (HCO_3^-) and hydrogen ions (H^+). The hydrogen ions that remain in the cells are neutralized, or buffered, when they combine with hemoglobin molecules. If they were not neutralized, the intracellular pH would become very acidic as H^+ ions accumulated. The bicarbonate ions diffuse out of the red blood cells into the plasma, where they become part of the carbonic acid–bicarbonate buffer system. As HCO_3^- follows its concentration gradient into the plasma, an electrical imbalance develops in the RBCs that draws Cl^- into them from the plasma. This exchange phenomenon is called the *chloride shift*.

Acids (more precisely, H^+) released into the blood by the body cells tend to lower the pH of the blood and to cause it to become acidic. On the other hand, basic substances that enter the blood tend to cause the blood to become more alkaline and the pH to rise. Both of these tendencies are resisted in large part by the carbonic acid–bicarbonate buffer system. If the H^+ concentration in the blood begins to increase, the H^+ ions combine with bicarbonate ions to form carbonic acid (a weak acid that does not tend to dissociate at physiological or acid pH) and are thus removed.

$$H^+ + HCO_3^- \rightarrow H_2CO_3$$

Likewise, as blood H^+ concentration drops below what is desirable and blood pH rises, H_2CO_3 dissociates to release bicarbonate ions and H^+ ions to the blood.

$$H_2CO_3 \rightarrow H^+ + HCO_3^-$$

The released H^+ lowers the pH again. The bicarbonate ions, being *weak* bases, are poorly functional under alkaline conditions and have little effect on blood pH unless and until blood pH drops toward acid levels.

In the case of excessively slow or shallow breathing (hypoventilation) or fast deep breathing (hyperventilation), the amount of carbonic acid in the blood can be greatly modified—increasing dramatically during hypoventilation and decreasing substantially during hyperventilation. In either situation, if the buffering ability of the blood is inadequate, respiratory acidosis or alkalosis can result. Therefore, maintaining the normal rate and depth of breathing is important for proper control of blood pH.

ACTIVITY 7

Demonstrating the Reaction Between Carbon dioxide (in Exhaled Air) and Water

1. Fill a beaker with 100 ml of distilled water.

2. Add 5 ml of 0.05 M NaOH and five drops of phenol red. Phenol red is a pH indicator that turns yellow in acidic solutions.

3. Blow through a straw into the solution.

What do you observe?

_____

_____

What chemical reaction is taking place in the beaker?

_____

_____

_____

4. Discard the straw in the autoclave bag. ▦

ACTIVITY 8

Observing the Operation of Standard Buffers

1. To observe the ability of a buffer system to stabilize the pH of a solution, obtain five 250-ml beakers and a wash bottle containing distilled water. Set up the following experimental samples:

Beaker 1:
(150 ml distilled water)   pH _____

Beaker 2:
(150 ml distilled water and
1 drop concentrated HCl)   pH _____

Beaker 3:
(150 ml distilled water and
1 drop concentrated NaOH)   pH _____

Beaker 4: (150 ml standard buffer solution
[pH 7] and 1 drop concentrated HCl)   pH _____

Beaker 5: (150 ml standard buffer solution
[pH 7] and 1 drop concentrated NaOH)   pH _____

2. Using a pH meter standardized with a buffer solution of pH 7, determine the pH of the contents of each beaker and record above. After *each and every* pH recording, the pH meter switch should be turned to **STANDBY,** and the electrodes rinsed thoroughly with a stream of distilled water from the wash bottle.

3. Add 3 more drops of concentrated HCl to beaker 4, stir,

and record the pH: _____

4. Add 3 more drops of concentrated NaOH to beaker 5,

stir, and record the pH: _____

How successful was the buffer solution in resisting pH changes when a strong acid (HCl) or a strong base (NaOH) was added?

_____ ▦

Exploring the Operation of the Carbonic Acid–Bicarbonate Buffer System

To observe the ability of the carbonic acid–bicarbonate buffer system of blood to resist pH changes, perform the following simple experiment.

1. Obtain two small beakers (50 ml), animal plasma, graduated cylinder, glass stirring rod, and a dropper bottle of 0.01 M HCl. Using the pH meter standardized with the buffer solution of pH 7.0, measure the pH of the animal plasma. Use only enough plasma to allow immersion of the electrodes and measure the volume used carefully.

pH of the animal plasma: _____

2. Add 2 drops of the 0.01 M HCl solution to the plasma; stir and measure the pH again.

pH of plasma plus 2 drops of HCl: _____

3. Turn the pH meter switch to **STANDBY,** rinse the electrodes, and then immerse them in a quantity of distilled water (pH 7) exactly equal to the amount of animal plasma used. Measure the pH of the distilled water.

pH of distilled water: _____

4. Add 2 drops of 0.01 M HCl, swirl, and measure the pH again.

pH of distilled water plus the two drops of HCl: _____

Is the plasma a good buffer? _____

What component of the plasma carbonic acid–bicarbonate buffer system was acting to counteract a change in pH when HCl was added?

_____

NAME _____

LAB TIME/DATE _____

Respiratory System Physiology

Mechanics of Respiration

1. For each of the following cases, check the column appropriate to your observations on the operation of the model lung.

	Diaphragm pushed up		Diaphragm pulled down	
Change	Increased	Decreased	Increased	Decreased
In internal volume of the bell jar (thoracic cage)				
In internal pressure				
In the size of the balloons (lungs)				
In direction of air flow	Into lungs	Out of lungs	Into lungs	Out of lungs

2. Base your answers to the following on your observations in question 1.

   Under what internal conditions does air tend to flow into the lungs? _____

   _____

   Under what internal conditions does air tend to flow out of the lungs? Explain why this is so. _____

   _____

3. Activation of the diaphragm and the external intercostal muscles begins the inspiratory process. What effect does contrac-

   tion of these muscles have on thoracic volume, and how is this accomplished?_____

   _____

   _____

4. What was the approximate increase in diameter of chest circumference during a quiet inspiration? _____ inches

   During forced inspiration? _____ inches

What temporary physiological advantage is created by the substantial increase in chest circumference during forced

inspiration? _____

_____

5. The presence of a partial vacuum between the pleural membranes is integral to normal breathing movements. What would happen if an opening were made into the chest cavity, as with a puncture wound?

_____

How is this condition treated medically? _____

Respiratory Sounds

6. Which of the respiratory sounds is heard during both inspiration and expiration? _____

Which is heard primarily during inspiration? _____

7. Where did you best hear the vesicular respiratory sounds? _____

Respiratory Volumes and Capacities—Spirometry or BIOPAC®

8. Write the respiratory volume term and the normal value that is described by the following statements.

Volume of air present in the lungs after a forceful expiration: _____

Volume of air that can be expired forcibly after a normal expiration: _____

Volume of air that is breathed in and out during a normal respiration: _____

Volume of air that can be inspired forcibly after a normal inspiration: _____

Volume of air corresponding to TV + IRV + ERV: _____

9. Record experimental respiratory volumes as determined in the laboratory. (Corrected values are for the recording spirometer only.)

Average TV: _____ ml   Average ERV: _____ ml

Corrected value for TV: _____ ml   Corrected value for ERV: _____ ml

Average IRV: _____ ml   Average VC: _____ ml

Corrected value for IRV: _____ ml   Corrected value for VC: _____ ml

MRV: _____ ml/min   % predicted VC: _____ %

FEV$_1$: _____ % FVC

10. Would your vital capacity measurement differ if you performed the test while standing? _____ While lying down?

    _____ Explain. _____

    _____

11. Which respiratory ailments can respiratory volume tests be used to detect? _____

    _____

    _____

12. Using an appropriate reference, complete the chart below.

		O_2	CO_2	N_2
% of composition of air	Inspired			
	Expired			

Factors Influencing Rate and Depth of Respiration

13. Where are the neural control centers of respiratory rhythm? _____ and _____

For questions 14–21, use your Activity 6 data (the pneumograph-physiograph recording or visual count).

14. In your data, what was the rate of quiet breathing?

    Initial testing _____ breaths/min

    Record observations of how the initial pneumograph recording was modified during the various testing procedures described below. Indicate the respiratory rate, and include comments on the relative depth of the respiratory peaks observed.

Test performed	Observations
Talking	
Yawning	
Laughing	
Standing	
Concentrating	
Swallowing water	
Coughing	
Lying down	
Running in place	

15. Record student data below.

Breath-holding interval after a deep inhalation: _____ sec   length of recovery period: _____ sec

Breath-holding interval after a forceful expiration: _____ sec   length of recovery period: _____ sec

After breathing quietly and taking a deep breath (which you held), was your urge to inspire *or* expire? _____

After exhaling and then holding one's breath, was the desire for inspiration *or* expiration? _____

Explain these results. (Hint: What reflex is involved here?) _____

_____

16. Observations after hyperventilation: _____

_____

17. Length of breath holding after hyperventilation: _____ sec

Why does hyperventilation produce apnea or a reduced respiratory rate? _____

_____

18. Observations for rebreathing air: _____

_____

Why does rebreathing air produce an increased respiratory rate? _____

_____

19. What was the effect of running in place (exercise) on the duration of breath holding? _____

Explain this effect. _____

_____

20. Record student data from the test illustrating the effect of respiration on circulation.

Radial pulse before beginning test: _____ /min   Radial pulse after testing: _____ /min

Relative pulse force before beginning test: _____   Relative force of radial pulse after testing: _____

Condition of neck and facial veins after testing: _____

Explain these data. _____

_____

21. Do the following factors generally increase (indicate with I) or decrease (indicate with D) the respiratory rate and depth?

increase in blood CO_2: _____   increase in blood pH: _____

decrease in blood O_2: _____   decrease in blood pH: _____

Did it appear that CO_2 or O_2 had a more marked effect on modifying the respiratory rate? _____

22. Where are sensory receptors sensitive to changes in blood pressure located? _____

_____

23. Where are sensory receptors sensitive to changes in O_2 levels in the blood located? _____

_____

24. What is the primary factor that initiates breathing in a newborn infant? _____

_____

25. Blood CO_2 levels and blood pH are related. When blood CO_2 levels increase, does the pH increase or decrease?

_____ Explain why. _____

_____

26. Which, if any, of the measurable respiratory volumes would likely be exaggerated in a person who is cardiovascularly fit, such as a runner or a swimmer?

_____

_____

Which, if any, of the measurable respiratory volumes would likely be exaggerated in a person who has smoked a lot for over twenty years?

_____

_____

Role of the Respiratory System in Acid-Base Balance of Blood

27. Define *buffer.* _____

28. How successful was the laboratory buffer (pH 7) in resisting changes in pH when the acid was added? _____

_____

When the base was added? _____

How successful was the buffer in resisting changes in pH when the additional aliquots (3 more drops) of the acid and base

were added to the original samples? _____

29. What buffer system operates in blood plasma? _____

Which member of the buffer system resists a *drop* in pH? _____ Which resists a *rise* in pH? _____

30. Explain how the carbonic acid–bicarbonate buffer system of the blood operates. _____

_____

_____

_____

31. What happened when the carbon dioxide in exhaled air mixed with water? _____

_____

What role does exhalation of carbon dioxide play in maintaining relatively constant blood pH? _____

_____

_____

Anatomy of the Digestive System

MATERIALS

- ☐ Dissectible torso model
- ☐ Anatomical chart of the human digestive system
- ☐ Prepared slides of the liver and mixed salivary glands; of longitudinal sections of the gastroesophageal junction and a tooth; and of cross sections of the stomach, duodenum, and ileum
- ☐ Compound microscope
- ☐ Three-dimensional model of a villus (if available)
- ☐ Jaw model or human skull
- ☐ Three-dimensional model of liver lobules (if available)
- ☐ *Human Digestive System* videotape
- ✂ For instructions on animal dissections, see the dissection exercises starting on page 697 in the cat, fetal pig, and rat editions of this manual.

OBJECTIVES

1. To state the overall function of the digestive system.
2. To identify on an appropriate diagram or torso model the organs of the alimentary canal, and to name their subdivisions if any.
3. To name and/or identify the accessory digestive organs.
4. To describe the general functions of the digestive system organs or structures.
5. To describe the general histologic structure of the alimentary canal wall and/or label a cross-sectional diagram of the wall with the following terms: mucosa, submucosa, muscularis externa, and serosa or adventitia.
6. To list and explain the specializations of the structure of the stomach and small intestine that contribute to their functional roles.
7. To list the major enzymes or enzyme groups produced by the salivary glands, stomach, small intestine, and pancreas.
8. To name human deciduous and permanent teeth, and to describe the anatomy of the generalized tooth.
9. To recognize (by microscopic inspection or by viewing an appropriate diagram or photomicrograph) the histologic structure of the following organs:

small intestine	tooth	liver
salivary glands	stomach	

PRE-LAB QUIZ

1. The digestive system
   a. eliminates undigested food
   b. provides the body with nutrients
   c. provides the body with water
   d. all of the above
2. Circle the correct term. <u>Digestion / Absorption</u> occurs when small molecules pass through epithelial cells into the blood for distribution to the body cells.
3. The _____ abuts the lumen of the alimentary canal and consists of epithelium, lamina propria, and muscularis mucosae.
   a. mucosa
   b. serosa
   c. submucosa
4. Circle the correct term. Approximately 25 cm long, the <u>esophagus / alimentary canal</u> conducts food from the pharynx to the stomach.
5. Wavelike contractions of the digestive tract that propel food along are called
   a. digestion   c. ingestion
   b. elimination   d. peristalsis

Text continues on next page.

6. The _____ is located on the left side of the abdominal cavity and is hidden by the liver and diaphragm.
   a. gallbladder
   b. large intestine
   c. small intestine
   d. stomach

7. Circle True or False. Nearly all nutrient absorption occurs in the small intestine.

8. Circle the correct term. The <u>ascending colon</u> / <u>descending colon</u> traverses down the left side of the abdominal cavity and becomes the sigmoid colon.

9. A tooth consists of two major regions, the crown and the
   a. dentin
   b. enamel
   c. gingiva
   d. root

10. Located inferior to the diaphragm, the _____ is the largest gland in the body, with four lobes.
    a. gallbladder
    b. liver
    c. pancreas
    d. thymus

The **digestive system** provides the body with the nutrients, water, and electrolytes essential for health. The organs of this system ingest, digest, and absorb food and eliminate the undigested remains as feces.

The digestive system consists of a hollow tube extending from the mouth to the anus, into which various accessory organs or glands empty their secretions (see Figure 38.2). Food material within this tube, the *alimentary canal,* is technically outside the body because it has contact only with the cells lining the tract. For ingested food to become available to the body cells, it must first be broken down *physically* (by chewing or churning) and *chemically* (by enzymatic hydrolysis) into its smaller diffusible molecules—a process called **digestion.** The digested end products can then pass through the epithelial cells lining the tract into the blood for distribution to the body cells—a process termed **absorption.** In one sense, the digestive tract can be viewed as a disassembly line, in which food is carried from one stage of its digestive processing to the next by muscular activity, and its nutrients are made available to the cells of the body en route.

The organs of the digestive system are traditionally separated into two major groups: the **alimentary canal,** or **gastrointestinal (GI) tract,** and the **accessory digestive organs.** The alimentary canal is approximately 9 meters long in a cadaver but is considerably shorter in a living person due to muscle tone. It consists of the mouth, pharynx, esophagus, stomach, and small and large intestines. The accessory structures include the teeth, which physically break down foods, and the salivary glands, gallbladder, liver, and pancreas, which secrete their products into the alimentary canal. These individual organs are described shortly.

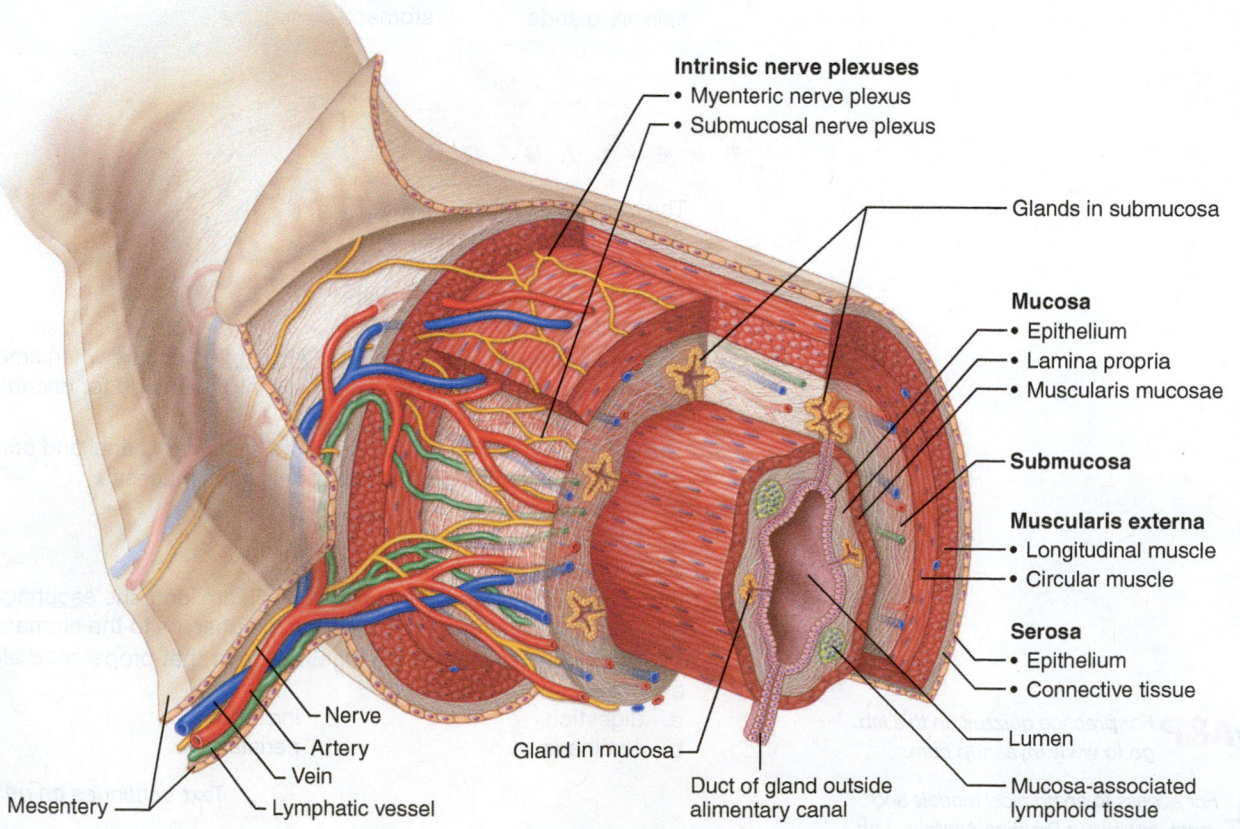

FIGURE 38.1 Basic structural pattern of the alimentary canal wall.

FIGURE 38.2 The human digestive system: alimentary tube and accessory organs. (Liver and gallbladder are reflected superiorly and to the right.)

General Histological Plan of the Alimentary Canal

Because the alimentary canal has a shared basic structural plan (particularly from the esophagus to the anus), it makes sense to review that general structure as we begin studying this group of organs. Then our descriptions of individual organs can focus on their specializations for unique functions in the digestive process.

Essentially the alimentary canal walls have four basic **tunics** (layers). From the lumen outward, these are the *mucosa,* the *submucosa,* the *muscularis externa,* and either a *serosa* or *adventitia* (Figure 38.1). Each of these tunics has a predominant tissue type and a specific function in the digestive process.

Mucosa (mucous membrane): The mucosa is the wet epithelial membrane abutting the alimentary canal lumen. It consists of a surface *epithelium* (in most cases, a simple columnar), a *lamina propria* (areolar connective tissue on which the epithelial layer rests), and a *muscularis mucosae* (a scant layer of smooth muscle fibers that enable local movements of the mucosa). The major functions of the mucosa are secretion (of enzymes, mucus, hormones, etc.), absorption of digested foodstuffs, and protection (against bacterial invasion). A particular mucosal region may be involved in one or all three functions.

Submucosa: The submucosa is moderately dense connective tissue containing blood and lymphatic vessels, scattered lymphoid follicles, and nerve fibers. Its intrinsic nerve supply is called the *submucosal plexus.* Its major functions are nutrition and protection.

Muscularis externa: The muscularis externa, also simply called the *muscularis,* typically is a bilayer of smooth muscle, with the inner layer running circularly and the outer layer running longitudinally. Another important intrinsic nerve plexus, the *myenteric plexus,* is associated with this tunic. By controlling the smooth muscle of the muscularis, this plexus is the major regulator of GI motility.

Serosa: The outermost covering of most of the alimentary canal is the serosa, also called the *visceral peritoneum.* It consists of mesothelium associated with a thin layer of areolar connective tissue. In areas *outside* the abdominopelvic cavity, the serosa is replaced by an **adventitia,** a layer of coarse fibrous connective tissue that binds the organ to surrounding tissues. (This is the case with the esophagus.) The serosa reduces friction as the mobile digestive system organs work and slide across one another and the cavity walls. The adventitia anchors and protects the surrounded organ.

Organs of the Alimentary Canal

ACTIVITY 1

Identifying Alimentary Canal Organs

The sequential pathway and fate of food as it passes through the alimentary canal organs are described in the next sections. Identify each structure in Figure 38.2 and on the torso model or anatomical chart of the digestive system as you work.

Oral Cavity or Mouth

Food enters the digestive tract through the **oral cavity,** or **mouth** (Figure 38.3). Within this mucous membrane–lined cavity are the gums, teeth, tongue, and openings of the ducts of the salivary glands. The **lips (labia)** protect the opening of the chamber anteriorly, the **cheeks** form its lateral walls, and the **palate,** its roof. The anterior portion of the palate is referred to as the **hard palate** because bone (the palatine processes of the maxillae and horizontal plates of the palatine bones) underlies it. The posterior **soft palate** is a fibromuscular structure that is unsupported by bone. The **uvula,** a fingerlike projection of the soft palate, extends inferiorly from its posterior margin. The soft palate rises to close off the oral cavity from the nasal and pharyngeal passages during swallowing. The floor of the oral cavity is occupied by the muscular **tongue,** which is largely supported by the *mylohyoid muscle* (Figure 38.4) and attaches to the hyoid bone, mandible, styloid processes, and pharynx. A membrane called the **lingual frenulum** secures the inferior midline of the tongue to the floor of the mouth. The space between the lips and cheeks and the teeth is the **vestibule;** the area that lies within the teeth and gums (gingivae) is the **oral cavity** proper. (The teeth and gums are discussed in more detail on pages 586–587.)

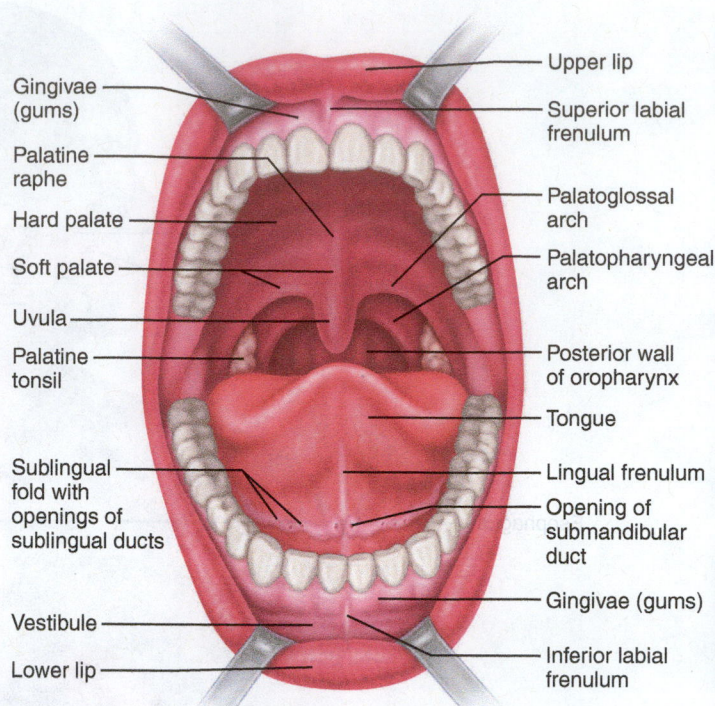

FIGURE 38.3 Anterior view of the oral cavity.

On each side of the mouth at its posterior end are masses of lymphoid tissue, the **palatine tonsils** (see Figure 38.3). Each lies in a concave area bounded anteriorly and posteriorly by membranes, the **palatoglossal arch** (anterior membrane) and the **palatopharyngeal arch** (posterior membrane). Another mass of lymphoid tissue, the **lingual tonsil** (see Figure 38.4), covers the base of the tongue, posterior to the oral cavity proper. The tonsils, in common with other lymphoid tissues, are part of the body's defense system.

Very often in young children, the palatine tonsils become inflamed and enlarge, partially blocking the entrance to the pharynx posteriorly and making swallowing difficult and painful. This condition is called **tonsillitis.** ■

Three pairs of salivary glands duct their secretion, saliva, into the oral cavity. One component of saliva, salivary amylase, begins the digestion of starchy foods within the oral cavity. (The salivary glands are discussed in more detail on page 587.)

As food enters the mouth, it is mixed with saliva and masticated (chewed). The cheeks and lips help hold the food between the teeth during mastication, and the highly mobile tongue manipulates the food during chewing and initiates swallowing. Thus the mechanical and chemical breakdown of food begins before the food has left the oral cavity. As noted in Exercise 26, the surface of the tongue is covered with papillae, many of which contain taste buds. Taste buds contain taste cells, receptors for taste sensation. So, in addition to its manipulative function, the tongue permits the enjoyment and appreciation of the food ingested.

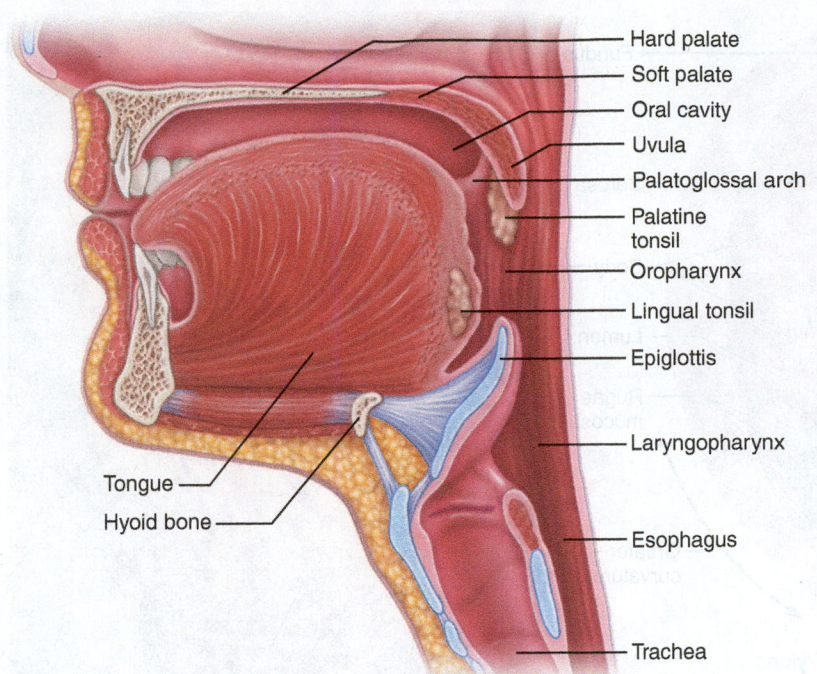

FIGURE 38.4 Sagittal view of the head showing oral cavity and pharynx.

Labels: Hard palate, Soft palate, Oral cavity, Uvula, Palatoglossal arch, Palatine tonsil, Oropharynx, Lingual tonsil, Epiglottis, Laryngopharynx, Esophagus, Trachea, Tongue, Hyoid bone

Pharynx

When the tongue initiates swallowing, the food passes posteriorly into the pharynx, a common passageway for food, fluid, and air (see Figure 38.4). The pharynx is subdivided anatomically into three parts—the **nasopharynx** (behind the nasal cavity), the **oropharynx** (behind the oral cavity extending from the soft palate to the epiglottis overlying the larynx), and the **laryngopharynx** (extending from the epiglottis to the base of the larynx), which is continuous with the esophagus.

The walls of the pharynx consist largely of two layers of skeletal muscles: an inner layer of longitudinal muscle (the levator muscles) and an outer layer of circular constrictor muscles, which initiate wavelike contractions that propel the food inferiorly into the esophagus. The mucosa of the oropharynx and laryngopharynx, like that of the oral cavity, contains a friction-resistant stratified squamous epithelium.

Esophagus

The **esophagus,** or gullet, extends from the pharynx through the diaphragm to the gastroesophageal sphincter in the superior aspect of the stomach. Approximately 25 cm long in humans, it is essentially a food passageway that conducts food to the stomach in a wavelike peristaltic motion. The esophagus has no digestive or absorptive function. The walls at its superior end contain skeletal muscle, which is replaced by smooth muscle in the area nearing the stomach. The **gastroesophageal sphincter,** a slight thickening of the smooth muscle layer at the esophagus-stomach junction, controls food passage into the stomach (see Figure 38.5). Since the esophagus is located in the thoracic rather than the abdominal cavity, its outermost layer is an *adventitia,* rather than the serosa.

Stomach

The **stomach** (Figures 38.2 and 38.5) is on the left side of the abdominal cavity and is hidden by the liver and diaphragm.

Different regions of the saclike stomach are the **cardiac region** or **cardia** (the area surrounding the cardiac orifice through which food enters the stomach from the esophagus), the **fundus** (the dome-shaped portion of the stomach, superolateral to the cardiac region), the **body** (midportion of the stomach, inferior to the fundus), and the funnel-shaped **pyloric region** (consisting of the superiormost *pyloric antrum,* the more narrow *pyloric canal,* and the terminal *pylorus,* which is continuous with the small intestine through the **pyloric valve** or **sphincter**).

The concave medial surface of the stomach is called the **lesser curvature;** its convex lateral surface is the **greater curvature.** Extending from these curvatures are two mesenteries, called *omenta.* The **lesser omentum** extends from the liver to the lesser curvature of the stomach. The **greater omentum,** a saclike mesentery, extends from the greater curvature of the stomach, reflects downward over the abdominal contents to cover them in an apronlike fashion, and then blends with the **mesocolon** attaching the transverse colon to the posterior body wall. Figure 38.7 (page 582) illustrates the omenta as well as the other peritoneal attachments of the abdominal organs.

The stomach is a temporary storage region for food as well as a site for mechanical and chemical breakdown of food. It contains a third (innermost) *obliquely* oriented layer of smooth muscle in its muscularis externa that allows it to churn, mix, and pummel the food, physically reducing it to smaller fragments. **Gastric glands** of the mucosa secrete hydrochloric acid (HCl) and hydrolytic enzymes (primarily pepsinogen, the inactive form of *pepsin,* a protein-digesting enzyme), which begin the enzymatic, or chemical, breakdown of protein foods. The *mucosal glands* also secrete a viscous mucus that helps prevent the stomach itself from being digested by the proteolytic enzymes. Most digestive activity occurs in the pyloric region of the stomach. After the food is processed in the stomach, it resembles a creamy mass (**chyme**), which enters the small intestine through the pyloric sphincter.

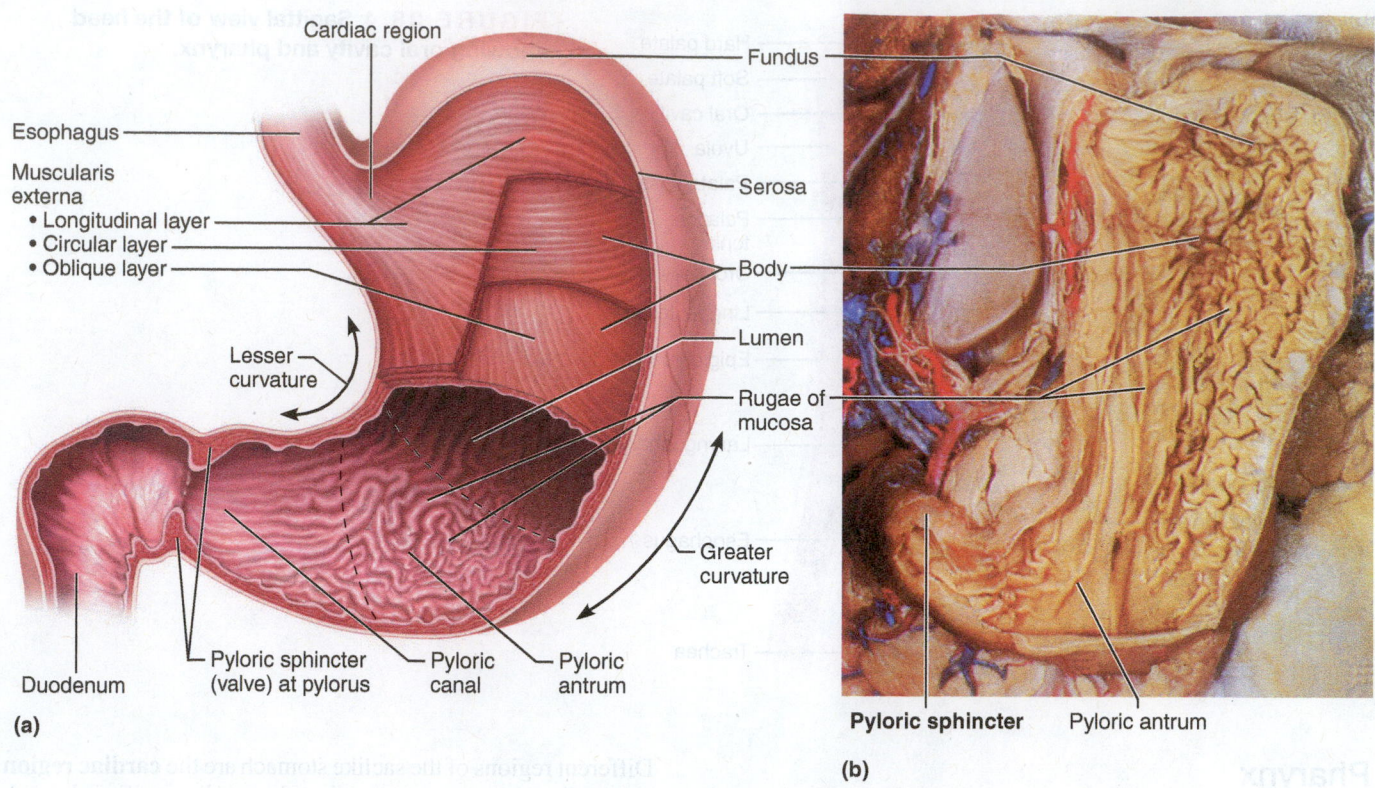

Cardiac region

Esophagus

Muscularis
externa
• Longitudinal layer
• Circular layer
• Oblique layer

Lesser
curvature

Duodenum

Pyloric sphincter
(valve) at pylorus

Pyloric
canal

Pyloric
antrum

Fundus

Serosa

Body

Lumen

Rugae of
mucosa

Greater
curvature

(a)

Pyloric sphincter   Pyloric antrum

(b)

Rugae

Gastric
pit

Gastric
pit

Gastric
gland

(c)

Gastric pits

Surface epithelium
(mucous cells)

Mucous neck cells

Parietal cell

Chief cell

Enteroendocrine cell

(d)

FIGURE 38.5 Anatomy of the stomach. (a) Gross internal
and external anatomy. **(b)** Photograph of internal aspect of
stomach. **(c, d)** Section of the stomach wall showing rugae and
gastric pits.

Studying the Histological Structure of Selected Digestive System Organs

To prepare for the histologic study you will be conducting now and later in the lab, obtain a microscope and the following slides: salivary glands (submandibular or sublingual); liver; cross sections of the duodenum, ileum, and stomach; and longitudinal sections of a tooth and the gastroesophageal junction.

1. **Stomach:** View the stomach slide first. Refer to Figure 38.6a as you scan the tissue under low power to locate the muscularis externa; then move to high power to more closely examine this layer. Try to pick out the three smooth muscle layers. How does the extra (oblique) layer of smooth muscle found in the stomach correlate with the stomach's churning movements?

_____

_____

_____

Identify the gastric glands and the gastric pits (see Figures 38.5 and 38.6b). If the section is taken from the stomach fundus and is appropriately stained, you can identify, in the gastric glands, the blue-staining **chief** (or **zymogenic) cells,** which produce pepsinogen, and the red-staining **parietal cells,** which secrete HCl. The enteroendocrine cells that release hormones are indistinguishable. Draw a small section of the stomach wall, and label it appropriately.

2. **Gastroesophageal junction:** Scan the slide under low power to locate the mucosal junction between the end of the esophagus and the beginning of the stomach, the gastroesophageal junction. Compare your observations to Figure 38.6c. What is the functional importance of the epithelial differences seen in the two organs?

_____

_____

_____

(a)

(b)

(c)

FIGURE 38.6 Histology of selected regions of the stomach and gastroesophageal junction.
(a) Stomach wall (30×). **(b)** Gastric pits and glands (120×).
(c) Gastroesophageal junction, longitudinal section (70×).

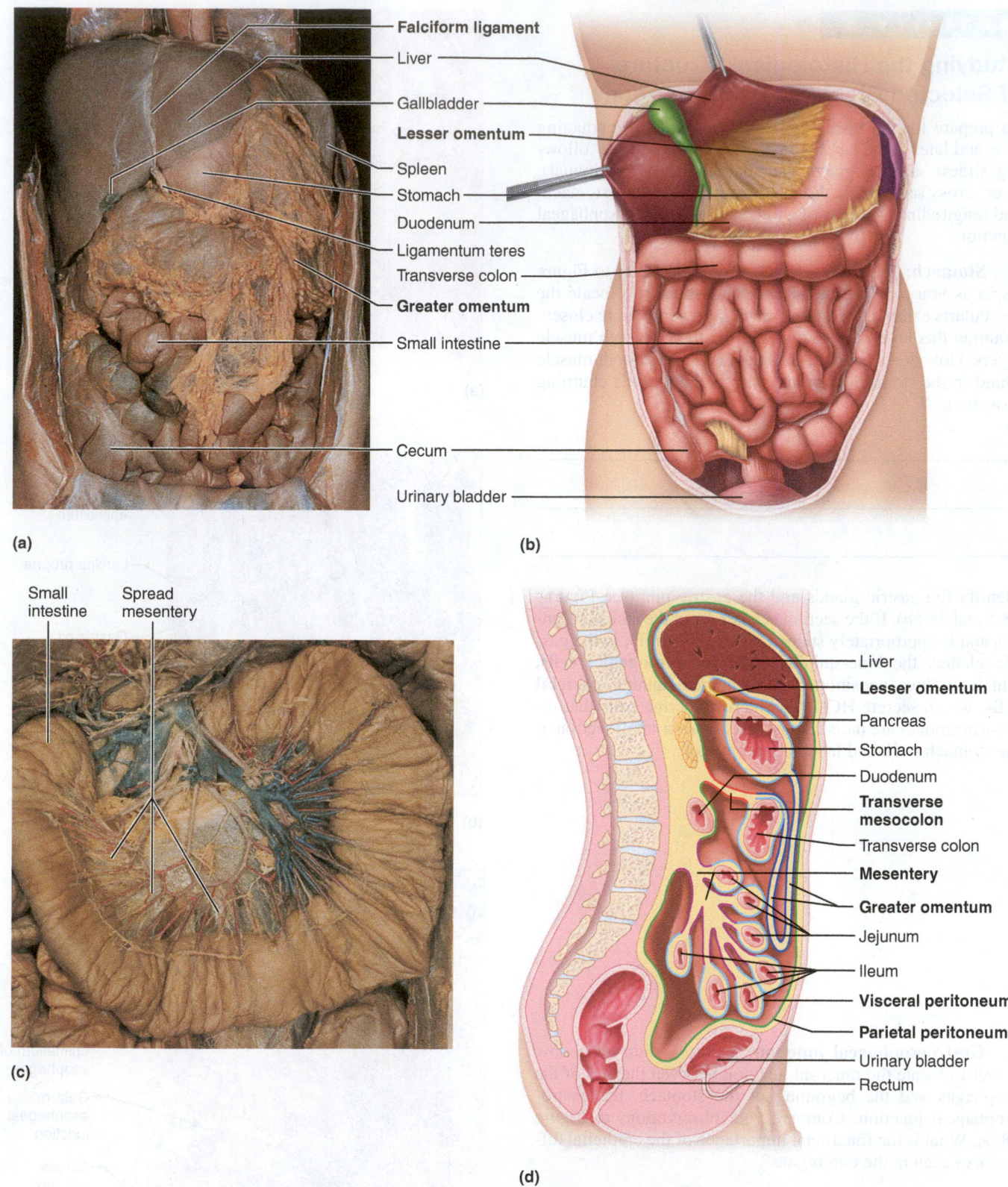

Falciform ligament
Liver
Gallbladder
Lesser omentum
Spleen
Stomach
Duodenum
Ligamentum teres
Transverse colon
Greater omentum
Small intestine
Cecum
Urinary bladder

(a)

(b)

Small intestine   Spread mesentery

(c)

Liver
Lesser omentum
Pancreas
Stomach
Duodenum
Transverse mesocolon
Transverse colon
Mesentery
Greater omentum
Jejunum
Ileum
Visceral peritoneum
Parietal peritoneum
Urinary bladder
Rectum

(d)

FIGURE 38.7 **Peritoneal attachments of the abdominal organs.** Superficial anterior views of abdominal cavity: **(a)** photograph with the greater omentum in place and **(b)** diagram showing greater omentum removed and liver and gallbladder reflected superiorly. **(c)** Mesentery of the small intestine. **(d)** Sagittal view of a male torso.

FIGURE 38.8 Structural modifications of the small intestine that increase its surface area for digestion and absorption. (a) Enlargement of a few circular folds, showing associated fingerlike villi. **(b)** Diagrammatic view of the structure of a villus. **(c)** Two absorptive cells that exhibit microvilli on their free (luminal) surface. **(d)** Photomicrograph of the mucosa showing villi (90×).

Labels in figure:
- Vein carrying blood to hepatic portal vessel
- Muscle layers
- Circular folds
- Villi
- Lumen
- Absorptive cells
- Lacteal
- Goblet cell
- Blood capillaries
- Mucosa associated lymphoid tissue
- Intestinal crypt
- Muscularis mucosae
- Duodenal gland
- Entero-endocrine cells
- Venule
- Lymphatic vessel
- Submucosa
- Microvilli (brush border)
- Villus
- Absorptive cells
- Intestinal crypt
- Goblet cells
- (a) (b) (c) (d)

Small Intestine

The **small intestine** is a convoluted tube, 6 to 7 meters (about 20 feet) long in a cadaver but only about 2 m (6 feet) long during life because of its muscle tone. It extends from the pyloric sphincter to the ileocecal valve. The small intestine is suspended by a double layer of peritoneum, the fan-shaped **mesentery,** from the posterior abdominal wall (see Figure 38.7), and it lies, framed laterally and superiorly by the large intestine, in the abdominal cavity. The small intestine has three subdivisions (see Figure 38.2): (1) the **duodenum** extends from the pyloric sphincter for about 25 cm (10 inches) and curves around the head of the pancreas; most of the duodenum lies in a retroperitoneal position. (2) The **jejunum,** continuous with the duodenum, extends for 2.5 m (about 8 feet). Most of the jejunum occupies the umbilical region of the abdominal cavity. (3) The **ileum**, the terminal portion of the small intestine, is about 3.6 m (12 feet) long and joins the large intestine at the **ileocecal valve.** It is located inferiorly and somewhat to the right in the abdominal cavity, but its major portion lies in the hypogastric region.

Brush border enzymes, hydrolytic enzymes bound to the microvilli of the columnar epithelial cells, and, more importantly, enzymes produced by the pancreas and ducted into the duodenum largely via the **main pancreatic duct** complete the enzymatic digestion process in the small intestine. Bile (formed in the liver) also enters the duodenum via the **bile duct** in the same area. At the duodenum, the ducts join to form the bulblike **hepatopancreatic ampulla** and empty their products into the duodenal lumen through the **major duodenal papilla**, an orifice controlled by a muscular valve called the **hepatopancreatic sphincter** (see Figure 38.15 on page 589).

Nearly all nutrient absorption occurs in the small intestine, where three structural modifications that increase the mucosa absorptive area appear—the microvilli, villi, and circular folds (Figure 38.8). **Microvilli** are minute projections of the surface plasma membrane of the columnar epithelial lining cells of the mucosa. **Villi** are the fingerlike projections of the mucosa tunic that give it a velvety appearance and texture. The

(a)

circular folds (**plicae circulares**) are deep, permanent folds of the mucosa and submucosa layers that force chyme to spiral through the intestine, mixing it and slowing its progress. These structural modifications, which increase the surface area, decrease in frequency and elaboration toward the end of the small intestine. Any residue remaining undigested and unabsorbed at the terminus of the small intestine enters the large intestine through the ileocecal valve. In contrast, the amount of lymphoid tissue in the submucosa of the small intestine (especially the aggregated lymphoid follicles called **Peyer's patches,** Figure 38.9b) increases along the length of the small intestine and is very apparent in the ileum. This reflects the fact that the remaining undigested food residue contains large numbers of bacteria that must be prevented from entering the bloodstream.

ACTIVITY 3

Observing the Histological Structure of the Small Intestine

1. **Duodenum:** Secure the slide of the duodenum (cross section) to the microscope stage. Observe the tissue under low power to identify the four basic tunics of the intestinal wall—that is, the **mucosa** (the lining and its three sublayers), the **submucosa** (areolar connective tissue layer deep to the mucosa), the **muscularis externa** (composed of circular and longitudinal smooth muscle layers), and the **serosa** (the outermost layer, also called the *visceral peritoneum*). Consult Figure 38.9a to help you identify the scattered mucus-producing **duodenal glands** (Brunner's glands) in the submucosa.

What type of epithelium do you see here? _____

_____

(b)

(c)

FIGURE 38.9 Histology of selected regions of the small and large intestines. Cross-sectional views. **(a)** Duodenum of the small intestine (15×). **(b)** Ileum of the small intestine (5×). **(c)** Large intestine (30×).

Examine the large leaflike *villi,* which increase the surface area for absorption. Notice the scattered mucus-producing goblet cells in the epithelium of the villi. Note also the **intestinal crypts** (crypts of Lieberkühn, see also Figure 38.8), invaginated areas of the mucosa between the villi containing the cells that produce intestinal juice, a watery mucus-containing mixture that serves as a carrier fluid for absorption of nutrients from the chyme. Sketch and label a small section of the duodenal wall, showing all layers and villi.

2. **Ileum:** The structure of the ileum resembles that of the duodenum, except that the villi are less elaborate (most of the absorption has occurred by the time the ileum is reached).

Left colic (splenic) flexure

Transverse mesocolon

Epiploic appendages

Descending colon

Cut edge of mesentery

Teniae coli

Sigmoid colon

Right colic (hepatic) flexure

Transverse colon

Superior mesenteric artery

Haustrum

Ascending colon

Ileum

Ileocecal valve

Cecum

Vermiform appendix

Rectum

Anal canal

External anal sphincter

FIGURE 38.10 The large intestine. (Section of the cecum removed to show the ileocecal valve.)

Secure a slide of the ileum to the microscope stage for viewing. Observe the villi, and identify the four layers of the wall and the large, generally spherical Peyer's patches (Figure 38.9b). What tissue composes Peyer's patches?

3. If a villus model is available, identify the following cells or regions before continuing: absorptive epithelium, goblet cells, lamina propria, slips of the muscularis mucosae, capillary bed, and lacteal. If possible, also identify the intestinal crypts.

Large Intestine

The **large intestine** (Figure 38.10) is about 1.5 m (5 feet) long and extends from the ileocecal valve to the anus. It encircles the small intestine on three sides and consists of the following subdivisions: **cecum, vermiform appendix, colon, rectum,** and **anal canal.**

The blind tubelike appendix, which hangs from the cecum, is a trouble spot in the large intestine. Since it is generally twisted, it provides an ideal location for bacte-

ria to accumulate and multiply. Inflammation of the appendix, or appendicitis, is the result.

The colon is divided into several distinct regions. The **ascending colon** travels up the right side of the abdominal cavity and makes a right-angle turn at the **right colic (hepatic) flexure** to cross the abdominal cavity as the **transverse colon.** It then turns at the **left colic (splenic) flexure** and continues down the left side of the abdominal cavity as the **descending colon,** where it takes an S-shaped course as the **sigmoid colon.** The sigmoid colon, rectum, and the anal canal lie in the pelvis anterior to the sacrum and thus are not considered abdominal cavity structures. Except for the transverse and sigmoid colons, which are secured to the dorsal body wall by mesocolons (see Figure 38.7), the colon is retroperitoneal.

The anal canal terminates in the **anus,** the opening to the exterior of the body. The anus, which has an external sphincter of skeletal muscle (the voluntary sphincter) and an internal sphincter of smooth muscle (the involuntary sphincter), is normally closed except during defecation when the undigested remains of the food and bacteria are eliminated from the body as feces.

Incisors
Central (6–8 mo)
Lateral (8–10 mo)
Canine (eyetooth) (16–20 mo)
Molars
First molar (10–15 mo)
Second molar (about 2 yr)

Deciduous (milk) teeth

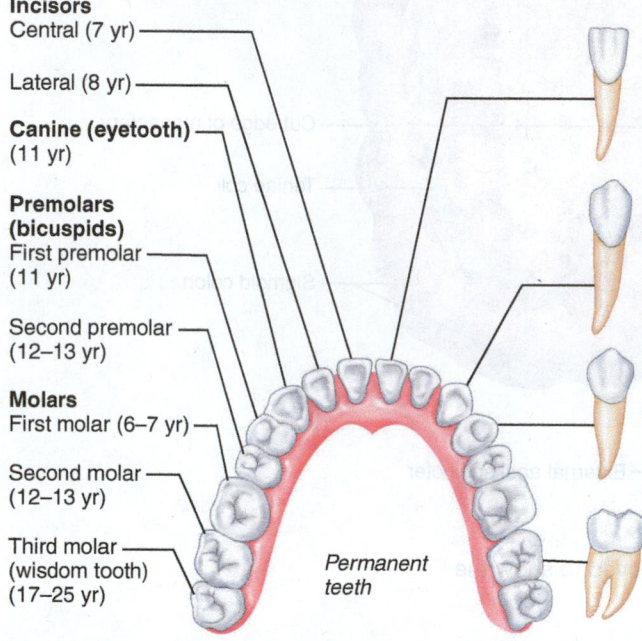

Incisors
Central (7 yr)
Lateral (8 yr)
Canine (eyetooth) (11 yr)
Premolars (bicuspids)
First premolar (11 yr)
Second premolar (12–13 yr)
Molars
First molar (6–7 yr)
Second molar (12–13 yr)
Third molar (wisdom tooth) (17–25 yr)

Permanent teeth

FIGURE 38.11 Human deciduous teeth and permanent teeth. (Approximate time of teeth eruption shown in parentheses.)

In the large intestine, the longitudinal muscle layer of the muscularis externa is reduced to three longitudinal muscle bands called the **teniae coli.** Since these bands are shorter than the rest of the wall of the large intestine, they cause the wall to pucker into small pocketlike sacs called **haustra.** Fat-filled pouches of visceral peritoneum, called *epiploic appendages,* hang from the colon's surface.

The major function of the large intestine is to consolidate and propel the unusable fecal matter toward the anus and eliminate it from the body. While it does that chore, it (1) provides a site for the manufacture, by intestinal bacteria, of some vitamins (B and K), which it then absorbs into the bloodstream; and (2) reclaims most of the remaining water from undigested food, thus conserving body water.

Watery stools, or **diarrhea,** result from any condition that rushes undigested food residue through the large intestine before it has had sufficient time to absorb the water (as in irritation of the colon by bacteria). Conversely, when food residue remains in the large intestine for extended periods (as with atonic colon or failure of the defecation reflex), excessive water is absorbed and the stool becomes hard and difficult to pass causing **constipation.** ■

Examining the Histological Structure of the Large Intestine

Large intestine: Secure a slide of the large intestine to the microscope stage for viewing. Observe the villi and note the numerous goblet cells (Figure 38.9c). Why do you think the large intestine produces so much mucus?

_____

_____ ■

Accessory Digestive Organs

Teeth

By the age of 21, two sets of teeth have developed (Figure 38.11). The initial set, called the **deciduous** (or **milk) teeth,** normally appears between the ages of 6 months and 2½ years. The first of these to erupt are the lower central incisors. The child begins to shed the deciduous teeth around the age of 6, and a second set of teeth, the **permanent teeth,** gradually replaces them. As the deeper permanent teeth progressively enlarge and develop, the roots of the deciduous teeth are resorbed, leading to their final shedding. During years 6 to 12, the child has mixed dentition—both permanent and deciduous teeth. Generally, by the age of 12, all of the deciduous teeth have been shed, or exfoliated.

Teeth are classified as **incisors, canines** (*eye teeth*), **premolars** (*bicuspids*)*,* and **molars.** Teeth names reflect differences in relative structure and function. The incisors are chisel-shaped and exert a shearing action used in biting. Canines are cone-shaped or fanglike, the latter description being much more applicable to the canines of animals whose teeth are used for the tearing of food. Incisors, canines, and premolars typically have single roots, though the first upper premolars may have two. The lower molars have two roots, but the upper molars usually have three. The premolars have two *cusps* (grinding surfaces); the molars have broad crowns with rounded cusps specialized for the fine grinding of food.

Dentition is described by means of a **dental formula,** which designates the numbers, types, and position of the teeth in one side of the jaw. (Because tooth arrangement is bilaterally symmetrical, it is only necessary to designate one side of the jaw.) The complete dental formula for the deciduous teeth from the medial aspect of each jaw and proceeding posteriorly is as follows:

$$\frac{\text{Upper teeth: 2 incisors, 1 canine, 0 premolars, 2 molars}}{\text{Lower teeth: 2 incisors, 1 canine, 0 premolars, 2 molars}} \times 2$$

This formula is generally abbreviated to read as follows:

$$\frac{2,1,0,2}{2,1,0,2} \times 2 = 20 \text{ (number of deciduous teeth)}$$

The 32 permanent teeth are then described by the following dental formula:

$$\frac{2,1,2,3}{2,1,2,3} \times 2 = 32 \text{ (number of permanent teeth)}$$

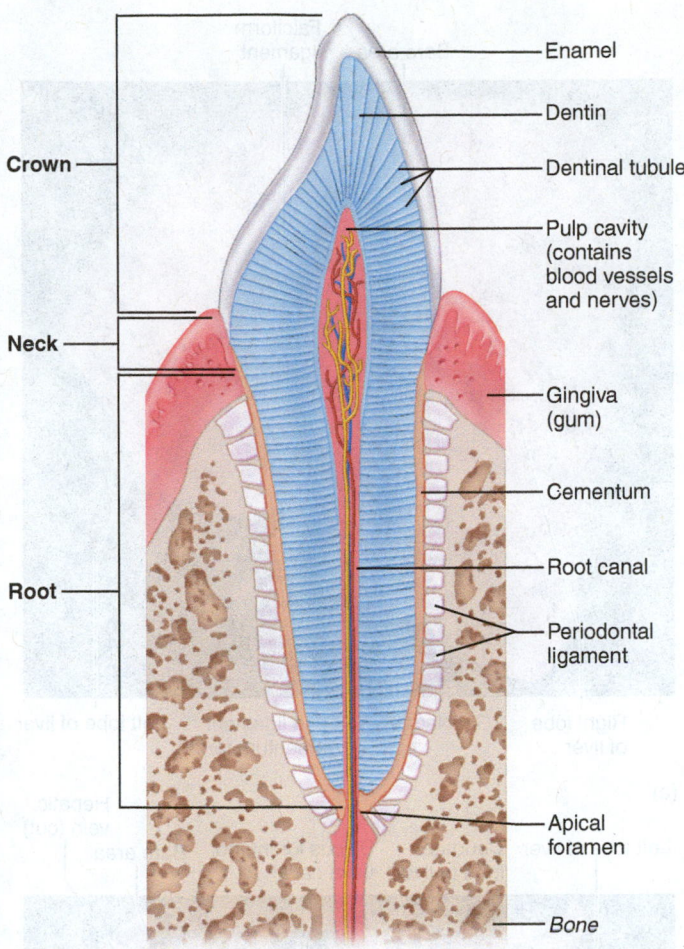

FIGURE 38.12 Longitudinal section of human canine tooth within its bony alveolus.

Labels (top to bottom, left): Crown, Neck, Root

Labels (top to bottom, right): Enamel, Dentin, Dentinal tubules, Pulp cavity (contains blood vessels and nerves), Gingiva (gum), Cementum, Root canal, Periodontal ligament, Apical foramen, *Bone*

Although 32 is designated as the normal number of permanent teeth, not everyone develops a full complement. In many people, the third molars, commonly called *wisdom teeth,* never erupt.

ACTIVITY 5

Identifying Types of Teeth

Identify the four types of teeth (incisors, canines, premolars, and molars) on the jaw model or human skull. ▇

A tooth consists of two major regions, the **crown** and the **root.** A longitudinal section made through a tooth shows the following basic anatomical plan (Figure 38.12). The crown is the superior portion of the tooth. The portion of the crown visible above the **gingiva,** or **gum,** is referred to as the *clinical crown.* The entire area covered by **enamel** is called the *anatomical crown.* Enamel is the hardest substance in the body and is fairly brittle. It consists of 95% to 97% inorganic

calcium salts and thus is heavily mineralized. The crevice between the end of the anatomical crown and the upper margin of the gingiva is referred to as the *gingival sulcus* and its apical border is the *gingival margin.*

That portion of the tooth embedded in the alveolar portion of the jaw is the root, and the root and crown are connected by a slight constriction, the **neck.** The outermost surface of the root is covered by **cementum,** which is similar to bone in composition and less brittle than enamel. The cementum attaches the tooth to the **periodontal ligament,** which holds the tooth in the alveolar socket and exerts a cushioning effect. **Dentin,** which composes the bulk of the tooth, is the bonelike material medial to the enamel and cementum.

The **pulp cavity** occupies the central portion of the tooth. **Pulp,** connective tissue liberally supplied with blood vessels, nerves, and lymphatics, occupies this cavity and provides for tooth sensation and supplies nutrients to the tooth tissues. **Odontoblasts,** specialized cells that reside in the outer margins of the pulp cavity, produce the dentin. The pulp cavity extends into distal portions of the root and becomes the **root canal.** An opening at the root apex, the **apical foramen,** provides a route of entry into the tooth for blood vessels, nerves, and other structures from the tissues beneath.

ACTIVITY 6

Studying Microscopic Tooth Anatomy

Observe a slide of a longitudinal section of a tooth, and compare your observations with the structures detailed in Figure 38.12. Identify as many of these structures as possible. ▇

Salivary Glands

Three pairs of major **salivary glands** (see Figure 38.2) empty their secretions into the oral cavity.

Parotid glands: Large glands located anterior to the ear and ducting into the mouth over the second upper molar through the parotid duct.

Submandibular glands: Located along the medial aspect of the mandibular body in the floor of the mouth, and ducting under the tongue to the base of the lingual frenulum.

Sublingual glands: Small glands located most anteriorly in the floor of the mouth and emptying under the tongue via several small ducts.

Food in the mouth and mechanical pressure (even chewing rubber bands or wax) stimulate the salivary glands to secrete saliva. Saliva consists primarily of *mucin* (a viscous glycoprotein), which moistens the food and helps to bind it together into a mass called a **bolus,** and a clear serous fluid containing the enzyme *salivary amylase.* Salivary amylase begins the digestion of starch (a large polysaccharide), breaking it down into disaccharides, or double sugars, and glucose. Parotid gland secretion is mainly serous; the submandibular is a mixed gland that produces both mucin and serous components; and the sublingual gland produces mostly mucin.

FIGURE 38.13 Histology of a mixed salivary gland.
Sublingual gland (180×).

Labels on figure: Mucous cells, Serous demilunes, Duct

ACTIVITY 7

Examining Salivary Gland Tissue

Examine salivary gland tissue under low power and then high power to become familiar with the appearance of a glandular tissue. Notice the clustered arrangement of the cells around their ducts. The cells are basically triangular, with their pointed ends facing the duct orifice. If possible, differentiate between mucus-producing cells, which look hollow or have a clear cytoplasm, and serous cells, which produce the clear, enzyme-containing fluid and have granules in their cytoplasm. The serous cells often form *demilunes* (caps) around the more central mucous cells. Figure 38.13 may be helpful in this task. ▪

Liver and Gallbladder

The **liver** (see Figure 38.2), the largest gland in the body, is located inferior to the diaphragm, more to the right than the left side of the body. As noted earlier, it hides the stomach from view in a superficial observation of abdominal contents. The human liver has four lobes and is suspended from the diaphragm and anterior abdominal wall by the **falciform ligament** (see Figure 38.14).

The liver is one of the body's most important organs, and it performs many metabolic roles. However, its digestive function is to produce bile, which leaves the liver through the **common hepatic duct** and then enters the duodenum through the **bile duct** (Figure 38.15). Bile has no enzymatic action but emulsifies fats (breaks up large fat particles into smaller ones), thus creating a larger surface area for more efficient lipase activity. Without bile, very little fat digestion or absorption occurs.

When digestive activity is not occurring in the digestive tract, bile backs up into the **cystic duct** and enters the **gallbladder,** a small, green sac on the inferior surface of the liver. It is stored there until needed for the digestive process. While in the gallbladder, bile is concentrated by the removal of water and some ions. When fat-rich food enters the duodenum, a hormonal stimulus causes the gallbladder to contract, releasing the stored bile and making it available to the duodenum.

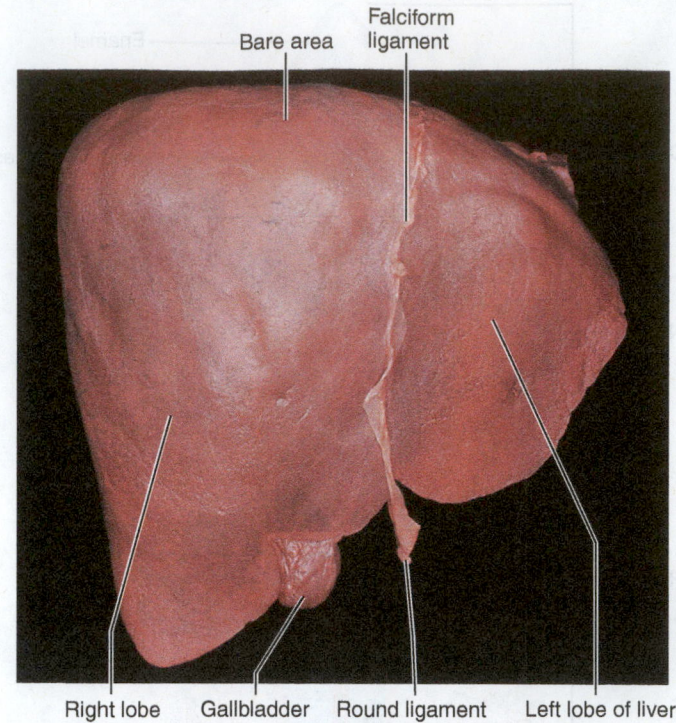

(a)

Labels: Bare area, Falciform ligament, Right lobe of liver, Gallbladder, Round ligament (ligamentum teres), Left lobe of liver

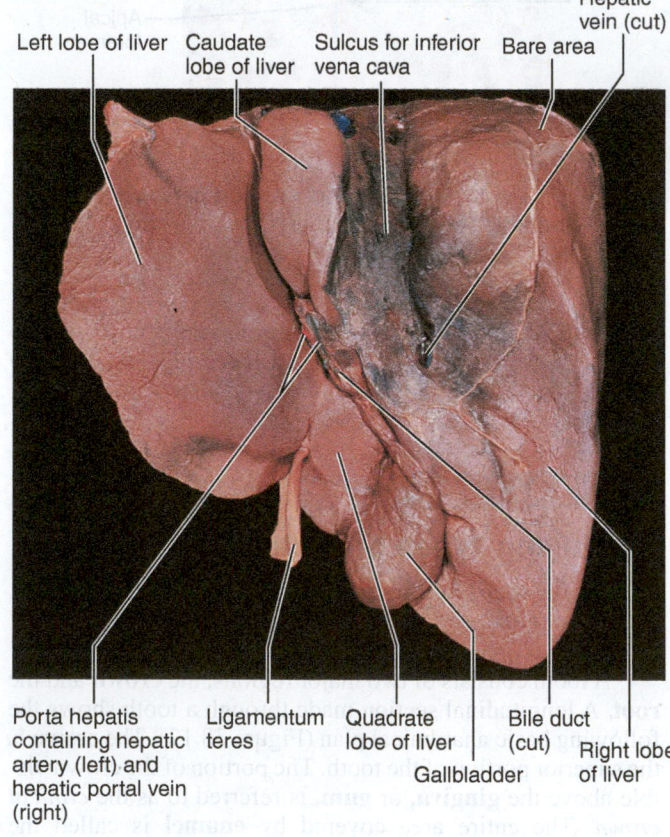

(b)

Labels: Left lobe of liver, Caudate lobe of liver, Sulcus for inferior vena cava, Bare area, Hepatic vein (cut), Porta hepatis containing hepatic artery (left) and hepatic portal vein (right), Ligamentum teres, Quadrate lobe of liver, Gallbladder, Bile duct (cut), Right lobe of liver

FIGURE 38.14 Gross anatomy of the human liver.
(a) Anterior view. **(b)** Posteroinferior aspect. The four liver lobes are separated by a group of fissures in this view.

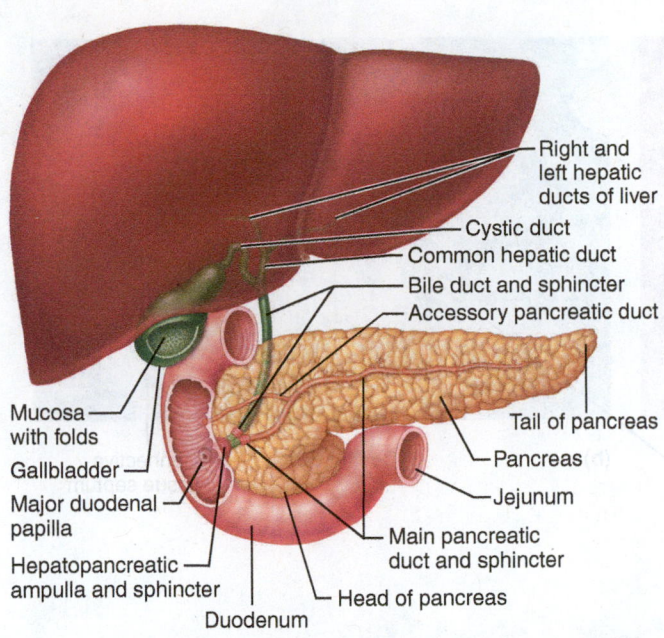

Right and left hepatic ducts of liver

Cystic duct

Common hepatic duct

Bile duct and sphincter

Accessory pancreatic duct

Tail of pancreas

Pancreas

Jejunum

Main pancreatic duct and sphincter

Head of pancreas

Duodenum

Hepatopancreatic ampulla and sphincter

Major duodenal papilla

Gallbladder

Mucosa with folds

FIGURE 38.15 Ducts of accessory digestive organs.

If the common hepatic or bile duct is blocked (for example, by wedged gallstones), bile is prevented from entering the small intestine, accumulates, and eventually backs up into the liver. This exerts pressure on the liver cells, and bile begins to enter the bloodstream. As the bile circulates through the body, the tissues become yellow, or jaundiced.

Blockage of the ducts is just one cause of jaundice. More often it results from actual liver problems such as **hepatitis** (an inflammation of the liver) or **cirrhosis,** a condition in which the liver is severely damaged and becomes hard and fibrous. Cirrhosis is almost guaranteed in those who drink excessive alcohol for many years. ■

As demonstrated by its highly organized anatomy, the liver (Figure 38.16) is very important in the initial processing of the nutrient-rich blood draining the digestive organs. Its structural and functional units are called **lobules.** Each lobule is a basically cylindrical structure consisting of cordlike arrays of **hepatocytes** or *liver cells,* which radiate outward from a central vein running upward in the longitudinal axis of the lobule. At each of the six corners of the lobule is a **portal triad** (portal tract), so named because three basic structures are always present there: a *portal arteriole* (a branch of the *hepatic artery,* the functional blood supply of the liver), a *portal venule* (a branch of the *hepatic portal vein* carrying nutrient-rich blood from the digestive viscera), and a *bile duct.* Between the liver cells are blood-filled spaces, or **sinusoids,** through which blood from the hepatic portal vein and hepatic artery percolates. Star-shaped **hepatic macrophages,** special phagocytic cells, also called **Kupffer cells,** line the sinusoids and remove debris such as bacteria from the blood as it flows past, while the hepatocytes pick up oxygen and nutrients. Much of the glucose transported to the liver from the diges-

tive system is stored as glycogen in the liver for later use, and amino acids are taken from the blood by the liver cells and utilized to make plasma proteins. The sinusoids empty into the central vein, and the blood ultimately drains from the liver via the *hepatic veins.*

Bile is continuously being made by the hepatocytes. It flows through tiny canals, the **bile canaliculi,** which run between adjacent cells toward the bile duct branches in the triad regions, where the bile eventually leaves the liver. Notice that the directions of blood and bile flow in the liver lobule are exactly opposite.

ACTIVITY 8

Examining the Histology of the Liver

Examine a slide of liver tissue and identify as many as possible of the structural features illustrated in Figure 38.16. Also examine a three-dimensional model of liver lobules if this is available. Reproduce a small pie-shaped section of a liver lobule in the space below. Label the hepatocytes, the Kupffer cells, sinusoids, a portal triad, and a central vein. ■

Pancreas

The **pancreas** is a soft, triangular gland that extends horizontally across the posterior abdominal wall from the spleen to the duodenum (see Figure 38.2). Like the duodenum, it is a retroperitoneal organ (see Figure 38.7). As noted in Exercise 27, the pancreas has both an endocrine function (it produces the hormones insulin and glucagon) and an exocrine (enzyme-producing) function. It produces a whole spectrum of hydrolytic enzymes, which it secretes in an alkaline fluid into the duodenum through the pancreatic duct. Pancreatic juice is very alkaline. Its high concentration of bicarbonate ion (HCO_3^-) neutralizes the acidic chyme entering the duodenum from the stomach, enabling the pancreatic and intestinal enzymes to operate at their optimal pH. (Optimal pH for digestive activity to occur in the stomach is very acidic and results from the presence of HCl; that for the small intestine is slightly alkaline.) See Figure 27.3c.

For instructions on animal dissections, see the dissection exercises starting on page 697 in the cat, rat, and fetal pig editions of this manual.

(a) Lobule

(b) Central vein

Connective tissue septum

Interlobular veins (to hepatic vein)

Central vein

Sinusoids

Plates of hepatocytes

Bile canaliculi

Bile duct (receives bile from bile canaliculi)

Fenestrated lining (endothelial cells) of sinusoids

Bile duct

Portal venule

Portal arteriole

Portal triad

Hepatic macrophages in sinusoid walls

Portal vein

(c)

FIGURE 38.16 Microscopic anatomy of the liver, diagrammatic view.
(a) Schematic view of the cut surface of the liver showing the hexagonal nature of its lobules. **(b)** Photomicrograph of one liver lobule (40X). **(c)** Enlarged three-dimensional view of one liver lobule. Arrows show direction of blood flow. Bile flows in the opposite direction toward the bile ducts.

NAME _____

LAB TIME/DATE _____

Anatomy of the Digestive System

General Histological Plan of the Alimentary Canal

1. The general anatomical features of the alimentary canal are listed below. Fill in the table to complete the information.

Wall layer	Subdivisions of the layer (if applicable)	Major functions
mucosa		
submucosa		
muscularis externa		
serosa or adventitia		

Organs of the Alimentary Canal

2. The tubelike digestive system canal that extends from the mouth to the anus is known as the _____

   canal or the _____ tract.

3. How is the muscularis externa of the stomach modified? _____

   _____

   How does this modification relate to the function of the stomach? _____

   _____

4. What transition in epithelial type exists at the gastroesophageal junction? _____

   _____

   How do the epithelia of these two organs relate to their specific functions? _____

   _____

5. Differentiate between the colon and the large intestine. _____

   _____

6. Match the items in column B with the descriptive statements in column A.

Column A

_____ 1. structure that suspends the small intestine from the posterior body wall

_____ 2. fingerlike extensions of the intestinal mucosa that increase the surface area for absorption

_____ 3. large collections of lymphoid tissue found in the submucosa of the small intestine

_____ 4. deep folds of the mucosa and submucosa that extend completely or partially around the circumference of the small intestine

_____, _____ 5. regions that break down foodstuffs mechanically

_____ 6. mobile organ that manipulates food in the mouth and initiates swallowing

_____ 7. conduit for both air and food

_____, _____, _____ 8. three structures continuous with and representing modifications of the peritoneum

_____ 9. the "gullet"; no digestive/absorptive function

_____ 10. folds of the gastric mucosa

_____ 11. sacculations of the large intestine

_____ 12. projections of the plasma membrane of a mucosal epithelial cell

_____ 13. valve at the junction of the small and large intestines

_____ 14. primary region of food and water absorption

_____ 15. membrane securing the tongue to the floor of the mouth

_____ 16. absorbs water and forms feces

_____ 17. area between the teeth and lips/cheeks

_____ 18. wormlike sac that outpockets from the cecum

_____ 19. initiates protein digestion

_____ 20. structure attached to the lesser curvature of the stomach

_____ 21. organ distal to the stomach

_____ 22. valve controlling food movement from the stomach into the duodenum

_____ 23. posterosuperior boundary of the oral cavity

_____ 24. location of the hepatopancreatic sphincter through which pancreatic secretions and bile pass

_____ 25. serous lining of the abdominal cavity wall

_____ 26. principal site for the synthesis of vitamin K by microorganisms

_____ 27. region containing two sphincters through which feces are expelled from the body

_____ 28. bone-supported anterosuperior boundary of the oral cavity

Column B

a. anus

b. appendix

c. circular folds

d. esophagus

e. frenulum

f. greater omentum

g. hard palate

h. haustra

i. ileocecal valve

j. large intestine

k. lesser omentum

l. mesentery

m. microvilli

n. oral cavity

o. parietal peritoneum

p. Peyer's patches

q. pharynx

r. pyloric valve

s. rugae

t. small intestine

u. soft palate

v. stomach

w. tongue

x. vestibule

y. villi

z. visceral peritoneum

7. Correctly identify all organs depicted in the diagram below.

8. You have studied the histological structure of a number of organs in this laboratory. Three of these are diagrammed below. Identify and correctly label each.

(a) _____

(b) _____

(c) _____

Accessory Digestive Organs

9. Correctly label all structures provided with leader lines in the diagram of a molar below. (Note: Some of the terms in the key for question 10 may be helpful in this task.)

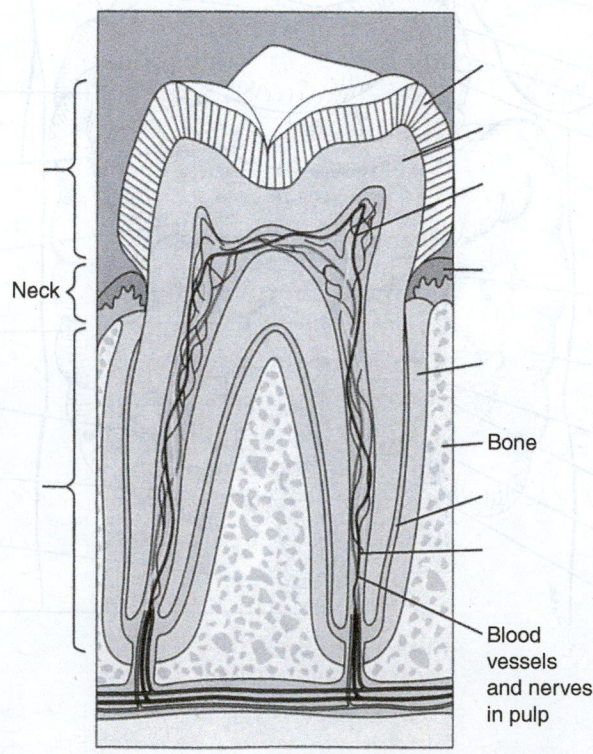

Neck

Bone

Blood
vessels
and nerves
in pulp

10. Use the key to identify each tooth area described below.   *Key:* a.   anatomical crown

_____ 1.   visible portion of the tooth in situ   b.   cementum

_____ 2.   material covering the tooth root   c.   clinical crown

_____ 3.   hardest substance in the body   d.   dentin

_____ 4.   attaches the tooth to bone and surrounding alveolar structures   e.   enamel

_____ 5.   portion of the tooth embedded in bone   f.   gingiva

_____ 6.   forms the major portion of tooth structure; similar to bone   g.   odontoblast

_____ 7.   produces the dentin   h.   periodontal ligament

_____ 8.   site of blood vessels, nerves, and lymphatics   i.   pulp

_____ 9.   entire portion of the tooth covered with enamel   j.   root

11. In the human, the number of deciduous teeth is _____; the number of permanent teeth is _____.

12. The dental formula for permanent teeth is $\dfrac{2,1,2,3}{2,1,2,3} \times 2$

Explain what this means. _____

_____

What is the dental formula for the deciduous teeth? _____ × _____ = _____

13. Which teeth are the "wisdom teeth"? _____

14. Various types of glands form a part of the alimentary tube wall or duct their secretions into it. Match the glands listed in column B with the function/locations described in column A.

Column A   **Column B**

_____ 1.   produce(s) mucus; found in the submucosa of the small intestine   a.   duodenal glands

_____ 2.   produce(s) a product containing amylase that begins starch   b.   gastric glands
breakdown in the mouth

    c.   intestinal crypts

_____ 3.   produce(s) a whole spectrum of enzymes and an alkaline fluid that is
secreted into the duodenum   d.   liver

_____ 4.   produce(s) bile that it secretes into the duodenum via the bile duct   e.   pancreas

_____ 5.   produce(s) HCl and pepsinogen   f.   salivary glands

_____ 6.   found in the mucosa of the small intestine; produce(s) intestinal juice

15. Which of the salivary glands produces a secretion that is mainly serous? _____

16. What is the role of the gallbladder? _____

17. Name three structures always found in the portal triad regions of the liver. _____,

_____, and _____

18. Where would you expect to find the Kupffer cells of the liver? _____

What is their function? _____

19. Why is the liver so dark red in the living animal? _____

_____

20. The pancreas has two major populations of secretory cells—those in the islets and the acinar cells. Which population serves

the digestive process? _____

Chemical and Physical Processes of Digestion: Wet Lab

MATERIALS

Part I: Enzyme Action

General Supply Area

- ☐ Hot plates
- ☐ 250-ml beakers
- ☐ Boiling chips
- ☐ Test tubes and test tube rack
- ☐ Wax markers
- ☐ Water bath set at 37°C (if not available, incubate at room temperature and double the time)
- ☐ Ice water bath
- ☐ Chart on chalkboard for recording class results

Activity 1: Starch Digestion

- ☐ Dropper bottle of distilled water
- ☐ Dropper bottles of the following:
  1% alpha-amylase solution*
  1% boiled starch solution, freshly prepared†
  1% maltose solution
  Lugol's iodine solution (IKI)
  Benedict's solution
- ☐ Spot plate

Activity 2: Protein Digestion

- ☐ Dropper bottles of 1% trypsin and 0.01% BAPNA solution

*The alpha-amylase must be a low-maltose preparation for good results.

†Prepare by adding 1 g starch to 100 ml distilled water; boil and cool; add a pinch of salt (NaCl). Prepare fresh daily.

Text continues on next page.

OBJECTIVES

1. To list the digestive system enzymes involved in the digestion of proteins, fats, and carbohydrates; to state their site of origin; and to summarize the environmental conditions promoting their optimal functioning.
2. To recognize the variation between different types of enzyme assays.
3. To name the end products of protein, fat, and carbohydrate digestion.
4. To perform the appropriate chemical tests to determine if digestion of a particular foodstuff has occurred.
5. To cite the function(s) of bile in the digestive process.
6. To discuss the possible role of temperature and pH in the regulation of enzyme activity.
7. To define *enzyme, catalyst, control, substrate,* and *hydrolase.*
8. To explain why swallowing is both a voluntary and a reflex activity.
9. To discuss the role of the tongue, larynx, and gastroesophageal sphincter in swallowing.
10. To compare and contrast segmentation and peristalsis as mechanisms of propulsion.

PRE-LAB QUIZ

1. Circle the correct term. Enzymes are <u>catalysts / substrates</u> that increase the rate of chemical reactions without becoming a part of the product.
2. A(n) _____ is a specimen or standard against which all experimental samples are compared.
   a. assay   b. control   c. substrate   d. trial
3. One enzyme that you will be studying today, produced by the salivary glands and secreted into the mouth, hydrolyzes starch to maltose. It is _____.
4. Circle True or False. When you use iodine to test for starch, a color change to blue-black indicates a positive starch test.
5. If Benedict's test in the starch assay produces a _____ precipitate, then your test will be recorded as positive for maltose.
   a. blue to black b. green to orangec. white
6. The enzyme _____, produced by the pancreas, is responsible for breaking down proteins.
   a. amylase   b. kinase   c. lipase   d. trypsin
7. Circle the correct term. The enzyme <u>pancreatic lipase / pepsin</u> hydrolyzes neutral fats to their component monoglycerides and fatty acids.
8. Circle True or False. Both smooth and skeletal muscles are involved in the physical processes of digestion.
9. _____ movements are local contractions that mix foodstuffs with digestive juices and increase the rate of absorption.
   a. Deglutition b. Elimination c. Peristaltic d. Segmental

myA&P For practice quizzes on this lab, go to www.myaandp.com.

597

Because nutrients can be absorbed only when broken down to their monomers, food digestion is a prerequisite to food absorption. You have already studied mechanisms of passive and active absorption in Exercise 5A and/or 5B. Before proceeding, review that material.

Chemical Digestion of Foodstuffs: Enzymatic Action

Enzymes are large protein molecules produced by body cells. They are biological **catalysts,** meaning that they increase the rate of a chemical reaction without themselves becoming part of the product. The digestive enzymes are hydrolytic enzymes, or **hydrolases.** Their **substrates,** or the molecules on which they act, are organic food molecules which they break down by adding water to the molecular bonds, thus cleaving the bonds between the subunits or monomers.

The various hydrolytic enzymes are highly specific in their action. Each enzyme hydrolyzes only one or a small group of substrate molecules, and specific environmental conditions are necessary for it to function optimally. Since digestive enzymes actually function outside the body cells in the digestive tract, their hydrolytic activity can also be studied in a test tube. Such an in vitro study provides a convenient laboratory environment for investigating the effect of such variations on enzymatic activity.

Figure 39A.1 is a flowchart of the progressive digestion of carbohydrates, proteins, fats, and nucleic acids. It summarizes the specific enzymes involved, their site of formation, and their site of action. Acquaint yourself with the flowchart before beginning this experiment, and refer to it as necessary during the laboratory session.

General Instructions for Activities 1–3

Work in groups of four, with each group taking responsibility for setting up and conducting one of the following experiments. In each of the digestive procedures being studied (starch, protein, and fat digestion) and in the amylase assay, you are directed to boil the contents of one or more test tubes. To do this, obtain a 250-ml beaker, boiling chips, and a hot plate from the general supply area. Place a few boiling chips into the beaker, add about 125 ml of water, and bring to a boil. Place the test tube for each specimen in the water for the number of minutes specified in the directions. You will also be using a 37°C and an ice water bath for parts of these experiments. You will need to use your time very efficiently in order to set up and perform each test properly.

Upon completion of the experiments, each group should communicate its results to the rest of the class by recording them in a chart on the chalkboard. All members of the class should observe the **controls** (the specimens or standards against which experimental samples are compared) as well as the positive and negative examples of all experimental results. Additionally, all members of the class should be able to explain the tests used and the results observed and anticipated for each experiment. Note that water baths and hot plates are at the general supply area.

ACTIVITY 1

Assessing Starch Digestion by Salivary Amylase

1. From the general supply area, obtain a test tube rack, 10 test tubes, and a wax marking pencil. From the Activity 1 supply area, obtain a dropper bottle of distilled water and dropper bottles of maltose, amylase, and starch solutions.

2. In this experiment you will investigate the hydrolysis of starch to maltose by **salivary amylase** (the enzyme produced by the salivary glands and secreted into the mouth), so you will need to be able to identify the presence of starch and maltose to determine to what extent the enzymatic activity has occurred. Thus controls must be prepared to provide a known standard against which comparisons can be made. Starch decreases and sugar increases as digestion occurs, according to the following formula:

$$\text{Starch} + \text{water} \xrightarrow{\text{amylase}} \text{maltose}$$

Two students should prepare the controls (tubes 1A to 3A) while the other two prepare the experimental samples (tubes 4A to 6A).

• Mark each tube with a wax pencil and load the tubes as indicated in the Salivary Amylase chart on page 600, using 3 drops (gtt) of each indicated substance.

• Place all tubes in a rack in the 37°C water bath for approximately 1 hour. Shake the rack gently from time to time to keep the contents evenly mixed.

• At the end of the hour, perform the amylase assay described below.

• While these tubes are incubating, proceed to Physical Processes: Mechanisms of Food Propulsion and Mixing (page 603). Be sure to monitor the time so as to complete this activity as needed.

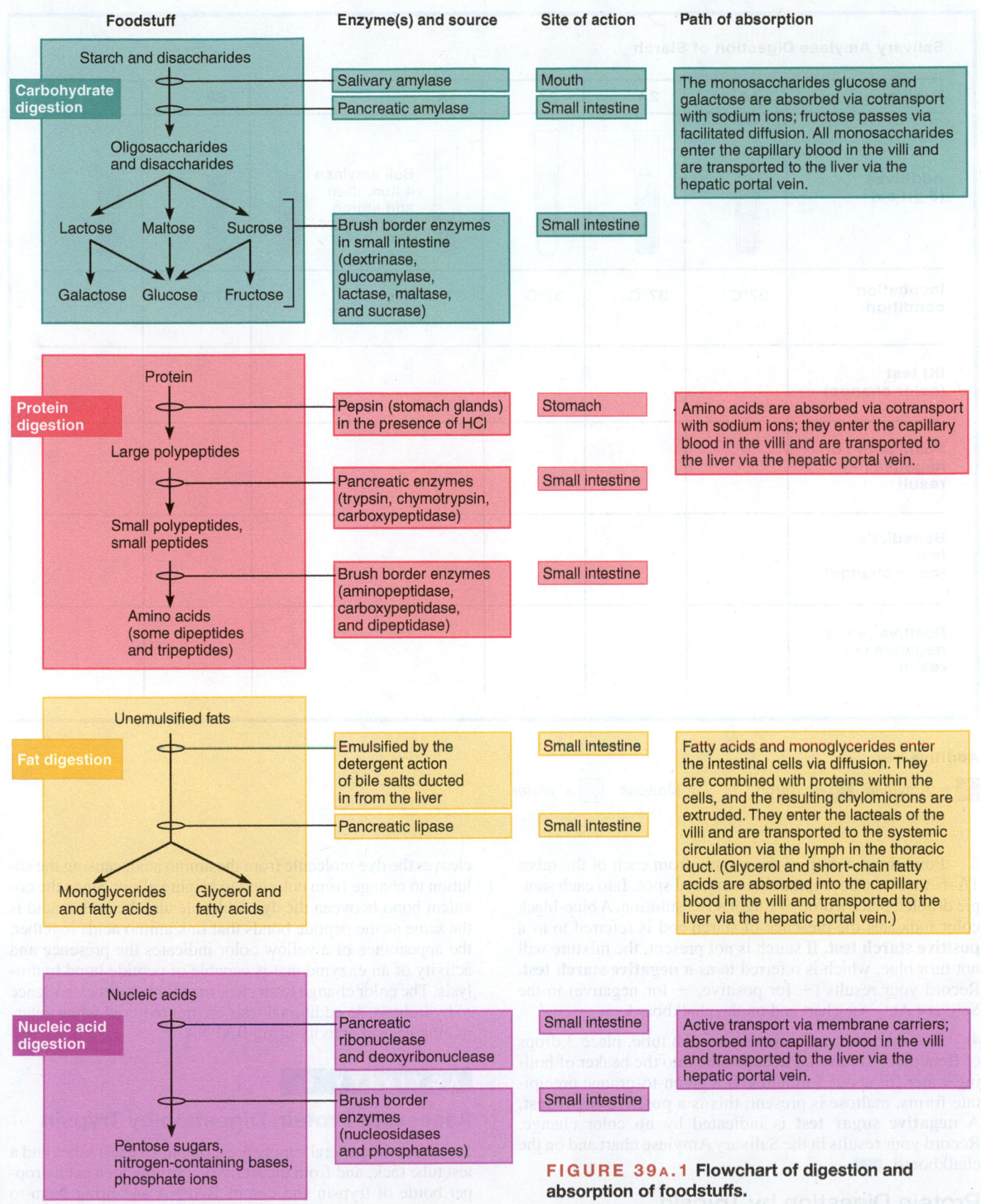

FIGURE 39A.1 **Flowchart of digestion and absorption of foodstuffs.**

Amylase Assay

1. After one hour, obtain a spot plate and dropper bottles of Lugol's solution (for the IKI, or iodine, test) and Benedict's solution from the Activity 1 supply area. Set up your boiling

water bath using a hot plate, boiling chips, and a 250-ml beaker obtained from the general supply area.

2. While the water is heating, mark six depressions of the spot plate 1A–6A (*A* for amylase) for sample identification.

Salivary Amylase Digestion of Starch

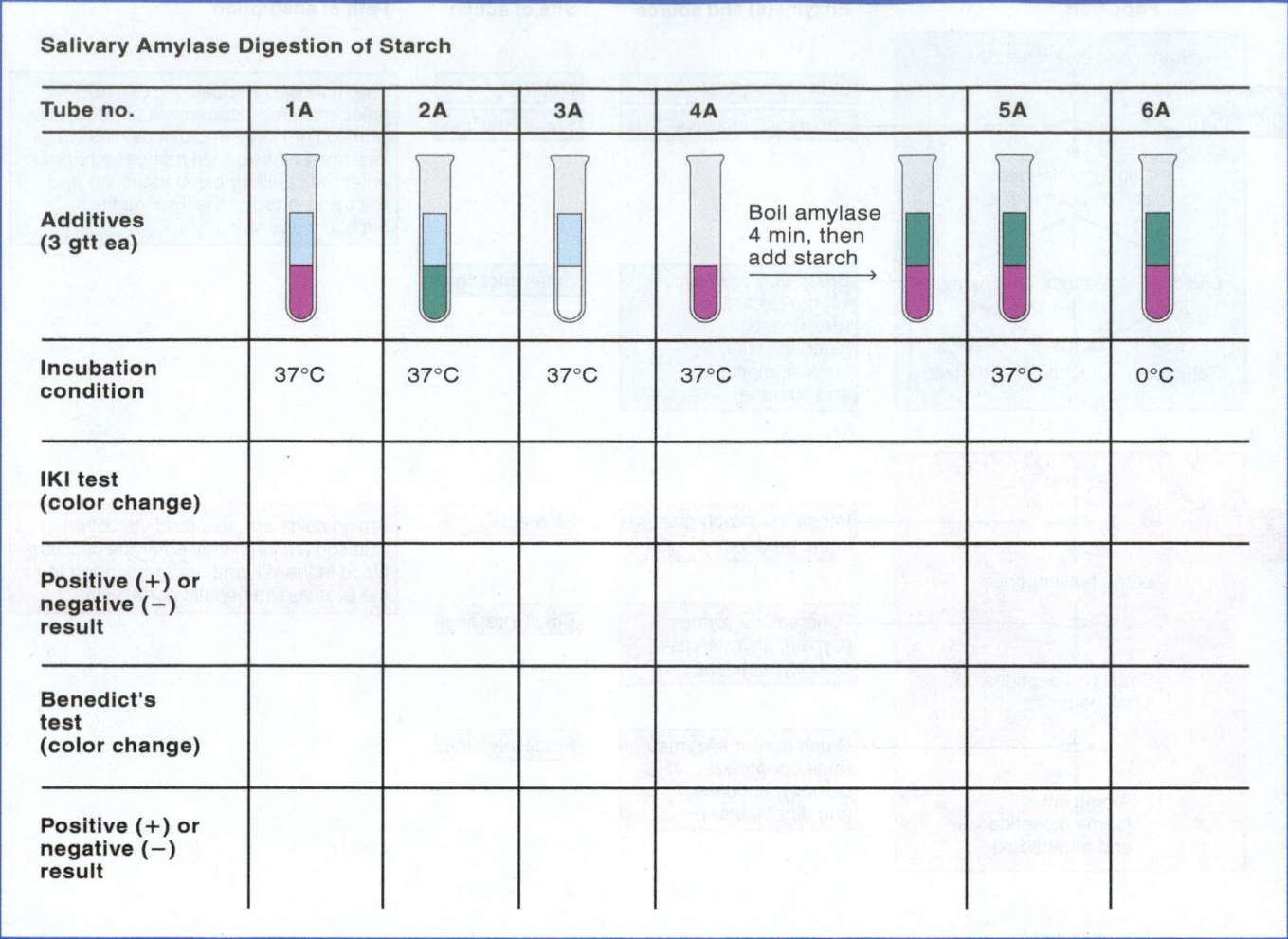

Tube no.	1A	2A	3A	4A		5A	6A
Additives (3 gtt ea)					Boil amylase 4 min, then add starch →		
Incubation condition	37°C	37°C	37°C	37°C		37°C	0°C
IKI test (color change)							
Positive (+) or negative (−) result							
Benedict's test (color change)							
Positive (+) or negative (−) result							

Additive key:

■ = Amylase   ■ = Starch   □ = Maltose   ■ = Water

3. Pour about a drop of the sample from each of the tubes 1A–6A into the appropriately numbered spot. Into each sample droplet, place a drop of Lugol's IKI solution. A blue-black color indicates the presence of starch and is referred to as a **positive starch test.** If starch is not present, the mixture will not turn blue, which is referred to as a **negative starch test.** Record your results (+ for positive, − for negative) in the Salivary Amylase chart and on the chalkboard.

4. Into the remaining mixture in each tube, place 3 drops of Benedict's solution. Put each tube into the beaker of boiling water for about 5 minutes. If a green-to-orange precipitate forms, maltose is present; this is a **positive sugar test.** A **negative sugar test** is indicated by no color change. Record your results in the Salivary Amylase chart and on the chalkboard. ▬

Protein Digestion by Trypsin

Trypsin, an enzyme produced by the pancreas, hydrolyzes proteins to small fragments (proteoses, peptones, and peptides). BAPNA (*N*-alpha-benzoyl-L-arginine-*p*-nitroanilide) is a synthetic trypsin substrate consisting of a dye covalently bound to an amino acid. Trypsin hydrolysis of BAPNA

cleaves the dye molecule from the amino acid, causing the solution to change from colorless to bright yellow. Since the covalent bond between the dye molecule and the amino acid is the same as the peptide bonds that link amino acids together, the appearance of a yellow color indicates the presence and activity of an enzyme that is capable of peptide bond hydrolysis. The color change from clear to yellow is direct evidence of hydrolysis, so additional tests are not required when determining trypsin activity using BAPNA.

ACTIVITY 2

Assessing Protein Digestion by Trypsin

1. From the general supply area, obtain five test tubes and a test tube rack, and from the Activity 2 supply area get a dropper bottle of trypsin and one of BAPNA and bring them to your bench.

2. Two students should prepare the controls (tubes 1T and 2T) while the other two prepare the experimental samples (tubes 3T to 5T).

Trypsin Digestion of Protein

Tube no.	1T	2T	3T	4T	5T
Additives (3 gtt ea)			Boil trypsin 4 min, then add BAPNA. →		
Incubation condition	37°C	37°C	37°C	37°C	0°C
Color change					
Positive (+) or negative (−) result					

Additive key:

■ = Trypsin   ■ = BAPNA   ■ = Water

- Mark each tube with a wax pencil and load the tubes as indicated in the Trypsin chart, using 3 drops (gtt) of each indicated substance.
- Place all tubes in a rack in the appropriate water bath for approximately 1 hour. Shake the rack occasionally to keep the contents well mixed.
- At the end of the hour, examine the tubes for the results of the trypsin assay (detailed below).
- While these tubes are incubating, proceed to Physical Processes: Mechanisms of Food Propulsion and Mixing (page 603).

Trypsin Assay

Since BAPNA is a synthetic colorigenic (color-producing) substrate, the presence of yellow color indicates a **positive hydrolysis test;** the dye molecule has been cleaved from the amino acid. If the sample mixture remains clear, a **negative hydrolysis test** has occurred.

Record the results in the Trypsin chart and on the chalkboard. ▪▪▪

Pancreatic Lipase Digestion of Fats and the Action of Bile

The treatment that fats and oils go through during digestion in the small intestine is a bit more complicated than that of carbohydrates or proteins—pretreatment with bile to physically emulsify the fats is required. Hence, two sets of reactions occur.

First:

$$\text{Fats/oils} \xrightarrow[\text{(emulsification)}]{\text{bile}} \text{minute fat/oil droplets}$$

Then:

$$\text{Fat/oil droplets} \xrightarrow[\text{(digestion)}]{\text{lipase}} \text{monoglycerides and fatty acids}$$

The term **pancreatin** describes the enzymatic product of the pancreas, which includes enzymes that digest proteins, carbohydrates, nucleic acids, and fats. It is used here to investigate the properties of **pancreatic lipase,** which hydrolyzes fats and oils to their component monoglycerides and two fatty acids (and occasionally to glycerol and three fatty acids).

The fact that some of the end products of fat digestion (fatty acids) are organic acids that decrease the pH provides an easy way to recognize that digestion is ongoing or completed. You will be using a pH indicator called *litmus blue* to follow these changes; it changes from blue to pink as the test tube contents become acid.

ACTIVITY 3

Demonstrating the Emulsification Action of Bile and Assessing Fat Digestion by Lipase

1. From the general supply area, obtain nine test tubes and a test tube rack, plus one dropper bottle of each of the solutions in the Activity 3 supply area.

2. Although *bile,* a secretory product of the liver, is not an enzyme, it is important to fat digestion because of its emulsifying

Pancreatic Lipase Digestion of Fats

Tube no.	1L	2L	3L	4L	5L	4B	5B
Additives (5 gtt ea)			Boil lipase 4 min, then add litmus cream. →				
Incubation condition	37°C	37°C	37°C	37°C	0°C	37°C	0°C
Color change							
Positive (+) or negative (−) result							

Additive key:

■ = Lipase   ■ = Litmus cream   ■ = Water   △ = Pinch bile salts

action (the physical breakdown of larger particles into smaller ones) on fats. Emulsified fats provide a larger surface area for enzymatic activity. To demonstrate the action of bile on fats, prepare two test tubes and mark them 1E and 2E (*E* for emulsified fats).

- To tube 1E, add 10 drops of water and 2 drops of vegetable oil.
- To tube 2E, add 10 drops of water, 2 drops of vegetable oil, and a pinch of bile salts.
- Cover each tube with a small square of Parafilm, shake vigorously, and allow the tubes to stand at room temperature.

After 10 to 15 minutes, observe both tubes. If emulsification has not occurred, the oil will be floating on the surface of the water. If emulsification has occurred, the fat droplets will be suspended throughout the water, forming an emulsion.

In which tube has emulsification occurred?_____

3.   Two students should prepare the controls (1L and 2L, *L* for lipase), while the other two students in the group set up the experimental samples (3L to 5L, 4B, and 5B, where *B* is for bile) as illustrated in the Pancreatic Lipase chart.

- Mark each tube with a wax pencil and load the tubes using 5 drops (gtt) of each indicated solution.
- Place a pinch of bile salts in tubes 4B and 5B.
- Cover each tube with a small square of Parafilm, and shake to mix the contents of the tube.
- Remove the Parafilm, and place all tubes in a rack in the appropriate water bath for approximately 1 hour.

Shake the test tube rack from time to time to keep the contents well mixed.

- At the end of the hour, perform the lipase assay (below).
- While these tubes are incubating proceed to Physical Processes: Mechanisms of Food Propulsion and Mixing (p. 603). Be sure to monitor the time so as to complete this activity when needed.

Lipase Assay

The basis of this assay is a pH change that is detected by a litmus powder indicator. Alkaline or neutral solutions containing litmus are blue but will turn reddish in the presence of acid. Since fats are digested to fatty acids (organic acids) during hydrolysis, they lower the pH of the sample they are in. Litmus cream (fresh cream providing the fat substrate to which litmus powder was added) will turn from blue to pink if the solution is acid. Because the effect of hydrolysis is directly seen, additional assay reagents are not necessary.

1.   To prepare a color control, add 0.1 *N* HCl drop by drop to tubes 1L and 2L (covering the tubes with a square of Parafilm after each addition and shaking to mix) until the cream turns pink.

2.   Record the color of the tubes in the Pancreatic Lipase chart and on the chalkboard. ■

ACTIVITY 4

Reporting Results and Conclusions

1.   Share your results with the class as directed in the General Instructions on page 598.

Bolus of food

Tongue

Pharynx

Epiglottis

Glottis

Trachea

Uvula

Bolus

Epiglottis

Esophagus

Bolus

① Upper esophageal sphincter is contracted. During the buccal phase, the tongue presses against the hard palate, forcing the food bolus into the oropharynx where the involuntary phase begins.

② The uvula and larynx rise to prevent food from entering respiratory passageways. The tongue blocks off the mouth. The upper esophageal sphincter relaxes, allowing food to enter the esophagus.

③ The constrictor muscles of the pharynx contract, forcing food into the esophagus inferiorly. The upper esophageal sphincter contracts (closes) after entry.

FIGURE 39A.2 Swallowing. The process of swallowing consists of voluntary (buccal) (step ①) and involuntary (pharyngeal-esophageal) phases (steps ②–③).

2. Suggest additional experiments, and carry out experiments if time permits.

3. Prepare a lab report for the experiments on digestion. See Getting Started on page xiv. ■

Physical Processes: Mechanisms of Food Propulsion and Mixing

Although enzyme activity is a very important part of the overall digestion process, foods must also be processed physically (by chewing and churning) and moved by mechanical means along the tract if digestion and absorption are to be completed. Just about any time organs exhibit mobility, muscles are involved, and movements of and in the gastrointestinal tract are no exception. Although we tend to think only of smooth muscles when visceral activities are involved, both skeletal and smooth muscles are involved in digestion. This fact is amply demonstrated by the simple activities that follow.

Deglutition (Swallowing)

Swallowing, or **deglutition,** which is largely the result of skeletal muscle activity, occurs in two phases: *buccal* (mouth) and *pharyngeal-esophageal*. The initial phase—the buccal (Figure 39A.2 step ①)—is voluntarily controlled and initiated by the tongue. Once begun, the process continues involuntarily in the pharynx and esophagus, through peristalsis, resulting in the delivery of the swallowed contents to the stomach (Figure 39A.2 steps ②–③).

ACTIVITY 5

Observing Movements and Sounds of Digestion

1. Obtain a pitcher of water, a stethoscope, a paper cup, an alcohol swab, and an autoclave bag in preparation for making the following observations.

2. While swallowing a mouthful of water, consciously note the movement of your tongue during the process. Record your observations.

_____

_____

_____

3. Repeat the swallowing process while your laboratory partner watches the externally visible movements of your larynx. (This movement is more obvious in a male, since males have a larger Adam's apple.) Record your observations.

_____

_____

What do these movements accomplish? _____

_____

_____

From
mouth

(a)

(b)

FIGURE 39A.3 Peristaltic and segmental movements of the digestive tract. (a) Peristalsis: neighboring segments of the intestine alternately contract and relax, moving food along the tract. **(b)** Segmentation: single segments of intestine alternately contract and relax. Because inactive segments exist between active segments, food mixing occurs to a greater degree than food movement. Peristalsis is superimposed on segmentation during digestion.

4.   Before donning the stethoscope, your lab partner should clean the earpieces with an alcohol swab. Then, he or she should place the diaphragm of the stethoscope over your abdominal wall, approximately 2.5 cm (1 inch) below the xiphoid process and slightly to the left, to listen for sounds as you again take two or three swallows of water. There should be two audible sounds—one when the water splashes against the gastroesophageal sphincter and the second when the peristaltic wave of the esophagus arrives at the sphincter and the sphincter opens, allowing water to gurgle into the stomach. Determine, as accurately as possible, the time interval between these two sounds and record it below.

Interval between arrival of water at the sphincter and the

opening of the sphincter: _____ sec

This interval gives a fair indication of the time it takes for the peristaltic wave to travel down the 25 cm (10 inches) of the esophagus. (Actually the time interval is slightly less than it seems, because pressure causes the sphincter to relax before the peristaltic wave reaches it.)

⚠ Dispose of the used paper cup in the autoclave bag. ▬

Segmentation and Peristalsis

Although several types of movements occur in the digestive tract organs, peristalsis and segmentation are most important as mixing and propulsive mechanisms (Figure 39A.3).

Peristaltic movements are the major means of propelling food through most of the digestive viscera. Essentially they are waves of contraction followed by waves of relaxation that squeeze foodstuffs through the alimentary canal, and they are superimposed on segmental movements.

Segmental movements are local constrictions of the organ wall that occur rhythmically. They serve mainly to mix the foodstuffs with digestive juices and to increase the rate of absorption by continually moving different portions of the chyme over adjacent regions of the intestinal wall. However, segmentation is also an important means of food propulsion in the small intestine, and slow segmenting movements called haustral contractions are frequently seen in the large intestine.

ACTIVITY 6

Viewing Segmental and Peristaltic Movements

If a videotape showing some of the propulsive movements is available, go to a viewing station to view it before leaving the laboratory. Alternatively, use the *Interactive Physiology*® module on the Digestive System to observe gut motility. ▬

Chemical and Physical Processes of Digestion: Wet Lab

Chemical Digestion of Foodstuffs: Enzymatic Action

1. Match the following definitions with the proper choices from the key.

   Key: a. catalyst   b. control   c. enzyme   d. substrate

   _____ 1. substance on which a catalyst works

   _____ 2. biologic catalyst; protein in nature

   _____ 3. increases the rate of a chemical reaction without becoming part of the product

   _____ 4. provides a standard of comparison for test results

2. List the three characteristics of enzymes. _____

   _____

   _____

3. The enzymes of the digestive system are classified as hydrolases. What does this mean?

   _____

   _____

4. Fill in the following chart about the various digestive system enzymes encountered in this exercise.

Enzyme	Organ producing it	Site of action	Substrate(s)	Optimal pH
Salivary amylase				
Trypsin				
Lipase (pancreatic)				

5. Name the end products of digestion for the following types of foods.

   proteins: _____ carbohydrates: _____

   fats: _____ and _____

6. You used several indicators or tests in the laboratory to determine the presence or absence of certain substances. Choose the correct test or indicator from the key to correspond to the condition described below.

    Key: a.   Lugol's iodine (IKI)   b.   Benedict's solution   c.   litmus   d.   BAPNA

_____ 1.   used to test for protein hydrolysis, which was indicated by a yellow color

_____ 2.   used to test for the presence of starch, which was indicated by a blue-black color

_____ 3.   used to test for the presence of fatty acids, which was evidenced by a color change from blue to pink

_____ 4.   used to test for the presence of reducing sugars (maltose, sucrose, glucose) as indicated by a blue to green or orange color change

7. What conclusions can you draw when an experimental sample gives both a positive starch test and a positive maltose test

after incubation? _____

Why was 37°C the optimal incubation temperature? _____

Why did very little, if any, starch digestion occur in test tube 4A? _____

_____

When starch was incubated with amylase at 0°C, did you see any starch digestion? _____

Why or why not? _____

_____

Assume you have made the statement to a group of your peers that amylase is capable of starch hydrolysis to maltose. If you

had not done control tube 1A, what objection to your statement could be raised? _____

_____

What if you had not done tube 2A? _____

8. In the exercise concerning trypsin function, why was an enzyme assay like Benedict's or Lugol's IKI (which test for the presence of a reaction product) not necessary? _____

Why was tube 1T necessary? _____

Why was tube 2T necessary? _____

Trypsin is a protease similar to pepsin, the protein-digesting enzyme in the stomach. Would trypsin work well in the

stomach? _____ Why? _____

9. In the procedure concerning pancreatic lipase digestion of fats and the action of bile salts, how did the appearance of tubes

1E and 2E differ? _____

_____

Explain the reason for the difference. _____

_____

Why did the litmus indicator change from blue to pink during fat hydrolysis? _____

_____

Why is bile not considered an enzyme? _____

How did the tubes containing bile compare with those not containing bile? _____

What role does bile play in fat digestion? _____

_____

10. The three-dimensional structure of a functional protein is altered by intense heat or nonphysiological pH even though peptide bonds may not break. Such inactivation is called denaturation, and denatured enzymes are nonfunctional. Explain why.

_____

_____

What specific experimental conditions resulted in denatured enzymes? _____

_____

11. Pancreatic and intestinal enzymes operate optimally at a pH that is slightly alkaline, yet the chyme entering the duodenum
from the stomach is very acid. How is the proper pH for the functioning of the pancreatic-intestinal enzymes ensured?

_____

_____

12. Assume you have been chewing a piece of bread for 5 or 6 minutes. How would you expect its taste to change during this

interval? _____

Why? _____

13. Note the mechanism of absorption (passive or active transport) of the following food breakdown products, and indicate by
a check mark (✔) whether the absorption would result in their movement into the blood capillaries or the lymph capillaries
(lacteals).

Substance	Mechanism of absorption	Blood	Lymph
Monosaccharides			
Fatty acids and glycerol			
Amino acids			
Water			
Na^+, Cl^-, Ca^{2+}			

14. People on a strict diet to lose weight begin to metabolize stored fats at an accelerated rate. How does this condition affect

blood pH? _____

15. Using a flowchart, trace the pathway of a ham sandwich (ham = protein and fat; bread = starch) from the mouth to the site of absorption of its breakdown products, noting where digestion occurs and what specific enzymes are involved.

16. Some of the digestive organs have groups of secretory cells that liberate hormones into the blood. These exert an effect on the digestive process by acting on other cells or structures and causing them to release digestive enzymes, expel bile, or increase the motility of the digestive tract. For each hormone below, note the organ producing the hormone and its effects on the digestive process. Include the target organs affected.

Hormone	Produced by	Target organ(s) and effects
Secretin		
Gastrin		
Cholecystokinin		

Physical Processes: Mechanisms of Food Propulsion and Mixing

17. Complete the following statements.

Swallowing, or __1__, occurs in two phases—the __2__ and __3__. One of these phases, the __4__ phase, is voluntary. During the voluntary phase, the __5__ is used to push the food into the back of the throat. During swallowing, the __6__ rises to ensure that its passageway is covered by the epiglottis so that the ingested substances don't enter the respiratory passageways. It is possible to swallow water while standing on your head because the water is carried along the esophagus involuntarily by the process of __7__. The pressure exerted by the foodstuffs on the __8__ sphincter causes it to open, allowing the foodstuffs to enter the stomach.

The two major types of propulsive movements that occur in the small intestine are __9__ and __10__. One of these movements, __11__, acts to continually mix the foods and to increase the absorption rate by moving different parts of the chyme mass over the intestinal mucosa, but it has less of a role in moving foods along the digestive tract.

1. _____

2. _____

3. _____

4. _____

5. _____

6. _____

7. _____

8. _____

9. _____

10. _____

11. _____

Anatomy of the Urinary System

MATERIALS

- ☐ Human dissectible torso model, three-dimensional model of the urinary system, and/or anatomical chart of the human urinary system
- ☐ Dissecting instruments and tray
- ☐ Pig or sheep kidney, doubly or triply injected
- ☐ Disposable gloves
- ☐ Three-dimensional models of the cut kidney and of a nephron (if available)
- ☐ Compound microscope
- ☐ Prepared slides of a longitudinal section of kidney and cross sections of the bladder

✂ For instructions on animal dissections, see the dissection exercises starting on page 697 in the cat, fetal pig, and rat editions of this manual.

OBJECTIVES

1. To describe the function of the urinary system.
2. To identify, on an appropriate diagram or torso model, the urinary system organs and to describe the general function of each.
3. To compare the course and length of the urethra in males and females.
4. To identify these regions of the dissected kidney (longitudinal section): hilum, cortex, medulla, medullary pyramids, major and minor calyces, pelvis, renal columns, and fibrous and perirenal fat capsules.
5. To trace the blood supply of the kidney from the renal artery to the renal vein.
6. To define the nephron as the physiological unit of the kidney, and to describe its anatomy.
7. To define *glomerular filtration, tubular reabsorption,* and *tubular secretion,* and to indicate the nephron areas involved in these processes.
8. To define *micturition,* and to explain pertinent differences in the control of the two bladder sphincters (internal and external).
9. To recognize microscopic or diagrammatic views of the histologic structure of the kidney and bladder.

PRE-LAB QUIZ

1. Circle the correct term. In its excretory role, the urinary system is primarily concerned with the removal of carbon-containing / nitrogenous wastes from the body.
2. The _____ perform(s) the excretory and homeostatic functions of the urinary system.
   - a. kidneys
   - b. ureters
   - c. urinary bladder
   - d. all of the above
3. Circle the correct term. The cortex / medulla of the kidney is segregated into triangular regions with a striped appearance.
4. Circle the correct term. As the renal artery approaches a kidney, it is divided into branches known as the segmental arteries / afferent arterioles.
5. What do we call the anatomical units responsible for the formation of urine? _____
6. This knot of coiled capillaries, found in the kidneys, forms the filtrate. It is the
   - a. arteriole
   - b. glomerulus
   - c. podocyte
   - d. tubule
7. The section of the renal tubule closest to the glomerular capsule is the
   - a. collecting duct
   - b. distal convoluted tubule
   - c. loop of Henle
   - d. proximal convoluted tubule
8. Circle the correct term. The afferent / efferent arteriole drains the glomerular capillary bed.
9. Circle True or False. During tubular reabsorption, components of the filtrate move from the bloodstream into the tubule.
10. Circle the correct term. The internal / external urethral sphincter consists of skeletal muscle and is voluntarily controlled.

Metabolism of nutrients by the body produces wastes (carbon dioxide, nitrogenous wastes, ammonia, and so on) that must be eliminated from the body if normal function is to continue. Although excretory processes involve several organ systems (the lungs excrete carbon dioxide and skin glands excrete salts and water), it is the **urinary system** that is primarily concerned with the removal of nitrogenous wastes from the body. In addition to this purely excretory function, the kidney maintains the electrolyte, acid-base, and fluid balances of the blood and is thus a major, if not *the* major, homeostatic organ of the body.

(a)

(b)

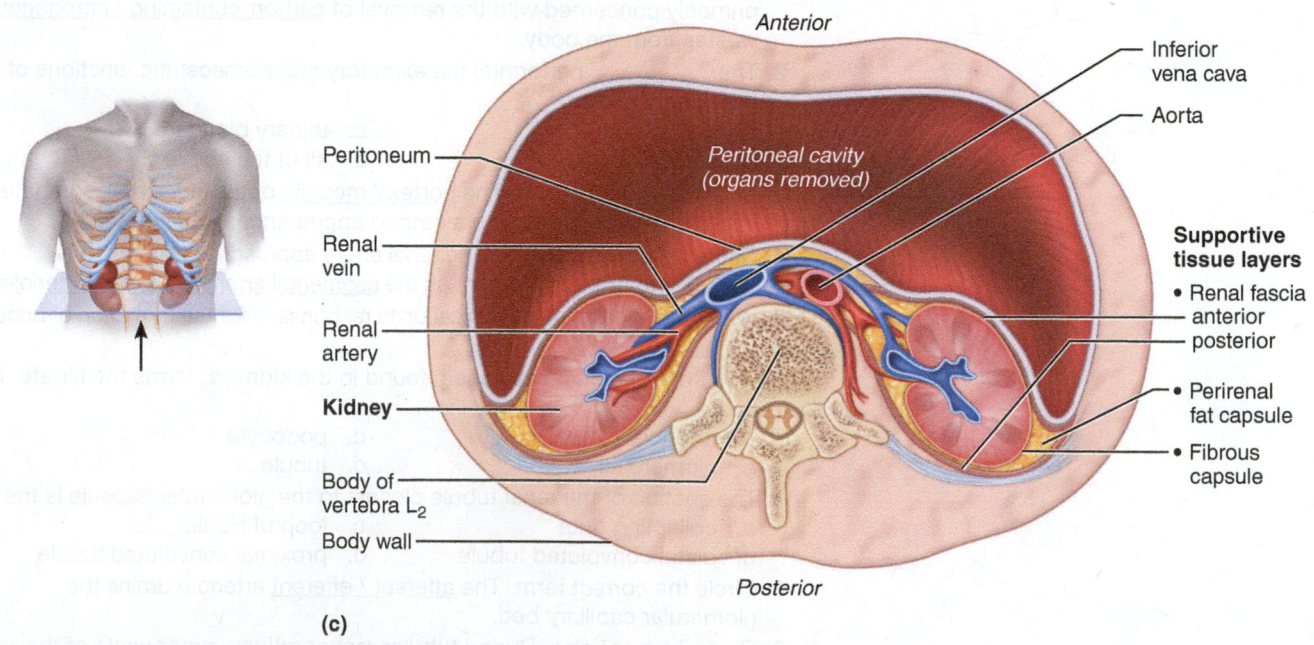

(c)

FIGURE 40.1 Organs of the urinary system. (a) Anterior view of the female urinary organs. Most unrelated abdominal organs have been removed. **(b)** Posterior in situ view showing the position of the kidneys relative to the twelfth rib pair. **(c)** Cross section of the abdomen viewed from inferior direction. Note the retroperitoneal position and supportive tissue layers of the kidneys.

Peritoneum

Ureter

Rugae

Detrusor muscle

Adventitia

Ureteric orifices

Trigone of bladder

Bladder neck

Internal urethral sphincter

Prostate

Prostatic urethra

Membranous urethra

External urethral sphincter

Urogenital diaphragm

Spongy urethra

Erectile tissue of penis

External urethral orifice

(a)

Trigone

Urethra

External urethral orifice

(b)

FIGURE 40.2 Detailed structure of the urinary bladder, urethral sphincters, and urethra. The anterior wall of the bladder has been reflected or omitted to reveal the position of the trigone. **(a)** Male. Note that the long male urethra has three regions: prostatic, membranous, and spongy. **(b)** Female.

ACTIVITY 1

Identifying Urinary System Organs

Examine the human torso model, a large anatomical chart, or a three-dimensional model of the urinary system to locate and study the anatomy and relationships of the urinary organs.

1.   Locate the paired kidneys on the dorsal body wall in the superior lumbar region. Notice that they are not positioned at exactly the same level. Because it is crowded by the liver, the right kidney is slightly lower than the left kidney. In a living person, a transparent membrane (the fibrous capsule), fat deposits (the *perirenal fat capsules*), and the fibrous renal fascia surround and hold the kidneys in place in a retroperitoneal position.

When the fatty material surrounding the kidneys is reduced or too meager in amount (in cases of rapid weight loss or in very thin individuals), the kidneys are less securely anchored and may drop to a more inferior position in the abdominal cavity. This phenomenon is called **ptosis.** ■

2.   Observe the **renal arteries** as they diverge from the descending aorta and plunge into the indented medial region (**hilum**) of each kidney. Note also the **renal veins,** which drain the kidneys (circulatory drainage) and the two **ureters,** which drain urine from the kidneys and conduct it by peristalsis to the bladder for temporary storage.

3.   Locate the **urinary bladder,** and observe the point of entry of the two ureters into this organ. Also locate the single **urethra,** which drains the bladder. The triangular region of the bladder delineated by these three openings (two ureteral and one urethral orifice) is referred to as the **trigone** (Figure 40.2).

To perform its functions, the kidney acts first as a blood filter, and then as a blood processor. It allows toxins, metabolic wastes, and excess ions to leave the body in the urine, while retaining needed substances and returning them to the blood. Malfunction of the urinary system, particularly of the kidneys, leads to a failure in homeostasis which, unless corrected, is fatal.

Gross Anatomy of the Human Urinary System

The urinary system (Figure 40.1) consists of the paired kidneys and ureters and the single urinary bladder and urethra. The **kidneys** perform the functions described above and manufacture urine in the process. The remaining organs of the system provide temporary storage reservoirs or transportation channels for urine.

FIGURE 40.3 Internal anatomy of the kidney. (a) Photograph of a right kidney. **(b)** Diagrammatic view showing the larger blood vessels supplying the kidney tissue.

Renal hilum

(a)

Renal cortex

Renal medulla

Major calyx

Papilla of pyramid

Renal pelvis

Minor calyx

Ureter

Renal pyramid in renal medulla

Renal column

Fibrous capsule

(b)

Cortical radiate vein

Cortical radiate artery

Arcuate vein

Arcuate artery

Interlobar vein

Interlobar artery

Segmental arteries

Renal vein

Renal artery

Renal pelvis

Ureter

---

4. Follow the course of the urethra to the body exterior. In the male, it is approximately 20 cm (8 inches) long, travels the length of the **penis,** and opens at its tip. Its three named regions—the *prostatic, membranous,* and *spongy urethrae*—are described in more detail in Exercise 42. The male urethra has a dual function: it is a urine conduit to the body exterior, and it provides a passageway for semen ejaculation. Thus in the male, the urethra is part of both the urinary and reproductive systems. In females, the urethra is very short, approximately 4 cm (1½ inches) long (see Figure 40.2). There are no common urinary-reproductive pathways in the female, and the female's urethra serves only to transport urine to the body exterior. Its external opening, the **external urethral orifice,** lies anterior to the vaginal opening.

DISSECTION:

Gross Internal Anatomy of the Pig or Sheep Kidney

1. In preparation for dissection, don gloves. Obtain a preserved sheep or pig kidney, dissecting tray, and instruments. Observe the kidney to identify the **fibrous capsule,** a smooth,

transparent membrane that adheres tightly to the external aspect of the kidney.

2. Find the ureter, renal vein, and renal artery at the hilum (indented) region. The renal vein has the thinnest wall and will be collapsed. The ureter is the largest of these structures and has the thickest wall.

3. Make a cut through the longitudinal axis (frontal section) of the kidney and locate the anatomical areas described below and depicted in Figure 40.3.

Kidney cortex: The superficial kidney region, which is lighter in color. If the kidney is doubly injected with latex, you will see a predominance of red and blue latex specks in this region indicating its rich vascular supply.

Medullary region: Deep to the cortex; a darker, reddish-brown color. The medulla is segregated into triangular regions that have a striped, or striated, appearance—the **medullary (renal) pyramids.** The base of each pyramid faces toward the cortex. Its more pointed *papilla,* or *apex,* points to the innermost kidney region.

Renal columns: Areas of tissue that are more like the cortex in appearance, which segregate and dip inward between the pyramids.

Cortex
Medulla

Renal
pelvis

(a)

Ureter

FIGURE 40.4 Structure of a nephron. (a) Wedge-shaped section of kidney tissue, indicating the position of the nephrons in the kidney. Note, however, that the section marked by the wedge contains hundreds of thousands of nephrons. **(b)** Detailed nephron anatomy and associated blood supply.

Parietal layer of glomerular capsule

Distal convoluted tubule

Basement membrane

Visceral layer of glomerular capsule

Fenestrated endothelium of the **glomerulus**

Proximal convoluted tubule

Cortex

Medulla

Blood vessels

Microvilli   Mitochondria

Highly infolded plasma membrane

Proximal convoluted tubule cells

Distal convoluted tubule cells

Loop of Henle
- Ascending limb
- Descending limb

Loop of Henle (thin-segment) cells

Collecting duct

Thick segment

Thin segment

Collecting duct cells

(b)

Renal pelvis: Extending inward from the hilum; a relatively flat, basinlike cavity that is continuous with the **ureter,** which exits from the hilum region. Fingerlike extensions of the pelvis should be visible. The larger, or primary, extensions are called the **major calyces** (singular: *calyx*); subdivisions of the major calyces are the **minor calyces.** Notice that the minor calyces terminate in cuplike areas that enclose the apexes of the medullary pyramids and collect urine draining from the pyramidal tips into the pelvis.

4.   If the preserved kidney is doubly or triply injected, follow the renal blood supply from the renal artery to the **glomeruli.** The glomeruli appear as little red and blue specks in the cortex region. (See Figure 40.4.)

Approximately a fourth of the total blood flow of the body is delivered to the kidneys each minute by the large **renal arteries.** As a renal artery approaches the kidney, it

breaks up into branches called **segmental arteries,** which enter the hilum. Each segmental artery, in turn, divides into several **interlobar arteries,** which ascend toward the cortex in the renal column areas. At the top of the medullary region, these arteries give off arching branches, the **arcuate arteries,** which curve over the bases of the medullary pyramids. Small **cortical radiate arteries** branch off the arcuate arteries and ascend into the cortex, giving off the individual **afferent arterioles,** which provide the capillary networks (glomeruli and peritubular capillary beds) that supply the nephrons, or functional units, of the kidney. Blood draining from the nephron capillary networks in the cortex enters the **cortical radiate veins** and then drains through the **arcuate veins** and the **interlobar veins** to finally enter the **renal vein** in the pelvis region. (There are no segmental veins.)

Dispose of the kidney specimen as your instructor specifies.

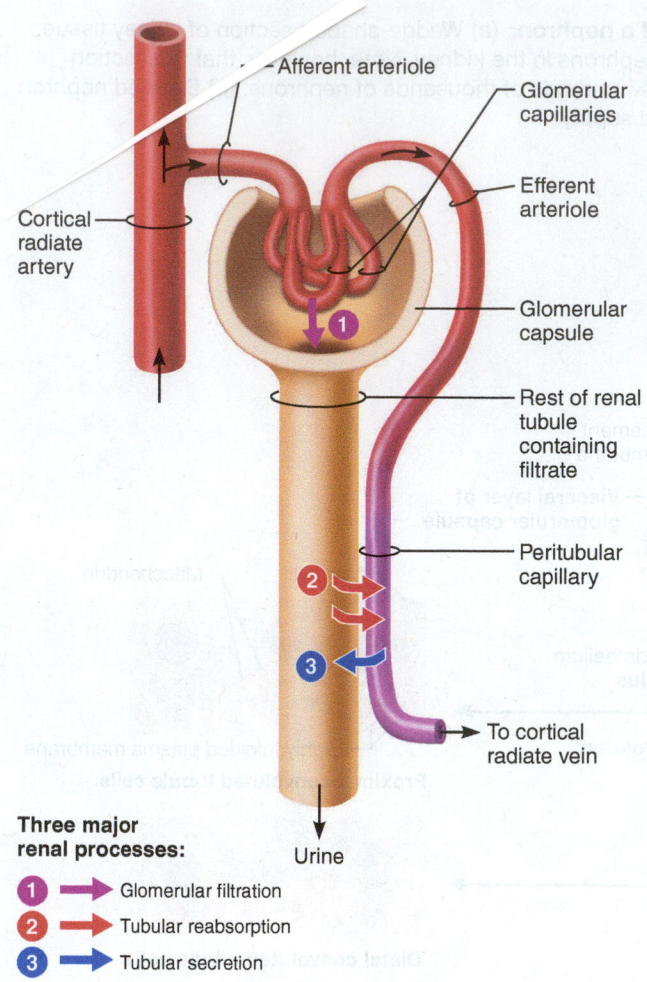

Three major renal processes:

1 → Glomerular filtration

2 → Tubular reabsorption

3 → Tubular secretion

FIGURE 40.5 A schematic, uncoiled nephron. A kidney actually has millions of nephrons acting in parallel. The three major renal processes by which the kidneys adjust the composition of plasma are **(1)** glomerular filtration, **(2)** tubular reabsorption, and **(3)** tubular secretion. Black arrows show the path of blood flow through the renal microcirculation.

Functional Microscopic Anatomy of the Kidney and Bladder

Kidney

Each kidney contains over a million nephrons, which are the anatomical units responsible for forming urine. Figure 40.4 depicts the detailed structure and the relative positioning of the nephrons in the kidney.

Each nephron consists of two major structures: a **glomerulus** (a capillary knot) and a renal tubule. During embryologic development, each **renal tubule** begins as a blind-ended tubule that gradually encloses an adjacent capillary cluster, or glomerulus. The enlarged end of the tubule encasing the glomerulus is the **glomerular (Bowman's) capsule,** and its inner, or visceral, wall consists of highly specialized

cells called **podocytes.** Podocytes have long, branching processes (*foot processes*) that interdigitate with those of other podocytes and cling to the endothelial wall of the glomerular capillaries, thus forming a very porous epithelial membrane surrounding the glomerulus. The glomerulus-capsule complex is sometimes called the **renal corpuscle.**

The rest of the tubule is approximately 3 cm (1.25 inches) long. As it emerges from the glomerular capsule, it becomes highly coiled and convoluted, drops down into a long hairpin loop, and then again coils and twists before entering a collecting duct. In order from the glomerular capsule, the anatomical areas of the renal tubule are: the **proximal convoluted tubule, loop of Henle** also called the **nephron loop** (descending and ascending limbs), and the **distal convoluted tubule.** The wall of the renal tubule is composed almost entirely of cuboidal epithelial cells, with the exception of part of the descending limb (and sometimes part of the ascending limb) of the loop of Henle, which is simple squamous epithelium. The lumen surfaces of the cuboidal cells in the proximal convoluted tubule have dense microvilli (a cellular modification that greatly increases the surface area exposed to the lumen contents, or filtrate). Microvilli also occur on cells of the distal convoluted tubule but in greatly reduced numbers, revealing its less significant role in reclaiming filtrate contents.

Most nephrons, called **cortical nephrons,** are located entirely within the cortex. However, parts of the loops of Henle of the **juxtamedullary nephrons** (located close to the cortex-medulla junction) penetrate well into the medulla. The **collecting ducts,** each of which receives urine from many nephrons, run downward through the medullary pyramids, giving them their striped appearance. As the collecting ducts approach the renal pelvis, they fuse together and empty the final urinary product into the minor calyces via the papillae of the pyramids.

The function of the nephron depends on several unique features of the renal circulation (see Figure 40.5). The capillary vascular supply consists of two distinct capillary beds, the *glomerulus* and the *peritubular capillary bed.* Vessels leading to and from the glomerulus, the first capillary bed, are both arterioles: the **afferent arteriole** feeds the bed while the **efferent arteriole** drains it. The glomerular capillary bed has no parallel elsewhere in the body. It is a high-pressure bed along its entire length. Its high pressure is a result of two major factors: (1) the bed is *fed and drained* by arterioles (arterioles are high-resistance vessels as opposed to venules, which are low-resistance vessels), and (2) the afferent feeder arteriole is larger in diameter than the efferent arteriole draining the bed. The high hydrostatic pressure created by these two anatomical features forces out fluid and blood components smaller than proteins from the glomerulus into the glomerular capsule. That is, it forms the filtrate that is processed by the nephron tubule.

The **peritubular capillary bed** arises from the efferent arteriole draining the glomerulus. This set of capillaries clings intimately to the renal tubule and empties into the cortical radiate veins that leave the cortex. The peritubular capillaries are *low-pressure,* porous capillaries adapted for absorption rather than filtration and readily take up the solutes and water reabsorbed from the filtrate by the tubule cells. The juxtamedullary nephrons have additional looping vessels, called the **vasa recta** (straight vessels), that parallel the long loops of Henle in the medulla. Hence, the two capillary beds of the nephron have very different, but complementary, roles: the glomerulus produces the filtrate, and the peritubular capillaries reclaim most of that filtrate.

Additionally, each nephron has a region called a **juxtaglomerular apparatus (JGA),** which plays an important role in forming concentrated urine. The JGA consists of (1) *juxtaglomerular (JG) cells* (also called *granular cells*), which function as blood pressure sensors in the walls of the afferent arterioles near the glomerulus, and (2) a *macula densa,* a specialized group of columnar chemoreceptor cells in the distal convoluted tubule abutting the JG cells (Figure 40.6a).

Urine formation is a result of three processes: *filtration, reabsorption,* and *secretion* (see Figure 40.5). **Filtration,** the role of the glomerulus, is largely a passive process in which a portion of the blood passes from the glomerular bed into the glomerular capsule. This filtrate then enters the proximal convoluted tubule where tubular reabsorption and secretion begin. During **tubular reabsorption,** many of the filtrate components move through the tubule cells and return to the blood in the peritubular capillaries. Some of this reabsorption is passive, such as that of water which passes by osmosis, but the reabsorption of most substances depends on active transport processes and is highly selective. Which substances are reabsorbed at a particular time depends on the composition of the blood and needs of the body at that time. Substances that are almost entirely reabsorbed from the filtrate include water, glucose, and amino acids. Various ions are selectively reabsorbed or allowed to go out in the urine according to what is required to maintain appropriate blood pH and electrolyte composition. Waste products (urea, creatinine, uric acid, and drug metabolites) are reabsorbed to a much lesser degree or not at all. Most (75% to 80%) of tubular reabsorption occurs in the proximal convoluted tubule. The rest occurs in other areas, especially the distal convoluted tubules and collecting ducts.

Tubular secretion is essentially the reverse process of tubular reabsorption. Substances such as hydrogen and potassium ions and creatinine move either from the blood of the peritubular capillaries through the tubular cells or from the tubular cells into the filtrate to be disposed of in the urine. This process is particularly important for the disposal of substances not already in the filtrate (such as drug metabolites), and as a device for controlling blood pH.

ACTIVITY 2

Studying Nephron Structure

1. Begin your study of nephron structure by identifying the glomerular capsule, proximal and distal convoluted tubule regions, and the loop of Henle on a model of the nephron. Then, obtain a compound microscope and a prepared slide of kidney tissue to continue with the microscope study of the kidney.

2. Hold the longitudinal section of the kidney up to the light to identify cortical and medullary areas. Then secure the slide on the microscope stage, and scan the slide under low power.

3. Move the slide so that you can see the cortical area. Identify a glomerulus, which appears as a ball of tightly packed material containing many small nuclei (Figures 40.6). It is usually delineated by a vacant-appearing region (corresponding to the space between the visceral and parietal layers of the glomerular capsule) that surrounds it.

4. Notice that the renal tubules are cut at various angles. Try to differentiate between the fuzzy cuboidal epithelium of the

(a)

(b)

FIGURE 40.6 Microscopic structure of kidney tissue.
(a) Detailed structure of the glomerulus (170×). **(b)** Low-power view of the renal cortex (50×).

proximal convoluted tubule, which has dense microvilli, and that of the distal convoluted tubule with sparse microvilli. Also identify the thin-walled loop of Henle. ◼

Bladder

Although urine production by the kidney is a continuous process, urine is usually removed from the body when voiding is convenient. In the meantime the **urinary bladder,** which receives urine via the ureters and discharges it via the urethra, stores it temporarily.

Voiding, or **micturition,** is the process in which urine empties from the bladder. Two sphincter muscles or valves (see Figure 40.2), the **internal urethral sphincter** (more superiorly located) and the **external urethral sphincter** (more inferiorly located) control the outflow of urine from the bladder. Ordinarily, the bladder continues to collect urine until about 200 ml have accumulated, at which time the stretching of the bladder wall activates stretch receptors. Impulses transmitted to the central nervous system subsequently produce reflex contractions of the bladder wall through parasympathetic

Circular layer

Longitudinal layer

Smooth muscle

Transitional epithelium

Adventitia

FIGURE 40.7 Structure of the ureter wall. Cross section of ureter (15×).

nervous system pathways (in other words, via the pelvic splanchnic nerves). As contractions increase in force and frequency, stored urine is forced past the internal sphincter, which is a smooth muscle involuntary sphincter, into the superior part of the urethra. It is then that a person feels the urge to void. The inferior external sphincter consists of skeletal muscle and is voluntarily controlled. If it is not convenient to void, the opening of this sphincter can be inhibited. Conversely, if the time is convenient, the sphincter may be relaxed and the stored urine flushed from the body. If voiding is inhibited, the reflex contractions of the bladder cease temporarily and urine continues to accumulate in the bladder. After another 200 to 300 ml of urine have been collected, the *micturition reflex* will again be initiated.

Lack of voluntary control over the external sphincter is referred to as **incontinence.** Incontinence is normal in children 2 years old or younger, as they have not yet gained control over the voluntary sphincter. In adults and older children, incontinence is generally a result of spinal cord injury, emotional problems, bladder irritability, or some other pathology of the urinary tract. ■

ACTIVITY 3

Studying Bladder Structure

1.   Return the kidney slide to the supply area, and obtain a slide of bladder tissue. Scan the bladder tissue. Identify its three layers: mucosa, muscular layer, and fibrous adventitia.

2.   Study the mucosa with its highly specialized transitional epithelium. The plump, transitional epithelial cells have the ability to slide over one another, thus decreasing the thickness of the mucosa layer as the bladder fills and stretches to accommodate the increased urine volume. Depending on the degree of stretching of the bladder, the mucosa may be three to eight cell layers thick. Compare the transitional epithelium of the mucosa to that shown in Figure 6A.3h (page 73).

3.   Examine the heavy muscular wall (detrusor muscle), which consists of three irregularly arranged muscular layers. The innermost and outermost muscle layers are arranged longitudinally; the middle layer is arranged circularly. Attempt to differentiate the three muscle layers.

4.   Draw a small section of the bladder wall, and label all regions or tissue areas.

5.   Compare your sketch of the bladder wall to the structure of the ureter wall shown in Figure 40.7. How are the two organs similar histologically?

_____

_____

_____

What is/are the most obvious differences?

_____

_____

For instructions on animal dissections, see the dissection exercises starting on page 697 in the cat, rat, and fetal pig editions of this manual.

Anatomy of the Urinary System

Gross Anatomy of the Human Urinary System

1. Complete the following statements.

The kidney is referred to as an excretory organ because it excretes __1__ wastes. It is also a major homeostatic organ because it maintains the electrolyte, __2__, and __3__ balance of the blood.

Urine is continuously formed by the __4__ and is routed down the __5__ by the mechanism of __6__ to a storage organ called the __7__. Eventually, the urine is conducted to the body __8__ by the urethra. In the male, the urethra is __9__ centimeters long and transports both urine and __10__. The female urethra is __11__ centimeters long and transports only urine.

Voiding or emptying the bladder is called __12__. Voiding has both voluntary and involuntary components. The voluntary sphincter is the __13__ sphincter. An inability to control this sphincter is referred to as __14__.

1. _____

2. _____

3. _____

4. _____

5. _____

6. _____

7. _____

8. _____

9. _____

10. _____

11. _____

12. _____

13. _____

14. _____

2. What is the function of the fat cushion that surrounds the kidneys in life? _____

_____

3. Define *ptosis*. _____

_____

4. Why is incontinence a normal phenomenon in the child under 1½ to 2 years old? _____

_____

What events may lead to its occurrence in the adult? _____

_____

_____

5. Complete the labeling of the diagram to correctly identify the urinary system organs.

Hepatic veins (cut)

Adrenal gland

Aorta

Iliac crest

Rectum

Gross Internal Anatomy of the Pig or Sheep Kidney

6. Match the appropriate structure in column B to its description in column A.

Column A

_____ 1. smooth membrane, tightly adherent to the kidney surface

_____ 2. portion of the kidney containing mostly collecting ducts

_____ 3. portion of the kidney containing the bulk of the nephron structures

_____ 4. superficial region of kidney tissue

_____ 5. basinlike area of the kidney, continuous with the ureter

_____ 6. a cup-shaped extension of the pelvis that encircles the apex of a pyramid

_____ 7. area of cortical tissue running between the medullary pyramids

Column B

a. cortex

b. medulla

c. minor calyx

d. fibrous capsule

e. renal column

f. renal pelvis

Functional Microscopic Anatomy of the Kidney and Bladder

7. Match each lettered structure in the diagram of the nephron (and associated renal blood supply) with the correct name in the numbered list.

_____	1. afferent arteriole
_____	2. arcuate artery
_____	3. arcuate vein
_____	4. collecting duct
_____	5. cortical radiate artery
_____	6. cortical radiate vein
_____	7. distal convoluted tubule
_____	8. efferent arteriole
_____	9. glomerular capsule
_____	10. glomerulus
_____	11. interlobar artery
_____	12. interlobar vein
_____	13. loop of Henle
_____	14. peritubular capillaries
_____	15. proximal convoluted tubule

8. Use the terms provided in question 7 to identify the following descriptions.

_____ 1. site of filtrate formation

_____ 2. primary site of tubular reabsorption

_____ 3. secondarily important site of tubular reabsorption

_____ 4. structure that conveys the processed filtrate (urine) to the renal pelvis

_____ 5. blood supply that directly receives substances from the tubular cells

_____ 6. its inner (visceral) membrane forms part of the filtration membrane

9. Explain *why* the glomerulus is such a high-pressure capillary bed. _____

_____

How does its high-pressure condition aid its function of filtrate formation? _____

_____

10. What structural modification of certain tubule cells enhances their ability to reabsorb substances from the filtrate?

_____

11. Explain the mechanism of tubular secretion, and explain its importance in the urine-formation process. _____

_____

_____

12. Compare and contrast the composition of blood plasma and glomerular filtrate. _____

_____

13. Trace a drop of blood from the time it enters the kidney via the renal artery until it leaves the kidney through the renal vein.

Renal artery → _____

_____

_____ → renal vein

14. Define _juxtaglomerular apparatus._ _____

_____

15. Label the figure using the key letters of the correct terms.

Key: a.   _juxtaglomerular cells_

     b.   cuboidal epithelium

     c.   macula densa

     d.   glomerular capsule (parietal layer)

     e.   distal convoluted tubule

16. Trace the anatomical pathway of a molecule of creatinine (metabolic waste) from the glomerular capsule to the urethra. Note each microscopic and/or gross structure it passes through in its travels. Name the subdivisions of the renal tubule.

Glomerular capsule → _____

_____

_____ → urethra

17. What is important functionally about the specialized epithelium (transitional epithelium) in the bladder?

_____

MATERIALS

- ☐ Disposable gloves
- ☐ Student urine samples collected at the beginning of the laboratory or "normal" artificial urine provided by the instructor*
- ☐ Numbered "pathological" urine specimens provided by the instructor*
- ☐ Wide-range pH paper
- ☐ Dipsticks: individual (Clinistix, Ketostix, Albustix, Hemastix) or combination (Chemstrip or Multistix)
- ☐ Urinometer
- ☐ Test tubes, test tube rack, and test tube holders
- ☐ 10-cc graduated cylinders
- ☐ Test reagents for sulfates: 10% barium chloride solution, dilute HCl (hydrochloric acid)
- ☐ Hot plate
- ☐ 500-ml beaker
- ☐ Test reagent for phosphates: dilute nitric acid, dilute ammonium molybdate
- ☐ Glass stirring rod
- ☐ Test reagent for chloride: 3.0% silver nitrate solution ($AgNO_3$), freshly prepared
- ☐ Clean microscope slide and coverslip
- ☐ Compound microscope
- ☐ Test reagent for urea: concentrated nitric acid in dropper bottles
- ☐ Test reagent for glucose (Clinitest tablets) and Clinitest color chart
- ☐ Medicine droppers

*Directions for making artificial urine are provided in the Instructor's Guide for this manual.

Text continues on next page.

OBJECTIVES

1. To list the physical characteristics of urine, and to indicate the normal pH and specific gravity ranges.
2. To list substances that are normal urinary constituents.
3. To conduct various urinalysis tests and procedures, and to use them to determine the substances present in a urine specimen.
4. To define the following urinary conditions:

calculi	ketonuria	pyuria
glycosuria	hematuria	casts
albuminuria	hemoglobinuria	

5. To explain the implications and possible causes of conditions listed in objective 4.

PRE-LAB QUIZ

1. Normal urine is usually pale yellow to amber in color, due to the presence of
    a. hemochrome
    b. melanin
    c. urochrome
2. Circle the correct term. The average pH value of urine is 6.0 / 11.0.
3. Circle True or False. Glucose can usually be found in all normal urine.
4. _____, like other blood proteins, is /are too large to pass through the glomerular filtration membrane and is/are normally not found in urine.
    a. Albumin
    b. Chloride
    c. Nitrates
    d. Sulfate
5. Circle the correct term. Hematuria / Ketonuria, the appearance of red blood cells in the urine, almost always indicates pathology of the urinary system.
6. The appearance of bile pigments in the urine, a condition known as _____, can be an indication of liver disease.
    a. albuminuria
    b. bilirubinuria
    c. ketonuria
    d. pyuria
7. Circle the correct term. Casts / Calculi are hardened cell fragments formed in the distal convoluted tubules and collecting ducts and flushed out of the urinary tract.
8. When determining the presence of inorganic constituents such as sulfates, phosphates, and chlorides, you will be looking for the "formation of a precipitate." What is a precipitate? _____
   _____

Blood composition depends on three major factors: diet, cellular metabolism, and urinary output. In 24 hours, the kidneys' 2 million nephrons filter 150 to 180 liters of blood plasma through their glomeruli into the tubules, where it is selectively processed by tubular reabsorption and secretion. In the same period, urinary output, which contains by-products of metabolism and excess ions, is 1.0 to 1.8 liters. In healthy individuals, the kidneys can maintain blood constancy despite wide variations in diet and metabolic activity. With certain pathological conditions, urine composition often changes dramatically.

myA&P For practice quizzes on this lab, go to www.myaandp.com.

621

☐ Timer (watch or clock with a second hand)
☐ Ictotest reagent tablets and test mat
☐ Flasks and laboratory buckets containing 10% bleach solution
☐ Disposable autoclave bags
☐ *Demonstration:* Instructor-prepared specimen of urine sediment set up for microscopic analysis

PEx PhysioEx™ 8.0 Computer Simulation on page PEx-145

Characteristics of Urine

To be valuable as a diagnostic tool, a urinalysis must be done within 30 minutes after the urine is voided or on refrigerated urine. Freshly voided urine is generally clear and pale yellow to amber in color. This normal yellow color is due to *urochrome,* a pigment metabolite arising from the body's destruction of hemoglobin (via bilirubin or bile pigments). As a rule, color variations from pale yellow to deeper amber indicate the relative concentration of solutes to water in the urine. The greater the solute concentration, the deeper the color. Abnormal urine color may be due to certain foods, such as beets, various drugs, bile, or blood.

The odor of freshly voided urine is slightly aromatic, but bacterial action gives it an ammonia-like odor when left standing. Some drugs, vegetables (such as asparagus), and various disease processes (such as diabetes mellitus) alter the characteristic odor of urine. For example, the urine of a person with uncontrolled diabetes mellitus (and elevated levels of ketones) smells fruity or acetone-like.

The pH of urine ranges from 4.5 to 8.0, but its average value, 6.0, is slightly acidic. Diet may markedly influence the pH of the urine. For example, a diet high in protein (meat, eggs, cheese) and whole wheat products increases the acidity of urine. Such foods are called *acid ash foods.* On the other hand, a vegetarian diet *(alkaline ash diet)* increases the alkalinity of the urine.* A bacterial infection of the urinary tract may also result in urine with a high pH.

Specific gravity is the relative weight of a specific volume of liquid compared with an equal volume of distilled water. The specific gravity of distilled water is 1.000, because 1 ml weighs 1 g. Since urine contains dissolved solutes, it weighs more than water, and its customary specific gravity ranges from 1.001 to 1.030. Urine with a specific gravity of 1.001 contains few solutes and is considered very dilute. Dilute urine commonly results when a person drinks excessive amounts of water, uses diuretics, or suffers from diabetes insipidus or chronic renal failure. Conditions that produce urine with a high specific gravity include limited fluid intake, fever, and kidney inflammation, called *pyelonephritis.* If urine becomes excessively concentrated, some of the substances normally held in solution begin to precipitate or crystallize, forming **kidney stones,** or **renal calculi.**

Normal constituents of urine (in order of decreasing concentration) include water; urea;* sodium,[†] potassium, phosphate, and sulfate ions; creatinine;* and uric acid.* Much smaller but highly variable amounts of calcium, magnesium, and bicarbonate ions are also found in the urine. Abnormally high concentrations of any of these urinary constituents may indicate a pathological condition.

Abnormal Urinary Constituents

Abnormal urinary constituents are substances not normally present in the urine when the body is operating properly. ■

Glucose

The presence of glucose in the urine, a condition called **glycosuria,** indicates abnormally high blood sugar levels. Normally, blood sugar levels are maintained between 80 and 100 mg/100 ml of blood. At this level all glucose in the filtrate is reabsorbed by the tubular cells and returned to the blood. Glycosuria may result from carbohydrate intake so excessive that normal physiological and hormonal mechanisms cannot clear it from the blood quickly enough. In such cases, the active transport reabsorption mechanisms of the renal tubules for glucose are exceeded—but only temporarily.

Pathological glycosuria occurs in conditions such as uncontrolled diabetes mellitus, in which the body cells are unable to absorb glucose from the blood because the pancreatic islet cells produce inadequate amounts of the hormone insulin, or there is some abnormality of the insulin receptors. Under such circumstances, the body cells increase their metabolism of fats, and the excess and unusable glucose spills out in the urine.

Albumin

Albuminuria, or the presence of albumin in urine, is an abnormal finding. Albumin is the single most abundant blood protein and is very important in maintaining the osmotic pressure of the blood. Albumin, like other blood proteins, is too large to pass through the glomerular filtration membrane. Thus, albuminuria is generally indicative of abnormally increased permeability of the glomerular membrane. Certain nonpathological conditions, such as excessive exertion, pregnancy, or overabundant protein intake, can temporarily increase the membrane permeability, leading to **physiological albuminuria.** Pathological conditions resulting in albuminuria include events that damage the glomerular membrane, such as kidney trauma due to blows, the ingestion of poisons or heavy metals, bacterial toxins, glomerulonephritis, and hypertension.

---

*Urea, uric acid, and creatinine are the most important nitrogenous wastes found in urine. Urea is an end product of protein breakdown; uric acid is a metabolite of purine breakdown; and creatinine is associated with muscle metabolism of creatine phosphate.

[†]Sodium ions appear in relatively high concentration in the urine because of reduced urine volume, not because large amounts are being excreted. Sodium is the major positive ion in the plasma; under normal circumstances, most of it is actively reabsorbed.

---

*The naming of foods as acid or alkaline *ash* derives from the fact that if an acid ash food is burned to ash, the pH of the ash is acidic. The ash of alkaline ash foods is alkaline.

Ketone Bodies

Ketone bodies (acetoacetic acid, beta-hydroxybutyric acid, and acetone) normally appear in the urine in very small amounts. **Ketonuria,** the presence of these intermediate products of fat metabolism in excessive amounts, usually indicates that abnormal metabolic processes are occurring. The result may be *acidosis* and its complications. Ketonuria is an expected finding during starvation, or diets very low in carbohydrates, when inadequate food intake forces the body to use its fat stores. Ketonuria coupled with a finding of glycosuria is generally diagnostic for diabetes mellitus.

Red Blood Cells

Hematuria, the appearance of red blood cells, or erythrocytes, in the urine, almost always indicates pathology of the urinary tract, because erythrocytes are too large to pass through the glomerular pores. Possible causes include irritation of the urinary tract organs by calculi (kidney stones), which produces frank bleeding; infection or tumors of the urinary tract; or physical trauma to the urinary organs. In healthy menstruating females, it may reflect accidental contamination of the urine sample with the menstrual flow.

Hemoglobin

Hemoglobinuria, the presence of hemoglobin in the urine, is a result of the fragmentation, or hemolysis, of red blood cells. As a result, hemoglobin is liberated into the plasma and subsequently appears in the kidney filtrate. Hemoglobinuria indicates various pathological conditions including hemolytic anemias, transfusion reactions, burns, poisonous snake bites, or renal disease.

Nitrites

The presence of urinary nitrites might indicate a bacterial infection, particularly *E. coli* or other gram-negative rods. Nitrites are valuable for early detection of bladder infections.

Bile Pigments

Bilirubinuria, the appearance of bilirubin (bile pigments) in urine, is an abnormal finding and usually indicates liver pathology, such as hepatitis, cirrhosis, or bile duct blockage. Bilirubinuria is signaled by a yellow foam that forms when the urine sample is shaken.

Urobilinogen is produced in the intestine from bilirubin and gives feces a brown color. Some urobilinogen is reabsorbed into the blood and either excreted back into the intestine by the liver or excreted by the kidneys in the urine. Complete absence of urobilinogen may indicate renal disease or obstruction of bile flow in the liver. Increased levels may indicate hepatitis A, cirrhosis, or biliary disease.

White Blood Cells

Pyuria is the presence of white blood cells or other pus constituents in the urine. It indicates inflammation of the urinary tract.

Casts

Any complete discussion of the varieties and implications of casts is beyond the scope of this exercise. However, because they always represent a pathological condition of the kidney or urinary tract, they should at least be mentioned. **Casts** are hardened cell fragments, usually cylindrical, which are formed in the distal convoluted tubules and collecting ducts and then flushed out of the urinary tract. Hyaline casts are formed from a mucoprotein secreted by tubule cells. These casts form when the filtrate flow rate is slow, the pH is low, or the salt concentration is high, all conditions which cause protein to denature. Red blood cell casts are typical in glomerulonephritis, as red blood cells leak through the filtration membrane and stick together in the tubules. White blood cell casts form when the kidney is inflamed, which is typically a result of pyelonephritis but sometimes occurs with glomerulonephritis. Degenerated renal tubule cells form granular or waxy casts. Broad waxy casts may indicate end-stage renal disease. Two cast types are shown in Figure 41A.1 (page 626).

ACTIVITY 1

Analyzing Urine Samples

In this part of the exercise, you will use prepared dipsticks and perform chemical tests to determine the characteristics of normal urine as well as to identify abnormal urinary components. You will investigate two or more urine samples. The first, designated as the *standard urine specimen* in the chart on page 625, will be either yours or a "normal" sample provided by your instructor. The second will be an unknown urine specimen provided by your instructor. Make the following determinations on both samples, and record your results by circling the appropriate item or description or by adding data to complete the chart. If you have more than one unknown sample, accurately identify each sample by number.

⚠️ *Obtain and wear disposable gloves throughout this laboratory session.* Although the instructor-provided urine samples are actually artificial urine (concocted in the laboratory to resemble real urine), you should still observe the techniques of safe handling of body fluids as part of your learning process. When you have completed the laboratory procedures: (1) dispose of the gloves, used pH paper strips, and dipsticks in the autoclave bag; (2) put used glassware in the bleach-containing laboratory bucket; (3) wash the lab bench down with 10% bleach solution.

Determination of the Physical Characteristics of Urine

1. Determine the color, transparency, and odor of your "normal" sample and one of the numbered pathological samples, and circle the appropriate descriptions in the Urinalysis Results chart.

2. Obtain a roll of wide-range pH paper to determine the pH of each sample. Use a fresh piece of paper for each test, and dip the strip into the urine to be tested two or three times before comparing the color obtained with the chart on the dispenser. Record your results in the chart. (If you will be using one of the combination dipsticks—Chemstrip or Multistix—this pH determination can be done later.)

3. To determine specific gravity, obtain a urinometer cylinder and float. Mix the urine well, and fill the urinometer cylinder about two-thirds full with urine.

4. Examine the urinometer float to determine how to read its markings. In most cases, the scale has numbered lines separated by a series of unnumbered lines. The numbered lines

give the reading for the first two decimal places. You must determine the third decimal place by reading the lower edge of the meniscus—the curved surface representing the urine-air junction—on the stem of the float.

5. Carefully lower the urinometer float into the urine. Make sure it is floating freely before attempting to take the reading. Record the specific gravity of both samples in the chart. _Do not dispose of this urine if the samples that you have are less than 200 ml in volume_ because you will need to make several more determinations.

Determination of Inorganic Constituents in Urine

Sulfates Using a 10-cc graduated cylinder, add 5 ml of urine to a test tube, and then add a few drops of dilute hydrochloric acid and 2 ml of 10% barium chloride solution. The appearance of a white precipitate (barium sulfate) indicates the presence of sulfates in the sample. Clean the graduated cylinder and the test tubes well after use. Record your results.

Phosphates Obtain a hot plate and a 500-ml beaker. To prepare the hot water bath, half fill the beaker with tap water and heat it on the hot plate. Add 5 ml of urine to a test tube, and then add three or four drops of dilute nitric acid and 3 ml of ammonium molybdate. Mix well with a glass stirring rod, and then heat gently in a hot water bath. Formation of a yellow precipitate indicates the presence of phosphates in the sample. Record your results.

Chlorides Place 5 ml of urine in a test tube, and add several drops of silver nitrate ($AgNO_3$). The appearance of a white precipitate (silver chloride) is a positive test for chlorides. Record your results.

Nitrites Use a combination dipstick to test for nitrites. Record your results.

Determination of Organic Constituents in Urine

Individual dipsticks or combination dipsticks (Chemstrip or Multistix) may be used for many of the tests in this section. If combination dipsticks are used, be prepared to take the readings on several factors (pH, protein [albumin], glucose, ketones, blood/hemoglobin, leukocytes, urobilinogen, bilirubin, and nitrites) at the same time. Generally speaking, results for all of these tests may be read _during_ the second minute after immersion, but readings taken after 2 minutes have passed should be considered invalid. Pay careful attention to the directions for method and time of immersion and disposal of excess urine from the strip, regardless of the dipstick used. If you are testing your own urine and get an unanticipated result, it is helpful to know that most of the combination dipsticks produce false positive or negative results for certain solutes when the subject is taking vitamin C, aspirin, or certain drugs.

Urea Put two drops of urine on a clean microscope slide and _carefully_ add one drop of concentrated nitric acid to the urine. Slowly warm the mixture on a hot plate until it begins to dry at the edges, but do not allow it to boil or to evaporate to dryness. When the slide has cooled, examine the edges of the preparation under low power to identify the rhombic or hexagonal crystals of urea nitrate, which form when urea and nitric acid react chemically. Keep the light low for best contrast. Record your results.

Glucose Use a combination dipstick or obtain a vial of Clinistix, and conduct the dipstick test according to the instructions on the vial. Record your results in the Urinalysis Results chart.

Because the Clinitest reagent is routinely used in clinical agencies for glucose determinations in pediatric patients (children), it is worthwhile to conduct this test as well. Obtain the Clinitest tablets and the associated color chart. You will need a timer (watch or clock with a second hand) for this test. Using a medicine dropper, put 5 drops of urine into a test tube; then rinse the dropper and add 10 drops of water to the tube. Add a Clinitest tablet. Wait 15 seconds and then compare the color obtained to the color chart. Record your results.

Albumin Use a combination dipstick or obtain the Albustix dipsticks, and conduct the determinations as indicated on the vial. Record your results.

Ketones Use a combination dipstick or obtain the Ketostix dipsticks. Conduct the determinations as indicated on the vial. Record your results.

Blood/Hemoglobin Test your urine samples for the presence of hemoglobin by using a Hemastix dipstick or a combination dipstick according to the directions on the vial. Usually a short drying period is required before making the reading, so read the directions carefully. Record your results.

Bilirubin Using a combination dipstick, determine if there is any bilirubin in your urine samples. Record your results.

Also conduct the Ictotest for the presence of bilirubin. Using a medicine dropper, place one drop of urine in the center of one of the special test mats provided with the Ictotest reagent tablets. Place one of the reagent tablets over the drop of urine, and then add two drops of water directly to the tablet. If the mixture turns purple when you add water, bilirubin is present. Record your results.

Leukocytes Use a combination dipstick to test for leukocytes. Record your results.

Urobilinogen Use a combination dipstick to test for urobilinogen. Record your results.

Clean up your area following the procedures on page 623. ▪

Urinalysis Results*

Observation or test	Normal values	Standard urine specimen	Unknown specimen (# _____)
Physical Characteristics			
Color	Pale yellow	Yellow: pale medium dark other _____	Yellow: pale medium dark other _____
Transparency	Transparent	Clear Slightly cloudy Cloudy	Clear Slightly cloudy Cloudy
Odor	Characteristic	Describe:	Describe:
		_____	_____
pH	4.5–8.0	_____	_____
Specific gravity	1.001–1.030	_____	_____
Inorganic Components			
Sulfates	Present	Present Absent	Present Absent
Phosphates	Present	Present Absent	Present Absent
Chlorides	Present	Present Absent	Present Absent
Nitrites	Absent	Present Absent	Present Absent
Organic Components			
Urea	Present	Present Absent	Present Absent
Glucose Dipstick: _____	Negative	Record results: _____	Record results: _____
Clinitest	Negative	_____	_____
Albumin Dipstick: _____	Negative	_____	_____
Ketone bodies Dipstick: _____	Negative	_____	_____
RBCs/hemoglobin Dipstick: _____	Negative	_____	_____
Bilirubin Dipstick: _____	Negative	_____	_____
Ictotest	Negative (no color change)	Negative Positive (purple)	Negative Positive (purple)
Leukocytes	Absent	Present Absent	Present Absent
Urobilinogen	Present	Present Absent	Present Absent

*Circle the appropriate description if provided; otherwise, record the results you observed. Identify dipsticks used.

Analyzing Urine Sediment Microscopically (Optional)

If your instructor so indicates, conduct a microscopic analysis of urine sediment (of "real" urine). The urine sample to be analyzed microscopically has been centrifuged to spin the more dense urine components to the bottom of a tube, and some of the sediment (mounted on a slide) has been stained with Sedi-stain to make the components more visible.

Go to the demonstration microscope to conduct this study. Using the lowest light source possible, examine the slide under low power to determine if any of the sediments illustrated in Figure 41A.1 can be seen.

Unorganized sediments: Chemical substances that form crystals or precipitate from solution; for example, calcium oxalates, carbonates, and phosphates; uric acid; ammonium ureates; and cholesterol. Also, if one has been taking antibiotics or certain drugs such as sulfa drugs, these may be detectable in the urine in crystalline form. Normal urine contains very small amounts of crystals, but conditions such as urinary retention or urinary tract infection may cause the appearance of much larger amounts (and their possible consolidation into calculi). The high-power lens may be needed to view the various crystals, which tend to be much more minute than the organized (cellular) sediments.

Organized sediments: Include epithelial cells (rarely of any pathological significance), pus cells (white blood cells), red blood cells, and casts. Urine is normally negative for organized sediments, and the presence of the last three categories mentioned, other than trace amounts, always indicates kidney pathology.

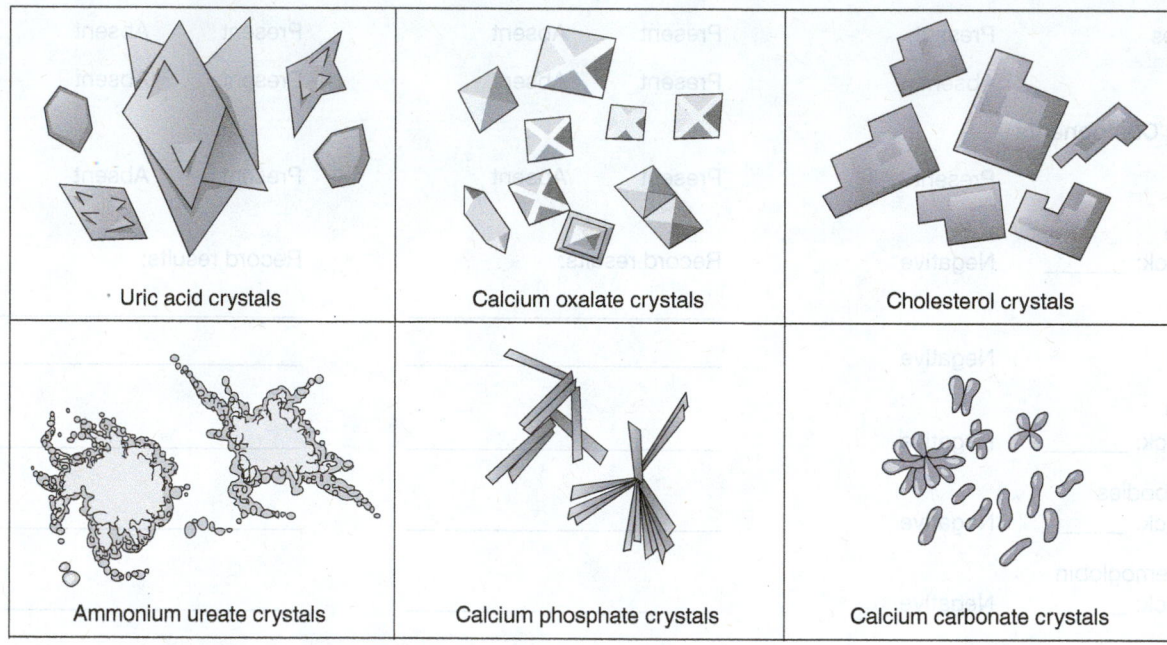

Uric acid crystals

Calcium oxalate crystals

Cholesterol crystals

Ammonium ureate crystals

Calcium phosphate crystals

Calcium carbonate crystals

(a) Unorganized sediments

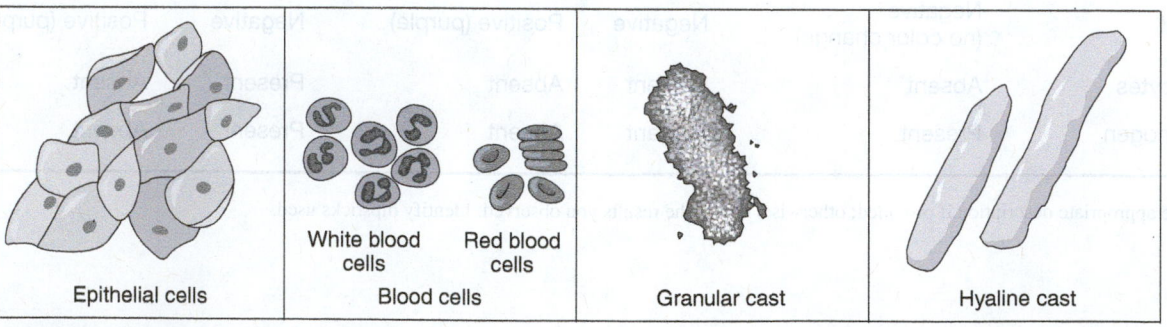

Epithelial cells

White blood cells

Red blood cells

Blood cells

Granular cast

Hyaline cast

(b) Organized sediments

FIGURE 41A.1 Examples of sediments. (a) Unorganized sediments. **(b)** Organized sediments.

Urinalysis

Characteristics of Urine

1. What is the normal volume of urine excreted in a 24-hour period? _____

2. Assuming normal conditions, note whether each of the following substances would be (a) in greater relative concentration in the urine than in the glomerular filtrate, (b) in lesser concentration in the urine than in the glomerular filtrate, or (c) absent from both the urine and the glomerular filtrate.

_____ 1. water   _____ 6. amino acids   _____ 11. uric acid

_____ 2. phosphate ions   _____ 7. glucose   _____ 12. creatinine

_____ 3. sulfate ions   _____ 8. albumin   _____ 13. pus (WBCs)

_____ 4. potassium ions   _____ 9. red blood cells   _____ 14. nitrites

_____ 5. sodium ions   _____ 10. urea

3. Explain why urinalysis is a routine part of any good physical examination. _____

_____

4. What substance is responsible for the normal yellow color of urine? _____

5. Which has a greater specific gravity: 1 ml of urine or 1 ml of distilled water? _____ Explain your answer. _____

_____

6. Explain the relationship between the color, specific gravity, and volume of urine. _____

_____

Abnormal Urinary Constituents

7. A microscopic examination of urine may reveal the presence of certain abnormal urinary constituents.

   Name three constituents that might be present if a urinary tract infection exists. _____,

   _____, and _____

8. How does a urinary tract infection influence urine pH? _____

   How does starvation influence urine pH? _____

9. All urine specimens become alkaline and cloudy on standing at room temperature. Explain why. _____

_____

10. Several specific terms have been used to indicate the presence of abnormal urine constituents. Identify each of the abnormalities described below by inserting a term from the key at the right that names the condition.

_____ 1. presence of erythrocytes in the urine

_____ 2. presence of hemoglobin in the urine

_____ 3. presence of glucose in the urine

_____ 4. presence of albumin in the urine

_____ 5. presence of ketone bodies (acetone and others) in the urine

_____ 6. presence of pus (white blood cells) in the urine

Key:

a. albuminuria

b. glycosuria

c. hematuria

d. hemoglobinuria

e. ketonuria

f. pyuria

11. What are renal calculi, and what conditions favor their formation? _____

_____

12. Glucose and albumin are both normally absent in the urine, but the reason for their exclusion differs. Explain the reason for

the absence of glucose. _____

Explain the reason for the absence of albumin. _____

13. The presence of abnormal constituents or conditions in urine may be associated with diseases, disorders, or other causes listed in the key. Select and list all conditions associated with each numbered item.

_____ 1. low specific gravity

_____ 2. high specific gravity

_____ 3. glucose

_____ 4. albumin

_____ 5. blood cells

_____ 6. hemoglobin

_____ 7. bilirubin

_____ 8. ketone bodies

_____ 9. casts

_____ 10. pus

Key:

a. cystitis (inflammation of the bladder)

b. diabetes insipidus

c. diabetes mellitus

d. eating a 5-lb box of sweets for lunch

e. glomerulonephritis

f. gonorrhea

g. hemolytic anemias

h. hepatitis, cirrhosis of the liver

i. kidney stones

j. pregnancy, exertion

k. pyelonephritis

l. starvation

14. Name the three major nitrogenous wastes found in the urine. _____,

_____, and _____

15. Explain the difference between organized and unorganized sediments. _____

_____

_____

42

Anatomy of the Reproductive System

MATERIALS

- ☐ Three-dimensional models or large laboratory charts of the male and female reproductive tracts
- ☐ Prepared slides of cross sections of the penis, seminal vesicles, epididymis, uterus showing endometrium (proliferative phase), and uterine tube
- ☐ Compound microscope

For instructions on animal dissections, see the dissection exercises starting on page 697 in the cat, fetal pig, and rat editions of this manual.

OBJECTIVES

1. To discuss the general function of the reproductive system.
2. To identify and name the structures of the male and female reproductive systems when provided with an appropriate model or diagram, and to discuss the general function of each.
3. To define *semen,* discuss its composition, and name the organs involved in its production.
4. To trace the pathway followed by a sperm from its site of formation to the external environment.
5. To name the exocrine and endocrine products of the testes and ovaries, indicating the cell types or structures responsible for the production of each.
6. To discuss the microscopic structure of the penis, seminal vesicles, epididymis, uterine (fallopian) tube, and uterus, and to relate structure to function.
7. To define *gonad, ejaculation,* and *erection.*
8. To discuss the function of the fimbriae and ciliated epithelium of the uterine tubes.
9. To identify the fundus, body, and cervical regions of the uterus.
10. To define *endometrium, myometrium*, and *ovulation*.
11. To discuss the reproduction-related function of female mammary glands.

PRE-LAB QUIZ

1. The essential organs of reproduction are the _____, which produce the germ cells.
   - a. accessory male glands
   - b. gonads
   - c. seminal vesicles
   - d. uterus
2. Circle the correct term. The paired oval testes lie in the <u>scrotum / prostate</u> outside the abdominopelvic cavity, where they are kept slightly cooler than body temperature.
3. After sperm are produced, they enter the first part of the duct system, the _____.
   - a. ductus deferens
   - b. ejaculatory duct
   - c. epididymis
   - d. urethra
4. The prostate, seminal vesicles, and bulbourethral glands produce _____, the liquid medium in which sperm leaves the body.
   - a. seminal fluid
   - b. testosterone
   - c. urine
   - d. water
5. Circle the correct term. The <u>interstitial cells / seminiferous tubules</u> produce testosterone, the hormonal product of the testis.
6. The endocrine products of the ovaries are estrogen and
   - a. luteinizing hormone
   - b. progesterone
   - c. prolactin
   - d. testosterone
7. Circle the correct term. The <u>labia majora / clitoris</u> are/is homologous to the penis.
8. The _____ is a pear-shaped organ that houses the embryo or fetus during its development.
   - a. bladder
   - b. cervix
   - c. uterus
   - d. vagina

Text continues on next page.

9. Circle the correct term. The <u>endometrium / myometrium</u>, the thick mucosal lining of the uterus, has a superficial layer that sloughs off periodically.

10. Circle the correct term. A developing egg is ejected from the ovary at the appropriate stage of maturity in an event known as <u>menstruation / ovulation</u>.

Other organ systems of the body function primarily to sustain the existing individual, but the reproductive system is unique. Most simply stated, the biological function of the **reproductive system** is to perpetuate the species.

The essential organs of reproduction are the **gonads,** the testes and the ovaries, which produce the germ cells. The reproductive role of the male is to manufacture sperm and to deliver them to the female reproductive tract. The female, in turn, produces eggs. If the time is suitable, the combination of sperm and egg produces a fertilized egg, which is the first cell of a new individual. Once fertilization has occurred, the female uterus provides a nurturing, protective environment in which the embryo, later called the fetus, develops until birth.

Gross Anatomy of the Human Male Reproductive System

The primary reproductive organs of the male are the **testes,** the male gonads, which have both an exocrine (sperm pro-

duction) and an endocrine (testosterone production) function. All other reproductive structures are conduits or sources of secretions, which aid in the safe delivery of the sperm to the body exterior or female reproductive tract.

ACTIVITY 1

Identifying Male Reproductive Organs

As the following organs and structures are described, locate them on Figure 42.1, and then identify them on a three-dimensional model of the male reproductive system or on a large laboratory chart. ▪

The paired oval testes lie in the **scrotum** outside the abdominopelvic cavity. The temperature there (approximately 94°F, or 34°C) is slightly lower than body temperature, a requirement for producing viable sperm.

The accessory structures forming the *duct system* are the epididymis, the ductus deferens, the ejaculatory duct, and the urethra. The **epididymis** is an elongated structure running up

FIGURE 42.1 Reproductive organs of the human male. (a) Sagittal view.

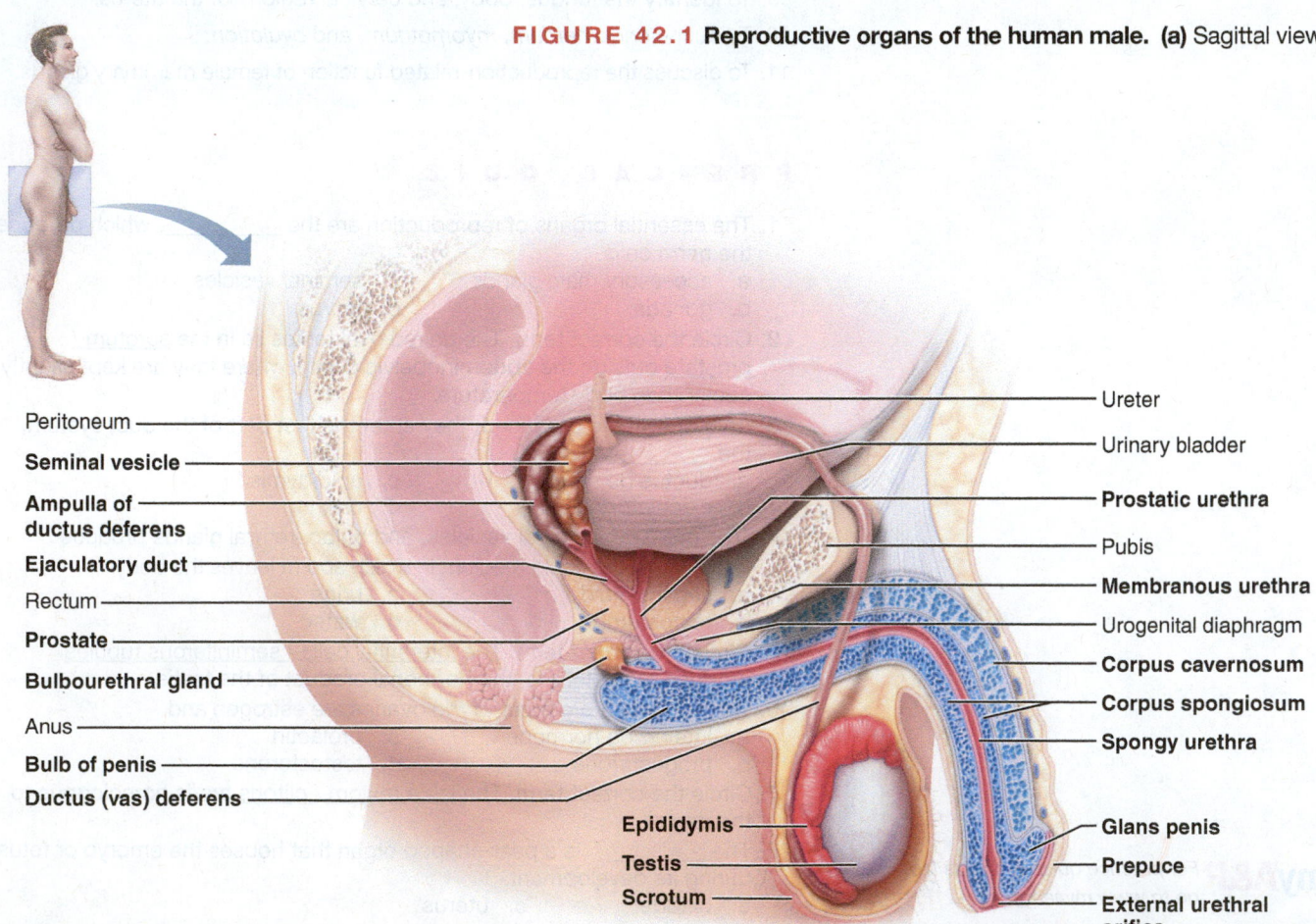

Peritoneum
Seminal vesicle
Ampulla of ductus deferens
Ejaculatory duct
Rectum
Prostate
Bulbourethral gland
Anus
Bulb of penis
Ductus (vas) deferens
Epididymis
Testis
Scrotum

Ureter
Urinary bladder
Prostatic urethra
Pubis
Membranous urethra
Urogenital diaphragm
Corpus cavernosum
Corpus spongiosum
Spongy urethra
Glans penis
Prepuce
External urethral orifice

(a)

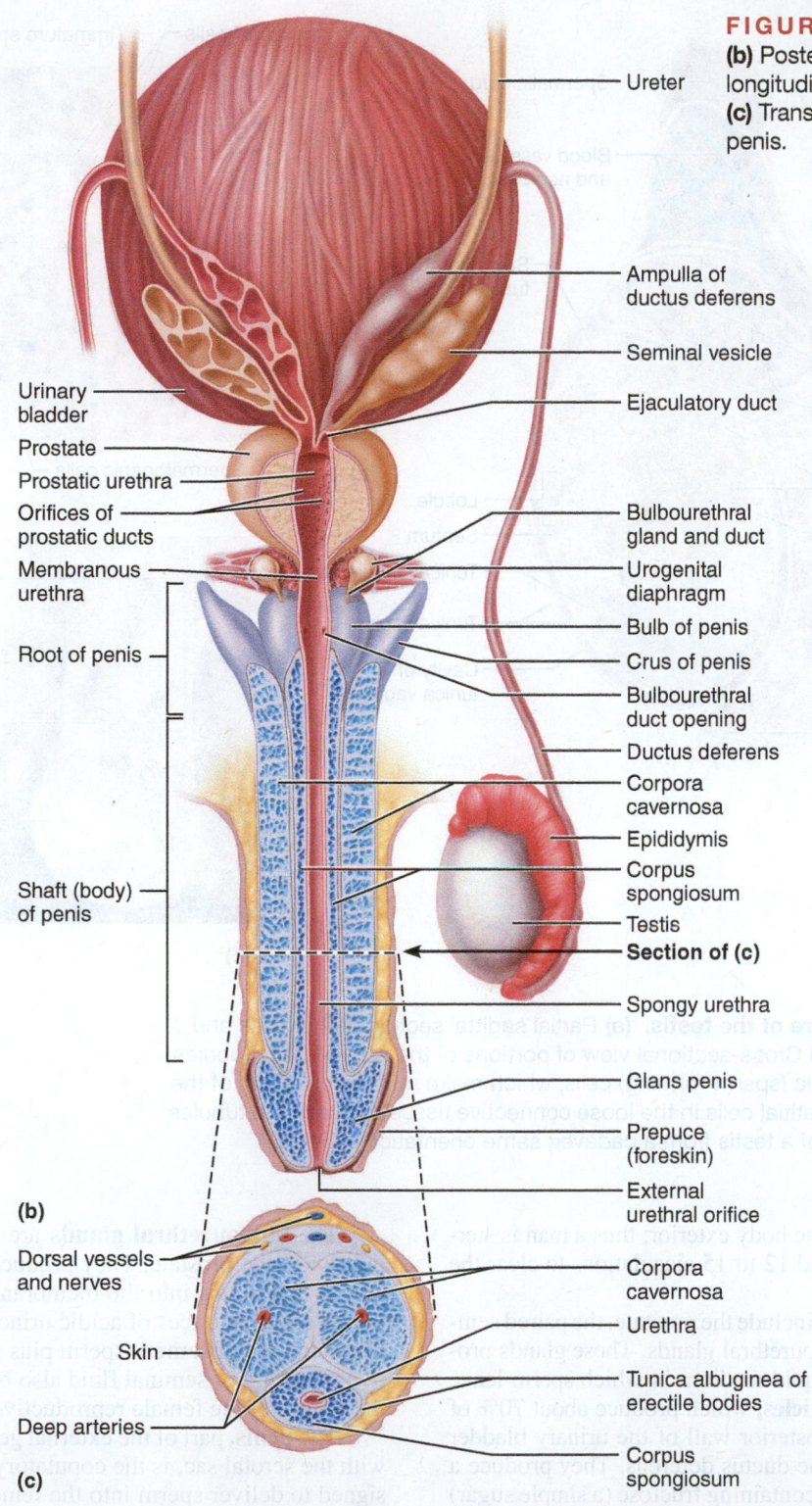

FIGURE 42.1 *(continued)*
(b) Posterior view showing a longitudinal section of the penis.
(c) Transverse section of the penis.

Ureter

Ampulla of ductus deferens

Seminal vesicle

Ejaculatory duct

Urinary bladder

Prostate

Prostatic urethra

Orifices of prostatic ducts

Bulbourethral gland and duct

Membranous urethra

Urogenital diaphragm

Root of penis

Bulb of penis

Crus of penis

Bulbourethral duct opening

Ductus deferens

Corpora cavernosa

Epididymis

Corpus spongiosum

Shaft (body) of penis

Testis

Section of (c)

Spongy urethra

Glans penis

Prepuce (foreskin)

External urethral orifice

(b)

Dorsal vessels and nerves

Corpora cavernosa

Urethra

Skin

Tunica albuginea of erectile bodies

Deep arteries

Corpus spongiosum

(c)

the posterolateral aspect of the testis and capping its superior aspect. The epididymis forms the first portion of the duct system and provides a site for immature sperm entering it from the testis to complete their maturation process. The **ductus deferens,** or **vas deferens** (sperm duct), arches superiorly from the epididymis, passes through the inguinal canal into the pelvic cavity, and courses over the superior aspect of the urinary bladder. In life, the ductus deferens is enclosed along with blood vessels and nerves in a connective tissue sheath called the **spermatic cord** (see Figure 42.2). The terminus of the ductus

deferens enlarges to form the region called the **ampulla,** which empties into the **ejaculatory duct.** During **ejaculation,** contraction of the ejaculatory duct propels the sperm through the prostate to the **prostatic urethra,** which in turn empties into the **membranous urethra** and then into the **spongy urethra,** which runs through the length of the penis to the body exterior.

The spermatic cord is easily palpated through the skin of the scrotum. When a *vasectomy* is performed, a small incision is made in each side of the scrotum, and each ductus deferens is cut through or cauterized. Although sperm are still produced,

FIGURE 42.2 Structure of the testis. (a) Partial sagittal section of the testis and associated epididymis. **(b)** Cross-sectional view of portions of the seminiferous tubules, showing the spermatogenic (sperm-forming) cells, which make up the epithelium of the tubule walls, and the interstitial cells in the loose connective tissue between the tubules (160×). **(c)** External view of a testis from a cadaver; same orientation as in (a).

they can no longer reach the body exterior; thus a man is sterile after this procedure (and 12 to 15 ejaculations to clear the conducting tubules).

The *accessory glands* include the prostate, the paired seminal vesicles, and the bulbourethral glands. These glands produce **seminal fluid,** the liquid medium in which sperm leave the body. The **seminal vesicles,** which produce about 70% of seminal fluid, lie at the posterior wall of the urinary bladder close to the terminus of the ductus deferens. They produce a viscous alkaline secretion containing fructose (a simple sugar) and other substances that nourish the sperm passing through the tract or that promote the fertilizing capability of sperm in some way. The duct of each seminal vesicle merges with a ductus deferens to form the ejaculatory duct (mentioned above); thus sperm and seminal fluid enter the urethra together.

The **prostate** encircles the urethra just inferior to the bladder. It secretes a milky fluid into the urethra, which plays a role in activating the sperm.

Hypertrophy of the prostate, a troublesome condition commonly seen in elderly men, constricts the urethra so that urination is difficult. ■

The **bulbourethral glands** are tiny, pea-shaped glands inferior to the prostate. They produce a thick, clear, alkaline mucus that drains into the membranous urethra. This secretion neutralizes traces of acidic urine in the urethra just prior to ejaculation of **semen** (sperm plus seminal fluid). The relative alkalinity of seminal fluid also buffers the sperm against the acidity of the female reproductive tract.

The **penis,** part of the external genitalia of the male along with the scrotal sac, is the copulatory organ of the male. Designed to deliver sperm into the female reproductive tract, it consists of a shaft, which terminates in an enlarged tip, the **glans penis** (see Figure 42.1a and b). The skin covering the penis is loosely applied, and it reflects downward to form a circular fold of skin, the **prepuce,** or **foreskin,** around the proximal end of the glans. (The foreskin is removed in the surgical procedure called *circumcision.*) Internally, the penis consists primarily of three elongated cylinders of erectile tissue, which engorge with blood during sexual excitement. This causes the penis to become rigid and enlarged so that it may more adequately serve as a penetrating device. This event is called **erection.** The paired dorsal cylinders are the

corpora cavernosa. The single ventral **corpus spongiosum** surrounds the penile urethra (see Figure 42.1c).

Microscopic Anatomy of Selected Male Reproductive Organs

Each **testis** is covered by a dense connective tissue capsule called the **tunica albuginea** (literally, "white tunic"). Extensions of this sheath enter the testis, dividing it into a number of lobes, each of which houses one to four highly coiled **seminiferous tubules,** the sperm-forming factories (Figure 42.2). The seminiferous tubules of each lobe converge to empty the sperm into another set of tubules, the **rete testis,** at the posterior of the testis. Sperm traveling through the rete testis then enter the epididymis, located on the exterior aspect of the testis, as previously described. Lying between the seminiferous tubules and softly padded with connective tissue are the **interstitial cells,** which produce testosterone, the hormonal product of the testis. Unless directed by your instructor to conduct a microscopic study of the testis here, you will conduct that study in Exercise 43.

ACTIVITY 2

Penis

Obtain a slide of a cross section of the penis. Scan the tissue under low power to identify the urethra and the cavernous bodies. Compare your observations to Figure 42.1c and Figure 42.3. Observe the lumen of the urethra carefully. What type of epithelium do you see?

_____

Explain the function of this type of epithelium.

_____

_____ ▬

FIGURE 42.3 Transverse section of the penis (3×).

Labels on figure:
- Corpora cavernosae
- Venous cavities
- Tunic albuginea (surrounds corpora)
- Lumen of urethra
- Corpus spongiosum

FIGURE 42.4 Cross-sectional view of a seminal vesicle with its elaborate network of mucosal folds. Vesicular secretion is seen in the lumen (7×).

Labels on figure:
- Mucosal folds
- Lumen of seminal tubule
- Muscular wall
- Connective tissue

ACTIVITY 3

Seminal Vesicle

Obtain a slide showing a cross-sectional view of the seminal vesicle. Examine the slide at low magnification to get an overall view of the highly folded mucosa of this gland. Switch to higher magnification, and notice that the folds of the vesicle protrude into the lumen where they divide further, giving the lumen a honeycomb look (Figure 42.4). Notice that the loose connective tissue lamina propria is underlain by smooth muscle fibers—first a circular layer, and then a longitudinal layer. Identify the vesicular secretion in the lumen, a viscous substance that is rich in sugar and prostaglandins. ▬

ACTIVITY 4

Epididymis

Obtain a slide of a cross section of the epididymis. Notice the abundant tubule cross sections resulting from the fact that the coiling epididymis tubule has been cut through many times in the specimen. Look for sperm in the lumen of the tubule. Examine the composition of the tubule wall carefully. Identify the *stereocilia* (not shown) of the pseudostratified columnar epithelial lining. These nonmotile microvilli absorb excess fluid and pass nutrients to the sperm in the lumen. Now identify the smooth muscle layer. What do you think the function of the smooth muscle is?

_____

_____ ▬

Gross Anatomy of the Human Female Reproductive System

The **ovaries** (female gonads) are the primary reproductive organs of the female. Like the testes of the male, the ovaries produce both an exocrine product (eggs, or ova) and endocrine products (estrogens and progesterone). The other accessory structures of the female reproductive system transport, house, nurture, or otherwise serve the needs of the reproductive cells and/or the developing fetus.

The reproductive structures of the female are generally considered in terms of internal organs and external organs, or external genitalia.

ACTIVITY 5

Identifying Female Reproductive Organs

As you read the descriptions of these structures, locate them on Figures 42.5 and 42.6 and then on the female reproductive system model or large laboratory chart. ■

External Genitalia

The **external genitalia (vulva)** consist of the mons pubis, the labia majora and minora, the clitoris, the urethral and vaginal orifices, the hymen, and the greater vestibular glands. The **mons pubis** is a rounded fatty eminence overlying the pubic symphysis. Running inferiorly and posteriorly from the mons pubis are two elongated, pigmented, hair-covered skin folds,

the **labia majora,** which are homologous to the scrotum. These enclose two smaller hair-free folds, the **labia minora.** (Terms indicating only one of the two folds in each case are *labium majus* and *minus,* respectively.) The labia minora, in turn, enclose a region called the **vestibule,** which contains many structures—

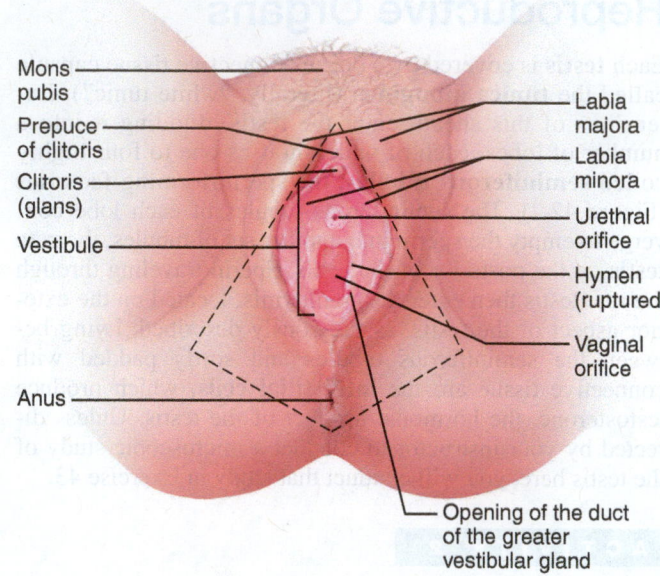

Mons pubis
Prepuce of clitoris
Clitoris (glans)
Vestibule
Anus
Labia majora
Labia minora
Urethral orifice
Hymen (ruptured)
Vaginal orifice
Opening of the duct of the greater vestibular gland

FIGURE 42.5 External genitalia of the human female. The region enclosed by dashed lines is the perineum.

Peritoneum
Uterosacral ligament
Perimetrium
Rectouterine pouch
Rectum
Posterior fornix
Cervix
Anterior fornix
Vagina
Anus
Urogenital diaphragm
Greater vestibular (Bartholin's) gland

Suspensory ligament of ovary
Infundibulum
Uterine tube
Ovary
Fimbriae
Uterus
Round ligament
Vesicouterine pouch
Urinary bladder
Pubic symphysis
Mons pubis
Urethra
Clitoris
External urethral orifice
Hymen
Labium minus
Labium majus

(a)

FIGURE 42.6 Internal reproductive organs of the human female. (a) Midsagittal section of the human female reproductive system.

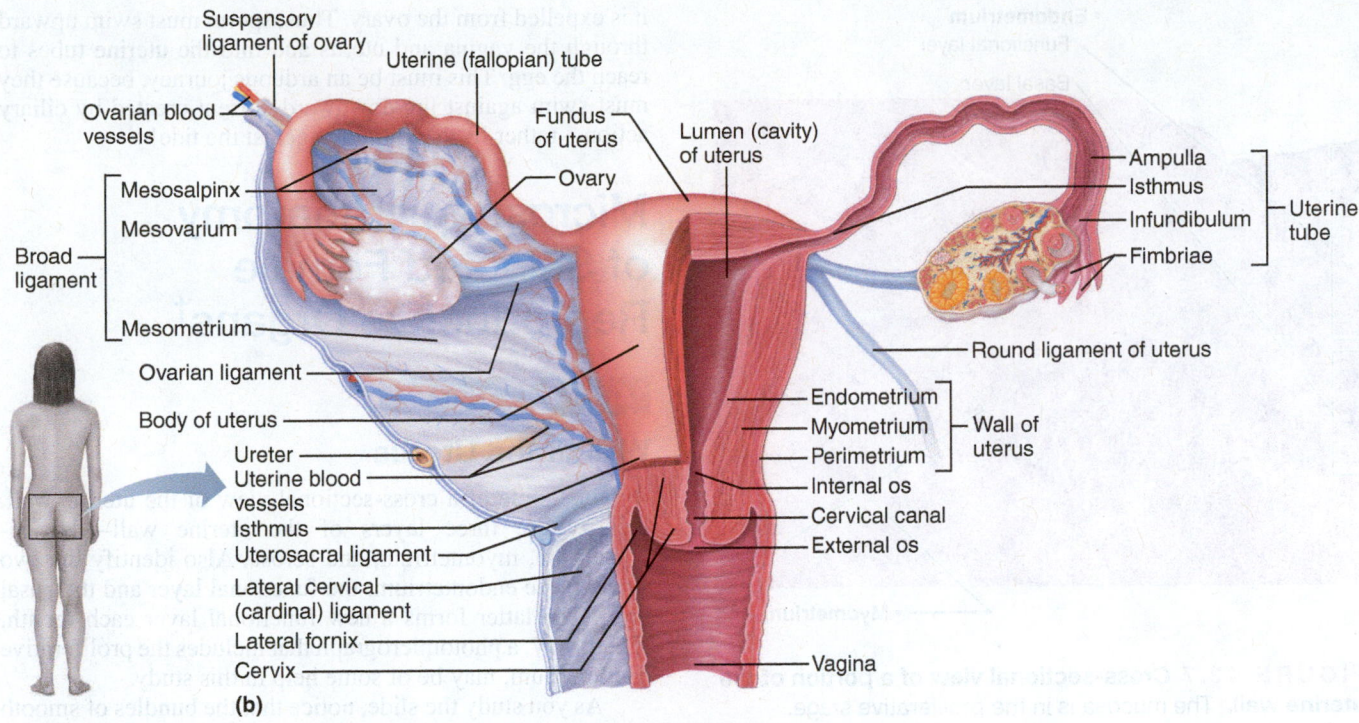

Suspensory ligament of ovary

Ovarian blood vessels

Mesosalpinx

Mesovarium

Broad ligament

Mesometrium

Ovarian ligament

Body of uterus

Ureter

Uterine blood vessels

Isthmus

Uterosacral ligament

Lateral cervical (cardinal) ligament

Lateral fornix

Cervix

(b)

Uterine (fallopian) tube

Fundus of uterus

Ovary

Lumen (cavity) of uterus

Ampulla

Isthmus

Infundibulum

Fimbriae

Uterine tube

Round ligament of uterus

Endometrium

Myometrium

Perimetrium

Wall of uterus

Internal os

Cervical canal

External os

Vagina

FIGURE 42.6 (continued) (b) Posterior view. The posterior walls of the vagina, uterus, and uterine tubes, and the broad ligament have been removed on the right side to reveal the shape of the lumen of these organs.

the clitoris, most anteriorly, followed by the urethral orifice and the vaginal orifice. The diamond-shaped region between the anterior end of the labial folds, the ischial tuberosities laterally, and the anus posteriorly is called the **perineum.**

The **clitoris** is a small protruding structure, homologous to the penis. Like its counterpart, it is composed of highly sensitive, erectile tissue. It is hooded by skin folds of the anterior labia minora, referred to as the **prepuce of the clitoris.** The urethral orifice, which lies posterior to the clitoris, is the outlet for the urinary system and has no reproductive function in the female. The vaginal opening is partially closed by a thin fold of mucous membrane called the **hymen** and is flanked by the pea-sized, mucus-secreting **greater vestibular glands.** These glands (see Figure 42.5) lubricate the distal end of the vagina during coitus.

Internal Organs

The internal female organs include the vagina, uterus, uterine tubes, ovaries, and the ligaments and supporting structures that suspend these organs in the pelvic cavity (see Figure 42.6). The **vagina** extends for approximately 10 cm (4 inches) from the vestibule to the uterus superiorly. It serves as a copulatory organ and birth canal and permits passage of the menstrual flow. The pear-shaped **uterus,** situated between the bladder and the rectum, is a muscular organ with its narrow end, the **cervix,** directed inferiorly. The major portion of the uterus is referred to as the **body;** its superior rounded region above the entrance of the uterine tubes is called the **fundus.** A fertilized egg is implanted in the uterus, which houses the embryo or fetus during its development.

In some cases, the fertilized egg may implant in a uterine tube or even on the abdominal viscera, creating an **ectopic pregnancy.** Such implantations are usually unsuccessful and may even endanger the mother's life because the uterine tubes cannot accommodate the increasing size of the fetus. ■

The **endometrium,** the thick mucosal lining of the uterus, has a superficial **functional layer,** or **stratum functionalis,** that sloughs off periodically (about every 28 days) in response to cyclic changes in the levels of ovarian hormones in the woman's blood. This sloughing-off process, which is accompanied by bleeding, is referred to as **menstruation,** or **menses.** The deeper **basal layer,** or **stratum basalis** (see Figure 42.7), forms a new functionalis after menstruation ends.

The **uterine,** or **fallopian, tubes** enter the superolateral region of the uterus and extend laterally for about 10 cm (4 inches) toward the ovaries in the peritoneal cavity. The distal ends of the tubes are funnel-shaped and have fingerlike projections called **fimbriae.** Unlike in the male duct system, there is no actual contact between the female gonad and the initial part of the female duct system—the uterine tube.

Because of this open passageway between the female reproductive organs and the peritoneal cavity, reproductive system infections, such as gonorrhea and other **sexually transmitted diseases (STDs),** can cause widespread inflammations of the pelvic viscera, a condition called **pelvic inflammatory disease (PID).** ■

The internal female organs are all retroperitoneal, except the ovaries. They are supported and suspended somewhat freely by ligamentous folds of peritoneum. The peritoneum takes an undulating course. From the pelvic cavity floor it

Endometrium
— Functional layer
— Basal layer

• Myometrium

FIGURE 42.7 Cross-sectional view of a portion of the uterine wall. The mucosa is in the proliferative stage.

moves superiorly over the top of the bladder, reflects over the anterior and posterior surfaces of the uterus, and then over the rectum, and up the posterior body wall. The fold that encloses the uterine tubes and uterus and secures them to the lateral body walls is the **broad ligament** (Figure 42.6b). The part of the broad ligament specifically anchoring the uterus is called the **mesometrium** and that anchoring the uterine tubes, the **mesosalpinx.** The **round ligaments,** fibrous cords that run from the uterus to the labia majora, and the **uterosacral ligaments,** which course posteriorly to the sacrum, also help attach the uterus to the body wall. The ovaries are supported medially by the **ovarian ligament** (extending from the uterus to the ovary), laterally by the **suspensory ligaments,** and posteriorly by a fold of the broad ligament, the **mesovarium.**

Within the ovaries, the female gametes (eggs) begin their development in saclike structures called *follicles.* The growing follicles also produce *estrogens.* When a developing egg has reached the appropriate stage of maturity, it is ejected from the ovary in an event called **ovulation.** The ruptured follicle is then converted to a second type of endocrine gland, called a *corpus luteum,* which secretes progesterone (and some estrogens).

The flattened almond-shaped ovaries lie adjacent to the uterine tubes but are not connected to them; consequently, an ovulated egg* enters the pelvic cavity. The waving fimbriae of the uterine tubes create fluid currents that, if successful, draw the egg into the lumen of the uterine tube, where it begins its passage to the uterus, propelled by the cilia of the tubule walls. The usual and most desirable site of fertilization is the uterine tube, because the journey to the uterus takes about 3 to 4 days and an egg is viable for up to 24 hours after

*To simplify this discussion, the ovulated cell is called an egg. What is actually expelled from the ovary is an earlier stage of development called a secondary oocyte. These matters are explained in more detail in Exercise 43.

it is expelled from the ovary. Thus, sperm must swim upward through the vagina and uterus and into the uterine tubes to reach the egg. This must be an arduous journey, because they must swim against the downward current created by ciliary action—rather like swimming against the tide!

Microscopic Anatomy of Selected Female Reproductive Organs†

ACTIVITY 6

Wall of the Uterus

Obtain a slide of a cross-sectional view of the uterine wall. Identify the three layers of the uterine wall—the endometrium, myometrium, and serosa. Also identify the two strata of the endometrium: the functional layer and the basal layer. The latter forms a new functional layer each month. Figure 42.7, a photomicrograph that includes the proliferative endometrium, may be of some help in this study.

As you study the slide, notice that the bundles of smooth muscle are oriented in several different directions. What is the function of the **myometrium** (smooth muscle layer) during the birth process?

_____

_____

ACTIVITY 7

Uterine Tube

Obtain a slide of a cross-sectional view of a uterine tube for examination. Using Figure 42.8 as a guide, notice the highly folded mucosa (the folds nearly fill the tubule lumen). Then switch to high power to examine the ciliated secretory epithelium.

— Serosa

— Smooth muscle

— Highly folded mucosa

— Lumen

FIGURE 42.8 Cross-sectional view of the uterine tube (7×).

†A microscopic study of the ovary is described in Exercise 43.

The Mammary Glands

The **mammary glands** exist within the breasts, of course, in both sexes, but they normally have a reproduction-related function only in females. Since the function of the mammary glands is to produce milk to nourish the newborn infant, their importance is more closely associated with events that occur when reproduction has already been accomplished. Periodic stimulation by the female sex hormones, especially estrogens, increases the size of the female mammary glands at puberty. During this period, the duct system becomes more elaborate, and fat is deposited—fat deposition being the more important contributor to increased breast size.

The rounded, skin-covered mammary glands lie anterior to the pectoral muscles of the thorax, attached to them by connective tissue. Slightly below the center of each breast is a pigmented area, the **areola,** which surrounds a centrally protruding **nipple** (Figure 42.9.)

Internally each mammary gland consists of 15 to 25 **lobes** which radiate around the nipple and are separated by fibrous connective tisse and adipose, or fatty, tissue. Within each lobe are smaller chambers called **lobules,** containing the glandular **alveoli** that produce milk during lactation. The alveoli of each lobule pass the milk into a number of **lactiferous ducts,** which join to form an expanded storage chamber, the **lactiferous sinus,** as they approach the nipple. The sinuses open to the outside at the nipple.

For instructions on animal dissections, see the dissection exercises starting on page 697 in the cat, fetal pig, and rat editions of this manual.

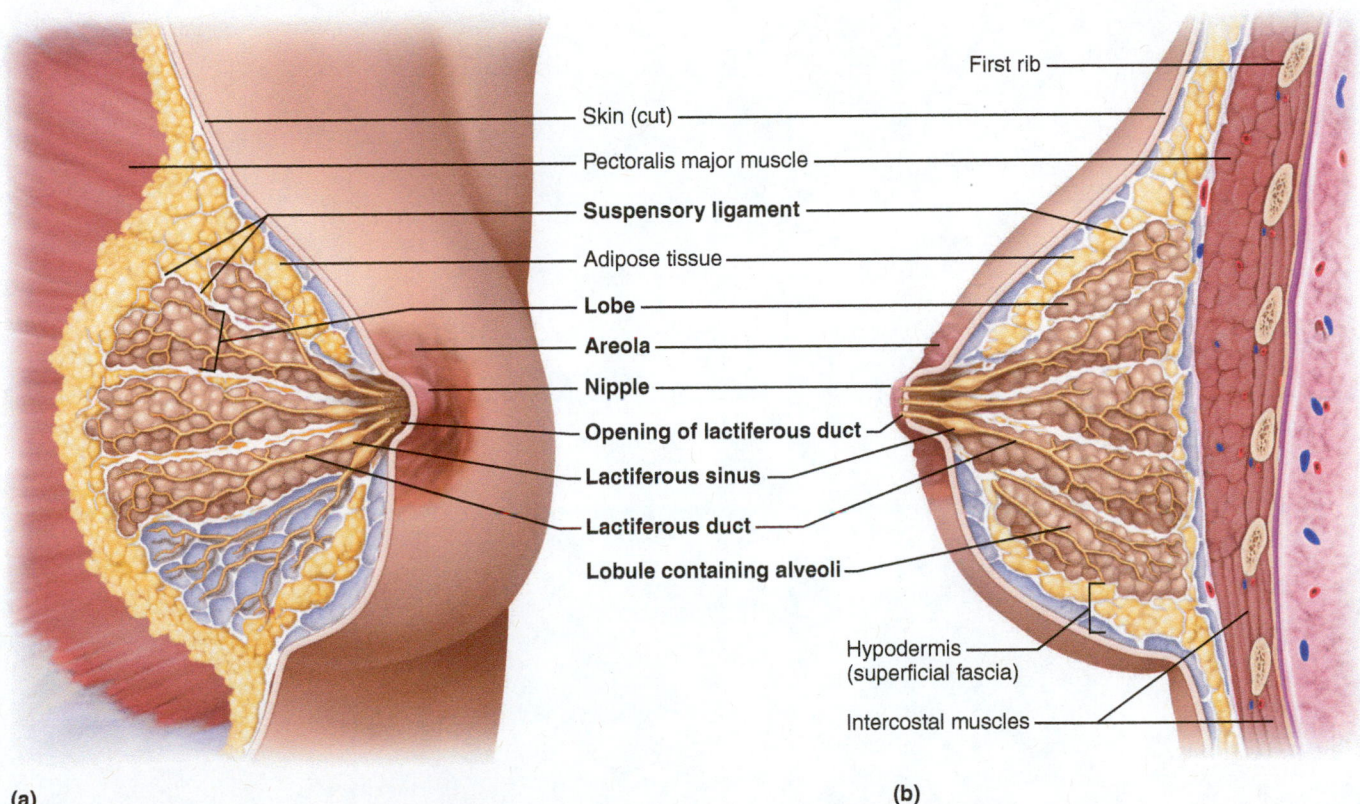

First rib

Skin (cut)

Pectoralis major muscle

Suspensory ligament

Adipose tissue

Lobe

Areola

Nipple

Opening of lactiferous duct

Lactiferous sinus

Lactiferous duct

Lobule containing alveoli

Hypodermis (superficial fascia)

Intercostal muscles

(a)   (b)

FIGURE 42.9 Anatomy of lactating mammary gland. (a) Anterior view of partially dissected breast. **(b)** Sagittal section of the breast.

Anatomy of the Reproductive System

Gross Anatomy of the Human Male Reproductive System

1. List the two principal functions of the testis. _____

   and _____

2. Identify all indicated structures or portions of structures on the diagrammatic view of the male reproductive system below.

3. A common part of any physical examination of the male is palpation of the prostate. How is this accomplished?

   (Think!) _____

4. How might enlargement of the prostate interfere with urination or the reproductive ability of the male?

   _____

   _____

5. Why are the testes located in the scrotum rather than inside the ventral body cavity?

   _____

   _____

6. Match the terms in column B to the descriptive statements in column A.

Column A

_____ 1. copulatory organ/penetrating device

_____ 2. muscular passageway conveying sperm to the ejaculatory duct; in the spermatic cord

_____ 3. transports both sperm and urine

_____ 4. sperm maturation site

_____ 5. location of the testis in adult males

_____ 6. loose fold of skin encircling the glans penis

_____ 7. portion of the urethra between the prostate and the penis

_____ 8. empties a secretion into the prostatic urethra

_____ 9. empties a secretion into the membranous urethra

Column B

a. bulbourethral glands

b. ductus (vas) deferens

c. epididymis

d. membranous urethra

e. penis

f. prepuce

g. prostate

h. prostatic urethra

i. scrotum

j. seminal vesicles

k. spongy urethra

7. Describe the composition of semen, and name all structures contributing to its formation. _____

_____

_____

8. Of what importance is the fact that seminal fluid is alkaline? _____

_____

9. What structures compose the spermatic cord? _____

_____

Where is it located? _____

10. Using the following terms, trace the pathway of sperm from the testes to the urethra: rete testis, epididymis, seminiferous tubule, ductus deferens.

_____ → _____ → _____ → _____

Gross Anatomy of the Human Female Reproductive System

11. Name the structures composing the external genitalia, or vulva, of the female. _____

_____

_____

12. On the diagram below of a frontal section of a portion of the female reproductive system, identify all indicated structures.

13. Identify the female reproductive system structures described below.

_____ 1. site of fetal development

_____ 2. copulatory canal

_____ 3. egg typically fertilized here

_____ 4. becomes erect during sexual excitement

_____ 5. duct extending superolaterally from the uterus

_____ 6. partially closes the vaginal canal; a membrane

_____ 7. produces oocytes, estrogens, and progesterone

_____ 8. fingerlike ends of the uterine tube

14. Do any sperm enter the pelvic cavity of the female? Why or why not? _____

_____

15. What is an ectopic pregnancy, and how can it happen? _____

_____

_____

16. Put the following vestibular-perineal structures in their proper order from the anterior to the posterior aspect: vaginal orifice, anus, urethral opening, and clitoris.

Anterior limit: _____ → _____ → _____ → _____

17. Assume a couple has just consummated the sex act and the sperm have been deposited in the vagina. Trace the pathway of the sperm through the female reproductive tract.

_____

18. Define *ovulation.* _____

Microscopic Anatomy of Selected Male and Female Reproductive Organs

19. The testis is divided into a number of lobes by connective tissue. Each of these lobes contains one to four _____

_____, which converge to empty sperm into another set of tubules called the

_____.

20. What is the function of the cavernous bodies seen in the penis? _____

_____

21. Name the three layers of the uterine wall from the inside out.

_____, _____, _____

Which of these is sloughed during menses? _____

Which contracts during childbirth? _____

22. What is the function of the stereocilia exhibited by the epithelial cells of the mucosa of the epididymis? _____

_____

23. On the diagram showing the sagittal section of the human testis, correctly identify all structures provided with leader lines.

The Mammary Glands

24. Match the key term with the correct description.

_____ glands that produce milk during lactation

_____ subdivisions of mammary lobes that contain alveoli

_____ enlarged storage chambers for milk

_____ ducts connecting alveoli to the storage chambers

_____ pigmented area surrounding the nipple

_____ releases milk to the outside

Key:

a. alveoli

b. areola

c. lactiferous duct

d. lactiferous sinus

e. lobule

f. nipple

25. Using the key terms, correctly identify breast structures.

Key: a. adipose tissue
b. areola
c. lactiferous duct
d. lactiferous sinus
e. lobule containing alveoli
f. nipple

Clavicle
1st rib
Pectoralis muscles
Intercostal muscles
Fibrous connective tissue stroma
Skin
6th rib

26. Describe the procedure for self-examination of the breasts. (Men are not exempt from breast cancer, you know!)

_____

_____

_____

_____

Physiology of Reproduction: Gametogenesis and the Female Cycles

MATERIALS

- ☐ Three-dimensional models illustrating meiosis, spermatogenesis, and oogenesis
- ☐ Sets of "pop it" beads in two colors with magnetic centromeres*
- ☐ Compound microscope
- ☐ Prepared slides of testis and human sperm
- ☐ *Demonstration:* microscopes set up to demonstrate the stages of oogenesis in *Ascaris megalocephala* listed below

  Slide 1: Primary oocyte with fertilization membrane, sperm nucleus, and aligned tetrads apparent

  Slide 2: Formation of the first polar body

  Slide 3: Secondary oocyte with dyads aligned

  Slide 4: Formation of the ovum and second polar body

  Slide 5: Fusion of the male and female pronuclei to form the fertilized egg
- ☐ Prepared slides of ovary and uterine endometrium (showing menstrual, proliferative, and secretory stages)

*Chromosome Simulation Lab Activity available from Ward's Natural Science

OBJECTIVES

1. To define *meiosis, gametogenesis, oogenesis, spermatogenesis, spermiogenesis, synapsis, haploid, diploid,* and *menses*.
2. To relate the stages of spermatogenesis to the cross-sectional structure of the seminiferous tubule.
3. To discuss the microscopic structure of the ovary; to be prepared to identify primary, secondary, and vesicular follicles and the corpus luteum; and to state the hormonal products of the last two structures.
4. To relate the stages of oogenesis to follicle development in the ovary.
5. To cite similarities and differences between mitosis and meiosis and between spermatogenesis and oogenesis.
6. To describe sperm anatomy, and to relate it to function.
7. To discuss the phases and control of the menstrual cycle.
8. To discuss the effect of FSH and LH on the ovary, and to describe the feedback relationship between anterior pituitary gonadotropins and ovarian hormones.
9. To describe the effect of FSH and LH on testicular function.

PRE-LAB QUIZ

1. Human gametes contain _____ chromosomes.
   a. 13   b. 23   c. 36   d. 46
2. The end product of meiosis is
   a. two diploid daughter cells   c. four diploid daughter cells
   b. two haploid daughter cells   d. four haploid daughter cells
3. Circle the correct terms. A grouping of four chromatids, known as a dyad / tetrad, occurs only during mitosis / meiosis.
4. _____ cells extend inward from the periphery of the seminiferous tubule and provide nourishment to the spermatids as they begin their transformation into sperm.
   a. Interstitial   c. Sustentacular
   b. Leydig
5. Circle the correct term. The acrosome / midpiece of the sperm contains enzymes involved in the penetration of the egg.
6. Circle the correct term. Within each ovary, the immature ovum develops in a saclike structure called a corpus / follicle.
7. As the primordial follicle grows and its epithelium changes from squamous to cuboidal cells, it becomes a(n) _____ and begins to produce estrogens.
   a. oocyte   c. primary follicle
   b. oogonia   d. primary ovum
8. Circle True or False. A sudden release of luteinizing hormone by the anterior pituitary triggers ovulation.

Text continues on next page.

myA&P For practice quizzes on this lab, go to www.myaandp.com.

645

9. Circle the correct term. The <u>corpus luteum / corpus albicans</u> is a solid glandular structure with a scalloped lumen that develops from a ruptured follicle.

10. The _____ phase of the female cycle occurs from days 1–5 and is signaled by the sloughing off of the thick functional layer of the endometrium.
   a. endometrial
   b. menstrual
   c. proliferative
   d. secretory

Every human being, so far, has developed from the union of gametes. Gametes, produced only in the testis or ovary, are unique cells. They have only half the normal chromosome number (designated as *n,* or the **haploid complement**) seen in all other body cells.

Meiosis

In humans, gametes have 23 chromosomes instead of the 46 present in other tissue cells. Theoretically, every gamete has a full set of genetic instructions, a conclusion borne out by the observation that some animals can develop from an egg that is artificially stimulated, as by a pinprick, rather than by sperm entry. (This is less true of the sperm, because some have an incomplete sex chromosome.)

Gametogenesis, the process of gamete formation, involves reduction of the chromosome number by half. This event is important to maintain the characteristic chromosomal number of the species generation after generation. Otherwise there would be a doubling of chromosome number with each succeeding generation, and the cells would become so chock-full of genetic material there would be little room for anything else.

Egg and sperm chromosomes that carry genes for the same traits are called **homologous chromosomes.** When the sperm and egg fuse to form the **zygote,** or fertilized egg, it is said to contain 23 pairs of homologous chromosomes, or the **diploid (2n)** chromosome number of 46. The zygote, once formed, then divides to produce the cells needed to construct the multicellular human body. All cells of the developing human body have a chromosome content exactly identical in quality and quantity to that of the fertilized egg. This is assured by the nuclear division process called **mitosis.** (Mitosis was considered in depth in Exercise 4. You may want to review it at this time.)

To produce gametes with the reduced (haploid) chromosomal number, **meiosis,** a specialized type of nuclear division, occurs in the ovaries and testes during gametogenesis. Before meiosis begins, the chromosomes are replicated in the *mother cell* or stem cell just as they are before mitosis. As a result, the mother cell briefly has double the normal diploid genetic complement. The stem cell then undergoes two consecutive nuclear divisions, termed *meiosis I and II,* or the first and second maturation divisions, *without replicating the chromosomes before the second division.* Cytokinesis produces four haploid daughter cells, rather than the two diploid daughter cells resulting from mitotic division.

The entire process of meiosis is complex and is dealt with here only to the extent necessary to reveal important differences between this type of nuclear division and mitosis. Essentially, each meiotic division involves the same phases and events seen in mitosis (prophase, metaphase, anaphase, and telophase), but during the first maturation division (meiosis I) an event not seen in mitosis occurs during prophase. The homologous chromosomes, each now a duplicated structure, begin to pair so that they become closely aligned along their entire length. This pairing is called **synapsis.** As a result,

23 **tetrads** (groupings of four chromatids) form, become attached to the spindle fibers, and begin to align themselves on the spindle equator. While in synapsis, the "arms" of adjacent homologous chromosomes coil around each other, forming many points of **crossover,** or **chiasmata.** (Perhaps this could be called the conjugal bed of the cell!) When anaphase of meiosis I begins, the homologues separate from one another, breaking and exchanging parts at points of crossover, and move apart toward opposite poles of the cell. The centromeres holding the "sister" *chromatids* (threads of chromatin), or **dyads,** together do *not* break at this point (Figure 43.1).

During the second maturation division, events parallel those in mitosis, except that the daughter cells do *not* replicate their chromosomes before this division, and each daughter cell has only half of the homologous chromosomes rather than a complete set. The crossover events and the way in which the homologues align on the spindle equator during the

Prophase of meiosis I; homologues synapse

Then form chiasmata

Anaphase of meiosis I; homologues separate

Daughter cells of meiosis I

Anaphase of meiosis II; centromeres break

Daughter cells of meiosis II

FIGURE 43.1 Events of meiosis involving one pair of homologous chromosomes. Male homologue is purple; female homologue is pink.

first maturation division introduce an immense variability in the resulting gametes, which explains why, barring identical twins, we are all genetically unique.

Identifying Meiotic Phases and Structures

1.   Obtain a model depicting the events of meiosis, and follow the sequence of events during the first and second maturation divisions. Identify prophase, metaphase, anaphase, and telophase in each. Also identify tetrads and chiasmata during the first maturation division and dyads (groupings of two chromatids connected by centromeres) in the second maturation division. Note ways in which the daughter cells resulting from meiosis I differ from the mother cell and how the gametes differ from both cell populations. (Use the key on the model, your textbook, or an appropriate reference as necessary to aid you in these observations.)

2.   Using strings of colored "pop it" beads with magnetic centromeres, demonstrate the phases of meiosis, including crossing over, for a cell with a diploid (2*n*) number of 4. Use one bead color for the male chromosomes and another color for the female chromosomes.

3.   Ask your instructor to verify the accuracy of your "creation" before returning the beads to the supply area.

Spermatogenesis

Human sperm production, or **spermatogenesis,** begins at puberty and continues without interruption throughout life. The average male ejaculation contains about a quarter billion sperm. Because only one sperm fertilizes an ovum, it seems that nature has tried to ensure that the perpetuation of the species will not be endangered for lack of sperm.

As explained in Exercise 42, spermatogenesis (the process of gametogenesis in males, Figure 43.2) occurs in the seminiferous tubules of the testes. The primitive stem cells or **spermatogonia,** found at the tubule periphery, divide extensively to build up the stem cell line. Before puberty, all divisions are mitotic divisions that produce more spermatogonia. At puberty, however, under the influence of follicle-stimulating hormone (FSH) secreted by the anterior pituitary gland, each mitotic division of a spermatogonium produces one spermatogonium and one **primary spermatocyte,** which is destined to undergo meiosis. As meiosis occurs, the dividing cells approach the lumen of the tubule. Thus the progression of meiotic events can be followed from the tubule periphery to the lumen. It is important to recognize that **spermatids,** haploid cells that are the actual product of meiosis, are not functional gametes. They are nonmotile cells and have too much excess baggage to function well in a reproductive capacity. Another process, called **spermiogenesis,** which follows meiosis, strips away the extraneous cytoplasm from the spermatid, converting it to a motile, streamlined **sperm.**

Examining Events of Spermatogenesis

1.   Obtain a slide of the testis and a microscope. Examine the slide under low power to identify the cross-sectional views of the cut seminiferous tubules. Then rotate the high power lens into

(a)

(b)

FIGURE 43.2 Spermatogenesis. (a) Flowchart of meiotic events and spermiogenesis. **(b)** Micrograph of an active seminiferous tubule (230×).

position and observe the wall of one of the cut tubules. As you work, refer to Figure 43.2 to make the following identifications.

2.   Scrutinize the cells at the periphery of the tubule. The cells in this area are the spermatogonia. About half of these will form primary spermatocytes, which begin meiosis.

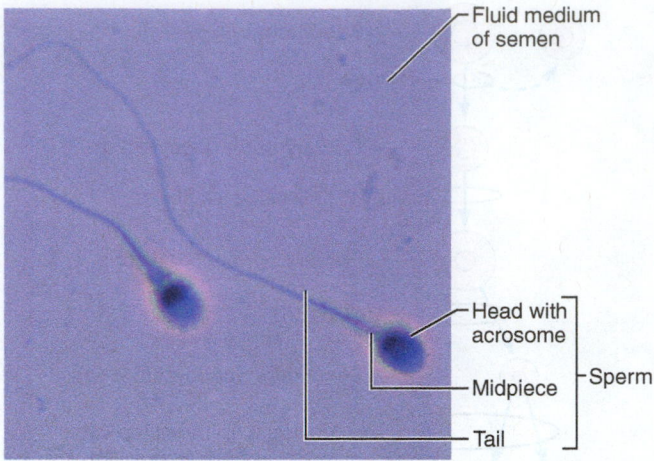

Fluid medium of semen

Head with acrosome

Midpiece — Sperm

Tail

FIGURE 43.3 Sperm in semen. In addition to sperm, semen contains fluids secreted by the accessory glands (1500×).

These are recognizable by their pale-staining nuclei with centrally located nucleoli. The remaining daughter cells resulting from mitotic divisions of spermatogonia stay at the tubule periphery to maintain the germ cell line.

3.   Observe the cells in the middle of the tubule wall. There you should see a large number of cells (spermatocytes) that are obviously undergoing a nuclear division process. Look for coarse clumps of chromatin or threadlike chromosomes (visible only during nuclear division) that have the appearance of coiled springs. Attempt to differentiate between the larger primary spermatocytes and the somewhat smaller secondary spermatocytes. Once formed, the secondary spermatocytes quickly undergo division and so are more difficult to find.

Can you see tetrads? _____

Is there evidence of crossover? _____

In which location would you expect to see cells containing tetrads, closer to the spermatogonia or closer to the lumen?

_____

Would these cells be primary or secondary spermatocytes?

_____

4.   Examine the cells at the tubule lumen. Identify the small round-nucleated spermatids, many of which may appear lopsided and look as though they are starting to lose their cytoplasm. See if you can find a spermatid embedded in an elongated cell type—a **sustentacular,** or **Sertoli, cell**—which extends inward from the periphery of the tubule. The sustentacular cells nourish the spermatids as they begin their transformation into sperm. Also in the adluminal area (area toward the lumen), locate immature sperm, which can be identified by their tails. The sperm develop directly from the spermatids by the loss of extraneous cytoplasm and the development of a propulsive tail.

5.   Identify the **interstitial cells,** or **Leydig cells,** lying external to and between the seminiferous tubules. LH (luteinizing hormone), also called *interstitial cell–stimulating hormone* in

males, prompts these cells to produce testosterone, which acts synergistically with FSH to stimulate sperm production.

In the next stage of sperm development, spermiogenesis, all the superficial cytoplasm is sloughed off, and the remaining cell organelles are compacted into the three regions of the mature sperm. At the risk of oversimplifying, these anatomical regions are the *head,* the *midpiece,* and the *tail,* which correspond roughly to the activating and genetic region, the metabolic region, and the locomotor region, respectively. The mature sperm is a streamlined cell equipped with an organ of locomotion and a high rate of metabolism that enable it to move long distances quickly to get to the egg. It is a prime example of the correlation of form and function.

The pointed sperm head contains the DNA, or genetic material, of the chromosomes. Essentially it is the nucleus of the spermatid. Anterior to the nucleus is the **acrosome,** which contains enzymes involved in sperm penetration of the egg.

In the midpiece of the sperm is a centriole which gives rise to the filaments that structure the sperm tail. Wrapped tightly around the centriole are mitochondria that provide the ATP needed for contractile activity of the tail.

The tail is a typical flagellum produced by a centriole. When powered by ATP, the tail propels the sperm.

6.   Obtain a prepared slide of human sperm, and view it with the oil immersion lens. Compare what you see to the photograph of sperm in Figure 43.3. Identify the head, acrosome, and tail regions. Deformed sperm, for example sperm with multiple heads or tails, are sometimes present in such preparations. Did you observe any?

_____ If so, describe them. _____

_____

_____

7.   Examine the model of spermatogenesis to identify the spermatogonia, the primary and secondary spermatocytes, the spermatids, and the functional sperm. ▇▇▇

Demonstration of Oogenesis in *Ascaris* (Optional)

Oogenesis (the process of producing an egg) in mammals is difficult to demonstrate. However, the process may be studied rather easily in the transparent eggs of *Ascaris megalocephala,* an invertebrate roundworm parasite found in the intestine of mammals. Since its diploid chromosome number is 4, the chromosomes are easily counted.

ACTIVITY 3

Examining Meiotic Events Microscopically

Go to the demonstration area where the slides are set up, and make the following observations:

1.   Scan the first demonstration slide to identify a *primary oocyte,* the cell type that begins the meiotic process. It will have what appears to be a relatively thick cell membrane; this is the *fertilization membrane* that the oocyte produces after sperm penetration. Find and study a primary oocyte that is undergoing the first maturation division. Look for a barrel-shaped spindle with two tetrads (two groups of four beadlike

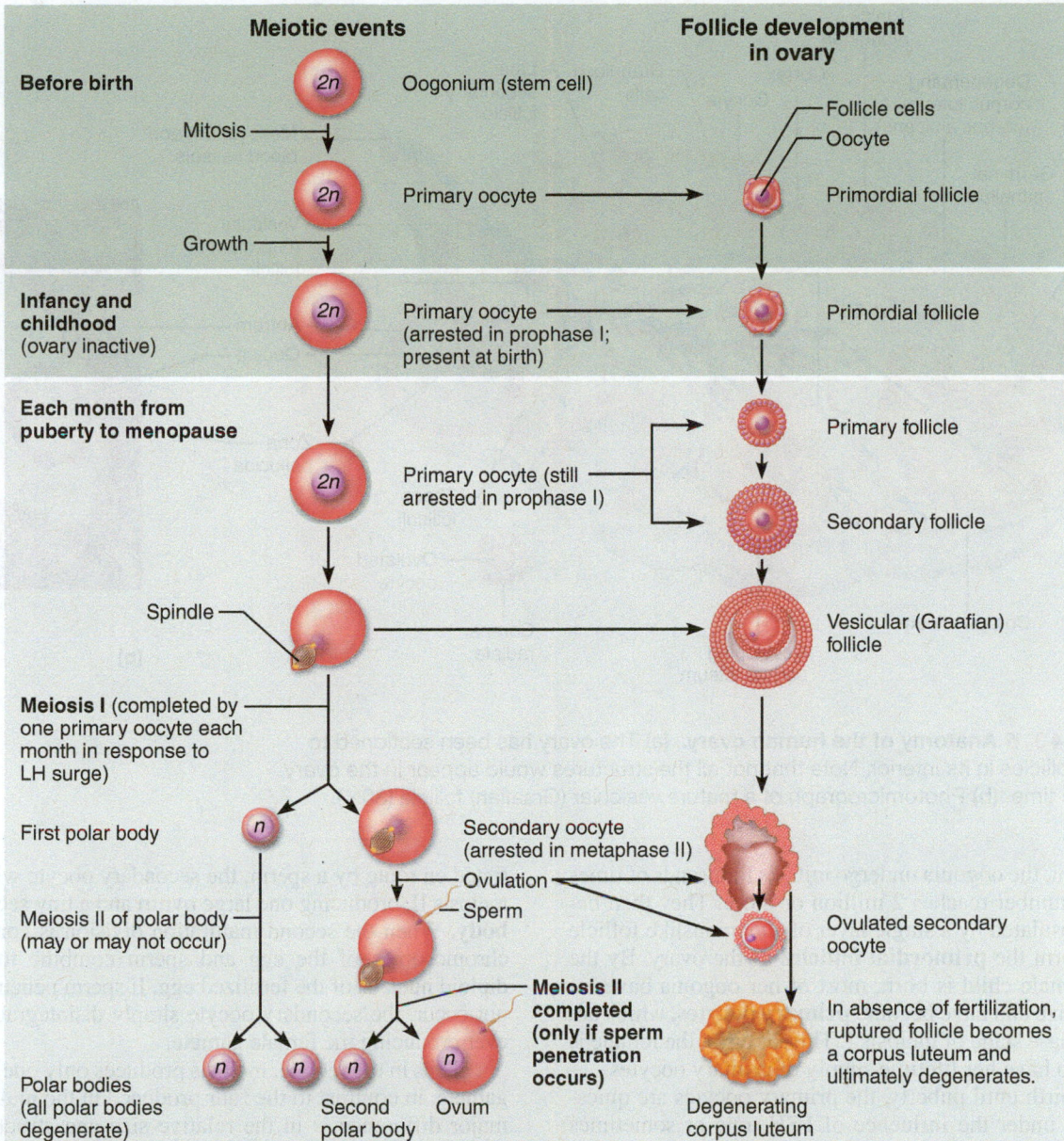

Meiotic events

Before birth
Mitosis
Growth

Infancy and childhood
(ovary inactive)

Each month from puberty to menopause

Spindle

Meiosis I (completed by one primary oocyte each month in response to LH surge)

First polar body

Meiosis II of polar body (may or may not occur)

Polar bodies (all polar bodies degenerate)

Second polar body

Ovum

Meiosis II completed (only if sperm penetration occurs)

Oogonium (stem cell)

Primary oocyte

Primary oocyte (arrested in prophase I; present at birth)

Primary oocyte (still arrested in prophase I)

Secondary oocyte (arrested in metaphase II)

Ovulation

Sperm

Follicle development in ovary

Follicle cells
Oocyte
Primordial follicle

Primordial follicle

Primary follicle

Secondary follicle

Vesicular (Graafian) follicle

Ovulated secondary oocyte

In absence of fertilization, ruptured follicle becomes a corpus luteum and ultimately degenerates.

Degenerating corpus luteum

FIGURE 43.4 Oogenesis. Left, flowchart of meiotic events. Right, correlation with follicular development and ovulation in the ovary.

chromosomes) in it. Most often the spindle is located at the periphery of the cell. (The sperm nucleus may or may not be seen, depending on how the cell was cut.)

2. Observe slide 2. Locate a cell in which half of each tetrad (a dyad) is being extruded from the cell surface into a smaller cell called the *first polar body*.

3. On slide 3, attempt to locate a *secondary oocyte* (a daughter cell produced during meiosis I) undergoing the second maturation division. In this view, you should see two dyads (two groups of two beadlike chromosomes) on the spindle.

4. On slide 4, locate a cell in which the *second polar body* is being formed. In this case, both it and the ovum will now contain two chromosomes, the haploid number for *Ascaris*.

5. On slide 5, identify a *fertilized egg* or a cell in which the sperm and ovum nuclei (actually *pronuclei*) are fusing to form a single nucleus containing four chromosomes. ▆

Human Oogenesis and the Ovarian Cycle

Once the adult ovarian cycle is established, gonadotropic hormones produced by the anterior pituitary influence the development of ova in the ovaries and their cyclic production of female sex hormones. Within an ovary, each immature ovum develops within a saclike structure called a *follicle*, where it is encased by one or more layers of smaller cells called **follicle cells** (when one layer is present) or **granulosa cells** (when there is more than one layer).

The process of **oogenesis**, or female gamete formation, which occurs in the ovary, is similar to spermatogenesis occurring in the testis, but there are some important differences. The process, schematically outlined in Figure 43.4, begins with primitive stem cells called **oogonia**, located in the ovarian cortices of the developing female fetus. During fetal

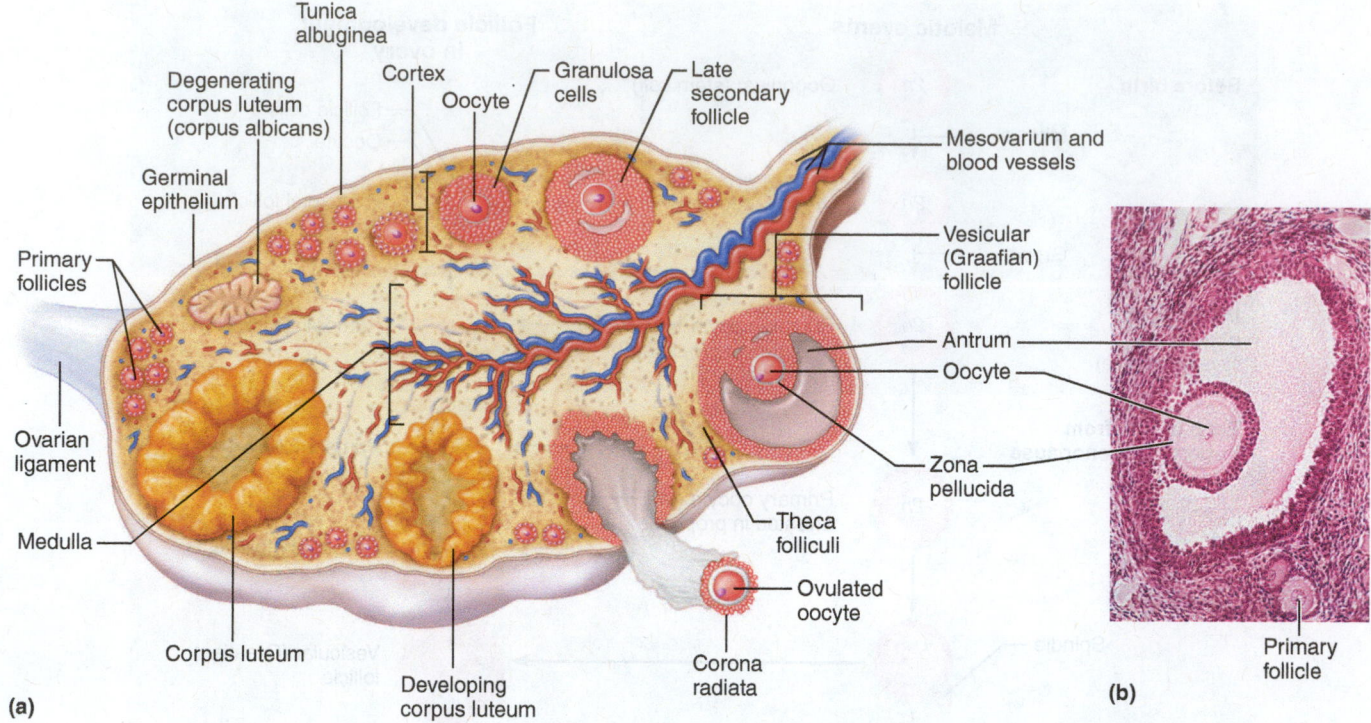

FIGURE 43.5 Anatomy of the human ovary. (a) The ovary has been sectioned to reveal the follicles in its interior. Note that not all the structures would appear in the ovary at the same time. **(b)** Photomicrograph of a mature vesicular (Graafian) follicle (30×).

development, the oogonia undergo mitosis thousands of times until their number reaches 2 million or more. They then become encapsulated by a single layer of squamouslike follicle cells and form the **primordial follicles** of the ovary. By the time the female child is born, most of her oogonia have increased in size and have become **primary oocytes,** which are in the prophase stage of meiosis I. Thus at birth, the female is presumed to have her lifetime supply of primary oocytes.

From birth until puberty, the primary oocytes are quiescent. Then, under the influence of FSH, one or sometimes more of the follicles begin to undergo maturation approximately every 28 days.

As a follicle grows, its epithelium changes from squamous to cuboidal cells and it comes to be called a **primary follicle** (see also Figure 43.5). The primary follicle begins to produce estrogens, and the primary oocyte completes its first maturation division, producing two haploid daughter cells that are very disproportionate in size. One of these is the **secondary oocyte,** which contains nearly all of the cytoplasm in the primary oocyte. The other is the tiny **first polar body.** The first polar body may then complete the second maturation division, producing two more polar bodies. These eventually disintegrate for lack of sustaining cytoplasm.

As the follicle containing the secondary oocyte continues to enlarge, blood levels of estrogens rise. Initially, estrogen exerts a negative feedback influence on the release of gonadotropins by the anterior pituitary. However, approximately in the middle of the 28-day cycle, as the follicle reaches the mature **vesicular,** or **Graafian, follicle** stage, rising estrogen levels become highly stimulatory and a sudden burstlike release of LH (and, to a lesser extent, FSH) by the anterior pituitary triggers ovulation. The secondary oocyte is extruded and begins its journey along the uterine tube to the uterus. If pene-

trated en route by a sperm, the secondary oocyte will undergo meiosis II, producing one large **ovum** and a tiny **second polar body.** When the second maturation division is complete, the chromosomes of the egg and sperm combine to form the diploid nucleus of the fertilized egg. If sperm penetration does not occur, the secondary oocyte simply disintegrates without ever producing the female gamete.

Thus in the female, meiosis produces only one functional gamete, in contrast to the four produced in the male. Another major difference is in the relative size and structure of the functional gametes. Sperm are tiny and equipped with tails for locomotion. They have few organelles and virtually no nutrient-containing cytoplasm; hence the nutrients contained in semen are essential to their survival. In contrast, the egg is a relatively large nonmotile cell, well stocked with cytoplasmic reserves that nourish the developing embryo until implantation can be accomplished. Essentially all the zygote's organelles are "delivered" by the egg.

Once the secondary oocyte has been expelled from the ovary, LH transforms the ruptured follicle into a **corpus luteum,** which begins producing progesterone and estrogen. Rising blood levels of the two ovarian hormones inhibit FSH release by the anterior pituitary. As FSH declines, its stimulatory effect on follicular production of estrogens ends, and estrogen blood levels begin to decline. Since rising estrogen levels triggered LH release by the anterior pituitary, falling estrogen levels result in declining levels of LH in the blood. Corpus luteum secretory function is maintained by high blood levels of LH. Thus as LH blood levels begin to drop toward the end of the 28-day cycle, progesterone production ends and the corpus luteum begins to degenerate and is replaced by scar tissue (**corpus albicans**). The graphs in Figure 43.7 depict the hormone relationships described here.

Necrotic (areas of dead and dying cells) fragments of functional layer of endometrium

(a)

Glands

Endometrium
- Functional layer

- Basal layer

Myometrium

(b)

Elaborated glands

Endometrium

Myometrium

(c)

FIGURE 43.6 Endometrial changes during the menstrual cycle. (a) Onset of menstruation (20×). **(b)** Early proliferative phase (20×). **(c)** Early secretory phase (all 20×).

Examining Oogenesis in the Ovary

Because many different stages of ovarian development exist within the ovary at any one time, a single microscopic prepa-ration will contain follicles at many different stages of devel-opment. Obtain a cross section of ovary tissue, and identify the following structures. Refer to Figure 43.5 as you work.

Germinal epithelium: Outermost layer of the ovary.

Primary follicle: One or a few layers of cuboidal follicle cells surrounding the larger central developing ovum.

Secondary (growing) follicles: Follicles consisting of sev-eral layers of follicle (granulosa) cells surrounding the central developing ovum, and beginning to show evidence of fluid accumulation and **antrum** (central cavity) formation. Follicle development may take more than one cycle.

Vesicular (Graafian) follicle: At this stage of development, the follicle has a large antrum containing fluid produced by the gran-ulosa cells. The developing secondary oocyte is pushed to one side of the follicle and is surrounded by a capsule of several lay-ers of granulosa cells called the **corona radiata** (radiating crown). When the secondary oocyte is released, it enters the uter-ine tubes with its corona radiata intact. The connective tissue stroma (background tissue) adjacent to the mature follicle forms a capsule, called the **theca folliculi,** that encloses the follicle.

Corpus luteum: A solid glandular structure or a structure containing a scalloped lumen that develops from the ruptured follicle. ▬

Comparing and Contrasting Oogenesis and Spermatogenesis

Examine the model of oogenesis, and compare it with the spermatogenesis model. Note differences in the size and structure of the functional gametes. ▬

The Menstrual Cycle

The **uterine cycle,** or **menstrual cycle,** is hormonally con-trolled by estrogens and progesterone secreted by the ovary. It is normally divided into three stages: menstrual, prolifera-tive, and secretory. The endometrial changes are described in Figure 43.7 and shown in Figure 43.6. Figure 43.7 shows how they correlate with hormonal and ovarian changes.

If fertilization has occurred, the embryo will produce a hormone much like LH, which will maintain the function of the corpus luteum. Otherwise, as the corpus luteum begins to deteriorate, lack of ovarian hormones in the blood causes blood vessels supplying the endometrium to kink and become spastic, setting the stage for menses to begin by the 28th day.

Although Figure 43.7d assumes a classic 28-day cycle, the length of the menstrual cycle is highly variable, some-times as short as 21 days or as long as 38.

Observing Histological Changes in the Endometrium During the Menstrual Cycle

Obtain slides showing the menstrual, secretory, and prolifer-ative phases of the uterine endometrium. Observe each care-fully, comparing their relative thicknesses and vascularity. As you work, refer to the corresponding photomicrographs in Figure 43.6. ▬

(a) Fluctuation of gonadotropin levels: Fluctuating levels of pituitary gonadotropins (follicle-stimulating hormone and luteinizing hormone) in the blood regulate the events of the ovarian cycle.

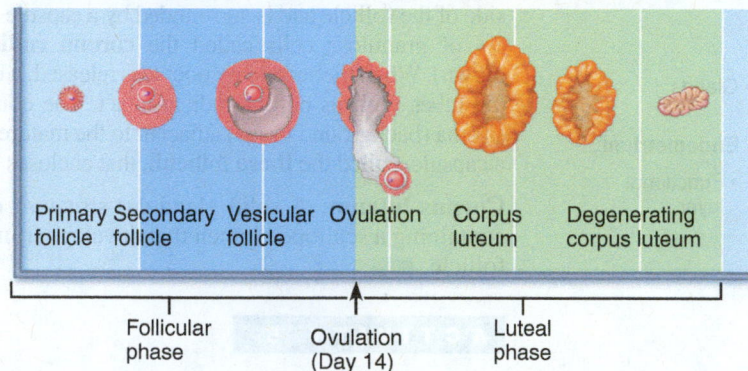

Primary follicle   Secondary follicle   Vesicular follicle   Ovulation   Corpus luteum   Degenerating corpus luteum

Follicular phase   Ovulation (Day 14)   Luteal phase

(b) Ovarian cycle: Structural changes in the ovarian follicles during the ovarian cycle are correlated with (d) changes in the endometrium of the uterus during the uterine cycle.

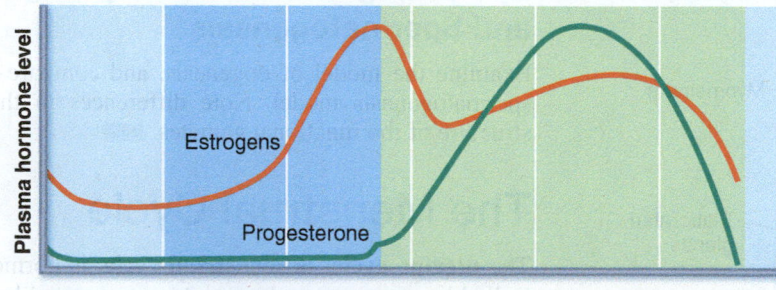

Estrogens

Progesterone

(c) Fluctuation of ovarian hormone levels: Fluctuating levels of ovarian hormones (estrogens and progesterone) cause the endometrial changes of the uterine cycle. The high estrogen levels are also responsible for the LH/FSH surge in (a).

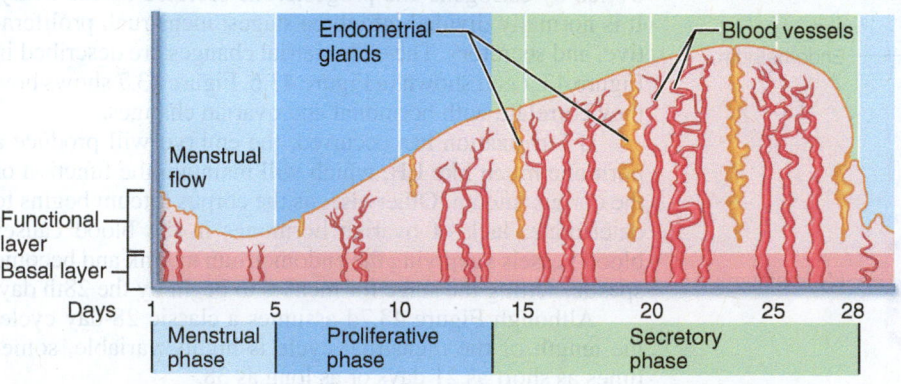

Endometrial glands   Blood vessels

Menstrual flow

Functional layer
Basal layer

Days   1   5   10   15   20   25   28

Menstrual phase   Proliferative phase   Secretory phase

(d) The three phases of the uterine cycle:
- Menstrual: Shedding of the functional layer of the endometrium. Approximately days 1–5.
- Proliferative: Rebuilding of the functional layer of the endometrium under influence of estrogens. Approximately days 6–14. Ovulation occurs at the end of this phase.
- Secretory: Begins immediately after ovulation under the influence of progesterone. The blood supply is enriched and glandular secretion of nutrients increases, events that prepare the endometrium to receive an embryo.

FIGURE 43.7 Correlation of anterior pituitary and ovarian hormones with structural changes in the ovary and uterus. The time bar applies to all parts of the figure.

Physiology of Reproduction: Gametogenesis and the Female Cycles

Meiosis

1. The following statements refer to events occurring during mitosis and/or meiosis. For each statement, decide if the event occurs in (a) mitosis only, (b) meiosis only, or (c) both mitosis and meiosis.

_____ 1. dyads are visible

_____ 2. tetrads are visible

_____ 3. product is two diploid daughter cells genetically identical to the mother cell

_____ 4. product is four haploid daughter cells quantitatively and qualitatively different from the mother cell

_____ 5. involves the phases prophase, metaphase, anaphase, and telophase

_____ 6. occurs throughout the body

_____ 7. occurs only in the ovaries and testes

_____ 8. provides cells for growth and repair

_____ 9. homologues synapse; chiasmata are seen

_____ 10. chromosomes are replicated before the division process begins

_____ 11. provides cells for perpetuation of the species

_____ 12. consists of two consecutive nuclear divisions, without chromosomal replication occurring before the second division

2. Describe the process of synapsis. _____

_____

3. How does crossover introduce variability in the daughter cells? _____

_____

4. Define *homologous chromosomes*. _____

_____

Spermatogenesis

5. The cell types seen in the seminiferous tubules are listed in the key. Match the correct cell type(s) with the descriptions given below.

Key: a. primary spermatocyte   c. spermatogonium   e. spermatid
       b. secondary spermatocyte   d. sustentacular cell   f. sperm

_____ 1. primitive stem cell   _____ 4. products of meiosis II

_____ 2. haploid   _____ 5. product of spermiogenesis

_____ 3. provides nutrients to   _____ 6. product of meiosis I
                 developing sperm

6. Why are spermatids not considered functional gametes? _____

_____

7. Differentiate between *spermatogenesis* and *spermiogenesis*. _____

_____

_____

8. Draw a sperm below, and identify the acrosome, head, midpiece, and tail. Then beside each label, note the composition and function of each of these sperm structures.

9. The life span of a sperm is very short. What anatomical characteristics might lead you to suspect this even if you didn't know

its life span? _____

Oogenesis, the Ovarian Cycle, and the Menstrual Cycle

10. The sequence of events leading to germ cell formation in the female begins during fetal development. By the time the child

is born, all viable oogonia have been converted to _____.

In view of this fact, how does the total germ cell potential of the female compare to that of the male?

_____

11. The female gametes develop in structures called *follicles*. What is a follicle? _____

_____

How are primary and vesicular follicles anatomically different? _____

_____

_____

What is a corpus luteum? _____

_____

12. What is the major hormone produced by the vesicular follicle? _____

By the corpus luteum? _____

13. Use the key to identify the cell type you would expect to find in the following structures.

Key: a. oogonium   b. primary oocyte   c. secondary oocyte   d. ovum

_____ 1. forming part of the primary follicle   _____ 3. in the mature vesicular follicle of the ovary
             in the ovary

                                                            _____ 4. in the uterine tube shortly after sperm penetration
_____ 2. in the uterine tube before fertilization

14. The cellular product of spermatogenesis is four _____; the final product of oogenesis is one

_____ and three _____. What is the function of this unequal cytoplasmic

division seen during oogenesis in the female? _____

_____

_____

What is the fate of the three tiny cells produced during oogenesis? _____

Why? _____

15. The following statements deal with anterior pituitary and ovarian hormones and with hormonal interrelationships. Name the
hormone(s) described in each statement.

_____ 1.	produced by primary follicles in the ovary
_____ 2.	ovulation occurs after its burstlike release
_____ and _____ 3.	exert negative feedback on the anterior pituitary relative to FSH secretion
_____ 4.	stimulates LH release by the anterior pituitary
_____ 5.	stimulates the corpus luteum to produce progesterone and estrogen
_____ 6.	maintains the hormonal production of the corpus luteum in a nonpregnant woman

16. Why does the corpus luteum deteriorate toward the end of the ovarian cycle? _____

_____

17. For each statement below dealing with hormonal blood levels during the female ovarian and menstrual cycles, decide whether the condition in column A is usually (a) greater than, (b) less than, or (c) essentially equal to the condition in column B.

Column A   **Column B**

_____ 1. amount of LH in the blood .... amount of LH in the blood at ovulation
during menses

_____ 2. amount of FSH in the blood on .... amount of FSH in the blood on day 20 of the cycle
day 6 of the cycle

_____ 3. amount of estrogen in the blood .... amount of estrogen in the blood at ovulation
during menses

_____ 4. amount of progesterone in the blood .... amount of progesterone in the blood on day 23
on day 14

_____ 5. amount of estrogen in the blood .... amount of progesterone in the blood on day 10
on day 10

18. What uterine tissue undergoes dramatic changes during the menstrual cycle? _____

19. When during the female menstrual cycle would fertilization be unlikely? Explain why. _____

_____

20. Assume that a woman could be an "on demand" ovulator like the rabbit, in which copulation stimulates the hypothalamic–anterior pituitary axis and causes LH release, and an oocyte was ovulated and fertilized on day 26 of her 28-day cycle. Why would a successful pregnancy be unlikely at this time?

_____

_____

_____

21. The menstrual cycle depends on events within the female ovary. The stages of the menstrual cycle are listed below. For each, note its approximate time span and the related events in the uterus; and then to the right, record the ovarian events occurring simultaneously. Pay particular attention to hormonal events.

Menstrual cycle stage	Uterine events	Ovarian events
Menstruation		
Proliferative		
Secretory		

44

Survey of Embryonic Development

MATERIALS

- ☐ Prepared slides of sea urchin development (zygote through larval stages)
- ☐ Compound microscope
- ☐ Three-dimensional human development models or plaques (if available)
- ☐ *Demonstration:* Phases of human development in *Life Before Birth: Normal Fetal Development,* Second Edition (by Marjorie A. England, 1996, Mosby-Wolfe)
- ☐ Disposable gloves
- ☐ *Demonstration:* Pregnant cat, rat, or pig uterus (one per laboratory session) with uterine wall dissected to allow student examination
- ☐ Three-dimensional model of pregnant human torso
- ☐ *Demonstration:* Fresh or formalin-preserved human placenta (obtained from a clinical agency)
- ☐ Prepared slide of placenta tissue

OBJECTIVES

1. To define *fertilization* and *zygote*.
2. To define and discuss the function of *cleavage* and *gastrulation*.
3. To name the three primary germ layers, and to discuss the importance of each.
4. To differentiate between the blastula and gastrula forms of the sea urchin and human when provided with appropriate models or diagrams.
5. To define *blastocyst* and/or *chorionic vesicle*.
6. To identify the following structures of a human chorionic vesicle when provided with an appropriate diagram, and to state the function of each.

   | inner cell mass | chorionic villi | yolk sac |
   | trophoblast | amnion | allantois |

7. To describe the process and timing of implantation in the human.
8. To define *decidua basalis* and *decidua capsularis*.
9. To state the germ-layer origin of several body organs and organ systems of the human.
10. To describe developmental direction.
11. To describe the gross anatomy and general function of the human placenta.

PRE-LAB QUIZ

1. Circle the correct term. The fertilized egg, or zygote / embryo, appears as a single cell surrounded by a fertilization membrane and a jellylike membrane.
2. The uniting of the egg and sperm nuclei is known as
   a. embryogensis
   b. fertilization
   c. implantation
   d. mitosis
3. Circle True or False. Cleavage is a series of mitotic divisions without any intervening growth periods that results in a multicellular embryonic body.
4. Circle the correct term. As a result of gastrulation, a three / four-layered embryo forms, with each layer corresponding to a primary germ layer.
5. The _____ gives rise to the epidermis of the skin and the nervous system.
   a. ectoderm
   b. endoderm
   c. mesoderm
6. By the ninth week of development, the embryo is referred to as a
   a. blastocyst
   b. blastomere
   c. fetus
   d. gastrula
7. Circle True or False. The placenta is composed solely of embryonic membranes.
8. Circle the correct term. The allantois / amnion encases the young embryonic body in a fluid-filled chamber that acts to protect the developing embryo against trauma.
9. What is the function of the placenta? _____

myA&P *For practice quizzes on this lab, go to www.myaandp.com.*

Because reproduction is such a familiar event, we tend to lose sight of the wonder of the process. One part of that process, the development of the embryo, is the concern of embryologists who study the changes in structure that occur from the time of fertilization until the time of birth.

Early development in all animals involves three basic types of activities, which are integrated to ensure the formation of a viable offspring: (1) an increase in cell number and subsequent cell growth; (2) cellular specialization; and (3) morphogenesis, the formation of functioning organ systems. This exercise first provides a rather broad overview of the changes in structure that take place during embryonic development in sea urchins. The pattern of changes in this marine animal provides a basis of comparison with developmental events in the human.

Developmental Stages of Sea Urchins and Humans

Microscopic Study of Sea Urchin Development

1. Obtain a compound microscope and a set of slides depicting embryonic development of the sea urchin. Draw simple diagrams of your observations as you work.

2. Observe the fertilized egg, or **zygote,** which appears as a single cell immediately surrounded by a fertilization membrane and a jellylike membrane. After an egg is penetrated by a sperm, the egg and the sperm nuclei fuse to form a single nucleus. This process is called **fertilization.** Within 2 to 5 minutes after sperm penetration, a fertilization membrane forms beneath the jelly coat to prevent the entry of additional sperm. Draw the zygote and label the fertilization and jelly membranes.

Zygote

3. Observe the cleavage stages. Once fertilization has occurred, the zygote begins to divide, forming a mass of successively smaller and smaller cells, called **blastomeres.** This series of mitotic divisions without intervening growth periods is referred to as **cleavage,** and it results in a multicellular embryonic body. As the division process continues, a solid ball of cells forms. (At the 32-cell stage, it is called the **morula,** and the embryo resembles a raspberry in form.) Then the cell mass hollows out to become the embryonic form called the **blastula,** which is a ball of cells surrounding a central cavity. The blastula is the final product of cleavage.

The cleavage stage of embryonic development provides a large number of building blocks (cells) with which to fashion the forming body. (If this is a little difficult to understand, consider trying to build a structure with a huge block of granite rather than with small bricks.)

In the spaces below, diagram the 2-, 4-, 8-, and 16-cell stages as you observe them.

2-cell stage   4-cell stage

8-cell stage   16-cell stage

Identify and sketch the blastula stage of cleavage—a ball of cells with an apparently lighter center due to the presence of the central cavity.

Blastula

4. Identify the **early gastrula** form (which follows the blastula in the developmental sequence). The gastrula looks as if one end of the blastula has been indented or pushed into the central cavity, forming a two-layered embryo. In time, a third layer of cells appears between the initial two cell layers. Thus, as a result of **gastrulation,** a three-layered embryo forms, each layer corresponding to a **primary germ layer** from which all body tissues develop. The innermost layer, the **endoderm,** and the middle layer, the **mesoderm,** form the internal organs; the outermost layer, the **ectoderm,** forms the surface tissues of the body.

Draw a gastrula below. Label the ectoderm and endoderm. If you can see the third layer of cells, the mesoderm, budding off between the other two layers, label that also.

Gastrula

5. Gastrulation in the sea urchin is followed by the appearance of the free-swimming larval form, in which the three germ layers have differentiated into the various tissues and organs of the animal's body.

The larvae exist for a few days in the unattached form and then settle to the ocean bottom to attach and develop into the sessile adult form. If time allows, observe the larval form on the prepared slides. Record your observations in a simple drawing below. ■

(a) Zygote
(fertilized egg)

(b) 4-cell stage
2 days

(c) Morula (a solid ball
of blastomeres).
3 days

(d) Early blastocyst
(Morula hollows out,
fills with fluid, and
"hatches" from the
zona pellucida).
4 days

Zona
pellucida

Sperm

Uterine
tube

Fertilization
(sperm
meets and
enters egg)

Oocyte
(egg)

Ovary

Ovulation

Degenerating
zona
pellucida

Blastocyst
cavity

(e) Implanting blastocyst
(Consists of a sphere
of trophoblast cells and
an eccentric cell cluster
called the inner cell
mass). 7 days

Trophoblast

Blastocyst
cavity

Inner cell
mass

Uterus

Endometrium

Cavity of
uterus

**FIGURE 44.1 Early embryonic development of
the human.** Sequential developmental changes from
fertilization to blastocyst and implantation in the uterus.

ACTIVITY 2

Examining the Stages
of Human Development

Examine the models or plaques of human development that
are on display. If these are not available, use Figures 44.1 and
44.2 for this study. Observe the models to identify the various
stages of human development and respond to the questions
posed below.

1.   Observe the fertilized egg, or zygote, which appears as a
single cell immediately surrounded by a jellylike *zona pellucida* and then a crown of granulosa cells (the *corona radiata*).

2.   Next, observe the cleavage stages.

Is the human cleavage process similar to that in the sea urchin?

_____

Why do you suppose this is so? _____

_____

Observe the blastula, the final product of cleavage, which
is called the **blastocyst** or **chorionic vesicle** in the human. Unlike the sea urchin, only a portion of the blastula cells in the
human contribute to the formation of the embryonic body—
those seen at one side of the blastocyst (Figure 44.1e) forming
the **inner cell mass (ICM).** The rest of the blastocyst—that
enclosing the central cavity and overriding the ICM—is re-

ferred to as the **trophoblast.** The trophoblast becomes an extraembryonic membrane called the **chorion,** which forms the
fetal portion of the **placenta.**

3.   Observe the *implanting* blastocyst shown on the model or
in the figures. By approximately the seventh day after ovulation,
a developing human embryo (blastocyst) is floating free in the
uterine cavity. About that time, it adheres to the uterine wall over
the ICM area, and implantation begins. The trophoblast cells secrete enzymes that erode the uterine mucosa at the point of attachment to reach the vascular supply in the submucosa. By the
fourteenth day after ovulation, implantation is completed and
the uterine mucosa has grown over the burrowed-in embryo.
The portion of the uterine wall beneath the ICM, destined to take
part in placenta formation, is called the **decidua basalis** and that
surrounding the rest of the blastocyst is called the **decidua capsularis.** Identify these regions.

By the time implantation has been completed, embryonic
development has progressed to the **gastrula stage,** and the three
primary germ layers are present and are beginning to differentiate (Figure 44.2). Within the next 6 weeks, virtually all of the
body organ systems will have been laid down at least in rudi-
mentary form by the germ layers. The outermost layer,
ectoderm, gives rise to the epidermis of the skin and the nervous
system. The deepest layer, the *endoderm,* forms the mucosa of
the digestive and respiratory tracts and associated glands.
Mesoderm, the middle layer, forms virtually everything lying

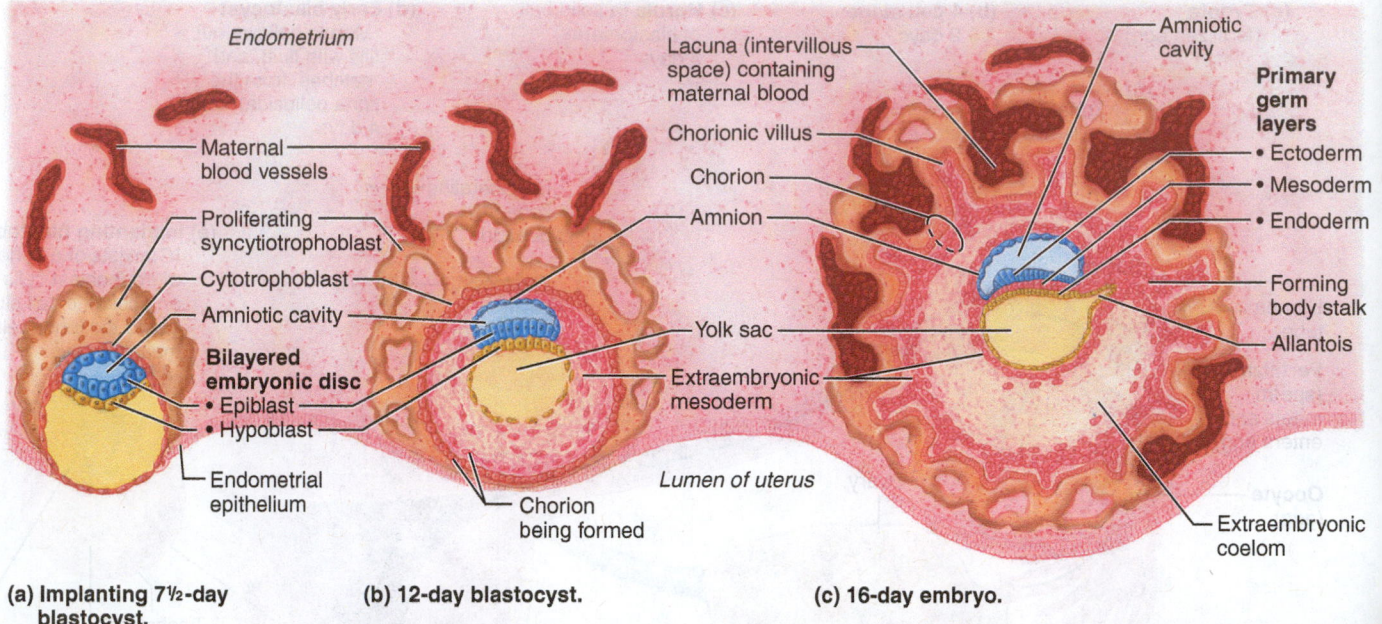

(a) Implanting 7½-day blastocyst.

(b) 12-day blastocyst.

(c) 16-day embryo.

FIGURE 44.2 Events of placentation, early embryonic development, and extraembryonic membrane formation.

between the two (skeleton, walls of the digestive organs, urinary system, skeletal muscles, circulatory system, and others).

All the groundwork has been completed by the eighth week. By the ninth week of development, the embryo is referred to as a **fetus,** and from this point on, the major activities are growth and tissue and organ specialization.

4.   Again observe the blastocyst to follow the formation of the embryonic membranes and the placenta (see Figure 44.2). Notice the villus extensions of the trophoblast. By the time implantation is complete, the trophoblast has differentiated into the chorion, and its large elaborate villi are lying in the blood-filled sinusoids in the uterine tissue. This composite of uterine tissue and **chorionic villi** is called the **placenta** (Figure 44.3), and all exchanges to and from the embryo occur through the chorionic membranes.

Three embryonic membranes (originating in the ICM) have also formed by this time—the amnion, the allantois, and the yolk sac (Figure 44.2). Attempt to identify each.

*   The **amnion** encases the young embryonic body in a fluid-filled chamber that protects the embryo against mechanical trauma and temperature extremes and prevents adhesions during rapid embryonic growth.

*   The **yolk sac** in humans has lost its original function, which was to pass nutrients to the embryo after digesting the yolk mass. The placenta has taken over that task; also, the human egg has very little yolk. However, the yolk sac is not totally useless. The embryo's first blood cells originate here, and the primordial germ cells migrate from it into the embryo's body to seed the gonadal tissue.

*   The **allantois,** which protrudes from the posterior end of the yolk sac, is also largely redundant in humans because of the placenta. In birds and reptiles, it is a repository for embryonic wastes. In humans, it is the struc-

(d) 4½-week embryo.

tural basis on which the mesoderm migrates to form the body stalk, or **umbilical cord,** which attaches the embryo to the placenta.

5.   Go to the demonstration area to view the photographic series, *Life Before Birth: Normal Fetal Development.* These photographs illustrate human development in a way you will long remember. After viewing them, respond to the following questions.

In your own words, what do the chorionic villi look like?

_____

_____

_____

What organs or organ systems appear *very* early in embryonic development?

_____

_____

Does development occur in a rostral to caudal (head to toe) direction, or vice versa?

_____

Does development occur in a distal to proximal direction, or vice versa?

_____

_____

Does spontaneous movement occur in utero? _____

How does the mother recognize this? _____

_____

_____

The very young embryo has been described as resembling "an astronaut suspended and floating in space." Do you think this definition is appropriate?

_____ Why or why not? _____

_____

_____

_____

What is vernix caseosa? _____

_____

_____

What is lanugo? _____

_____

_____

In Utero Development

ACTIVITY 3

Identifying Fetal Structures

1. Put on disposable gloves. Go to the appropriate demonstration area and observe the fetuses in the **Y**-shaped animal (cat, rat, or pig) uterus. Identify the following fetal or fetal-related structures:

• **Placenta** (a composite structure formed from the uterine mucosa and the fetal chorion).

Describe its appearance. _____

_____

_____

_____

• **Umbilical cord.** Describe its relationship to the placenta and fetus.

_____

_____

_____

• **Amniotic sac.** Identify the transparent amnion surrounding a fetus. Open one amniotic sac and note the amount, color, and consistency of the fluid.

_____

_____

_____

Remove a fetus and observe the degree of development of the head, body, and extremities. Is the skin thick or thin?

_____

What is the basis for your response? _____

_____

_____

2. Observe the model of a pregnant human torso. Identify the placenta. How does it differ in shape from the animal placenta observed?

_____

_____

_____

Identify the umbilical cord. In what region of the uterus does implantation usually occur, as indicated by the position of the placenta?

_____

_____

What might be the consequence if it occurred lower?

_____

_____

_____

Why would a feet-first position (breech presentation) be less desirable than the positioning of the model?

_____

_____

_____

Gross and Microscopic Anatomy of the Placenta

The placenta is a remarkable temporary organ. Composed of maternal and fetal tissues, it is responsible for providing nutrients and oxygen to the embryo and fetus while removing carbon dioxide and metabolic wastes.

ACTIVITY 4

Studying Placental Structure

1. Notice that the human placenta on display has two very different-appearing surfaces—one smooth and the other spongy, roughened, and torn-looking.

Which is the fetal side? _____

What is the basis for your conclusion? _____

_____

_____

_____

Identify the umbilical cord. Within the cord, identify the umbilical vein and two umbilical arteries. What is the function of the umbilical vein?

_____

_____

The umbilical arteries? _____

_____

_____

2. Obtain a microscope slide of placental tissue. Observe the tissue carefully, comparing it to Figure 44.3. Identify the *intervillous spaces* (maternal sinusoids), which are blood-filled in life. Identify the villi, and notice their rich vascular supply. Draw a small representative diagram of your observations below and label it appropriately. ■

FIGURE 44.3 Diagrammatic representation of the structure of the placenta for a 13-week fetus.

NAME _____

LAB TIME/DATE _____

Survey of Embryonic Development

Developmental Stages of Sea Urchins and Humans

1. Define *zygote*. _____

2. Describe how you were able to tell by observation when a sea urchin egg was fertilized. _____

_____

3. Use the key choices to identify the embryonic stage or process described below.

Key: a. blastula   c. fertilization   e. morula
      b. cleavage   d. gastrulation   f. zygote

_____ 1. fusion of male and female pronuclei

_____ 2. solid ball of embryonic cells

_____ 3. process of rapid mitotic cell division without intervening growth periods

_____ 4. combination of egg and sperm

_____ 5. process involving cell rearrangements to form the three primary germ layers

_____ 6. embryonic stage in which the embryo consists of a hollow ball of cells

4. What is the importance of cleavage in embryonic development? _____

_____

How is cleavage different from mitotic cell division, which occurs later in life? _____

_____

_____

5. The cells of the human blastula (blastocyst) have various fates. Which blastocyst structures have the following fates?

_____ 1. produces the embryonic body

_____ 2. becomes the chorion and cooperates with uterine tissues to form the placenta

_____ 3. produces the amnion, yolk sac, and allantois

_____ 4. produces the primordial germ cells

_____ 5. an embryonic membrane that provides the structural basis for the body stalk or umbilical cord

6. Using the letters on the diagram, correctly identify each of the following maternal or embryonic structures.

_____ amnion	_____ chorion	_____ decidua basalis	_____ endoderm
_____ body stalk	_____ chorionic villi	_____ decidua capsularis	_____ mesoderm
		_____ ectoderm	_____ uterine cavity

7. Explain the process and importance of gastrulation. _____

_____

_____

8. What is the function of the amnion and the amniotic fluid? _____

_____

_____

9. Describe the process of implantation, noting the role of the trophoblast cells. _____

_____

_____

10. How many days after fertilization is implantation generally completed? _____ What event in the female menstrual cycle

ordinarily occurs just about this time if implantation does not occur? _____

_____

11. What name is given to the part of the uterine wall directly under the implanting embryo? _____

That surrounding the rest of the embryonic structure? _____

12. Using an appropriate reference, find out what *decidua* means and state the definition. _____

_____

How is this terminology applicable to the deciduas of pregnancy? _____

_____

13. Referring to the illustrations and text of *Life Before Birth: Normal Fetal Development,* answer the following:

Which two organ systems are extensively developed in the *very young* embryo?

_____ and _____

Describe the direction of development by circling the correct descriptions below:

proximal-distal   distal-proximal   caudal-rostral   rostral-caudal

Does bodily control during infancy develop in the same directions? Think! Can an infant pick up a common pin (pincer grasp) or wave his arms earlier? Is arm-hand or leg-foot control achieved earlier?

_____

14. Note whether each of the following organs or organ systems develops from the (a) ectoderm, (b) endoderm, or (c) mesoderm. Use an appropriate reference as necessary.

_____ 1.   skeletal muscle   _____ 4.   respiratory mucosa   _____ 7.   nervous system

_____ 2.   skeleton   _____ 5.   circulatory system   _____ 8.   serosa membrane

_____ 3.   lining of gut   _____ 6.   epidermis of skin   _____ 9.   liver, pancreas

In Utero Development

15. Make the following comparisons between a human and the pregnant dissected animal structures.

Comparison object	Human	Dissected animal
Shape of the placenta		
Shape of the uterus		

16. Where in the human uterus do implantation and placentation ordinarily occur? _____

_____

17. Describe the function(s) of the placenta. _____

_____

What embryonic membranes has the placenta more or less "put out of business"? _____

_____

18. When does the human embryo come to be called a fetus? _____

19. What is the usual and most desirable fetal position in utero? _____

Why is this the most desirable position? _____

_____

_____

_____

Gross and Microscopic Anatomy of the Placenta

20. Describe fully the gross structure of the human placenta as observed in the laboratory. _____

_____

_____

21. What is the tissue origin of the placenta: fetal, maternal, or both? _____

22. What placental barriers must be crossed to exchange materials? _____

_____

Principles of Heredity

MATERIALS

- ☐ Pennies (for coin tossing)
- ☐ PTC (phenylthiocarbamide) taste strips
- ☐ Sodium benzoate taste strips
- ☐ Chart drawn on chalkboard for tabulation of class results of human phenotype/genotype determinations

Activity 5: Blood typing

- ☐ Anti-A and Anti-B sera
- ☐ Clean microscope slides
- ☐ Toothpicks
- ☐ Wax pencils
- ☐ Sterile lancets
- ☐ Alcohol swabs
- ☐ Beaker containing 10% bleach solution
- ☐ Disposable autoclave bag

Activity 6: Hemoglobin phenotyping

- ☐ Electrophoresis equipment and power supply
- ☐ 1.2% agarose gels
- ☐ 1X TBE (Tris-Borate/EDTA) buffer pH 8.4
- ☐ Micropipette or variable automicropipette with tips
- ☐ Marking pen
- ☐ Safety goggles (student-provided)
- ☐ Metric ruler
- ☐ Plastic baggies
- ☐ Disposable gloves
- ☐ Coomassie protein stain solution
- ☐ Coomassie de-stain solution
- ☐ Distilled water
- ☐ Staining tray
- ☐ 100-ml graduated cylinder
- ☐ Hemoglobin samples dissolved in TBE solubilizing buffer with bromophenol blue:
  - HbA, labeled
  - HbS, labeled
  - HbA + HbS, labeled
  - Unknown samples of each of the above

OBJECTIVES

1. To define *allele, heterozygous, homozygous, dominance, recessiveness, genotype, phenotype,* and *incomplete dominance.*
2. To gain practice working out simple genetics problems using a Punnett square.
3. To become familiar with basic laws of probability.
4. To observe selected human phenotypes, and to determine their genotype basis.
5. To separate variants of hemoglobin using agarose gel electrophoresis.

PRE-LAB QUIZ

1. Circle the correct term. Genes that code for the same genetic trait are <u>alleles</u> / sister chromatids.
2. Circle True or False. A heterozygous individual will have two of the same alleles in a chromosome pair.
3. The allele with less potency, which is present but not expressed, is the _____ allele.
   a. dominant
   b. genotypic
   c. homozygous
   d. recessive
4. Circle the correct term. The physical appearance of an individual's genetic makeup, the characteristics that we can see, is that person's <u>gentotype / phenotype</u>.
5. A _____ is used to demonstrate the genotypes of potential offspring that might result from mating.
   a. karyotype
   b. phenotype cross
   c. Punnett square
6. A condition known as _____ can result when heterozygous individuals exhibit a phenotype intermediate between homozygous individuals, and both alleles are expressed in the offspring.
   a. incomplete dominance
   b. sex-linked inheritance
   c. total dominance
   d. total heterozygosity
7. Circle the correct term. Possession of the <u>X / Y</u> chromosome determines maleness.
8. Circle True or False. The Y chromosome is only about one-third the size of the X chromosome, and it lacks many of the genes that are found on the X.
9. Circle True or False. Males are more likely to suffer from hemophilia because it is a result of receiving the sex-linked gene from the father.

The field of genetics is bristling with excitement. Complex gene-splicing techniques have allowed researchers to precisely isolate genes coding for specific proteins and then to use those genes to harvest large amounts of specific proteins and even to cure some dreaded human diseases. At present, growth hormone, insulin, erythropoietin, and interferon produced by these genetic engineering techniques are available for clinical use, and the list is growing daily.

Comprehending the genetics involved in such studies requires arduous training. However, anyone can gain a basic understanding and appreciation of how genes regulate our various traits (dimples and hair color, for example). The focus of this exercise is to provide a "genetics sampler" or relatively simple introduction to the principles of heredity.

Introduction to the Language of Genetics

In humans all cells, except eggs and sperm, contain 46 chromosomes, that is, the diploid number. This number is established when fertilization occurs and the egg and sperm fuse, combining the 23 chromosomes (or haploid complement) each is carrying. The diploid chromosomal number is maintained throughout life in nearly all cells of the body by the precise process of mitosis. As explained in Exercise 43, the diploid chromosomal number actually represents two complete (or nearly complete) sets of genetic instructions—one from the egg and the other from the sperm—or 23 pairs of *homologous chromosomes*.

Genes coding for the same traits on each pair of homologous chromosomes are called **alleles.** The alleles may be identical or different in their influence. For example, the pair of alleles coding for hairline shape on your forehead may specify either straight across or widow's peak. When both alleles in a homologous chromosome pair have the same expression, the individual is **homozygous** for that trait. When the alleles differ in their expression, the individual is **heterozygous** for the given trait; and often only one of the alleles, called the **dominant gene,** will exert its effects. The allele with less potency, the **recessive gene,** will be present but suppressed. Whereas dominant genes, or alleles, exert their effects in both homozygous and heterozygous conditions, as a rule recessive alleles *must* be present in double dose (homozygosity) to exert their influence.

An individual's actual genetic makeup, that is, whether he is homozygous or heterozygous for the various alleles, is called **genotype.** The manner in which genotype is expressed (for example, the presence of a widow's peak [see Figure 45.2 on page 672] or not, blue versus brown eyes) is referred to as **phenotype.**

The complete story of heredity is much more complex than just outlined, and in actuality the expression of many traits (for example, eye color) is determined by the interaction of many allele pairs. However, our emphasis here will be to investigate only the less complex aspects of genetics.

Dominant-Recessive Inheritance

One of the best ways to master the terminology and learn the principles of heredity is to work out the solutions to some genetic crosses in much the same manner Gregor Mendel did in his classic experiments on pea plants. (Mendel, an Austrian monk of the mid-1800s, found evidence in these experiments that each gamete contributes just one allele to each pair in the zygote.)

To work out the various simple monohybrid (one pair of alleles) crosses in this exercise, you will be given the genotype of the parents. You will then determine the possible genotypes of their offspring by using a grid called the *Punnett square,* and you will record the percentages of both genotype and phenotype. To illustrate the procedure, an example of one of Mendel's pea plant crosses is outlined next.

Alleles: *T* (determines *tallness;* dominant)
 t (determines *dwarfism;* recessive)

Genotypes of parents: TT (♂) $\times$ tt (♀)

Phenotypes of parents: Tall $\times$ dwarf

To use the Punnett, or checkerboard, square, write the alleles (actually gametes) of one parent across the top and the gametes of the other parent down the left side. Then combine the gametes across and down to achieve all possible combinations, as follows:

Results: Genotypes 100% *Tt* (all heterozygous)
 Phenotypes 100% tall (because *T*, which determines tallness, is dominant and all contain the *T* allele)

ACTIVITY 1

Working Out Crosses Involving Dominant and Recessive Genes

For each of the following crosses, draw your own Punnett square and use the technique outlined above to determine the genotypes and phenotypes of the offspring.

1. Genotypes of parents: Tt (♂) $\times$ tt (♀)

% of each genotype: _____

% of each phenotype: _____% tall, _____% dwarf

2. Genotypes of parents: Tt (♂) $\times$ Tt (♀)

% of each genotype: _____

% of each phenotype: _____% tall, _____% dwarf

3. Genotypes of parents: TT (♂) $\times$ Tt (♀)

% of each genotype: _____

% of each phenotype: _____% tall, _____% dwarf

Incomplete Dominance

The concepts of dominance and recessiveness are somewhat arbitrary and artificial in some instances because so-called dominant genes may be expressed differently in homozygous and heterozygous individuals. This produces a condition called **incomplete dominance,** or *intermediate inheritance*. In such cases, both alleles express themselves in the off-spring. The crosses are worked out in the same manner as indicated previously, but heterozygous offspring exhibit a phenotype intermediate between that of the homozygous individuals. Some examples follow.

ACTIVITY 2

Working Out Crosses Involving Incomplete Dominance

1. The inheritance of flower color in snapdragons illustrates the principle of incomplete dominance. The genotype *RR* is expressed as a red flower, *Rr* yields pink flowers, and *rr* produces white flowers. Work out the following crosses to determine the expected phenotypes and both genotypic and phenotypic percentages.

a. Genotypes of parents: *RR* × *rr*

% of each genotype: _____

% of each phenotype: _____

b. Genotypes of parents: *Rr* × *rr*

% of each genotype: _____

% of each phenotype: _____

_____

c. Genotypes of parents: *Rr* × *Rr*

% of each genotype: _____

% of each phenotype: _____

_____

2. In humans, the inheritance of sickle cell anemia/trait is determined by a single pair of alleles that exhibit incomplete dominance. Individuals homozygous for the sickling gene *(s)* have *sickle cell anemia* (SCA). In double dose *(ss),* the sickling gene causes production of a very abnormal hemoglobin, which crystallizes and becomes sharp and spiky under conditions of oxygen deficit. This, in turn, leads to clumping and hemolysis of red blood cells in the circulation, which causes a great deal of pain and can be fatal. Heterozygous individuals *(Ss)* have the *sickle cell trait* (SCT); they make both normal and sickling hemoglobin. Usually these individuals are healthy, but prolonged decreases in blood oxygen levels can lead to a sickle cell crisis. Individuals with the genotype *SS* form normal hemoglobin. Work out the following crosses:

a. Parental genotypes: *SS* × *ss*

% of each genotype: _____

% of each phenotype: _____

b. Parental genotypes: *Ss* × *Ss*

% of each genotype: _____

% of each phenotype: _____

c. Parental genotypes: *ss* × *Ss*

% of each genotype: _____

% of each phenotype: _____

Sex-Linked Inheritance

Of the 23 pairs of homologous chromosomes, 22 pairs are referred to as **autosomes.** Autosomes contain genes that determine most body (somatic) characteristics. The 23rd pair, the **sex chromosomes,** determine the sex of an individual, that is, whether an individual will be male or female. Normal females possess two sex chromosomes that look alike, the X chromosomes. Males possess two dissimilar sex chromosomes, referred to as X and Y. Possession of the Y chromosome determines maleness. A photomicrograph of a male's chromosome complement (male karyotype) is shown in Figure 45.1. The Y sex chromosome is only

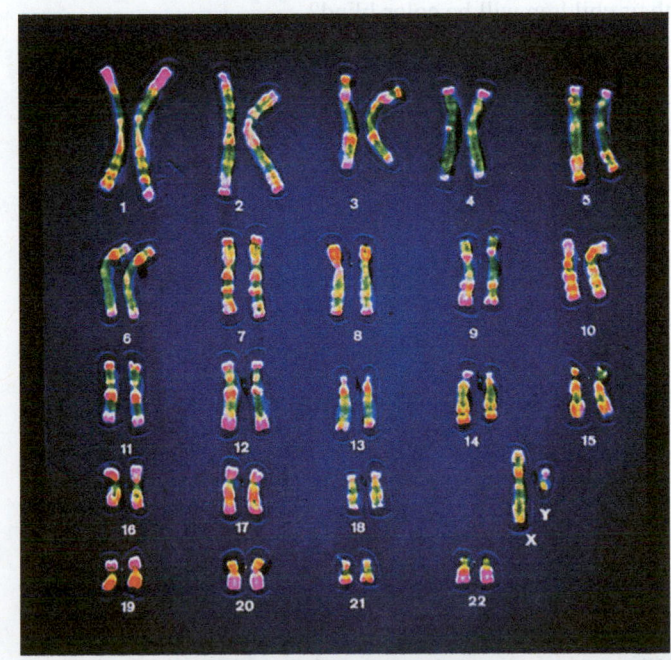

FIGURE 45.1 Karyotype (chromosomal complement) of human male. Each pair of homologous chromosomes is numbered except the sex chromosomes, which are identified by their letters, X and Y.

about a third the size of the X sex chromosome, and it lacks many of the genes (directing characteristics other than sex) that are found on the X.

Genes present *only* on the X sex chromosome are called *sex-linked* (or X-linked) genes. Some examples of sex-linked genes include those that determine normal color vision (or, conversely, color blindness), and normal clotting ability (as opposed to hemophilia, or bleeder's disease). The alleles that determine color blindness and hemophilia are recessive alleles. In females, *both* X chromosomes must carry the recessive alleles for a woman to express either of these conditions, and thus they tend to be infrequently seen. However, should a male receive a sex-linked recessive allele for these conditions, he will exhibit the recessive phenotype because his Y chromosome does not contain alleles for that gene.

The critical point to understand about sex-linked inheritance is the *absence* of male to male (that is, father to son) transmission of sex-linked genes. The X of the father *will* pass to each of his daughters but to none of his sons. Males always inherit sex-linked conditions from their mothers (via the X chromosome); they may inherit holandric conditions (from alleles on the Y chromosome) from their fathers.

ACTIVITY 3

Working Out Crosses Involving Sex-Linked Inheritance

1. A heterozygous woman carrying the recessive gene for color blindness marries a man who is color-blind. Assume the dominant gene is X^C (allele for normal color vision) and the recessive gene is X^c (determines color blindness). The mother's genotype is $X^C X^c$ and the father's $X^c Y$. Do a Punnett square to determine the answers to the following questions.

According to the laws of probability, what percentage of all their children will be color-blind?

_____%

What is the percentage of color-blind individuals by sex?

_____% males; _____% females

What percentage will be carriers? _____%

What is the sex of the carriers? _____

2. A heterozygous woman carrying the recessive gene for hemophilia marries a man who is not a hemophiliac. Assume the dominant gene is X^H and the recessive gene is X^h. The woman's genotype is $X^H X^h$ and her husband's genotype is $X^H Y$. What is the potential percentage and sex of their offspring who will be hemophiliacs?

_____% males; _____% females

What percentage can be expected to neither exhibit nor carry the allele for hemophilia?

_____% males; _____% females

What is the anticipated sex and percentage of individuals who will be carriers for hemophilia?

_____%; _____sex ▰

Probability

Segregation (or parceling out) of chromosomes to daughter cells (gametes) during meiosis and the combination of egg and sperm are random or chance events. Hence, the possibility that certain genomes will arise and be expressed is based on the laws of probability. The randomness of gene recombination from each parent determines individual uniqueness and explains why siblings, however similar, never have totally corresponding traits (unless, of course, they are identical twins). The Punnett square method that you have been using to work out the genetics problems actually provides information on the *probability* of the appearance of certain genotypes considering all possible events. Probability (*P*) is defined as:

$$P = \frac{\text{number of specific events or cases}}{\text{total number of events or cases}}$$

If an event is certain to happen, its probability is 1. If it happens one out of every two times, its probability is ½; if one out of four times, its probability is ¼, and so on.

When figuring the probability of separate events occurring together (or consecutively), the probability of each event must be multiplied together to get the final probability figure. For example, the probability of a penny coming up "heads" in each toss is ½ (because it has two sides—heads and tails). But the probability of a tossed penny coming up heads four times in a row is $\frac{1}{2} \times \frac{1}{2} \times \frac{1}{2} \times \frac{1}{2} = \frac{1}{16}$.

ACTIVITY 4

Exploring Probability

1. Obtain two pennies and perform the following simple experiment to explore the laws of probability.

a. Toss one penny into the air ten times, and record the number of heads (H) and tails (T) observed.

_____ heads _____ tails

Probability: _____/10 tails; _____/10 heads

b. Now simultaneously toss two pennies into the air for 24 tosses, and record the results of each toss below. In each case, report the probability in the lowest fractional terms.

# of HH: _____ Probability: _____

# of HT: _____ Probability: _____

# of TT: _____ Probability: _____

Does the first toss have any influence on the second?

_____

Does the third toss have any influence on the fourth?

_____

c. Do a Punnett square using HT for the "alleles" of one "parental" coin and HT for the "alleles" of the other.

Probability of HH: _____

Probability of HT: _____.

Probability of TT: _____

How closely do your coin-tossing results correlate with the percentages obtained from the Punnett square results?

_____

_____

2. Determine the probability of having a boy or girl off-spring for each conception.

Parental genotypes: XY × XX

Probability of males: _____%

Probability of females: _____%

3. Dad wants a baseball team! What are the chances of his having nine sons in a row?

_____ (Sorry, Dad! Let the girls play.) ▮

Genetic Determination of Selected Human Characteristics

Most human traits are determined by multiple alleles or the interaction of several gene pairs. However, a few visible human traits or phenotypes can be traced to a single gene pair. It is some of these that will be investigated here.

ACTIVITY 5

Using Phenotype to Determine Genotype

For each of the characteristics described here, determine (as best you can) both your own phenotype and genotype, and record this information on the following chart. Since it is impossible to know if you are homozygous or heterozygous for a nondetrimental trait when you exhibit its dominant expression, you are to record your genotype as A—(or B—, and so on, depending on the letter used to indicate the alleles) in such cases. As you will see, all the traits examined here are non-harmful characteristics. Generally speaking, in humans dominant gene disorders are presumed to be heterozygous (one dominant and one recessive allele), because having two such defective mutated alleles is usually not compatible with life.

Record of Human Genotypes/Phenotypes

Characteristic	Phenotype	Genotype
PTC taste (P,p)		
Sodium benzoate taste (S,s)		
Sex (X,Y)		
Dimples (D,d)		
Widow's peak (W,w)		
Proximal finger hair (H,h)		
Freckles (F,f)		
Blaze (B,b)		
ABO blood type (I^A,I^B,i)		

On the other hand, if you exhibit the recessive trait, you are homozygous for the recessive allele and should record it accordingly as *aa* (*bb*, *cc*, and so on). When you have completed your observations, also record your data on the chalkboard chart for tabulation of class results.

PTC taste: Obtain a PTC taste strip. PTC, or phenylthiocarbamide, is a harmless chemical that some people can taste and others find tasteless. Chew the strip. If it tastes slightly bitter, you are a "taster" and possess the dominant gene (*P*) for this trait. If you cannot taste anything, you are a nontaster and are homozygous recessive (*pp*) for the trait. Approximately 70% of the people in the United States are tasters.

Sodium benzoate taste: Obtain a sodium benzoate taste strip and chew it. A different pair of alleles (from that determining PTC taste) determines the ability to taste sodium benzoate. If you can taste it, you have at least one of the dominant alleles (*S*). If not, you are homozygous recessive (*ss*) for the trait. Also record whether sodium benzoate tastes salty, bitter, or sweet to you (if a taster). Even though PTC and sodium benzoate taste are inherited independently, they interact to determine a person's taste sensations. Individuals who find PTC bitter and sodium benzoate salty tend to like sauerkraut, buttermilk, spinach, and other slightly bitter or salty foods.

Sex: The genotype XX determines the female phenotype, whereas XY determines the male phenotype.

Dimpled cheeks: The presence of dimples in one or both cheeks is due to a dominant gene (*D*). Absence of dimples indicates the homozygous recessive condition (*dd*).

Widow's peak: A distinct downward V-shaped hairline at the middle of the forehead is referred to as a widow's peak. It is determined by a dominant allele (*W*), whereas the straight or continuous forehead hairline is determined by the homozygous recessive condition (*ww*) (see Figure 45.2).

Dominant traits   **Recessive traits**

Widow's peak   Straight hairline

Finger hair   No finger hair

Freckles   No freckles

FIGURE 45.2 Selected examples of human phenotypes.

Proximal finger hair: Critically examine the dorsum of the proximal segment (phalanx) of fingers 3 and 4. If no hair is obvious, you are recessive *(hh)* for this condition. If hair is seen, you have the dominant gene *(H)* for this trait (which, however, is determined by multigene inheritance) (see Figure 45.2).

Freckles: Freckles are the result of a dominant gene. Use *F* as the dominant allele and *f* as the recessive allele (see Figure 45.2).

Blaze: A lock of hair different in color from the rest of scalp hair is called a blaze; it is determined by a dominant gene. Use *B* for the dominant gene and *b* for the recessive gene.

Blood type: Inheritance of the ABO blood type is based on the existence of three alleles designated as I^A, I^B, and *i*. Both I^A and I^B are dominant over *i*, but neither is dominant over the other. Thus the possession of I^A and I^B will yield type AB blood, whereas the possession of the I^A and *i* alleles will yield type A blood, and so on as explained in Exercise 29A. There

TABLE 45.1	Blood Groups
ABO blood group	Genotype
A	$I^A I^A$ or $I^A i$
B	$I^B I^B$ or $I^B i$
AB	$I^A I^B$
O	*ii*

are four ABO blood groups or phenotypes, A, B, AB, and O, and their correlation to genotype is indicated in Table 45.1.

Assuming you have previously typed your blood, record your phenotype and genotype in the chart on page 671. If not, type your blood following the instructions on pages 434–435, and then enter your results in the table.

 Dispose of any blood-soiled supplies by placing the glassware in the bleach-containing beaker and all other items in the autoclave bag.

Once class data have been tabulated, scrutinize the results. Is there a single trait that is expressed in an identical manner by all members of the class?

Because all human beings have 23 pairs of homologues and each pair segregates independently at meiosis, the number of possible combinations at segregation is more than 8 million! On the basis of this information, what would you guess are the chances of any two individuals in the class having identical phenotypes for all 14 traits investigated?

Hemoglobin Phenotype Identification Using Agarose Gel Electrophoresis

Agarose gel electrophoresis separates molecules based on charge. In the appropriate buffer with an alkaline pH, hemoglobin molecules will move toward the anode of the apparatus at different speeds, based on the number of negative charges on the molecules. Agarose gel provides a medium for travel and slows the migration down a bit.

Sickle cell anemia slides were observed in Exercise 29A and the trait/disease is discussed earlier in this exercise. The beta chains of hemoglobin S (HbS) contain a base substitution where a valine replaces glutamic acid. As a result of the substitution, HbS has fewer negative charges than the predominant form of adult hemoglobin (HbA) and can be separated from HbA using agarose gel electrophoresis.

FIGURE 45.3 Agarose gel electrophoresis equipment and power supply.

Using Agarose Gel Electrophoresis to Identify Normal Hemoglobin, Sickle Cell Anemia, and Sickle Cell Trait

1. You will need an electrophoresis unit and power supply (Figure 45.3), a 1.2% agarose gel with eight wells, 1X TBE buffer, micropipettes or a variable automatic micropipette (2–20 µl) with tips, samples of hemoglobin (marked AA, AS, SS, and unknown #_____) dissolved in TBE solubilizing buffer containing bromophenol blue, a marking pen, safety goggles, metric ruler, plastic baggie, and disposable gloves.

2. Record the number of your unknown sample._____

3. Place the agarose gel into the electrophoresis unit.

4. Using a micropipette, carefully add 15 µl of hemoglobin sample AA to wells number 1 and 5, AS to wells 2 and 6, SS to wells 3 and 7, and the unknown samples to wells 4 and 8.

5. Slowly add electrophoresis buffer until the gels are covered with about 0.25 cm of buffer.

6. The electrophoresis unit runs with high voltage. Do not attempt to open it while the power supply is attached. Close and lock the electrophoresis unit, and connect the unit to the power source, red to red and black to black.

7. Run the unit about 50 minutes at 120 volts until the bromophenol blue is about 0.25 cm from the anode.

8. Turn the power supply **OFF**. Disconnect the cables.

9. Open the electrophoresis unit, carefully remove the gel, and slide the gel into a plastic baggie. You should be able to see the hemoglobin bands on the gel. Mark each of the bands on the gel with the marking pen.

Alternatively the gels may be stained with Coomassie blue. Obtain a flask of Coomassie blue stain, a flask of de-staining solution, a flask of distilled water, a staining tray, and a 100-ml graduated cylinder, and do the following:

  a. Carefully remove the gel from the plastic plate, and place the gel into a staining dish.

  b. Add about 30 ml of stain (enough stain to cover the gel), and be sure the agarose is not stuck to the dish.

  c. Allow the gel to remain in the stain for at least an hour (more time might be necessary) and then remove the stain. Rinse the gel and dish with distilled water.

  d. Add about 100 ml of de-staining solution. Change the solution after a day. If the background stain has been reduced enough to see the bands, place the staining dish over a light source, and observe the bands. If the stain is still too dark, repeat the de-staining process until the bands can be observed.

  e. To store the gels, refrigerate in a baggie with a small amount of de-stain solution or dry on a glass plate.

10. Draw the banding patterns for samples 1 through 8 in the figure for question 16 in the Review Sheet, page 678. Based on the banding patterns of the known samples, what are the genotypes of your unknown samples? Record on the chart.

11. Rinse the electrophoresis unit in distilled or de-ionized water, and clean the glass plates with soap and water. ▬

Principles of Heredity

Introduction to the Language of Genetics

1. Match the key choices with the definitions given below.

Key: a. alleles   d. genotype   g. phenotype
     b. autosomes   e. heterozygous   h. recessive
     c. dominant   f. homozygous   i. sex chromosomes

_____ 1. actual genetic makeup

_____ 2. chromosomes determining maleness/femaleness

_____ 3. situation in which an individual has identical alleles for a particular trait

_____ 4. genes not expressed unless they are present in homozygous condition

_____ 5. expression of a genetic trait

_____ 6. situation in which an individual has different alleles making up his genotype for a particular trait

_____ 7. genes for the same trait that may have different expressions

_____ 8. chromosomes regulating most body characteristics

_____ 9. the more potent gene allele; masks the expression of the less potent allele

Dominant-Recessive Inheritance

2. In humans, farsightedness is inherited by possession of a dominant allele *(A)*. If a man who is homozygous for normal vision *(aa)* marries a woman who is heterozygous for farsightedness *(Aa)*, what proportion of their children would be expected to be

farsighted? _____%

3. A metabolic disorder called phenylketonuria (PKU) is due to an abnormal recessive gene *(p)*. Only homozygous recessive individuals exhibit this disorder. What percentage of the offspring will be anticipated to have PKU if the parents are *Pp* and

pp? _____%

4. A man obtained 32 spotted and 10 solid-color rabbits from a mating of two spotted rabbits.

Which trait is dominant? _____ Recessive? _____

What is the probable genotype of the rabbit parents? _____ × _____

5. Assume that the allele controlling brown eyes (B) is dominant over that controlling blue eyes (b) in human beings. (In actu-ality, eye color in humans is an example of polygenic inheritance, which is much more complex than this.) A blue-eyed man marries a brown-eyed woman, and they have six children, all brown-eyed. What is the most likely genotype of the father?

_____ Of the mother? _____ If the seventh child had *blue* eyes, what could you conclude about the parents' genotypes?

_____

_____

Incomplete Dominance

6. Tail length on a bobcat is controlled by incomplete dominance. The alleles are *T* for normal tail length and *t* for tail-less.

What name could/would you give to the tails of heterozygous *(Tt)* cats? _____

How would their tail length compare with that of *TT* or *tt* bobcats? _____

7. If curly-haired individuals are genotypically *CC*, straight-haired individuals are *cc*, and wavy-haired individuals are het-erozygotes *(Cc)*, what percentage of the various phenotypes would be anticipated from a cross between a *CC* woman and a *cc* man?

_____% curly   _____% wavy   _____% straight

Sex-Linked Inheritance

8. What does it mean when someone says a particular characteristic is sex-linked? _____

_____

9. You are a male, and you have been told that hemophilia "runs in your genes." Whose ancestors, your mother's or your

father's, should you investigate? _____ Why? _____

_____

_____

10. An $X^C X^c$ female marries an $X^C Y$ man. Do a Punnett square for this match.

What is the probability of producing a color-blind son? _____

A color-blind daughter? _____

A daughter who is a carrier for the color-blind allele? _____

11. Why are consanguineous marriages (marriages between blood relatives) prohibited in most cultures?

_____

_____

Probability

12. What is the probability of having three daughters in a row? _____

13. A man and a woman, each of seemingly normal intellect, marry. Although neither is aware of the fact, each is a heterozygote

for the allele for mental retardation. Is the allele for mental retardation dominant or recessive? _____

What are the chances of their having one mentally retarded child? _____

What are the chances that all their children (they plan a family of four) will be mentally retarded? _____

Genetic Determination of Selected Human Characteristics

14. Look back at your data to complete this section. For each of the situations described here, determine if an offspring with the characteristics noted is possible with the parental genotypes listed. Check (✓) the appropriate column.

Parental genotypes	Phenotype of child	Possibility	
		Yes	No
Ff × ff	Freckles		
DD × dd	Dimples		
HH × Hh	Proximal finger hair		
$I^A i \times I^B i$	Type O blood		
$I^A I^B \times ii$	Type B blood		

15. You have dimples, and you would like to know if you are homozygous or heterozygous for this trait. You have six brothers and sisters. By observing your siblings, how could you tell, with some degree of certainty, that you are a heterozygote?

_____

_____

_____

Using Agarose Gel Electrophoresis
to Identify Hemoglobin Phenotypes

16. Draw the banding patterns you obtained on the figure below. Indicate the genotype of each band.

Sample genotype	Well	Banding pattern
1. _____	1. ☐	
2. _____	2. ☐	
3. _____	3. ☐	
4. _____	4. ☐	
5. _____	5. ☐	
6. _____	6. ☐	
7. _____	7. ☐	
8. _____	8. ☐	

17. What is the genotype of sickle cell anemia? _____ Sickle cell trait? _____

18. Why does sickle cell hemoglobin behave differently from normal hemoglobin during agarose gel electrophoresis?

_____

_____

Surface Anatomy Roundup

MATERIALS

- ☐ Articulated skeletons
- ☐ Three-dimensional models or charts of the skeletal muscles of the body
- ☐ Hand mirror
- ☐ Stethoscope
- ☐ Alcohol swabs
- ☐ Washable markers

OBJECTIVES

1. To define *surface anatomy* and explain why it is an important field of study, and to define *palpation*.
2. To describe and palpate the major surface features of the cranium, face, and neck.
3. To describe the easily palpated bony and muscular landmarks of the back, and to locate the vertebral spines on the living body.
4. To list the bony surface landmarks of the thoracic cage, explain how they relate to the major soft organs of the thorax, and explain how to find the second to eleventh ribs.
5. To name and palpate the important surface features on the anterior abdominal wall, and to explain how to palpate a full bladder.
6. To define and explain the following: *linea alba, umbilical hernia,* examination for an inguinal hernia, *linea semilunaris,* and *McBurney's point*.
7. To locate and palpate the main surface features of the upper limb.
8. To explain the significance of the antecubital fossa, pulse points in the distal forearm, and the anatomical snuff box.
9. To describe and palpate the surface landmarks of the lower limb.
10. To explain exactly where to administer an injection in the gluteal region and in the other major sites of intramuscular injection.

PRE-LAB QUIZ

1. Why is it useful to study surface anatomy?
   a. You can easily locate deep muscle insertions.
   b. You can relate external surface landmarks to the location of internal organs.
   c. You can study cadavers more easily.
   d. You really can't learn that much by studying surface anatomy; it's a gimmick.
2. Circle the correct term. <u>Palpation / Dissection</u> allows you to feel internal structures through the skin.
3. The galea aponeurotica binds to the subcutaneous tissue of the cranium to form the
   a. mastoid process   c. true scalp
   b. occipital protuberance   d. xiphoid process
4. The _____ is the most prominent neck muscle and also the neck's most important landmark.
   a. buccinator   c. masseter
   b. epicranius   d. sternocleidomastoid
5. The three boundaries of the _____ are the trapezius medially, the latissimus dorsi inferiorly, and the scapula laterally.
   a. torso triangle   c. triangle of back muscles
   b. triangle of ausculation   d. triangle of Burney
6. Circle True or False. The lungs do not fill the inferior region of the pleural cavity.

Text continues on next page.

7. Circle True or False. With the exception of a full bladder, most internal pelvic organs are not easily palpated through the skin of the body surface.

8. On the dorsum of your hand is a grouping of superficial veins known as the _____, which provides a site for drawing blood and inserting intravenous catheters.
   a. anatomical snuff box
   b. dorsal venous network
   c. radial and ulnar veins
   d. palmar arches

9. Circle True or False. To avoid harming major nerves and blood vessels, clinicians who administer intramuscular injections in the gluteal region of adults use the gluteus medius muscle.

10. The large femoral artery and vein descend vertically through the _____, formed by the border of the inguinal ligament, the medial border of the adductor longus muscle, and the medial border of the sartorius muscle.
    a. femoral triangle
    b. lateral condyle
    c. medial condyle
    d. quadriceps

Surface anatomy is a valuable branch of anatomical and medical science. True to its name, **surface anatomy** does indeed study the *external surface* of the body, but more importantly, it also studies *internal organs* as they relate to external surface landmarks and as they are seen and felt through the skin. Feeling internal structures through the skin with the fingers is called **palpation** (literally, "touching").

Surface anatomy is living anatomy, better studied in live people than in cadavers. It can provide a great deal of information about the living skeleton (almost all bones can be palpated) and about the muscles and blood vessels that lie near the body surface. Furthermore, a skilled examiner can learn a good deal about the heart, lungs, and other deep organs by performing a surface assessment. Thus, surface anatomy serves as the basis of the standard physical examination. For those planning a career in the health sciences or physical education, a study of surface anatomy will show you where to take pulses, where to insert tubes and needles, where to locate broken bones and inflamed muscles, and where to listen for the sounds of the lungs, heart, and intestines.

We will take a regional approach to surface anatomy, exploring the head first and proceeding to the trunk and the limbs. You will be observing and palpating your own body as you work through the exercise, because your body is the best learning tool of all. To aid your exploration of living anatomy, skeletons and muscle models or charts are provided around the lab so that you can review the bones and muscles you will encounter. For skin sites you are asked to mark that you cannot reach on your own body, it probably would be best to choose a male student as a subject.

ACTIVITY 1

Palpating Landmarks of the Head

The head (Figures 46.1 and 46.2) is divided into the cranium and the face.

Superciliary arch

Zygomatic arch

External occipital protuberance

Superficial temporal artery (pulse point)

Mastoid process

Temporomandibular joint

Ramus of mandible

Angle of mandible

Facial artery (pulse point)

(a)

External acoustic meatus

Tragus

Lobule

Helix

(b)

FIGURE 46.1 Surface anatomy of the head. (a) Lateral aspect. **(b)** Close-up of an auricle.

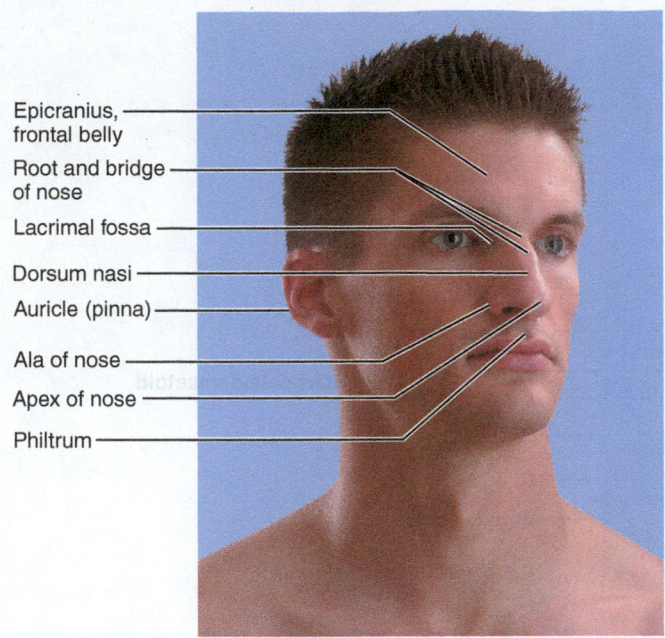

Epicranius, frontal belly
Root and bridge of nose
Lacrimal fossa
Dorsum nasi
Auricle (pinna)
Ala of nose
Apex of nose
Philtrum

FIGURE 46.2 Surface structures of the face.

Cranium

1. Run your fingers over the superior surface of your head. Notice that the underlying cranial bones lie very near the surface. Proceed to your forehead and palpate the **superciliary arches** (brow ridges) directly superior to your orbits (see Figure 46.1).

2. Move your hand to the posterior surface of your skull, where you can feel the knoblike **external occipital protuberance.** Run your finger directly laterally from this projection to feel the ridgelike *superior nuchal line* on the occipital bone. This line, which marks the superior extent of the muscles of the posterior neck, serves as the boundary between the head and the neck. Now feel the prominent **mastoid process** on each side of the cranium just posterior to your ear.

3. The **frontal belly** of the epicranius (see Figure 46.2) inserts superiorly onto the broad aponeurosis called the *galea aponeurotica* (Table 15.1, pages 202 and 204) that covers the superior surface of the cranium. This aponeurosis binds tightly to the overlying subcutaneous tissue and skin to form the true **scalp.** Push on your scalp, and confirm that it slides freely over the underlying cranial bones. Because the scalp is only loosely bound to the skull, people can easily be "scalped" (in industrial accidents, for example). The scalp is richly vascularized by a large number of arteries running through its subcutaneous tissue. Most arteries of the body constrict and close after they are cut or torn, but those in the scalp are unable to do so because they are held open by the dense connective tissue surrounding them.

What do these facts suggest about the amount of bleeding that accompanies scalp wounds?

_____

_____

Face

The surface of the face is divided into many different regions, including the *orbital, nasal, oral* (mouth), and *auricular* (ear) areas.

1. Trace a finger around the entire margin of the bony orbit. The **lacrimal fossa,** which contains the tear-gathering lacrimal sac, may be felt on the medial side of the eye socket.

2. Touch the most superior part of your nose, its **root,** which lies between the eyebrows (see Figure 46.2). Just inferior to this, between your eyes, is the **bridge** of the nose formed by the nasal bones. Continue your finger's progress inferiorly along the nose's anterior margin, the **dorsum nasi,** to its tip, the **apex.** Place one finger in a nostril and another finger on the flared winglike **ala** that defines the nostril's lateral border. Then feel the **philtrum,** the shallow vertical groove on the upper lip below the nose.

3. Grasp your **auricle,** the shell-like part of the external ear that surrounds the opening of the **external acoustic meatus** (Figure 46.1). Now trace the ear's outer rim, or **helix,** to the **lobule** (earlobe) inferiorly. The lobule is easily pierced, and since it is not highly sensitive to pain, it provides a convenient place to hang an earring or obtain a drop of blood for clinical blood analysis. Feel the **tragus,** the stiff projection just anterior to the external acoustic meatus. Next, place a finger on your temple just anterior to the auricle. There, you will be able to feel the pulsations of the **superficial temporal artery,** which ascends to supply the scalp (Figure 46.1).

4. Run your hand anteriorly from your ear toward the orbit, and feel the **zygomatic arch** just deep to the skin. This bony arch is easily broken by blows to the face. Next, place your fingers on the skin of your face, and feel it bunch and stretch as you contort your face into smiles, frowns, and grimaces. You are now monitoring the action of several of the subcutaneous **muscles of facial expression** (Table 15.1, pages 202 and 204).

5. On your lower jaw, palpate the parts of the bony **mandible:** its anterior body and its posterior ascending **ramus.** Press on the skin over the mandibular ramus, and feel the **masseter muscle** bulge when you clench your teeth. Palpate the anterior border of the masseter, and trace it to the mandible's inferior margin. At this point, you will be able to detect the pulse of your **facial artery** (Figure 46.1). Finally, to feel the **temporomandibular joint,** place a finger directly anterior to the external acoustic meatus of your ear, and open and close your mouth several times. The bony structure you feel moving is the *head of the mandible.* ▬

ACTIVITY 2

Palpating Landmarks of the Neck

Bony Landmarks

1. Run your fingers inferiorly along the back of your neck, in the posterior midline, to feel the *spinous processes* of the cervical vertebrae. The spine of C_7, the *vertebra prominens,* is especially prominent.

2. Now, beginning at your chin, run a finger inferiorly along the anterior midline of your neck (Figure 46.3). The first hard structure you encounter will be the U-shaped **hyoid bone,**

FIGURE 46.3 Anterior surface of the neck. A diagram of the underlying skeleton of the larynx is superimposed on a photograph of the neck.

which lies in the angle between the floor of the mouth and the vertical part of the neck. Directly inferior to this, you will feel the **laryngeal prominence** (Adam's apple) of the thyroid cartilage. Just inferior to the laryngeal prominence, your finger will sink into a soft depression (formed by the **cricothyroid ligament**) before proceeding onto the rounded surface of the **cricoid cartilage.** Now swallow several times, and feel the whole larynx move up and down.

3.   Continue inferiorly to the trachea. Attempt to palpate the *isthmus of the thyroid gland,* which feels like a spongy cushion over the second to fourth tracheal rings (see Figure 46.3). Then, try to palpate the two soft lateral *lobes* of your thyroid gland along the sides of the trachea.

4.   Move your finger all the way inferiorly to the root of the neck, and rest it in the **jugular notch,** the depression in the superior part of the sternum between the two clavicles. By pushing deeply at this point, you can feel the cartilage rings of the trachea.

Muscles

The **sternocleidomastoid** is the most prominent muscle in the neck and the neck's most important surface landmark. You can best see and feel it when you turn your head to the side.

Obtain a hand mirror, hold it in front of your face, and turn your head sharply from right to left several times. You will be able to see both heads of this muscle, the **sternal head** medially and the **clavicular head** laterally (Figure 46.3). Several important structures lie beside or beneath the sternocleidomastoid:

• The *cervical lymph nodes* lie both superficial and deep to this muscle. (Swollen cervical nodes provide evidence of infections or cancer of the head and neck.)

• The *common carotid artery* and *internal jugular vein* lie just deep to the sternocleidomastoid, a relatively superficial location that exposes these vessels to danger in slashing wounds to the neck.

• Just lateral to the inferior part of the sternocleidomastoid is the large **subclavian artery** on its way to supply the upper limb. By pushing on the subclavian artery at this point, one can stop the bleeding from a wound anywhere in the associated limb.

• Just anterior to the sternocleidomastoid, superior to the level of your larynx, you can feel a carotid pulse—the pulsations of the **external carotid artery** (Figure 46.4).

• The *external jugular vein* descends vertically, just superficial to the sternocleidomastoid and deep to the skin (Figure 46.3). To make this vein "appear" on your neck, stand before the mirror, and gently compress the skin superior to your clavicle with your fingers.

Triangles of the Neck

The sternocleidomastoid muscles divide each side of the neck into the posterior and anterior triangles (Figure 46.4a).

1.   The **posterior triangle** is defined by the sternocleidomastoid anteriorly, the trapezius posteriorly, and the clavicle inferiorly. Palpate the borders of the posterior triangle.

The **anterior triangle** is defined by the inferior margin of the mandible superiorly, the midline of the neck anteriorly, and the sternocleidomastoid posteriorly.

2.   The contents of these two triangles are shown in Figure 46.4b. The posterior triangle contains many important nerves and blood vessels, including the **accessory nerve** (cranial nerve XI), most of the **cervical plexus,** and the **phrenic nerve.** In the inferior part of the triangle are the **external jugular vein,** the trunks of the **brachial plexus,** and the **subclavian artery.** These structures are relatively superficial and are easily cut or injured by wounds to the neck.

In the neck's anterior triangle, important structures include the **submandibular gland,** the **suprahyoid** and **infrahyoid muscles,** and parts of the **carotid arteries** and **jugular veins** that lie superior to the sternocleidomastoid.

• Palpate your carotid pulse.

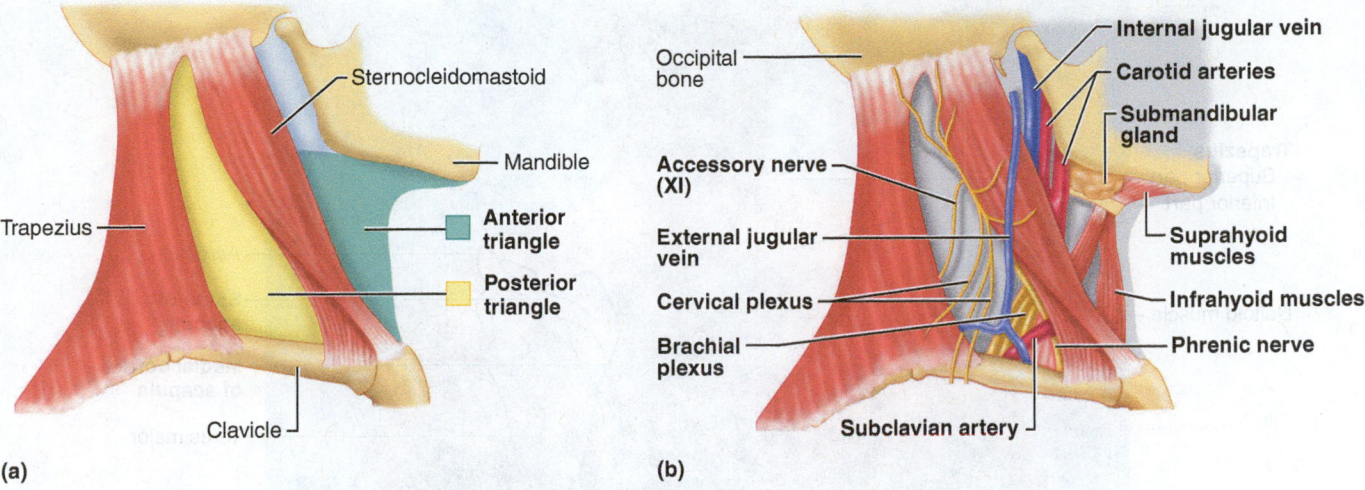

FIGURE 46.4 Anterior and posterior triangles of the neck. (a) Boundaries of the triangles. **(b)** Some contents of the triangles.

A wound to the posterior triangle of the neck can lead to long-term loss of sensation in the skin of the neck and shoulder, as well as partial paralysis of the sternocleidomastoid and trapezius muscles. Explain these effects. ■

_____

_____

ACTIVITY 3

Palpating Landmarks of the Trunk

The trunk of the body consists of the thorax, abdomen, pelvis, and perineum. The *back* includes parts of all of these regions, but for convenience it is treated separately.

The Back

Bones

1. The vertical groove in the center of the back is called the **posterior median furrow** (Figure 46.5). The *spinous processes* of the vertebrae are visible in the furrow when the spinal column is flexed.

- Palpate a few of these processes on your partner's back (C_7 and T_1 are the most prominent and the easiest to find).

- Also palpate the posterior parts of some ribs, as well as the prominent **spine of the scapula** and the scapula's long **medial border.**

  The scapula lies superficial to ribs 2 to 7; its **inferior angle** is at the level of the spinous process of vertebra T_7. The medial end of the scapular spine lies opposite the T_3 spinous process.

2. Now feel the **iliac crests** (superior margins of the iliac bones) in your own lower back. You can find these crests effortlessly by resting your hands on your hips. Locate the most superior point of each crest, a point that lies roughly halfway between the posterior median furrow and the lateral side of the body (see Figure 46.5). A horizontal line through these two superior points, the **supracristal line,** intersects L_4, pro-

viding a simple way to locate that vertebra. The ability to locate L_4 is essential for performing a *lumbar puncture*, a procedure in which the clinician inserts a needle into the vertebral canal of the spinal column directly superior or inferior to L_4 and withdraws cerebrospinal fluid.

3. The *sacrum* is easy to palpate just superior to the cleft in the buttocks. You can feel the *coccyx* in the extreme inferior part of that cleft, just posterior to the anus.

Muscles The largest superficial muscles of the back are the **trapezius** superiorly and **latissimus dorsi** inferiorly (Figure 46.5). Furthermore, the deeper **erector spinae** muscles are very evident in the lower back, flanking the vertebral column like thick vertical cords.

1. Shrug your shoulders to feel the trapezius contracting just deep to the skin.

2. Feel your partner's erector spinae muscles contract and bulge as he straightens his spine from a slightly bent-over position.

The superficial muscles of the back fail to cover a small area of the rib cage called the **triangle of auscultation** (see Figure 46.5). This triangle lies just medial to the inferior part of the scapula. Its three boundaries are formed by the trapezius medially, the latissimus dorsi inferiorly, and the scapula laterally. The physician places a stethoscope over the skin of this triangle to listen for lung sounds (*auscultation* = listening). To hear the lungs clearly, the doctor first asks the patient to fold the arms together in front of the chest and then flex the trunk.

What do you think is the precise reason for having the patient take this action?

_____

_____

3. Have your partner assume the position just described. After cleaning the earpieces with an alcohol swab, use the stethoscope to auscultate the lung sounds. Compare the clarity of the

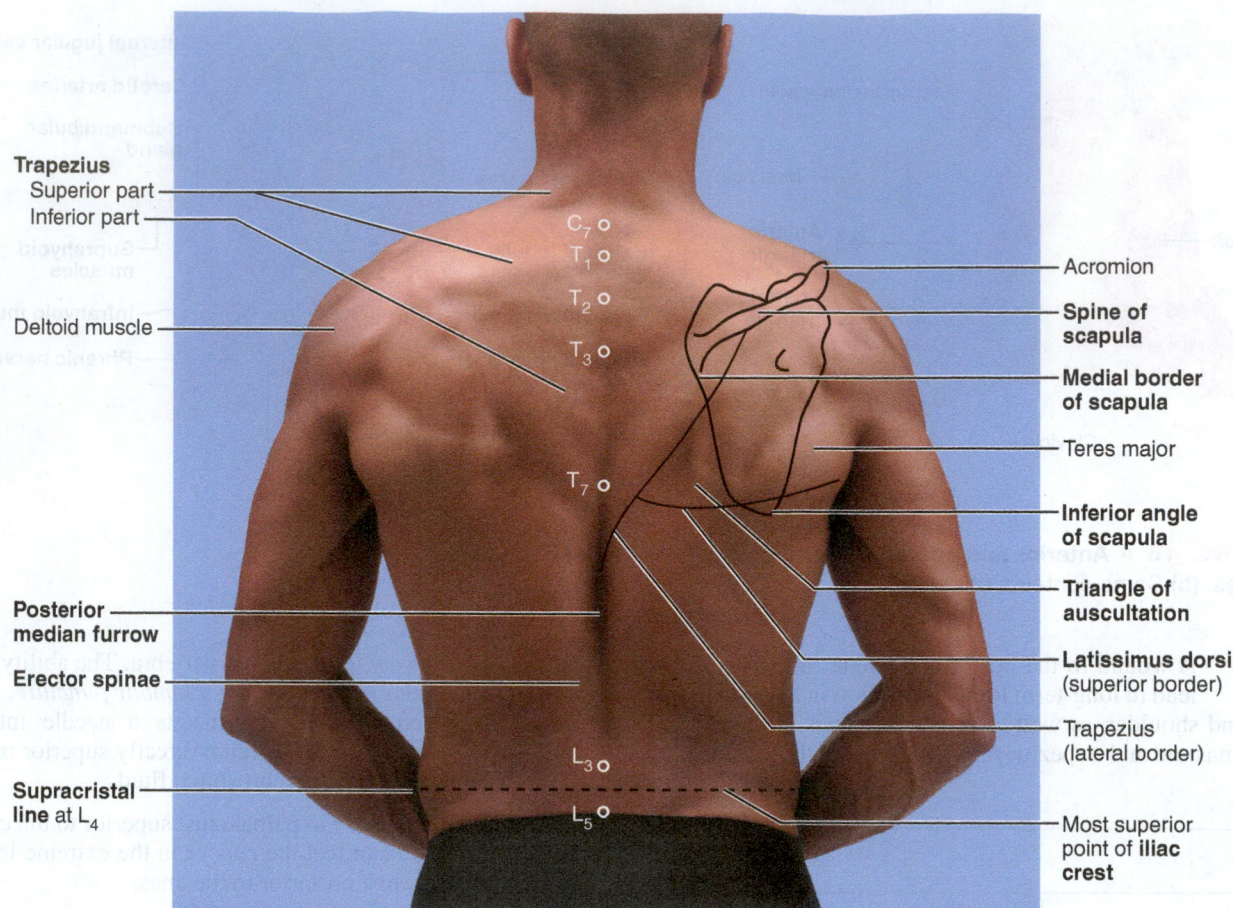

Trapezius
Superior part
Inferior part

Deltoid muscle

C_7
T_1
T_2
T_3

T_7

Acromion

Spine of scapula

Medial border of scapula

Teres major

Inferior angle of scapula

Triangle of auscultation

Latissimus dorsi (superior border)

Trapezius (lateral border)

Posterior median furrow

Erector spinae

Supracristal line at L_4

L_3
L_5

Most superior point of **iliac crest**

FIGURE 46.5 Surface anatomy of the back.

lung sounds heard over the triangle of auscultation to that over other areas of the back.

The Thorax
Bones

1. Start exploring the anterior surface of your partner's bony *thoracic cage* (Figures 46.6 and 46.7) by defining the extent of the *sternum*. Use a finger to trace the sternum's triangular *manubrium* inferior to the jugular notch, its flat *body*, and the tongue-shaped **xiphoid process.** Now palpate the ridgelike **sternal angle**, where the manubrium meets the body of the sternum. Locating the sternal angle is important because it directs you to the second ribs (which attach to it). Once you find the second rib, you can count down to identify every other rib in the thorax (except the first and sometimes the twelfth rib, which lie too deep to be palpated). The sternal angle is a highly reliable landmark—it is easy to locate, even in overweight people.

2. By locating the individual ribs, you can mentally "draw" a series of horizontal lines of "latitude" that you can use to map and locate the underlying visceral organs of the thoracic cavity. Such mapping also requires lines of "longitude," so let us construct some vertical lines on the wall of your partner's trunk. As he lifts an arm straight up in the air, extend a line inferiorly from the center of the axilla onto his lateral thoracic

wall. This is the **midaxillary line** (see Figure 46.6a). Now estimate the midpoint of his **clavicle,** and run a vertical line inferiorly from that point toward the groin. This is the **midclavicular line,** and it will pass about 1 cm medial to the nipple.

3. Next, feel along the V-shaped inferior edge of the rib cage, the **costal margin.** At the **infrasternal angle,** the superior angle of the costal margin, lies the **xiphisternal joint.** Deep to the xiphisternal joint, the heart lies on the diaphragm.

4. The thoracic cage provides many valuable landmarks for locating the vital organs of the thoracic and abdominal cavities. On the anterior thoracic wall, ribs 2–6 define the superior-to-inferior extent of the female breast, and the fourth intercostal space indicates the location of the **nipple** in men, children, and small-breasted women. The right costal margin runs across the anterior surface of the liver and gallbladder. Surgeons must be aware of the inferior margin of the *pleural cavities* because if they accidentally cut into one of these cavities, a lung collapses. The inferior pleural margin lies adjacent to vertebra T_{12} near the posterior midline (see Figure 46.6b) and runs horizontally across the back to reach rib 10 at the midaxillary line. From there, the pleural margin ascends to rib 8 in the midclavicular line (see Figure 46.6a) and to the level of the xiphisternal joint near the anterior midline. The *lungs* do not fill the inferior region of the pleural cavity. Instead, their inferior borders run at a level that is

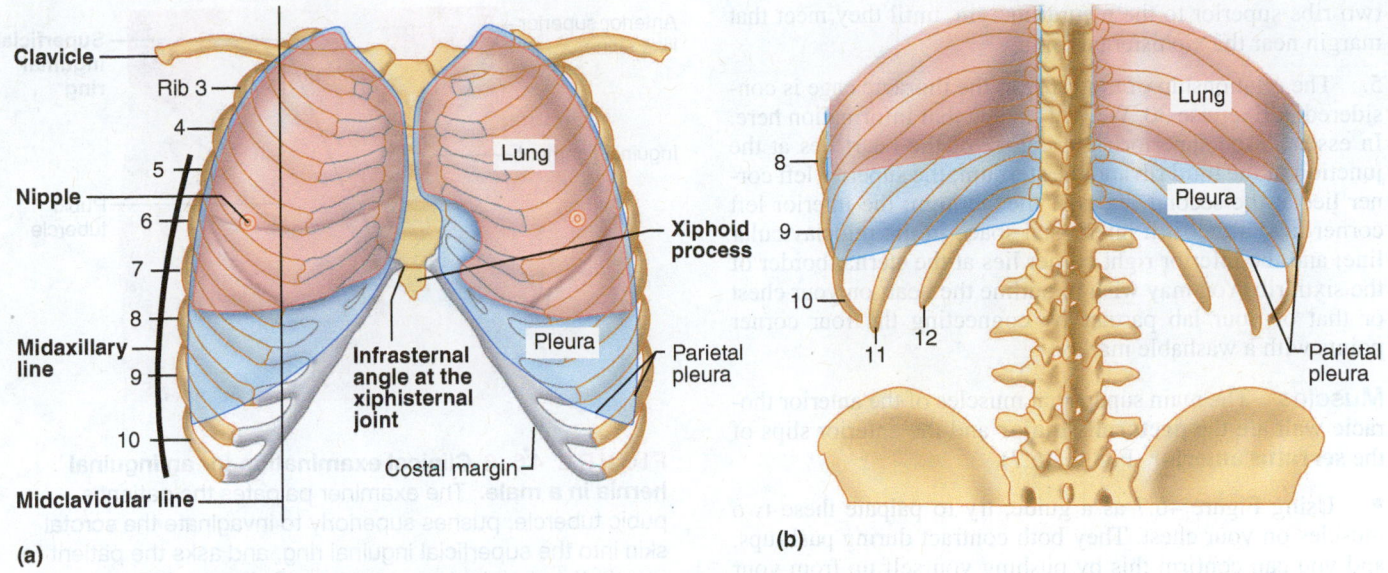

FIGURE 46.6 The bony rib cage as it relates to the underlying lungs and pleural cavities. Both the pleural cavities (blue) and the lungs (pink) are outlined. **(a)** Anterior view. **(b)** Posterior view.

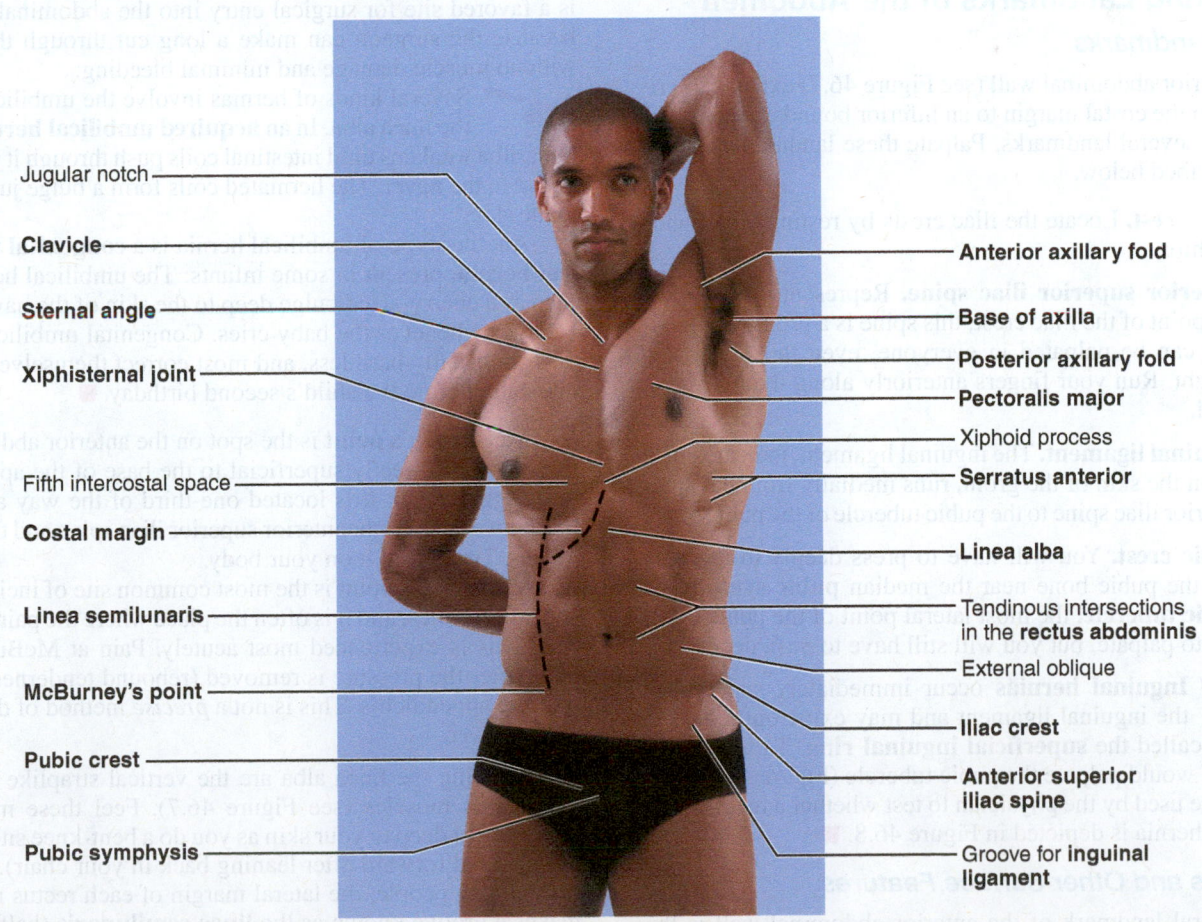

FIGURE 46.7 The anterior thorax and abdomen.

two ribs superior to the pleural margin, until they meet that margin near the xiphisternal joint.

5. The relationship of the *heart* to the thoracic cage is considered in Exercise 30. We will review that information here. In essence, the superior right corner of the heart lies at the junction of the third rib and the sternum; the superior left corner lies at the second rib, near the sternum; the inferior left corner lies in the fifth intercostal space in the midclavicular line; and the inferior right corner lies at the sternal border of the sixth rib. You may wish to outline the heart on your chest or that of your lab partner by connecting the four corner points with a washable marker.

Muscles The main superficial muscles of the anterior thoracic wall are the **pectoralis major** and the anterior slips of the **serratus anterior** (Figure 46.7).

- Using Figure 46.7 as a guide, try to palpate these two muscles on your chest. They both contract during push-ups, and you can confirm this by pushing yourself up from your desk with one arm while palpating the muscles with your opposite hand. ■

FIGURE 46.8 Clinical examination for an inguinal hernia in a male. The examiner palpates the patient's pubic tubercle, pushes superiorly to invaginate the scrotal skin into the superficial inguinal ring, and asks the patient to cough. If an inguinal hernia exists, it will push inferiorly and touch the examiner's fingertip.

ACTIVITY 4

Palpating Landmarks of the Abdomen

Bony Landmarks

The anterior abdominal wall (see Figure 46.7) extends inferiorly from the costal margin to an inferior boundary that is defined by several landmarks. Palpate these landmarks as they are described below.

1. **Iliac crest.** Locate the iliac crests by resting your hands on your hips.

2. **Anterior superior iliac spine.** Representing the most anterior point of the iliac crest, this spine is a prominent landmark. It can be palpated in everyone, even those who are overweight. Run your fingers anteriorly along the iliac crest to its end.

3. **Inguinal ligament.** The inguinal ligament, indicated by a groove on the skin of the groin, runs medially from the anterior superior iliac spine to the pubic tubercle of the pubic bone.

4. **Pubic crest.** You will have to press deeply to feel this crest on the pubic bone near the median **pubic symphysis.** The **pubic tubercle,** the most lateral point of the pubic crest, is easier to palpate, but you will still have to push deeply.

Inguinal hernias occur immediately superior to the inguinal ligament and may exit from a medial opening called the **superficial inguinal ring.** To locate this ring, one would palpate the pubic tubercle (Figure 46.8). The procedure used by the physician to test whether a male has an inguinal hernia is depicted in Figure 46.8. ■

Muscles and Other Surface Features

The central landmark of the anterior abdominal wall is the *umbilicus* (navel). Running superiorly and inferiorly from the umbilicus is the **linea alba** (white line), represented in the skin of lean people by a vertical groove (see Figure 46.7). The linea alba is a tendinous seam that extends from the xiphoid

process to the pubic symphysis, just medial to the rectus abdominis muscles (Table 15.3, pages 207–208). The linea alba is a favored site for surgical entry into the abdominal cavity because the surgeon can make a long cut through this line with no muscle damage and minimal bleeding.

Several kinds of hernias involve the umbilicus and the linea alba. In an **acquired umbilical hernia,** the linea alba weakens until intestinal coils push through it just superior to the navel. The herniated coils form a bulge just deep to the skin.

Another type of umbilical hernia is a **congenital umbilical hernia,** present in some infants: The umbilical hernia is seen as a cherry-sized bulge deep to the skin of the navel that enlarges whenever the baby cries. Congenital umbilical hernias are usually harmless, and most correct themselves automatically before the child's second birthday. ■

1. **McBurney's point** is the spot on the anterior abdominal skin that lies directly superficial to the base of the appendix (see Figure 46.7). It is located one-third of the way along a line between the right anterior superior iliac spine and the umbilicus. Try to find it on your body.

McBurney's point is the most common site of incision in appendectomies, and it is often the place where the pain of appendicitis is experienced most acutely. Pain at McBurney's point after the pressure is removed (rebound tenderness) can indicate appendicitis. This is not a *precise* method of diagnosis, however.

2. Flanking the linea alba are the vertical straplike **rectus abdominis** muscles (see Figure 46.7). Feel these muscles contract just deep to your skin as you do a bent-knee sit-up (or as you bend forward after leaning back in your chair). In the skin of lean people, the lateral margin of each rectus muscle makes a groove known as the **linea semilunaris** (half-moon line). On your right side, estimate where your linea semilunaris crosses the costal margin of the rib cage. The *gallbladder* lies just deep to this spot, so this is the standard point of incision for gallbladder surgery. In muscular people, three horizontal grooves can be seen in the skin covering the

Deltoid

Biceps brachii

Medial bicipital
furrow

Medial epicondyle
of the humerus

Olecranon
process

Clavicle

Acromioclavicular
joint

Greater
tubercle
of the
humerus

Cephalic
vein

FIGURE 46.9 Shoulder and arm.

rectus abdominis. These grooves represent the **tendinous insertions** (or **intersections** or **inscriptions**), fibrous bands that subdivide the rectus muscle. Because of these subdivisions, each rectus abdominis muscle presents four distinct bulges. Try to identify these insertions on yourself or your partner.

3. The only other major muscles that can be seen or felt through the anterior abdominal wall are the lateral **external obliques**. Feel these muscles contract as you cough, strain, or raise your intra-abdominal pressure in some other way.

4. Recall that the anterior abdominal wall can be divided into four quadrants (see Figure 1.7a). A clinician listening to a patient's **bowel sounds** places the stethoscope over each of the four abdominal quadrants, one after another. Normal bowel sounds, which result as peristalsis moves air and fluid through the intestine, are high-pitched gurgles that occur every 5 to 15 seconds.

● Use the stethoscope to listen to your own or your partner's bowel sounds.

Abnormal bowel sounds can indicate intestinal disorders. Absence of bowel sounds indicates a halt in intestinal activity, which follows long-term obstruction of the intestine, surgical handling of the intestine, peritonitis, or other conditions. Loud tinkling or splashing sounds, by contrast, indicate an increase in intestinal activity. Such loud sounds may accompany gastroenteritis (inflammation and upset of the GI tract) or a partly obstructed intestine. ■

The Pelvis and Perineum

The bony surface features of the *pelvis* are considered with the bony landmarks of the abdomen (page 686) and the gluteal region (page 690). Most *internal* pelvic organs are not palpable through the skin of the body surface. A full *bladder,*

however, becomes firm and can be felt through the abdominal wall just superior to the pubic symphysis. A bladder that can be palpated more than a few centimeters above this symphysis is retaining urine and dangerously full, and it should be drained by catheterization. ■

ACTIVITY 5

Palpating Landmarks of the Upper Limb

Axilla

The **base of the axilla** is the groove in which the underarm hair grows (see Figure 46.7). Deep to this base lie the axillary *lymph nodes* (which swell and can be palpated in breast cancer), the large *axillary vessels* serving the upper limb, and much of the brachial plexus. The base of the axilla forms a "valley" between two thick, rounded ridges, the **axillary folds.** Just anterior to the base, clutch your **anterior axillary fold,** formed by the pectoralis major muscle. Then grasp your **posterior axillary fold.** This fold is formed by the latissimus dorsi and teres major muscles of the back as they course toward their insertions on the humerus.

Shoulder

1. Again locate the prominent spine of the scapula posteriorly. Follow the spine to its lateral end, the flattened **acromion** on the shoulder's summit. Then, palpate the **clavicle** anteriorly, tracing this bone from the sternum to the shoulder. Notice the clavicle's curved shape.

2. Now locate the junction between the clavicle and the acromion on the superolateral surface of your shoulder, at the **acromioclavicular joint.** To find this joint, thrust your arm anteriorly repeatedly until you can palpate the precise point of pivoting action.

Triceps brachii
Lateral head
Long head
Tendon
Medial head

Lateral epicondyle of the humerus

Dimple in which **head of radius** is felt

Head of ulna

FIGURE 46.10 Surface anatomy of the upper limb, posterior view.

3. Next, place your fingers on the **greater tubercle** of the humerus. This is the most lateral bony landmark on the superior surface of the shoulder. It is covered by the thick **deltoid muscle,** which forms the rounded superior part of the shoulder. Intramuscular injections are often given into the deltoid, about 5 cm (2 inches) inferior to the greater tubercle (refer to Figure 46.17a, page 691).

Arm

Remember, according to anatomists, the arm runs only from the shoulder to the elbow, and not beyond.

1. In the arm, palpate the humerus along its entire length, especially along its medial and lateral sides.

2. Feel the **biceps brachii** muscle contract on your anterior arm when you flex your forearm against resistance. The medial boundary of the biceps is represented by the **medial bicipital furrow** (see Figure 46.9). This groove contains the large *brachial artery,* and by pressing on it with your fingertips you can feel your *brachial pulse.* Recall that the brachial artery is the artery routinely used in measuring blood pressure with a sphygmomanometer.

3. All three heads of the **triceps brachii** muscle (lateral, long, and medial) are visible through the skin of a muscular person (Figure 46.10).

Elbow Region

1. In the distal part of your arm, near the elbow, palpate the two projections of the humerus, the **lateral** and **medial epicondyles** (Figures 46.9 and 46.10). Midway between the epicondyles, on the posterior side, feel the **olecranon process** of the ulna, which forms the point of the elbow.

2. Confirm that the two epicondyles and the olecranon all lie in the same horizontal line when the elbow is extended. If these three bony processes do not line up, the elbow is dislocated.

3. Now feel along the posterior surface of the medial epicondyle. You are palpating your ulnar nerve.

4. On the anterior surface of the elbow is a triangular depression called the **antecubital fossa,** or **cubital fossa** (Figure 46.11). The triangle's superior *base* is formed by a horizontal line between the humeral epicondyles; its two inferior sides are defined by the **brachioradialis** and **pronator teres** muscles (see Figure 46.11b). Try to define these boundaries on your own limb. To find the brachioradialis muscle, flex your forearm against resistance, and watch this muscle bulge through the skin of your lateral forearm. To feel your pronator teres contract, palpate the antecubital fossa as you pronate your forearm against resistance. (Have your partner provide the resistance.)

Superficially, the antecubital fossa contains the **median cubital vein** (see Figure 46.11a). Clinicians often draw blood from this superficial vein and insert intravenous (IV) catheters into it to administer medications, transfused blood, and nutrient fluids. The large **brachial artery** lies just deep to the median cubital vein (see Figure 46.11b), so a needle must be inserted into the vein from a shallow angle (almost parallel to the skin) to avoid puncturing the artery. Other structures that lie deep in the fossa are also shown in Figure 46.11b.

5. The median cubital vein interconnects the larger **cephalic** and **basilic veins** of the upper limb. These veins are visible through the skin of lean people (see Figure 46.11a). Examine your arm to see if your cephalic and basilic veins are visible.

Forearm and Hand

The two parallel bones of the forearm are the medial *ulna* and the lateral *radius.*

1. Feel the ulna along its entire length as a sharp ridge on the posterior forearm (confirm that this ridge runs inferiorly from the olecranon process). As for the radius, you can feel its distal half, but most of its proximal half is covered by muscle. You can, however, feel the rotating **head** of the radius. To do this, extend your forearm, and note that a dimple forms on the posterior lateral surface of the elbow region (see Figure 46.10). Press three fingers into this dimple, and rotate your free hand as if you were turning a doorknob. You will feel the head of the radius rotate as you perform this action.

2. Both the radius and ulna have a knoblike **styloid process** at their distal ends. Figure 46.12 shows a way to locate these processes. Do not confuse the ulna's styloid process with the conspicuous **head of the ulna,** from which the styloid process stems. Confirm that the styloid process of the radius lies about 1 cm (0.4 inch) distal to that of the ulna.

Colles' fracture of the wrist is an impacted fracture in which the distal end of the radius is pushed proximally into the shaft of the radius. This sometimes occurs

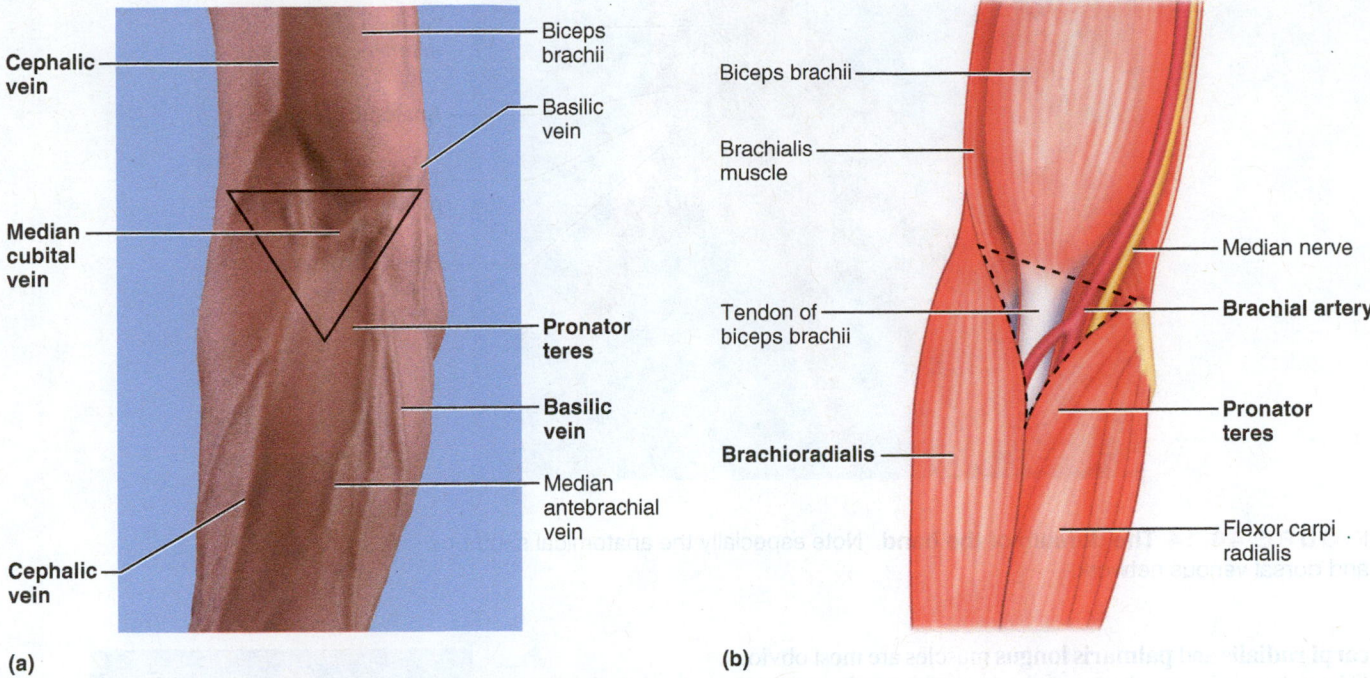

(a)

(b)

FIGURE 46.11 The antecubital (cubital) fossa on the anterior surface of the right elbow (outlined by the triangle). (a) Photograph. **(b)** Diagram of deeper structures in the fossa.

FIGURE 46.12 A way to locate the styloid processes of the ulna and radius. The right hand is palpating the left hand in this picture. Note that the head of the ulna is not the same as its styloid process. The styloid process of the radius lies about 1 cm distal to the styloid process of the ulna.

when someone falls on outstretched hands, and it most often happens to elderly women with osteoporosis. Colles' fracture bends the wrist into curves that resemble those on a fork. ■

Can you deduce how physicians use palpation to diagnose a Colles' fracture?

FIGURE 46.13 The anterior surface of the distal forearm and fist. The tendons of the flexor muscles guide the clinician to several sites for pulse taking.

3. Next, feel the major groups of muscles within your forearm. Flex your hand and fingers against resistance, and feel the anterior *flexor muscles* contract. Then extend your hand at the wrist, and feel the tightening of the posterior *extensor muscles*.

4. Near the wrist, the anterior surface of the forearm reveals many significant features (Figure 46.13). Flex your fist against resistance; the tendons of the main wrist flexors will bulge the skin of the distal forearm. The tendons of the **flexor**

FIGURE 46.14 The dorsum of the hand. Note especially the anatomical snuff box and dorsal venous network.

carpi radialis and **palmaris longus** muscles are most obvious. (The palmaris longus, however, is absent from at least one arm in 30% of all people, so your forearm may exhibit just one prominent tendon instead of two.) The **radial artery** lies just lateral to (on the thumb side of) the flexor carpi radialis tendon, where the pulse is easily detected (Figure 46.13). Feel your radial pulse here. The *median nerve* (which innervates the thumb) lies deep to the palmaris longus tendon. Finally, the **ulnar artery** lies on the medial side of the forearm, just lateral to the tendon of the **flexor carpi ulnaris.** Using Figure 46.13 as a guide, locate and feel your ulnar arterial pulse.

5.   Extend your thumb and point it posteriorly to form a triangular depression in the base of the thumb on the back of your hand. This is the **anatomical snuff box** (Figure 46.14). Its two elevated borders are defined by the tendons of the thumb extensor muscles, **extensor pollicis brevis** and **extensor pollicis longus.** The radial artery runs within the snuff box, so this is another site for taking a radial pulse. The main bone on the floor of the snuff box is the scaphoid bone of the wrist, but the styloid process of the radius is also present here. (If displaced by a bone fracture, the radial styloid process will be felt outside of the snuff box rather than within it.) The "snuff box" took its name from the fact that people once put snuff (tobacco for sniffing) in this hollow before lifting it up to the nose.

6.   On the dorsum of your hand, observe the superficial veins just deep to the skin. This is the **dorsal venous network,** which drains superiorly into the cephalic vein. This venous network provides a site for drawing blood and inserting intravenous catheters and is preferred over the median cubital vein for these purposes. Next, extend your hand and fingers, and observe the tendons of the **extensor digitorum** muscle.

7.   The anterior surface of the hand also contains some features of interest (Figure 46.15). These features include the *epidermal ridges* (fingerprints) and many **flexion creases** in the skin. Grasp your **thenar eminence** (the bulge on the palm that contains the thumb muscles) and your **hypothenar eminence** (the bulge on the medial palm that contains muscles that move the little finger).

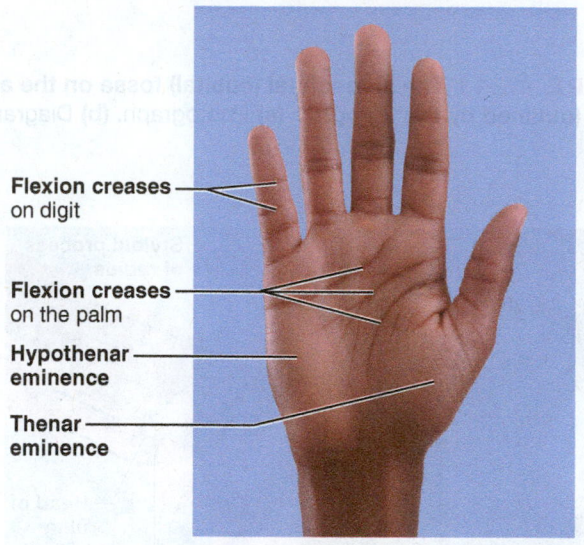

FIGURE 46.15 The palmar surface of the hand.

ACTIVITY 6

Palpating Landmarks of the Lower Limb
Gluteal Region

Dominating the gluteal region are the two *prominences* (cheeks) of the buttocks. These are formed by subcutaneous fat and by the thick **gluteus maximus** muscles. The midline groove between the two prominences is called the **natal cleft** (*natal* = rump) or **gluteal cleft.** The inferior margin of each prominence is the horizontal **gluteal fold,** which roughly corresponds to the inferior margin of the gluteus maximus.

1.   Try to palpate your **ischial tuberosity** just above the medial side of each gluteal fold (it will be easier to feel if you sit down or flex your thigh first). The ischial tuberosities are the robust inferior parts of the ischial bones, and they support the body's weight during sitting.

FIGURE 46.16 The gluteal region. The region extends from the iliac crests superiorly to the gluteal folds inferiorly. Therefore, it includes more than just the prominences of the buttock.

2. Next, palpate the **greater trochanter** of the femur on the lateral side of your hip (Figure 46.16). This trochanter lies just anterior to a hollow and about 10 cm (one hand's breadth, or 4 inches) inferior to the iliac crest. To confirm that you have found the greater trochanter, alternately flex and extend your thigh. Because this trochanter is the most superior point on the lateral femur, it moves with the femur as you perform this movement.

3. To palpate the sharp **posterior superior iliac spine** (see Figure 46.16), locate your iliac crests again, and trace each to its most posterior point. You may have difficulty feeling this spine, but it is indicated by a distinct dimple in the skin that is easy to find. This dimple lies two to three finger breadths lateral to the midline of the back. The dimple also indicates the position of the *sacroiliac joint*, where the hip bone attaches to

the sacrum of the spinal column. (You can check *your* "dimples" out in the privacy of your home.)

The gluteal region is a major site for administering intramuscular injections. When giving such injections, extreme care must be taken to avoid piercing a major nerve that lies just deep to the gluteus maximus muscle. Can you guess what nerve this is?

It is the thick *sciatic nerve,* which innervates much of the lower limb. Furthermore, the needle must avoid the gluteal nerves and gluteal blood vessels, which also lie deep to the gluteus maximus.

To avoid harming these structures, the injections are most often applied to the **gluteus** *medius* (not maximus) muscle superior to the cheeks of the buttocks, in a safe area called the **ventral gluteal site** (Figure 46.17b). To locate this site, mentally

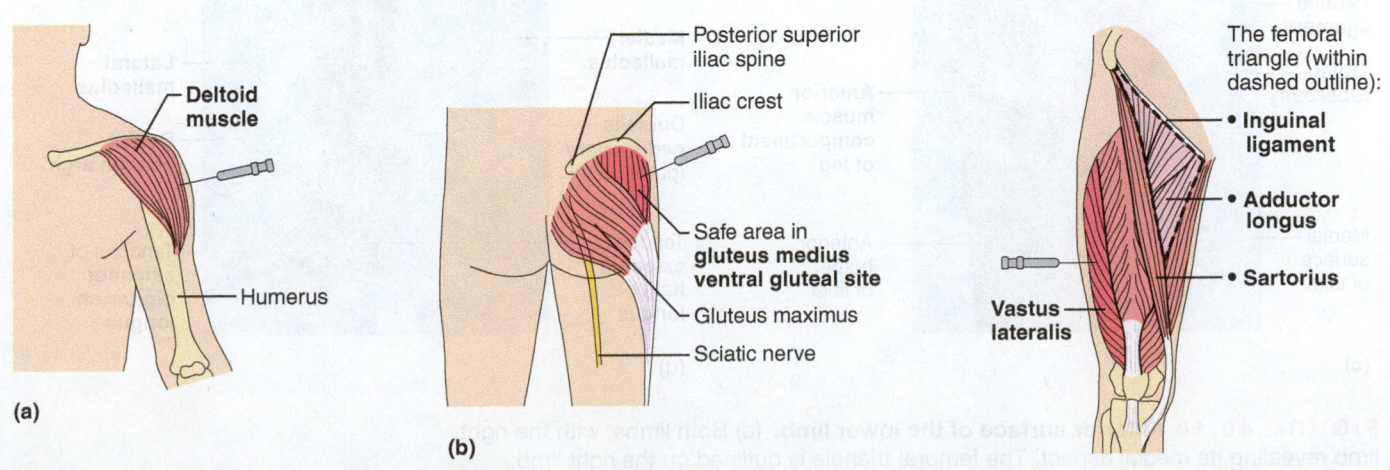

FIGURE 46.17 Three major sites of intramuscular injections. (a) Deltoid muscle of the arm. **(b)** Ventral gluteal site (gluteus medius). **(c)** Vastus lateralis in the lateral thigh. The femoral triangle is also shown.

(a)

(b)

(c)

(d)

FIGURE 46.18 Anterior surface of the lower limb. (a) Both limbs, with the right limb revealing its medial aspect. The femoral triangle is outlined on the right limb. **(b)** Enlarged view of the left thigh. **(c)** The left knee region. **(d)** The dorsum of the left foot.

Hamstring muscles
Biceps femoris
Semitendinosus
Semimembranosus
Popliteal fossa

Gastrocnemius
Medial head
Lateral head
Soleus
Calcaneal (Achilles) tendon

Calcaneus

FIGURE 46.19 Posterior surface of the lower limb. Notice the diamond-shaped popliteal fossa posterior to the knee.

draw a line laterally from the posterior superior iliac spine (dimple) to the greater trochanter; the injection would be given 5 cm (2 inches) superior to the midpoint of that line. Another safe way to locate the ventral gluteal site is to approach the lateral side of the patient's left hip with your extended right hand (or the right hip with your left hand). Then, place your thumb on the anterior superior iliac spine and your index finger as far posteriorly on the iliac crest as it can reach. The heel of your hand comes to lie on the greater trochanter, and the needle is inserted in the angle of the V formed between your thumb and index finger about 4 cm (1.5 inches) inferior to the iliac crest.

Gluteal injections are not given to small children because their "safe area" is too small to locate with certainty and because the gluteal muscles are thin at this age. Instead, infants and toddlers receive intramuscular shots in the prominent **vastus lateralis** muscle of the thigh.

Thigh

The thigh is pictured in Figures 46.18 and 46.19. Much of the femur is clothed by thick muscles, so the thigh has few palpable bony landmarks.

1. Distally, feel the **medial** and **lateral condyles of the femur** and the **patella** anterior to the condyles (see Figure 46.18c and a).

2. Next, palpate your three groups of thigh muscles—the **quadriceps femoris muscles** anteriorly, the **adductor muscles** medially, and the **hamstrings** posteriorly (see Figures 46.18a and b and 46.19). The **vastus lateralis,** the lateral muscle of the quadriceps group, is a site for intramuscular injections. Such injections are administered about halfway down the length of this muscle (see Figure 46.17c).

3. The anterosuperior surface of the thigh exhibits a three-sided depression called the **femoral triangle** (see Figure 46.18a). As shown in Figure 46.17c, the superior border of this triangle is formed by the **inguinal ligament,** and its two inferior borders are defined by the **sartorius** and **adductor longus** muscles. The large *femoral artery* and *vein* descend vertically through the center of the femoral triangle. To feel the pulse of your femoral artery, press inward just inferior to your midinguinal point (halfway between the anterior superior iliac spine and the pubic tubercle). Be sure to push hard, because the artery lies somewhat deep. By pressing very hard on this point, one can stop the bleeding from a hemorrhage in the lower limb. The femoral triangle also contains most of the *inguinal lymph nodes* (which are easily palpated if swollen).

Leg and Foot

1. Locate your patella again, then follow the thick **patellar ligament** inferiorly from the patella to its insertion on the superior tibia (see Figure 46.18c). Here you can feel a rough projection, the **tibial tuberosity.** Continue running your fingers inferiorly along the tibia's sharp **anterior border** and its flat **medial surface**—bony landmarks that lie very near the surface throughout their length.

2. Now, return to the superior part of your leg, and palpate the expanded **lateral** and **medial condyles of the tibia** just inferior to the knee. (You can distinguish the tibial condyles from the femoral condyles because you can feel the tibial condyles move with the tibia during knee flexion.) Feel the bulbous **head of the fibula** in the superolateral region of the leg (see Figure 46.18c). Try to feel the *common fibular nerve* (nerve to the anterior leg and foot) where it wraps around the fibula's *neck* just inferior to its head. This nerve is often bumped against the bone here and damaged.

3. In the most distal part of the leg, feel the **lateral malleolus** of the fibula as the lateral prominence of the ankle (see Figure 46.18d). Notice that this lies slightly inferior to the **medial malleolus** of the tibia, which forms the ankle's medial prominence. Place your finger just posterior to the medial malleolus to feel the pulse of your *posterior tibial artery*.

4. On the posterior aspect of the knee is a diamond-shaped hollow called the **popliteal fossa** (see Figure 46.19). Palpate the large muscles that define the four borders of this fossa: The **biceps femoris** forming the superolateral border, the **semitendinosus** and **semimembranosus** defining the superomedial border, and the two heads of the **gastrocnemius** forming the inferior border. The *popliteal artery* and *vein* (main vessels to the leg) lie deep within this fossa. To feel a popliteal pulse, flex your leg at the knee and push your fingers firmly into the popliteal fossa. If a physician is unable to

feel a patient's popliteal pulse, the femoral artery may be narrowed by atherosclerosis.

5. Observe the dorsum (superior surface) of your foot. You may see the superficial **dorsal venous arch** overlying the proximal part of the metatarsal bones (Figure 46.18d). This arch gives rise to both saphenous veins (the main superficial veins of the lower limb). Visible in lean people, the *great saphenous vein* ascends along the medial side of the entire

limb (see Figure 32.8, page 479). The *small saphenous vein* ascends through the center of the calf.

As you extend your toes, observe the tendons of the **extensor digitorum longus** and **extensor hallucis longus** muscles on the dorsum of the foot. Finally, place a finger on the extreme proximal part of the space between the first and second metatarsal bones. Here you should be able to feel the pulse of the **dorsalis pedis artery.**

Surface Anatomy Roundup

_____ 1. A blow to the cheek is most likely to break what superficial bone or bone part? (a) superciliary arches, (b) the philtrum, (c) zygomatic arch, (d) the tragus

_____ 2. Rebound tenderness (a) occurs in appendicitis, (b) is whiplash of the neck, (c) is a sore foot from playing basketball, (d) occurs when the larynx falls back into place after swallowing.

_____ 3. The anatomical snuff box (a) is in the nose, (b) contains the styloid process of the radius, (c) is defined by tendons of the flexor carpi radialis and palmaris longus, (d) cannot really hold snuff.

_____ 4. Some landmarks on the body surface can be seen or felt, but others are abstractions that you must construct by drawing imaginary lines. Which of the following pairs of structures is abstract and invisible? (a) umbilicus and costal margin, (b) anterior superior iliac spine and natal cleft, (c) linea alba and linea semilunaris, (d) McBurney's point and midaxillary line, (e) philtrum and sternocleidomastoid

_____ 5. Many pelvic organs can be palpated by placing a finger in the rectum or the vagina, but only one pelvic organ is readily palpated through the skin. This is the (a) nonpregnant uterus, (b) prostate gland, (c) full bladder, (d) ovaries, (e) rectum.

_____ 6. A muscle that contributes to the posterior axillary fold is the (a) pectoralis major, (b) latissimus dorsi, (c) trapezius, (d) infraspinatus, (e) pectoralis minor, (f) a and e.

_____ 7. Which of the following is not a pulse point? (a) anatomical snuff box, (b) inferior margin of mandible anterior to masseter muscle, (c) center of distal forearm at palmaris longus tendon, (d) medial bicipital furrow on arm, (e) dorsum of foot between the first two metatarsals

_____ 8. Which pair of ribs inserts on the sternum at the sternal angle? (a) first, (b) second, (c) third, (d) fourth, (e) fifth

_____ 9. The inferior angle of the scapula is at the same level as the spinous process of which vertebra? (a) C_5, (b) C_7, (c) T_3, (d) T_7, (e) L_4

_____ 10. An important bony landmark that can be recognized by a distinct dimple in the skin is the (a) posterior superior iliac spine, (b) styloid process of the ulna, (c) shaft of the radius, (d) acromion.

_____ 11. A nurse missed a patient's median cubital vein while trying to withdraw blood and then inserted the needle far too deeply into the cubital fossa. This error could cause any of the following problems, except this one: (a) paralysis of the ulnar nerve, (b) paralysis of the median nerve, (c) bruising the insertion tendon of the biceps brachii muscle, (d) blood spurting from the brachial artery.

_____ 12. Which of these organs is almost impossible to study with surface anatomy techniques? (a) heart, (b) lungs, (c) brain, (d) nose

_____ 13. A preferred site for inserting an intravenous medication line into a blood vessel is the (a) medial bicipital furrow on arm, (b) external carotid artery, (c) dorsal venous arch of hand, (d) popliteal fossa.

_____ 14. One listens for bowel sounds with a stethoscope placed (a) on the four quadrants of the abdominal wall; (b) in the triangle of auscultation; (c) in the right and left midaxillary line, just superior to the iliac crests; (d) inside the patient's bowels (intestines), on the tip of an endoscope.

695

Dissection and Identification of Rat Muscles

MATERIALS

- ☐ Disposable gloves
- ☐ Safety glasses
- ☐ Lab coat or apron
- ☐ Dissecting instruments, pins, and tray
- ☐ Preserved and latex-injected rat
- ☐ Name tag and plastic bag
- ☐ Paper towels
- ☐ Container for disposal of dissection material

OBJECTIVES

1. To name and locate muscles on a dissected rat.
2. To recognize similarities and differences between rat and human musculature.

The skeletal muscles of all mammals are named in a similar fashion. However, some muscles that are separate in lower animals are fused in humans, and some muscles present in lower animals are lacking in humans. This exercise involves dissection of the rat musculature, in conjunction with the study of human muscles, to enhance your knowledge of the human musculature system. Since the aim is to become familiar with the muscles of the human body, you should pay particular attention to the similarities between rat and human muscles. There are many more muscles in the rat than those studied here. Because of the small size of the specimens, only those muscles easily found and with major counterparts in humans will be examined. See Exercise 15 of this manual for a discussion of the anatomy of the human muscular system.

ACTIVITY 1

Examining the Surface Anatomy of the Rat

1. Obtain all the materials needed to commence the dissection. Label the name tag with a pencil (ink runs when wet). Put on gloves and a lab coat or apron to protect your clothing. Take a dissecting tray and obtain the preserved specimen. Bring the rat to the sink and rinse off any residual shipping fluid with cold tap water. The shipping solution will be cleared off the specimen with the initial rinse in tap water. You will use three tools when performing the dissection: scissors, forceps, and the blunt probe. The use of scalpels or teasing needles is unnecessary and usually results in cutting or damaging more of the specimen than intended. Scalpels are also inherently dangerous.

2. Lay the specimen on its dorsal side and examine it for the following external features:

a. Head

- **Nares:** Nose
- **Vibrissae:** Hairlike "whiskers"
- **Incisors:** Front teeth
- **Forelegs and hindlegs**
- **Anus:** Posterior external opening of the digestive tract
- **Tail:** Posterior projection from the body trunk

b. On a male rat, identify:

- **Prepuce:** Covering of the end of the urethra
- **Urethral opening**
- **Scrotum:** Contains the suspended testes

c. On a female rat, identify:

- **Mammary papillae:** The nipples on humans
- **Urethral/vaginal Opening:** Common opening on rats, separate on humans
- **Clitoris:** Contains erectile tissue as does the penis ▉

Preparing the Rat for Dissection

1. See Figure D1.1 for an illustration of the incisions to be made to skin the rat. Don gloves and place the rat on its dorsal

side and begin skinning the animal. Stretch the fore and hind legs flat; tie them down if necessary. If the animal was injected along the midline, use this incision as a starting point and continue the cut, using scissors. Pick up the skin with the forceps to facilitate cutting. Cut cranially to the mandible and caudally to the pubic region. To separate the skin from the underlying musculature, insert the closed scissors or blunt probe and sweep the instrument to each side, breaking the connective tissues holding the skin to the underlying musculature. Cut any superficial muscles connected to the skin.

2. Make a cut around the head, leaving the skin on the most cranial part of the head. Make a cut across the initial cut at chest level, from one front paw to the other. Cut around the paws, separating the skin from the underlying tissues as you go. Be careful not to cut through the genitalia, but around the structures. Separate the skin from the body and put the skin aside. You will use the skin to wrap the specimen between exercises, along with a paper towel dampened with embalming fluid or other specimen preservative that inhibits mold (available from your supply company), before placing the rat in a labeled plastic bag.

3. If the animal was originally soaking in transport fluid in a bucket, it may have acquired fluid in its abdominal cavity. This needs to be eliminated. Bring the specimen to the sink. Use the closed scissors to make a hole about five millimeters wide in the side of the animal and expel excess fluid into the sink or other suitable container.

4. Eliminate any residual latex that may have leaked from the blood vessel injection. This latex will make it difficult to view body structures and should be removed.

5. If the muscle dissection exercises are to be done at a later laboratory session, follow the cleanup instructions notes in the box below. Prepare your rat for storage in this way every time you use it. ▉

FIGURE D1.1 Incisions to be made in skinning the rat.

Preparing the Dissection Animal for Storage

Before leaving the lab, prepare your animal for storage:

1. To prevent the internal organs from drying out, wrap the animal in its skin, dampen a layer of folded paper towels with specimen preservative as directed by your instructor, and wrap them around the animal. (Do not use *water-soaked* paper towels, which encourages mold growth.) Make sure that the dissected areas are completely covered.

2. Place the animal in its plastic storage bag. Close the bag with an elastic band or twine.

3. Make sure that your name tag is still legible and attach it to the storage bag. Place the animal in its designated container.

4. Clean all dissecting equipment with soapy water, rinse, dry, and return to the storage area. Wash down the lab bench and properly dispose of organic debris and your gloves before leaving the laboratory.

Dissecting Head, Neck, and Trunk Muscles

When doing the muscle dissection, you will need to separate each muscle from its neighbors. Connective tissue covers and connects the muscles. This must be broken to view the muscles clearly. To separate the individual muscles, identify the parallel fibers making up each muscle of interest. Use the blunt probe to trace along the borders of each muscle to separate it cleanly from the adjoining muscles. It should be possible to lift each muscle with the forceps when the muscles are separated. To view deeper muscles, cut the overlying muscle through the belly of the muscle about halfway between its origin and insertion (leave the muscle on the other side of the body intact). Reflect the cut ends and continue separating the muscles with the blunt probe.

Head and Neck Muscles

1. Extend the initial cut cranially to the bottom teeth. Using Figure D1.2 as a guide, clear the skin from the area, including

the sides of the head over to the ears. Do not remove the skin but pin it out of the way. Be careful in the area around the salivary glands in the neck, as these will be examined later, in Dissection Exercise 5.

The **temporalis** is a large muscle located on the lateral side of the cranium, between the ear and eye of the rat. It originates on both the parietal and temporal bone and inserts at the coronoid process of the mandible; it elevates the mandible.

The two large **masseter** muscles are at the lateral area of the head. These are the muscles that become prominent when humans clench their jaws. The masseter muscles originate on the zygomatic process and insert at the masseteric fossa of the mandible; they help elevate the mandible. The cranial parts of the **digastric** muscles are in the midline of the lower jaw, running parallel to the mandible. The caudal parts of the digastric muscles are below the cranial portions and angle away from the midline, laterally toward the neck. The digastric muscles originate on the paraoccipital process and mastoid process and insert on the ventral surface of the mandible; they help depress the mandible. The **mylohyoid** muscles are deep to the cranial digastric muscle, with muscle fibers parallel to

(a)

FIGURE D1.2 Superficial muscles of the anterior neck of the rat. (a) Photograph.

Digastric
(cranial)

Masseter

Digastric
(caudal)

Omohyoid

Sternothyroid

Mylohyoid

Hyoid bone

Sternohyoid

Sternomastoid

Cleidocervicularis

(b)

FIGURE D1.2 *(continued)* **Superficial muscles of the anterior neck of the rat.**
(b) Diagrammatic view.

the digastric muscle. After separating the muscles from the surrounding tissue, cut the right cranial digastric muscle to expose the mylohyoid muscle on that side. Leave the other cranial digastric muscle intact for later study. The mylohyoid muscles originate on the medial surfaces of the mandible. They insert at the hyoid bone and draw the hyoid forward.

2. There are three layers of muscles along the midline of the neck. The most superficial and medial is the pair of **sternohyoid** muscles (see Figure D1.2b). The sternohyoid muscles originate at the cartilage of the first rib and insert at the hyoid bone; they draw the hyoid caudally. Running parallel and immediately inferior to the sternohyoid muscles are the **omohyoid** muscles. After separating the muscles from the surrounding tissue, cut the right cranial sternohyoid muscle to expose the omohyoid muscle on that side. Leave the other sternohyoid muscle intact for later study. The omohyoid muscles originate at the rostral border of the scapula and insert on the hyoid bone, and they draw the hyoid caudally and laterally. Gently pull the omohyoid muscle to the side and expose the deep **sternothyroid** muscle running laterally to the trachea, which is deep to the omohyoid muscle. The sternothyroid mus-

cles originate at the cartilage of the first rib and insert on the thyroid cartilage of the larynx; they pull the larynx caudally.

3. Observe the **sternomastoid** muscles, which are lateral to the midline muscles of the neck and angle medially toward the sternum. The sternomastoid muscles originate on the manubrium of the sternum and insert on the occipital bone; they help to rotate the head laterally.

4. Observe the cleidocervicularis muscles, which are lateral to the sternomastoid muscles. They originate on the occipital bone and the midline of the neck, and they insert on the clavicle. These draw the clavicle cranially. The sternomastoid and cleidocervicularis muscles are fused in the human to one pair of muscles that assist in rotating the head or raising the clavicle cranially, as in shrugging the shoulders.

What is the name of the single muscle in humans that is analogous to the sternomastoid and cleidocervicularis muscles in the rat?

_____

Acromiodeltoid

Biceps brachii

Brachialis

Triceps brachii

Serratus ventralis

Rectus abdominis

Internal oblique

Pectoralis superficialis

Pectoralis profundus

External oblique

(a)

FIGURE D1.3 **Superficial muscles of the thorax and abdominal wall, ventral view.** **(a)** Photograph.

Thoracic and Abdominal Muscles

1. In the rat, two major chest muscles are the **pectoralis superficialis** and the **pectoralis profundus** (see Figure D1.3). Identify the pectoralis superficialis muscle, which is a large, triangular superficial muscle covering most of the chest area. The pectoralis profundus muscle is located deep and caudal to the previous muscle; observe it along the lateral edge of the pectoralis superficialis muscle. Both muscles originate at the sternum and insert on the proximal humerus. They both adduct the foreleg.

In humans, what muscles are analogous to the pectoralis superficialis and pectoralis profundus muscles?

How do the origin and insertion of the pectoralis superficialis and pectoralis profundus muscles in the rat differ from those of the pectoral muscles of humans?

2. Try to identify the two serratus muscles. One is deep to the pectoralis muscles and is called the **serratus ventralis.** This muscle originates on the first seven ribs, inserts on the vertebral border of the scapula, and depresses the scapula. The other serratus muscle, the **serratus dorsalis** (Figure D1.4), is found on the dorsal surface of the rat, at the same level on the thorax as its counterpart. This muscle originates on the spinous process of vertebrae, inserts on the first nine ribs, and draws the ribs dorsally. The term *serratus* is derived from the fact that both muscles connect to a series of ribs, giving them a serrated appearance.

3. Observe the deltoid group. Major muscles of the shoulder are the **spinodeltoid** (Figure D1.4) and **acromiodeltoid** muscles. The spinodeltoid is caudal to the acromiodeltoid. Its origin is at the spine of the scapula, and its insertion is on the deltoid tuberosity. The acromiodeltoid muscle is triangular and lies anterior and superficial to the spinodeltoid. Both muscles flex and rotate the humerus medially. These muscles are fused into one muscle in humans.

Acromiodeltoid

Biceps brachii

Brachialis

Triceps brachii

Serratus ventralis

Rectus abdominis

Internal oblique

Pectoralis superficialis

Pectoralis profundus

External oblique

(b)

FIGURE D1.3 *(continued)* **Superficial muscles of the thorax and abdominal wall, ventral view. (b)** Diagrammatic view. Note the location of the two pectoralis muscles. (Compare to human thoracic and abdominal muscles, anterior view, Figure 15.2.)

In humans, what muscles are analogous to the deltoid group?

_____

Muscles of the Abdominal Wall

- Place the specimen on its dorsal surface and examine the muscles in the abdominal area (see Figure D1.3). Four muscles, three of them major ones, make up the ventral abdominal wall. The most superficial muscle is the **rectus abdominis** muscle, which lies adjacent and just lateral to the linea alba. The muscle originates at the pubic tubercle and inserts on the bottommost costal cartilages and xyphoid process. It compresses the abdomen and flexes the trunk. Identify two sheet-like oblique muscles, the **external oblique** and the **internal oblique.** Both muscles have origins in the lumbodorsal fascia and insertions by way of aponeuroses connecting to the linea alba, and both compress the abdomen. The external oblique muscle is found at the lateral side of the abdomen, with fibers that run from the side, down toward the linea alba. To find the

internal oblique muscle, carefully cut a small square hole in the external oblique muscle and deflect the external muscle to the side. The internal oblique muscle is deep to the external oblique, and its fibers run from the linea alba toward the side of the abdomen. These fibers are oriented at a 90° angle to the external oblique muscle fibers. In humans, there are pronounced tendinous bands separating the superficial abdominal muscles into distinct segments.

Which abdominal muscle is specifically referred to as the "six pack" muscle in humans?

_____

_____

A fourth abdominal muscle, the transverse abdominis muscle, is difficult to find in the rat. This is the deepest one of the four and runs across the abdomen, perpendicular to the rectus abdominis muscle. ▬

Acromiotrapezius

Spinodeltoid

Spinotrapezius

Latissimus dorsi

Serratus dorsalis

Supraspinatus

Infraspinatus

Teres major

(a)

FIGURE D1.4 Superficial muscles of the anterodorsal aspect of the shoulder, trunk, and neck of the rat. (a) Photograph.

ACTIVITY 4

Dissecting Forelimb Muscles

1.   Move out onto the forelimb (Figure D1.3) and locate the **brachialis** muscle on its anterior surface. The brachialis originates on the dorsal border of the humerus and inserts on the medial surface of the ulna; it flexes the foreleg. The **biceps brachii** muscle is found in the same anterior area of the foreleg. The biceps muscle originates on the cranial border of the glenoid cavity, inserts on the radial tuberosity, and also flexes the foreleg.

When you ask children to "make a muscle," what muscle are they trying to show off?

The **triceps brachii** is a major muscle of the medial portion on the dorsal surface of the foreleg. Although it has three heads, only the long and lateral heads are easily visible on the rat. The triceps muscle originates on the scapula and lateral surface of the humerus, and it inserts at the olecranon process of the ulna. The triceps extends the foreleg. It is a major antagonist to the brachialis and biceps brachii muscles.

2.   Place the rat on its ventral surface and examine the muscles of the cranial portion of its back (Figure D1.4). Although humans have a single trapezius muscle, rats have three. Locate the three trapezius muscles on the rat. The **acromiotrapezius** is a superficial muscle at the back of the neck at the level of the ears. It originates on the spinous processes of the cervical and the first four thoracic vertebrae. It inserts on the acromion and spinous processes of the scapula. The muscle draws the scapula

Acromiotrapezius

Spinodeltoid

Spinotrapezius

Latissimus dorsi

Serratus dorsalis

Supraspinatus

Infraspinatus

Teres major

(b)

FIGURE D1.4 *(continued)* **Superficial muscles of the anterodorsal aspect of the shoulder, trunk, and neck of the rat. (b)** Diagrammatic view. (Compare to human thoracic muscles, posterior view, Figure 15.3)

medially. The **spinotrapezius** muscle is lower on the back of the rat. It originates on the spinous processes of the fourth thoracic to the third lumbar vertebrae and inserts on the spines of the scapula. The spinotrapezius muscle draws the scapula caudally. There is a small, narrow third trapezius muscle called the clavotrapezius. This muscle is deep to the acromiotrapezius and will not be identified on the rat. The clavotrapezius originates on the occipital bone and inserts on the clavicle. It draws the clavicle cranially.

3.   Immediately lateral to the spinotrapezius muscle, locate the **latissimus dorsi** muscle, on both sides of the animal. This originates in an extended aponeurosis called the lumbodorsal fascia of the trunk and inserts on the deltoid ridge of the humerus. It flexes the humerus.

4.   Below the spinotrapezius are two additional muscles connected to the scapula. Deflect the spinotrapezius on one side

and gently expose the scapula's spinous process using the blunt probe. The muscle attached to the superior portion of the spinous process is the **supraspinatus** muscle. This muscle originates at the spine of the scapula, inserts on the greater tubercle of the humerus, and abducts the humerus. The muscle attached to the inferior border of the spine is the **infraspinatus** muscle. This muscle originates at the spinous process, inserts on the greater tubercle of the humerus, and extends the humerus.

5.   Identify the **teres major,** a muscle along the caudal border of the scapula. This is a thick, triangular muscle adjacent to the infraspinatus muscle. It originates at the axillary and posterior borders of the scapula and inserts on the proximal, medial end of the humerus. The teres major flexes the shoulder and adducts the foreleg. This muscle extends the arm in humans.

Rectus femoris
Vastus medialis
Gracilis cranialis
Semimembranosus
Gracilis caudalis
Semitendinosus

Adductor longus
Adductor magnus
Adductor brevis

(a)

FIGURE D1.5 **Superficial muscles of the anteromedial thigh of the rat.**
(a) Photograph.

ACTIVITY 5

Dissecting the Hindlimb Muscles

1. With the rat on its dorsal surface, examine the muscles of the upper thigh (see Figure D1.5). Spread the hindlimbs apart and, as before, thoroughly clean the superficial connective tissue from the muscles and separate the muscles using the blunt probe. Use the blood vessel that runs down the middle of the thigh as a convenient anatomical landmark. The muscle immediately above the blood vessels is the **vastus medialis.** This muscle originates on the posterior shaft of the femur, inserts on the patella and the head of the tibia, and extends the hindleg. Cranial to the vastus medialis is the **rectus femoris** muscle. This muscle originates on the ileum, inserts on the tibial crest, and also extends the foreleg. An extension of this muscle is found above the rectus femoris, called the tensor fasciae latae in humans. This muscle is an extension of the gluteus superficialis studied later.

2. Below the blood vessels and close to the midline, locate three adductor muscles. All three originate on the pubic symphysis. The **adductor longus** and **adductor brevis** muscles insert on the linea aspera of the femur, while the **adductor magnus** inserts on the patellar ligament. All three muscles adduct the thigh.

3. Locate the **gracilis** muscle running from the midline to the femoral artery and vein, visible in the hindlinb and below

the adductor longus. It is composed of two muscles in the rat, although it is only one in humans. The gracilis cranialis is larger, originates on the pubic symphysis, and inserts on the shaft of the tibia. The gracilis caudalis originates on the ischium and inserts on the tibial tuberosity. Both gracilis muscles aid in adducting the thigh.

How does this compare with the human gracilis?

_____

_____

Carefully separate the gracilis muscles to view the **semimembranosus** muscle below and posterior to the gracilis. This muscle can also be seen on the dorsal side of the thigh, below the biceps femoris muscle. The semimembranosus muscle originates from the ischium, sacrum, and first caudal vertebrae; inserts on the medial surface of the tibia; and extends the hindleg.

How does the semimembranosus compare with its human homologue?

_____

_____

The next muscle caudal to the gracilis caudalis is the **semitendinosus** muscle. This muscle has its origin on the sacral and caudal vertebrae, and its insertion on the tibia. It also extends the thigh.

Rectus femoris

Vastus medialis

Gracilis cranialis

Semimembranosus

Gracilis caudalis

Semitendinosus

Adductor longus

Adductor magnus

Adductor brevis

(b)

FIGURE D1.5 *(continued)* **Superficial muscles of the anteromedial thigh of the rat. (b)** Diagrammatic view.

4. Turn the specimen over and expose its dorsal surface (see Figure D1.6). The most prominent muscle on the upper dorsal thigh is the **gluteus superficialis** muscle. It has its origin on the ileum and sacrum and its insertion on the femur near the greater trochanter; it abducts the thigh. The gluteus superficialis muscle in the rat includes three separate muscles found in the human, the tensor fasciae latae, sartorius, and gluteus maximus muscles.

Cut either end of the gluteus superficialis on one side of the rat and deflect the muscle to view the thick **gluteus medius** below. This muscle has its origin on the lateral surface of the ileum and its insertion on the greater trochanter of the femur. It also helps to abduct the thigh. A third gluteus muscle, called the gluteus profundus, is too difficult to dissect in the rat. This muscle is called the gluteus minimus in humans.

5. The next superficial muscle is the **biceps femoris** muscle. This muscle originates on the ischial tuberosity, inserts on the dorsal border of the tibia and patella, and also abducts and extends the thigh and flexes the hindleg.

Carefully cut the biceps femoris on one side and deflect it to expose the **vastus lateralis** muscle below. This muscle originates on the greater trochanter of the femur and inserts on the patellar ligament; it extends the hindleg.

What muscles are collectively referred to as the quadriceps femoris in humans?

How do muscles of the anterior quadrant of the thigh differ between humans and rats?

6. Further down on the leg is the most prominent muscle on the dorsal side of the lower leg, the **gastrocnemius** muscle. This muscle has two origins, the lateral head from the lateral epicondyle of the femur and the medial head from the medial condyle of the femur. The muscle inserts on the calcaneus by way of the calcaneal tendon. It plantarflexes the foot.

Using the blunt probe, carefully deflect the gastrocnemius muscle to the side to view the **soleus** muscle beneath (not shown). This muscle originates from the head of the femur and also inserts on the calcaneus by way of the calcaneus tendon. It extends the foot.

7. Locate the **tibialis cranialis** muscle (not shown) extending along the proximal surface of the tibia. This muscle originates along the lateral shaft of the tibia and inserts on the first metatarsal. This muscle is called the tibialis anterior in humans.

8. Prepare your rat for storage and clean the area as instructed in the box on page 698 before leaving the laboratory. ▬

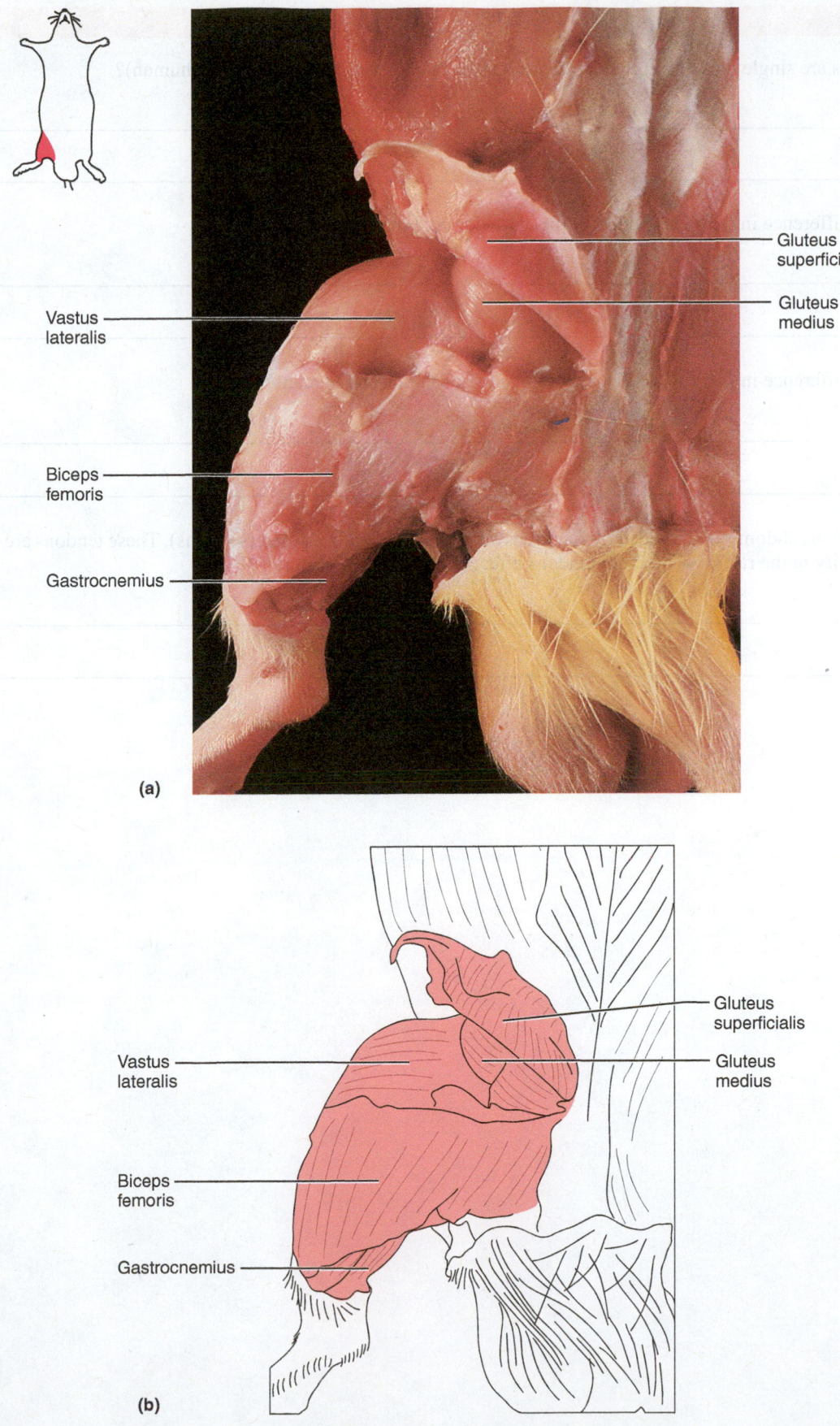

(a)

(b)

FIGURE D1.6 Muscles of the posterolateral thigh in the rat. (a) Photograph.
(b) Diagrammatic view.

1. What muscles are single muscles in one species and more than one in the other (rat and human)?

_____

_____

2. What is the difference in range of motion of the deltoid muscles in rats and humans?

_____

_____

3. What is the difference in function of the pectoralis muscles in rats and humans?

_____

_____

4. The human rectus abdominis is divided by four transverse tendons (tendinous intersections). These tendons are absent or difficult to identify in the rat. How do these tendons affect human upright posture?

_____

_____

Dissection and Identification of Selected Endocrine Organs of the Rat

OBJECTIVES

1. To name and locate selected endocrine glands on a dissected rat.
2. To recognize similarities and differences between selected rat and human endocrine glands.

This exercise involves dissection and identification of selected rat endocrine glands, in conjunction with the study of the human systems, to enhance your knowledge of the human endocrine system. Since the aim is to become familiar with the endocrine glands of the human body, you should pay particular attention to the similarities between rat and human endocrine glands.

ACTIVITY 1

Opening the Ventral Body Cavity

1. Don gloves, remove the specimen from the plastic bag, and remove the skin and place it aside. Open the scissors and insert one end into the thoracic cavity below the ribs and alongside the sternum. Cut cranially to the neck. Remove the cartilage at the top of the sternum to facilitate opening the rib cage. Reverse the scissors and cut toward the caudal end of the animal, stopping at the pubic symphysis. Carefully cut through the diaphragm. Make lateral cuts through the abdominal wall along the caudal edges of the ribs, deflect the rib cage to the side, and pin it in place. Make additional, lateral cuts at the caudal end of the abdominal cavity, deflect the abdominal wall to the side, and pin it in place. Identify the ventral body organs shown in Figure D2.1.

2. If the specimen has been double-injected with latex, the arteries will be red and the veins blue. If the animal has been triple-injected, the hepatic portal veins, connecting the stomach and intestines to the liver, will be yellow. Eliminate any excess latex that may have come from ruptured vessels. Veins tend to have thinner walls than arteries, and some may have ruptured during processing at the vendor's facility. Eliminate any excess adipose tissue in the body cavities as it may interfere with the viewing of the blood vessels and other internal organs. ■■

Larynx

Trachea

Lung

Heart

Liver

Small intestine

Large intestine

Urinary bladder

Scrotum

FIGURE D2.1 Ventral body organs of the rat.

Trachea

Thymus gland

Thyroid gland

Level of diaphragm

Pancreas

Adrenal gland

Kidney

Ovary (female)

Testis (male)

FIGURE D2.2 Endocrine organs in the rat.

Identifying Selected Endocrine Glands

The endocrine system and the nervous system control body activities. The endocrine system secretes hormones that act on specific sites within the body to stimulate or inhibit organ functions and assist in maintaining homeostasis. The major endocrine glands of the human body are discussed in Exercises 27 and 28A. Although all the glands in humans are also present in rats, not all of them can be easily dissected in such a small animal. The more prominent glands have been selected for dissection: the thyroid, parathyroid, thymus, pancreas, ovaries, and testes. A schematic showing the relative positioning of several of the animal's endocrine organs is provided in Figure D2.2.

Thyroid and Parathyroid Glands

1. Place the rat on its dorsal side and examine the neck. Follow the trachea caudally from the lower jaw to the larynx and identify the thyroid cartilage. You may need to remove connective tissue from the area to see the thyroid cartilage clearly. Use the blunt probe for this activity. This cartilage is the part of the larynx that protrudes slightly in humans and is more evident in males. Identify the **thyroid gland** immediately caudal to the thyroid cartilage. It resembles a bow tie, with the wings of the tie at the sides of the trachea and the central portion, called the isthmus, lying across the trachea and connecting the wings, or lobes of the gland (see Figure D2.3). As in humans, the thyroid in rats makes two versions of a hormone to regulate body metabolism and another hormone to regulate blood calcium levels. The metabolic regulators are triiodothyronine and thyroxine, or T_3 and T_4. They increase metabolism throughout most of the body. The hormone related to calcium levels is calcitonin. It lowers blood calcium levels.

What is the common name for the protrusion of the thyroid cartilage in humans?

_____

2. Examine the cranial portions of the lobes of the thyroid gland. Use a magnifying glass or dissecting microscope to identify the slightly lighter appearing, round **parathyroid glands** at the tip of the lobe. This pair of glands monitors blood calcium and produces parathyroid hormone (PTH) to increase blood calcium levels when necessary.

Thymus Gland

• Follow the trachea caudally into the thoracic cavity. A large, centrally located mass is cranial to the heart and may overlay part of the pericardium. This is the **thymus gland.** The thymus produces several families of hormones, including thymosins which assist the immune system in initially producing a subset of lymphocytes called T cells and in the immune response. The thymus in the rat is proportionately larger than the gland in humans.

Pancreas

• The **pancreas** (Figure D2.4) is located caudal to the liver, in the area of the stomach and duodenum. These organs are discussed in Dissection Exercise 5. Locate the pancreas behind and slightly below the stomach in the curvature where the duodenum joins the stomach and extending across the posterior portion of the abdomen. It is a lightly colored and poorly encapsulated organ. Its consistency resembles that of cottage cheese. The pancreas is an organ with both endocrine and exocrine functions. The hormones produced by the pancreas include insulin and glucagon. They are involved in the control of blood levels of glucose. Insulin lowers blood glucose, and glucagon helps to raise glucose levels. The cells producing the

FIGURE D2.3 Organs of the neck region of the rat, including the thyroid and thymus.

endocrine hormones of the pancreas are located in isolated, encapsulated areas of the organ called islets of Langerhans. These can be seen only microscopically.

Adrenal Gland

- Locate the adrenal glands (Figure D2.2), cranial to the kidneys, closer to the midline and the descending, abdominal aorta. They may be confused with lymph nodes that are usually in the same area. Locate the adrenal artery and vein identified in Dissection Exercise 3 to help you differentiate between a lymph node and the adrenal gland. The gland consists of a cortex and medulla. The cortex produces steroid-based hormones related to a variety of body functions. The medulla produces epinephrine and norepinephrine as hormones. The adrenal gland in humans is located on the cranial surface of the kidney and is not as well encapsulated as it is in the rat.

Ovaries

- Continue caudally through the abdominal cavity of a female rat to the kidneys. Locate the **ovaries** slightly caudal and lateral to the kidneys, on each side of the cavity at the distal end of the uterine horn (see Figure D7.2). Remove the layer of fat covering the ovaries. A capsule surrounds the ovaries. This capsule, called the ovarian bursa, is discussed in Dissec-

tion Exercise 7. The ovaries are both exocrine and endocrine glands. Their exocrine function produces eggs or ova ready for fertilization. Their endocrine function produces the hormones estrogen and progesterone during specific phases of the animal's reproductive cycle. The function of these hormones is the same in humans and rats.

Testes

1. Place a male rat on its dorsal surface and locate the scrotum. This is viewed externally below the pubic area (see Figure D2.1). Make a cut through the ventral wall of the scrotum on one side to expose the **testes** within the sac (see Figure D7.1). The testes are elongated, oval, and brown in color. They are enclosed in a membrane called the cremasteric pouch. Additional details of the anatomy are in Dissection Exercise 7. The testes also have both exocrine and endocrine functions. As with the ovaries, the testes produce the reproductive cells of the male, the sperm. Mixed in with the developing sperm cells are the interstitial cells of Leydig. Under proper stimulation, these produce the hormone testosterone. Another type of cell, sustentacular or Sertoli cells, make the hormone inhibin, which limits sperm production.

2. Prepare your rat for storage and clean the area as instructed in the box on page 698. ▬

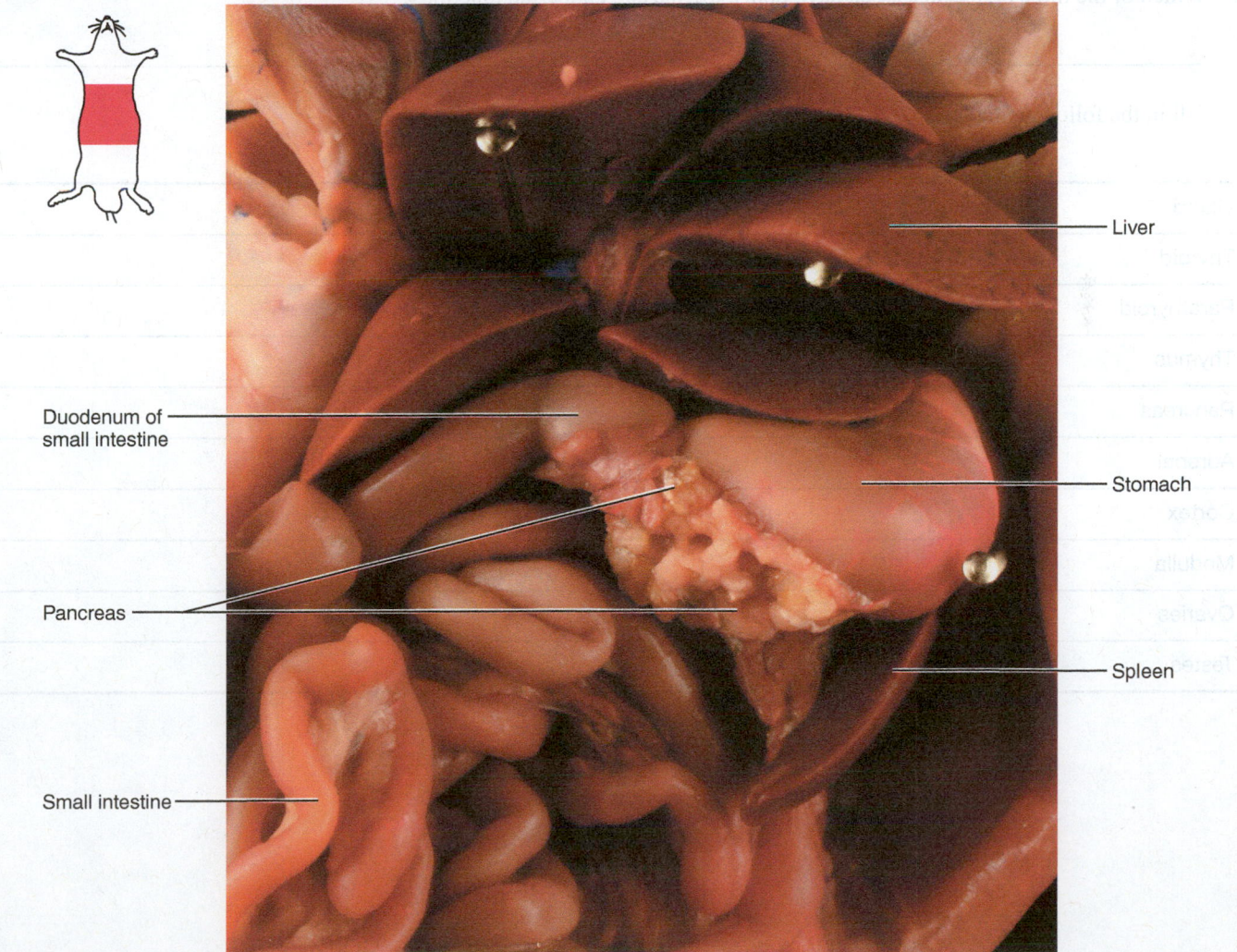

FIGURE D2.4 Organs of the abdominal region of the rat, including the pancreas.

Liver

Duodenum of small intestine

Stomach

Pancreas

Spleen

Small intestine

DISSECTION REVIEW

1. How do the locations of the endocrine organs in the rat compare with those in the human? _____

_____

2. How many parathyroid glands are found in humans?

3. Compare the relative size of the thymus in rats and humans. Does the difference indicate anything about the species' immune systems?

_____

_____

4. Which hormones aid in regulating blood calcium levels? Where are they made?

_____

_____

5. Which of the three organs discussed have both exocrine and endocrine functions?

_____

6. Fill in the following table:

Gland	Location	Hormone(s)
Thyroid		
Parathyroid		
Thymus		
Pancreas		
Adrenal		
Cortex		
Medulla		
Ovaries		
Testes		

Dissection of the Blood Vessels of the Rat

OBJECTIVES

1. To identify major organs related to the circulatory system of the rat.
2. To identify important blood vessels of the dissected rat.
3. To recognize similarities and differences between the circulatory systems of the rat and human.

To identify the blood vessels of the rat, you must open the ventral body cavity. If Dissection Exercise 2 was conducted, you have already opened your animal's ventral body cavity and identified many of its organs. If Dissection Exercise 2 was not conducted, don gloves and open the ventral body cavity by following the instructions in that exercise for Activity 1 on page 709. See Exercise 32 of this manual for a discussion of the anatomy of the human blood vessels.

ACTIVITY 1

Dissecting the Heart and Major Blood Vessels Related to the Heart

1. Carefully deflect, but do not remove, the portion of the thymus gland that covers the heart.

2. Remove the slightly opaque sac that surrounds the heart. This is the **pericardium,** the outer covering of the heart. The bottom portion of the heart is made up of two chambers called ventricles. They propel blood away from the heart when the muscle contracts. Remember that right and left on models, specimens, and patients are designated according to their orientation, not the viewer's. The **right ventricle** delivers blood to the lungs in the pulmonary system, and the **left ventricle** delivers blood to the systemic system. The darker-appearing folds of tissue above the ventricles are called the **auricles.** These are extensions of the atria that make up the two top chambers of the heart. The **right atrium** receives blood from the systemic circulation, and the **left atrium** receives blood from the lungs (pulmonary circulation). Use a hand lens or dissecting microscope to view the cardiac vessels in the interventricular septum, the division between the two ventricles. See Figure D3.1.

Which wall of the heart is the thickest? Right or left atrium, right or left ventricle?

_____

_____

External jugular vein

Internal jugular vein

Right cranial vena cava

Brachiocephalic artery

Aortic arch

Brachial artery

Basilic vein

Axillary vein

Left cranial vena cava

Left common carotid artery

Left subclavian artery

Caudal vena cava

(a)

External jugular vein

Internal jugular vein

Right cranial vena cava

Brachiocephalic artery

Aortic arch

Brachial artery

Basilic vein

Axillary vein

Left cranial vena cava

Left common carotid artery

Left subclavian artery

Caudal vena cava

(b)

FIGURE D3.1 Arteries and veins of the thoracic and abdominopelvic cavity of the rat. (a) Photograph. **(b)** Diagrammatic view.

3.   The rat has three blood vessels returning systemic blood to the right atrium. Blood coming from regions above the heart drain into the **right and left cranial venae cavae.** The cranial venae cavae can be seen immediately behind and above the two auricles. Blood coming from below the heart level drains into the **caudal vena cava.** This can be seen behind and below the right auricle.

4.   Deflect the heart to the left and view the two pairs of **pulmonary veins** attached to the posterior portion of the left atrium. These vessels carry blood from the lungs back to the heart. Use a hand lens or dissecting microscope if needed.

5.   Locate the **aorta's** connection to the heart. This vessel originates from the left ventricle but appears to be leaving the heart behind the right auricle. It is usually not possible to view the colored latex within the vessel, because this is the thickest-walled blood vessel in the body. The aorta will appear white, not red from the latex injection. The **aortic arch** begins at the top of the heart (anatomically the base; the apex is the point at the bottom) and branches into other arteries. The aorta proceeds through the thorax and abdomen as the thoracic and abdominal descending aorta until it disappears as it branches.

6.   With the heart deflected, locate the **pulmonary trunk** branching into the **right** and **left pulmonary arteries** before they enter the lobes of the lungs. ▪

ACTIVITY 2

Dissecting the Spleen

•   The **spleen** (see Figure D2.4) is another major organ related to the circulatory system. It is a darker red organ lateral to the stomach and slightly dorsal to it. It is thin and well encapsulated, and it may wrap around part of the stomach to the ventral side of the body. Most of the body's red blood cells die in this organ at the end of their lifespan. Some lymphocytes are produced in this organ, and some blood is stored here in reserve. ▪

ACTIVITY 3

Dissecting Blood Vessels Cranial to the Heart

1.   Examine the aortic arch and, using the blunt probe, carefully clear out any connective tissues that may mask the blood vessels. You may need to work with another student on the vessels cranial to the heart. The veins are superficial to the arteries in this area. It will be difficult to study the veins later, if you remove them. If one person removes the overlapping veins to view the arteries while another person leaves the veins in place, you will both be able to study the vessels in place. Trace the blood vessels from the aorta. When they branch, they acquire another name. See Figure D3.1.

2.   There are three branches off the aorta cranial to the heart: the **brachiocephalic artery, left common carotid artery,** and **left subclavian artery.** Trace the path of the brachiocephalic artery as it branches into the **right subclavian artery** and the **right common carotid artery** (not shown). The two common carotid arteries travel along the sides of the trachea in the neck.

The right subclavian artery is short and branches into vessels that go into the shoulder; the first one is the **axillary artery.** Trace its path as it branches into the **brachial artery,** which proceeds into the upper arm. The vein corresponding to the brachial artery is the **basilic vein.** These two vessels are found parallel to each other through the limb.

Many times, arteries and veins share the same name, but occasionally the names are different, as listed here. The left subclavian artery also branches into the axillary artery and then branches into the brachial artery on the left. The basilic vein on the left follows the brachial artery. Just before the left subclavain artery branches into the axillary artery, there is a small branching that produces the **internal thoracic artery.** This angles in a caudal direction and follows along the side of the sternum. Trace the artery along the cut that was made to open up the thorax. The corresponding vein follows the same path in the tissue. Branches of this artery and vein become the **intercostal arteries** and **veins** that can be seen between the ribs on the dorsal side of the chest wall.

3.   Follow the cranial venae cavae to the branching that produces the **right and left subclavian veins** (not shown). These veins proceed into the shoulder and branch to produce **axillary veins** on each side, then branch again into the basilic veins listed above. Further into the shoulder, the basilic vein becomes the brachial vein after the vessel branches to produce the medial cubital vein leading into the foreleg. The brachial vein continues into the foreleg, along with the brachial artery.

When the subclavian veins branch, they produce the **internal** and **external jugular veins,** which proceed along the sides of the neck, lateral to the two common carotid arteries.

What major blood vessels pass into the arm of humans or the foreleg of the rat?

_____ ▪

FIGURE D3.2 Arteries and veins of the abdominal cavity of the rat.
(a) Photograph. (b) Diagrammatic view, including of the anteromedial thigh.

Dissecting Blood Vessels Caudal to the Heart

1. Follow the aorta past the aortic arch to its descending portion. Deflect the heart to the right and locate the **azygos vein** (not shown) as it passes posterior to the heart to link up with the caudal vena cava. This vein drains tissues on the dorsal side of the rib cage. Humans have two veins, the azygos and a hemiazygos, for the same functions.

2. Six major arteries are connected to the abdominal descending aorta below the diaphragm. See Figure D3.2. Follow the thoracic aorta to the diaphragm and identify the artery immediately below it, the single **celiac artery.** The celiac artery attaches to the ventral surface of the aorta. This artery branches into the gastric and hepatic arteries, not studied here. A pair of small arteries leave the aorta laterally in the area of the celiac artery; these are the adrenal arteries. The next succeeding major artery is the single **cranial mesenteric artery,** which supplies arterial blood to the small and large intestines. This artery attaches on the dorsal surface of the aorta. The largest arteries in this sequence are found next. These are the pair of **renal arteries.** The **renal veins** are found parallel to these arteries, although they course to connect with the caudal vena cava, running parallel to the aorta in this area. A pair of small, thready arteries called the **testicular** or **ovarian arteries** connect immediately below the renal arteries on the ventral surface of the aorta. These arteries continue to the reproductive structures of the testes or the ovaries. A pair of arteries branch off the sides of the aorta below the gonadal arteries. These are the **circumflex arteries** (not shown). Veins of the same name are found parallel to these arteries. The iliolumbar vessels go directly lateral into the abdominal wall. These veins and arteries branch off the iliac vessels in the human. The last major artery to attach to the aorta is the single **caudal mesenteric artery.** It occurs before the aorta branches into the iliac arteries leading to the leg. The caudal mesenteric artery provides blood to the large intestine and rectum.

3. If the specimen has been triple-injected, find the blood vessels that appear yellow in the abdominal cavity, caudal to the liver. If it has not been triple-injected, these vessels may be colorless or blue. These are the vessels of the **hepatic portal system** (not shown). These are veins that drain the blood from the digestive system and transport it to the liver. The combined vein that drains the stomach, spleen, and pancreas is called the **gastrosplenic vein.** This vein connects to the hepatic portal vein in the area of the stomach. Deflect the stomach to the right and follow the venous drainage from the organ to this vein. There are also **cranial** and **caudal mesenteric veins** that drain the digestive tract. These mesenteric veins can be seen best in the mesentery between parts of the intestines. ▄

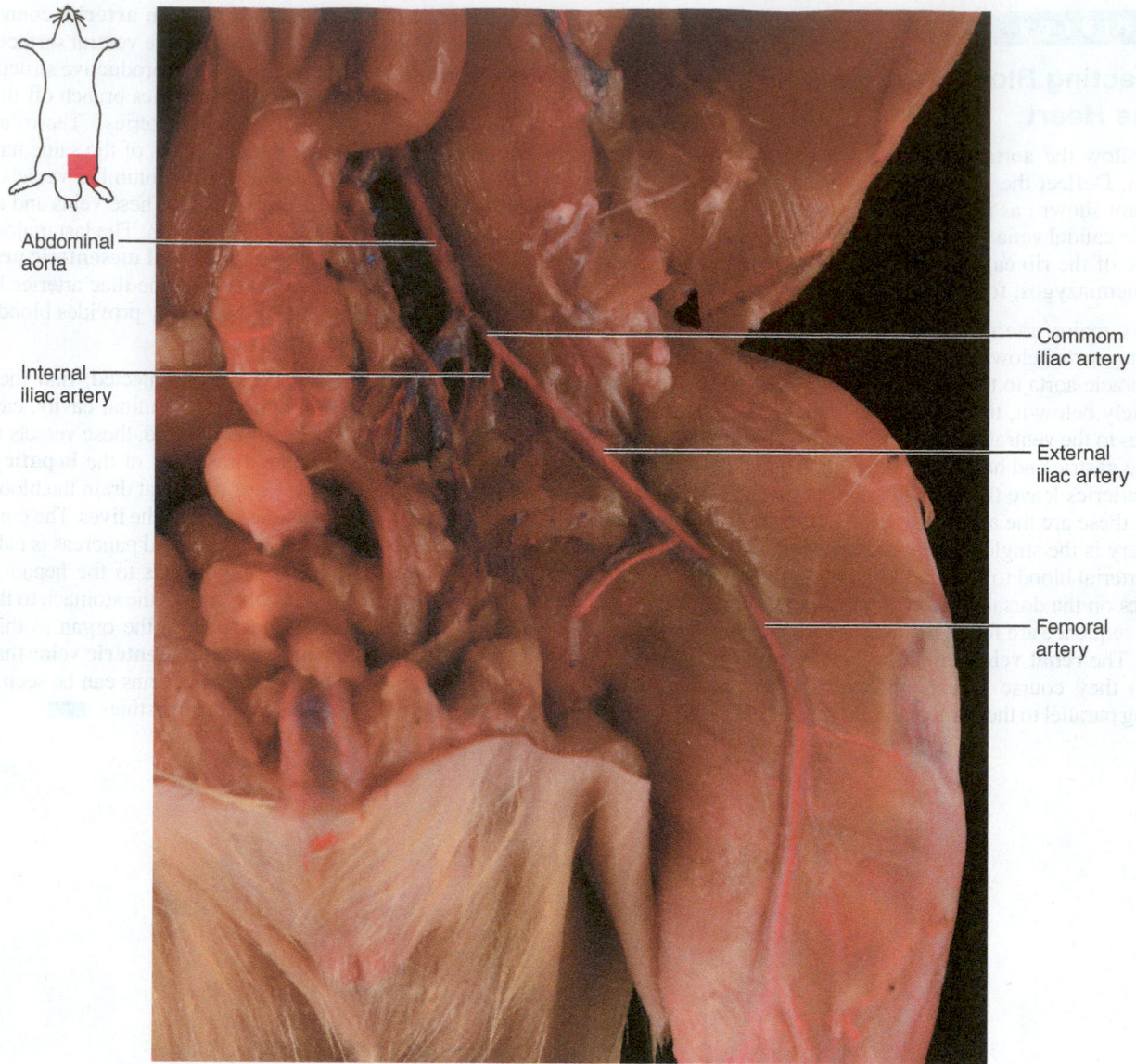

Abdominal aorta

Internal iliac artery

Commom iliac artery

External iliac artery

Femoral artery

FIGURE D3.3 Arteries and veins of the anteromedial thigh of the rat.

ACTIVITY 5

Dissecting Blood Vessels of the Proximal Hindlimb

1.   Dissect the proximal region of one hindlimb to expose the blood vessels as far as the knee. Remove connective tissue surrounding the vessels and separate them from the muscle tissue (if you did not do this in Dissection Exercise 1). See Figure D3.3.

Branching at the end of the descending aorta produces the first of three iliac arteries. The first is a pair of **common iliac arteries** that branch into the **internal** and **external** iliac arteries in each leg. Follow the external iliac artery to the next branch where the **femoral artery** is produced.

2.   Once you have completed your dissection, properly clean your dissecting instruments, tray, and lab bench, and prepare your rat for storage as instructed in the box on page 698. ∎

1. Which major blood vessels attached to the heart carry oxygen-rich blood?

    _____

2. What differences did you observe between the origin of the common carotid arteries in the rat and in the human?

    _____

3. How does the venous drainage from the head and neck to the heart differ between humans and rats?

    _____

    _____

4. How do the relative sizes of the external and internal jugular veins differ in the human and the rat?

    _____

5. What characteristic of the hepatic portal system is unique in the body?

    _____

6. Define the following terms:

    ascending aorta: _____

    aortic arch: _____

    descending thoracic aorta: _____

    descending abdominal aorta: _____

Dissection of the Respiratory System of the Rat

MATERIALS

- Disposable gloves
- Lab coat or apron
- Safety glasses
- Dissecting instruments, pins, and tray
- Magnifying glass or dissecting microscope
- Preserved rat
- Name tag and plastic bag
- Paper towels
- Container for disposal of dissection material

OBJECTIVES

1. To name and locate components of the respiratory system on a dissected rat.
2. To recognize similarities and differences between rat and human respiratory systems.

This exercise involves dissection and identification of components of the respiratory system of rats in conjunction with the study of the human systems, to enhance your knowledge of the human respiratory system. Since the aim is to become familiar with the respiratory system of the human body, you should pay particular attention to the similarities between rat and human respiratory anatomy.

The respiratory system allows the exchange of gases with the external environment. Carbon dioxide is exhaled, and oxygen is taken in from the air brought into the lungs. The system is usually divided into upper and lower portions in humans and into cranial and caudal portions in quadripeds, such as the rat. The respiratory system of the human body is discussed in Exercises 36 and 37A of this manual.

ACTIVITY 1

Identifying Cranial Respiratory Structures

1. The cranial portion of the system extends from the external nares through the trachea. The cranial structures in the head of the rat cannot be easily dissected. They are best seen with a midsagittal cut through the head (Figure D4.1). Notice that air first enters the respiratory system through the opening at the nose, or external nares, and enters the **nasal cavity.** As in the human, the air passage is split by the nasal septum. The turbinate bones form baffles in the passageway that allow the air to be warmed and moistened before it proceeds further into the respiratory system through the internal nares.

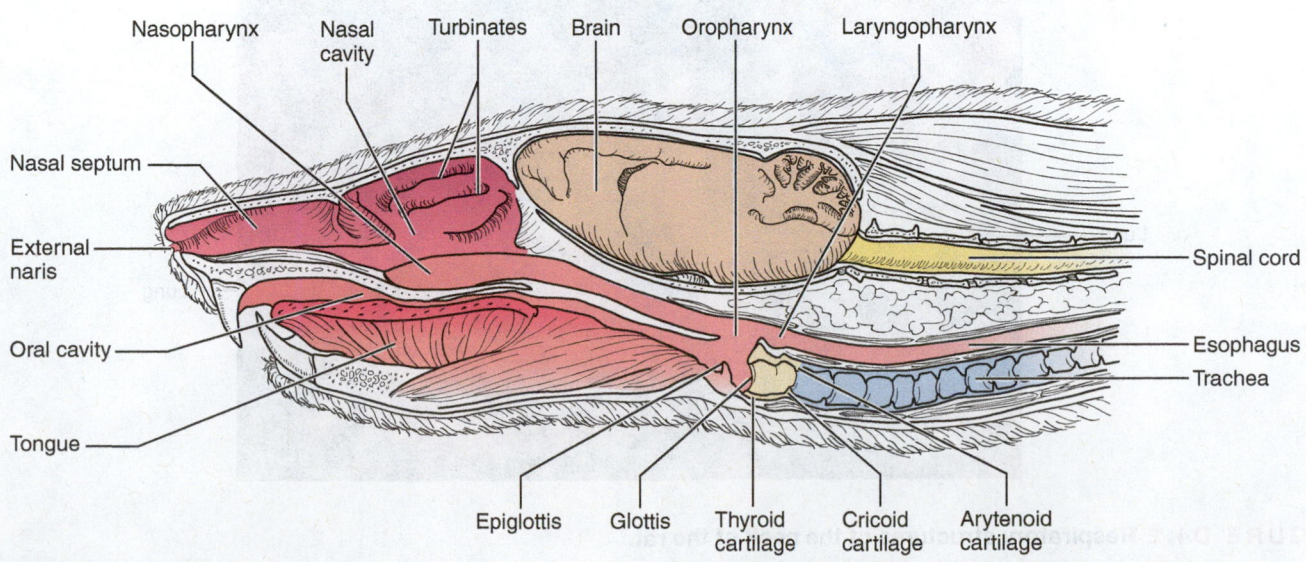

FIGURE D4.1 Midsagittal view of the respiratory structures of the head of the rat.

2.   Next the air enters the **pharynx,** which has three segments. The first is the nasopharynx, which receives the air from the nasal cavity. Notice that the air passes over the soft palate and down the posterior portion of the oral cavity, called the oropharynx. The soft palate is present in mammals, but not in other animals. The air then passes to the last part of the pharynx, the laryngopharynx, and on to the larynx (see Figure D4.1).

How do animals without a soft palate breathe and swallow?

_____

_____

3.   Place the rat on its dorsal side and examine the neck. If you did not dissect this area in Dissection Exercise 2, proceed caudally from the lower jaw to the **larynx** and identify the

thyroid cartilage. You may need to remove connective tissue from the area to see it clearly. Use the blunt probe for this activity. This cartilage is the part of the larynx that protrudes slightly in humans and is more evident in males (Figure D4.2). The larynx is composed of five cartilages, three single cartilages and one pair. Starting at the thyroid cartilage, proceed cranially to the **epiglottis,** a small triangular structure. The base of the epiglottis is attached to the thyroid cartilage. The epiglottis functions like a flap to cover the opening to the larynx during swallowing. This opening is called the **glottis.** If the epiglottis is not covering the glottis during a swallow, food or water may enter the larynx.

Refer again to the thyroid cartilage and examine the cricoid cartilage caudal to it. There will be a small, ovoid gap with soft tissue between these portions of the larynx. The cricoid cartilage encircles the larynx and attaches to the top cartilage ring of the trachea.

FIGURE D4.2 Respiratory structures of the neck of the rat.

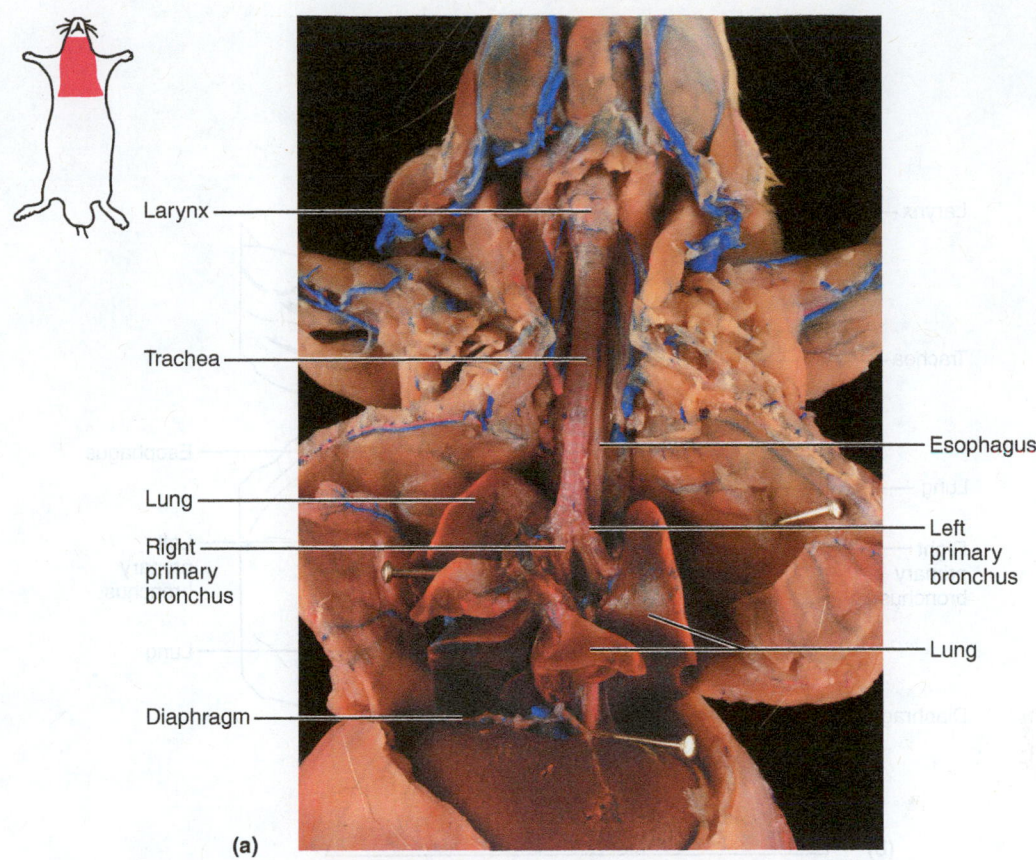

Larynx

Trachea

Lung

Right primary bronchus

Diaphragm

Esophagus

Left primary bronchus

Lung

(a)

FIGURE D4.3 Respiratory system of the rat. (a) Photograph.

The paired arytenoid cartilages are dorsal to the epiglottis-thyroid cartilage junction and may not easily be seen. The two arytenoids provide the site of attachment for the true vocal cords.

4. The caudal end of the larynx attaches to the **trachea.** Follow the tube caudally from the laryngeal cartilages to the top of the sternum. The thoracic cavity should have been dissected in earlier exercises. The tube is maintained open by C-shaped cartilages that alternate with soft tissue throughout the trachea. The opening of the C-shaped cartilages faces dorsally. The trachea is lined with a vascular tissue that has a pseudostratified, ciliated, columnar epithelium, which is called the respiratory epithelium. Carefully remove a half centimeter of the trachea and examine it through a hand lens or a dissecting microscope. Identify the cartilage and view the tissue lining the tube. ▬▬

ACTIVITY 2

Identifying Caudal Respiratory Structures

1. Examine the caudal respiratory structures of the rat, which are in the thoracic cavity and extend from a branching of the trachea into the bronchi through the lungs. The di-aphragm is also considered a caudal respiratory structure. The lining of the thoracic cavity is a thin membrane called the parietal pleura. The lungs are covered with another thin membrane called the visceral pleura. The space in between the pleurae allows the lungs to expand and contract during breathing. The membranes are normally kept moistened to prevent friction during the movement of the lungs within the thorax. Another set of serous membranes surrounds the heart, where they are called parietal and visceral pericardia.

2. Carefully separate the tissue around the base of the trachea to expose the branching of the trachea into the primary **bronchi** (see Figure D4.3). These bronchi branch further into secondary and tertiary bronchi as they penetrate the lung tissue. These tubes also have cartilage maintaining the opening, although the cartilage here is not C-shaped. The bronchi branch into progressively smaller tubes until they become terminal and then respiratory bronchioles attached to alveoli, where gas exchange takes place. The bronchi/bronchiole component of the system is lined with respiratory epithelium. It contains goblet cells, which contribute mucus that traps airborne particles in the bronchiole tree. The alveoli are made up of single layers of squamous epithelial cells to facilitate gas diffusion. This epithelium has no cilia or goblet cells.

Larynx

Trachea

Lung

Right primary bronchus

Diaphragm

Esophagus

Left primary bronchus

Lung

(b)

FIGURE D4.3 (continued) Respiratory system of the rat.
(b) Diagrammatic view.

3. The lungs are divided into five lobes. In the rat, there are four lobes on the right side and one on the left. There are several synonyms for the names of the lobes on the right side. They are listed here:

a. Cephalic, anterior, cranial

b. Middle, medial

c. Posterior, caudal

d. Postcaval, accessory

The postcaval or accessory lobe is located deep and medial to the other lobes and is not easily visible. This lobe is missing in humans. The tapered, cranial portion of the lung is called the apex, and the concave, caudal portion is called the base of the lung. The medial surface is called the mediastinal surface, and the side facing the ribs is the costal surface.

How does the distribution of the lobes of the lungs differ between rats and humans?

Remove the left lobe and cut it open. Examine it through a hand lens or dissecting microscope. Identify blood vessels, bronchi, bronchioles, and alveoli. The alveoli will be filled with fluid in this specimen instead of air.

4. Examine the **diaphragm** that forms the boundary between the thoracic and abdominal cavities. This muscle seals the thoracic cavity, making it airtight. In a relaxed state, it resembles an open umbrella, with the ligament forming the center pole of the umbrella. The diaphragm of a preserved specimen will be flat. Only mammals have diaphragms.

5. Prepare your rat for storage and clean the area as instructed in the box on page 698. ▉

1. What happens when we try to talk and swallow at the same time? Why?

   _____

   _____

2. What additional cartilages are found in the human larynx that are not found in the rat?

   _____

3. Why is it important that the trachea be maintained open?

   _____

   _____

4. Why do humans not have a postcaval or accessory lobe?

   _____

5. What is the advantage of having a diaphragm?

   _____

   _____

6. Describe the appearance of lung tissue under the dissection microscope.

   _____

   _____

Dissection of the Digestive System of the Rat

MATERIALS

- [ ] Disposable gloves
- [ ] Lab coat or apron
- [ ] Safety glasses
- [ ] Dissecting instruments and tray
- [ ] Rat specimen from previous dissections
- [ ] Hand lens or dissecting microscope
- [ ] Paper towels

OBJECTIVES

1. To identify on a dissected rat the organs composing the digestive tract, and to name their subdivisions if any.
2. To name and identify the accessory organs of the digestive tract, and to indicate their functions.

Don gloves and obtain your dissection specimen. Take the animal out of the plastic storage bag, and remove the paper toweling. Rinse the rat in cold tap water if necessary and pat dry. The thoracic and abdominal cavities should be exposed from previous dissections. If not, refer to Dissection Exercise 2, Activity 1, page 709, for instructions on opening these cavities.

ACTIVITY 1

Identifying Digestive Components of the Head and Neck

1. Place the rat on its dorsal suface. If the underside of the head is not exposed, use scissors to make a cut through the skin on the center of the neck and, using the blunt probe, separate the skin from the underlying tissues to expose the neck region. Identify the two **salivary glands,** the **sublingual gland,** and the **submaxillary or mandibular gland** (Figure D5.1). Locate the mandibular lymph nodes in the same area. The lymph nodes may be confused with the salivary glands.

Turn the rat on its side. Using the blunt probe, separate the skin from the side of the skull and make a cut with scissors from the anterior mandible posterior to the ear. Expose the underlying tissue with the blunt probe. Identify the **parotid gland** as a large, poorly encapsulated, triangular gland just caudal to the ear (Figure D5.2). The parotid duct crosses the gland to enter the mouth. The duct is larger than the portion of the facial nerve that crosses in the same area. An extraorbital lacrimal gland will be in the same area, usually anterior to the parotid gland. The extraorbital lacrimal gland makes tears, not saliva, and is not present in humans (see Figure D5.2).

2. Using scissors, cut through the masseter muscles on both sides of the mouth and extend the mandible caudally, fully opening the mouth. Examine the **teeth** of both upper and lower jaw.

The rat has two pairs of prominent incisors at the front of its mouth. These teeth continually grow through the animal's life, possibly reaching over two centimeters long. Look for a line of molars along the sides of the hard palate.

The dental formula for rats is the same for upper and lower teeth. It is 2 incisors and 6 molars $\left(\dfrac{1\text{I}, 3\text{M}}{1\text{I}, 3\text{M}} \times 2\right)$, producing a total of 16 teeth. What is the dental formula in adult humans?

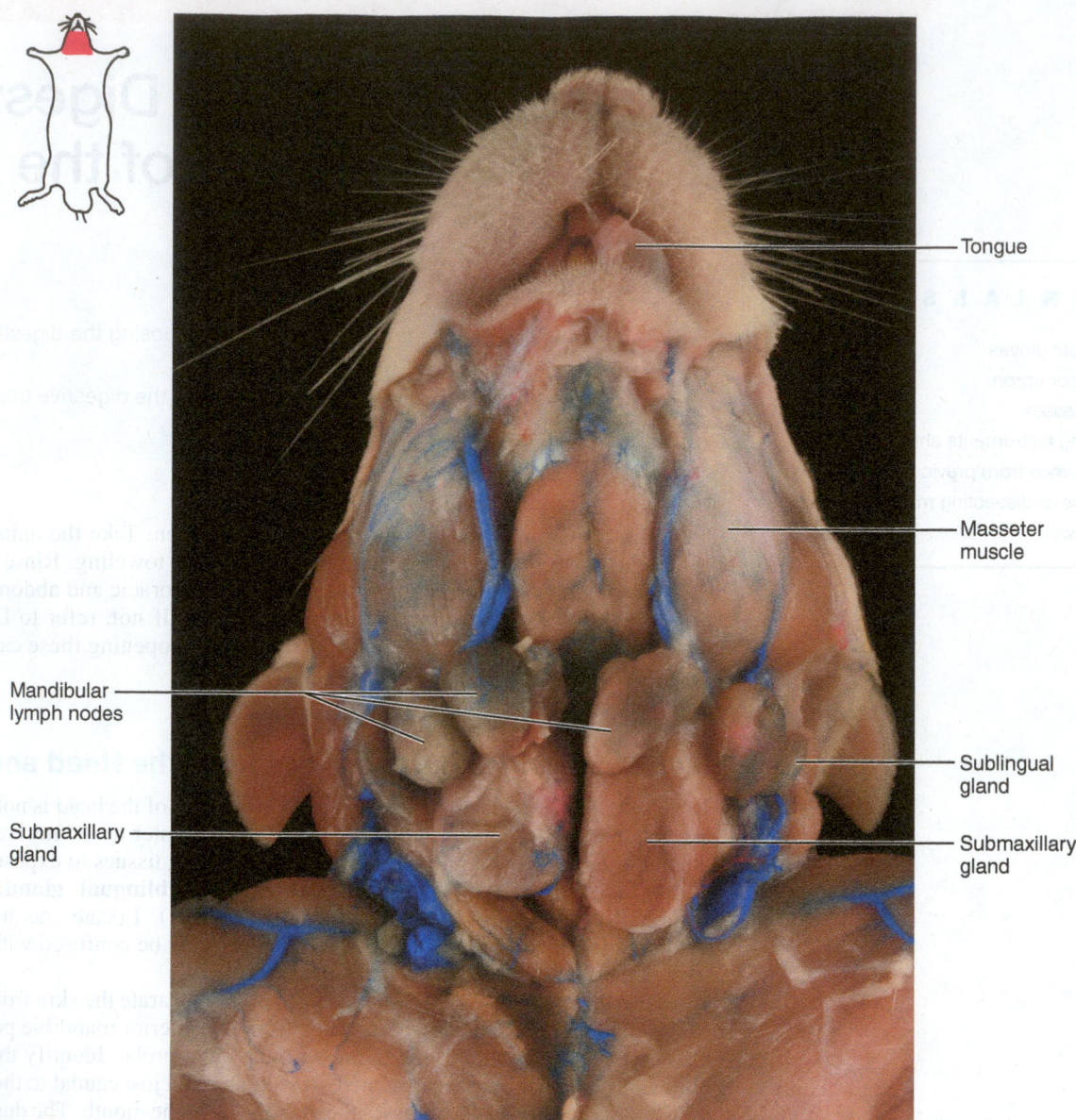

Tongue

Masseter muscle

Sublingual gland

Submaxillary gland

Mandibular lymph nodes

Submaxillary gland

FIGURE D5.1 **Submaxillary and sublingual salivary glands of the rat.**

3.   Elevate the **tongue** to locate the two vertical membranes that attach the tongue to floor of the mouth. These are called the lingual frenula. Flatten out the tongue and view its surface with the hand lens or dissecting microscope to view the papillae on its surface. Fungiform papillae are on the anterior surface, filiform papillae are between the molars, and circumvallate papillae are at the base of the tongue.

Diagram the locations of the papillae on the tongue, as seen through the lens or microscope.

4.   Locate the hard palate. It is the anteriormost, hard, ridged roof of the mouth. The hard palate has a line of molars along

both sides. Locate the **soft palate,** posterior to the **hard palate.** This makes up the back of the roof of the mouth. This soft tissue is raised up to close off the nasopharynx during swallowing. Locate the **glottis** at the opening to the larynx and the **epiglottis** protecting it.

Why is it important for the soft palate to raise while swallowing?

_____

_____

5.   With the rat on its dorsal surface, locate the trachea, seen in the Dissection Exercise 4. Using a blunt probe, deflect the trachea to the left and separate it from the tube underneath. This muscular tube is the **esophagus.** Follow the esophagus as far as possible, posterior to the heart (if it is still in place from Exercise 4) and through the diaphragm (seen in Exercise 4) to the stomach in the abdomen. ▪

(a)

Temporalis muscle

Extraorbital lacrimal gland

Parotid gland

Parotid duct

Facial nerve

(b)

Temporalis muscle

Extraorbital lacrimal gland

Parotid gland

Parotid duct

Facial nerve

FIGURE D5.2 Parotid salivary gland of the rat. (a) Photograph. **(b)** Diagrammatic view.

Identifying Digestive Components of the Abdomen

1. Using the flat end of the forceps, gently deflect the liver laterally to expose the **stomach** located caudal to the liver, at the junction of the stomach with the esophagus (Figure D5.3). Cut the stomach open and use the hand lens or dissecting microscope to view the gross folds of the stomach, called **rugae,** that increase the surface area of the organ when the stomach is empty. As the stomach fills, the rugae gradually disappear and are no longer visible. You may also have to remove stomach contents to see the rugae.

Describe the rugae as seen through the lens or microscope.

_____

_____

Locate the **cardiac sphincter** at the esophagus-stomach junction. Find the stomach-duodenum junction and identify the **pyloric sphincter.** Follow the stomach past the cardiac sphincter to an area of the stomach that extends cranial to it to locate the **fundus** of the stomach. This is a major portion of the stomach in the rat. The fundus in humans is smaller. Look at the stomach from above to identify the **lesser** and **greater curvatures** of the stomach. If possible, identify the lesser omentum connecting the stomach to the liver. This may have been inadvertently removed during the dissection.

2. **Small Intestine—Duodenum:** Trace the stomach to its distal end and identify the first portion of the small intestine, called the **duodenum.** The duodenum is the shortest portion of the small intestine. A common duct empties into the duodenum, carrying secretions from the pancreas and bile from the liver.

   Examine the loose, filmy tissue with blood vessels that connects the parts of the intestines. This is called the **mesentery.**

3. **Small Intestine—Jejunum:** Follow along the small intestine to the **jejunum.** This is the middle of the small intestine.

4. **Small Intestine—Ileum:** Go to the juncture of the small and large intestine discussed below. The last portion of the small intestine is the **ileum.** The jejunum and ileum are approximately the same length and cannot be easily distinguished in their gross anatomy. The three portions of the small intestine can be positively identified microscopically.

5. **Large Intestine—Colon:** Using the blunt probe, follow along the tube from the pyloric sphincter of the stomach through the portions of the small intestine to the large intestine at the ileocecal junction. Cut into the junction to view the ileocecal valve. Use a hand lens or a dissecting microscope to view the valve. Continue to follow the ascending colon up the right, lateral side of the rat to the stomach and down the left lateral side with the descending colon.

   Present at the junction of the small and large intestines is a structure called the **cecum.** This is an out-pouching of the tube that is prominent in the rat, but reduced in size in humans. Rats do not have an appendix. The colon has two principal parts, the **ascending** and **descending** portions. Intestinal contents pass into the **rectum** for elimination from the body.

What are the parts of the large intestine in humans?

_____

6. **Large Intestine—Colon—Rectum:** Follow the descending **colon** caudally to the short **rectum.** The last portion of the large intestine, which is short and straight, carries the contents to the end of the tube for elimination.

   In the female rat, the rectum is beneath the vagina and urethra. Cut the pubic bones and carefully dissect the three tubes in this area. Carefully deflect the vagina and urethra laterally to view the rectum. You may choose to wait to examine the rectum until Dissection Exercise 7. Dissecting this area now may damage the specimen's reproductive structures.

7. **Anus:** Follow the rectum to the exterior wall. Examine the exterior of the rat to identify the anus, through which fecal material is eliminated. ■■■

Accessory Digestive Organs in the Abdomen

1. **Liver:** Locate the rat's liver immediately caudal to the diaphragm (Figure D5.3). It is dark brown and has four lobes held together by loose connective tissue. The lobes are the median/cystic lobe, the right and left lobes, and the small caudate lobe. The rat does not have a gallbladder for storing bile. Bile produced by the liver passes into the duodenum by way of the **bile duct.**

2. **Pancreas:** Locate the **pancreas** dorsal and caudal to the stomach at the curvature where the stomach and duodenum join. It is a lightly colored and poorly encapsulated organ. This organ has a consistency resembling that of cottage cheese. The rat's pancreas has two parts. The ventral component is distal to the stomach wall, while the dorsal component is found in the mesentery at the duodenum. The pancreas is an organ with both endocrine and exocrine functions. Its exocrine secretions aid digestion and enter the duodenum with the bile through the same opening.

3. Prepare your rat for storage and clean the area as instructed in the box on page 698. ■■■

(a)

(b)

FIGURE D5.3 Digestive organs of the rat. (a) Photograph. **(b)** Diagrammatic view.

1. How do the variety of teeth in rats and humans reflect their diets?

    _____

    _____

2. How do the papillae of the tongue differ between rats and humans?

    _____

    _____

3. The liver in humans also has four lobes. What are their names?

    _____

Dissection of the Urinary System of the Rat

OBJECTIVES

1. To name and locate components of the urinary system on a dissected rat, and to describe the general function of each.

2. To recognize similarities and differences between rat and human urinary systems.

This exercise involves dissection and identification of components of the urinary system of rats, in conjunction with the study of the human systems, to enhance your knowledge of the human urinary system. Since the aim is to become familiar with the urinary system of the human body, you should pay particular attention to the similarities between rat and human urinary anatomy.

Functions of the urinary system include eliminating nitrogenous wastes and controlling water and electrolyte balances and blood pressure. Large amounts of blood are constantly filtered throughout the day. Most of the water component of the filtered fluid is reabsorbed, and the remainder is highly concentrated to form urine. Water balance in the body is controlled by the degree of concentration of the fluid. Electrolyte balance is both an active and passive phenomenon involving the entire kidney. Both processes involve hormones from other parts of the body. Adequate blood pressure is ensured to maintain the appropriate blood supply to the kidney. The urinary system of the human body is discussed in Exercise 40 of this manual.

ACTIVITY 1

Dissecting the Kidney of the Rat

• Don gloves and use the blunt end of the forceps to deflect the abdominal organs to the left. Pin them in place if possible. Identify the **kidneys** about halfway down the cavity on each side of the abdomen. The kidneys are found at the level of the third to fifth vertebrae. The right kidney is slightly more cranial than the left one in the rat (Figures D6.1 and D6.2). Note that the kidney is kept against the posterior wall of the cavity by a portion of the peritoneal membrane. This is called a retroperitoneal arrangement. Using a blunt probe, remove the fat covering the kidney. Another layer of fat is found between the kidney and the abdominal wall. A separate structure resembling a lymph node lies cranial to the kidneys. This is the rat's adrenal gland, discussed in Dissection Exercise 2. Blood, lymphatic vessels, and the ureters are attached to the kidney at the hilum, which is found at the inner curve of the organ. Carefully make a cut along the frontal plane of a kidney and examine it with a hand lens or dissecting microscope. Identify the outer cortex and inner medulla of the kidney.

Describe the texture and density of the renal cortex and medulla as seen in the rat kidney:

_____

_____

The renal pelvis may be visible as an open area of the organ at the hilum. Other anatomical structures cannot be seen at this level. ▬

(a)

(b)

FIGURE D6.1 Urinary system of the male rat. (a) Photograph. **(b)** Diagrammatic view.

Kidney

Ureter

Urinary bladder

(a)

(b)

Kidney

Ureter

Urinary bladder

FIGURE D6.2 Urinary system of the female rat. (a) Photograph. **(b)** Diagrammatic
view.

Dissecting the Ureters, Bladder, and Urethra of the Rat

1. Locate the **ureter** at the hilum of the kidney. It is a colorless tube that is not filled with latex as the blood vessels are. Use the blunt probe to separate the ureter from the surrounding fat and other tissues and follow it caudally to the bladder.

2. The urinary **bladder** will appear small and hard due to the preservation of the specimen. In a live animal, it can expand to five times larger. The bladder is held in place by medial and lateral ligaments.

Make a cut along the frontal plane of the bladder and examine the interior with a hand lens or dissecting microscope. Notice the two openings for the ureters and the single exit point connected to the urethra. The triangle formed by these openings is called the trigone. The interior of the bladder ap-

pears wrinkled due to folds in the wall similar to the rugae of the stomach. These folds and the transitional epithelium of the bladder allow for the expansion during filling.

3. The single **urethra** carries urine from the bladder to the exterior opening for elimination. The urethra in male rats is involved with the reproductive structures of the animal and will be discussed in Dissection Exercise 7. ■

Locating the External Urethral Opening

1. Refer to Dissection Exercise 1 of the manual for the surface anatomy of the rat and identification of the **external urethral openings**.

2. Prepare your rat for storage and clean the area as instructed in the box on page 698. ■

DISSECTION REVIEW

1. What is the difference between the fluid filtered in the kidney and in the urine?

_____

_____

2. What are some major functions of the urinary system?

_____

3. What is the function of the layers of fat surrounding the kidney?

_____

_____

4. What two anatomical adaptions are present in the bladder to facilitate expansion?

_____

5. How does the site of urethral emptying in the female rat differ from its termination point in the human female?

_____

_____

Dissection of the Reproductive System of the Rat

OBJECTIVES

1. To name and locate components of the male and female reproductive systems on a dissected rat.
2. To recognize and discuss pertinent differences between the reproductive structures of the human and the dissected rat.

This exercise involves dissection and identification of components of the male and female reproductive systems of rats, in conjunction with the study of the human systems, to enhance your knowledge of the human reproductive system. Since the aim is to become familiar with the reproductive system of the human body, you should pay particular attention to the similarities between rat and human reproductive anatomy.

The reproductive systems function to produce the gametes or sex cells of the body, the sperm and ova, and to provide the structures for delivering these to the appropriate areas for the development of offspring. Structures in these systems also produce the hormones that are necessary for reproduction. The hormonal contributions of the testes and ovaries were discussed in Dissection Exercise 3. The reproductive system of the human body is discussed in Exercise 42 of this manual.

ACTIVITY 1

Identifying Organs of the Male Reproductive System of the Rat

The following instructions assume that the abdominal cavity has been opened in previous dissection exercises.

1. The reproductive structures of the male rat are found in the lower abdominopelvic area, from the urinary bladder to the pubic symphysis, and outside the body in the **scrotum.** The scrotum contains the testes, epididymis, and the origin of the paired tubes delivering the sperm, the ductus (vas) deferens. If the testes were not exposed in Dissection Exercise 3, don gloves, place a male rat on its dorsal surface, and locate the scrotum. This is viewed externally below the pubic area (Figure D2.1). Make a cut through the ventral wall of the scrotum on one side to expose the **testes** within the sac (Figure D7.1). The testes are elongated, oval, and brown in color. They are enclosed in a membrane called the cremasteric pouch. The testes have both exocrine and endocrine functions. The testes produce the sex cells of the male, the sperm. Spermatogenesis occurs at temperatures lower than body temperature, so the site of this production is located outside the body. The sperm are produced within the walls of coiled tubes called the seminiferous tubules.

Why must the testes be located outside the body?

_____

_____

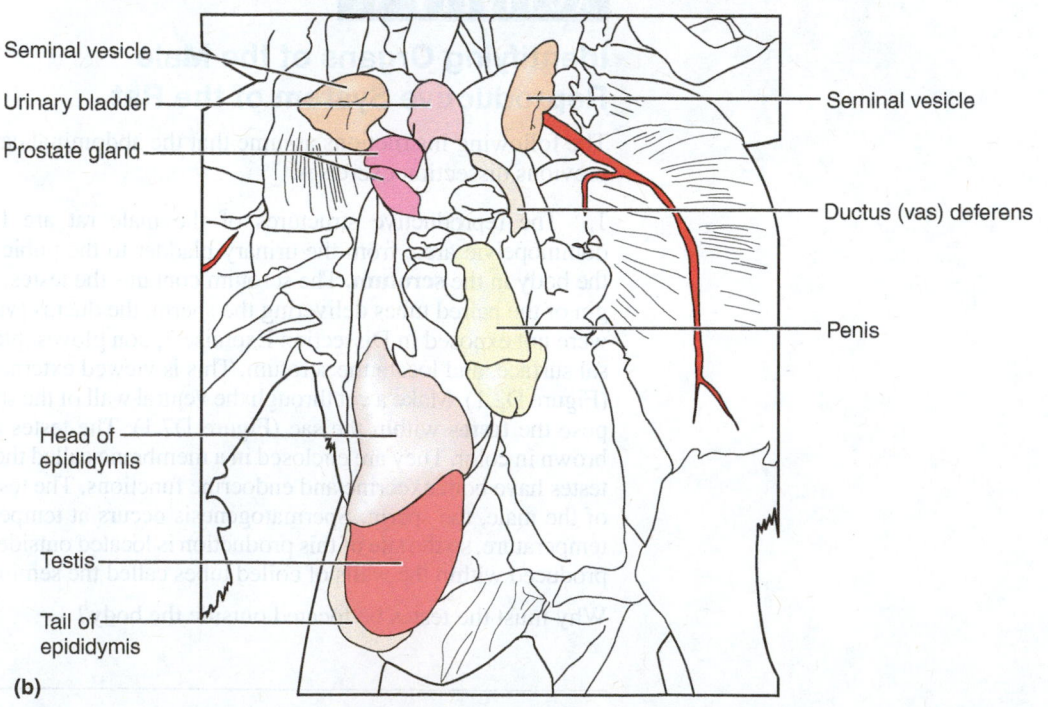

Seminal vesicle

Urinary bladder

Prostate gland

Seminal vesicle

Ductus (vas) deferens

Penis

Head of epididymis

Testis

Tail of epididymis

(a)

Seminal vesicle

Urinary bladder

Prostate gland

Seminal vesicle

Ductus (vas) deferens

Penis

Head of epididymis

Testis

Tail of epididymis

(b)

FIGURE D7.1 Reproductive system of the male rat. (a) Photograph.
(b) Diagrammatic view.

Carefully cut through the cremasteric pouch of one of the testes. Make a frontal cut through a testis and examine it with a hand lens or a dissecting microscope to view the seminiferous tubules. They are located in sections of the testes that resemble wedges. Other cells are mixed in with the developing sperm cells. These are discussed in Dissection Exercise 2.

2.   Examine the dorsal side of the testes and locate the **epididymis** (see Figure D7.1). This receives and stores the sperm from the testes. Connected to the epididymis is the **ductus (vas) deferens.** This tube carries the sperm into the body. The ductus deferens leaves the scrotum in a structure called the spermatic cord. The cord also contains the spermatic artery and vein, lymphatics, and several nerves. The ductus deferens is thin, colorless, and easily damaged.

3.   Follow the ductus deferens into the pelvic region to its connection to the urethra just below the bladder. Two prominent, leaf-shaped glands called the **seminal vesicles** are found in this area. They will appear to flare out from the urethral-bladder junction. The glands are scalloped on the lateral edge and have other glands, the coagulating glands, attached on their medial borders. The seminal vesicles contribute fluids to the semen. The coagulating glands contribute chemicals that cause the coagulation of the semen after ejaculation. Near the junction of the ductus deferens and the urethra is the brownish colored **prostate** gland. This is really two glands in the rat that encircle the first part of the urethra, just below the bladder. The prostate is made up of a mixture of smooth muscle and glandular tissue and contributes fluid and force to the ejaculated semen.

Name the structures that produce and deliver semen.

_____

_____

4.   Examine the **urethra,** a common tube that carries semen or urine. A smooth muscle sphincter at the opening of the bladder at the beginning of the urethra closes completely during ejaculation, preventing urine from entering the tube. The urethra is divided into three parts. The first, the prostatic urethra, extends through the prostate glands. The walls of this part of the tube have numerous openings through which prostatic secretions enter the urethra. The ductus deferens joins the urethra in this area, as do secretions from the other glands mentioned. The second portion is called the membranous or urogenital urethra. This extends to the base of the penis. The last part of the urethra is the spongy urethra. This extends through the penis and opens at the urogenital orifice.

5.   The **penis** is an excretory organ for the urinary tract and a copulatory organ for the reproductive tract. Three cylindrical masses of erectile tissue extend through the length of the penis. There are two dorsal tubes of tissue called corpora cavernosa and one ventral tube called the corpus spongiosum. The urethra runs through the corpus spongiosum. These cylinders engorge with blood, causing the penis to become erect and stiff during copulation. Rats have an additional aid to copulation in the form of a bone called the baculum or os penis, found in the distal end of the penis. It aids in the erection of the organ. Make a cross-sectional cut through the penis and examine it with a hand lens or dissecting microscope to view the three cylinders of tissue and the urethra. ▆▆

Ovary

Uterine horn

Colon

Uterine body

Urinary bladder

Urethra

Rectum

Vagina

(a)

Ovary

Uterine horn

Colon

Uterine body

Urinary bladder

Urethra

Rectum

Vagina

(b)

FIGURE D7.2 Reproductive system of the female rat. (a) Photograph.
(b) Diagrammatic view.

ACTIVITY 2

Identifying Organs of the Female Reproductive System of the Rat

1.   The reproductive structures of the female rat are found in the abdominopelvic area from the level of the kidneys through the pubic symphysis to the exterior of the body (Figure D7.2). If the ovaries were not exposed in Dissection Exercise 3, locate the **ovaries** slightly caudal and lateral to the kidneys, on each side of the cavity. Remove the layer of fat covering the ovaries. The ovaries are both exocrine and endocrine glands. Their exocrine function produces eggs or ova ready for fertilization. A capsule called the ovarian bursa surrounds the ovaries. The ovarian bursa in the rat is a continuation of the uterine tubes (also called oviducts or fallopian tubes). The bursa forms a sac that encircles the ovary and helps the released egg enter the uterine tube for transport to the uterus. This connection between the ovary and uterine tube is absent in humans. The uterine tubes in rats are short, thin, and difficult to view.

   Make a frontal cut through one ovary and view it with a hand lens or a dissecting microscope.

Observe any differences in the outer layers of cells. What do they represent?

_____

2.   The **uterus** of a rat is shaped like a capital Y, but with elongated arms, called a bipartite or bicornuate type of arrangement. Two separate tubes or horns of the organ extend from the short uterine tubes to the mid-ventral area of the pelvic region. Developing offspring implant in the uterine horns, enabling the rat to have a litter of offspring with each pregnancy. The **uterine horns** extend through the central portion of the uterus, called the **uterine body,** to connect with the **vagina.** The tubes unite at the cervical entry to the vagina. Follow the vagina to the **vaginal opening** at the body surface.

3.   Three tubes extend from the area of the uterus to the body's exterior. The bottom tube is the rectum, carrying semisolid waste from the intestines. The middle tube is the vagina, which is a copulatory organ and the tube used to deliver offspring. The **urethra** carries urine from the bladder to the exterior opening for elimination. The urethral opening is located cranial to the vaginal opening on the exterior of the animal. The urethra in the female rat passes through a small, round structure called the clitoris.

What is the difference in the location of the clitoris between humans and rats?

_____

_____

4.   Prepare your rat for storage and clean the area as instructed in the box on page 698. ▉

DISSECTION REVIEW

1. What is found in the spermatic cord?

2. What is the difference between human and rat prostate structure?

3. How do eggs enter the uterine tubes of humans?

4. How does the rat's uterus facilitate multiple births?

physioEX
VERSION 8

PhysioEx™ 8.0 by
Peter Zao, North Idaho College
Timothy Stabler, Indiana University Northwest
Lori Smith, American River College
Greta Peterson, Middlesex Community College
Marcia C. Gibson, University of Wisconsin–Madison (Histology Review Supplement)
Nina Zanetti, Siena College
Andrew Lokuta, University of Wisconsin–Madison

PhysioEx™ version 8.0 consists of 12 exercises containing 79 physiology lab activities that may be used to supplement or replace wet labs. This easy-to-use software allows you to repeat labs as often as you like, perform experiments without harming live animals, and conduct experiments that may be difficult to perform in a wet lab environment due to time, cost, or safety concerns. You also have the flexibility to change the parameters of an experiment and observe how outcomes are affected. In addition, PhysioEx includes an extensive histology tutorial that allows you to study histology images at various magnifications. This manual will walk you through each lab step by step. You will also find Review Sheets following each exercise to test your understanding of the key concepts in each lab.

New to Version 8.0

Note to instructors: If you have used previous versions of PhysioEx, here is a summary of the updates you will find to Exercise 28B: Endocrine System Physiology in PhysioEx 8.0.

- New data in Activities 1–4, Hormones and Metabolism, to demonstrate a more dramatic difference in metabolic rate.

- An examination of how estrogen and calcitonin affect bone density in Activity 5, Hormone Replacement Therapy.

- A glucose tolerance test in Activity 7, Insulin and Diabetes, Part II, to strengthen the correlation between types of diabetes and diagnosis.

- A new activity, Measuring Cortisol and Adrenocorticotropic Hormone (Activity 8), that explores the relationship between the levels of these two hormones and a variety of endocrine disorders.

PhysioEx 8.0 also includes revisions to the Blood Typing, BMR Measurement, Cardiovascular Physiology, and Cell Transport videos. All seven videos are available on the CD-ROM.

Topics in This Edition

Exercise 5B

Cell Transport Mechanisms and Permeability: Computer Simulation. Explores how substances cross the cell's membrane. Simple and facilitated diffusion, osmosis, filtration, and active transport are covered.

Exercise 6B

Histology Atlas and Review Supplement. Includes over 200 histology images, viewable at various magnifications, with accompanying descriptions and labels.

Exercise 16B

Skeletal Muscle Physiology: Computer Simulation. Provides insights into the complex physiology of skeletal muscle. Electrical stimulation, isometric contractions, and isotonic contractions are investigated.

Exercise 18B

Neurophysiology of Nerve Impulses: Computer Simulation. Investigates stimuli that elicit action potentials, stimuli that inhibit action potentials, and factors affecting nerve conduction velocity.

Exercise 28B

Endocrine System Physiology: Computer Simulation. Investigates the relationship between hormones and metabolism; the effect of estrogen replacement therapy; the diagnosis of diabetes; and the relationship between the levels of cortisol and adrenocorticotropic hormone and a variety of endocrine disorders.

Exercise 29B

Blood Analysis: Computer Simulation. Covers hematocrit determination, erythrocyte sedimentation rate determination, hemoglobin determination, blood typing, and total cholesterol determination.

Exercise 33B

Cardiovascular Dynamics: Computer Simulation. Topics of inquiry include vessel resistance and pump (heart) mechanics.

Exercise 34B

Frog Cardiovascular Physiology: Computer Simulation. Variables influencing heart activity are examined. Topics include setting up and recording baseline heart activity, the refractory period for cardiac muscle, and an investigation of physical and chemical factors that affect enzyme activity.

Exercise 37B

Respiratory System Mechanics: Computer Simulation. Investigates physical and chemical aspects of pulmonary function. Students collect data simulating normal lung volumes. Includes a new activity on comparative spirometry. Other activities examine factors such as airway resistance and the effect of surfactant on lung function.

Exercise 39B

Chemical and Physical Processes of Digestion: Computer Simulation. Turns the student's computer into a virtual chemistry lab where enzymes, reagents, and incubation conditions can be manipulated (in compressed time) to examine factors that affect enzyme activity.

Exercise 41B

Renal Physiology—The Function of the Nephron: Computer Simulation. Simulates the function of a single nephron. Topics include factors influencing glomerular filtration, the effect of hormones on urine function, and glucose transport maximum.

Exercise 47

Acid-Base Balance: Computer Simulation. Topics include respiratory and metabolic acidosis/alkalosis, as well as renal and respiratory compensation.

Getting Started

To use PhysioEx, your computer should meet the following minimum requirements (regardless of whether you are using the CD or accessing PhysioEx via the Web):

Windows:

- OS: Windows® XP, Vista™
- Resolution: 1024 × 768
- Latest version of Adobe® Flash® Player
- Latest version of Adobe Reader®
- Browsers: Internet Explorer 6.0 (XP only); Internet Explorer 7.0; Firefox 2.0
- Internet Connection: 56K modem minimum for website
- Printer

Macintosh:

- OS: 10.3.x, 10.4.x
- Resolution: 1024 × 768
- Latest version of Adobe Flash Player
- Latest version of Adobe Reader
- Browsers: Safari 1.3 (10.3.x only); Safari 2.0 (10.4.x only); Firefox 2.0
- Internet Connection: 56K modem minimum for website
- Printer

Instructions for Getting Started—Mac Users (CD Version)

1. Put the PhysioEx CD in the CD-ROM drive. Double-click the PhysioEx CD icon on your desktop, and then double-click the StartHere.html file.

2. Although you do not need a live Internet connection to run PhysioEx, you do need to have a browser (such as Firefox or Safari) installed on your computer.

3. Click **License Agreement** to read the License Agreement, then close the License Agreement window.

4. In the PhysioEx window, click **Enter.**

Instructions for Getting Started—Windows Users (CD Version)

1. Put the PhysioEx CD in the CD-ROM drive. The program should launch automatically. If autorun is disabled on your machine, double-click the My Computer icon on your Windows desktop, double-click the PhysioEx CD icon, and then double-click the StartHere.html file.

2. Although you do not need a live Internet connection to run PhysioEx, you do need to have a browser (such as Firefox or Internet Explorer) installed on your computer.

3. Click **License Agreement** to read the License Agreement.

4. In the PhysioEx window, click **Enter.**

Instructions for Getting Started—Web Users

Follow the instructions for accessing www.myaandp.com that appear at the very front of your lab manual.

Technical Support

If you need technical support, please contact the Benjamin Cummings Product Support Center at http://247.aw.com.

Cell Transport Mechanisms and Permeability: Computer Simulation

OBJECTIVES

1. To define the following terms: *differential permeability, passive* and *active processes* of transport, *diffusion (simple diffusion, facilitated diffusion,* and *osmosis), solute pump, pinocytosis,* and *phagocytosis.*

2. To describe the processes that account for the movement of substances across the plasma membrane, and to indicate the driving force for each.

3. To determine which way substances will move passively through a differentially permeable membrane (given the appropriate information on concentration differences).

T he molecular composition of the plasma membrane allows it to be selective about what passes through it. It allows nutrients to enter the cell but keeps out undesirable substances. By the same token, valuable cell proteins and other substances are kept within the cell, and excreta, or wastes, pass to the exterior. This property is known as **differential,** or **selective, permeability.** Transport through the plasma membrane occurs in two basic ways. In **active processes,** the cell provides energy (ATP) to power the transport. In the other, **passive processes,** the transport process is driven by concentration or pressure differences between the interior and exterior of the cell.

Passive Processes

The two key passive processes of membrane transport are diffusion and filtration. Diffusion is an important transport process for every cell in the body. By contrast, filtration usually occurs only across capillary walls. Each of these will be considered in turn.

Diffusion

Recall that all molecules possess *kinetic energy* and are in constant motion. As molecules move about randomly at high speeds, they collide and ricochet off one another, changing direction with each collision. For a given temperature, all matter has about the same average kinetic energy. Because kinetic energy is directly related to both mass and velocity ($KE = \frac{1}{2} mv^2$), smaller molecules tend to move faster.

When a **concentration gradient** (difference in concentration) exists, the net effect of this random molecular movement is that the molecules eventually become evenly distributed throughout the environment—in other words, the process called diffusion occurs. Hence, **diffusion** is the movement of molecules from a region of their higher concentration to a region of their lower concentration. Diffusion's driving force is the kinetic energy of the molecules themselves.

The diffusion of particles into and out of cells is modified by the plasma membrane, which constitutes a physical barrier. In general, molecules diffuse passively through the plasma membrane if they are small enough to pass through its pores (and are aided by an electrical and/or concentration gradient), or if they can dissolve in the lipid portion of the membrane as in the case of CO_2 and O_2.

The diffusion of solute particles dissolved in water through a differentially permeable membrane is called **simple diffusion.** The diffusion of water through a differentially permeable membrane is called **osmosis.** Both simple diffusion and osmosis involve movement of a substance from an area of its higher concentration to one of its lower concentration, that is, down its concentration gradient.

Solute Transport Through Nonliving Membranes

This computerized simulation provides information on the passage of water and solutes through semipermeable membranes, which may be applied to the study of transport mechanisms in living membrane-bounded cells.

ACTIVITY 1

Simulating Dialysis (Simple Diffusion)

Choose **Exercise 5B: Cell Transport Mechanisms and Permeability** from the drop-down menu and click **GO.** Watch the **Cell Transport** video to see an actual dialysis experiment performed. Then click **Simple Diffusion.** The opening screen will appear in a few seconds (Figure 5B.1). The primary features on the screen when the program starts are a pair of glass beakers perched atop a solutions dispenser, a dialysis membranes cabinet at the right side of the screen, and a data collection unit at the bottom of the display.

The beakers are joined by a membrane holder, which can be equipped with any of the dialysis membranes from the cabinet. Each membrane is represented by a thin colored line suspended in a gray supporting frame. The solute concentration of dispensed solutions is displayed at the side of each beaker. As you work through the experiments, keep in mind that membranes are three-dimensional; thus what appears as a slender line is actually the edge of a membrane sheet.

The solutions you can dispense are listed beneath each beaker. You can choose more than one solution, and you can control the amount to be dispensed by clicking (+) to increase concentration or (−) to decrease concentration. You can then deliver the chosen solutions to their beaker by clicking the **Dispense** button on the same side. Clicking the **Start** button opens the membrane holder and begins the experiment. The **Start** button will become a **Pause** button after you click it once. To clean the beakers and prepare them for the next run, click **Flush.** Clicking **Pause** and then **Flush** during a run stops the experiment and prepares the beakers for another run. You can adjust the timer for any interval between 5 and 300 minutes; the elapsed time is shown in the small window to the right of the timer.

To move dialysis membranes from the cabinet to the membrane holder, click and hold the mouse on the selected membrane, drag it into position between the beakers, and then release the mouse button to drop it into place. Each membrane possesses a different molecular weight cutoff (MWCO), indicated by the number below it. You can think of MWCO in terms of pore size; the larger the MWCO number, the larger the pores in the membrane.

The **Run Number** window in the data collection unit at the bottom of the screen displays each experimental trial (run). When you click the **Record Data** button, your data is recorded in the computer's memory and is displayed in the data grid at the bottom of the screen. Data displayed in the data grid include the solute (Solute) and membrane (MWCO) used in a run, the starting concentrations in the left and right beakers (Start Conc. L. and Start Conc. R.), and the average diffusion rate (Avg. Diff. Rate). If you are not satisfied with a run, you can click **Delete Run.** *Note:* Remember that sodium chloride (NaCl) does not move as a molecule. It dissociates to Na$^+$ and Cl$^-$ ions in water.

1. Click and hold the mouse on the 20 MWCO membrane, and drag it to the membrane holder between the beakers. Release the mouse button to lock the membrane into place.

2. Now increase the NaCl concentration to be dispensed by clicking the (+) button under the left beaker until the display window reads 9.00 m*M*. Click **Dispense** to fill the left beaker with 9.00 m*M* NaCl solution.

3. Click the **Deionized Water** button under the right beaker and then click **Dispense** to fill the right beaker with deionized water.

4. Adjust the timer to 60 minutes (compressed time), then click the **Start** button. When Start is clicked, the barrier between the beakers descends, allowing the solutions in each beaker to have access to the dialysis membrane separating them. Recall that the Start button becomes a Pause button that allows you to momentarily halt the progress of the experiment so you can see instantaneous diffusion or transport rates.

5. Watch the concentration windows at the side of each beaker for any activity. A level above zero in NaCl concentration in the right beaker indicates that Na$^+$ and Cl$^-$ ions are diffusing from the left into the right beaker through the semipermeable dialysis membrane. Record your results in Chart 1. Record (—) for no diffusion. If diffusion occurred,

CHART 1	Dialysis Results (average diffusion rate in m*M*/min)			
	Membrane (MWCO)			
Solute	20	50	100	200
NaCl				
Urea				
Albumin				
Glucose				

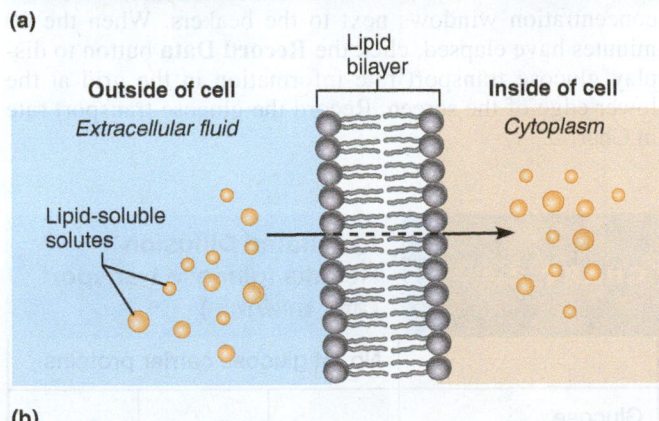

(a)

Outside of cell | Lipid bilayer | **Inside of cell**

Extracellular fluid | *Cytoplasm*

Lipid-soluble solutes

(b)

FIGURE 5B.1 Simple diffusion. (a) Opening screen of the Simple Diffusion experiment. **(b)** Simple diffusion through the phospholipid bilayer.

record the average diffusion rate in Chart 1. Click the **Record Data** button to keep your data in the computer's memory.

6. Click the 20 MWCO membrane (in the membrane holder) again to automatically return it to the membranes cabinet and then click **Flush** beneath each beaker to prepare for the next run.

7. Drag the next membrane (50 MWCO) to the holder and repeat steps 2 through 6. Continue the runs until you have tested all four membranes. (Remember: Click **Flush** beneath each beaker between runs.)

8. Now repeat the same experiment three times for urea, albumin, and glucose, respectively. In step 2 you will be

dispensing first urea, then albumin, and finally glucose, instead of NaCl.

9.   Click **Tools → Print Data** to print your data.

Which solute(s) were able to diffuse into the right beaker from the left?

_____

Which solute(s) did not diffuse?

_____

If the solution in the left beaker contained both urea and albumin, which membrane(s) could you choose to selectively remove the urea from the solution in the left beaker? How would you carry out this experiment?

_____

_____

_____

_____

Assume that the solution in the left beaker contained NaCl in addition to the urea and albumin. How could you set up an experiment so that you removed the urea but left the NaCl concentration unchanged? *Hint:* Assume that you also have control of the contents in the right beaker.

_____

_____

_____

Facilitated Diffusion

Some molecules are lipid insoluble or too large to pass through plasma membrane pores; instead, they pass through the membrane by a passive transport process called **facilitated diffusion.** In this form of transport, solutes combine with carrier protein molecules in the membrane and are then transported *along* or *down* their concentration gradient. Because facilitated diffusion relies on carrier proteins, solute transport varies with the number of available membrane transport proteins.

ACTIVITY 2

Simulating Facilitated Diffusion

Click the **Experiment** menu and then choose **Facilitated Diffusion.** The opening screen will appear in a few seconds

(Figure 5B.2). The basic screen layout is similar to that of the previous experiment with only a few modifications to the equipment. You will notice that only NaCl and glucose solutes are available in this experiment, and you will see a Membrane Builder on the right side of the screen.

The (+) and (−) buttons underneath each beaker adjust solute concentration in the solutions to be delivered into each beaker. Similarly, the buttons in the Membrane Builder allow you to control the number of carrier proteins implanted in the membrane when you click the **Build Membrane** button.

In this experiment, you will investigate how glucose transport is affected by the number of available carrier molecules.

1.   The Glucose Carriers window in the Membrane Builder should read 500. If not, adjust to 500 by using the (+) or (−) button.

2.   Now click **Build Membrane** to insert 500 glucose carrier proteins into the membrane. You should see the membrane appear as a slender line encased in a support structure within the Membrane Builder. Remember that we are looking at the edge of a three-dimensional membrane.

3.   Click on the membrane and hold the mouse button down as you drag the membrane to the membrane holder between the beakers. Release the mouse to lock the membrane into place.

4.   Adjust the glucose concentration to be delivered to the left beaker to 2.00 m*M* by clicking the (+) button next to the Glucose window until it reads 2.00.

5.   To fill the left beaker with the glucose solution, click the **Dispense** button just below the left beaker.

6.   Click the **Deionized Water** button below the right beaker, and then click the **Dispense** button. The right beaker will fill with deionized water.

7.   Set the timer to 60 minutes, and click **Start.** Watch the concentration windows next to the beakers. When the 60 minutes have elapsed, click the **Record Data** button to display glucose transport rate information in the grid at the lower edge of the screen. Record the glucose transport rate in Chart 2.

CHART 2	Facilitated Diffusion Results (glucose transport rate, m*M*/min)		
	No. of glucose carrier proteins		
Glucose concentration (m*M*)	500	700	900
2.00			
8.00			

FIGURE 5B.2 Opening screen of the Facilitated Diffusion experiment.

8. Click the **Flush** button beneath each beaker to remove any residual solution.

9. Click the membrane's holder to return it to the Membrane Builder. Increase the glucose carriers, and repeat steps 2 through 8 using membranes with 700 and then 900 glucose carrier proteins. Record the glucose transport rate in Chart 2 each time.

10. Repeat steps 1 through 9 at 8.00 m*M* glucose concentration. Record your results in Chart 2.

11. Click **Tools → Print Data** to print your data.

What happened to the rate of facilitated diffusion as the number of protein carriers increased? Explain your answer.

_____

_____

_____

What do you think would happen to the transport rate if you put the same concentration of glucose into both beakers instead of deionized water in the right beaker?

_____

_____

_____

Should NaCl have an effect on glucose diffusion? Explain your answer. Use the simulation to see if it does.

_____

_____

_____

FIGURE 5B.3 Opening screen of the Osmosis experiment.

Osmosis

A special form of diffusion, the diffusion of water through a semipermeable membrane, is called **osmosis.** Because water can pass through the pores of most membranes, it can move from one side of a membrane to another relatively unimpeded. Osmosis occurs whenever there is a difference in water concentration on the two sides of a membrane.

If we place distilled water on both sides of a membrane, *net* movement of water will not occur; however, water molecules would still move between the two sides of the membrane. In such a situation, we would say that there is no *net* osmosis. The concentration of water in a solution depends on the number of solutes present. Therefore, increasing the solute concentration coincides with a decrease in water concentration. Because water moves down its concentration gradient, it will always move toward the solution with the highest concentration of solutes. Similarly, solutes also move down their concentration gradient. If we position a *fully* permeable membrane (permeable to solutes and water) between two solutions of differing concentrations, then all substances—solutes and water—will diffuse freely, and an equilibrium

will be reached between the two sides of the membrane. However, if we use a semipermeable membrane that is impermeable to the solutes, then we have established a condition where water will move but solutes will not. Consequently, water will move toward the more concentrated solution, resulting in a volume increase. By applying this concept to a closed system where volumes cannot change, we can predict that the pressure in the more concentrated solution would rise.

ACTIVITY 3

Simulating Osmotic Pressure

Click the **Experiment** menu, and then select **Osmosis.** The opening screen will appear in a few seconds (Figure 5B.3). The most notable difference in this experiment screen concerns meters atop the beakers that measure pressure changes in the beaker they serve. As before, (+) and (−) buttons control solute concentrations in the dispensed solutions.

1. Drag the 20 MWCO membrane to the holder between the two beakers.

2. Adjust the NaCl concentration to 8.00 m*M* in the left beaker, and then click the **Dispense** button.

3. Click **Deionized Water** under the right beaker, and then click **Dispense.**

4. Set the timer to 60 minutes, and then click **Start** to run the experiment. Pay attention to the pressure displays. At the end of the run, click the **Record Data** button to retain your data in the computer's memory, and also record the osmotic pressure in Chart 3.

5. Click the membrane to return it to the membrane cabinet.

6. Repeat steps 1 through 5 with the 50, 100, and 200 MWCO membranes.

Do you see any evidence of pressure changes in either beaker, using any of the four membranes? If so, which membrane(s)?

_____

Does NaCl appear in the right beaker? If so, which membrane(s) allowed it to pass?

_____

_____

7. Now perform the same experiment for albumin and glucose by repeating steps 1 through 6 for each solute. For albumin, dispense 9.00 m*M* albumin in step 2 (instead of NaCl). For glucose, dispense 10.00 m*M* glucose in step 2 (instead of NaCl).

8. Click **Tools → Print Data** to print your data.

Answer the following questions using the results you recorded in Chart 3. Use the simulation if you need help formulating a response.

CHART 3	Osmosis Results (pressure in mm Hg)			
	Membrane (MWCO)			
Solute	20	50	100	200
Na+Cl⁻				
Albumin				
Glucose				

Explain the relationship between solute concentration and osmotic pressure.

_____

_____

Will osmotic pressure be generated if solutes are able to diffuse? Explain your answer.

_____

_____

Because the albumin molecule is much too large to pass through a 100 MWCO membrane, you should have noticed the development of osmotic pressure in the left beaker in the albumin run using the 100 MWCO membrane. What do you think would happen to the osmotic pressure if you replaced the deionized water in the right beaker with 9.00 m*M* albumin in that run? (Both beakers would contain 9.00 m*M* albumin.)

_____

_____

What would happen if you doubled the albumin concentration in the left beaker using any membrane?

_____

In the albumin run using the 200 MWCO membrane, what would happen to the osmotic pressure if you put 10 m*M* glucose in the right beaker instead of deionized water? Explain your answer.

_____

_____

What if you used the 100 MWCO membrane in the albumin/glucose run described in the previous question?

_____

Simulating Filtration

Filtration is the process by which water and solutes pass through a membrane (such as a dialysis membrane) from an area of higher hydrostatic (fluid) pressure into an area of lower hydrostatic pressure. Like diffusion, it is a passive process. For example, fluids and solutes filter out of the capillaries in the kidneys into the kidney tubules because blood pressure in the capillaries is greater than the fluid pressure in the tubules. Filtration is not a selective process. The amount

FIGURE 5B.4 Opening screen of the Filtration experiment.

of filtrate—fluids and solutes—formed depends almost entirely on the pressure gradient (the difference in pressure on the two sides of the membrane) and on the size of the membrane pores.

Click the **Experiment** menu, and then choose **Filtration.** The opening screen will appear in a few seconds (Figure 5B.4). The basic screen elements resemble the other simulations but in a different arrangement. The top beaker can be pressurized to force fluid through the filtration membrane into the bottom beaker. Any of the filtration membranes can be positioned in the holder between the beakers by drag-and-drop as in the previous experiments. The solutions you can dispense are listed to the right of the top beaker and are adjusted by clicking the (+) and (−) buttons. You can then deliver the selected solutions to the top beaker by clicking **Dispense.** Click **Flush** to clean and prepare the top beaker for the next run. You can adjust the timer for any interval between 5 and 300; the elapsed time is shown in the window to the right of the timer. When you click the **Record Data** button, your data is recorded in the computer's memory and is displayed in the data grid at the bottom of the screen.

Solute concentrations in the filtrate are automatically monitored by the *Filtration Rate Analysis unit* to the right of the bottom beaker. After a run you can detect the presence of any solute remaining on a membrane by using the *Membrane Residue Analysis* unit located above the membranes cabinet.

1. Click and hold the mouse on the 20 MWCO membrane, and drag it to the holder below the top beaker. Release the mouse button to lock the membrane into place.

2. Now adjust the NaCl, urea, glucose, and powdered charcoal windows to 5.00 mg/ml each, and then click **Dispense.**

3. If necessary, adjust the pressure unit atop the beaker until its window reads 50 mm Hg.

4. Set the timer to 60 minutes, and then click **Start.** When you click the Start button, the membrane holder below the top beaker retracts, and the solution will flow through the membrane into the beaker below.

5. Watch the Filtration Rate box for any activity. A rise in detected solute concentration indicates that the solute particles are

CHART 4	Filtration Results				
		Membrane (MWCO)			
Solute		20	50	100	200
NaCl	Filtration rate (ml/min)				
	In filtrate (mg/ml)				
	Membrane residue (+/−)				
Urea	In filtrate (mg/ml)				
	Membrane residue (+/−)				
Glucose	In filtrate (mg/ml)				
	Membrane residue (+/−)				
Powdered charcoal	In filtrate (mg/ml)				
	Membrane residue (+/−)				

moving through the filtration membrane. At the end of the run, record the filtration *rate* and the amount of each solute present in the *filtrate* (mg/ml) in Chart 4.

6. Now drag the 20 MWCO membrane to the holder in the Membrane Residue Analysis unit. Click **Start Analysis** to begin analysis (and cleaning) of the membrane. Record your results for solute *residue* presence on the membrane (+ for present, − for not present) in Chart 4, and click the **Record Data** button to keep your data in the computer's memory.

7. Click the 20 MWCO membrane again to automatically return it to the membranes cabinet, and then click **Flush** to prepare for the next run.

8. Repeat steps 1 through 7 three times using 50, 100, and 200 MWCO membranes, respectively.

9. Click **Tools → Print Data** to print your data.

How did the membrane's MWCO affect the filtration rate?

_____

_____

Which solute did not appear in the filtrate using any of the membranes?

_____

What would happen if you increased the driving pressure? Use the simulation to arrive at an answer.

_____

_____

Explain how you can increase the filtration rate through living membranes.

_____

_____

_____

By examining the filtration results, we can predict that the molecular weight of glucose must be

greater than _____ but less than _____. ▮

Active Transport

Whenever a cell expends cellular energy (ATP) to move substances across its membrane, the process is referred to as an *active transport process*. Substances moved across cell membranes by active means are generally unable to pass by diffusion. There are several possible reasons why substances may not be able to pass through a membrane by diffusion: they may be too large to pass through the membrane channels, they may not be lipid soluble, or they may have to move against rather than with a concentration gradient.

In one type of active transport, substances move across the membrane by combining with a protein carrier molecule; the process resembles an enzyme-substrate interaction. ATP provides the driving force, and in many cases the substances move against concentration or electrochemical gradients or both. Some of the substances that are moved into the cells by such carriers, commonly called **solute pumps,** are amino acids and some sugars. Both solutes are lipid insoluble and too large to pass through the membrane channels but are necessary for cell life. On the other hand, sodium ions (Na^+) are ejected from the cells by active transport. There is more Na^+ outside the cell than inside, so the Na^+ tends to remain in the cell unless actively transported out. In the body, the most common type of solute pump is the coupled Na^+-K^+ (sodium-potassium) pump that moves Na^+ and K^+ in opposite directions across cellular membranes. Three Na^+ are ejected for every two K^+ entering the cell.

Engulfment processes such as pinocytosis and phagocytosis also require ATP. In **pinocytosis,** the cell membrane sinks beneath the material to form a small vesicle, which then pinches off into the cell interior. Pinocytosis is most common for taking in liquids containing protein or fat.

In **phagocytosis** (cell eating), parts of the plasma membrane and cytoplasm expand and flow around a relatively large or solid material such as bacteria or cell debris and engulf it, forming a membranous sac called a *phagosome.* The phagosome is then fused with a *lysosome,* and its contents are digested. In the human body, phagocytic cells are mainly found among the white blood cells and macrophages that act as scavengers and help protect the body from disease-causing microorganisms and cancer cells.

You will examine various factors influencing the function of solute pumps in the following experiment.

ACTIVITY 5

Simulating Active Transport

Click the **Experiment** menu and then choose **Active Transport.** The opening screen will appear in a few seconds (Figure 5B.5). This experiment screen resembles the osmosis experiment screen except that an ATP dispenser is substituted for the pressure meters atop the beakers. The (+) and (−) buttons control NaCl, KCl, and glucose concentrations in the dispensed solutions. You will use the Membrane Builder to build membranes containing glucose (facilitated diffusion) carrier proteins and active transport Na^+-K^+ (sodium-potassium) pumps.

In this experiment, we will assume that the left beaker represents the cell's interior and the right beaker represents the extracellular space. The Membrane Builder will insert the Na^+-K^+ (sodium-potassium) pumps into the membrane so Na^+ will be pumped toward the right (out of the cell) while K^+ is simultaneously moved to the left (into the cell).

1. In the Membrane Builder, adjust the number of glucose carriers and the number of sodium-potassium pumps to 500.

2. Click **Build Membrane,** and then drag the membrane to its position in the membrane holder between the beakers.

3. Adjust the NaCl concentration to be delivered to the left beaker to 9.00 mM, then click the **Dispense** button.

4. Adjust the KCl concentration to be delivered to the right beaker to 6.00 mM, then click **Dispense.**

5. Adjust the ATP dispenser to 1.00 mM, then click **Dispense ATP.** This action delivers the chosen ATP concentration to both sides of the membrane.

6. Adjust the timer to 60 min, and then click **Start.** Click **Record Data** after each run.

7. Click **Tools → Print Data** to print your data.

Watch the solute concentration windows at the side of each beaker for any changes in Na^+ and K^+ concentrations. The Na^+ transport rate stops before transport has completed. Why do you think that this happens?

_____

_____

What would happen if you did not dispense any ATP?

_____

_____

8. Click either **Flush** button to clean both beakers. Repeat steps 3 through 6, adjusting the ATP concentration to 3.00 mM in step 5. Click **Record Data** after each run.

Has the amount of Na^+ transported changed?

_____

_____

What would happen if you decreased the number of sodium-potassium pumps?

_____

_____

Explain how you could show that this phenomenon is not just simple diffusion. (Hint: Adjust the Na^+ concentration in the right beaker.)

_____

_____

_____

9. Click either **Flush** button to clean both beakers. Now repeat steps 1 through 6, dispensing 9.00 mM NaCl into the left beaker and 10.00 mM NaCl into the right beaker (instead of 6.00 mM KCl). Is Na^+ transport affected by this change? Explain your answer.

_____

_____

_____

FIGURE 5B.5 Opening screen of the Active Transport experiment.

What would happen to the rate of ion transport if we increased the number of sodium-potassium pump proteins?

_____

Would Na^+ and K^+ transport change if we added glucose solution?

_____

10. Click **Tools → Print Data** to print your recorded data.

Try adjusting various membrane and solute conditions and attempt to predict the outcome of experimental trials. For example, you could dispense 10 mM glucose into the right beaker instead of deionized water. ▮

Cell Transport Mechanisms and Permeability: Computer Simulation

NAME _____

LAB TIME/DATE _____

Simple Diffusion

1. The following refer to Activity 1: Simulating Dialysis (Simple Diffusion).

   Which solute(s) were able to pass through the 20 MWCO membrane?

   _____

   According to your results, which solute had the highest molecular weight? _____

   Which solute displayed the highest rate of diffusion through the 200 MWCO membrane? _____

   Using the data from Chart 1, explain the relationship between the rate of diffusion and the size of the solute.

   _____

Facilitated Diffusion

2. The following refer to Activity 2: Simulating Facilitated Diffusion.

   Did any of the substances travel against their concentration gradient? Explain why or why not.

   _____

   _____

   Using your results from Chart 2, what was the fastest rate of facilitated diffusion recorded? _____ Describe

   the conditions that were used to achieve this rate. _____

   _____

   Name two ways to increase the rate of glucose transport. _____

   _____

   Did NaCl affect glucose transport? _____

   Did NaCl require a transport protein for diffusion? Why or why not? _____

   _____

Osmotic Pressure

3. The following refer to Activity 3: Simulating Osmotic Pressure.

   For NaCl, which MWCO membrane(s) provided for the net movement of water without movement of NaCl?

   _____

   Explain how you determined this. (*Hint*: Correlate your results to the data in Chart 3.) _____

   _____

   For glucose, which MWCO membrane(s) provided for the net movement of glucose without net movement of water?

   _____

   Explain how you determined this. _____

   _____

   Is osmotic pressure generated if solutes diffuse freely? _____

   Explain how the solute concentration affects osmotic pressure. _____

   _____

Filtration

4. The following refer to Activity 4: Simulating Filtration.

   Using your results in Chart 4, which MWCO membrane had the greatest filtration rate? _____

   Explain the relationship between pore size and filtration rate. _____

   _____

   Which solute did not appear in the filtrate using any of the membranes? _____

   What is your prediction of the molecular weight of glucose compared to the other solutes in the solution? _____

   What happened when you increased the driving pressure? _____

   _____

   Explain why fluid flows from the capillaries of the kidneys into the kidney tubules.

   _____

   _____

   How do you think a decrease in blood pressure would affect filtration in the kidneys? _____

   _____

5. The following refer to Activity 5: Simulating Active Transport.

With 1 m*M* ATP added to the cell interior (left beaker) and the extracellular space (right beaker), was all of the Na$^+$ moved

into the extracellular space? Why or why not?_____

_____

Describe the effect of decreasing the number of sodium-potassium pumps. _____

Describe how you were able to show that the movement of sodium was due to active transport. _____

_____

Histology Atlas and Review Supplement

Exit   **Go To**   **Experiment**   **Tools**   **Help**

Sort by : System

▼ 📂 Cardiovascular
  📄 Aorta, Elastic Tissue, medium
  📄 Artery and Vein, medium
▼ 📂 📄 Artery and Vein, oil
  📄 Artery, high
  📄 Artery, medium
  📄 Blood Vessel, Endothelium, o
  📄 Blood, Basophil, oil
  📄 Blood, Eosinophil, oil
  📄 Blood, high
  📄 Blood, Lymphocyte, oil
  📄 Blood, Monocyte, oil
  📄 Blood, Neutrophil, oil
  📄 Cardiac Muscle, high
  📄 Cardiac Muscle, medium
  📄 Cardiac Muscle, oil
  📄 Cardiac Muscle, Purkinje Fibe
  📄 Elastic Tissue, Artery, high
  📄 Simple Squamous Epithelium
  📄 Skin, Capillaries, high
▶ 📁 Digestive
▶ 📁 Endocrine
▶ 📁 Integumentary
▶ 📁 Lymphatic
▶ 📁 Muscular
▶ 📁 Nervous

Blood Vessel, Endothelium, oil   Move the slide around by clicking and dragging below.

Lumen

Endothelium

Nuclei of endothelial cells

Connective tissue

Labels : ⦿ On ◯ Off

The innermost layer of the wall of all blood vessels is lined with endothelium, which is a layer of simple squamous epithelium. Note the flattened nuclei of the endothelial cells. Numerous round blood cells and one white blood cell (with dark, lobed nucleus) appear in the lumen of this blood vessel.

E xamining a specimen using a microscope accomplishes two goals: first, it gives you an understanding of the cellular organization of tissues, and second—perhaps even more importantly—it hones your observational skills. Because developing these skills is crucial in the understanding and eventual mastery of the scientific method, using this histology tutorial is not intended as a substitute for using the microscope. Instead, use it to gain an overall appreciation of the specimens and then make your own observations using your microscope.

You can use the Histology Atlas independently of this lab manual to explore the different tissue types found in the human body. Or, you can use it in conjunction with the printable Histology Review Supplement worksheets found in Exercise 6B on myA&P, for a review of histology slides specific to topics covered in the PhysioEx lab simulations.

To begin, choose **Exercise 6B: Histology Atlas and Review Supplement** from the drop-down menu and click **GO.** Then click **Histology Atlas** to browse the library of histology images. There are four main components of the tutorial. The *Sort by* drop-down menu is located at the top left. After you select a sorting option, the *slide menu* below will display all the folders and slide listings that are available. The *image viewer* is located on the right side with the *description box* directly below it.

Sorting and Locating Slides

You can search for slides by selecting any of the four sorting options from the *Sort by* drop-down menu. Click on the white menu bar to select from the following sorting options:

- **A-Z** Organizes slides alphabetically by title. Contains all of the slide listings in the tutorial.

- **System** Organizes slides into folders based on the body system they represent.

- **Tissue Type** Organizes slides into folders based on the tissue type(s) they represent.

- **Histology Review** Calls up the images used in the Histology Review Supplement worksheets that are available on the PhysioEx web site.

Certain histology images demonstrate more than one system or tissue type; therefore, an image might be found in multiple locations with different titles, labels, and descriptions, depending on the categories it is listed under.

All slide listings include magnification information at the end of the title. Because the exact magnification is variable depending on screen resolution, we have provided approximate magnifications instead:

- **Low** originally photographed at **40×**

- **Medium** originally photographed at **100×**

- **High** originally photographed at **400×**

- **Oil (immersion)** originally photographed at **1000×**

Viewing Slides and Labels

Click any listing in the *slide menu* to call up an image and description in the viewing area. The image may take a few seconds to load if you are using the web version. You can move the slide around in the viewer by clicking and dragging directly on the image.

You can show or hide the labels at any time by selecting the **On** or **Off** buttons in the *Labels* menu below the viewer. If a label appears to be out of the viewing area, keep in mind that you can see more of the image by clicking and dragging it in the *image viewer*.

Skeletal Muscle Physiology: Computer Simulation

OBJECTIVES

1. To define these terms used in describing muscle physiology: *multiple motor unit summation, maximal stimulus, treppe, wave summation,* and *tetanus.*

2. To identify two ways that the mode of stimulation can affect muscle force production.

3. To plot a graph relating stimulus strength and twitch force to illustrate graded muscle response.

4. To explain how slow, smooth, sustained contraction is possible in a skeletal muscle.

5. To graphically understand the relationships between passive, active, and total forces.

6. To identify the conditions under which muscle contraction is isometric or isotonic.

7. To describe in terms of length and force the transitions between isometric and isotonic conditions during a single muscle twitch.

8. To describe the effects of resistance and starting length on the initial velocity of shortening.

9. To explain why muscle force remains constant during isotonic shortening.

10. To explain experimental results in terms of muscle structure.

Skeletal muscles are composed of hundreds to thousands of individual cells, each doing their share of work in the production of force. As their name suggests, skeletal muscles move the skeleton. Skeletal muscles are remarkable machines; while allowing us the manual dexterity to create magnificent works of art, they are also capable of generating the brute force needed to lift a 100-lb. sack of concrete. When a skeletal muscle from an experimental animal is electrically stimulated, it behaves in the same way as a stimulated muscle in the intact body, that is, in vivo. Hence, such an experiment gives us valuable insight into muscle behavior.

This set of computer simulations demonstrates many important physiological concepts of skeletal muscle contraction. The program graphically provides all the equipment and materials necessary for you, the investigator, to set up experimental conditions and observe the results. In student-conducted laboratory investigations, there are many ways to approach a problem, and the same is true of these simulations. The instructions will guide you in your investigation, but you should also try out alternative approaches to gain insight into the logical methods used in scientific experimentation.

Try this approach: As you work through the simulations for the first time, follow the instructions closely and answer the questions posed as you go. Then try asking "What if . . . ?" questions to test the validity of your hypotheses. The major advantages of these computer simulations are that the muscle cannot be accidentally damaged, lab equipment will not break down at the worst possible time, and you will have ample time to think critically about the processes being investigated.

Because you will be working with a simulated muscle and an oscilloscope display, you need to watch both carefully during the experiments. Think about what is happening in each situation. You need to understand how you are experimentally manipulating the muscle in order to understand your results.

Electrical Stimulation

A contracting skeletal muscle will produce force and/or shortening when nervous or electrical stimulation is applied. The force generated by a whole muscle reflects the number of motor units firing at a given time. Strong muscle contraction implies that many motor units are activated and each unit has maximally contracted. Weak contraction means that few motor units are active; however, the activated units are maximally contracted. By increasing the number of motor units firing, we can produce a steady increase in muscle force, a process called **recruitment** or **multiple motor unit summation.**

Regardless of the number of motor units activated, a single contraction of skeletal muscle is called a muscle twitch (Figure 16B.1b). A tracing of a muscle twitch is divided into three phases: latent, contraction, and relaxation. The **latent period** is a short period between the time of stimulation and the beginning of contraction. Although no force is generated during this interval, chemical changes occur intracellularly in preparation for contraction, such as the release of calcium from the sarcoplasmic reticulum. During contraction, the myofilaments slide past each other, and the muscle shortens. Relaxation takes place when contraction has ended and the muscle returns to its normal resting state and length.

The first activity you will conduct simulates an **isometric,** or **fixed length, contraction** of an isolated skeletal muscle. This activity allows you to investigate how the strength and frequency of an electrical stimulus affect whole muscle function. Note that these simulations involve indirect stimulation by an electrode placed on the surface of the muscle. This differs from the situation in vivo where each fiber in the muscle receives direct stimulation via a nerve ending. In other words, increasing the intensity of the electrical stimulation mimics how the nervous system increases the number of motor units activated.

Single Stimulus

Choose **Exercise 16B: Skeletal Muscle Physiology** from the drop-down menu and click **GO.** Before you perform the activities, watch the **Skeletal Muscle** video to gain an appreciation for the preparation required for these experiments. Then click **Single Stimulus.** The opening screen will appear in a few seconds (Figure 16B.1a). The oscilloscope display, the grid at the top of the screen, is the most important part of the screen because it graphically displays the contraction data for analysis. Time is displayed on the horizontal axis. A full sweep is initially set at 200 msec. However, you can adjust the sweep time from 200 msec to 1000 msec by clicking and dragging the **200** msec button at the lower right corner of the oscilloscope display to the left to a new position on the time axis. The force (in grams) produced by muscle contraction is displayed on the vertical axis. Clicking the **Clear Tracings** button at the bottom right of the oscilloscope erases all muscle twitch tracings from the oscilloscope display.

The *electrical stimulator* is the equipment seen just beneath the oscilloscope display. Clicking **Stimulate** delivers the electrical shock to the muscle through the electrodes lying on the surface of the muscle. Stimulus voltage is set by clicking the (+) or (−) buttons next to the voltage window. Three small windows to the right of the Stimulate button display the force measurements. *Active force* is produced during muscle contraction, while *passive force* results from the muscle being stretched (much like a rubber band). The *total force* is the sum of active and passive forces. The red arrow at the left of the oscilloscope display is an indicator of passive force. After the muscle is stimulated, the **Measure** button at the right edge of the electrical stimulator becomes active. When you click the Measure button, a vertical orange line appears at the left edge of the oscilloscope display. Clicking the arrow buttons below the Measure button moves the orange line horizontally across the screen. The Time window displays the difference in time between the zero point on the X-axis and the intersection between the orange measure line and the muscle twitch tracing.

The muscle is suspended in the support stand to the left of the oscilloscope display. The hook through the upper tendon of the muscle is part of the force transducer, which measures the force produced by the muscle. The hook through the lower tendon secures the muscle in place. The weight cabinet just below the muscle support stand is not active in this experiment; it contains weights you will use in the isotonic contraction part of the simulation. You can adjust the starting length of the muscle by clicking the (+) or (−) buttons located next to the Muscle Length display window.

When you click the **Record Data** button in the data collection unit below the electrical stimulator, your data is recorded in the computer's memory and is displayed in the data grid at the bottom of the screen. Data displayed in the data grid include the voltage, muscle length, and active, passive, and total force measurements. If you are not satisfied with a single run, you can click **Delete Line** to erase a single line of data. To start over from the beginning and remove all data, Click the **Clear Table** button.

ACTIVITY 1

Practicing Generating a Tracing

1. Click the **Stimulate** button once. Because the beginning voltage is set to zero, no muscle activity should result. You will see a blue line moving across the bottom of the oscilloscope display. This blue line will indicate muscle force in the experiments. If the tracings move too slowly across the screen, click and hold the **200** button at the lower right corner of the oscilloscope and drag it to the left to the 40 msec mark and release it. This action resets the total sweep time to 1000 msec to speed up the display time.

2. Click and hold the (+) button beneath the Stimulate button until the voltage window reads 3.0 volts. Click **Stimulate** once. You will see the muscle react, and a contraction tracing will appear on the screen. Notice that the muscle tracing color alternates between blue and yellow each time you click the Stimulate button to enhance the visual difference between twitch tracings. You can click the **Clear Tracings** button as needed to clean up the oscilloscope display. To retain your data, click the **Record Data** button at the end of each stimulus.

3. Change the voltage to 5.0 volts, and click **Stimulate** again. Notice how the force of contraction also changes. Identify the latent, contraction, and relaxation phases in the tracings.

4. You may print your data by clicking **Tools → Print Data.** You may also print out hard copies of the graphs you generate by clicking **Tools → Print Graph.**

Feel free to experiment with anything that comes to mind to get a sense of how whole muscle responds to an electrical stimulus. ▬

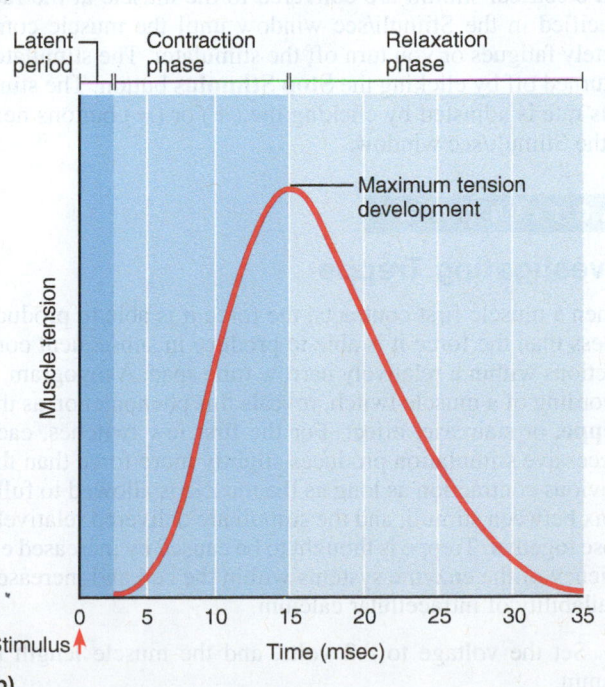

FIGURE 16B.1 **Single stimulus and muscle twitch.**
(a) Opening screen of the Single Stimulus experiment. **(b)** The muscle twitch: myogram of an isometric twitch contraction.

ACTIVITY 2

Determining the Latent Period

1. Click **Clear Tracings** to erase the oscilloscope display. The voltage should be set to 5.0 volts.

2. Drag the **200** msec button to the right edge of the oscilloscope.

3. Click the **Stimulate** button once, and allow the tracing to complete.

4. When you measure the length of the latent period from a printed graph, you measure the time between the application of the stimulus and the beginning of the first observable response (increase in force). The computer can't "look ahead," anticipating the change in active force. To measure the length of the latent period using the computer, click the **Measure** button. Then click the right arrow button next to the **Time** window repeatedly until you notice the first increase in the Active Force window. This takes you beyond the actual length of the latent period. Now click the left arrow button next to the **Time** window until the Active Force window again reads zero. At this point the computer is measuring the time between the application of the stimulus and the last point where the active force is zero (just prior to contraction).

How long is the latent period? _____ msec

What occurs in the muscle during this apparent lack of activity?

_____

_____ ▬

The Graded Muscle Response to Increased Stimulus Intensity

As the stimulus to a muscle is increased, the amount of force produced by the muscle also increases. As more voltage is delivered to the whole muscle, more muscle fibers are activated, and the total force produced by the muscle is increased. Maximal contraction occurs when all the muscle cells have been activated. Any stimulation beyond this voltage will not increase the force of contraction. This experiment mimics muscle activity in vivo, where the recruitment of additional motor units increases the total force produced. This phenomenon is called *multiple motor unit summation* or *recruitment*.

ACTIVITY 3

Investigating Graded Muscle Response to Increased Stimulus Intensity

1. Click **Clear Tracings** if there are tracings on your screen.

2. Set the voltage to 0.0, and click **Stimulate.**

3. Click **Record Data.** If you decide to redo a single stimulus, choose the data line in the grid and click **Delete Line** to erase that single line of data. If you want to repeat the entire experiment, click the **Clear Table** button to erase all data recorded to that point.

4. Repeat steps 2 and 3, increasing the voltage by 0.5 each time until you reach the maximum voltage of 10.0. Be sure to select **Record Data** each time.

5. Observe the twitch tracings. Click the **Tools** menu and then choose **Plot Data.**

6. Use the slider bars to display Active Force on the Y-axis and Voltage on the X-axis.

7. Use your graph to answer the following questions:

What is the minimal, or threshold, stimulus? _____ V

What is the maximal stimulus? _____ V

How can you explain the increase in force that you observe?

_____

_____

8. Click **Print Plot** at the top left corner of the Plot Data window to print a hard copy of the graph. When finished, click the X at the top right of the plot window.

9. Click **Tools → Print Data** to print your data. ▬

Multiple Stimulus

Choose **Multiple Stimulus** from the **Experiment** menu. The opening screen will appear in a few seconds (Figure 16B.2).

The only significant change to the on-screen equipment is found in the electrical stimulator. The measuring equipment has been removed and other controls have been added: The **Multiple Stimulus** button is a toggle that allows you to alternately start and stop the electrical stimulator. When you first click Multiple Stimulus, its name changes to Stop Stimulus, and electrical stimuli are delivered to the muscle at the rate specified in the Stimuli/sec window until the muscle completely fatigues or you turn off the stimulator. The stimulator is turned off by clicking the **Stop Stimulus** button. The stimulus rate is adjusted by clicking the $(+)$ or $(-)$ buttons next to the Stimuli/sec window.

ACTIVITY 4

Investigating Treppe

When a muscle first contracts, the force it is able to produce is less than the force it is able to produce in subsequent contractions within a relatively narrow time span. A myogram, a recording of a muscle twitch, reveals this phenomenon as the **treppe,** or staircase, effect. For the first few twitches, each successive stimulation produces slightly more force than the previous contraction as long as the muscle is allowed to fully relax between stimuli, and the stimuli are delivered relatively close together. Treppe is thought to be caused by increased efficiency of the enzyme systems within the cell and increased availability of intracellular calcium.

1. Set the voltage to 8.2 volts, and the muscle length to 75 mm.

2. Drag the **200** msec button to the center of the X-axis time range.

FIGURE 16B.2 Opening screen of the Multiple Stimulus experiment.

3. Be sure that you fully understand the following three steps before you proceed.

- Click **Single Stimulus.** Watch the twitch tracing carefully.

- After the tracing shows that the muscle has completely relaxed, immediately click **Single Stimulus** again.

- When the second twitch completes, click **Single Stimulus** once more and allow the tracing to complete.

4. Click **Tools → Print Graph.**

What happens to force production with each subsequent stimulus?

_____

_____

Investigating Wave Summation

As demonstrated in Activity 3 with single stimuli, multiple motor unit summation is one way to increase the amount of force produced by muscle. Multiple motor unit summation relied on increased stimulus *intensity* in that simulation. Another way to increase force is by wave, or temporal, summation. **Wave summation** is achieved by increasing the stimulus *frequency*, or rate of stimulus delivery to the muscle. Wave summation occurs because the muscle is already in a partially contracted state when subsequent stimuli are delivered.

Tetanus can be considered an extreme form of wave summation that results in a steady, sustained contraction. In effect, the muscle does not have any chance to relax because it is being stimulated at such a high frequency. This fuses the force peaks so that we observe a smooth tracing.

1. Click **Clear Tracings** to erase the oscilloscope display.

2. Set and keep the voltage at the maximal stimulus (8.2 volts) and the muscle length at 75 mm.

3. Drag the **200** msec button to the right edge of the oscilloscope display unless you are using a slow computer.

4. Click **Single Stimulus,** and then click **Single Stimulus** again when the muscle has relaxed about halfway. In this experiment, unlike the previous one, you will not allow the muscle to completely relax.

You may click **Tools → Print Graph** any time you want to print graphs generated during this activity.

Is the peak force produced in the second contraction greater

than that produced by the first stimulus? _____

5. Try stimulating again at greater frequencies by clicking the **Single Stimulus** button several times in rapid succession.

Is the total force production even greater? _____

6. In order to produce smooth, sustained muscle contraction at Active Force = 2 gms, do you think you will need to increase or decrease the voltage?

_____

_____

Change the voltage to test your hypothesis and try rapidly clicking **Single Stimulus** several times.

At what voltage were you able to achieve Active Force = 2 gms?

_____

_____

7. How does the frequency of stimulation affect the amount of force generated by the muscle? *Hint:* Compare the force generated from a single click and from rapidly clicking **Single Stimulus** several times.

_____

_____

ACTIVITY 6

Investigating Fusion Frequency/Tetanus

1. Click **Clear Tracings** to erase the oscilloscope display.

2. Set the voltage to 8.2 volts, and the muscle length to 75 mm.

3. Adjust the stimulus rate to 30 stimuli/sec.

4. The following steps constitute a single "run." Become familiar with the procedure for completing a run before continuing.

- Click **Multiple Stimulus.**
- When the tracing is close to the right side of the screen, click **Stop Stimulus** to turn off the stimulator.
- Click **Record Data** to retain your data in the grid at the bottom of the screen and in the computer's memory. Click **Tools → Print Graph** to print a hard copy of your graph at any point during this activity.

If you decide to redo a single run, choose the data line in the grid and click **Delete Line** to erase that single line of data. If you want to repeat the entire experiment, click the **Clear Table** button to erase all data recorded thus far.

Describe the appearance of the tracing.

_____

_____

_____

5. Repeat steps 3 and 4, increasing the stimulation rate by 10 stimuli/sec each time up to 150 stimuli/sec.

How do the tracings change as the stimulus rate is increased?

_____

_____

6. When you have finished observing the twitch tracings, click the **Tools** menu, and then choose **Plot Data.**

7. Set the Y-axis slider to display Active Force and the X-axis slider to display Stimuli/sec.

From your graph, estimate the stimulus rate above which there appears to be no significant increase in force.

_____stimuli/sec

This rate is the *fusion frequency,* also called tetanus.

8. Click **Print Plot** at the top left of the Plot Data window. When finished, click the X at the top right of the plot window.

9. Reset the stimulus rate to the fusion frequency identified in step 7.

10. Try to produce a smooth contraction at Force = 2 gms and Force = 3 gms by adjusting only the stimulus intensity, or voltage, using the following procedure.

- Decrease the voltage to a starting point of 1.0 volt, and click **Multiple Stimulus.**
- Click **Stop Stimulus** to turn off the stimulator when the tracing is near the right side of the oscilloscope display.
- If the force produced is not smooth and continuous at the desired level of force, increase the voltage in 0.1-volt increments and stimulate as above until you achieve a smooth force at 2 gms and again at 3 gms.

What stimulus intensity produced smooth force at Force = 2 gms?

_____ V

Which intensity produced smooth contraction at Force = 3 gms?

_____ V

Explain what must happen to the intensity and frequency of the stimulus to achieve smooth contraction at different force levels.

_____

_____

_____

_____

_____

_____ ▬

Investigating Muscle Fatigue

A prolonged period of sustained contraction will result in **muscle fatigue,** a condition in which the tissue has lost its ability to contract. Fatigue results when a muscle cell's ATP consumption is faster than its production. Consequently, increasingly fewer ATP molecules are available for the contractile parts within the muscle cell.

1. Click **Clear Tracings** to erase the oscilloscope display.

2. Set the voltage to 8.2 volts, and the muscle length to 75 mm.

3. Adjust the stimulus rate to 120 stimuli/sec.

4. Click **Multiple Stimulus,** allow the tracing to sweep through three screens, and then click **Stop Stimulus** to stop the stimulator.

Click **Tools → Print Graph** at any time to print graphs during this activity. Click **Tools → Print Data** to print your data.

Why does the force begin to decrease with time? Note that a decrease in force indicates muscle fatigue.

_____

_____

5. Click **Clear Tracings** to erase the oscilloscope display. Keep the same settings as before.

6. You will be clicking **Multiple Stimulus** on and off three times to demonstrate fatigue with recovery. Read the steps below before proceeding.

*   Click **Multiple Stimulus.**

*   When the tracing reaches the middle of the screen, briefly turn off the stimulator by clicking **Stop Stimulus,** then immediately click **Multiple Stimulus** again.

*   You will see a dip in the force tracing where you turned the stimulator off and then on again. The force tracing will continue to drop as the muscle fatigues.

*   Before the muscle fatigues completely, repeat the on/off cycle twice more without clearing the screen.

Turning the stimulator off allows a small measure of recovery. The muscle will produce force for a longer period if the stimulator is briefly turned off than if the stimulations were allowed to continue without interruption. Explain why.

7. To see the difference between continuous multiple stimulation and multiple stimulation with recovery, click **Multiple Stimulus** and let the tracing fall without interruption to zero force. This tracing will follow the original myogram exactly until the first "dip" is encountered, after which you will notice a difference in the amount of force produced between the two runs.

Describe the difference between the current tracing and the myogram generated in step 6.

_____

_____

_____

_____

_____

_____

_____ ▬

Isometric Contraction

Isometric contraction is the condition in which muscle length does not change regardless of the amount of force generated by the muscle (*iso* = same, *metric* = length). This is accomplished experimentally by keeping both ends of the muscle in a fixed position while stimulating it electrically. Resting length (length of the muscle before contraction) is an important factor in determining the amount of force that a muscle can develop. **Passive force** is generated by stretching the muscle and is due to the elastic properties of the tissue itself. This passive force is largely due to the protein titin, which acts as a molecular bungee cord. **Active force** is generated by the physiological contraction of the muscle. Think of the muscle as having two force properties: it exerts passive force when it is stretched (like a rubber band exerts passive force) and active force when it contracts. Total force is the sum of passive and active forces, and it is what we experimentally measure.

This simulation allows you to set the resting length of the experimental muscle and stimulate it with individual maximal stimulus shocks. A graph relating the forces generated to the length of the muscle will be automatically plotted as you stimulate the muscle. The results of this simulation can then be applied to human muscles in order to understand how optimum resting length will result in maximum force production. In order to understand why muscle tissue behaves as it does, it is necessary to comprehend contraction at the cellular level. *Hint:* If you have difficulty understanding the results of this exercise, review the sliding filament model of muscle contraction. Then think in terms of sarcomeres that are too short, those that are too long, and those that have the ideal length-tension relationship.

FIGURE 16B.3 Opening screen of the Isometric Contraction experiment.

Choose **Isometric Contraction** from the **Experiment** menu. The opening screen will appear in a few seconds (Figure 16B.3). Notice that the oscilloscope is now divided into two parts. The left side of the scope displays the muscle twitch tracing. The active, passive, and total force data points are plotted on the right side of the screen.

Investigating Isometric Contraction

1. Set the voltage to the maximal stimulus (8.2 volts), and the muscle length to 75 mm.

2. To see how the equipment works, stimulate once by clicking **Stimulate.** You should see a single muscle twitch tracing on the left oscilloscope display and three data points representing active, passive, and total force on the right display. The yellow box represents the total force, and the red dot it contains symbolizes the superimposed active force. The green square represents the passive force data point.

3. Try adjusting the muscle length by clicking the (+) or (−) buttons located next to the Muscle Length window, and watch the effect on the muscle.

4. When you feel comfortable with the equipment, click **Clear Tracings** and **Clear Plot.**

5. Now stimulate at different muscle lengths using the following procedure.

- Shorten the muscle to a length of 50 mm by clicking the (−) button next to the Muscle Length window.

- Click **Stimulate** and, when the tracing is complete, click **Record Data.**

- Repeat the **Stimulate** and **Record Data** sequence, increasing the muscle length by 2 mm each time until you reach the maximum muscle length of 100 mm.

6. Carefully examine the active, passive, and total force plots in the right oscilloscope display.

7. Click **Tools → Print Data** to print your data.

What happens to the passive and active forces as the muscle length is increased from 50 mm to 100 mm?

Passive force:

_____

_____

Active force:

_____

_____

_____

Total force:

_____

_____

_____

Explain the dip in the total force curve. (*Hint:* Keep in mind you are measuring the sum of active and passive forces.)

_____

_____

_____

_____

Isotonic Contraction

During **isotonic contraction**, muscle length changes, but the force produced stays the same (*iso* = same, *tonic* = force). Unlike the isometric exercise in which both ends of the muscle are held in a fixed position, one end of the muscle remains free in the isotonic contraction exercise. Different weights can then be attached to the free end while the other end is fixed in position on the force transducer. If the weight is not too great, the muscle will be able to lift it with a certain velocity. You can think of lifting an object from the floor as an example: if the object is light it can be lifted quickly (high velocity), whereas a heavier weight will be lifted with a slower velocity. Try to transfer the idea of what is happening in the simulation to the muscles of your arm when you lift a weight. The two important variables in this exercise are starting length of the muscle and resistance (weight) applied. You have already examined the effect of starting length on muscle force production in the previous exercise. Now you will change both muscle length and resistance to investigate how such changes affect the speed of skeletal muscle shortening. Both variables can be independently altered, and the results are graphically presented on the screen.

Choose **Isotonic Contraction** from the **Experiment** menu. The opening screen will appear in a few seconds (Figure 16B.4). The general operation of the equipment is the same as in the previous experiments. In this simulation, the weight cabinet doors are open. You will attach weights to the lower tendon of the muscle by clicking and holding the mouse on any weight in the cabinet and then dragging-and-

dropping the weight's hook onto the lower tendon. The Muscle Length window displays the length achieved when the muscle is stretched by hanging a weight from its lower tendon. You can click the (+) and (−) buttons next to the Platform Height window to change the position of the platform on which the weight rests. Click on the weight again to automatically return it to the weight cabinet. The electrical stimulator displays the initial velocity of muscle shortening in the Velocity window to the right of the Voltage control.

ACTIVITY 9

Investigating the Effect of Load on Skeletal Muscle

1.   Set the voltage to the maximal stimulus (8.2 volts).

2.   Drag-and-drop the 0.5-g weight onto the muscle's lower tendon.

3.   Platform height should be 75 mm.

4.   Click **Stimulate** and simultaneously watch the muscle action and the oscilloscope tracing.

5.   Click the **Record Data** button to retain and display the data in the grid.

What do you see happening to the muscle during the flat part of the tracing? Click **Stimulate** to repeat if you wish to see the muscle action again.

_____

_____

Does the force the muscle produces change during the flat part of the tracing (increase, decrease, or stay the same)?

_____

6.   Return the 0.5-g weight to the cabinet. Drag the 1.5-g weight to the muscle. Click **Stimulate,** and then click **Record Data.**

Which of the two weights used so far results in the highest initial velocity of shortening?

Weight _____ g

Velocity _____ mm/sec

7.   Repeat step 6 for the remaining two weights.

Weight _____ g

Velocity _____ mm/sec

Weight _____ g

Velocity _____ mm/sec

8.   Choose **Plot Data** from the **Tools** menu.

FIGURE 16B.4 Opening screen of the Isotonic Contraction experiment.

9. Set Weight as the X-axis and Total Force as the Y-axis by dragging the slider bars. Click **Print Plot** if you wish to print the graph.

What does the plot reveal about the relationship between resistance and the initial velocity of shortening?

_____

_____

_____

10. Close the plot window. If you wish, click **Tools → Print Data** to print your data.

11. Click **Clear Table** in the data control unit at the bottom of the screen. Click **Yes** when you are asked if you want to erase all data in the table.

12. Return the current weight to the weight cabinet.

13. Attach the 1.5-g weight to the muscle and run through the range of starting lengths from 60–90 mm in 5-mm increments. Be sure to click **Record Data** after each stimulus.

14. After all runs have been completed, choose **Plot Data** from the **Tools** menu.

15. Set Length as the X-axis and Velocity as the Y-axis by dragging the slider bars. Click **Print Plot** if you wish to print the graph.

Describe the relationship between starting length and initial velocity of shortening.

_____

_____

_____

_____

Histology Review Supplement

For a review of skeletal muscle tissue, go to **Exercise 6B: Histology Atlas and Review** on **myA&P** to print out the **Skeletal Muscle Tissue Review** worksheet.

Skeletal Muscle Physiology: Computer Simulation

NAME _____

LAB TIME/DATE _____

Electrical Stimulation

1. Name each phase of a typical muscle twitch, and, on the following line, describe what is happening in each phase.

a. _____

_____

b. _____

_____

c. _____

_____

2. In Activity 2, how long was the latent period? _____ msec

Describe the chemical changes that are occurring during this period. _____

_____

_____

The Graded Muscle Response to Increased Stimulus Intensity

3. From Activity 3, describe the effect of increasing the voltage. What happened to the force generated, and why did this change

occur? _____

_____

_____

4. How does this change occur in vivo? _____

_____

_____

5. In Activity 4, you looked at the effect of stimulating the muscle multiple times in a short period with complete relaxation between the stimuli.

Describe the force of contraction with each subsequent stimulus. _____

_____

6. Describe the chemical changes that are thought to correlate to this change in vivo.

_____

_____

7. In Activity 5, what was the effect of increasing the frequency of stimulation?

_____

_____

8. Compare and contrast wave summation with recruitment (multiple motor unit summation). How are they similar? How was each achieved in the simulation?

_____

_____

_____

9. Explain how wave summation and recruitment are achieved in vivo.

_____

_____

10. For Activity 6, explain how you were able to achieve smooth contraction at a given force level. _____

_____

11. In Activity 7, explain why the force of the muscle decreased over time during uninterrupted stimulation. Describe the

multiple causes of this phenomenon, which occurs in vivo with prolonged use of a muscle. _____

_____

_____

Isometric Contraction

12. In Activity 8, at what length of the muscle does the passive force start to increase?

_____

13. Explain what happens to the active force with an increase in the muscle length.

_____

14. Explain what happens to the active force with a decrease in the muscle length.

_____

15. Explain what is happening in the sarcomere that results in the changes in total force when the muscle length changes.

_____

_____

Isotonic Contraction

16. In Activity 9, which weight resulted in the highest initial velocity of shortening? _____

17. Explain the relationship between the amount of resistance and the initial velocity of shortening.

_____

18. Explain why it will take you longer to perform 10 repetitions lifting a 20-pound weight than it would to perform the same

number of repetitions with a 5-pound weight. _____

_____

Neurophysiology of Nerve Impulses: Computer Simulation

OBJECTIVES

1. To define the following terms: *irritability, conductivity, resting membrane potential, polarized, sodium-potassium pump, threshold stimulus, depolarization, action potential, repolarization, hyperpolarization, absolute refractory period, relative refractory period, nerve impulse, compound nerve action potential,* and *conduction velocity.*

2. To list at least four different stimuli capable of generating an action potential.

3. To list at least two agents capable of inhibiting an action potential.

4. To describe the relationship between nerve size and conduction velocity.

5. To describe the relationship between nerve myelination and conduction velocity.

Neurons have two major physiological properties: **excitability,** or the ability to respond to stimuli and convert them into nerve impulses, and **conductivity,** the ability to transmit an impulse (in this case, to take the neural impulse and pass it along the cell membrane). In the resting neuron (that is, a neuron that does not have any neural impulses), the exterior of the cell membrane is positively charged and the interior is negatively charged relative to the outside. This difference in electrical charge across the plasma membrane is referred to as the **resting membrane potential,** and the membrane is said to be **polarized.** The **sodium-potassium pump** in the membrane maintains the difference in electrical charge established by diffusion of ions. This active transport mechanism moves 3 sodium ions (Na^+) out of the cell while moving in 2 potassium ions (K^+). Therefore, the major cation (positively charged ion) outside the cell in the extracellular fluid is Na^+, and the major cation inside the cell is K^+. The inner surface of the cell membrane is more negative than the outer surface, mainly because of intracellular proteins, which, at body pH, tend to be negatively charged.

The resting membrane potential can be measured with a voltmeter by putting a recording electrode just inside the cell membrane with a reference, or ground,

Voltmeter

−70mV

Plasma membrane

Microelectrode outside cell

Microelectrode inside cell

Axon

Neuron

FIGURE 18B.1
Resting membrane potential is measured with a voltmeter.

FIGURE 18B.2 The nerve impulse. (a) Resting membrane potential (−70 mV). There is an excess of positive ions outside the cell, with Na⁺ the predominant ion in extracellular fluid and K⁺ the predominant intracellular ion. The plasma membrane has a low permeability to Na⁺. **(b)** Depolarization—reversal of the resting potential. Application of a stimulus changes the membrane permeability, and Na⁺ ions diffuse rapidly into the cell. **(c)** Generation of the action potential or nerve impulse. If the stimulus is of adequate intensity, the depolarization wave spreads rapidly along the entire length of the membrane. **(d)** Repolarization—reestablishment of the resting potential. The negative charge on the internal plasma membrane surface and the positive charge on its external surface are reestablished by diffusion of K⁺ out of the cell, proceeding in the same direction as in depolarization. **(e)** The original ionic concentrations of the resting state are restored by the sodium-potassium pump. **(f)** A tracing of an action potential.

electrode outside the membrane (Figure 18B.1). In the giant squid axon (on which most early neural research was conducted), or in the frog axon that will be used in this exercise, the resting membrane potential is measured at –70 millivolts (mV). (In humans, the resting membrane potential typically measures between– 40 mV and –90mV.)

The Nerve Impulse

When a neuron is activated by a stimulus of adequate intensity, known as a **threshold stimulus,** the membrane at its *trigger zone,* typically the axon hillock, briefly becomes more permeable to Na⁺ ions (sodium ion channels in the cell membrane open). Na+ rushes into the cell, increasing the number of positive ions inside the cell and changing the membrane polarity. The interior surface of the membrane becomes less negative and the exterior surface becomes less positive, a phenomenon called **depolarization** (Figure 18B.2b). When depolarization reaches a certain point called **threshold,** an **action potential** is initiated (Figure 18B.2c) and the polarity of the membrane reverses.

When the membrane depolarizes, the resting membrane potential of -70 mV becomes less negative. When the membrane potential reaches 0 mV, indicating that there is no charge difference across the membrane, the sodium ion channels start to close, and potassium ion channels open. By the time the sodium ion channels finally close, the membrane potential has reached $+35$ mV. The opening of the potassium ion channels allows K^+ to flow out of the cell down its electrochemical gradient—remember, ions of like charge are repelled from each other. The flow of K^+ out of the cell causes the membrane potential to move in a negative direction. This is referred to as **repolarization** (Figure 18B.2d). This repolarization occurs within a millisecond of the initial sodium influx and reestablishes the resting membrane potential. Actually, by the time the potassium ion channels close, the cell membrane has undergone a **hyperpolarization,** slipping to perhaps -75 mV. With the channels closed, the membrane potential is quickly returned to the normal resting membrane potential.

When the sodium ion channels are open, the membrane is totally insensitive to additional stimuli, regardless of the force of stimulus. The cell is in what is called the **absolute refractory period.** During repolarization, the membrane may be stimulated if a very strong stimulus is used. This period is called the **relative refractory period.**

The action potential, once started, is self-propagating, spreading rapidly along the neuron membrane. The action potential is a *phenomenon*, *all-or-none*, in which the neuron membrane either depolarizes to threshold and the action potential is generated, or it does not. In neurons, the action potential is also called a **nerve impulse.** When it reaches the axon terminal, it triggers the release of neurotransmitters into the synaptic cleft. Depending on the situation, the neurotransmitter will either excite or inhibit the postsynaptic neuron.

To study nerve physiology, we will use a frog nerve and several electronic instruments. The first instrument is the *electronic stimulator*. Nerves can be stimulated by chemicals, touch, or electric shock. The electronic stimulator administers an electric shock that is pure direct current (DC) and allows duration, frequency, and voltage of the shock to be precisely controlled. The stimulator has two output terminals; the positive terminal is red and the negative terminal is black. Voltage leaves the stimulator via the red terminal, passes through the item to be stimulated (in this case, the nerve), and returns to the stimulator at the black terminal to complete the circuit.

The second instrument is the **oscilloscope,** an instrument that measures voltage changes over a period of time. The face of the oscilloscope is similar to a black-and-white television screen. The screen of the oscilloscope is the front of a tube with a filament at the other end. The filament is heated and gives off a beam of electrons that passes to the front of the tube. Electronic circuitry allows the electron beam to be brought across the screen in preset time intervals. When the electrons hit the phosphorescent material on the inside of the screen, a spot on the screen glows. When we apply a stimulus to a nerve, the oscilloscope screen will display one of the following three results: no response, a flat line, or a graph with

a peak. A graph with a peak indicates that an action potential has been generated.

While performing the following experiments, keep in mind that you are working with a nerve, which consists of many neurons—you are not working with just a single neuron. The action potential you will see on the oscilloscope screen reflects the cumulative action potentials of all the neurons in the nerve, called a **compound nerve action potential.** Although an action potential follows the all-or-none law within a single neuron, it does not necessarily follow this law within an entire nerve. When you electrically stimulate a nerve at a given voltage, the stimulus may result in the depolarization of most of the neurons but not necessarily all of them. To achieve depolarization of *all* of the neurons, a higher stimulus voltage may be needed.

Eliciting (Generating) a Nerve Impulse

In the following experiments, you will investigate what kinds of stimuli trigger an action potential. To begin, select **Exercise 18B: Neurophysiology of Nerve Impulses** from the drop-down menu and click **GO.** Before you perform the activities, watch the **Nerve Impulses** video to see how ambient activitiy is measured. Then click **Eliciting a Nerve Impulse.** The opening screen will appear in a few seconds (Figure 18B.3). Note that a sciatic nerve from a frog has been placed into the nerve chamber. Leads go from the stimulator output to the nerve chamber, the vertical box on the left side. Leads also go from the nerve chamber to the oscilloscope. Notice that these leads are red and black. The current travels along the red lead to the nerve. When the nerve depolarizes, it will generate an electrical current that travels along the red wire to the oscilloscope and back to the nerve along the black wire.

ACTIVITY 1

Electrical Stimulation

1. Set the voltage at 1.0 V by clicking the (+) button next to the **Voltage** display.

2. Click **Single Stimulus.**

Do you see any kind of response on the oscilloscope screen?

_____

If you saw no response, or a flat line indicating no action potential, click the **Clear** button on the oscilloscope, increase the voltage, and click **Single Stimulus** again until you see a trace (deflection of the line) that indicates an action potential.

What was the *threshold voltage,* that is, the voltage at which

you first saw an action potential? _____ V

Click **Record Data** on the data collection box to record your results.

3. If you wish to print your graph, click **Tools** and then **Print Graph.** You may do this each time you generate a graph on the oscilloscope screen.

FIGURE 18B.3 Opening screen of the Eliciting a Nerve Impulse experiment.

4.   Increase the voltage by 0.5 V, and click **Single Stimulus.**

How does this tracing compare to the one trace that was generated at the threshold voltage? (Hint: Look very carefully at the tracings.)

_____

_____

What reason can you give for the change?

_____

_____

_____

Click **Record Data** on the data collection box to record your results.

5.   Continue to increase the voltage by 0.5 V and to click **Single Stimulus** until you find the point beyond which no further increase occurs in the peak of the action potential trace.

Record this maximal voltage here: _____ V

Click **Record Data** to record your results. ■

Now that we have seen that an electrical impulse can cause an action potential, let's try some other methods of stimulating a nerve.

Mechanical Stimulation

1.   Click the **Clear** button on the oscilloscope.

2.   Using the mouse, click the glass rod located on the bottom shelf on the left side of the screen, and drag it over to the nerve. When the glass rod is over the nerve, release the mouse

button to indicate that the rod is now touching the nerve. What do you see on the oscilloscope screen?

_____

How does this tracing compare with the other tracings that you have generated?

_____

_____

Click **Record Data** to record your results. Leave the graph on the screen so that you can compare it to the graph you will generate in the next activity. ▬

ACTIVITY 3

Thermal Stimulation

Click on the glass rod and drag it to the heater, releasing the mouse button. Click the **Heat** button. When the rod turns red, indicating that it has been heated, click and drag the rod over the nerve and release the mouse button. What happens?

_____

_____

How does this trace compare to the trace that was generated with the unheated glass rod?

_____

_____

What explanation can you provide for this?

_____

_____

Click **Record Data** to record your results. Then click **Clear** to clear the oscilloscope screen for the next activity. ▬

ACTIVITY 4

Chemical Stimulation

1. Click and drag the dropper from the bottle of sodium chloride (salt solution) over to the nerve in the chamber and then release the mouse button to dispense drops.

Does this generate an action potential? _____

2. Look back at Activity 1 for the voltage you determined. Set the voltage at that level, and click **Single Stimulus** to stimulate the nerve.

Does this tracing differ from the original threshold stimulus

tracing? _____

Click **Record Data** to record your results.

3. Click the **Clean** button on top of the nerve chamber. This will return the nerve to its original (nonsalted) state. Click **Clear** to clear the oscilloscope screen.

4. Click and drag the dropper from the bottle of hydrochloric acid over to the nerve, and release the mouse button to dispense drops.

Does this generate an action potential? _____

Does this tracing differ from the one generated by the original

threshold stimulus? _____

Click **Record Data** to record your results.

5. Click the **Clean** button on the nerve chamber to clean the chamber and return the nerve to its untouched state.

6. Click **Tools → Print Data** to print the data you have recorded for this experiment.

To summarize your experimental results, what kinds of stimuli can elicit an action potential?

_____

_____

_____ ▬

Inhibiting a Nerve Impulse

Numerous physical factors and chemical agents can impair the ability of nerve fibers to function. For example, deep pressure and cold temperature both block nerve impulse transmission by preventing local blood supply from reaching the nerve fibers. Local anesthetics, alcohol, and numerous other chemicals are also effective in blocking nerve transmission. In this experiment, we will study the effects of various agents on nerve transmission.

To begin, click the **Experiment** menu and select **Inhibiting a Nerve Impulse.** The display screen for this activity (Figure 18B.4) is similar to the screen in the first activity. To the left are bottles of several agents that you will test on the nerve. Keep the tracings you printed out from the first activity close at hand for comparison.

FIGURE 18B.4 Opening screen of the Inhibiting a Nerve Impulse experiment.

Testing the Effects of Ether

1.   Using the mouse, click and drag the dropper from the bottle of ether over to the nerve between the stimulating electrodes and recording electrodes. Release the mouse button to dispense drops.

2.   Look back at Activity 1 for the voltage you determined. Set the voltage at that level, and click **Single Stimulus** to stimulate the nerve. What sort of trace do you see?

_____

_____

What has happened to the nerve? _____

_____

_____

Click **Record Data** to record your results.

3.   Click the **Time (min)** button on the oscilloscope. This button toggles the time scale between minutes and milliseconds. The screen will now display activity over the course of 10 minutes (the space between each vertical line representing 1 minute). Because of the change in time scale, an action potential will look like a sharp vertical spike on the screen.

4.   Click the (+) button under **Interval between Stimuli** on the stimulator until the timer is set for 2.0 minutes. This will set the stimulus to stimulate the nerve every 2 minutes. Click **Stimulate** to start the stimulations. Watch the **Elapsed Time** display. With the change in time scale, the action potential will look like a straight vertical line.

How long does it take for the nerve to return to normal?

_____

5.   Click the **Stop** button to stop this action and to return the Elapsed Time to 0.0.

6. Click the **Time (msec)** button on the oscilloscope to return it to its normal millisecond display.

7. Click **Clear** to clear the oscilloscope for the next activity.

8. Click the (−) button under **Interval between Stimuli** until it is reset to 0.00. ▬

Testing the Effects of Curare

Curare is a well-known plant extract that South American Indians used to paralyze their prey. It is an alpha-toxin that binds to acetylcholine binding sites on the postsynaptic cell membrane, preventing the acetylcholine from acting. Curare blocks synaptic transmission by preventing the flow of neural impulses from neuron to neuron.

1. Click and drag the dropper from the bottle of curare and position the dropper on the nerve in between the stimulating and recording electrodes. Release the mouse button to dispense drops.

2. Look back at Activity 1 for the voltage you determined. Set the voltage at that level, and click Single Stimulus to stimulate the nerve. Does this generate an action potential?

_____

What explains this effect? _____

What do you think would be the overall effect of curare on the organism?

_____

_____

Click **Record Data** to record your results.

3. Click on the **Clean** button on the nerve chamber to remove the curare and return the nerve to its original untouched state.

4. Click **Clear** to clear the oscilloscope screen for the next activity. ▬

Testing the Effects of Lidocaine

Note: Lidocaine is a sodium-channel antagonist that prevents sodium channels from opening.

1. Click and drag the dropper from the bottle of lidocaine and position it over the nerve between the stimulating and recording electrodes. Release the mouse button to dispense drops. Does this generate a trace?

2. Look back at Activity 1 for the voltage you determined. Set the voltage at that level, and click **Single Stimulus** to stimulate the nerve. What sort of tracing do you see?

_____

Why does lidocaine have this effect on nerve fiber transmission?

_____

_____

Click **Record Data** to record your results. Click **Tools → Print Data** if you wish to print your data.

3. Click the **Clean** button on the nerve chamber to remove the lidocaine and return the nerve to its original untouched state. ▬

Nerve Conduction Velocity

As has been pointed out, one of the major physiological properties of neurons is conductivity: the ability to transmit the nerve impulse to other neurons, muscles, or glands. The nerve impulse, or propagated action potential, occurs when Na^+ floods into the neuron, causing the membrane to depolarize. Although this event is spoken of in electrical terms and is measured using instruments that measure electrical events, the **conduction velocity,** that is, the velocity of the action potential along a neural membrane, does not occur at the speed of light. Rather, this event is much slower. In certain nerves in the human, the velocity of an action potential may be as fast as 120 meters per second. In other nerves, conduction speed is much slower, occurring at a speed of less than 3 meters per second.

To see the setup for this experiment, click the **Experiment** menu and select **Nerve Conduction Velocity** (Figure 18B.5). In this exercise, you will use the oscilloscope and stimulator along with a third instrument, the bio-amplifier. The **bio-amplifier** is used to amplify any membrane depolarization so that the oscilloscope can easily record the event. Normally, when a membrane depolarization sufficient to initiate an action potential is looked at, the interior of the cell membrane goes from −70 mV to about +40 mV. This is easily registered and viewable on an oscilloscope without the aid of an amplifier. However, in this experiment, it is the change in the membrane potential on the *outside* of the nerve that is being observed. The change that occurs here during depolarization will be so minuscule that it must be amplified in order to be visible on the oscilloscope.

A nerve chamber (similar to the one used in the previous two experiments) will be used. The design is basically a plastic box with platinum electrodes running across it. The nerve will be laid on these electrodes. Two electrodes will be used to bring the impulse from the stimulator to the nerve and three will be used for recording the membrane depolarization.

FIGURE 18B.5 Opening screen of the Nerve Conduction Velocity experiment.

In this experiment, you will determine and compare the conduction velocities of different types of nerves. You will examine four nerves: an earthworm nerve, a frog nerve, and two rat nerves. The earthworm nerve is the smallest of the four. The frog nerve is a medium-sized myelinated nerve. Rat nerve 1 is a medium-sized unmyelinated nerve. Rat nerve 2 is a large, myelinated nerve—the largest nerve in this group. You will observe the effects of size and myelination on nerve conductivity.

The basic layout of the materials is shown in Figure 18B.5. The two wires (red and black) from the stimulator connect with the top right side of the nerve chamber. Three recording wires (red, black, and a bare wire cable) are attached to connectors on the other end of the nerve chamber and go to the bio-amplifier. The bare cable serves as a ground reference for the electrical circuit and provides the reference for comparison of any change in membrane potential. The bio-amplifier is connected to the oscilloscope so that any amplified membrane changes can be observed. The stimulator

output, called the *pulse*, has been connected to the oscilloscope so that when the nerve is stimulated, the tracing will start across the oscilloscope screen. Thus, the time from the start of the trace on the left side of the screen (when the nerve was stimulated) to the actual nerve deflection (from the recording electrodes) can be accurately measured. This amount of time, usually in milliseconds, is critical for determining conduction velocity.

ACTIVITY 8

Measuring Nerve Conduction Velocity

1. On the stimulator, click the **Pulse** button.

2. Turn the bio-amplifier on by clicking the horizontal bar on the bio-amplifier and dragging it to the **On** setting.

On the left side of the screen are the four nerves that will be studied. You will study the earthworm, a frog nerve, and two rat nerves of different sizes. The earthworm as a whole is used because it has a nerve running down its ventral surface. A frog nerve is used as the frog has long been the animal of choice in many physiology laboratories. The rat nerves are used so that you may compare (a) the conduction velocity of different sized nerves and (b) the conduction velocity of a myelinated versus unmyelinated nerve. Remember that the frog nerve is myelinated and that rat nerve 1 is the same size as the frog nerve but unmyelinated. Rat nerve 2, the largest nerve of the bunch, is myelinated.

3. Using the mouse, click and drag the dropper from the bottle of ethanol over the earthworm and release the mouse button to dispense drops of ethanol. This will narcotize the worm so it does not move around during the experiment but will not affect nerve conduction velocity. The alcohol is at a low enough percentage that the worm will be fine and back to normal within 15 minutes.

4. Click and drag the earthworm into the nerve chamber. Be sure the worm is over both of the stimulating electrodes and all three of the recording electrodes.

5. Using the (+) button next to the **Voltage** display, set the voltage to 1.0 V. Then click **Stimulate** to stimulate the nerve. Do you see an action potential? If not, increase the voltage by increments of 1.0 V until a trace is obtained.

At what threshold voltage do you first see an action potential

generated? _____ V

6. Next, click the **Measure** button located on the stimulator. You will see a vertical yellow line appear on the far left edge of the oscilloscope screen. Now click the (+) button under the Measure button. This will move the yellow line to the right. This line lets you measure how much time has elapsed on the graph at the point that the line is crossing the graph. You will see the elapsed time appear on the **Time (msec)** display on the stimulator. Keep clicking (+) until the yellow line is exactly at the point in the graph where the graph ceases being a flat line and first starts to rise.

7. Once you have the yellow line positioned at the start of the graph's ascent, note the time elapsed at this point. Click **Record Data** to record the elapsed time on the data collection graph. PhysioEx will automatically compute the conduction velocity based on this data. Note that the data collection box includes a **Distance (mm)** column and that the distance is always 43 mm. This is the distance from the red stimulating wire to the red recording wire. In a wet lab, you would have to measure the distance yourself before you could proceed with calculating the conduction velocity.

It is important that you have the yellow vertical measuring line positioned at the start of the graph's rise before you click **Record Data**—otherwise, the conduction velocity calculated for the nerve will be inaccurate.

8. Fill in the data in the Earthworm column on Chart 1.

9. Click and drag the earthworm to its original place. Click **Clear** to clear the oscilloscope screen.

10. Repeat steps 4 through 9 for the remaining nerves. Remember to click **Record Data** after each experimental run and to fill in the chart for question 8.

11. Click **Tools → Print Data** to print your data.

CHART 1				
Nerve	Earthworm (small nerve)	Frog (medium nerve, myelinated)	Rat nerve 1 (medium nerve, unmyelinated)	Rat nerve 2 (large nerve, myelinated)
Threshold voltage				
Elapsed time from stimulation to action potential				
Conduction velocity				

Which nerve in the group has the slowest conduction velocity?

_____

What was the speed of the nerve? _____

Which nerve in the group of four has the fastest conduction velocity?

_____

_____

What was the speed of the nerve? _____

What is the relationship between nerve size and conduction velocity? _____

_____

_____

_____

_____

_____

Based on the results, what is your conclusion regarding conduction velocity and whether the nerve is myelinated or not?

_____

_____

_____

_____

What is the major reason for the differences seen in conduction velocity between the myelinated nerves and the

unmyelinated nerves? _____

_____

_____

Histology Review Supplement

For a review of nervous tissue, go to **Exercise 6B: Histology Atlas and Review** on **myA&P** to print out the **Nervous Tissue Review** worksheet.

NAME _____

LAB TIME/DATE _____

Neurophysiology of Nerve Impulses: Computer Simulation

Eliciting (Generating) a Nerve Impulse

1. Why don't the terms *depolarization* and *action potential* mean the same thing?

_____

_____

_____

2. What was the threshold voltage in Activity 1? _____

3. What was the effect of increasing the voltage? How does this change correlate to changes in the nerve? _____

_____

_____

4. How did the action potential generated with the unheated rod compare to that generated with the heated rod? _____

5. Describe the types of stimuli that generated an action potential. _____

_____

_____

6. If you were to spend a lot of time studying nerve physiology in the laboratory, what type of stimulus would you use and why?

_____

_____

7. Why does the addition of sodium chloride elicit an action potential? Hint: Think about the sodium permeability of the neuron

(Figure 18B.2e). _____

_____

_____

Inhibiting a Nerve Impulse

8. What was the effect of ether on eliciting an action potential? _____

_____

9. Does the addition of ether to the nerve cause any permanent alteration in neural response?

_____

10. What was the effect of curare on eliciting an action potential?

_____

11. Explain the reason for your answer to question 10 above.

_____

12. What was the effect of lidocaine on eliciting an action potential?

_____

Nerve Conduction Velocity

13. What is the relationship between size of the nerve and conduction velocity? _____

_____

_____

14. Keeping your answer to question 13 in mind, how might you draw an analogy between the nerves in the human body and electrical wires?

_____

15. How does myelination affect nerve conduction velocity? Explain, using your data from Chart 1. _____

_____

_____

_____

16. If any of the nerves used were reversed in their placement on the stimulating and recording electrodes, would any differences be seen in conduction velocity? Explain.

_____

_____

_____

Endocrine System Physiology: Computer Simulation

O B J E C T I V E S

1. To define the following terms: *metabolism, hormone replacement therapy, type 1 diabetes, type 2 diabetes,* and *glucose standard curve.*
2. To explain the role of thyroxine in maintaining an animal's metabolic rate.
3. To explain the effects of thyroid-stimulating hormone on an animal's metabolic rate.
4. To understand how estrogen affects bone density.
5. To explain how hormone replacement therapy works.
6. To explain how fasting plasma glucose is used to diagnose diabetes.
7. To understand how levels of cortisol and ACTH can be used to diagnose endocrine diseases.

The endocrine system exerts many complex and interrelated effects on the body as a whole, as well as on specific tissues and organs. Studying the effects of hormones on the body is difficult to do in a wet lab because experiments often take days, weeks, or even months to complete and are expensive. In addition, live animals may need to be sacrificed, and technically difficult surgical procedures are sometimes necessary. This computer simulation allows you to study the effects of given hormones on the body by using "virtual" animals rather than live ones. You can carry out delicate surgical techniques with the click of a button and complete experiments in a fraction of the time that it would take in an actual wet lab environment.

Hormones and Metabolism

Metabolism is the broad term used for all biochemical reactions occurring in the body. Metabolism involves *catabolism,* a process by which complex materials are broken down into simpler substances, usually with the aid of enzymes found in the body cells. Metabolism also involves *anabolism,* in which the smaller materials are built up by enzymes into larger, more complex molecules. When larger molecules are made, energy is stored in the various bonds formed. When bonds are broken in catabolism, energy that was stored in the bonds is released for use by the cell. Some of the energy liberated may go into the formation of ATP, the energy-rich material used by the body to run itself. However, not all of the energy liberated goes into this pathway; some is given off as body heat. Humans are *homeothermic* animals, meaning they have a fixed body temperature. Maintaining this temperature is important to maintaining the metabolic pathways found in the body.

The most important hormone in maintaining metabolism and body heat is *thyroxine,* the hormone of the thyroid gland, which is found in the neck. The thyroid gland secretes thyroxine, but the production of thyroxine is really controlled by the pituitary gland, which secretes *thyroid-stimulating hormone (TSH).* TSH is carried by the blood to the thyroid gland (its *target tissue*) and causes the thyroid to produce more thyroxine. So, in an indirect way, an animal's metabolic rate is the result of pituitary hormones.

In the following experiments, you will investigate the effects of thyroxine and TSH on an animal's metabolic rate (see Figure 28B.1b). To begin, select **Exercise 28B: Endocrine System Physiology** from the drop-down menu and click **GO.**

(a)

(b)

FIGURE 28B.1 Metabolism and the thyroid gland. (a) Opening screen of the Metabolism experiment. **(b)** The regulation of thyroid secretion. + indicates stimulation of release, − indicates inhibition of release, T$_3$ = triiodothyronine, T$_4$ = thyroxine, TRH = thyrotropin-releasing hormone, TSH = thyroid-stimulating hormone.

Before you perform the activities, watch the **BMR Measurement** video to see an experiment in which basal metabolic rate is measured. Then click **Metabolism.** The opening screen will appear in a few seconds (see Figure 28B.1a). Select **Balloons On/Off** from the **Help** menu for help identifying the equipment onscreen (you will see labels appear as you roll the cursor over each piece of equipment). Select **Balloons On/Off** to turn this feature off before you begin the experiments.

Study the screen. You will see a jar-shaped chamber to the left, connected to a *respirometer-manometer apparatus* (consisting of a U-shaped tube, a syringe, and associated tubing). You will be placing animals—in this case, rats—in the chamber to gather information about how thyroxine and TSH affect their metabolic rates. Note that the chamber also includes a weight scale, and under the timer is a weight display. Next to the chamber is a timer for setting and timing the length of a given experiment.

Two tubes are connected to the top of the chamber. The left tube has a clamp that can be opened or closed. Leaving the clamp open allows outside air into the chamber; closing the clamp creates a closed, airtight system. The other tube leads to a *T-connector*. One branch of the T leads to a fluid-containing, U-shaped tube, called a *manometer*. As an animal uses up the air in the closed system, this fluid rises in the left side of the U-shaped tube and falls in the right.

The other branch of the T-connector leads to a syringe filled with air. Using the syringe to inject air into the tube, you will measure the amount of air that is needed to return the fluid columns to their original levels. This measurement will be equal to the amount of oxygen used by the animal during the elapsed time of the experiment. Soda lime, found at the bottom of the chamber, absorbs the carbon dioxide given off by the animal so that the amount of oxygen used can easily be measured. The amount of oxygen used by the animal, along with its weight, will be used to calculate the animal's metabolic rate.

Also on the screen are three white rats in their individual cages. These are the specimens you will use in the following experiments. One rat is *normal;* the second is *thyroidectomized* (abbreviated on the screen as *Tx*), meaning that its thyroid has been removed; and the third is *hypophysectomized* (abbreviated on the screen as *Hypox*), meaning that its pituitary gland has been removed. The pituitary gland is also known as the *hypophysis,* and removal of this organ is called a *hypophysectomy.*

To the top left of the screen are three syringes with various chemicals inside: propylthiouracil, thyroid-stimulating hormone (TSH), and thyroxine. TSH and thyroxine have been previously mentioned; propylthiouracil is a drug that inhibits the production of thyroxine. You will perform four experiments on each animal to: (1) determine its baseline metabolic rate, (2) determine its metabolic rate after it has been injected with thyroxine, (3) determine its metabolic rate after it has been injected with TSH, and (4) determine its metabolic rate after it has been injected with propylthiouracil.

You will be recording all of your data on Chart 1. You may also record your data on-screen by using the equipment in the lower part of the screen, called the *data collection unit.* This equipment records and displays data you accumulate during the experiments. Check that the data set for **Normal** is highlighted in the **Data Sets** window; you will be experimenting with the normal rat first. The **Record Data** button lets you record data after an experimental trial. Clicking the

Delete Line or **Clear Data Set** button erases any data you want to delete.

A C T I V I T Y 1

Determining Baseline Metabolic Rates

First, you will determine the baseline metabolic rate for each rat.

1. Using the mouse, click and drag the **normal** rat into the chamber and place it on top of the scale. When the animal is in the chamber, release the mouse button.

2. Be sure the clamp on the left tube (on top of the chamber) is open, allowing air to enter the chamber. If the clamp is closed, click it to open it.

3. Be sure the indicator next to the T-connector reads "Chamber and manometer connected." If not, click the **T-connector knob.**

4. Click on the **Weigh** button in the box to the right of the chamber to weigh the rat. Record this weight in the Baseline section of Chart 1 in the row labeled "Weight."

5. Click the (+) button on the **Timer** so that the Timer display reads 1 minute.

6. Click the clamp to close it. This prevents any outside air from entering the chamber and ensures that the rat is breathing only the oxygen inside the closed system.

7. Click **Start** on the Timer display. You will see the elapsed time appear in the "Elapsed Time" display. Watch what happens to the water levels in the U-shaped tube.

8. At the end of the 1-minute period, the timer will automatically stop. When it stops, click the **T-connector knob** so that the indicator reads "Manometer and syringe connected."

9. Click the clamp to open it so that the rat can once again breathe outside air.

10. Look at the difference between the levels in the left and right arms of the U-shaped tube. To estimate the volume of O_2 that you need to inject to equalize the levels, count the divider lines on both sides. Then click the (+) button next to the **ml O_2** display until the display shows your estimate. Click **Inject** and watch what happens to the fluid in the two arms. When the volume is equalized, the word "Level" will appear between the arms and stay on the screen. If too little was injected, click (+) and then **Inject** until the arms are level. If too much was injected, the word "Level" will flash and then disappear. You will then have to click the **Reset** button and try a lower volume. (The total amount injected to equalize the arm levels is equivalent to the amount of oxygen that the rat used up during 1 minute in the closed chamber.) Record this measurement in the Baseline section of Chart 1 in the row labeled "ml O_2 used in 1 minute."

11. Determine the oxygen consumption per hour for the rat. Use the following formula:

$$\frac{\text{ml } O_2 \text{ consumed}}{1 \text{ minute}} \times \frac{60 \text{ minutes}}{1 \text{ hr}} = \text{ml } O_2/\text{hr}$$

Record this data in the Baseline section of Chart 1 in the row labeled "ml O_2 used per hour."

CHART 1   Effects of Hormones on Metabolic Rate

	Normal rat	Thyroidectomized rat	Hypophysectomized rat
Baseline			
Weight	_____ grams	_____ grams	_____ grams
ml O₂ used in 1 minute	_____ ml	_____ ml	_____ ml
ml O₂ used per hour	_____ ml	_____ ml	_____ ml
Metabolic rate	_____ ml O₂/kg/hr	_____ ml O₂/kg/hr	_____ ml O₂/kg/hr
With thyroxine			
Weight	_____ grams	_____ grams	_____ grams
ml O₂ used in 1 minute	_____ ml	_____ ml	_____ ml
ml O₂ used per hour	_____ ml	_____ ml	_____ ml
Metabolic rate	_____ ml O₂/kg/hr	_____ ml O₂/kg/hr	_____ ml O₂/kg/hr
With TSH			
Weight	_____ grams	_____ grams	_____ grams
ml O₂ used in 1 minute	_____ ml	_____ ml	_____ ml
ml O₂ used per hour	_____ ml	_____ ml	_____ ml
Metabolic rate	_____ ml O₂/kg/hr	_____ ml O₂/kg/hr	_____ ml O₂/kg/hr
With propylthiouracil			
Weight	_____ grams	_____ grams	_____ grams
ml O₂ used in 1 minute	_____ ml	_____ ml	_____ ml
ml O₂ used per hour	_____ ml	_____ ml	_____ ml
Metabolic rate	_____ ml O₂/kg/hr	_____ ml O₂/kg/hr	_____ ml O₂/kg/hr

12. Now that you have the amount of oxygen used per hour, determine the metabolic rate per kilogram of body weight by using the following formula. (Note that you will need to convert the weight data from g to kg before you can use the formula.)

$$\text{Metabolic rate} = \frac{\text{ml } O_2/\text{hr}}{\text{wt. in kg}} = \underline{\quad} \text{ml } O_2/\text{kg/hr}$$

Record this data in the Baseline section of Chart 1 in the row labeled "Metabolic rate."

13. Click **Record Data.**

14. Click and drag the rat from the chamber back to its cage.

15. Click the **Reset** button in the box labeled Apparatus.

16. Now repeat steps 1–15 for the **thyroidectomized (Tx)** and **hypophysectomized (Hypox)** rats. Record your data in

the Baseline section of Chart 1 in the appropriate column for each rat. Note that when you put the Tx vat in the chamber, the simulation highlights **Tx** under **Data Sets** (on the data collection box); likewise, it highlights **Hypox** when you move the hypophysectomized rat.

Which rat had the fastest baseline metabolic rate?

_____

_____

_____

Why did the metabolic rates differ? _____

_____

_____

_____

ACTIVITY 2

Determining the Effect of Thyroxine on Metabolic Rate

Next, you will investigate the effects of thyroxine injections on the metabolic rates of all three rats.

Note that in a wet lab environment, you would normally need to inject thyroxine (or any other hormone) into a rat *daily* for a minimum of 1–2 weeks for any response to be seen. However, in the following simulations, you will inject the rat only once and be able to witness the same results as if you had administered multiple injections over the course of several weeks. In addition, by clicking the **Clean** button while a rat is inside its cage, you can magically remove all residue of any previously injected hormone from the rat and perform a new experiment on the same rat. In a real wet lab environment, you would need to either wait weeks for hormonal residue to leave the rat's system or use a different rat.

1. Choose and click on a rat to test. You will eventually test all three, and it doesn't matter in what order you test them. Do not drag the rat to the chamber yet. Under **Data Sets,** the simulation will highlight **Normal, Tx,** or **Hypox** depending on which rat you use.

2. Click the **Reset** button in the box labeled Apparatus.

3. Click the syringe labeled **thyroxine** and drag it over to the rat. Release the mouse button. This will cause thyroxine to be injected into the rat.

4. Click and drag the rat into the chamber. Perform steps 1–12 of Activity 1 again, except this time record your data in the With Thyroxine section of Chart 1.

5. Click **Record Data.**

6. Click and drag the rat from the chamber back to its cage, and click **Clean** to cleanse it of all traces of thyroxine.

7. Now repeat steps 1–6 for the remaining rats. Record your data in the With Thyroxine section of Chart 1 in the appropriate column for each rat.

What was the effect of thyroxine on the normal rat's metabolic rate? How does it compare to the normal rat's baseline metabolic rate?

_____

_____

_____

Why was this effect seen? _____

_____

_____

What was the effect of thyroxine on the thyroidectomized rat's metabolic rate? How does it compare to the thyroidectomized rat's baseline metabolic rate?

_____

_____

_____

Why was this effect seen? _____

_____

_____

What was the effect of thyroxine on the hypophysectomized rat's metabolic rate? How does it compare to the hypophysectomized rat's baseline metabolic rate?

_____

_____

_____

Why was this effect seen? _____

_____

ACTIVITY 3

Determining the Effect of TSH on Metabolic Rate

Now you will investigate the effects of TSH injections on the metabolic rates of the three rats. Select a rat to experiment on first, and then proceed.

1. Under **Data Sets,** highlight **Normal, Tx,** or **Hypox,** depending on which rat you are using.

2. Click the **Reset** button in the box labeled Apparatus.

3. Click and drag the syringe labeled **TSH** over to the rat and release the mouse button, injecting the rat.

4. Click and drag the rat into the chamber. Perform steps 1–12 of Activity 1 again. Record your data in the With TSH section of Chart 1.

5. Click **Record Data.**

6. Click and drag the rat from the chamber back to its cage, and click **Clean** to cleanse it of all traces of TSH.

7. Now repeat this activity for the remaining rats. Record your data in the With TSH section of the chart in the appropriate column for each rat.

What was the effect of TSH on the normal rat's metabolic rate? How does it compare to the normal rat's baseline metabolic rate?

_____

_____

_____

Why was this effect seen? _____

_____

What was the effect of TSH on the thyroidectomized rat's metabolic rate? How does it compare to the thyroidectomized rat's baseline metabolic rate?

_____

_____

_____

Why was this effect seen? _____

_____

What was the effect of TSH on the hypophysectomized rat's metabolic rate? How does it compare to the hypophysectomized rat's baseline metabolic rate?

_____

_____

_____

Why was this effect seen? _____

_____

ACTIVITY 4

Determining the Effect of Propylthiouracil on Metabolic Rate

Next, you will investigate the effects of propylthiouracil injections on the metabolic rates of the three rats. Keep in mind that propylthiouracil is a drug that inhibits the production of thyroxine by blocking the attachment of iodine to the amino acid tyrosine and interfering with the conversion of thyroxine to triiodothyronine. Select a rat to experiment on first, and then proceed.

1.   Under **Data Sets,** the simulation will highlight **Normal, Tx,** or **Hypox,** depending on which rat you are using.

2.   Click the **Reset** button in the box labeled Apparatus.

3.   Click and drag the syringe labeled **propylthiouracil** over to the rat and release the mouse button, injecting the rat.

4.   Click and drag the rat into the chamber. Perform steps 1–12 of Activity 1 again, except this time record your data in the With Propylthiouracil section of Chart 1.

5.   Click **Record Data.**

6.   Click and drag the rat from the chamber back to its cage, and click **Clean** to cleanse the rat of all traces of propylthiouracil.

7.   Now repeat this activity for the remaining rats. Record your data in the With Propylthiouracil section of Chart 1 in the appropriate column for each rat.

What was the effect of propylthiouracil on the normal rat's metabolic rate? How does it compare to the normal rat's baseline metabolic rate?

_____

_____

Why was this effect seen? _____

_____

What was the effect of propylthiouracil on the thyroidectomized rat's metabolic rate? How does it compare to the thyroidectomized rat's baseline metabolic rate?

_____

_____

Why was this effect seen? _____

_____

What was the effect of propylthiouracil on the hypophysectomized rat's metabolic rate? How does it compare to the hypophysectomized rat's baseline metabolic rate?

_____

_____

_____

Why was this effect seen? _____

_____

8.   If you wish, click **Tools → Print Data** to print all of your recorded data for this experiment.

FIGURE 28B.2 Opening screen of the Hormone Replacement Therapy experiment.

Hormone Replacement Therapy

Follicle-stimulating hormone (FSH) stimulates ovarian follicle growth. While the follicles are developing, they produce the hormone *estrogen.* As the female enters menopause, the ovaries stop producing estrogen. One of the symptoms of menopause is loss of bone density, which can result in osteoporosis and bone fractures. Postmenopausal treatments to prevent osteoporosis include the administration of estrogen to increase bone density. Calcitonin is a hormone that inhibits osteoclast activity and stimulates calcium uptake for deposit in bone.

In this experiment we will use three ovariectomized rats because they are no longer producing estrogen due to the removal of their ovaries. The three rats were chosen because each has a baseline T score of −2.6, indicating osteoporosis. T scores are interpreted as follows: normal = +1 to −0.99; osteopenia (bone thinning) = −1.0 to −2.49; osteoporosis = −2.5 and below. You will administer either estrogen therapy or calcitonin therapy, two types of **hormone replacement therapy.** The third rat will serve as an untreated control and receive daily injections of saline. The vertebral bone density

(VBD) of each rat will be measured with dual X-ray absorptiometry (DXA) to obtain the T score.

Start by selecting **Hormone Replacement Therapy** from the **Experiment** menu. A new screen will appear (Figure 28B.2) with three ovariectomized rats in cages. (Note that if this were a wet lab, the ovariectomies would have been performed on the rats a month prior to the rest of the experiment in order to ensure that no residual hormones remained in the rats' systems.) Also on screen are a bottle of saline, a bottle of estrogen, a bottle of calcitonin, a clock, and a dual X-ray absorptiometry bone density scanner.

Hormone Replacement Therapy

1. Click the syringe, drag it to the bottle of **saline,** and release the mouse button. The syringe will automatically fill with 1 ml of saline.

2. Click and hold the syringe, drag it to the **control** rat, and place the tip of the needle in the rat's lower abdominal area. Injections into this area are considered *intraperitoneal* and will quickly be picked up by the abdominal blood vessels.

Release the mouse button—the syringe will empty into the rat and automatically return to its holder. Click **Clean** on the syringe holder to clean the syringe of all residue.

3. Click the syringe again, this time dragging it to the bottle of **estrogen**, and release the mouse button. The syringe will automatically fill with 1 ml of estrogen.

4. Click and hold the syringe, drag it to the **estrogen-treated** rat, and place the tip of the needle in the rat's lower abdominal area. Release the mouse button—the syringe will empty into the rat and automatically return to its holder. Click **Clean** on the syringe holder to clean the syringe of all residue.

5. Click the syringe again, this time dragging it to the bottle of **calcitonin,** and release the mouse button. The syringe will automatically fill with 1 ml of calcitonin.

6. Click and hold the syringe, drag it to the **calcitonin-treated** rat, and place the tip of the needle in the rat's lower abdominal area. Release the mouse button—the syringe will empty into the rat and automatically return to its holder. Click **Clean** on the syringe holder to clean the syringe of all residue.

7. Click the **clock.** You will notice the hands sweep the clock face twice, indicating that 24 hours have passed.

8. Repeat steps 1–7 until each rat has received a total of 7 injections over the course of 7 days (1 injection per day). Note that the **# of injections** displayed below each rat cage records how many injections the rat has received. The control rat should receive 7 injections of saline, the estrogen-treated rat should receive 7 injections of estrogen, and the calcitonin-treated rat should receive 7 injections of calcitonin.

9. You are now ready to measure the effect of each of the solutions. First, predict the effect that each solution will have on the rat's vertebral bone density.

Saline injections _____

_____

Estrogen injections _____

_____

Calcitonin injections _____

_____

10. A gaseous anesthetic will be applied to immobilize the rats for imaging. Click the **Anesthesia** button for the control rat to immobilize the rat.

11. Click the **control** rat and drag it to the exam table. Release the mouse to release the rat.

12. Click the **Scan** button to activate the scanner. Record the T score:

T score (control): _____

13. Click **Record Data.**

14. Click and drag the rat to return it to its cage.

15. Repeat steps 10–14 for the **estrogen-treated** rat.

T score (estrogen): _____

16. Repeat steps 10–14 for the **calcitonin-treated** rat.

T score (calcitonin): _____

17. Click **Tools → Print Data** to print your recorded data for this experiment.

Recall that the baseline value for all three rats was −2.6. T scores are interpreted as follows: normal = +1 to −0.99; osteopenia (bone thinning) = −1.0 to −2.49; osteoporosis = −2.5 and below.

What effect did the administration of estrogen injections have on the estrogen-treated rat?

_____

_____

What effect did the administration of calcitonin injections

have on the calcitonin-treated rat? _____

_____

How did these results compare with your predictions?

_____

_____

_____

Insulin and Diabetes

Insulin is produced by the beta cells of the endocrine portion of the pancreas. It is vital to the regulation of blood glucose levels because it enables the body's cells to absorb glucose from the bloodstream (see Figure 28B.4b). When insulin is not produced by the pancreas, **type 1 diabetes mellitus** results. When insulin is produced by the pancreas but the body fails to respond to it, **type 2 diabetes mellitus** results. In either case, glucose remains in the bloodstream, unable to be taken up by the body's cells to serve as the primary fuel for metabolism.

The following experiment is divided into two parts. In Part I, you will obtain a *glucose standard curve,* which will be explained shortly. In Part II, you will use the standard curve

FIGURE 28B.3 Opening screen of the Insulin and Diabetes experiment, Part I.

to measure fasting plasma glucose levels in patients to diagnose diabetes mellitus.

Part I

ACTIVITY 6

Obtaining a Glucose Standard Curve

To begin, select **Insulin and Diabetes-Part 1** from the **Experiment** menu (see Figure 28B.3).

Select **Balloons On/Off** from the **Help** menu for help identifying the equipment on-screen. (You will see labels appear as you move the cursor over each piece of equipment.) Select **Balloons On/Off** to turn this feature off before you begin the experiments.

On the right side of the opening screen is a special spectrophotometer. The **spectrophotometer** is one of the most widely used research instruments in biology. It is used to measure the amounts of light of different wavelengths absorbed and transmitted by a pigmented solution. Inside the spectrophotometer is a source for white light, which is separated into various wavelengths (or colors) by a prism. The user selects a wavelength (color), and light of this color passes through a special tube, or *cuvette*, containing the sample being tested. (For this experiment, the spectrophotometer light source will be preset for a wavelength of 450 nanometers, or nm.) The light transmitted by the sample then passes onto a photoelectric tube, which converts the light energy into an electrical current. This current is measured by a meter. Alternatively, the light may be measured before the sample is put into the light path, and the amount of light absorbed—called **optical density**—is measured. Using either method, the change in light transmitted or light absorbed can be used to measure the amount of a given substance in the sample being tested.

In Part II, you will use the spectrophotometer to determine how much glucose is present in blood samples taken from two rats. Before using the spectrophotometer, you must obtain a **glucose standard curve** so that you have a point of reference for converting optical density readings into glucose readings, which will be measured in mg/deciliter (mg/dl). To do this, you will prepare five test tubes that contain known amounts of glucose: 30 mg/dl, 60 mg/dl, 90 mg/dl, 120 mg/dl, and 150 mg/dl, respectively. You will then use the spectrophotometer to determine the corresponding optical density readings for each of these known amounts of glucose. Information obtained in Part I will be used to perform Part II.

Also on the screen are three dropper bottles, a test tube washer, a test tube dispenser (on top of the washer), and a test tube incubation unit with numbered cradles that you will need to prepare the samples for analysis.

1. Click and drag the test tube (on top of the test tube washer) into slot 1 of the incubation unit. You will see another test tube pop up from the dispenser. Click and drag this second test tube into slot 2 of the incubation unit. Repeat until you have dragged a total of five test tubes into the five slots in the incubation unit.

2. Click and hold the mouse button on the dropper cap of the **glucose standard** bottle. Drag the dropper cap over to tube 1. Release the mouse button to dispense the glucose. You will see that one drop of glucose solution is dropped into the tube.

3. The dropper will automatically slide over to each of the remaining samples. Notice that each subsequent tube will automatically receive one additional drop of glucose standard (i.e., tube 2 will receive two drops, tube 3 will receive three drops, tube 4 will receive four drops, and tube 5 will receive five drops).

4. Click and hold the mouse button on the dropper cap of the **deionized water** bottle. Drag the dropper cap over to tube 1. Release the mouse button to dispense the water. Notice that four drops of water are automatically added to the first tube.

5. The dropper will automatically slide over to each of the remaining samples. Notice that each subsequent tube will receive one drop *fewer* than the previous tube (i.e., tube 2 will receive three drops, tube 3 will receive two drops, tube 4 will receive one drop, and tube 5 will receive *no* drops of water).

6. Click the **Mix** button of the incubator to mix the contents of the tubes.

7. Click the **Centrifuge** button. The tubes will descend into the incubator and be centrifuged.

8. When the tubes resurface, click the **Remove Pellet** button. Any pellets from the centrifuging process will be removed from the test tubes.

9. Click and hold the mouse button on the dropper cap of the **enzyme color reagent** bottle. Still holding the mouse button down, drag the dropper cap over to tube 1. When you release the mouse, you will note that five drops of reagent are added to the tube.

10. The dropper will automatically slide over to each of the remaining samples.

11. Now click **Incubate.** The tubes will descend into the incubator, incubate, and then resurface.

12. Using the mouse, click **Set Up** on the spectrophotometer. This will warm up the instrument and get it ready for your readings.

13. Click and drag tube 1 into the spectrophotometer (above the **Set Up** button) and release the mouse button. The tube will lock into place.

14. Click **Analyze.** You will see a spot appear on the screen and values appear in the **Optical Density** and **Glucose** displays.

15. Click **Record Data** on the data collection unit.

16. Click and drag the tube into the test tube washer.

17. Repeat steps 13–16 for the remaining test tubes.

18. When all five tubes have been analyzed, click the **Graph** button. This is the glucose standard graph, which you will use in Part II of the experiment. Click **Tools → Print Data** to print your recorded data. ■

Part II

Measuring Fasting Plasma Glucose

Select **Insulin and Diabetes-Part 2** from the **Experiment** menu.

A new screen will appear (Figure 28b.4a). Four reagents and five patient samples are present. To undergo the fasting plasma glucose (FPG) test, patients must fast for a minimum of 8 hours prior to the blood draw. Plasma samples will be measured in the spectrophotometer, and the glucose standard curve generated in Part I will be used to determine fasting plasma glucose levels in the five patient samples. A patient with two separate FPG tests greater than or equal to 126 mg/dl is diagnosed with diabetes. FPG values between 110 and 126 mg/dl are indicative of impairment or borderline impairment of glucose uptake by cells. FPG values less than 110 mg/dl are normal.

If the FPG is borderline, another test, the oral glucose tolerance test (OGTT), is performed. In this test, the patient also fasts for 8 hours. The patient then ingests a concentrated glucose solution, and blood is drawn and tested at periodic intervals. Glucose and sometimes insulin levels are measured. The 2-hour glucose level should be below 140 mg/dl. A 2-hour OGTT level between 140 and 200 mg/dl indicates impaired glucose tolerance, and a level above 200 mg/dl confirms the diabetes diagnosis. Individuals with impaired fasting glucose values and impaired glucose tolerance are at a higher risk of developing type 2 diabetes. If a patient is pregnant, an FPG value greater than 110 mg/dl could indicate gestational diabetes and a strict diet should be followed for the remainder of the pregnancy.

1. Click and drag a test tube (on top of the test tube washer) into slot 1 of the incubation unit. You will see another test tube pop up from the dispenser. Click and drag the second test tube into slot 2 of the incubation unit. Repeat until you have dragged a total of five test tubes into the five slots in the incubation unit.

2. Click and hold the mouse button on the dropper cap of **Sample 1** and then drag the dropper to the first test tube. The dropper will automatically dispense 3 drops of blood into the test tube and automatically return to the vial.

3. Repeat step 2 for the remaining patient samples.

4. Click and hold the mouse button on the dropper cap of the **deionized water** bottle. Drag the dropper cap over to test tube 1. Release the mouse to dispense the water. Five drops of water will be dispensed into the tube.

5. The dropper will automatically slide over to the remaining tubes and will add five drops to each tube. The

FIGURE 28B.4 Insulin and diabetes. (a) Opening screen of the Insulin and Diabetes experiment, Part II.

dropper will automatically return to the vial when the dispensing is complete.

6. Click and hold the mouse button on the dropper of **barium hydroxide.** Drag the dropper cap over to test tube 1. Release the mouse button to dispense the barium hydroxide. Five drops of the solution will be dispensed.

7. The dropper will automatically slide over to the remaining tubes and will add five drops to each tube. The dropper will automatically return to the vial when the dispensing is complete. (Barium hydroxide is used for clearing proteins and cells so that clear glucose readings may be obtained.)

8. Click and hold the mouse button on the dropper of the **heparin** bottle. Drag the dropper cap over to tube 1. Release the mouse button to dispense the heparin.

9. The dropper will automatically slide over to the remaining tubes and will add one drop to each tube. The dropper will automatically return to the vial when the dispensing is complete. (Heparin is an anticoagulant that prevents blood clotting.)

10. Click the **Mix** button of the incubator to mix the contents of the tubes.

11. Click the **Centrifuge** button. The tubes will descend into the incubator, be centrifuged, and then resurface.

12. Click the **Remove Pellet** button to remove any pellets from the centrifugation process.

13. Click and hold the mouse button on the dropper of the **enzyme color reagent** bottle. Drag the dropper cap to test tube 1. Release the mouse to dispense the reagent.

14. The dropper will automatically slide over to the remaining tubes and will add five drops to each tube. The dropper will automatically return to the vial when the dispensing is complete.

15. Click **Incubate.** The tubes will descend into the incubator, incubate, and then resurface.

16. Click **Set Up** on the spectrophotometer to warm up the instrument and get it ready for your readings.

17. Click **Graph Glucose Standard.** The graph from Part I of the experiment will appear on the monitor.

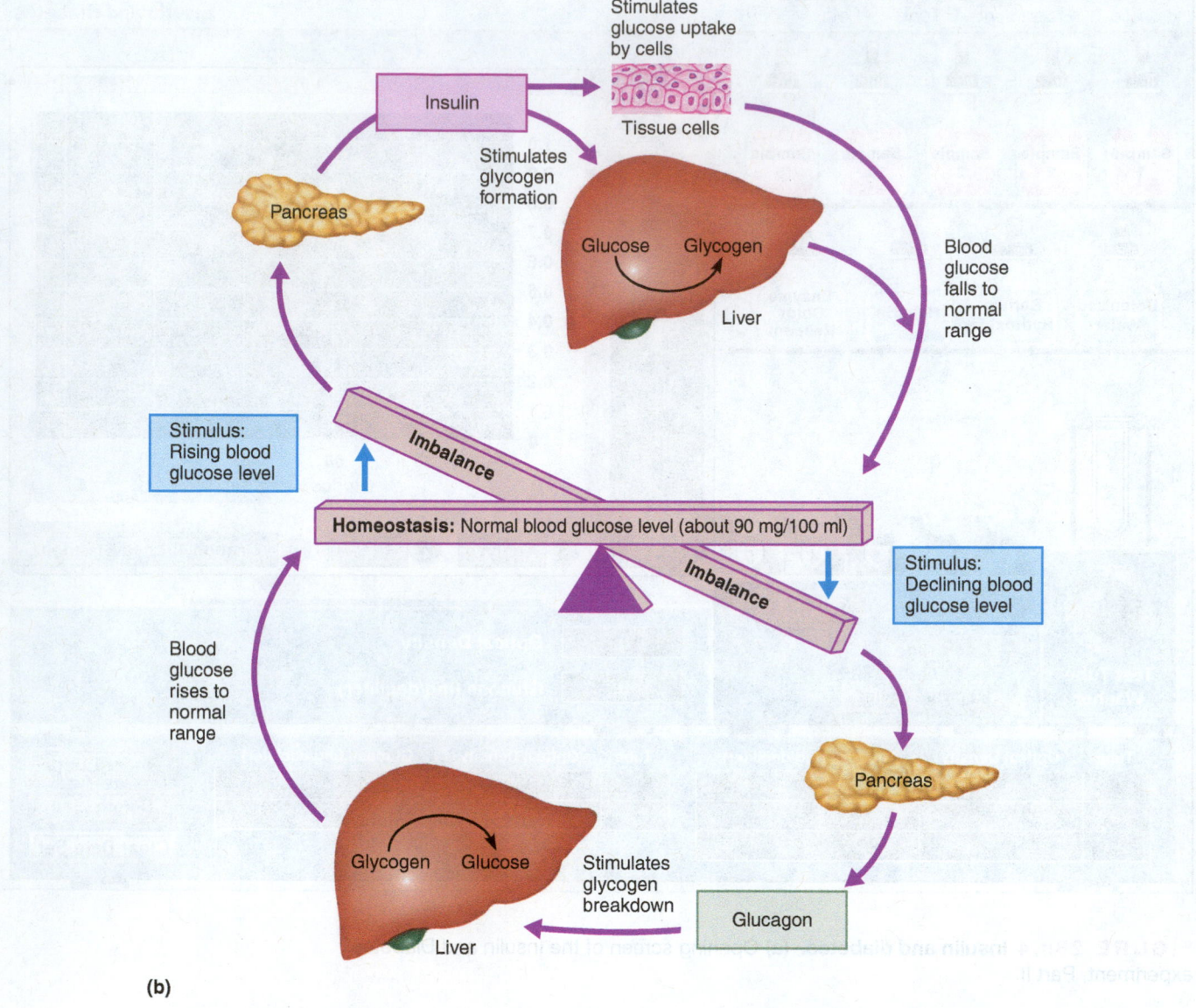

(b)

FIGURE 28B.4 (continued) Insulin and diabetes. (b) Regulation of blood sugar levels by insulin and glucagon.

18. Click and drag tube 1 to the spectrophotometer and release the mouse button. The tube will lock into place.

19. Click **Analyze.** You will see a horizontal line appear on the screen and a value appear in the **Optical Density** display.

20. Drag the movable ruler (the vertical line on the far right of the spectrophotometer monitor) over to where the horizontal line (from step 19) crosses the glucose standard line. Watch what happens to the **Glucose** display as you move the movable ruler to the left.

What is the glucose reading where the horizontal line crosses the glucose standard line?

Sample 1: glucose concentration of _____ mg/deciliter

This is your glucose reading for the patient being tested.

21. Click **Record Data** on the data collection unit.

22. Click and drag the test tube from the spectrophotometer into the test tube washer, then click **Clear** under the display.

23. Repeat steps 17–22 for the remaining test tubes. Record your glucose readings for each test tube here:

Sample 2: glucose concentration of _____ mg/deciliter

Sample 3: glucose concentration of _____ mg/deciliter

Sample 4: glucose concentration of _____ mg/deciliter

Sample 5: glucose concentration of _____ mg/deciliter

For which patient(s) were the glucose reading(s) in the normal

range? _____
_____

For which patient(s) were the fasting plasma glucose reading(s)

in the diabetic range? _____
_____

For which patient(s) were the fasting plasma glucose reading(s) in the impaired range?

_____
_____

What recommendations would you make to a patient with an impaired FPG value who also tested in the impaired range with the oral glucose tolerance test?

_____
_____

Patient 3 is pregnant; how might this change the diagnosis? What recommendations would you make to this patient?

_____
_____
_____

Measuring Cortisol and Adrenocorticotropic Hormone

Cortisol, a hormone secreted by the adrenal cortex, is key to the long-term regulation of stress. Cortisol release is stimulated by adrenocorticotropic hormone (ACTH), a hormone released by the anterior pituitary. ACTH release is stimulated by a hypothalamic hormone, corticotropin-releasing hormone (CRH). Increased levels of cortisol negatively feed back to inhibit the release of both ACTH and CRH. See Figure 28B.5b for the regulation of cortisol secretion.

Increased cortisol in the blood, or hypercortisolism, is referred to as Cushing's syndrome if it is due to an adrenal tumor. Hypercortisolism caused by a pituitary tumor also causes levels of ACTH to increase and is referred to as Cushing's disease. Cushing's syndrome can also be iatrogenic; that is, physician induced. This occurs when glucocorticoid hormones such as prednisone are administered for the treatment of rheumatoid arthritis, asthma, or lupus and is often referred to as "steroid diabetes" because it results in hyperglycemia.

Hypocortisolism can be due to adrenal insufficiency. In primary adrenal insufficiency, also known as Addison's disease, the low cortisol is directly due to gradual destruction of the adrenal cortex, and ACTH levels are typically elevated as a compensatory effect. Secondary adrenal insufficiency also

TABLE 28B.1	Cortisol and ACTH Disorders	
	Cortisol level	ACTH level
Cushing's syndrome (primary hypercortisolism)	High	Low
Cushing's disease (secondary hypercortisolism)	High	High
Iatrogenic Cushing's syndrome	High	Low
Addison's disease (primary adrenal insufficiency)	Low	High
Secondary adrenal insufficiency (hypopituitarism)	Low	Low

results in low levels of cortisol, usually due to damage to the pituitary gland. Levels of ACTH are also low in secondary adrenal insufficiency.

A variety of endocrine disorders are related to both high and low levels of cortisol and adrenocorticotropic hormone. Table 28B.1 summarizes these endocrine disorders.

Start by selecting **Measuring Cortisol and Adrenocorticotropic Hormone** from the **Experiment** menu. A new screen will appear (Figure 28B.5a) with five patient plasma samples and an HPLC (high-performance liquid chromatography) column that will be used to simulate the measurement of cortisol and adrenocorticotropic hormone (ACTH). There is a syringe that will be used to inject the samples into the HPLC injector for analysis. The **Cortisol** and **ACTH** buttons are used to prepare the column with solvents used to separate the two different hormones. The detector will measure the amount of the hormone and convert it into a concentration value.

1. Start the experiment by clicking the **Cortisol** button. This will prepare the column for the separation and measurement of cortisol.

2. Click and hold the syringe and drag it over to the first patient sample. Then release the mouse. The syringe will fill with plasma.

3. Click and hold the syringe again and drag it over to the **HPLC injector.** Then release the mouse. The sample will enter the tubing and flow through the column. The detector will display the concentration of cortisol in the first patient sample.

4. Click **Record Data.**

5. Click the **Clean** button under the syringe to prepare it for the next sample.

6. Click the **Clean Column** button near the top of the screen to remove residual cortisol from the column.

7. Repeat steps 2–6 for the remaining four patient samples.

8. Next, prepare the column for ACTH separation and measurement by clicking the **ACTH** button.

9. Click and hold the syringe and drag it over to the first patient sample. Then release the mouse. The syringe will fill with plasma.

10. Click and hold the syringe again and drag it over to the HPLC injector. Then release the mouse. The sample will enter the tubing and flow through the column. The detector will display the concentration of ACTH in the first patient sample.

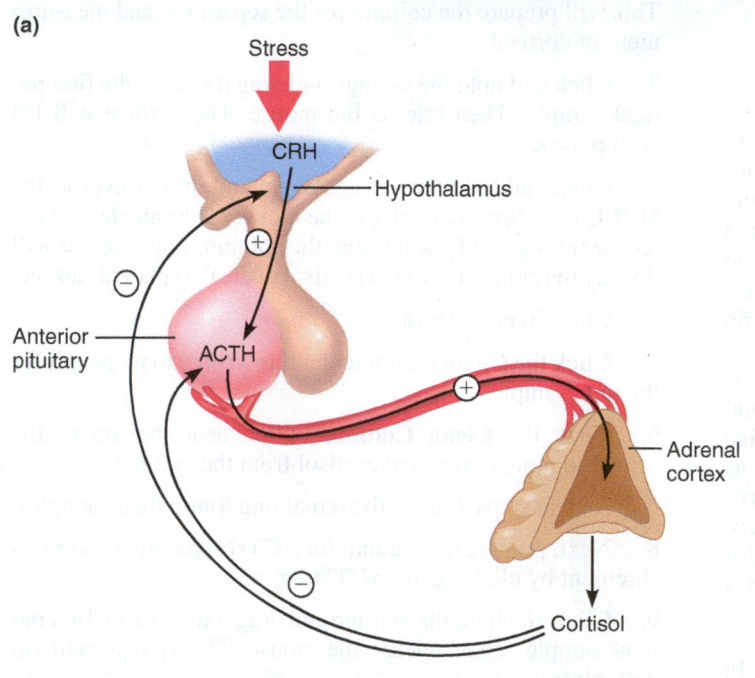

(a)

(b)

FIGURE 28B.5 Following the cortisol release pathway. (a) Opening screen of the Measuring Cortisol and ACTH experiment. **(b)** The regulation of cortisol secretion. + indicates stimulation of release, − indicates inhibition of release, CRH = corticotropin-releasing hormone, ACTH = adrenocorticotropic hormone.

TABLE 28B.2	Abnormal Morning Cortisol, ACTH Levels	
	High	Low
Cortisol	≥23 mcg/dl	<5 mcg/dl
ACTH	≥80 pg/ml	<20 pg/ml

Note: 1 mcg = 1μg = 1 microgram

11. Click **Record Data.**

12. Click the **Clean** button under the syringe to prepare it for the next sample.

13. Click the **Clean Column** button near the top of the screen.

14. Repeat steps 9–13 for the remaining four patient samples.

15. Select a row in the Data Set and choose **High** or **Low** based on the breakpoints shown in Table 28B.2 for cortisol and ACTH in plasma from a morning blood draw.

16. Click **Tools → Print Data** to print your recorded data for this experiment.

17. Record your results for each patient here and circle High or Low:

Patient 1: Cortisol _____ mcg/dl   High/Low

ACTH _____ pg/ml   High/Low

Patient 2: Cortisol _____ mcg/dl   High/Low

ACTH _____ pg/ml   High/Low

Patient 3: Cortisol _____ mcg/dl   High/Low

ACTH _____ pg/ml   High/Low

Patient 4: Cortisol _____ mcg/dl   High/Low

ACTH _____ pg/ml   High/Low

Patient 5: Cortisol _____ mcg/dl   High/Low

ACTH _____ pg/ml   High/Low

Endocrine System Physiology: Computer Simulation

NAME _____

LAB TIME/DATE _____

Metabolism

The following questions refer to Activity 1: Determining Baseline Metabolic Rates.

1. Which rat had the fastest baseline metabolic rate? _____

_____

2. Compare the baseline metabolic rates for the thyroidectomized rat and the normal rat and explain your results. _____

3. Compare the baseline metabolic rates for the hypophysectomized rat and the normal rat and explain your results. _____

_____

The following questions refer to Activity 2: Determining the Effect of Thyroxine on Metabolic Rate.

4. What effect did administering thyroxine have on each of the rats? _____

_____

_____

_____

5. Explain why thyroxine had these effects. _____

_____

_____

The following questions refer to Activity 3: Determining the Effect of TSH on Metabolic Rate.

6. Was there a change in the metabolic rate of the thyroidectomized rat with the administration of TSH? Explain your results. ____

_____

_____

7. Did the results for the thyroidectomized rat indicate hyperthyroidism or hypothyroidism? _____

_____

The following questions refer to Activity 4: Determining the Effect of Propylthiouracil on Metabolic Rate.

8. Describe the effect of administering propylthiouracil on each of the rats, and explain why it had this effect. _____

_____

_____

9. Do you think the drug propylthiouracil is used to treat hypothyroidism or hyperthyroidism? Explain your answer. _____

_____

Hormone Replacement Therapy

The following questions refer to Activity 5: Hormone Replacement Therapy.

10. Explain why ovariectomized rats were used in this experiment and correlate this to their baseline T score. _____

_____

_____

11. Recap your predictions regarding the effects of calcitonin and estrogen on bone density and explain why you made those

predictions. _____

_____

_____

12. Why was one of the ovariectomized rats injected with saline? _____

_____

13. What effect did the administration of estrogen injections have on the estrogen-treated rat? _____

_____

14. What effect did the administration of calcitonin injections have on the calcitonin-treated rat? _____

_____

15. How did your results compare to your predictions? _____

_____

_____

Insulin and Diabetes

The following question refers to Activity 6: Obtaining a Glucose Standard Curve.

16. What is a glucose standard curve, and how can you use this tool to determine a concentration of glucose? _____

_____

The following questions refer to Activity 7: Measuring Fasting Plasma Glucose.

17. Which patient(s) had glucose reading(s) in the normal range? _____

_____

18. Which patient(s) had glucose reading(s) in the diabetic range? _____

_____

19. Which patient(s) had glucose reading(s) in the impaired range? _____

_____

20. Describe the diagnosis for Patient 3. _____

_____

The following questions refer to Activity 8: Measuring Cortisol and Adrenocorticotropic Hormone.

21. Which patient would most likely be diagnosed with Cushing's disease? Why?

_____

_____

22. Which two patients have hormone levels characteristic of Cushing's syndrome?

_____

23. Patient 2 is being treated for rheumatoid arthritis with prednisone. How does this change the diagnosis? _____

_____

24. Which patient would most likely be diagnosed with Addison's disease? Why?

_____

_____

Blood Analysis: Computer Simulation

O B J E C T I V E S

1. To become familiar with the "normal" values obtained with selected blood tests.
2. To understand how common laboratory procedures for examining blood can indicate pathology, or a state of disease.
3. To learn how the following blood tests are performed:
   hematocrit (packed cell volume) determination
   erythrocyte sedimentation rate
   hemoglobin determination
   blood typing
   total blood cholesterol determination
4. To understand what each of these procedures is measuring in a sample of blood.
5. To realize the importance of proper disposal of laboratory equipment that has come in contact with blood.
6. To understand the importance of matching blood types for blood transfusions.

Blood transports soluble substances to and from all cells of the body. Blood cells are also important in defense against pathogens. Laboratory analysis of the blood gives important information about how well these functions are being carried out.

This lab exercise consists of five common laboratory tests performed on blood: hematocrit determination; erythrocyte sedimentation rate; hemoglobin determination; blood typing; and total cholesterol determination.

Hematocrit Determination

Hematocrit refers to the percentage of red blood cells (RBCs) in a sample of whole blood. A hematocrit of 48 means that 48% of the volume of blood is red blood cells. Since the function of red blood cells is the transport of oxygen to the cells of the body, the higher the hematocrit, the more red blood cells are available to carry oxygen.

Hematocrit values are determined by spinning a microcapillary tube filled with a whole blood sample in a special microhematocrit centrifuge. This procedure separates the blood cells from the blood plasma and leaves a "buffy coat" layer of white blood cells between the heavier red blood cell layer and the lighter plasma.

The hematocrit value can be determined after centrifuging by measuring the height of the layer of red cells in millimeters and dividing that number by the height of the initial column of blood to obtain the percentage of red blood cells.

The percentage of white blood cells (WBCs) can also be determined after centrifuging by comparing the height of the buffy coat to the initial height of the blood column.

The average hematocrit value for males is 47%, and the average for females is 42%. The normal upper limit is 55%. A lower-than-normal hematocrit indicates *anemia*. A higher-than-normal hematocrit indicates *polycythemia*.

FIGURE 29B.1 Opening screen of the Hematocrit Determination experiment.

Anemia is a condition in which insufficient oxygen is transported to the body's cells. There are many possible causes for anemia, including inadequate numbers of red blood cells, decreased amount of the oxygen-carrying pigment hemoglobin, and abnormal hemoglobin. The heme portion of hemoglobin molecules contains an atom of iron. If adequate iron is not available, the body cannot manufacture hemoglobin. This results in a condition called *iron-deficiency anemia*. *Aplastic anemia* is the result of the failure of the bone marrow to produce adequate blood cells. *Pernicious anemia* is due to a lack of vitamin B$_{12}$, which is necessary for cell division. Intrinsic factor, produced by the stomach, allows absorption of vitamin B$_{12}$. Individuals who do not produce adequate intrinsic factor, or individuals who do not have adequate vitamin B$_{12}$ in their diet, will suffer from pernicious anemia. *Sickle cell anemia* is an inherited condition in which the protein portion of hemoglobin molecules is folded incorrectly. As a result, oxygen molecules cannot fit with the misshapen hemoglobin, and anemia results.

Polycythemia refers to a significant increase in red blood cells. There are many possible causes of polycythemia, including living at high altitudes, strenuous athletic training, and tumors in the bone marrow.

In the following activity, we will simulate the blood test that is used to determine hematocrit. From the drop-down menu, select **Experiment 29B: Blood Analysis** and click **GO.** Before you perform the activities, watch the video **Blood Typing** to see how similar the simulation is to actual blood typing. Then click **Hematocrit Determination.** You will see the opening screen for the Hematocrit Determination experiment (Figure 29B.1).

To familiarize yourself with the equipment, select **Help** from the menu bar and then select **Balloons On/Off.** This feature allows you to scroll around the screen and view equipment labels. You can turn the feature off by returning to **Help** and then selecting **Balloons On/Off.**

In the upper right portion of the screen is a dispenser containing six thin tubes, which are *heparinized capillary tubes.* Heparin is a substance that keeps blood from clotting. Below the capillary tubes are six test tubes containing samples of blood to be tested. When a capillary tube is dragged to a test tube of blood, it partially fills by fluid capillary action.

To the left of the samples of blood is a container of *capillary tube sealer* (a clay material, shown on-screen as an orange-yellow substance). The capillary tubes must be sealed on one end with this tube sealer so that the blood sample can be centrifuged without spraying out the blood.

When the tubes have been sealed, they are moved to slots in the *microhematocrit centrifuge*. When you click the **Start** button, the centrifuge will rotate at 14,500 revolutions per minute.

After the centrifuge stops and opens, the capillary tubes are moved, one at a time, next to the metric ruler on the upper left of the screen. When you click the **Record Data** button next to the data table at the bottom of the screen, the following information about the sample will be recorded: the height of the column of blood in millimeters, the height of the red blood cell layer, the height of the buffy coat (white blood cells), the hematocrit (percentage of red blood cells) and the percentage of white blood cells.

In the lower left corner of the screen is a contaminated disposal container. Every piece of glassware that has come in contact with the blood must be disposed of by dragging it to this container for proper disposal.

A C T I V I T Y 1

Hematocrit Determination

The following individuals have contributed their blood for this test:

Sample 1: healthy male, living in Boston

Sample 2: healthy female, living in Boston

Sample 3: healthy male, living in Denver

Sample 4: healthy female, living in Denver

Sample 5: male with aplastic anemia

Sample 6: female with iron-deficiency anemia

1. Click and drag one heparinized capillary tube over to the test tube containing blood sample 1. Make sure the capillary tube is touching the blood. The capillary tube will fill itself by fluid capillary action.

2. Drag the capillary tube containing sample 1 to the container of capillary tube sealer to "seal" one end of the tube.

3. Drag the capillary tube to the microhematocrit centrifuge.

4. Repeat steps 1–3 for the remaining five samples of blood.

5. Set the timer for the centrifuge for 5 minutes by clicking the (+) button, and then click the **Start** button.

6. When the centrifuge stops and opens, click and drag capillary tube 1 to the metric ruler.

7. Click **Record Data** to record the information about sample 1.

8. Click and drag capillary tube 1 to the contaminated disposal container.

9. Repeat steps 6–8 for the remaining five capillary tubes in the centrifuge.

10. Click **Tools,** then **Print Data** to print the data from the table (or fill in Chart 1).

If you wish to restart or repeat the lab, click the **Reset** button next to the data table.

CHART 1	Blood Analysis Results				
Blood Sample	Total Height of Column of Blood (mm)	Height of Red Blood Cell Layer (mm)	Height of Buffy Coat (White Blood Cells) (mm)	Hematocrit	% WBC
Healthy male, living in Boston					
Healthy female, living in Boston					
Healthy male, living in Denver					
Healthy female, living in Denver					
Male with aplastic anemia					
Female with iron-deficiency anemia					

What is the hematocrit value of a healthy male living at sea level in Boston?

_____

What is the hematocrit value of a healthy male living at one mile elevation in Denver?

_____

Is there as much oxygen in the air in Denver as there is in Boston?

_____

How do your kidneys respond to a decrease in blood oxygen? (Review this section in your textbook if necessary.)

_____

_____

If your bone marrow is producing an elevated number of red blood cells, what happens to your hematocrit?

_____

_____

What is the hematocrit value of the male with aplastic anemia?

_____

_____

Would the red blood cell count for an individual with aplastic anemia be higher, lower, or the same as the red blood cell count of a healthy individual?

_____

_____

What is the hematocrit value of a healthy female living in Boston?

_____

_____

Explain the difference in hematocrit values obtained from a healthy female living in Boston and a female with iron-deficiency anemia.

_____

_____

Erythrocyte Sedimentation Rate

The **erythrocyte sedimentation rate (ESR)** measures the settling of red blood cells in a vertical, stationary tube of blood during one hour.

In a healthy individual, red blood cells do not settle very much in an hour. In some disease conditions, increased pro-duction of fibrinogen and immunoglobulins cause the red blood cells to clump together, stack up, and form a column (called a *rouleaux formation*). Grouped like this, red blood cells are heavier and settle faster.

This test is not a very specific or diagnostic test, but it can be used to follow the progression of certain disease conditions such as sickle cell anemia, certain cancers, and inflammatory diseases such as rheumatoid arthritis. When the disease worsens, the ESR increases; and when the disease improves, the ESR decreases. The ESR is elevated in iron-deficiency anemia. Sometimes a menstruating female will develop anemia and show an increase in ESR.

The ESR can be used to evaluate a patient with chest pains: the ESR is elevated in established myocardial infarction (heart attack) but normal in angina pectoris. Similarly, it can be useful in screening a female patient with severe abdominal pains because the ESR is not elevated within the first 24 hours of acute appendicitis but is elevated in the early stage of acute pelvic inflammatory disease (PID) or ruptured ectopic pregnancy.

Click **Experiment** on the menu bar, then select **Erythrocyte Sedimentation Rate.** You will see the opening screen for the Erythrocyte Sedimentation Rate lab (Figure 29B.2). Use the **Balloons On/Off** feature from the **Help** menu to familiarize yourself with the equipment on the screen.

In the upper left portion of the screen is a shelf with six samples of blood that have been treated with the anticoagulant heparin. Also on the shelf is a dropper bottle of sodium citrate. The sodium citrate is used to bind with calcium to prevent the blood samples from clotting so they can easily be poured into the narrow sedimentation rate tubes (used later in the lab).

Below the shelf is a test tube dispenser and a test tube rack. To the right of the test tube rack is a cabinet that contains six sedimentation tubes. This cabinet will open when all six blood samples have been added to the test tubes and diluted with sodium citrate. Below this cabinet is a timer, a window showing elapsed time, and a **Start** button to start the timer.

In the upper right portion of the screen is a magnifying chamber that will help you read the millimeter markings on the sedimentation tubes.

In the lower right portion of the screen is a contaminated disposal container. All glassware that has come in contact with the blood must be placed in this container for proper disposal.

When you click the **Record Data** button next to the data table at the bottom of the screen, the following information about the sample will be recorded: the distance that the RBCs have settled, time elapsed, and sedimentation rate.

A C T I V I T Y 2

Erythrocyte Sedimentation Rate

The following individuals have contributed their blood for this test:

Sample 1: healthy individual

Sample 2: menstruating female

Sample 3: person with sickle cell anemia

Sample 4: person with iron-deficiency anemia

Sample 5: person suffering from a myocardial infarction

Sample 6: person suffering from angina pectoris

FIGURE 29B.2 Opening screen of the Erythrocyte Sedimentation Rate experiment.

1. Individually click and drag six test tubes from the dispenser to the test tube rack.

2. Click the dropper for blood sample 1 and drag it to the first test tube. One milliliter of blood will be dispensed into the tube.

3. Repeat step 2 for the remaining five samples of blood, using a different test tube for each sample.

4. Click the dropper for the **3.8% sodium citrate** and drag it over the test tube containing blood sample 1; 0.5 milliliter of sodium citrate will be dispensed into the tube.

5. The dropper will automatically slide over to each of the remaining samples.

6. Click the **Mix** button. The samples will automatically mix for a few seconds.

7. After the samples have been mixed, the cabinet with six sedimentation tubes will open.

8. Click the tube containing blood sample 1. Notice that the pointer is now a small test tube pointed to the left.

9. While still holding the mouse button down, move the pointer to the first sedimentation tube in the cabinet.

The contents of the small test tube will be poured into the sedimentation tube.

10. Click and drag the now empty test tube to the contaminated disposal container.

11. Repeat steps 8–10 with the other five samples of blood.

12. When the six sedimentation tubes are filled, set the timer for 60 minutes by clicking the (+) button, and then click the **Start** button.

13. After 60 minutes have elapsed, drag sedimentation tube 1 to the magnifying chamber at the top right of the screen. Examine the tube. The tube is marked in millimeters, and the distance between two marks is 5 mm. How many millimeters has the blood settled?

_____

What is in the beige-colored portion of the tube? _____

14. Click the **Record Data** button next to the data table. The distance in millimeters that the red blood cells have settled,

the elapsed time, and the sedimentation rate will be entered in the table.

15. Drag the sedimentation tube to the contaminated disposal container.

16. Repeat steps 13–15 with the other five sedimentation tubes.

17. Click **Tools,** then **Print Data** to print the data from the table, or fill in Chart 2.

Did the person with sickle cell anemia show an elevated ESR?

_____

_____

How did the ESR for a person with iron-deficiency anemia compare to the ESR for a healthy individual?

_____

_____

Explain the ESR for sample 2, the menstruating female.

_____

_____

Explain the ESRs for samples 5 and 6 (the patients suffering from myocardial infarction and angina pectoris, respectively.)

_____

_____

Hemoglobin

Hemoglobin (Hb), a protein found in red blood cells, is necessary for the transport of oxygen from the lungs to the body's cells. Anemia results when insufficient oxygen is carried in the blood.

Hemoglobin molecules consist of four polypeptide chains of amino acids, the "globin" part of the molecule. Each polypeptide chain has a heme unit—a group of atoms, which includes an atom of iron. When the polypeptide chain folds up correctly, it has an appropriate shape to bind with a molecule of oxygen. So, each hemoglobin molecule can carry four molecules of oxygen. Oxygen combined with hemoglobin forms oxyhemoglobin, which has a bright red color.

A quantitative hemoglobin determination is useful for determining the classification and possible causes of anemia and gives useful information on some other disease conditions. For example, a person can have anemia with a normal red blood cell count, if there is inadequate hemoglobin in the red blood cells.

Normal blood contains an average of 12 to 18 grams of hemoglobin per 100 milliliters of blood. A healthy male has 13.5 to 18 g/100 ml; a healthy female has 12 to 16 g/100 ml. Hemoglobin values increase in patients with polycythemia, congestive heart failure, and chronic obstructive pulmonary disease (COPD). They also increase at high altitudes. Hemoglobin values decrease in patients with anemia, hyperthyroidism, cirrhosis of the liver, renal disease, systemic lupus erythematosus, and severe hemorrhage.

The hemoglobin content of a sample of blood can be determined by stirring the blood with a wooden stick to rupture, or lyse, the cells. The intensity of the color of the lysed blood

CHART 2	Erythrocyte Sedimentation Rate Results		
Blood Sample	Distance RBCs Have Settled (mm)	Elapsed Time	Sedimentation Rate
Healthy individual			
Menstruating female			
Person with sickle cell anemia			
Person with iron-deficiency anemia			
Person suffering from a myocardial infarction			
Person suffering from angina pectoris			

FIGURE 29B.3 Opening screen of the Hemoglobin Determination experiment.

is a result of the amount of hemoglobin present. A *hemoglobinometer* compares the color of the sample to standard values to determine the hemoglobin content of the sample. The hemoglobinometer transmits green light through the hemolyzed blood sample. The amount of light that passes through the sample is compared to standard color intensities. Green light is used because the human eye is able to easily detect subtle differences in green colors.

From the **Experiment** menu, select **Hemoglobin Determination.** You will see the opening screen for the Hemoglobin Determination lab (Figure 29B.3). Use the **Balloons On/Off** feature from the **Help** menu to familiarize yourself with the equipment on the screen.

In the upper right portion of the screen is a shelf with five samples of blood.

In the middle of the screen is a lab table and a container of hemolysis sticks. The hemolysis sticks will be used to stir the blood samples to lyse the red blood cells, thereby releasing their hemoglobin.

At the bottom left of the screen is a blood chamber dispenser that provides a slide with a depression to receive the blood sample.

Above the blood chamber dispenser is a hemoglobinometer. The hemoglobinometer has a black rectangular slot to receive the blood chamber and an **Eject** button to remove the blood chamber. When the loaded blood chamber is inserted into the slot, the hemoglobinometer view will change to show a split screen that compares the color of the hemolyzed blood sample to a standard color for which given levels of hemoglobin are already known. A window on the hemoglobinometer displays the grams of hemoglobin per 100 milliliters of blood. You can move the small handle on the top right of the hemoglobinometer until the colors shown on the device match the colors of the sample of blood to be tested.

When you click the **Record Data** button next to the data table at the bottom of the screen, the grams of hemoglobin per 100 milliliters of blood will be recorded.

In the lower right portion of the screen is a contaminated disposal container. All glassware and hemolysis sticks that have come in contact with the blood must be placed in this container for proper disposal.

ACTIVITY 3

Hemoglobin (Hb) Determination

The following individuals have contributed their blood for this test:

Sample 1: healthy male

Sample 2: healthy female

Sample 3: female with iron-deficiency anemia

Sample 4: male with polycythemia

Sample 5: female Olympic athlete

1.   Click and drag a clean blood chamber slide from the blood chamber dispenser to the lab table.

2.   Click the dropper for blood sample 1 and drag it over to the depression on the blood chamber slide. A drop of blood will be dispensed into the depression.

3.   Click a hemolysis stick and drag it to the drop of blood. The stick will stir the blood sample for 45 seconds, lysing the red blood cells and releasing their hemoglobin.

4.   Drag the hemolysis stick to the contaminated disposal container.

5.   Drag the blood chamber slide to the dark rectangular slot on the hemoglobinometer.

6.   You will see a pop-up window appear, displaying the view inside the hemoglobinometer. The left half of the circular field shows the intensity of green light transmitted by blood sample 1. The right half of the circular field shows the intensity of green light for known levels of hemoglobin present in blood.

7.   Click and hold the lever on the top right of the hemoglobinometer, and slowly drag it downward until the right half of the field matches the shade of green on the left side of the field.

8.   Click the **Record Data** button next to the data table to record the grams of hemoglobin per 100 milliliters of blood for blood sample 1. Click **X** to close the pop-up window.

9.   Click the **Eject** button to remove the blood chamber with blood sample 1 from the hemoglobinometer.

10.   Drag the blood sample 1 chamber to the contaminated disposal container.

11.   Repeat steps 1–10 for the remaining samples of blood.

Fill in Chart 3, using the grams of hemoglobin per 100 milliliters of blood that you obtained in this exercise. Use the packed cell volume (PCV) data provided in Chart 3 to calculate the ratio of PCV to Hb.

An individual might have a normal or near normal hematocrit value (packed cell volume) and still suffer from anemia if the red blood cells do not contain adequate hemoglobin. A normal ratio of packed cell volume to grams of hemoglobin is approximately 3:1.

What is the hematocrit value for the healthy male?

_____

What is the hematocrit value for the healthy female?

_____

What does the ratio of PCV to Hb tell you about the red blood cells of the female with iron-deficiency anemia?

_____

Does the male with polycythemia have a normal ratio of PCV

to Hb? _____

CHART 3	Hemoglobin Determination		
Blood Sample	Hb in grams per 100 ml of blood	Hematocrit (PCV)	Ratio of PCV to Hb
Healthy male		48	
Healthy female		44	
Female with iron-deficiency anemia		40	
Male with polycythemia		60	
Female Olympic athlete		60	

Based on these results, do you think his red blood cells contain adequate quantities of hemoglobin molecules? Why?

_____

_____

Does the female Olympic athlete have a normal ratio of PCV

to Hb? _____

Based on these results, do you think her red blood cells contain adequate quantities of hemoglobin molecules? Why?

_____

_____ ▬

Blood Typing

All of the cells in the human body, including the red blood cells, are surrounded by a *plasma (cell) membrane*. The plasma membrane contains genetically determined glycoproteins, called antigens, that identify the cells. On red blood cell membranes, these antigens are called *agglutinogens*.

It is important to determine blood types before performing blood transfusions in order to avoid mixing incompatible blood. Although many different antigens are present on red blood cell membranes, the ABO and Rh antigens cause the most vigorous and potentially fatal transfusion reactions. If a blood transfusion recipient has antibodies (called *agglutinins*) to the antigens present on the transfused cells, the red blood cells will be clumped together, or *agglutinated,* and then lysed. This results in a potentially life-threatening blood transfusion reaction.

The ABO blood groups are determined by the presence or absence of two antigens: type A and type B (see Figure 29B.4b). These antigens are genetically determined so a person has two copies (alleles) of the gene for these proteins, one copy from each parent. The presence of these antigens is due to a dominant gene, and their absence is due to a recessive gene.

- A person with type A blood can have two gene alleles for the A antigen, or that person could have one gene allele for type A antigen and the other allele for the absence of either A or B antigen.

- A person with type B blood can have two gene alleles for the B antigen, or that person could have one gene allele for type B antigen and the other allele for the absence of either A or B antigen.

- A person with type AB blood has one gene allele for the A antigen and the other allele for the B antigen.

- A person with type O blood will have inherited two recessive gene alleles and has neither type A nor type B antigen.

Antibodies to the A and B antigens are found preformed in the blood plasma. A person has antibodies only for the antigens not on his or her red blood cells, so a person with type A blood will have anti-B antibodies. This is summarized in Chart 4.

CHART 4	ABO Blood Types	
Blood Type	Antigens on RBCs	Antibodies Present in Plasma
A	A	anti-B
B	B	anti-A
AB	A and B	none
O	none	anti-A and anti-B

The Rh factor is another genetically determined protein that may be present on red blood cell membranes. Approximately 85% of the population is Rh positive and has this protein. Antibodies to the Rh factor are not found preformed in the plasma. These antibodies are produced only after exposure to the Rh factor by persons who are Rh negative.

Separate drops of a blood sample are mixed with antisera containing antibodies to the types A and B antigens and antibodies to the Rh factor. An agglutination reaction (showing clumping) indicates the presence of the agglutinogen.

In this experiment, you will conduct blood typing tests on six blood samples. From the **Experiment** menu, select **Blood Typing.** You will see the opening screen for the Blood Typing lab (Figure 29B.4a). Use the **Balloons On/Off** feature from the **Help** menu to familiarize yourself with the equipment on the screen.

In the upper right portion of the screen is a shelf with six samples of blood.

In the upper left portion of the screen is a shelf containing bottles of anti-A serum (blue color), anti-B serum (yellow color), and anti-Rh serum (white color). These bottles contain antibodies to the A antigen, B antigen, and Rh antigen, respectively.

In the center of the screen is a lab table for performing the blood typing. To the left of the lab table is a blood typing slide dispenser.

Above the blood typing slide dispenser is a container of stirring sticks. These sticks are color coded: the blue stick is to be used with the anti-A serum, the yellow stick is to be used with the anti-B serum, and the white stick is to be used with the anti-Rh serum.

To the right of the lab table is a *light box* for viewing the blood type samples. When you click the **Light** button, the screen above unrolls to display the blood types.

To the left of the light box is a data table to record your results.

(a)

A antigen   B antigen

Type A   **Type B**   **Type AB**   **Type O**

(b) **Blood type surface antigens**

FIGURE 29B.4 Blood typing. (a) Opening screen of the Blood Typing experiment. **(b)** Antigens determining ABO blood type, found on the surface of red blood cells.

In the bottom right portion of the screen is a contaminated disposal container. All glassware and sticks that have come in contact with blood must be placed in this container for proper disposal.

ACTIVITY 4

Blood Typing

Six individuals with different blood types have donated their blood for this exercise.

1. Click and drag a blood typing slide from the blood typing slide dispenser to the lab table. Note that the three wells on the slide are labeled "A," "B," and "Rh."

2. Click the dropper for blood sample 1 and drag it over the well labeled A on the blood typing slide. A drop of blood will be dispensed into the well.

3. The dropper will automatically slide over to each of the remaining wells.

4. Click the dropper for anti-A serum and drag it over the well labeled A on the blood typing slide. A drop of anti-A serum will be dispensed into the well.

5. Repeat step 4 with the anti-B serum. Be sure to dispense it into the well labeled B.

6. Repeat step 4 with the anti-Rh serum. Be sure to dispense it into the well labeled Rh.

7. Obtain a blue-tipped stirring stick, and drag it to well A. It will mix the blood and anti-A serum.

8. Dispose of the stirring stick in the contaminated disposal container.

9. Select a yellow-tipped stirring stick and drag it to well B.

10. Dispose of the stirring stick in the contaminated disposal container.

11. Select a white-tipped stirring stick and drag it to well Rh.

12. Dispose of the stirring stick in the contaminated disposal container.

13. Drag the blood typing slide to the light box and click the **Light** button. The screen will unroll, displaying the results of the blood typing.

14. Examine the results labeled A on the screen. If coagulation (agglutination, or "clumpiness") is present, click **Positive.** If no coagulation is present (the sample will look smooth), click **Negative.**

15. Repeat step 14 for the results labeled B and Rh. In each case, choose **Positive** if the sample is coagulated and **Negative** if the sample is not coagulated.

16. Click the **Record Data** button on the data table to record the results of blood sample 1.

17. Click and drag the blood typing slide to the contaminated disposal container.

18. Click the **X** at the top right of the scroll to close the scroll.

19. Repeat steps 1–18 for the remaining samples of blood.

Using the data you have collected in this activity, fill in Chart 5. (Indicate coagulation as either "positive" or "negative.") Determine the blood type of each sample and fill in the last

column. For Rh positive or negative, add + or − to the blood type; for example, AB+.

If the anti-A antibody causes the blood to coagulate, which antigen would be present on the blood cells?

_____

If a person has type AB blood, which antigens are present on the red blood cells?

_____

Which antibodies are present in the plasma of a person with type AB blood?

_____

Does a person with type O blood have A or B antigens on the red blood cells?

_____

Blood Cholesterol

Cholesterol is a lipid substance that is essential for life. It is an important component of all cell membranes and is the basis for making steroid hormones, vitamin D, and bile salts.

Cholesterol is produced in the human liver and is present in foods of animal origin, such as milk, meat, and eggs. Since cholesterol is a water-insoluble lipid, it needs to be wrapped in protein packages, called lipoproteins, to travel in the watery blood from the liver and digestive organs to the cells of the body.

CHART 5	Blood Typing Results			
Blood Sample	Agglutination with Anti-A Serum	Agglutination with Anti-B Serum	Agglutination with Anti-Rh Serum	Blood Type
1				
2				
3				
4				
5				
6				

FIGURE 29B.5 Opening screen of the Total Cholesterol Determination experiment.

One type of lipoprotein package, called LDL (low-density liproprotein), has been identified as a potential source of damage to the interior of arteries because it can contribute to atherosclerosis, the buildup of plaque, in these blood vessels. A total blood cholesterol determination does not measure the level of LDLs, but it does provide valuable information about the total amount of cholesterol in the blood.

Less than 200 milligrams of total cholesterol per deciliter of blood is considered desirable. Between 200 and 239 mg/dl is considered borderline high cholesterol. Over 240 mg/dl is considered high blood cholesterol and is associated with increased risk of cardiovascular disease. Abnormally low blood levels of cholesterol (total cholesterol lower than 100 mg/dl) can also be a problem. Low levels may indicate hyperthyroidism (overactive thyroid gland), liver disease, inadequate absorption of nutrients from the intestine, or malnutrition. Other reports link hypocholesterolemia (low blood cholesterol) to depression, anxiety, and mood disturbances, which are thought to be controlled by the level of available serotonin, a neurotransmitter. There is evidence of a relationship between low levels of blood cholesterol and low levels of serotonin in the brain.

In this test for total blood cholesterol, a sample of blood is mixed with enzymes that produce a colored reaction with cholesterol. The intensity of the color indicates the amount of cholesterol present. The cholesterol tester compares the color of the sample to the colors of known levels of cholesterol (standard values).

From the **Experiment** menu, select **Total Cholesterol Determination.** You will see the opening screen for the Total Cholesterol Determination lab (Figure 29B.5). Use the **Balloons On/Off** feature from the **Help** menu to familiarize yourself with the equipment on the screen.

In the upper right portion of the screen is a dispenser of *lancets,* sharp needlelike instruments that are used to prick the finger to obtain a drop of blood.

Beneath the lancet dispenser is a patient's finger. You can specify a new patient by clicking the **Next Patient** button beneath the finger.

On top of the data table is a container of alcohol wipes for cleaning the fingertip before it is punctured with the lancet.

The left portion of the screen shows a cabinet containing a *color wheel* that is divided into sections showing different intensities of green. Each shade of green corresponds to a range of total cholesterol levels. Below the cabinet is a timer that can be set for 1 to 3 minutes.

In the upper left portion of the screen is a cholesterol strip dispenser. These cholesterol strips contain chemicals that convert, by a series of reactions, the cholesterol in the blood sample into a green-colored solution. These reactions take 3 minutes. By matching the color of the cholesterol strip to a color on the color wheel, you can determine the cholesterol level of a given blood sample. Higher levels of cholesterol will result in a deeper green color.

The bottom of the screen has a data table for recording the total cholesterol level of the blood samples.

In the lower right portion of the screen is a contaminated disposal container. Dispose of any piece of equipment that has come into contact with the blood by dragging it to this contaminated disposal container.

ACTIVITY 5

Total Cholesterol Determination

1. Click and drag an alcohol wipe over the end of patient 1's finger.

2. Click and drag a lancet to the tip of the finger. The lancet will prick the finger to obtain a drop of blood.

3. Drag the lancet to the contaminated disposal container.

4. Drag a cholesterol strip to the finger to transfer the blood to the strip.

5. Drag the cholesterol strip to the rectangular area to the right of the color wheel.

6. Set the timer for 3 minutes, and click **Start.** Notice that the strip begins to change color.

7. After 3 minutes, decide which color on the color wheel most closely matches the color on the cholesterol test strip. Click that color. It is sometimes difficult to match the color on the cholesterol strip with the appropriate color on the color wheel. If the color you have chosen is not an exact match, you will see a pop-up window asking you to try again.

8. Click **Record Data** to record this information in the data table.

9. Drag the cholesterol test strip for patient 1 to the contaminated disposal container. Record your results in Chart 6.

10. There are a total of four patients. Click **Next Patient** and repeat steps 1–9 until you have collected data for all four patients.

What health problems might be in store for patient 2, based on these results?

_____

What advice about diet and exercise would you give patient 4?

_____

CHART 6	Total Cholesterol Determination	
Blood Sample	Approximate Total Cholesterol	Cholesterol Level
1		
2		
3		
4		

Blood Analysis: Computer Simulation

NAME _____

LAB TIME/DATE _____

Hematocrit Determination

The following questions refer to Activity 1: Hematocrit Determination.

1. List the following values from Chart 1:

   Hematocrit value for healthy male living at sea level in Boston = _____

   Hematocrit value for healthy female living at sea level in Boston = _____

2. Were the values listed in question 1 within normal range? _____

3. Describe the difference between the male and the female hematocrit for an individual living in Boston. _____

   _____

4. List the following values from Chart 1:

   Hematocrit value for healthy male living in Denver = _____

   Hematocrit value for healthy female living in Denver = _____

5. How did these values differ from the values for Boston? _____

   _____

6. Describe the effect of living at high elevations on a person's hematocrit. _____

   _____

7. Describe how the kidneys respond to a decrease in oxygen and what effect this has on hematocrit. _____

   _____

8. List the following values from Chart 1:

   Hematocrit value for male with aplastic anemia = _____

   % WBC for male with aplastic anemia = _____

9. Were the values listed in question 8 within the normal range? Why or why not? _____

   _____

   _____

10. List the following value from Chart 1:

    Hematocrit for female with iron-deficiency anemia = _____

11. Was the value in question 10 normal or not? Explain. _____

    _____

Erythrocyte Sedimentation Rate

The following questions refer to Activity 2: Erythrocyte Sedimentation Rate.

12. Describe the effect that sickle cell anemia has on the sedimentation rate. _____

    _____

13. Why do you think that it has this effect? Hint: Sickle cell anemia alters the shape of red blood cells. _____

    _____

14. Record the sedimentation rate for a menstruating female. _____

15. How did this value compare to the healthy individual? Why? _____

    _____

16. What was the sedimentation rate for the iron-deficient individual? _____

17. What effect does iron deficiency have on ESR? _____

    _____

18. Record the following values from Chart 2:

    ESR for person suffering from a myocardial infarction = _____

    ESR for person suffering from angina pectoris = _____

19. Compare the values in question 18 and explain how they might be used to monitor heart conditions._____

    _____

20. List some other conditions that ESR is used to monitor. _____

    _____

Hemoglobin

The following questions refer to Activity 3: Hemoglobin (Hb) Determination.

21. Describe the ratio of packed cell volume to Hb (hemoglobin) obtained for the healthy male and female subjects. _____

    _____

22. Describe the ratio of packed cell volume to Hb (hemoglobin) for the female with iron-deficiency anemia. _____

23. Is the female with iron-deficiency anemia deficient in hemoglobin? _____

24. Is the male with polycythemia deficient in hemoglobin? _____

25. Is the female Olympic athlete deficient in hemoglobin? _____

26. List conditions in which Hb would decrease. _____

    _____

27. List conditions in which Hb would increase. _____

    _____

Blood Typing

The following questions refer to Activity 4: Blood Typing.

28. Which blood sample contained the rarest blood type? _____

29. Which blood sample contained the universal donor? _____

30. Which blood sample contained the universal recipient? _____

31. Which blood sample did not coagulate with any of the antibodies tested? _____

    Why? _____

32. What antibodies would be found in the plasma of blood sample 1? _____

33. When an individual is transfused with blood that is compatible but not the same type, it is important to separate packed cells

    from the plasma and administer only the packed cells. Why do you think this is done? _____

    _____

34. List which blood samples in this experiment represent people who could donate blood to a person with type B⁺. _____

    _____

Blood Cholesterol

The following questions refer to Activity 5: Total Cholesterol Determination.

35. Which patient had desirable cholesterol levels? _____

36. Which patient(s) had an elevated cholesterol level? _____

37. Describe the risks for the patient identified in question 36. _____

38. Which advice would you give patient 4? Why? _____

_____

39. Describe some reasons why a patient might have abnormally low blood cholesterol.

_____

_____

Cardiovascular Dynamics: Computer Simulation

1. To define the following terms: *blood flow, peripheral resistance, viscosity, systole, diastole, end diastolic volume, end systolic volume, stroke volume,* and *cardiac output.*

2. To explore cardiovascular dynamics using an experimental setup to simulate a human body function.

3. To understand that heart and blood vessel functions are highly coordinated.

4. To recognize that pressure differences provide the driving force that moves blood through the blood vessels.

5. To recognize that body tissues may differ in their blood demands at a given time.

6. To identify the most important factors in control of blood flow.

7. To recognize that changing blood vessel diameter can alter the pumping ability of the heart.

8. To examine the effect of stroke volume on blood flow.

The physiology of human blood circulation can be divided into two distinct but remarkably harmonized processes: (1) the pumping of blood by the heart, and (2) the transport of blood to all body tissues via the vasculature, or blood vessels. Blood supplies all body tissues with the substances needed for survival, so it is vital that blood delivery is ample for tissue demands.

The Mechanics of Circulation

To understand how blood is transported throughout the body, let's examine three important factors influencing how blood circulates through the cardiovascular system: blood flow, blood pressure, and peripheral resistance.

Blood flow is the amount of blood moving through a body area or the entire cardiovascular system in a given amount of time. Total blood flow is determined by cardiac output (the amount of blood the heart is able to pump per minute); however, blood flow to specific body areas can vary dramatically in a given time period. Organs differ in their requirements from moment to moment, and blood vessels constrict or dilate to regulate local blood flow to various areas in response to the tissues' immediate needs. Consequently, blood flow can increase to some regions and decrease to other areas at the same time.

Blood pressure is the force blood exerts against the wall of a blood vessel. Owing to cardiac activity, pressure is highest at the heart end of any artery. Because of the effect of peripheral resistance, which will be discussed shortly, pressure within the arteries (or any blood vessel) drops as the distance (vessel length) from the heart increases. This pressure gradient causes blood to move from and then back to the heart, always moving from high- to low-pressure areas.

Peripheral resistance is the opposition to blood flow resulting from the friction developed as blood streams through blood vessels. Three factors affect vessel resistance: blood viscosity, vessel radius, and vessel length.

Blood viscosity is a measure of the "thickness" of the blood, and is caused by the presence of proteins and formed elements in the plasma (the fluid part of the blood). As the viscosity of a fluid increases, its flow rate through a tube decreases.

Blood viscosity in healthy people normally does not change, but certain conditions, such as too many or too few blood cells, may modify it.

Controlling *blood vessel radius* (one-half of the diameter) is the principal method of blood flow control. This is accomplished by contracting or relaxing the smooth muscle within the blood vessel walls. To see why radius has such a pronounced effect on blood flow, consider the physical relationship between blood and the vessel wall. Blood in direct contact with the vessel wall flows relatively slowly because of the friction, or drag, between the blood and the lining of the vessel. In contrast, fluid in the center of the vessel flows more freely because it is not rubbing against the vessel wall. Now picture a large- and a small-radius vessel: proportionately more blood is in contact with the wall of the small vessel; hence blood flow is notably impeded as vessel radius decreases.

Although *vessel length* does not ordinarily change in a healthy person, any increase in vessel length causes a corresponding flow decrease. This effect is principally caused by friction between blood and the vessel wall. Consequently, given two blood vessels of the same diameter, the longer vessel will have more resistance, and thus a reduced blood flow.

The Effect of Blood Pressure and Vessel Resistance on Blood Flow

Blood flow is directly proportional to blood pressure because the pressure difference (Δ pressure) between the two ends of a vessel is the driving force for blood flow. Peripheral resistance is the force that opposes blood flow. This relationship is represented in the following equation:

$$\text{Blood flow (ml/min)} = \frac{\Delta \text{ pressure}}{\text{peripheral resistance}}$$

Three factors contribute to peripheral resistance: viscosity (V), blood vessel length (L), and the radius of the blood vessel (r). These relationships are expressed in the following equation:

$$\text{Peripheral resistance} = \frac{8(V)(L)}{\pi r^4}$$

From this equation, we can see that the viscosity of the blood and the length of the blood vessel are directly proportional to peripheral resistance. The peripheral resistance is inversely proportional to the fourth power of the vessel radius.

If we combine the two equations, we get the following result:

$$\text{Blood flow (ml/min)} = \frac{\Delta \text{ pressure } \pi r^4}{8(V)(L)}$$

From this combination, we can see that blood flow is directly proportional to the fourth power of vessel radius, which means that small changes in vessel radius result in dramatic changes in blood flow.

Vessel Resistance

Imagine for a moment that you are one of the first cardiovascular researchers interested in the physics of blood flow. Your first task as the principal investigator for this project is to plan an effective experimental design simulating a simple fluid pumping system that can be related to the mechanics of the cardiovascular system. The initial phenomenon you study is how fluids, including blood, flow through tubes or blood vessels. Questions you might ask include:

1. What role does pressure play in the flow of fluid?

2. How does peripheral resistance affect fluid flow?

The equipment required to solve these and other questions has already been designed for you in the form of a computerized simulation, which frees you to focus on the logic of the experiment. The first part of the computer simulation indirectly investigates the effects of pressure, vessel radius, viscosity, and vessel length on fluid flow. The second part of the experiment explores the effects of several variables on the output of a single-chamber pump. Follow the specific guidelines in the exercise for collecting data. As you do so, also try to imagine alternative methods of achieving the same experimental goal.

Choose **Exercise 33B: Cardiovascular Dynamics** from the drop-down menu and click **GO.** Then click **Vessel Resistance.** The opening screen will appear in a few seconds (Figure 33B.1). Select **Balloons-On/Off** from the **Help** menu for help identifying the equipment on-screen (you will see labels appear as you move the cursor over each piece of equipment). Select **Balloons On/Off** to turn this feature off before you begin the experiments.

The primary features on the screen when the program starts are a pair of glass beakers perched atop a simulated electronic device called the *equipment control unit,* which is used to set experimental parameters and to operate the equipment. When you click the **Start** button (beneath the left beaker), the simulated blood flows from the left beaker (source) to the right beaker (destination) through the connecting tube. To relate this to the human body, think of the left beaker as the left side of your heart, the tube as your aorta, and the right beaker as any organ to which blood is flowing.

Click the **Refill** button to refill the source beaker after an experimental trial. You can adjust experimental parameters by clicking the plus (+) or minus (−) buttons to the right of each display window.

The equipment in the lower part of the screen is called the *data collection unit.* This equipment records and displays data you accumulate during the experiments. The data set for the first experiment (Radius) is highlighted in the **Data Sets** window. You can add or delete a data set by clicking the appropriate button to the right of the **Data Sets** window. The **Record Data** button in the lower right part of the screen activates automatically after an experimental trial. Clicking the **Delete Line** or **Clear Data Set** buttons erases any data you want to delete.

You will record the data you accumulate in the experimental values grid in the lower middle part of the screen.

ACTIVITY 1

Studying the Effect of Flow Tube Radius on Fluid Flow

Our initial study will examine the effect of flow tube radius on fluid flow.

1. Open the **Vessel Resistance** window if it isn't already open.

The Radius line in the data collection unit should be highlighted in bright blue. If it is not, choose it by clicking the

FIGURE 33B.1 Opening screen of the Vessel Resistance experiment.

Radius line. The data collection unit will now record flow variations due to changing flow tube radius.

If the data grid is not empty, click **Clear Data Set** to discard all previous values.

If the left beaker is not full, click **Refill.**

2. Adjust the flow tube radius to 1.5 mm and the viscosity to 1.0 by clicking the appropriate (+) or (−) button. During the course of this part of the experiment, maintain the other experiment conditions at:

100 mm Hg driving pressure (top left)

50-mm flow tube length (middle right)

3. Click **Start,** and watch the fluid move into the right beaker. (Fluid moves slowly under some conditions—be patient!) Pressure (currently set to 100 mm Hg) propels fluid from the left beaker to the right beaker through the flow tube. The flow rate is displayed in the Flow window when the left beaker has finished draining. Now click **Record Data** to display the flow rate and experimental parameters in the experi-

mental values grid (and retain the data in the computer's memory for printing and saving). Click **Refill** to replenish the left beaker.

4. Increase the radius in 0.5-mm increments, and repeat step 3 until the maximum radius (6.0 mm) is achieved. Be sure to click **Record Data** after each fluid transfer. If you make an error and want to delete a data value, click the data line in the experimental values grid and then click **Delete Line.**

5. View your data graphically by choosing **Plot Data** from the **Tools** menu. Choose **Radius** as the data set to be graphed, and then use the slider bars to select the radius data to be plotted on the X-axis and the flow data to be plotted on the Y-axis. You can highlight individual data points by clicking a line in the data grid. When you finish, click the close box at the top of the plot window.

What happened to the fluid flow rate as the radius of the flow tube was increased?

_____

_____

Circle the correct term within the parentheses: Because fluid flow is proportional to the fourth power of the radius, (increases / decreases) in tube radius cause (increases / decreases) in fluid flow.

Is the relationship between the fluid flow rate and the flow tube radius linear or exponential? _____

In this experiment, a simulated motor changes the diameter of the flow tube. Explain how our blood vessels alter blood flow.

_____

_____

_____

_____

After a heavy meal when we are relatively inactive, we might expect blood vessels in the skeletal muscles to be somewhat

_____, whereas blood vessels in the digestive

organs are probably _____. ▮

ACTIVITY 2

Studying the Effect of Viscosity on Fluid Flow

With a viscosity of 3 to 4, blood is much more viscous than water (1.0 viscosity). Although viscosity is altered by factors such as dehydration and altered blood cell numbers, a body in homeostatic balance has a relatively stable blood consistency. Nonetheless it is useful to examine the effects of viscosity changes on fluid flow because we can then predict what might occur in the human cardiovascular system during certain homeostatic imbalances.

1. Set the starting conditions as follows:
- 100 mm Hg driving pressure
- 5.0-mm flow tube radius
- 1.0 viscosity
- 50-mm flow tube length

2. Click the **Viscosity** data set in the data collection unit. (This action prepares the experimental values grid to record the viscosity data.)

3. **Refill** the left beaker if you have not already done so.

4. Click **Start** to begin the experiment. After all the fluid has drained into the right beaker, click **Record Data** to record this data point, and then click **Refill** to replenish the left beaker.

5. In 1.0-unit increments, increase the fluid viscosity by clicking (+) next to the **Viscosity** window, and repeat step 4 until the maximum viscosity (10.0) is reached.

6. View your data graphically by choosing **Plot Data** from the **Tools** menu. Choose **Viscosity** as the data set to be graphed, and then use the slider bars to plot the viscosity data on the X-axis and the flow data on the Y-axis. You can highlight individual data points by clicking a line in the data grid. When finished, click the close box at the top of the plot window.

How does fluid flow change as viscosity is modified?

_____

_____

_____

Is fluid flow versus viscosity an inverse or direct relationship?

_____

Is the effect of viscosity greater or less than the effect of radius on fluid flow?

_____

_____

Predict the effect of anemia (e.g., fewer red blood cells than normal) on blood flow.

_____

_____

What might happen to blood flow if we increased the number of blood cells?

_____

_____

_____

Blood viscosity would _____ in conditions of

dehydration, resulting in _____ blood flow. ▮

ACTIVITY 3

Studying the Effect of Flow Tube Length on Fluid Flow

With the exception of the normal growth that occurs until the body reaches full maturity, blood vessel length does not significantly change. In this activity you will investigate the physical relationship between vessel length and blood movement; specifically, how blood flow changes in flow tubes (vessels) of constant radius but of different lengths.

1. Set the starting conditions as follows:

- 100 mm Hg driving pressure
- 5.0-mm flow tube radius
- 3.5 viscosity
- 10-mm flow tube length

2. Click the **Length** data set in the data collection unit. (This action prepares the experimental values grid to display the length data.)

3. Click **Refill** to refill the left beaker if you have not already done so.

4. Click **Start** to begin the experiment. After all the fluid has drained into the right beaker, click **Record Data** to record this data point, and then click **Refill** to refill the left beaker.

5. In 5-mm increments, increase the flow tube length by clicking (+) next to the **Length** window, and repeat step 4 until the maximum length (50 mm) has been reached.

6. View your data graphically by choosing **Plot Data** from the **Tools** menu. Choose **Length** as the data set to be graphed, and then use the slider bars to select the length data to be plotted on the X-axis and the flow data to be plotted on the Y-axis. You can highlight individual data points by clicking a line in the grid. When finished, click the close box at the top of the plot window.

How does flow tube length affect fluid flow?

_____

_____

_____

What effect do you think obesity would have on blood flow? Hint: Relate obesity to changes in blood vessel length.

_____

_____

_____

ACTIVITY 4

Studying the Effect of Pressure on Fluid Flow

The pressure difference between the two ends of a blood vessel is the driving force behind blood flow. In comparison, our experimental setup pressurizes the left beaker, thereby providing the driving force that propels fluid through the flow tube to the right beaker. You will examine the effect of pressure on fluid flow in this part of the experiment.

1. Set the starting conditions as follows:

- 25 mm Hg driving pressure
- 5.0-mm flow tube radius
- 3.5 viscosity
- 50-mm flow tube length

2. Click the **Pressure** data set in the data collection unit. (This action prepares the experimental values grid for the pressure data.)

3. Click **Refill** to refill the left beaker if you have not already done so.

4. Click **Start** to begin the experiment. After all the fluid has moved into the right beaker, click **Record Data** to record this data point. Click **Refill** to refill the left beaker.

5. In increments of 25 mm Hg, increase the driving pressure by clicking (+) next to the **Pressure** window, and repeat step 4 until the maximum pressure (225 mm Hg) has been reached.

6. View your data graphically by choosing **Plot Data** from the **Tools** menu. Choose **Pressure** as the data set to be graphed, and then use the slider bars to plot the pressure data on the X-axis and the flow data on the Y-axis. You can highlight individual data points by clicking a line in the data grid. When finished, click the close box at the top of the plot window.

How does driving pressure affect fluid flow?

_____

_____

_____

How does this plot differ from the plots for tube radius, viscosity, and tube length?

_____

_____

_____

Although changing pressure could be used to control blood flow, explain why this approach would not be as effective as altering blood vessel radius.

_____

_____

_____

7.   Click **Tools** → **Print Data** to print your recorded data for this experiment. ▮

Pump Mechanics

In the human body, the heart beats approximately 70 strokes each minute. Each heartbeat consists of a filling interval, during which blood moves into the chambers of the heart, and an ejection period when blood is actively pumped into the great arteries. The pumping activity of the heart can be described in terms of the phases of the cardiac cycle. Heart chambers fill during **diastole** (relaxation of the heart) and pump blood out during **systole** (contraction of the heart). As you can imagine, the length of time the heart is relaxed is one factor that determines the amount of blood within the heart at the end of the filling interval. Up to a point, increasing ventricular filling time results in a corresponding increase in ventricular volume. The volume in the ventricles at the end of diastole, just before cardiac contraction, is called the **end diastolic volume,** or **EDV.**

Blood moves from the heart into the arterial system when systolic pressure increases above the residual pressure (from the previous systole) in the great arteries leaving the heart. Although ventricular contraction causes blood ejection, the heart does not empty completely; a small quantity of blood—the **end systolic volume,** or **ESV**—remains in the ventricles at the end of systole.

Because the oxygen requirements of body tissue change depending on activity levels, we would expect the **cardiac output** (amount of blood pumped by each ventricle per minute) to vary correspondingly. We can calculate the **stroke volume** (**SV,** the amount of blood pumped per contraction of each ventricle) by subtracting the end systolic volume from the end diastolic volume (SV = EDV – ESV). We then compute cardiac output by multiplying the stroke volume by heart rate.

The human heart is a complex four-chambered organ, consisting of two individual pumps (the right and left sides) connected together in series. The right heart pumps blood through the lungs into the left heart, which in turn delivers blood to the systems of the body. Blood then returns to the right heart to complete the circuit.

Using the Pump Mechanics part of the PhysioEx program you will explore the operation of a simple one-chambered pump and apply the physical concepts in the simulation to the operation of either of the two pumps composing the human heart.

In this experiment you can vary the starting and ending volumes of the pump (analogous to EDV and ESV, respectively), driving and resistance pressures, and the diameters of the flow tubes leading to and from the pump chamber. As you proceed through the exercise, try to apply the ideas of ESV, EDV, cardiac output, stroke volume, and blood flow to the on-screen simulated pump system. For example, imagine that the flow tube leading to the pump from the left represents the pulmonary veins, and the flow tube exiting the pump to the right represents the aorta. The pump would then represent the left side of the heart.

Select **Pump Mechanics** from the **Experiment** menu. The equipment for the Pump Mechanics experiment appears. Figure 33B.2 shows the opening screen with labels added.

As in the previous experiment, there are two simulated electronic control units on the computer's screen. The upper apparatus is the _equipment control unit,_ which is used to adjust experiment parameters and to operate the equipment. The lower apparatus is the _data collection unit,_ in which you will record the data you accumulate.

This equipment differs slightly from that used in the Vessel Resistance experiment. There are still two beakers: the _source_ beaker on the left and the _destination_ beaker on the right. Now the pressure in each beaker is individually controlled by the small pressure units on top of the beakers. Between the two beakers is a simple pump, which can be thought of as one side of the heart, or even as a single ventricle (e.g., left ventricle). The left beaker and flow tube are analogous to the venous side of human blood flow, and arterial circulation is simulated by the right flow tube and beaker. One-way valves in the flow tubes supplying the pump ensure fluid movement in one direction—from the left beaker into the pump, and then into the right beaker. If you imagine that the pump represents the left ventricle, then think of the valve to the left of the pump as the bicuspid valve and the valve to the right of the pump as the aortic semilunar valve. The pump is driven by a pressure unit mounted on its cap. An important distinction between the pump's pressure unit and the pressure units atop the beakers is that the pump delivers pressure only during its downward stroke. Upward pump strokes are driven by pressure from the left beaker (the pump does not exert any resistance to flow from the left beaker during pump filling). In contrast, pressure in the right beaker works against the pump pressure, which means that the net pressure driving the fluid into the right beaker is calculated (automatically) by subtracting the right beaker pressure from the pump pressure. The resulting pressure difference between the pump and the right beaker is displayed in the experimental values grid in the data collection unit as **Press.Dif.R.**

Clicking the **Auto Pump** button will cycle the pump through the number of strokes indicated in the Max. strokes window. Clicking the **Single** button cycles the pump through one stroke. During the experiment, the pump and flow rates are automatically displayed when the number of pump strokes is five or greater. You control the radius of each flow tube individually by clicking the appropriate button. Click (+) to increase flow tube radius or (−) to decrease flow tube radius.

The pump's stroke volume (the amount of fluid ejected in one stroke) is automatically computed by subtracting its ending volume from the starting volume. You can adjust starting and ending volumes, and thereby stroke volume, by clicking the appropriate (+) or (−) button in the equipment control unit.

The data collection unit records and displays data you accumulate during the experiments. The data set for the first experiment (**Rad.R.,** which represents right flow tube radius) is

FIGURE 33B.2 Opening screen of the Pump Mechanics experiment with labels added.

highlighted in the **Data Sets** window. You can add or delete a data set by clicking the appropriate button to the right of the **Data Sets** window. Clicking **Delete Data Set** erases the data set itself, including all the data it contained. The **Record Data** button at the right edge of the screen activates automatically after an experimental trial. When clicked, the **Record Data** button displays the flow rate data in the experimental values grid and saves it in the computer's memory. Clicking the **Delete Line** or **Clear Data Set** button erases any data you want to delete.

A C T I V I T Y   5

Studying the Effect of Radius on Pump Activity

Although you will be manipulating the radius of only the right flow tube in this part of the exercise, try to predict the consequence of altering the left flow tube radius as you collect the experimental data. (Remember that the left flow tube simulates the pulmonary veins and the right flow tube simulates the aorta, as labeled in Figure 33B.2.)

1. Open the **Pump Mechanics** window if it isn't already open.

Click the **Rad.R.** data set to activate it. The data collection unit is now ready to record flow variations due to changing flow tube radius.

If the experimental values grid is not empty, click **Clear Data Set** to discard all previous values.

If the left beaker is not full, click **Refill.**

2. Adjust the **right** flow tube radius to 2.5 mm, and the **left** flow tube radius to 3.0 mm by clicking and holding the appropriate button. During the entire radius part of the experiment, maintain the other experiment conditions at:

- 40 mm Hg for left beaker pressure (this pressure drives fluid into the pump, which offers no resistance to filling)

- 120 mm Hg for pump pressure (pump pressure is the driving force that propels fluid into the right beaker)

- 80 mm Hg for right beaker pressure (this pressure is the resistance to the pump's pressure)

- 120-ml Start volume in pump (analogous to EDV)

- 50-ml End volume in pump (analogous to ESV)

- 10 strokes in the Max. strokes window

Notice that the displayed 70-ml stroke volume is automatically calculated. Before starting, click the **Single** button one or two times and watch the pump action.

To be sure you understand how this simple mechanical pump can be thought of as a simulation of the human heart, complete the following statements by circling the correct term within the parentheses:

a. When the piston is at the bottom of its travel, the volume remaining in the pump is analogous to the (EDV / ESV) of the heart.

b. The amount of fluid ejected into the right beaker by a single pump cycle is analogous to (stroke volume / cardiac output) of the heart.

c. The volume of blood in the heart just before systole is called the (EDV / ESV) and is analogous to the volume of fluid present in the simulated pump when it is at the (top / bottom) of its stroke.

3. Click the **Auto Pump** button in the equipment control unit to start the pump. After the 10 stroke volumes have been delivered, the Flow and Rate windows will automatically display the experimental results. Now click **Record Data** to display the figures you just collected in the experimental values grid. Click **Refill** to replenish the left beaker.

4. Increase the *right* flow tube radius in 0.5-mm increments, and repeat step 3 above until the maximum radius (6.0 mm) is achieved. Be sure to click **Record Data** after each trial.

5. When you have completed the experiment, view your data graphically by choosing **Plot Data** from the **Tools** menu. Choose **Rad.R.** as the data set to be graphed, and then use the slider bars to plot the Rad.R. data on the X-axis and the flow data on the Y-axis. You can highlight individual data points by clicking a line in the data grid.

The total flow rates you just determined depend on the flow rate into the pump from the left and on the flow rate out of the pump toward the right. Consequently, the shape of the plot is different from what you might predict after viewing the vessel resistance radius graph.

Try to explain why this graph differs from the radius plot in the Vessel Resistance experiment. Remember that the flow rate into the pump did not change, whereas the flow rate out of the pump varied according to your radius manipulations.

_____

_____

_____

When you have finished, click the close box at the top of the plot window.

Complete the following statements by circling the correct term within the parentheses.

a. As the right flow tube radius is increased, fluid flow rate (increases / decreases). This is analogous to (dilation / constriction) of blood vessels in the human body.

b. Even though the pump pressure remains constant, the pump rate (increases / decreases) as the radius of the right flow tube is increased. This happens because the resistance to fluid flow is (increased / decreased).

Apply your observations of the simulated mechanical pump to complete the following statements about human heart function. If you are not sure how to formulate your response, use the simulation to arrive at an answer. Circle the correct term within the parentheses.

c. The heart must contract (more / less) forcefully to maintain cardiac output if the resistance to blood flow in the vessels exiting the heart is increased.

d. Increasing the resistance of (that is, constricting) the blood vessels entering the heart would (increase / decrease) the time needed to fill the heart chambers.

What do you think would happen to the flow rate and the pump rate if the left flow tube radius is changed (either increased or decreased)?

_____

_____

_____ ▬

Studying the Effect of Stroke Volume on Pump Activity

The heart of a person at rest pumps about 60% of the blood in its chambers, and the other 40% remains in the chambers after systole. The 60% of blood ejected by the heart is called the stroke volume and is the difference between EDV and ESV. Even though our simple pump in this experiment does not work exactly like the human heart, you can apply the concepts to basic cardiac function. In this experiment, you will examine how the activity of the simple pump is affected by changing the pump's starting and ending volumes.

1. Click the **Str.V.** (stroke volume) data set to activate it. If the experimental values grid is not empty, click **Clear Data Set** to discard all previous values. If the left beaker is not full, click **Refill.**

2. Adjust the stroke volume to 10 ml by setting the **Start** volume (EDV) to 120 ml and the **End** volume (ESV) to 110 ml (stroke volume = start volume − end volume). During the entire stroke volume part of the experiment, keep the other experimental conditions at:

- 40 mm Hg for left beaker pressure

- 120 mm Hg for pump pressure

- 80 mm Hg for right beaker pressure
- 3.0 mm for flow tube radius, both left and right
- 10 strokes in the Max. strokes window

3. Click the **Auto Pump** button to start the experiment. After 10 stroke volumes have been delivered, the Flow and Rate windows will display the experimental results given the current parameters. Click **Record Data** to display the figures you just collected in the experimental values grid. Click **Refill** to replenish the left beaker.

4. Increase the stroke volume in 10-ml increments (by decreasing the End volume) and repeat step 3 until the maximum stroke volume (120 ml) is achieved. Be sure to click the **Record Data** button after each trial. Watch the pump action during each stroke to see how you can apply the concepts of starting and ending pump volumes to EDV and ESV of the heart.

5. View your data graphically by choosing **Plot Data** from the **Tools** menu. Choose **Str.V.** as the data set to be graphed, and then use the slider bars to plot the Str.V. data on the X-axis and the pump rate data on the Y-axis. Answer the following questions. When you have finished, click the close box at the top of the plot window.

What happened to the pump's rate as its stroke volume was increased?

_____

_____

_____

Using your simulation results as a basis for your answer, explain why an athlete's resting heart rate might be lower than that of the average person.

_____

_____

_____

Applying the simulation outcomes to the human heart, predict the effect of increasing the stroke volume on cardiac output (at any given rate).

_____

_____

_____

ACTIVITY 7

Studying Combined Effects

In this section, you will set up your own experimental conditions to answer the following questions. Carefully examine each question and decide how to set experimental parameters

to arrive at an answer. You can examine your previously collected data if you need additional information. Record several data points for each question as evidence for your answer (unless the question calls for a single pump stroke).

Click the **Add Data Set** button in the data collection unit. Next, create a new data set called Combined. Your newly created data set will be displayed beneath Str.V. Now click the **Combined** line to activate the data set. As you collect the supporting data for the following questions, be sure to click **Record Data** each time you have a data point you wish to keep for your records.

How is the flow rate affected when the right flow tube radius is kept constant (at 3.0 mm) and the left flow tube radius is modified (either up or down)?

_____

_____

_____

_____

How does decreasing left flow tube radius affect pump chamber filling time? Does it affect the ability of the pump to empty?

_____

_____

_____

You have already examined the effect of changing the pump's end volume as a way of manipulating stroke volume. What effect will decreasing stroke volume have on the pump rate?

_____

_____

_____

Try manipulating the pressure delivered to the left beaker. How does changing the left beaker pressure affect flow rate? (This change would be similar to changing pulmonary vein pressure.)

_____

_____

_____

If the left beaker pressure is decreased to 10 mm Hg, how is pump-filling time affected?

_____

_____

_____

What happens to the pump rate if the filling time is shortened?

_____

_____

What happens to fluid flow when the right beaker pressure equals the pump pressure?

_____

_____

_____

ACTIVITY 8

Studying Compensation

In this activity you will explore the concept of cardiovascular compensation. Click the **Add Data Set** button in the data collection unit. Next, create a new data set called **Comp.** Your newly created data set will be displayed beneath Combined. Now click the **Comp.** line to activate the data set. As you collect the supporting data for the following questions, be sure to click **Record Data** each time you have a data point you wish to keep for your records.

Adjust the experimental conditions to the following:

- 40 mm Hg for left beaker pressure
- 120 mm Hg for pump pressure
- 80 mm Hg for right beaker pressure
- 3.0 mm for left and right flow tube radius
- 10 strokes in the Max. strokes window
- 120-ml Start volume in pump
- 50-ml End volume in pump

Click **Auto Pump,** and then record your flow rate data. Let's declare the value you just obtained to be the "normal" flow rate for the purpose of this exercise.

Now decrease the right flow tube radius to 2.5 mm, and run another trial. How does this flow rate compare with "normal"?

_____

_____

Leave the right flow tube radius at 2.5 mm radius, and try to adjust one or more other conditions to return flow to "nor-

mal." Think logically about what condition(s) might compensate for a decrease in flow tube radius. How were you able to accomplish this? (Hint: There are several ways.)

_____

_____

_____

Circle the correct term within the parentheses: Decreasing the right flow tube radius is similar to a partial (leakage / blockage) of the aortic valve or (increased / decreased) resistance in the arterial system.

Explain how the human heart might compensate for such a condition.

_____

_____

_____

To increase (or decrease) blood flow to only one particular body system (e.g., digestive), would it be better to adjust heart rate or blood vessel diameter? Explain.

_____

_____

_____

_____

Complete the following statements by circling the correct response. (If necessary, use the pump simulation to help you with your answers.)

a. If we decreased overall peripheral resistance in the human body (as in an athlete), the heart would need to generate (more / less) pressure to deliver an adequate amount of blood flow, and arterial pressure would be (higher / lower).

b. If the diameter of the arteries of the body were partly filled with fatty deposits, the heart would need to generate (more / less) force to maintain blood flow, and pressure in the arterial system would be (higher / lower) than normal.

Click **Tools → Print Data** to print your recorded data for this experiment. ▬▬

Histology Review Supplement

For a review of cardiovascular tissue, go to **Exercise 6B: Histology Atlas and Review** on **myA&P** to print out the **Cardiovascular Tissue Review** worksheet.

NAME _____

LAB TIME/DATE _____

Cardiovascular Dynamics: Computer Simulation

Vessel Resistance

The following questions refer to Activity 1: Studying the Effect of Flow Tube Radius on Fluid Flow.

1. At which radius was the fluid flow rate the highest? _____

2. What was the flow rate at this radius? _____

3. Describe the relationship between flow rate and radius size. _____

_____

4. What happens to blood vessels in the body if increased blood flow is needed? _____

_____

The following questions refer to Activity 2: Studying the Effect of Viscosity on Fluid Flow.

5. At what viscosity level was the fluid flow rate the highest? _____

6. Describe the relationship between flow rate and viscosity. _____

_____

7. Was the effect of viscosity greater or less than the effect of radius on fluid flow? Why? _____

_____

8. What effect would anemia have on blood flow? Why? _____

_____

The following questions refer to Activity 3: Studying the Effect of Flow Tube Length on Fluid Flow.

9. At what flow tube length was the flow rate the highest? _____

10. Describe the relationship between flow tube length and fluid flow rate. _____

_____

11. What effect do you think obesity would have on blood flow? Why? _____

_____

_____

The following questions refer to Activity 4: Studying the Effect of Pressure on Fluid Flow.

12. What effect did increased pressure have on the fluid flow rate? _____

_____

13. In the body, where does the driving pressure for fluid flow come from? _____

_____

Pump Mechanics

The following questions refer to Activity 5: Studying the Effect of Radius on Pump Activity.

14. What happened to the flow rate as the right vessel radius was increased? _____

_____

15. What happened to the rate (strokes/min) as the right vessel radius was increased? _____

Why did this occur? _____

_____

The following questions refer to Activity 6: Studying the Effect of Stroke Volume on Pump Activity.

16. At what stroke volume tested was the pump rate the lowest? _____

17. Describe the relationship between stroke volume and pump rate. _____

_____

18. Use the relationship in question 17 to explain why an athlete's resting heart rate would be lower than that of a sedentary

individual. _____

_____

The following questions refer to Activity 7: Studying Combined Effects.

19. How did decreasing the left flow tube radius affect pump chamber filling time? Hint: Look at the change in flow rate and

relate this to filling time. _____

_____

20. When the left beaker pressure was decreased to 10 mm Hg, what happened to the filling time? _____

The following questions refer to Activity 8: Studying Compensation.

21. With the right flow tube radius decreased to 2.5 mm, what conditions did you change to bring the flow rate back to

    normal? _____

    _____

22. A decreased tube radius is analogous to atherosclerosis (plaque formation in vessels). Describe what effect this would have

    on resistance in the arterial system and how the human heart might compensate for this change. _____

    _____

Frog Cardiovascular Physiology: Computer Simulation

OBJECTIVES

1. To list the properties of cardiac muscle as automaticity and rhythmicity, and to define each.

2. To explain the statement, "Cardiac muscle has an intrinsic ability to beat."

3. To compare the relative length of the refractory period of cardiac muscle with that of skeletal muscle, and to explain why it is not possible to tetanize cardiac muscle.

4. To define *extrasystole,* and to explain at what point in the cardiac cycle (and on an ECG tracing) an extrasystole can be induced.

5. To describe the effect of the following on heart rate: vagal stimulation; cold; heat; pilocarpine; atropine; epinephrine; digitalis; and potassium, sodium, and calcium ions.

6. To define *vagal escape* and discuss its value.

7. To define *ectopic pacemaker.*

Investigation of human cardiovascular physiology is very interesting, but many areas obviously do not lend themselves to experimentation. It would be tantamount to murder to inject a human subject with various drugs to observe their effects on heart activity or to expose the human heart in order to study the length of its refractory period. However, this type of investigation can be done on frogs or computer simulations and provides valuable data because the physiological mechanisms in these animals, or programmed into the computer simulation, are similar if not identical to those in humans.

In this exercise, you will conduct the cardiac investigations just mentioned.

Special Electrical Properties of Cardiac Muscle: Automaticity and Rhythmicity

Cardiac muscle differs from skeletal muscle both functionally and in its fine structure. Skeletal muscle must be electrically stimulated to contract. In contrast, heart muscle can and does depolarize spontaneously in the absence of external stimulation. This property, called **automaticity,** is due to plasma membranes that have reduced permeability to potassium ions but still allow sodium ions to slowly leak into the cells. This leakage causes the muscle cells to slowly depolarize until the action potential threshold is reached and *fast calcium channels* open, allowing Ca^{2+} entry from the extracellular fluid. Shortly thereafter, contraction occurs.

The spontaneous depolarization-repolarization events occur in a regular and continuous manner in cardiac muscle, a property referred to as **rhythmicity.**

In the following experiment, you will observe these properties of cardiac muscle in a computer simulation. Additionally, your instructor may demonstrate this procedure using a real frog.

Nervous Stimulation of the Heart

Both the parasympathetic and sympathetic nervous systems innervate the heart. Stimulation of the sympathetic nervous system increases the rate and force of contraction of the heart. Stimulation of the parasympathetic nervous system (vagal nerves) decreases the depolarization rhythm of the sinoatrial node and slows transmission of excitation through the atrioventricular node. If vagal stimulation is excessive, the heart will stop beating. After a short time, the ventricles will begin to beat again. This is referred to as **vagal escape** and may be the result of sympathetic reflexes or initiation of a rhythm by the Purkinje fibers.

Baseline Frog Heart Activity

The heart's effectiveness as a pump is dependent on intrinsic (within the heart) and extrinsic (external to the heart) controls. In Activities 1–3, you will investigate some of these factors.

The nodal system, in which the "pacemaker" imposes its depolarization rate on the rest of the heart, is one intrinsic factor that influences the heart's pumping action. If its impulses fail to reach the ventricles (as in heart block), the ventricles continue to beat but at their own inherent rate, which is much slower than that usually imposed on them. Although heart contraction does not depend on nerve impulses, its rate can be modified by extrinsic impulses reaching it through the autonomic nerves. Cardiac activity is also modified by various chemicals, hormones, ions, and metabolites. The effects of several of these factors are examined in Activities 4–9.

The frog heart has two atria and a single, incompletely divided ventricle. The pacemaker is located in the sinus venosus, an enlarged region between the venae cavae and the right atrium. The sinoatrial (SA) node of mammals may have evolved from the sinus venosus.

Choose **Exercise 34B: Frog Cardiovascular Physiology** from the drop-down menu and click **GO.** Then click **Electrical Stimulation.** The opening screen will appear in a few seconds (Figure 34B.1). When the program starts, you will see a tracing of the frog's heartbeat on the *oscilloscope display* in the upper right part of the screen. Because the simulation automatically adjusts itself to your computer's speed, you may not see the heart tracing appear in real time. If you want to increase the speed of the tracing (at the expense of tracing quality), click the **Tools** menu, choose **Modify Display,** and then select **Increase Speed.**

FIGURE 34B.1 Opening screen of the Electrical Stimulation experiment.

To familiarize yourself with the equipment, choose **Balloons On/Off** from the **Help** menu. This feature allows you to scroll around the screen and view equipment labels. You can turn off this feature by returning to the **Help** menu and selecting **Balloons On/Off.**

The oscilloscope display shows the ventricular contraction rate in the Heart Rate window. The *heart activity window* to the right of the Heart Rate display provides the following messages:

- Heart Rate Normal—displayed when the heart is beating under resting conditions.

- Heart Rate Changing—displayed when the heart rate is increasing or decreasing.

- Heart Rate Stable—displayed when the heart rate is steady, but higher or lower than normal. For example, if you applied a chemical that increased heart rate to a stable but higher-than-normal rate, you would see this message.

The *electrical stimulator* is below the oscilloscope display. In the experiment, clicking **Single Stimulus** delivers a single electrical shock to the frog heart. Clicking **Multiple Stimulus** delivers repeated electrical shocks at the rate indicated in the Stimuli/sec window just below the Multiple Stimulus button. When the **Multiple Stimulus** button is clicked, it changes to a **Stop Stimulus** button that allows you to stop electrical stimulation as desired. Clicking the (+) or (−) buttons next to the Stimuli/sec window adjusts the stimulus rate. The voltage delivered when Single Stimulus or Multiple Stimulus is clicked is displayed in the **Voltage** window just below the Single Stimulus button. The simulation automatically adjusts the voltage for the experiment. The postlike apparatus extending upward from the electrical stimulator is the *electrode holder* into which you will drag-and-drop electrodes from the supply cabinet in the bottom left corner of the screen.

The left side of the screen contains the apparatus that sustains the frog heart. The heart has been lifted away from the body of the frog by a hook passed through the apex of the heart. Although the frog cannot be seen because it is in the dissection tray, its heart has not been removed from its circulatory system. A thin string connects the hook in the heart to the force transducer at the top of the support bracket. As the heart contracts, the string exerts tension on the force transducer, which converts the contraction into the oscilloscope tracing. The slender white strand extending from the heart toward the right side of the dissection tray is the vagus nerve. In the simulation, room-temperature (23°C) frog Ringer's solution continuously drips onto the heart to keep it moist and responsive so that a regular heart beat is maintained.

The two *electrodes* you will use during the experiment are located in the supply cabinet beneath the dissection tray. The **Direct Heart Stimulation** electrode is used to stimulate the ventricular muscle directly. The **Vagus Nerve Stimulation** electrode is used to stimulate the vagus nerve. To position either electrode, click and drag the electrode to the two-pronged plug in the electrode holder and then release the mouse button.

ACTIVITY 1

Recording Baseline Frog Heart Activity

1. Before beginning to stimulate the frog heart experimentally, watch several heartbeats. Be sure you can distinguish atrial and ventricular contraction (Figure 34B.2a).

2. Record the number of ventricular contractions per minute displayed in the Heart Rate window under the oscilloscope.

_____ bpm (beats per minute) ■

ACTIVITY 2

Investigating the Refractory Period of Cardiac Muscle

In Exercise 16B you saw that repeated rapid stimuli could cause skeletal muscle to remain in a contracted state. In other words, the muscle could be tetanized. This was possible because of the relatively short refractory period of skeletal muscle. In this experiment you will investigate the refractory period of cardiac muscle and its response to stimulation.

1. Click and hold the mouse button on the **Direct Heart Stimulation** electrode, and drag it to the electrode holder.

2. Release the mouse button to lock the electrode in place. The electrode will touch the ventricular muscle tissue.

3. Deliver single shocks in succession by clicking **Single Stimulus** rapidly. You may need to practice to acquire the correct technique.

Watch for **extrasystoles,** which are extra beats that show up riding on the ventricular contraction peak. Also note the compensatory pause, which allows the heart to get back on schedule after an extrasystole (Figure 34B.2b).

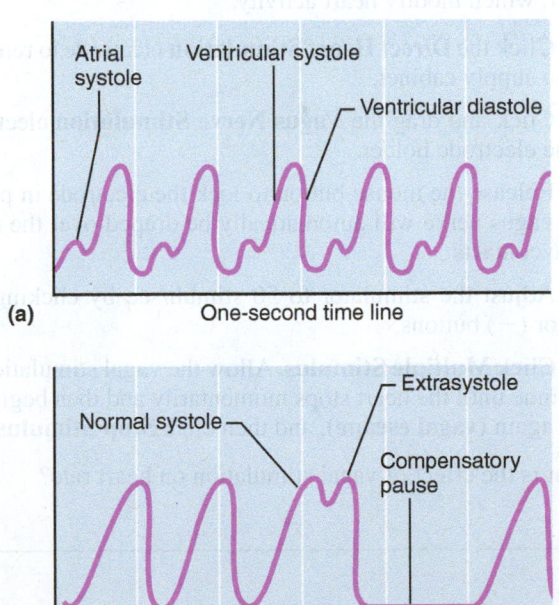

FIGURE 34B.2 Recording of contractile activity of a frog heart. (a) Normal heartbeat. **(b)** Induction of an extrasystole.

On the basis of the recording, during which portion of the cardiac cycle was it possible to induce an extrasystole? Use Figures 34B.2a and b to help you decide.

_____

_____

4.   Attempt to tetanize the heart by clicking **Multiple Stimulus.** Electrical shocks will be delivered to the muscle at a rate of 20 stimuli/sec. What is the result?

_____

_____

Considering the function of the heart, why is it important that the heart muscle cannot be tetanized?

_____

_____

5.   Click **Stop Stimulus** to stop the electrical stimulation. �in

ACTIVITY 3

Examining the Effect of Vagus Nerve Stimulation

The vagus nerve carries parasympathetic impulses to the heart, which modify heart activity.

1.   Click the **Direct Heart Stimulation** electrode to return it to the supply cabinet.

2.   Click and drag the **Vagus Nerve Stimulation** electrode to the electrode holder.

3.   Release the mouse button to lock the electrode in place. The vagus nerve will automatically be draped over the electrode contacts.

4.   Adjust the stimulator to 50 stimuli/sec by clicking the (+) or (−) buttons.

5.   Click **Multiple Stimulus.** Allow the vagal stimulation to continue until the heart stops momentarily and then begins to beat again (**vagal escape**), and then click **Stop Stimulus.**

What is the effect of vagal stimulation on heart rate?

_____

_____

_____

The phenomenon of vagal escape demonstrates that many factors are involved in heart regulation and that any deleterious factor (in this case, excessive vagal stimulation) will be overcome, if possible, by other physiological mechanisms such as activation of the sympathetic division of the autonomic nervous system (ANS). ▬

Assessing Physical and Chemical Modifiers of Heart Rate

Now that you have observed normal frog heart activity, you will have an opportunity to investigate the effects of various modifying factors on heart activity. After removing the agent in each activity, allow the heart to return to its normal rate before continuing with the testing.

Choose **Modifiers of Heart Rate** from the **Experiment** menu. The opening screen will appear in a few seconds (Figure 34B.3). The appearance and functionality of the *oscilloscope display* is the same as it was in the Electrical Stimulation experiment. The *solutions shelf* above the oscilloscope display contains the chemicals you'll use to modify heart rate in the experiment. You can choose the temperature of the Ringer's solution dispensed by clicking the appropriate button in the Ringer's dispenser at the left part of the screen. The doors to the supply cabinet are closed during this experiment because the electrical stimulator is not used.

When you click **Record Data** in the *data control unit* below the oscilloscope, your data is stored in the computer's memory and is displayed in the data grid at the bottom of the screen; data displayed include the solution used and the resulting heart rate. If you are not satisfied with a trial, you can click **Delete Line.** Click **Clear Table** if you wish to repeat the entire experiment.

ACTIVITY 4

Assessing the Effect of Temperature

Predict what effect a decrease in temperature will have on heart rate and write your prediction below.

_____

_____

1.   Click the **5°C Ringer's** button to bathe the frog heart in cold Ringer's solution. Watch the recording for a change in cardiac activity.

2.   When the heart activity window displays the message Heart Rate Stable, click **Record Data** to retain your data in the data grid.

What change occurred with the cold (5°C) Ringer's solution? Compare to the baseline value recorded in Activity 1.

_____

_____

Did this change match your prediction? _____

3.   Now click the **23°C Ringer's** button to flood the heart with fresh room-temperature Ringer's solution.

4.   After you see the message Heart Rate Normal in the heart activity window, click the **32°C Ringer's** button.

5.   When the heart activity window displays the message Heart Rate Stable, click **Record Data** to retain your data.

FIGURE 34B.3 Opening screen of the Modifiers of Heart Rate experiment.

What change occurred with the warm (32°C) Ringer's solution?

_____

_____

Record the heart rate at the two temperatures below.

_____ bpm at 5°C; _____ bpm at 32°C

What can you say about the effect of temperature on heart rate?

_____

_____

_____

6. Click the **23°C Ringer's** button to flush the heart with fresh Ringer's solution. Watch the heart activity window for the message Heart Rate Normal before beginning the next test. ■

ACTIVITY 5

Assessing the Effect of Pilocarpine

1. Click and hold the mouse on the **pilocarpine** dropper cap.

2. Drag the dropper cap to a point about an inch above the heart, and release the mouse button.

3. Pilocarpine solution will be dispensed onto the heart, and the dropper cap will automatically return to the pilocarpine bottle.

4. Watch the heart activity window for the message Heart Rate Stable, indicating that the heart rate has stabilized under the effects of pilocarpine.

5. After the heart rate stabilizes, record the heart rate in the space provided below, and click **Record Data** to retain your data in the grid.

_____ bpm

What happened when the heart was bathed in the pilocarpine solution?

_____

6.   Click the **23°C Ringer's** button to flush the heart with fresh Ringer's solution. Watch the heart activity window for the message Heart Rate Normal, an indication that the heart is ready for the next test. ■■■

Pilocarpine simulates the effect of parasympathetic nerve (hence, vagal) stimulation by enhancing acetylcholine release; such drugs are called parasympathomimetic drugs.

ACTIVITY 6

Assessing the Effect of Atropine

1.   Drag-and-drop the **atropine** dropper cap to a point about an inch above the heart.

2.   Atropine solution will automatically drip onto the heart, and the dropper cap will return to its position in the atropine bottle.

3.   Watch the heart activity window for the message Heart Rate Stable.

4.   After the heart rate stabilizes, record the heart rate in the space below, and click **Record Data** to retain your data in the grid.

_____ bpm

What is the effect of atropine on the heart?

_____

Atropine is a drug that blocks the effect of the neurotransmitter acetylcholine, liberated by the parasympathetic nerve endings. Do your results accurately reflect this effect of atropine?

_____

Are pilocarpine and atropine agonists or antagonists with respect to each other in their effects on heart activity?

_____

5.   Click the **23°C Ringer's** button to flush the heart with fresh Ringer's solution. Watch the heart activity window for the message Heart Rate Normal before beginning the next test. ■■■

ACTIVITY 7

Assessing the Effect of Epinephrine

1.   Drag-and-drop the **epinephrine** dropper cap to a point about an inch above the heart.

2.   Epinephrine solution will be dispensed onto the heart, and the dropper cap will return to the epinephrine bottle.

3.   Watch the heart activity window for the message Heart Rate Stable.

4.   After the heart rate stabilizes, record the heart rate in the space provided below, and click **Record Data** to retain your data in the grid.

_____ bpm

What happened when the heart was bathed in the epinephrine solution?

_____

Which division of the autonomic nervous system does its effect imitate?

_____

5.   Click the **23°C Ringer's** button to flush the heart with fresh Ringer's solution. Watch the heart activity window for the message Heart Rate Normal, meaning that the heart is ready for the next test. ■■■

ACTIVITY 8

Assessing the Effect of Digitalis

1.   Drag-and-drop the **digitalis** dropper cap to a point about an inch above the heart.

2.   Digitalis solution will automatically drip onto the heart, and then the dropper will return to the digitalis bottle.

3.   Watch the heart activity window to the right of the Heart Rate window for the message Heart Rate Stable.

4.   After the heart rate stabilizes, record the heart rate in the space provided below, and click **Record Data** to retain your data in the grid.

_____ bpm

What is the effect of digitalis on the heart?

_____

5.   Click the **23°C Ringer's** button to flush the heart with fresh Ringer's solution. Watch the heart activity window for the message Heart Rate Normal, then proceed to the next test. ■■■

Digitalis (also known as digoxin and digitoxin) is a drug commonly prescribed for heart patients with congestive heart failure. It slows heart rate and strengthens the force of contraction of the heart, providing more time for venous return and decreasing the workload on the weakened heart. These effects are thought to be due to inhibition of the sodium-potassium pump and enhancement of Ca^{2+} entry into myocardial fibers.

A C T I V I T Y   9

Assessing the Effect of Various Ions

To test the effect of various ions on the heart, apply the desired solution using the following method.

1. Drag-and-drop the **calcium ions** dropper cap to a point about an inch above the heart.

2. Calcium ions will automatically be dripped onto the heart, and the dropper cap will return to the calcium ions bottle.

3. Watch the heart activity window for the message Heart Rate Stable.

4. When you see Heart Rate Stable on the screen, record the heart rate in the space provided below step 6, and click **Record Data** to retain your data in the grid.

5. Click the **23°C Ringer's** button to flush the heart with fresh Ringer's solution. Watch the heart activity window for the message Heart Rate Normal, which means that the heart is ready for the next test.

6. Repeat steps 1–5 for **sodium ions** and then **potassium ions.**

Effect of Ca²⁺:

Does the heart rate stabilize and remain stable?

_____

Describe your observations of the rhythm of the heartbeat.

_____

_____

Effect of Na⁺:

Does the heart rate stabilize and remain stable?

_____

Describe your observations of the rhythm of the heartbeat.

_____

_____

Effect of K⁺:

Describe what happened to the recording.

_____

_____

Describe your observations of the rhythm of the heartbeat.

_____

_____

Potassium ion concentration is normally higher within cells than in the extracellular fluid. *Hyperkalemia* decreases the resting potential of plasma membranes, thus decreasing the force of heart contraction. In some cases, the conduction rate of the heart is so depressed that **ectopic pacemakers** (pacemakers appearing erratically and at abnormal sites in the heart muscle) appear in the ventricle, and fibrillation may occur.

Was there any evidence of premature beats in the recording of potassium ion effects?

_____

Was arrhythmia produced with any of the ions tested?

_____ If so, which? _____

7. Click **Tools → Print Data** to print your recorded data for this experiment. ▬

Histology Review Supplement

For a review of cardiovascular tissue, go to **Exercise 6B: Histology Atlas and Review** on **myA&P** to print out the **Cardiovascular Tissue Review** worksheet.

Frog Cardiovascular Physiology: Computer Simulation

NAME _____

LAB TIME/DATE _____

Baseline Frog Heart Activity

The following questions refer to Activity 1: Recording Baseline Frog Heart Activity.

1. What was the baseline heart rate for the frog? _____

2. Which wave is larger, the one for atrial contraction or the one for ventricular contraction? _____

   Why? _____

   _____

The following questions refer to Activity 2: Investigating the Refractory Period of Cardiac Muscle.

3. At what time during the contraction cycle was it possible to induce an extrasystole?

   _____

4. By clicking the Multiple Stimulus button and delivering 20 stimuli/sec, were you able to achieve tetanus? Why or why

   not? _____

   _____

The following questions refer to Activity 3: Examining the Effect of Vagus Nerve Stimulation.

5. What happens to the heart rate with vagal stimulation? _____

   _____

6. What happens during vagal escape? _____

   _____

Assessing Physical and Chemical Modifiers of Heart Rate

The following questions refer to Activity 4: Assessing the Effect of Temperature.

7. List the frog heart rate for the following conditions:

_____ bpm with 5°C Ringer's solution

_____ bpm with 32°C Ringer's solution

8. Describe the effect of temperature on heart rate. _____

_____

9. Did this effect match your prediction? Explain. _____

_____

The following questions refer to Activity 5: Assessing the Effect of Pilocarpine.

10. What was the heart rate after treatment with pilocarpine?

_____ bpm with pilocarpine

11. Did this effect match your prediction? Explain. _____

_____

The following questions refer to Activity 6: Assessing the Effect of Atropine.

12. What was the heart rate after treatment with atropine?

_____ bpm with atropine

13. Are the effects of pilocarpine and atropine the same or opposite?

_____

The following questions refer to Activity 7: Assessing the Effect of Epinephrine.

14. What was the heart rate after treatment with epinephrine?

_____ bpm with epinephrine

15. Did this effect match your prediction? Explain. _____

_____

16. What division of the autonomic nervous system does the addition of epinephrine imitate? _____

_____

The following questions refer to Activity 8: Assessing the Effect of Digitalis.

17. What was the heart rate after treatment with digitalis?

_____ bpm with digitalis

18. Describe the effect that digitalis had on the heart. _____

_____

The following questions refer to Activity 9: Assessing the Effect of Various Ions.

19. Which ions resulted in arrhythmia of the frog heart? _____

_____

20. Which ion had the greatest effect on the frog heart? Explain. _____

_____

_____

Respiratory System Mechanics: Computer Simulation

OBJECTIVES

1. To define the following terms:
   ventilation, inspiration, expiration, forced expiration, tidal volume, expiratory reserve volume, inspiratory reserve volume, residual volume, vital capacity, forced expiratory volume, minute respiratory volume, surfactant, and *pneumothorax.*
2. To describe the role of muscles and volume changes in the mechanics of breathing.
3. To understand that the lungs do not contain muscle and that respirations are therefore caused by external forces.
4. To explore the effect of changing airway resistance on breathing.
5. To study the effect of surfactant on lung function.
6. To examine the factors that cause lung collapse.
7. To understand the effects of hyperventilation, rebreathing, and breath holding on the CO_2 level in the blood.

The two phases of **pulmonary ventilation** or **breathing** are **inspiration,** during which air is taken into the lungs, and **expiration,** during which air is expelled from the lungs. Inspiration occurs as the external intercostal muscles and the diaphragm contract. The diaphragm, normally a dome-shaped muscle, flattens as it moves inferiorly while the external intercostal muscles between the ribs lift the rib cage. These cooperative actions increase the thoracic volume. Because the increase in thoracic volume causes a partial vacuum, air rushes into the lungs. During normal expiration, the inspiratory muscles relax, causing the diaphragm to rise and the chest wall to move inward. The thorax returns to its normal shape because of the elastic properties of the lung and thoracic wall. As in a deflating balloon, the pressure in the lungs rises, forcing air out of the lungs and airways. Although expiration is normally a passive process, abdominal wall muscles and the internal intercostal muscles can contract to force air from the lungs. Blowing up a balloon is an example where such **forced expiration** would occur.

Simulating Spirometry: Measuring Respiratory Volumes and Capacities

This computerized simulation allows you to investigate the basic mechanical function of the respiratory system as you determine lung volumes and capacities. You can then apply the concepts you will learn by studying this simulated mechanical lung to the operation of the human respiratory system.

Normal quiet breathing moves about 500 ml (0.5 liter) of air (the tidal volume) in and out of the lungs with each breath, but this amount can vary according to a person's size, sex, age, physical condition, and immediate respiratory needs. The terms used for the normal respiratory volumes are defined next. The values are for the normal adult male and are approximate.

Normal Respiratory Volumes

Tidal volume (TV): Amount of air inhaled or exhaled with each breath under resting conditions (500 ml)

Expiratory reserve volume (ERV): Amount of air that can be forcefully exhaled after a normal tidal volume exhalation (1200 ml)

Inspiratory reserve volume (IRV): Amount of air that can be forcefully inhaled after a normal tidal volume inhalation (3100 ml)

Residual volume (RV): Amount of air remaining in the lungs after complete exhalation (1200 ml)

Vital capacity (VC): Maximum amount of air that can be exhaled after a normal maximal inspiration (4800 ml)

$$VC = TV + IRV + ERV$$

Total lung capacity (TLC): Sum of vital capacity and residual volume

Pulmonary Function Tests

Forced vital capacity (FVC): Amount of air that can be expelled when the subject takes the deepest possible breath and exhales as completely and rapidly as possible

Forced expiratory volume (FEV$_1$): Measures the percentage of the vital capacity that is exhaled during 1 second of the FVC test (normally 75% to 85% of the vital capacity)

Choose **Exercise 37B: Respiratory System Mechanics** from the drop-down menu and click **GO.** Before you perform the activities, watch the **Water-Filled Spirometer** video to see the experiment performed with a human subject. Then click **Respiratory Volumes.** The opening screen for the Respiratory Volumes experiment will appear in a few seconds (Figure 37B.1a). The main features on the screen when the program starts are a pair of *simulated lungs within a bell jar* at the left side of the screen, an *oscilloscope* in the upper right part of the screen, a *data display* area beneath the oscilloscope, and a *data control unit* at the bottom of the screen.

The black rubber "diaphragm" sealing the bottom of the glass bell jar is attached to a rod in the pump just below the jar. The rod moves the rubber diaphragm up and down to change the pressure within the bell jar (comparable to the intrapleural pressure in the body). As the diaphragm moves inferiorly, the resulting volume increase creates a partial vacuum in the bell jar because of lowered pressure. This partial vacuum causes air to be sucked into the tube at the top of the bell jar and then into the simulated lungs.

Conversely, as the diaphragm moves up, the rising pressure within the bell jar forces air out of the lungs. The partition between the two lungs compartmentalizes the bell jar into right and left sides. The lungs are connected to an airflow tube whose diameter you can adjust by clicking the (+) and (−) buttons next to the Radius window in the equipment atop the bell jar. The volume of each breath that passes through the single airflow tube above the bell jar is displayed in the Flow window. Clicking **Start** below the bell jar begins a trial run in which the simulated lungs will "breathe" in normal tidal volumes and the oscilloscope will display the tidal tracing. When you click **ERV,** the program will simulate forced exhalation using the contraction of the internal intercostal muscles and

abdominal wall muscles, and the expiratory reserve volume will be displayed in the Exp. Res. Vol. window below the oscilloscope. When you click **FVC,** the lungs will first inhale maximally and then exhale fully to demonstrate forced vital capacity. After ERV and FVC have been measured, the remaining lung values will be calculated and displayed in the small windows below the oscilloscope.

The data control equipment in the lower part of the screen records and displays data accumulated during the experiments. When you click **Record Data,** your data are recorded in the computer's memory and displayed in the data grid. Data displayed in the data grid include the Radius, Flow, TV (tidal volume), ERV (expiratory reserve volume), IRV (inspiratory reserve volume), RV (residual volume), VC (vital capacity), FEV$_1$ (forced expiratory volume—1 second), TLC (total lung capacity), and Pump Rate. Clicking **Delete Line** allows you to discard the data for a single run; clicking **Clear Table** erases the entire experiment to allow you to start over.

If you need help identifying any piece of equipment, choose **Balloons On/Off** from the **Help** menu, and move the pointer onto any piece of equipment visible on the computer's screen. As the pointer touches the object, a pop-up window will identify the equipment. To close the pop-up window, move the pointer away from the equipment. Choose **Balloons On/Off** to turn off this Help feature.

ACTIVITY 1

Measuring Respiratory Volumes

Your first experiment will establish the baseline respiratory values.

1. If the grid in the data control unit is not empty, click **Clear Table** to discard all previous data.

2. Adjust the radius of the airways to 5.00 mm by clicking the appropriate button next to the Radius window.

3. Click **Start,** and allow the tracing to complete. Watch the simulated lungs begin to breathe as a result of the "contraction and relaxation" of the diaphragm. Simultaneously, the oscilloscope will display a tracing of the tidal volume for each breath. The Flow window atop the bell jar indicates the tidal volume for each breath, and the Tidal Vol. window below the oscilloscope shows the average tidal volume. The Pump Rate window displays the number of breaths per minute.

4. Click **Clear Tracings.**

5. Now click **Start** again. After a second or two, click **ERV,** wait 2 seconds, and then click **FVC** to complete the measurement of respiratory volumes. The expiratory reserve volume, inspiratory reserve volume, and residual volume will be automatically calculated and displayed from the tests you have performed so far. Also, the equipment calculates and displays the total lung capacity.

6. Compute the **minute respiratory volume (MRV)** using the following formula:

$$MRV = TV \times BPM \text{ (breaths per minute)}$$
$$MRV \text{_____ ml/min}$$

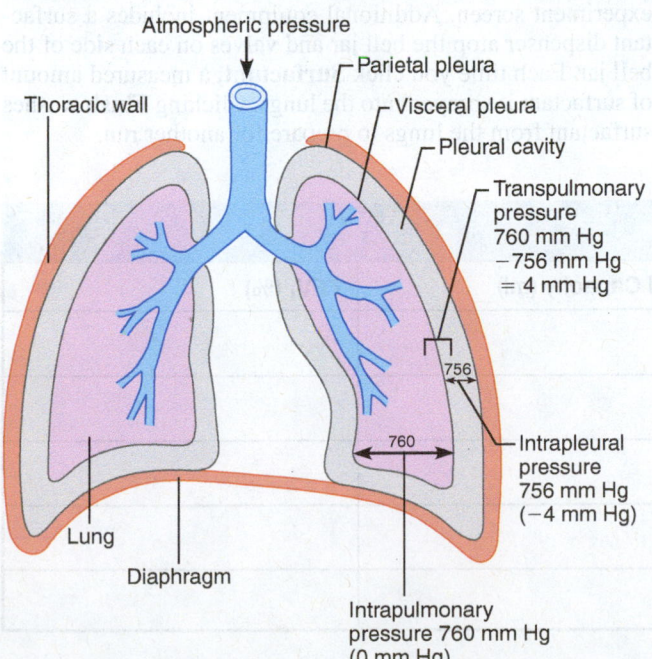

(a)

FIGURE 37B.1 Respiratory Volumes. (a) Opening screen of the Respiratory Volumes experiment. **(b)** Intrapulmonary and intrapleural pressure relationships.

7.   Does expiratory reserve volume include tidal volume?

_____ Explain your answer. _____

_____

_____

8.   Now click **Record Data** to record the current experimental data in the data grid. Then click **Clear Tracings.**

9.   If you want to print a tracing at any time, click **Tools** and then **Print Graph.** ■

Examining the Effect of Changing Airway Resistance on Respiratory Volumes

Lung diseases are often classified as obstructive or restrictive. With an **obstructive** problem, expiratory flow is affected, whereas a **restrictive** problem might indicate reduced inspiratory volume. Although they are not diagnostic, pulmonary function tests such as FEV_1 can help a clinician determine the difference between obstructive and restrictive problems. FEV_1 is the forced volume exhaled in 1 second. In obstructive disorders like chronic bronchitis and asthma, airway resistance is increased and FEV_1 will be low. Here you will explore what effect changing the diameter of the airway has on pulmonary function.

1.   Do *not* clear the data table from the previous experiment.

2.   Adjust the radius of the airways to 4.50 mm by clicking the $(-)$ button next to the Radius window.

3.   Click **Start** to begin respirations.

4.   Click **FVC.** As you saw in the previous test, the simulated lungs will inhale maximally and then exhale as forcefully as possible. FEV_1 will be displayed in the FEV_1 window below the oscilloscope.

5.   When the lungs stop respiring, click **Record Data** to record the current data in the data grid.

6.   Decrease the radius of the airways in 0.50-mm decrements and repeat steps 4 and 5 until the minimum radius (3.00 mm) is achieved. Be sure to click **Record Data** after each trial. Click **Clear Tracings** between trials. If you make an error and want to delete a single value, click the data line in the data grid and then click **Delete Line.**

7.   A useful way to express FEV_1 is as a percentage of the forced vital capacity. Copy the FEV_1 and vital capacity values from the computer screen to Chart 1, and then calculate the FEV_1 (%) by dividing the FEV_1 volume by the vital capacity volume and multiplying by 100. Record the FEV_1 (%) in Chart 1.

What happened to the FEV_1 (%) as the radius of the airways

was decreased? _____

Explain your answer. _____

_____

_____

8.   Click **Tools → Print Data** to print your data. ■

Simulating Factors Affecting Respirations

This part of the computer simulation allows you to explore the action of surfactant on pulmonary function and the effect of changing the intrapleural pressure.

Choose **Factors Affecting Respirations** from the **Experiment** menu. The opening screen will appear in a few seconds (Figure 37B.2). The basic features on the screen when the program starts are the same as in the Respiratory Volumes experiment screen. Additional equipment includes a surfactant dispenser atop the bell jar and valves on each side of the bell jar. Each time you click **Surfactant,** a measured amount of surfactant is sprayed into the lungs. Clicking **Flush** washes surfactant from the lungs to prepare for another run.

CHART 1	FEV$_1$ as % of VC		
Radius (mm)	FEV$_1$ (ml)	Vital Capacity (ml)	FEV$_1$ (%)
5.00			
4.50			
4.00			
3.50			
3.00			

FIGURE 37B.2 Opening screen of the Factors Affecting Respirations experiment.

Clicking the valve button (which currently reads **Valve closed**) allows the pressure within that side of the bell jar to equalize with the atmospheric pressure. Click **Reset,** to prepare the lungs for another run.

Data accumulated during a run are displayed in the windows below the scilloscope. When you click **Record Data,** that data are recorded in the computer's memory and displayed in the data grid. Data displayed in the data grid include the Radius, Pump Rate, the amount of Surfactant, Pressure Left (pressure in the left lung), Pressure Right (pressure in the right lung), Flow Left (airflow in the left lung), Flow Right (airflow in the right lung), and Total Flow. Click **Delete Line** to discard data values for a single run, and click **Clear Table** to erase the entire experiment to allow you to start over.

ACTIVITY 3

Examining the Effect of Surfactant

At any gas-liquid boundary, the molecules of the liquid are attracted more strongly to each other than they are to the air molecules. This unequal attraction produces tension at the liquid surface called *surface tension*. Because surface tension

resists any force that tends to increase surface area, it acts to decrease the size of hollow spaces, such as the alveoli or microscopic air spaces within the lungs. If the film lining the air spaces in the lung were pure water, it would be very difficult, if not impossible, to inflate the lungs. However, the aqueous film covering the alveolar surfaces contains **surfactant,** a detergent-like lipoprotein that decreases surface tension by reducing the attraction of water molecules for each other. You will explore the action of surfactant in this experiment.

1.   If the data grid is not empty, click **Clear Table** to discard all previous data values.

2.   Adjust the airway radius to 5.00 mm by clicking the appropriate button next to the Radius window.

3.   If necessary, click **Flush** to clear the simulated lungs of existing surfactant.

4.   Click **Start,** and allow a baseline run without added surfactant to complete.

5.   When the run completes, click **Record Data.**

6.   Now click **Surfactant** twice.

7. Click **Start** to begin the surfactant run.

8. When the lungs stop respiring, click **Record Data** to display the data in the grid.

What happened to the FEV$_1$ (%) as the radius of the airways

was decreased? _____

_____

How has the airflow changed compared to the baseline run?

_____

_____

Premature infants often have difficulty breathing. Explain why this might be so. (Use your text as needed.)

_____

_____

ACTIVITY 4

Investigating Intrapleural Pressure

The pressure within the pleural cavity, **intrapleural pressure,** is less than the pressure within the alveoli. This negative pressure condition is caused by two forces, the tendency of the lung to recoil because of its elastic properties and the surface tension of the alveolar fluid. These two forces act to pull the lungs away from the thoracic wall, creating a partial vacuum in the pleural cavity (see Figure 37B.1b). Because the pressure in the intrapleural space is lower than atmospheric pressure, any opening created in the thoracic wall equalizes the intrapleural pressure with the atmospheric pressure by allowing air to enter the pleural cavity, a condition called **pneumothorax.** Pneumothorax allows lung collapse, a condition called **atelectasis.**

In the simulated respiratory system on the computer screen, the intrapleural space is the space between the wall of the bell jar and the outer wall of the lung it contains. The pressure difference between inspiration and expiration for the left lung is displayed in the Pressure Left window below the oscilloscope; the Pressure Right window gives the data for the right lung.

1. Do *not* discard your previous data.

2. Click **Clear Tracings** to clean up the screen, and then click **Flush** to clear the lungs of surfactant from the previous run.

3. Adjust the radius of the airways to 5.00 mm by clicking the appropriate button next to the Radius window.

4. Click **Start,** and allow one screen of respirations to complete. Notice the negative pressure condition displayed below the oscilloscope when the lungs inflate.

5. When the lungs stop respiring, click **Record Data** to display the data in the grid.

6. Now click the valve button (which currently reads **Valve closed**) on the left side of the bell jar above the Start button to open the valve.

7. Click **Start** to begin the run.

8. When the run completes, click **Record Data** again.

What happened to the lung in the left side of the bell jar?

_____

_____

How did the pressure in the left lung differ from that in the right lung?

_____

Explain your reasoning. _____

_____

_____

How did the total air flow in this trial compare with that in the previous trial in which the pleural cavities were intact?

_____

_____

What do you think would happen if the two lungs were in a single large cavity instead of separate cavities?

_____

_____

9. Now close the valve you opened earlier by clicking it again, and then click **Start** to begin a new trial.

10. When the run completes, click **Record Data** to display the data in the grid.

Did the deflated lung reinflate? _____

Explain your answer. _____

_____

_____

11. Click the **Reset** button atop the bell jar. This action draws the air out of the intrapleural space and returns it to normal resting condition.

12. Click **Start,** and allow the run to complete.

13. When the run completes, click **Record Data** to display the data in the grid.

14. Click **Tools → Print Data** to print data.

Why did lung function in the deflated (left) lung return to normal after you clicked Reset?

_____

_____ ▬

Simulating Variations in Breathing

This part of the computer simulation allows you to examine the effects of hyperventilation, rebreathing, and breath holding on CO_2 level in the blood.

Choose **Variations in Breathing** from the **Experiment** menu. The opening screen will appear in a few seconds (Figure 37B.3). The basic features on the screen when the program starts are the same as in the lung volumes screen. The buttons beneath the oscilloscope control the various possible breathing patterns. Clicking **Hyperventilation** causes the lungs to breathe faster than normal. A small bag automatically covers the airway tube when you click **Rebreathing.** Clicking **Breath Holding** causes the lungs to stop respiring. Click **Normal Breathing** at any time to resume normal tidal cycles. The window next to the Start button displays the breathing pattern being performed by the simulated lungs.

The windows below the oscilloscope display the P_{CO_2} (partial pressure of CO_2) of the air in the lungs, Maximum P_{CO_2}, Minimum P_{CO_2}, and Pump Rate.

Data accumulated during a run are displayed in the windows below the oscilloscope. When you click **Record Data,** those data are recorded in the computer's memory and displayed in the data grid. Data displayed in the data grid include the Condition, P_{CO_2}, Maximum P_{CO_2}, Minimum P_{CO_2}, Pump Rate, Radius, and Total Flow. Clicking **Delete Line** allows you to discard data values for a single run, and clicking **Clear Table** erases the entire experiment to allow you to start over.

FIGURE 37B.3 Opening screen of the Variations in Breathing experiment.

Exploring Various Breathing Patterns

You will establish the baseline respiratory values in the first part of this experiment.

1.   If the grid in the data control unit is not empty, click **Clear Table** to discard all previous data.

2.   Adjust the radius of the airways to 5.00 mm by clicking the appropriate button next to the Radius window. Now, read through steps 3–5 before attempting to execute them.

3.   Click **Start,** and notice that it changes to **Stop** to allow you to stop the respiration. Watch the simulated lungs begin to breathe as a result of the external mechanical forces supplied by the pump below the bell jar. Simultaneously, the oscilloscope will display a tracing of the tidal volume for each breath.

4.   After 2 seconds, click the **Hyperventilation** button and watch the P_{CO_2} displays. The breathing pattern will change to short, rapid breaths. The P_{CO_2} of the air in the lungs will be displayed in the small window to the right of the Hyperventilation button.

5.   Watch the oscilloscope display and the P_{CO_2} window, and click **Stop** before the tracing reaches the end of the screen.

What happens to P_{CO_2} during rapid breathing? Explain your answer.

_____

_____

_____

6.   Click **Record Data.**

7.   Now click **Clear Tracings** to prepare for the next run.

Rebreathing

When you click **Rebreathing,** a small bag will appear over the end of the air tube to allow the air within the lungs to be repeatedly inspired and expired.

1.   Click **Start,** wait 2 seconds, and then click **Rebreathing.**

2.   Watch the breathing pattern on the oscilloscope, and notice the P_{CO_2} during the course of the run. Click **Stop** when the tracing reaches the right edge of the oscilloscope.

What happens to P_{CO_2} during the entire time of the rebreathing activity?

_____

_____

Did the depth of the breathing pattern change during rebreathing? (Carefully examine the tracing for rate and depth changes; the changes can be subtle.) Explain your observations.

_____

_____

_____

_____

3.   Click **Record Data,** and then click **Clear Tracings** to prepare for the next run.

Breath Holding

Breath holding can be considered an extreme form of rebreathing in which there is no gas exchange between the outside atmosphere and the air within the lungs.

1.   Click **Start,** wait a second or two, and then click **Breath Holding.**

2.   Let the breath-holding activity continue for about 5 seconds, and then click **Normal Breathing.**

3.   Click **Stop** when the tracing reaches the right edge of the oscilloscope.

What happened to the P_{CO_2} during breath holding?

_____

What happened to the breathing pattern when normal respirations resume?

_____

_____

4.   Click **Record Data.**

5.   Click **Tools → Print Data** to print your data. ▰

Comparative Spirometry

In Activity 1, you measured normal respiratory volumes and capacities. In this activity, you will explore what happens to these values when pathophysiology develops or during episodes of aerobic exercise. Using a water-filled spirometer and knowledge of respiratory mechanics, you can predict, document, and explain changes to these values in each condition.

Normal Breathing

1.   Click the **Experiment** menu, and then click **Comparative Spirometry.** The opening screen will appear in a few seconds (see Figure 37B.4).

2. For the patient's type of breathing, select the **Normal** option from the drop-down menu in the **Patient Type** box. These values will serve as a basis of comparison in the diseased conditions.

3. Select the patient's breathing pattern as **Unforced Breathing** from the **Breathing Pattern Option** box.

4. After you make these selections, click the **Start** button and watch as the drum starts turning and the spirogram develops on the paper rolling off the drum across the screen, left to right.

5. When half the screen is filled with unforced tidal volumes and the trace has paused, select the **Forced Vital Capacity** button in the Breathing Pattern Options box.

6. Click the **Start** button and the trace will continue with the FVC maneuver. The trace ends as the paper rolls to the right edge of the screen.

7. Now click the individual measure buttons that appear in the data table above each data column to measure the lung volume and lung capacity data. Note that when a measure button is selected, two things happen simultaneously: (1) a

bracket appears on the spirogram to indicate where that measurement originates on the spirogram, and (2) the value in milliliters appears in the data table. Also note that when you select the FEV_1 measure button, the final column labeled FEV_1/FVC will be automatically calculated and appear in the data table. The calculation is $(FEV_1/FVC) \times 100\%$, and the result will appear as a percentage in the data table.

What do you think is the clinical importance of the FVC and FEV_1 values?

_____

_____

Why do you think the ratio of these two values is important to

the clinician diagnosing respiratory diseases? _____

_____

_____

$FEV_1/FVC \times 100\% = $ _____

FIGURE 37B.4 Opening screen of the Comparative Spirometry experiment.

Emphysema Breathing

In a person with emphysema, there is a significant loss of intrinsic elastic recoil in the lung tissue. This loss of elastic recoil occurs as the disease destroys the walls of the alveoli. Airway resistance is also increased as the lung tissue in general becomes more flimsy and exerts less mechanical tethering on the surrounding airways. Thus the lung becomes overly compliant and expands easily. Conversely, a great effort is required to exhale as the lungs can no longer passively recoil and deflate. A noticeable and exhausting muscular effort is required for each exhalation. Thus a person with emphysema exhales slowly.

1.   Using this information, predict what lung values will change in the spirogram when the patient with emphysema breathing is selected. Assume that significant disease has developed, and thus a loss of elastic recoil has occurred in this patient's lungs.

2.   Select **Emphysema** from the drop-down menu in the **Patient Type** box.

3.   Select the patient's breathing pattern as **Unforced Breathing** from the **Breathing Pattern** box.

4.   After you make these selections and the existing spirogram screen clears, click the **Start** button and watch as the drum starts turning and a new spirogram develops on the paper rolling off the drum.

5.   Repeat steps 5–7 of the Normal Breathing section in this activity.

6.   Now consider the accuracy of your predictions (what changed versus what you expected to change). Compared to the values for normal breathing:

Is the FVC reduced or increased? _____

Is the FEV_1 reduced or increased? _____

Which of these two changed more? _____

Explain the physiological reasons for the lung volumes and capacities that changed in the spirogram for this condition.

_____

_____

_____

Acute Asthma Attack Breathing

During an acute asthma attack, bronchiole smooth muscle will spasm and thus the airways become constricted (that is, they have a reduced diameter). They also become clogged with thick mucous secretions. These two facts lead to significantly increased airway resistance. Underlying these symptoms is an airway inflammatory response brought on by triggers such as allergens (e.g., dust and pollen), extreme temperature changes, and even exercise. As in emphysema, the airways collapse and pinch closed before a forced expiration is completed. Thus the volumes and peak flow rates are significantly reduced during an asthma attack. However, the elastic recoil is not diminished in an acute asthma attack.

1.   Using this information, predict what lung values will change in the spirogram when you select the patient who is having an acute asthma attack. Assume that significantly decreased airway radius and increased airway resistance have developed in this patient's lungs.

2.   Select **Asthmatic** from the drop-down menu in the **Patient Type** box.

3.   Select the patient's breathing pattern as **Unforced Breathing** from the **Breathing Pattern** box.

4.   After you make these selections and the existing spirogram screen clears, click the **Start** button and watch as the drum starts turning, and a new spirogram develops as the paper rolls off the drum.

5.   Repeat steps 5–7 of the Normal Breathing section in this activity.

6.   Now consider the accuracy of your predictions (what changed versus what you expected to change). Compared to the values for normal breathing:

Is the FVC reduced or increased? _____

Is the FEV_1 reduced or increased? _____

Which of these two changed more? _____

Explain the physiological reasons for the lung volumes and capacities that changed in the spirogram for this condition.

_____

_____

How is this condition similar to having emphysema? How is

it different? _____

_____

Emphysema and asthma are called *obstructive* lung diseases as they limit expiratory flow and volume. How would a spirogram look for someone with a *restrictive* lung disease, such as pulmonary fibrosis?

_____

What volumes and capacities would change in this case, and would these values be increased or decreased?

_____

_____

In an acute asthma attack, the compliance of the lung is decreased, not increased as it was for emphysema, and air flows freely through the bronchioles. Therefore, will the FEV_1/FVC percentage be less than normal, equal to normal, or

higher than normal? _____

Acute Asthma Attack Breathing with Inhaler Medication Applied

When an acute asthma attack occurs, many people seek relief from the symptoms by using an inhaler. This device atomizes the medication and allows for direct application onto the afflicted airways. Usually the medication includes a smooth muscle relaxant (e.g., a beta-2 agonist or an acetylcholine antagonist) that relieves the bronchospasms and induces bronchiole dilation. The medication may also contain an anti-inflammatory agent such as a corticosteroid that suppresses the inflammatory response. Airway resistance is reduced by the use of the inhaler.

1. Using this information, predict what lung values will change in the spirogram when the patient who is having an acute asthma attack applies the inhaler medication. By how much will the values change (will they return to normal)?

2. Select **Plus Inhaler** from the drop-down menu in the **Patient Type** box.

3. Select the patient's breathing pattern as **Unforced Breathing** from the **Breathing Pattern** box.

4. After you make these selections and the existing spirogram screen clears, click the **Start** button and watch as the drum starts turning, and a new spirogram develops as the paper rolls off the drum.

5. Repeat steps 5–7 of the Normal Breathing section.

6. Now consider the accuracy of your predictions (what changed versus what you expected to change). Compared to the values for the patient experiencing asthma symptoms:

Has the FVC reduced or increased? Is it "normal"? _____

Has the FEV_1 reduced or increased? Is it "normal"? _____

Which of these two changed more? _____

Explain the physiological reasons for the lung volumes and capacities that changed in the spirogram with the application

of the medication. _____

_____

How much of an increase in FEV_1 do you think is required for it to be considered significantly improved by the medication?

_____

_____

Breathing During Exercise

During moderate aerobic exercise, the human body has an increased metabolic demand, which is met in part by changes in respiration. During heavy exercise, further changes in respiration are required to meet the extreme metabolic demands of the body.

a. In moderate aerobic exercise, which do you predict will change more, the ERV or the IRV? _____

b. Do you predict that the respiratory rate will change significantly in moderate exercise? _____

c. Comparing heavy exercise to moderate exercise, what values do you predict will change when the body's significantly increased metabolic demands are being met by the respiratory system? _____

_____

d. During heavy exercise, what will happen to the lung volumes and capacities that have been considered thus far?

_____

e. Will the respiratory rate change? If so, how? _____

1. Select **Moderate Exercise** from the drop-down menu in the **Patient Type** box. The existing spirogram clears.

2. Click the **Start** button and watch as the drum starts turning and a new spirogram develops. Half of the screen will fill with breathing volumes and capacities for moderate exercise.

3. When the trace pauses, click the individual measure buttons that appear in the data table above each data column to measure the lung volume and lung capacity data.

4. Select **Heavy Exercise** from the drop-down menu in the **Patient Type** box.

5. Click the **Start** button. The trace will continue with the breathing pattern for heavy exercise. The trace ends as the paper rolls to the right edge of the screen.

6. Now click the individual measure buttons that appear in the data table above each data column to measure the lung volume and lung capacity data.

7. Now consider the accuracy of your predictions (what changed versus what you expected to change).

Which volumes changed the most and when? _____

Compare the respiratory rate during moderate exercise with

that seen during heavy exercise. _____

Histology Review Supplement

For a review of respiratory tissue, go to **Exercise 6B: Histology Atlas and Review** on **myA&P** to print out the **Respiratory Tissue Review** worksheet.

Respiratory System Mechanics: Computer Simulation

NAME _____

LAB TIME/DATE _____

Pulmonary Function Tests

The following questions refer to Activity 1: Measuring Respiratory Volumes.

1. What activity are you simulating when you click the ERV button? _____

   What additional muscles are used in this activity? _____

2. What was the MRV calculated in Activity 1? _____

3. What does the pump rate simulate? _____

   _____

The following questions refer to Activity 2: Examining the Effect of Changing Airway Resistance on Respiratory Volumes.

4. How did changing the radius effect FEV_1 (%)? _____

   _____

5. What was the FEV_1 at a radius of 5.00 mm? _____

6. Do the results suggest that there is an obstructive or restrictive problem? Explain.

   _____

Simulating Factors Affecting Respirations

The following questions refer to Activity 3: Examining the Effect of Surfactant.

7. What effect does the addition of surfactant have on the airflow? _____

   _____

8. Why does surfactant affect airflow? _____

   _____

9. Why do premature infants have difficulty breathing? _____

   _____

The following questions refer to Activity 4: Investigating Intrapleural Pressure.

10. What effect does opening the valve have on the left lung? Why does this happen?

_____

_____

11. What condition does opening the valve simulate? _____

_____

12. What is the value of the pressure in the left lung when the valve is opened? _____

_____

13. What happened to the total flow when the valve was opened? _____

_____

14. In the last part of this activity, you clicked the Reset button. What procedure would be used with real lungs? _____

Simulating Variations in Breathing

The following questions refer to Activity 5: Exploring Various Breathing Patterns.

15. What was the value of the P_{CO_2} with rapid breathing? _____

How does this compare to the value with normal breathing? Explain any differences.

_____

16. What was the value of the P_{CO_2} with rebreathing? _____

Explain any difference. _____

17. What happened to the rate of respirations with rebreathing? _____

_____

Why do you think this happened? (Hint: Think about the effects of chemoreceptors in the body). _____

18. What was the value of the P_{CO_2} with breath holding? Explain any difference.

_____

_____

19. Was there a change in the rate of respirations when breathing was resumed?

_____

The following questions refer to Activity 6: Comparative Spirometry.

20. What was the value obtained for the $(FEV_1/FVC) \times 100\%$ with "normal breathing"?

_____

21. What effect did "emphysema breathing" have on FVC and FEV_1?

_____

22. In "emphysema breathing" which of the two values, FVC and FEV_1 changed the most? _____

23. What effect did "acute asthma attack breathing" have on FVC and FEV_1?

_____

24. In "acute asthma attack breathing" which of the two values, FVC and FEV_1 changed the most? _____

25. Describe the effect that the inhaler medication had on the FVC and FEV_1.

_____

26. Did the values return to "normal"? Explain. _____

_____

27. During "moderate exercise breathing," which volumes changed the most?

_____

28. During "heavy exercise breathing," which volumes changed the most?

_____

Chemical and Physical Processes of Digestion: Computer Simulation

OBJECTIVES

1. To list the digestive system enzymes involved in the digestion of proteins, fats, and carbohydrates; to state their site of origin; and to summarize the environmental conditions promoting their optimal functioning.

2. To recognize the variation between different types of enzyme assays.

3. To name the end products of digestion of proteins, fats, and carbohydrates.

4. To perform the appropriate chemical tests to determine if digestion of a particular food has occurred.

5. To cite the function(s) of bile in the digestive process.

6. To discuss the possible role of temperature and pH in the regulation of enzyme activity.

7. To define *enzyme*, *catalyst*, *hydrolase*, *substrate*, and *control*.

8. To explain why swallowing is both a voluntary and a reflex activity.

9. To discuss the role of the tongue, larynx, and gastroesophageal sphincter in swallowing.

10. To compare and contrast segmentation and peristalsis as mechanisms of propulsion.

The digestive system is a physiological marvel, composed of finely orchestrated chemical and physical activities. The food we ingest must be broken down into smaller subunits for us to absorb the nutrients we need, and digestion involves a complex sequence of mechanical and chemical processes designed to achieve this goal as efficiently as possible. As food passes through the gastrointestinal tract, it is progressively broken down by the mechanical action of smooth muscle and the chemical action of enzymes until most nutrients have been extracted and absorbed into the blood.

Chemical Digestion of Foodstuffs: Enzymatic Action

Nutrients can be absorbed only when broken down into their monomer form, so food digestion is a prerequisite to food absorption.

Enzymes are large protein molecules produced by body cells. They are biological **catalysts** that increase the rate of a chemical reaction without becoming part of the product. The digestive enzymes are hydrolytic enzymes, or **hydrolases,** which break down organic food molecules, or **substrates,** by adding water to the molecular bonds, thus cleaving the bonds between the subunits or monomers.

A hydrolytic enzyme is highly specific in its action. Each enzyme hydrolyzes one or, at most, a small group of substrate molecules, and specific environmental conditions are necessary for an enzyme to function optimally. For example, in extreme environments such as high temperature, an enzyme can unravel or denature because the high temperature disrupts the three-dimensional structure of the protein.

Because digestive enzymes actually function outside the body cells in the digestive tract lumen, their hydrolytic activity can also be studied in a test tube. See Figure 39B.1b for an overview of chemical digestion sites in the body. Such in vitro studies provide a convenient laboratory environment for investigating the effect of various factors on enzymatic activity.

Carbohydrate Digestion

In this experiment you will investigate the hydrolysis of starch to maltose by salivary amylase, the enzyme produced by the salivary glands and secreted into the mouth. To detect whether or not enzymatic action has occurred, you need to identify the presence of these substances and determine to what extent hydrolysis has occurred. Thus, **controls** must be prepared to provide a known standard against which comparisons can be made. The controls will vary for each experiment and will be discussed in each enzyme section in this exercise.

Starch decreases and sugar increases as digestion proceeds according to the following equation:

$$\text{Starch} + \text{water} \xrightarrow{\text{amylase}} \times \text{maltos}$$

Because the chemical changes that occur as starch is digested to maltose cannot be seen by the naked eye, you need to conduct an *enzyme assay,* the chemical method of detecting the presence of digested substances. You will perform two enzyme assays on each sample. The IKI assay detects the presence of starch, and the Benedict's assay tests for the presence of reducing sugars, such as glucose or maltose, which are the digestion products of starch. Normally a caramel-colored solution, IKI turns blue-black in the presence of starch. Benedict's reagent is a bright blue solution that changes to green to orange to reddish-brown with increasing amounts of maltose. It is important to understand that enzyme assays indicate only the presence or absence of substances. It is up to you to analyze the results of the experiments to decide if enzymatic hydrolysis has occurred.

Choose **Exercise 39B: Chemical and Physical Processes of Digestion** from the drop-down menu and click **GO.** Then click **Amylase.** The opening screen will appear in a few seconds (Figure 39B.1a). To familiarize yourself with the equipment, choose **Balloons On/Off** from the **Help** menu. This feature allows you to scroll around the screen and view equipment labels. You can turn off this feature by

(a)

FIGURE 39B.1 Chemical digestion. (a) Opening screen of the Amylase experiment.

Salivary glands:
produce salivary amylase
for the digestion of
starch.

Stomach glands:
produce pepsin (in the
presence of HCl) for
the digestion of proteins.

Liver:
produces bile for the
emulsification of fats
(ducted to the small
intestine).

Pancreas:
produces pancreatic
lipase for the digestion
of fats, and pancreatic
amylase for the digestion
of starch (enzymes are
ducted to the small
intestine).

Small intestine:
produces enzymes
for digestion of
starch and proteins.

(b)

FIGURE 39B.1 (continued) (b) A few sites of chemical digestion and the organs that
produce the enzymes of chemical digestion.

returning to the **Help** menu and selecting **Balloons On/Off.**
The *solutions shelf* in the upper right part of the screen contains the substances to be used in the experiment. The
incubation unit beneath the solutions shelf contains a rack of
test tube holders and the apparatus needed to run the experiments. To load test tubes from the *test tube washer* on the
left part of the screen into the rack in the incubation unit,
click and hold the mouse button on the first tube, and then
release (drag-and-drop) it into any position in the rack. To
dispense the substances in the dropper bottles on the solutions shelf, drag-and-drop the dropper cap to a position over
any test tube in the rack and then release it. During each dispensing event, five drops of solution drip into the test tube;
then the dropper cap automatically returns to its position in
the bottle.

Each test tube holder in the incubation unit not only supports but also allows you to boil the contents of a single test
tube. Clicking the numbered button at the base of a test tube
holder causes that single tube to descend into the incubation
unit. To boil the contents of all tubes inside the incubation unit,
click **Boil.** After they have been boiled, the tubes automatically
rise. You can adjust the incubation temperature for the experiment by clicking the (+) or (−) buttons next to the Temperature window. Set the incubation time by clicking the (+) or (−)
buttons next to the Timer window. Clicking the **Incubate** button starts the timer and causes the entire rack of tube holders to
descend into the incubation unit where the tubes will be incubated at the indicated temperature and time. While incubating,
the tubes are automatically agitated to ensure that their contents

are well mixed. During the experiment, elapsed time is displayed in the Elapsed Time window.

The cabinet doors in the *assay cabinet* above the test tube washer are closed at the beginning of the experiment, but they automatically open when the set time for incubation has elapsed. The assay cabinet contains the reagents and glassware needed to assay your experimental samples.

When you click the **Record Data** button in the *data control unit* at the bottom of the screen, your data is recorded in the computer's memory and displayed in the data grid at the bottom of the screen. Data displayed in the grid include the tube number, the three substances (additives) dispensed into each tube, whether or not a sample was boiled, the time and incubation temperature, and (+) or (−) marks indicating enzyme assay results. If you are not satisfied with a single run, you can click **Delete Run** to erase an experiment.

Once an experimental run is completed and you have recorded your data, discard the test tubes to prepare for a new run by dragging the used tubes to the large opening in the test tube washer. The test tubes will automatically be prepared for the next experiment.

The enzymes used in this simulation and their secreting organs are summarized in Figure 39B.1b.

A C T I V I T Y   1

Assessing Starch Digestion by Salivary Amylase

Incubation

1. Individually drag seven test tubes to the test tube holders in the incubation unit.

2. Note that Chart 1 lists the substances and conditions for each test tube. Prepare tubes 1 through 7 with the substances indicated in Chart 1 below using the following approach.

- Click and hold the mouse button on the dropper cap of the desired substance on the solutions shelf.

- While still holding down the mouse button, drag the dropper cap to the top of the desired test tube.

- Release the mouse button to dispense the substance. The dropper cap automatically returns to its bottle.

3. When all tubes are prepared, click the number (**1**) under the first test tube. The tube will descend into the incubation unit. All other tubes should remain in the raised position.

4. Click **Boil** to boil tube 1. After boiling for a few moments, the tube will automatically rise.

5. Now adjust the incubation temperature to 37°C and the timer to 60 min (compressed time) by clicking the (+) or (−) buttons.

6. Click **Incubate** to start the run. The incubation unit will gently agitate the test tube rack, evenly mixing the contents of all test tubes throughout the incubation. Notice that the computer compresses the 60-minute time period into 60 seconds of real time, so what would be a 1-hour incubation in real life will take only 1 minute in the simulation. When the incubation time elapses, the test tube rack will automatically rise, and the doors to the assay cabinet will open.

Assays

After the assay cabinet doors open, notice the two reagents in the assay cabinet. IKI tests for the presence of starch and Benedict's detects the presence of reducing sugars such as glucose or maltose, the digestion products of starch. Below the reagents are seven small assay tubes into which you will dispense a small amount of test solution from the incubated samples in the incubation unit, plus a drop of IKI.

1. Click and hold the mouse on the first tube in the incubation unit. Notice that the pointer is now a miniature test tube tilted to the left.

2. While still holding down the mouse button, move the pointer to the first small assay tube on the left side of the

CHART 1	Salivary Amylase Digestion of Starch						
Tube no.	1	2	3	4	5	6	7
Additives	Amylase Starch pH 7.0 buffer	Amylase Starch pH 7.0 buffer	Amylase D.I. water pH 7.0 buffer	D.I. water Starch pH 7.0 buffer	D.I. water Maltose pH 7.0 buffer	Amylase Starch pH 2.0 buffer	Amylase Starch pH 9.0 buffer
Incubation condition	Boil first, then incubate at 37°C for 60 minutes	37°C	37°C	37°C	37°C	37°C	37°C
IKI test							
Benedict's test							

Note: D.I. water = deionized water

assay cabinet. Release the mouse button. Watch the first test tube automatically decant approximately half of its contents into the first assay tube on the left.

3.   Repeat steps 1 and 2 for the remaining tubes in the incubation unit, moving to a fresh assay tube each time.

4.   Next, click and hold the mouse on the IKI dropper cap and drag it to the first assay tube. Release the mouse button to dispense a drop of IKI into the first assay tube on the left. You will see IKI drip into the tube, which may cause a color change in the solution. A blue-black color indicates a **positive starch test.** If starch is not present, the mixture will look like diluted IKI, a **negative starch test.** Intermediate starch amounts result in a pale gray color. The dropper will automatically move across and dispense IKI to the remaining tubes.

5.   Record your results (+ for positive, − for negative) in Chart 1.

6.   Dispense Benedict's reagent into the remaining mixture in each tube in the incubation unit by dragging-and-dropping the Benedict's dropper cap to the first tube. Repeat this for the remaining test tubes on top of the incubator.

7.   After Benedict's reagent has been delivered to each tube in the incubation unit, click **Boil.** The entire tube rack will descend into the incubation unit, which will automatically boil the tube contents for a few moments.

8.   When the rack of tubes rises, inspect the tubes for color change. A green-to-reddish color indicates that a reducing sugar is present; this is a **positive sugar test.** An orange-colored sample contains more sugar than a green sample. A reddish-brown color indicates even more sugar. A negative sugar test is indicated by no color change from the original bright blue. Record your results in Chart 1. Use a (+) for a green sample, a (++) for a reddish-brown sample, and a (−) for a blue sample.

9.   Click **Record Data** to display your results in the grid and retain your data in the computer's memory for later analysis. To repeat the experiment, drag all test tubes to the test tube washer and start again.

10.   Answer the following questions, referring to the chart (or the data grid in the simulation) as necessary. Hint: Closely examine the IKI and Benedict's results for each tube.

What do tubes 2, 6, and 7 reveal about pH and amylase activity? Hint: What variable was changed in the procedure?

_____

_____

Which pH buffer allowed the highest amylase activity?

_____

Which tube indicates that the amylase was not contaminated

with maltose? _____

Which tubes indicate that the deionized water did not contain

contaminating starch or maltose? _____

If we left out control tubes 3, 4, or 5, what objections could be raised to the statement: "Amylase digests starch to maltose"? (Hint: Think about the purity of the chemical solutions.)

_____

_____

_____

Would the amylase present in saliva be active in the stomach? Explain your answer.

_____

_____

What effect does boiling have on enzyme activity?

_____

_____

ACTIVITY 2

Assessing Cellulose Digestion

If any test tubes are still in the incubator, drag them to the test tube washer before beginning this activity. In this activity, we will test to see whether amylase digests *cellulose.*

Incubation

1.   Individually drag seven test tubes to the test tube holders in the incubation unit.

2.   Prepare tubes 1 through 7 with the substances indicated in Chart 2 on the next page using the following approach:

- Click and hold the mouse button on the dropper cap of the desired substance on the solutions shelf.

- While holding the mouse button down, drag the dropper cap to the top of the desired test tube.

- Release the mouse button to dispense the substance. The dropper cap automatically returns to its bottle.

3.   When all tubes are prepared, click the number (**1**) under the first test tube. The tube will descend into the incubation unit.

4.   Click **Freeze.** The tube's contents will be subjected to a temperature of −25°C. The tube will then automatically rise, with the contents of the tube frozen.

5.   Adjust the incubation temperature to 37°C and the timer to 60 minutes by clicking the appropriate (+) or (−) buttons.

6.   Click **Incubate** to start the run. The incubation unit will gently agitate the tubes as they incubate to thoroughly mix the tubes' contents. At the end of the incubation period, the tubes will ascend to their original positions on top of the incubator, and the doors to the assay cabinet will open.

Assays

When the assay cabinet opens, notice the two reagents in the cabinet. They are the same ones as in the previous activity: IKI will test for the presence of starch, and Benedict's solution will test for the presence of maltose. IKI turns blue-black in the presence of cellulose as well as starch. On the floor of the cabinet are seven small tubes that you will use to test the results of your experiment. The procedure will be identical to the one from the previous activity:

1. Click and hold the mouse on the first tube in the incubation unit. Notice that the pointer is now a miniature test tube tilted to the left.

2. While still holding the mouse button down, move the pointer to the first small assay tube on the left side of the assay cabinet. Release the mouse button.

3. Repeat steps 1 and 2 for the remaining tubes in the incubation unit, moving to a fresh assay tube each time.

4. Next, click and hold the mouse on the IKI dropper cap, and drag it to the first assay tube. Release the mouse button to dispense a drop of IKI into the first assay tube on the left. You will see IKI drip into the tube, which may cause a color change in the solution. A blue-black color indicates the presence of starch. If there is only a small amount of starch, you may see a pale gray color. If starch is not present, the mixture will look like diluted IKI. The dropper will automatically move across and dispense IKI to the remaining tubes.

5. Note the color of each tube. Record your results in Chart 2.

6. Dispense Benedict's reagent into the remaining mixture in each tube in the incubation unit by dragging-and-dropping the Benedict's dropper cap to the first tube. Repeat this for the remaining test tubes on top of the incubator.

7. After Benedict's reagent has been delivered to each tube in the incubation unit, click **Boil.** The entire tube rack will de-

scend into the incubation unit and automatically boil the tube contents for a few moments.

8. When the rack of tubes rises, inspect the tubes for color change. A green to reddish color indicates that a reducing sugar is present for a positive sugar test. An orange sample indicates more sugar than the green color, and a reddish-brown indicates the highest amounts of sugar. If there has been no color change from the original blue, no sugar is pres-ent in the tube. Record your results in Chart 2. Use a (+) for a green sample, a (++) for a reddish-brown sample, and a (−) for a blue sample.

9. Click **Record Data** to display your results in the grid and retain your data in the computer's memory for later analysis. To repeat the experiment, drag all test tubes to the test tube washer and start again.

10. Answer the following questions, referring to the chart.

Which tubes showed that starch or cellulose was still present?

_____

Which tubes tested positive for the presence of reducing sugars?

_____

What was the effect of freezing tube 1?

_____

How does the effect of freezing differ from the effect of boiling?

_____

_____

CHART 2	Enzyme Digestion of Starch and Cellulose						
Tube no.	1	2	3	4	5	6	7
Additives	Amylase Starch pH 7.0 buffer	Amylase Starch pH 7.0 buffer	Amylase Glucose pH 7.0 buffer	Amylase Cellulose pH 7.0 buffer	Amylase Cellulose D.I. water	Peptidase Starch pH 7.0 buffer	Bacteria Cellulose pH 7.0 buffer
Incubation condition	Freeze first, then incubate at 37°C for 60 minutes	37°C 60 min	37°C 60 min	37°C 60 min	37°C 60 min	37°C 60 min	37°C 60 min
IKI test							
Benedict's test							

Note: D.I. water = deionized water

Does amylase use cellulose as a substrate? Hint: Look at the results for tube 4.

_____

What effect did the addition of bacteria have on the digestion of cellulose?

_____

What was the effect of the different enzyme, peptidase, used in tube 6? Explain your answer, based on what you know about the substrate of peptidase?

_____

_____

11. Click **Tools** → **Print Data** to print your recorded data. ▬▬

Protein Digestion by Pepsin

The chief cells of the stomach glands produce pepsin, a protein-digesting enzyme. Pepsin hydrolyzes proteins to small fragments (polypeptides and a few free amino acids). In this experiment, you will use BAPNA, a synthetic "protein" that is transparent and colorless when in solution. However, if an active, protein-digesting enzyme such as pepsin is present, the solution will become yellow. You can use this characteristic to detect pepsin activity: the solution turns yellow if the enzyme digests the BAPNA substrate; it remains colorless if pepsin is not active or not present. One advantage of using a synthetic substrate is that you do not need any additional indicator reagents to see enzyme activity.

Choose **Pepsin** from the **Experiment** menu. The opening screen will appear in a few seconds (Figure 39B.2). The solutions shelf, test tube washer, and incubation equipment are the same as in the amylase experiment; only the solutions have changed.

Data displayed in the grid include the tube number, the three substances dispensed into each tube, a (+) or (−) mark indicating whether or not a sample was boiled, the time and temperature of the incubation, and the optical density measurement indicating enzyme assay results.

ACTIVITY 3

Assessing Protein Digestion by Pepsin

Pepsin Incubation

1. Individually drag six test tubes to the test tube holders in the incubation unit.

2. Prepare the tubes with the substances indicated in Chart 3 below using the following method.

- Click and hold the mouse button on the dropper cap of the desired substance and drag the dropper cap to the top of the desired test tube.

- Release the mouse button to dispense the substance.

3. Once all tubes are prepared, click the number (1) under the first test tube. The tube will descend into the incubation unit. All other tubes should remain in the raised position.

4. Click **Boil** to boil tube 1. After boiling for a few moments, the tube will automatically rise.

5. Adjust the incubation temperature to 37°C and the timer to 60 minutes (compressed time) by clicking the (+) or (−) button.

6. Click **Incubate** to start the run. The incubation unit will gently agitate the test tube rack, evenly mixing the contents of all test tubes throughout the incubation. The computer is compressing the 60-minute time period into 60 seconds of real time. When the incubation time elapses, the test tube rack will automatically rise, and the doors to the assay cabinet will open.

Pepsin Assay

After the assay cabinet doors open, you will see an instrument called a spectrophotometer, which you will use to measure how much yellow dye was liberated by pepsin digestion of

BAPNA. When you drag a test tube to the holder in the spectrophotometer and click the **Analyze** button, the instrument will shine a light through a specimen to measure the amount of light absorbed by the sample within the tube. The measure of the amount of light absorbed by the solution is known as its *optical density*. A colorless solution does not absorb light, whereas a colored solution has a relatively high light absorbance. For example, a colorless solution has an optical density of 0.0. A colored solution, however, absorbs some of the light emitted by the spectrophotometer, resulting in an optical density reading greater than zero.

In this experiment a yellow-colored solution is a direct indication of the amount of BAPNA digested by pepsin. Although you can visually estimate the yellow color produced by pepsin digestion of BAPNA, the spectrophotometer precisely measures how much BAPNA digestion occurred in the experiment.

1. Click and hold the mouse on the first tube in the incubation unit and drag it to the holder in the spectrophotometer.

2. Release the mouse button to drop the tube into the holder.

3. Click **Analyze.** You will see light shining through the solution in the test tube as the spectrophotometer measures its optical density. The optical density of the sample will be displayed in the optical density window below the Analyze button.

4. Record the optical density in Chart 3.

5. Drag the tube to its original position in the incubation unit and release the mouse button.

6. Repeat steps 1 through 5 for the remaining test tubes in the incubation unit.

7. Click **Record Data** to display your results in the grid and retain your data in the computer's memory for later analysis. To repeat the experiment, you must drag all test tubes to the test tube washer and start again.

8. Answer the following questions, referring to Chart 3 (or the data grid in the simulation) as necessary.

Which pH provided the highest pepsin activity? _____

CHART 3	Pepsin Digestion of Protein					
Tube no.	1	2	3	4	5	6
Additives	Pepsin BAPNA pH 2.0 buffer	Pepsin BAPNA pH 2.0 buffer	Pepsin D.I. water pH 2.0 buffer	D.I. water BAPNA pH 2.0 buffer	Pepsin BAPNA pH 7.0 buffer	Pepsin BAPNA pH 9.0 buffer
Incubation condition	Boil first, then incubate at 37°C for 60 minutes	37°C 60 min	37°C 60 min	37°C 60 min	37°C 60 min	37°C 60 min
Optical density	>					

Note: D.I. water = deionized water

Would pepsin be active in the mouth? Explain your answer.

_____

_____

How did the results of tube 1 compare with those of tube 2?

_____

Tubes 1 and 2 contained the same substances. Explain why their optical density measurements were different.

_____

_____

Did the pepsin or deionized water contain any contaminating digested BAPNA? Which tubes confirm this?

_____

_____

What do you think would happen if you reduced the incubation time to 30 minutes? Use the simulation to help you answer this question if you are not sure.

_____

_____

What do you think would happen if you decreased the temperature of incubation to 10°C? Use the simulation to help you answer this question if you are not sure.

_____

_____

9.   Click **Tools → Print Data** to print your recorded data. ▮

Fat Digestion by Pancreatic Lipase and the Action of Bile

The treatment that fats and oils undergo during digestion in the small intestine is a bit more complicated than that of carbohydrates or proteins. Fats and oils require pretreatment with bile to physically emulsify the fats. As a result, two sets of reactions must occur. First:

Fats/oils $\xrightarrow[\text{(emulsification)}]{\text{bile}}$ minute fat/oil droplets

Then:

Fat/oil droplets $\xrightarrow{\text{lipase}}$ monoglycerides and fatty acids

Lipase hydrolyzes fats and oils to their component monoglycerides and two fatty acids. Occasionally lipase hydrolyzes fats and oils to glycerol and three fatty acids.

The fact that some of the end products of fat digestion (fatty acids) are organic acids that decrease the pH provides an easy way to recognize that digestion is ongoing or completed. You will be using a pH meter in the assay cabinet to record the drop in pH as the test tube contents become acid.

Choose **Lipase** from the **Experiment** menu. The opening screen will appear in a few seconds (Figure 39B.3). The solutions shelf, test tube washer, and incubation equipment are the same as in the previous two experiments; only the solutions have changed.

Data displayed in the grid include the tube number, the four reagents dispensed into each tube, a (+) or (−) mark indicating whether or not a sample was boiled, the time and temperature of the incubation, and the pH measurement indicating enzyme assay results.

ACTIVITY 4

Assessing Fat Digestion by Pancreatic Lipase and the Action of Bile

Lipase Incubation

1.   Individually drag 6 test tubes to the test tube holders in the incubation unit.

2.   Prepare the tubes with the solutions indicated in Chart 4 on page PEx-139 by using the following method.

•   Click and hold the mouse button on the dropper cap of the desired substance.

•   While holding the mouse button down, drag the dropper cap to the top of the desired test tube.

•   Release the mouse button to dispense the substance.

3.   Adjust the incubation temperature to 37°C and the timer to 60 minutes (compressed time) by clicking the (+) or (−) button.

4.   Click **Incubate** to start the run. The incubation unit will gently agitate the test tube rack, evenly mixing the contents of all test tubes throughout the incubation. The computer is compressing the 60-minute time period into 60 seconds of real time. When the incubation time elapses, the test tube rack automatically rises, and the doors to the assay cabinet open.

Lipase Assay

After the assay cabinet doors open, you will see a pH meter that you will use to measure the relative acidity of your test solutions. When you drag a test tube to the holder in the pH meter and click the Measure pH button, a probe will descend into the sample, take a pH reading, and then retract. The pH of the sample will be displayed in the pH window below the Measure pH button. A solution containing fatty acids liberated from fat by the action of lipase will exhibit a lower pH than one without fatty acids.

1.   Click and hold the mouse on the first tube in the incubation unit, and drag it to the holder in the pH meter. Release the mouse button to drop the tube into the holder.

FIGURE 39B.3 Opening screen of the Lipase experiment.

2. Click **Measure pH.**

3. In Chart 4, record the pH displayed in the pH window.

4. Drag the test tube in the pH meter to its original position in the incubation unit, and release the mouse button.

5. Repeat steps 1 through 4 for the remaining test tubes in the incubation unit.

6. Click **Record Data** to display your results in the grid and retain your data in the computer's memory for later analysis. To repeat the experiment, you must drag all test tubes to the test tube washer and begin again.

7. Answer the following questions, referring to Chart 4 (or the data grid in the simulation) as necessary.

Explain the difference in activity between tubes 1 and 2.

_____

_____

Can you determine whether fat hydrolysis has occurred in

tube 6? _____ Explain your answer. _____

_____

Which pH resulted in maximum lipase activity? _____

Can you determine whether fat hydrolysis has occurred in tube 5? _____

_____

In theory, would lipase be active in the mouth? _____

Would it be active in the stomach? _____

Explain your answers. _____

_____

CHART 4	Pancreatic Lipase Digestion of Fats and the Action of Bile					
Tube no.	1	2	3	4	5	6
Additives	Lipase Vegetable oil Bile salts pH 7.0 buffer	Lipase Vegetable oil D.I. water pH 7.0 buffer	Lipase D.I. water Bile salts pH 9.0 buffer	D.I. water Vegetable oil Bile salts pH 7.0 buffer	Lipase Vegetable oil Bile salts pH 2.0 buffer	Lipase Vegetable oil Bile salts pH 9.0 buffer
Incubation condition	37°C 60 min	37°C 60 min	37°C 60 min	37°C 60 min	37°C 60 min	37°C 60 min
pH						

Note: D.I. = deionized water

What is the substrate, and what subunit is formed in this experiment? _____

_____

8. Click **Tools → Print Data** to print your recorded data. ▪️

Physical Processes: Mechanisms of Food Propulsion and Mixing

Although enzyme activity is an essential part of the overall digestion process, food must also be processed physically by churning and chewing and moved by mechanical means along the tract if digestion and absorption are to be completed. Just about any time organs exhibit mobility, muscles are involved, and movements of and in the gastrointestinal tract are no exception. Although we tend to think only of smooth muscles for visceral activities, both skeletal and smooth muscles are necessary in digestion. This fact is demonstrated by the simple trials in the next activity. Obtain the following materials:

- Water pitcher
- Paper cups
- Stethoscope
- Alcohol swabs
- Disposable autoclave bag

ACTIVITY 5

Studying Mechanisms of Food Propulsion and Mixing: Deglutition (Swallowing)

Swallowing, or *deglutition,* which is largely the result of skeletal muscle activity, occurs in two phases: *buccal* (mouth) and *pharyngeal-esophageal.* The initial phase—the buccal—is voluntarily controlled and initiated by the tongue. Once begun, the process continues involuntarily in the pharynx and esophagus, through peristalsis, resulting in the delivery of the swallowed contents to the stomach.

1. While swallowing a mouthful of water from a paper cup, consciously note the movement of your tongue during the process. Record your observations.

_____

_____

_____

2. Repeat the swallowing process while your laboratory partner watches the externally visible movements of your larynx. This movement is more obvious in a male, who has a larger Adam's apple. Record your observations.

_____

_____

What do these movements accomplish? _____

_____

_____

3. Your lab partner should clean the ear pieces of a stethoscope with an alcohol swab and don the stethoscope. Then your lab partner should place the diaphragm of the stethoscope on your abdominal wall, approximately 1 inch below the xiphoid process and slightly to the left, to listen for sounds as you again take two or three swallows of water. There should be two audible sounds. The first sound occurs when the water splashes against the gastroesophageal sphincter. The second occurs when the peristaltic wave of the esophagus arrives at the sphincter and the sphincter opens, allowing water to gurgle into the stomach. Determine, as accurately as possible, the time interval between these two sounds and record it below.

Interval between arrival of water at the sphincter and the opening of the sphincter:

_____ sec

This interval gives a fair indication of the time it takes for the peristaltic wave to travel down the 10-inch-long esophagus. Actually the time interval is slightly less than it seems because pressure causes the sphincter to relax before the peristaltic wave reaches it.

Dispose of the used paper cup in the autoclave bag. ▬

Segmentation and Peristalsis

Although several types of movement occur in the digestive tract organs, segmentation and peristalsis are most important as mixing and propulsive mechanisms.

Segmental movements are local constrictions of the organ wall that occur rhythmically. They serve mainly to mix the foodstuffs with digestive juices and to increase the rate of absorption by continually moving different portions of the chyme over adjacent regions of the intestinal wall. However, segmentation is an important means of food propulsion in the small intestine, and slow segmenting movements called haustral contractions are common in the large intestine.

Peristaltic movements are the major means of propelling food through most of the digestive viscera. Essentially they are waves of contraction followed by waves of relaxation that squeeze foodstuffs through the alimentary canal, and they are superimposed on segmental movements.

Histology Review Supplement

For a review of digestive tissue, go to **Exercise 6B: Histology Atlas and Review** on **myA&P** to print out the **Digestive Tissue Review** worksheet.

NAME _____

LAB TIME/DATE _____

Chemical and Physical Processes of Digestion: Computer Simulation

Carbohydrate Digestion

The following questions refer to Activity 1: Assessing Starch Digestion by Salivary Amylase.

1. At what pH did you see the highest activity of salivary amylase? _____ Why?

_____

2. How do you know that the amylase did not have any contaminating maltose?

_____

_____

3. What effect did boiling have on enzyme activity? Why? _____

_____

_____

4. Describe the substrate and the subunit product of amylase. _____

_____

The following questions refer to Activity 2: Assessing Cellulose Digestion.

5. Does amylase use cellulose as a substrate? Explain. _____

_____

6. Did freezing have an effect on the activity of amylase? Explain. _____

_____

7. Do you think that the bacterial suspension contained the enzyme cellulase (an enzyme that digests cellulose)? Why or why not?

_____

_____

8. What is the substrate of peptidase? Explain, based upon your results. _____

_____

Protein Digestion by Pepsin

The following questions refer to Activity 3: Assessing Protein Digestion by Pepsin.

9. At which pH did you see the highest activity of pepsin? _____ How does this correlate to the location of pepsin in the

body? _____

_____

10. What effect did boiling have on pepsin? _____

_____

11. Was there any digested BAPNA contaminating the pepsin or deionized (DI) water? _____

How can you tell? _____

_____

12. What is the substrate in this experiment? _____

What is the usual substrate for pepsin, and what subunits are formed with pepsin activity?

_____

_____

13. What was the effect of decreasing the incubation time on the optical density results?

_____

14. What effect would decreased incubation temperature have on pepsin activity? Why?

_____

_____

15. What was the significance of using 37°C for the incubation? _____

_____

Fat Digestion by Pancreatic Lipase and the Action of Bile

The following questions refer to Activity 4: Assessing Fat Digestion by Pancreatic Lipase and the Action of Bile.

16. Describe the activity of lipase with and without the addition of bile salts. Refer to Chart 4 for pH values. _____

_____

17. Is the activity of bile a chemical or a physical process? Explain. _____

_____

18. What pH resulted in the maximum pancreatic lipase activity? _____

How does this optimal pH correlate to the enzyme's location in the body? _____

_____

19. Explain whether or not we can determine fat hydrolysis in tube 5. Why or why not?

_____

_____

20. What is the substrate in this experiment? _____

What subunits does lipase form? _____

Physical Process: Mechanisms of Food Propulsion and Mixing

The following questions refer to Activity 5: Studying Mechanisms of Food Propulsion and Mixing: Deglutition (Swallowing).

21. Explain the significance of the movement of the tongue during swallowing. _____

_____

22. Describe three events that occur during the pharyngeal-esophageal phase of deglutition. _____

_____

_____

23. What was the time interval that you recorded between the first and second sound?

_____

Renal System Physiology: Computer Simulation

OBJECTIVES

1. To define the following terms: *glomerulus, glomerular capsule, renal corpuscle, renal tubule, nephron, proximal convoluted tubule, loop of Henle,* and *distal convoluted tubule.*
2. To describe the blood supply to each nephron.
3. To identify the regions of the nephron involved in glomerular filtration and tubular reabsorption.
4. To study the factors affecting glomerular filtration.
5. To explore the concept of carrier transport maximum.
6. To understand how the hormones aldosterone and ADH affect the function of the kidney.
7. To describe how the kidneys can produce urine that is four times more concentrated than the blood.

Metabolism produces wastes that must be eliminated from the body. This excretory function is the job of the renal system, most importantly the paired kidneys. Each kidney consists of about one million nephrons that carry out two crucial services, blood filtration and fluid processing.

Microscopic Structure and Function of the Kidney

Each of the million or so **nephrons** in each kidney is a microscopic tubule consisting of two major parts: a glomerulus and a renal tubule. The **glomerulus** is a tangled capillary knot that filters fluid from the blood into the lumen of the renal tubule. The function of the **renal tubule** is to process that fluid, also called the **filtrate.** The beginning of the renal tubule is an enlarged end called the **glomerular capsule,** which surrounds the glomerulus and serves to funnel the filtrate into the rest of the renal tubule. Collectively, the glomerulus and the glomerular capsule are called the **renal corpuscle.**

As the rest of the renal tubule extends from the glomerular capsule, it becomes twisted and convoluted, then dips sharply down to form a hairpin loop, and then coils again before entering a collecting duct. Starting at the glomerular capsule, the anatomical parts of the renal tubule are as follows: the **proximal convoluted tubule, the loop of Henle** (nephron loop), and the **distal convoluted tubule.**

Two arterioles supply each glomerulus: an afferent arteriole feeds the glomerular capillary bed and an efferent arteriole drains it. These arterioles are responsible for blood flow through the glomerulus. Constricting the afferent arteriole lowers the downstream pressure in the glomerulus, whereas constricting the efferent arteriole increases the pressure in the glomerulus. In addition, the diameter of the efferent arteriole is smaller than the diameter of the afferent arteriole, restricting blood flow out of the glomerulus. Consequently, the pressure in the glomerulus forces fluid through the endothelium of the glomerulus into the lumen of the surrounding glomerular capsule. In essence, everything in the blood except the cells and proteins are filtered through the glomerular wall. From the capsule, the filtrate moves into the rest of the renal tubule for processing. The job of the tubule is to reabsorb all the beneficial substances from its lumen while allowing the wastes to travel down the tubule for elimination from the body.

The nephron performs three important functions to process the filtrate into urine: glomerular filtration, tubular reabsorption, and tubular secretion. **Glomerular filtration** is a passive process in which fluid passes from the lumen of the glomerular capillary into the glomerular capsule of the renal tubule. **Tubular reabsorption** moves most of the filtrate back into the blood, leaving principally salt water plus the wastes in the lumen of the tubule. Some of the desirable or needed solutes are actively reabsorbed, and others move passively from the lumen of the tubule into the interstitial spaces. **Tubular secretion** is essentially the reverse of tubular reabsorption and is a process by which the kidneys can rid the blood of additional unwanted substances such as creatinine and ammonia.

The reabsorbed solutes and water that move into the interstitial space between the nephrons need to be returned to the blood, or the kidneys will rapidly swell like balloons. The peritubular capillaries surrounding the renal tubule reclaim the reabsorbed substances and return them to general circulation. Peritubular capillaries arise from the efferent arteriole exiting the glomerulus and empty into the veins leaving the kidney.

Simulating Glomerular Filtration

This computerized simulation allows you to explore one function of a single simulated nephron, glomerular filtration. You can then apply the concepts you will learn by studying a single nephron to the function of the kidney as a whole.

Choose **Exercise 41B: Renal System Physiology** from the drop-down menu and click **GO.** Then click **Simulating Glomerular Filtration.** The opening screen for the Simulating Glomerular Filtration experiment will appear in a few seconds (Figure 41B.1). The main features on the screen when the program starts are a *simulated blood supply* at the left side of the screen, a *simulated nephron* within a supporting tank on the right side, and a *data control unit* at the bottom of the display.

The left beaker is the "blood" source representing the general circulation supplying the nephron. You can adjust the "blood pressure" in the beaker by clicking the (+) and (−) buttons on top of the beaker. A tube with an adjustable radius called the *afferent flow* tube connects the left beaker to the simulated

FIGURE 41B.1 Opening screen of the Simulating Glomerular Filtration experiment.

glomerulus. Another adjustable tube called the *efferent flow* tube drains the glomerulus. The afferent flow tube represents the afferent arteriole feeding the glomerulus of each nephron, and the efferent flow tube represents the efferent arteriole draining the glomerulus. The outflow of the nephron empties into a collecting duct, which in turn drains into another small beaker at the bottom right of the screen. Clicking the valve at the end of the collecting duct (which currently reads **valve open**) stops the flow of fluid through the nephron and collecting duct.

The **Glomerular Pressure** window on top of the nephron tank displays the pressure within the glomerulus. The **Glomerular Filt. Rate** window indicates the flow rate of the fluid moving from the lumen of the glomerulus into the lumen of the renal tubule.

The concentration gradient bathing the nephron is fixed at 1200 milliosmoles (mosm). Clicking **Start** begins the experiment. Clicking **Refill** resets the equipment to begin another run.

The equipment in the lower part of the screen is called the *data control unit*. This equipment records and displays data you accumulate during the experiments. The data set for the first experiment (Afferent) is highlighted in the **Data Sets** window. You can add or delete a data set by clicking the appropriate button to the right of the Data Sets window. When you click **Record Data**, your data is recorded in the computer's memory and displayed in the data grid. Data displayed in the data grid include the afferent radius, efferent radius, beaker pressure, glomerular pressure, glomerular filtration rate, and urine volume. Clicking **Delete Line** allows you to discard data values for a single run, and clicking **Clear Data Set** erases the entire experiment to allow you to start over.

If you need help identifying any piece of equipment, choose **Balloons On/Off** from the **Help** menu and move the pointer onto any piece of equipment visible on the computer's screen. As the pointer touches the object, a pop-up window appears identifying the equipment. To close the pop-up window, move the pointer away from the equipment. Choose **Balloons On/Off** to turn off this Help feature.

ACTIVITY 1

Investigating the Effect of Flow Tube Radius on Glomerular Filtration

Your first experiment will examine the effects of flow tube radii and pressures on the rate of glomerular filtration. Click **Start** to see the on-screen action. Continue when you understand how the simulation operates. Click **Refill** to reset the experiment.

1. The **Afferent** line in the **Data Sets** window of the data control unit should be highlighted in bright blue. If it is not, choose it by clicking the **Afferent** line. The data control unit will now record filtration rate variations due to changing afferent flow tube radius.

2. If the data grid is not empty, click **Clear Data Set** to discard all previous data.

3. Adjust the afferent radius to 0.35 mm and the efferent radius to 0.40 mm by clicking the appropriate (+) or (−) buttons.

4. If the left beaker is not full, click **Refill.**

5. Keep the beaker pressure at 90 mm Hg during this part of the experiment.

6. Click **Start,** and watch the blood flow. Simultaneously, filtered fluid will be moving through the nephron and into the collecting duct. The Glomerular Filtration Rate window will display the fluid flow rate into the renal tubule when the left beaker has finished draining.

7. Now click **Record Data** to record the current experiment data in the data grid. Click **Refill** to replenish the left beaker and prepare the nephron for the next run.

8. Increase the afferent radius in 0.05-mm increments and repeat steps 6 and 7 until the maximum radius (0.60 mm) is achieved. Be sure to click **Record Data** after each trial. If you make an error and want to delete a single value, click the data line in the data grid and then click **Delete Line.**

What happens to the glomerular filtration rate as the afferent radius is increased?

_____

_____

_____

What happens to the glomerular pressure as the afferent radius is increased?

_____

_____

_____

Predict what effect increasing or decreasing the efferent radius will have on glomerular filtration rate. Use the simulation to check your prediction and record your results.

_____

_____

_____

ACTIVITY 2

Studying the Effect of Pressure on Glomerular Filtration

Both the blood pressure supplying the glomerulus and the pressure in the renal tubule have a significant impact on the glomerular filtration rate. In this activity, the data control unit will record filtration rate variations due to changing pressure.

1. Click the **Pressure** line in the **Data Sets** window of the data control unit.

2. If the data grid is not empty, click **Clear Data Set** to discard all previous data.

3. If the left beaker is not full, click **Refill.**

4. Adjust the pressure in the left beaker to 70 mm Hg by clicking the appropriate (+) or (−) button.

5. During this part of the experiment, maintain the afferent flow tube radius at 0.55 mm and the efferent flow tube radius at 0.45 mm.

6. Click **Start,** and watch the blood flow. Filtrate will move through the nephron into the collecting duct. At the end of the run, the Glomerular Filtration Rate window will display the filtrate flow rate into the renal tubule.

7. Now click **Record Data** to record the current experiment data in the data grid. Click **Refill** to replenish the left beaker.

8. Increase the pressure in the left beaker in increments of 10 mm Hg and repeat steps 6 and 7 until the maximum pressure (100 mm Hg) is achieved. Be sure to click **Record Data** after each trial. If you make an error and want to delete a single value, click the data line in the data grid and then click **Delete Line.**

What happened to the glomerular filtration rate as the beaker pressure was increased?

_____

_____

What was the effect on glomerular pressure as beaker pressure increased?

_____

_____

_____ ▬

ACTIVITY 3

Exploring Intrinsic Controls: Renal Autoregulation

So far, you have examined the effects of flow tube radius and pressure on glomerular filtration rate. In this experiment you will be altering both variables to explore the combined effects on glomerular filtration rate and to see how one can compensate for the other to maintain an adequate glomerular filtration rate.

1. Click **Combined** in the **Data Sets** window of the data control unit.

2. If the data grid is not empty, click **Clear Data Set** to discard all previous data.

3. If the left beaker is not full, click **Refill.**

4. Set the starting conditions at:

• 100 mm Hg beaker pressure

• 0.55 mm afferent radius

• 0.45 mm efferent radius

5. Click **Start.**

6. Now click **Record Data** to record the current baseline data in the data grid.

7. Click **Refill.**

8. Set the starting conditions at:

• 80 mm Hg beaker pressure

• 0.55 mm afferent radius

• 0.45 mm efferent radius

9. Record the glomerular filtration rate at a beaker pressure

of 80 mm Hg: _____

10. If the left beaker is not full, click **Refill.**

11. Adjust the pressure in the left beaker to 85 mm Hg by clicking the appropriate (+) or (−) button.

12. Maintain the starting conditions for the afferent flow tube radius and the efferent flow tube radius.

13. Record the glomerular filtration rate at a beaker pressure

of 85 mm Hg: _____

14. What variables other than beaker pressure could you change to return the glomerular filtration rate to "normal" (the value when beaker pressure is 80 mm Hg)? Circle the correct change in each set of parentheses: (increase / decrease) in the afferent radius, (increase / decrease) in the efferent radius.

15. Test your predictions. Hint: Try small changes of each variable one at a time.

16. List the value of each variable that results in a glomerular filtration rate approximately the same as its starting value when beaker pressure is 85 mm Hg.

Afferent radius _____ mm

Efferent radius _____ mm

17. Click **Tools → Print Data** to print your recorded data. ▬

Simulating Urine Formation

This part of the computer simulation allows you to explore some aspects of urine formation by manipulating the interstitial solute concentration. Other activities include investigating the effects of aldosterone and ADH (antidiuretic hormone) and the role that glucose carrier proteins play in renal function.

Choose **Simulating Urine Formation** from the **Experiment** menu. The opening screen will appear in a few seconds (Figure 41B.2a). The basic features on the screen when the program starts are similar to the glomerular filtration screen. Most of the vascular controls have been moved off-screen to the left because they will not be needed in this set of experiments. Additional equipment includes *supply shelves* at the right side of the screen, a *glucose carrier control* located at the top of the nephron tank, and a *concentration probe* at the bottom left of the screen.

You can adjust the maximum concentration of the interstitial gradient to be dispensed into the tank surrounding the nephron by clicking the (+) and (−) buttons next to the Conc. Grad. window. Click **Dispense** to fill the tank through the jets at the bottom of the tank with the chosen solute gradient. Click **Start** to begin a run. While the experiment is running, you can drag the concentration probe over the nephron to display the solute concentration within.

Hormone is dispensed by dragging a hormone dropper cap to the gray cap button in the nephron tank at the top of the collecting duct and then releasing the mouse button.

Use the (+) and (−) buttons in the glucose carrier control to adjust the number of glucose carriers that will be inserted into the simulated proximal convoluted tubule when you click the **Add Carriers** button.

Data displayed in the data grid will depend on which experiment is being conducted. Clicking **Delete Line** allows you to discard data values for a single run, and clicking **Clear Data Set** erases the entire experiment to allow you to start over.

FIGURE 41ʙ.2 Urine formation. (a) Opening screen of the Simulating Urine Formation experiment.

Exploring the Role of the Solute Gradient on Maximum Urine Concentration Achievable

In the process of urine formation, solutes and water move from the lumen of the nephron into the interstitial spaces. The passive movement of solutes and water from the lumen of the renal tubule into the interstitial spaces relies in part on the total solute gradient surrounding the nephron. When the nephron is permeable to solutes or water, an equilibrium will be reached between the interstitial fluid and the contents of the nephron. Antidiuretic hormone (ADH) increases the water permeability of the distal convoluted tubule and the collecting duct, allowing water to flow to areas of higher solute concentration, usually from the lumen of the nephron into the surrounding interstitial area. You will explore the process of passive reabsorption in this experiment. While doing this part of the simulation, assume that when ADH is present the conditions favor the formation of the most concentrated urine possible. (Figure 41ʙ.2b and c).

1. **Gradient** in the **Data Sets** window of the data control unit should be highlighted in bright blue. If it is not, then click **Gradient.**

2. If the data grid is not empty, click **Clear Data Set** to discard all previous data.

3. Click and hold the mouse button on the **ADH** bottle cap and drag it to the gray cap at the top right side of the nephron tank. Release the mouse button to dispense ADH onto the collecting duct.

4. Adjust the maximum total solute concentration of the gradient (**Conc. Grad.**) to 300 mosm by clicking the appropriate (+) or (−) button. Because the blood solute concentration is also 300 mosm, there is no osmotic difference between the lumen of the nephron and the surrounding interstitial fluid.

5. Click **Dispense.**

6. Click **Start** to begin the experiment. Filtrate will move through the nephron and then drain into the beaker below the collecting duct.

Key:

→ (red) Active transport
→ (blue) Passive transport

FIGURE 41B.2 *(continued)* **Urine formation.** **(b)** Mechanisms for forming dilute urine **(c)** and concentrated urine.

7.   While the experiment is running, watch the **Probe.** When it turns red, click and hold the mouse on it, and drag it to the urine beaker. Observe the total solute concentration in the **Concentration** window.

8.   Now click **Record Data** to record the current experiment data in the data grid.

9.   Increase the maximum concentration of the gradient in 300-mosm increments, and repeat steps 3 through 8 until 1200 mosm is achieved. Be sure to click **Record Data** after each trial. If you make an error and want to delete a single value, click the data line in the data grid and then click **Delete Line.**

What happened to the urine concentration as the gradient concentration was increased?

_____

_____

_____

What happened to the volume of urine?

_____

_____

What factor limits the maximum possible urine concentration?

_____

_____

Was equilibrium achieved?

_____

_____

ACTIVITY 5

Studying the Effect of Glucose Carrier Proteins on Glucose Reabsorption

Because carrier proteins are needed to move glucose from the lumen of the nephron into the interstitial spaces, there is a limit to the amount of glucose that can be reabsorbed. When all glucose carriers are bound with the glucose they are transporting, excess glucose is eliminated in urine. In this experiment, you will examine the effect of varying the number of glucose transport proteins in the proximal convoluted tubule.

1. Click **Glucose** in the **Data Sets** window of the data control unit.

2. If the data grid is not empty, click **Clear Data Set** to discard all previous data.

3. Set the concentration gradient (**Conc. Grad.**) to 1200 mosm.

4. Click **Dispense.**

5. Adjust the number of glucose carriers to 100 (an arbitrary figure) by clicking the appropriate (+) or (−) button.

6. Click **Add Carriers.** This action inserts the specified number of glucose carrier proteins per unit area into the membrane of the proximal convoluted tubule.

7. Click **Start** to begin the run after the carriers have been added.

8. Click **Record Data** to record the current experimental data in the data grid. Glucose presence in the urine will be displayed in the data grid.

9. Now increase the number of glucose carrier proteins in the proximal convoluted tubule in increments of 100 glucose carriers, and repeat steps 6 through 8 until the maximum number of glucose carrier proteins (500) is achieved. Remember to click **Add Carriers** each time. Be sure to click **Record Data** after each trial. If you make an error and want to delete a single value, click the data line in the data grid and then click **Delete Line.**

What happened to the amount of glucose present in the urine as the number of glucose carriers was increased?

_____

_____

The amount of glucose present in normal urine is minimal because there are normally enough glucose carriers present to handle the "traffic." Predict the consequence in the urine if there was more glucose than could be transported by the available number of glucose carrier proteins.

_____

_____

Explain why you would expect to find glucose in the urine of a diabetic person.

_____

_____

Testing the Effect of Hormones on Urine Formation

The concentration of the urine excreted by our kidneys changes depending on our immediate needs. For example, if a person

consumes a large quantity of water, the excess water will be eliminated, producing dilute urine. On the other hand, under conditions of dehydration, there is a clear benefit in being able to produce urine as concentrated as possible, thereby retaining precious water. Although the medullary gradient makes it possible to excrete concentrated urine, urine dilution or concentration is ultimately under hormonal control. In this experiment, you will investigate the effects of two different hormones on renal function, aldosterone produced by the adrenal gland and ADH manufactured by the hypothalamus and stored in the posterior pituitary gland. Aldosterone works to reabsorb sodium ions (and thereby water) at the expense of losing potassium ions; its site of action is the distal convoluted tubule. ADH makes the distal tubule and collecting duct more permeable to water, thereby allowing the body to reabsorb more water from the filtrate when it is present.

1. Click **Hormone** in the **Data Sets** window of the data control unit.

2. If the data grid is not empty, click **Clear Data Set** to discard all previous data.

3. During this part of the experiment, keep the concentration gradient at 1200 mosm.

4. Click **Dispense** to add the gradient, and then click **Start** to begin the experiment.

5. Now click **Record Data** to record the current experiment data in the data grid.

You will use this baseline data to compare with the conditions of the filtrate under the control of the two hormones.

Baseline urine volume _____

6. Keeping all experiment conditions the same as before, do the following:

• Drag the **Aldosterone** dropper cap to the gray cap on the top right side of the nephron tank, and release the mouse to automatically dispense aldosterone into the tank surrounding the distal convoluted tubule and collecting duct.

• Click **Start,** and allow the run to complete.

• Click **Record Data.**

Urine volume with aldosterone present _____

In this run, how does the volume of urine differ from the previously measured baseline volume?

_____

_____

Explain the difference in the total amount of potassium in the urine between this run and the baseline run.

_____

_____

7. Drag the **ADH** bottle cap to the gray cap on the top right side of the nephron tank, and release it to dispense ADH.

- Click **Start,** and allow the run to complete.
- Click **Record Data.**

In this run, how does the volume of urine differ from the baseline measurement?

_____

_____

Is there a difference in the total amount of potassium in this run and the total amount of potassium in the baseline run? Explain your answer. (Hint: The urine volume with ADH present is about one-tenth the urine volume when it is not present.)

_____

_____

Are the effects of aldosterone and ADH similar or antagonistic? _____

Consider this situation: we want to reabsorb sodium ions but do not want to increase the volume of the blood by reabsorbing water from the filtrate. Assuming that aldosterone and ADH are both present, how would you adjust the hormones to accomplish the task?

_____

_____

_____

8. Click **Tools → Print Data** to print your recorded data.

Histology Review Supplement

For a review of renal tissue, go to **Exercise 6B: Histology Atlas and Review** on **myA&P** to print out the **Renal Tissue Review worksheet.**

NAME _____

LAB TIME/DATE _____

Renal System Physiology: Computer Simulation

Simulating Glomerular Filtration

The following questions refer to Activity 1: Investigating the Effect of Flow Tube Radius on Glomerular Filtration.

1. Describe the effect of increasing the afferent radius on glomerular filtration rate and glomerular pressure.

   _____

   _____

2. Describe the effect of decreasing the efferent radius on glomerular filtration rate and glomerular pressure.

   _____

   _____

3. Describe the effect of increasing the efferent radius on glomerular filtration rate and glomerular pressure.

   _____

   _____

The following questions refer to Activity 2: Studying the Effect of Pressure on Glomerular Filtration.

4. Describe the effect of increasing the beaker pressure on glomerular filtration rate.

   _____

5. Describe the effect of increasing the beaker pressure on glomerular pressure.

   _____

6. In the absence of any regulatory mechanisms, what effect do you think an increase in blood pressure would have on

   glomerular filtration rate? _____

   _____

The following questions refer to Activity 3: Exploring Intrinsic Controls: Renal Autoregulation.

7. What was the glomerular filtration rate at 80 mm Hg beaker pressure, 0.55 mm afferent radius, and 0.45 mm efferent radius?

_____

8. With the beaker pressure increased to 85 mm Hg, at what afferent radius was the glomerular filtration rate in question 7

restored? _____

9. With the beaker pressure increased to 85 mm Hg, at what efferent radius was the glomerular filtration rate in question 7

restored? _____

10. In the body, what mechanisms play a role in maintaining glomerular filtration rate with fluctuating blood pressure?

_____

_____

Simulating Urine Formation

The following questions refer to Activity 4: Exploring the Role of the Solute Gradient on Maximum Urine Concentration Achievable.

11. As you increased the concentration gradient of the interstitial fluid, what happened to the concentration of the urine?

_____

12. What happened to the volume of the urine as you increased the concentration gradient of the interstitial fluid?

_____

13. What effect does the concentration gradient of the interstitial fluid have on the maximum urine concentration?

_____

The following questions refer to Activity 5: Studying the Effect of Glucose Carrier Proteins on Glucose Reabsorption.

14. What happens to the concentration of glucose in the urine as the number of glucose carriers increases?

_____

15. Glucose can be elevated in the blood of a diabetic person. Relate this information to glucose in the urine and glucose carriers.

_____

_____

The following questions refer to Activity 6: Testing the Effects of Hormones on Urine Formation.

16. What was the volume of urine in the presence of aldosterone? _____

How did aldosterone affect the urine volume? _____

17. What happened to the concentration of potassium in the urine in the presence of aldosterone? _____

18. What was the volume of the urine in the presence of ADH? _____

How did ADH affect the urine volume? _____

19. Why did the concentration of potassium change in the presence of ADH without a change in the excretion of potassium?

_____

_____

20. Does ADH favor the formation of dilute or concentrated urine? Explain.

_____

_____

Acid-Base Balance: Computer Simulation

O B J E C T I V E S

1. To define *pH*, and to identify the normal range of human blood pH levels.

2. To define *acid* and *base*, and to explain what characterizes each of the following: *strong acid*, *weak acid*, *strong base*, and *weak base*.

3. To explain how chemical and physiological buffering systems help regulate the body's pH levels.

4. To define the conditions of *acidosis* and *alkalosis*.

5. To explain the difference between *respiratory acidosis and alkalosis* and *metabolic acidosis and alkalosis*.

6. To understand the causes of respiratory acidosis and alkalosis.

7. To explain how the renal system compensates for respiratory acidosis and alkalosis.

8. To understand the causes of metabolic acidosis and alkalosis.

9. To explain how the respiratory system compensates for metabolic acidosis and alkalosis.

The term **pH** is used to denote the hydrogen ion concentration, [H$^+$], in body fluids. The pH values are the reciprocal of [H$^+$] and follow the formula

$$pH = log(1/[H^+])$$

At a pH of 7.4, [H$^+$] is about 40 nanomoles (n*M*) per liter. Because the relationship is reciprocal, [H$^+$] is higher at *lower* pH values (indicating higher acid levels) and lower at *higher* pH values (indicating lower acid levels).

The pH of a body's fluids is also referred to as its **acid-base balance.** An **acid** is a substance that releases H$^+$ in solution (such as in body fluids). A **base,** often a hydroxyl ion (OH$^-$) or bicarbonate ion (HCO$_3^-$), is a substance that binds to H$^+$. A *strong acid* is one that completely dissociates in solution, releasing all of its hydrogen ions and thus lowering the solution's pH level. A *weak acid* dissociates incompletely and does not release all of its hydrogen ions in solution. A *strong base* has a strong tendency to bind to H$^+$, which has the effect of raising the pH value of the solution. A *weak base* binds less of the H$^+$, having a lesser effect on solution pH.

The body's pH levels are very tightly regulated. Blood and tissue fluids normally have pH values between 7.35 and 7.45. Under pathological conditions, blood pH values as low as 6.9 or as high as 7.8 have been recorded; however, values higher or lower than these cannot sustain human life. The narrow range of 7.35–7.45 is remarkable when one considers the vast number of biochemical reactions that take place in the body. The human body normally produces a large amount of H$^+$ as the result of metabolic processes, ingested acids, and the products of fat, sugar, and amino acid metabolism. The regulation of a relatively constant internal pH environment is one of the major physiological functions of the body's organ systems.

To maintain pH homeostasis, the body utilizes both *chemical* and *physiological* buffering sytems. Chemical buffers are composed of a mixture of weak acids and weak bases. They help regulate body pH levels by binding H$^+$ and removing it from solution as its concentration begins to rise or by releasing H$^+$

into solution as its concentration begins to fall. The body's three major chemical buffering systems are the *bicarbonate, phosphate,* and *protein buffer systems.* We will not focus on chemical buffering systems in this lab, but keep in mind that chemical buffers are the fastest form of compensation and can return pH to normal levels within a fraction of a second.

The body's two major physiological buffering systems are the renal and respiratory systems. The renal system is the slower of the two, taking hours to days to do its work. The respiratory system usually works within minutes but cannot handle the amount of pH change that the renal system can. These physiological buffer systems help regulate body pH by controlling the output of acids, bases, or carbon dioxide (CO_2) from the body. For example, if there is too much acid in the body, the renal system may respond by excreting more H^+ from the body in urine. Similarly, if there is too much carbon dioxide in the blood, the respiratory system may respond by breathing faster to expel the excess carbon dioxide. Carbon dioxide levels have a direct effect on pH levels because the addition of carbon dioxide to the blood results in the generation of more H^+. The following reaction shows what happens in the respiratory system when carbon dioxide combines with water in the blood:

$$H_2O + CO_2 \rightleftharpoons H_2CO_3 \rightleftharpoons H^+ + HCO_3^-$$
$$\text{carbonic acid} \qquad \text{bicarbonate ion}$$

This is a reversible reaction and is useful for remembering the relationships between CO_2 and H^+. Note that as more CO_2 accumulates in the blood (which frequently is caused by reduced gas exchange in the lungs), the reaction moves to the right and more H^+ is produced, lowering the $\rightleftharpoons$ pH:

$$H_2O + CO_2 \rightarrow H_2CO_3 \rightarrow H^+ + HCO_3^-$$
$$\text{carbonic acid} \qquad \text{bicarbonate ion}$$

Conversely, as $[H^+]$ increases, more carbon dioxide will be present in the blood:

$$H_2O + CO_2 \leftarrow H_2CO_3 \leftarrow H^+ + HCO_3^-$$
$$\text{carbonic acid} \qquad \text{bicarbonate ion}$$

Disruptions of acid-base balance occur when the body's pH levels fall below or above the normal pH range of 7.35–7.45. When pH levels fall below 7.35, the body is said to be in a state of **acidosis.** When pH levels rise above 7.45, the body is said to be in a state of **alkalosis. Respiratory acidosis** and **respiratory alkalosis** are the result of the respiratory system accumulating too much or too little carbon dioxide in the blood. **Metabolic acidosis** and **metabolic alkalosis** refer to all other conditions of acidosis and alkalosis (i.e., those not caused by the respiratory system). The experiments in this lab will focus on these disruptions of acid-base balance and on the physiological buffer systems (renal and respiratory) that compensate for such imbalances (Figure 47.1b and c).

Respiratory Acidosis and Alkalosis

Respiratory acidosis is the result of impaired respiration, or *hypoventilation,* which leads to the accumulation of too much carbon dioxide in the blood. The causes of impaired respiration include airway obstruction, depression of the respiratory center in the brain stem, lung disease, and drug overdose. Recall that carbon dioxide acts as an acid by forming carbonic acid when it combines with water in the body's blood. The carbonic acid then forms hydrogen ions plus bicarbonate ions:

$$H_2O + CO_2 \rightarrow H_2CO_3 \rightarrow H^+ + HCO_3^-$$
$$\text{carbonic acid} \qquad \text{bicarbonate ion}$$

Because hypoventilation results in elevated carbon dioxide levels in the blood, the H^+ levels increase, and the pH value of the blood decreases.

Respiratory alkalosis is the condition of too little carbon dioxide in the blood. It is commonly the result of traveling to a high altitude (where the air contains less oxygen) or hyperventilation, which may be brought on by fever or anxiety. Hyperventilation removes more carbon dioxide from the blood, reducing the amount of H^+ in the blood and thus increasing the blood's pH level.

In this first set of activities, we focus on the causes of respiratory acidosis and alkalosis. From the drop-down menu, select **Exercise 47: Acid/Base Balance** and click **GO.** Then click **Respiratory Acidosis/Alkalosis.** You will see the opening screen for the Respiratory Acidosis/Alkalosis experiment (Figure 47.1a). To familiarize yourself with the equipment, choose **Balloons On/Off** from the **Help** menu. This feature allows you to scroll around the screen and view equipment labels. You can turn off this feature by returning to the **Help** menu and selecting **Balloons On/Off.**

If you have already completed Exercise 37B on respiratory system mechanics, this screen should look familiar. At the left is a pair of *simulated lungs,* which look like balloons, connected by a tube that looks like an upside-down Y. Air flows in and out of this tube, which simulates the trachea and other air passageways into the lungs. Beneath the "lungs" is a black platform simulating the diaphragm. The long, U-shaped tube containing red fluid represents blood flowing through the lungs. At the top left of the U-shaped tube is a pH meter that will measure the pH level of the blood once the experiment is begun. To the right is an *oscilloscope monitor,* which will graphically display respiratory volumes. Note that respiratory volumes are measured in liters (l) along the Y-axis, and time in seconds is measured along the X-axis. Below the monitor are three buttons: **Normal Breathing, Hyperventilation,** and **Rebreathing.** Clicking any one of these buttons will induce the given pattern of breathing. Next to these buttons are three data displays for P_{CO_2} (partial pressure of carbon dioxide in the blood)—these will give us the levels of carbon dioxide in the blood over the course of an experimental run. At the very bottom of the screen is the *data collection grid,* where you may record and view your data after each activity.

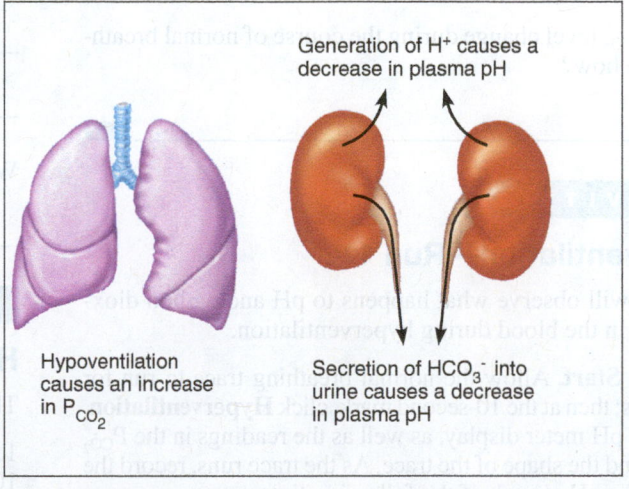

FIGURE 47.1 Maintaining acid-base balance. (a) Opening screen of the Respiratory Acidosis/Alkalosis experiment. **(b)** Compensatory mechanisms for acidosis. **(c)** Compensatory mechanisms for alkalosis.

ACTIVITY 1

Normal Breathing

We will begin by observing what happens during normal breathing in order to establish baseline data.

1. Click **Start.** Notice that the **Normal Breathing** button dims, indicating that the simulated lungs are "breathing" normally. Also notice the reading in the pH meter at the top left, the readings in the P_{CO_2} displays, and the shape of the trace that starts running across the oscilloscope screen. As the trace runs, record the readings for pH at each of the following times:

At 20 seconds, pH = _____

At 40 seconds, pH = _____

At 60 seconds, pH = _____

2. Allow the trace to run all the way to the right side of the oscilloscope screen. At this point, the run will automatically end.

3. Click **Record Data** at the bottom left to record your results.

4. Select **Print Graph** in the **Tools** menu.

5. Click **Clear Tracings** to clear the oscilloscope screen.

Did the pH level of the blood change at all during normal breathing? If so, how?

_____

Was the pH level always within the normal range for the human body?

_____

Did the P_{CO_2} level change during the course of normal breathing? If so, how?

_____

ACTIVITY 2A

Hyperventilation—Run 1

Next, we will observe what happens to pH and carbon dioxide levels in the blood during hyperventilation.

1. Click **Start.** Allow the normal breathing trace to run for 10 seconds; then at the 10-second mark, click **Hyperventilation.** Watch the pH meter display, as well as the readings in the P_{CO_2} displays and the shape of the trace. As the trace runs, record the readings for pH at each of the following times:

At 20 seconds, pH = _____

At 40 seconds, pH = _____

At 60 seconds, pH = _____

Maximum pH = _____

2. Allow the trace to run all the way across the oscilloscope screen and end.

3. Click **Record Data.**

4. Select **Print Graph** from the **Tools** menu.

5. Click **Clear Tracings** to clear the oscilloscope screen.

Did the pH level of the blood change at all during this run? If so, how?

_____

Was the pH level always within the normal range for the human body?

_____

If not, when was the pH value outside of the normal range, and what acid-base imbalance did this pH value indicate?

_____

Did the P_{CO_2} level change during the course of this run? If so, how?

_____

If you observed an acid-base imbalance during this run, how would you expect the renal system to compensate for this condition?

_____

How did the hyperventilation trace differ from the trace for normal breathing? Did the tidal volumes change?

_____

_____

What might cause a person to hyperventilate?

_____

ACTIVITY 2B

Hyperventilation—Run 2

This activity is a variation on Activity 2a.

1. Click **Start.** Allow the normal breathing trace to run for 10 seconds, then click **Hyperventilation** at the 10-second mark. Allow the hyperventilation trace to run for 10 seconds, then click **Normal Breathing** at the 20-second mark. Allow the trace to finish its run across the oscilloscope screen. Observe the changes in the pH meter and the P_{CO_2} displays.

2. Click **Record Data.**

3. Select **Print Graph** from the **Tools** menu.

4. Click **Clear Tracings** to clear the oscilloscope screen.

Describe the trace after the 20-second mark when you stopped the hyperventilation. Did the breathing return to normal immediately? Explain your observation.

_____

_____

_____

_____ ▬

ACTIVITY 3

Rebreathing

Rebreathing is the action of breathing in air that was just expelled from the lungs. Breathing into a paper bag is an example of rebreathing. In this activity, we will observe what happens to pH and carbon dioxide levels in the blood during rebreathing.

1.   Click **Start.** Allow the normal breathing trace to run for 10 seconds; then at the 10-second mark, click **Rebreathing.** Watch the pH meter display, as well as the readings in the P_{CO_2} displays and the shape of the trace. As the trace runs, record the readings for pH at each of the following times:

At 20 seconds, pH = _____

At 40 seconds, pH = _____

At 60 seconds, pH = _____

2.   Allow the trace to run all the way across the oscilloscope screen and end.

3.   Click **Record Data.**

4.   Select **Print Graph** from the **Tools** menu.

5.   Click **Clear Tracings** to clear the oscilloscope screen.

Did the pH level of the blood change at all during this run? If so, how?

_____

Was the pH level always within the normal range for the human body?

_____

If not, when was the pH value outside of the normal range, and what acid-base imbalance did this pH value indicate?

_____

Did the P_{CO_2} level change during the course of this run? If so, how?

_____

If you observed an acid-base imbalance during this run, how would you expect the renal system to compensate for this condition?

_____

How did the rebreathing trace differ from the trace for normal breathing? Did the tidal volumes change?

_____

_____

Give examples of respiratory problems that would result in pH and P_{CO_2} patterns similar to what you observed during rebreathing.

_____

_____

6.   To print out all of the recorded data from this activity, click **Tools** and then **Print Data.** ▬

In the next set of activities, we will focus on the body's primary mechanism of compensating for respiratory acidosis or alkalosis: renal compensation.

Renal System Compensation

The kidneys play a major role in maintaining fluid and electrolyte balance in the body's internal environment. By regulating the amount of water lost in the urine, the kidneys defend the body against excessive hydration or dehydration. By regulating the excretion of individual ions, the kidneys maintain normal electrolyte patterns of body fluids. By regulating the acidity of urine and the rate of electrolyte excretion, the kidneys maintain plasma pH levels within normal limits. Renal compensation is the body's primary method of compensating for conditions of respiratory acidosis or respiratory alkalosis. (Although the renal system also compensates for metabolic acidosis or metabolic alkalosis, a more immediate mechanism for compensating for metabolic acid-base imbalances is the respiratory system, as we will see in a later experiment.)

The activities in this section examine how the renal system compensates for respiratory acidosis or alkalosis. The primary variable we will be working with is P_{CO_2}. We will observe how increases and decreases in P_{CO_2} affect the levels of $[H^+]$ and $[HCO_3^-]$ that the kidneys excrete in urine.

Click **Experiment** at the top of the screen, and select **Renal System Compensation.** You will see the screen shown in Figure 47.2. If you completed Exercise 41B on renal physiology, this screen should look familiar. There are two beakers on the left side of the screen, one of which is filled with blood, simulating the body's blood supply to the kidneys. Notice that the P_{CO_2} level is currently set to 40 and that the corresponding blood pH value is 7.4—both normal values. By clicking **Start,** you will initiate the process of delivering blood to the simulated nephron at the right side of the screen. As blood flows through the glomerulus of the nephron, you will see the filtration from the plasma of everything except proteins and cells

FIGURE 47.2 Opening screen of the Renal Compensation experiment.

(note that the moving red dots in the animation do *not* include red blood cells). Blood will then drain from the glomerulus to the beaker at the right of the original beaker. At the end of the nephron tube, you will see the collection of urine in a small beaker. Keep in mind that although only one nephron is depicted here, there are actually over a million nephrons in each human kidney. Below the urine beaker are displays for H+ and HCO3⁻, which will tell us the relative levels of these ions present in the urine.

ACTIVITY 4

Renal Response to Normal Acid-Base Balance

1. Increase or decrease P_{CO_2} by clicking the (+) or (−) buttons. (Notice that as P_{CO_2} changes, so does the blood pH level.)

2. Click **Start,** and allow the run to finish.

3. At the end of the run, click **Record Data.**

At normal P_{CO_2} and pH levels, was the level of H+ present in the urine normal? _____

What level of [HCO3⁻] was present in the urine? _____

Why does the blood pH value change as P_{CO_2} changes?

_____

_____

How does the blood pH value change as P_{CO_2} changes?

_____

_____

4. Click **Refill** to prepare for the next activity. ▬

Renal Response to Respiratory Alkalosis

In this activity, we will simulate respiratory alkalosis by setting P_{CO_2} to values lower than normal (thus, blood pH will be *higher* than normal). We will then observe the renal system's response to these conditions.

1. Set P_{CO_2} to 35 by clicking the (−) button. Notice that the corresponding blood pH value is approximately 7.5.

2. Click **Start.**

3. At the end of the run, click **Record Data.**

4. Click **Refill.**

5. Repeat steps 1 through 4, setting P_{CO_2} to increasingly lower values (that is, set P_{CO_2} to 30 and then 20, the lowest value allowed).

What level of [H⁺] was present in the urine at each of these P_{CO_2} and pH levels?

_____

What level of [HCO₃⁻] was present in the urine at each of these P_{CO_2} and pH levels?

_____

Recall that it may take hours or even days for the renal system to respond to disruptions in acid-base balance. Assuming that enough time has passed for the renal system to fully compensate for respiratory alkalosis, would you expect P_{CO_2} levels to increase or decrease? Would you expect blood pH levels to increase or decrease?

_____

_____

Recall your activities in the first experiment on respiratory acidosis and alkalosis. Which type of breathing resulted in P_{CO_2} levels closest to the ones we experimented with in this activity—normal breathing, hyperventilation, or rebreathing?

_____

Explain why this type of breathing resulted in alkalosis.

_____

_____

_____

Renal Response to Respiratory Acidosis

In this activity, we will simulate respiratory acidosis by setting the P_{CO_2} values higher than normal (thus, blood pH will

be *lower* than normal). We will then observe the renal system's response to these conditions.

1. Make sure the left beaker is filled with blood. If not, click **Refill.**

2. Set P_{CO_2} to 60 by clicking the (+) button. Notice that the corresponding blood pH value is 7.3.

3. Click **Start.**

4. At the end of the run, click **Record Data.**

5. Click **Refill.**

6. Repeat steps 1 through 5, setting P_{CO_2} to increasingly higher values (that is, set P_{CO_2} to 75 and then 90, the highest value allowed).

What level of [H⁺] was present in the urine at each of these P_{CO_2} and pH levels?

_____

What level of [HCO₃⁻] was present in the urine at each of these P_{CO_2} and pH levels?

_____

Recall that it may take hours or even days for the renal system to respond to disruptions in acid-base balance. Assuming that enough time has passed for the renal system to fully compensate for respiratory acidosis, would you expect P_{CO_2} levels to increase or decrease? Would you expect blood pH levels to increase or decrease?

_____

_____

Recall your activities in the first experiment on respiratory acidosis and alkalosis. Which type of breathing resulted in P_{CO_2} levels closest to the ones we experimented with in this activity—normal breathing, hyperventilation, or rebreathing?

_____

Explain why this type of breathing resulted in acidosis.

_____

_____

_____

7. Before going on to the next activity, select **Tools** and then **Print Data** to save a hard copy of your data results.

Metabolic Acidosis and Alkalosis

Conditions of acidosis or alkalosis that do not have respiratory causes are termed *metabolic acidosis* or *metabolic alkalosis.*

Metabolic acidosis is characterized by low plasma HCO_3^- and pH. The causes of metabolic acidosis include:

- *Ketoacidosis,* a buildup of keto acids that can result from diabetes mellitus

- *Salicylate poisoning,* a toxic condition resulting from ingestion of too much aspirin or oil of wintergreen (a substance often found in laboratories)

- The ingestion of too much alcohol, which metabolizes to acetic acid

- Diarrhea, which results in the loss of bicarbonate with the elimination of intestinal contents

- Strenuous exercise, which may cause a buildup of lactic acid from anaerobic muscle metabolism

Metabolic alkalosis is characterized by elevated plasma HCO_3^- and pH. The causes of metabolic alkalosis include:

- Alkali ingestion, such as antacids or bicarbonate

- Vomiting, which may result in the loss of too much H^+

- Constipation, which may result in reabsorption of elevated levels of HCO_3^-

Increases or decreases in the body's normal metabolic rate may also result in metabolic acidosis or alkalosis. Recall that carbon dioxide—a waste product of metabolism—mixes with water in plasma to form carbonic acid, which in turn forms H^+:

$$H_2O + CO_2 \rightarrow \underset{\substack{\text{carbonic} \\ \text{acid}}}{H_2CO_3} \rightarrow H^+ + \underset{\substack{\text{bicarbonate} \\ \text{ion}}}{HCO_3^-}$$

Therefore, an increase in the normal rate of metabolism would result in more carbon dioxide being formed as a metabolic waste product, resulting in the formation of more H^+—and thereby lowering plasma pH and potentially causing acidosis. Other acids that are also normal metabolic waste products, such as ketone bodies and phosphoric, uric, and lactic acids, would likewise accumulate with an increase in metabolic rate. Conversely, a decrease in the normal rate of metabolism would result in less carbon dioxide being formed as a metabolic waste product, resulting in the formation of less H^+—raising plasma pH and potentially causing alkalosis. Many factors can affect the rate of cell metabolism. For example, fever, stress, or the ingestion of food all cause the rate of cell metabolism to increase. Conversely, a fall in body temperature or a decrease in food intake causes the rate of cell metabolism to decrease.

The respiratory system compensates for metabolic acidosis or alkalosis by expelling or retaining carbon dioxide in the blood. During metabolic acidosis, respiration increases to expel carbon dioxide from the blood and decrease $[H^+]$ in order to raise the pH level. During metabolic alkalosis, respiration decreases to promote the accumulation of carbon dioxide in the blood, thus increasing $[H^+]$ and decreasing the pH level.

The renal system also compensates for metabolic acidosis and alkalosis by conserving or excreting bicarbonate ions. However, in this set of activities we will focus on respiratory compensation of metabolic acidosis and alkalosis.

To begin, click **Experiment** at the top of the screen, and select **Metabolic Acidosis/Alkalosis.** The screen shown in Figure 47.3 will appear. This screen is similar to the screen from the first experiment; the main differences are the addition of a box representing the heart; tubes showing the double circulation of the heart; and a box representing the body's cells. The default "normal" metabolic rate has been set to 50 kcal/hr—an arbitrary value, given that normal metabolic rates vary widely from individual to individual. The (+) and (−) buttons in the Body Cells box allow you to increase or decrease the body's metabolic rate. In the following activities, you will observe the respiratory response to acidosis or alkalosis brought on by increases or decreases in the body's metabolic rate.

ACTIVITY 7

Respiratory Response to Normal Metabolism

Begin by observing respiratory activity at normal metabolic conditions. This data will serve as a baseline against which to compare data in Activities 8 and 9.

1. Make sure the **Metabolic Rate** is set to 50, which for the purposes of this experiment we will consider the normal value.

2. Click **Start** to begin the experiment. Notice the arrows showing the direction of blood flow. A graph displaying respiratory activity will appear on the oscilloscope screen.

3. After the graph has reached the end of the screen, the experiment will automatically stop. Note the data in the displays below the oscilloscope screen:

- The **BPM** display gives you the *breaths per minute*—the rate at which respiration occurred.

- **Blood pH** tells you the pH value of the blood.

- **P_{CO_2}** (shown as P_{CO_2} in the text) tells you the partial pressure of carbon dioxide in the blood.

- **H^+ and HCO_3^- tell you the levels of each of these ions.**

4. Click **Record Data.**

5. Click **Tools** and then **Print Graph** to print your graph.

What is the respiratory rate (BMP)? _____

What is the blood pH? _____

Are the blood pH and P_{CO_2} values within normal ranges?

_____

6. Click **Clear Tracings** before proceeding to the next activity. ▮

FIGURE 47.3 Opening screen of the Metabolic Acidosis/Alkalosis experiment.

Respiratory Response
to Increased Metabolism

1.   Increase the **Metabolic Rate** to 60 using the (+) **button.**

2.   Click **Start** to begin the experiment.

3.   Allow the graph to reach the end of the oscilloscope screen. Note the data in the displays below the oscilloscope screen.

4.   Click **Record Data.**

5.   Click **Tools** and then **Print Graph** to print your graph.

6.   Repeat steps 1 through 5 with the **Metabolic Rate** set at 70, and then 80.

As the body's metabolic rate increased:

How did respiration change with respect to BPM and tidal volume?

_____

How did blood pH change?

_____

How did P_{CO_2} change?

_____

How did [H$^+$] change?

_____

How did [HCO_3^-] change?

_____

Explain why these changes took place as metabolic rate increased. Hint: Start with the formation of excess CO_2 waste and explain the changes.

_____

_____

Which metabolic rates caused pH levels to decrease to a condition of metabolic acidosis?

_____

_____

What were the pH values at each of these rates?

_____

_____

By the time the respiratory system fully compensated for acidosis, how would you expect the pH values to change?

_____

_____

7.   Click **Clear Tracings** before proceeding to the next activity. ■

Respiratory Response to Decreased Metabolism

1.   Decrease the **Metabolic Rate** to 40.

2.   Click **Start** to begin the experiment.

3.   Allow the graph to reach the end of the oscilloscope screen. Note the data in the displays below the oscilloscope screen.

4.   Click **Record Data.**

5.   Click **Tools** and then **Print Graph** in order to print your graph.

6.   Repeat steps 1 through 5 with the **Metabolic Rate** set at 30, and then 20.

As the body's metabolic rate decreased:

How did respiration change?

_____

How did blood pH change?

_____

How did P_{CO_2} change?

_____

How did [H^+] change?

_____

How did [HCO_3^-] change?

_____

Explain why these changes took place as the metabolic rate decreased.

_____

_____

_____

Which metabolic rates caused pH levels to increase to a condition of metabolic alkalosis?

_____

_____

What were the pH values at each of these rates?

_____

_____

By the time the respiratory system fully compensated for acidosis, how would you expect the pH values to change?

_____

7.   Click **Tools → Print Data** to print your recorded data. ■

Acid-Base Balance: Computer Simulation

NAME _____

LAB TIME/DATE _____

Respiratory Acidosis and Alkalosis

The following questions refer to Activity 1: Normal Breathing.

1. What was the pH level during normal breathing? _____

2. Was this pH within the normal pH range? _____

The following questions refer to Activity 2: Hyperventilation.

3. In run 1, what was the maximum pH recorded with hyperventilation? _____

4. What acid-base imbalance occurred with hyperventilation? _____

_____

5. What happened to the tidal volume during hyperventilation? _____

_____

6. Describe the trace when hyperventilation stopped in run 2. _____

_____

The following questions refer to Activity 3: Rebreathing. _____

7. What was the effect on pH over time with rebreathing? _____

_____

8. Did rebreathing result in acidosis or alkalosis? Why? Hint: Specifically relate this to the level of CO_2.

_____

_____

9. List some potential causes that would mimic the patterns of pH and CO_2 levels seen in this rebreathing simulation.

_____

Renal System Compensation

The following questions refer to Activity 4: Renal Response to Normal Acid-Base Balance.

10. Describe how the pH of the blood changes with an increase in the level of CO_2.

_____

11. Why does this change occur? _____

The following questions refer to Activity 5: Renal Response to Respiratory Alkalosis.

12. What happened to the level of H^+ in the urine as the level of CO_2 decreased? _____

_____

13. Explain how the renal system compensates for respiratory alkalosis. _____

_____

14. Which type of breathing results in respiratory alkalosis? _____

The following questions refer to Activity 6: Renal Response to Respiratory Acidosis.

15. Explain how the renal system compensates for respiratory acidosis. _____

_____

16. Which type of breathing results in respiratory acidosis? _____

Metabolic Acidosis and Alkalosis

The following questions refer to Activity 8: Respiratory Response to Increased Metabolism.

17. What waste product is increased with an increased rate of metabolism? _____

18. Which metabolic rates results in metabolic acidosis? _____

19. List some other potential causes of metabolic acidosis. _____

_____

The following questions refer to Activity 9: Respiratory Response to Decreased Metabolism.

20. Which metabolic rates resulted in metabolic alkalosis? _____

21. List some other potential causes of metabolic alkalosis. _____

_____

The Metric System

Measurement	Unit and abbreviation	Metric equivalent	Metric to English conversion factor	English to metric conversion factor
Length	1 kilometer (km)	$= 1000$ (10^3) meters	1 km = 0.62 mile	1 mile = 1.61 km
	1 meter (m)	$= 100$ (10^2) centimeters	1 m = 1.09 yards	1 yard = 0.914 m
		$= 1000$ millimeters	1 m = 3.28 feet	1 foot = 0.305 m
			1 m = 39.37 inches	
	1 centimeter (cm)	$= 0.01$ (10^{-2}) meter	1 cm = 0.394 inch	1 foot = 30.5 cm
				1 inch = 2.54 cm
	1 millimeter (mm)	$= 0.001$ (10^{-3}) meter	1 mm = 0.039 inch	
	1 micrometer (μm) [formerly micron (μ)]	$= 0.000001$ (10^{-6}) meter		
	1 nanometer (nm) [formerly millimicron (mμ)]	$= 0.000000001$ (10^{-9}) meter		
	1 angstrom (Å)	$= 0.0000000001$ (10^{-10}) meter		
Area	1 square meter (m^2)	$= 10,000$ square centimeters	1 m^2 = 1.1960 square yards	1 square yard = 0.8361 m^2
			1 m^2 = 10.764 square feet	1 square foot = 0.0929 m^2
	1 square centimeter (cm^2)	$= 100$ square millimeters	1 cm^2 = 0.155 square inch	1 square inch = 6.4516 cm^2
Mass	1 metric ton (t)	$= 1000$ kilograms	1 t = 1.103 ton	1 ton = 0.907 t
	1 kilogram (kg)	$= 1000$ grams	1 kg = 2.205 pounds	1 pound = 0.4536 kg
	1 gram (g)	$= 1000$ milligrams	1 g = 0.0353 ounce	1 ounce = 28.35 g
			1 g = 15.432 grains	
	1 milligram (mg)	$= 0.001$ gram	1 mg = approx. 0.015 grain	
	1 microgram (μg)	$= 0.000001$ gram		
Volume (solids)	1 cubic meter (m^3)	$= 1,000,000$ cubic centimeters	1 m^3 = 1.3080 cubic yards	1 cubic yard = 0.7646 m^3
			1 m^3 = 35.315 cubic feet	1 cubic foot = 0.0283 m^3
	1 cubic centimeter (cm^3 or cc)	$= 0.000001$ cubic meter $= 1$ milliliter	1 cm^3 = 0.0610 cubic inch	1 cubic inch = 16.387 cm^3
	1 cubic millimeter (mm^3)	$= 0.000000001$ cubic meter		
Volume (liquids and gases)	1 kiloliter (kl or kL)	$= 1000$ liters	1 kL = 264.17 gallons	1 gallon = 3.785 L
	1 liter (l or L)	$= 1000$ milliliters	1 L = 0.264 gallons	1 quart = 0.946 L
			1 L = 1.057 quarts	
	1 milliliter (ml or mL)	$= 0.001$ liter $= 1$ cubic centimeter	1 ml = 0.034 fluid ounce	1 quart = 946 ml
				1 pint = 473 ml
			1 ml = approx. $\frac{1}{4}$ teaspoon	1 fluid ounce = 29.57 ml
			1 ml = approx. 15–16 drops (gtt.)	1 teaspoon = approx. 5 ml
	1 microliter (μl or μL)	$= 0.000001$ liter		
Time	1 second (s or sec)	$= \frac{1}{60}$ minute		
	1 millisecond (ms or msec)	$= 0.001$ second		
Temperature	Degrees Celsius (°C)		$°F = \frac{9}{5}(°C) + 32$	$°C = \frac{5}{9}(°F - 32)$

Credits

ILLUSTRATIONS

All illustrations are by Imagineering STA Media Services unless otherwise noted.

Exercise 1
1.1: Imagineering STA Media Services/Precision Graphics. 1.2, 1.4: Precision Graphics. 1.7: Adapted from Marieb and Mallatt, *Human Anatomy*, 3e, F1.10, © Benjamin Cummings, 2003.

Exercise 3
3.2–3.4, Activity 3: Precision Graphics.

Exercise 4
4.3: Tomo Narashima.

Exercise 5
5A.1: Precision Graphics.

Exercise 6
6A.2: Precision Graphics.

Exercise 7
7.1, 7.2, 7.7: Electronic Publishing Services, Inc.

Exercise 10
10.1–10.6, 10.8: Nadine Sokol.

Exercise 11
Table 11.1: Laurie O'Keefe.

Exercise 12
12.2a,b: Nadine Sokol.

Exercise 13
13.5: Precision Graphics.

Exercise 14
14.5: Electronic Publishing Services, Inc.

Exercise 15
15.1: Imagineering/Adapted from Martini, *Fundamentals of Anatomy & Physiology*, 4e, F11.1, Upper Saddle River, NJ: Prentice-Hall, © Frederic H. Martini, 1998.

Exercise 16
16A.1–16A.3: Precision Graphics. 16A.7–16A.9, 16A.13–16A.18, 16A.U1: Biopac Systems.

Exercise 17
17.1: Imagineering STA Media Services/Precision Graphics. 17.2, 17.5: Precision Graphics. 17.8a: Electronic Publishing Services, Inc.

Exercise 18
18A.2–18A.4: Precision Graphics.

Exercise 19
19.1, 19.5, 19.7–19.9: Electronic Publishing Services, Inc. 19.11b,c, 19.13a: Precision Graphics.

Exercise 20
20.4–20.7: Biopac Systems.

Exercise 21
21.2b: Electronic Publishing Services, Inc. 21.16–21.22: Biopac Systems.

Exercise 22
22.1: Electronic Publishing Services, Inc. 22.8, 22.9: Biopac Systems.

Exercise 24
24.1, 24.3a, 24.4a: Electronic Publishing Services, Inc. 24.7: Shirley Bortoli. 24.10, 24.11: Precision Graphics.

Exercise 25
25.1–25.3: Electronic Publishing Services, Inc./Precision Graphics.

Exercise 26
26.1, 26.2: Electronic Publishing Services, Inc.

Exercise 29
29A.2, 29A.5: Precision Graphics.

Exercise 30
30.1: Electronic Publishing Services, Inc./Precision Graphics. 30.2, 30.3a, 30.6: Electronic Publishing Services, Inc. 30.8: Precision Graphics.

Exercise 31
31.1: Electronic Publishing Services, Inc. 31.2, 31.4: Precision Graphics. 31.7–31.12: Biopac Systems.

Exercise 32
32.1: Adapted from Tortora and Grabowski, *Principles of Anatomy and Physiology*, 9e, F21.1, New York: Wiley, © Biological Sciences Textbooks and Sandra Reynolds Grabowski, 2000. 32.2, 32.3a, 32.4–32.12, 32.14: Electronic Publishing Services, Inc. 32.3b,c: Kristin Mount.

Exercise 33
33A.2: Precision Graphics. 33A.6–33A.8: Biopac Systems. 33A.9: Precision Graphics.

Exercise 34
34A.1, 34A.2, 34A.4: Precision Graphics. 34A.5: Biopac Systems. 34A.6a,b: Electronic Publishing Services, Inc.

Exercise 35
35A.8: Precision Graphics.

Exercise 36
36.1–36.5, 36.7: Electronic Publishing Services, Inc.

Exercise 37
37A.5, 37A.6: Precision Graphics. 37A.11, 37A.13, 37A.14: Biopac Systems.

Exercise 38
38.1–38.5, 38.8–38.10, 38.15: Electronic Publishing Services, Inc. 38.16: Electronic Publishing Services, Inc./Precision Graphics.

Exercise 39
Tables: Precision Graphics.

Exercise 40
40.1a, 40.2: Electronic Publishing Services, Inc.

Exercise 41
41A.1: Precision Graphics.

Exercise 42
42.1, 42.2a, 42.6: Electronic Publishing Services, Inc.

Exercise 43
43.1: Precision Graphics. 43.2: Electronic Publishing Services, Inc.

Exercise 44
44.1: Electronic Publishing Services, Inc.

Exercise 46
46.17: Precision Graphics.

Cat Dissection Exercises
CD1.1, CD3.1, CD3.3, CD7.1: Precision Graphics. CD2.1a, CD2.2a, CD3.2, CD4.2, CD4.3, CD6.1, CD7.2a, CD8.2a, CD9.1a: Kristin Mount.

Fetal Pig Dissection Exercises
Kristen Mount.

Rat Dissection Exercises
Imagineering STA Media Services.

PhysioEx Exercises
Opening Screens: Cadre Design. 18B.2, 34B.2: Precision Graphics.

PHOTOGRAPHS

Exercise 1
1.3 top: Jenny Thomas, Pearson Science. 1.3a: Howard Sochurek. 1.3b: James Cavallini/Photo Researchers. 1.3c: CNRI/Science Photo Library/Photo Researchers. 1.6b: Custom Medical Stock Photography.

Exercise 2
2.1–2.4a, 2.5b,c: Elena Dorfman, Pearson Science. 2.4b,c, 2.5a, 2.6a–c: David L. Bassett. 2.7: Cordelia Molloy/Photo Researchers, Inc.

Exercise 3

3.1: Leica. 3.5: Victor P. Eroschencko, Pearson Science.

Exercise 4

4.1: Don Fawcett and Science Source/Photo Researchers. 4.4a–f: Ed Reschke.

Exercise 5

5A.2a–c: Richard Megna/Fundamental Photographs. 5A.3a–c: David M. Philips/Photo Researchers.

Exercise 6

6A.3a: William Karkow/Pearson Education. 6A.3b,f,h, 6A.5d,j,k: Allen Bell, University of New England. Pearson Science. 6A.3c,e, 6A.5c,f,i: Nina Zanetti, Pearson Science. 6A.3d, 6A.5a,b,g,h,l, 6A.7b: Ed Reschke. 6A.3g: R. G. Kessel and R. H. Kardon/ Visuals Unlimited. 6A.5e: Ed Reschke/ Peter Arnold. 6A.6: Biophoto Associates/ Photo Researchers. 6A.7a: Eric Graves/ Photo Researchers. 6A.7c: Victor P. Eroschencko.

Exercise 7

7.2a: Ed Reschke/Peter Arnold. 7.3: Pearson Science. 7.5d: Manfred Kage/ Peter Arnold. 7.6a: Victor P. Eroschencko. 7.6b: From *Gray's Anatomy* by Henry Gray, © Churchill Livingstone, UK. 7.7a: Ed Reschke/Photolibrary/Peter Arnold, Inc. 7.7b: Lisa Lee/Pearson Education. 7.RS.2: Marian Rice.

Exercise 8

8.2a–c: Steve Downing. 8.3: Pearson Science.

Exercise 9

9.4c: Ed Reschke/Peter Arnold. 9.5: Ed Reschke. 9.RS.2: Alan Bell, Pearson Science.

Exercise 10

10.4a,b, 10.5: Ralph T. Hutchings. 10.6c: Elena Dorfman, Pearson Science. 10.9c: From the David Bassett *Atlas of Human Anatomy*. 10.17b: Dissection by Shawn Miller, photography by Mark Nielsen and Alexa Doig. 10.18c: Pearson Science.

Exercise 11

11.5b: National Library of Medicine. Table 11.1: From *A Stereoscopic Atlas of Human Anatomy* by David L. Bassett.

Exercise 12

12.1: Jack Scanlon, Holyoke Community College, MA. 12.2c,d: R. T. Hutchings.

Exercise 13

13.6c: From *A Stereoscopic Atlas of Human Anatomy* by David L. Bassett. 13.7d: Pearson Education. 13.8a: Mark Nielsen, University of Utah; Pearson Science. 13.8c: Video Surgery/Photo Researchers.

Exercise 14

14.1a: Marian Rice. 14.3, 14.6: Victor P. Eroschencko, Pearson Science. 14.4: Lisa Lee/Pearson Education

Exercise 15

15.4b: From *A Stereoscopic Atlas of Human Anatomy* by David L. Bassett. 15.5a, 15.8b, 15.9a: Dissection by Shawn Miller, photography by Mark Nielsen and Alexa Doig. 15.11f, Karen Krabbenhoft/ Pearson Science. 15.13b: From the David Bassett *Atlas of Human Anatomy*.

Exercise 17

17.2c: David M. Phillips/Photo Researchers, Inc. 17.3c: Don Fawcett/Photo Researchers. 17.4: Eroschencko's Interactive Histology. 17.6a: Michael Abby/Photo Researchers, Inc. 17.6b: Thomas Deerinck, NCMIR/SPL/ Photo Researchers. 17.6c: Nina Zanetti, Pearson Science. 17.8b: Victor P. Eroschencko, Pearson Science.

Exercise 19

19.2c: Robert A. Chase. 19.3: Pearson Education. 19.4a: Ralph T. Hutchings. 19.5b, 19.6a,b, 19.7c: From *A Stereoscopic Atlas of Human Anatomy* by David L. Bassett. 19.10: A. Glauberman/ Photo Researchers. 19.11a,d: Sharon Cummings, University of California, Davis; Pearson Science. 19.12, 19.13b, 19.14: Elena Dorfman, Pearson Science.

Exercise 20

20.1a: Alexander Tsiaras/Science Source/Photo Researchers.

Exercise 21

21.1b: From *A Stereoscopic Atlas of Human Anatomy* by David L. Bassett. 21.1c,d: L. Bassett/Visuals Unlimited. 21.4: Victor P. Eroschencko, Pearson Science. 21.7b: Ralph T. Hutchings.

Exercise 22

22.4–22.6: Richard Tauber, Pearson Science.

Exercise 23

23.1b: Kilgore College Biology Dept., Kilgore, Texas. 23.1c,d, 23.2b: Victor P. Eroschencko, Pearson Science.

Exercise 24

24.3b: From *A Stereoscopic Atlas of Human Anatomy* by David L Bassett. 24.4b: Ed Reschke/Peter Arnold. 24.5: Elena Dorfman, Pearson Science. 24.6b: Stephen Spector; courtesy of Charles Thomas, Kansas University Medical Center; Pearson Science. 24.12a,b: Richard Tauber, Pearson Science. 24.13: Charles Klettke/Pearson Education

Exercise 25

25.4: Victor P. Eroschencko, Pearson Science. 25.6a–c: Richard Tauber, Pearson Science. 25.8: I. M. Hunter-Duvar, Department of Otolaryngology, The Hospital for Sick Children, Toronto.

Exercise 26

26.1b, 26.3: Victor P. Eroschencko, Pearson Science. 26.2d: Pearson Education.

Exercise 27

27.3a: Michael Ross/Photo Researchers. 27.3b,d: Victor P. Eroschencko, Pearson Science. 27.3c: Lisa Lee/Pearson Science. 27.3e: Benjamin Widrevitz, Natural Sciences Division, College of DuPage, Glen Ellyn, IL. 27.3f: Ed Reschke/Peter Arnold.

Exercise 29A

29A.3: Ed Reschke/Peter Arnold. 29A.4a–e: Nina Zanetti, Pearson Science. 29A.6a-c, 29A.7a–d: Elena Dorfman, Pearson Science. 29A.8: Meckes and Ottawa/Photo Researchers. 29A.9: Pearson Science.

Exercise 30

30.3b, 30.3d: From A *Stereoscopic Atlas of Human Anatomy* by David L. Bassett. 30.3c: Lennart Nilsson, *The Body Victorious*, New York: Dell, © Boehringer Ingelheim International GmbH. 30.7: Ed Reschke. 30.8a,b, 30.9: Wally Cash, Kansas State University; Pearson Science. 30.RS.3: Ed Reschke.

Exercise 32

32.1a: Ed Reschke/Photolibrary, Inc. 32.3c: David L. Bassett.

Exercise 35A

35A.2: Ed Reschke/Peter Arnold. 35A.4b: Biophoto Associates/Photo Researchers. 35A.5c: LUMEN Histology, Loyola University Medical Education Network. 35A.6: Biophoto Associates/Photo Researchers, Inc..

Exercise 36

36.1a, 36.5b: From *A Stereoscopic Atlas of Human Anatomy* by David L. Bassett. 36.5a: Richard Tauber, Pearson Science. 36.6b: CNRI/Science Photo Library/Photo Researchers, Inc. 36.7a: Ed Reschke/Peter Arnold. 36.7b: Carolina Biological Supply/ Phototake.

Exercise 37A

37A.3, 37A.4a,b: Elena Dorfman, Pearson Science.

Exercise 38

38.5b: From *Color Atlas of Histology* by Leslie P. Garner and James L. Hiatt,

© Williams and Wilkins, 1990. 38.6a, 38.9a: Nina Zanetti, Pearson Science. 38.6b, 38.13: Victor P. Eroschencko, Pearson Science. 38.6c: Roger C. Wagner, Dept. of Biological Sciences, University of Delaware. 38.7a,c, 38.14a,b, 38.16b: From *A Stereoscopic Atlas of Human Anatomy* by David L. Bassett. 38.8d: LUMEN Histology, Loyola University Medical Education Network. 38.9b: Steve Downing. 38.9c: University of Kansas Medical Center, Department of Anatomy and Cell Biology.

Exercise 40
40.1b: Richard Tauber, Pearson Science. 40.3a: Ralph T. Hutchings. 40.6a,b, 40.7: Victor P. Eroschencko, Pearson Science.

Exercise 42
42.2b: Ed Reschke. 42.2c: From *A Stereoscopic Atlas of Human Anatomy* by David L. Bassett. 42.3: Harry Plymale. 42.4: Roger C. Wagner, University of Delaware. 42.7: Lisa Lee/Pearson Education. 42.8: Victor P. Eroschencko, Pearson Science.

Exercise 43
43.2.b: Pearson Science. 43.3: Michael Abby/Photo Researchers, Inc. 43.5b: Ed Reschke. 43.6a–c: Victor P. Eroschencko, Pearson Science.

Exercise 45
45.1: CNRI/SPL/Photo Researchers. 45.2.1: Llewellyn/Uniphoto Picture Agency. 45.2.2: photos.com. 45.2.3, 45.2.4: Ogust/Image Works. 45.2.5: Boisvieux/Explorer/Photo Researchers. 45.2.6: Anthony Loveday, Pearson Science. 45.3: Carolina Biological Supply.

Exercise 46
46.1a,b, 46.3, 46.5, 46.7, 46.9–46.16, 46.18a–d, 46.19: John Wilson White, Pearson Science. 46.2: Jenny Thomas, Pearson Science.

Cat Dissection Exercises
CD1.2–CD1.13, CD2.3b CD4.1, CD4.4b, CD4.5, CD6.2, CD6.3, CD7.3, CD7.4, CD7.5b, CD8.1b, CD9.2b: Shawn Miller (dissection) and Mark Nielsen (photography), Pearson Science. CD2.1b, CD9.1b: Paul Waring, Pearson Science. CD2.2b, CD7.2b, CD8.2b: Elena Dorfman, Pearson Science. CD3.3b,c: Yvonne Baptiste-Szymanski, Pearson Science.

Fetal Pig Dissection Exercises
PD1.1, PD1.2: Jack Scanlon, Holyoke Community College, Pearson Science. PD1.3b, PD1.4b, PD1.5b, PD1.6b, PD1.7b, PD1.8b, PD2.1, PD4.1b, PD4.2b, PD4.3b, PD4.4b, PD5.1, PD5.2b, PD6.1b, PD6.2b, PD7.1b, PD7.2b, PD8.1b, PD8.2b: Elena Dorfman, Pearson Science. PD3.2b,c: Charles J. Venglarik, Pearson Science.

Rat Dissection Exercises
Robert J. Sullivan, Pearson Science.

TRADEMARK ACKNOWLEDGMENTS

3M is a trademark of 3M.
Adrenaline is a registered trademark of King Pharmaceuticals.
Albustix, Clinistix, Clinitest, Hemastix, Ictotest, Ketostix, and Multistix are registered trademarks of Bayer.
Betadine is a registered trademark of Purdue Products L. P.
Chemstrip is a registered trademark of Roche Diagnostics.
Coban is a trademark of 3M.
Harleco is a registered trademark of EMD Chemicals Inc.
Hefty® Baggies® is a registered trademark of Pactiv Corporation.
Landau is a registered trademark of Landau Uniforms.
Lycra is a registered trademark of INVISTA.
Macintosh, Power Macintosh and Mac OS X are registered trademarks of Apple Computer, Inc.
Novocain is a registered trademark of Sterling Drug, Inc.
Parafilm is a registered trademark of Pechiney Incorporated.
Sedi-stain is a registered trademark of Becton, Dickinson and Company.
Speedo is a registered trademark of Speedo International.
VELCRO® is a registered trademark of VELCRO Industries B. V.
Wampole is a registered trademark of Wampole Laboratories.
Windows is either a registered trademark or trademark of Microsoft Corporation in the United States and/or other countries.